Collins gem

RUSSIAN DICTIONARY

A

HarperCollins Publishers
Westerhill Road
Bishopbriggs
Glasgow
G64 2QT
Great Britain

Fifth Edition 2018

10 9 8 7 6 5 4 3 2 1

ISBN 978-0-00-827080-3

www.collinsdictionary.com

A catalogue record for this book is available from the British Library

Typeset by Thomas Callan and Davidson Publishing Solutions, Glasgow

Printed and bound in China by RR Donnelley APS

Acknowledgements
We would like to thank those authors and publishers who kindly gave permission for copyright material to be used in the Collins Corpus. We would also like to thank Times Newspapers Ltd for providing valuable data.

If you would like to comment on any aspect of this book, please contact us at the given address or online.
E-mail: dictionaries@harpercollins.co.uk
facebook.com/collinsdictionary
@collinsdict

СОДЕРЖАНИЕ

CONTENTS

ВВЕДЕНИЕ

Мы рады, что вы выбрали словарь, подготовленный издательством Collins. Мы надеемся, что он окажется вам полезен, где бы вы им ни пользовались – дома, на отдыхе или на работе.

В настоящем введении излагаются некоторые советы по эффективному использованию данного издания: его обширного словника и сведений, содержащихся в каждой словарной статье. Данная информация поможет вам не только читать и понимать современный английский, но также овладеть устной речью.

INTRODUCTION

We are delighted that you have decided to use the Collins Russian Dictionary and hope that you will enjoy and benefit from using it at home, on holiday or at work.

This introduction gives you a few tips on how to get the most out of your dictionary – not simply from its wide-ranging wordlist but also from the information provided in each entry. This will help you to read and understand modern Russian, as well as communicate and express yourself in the language.

О ПОЛЬЗОВАНИИ СЛОВАРЁМ

Заглавные слова
Заглавными называются слова, начинающие словарную статью. Они напечатаны жирным шрифтом и расположены в алфавитном порядке. При многих из них приводятся словосочетания и сращения. Они напечатаны жирным шрифтом меньшего размера.

Перевод
Перевод заглавных слов напечатан обычным шрифтом. Варианты перевода, разделённые запятой, синонимичны. Различные значения многозначного слова разделены точкой с запятой.

Переводы для значений производных слов часто разделены только точкой с запятой, и перед ними даётся одна помета типа (*см прил*). Это означает, что последовательное разделение значений рассматриваемого слова и его переводов даётся при слове, от которого это слово образовано. Например, **careful/carefully**.

В случаях, когда точный перевод невозможен, даётся приблизительный эквивалент. Он обозначается знаком ≈. Если же таковой отсутствует, то приводится толкование.

Пометы
Пометы служат для разделения значений многозначного слова. Их цель – помочь читателю выбрать перевод, наиболее подходящий в том или ином контексте. Пометы напечатаны курсивом и заключены в круглые скобки.

При заглавных словах даны необходимые стилистические пометы. Нецензурные слова помечены восклицательным знаком (!).

Произношение
В англо-русской части словаря все заглавные слова снабжены транскрипцией. Транскрипция не даётся для производных слов, о произношении которых можно судить, исходя из произношения исходного слова, например, **enjoy/ enjoyment**. Список фонетических знаков приводится на страницах xvii–xviii.

В русско-английской части все русские слова снабжены знаком ударения. Омографы (слова, имеющие одинаковое написание, но различное ударение и значение) приводятся как отдельные заглавные слова в том порядке, в котором в них проставлено ударение, например, первым даётся слово **за́мок**, затем – **замóк**. Более подробную информацию о принципах русского произношения читатель может найти в разделе на страницах xvi–xvii.

Служебные слова

В словаре уделяется особое внимание русским и английским словам, которые обладают сложной грамматической струкктрой. Таковыми являются в первую очередь служебные слова, вспомогательные глаголы, местоимения, частицы итп. Они обозначены пометой **KEYWORD** или **КЛЮЧЕВОЕ СЛОВО**.

Английские фразовые глаголы

Фразовыми глаголами называются устойчивые сочетания глагола с элементами **in, up** итп, типа **blow up, cut down** итп. Они приводятся при базовых глаголах, таких как **blow, cut**, и расположены в алфавитном порядке.

Употребление *or/или*, косой черты и скобок

Между взаимозаменяемыми вариантами перевода фраз в англо-русской части употребляется союз "*or*", в русско-английской – "*или*". Косая черта (/) означает, что приведённые варианты перевода не являются взаимозаменяемыми. В круглые скобки заключаются возможные, но необязательные в данном выражении слова.

USING THE DICTIONARY

Headwords

The **headword** is the word you look up in a dictionary. They are listed in alphabetical order, and printed in bold type. Each headword may contain phrases, which are in smaller bold type. The two headwords appearing at the top of each page indicate the first (if it appears on a left-hand page) and last word (if it appears on a right-hand page) of the page in question.

Where appropriate, words related to headwords are grouped in the same entry (eg. **enjoy**, **enjoyment**) in smaller bold type than the headword.

Translations

The translations of the headword are printed in ordinary roman type. Translations separated by a comma are interchangeable, while those separated by a semi-colon are not interchangeable. Where it is not possible to give an exact translation equivalent, an approximate (cultural) equivalent is given, preceded by ≈. If this isn't possible either, then a gloss is given to explain the source item.

Indicators

Indicators are pieces of information given in italic type and in brackets. They offer contexts in which the headword might appear, or provide synonyms, guiding you to the most appropriate translation.

Colloquial and informal language in the dictionary is marked at the headword. Rude or offensive translations are also marked with (!).

Pronunciation

On the English-Russian side of the dictionary you will find the phonetic spelling of the word in square brackets after the headword, unless the word is grouped under another headword and the pronunciation can be easily derived eg. **enjoy/ enjoyment**. A list of the symbols used is given on pages xvii–xviii.

For Russian-English, stress is given on all Russian words as a guide to pronunciation. Words which are spelt in the same way, but have different stress positions are treated as separate entries, the order following the order of the stress eg. **за́мок** comes before **замо́к**. The section on pages xvi–xvii explains Russian phonetics in more detail.

Keywords

In the dictionary, special status is given to "key" Russian and English words. These words can be grammatically complex, often having many different usages, and are labelled KEYWORD in English and КЛЮЧЕВОЕ СЛОВО in Russian.

"You" in phrases

The Russian formal form is used to translate "you/your" and imperative phrases, unless the phrase is very colloquial and the informal form would be more natural.

Use of *or*/*или*, oblique and brackets

"*or*" on the English–Russian side, and "*или*" on the Russian–English side are used between interchangeable parts of a translation or phrase, whereas the oblique (/) is used between non-interchangeable alternatives. Round brackets are used to show the optional parts of the translation or phrase.

American variants

American spelling variants are generally shown at the British headword eg. **colour/color** and may also be shown as a separate entry. Variant forms are generally shown as separate headwords eg. **trousers/pants**, unless the British and American forms are alphabetically adjacent, when the American form is only shown separately if phonetics are required eg. **cut-price/cut-rate**.

Russian reflexive verbs

Russian reflexive verbs eg. **мы́ться**, **кра́ситься** are listed under the basic verb eg. **мыть, кра́сить**.

STYLE AND LAYOUT OF THE DICTIONARY

RUSSIAN–ENGLISH

Inflectional and grammatical information

Inflectional information is shown in the dictionary in brackets straight after the headword and before the part of speech eg. **стол (-á)** *м.*

Grammatical information is shown after the part of speech and refers to the whole entry eg. **зави́д|овать (-ую;** *pf* **позави́довать)** *несов +dat.* Note that transitive verbs are labelled *перех* and intransitive verbs have no label other than aspect. Where grammatical information eg. *no pf* is given in the middle of the entry, it then governs all of the following senses.

Use of the hairline (|)

The hairline is used in headwords to show where the inflection adds on eg. **кни́г|а (-и)**.

Stress

Stress changes are shown where they occur, the last form given being indicative of the rest of the pattern eg. **игр|á (-ы́;** *nom pl* **-ы)**. In this example the stress is on the last syllable in the singular moving to the first syllable throughout the plural.

Nouns, numerals and pronouns

In order to help you determine the declension and stress pattern of nouns, numerals and pronouns, we have shown the genitive in each case. This is given as the first piece of information after the headword and is not labelled eg. **стол (-á)**. Where the headword has further irregularities in declension these are shown at the headword and labelled eg. **я́блок|о (-а;** *nom pl* **-и)**.

Verbs

The majority of verbs are dealt with in aspectual pairs, and the translation is shown at the base form of the pair. The other aspect is generally shown separately and cross-referred to the base form. To help you see how a verb conjugates, inflections are shown immediately after the headword.

In phrases both aspects are shown if both work in the context.

The past tense is shown at the headword if it is irregularly formed.

Inflections given as separate entries

Some irregular inflected forms are also shown at their alphabetical position and cross-referred to the base headword.

Spelling rules

The following spelling rules apply to Russian:

- after **ж, ч, ш, щ, г, к** and **х, ы** is replaced by **и, я** by **а** and **ю** by **у**.
- after **ж, ч, ш, щ** and **ц, е** replaces an unstressed **о**.

Latin letters in Russian

With the increase in popularity of

the internet, some words in Russian are now normally spelt with Latin rather than Cyrillic characters eg. **SMS**, **MP3-плéер**. These words are listed in alphabetical order of their Cyrillic transliterations, so for example **MP3** and **MP3-плéер** are listed between **моя́** and **мрак**.

ENGLISH–RUSSIAN

Gender

The gender of Russian noun translations is only shown for:
- nouns ending in **-ь**
- neuter nouns ending in **-я**
- masculine nouns ending in **-а**
- nouns with a common gender
- indeclinable nouns
- substantivized adjectives
- plural noun translations if a singular form exists.

Feminine forms

The feminine forms of masculine nouns are shown as follows:
- the feminine ending adds on to the masculine form eg. учи́тель(ница)
- the feminine ending substitutes part of the masculine form, the last common letter of both forms being shown before the feminine ending (unless it is a substantivized adjective) eg. актёр(три́са)
- the feminine form is given in full eg. чех (чéшка).

Adjectives

Russian translations of adjectives are always given in the masculine, unless the adjective relates only to a feminine noun eg. берéменная.

Verbs

Imperfective and perfective aspects are shown in translation where they both apply eg. **to do** дéлать (сдéлать *pf*). If only one aspect is shown, it means that only one aspect works for this sense. The same applies to translations of infinitive phrases eg. **to buy sth** покупа́ть (купи́ть *pf*) что-н.

Where the English phrases contains the construction "to do" standing for any verb, it has been translated by *+infin/+impf infin/+pf infin*, depending on which aspects of the Russian verb work in the context.

Where the English phrase contains the past tense of a verb in the 1st person singular, the Russian translation gives only the masculine form eg. **I was glad** я был рад.

Prepositions

Unless bracketed, prepositions and cases which follow verbs, adjectives etc are obligatory as part of the translation eg. **to inundate with** зава́ливать (завали́ть *pf*) *+instr*.

Where they are separated by *or* they are interchangeable.

An oblique (/) is used to separate prepositions when the preposition depends on the following noun not the preceding verb eg. идти́ в/на.

RUSSIAN ABBREVIATIONS

aviation	***Авиа***	авиация
automobiles	***Авт***	автомобильное дело
administration	***Админ***	администрация
anatomy	***Анат***	анатомия
architecture	***Архит***	архитектура
impersonal	***безл***	безличный
biology	***Био***	биология
botany	***Бот***	ботаника
parenthesis	***вводн сл***	вводное слово
military	***Воен***	военный термин
reflexive	***возв***	возвратный глагол
geography	***Гео***	география
geometry	***Геом***	геометрия
verb	***глаг***	глагол
offensive	***груб!***	грубо
singular	***ед***	единственное число
feminine	***ж***	женский род
zoology	***Зоол***	зоология
history	***Ист***	история
et cetera	***итп***	и тому подобное
predicate	***как сказ***	как сказуемое
commercial	***Комм***	коммерция
computing	***Комп***	компьютер
somebody	***кто-н***	кто-нибудь
culinary	***Кулин***	кулинария
linguistics	***Линг***	лингвистика
masculine	***м***	мужской род
mathematics	***Мат***	математика
medicine	***Мед***	медицина
exclamation	***межд***	междометие
pronoun	***мест***	местоимение
plural	***мн***	множественное число
nautical	***Мор***	морской термин
music	***Муз***	музыка
adverb	***нареч***	наречие
invariable	***неизм***	неизменяемое
intransitive	***неперех***	непереходный глагол
indeclinable	***нескл***	несклоняемое
imperfective	***несов***	несовершенный вид
figurative	***перен***	в переносном значении
transitive	***перех***	переходный
subject	***подлеж***	подлежащее
politics	***Полит***	политика

superlative	***превос***	превосходная степень
preposition	***предл***	предлог
pejorative	***пренебр***	пренебрежительное
adjective	***прил***	прилагательное
possessive	***притяж***	притяжательный
school	***Просвещ***	просвещение
psychology	***Психол***	психология
informal	***разг***	разговорное
religion	***Рел***	религия
agriculture	***С.-Х.***	сельское хозяйство
see	***см***	смотри
collective	***собир***	собирательное
perfective	***сов***	совершенный вид
abbreviation	***сокр***	сокращение
neuter	***ср***	средний род
comparative	***сравн***	сравнительная степень
construction	***Строит***	строительство
noun	***сущ***	имя существительное
television	***Тел***	телевидение
technology	***Тех***	техника
printing	***Типог***	типографский термин
diminutive	***уменьш***	уменьшительное
physics	***Физ***	физика
photography	***Фото***	фотография
chemistry	***Хим***	химия
particle	***част***	частица
somebody's	***чей-н***	чей-нибудь
numeral	***чис***	числительное
something	***что-н***	что-нибудь
economics	***Экон***	экономика
electricity	***Элек***	электроника
law	***Юр***	юридический термин
registered trademark	®	зарегистрированный торговый знак
introduces a cultural equivalent	≈	вводит культурный эквивалент

АНГЛИЙСКИЕ СОКРАЩЕНИЯ

сокращение	***abbr***	abbreviation
винительный падеж	***acc***	accusative
прилагательное	***adj***	adjective
администрация	***Admin***	administration
наречие	***adv***	adverb

сельское хозяйство	***Agr***	agriculture
анатомия	***Anat***	anatomy
архитектура	***Archit***	architecture
автомобильное дело	***Aut***	automobiles
вспомогательный глагол	***aux vb***	auxiliary verb
авиация	***Aviat***	aviation
биология	***Bio***	biology
ботаника	***Bot***	botany
британский английский	***Brit***	British English
химия	***Chem***	chemistry
коммерция	***Comm***	commerce
компьютер	***Comput***	computing
союз	***conj***	conjunction
строительство	***Constr***	construction
сращение	***cpd***	compound
кулинария	***Culin***	culinary
дательный падеж	***dat***	dative
склоняется	***decl***	declines
определённый артикль	***def art***	definite article
уменьшительное	***dimin***	diminutive
экономика	***Econ***	economics
электроника	***Elec***	electricity
особенно	***esp***	especially
и тому подобное	***etc***	et cetera
междометие	***excl***	exclamation
женский род	***f***	feminine
в переносном значении	***fig***	figurative
родительный падеж	***gen***	genitive
география	***Geo***	geography
геометрия	***Geom***	geometry
безличный	***impers***	impersonal
несовершенный вид	***impf***	imperfective
несклоняемое	***ind***	indeclinable
неопределённый артикль	***indef art***	indefinite article
разговорное	***inf***	informal
грубо	***inf!***	offensive
инфинитив	***infin***	infinitive
творительный падеж	***instr***	instrumental
неизменяемое	***inv***	invariable
неправильный	***irreg***	irregular
лингвистика	***Ling***	linguistics
местный падеж	***loc***	locative
мужской род	***m***	masculine
субстантивированное прилагательное	***m/f/nt adj***	adjectival noun
математика	***Math***	mathematics
медицина	***Med***	medicine

военный термин	***Mil***	military
музыка	***Mus***	music
имя существительное	***n***	noun
морской термин	***Naut***	nautical
существительное во множественном числе	***npl***	plural noun
средний род	***nt***	neuter
числительное	***num***	numeral
себя	***o.s.***	oneself
пренебрежительное	***pej***	pejorative
совершенный вид	***pf***	perfective
фотография	***Phot***	photography
физика	***Phys***	physics
физиология	***Physiol***	physiology
множественное число	***pl***	plural
политика	***Pol***	politics
страдательное причастие	***pp***	past participle
предлог	***prep***	preposition
местоимение	***pron***	pronoun
предложный падеж	***prp***	prepositional
психология	***Psych***	psychiatry
прошедшее время	***pt***	past tense
религия	***Rel***	religion
кто-нибудь	***sb***	somebody
просвещение	***Scol***	school
единственное число	***sg***	singular
что-нибудь	***sth***	something
подлежащее	***subj***	subject
превосходная степень	***superl***	superlative
техника	***Tech***	technology
телесвязь	***Tel***	telecommunications
театр	***Theat***	theatre
телевидение	***TV***	television
типографский термин	***Typ***	printing
американский английский	***US***	American English
обычно	***usu***	usually
глагол	***vb***	verb
непереходный глагол	***vi***	intransitive verb
звательный падеж	***voc***	vocative
фразовый глагол	***vt fus***	phrasal verb
переходный глагол	***vt***	transitive verb
зоология	***Zool***	zoology
зарегистрированный торговый знак	®	registered trademark
вводит культурный эквивалент	≈	introduces a cultural equivalent

RUSSIAN PRONUNCIATION

Vowels and diphthongs

Letter	Symbol	Russian example	English example/explanation
А,а	[a]	дать	**a**fter
Е,е	[ɛ]	сел	g**e**t
Ё,ё	[jo]	ёлка, моё	**ya**wn
И,и	[i]	их, ни́ва	sh**ee**t
Й,й	[j]	йод, мой	**y**ield
Ó,ó	[o]	кот	d**o**t
О,о	[ʌ]	ного́	c**u**p
У,у	[u]	ум	sh**oo**t
Ы,ы	[+]	сын	*pronounced like "ee", but with the tongue arched further back in the mouth*
Э,э	[æ]	э́то	c**a**t
Ю,ю	[ju]	юг	**yo**u, **you**th
Я,я	[ja]	я́сно	**ya**k

Consonants

Letter	Symbol	Russian example	English example/explanation
Б,б	[b]	банк	**b**ut
В,в	[v]	вот	**v**at
Г,г	[g]	гол	**g**ot
Д,д	[d]	дом	**d**og
Ж,ж	[ʒ]	жена́	mea**s**ure
З,з	[z]	за́втра	do**z**e
К,к	[k]	кот	**c**at
Л,л	[l]	ло́дка	**l**ot
М,м	[m]	мать	**m**at
Н,н	[n]	нас	**n**o
П,п	[p]	пасть	**p**ut
Р,р	[r]	рот	*pronounced like rolled Scots "r"*
С,с	[s]	сад	**s**at
Т,т	[t]	ток	**t**op
Ф,ф	[f]	фо́рма	**f**at
Х,х	[x]	ход	*pronounced like Scots "ch" in "loch"*
Ц,ц	[ts]	цель	bi**ts**
Ч,ч	[tʃ]	ча́сто	**ch**ip
Ш,ш	[ʃ]	шу́тка	**sh**oot
Щ,щ	[ʃʃ]	щит	fre**sh sh**eets

Russian vowels are inherently short. Russian stressed vowels tend to be slightly longer than unstressed vowels. In unstressed positions all vowels are "reduced". Unstressed "**о**" sounds like "**а**" eg. **городá** [gərʌ'da], except in some loanwords and acronyms eg. **рáдио** ['raḑio], **госбáнк** [gos'bank]. Unstressed "**е**" is pronounced like "**bit**" eg. **селó** [şi'lo]. The same is true of "**я**" before stressed syllables eg. **пяти́** [pi'ţi], and of "**а**" when it follows "**ч**" or "**щ**" eg. **щади́ть** [ʃʃi'ḑiţ].

The letter "**ё**" is used only in grammar books, dictionaries etc to avoid ambiguity eg. **нéбо** and **нёбо**.

Latin characters in Russian are pronounced as if they were their Cyrillic equivalents, so for example **MP3** is pronounced [ɛmpɛtri]

АНГЛИЙСКОЕ ПРОИЗНОШЕНИЕ

Гласные и дифтонги

Знак	Английский пример	Русское соответствие/описание
[ɑ:]	f**a**ther	м**á**ма
[ʌ]	b**u**t, c**o**me	**а**льянс
[æ]	m**a**n, c**a**t	**э́**тот
[ə]	fath**er**, **a**go	р**á**на
[ə:]	b**ir**d, h**ea**rd	Ф**ё**дор
[ɛ]	g**e**t, b**e**d	ж**е**ст
[ɪ]	**i**t, b**i**g	к**и**т
[i:]	t**ea**, s**ea**	**и́**ва
[ɔ]	h**o**t, w**a**sh	х**о**д
[ɔ:]	s**aw**, **a**ll	**о́**чень
[u]	p**u**t, b**oo**k	б**у**к
[u:]	t**oo**, y**ou**	**у́**лица
[aɪ]	fl**y**, h**igh**	**лáй**
[au]	h**ow**, h**ou**se	**áу**т
[ɛə]	th**ere**, b**ear**	*произнóсится как сочетáние "э" и крáткого "а"*
[eɪ]	d**ay**, ob**ey**	**эй**
[ɪə]	h**ere**, h**ear**	*произнóсится как сочетáние "и" и крáткого "а"*
[əu]	g**o**, n**o**te	**óу**
[ɔɪ]	b**oy**, **oi**l	б**ой**

[uə]	poor, **sure**	*произно́сится как сочета́ние "у" и кра́ткого "а"*
[juə]	p**ure**	*произно́сится как сочета́ние "ю" и кра́ткого "а"*

Согласные

[b]	**b**ut	**б**ал
[d]	**d**ot	**д**ом
[g]	**g**o, **g**et, bi**g**	**г**ол, ми**г**
[dʒ]	**g**in, **j**u**dge**	**дж**и́нсы, и́ми**дж**
[ŋ]	si**ng**	*произно́сится как ру́сское "н", но не ко́нчиком языка́, а за́дней ча́стью его́ спи́нки*
[h]	**h**ouse, **h**e	**х**а́ос, **х**и́мия
[j]	**y**oung, **y**es	**й**од, **Й**е́мен
[k]	**c**ome, mo**ck**	**к**а́мень, ро**к**
[r]	**r**ed, t**r**ead	**р**от, т**р**ава́
[s]	**s**and, ye**s**	**с**ад, ри**с**
[z]	ro**s**e, **z**ebra	ро́**з**а, **з**е́бра
[ʃ]	**sh**e, ma**ch**ine	**ш**и́на, ма**ш**и́на
[tʃ]	**ch**in, ri**ch**	**ч**ин, кули́**ч**
[v]	**v**alley	**в**альс
[w]	**w**ater, **wh**ich	**уо́**тергейт, **уи**к-э́нд
[ʒ]	vi**s**ion	ва́**ж**ный
[θ]	**th**ink, my**th**	*произно́сится как ру́сское "с", но ко́нчик языка́ нахо́дится ме́жду зуба́ми*
[ð]	**th**is, **th**e	*произно́сится как ру́сское "з", но ко́нчик языка́ нахо́дится ме́жду зуба́ми*
[f]	**f**ace	**ф**а́кт
[l]	**l**ake, **l**ick	**л**ай, **л**ом
[m]	**m**ust	**м**ат
[n]	**n**ut	**н**ет
[p]	**p**at, **p**ond	**п**ар, **п**от
[t]	**t**ake, ha**t**	э**т**о**т**, не**т**
[x]	lo**ch**	**х**од

a

КЛЮЧЕВОЕ СЛОВО

а *союз* **1** but; **он согласи́лся, а я отказа́лась** he agreed, but I refused
2 (*выражает присоединение*) and
3 (*во фразах*): **а (не) то** or (else); **а вот** but
▷ *част* (*обозначает отклик*): **иди́ сюда́! — а, что тако́е!** come here! — yes, what is it?; **а как же** (*разг*) of course, certainly
▷ *межд* ah; (*выражает ужас, боль*) oh; **а ну** (*разг*) go on; **а ну́ его!** (*разг*) stuff him!

абажу́р (**-а**) *м* lampshade
абза́ц (**-а**) *м* paragraph
абитурие́нт (**-а**) *м* *entrant to university, college etc*
абонеме́нт (**-а**) *м* season ticket
або́рт (**-а**) *м* abortion
абрико́с (**-а**) *м* (*плод*) apricot
абсолю́тный *прил* absolute
абстра́ктный *прил* abstract
абсу́рдный *прил* absurd
авантю́р|а (**-ы**) *ж* adventure
авари́йный *прил* emergency; (*дом*) unsafe; **авари́йный сигна́л** alarm signal
ава́ри|я (**-и**) *ж* accident; (*повреждение*) breakdown
а́вгуст (**-а**) *м* August
а́виа *нескл* (*авиапочта*) air mail
авиакомпа́ни|я (**-и**) *ж* airline
авиано́с|ец (**-ца**) *м* aircraft carrier
Австра́ли|я (**-и**) *ж* Australia
А́встри|я (**-и**) *ж* Austria
автоба́з|а (**-ы**) *ж* depot
автобиогра́фи|я (**-и**) *ж* autobiography
авто́бус (**-а**) *м* bus
автовокза́л (**-а**) *м* bus station
авто́граф (**-а**) *м* autograph
авто-: **автозаво́д** (**-а**) *м* car (*Brit*) *или* automobile (*US*) plant; **автозапра́вочн|ая** (**-ой**) *ж* (*также* **автозапра́вочная ста́нция**) filling station; **автомагистра́л|ь** (**-и**) *ж* motorway (*Brit*), expressway (*US*); **автомаши́н|а** (**-ы**) *ж* (motor)car, automobile (*US*); **автомеха́ник** (**-а**) *м* car mechanic; **автомоби́л|ь** (**-я**) *м* (motor)car, automobile (*US*); **легково́й автомоби́ль** (passenger) car
автоно́мный *прил* autonomous
автоотве́тчик (**-а**) *м* answering machine, answer phone, voice mail
а́втор (**-а**) *м* author
авторите́т (**-а**) *м* authority
автору́ч|ка (**-ки**; *gen pl* **-ек**) *ж* fountain pen
автостра́д|а (**-ы**) *ж* motorway (*Brit*), expressway (*US*)

аге́нт (**-а**) *м* agent; **аге́нтств|о** (**-а**) *ср* agency
агити́р|овать (**-ую**) *несов*: **агити́ровать** (**за** *+acc*) to campaign (for)
аго́ни|я (**-и**) *ж* death throes *мн*
агрега́т (**-а**) *м* machine
агре́сси|я (**-и**) *ж* aggression
ад (**-а**) *м* hell
адапти́р|оваться (**-уюсь**) *(не) сов возв* to adapt
адвока́т (**-а**) *м* counsel; (*в суде*) ≈ barrister (*Brit*), ≈ attorney (*US*)
адеква́тный *прил* adequate
администра́ци|я (**-и**) *ж* administration; (*гостиницы*) management
а́дрес (**-а**; *nom pl* **-а́**) *м* address; **а́дресный** *прил*: **а́дресный стол** *residents' registration office*; **адрес|ова́ть** (**-у́ю**) *(не)сов перех*: **адресова́ть что-н кому́-н** to address sth to sb
ажу́рный *прил* lace
аза́рт (**-а**) *м* ardour (*Brit*), ardor (*US*)
а́збук|а (**-и**) *м* alphabet; (*букварь*) first reading book
Азербайджа́н (**-а**) *м* Azerbaijan
А́зи|я (**-и**) *ж* Asia
азо́т (**-а**) *м* nitrogen
ай *межд* (*выражает боль*) ow, ouch
а́йсберг (**-а**) *м* iceberg
акаде́ми|я (**-и**) *ж* academy
акваре́л|ь (**-и**) *ж* watercolours *мн* (*Brit*), watercolors *мн* (*US*); (*картина*) watercolo(u)r
аква́риум (**-а**) *м* aquarium, fish tank
аккомпани́р|овать (**-ую**) *несов +dat* to accompany
акко́рд (**-а**) *м* chord
аккура́тный *прил* (*посещение*) regular; (*работник*) meticulous; (*работа*) accurate; (*костюм*) neat
акселера́тор (**-а**) *м* accelerator
акт (**-а**) *м* act; (*документ*) formal document
актёр (**-а**) *м* actor
акти́в (**-а**) *м* assets *мн*
акти́вный *прил* active
актри́с|а (**-ы**) *ж* actress
актуа́льный *прил* topical; (*задача*) urgent
аку́л|а (**-ы**) *ж* shark
акуше́р|ка (**-ки**; *gen pl* **-ок**) *ж* midwife
акце́нт (**-а**) *м* accent
акци́з (**-а**) *м* excise (tax)
акционе́р (**-а**) *м* shareholder
а́кци|я (**-и**) *ж* (*Комм*) share; (*действие*) action
а́либи *ср нескл* alibi
алиме́нт|ы (**-ов**) *мн* alimony *ед*, maintenance *ед*
алкого́лик (**-а**) *м* alcoholic
алкого́л|ь (**-я**) *м* alcohol
аллерги́|я (**-и**) *ж* allergy
алле́|я (**-и**) *ж* alley
алло́ *межд* hello
алма́з (**-а**) *м* diamond
алфави́т (**-а**) *м* alphabet
альбо́м (**-а**) *м* album
альт (**-а́**) *м* (*инструмент*) viola
альтернати́в|а (**-ы**) *ж* alternative
алья́нс (**-а**) *м* alliance
алюми́ни|й (**-я**) *м* aluminium (*Brit*), aluminum (*US*)
амбулато́ри|я (**-и**) *ж* doctor's surgery (*Brit*) *или* office (*US*)
Аме́рик|а (**-и**) *ж* America
америка́нск|ий *прил* American
амнисти́р|овать (**-ую**) *(не)сов перех* to grant (an) amnesty to
амни́сти|я (**-и**) *ж* amnesty
амора́льный *прил* immoral
амортиза́тор (**-а**) *м* (*Tex*) shock absorber
а́мпул|а (**-ы**) *ж* ampoule (*Brit*), ampule (*US*)

АН *ж сокр* (= *Акаде́мия нау́к*) Academy of Sciences
ана́лиз (**-а**) *м* analysis
анализи́р|овать (**-ую**; *perf* **проанализи́ровать**) *несов перех* to analyse (*Brit*), analyze (*US*)
анали́тик (**-а**) *м* analyst
аналоги́чный *прил* analogous
анало́ги|я (**-и**) *ж* analogy; **по анало́гии** (**с** *+instr*) in a similar way (to)
анана́с (**-а**) *м* pineapple
ана́рхи|я (**-и**) *ж* anarchy
анато́ми|я (**-и**) *ж* anatomy
а́нгел (**-а**) *м* (*также разг*) angel
анги́н|а (**-ы**) *ж* tonsillitis
англи́йский *прил* English; **англи́йский язы́к** English
англича́н|ин (**-ина**; *nom pl* **-е**, *gen pl* **-**) *м* Englishman (*мн* Englishmen)
А́нгли|я (**-и**) *ж* England
анекдо́т (**-а**) *м* joke
анеми́|я (**-и**) *ж* anaemia (*Brit*), anemia (*US*)
анестезио́лог (**-а**) *м* anaesthetist (*Brit*), anesthiologist (*US*)
анестези́|я (**-и**) *ж* anaesthesia (*Brit*), anesthesia (*US*)
анке́т|а (**-ы**) *ж* (*опросный лист*) questionnaire; (*бланк для сведений*) form; (*сбор сведений*) survey
анони́мный *прил* anonymous
Антаркти́д|а (**-ы**) *ж* Antarctica
Анта́рктик|а (**-и**) *ж* the Antarctic
анте́нн|а (**-ы**) *ж* aerial (*Brit*), antenna (*US*); **анте́нна косми́ческой свя́зи** satellite dish
антибио́тик (**-а**) *м* antibiotic
антиви́русный *прил* antivirus; **антиви́русное програ́ммное обеспече́ние** antivirus software
антиква́рный *прил* antique
анти́чный *прил* classical; **анти́чный мир** the Ancient World
антра́кт (**-а**) *м* interval
аню́тины *прил*: **аню́тины гла́зки** pansy *ед*
А/О *ср сокр* (= *акционе́рное о́бщество*) joint-stock company
апа́ти|я (**-и**) *ж* apathy
апелли́р|овать (**-ую**) *(не)сов* (*Юр*) to appeal
апелля́ци|я (**-и**) *ж* (*также Юр*) appeal
апельси́н (**-а**) *м* orange
аплоди́р|овать (**-ую**) *несов +dat* to applaud
аплодисме́нт|ы (**-ов**) *мн* applause *ед*
аппара́т (**-а**) *м* apparatus; (*Физиология*) system; (*штат*) staff
аппарату́р|а (**-ы**) *ж собир* equipment
аппендици́т (**-а**) *м* appendicitis
аппети́т (**-а**) *м* appetite; **прия́тного аппети́та!** bon appétit!
апре́л|ь (**-я**) *м* April
апте́к|а (**-и**) *ж* pharmacy; **апте́кар|ь** (**-я**) *м* pharmacist
ара́б (**-а**) *м* Arab; **ара́бский** *прил* (*страны*) Arab; **ара́бский язы́к** Arabic
ара́хис (**-а**) *м* peanut
арби́тр (**-а**) *м* (*в спорах*) arbitrator; (*в футболе*) referee
арбитра́ж (**-а**) *м* arbitration
арбу́з (**-а**) *м* watermelon
аргуме́нт (**-а**) *м* argument; **аргументи́р|овать** (**-ую**) *(не)сов перех* to argue
аре́н|а (**-ы**) *ж* arena; (*цирка*) ring
аре́нд|а (**-ы**) *ж* (*наём*) lease; **аре́ндн|ый** *прил* lease; **аре́ндная пла́та** rent; **аренд|ова́ть** (**-у́ю**) *(не)сов перех* to lease
аре́ст (**-а**) *м* (*преступника*) arrest; **аресто́ванн|ый** (**-ого**) *м* person

held in custody; **арест|ова́ть** (**-у́ю**; *impf* **аресто́вывать**) *сов перех* (*преступника*) to arrest
арифме́тик|а (**-и**) *ж* arithmetic
а́р|ка (**-ки**; *gen pl* **-ок**) *ж* arch
А́рктик|а (**-и**) *ж* the Arctic
армату́р|а (**-ы**) *ж* steel framework
арме́йский *прил* army
Арме́ни|я (**-и**) *ж* Armenia
а́рми|я (**-и**) *ж* army
армяни́н (**-а**; *nom pl* **армя́не**, *gen pl* **армя́н**) *м* Armenian
арома́т (**-а**) *м* (*цветов*) fragrance; (*кофе итп*) aroma
арте́ри|я (**-и**) *ж* (*также перен*) artery
арти́кл|ь (**-я**) *м* (*Линг*) article
арти́ст (**-а**) *м* actor
арти́ст|ка (**-ки**; *gen pl* **-ок**) *ж* actress
артри́т (**-а**) *м* arthritis
а́рф|а (**-ы**) *ж* harp
архео́лог (**-а**) *м* archaeologist (*Brit*), archeologist (*US*)
архи́в (**-а**) *м* archive
архиепи́скоп (**-а**) *м* archbishop
архите́ктор (**-а**) *м* architect; **архитекту́р|а** (**-ы**) *ж* architecture
аспе́кт (**-а**) *м* aspect
аспира́нт (**-а**) *м* postgraduate (*doing PhD*); **аспиранту́р|а** (**-ы**) *ж* postgraduate studies *мн* (*leading to PhD*)
аспири́н (**-а**) *м* aspirin
ассамбле́|я (**-и**) *ж* assembly
ассигн|ова́ть (**-у́ю**) *(не)сов перех* to allocate
ассимили́р|оваться (**-уюсь**) *(не)сов возв* to become assimilated
ассисте́нт (**-а**) *м* assistant; (*в вузе*) assistant lecturer
ассортиме́нт (**-а**) *м* range
ассоциа́ци|я (**-и**) *ж* association
ассоции́р|овать (**-ую**) *(не)сов перех* to associate
а́стм|а (**-ы**) *ж* asthma
астроло́ги|я (**-и**) *ж* astrology
астрономи́ческий *прил* (*также перен*) astronomic(al)
ата́к|а (**-и**) *ж* attack; **атак|ова́ть** (**-у́ю**) *(не)сов перех* to attack
атама́н (**-а**) *м* ataman (*Cossack leader*)
атеи́ст (**-а**) *м* atheist
ателье́ *ср нескл* studio; (*мод*) tailor's shop; **телевизио́нное ателье́** television repair shop; **ателье́ прока́та** rental shop
атланти́ческий *прил*: **Атланти́ческий океа́н** the Atlantic (Ocean)
а́тлас (**-а**) *м* atlas
атле́тик|а (**-и**) *ж*: **лёгкая атле́тика** track and field events; **тяжёлая атле́тика** weight lifting
атмосфе́р|а (**-ы**) *ж* atmosphere
а́том (**-а**) *м* atom
АТС *ж сокр* (= *автомати́ческая телефо́нная ста́нция*) automatic telephone exchange
аттеста́т (**-а**) *м* certificate; **аттеста́т зре́лости** ≈ GCSE

Аттеста́т зре́лости

Certificate of Secondary Education. This was formerly obtained by school-leavers after sitting their final exams. This system has now been replaced by the **ЕГЭ**.

аттест|ова́ть (**-у́ю**) *(не)сов перех* to assess
аттракцио́н (**-а**) *м* (*в цирке*) attraction; (*в парке*) amusement
ауди́т (**-а**) *м* audit
аудито́ри|я (**-и**) *ж* lecture hall ▷ *собир* (*слушатели*) audience
аукцио́н (**-а**) *м* auction

áут (**-а**) *м* (*в теннисе*) out; (*в футболе*): **мяч в áуте** the ball is out of play
афи́ш|а (**-и**) *ж* poster
Áфрик|а (**-и**) *ж* Africa
ах *межд*: **ах!** oh!, ah!; **ах да!** (*разг*) ah yes!
АЦАЛ *ж сокр* (= *асимметри́чная цифровáя абонéнтская ли́ния*) ADSL (= *Asymmetric Digital Subscriber Line*)
аэрóбик|а (**-и**) *ж* aerobics
аэровокзáл (**-а**) *м* air terminal (*esp Brit*)
аэрозóл|ь (**-я**) *м* aerosol, spray
аэропóрт (**-а**; *loc sg* **-ý**) *м* airport
АЭС *ж сокр* (= *áтомная электростáнция*) atomic power station

б

б *част см* **бы**
бáб|а (**-ы**) *ж* (*разг*) woman; **бáб|а-яг|á** (**-ы, -и́**) *ж* Baba Yaga (*old witch in Russian folk-tales*); **бáб|ка** (**-ки**; *gen pl* **-ок**) *ж* grandmother
бáбоч|ка (**-ки**; *gen pl* **-ек**) *ж* butterfly; (*галстук*) bow tie
бáбуш|ка (**-ки**; *gen pl* **-ек**) *ж* grandmother, grandma
багáж (**-á**) *м* luggage (*Brit*), baggage (*US*); **багáжник** (**-а**) *м* (*в автомобиле*) boot (*Brit*), trunk (*US*); (*на велосипеде*) carrier
багрóвый *прил* crimson
бадминтóн (**-а**) *м* badminton
бáз|а (**-ы**) *ж* basis; (*Воен, Архит*) base; (*для туристов*) centre (*Brit*), center (*US*); (*товаров*) warehouse
базáр (**-а**) *м* market; (*книжный*) fair; (*перен*: *разг*) racket
бази́р|овать (**-ую**) *несов перех*:

бази́ровать что-н на *+prp* to base sth on; **бази́роваться** *несов возв*: **бази́роваться (на** *+prp*) to be based (on)
байда́р|ка (**-ки**; *gen pl* **-ок**) *ж* canoe
Байка́л (**-а**) *м* Lake Baikal
бак (**-а**) *м* tank
бакале́|я (**-и**) *ж* grocery section; (*товары*) groceries *мн*
ба́кен (**-а**) *м* buoy
бакенба́рд|ы (-) *мн* sideburns
баклажа́н (**-а**; *gen pl* **—** *или* **-ов**) *м* aubergine (*Brit*), eggplant (*US*)
бакс (**-а**) *м* (*разг*) dollar
бал (**-а**; *loc sg* **-ý**, *nom pl* **-ы́**) *м* ball
балала́|йка (**-йки**; *gen pl* **-ек**) *ж* balalaika
бала́нс (**-а**) *м* balance; **баланси́р|овать** (**-ую**) *несов*: **баланси́ровать (на** *+prp*) to balance (on)
балери́н|а (**-ы**) *ж* ballerina
бале́т (**-а**) *м* ballet
ба́л|ка (**-ки**; *gen pl* **-ок**) *ж* beam
Балка́н|ы (-) *мн* the Balkans
балко́н (**-а**) *м* (*Архит*) balcony; (*Театр*) circle (*Brit*), balcony (*US*)
балл (**-а**) *м* mark; (*Спорт*) point
балло́н (**-а**) *м* (*газовый*) cylinder; (*для жидкости*) jar
баллоти́р|овать (**-ую**) *несов перех* to vote for; **баллоти́роваться** *несов возв*: **баллоти́роваться в** *+acc* *или* **на пост** *+gen* to stand (*Brit*) *или* run (*US*) for
бал|ова́ть (**-ýю**; *perf* **избалова́ть**) *несов перех* to spoil; **балова́ться** *несов возв* (*ребёнок*) to be naughty
балти́йск|ий *прил*: **Балти́йское мо́ре** the Baltic (Sea)
ба́льн|ый *прил*: **ба́льное пла́тье** ball gown
ба́мпер (**-а**) *м* bumper
бана́н (**-а**) *м* banana
ба́нд|а (**-ы**) *ж* gang
бандеро́л|ь (**-и**) *ж* package
банк (**-а**) *м* bank
ба́н|ка (**-ки**; *gen pl* **-ок**) *ж* jar; (*жестяная*) tin (*Brit*), can (*US*)
банке́т (**-а**) *м* banquet
банки́р (**-а**) *м* banker
банкно́т (**-а**; *gen pl* **-**) *м* banknote
ба́нковский *прил* bank
банкома́т (**-а**) *м* cash machine
банкро́т (**-а**) *м* bankrupt
банкро́тств|о (**-а**) *ср* bankruptcy
бант (**-а**) *м* bow
ба́н|я (**-и**; *gen pl* **-ь**) *ж* bathhouse
бар (**-а**) *м* bar
бараба́н (**-а**) *м* drum; **бараба́н|ить** (**-ю, -ишь**) *несов* to drum
бара́к (**-а**) *м* barracks *мн*
бара́н (**-а**) *м* sheep; **бара́нин|а** (**-ы**) *ж* mutton; (*молодая*) lamb
барахл|о́ (**-а́**) *ср собир* junk
барахо́л|ка (**-ки**; *gen pl* **-ок**) *ж* flea market
барда́к (**-а́**) *м* (*груб!*: *беспорядок*) hell broke loose (*!*)
ба́рж|а (**-и**) *ж* barge
ба́рмен (**-а**) *м* barman (*мн* barmen), bartender (*US*)
баро́метр (**-а**) *м* barometer
баррика́д|а (**-ы**) *ж* barricade
барсу́к (**-а́**) *м* badger
ба́рхат (**-а**) *м* velvet
барье́р (**-а**) *м* (*в беге*) hurdle; (*на скачках*) fence; (*перен*) barrier
бас (**-а**; *nom pl* **-ы́**) *м* bass
баскетбо́л (**-а**) *м* basketball
бассе́йн (**-а**) *м* (swimming) pool; (*реки, озера итп*) basin
баст|ова́ть (**-ýю**) *несов* to be on strike
батаре́|йка (**-йки**; *gen pl* **-ек**) *ж* (*Элек*) battery

батаре́|я (**-и**) *ж* (*отопительная*) radiator; (*Воен, Элек*) battery
бато́н (**-а**) *м* (white) loaf (*long or oval*)
ба́тюш|ка (**-ки**; *gen pl* **-ек**) *м* father
бахром|а́ (**-ы́**) *ж* fringe (*Brit*), bangs *мн* (*US*)
ба́ш|ня (**-ни**; *gen pl* **-ен**) *ж* tower
баю́ка|ть (**-ю**) *несов перех* to lull to sleep
working баян (**-а**) *м* bayan (*kind of concertina*)
бди́тельный *прил* vigilant
бег (**-а**) *м* run, running; **на бегу́** hurriedly; *см также* **бега́**
бег|а́ (**-о́в**) *мн* the races *мн*
бе́га|ть (**-ю**) *несов* to run
бегемо́т (**-а**) *м* hippopotamus, hippo (*inf*)
беги́(те) *несов см* **бежа́ть**
бегов|о́й *прил* (*лошадь*) race; **бегова́я доро́жка** running track
бего́м *нареч* quickly; (*перен*: *разг*) in a rush
бе́гств|о (**-а**) *ср* flight; (*из плена*) escape
бегу́ *итп несов см* **бежа́ть**
бегу́н (**-а́**) *м* runner
бегу́н|ья (**-ьи**; *gen pl* **-ий**) *ж* runner
бед|а́ (**-ы́**; *nom pl* **-ы**) *ж* tragedy; (*несчастье*) misfortune, trouble; **про́сто беда́!** it's just awful!; **не беда́!** (*разг*) (it's) nothing!, not to worry!
бедне́|ть (**-ю**; *perf* **обедне́ть**) *несов* to become poor
бе́дност|ь (**-и**) *ж* poverty; **бе́дный** *прил* poor
бедня́г|а (**-и**) *м/ж* (*разг*) poor thing
бедня́к (**-а́**) *м* poor man
бедр|о́ (**-а́**; *nom pl* **бёдра**, *gen pl* **бёдер**) *ср* thigh; (*таз*) hip
бе́дственный *прил* disastrous; **бе́дстви|е** (**-я**) *ср* disaster; **бе́дств|овать** (**-ую**) *несов* to live in poverty
бе|жа́ть (*см Table 20*) *несов* to run; (*время*) to fly
бе́жевый *прил* beige
бе́жен|ец (**-ца**) *м* refugee
без *предл +gen* without; **без пяти́/десяти́ мину́т шесть** five to/ten to six
безала́берный *прил* (*разг*) sloppy
безалкого́льный *прил* nonalcoholic, alcohol-free; **безалкого́льный напи́ток** soft drink
безбиле́тник (**-а**) *м* fare dodger
безбо́жный *прил* (*разг*) shameless
безве́тренный *прил* calm
безвку́сный *прил* tasteless
безвла́сти|е (**-я**) *ср* anarchy
безвы́ходный *прил* hopeless
безгра́мотный *прил* illiterate; (*работник*) incompetent
безде́йств|овать (**-ую**) *несов* to stand idle; (*человек*) to take no action
безде́льнича|ть (**-ю**) *несов* (*разг*) to loaf *или* lounge about
бездо́мный *прил* (*человек*) homeless; (*собака*) stray
безду́мный *прил* thoughtless
безду́шный *прил* heartless
безе́ *ср нескл* meringue
безжа́лостный *прил* ruthless
беззабо́тный *прил* carefree
беззасте́нчивый *прил* shameless
беззащи́тный *прил* defenceless (*Brit*), defenseless (*US*)
безли́чный *прил* impersonal
безмо́лвный *прил* silent
безмяте́жный *прил* tranquil

безнадёжный *прил* hopeless
безнра́вственный *прил* immoral
безо *предл* = **без**
безоби́дный *прил* harmless
безобра́зный *прил* ugly; (*поступок*) outrageous, disgraceful
безогово́рочный *прил* unconditional
безопа́сност|ь (**-и**) *ж* safety; (*международная*) security
безопа́сный *прил* safe
безору́жный *прил* unarmed
безотве́тственный *прил* irresponsible
безотка́зный *прил* reliable
безотлага́тельный *прил* urgent
безотноси́тельно *нареч*: **безотноси́тельно к** *+dat* irrespective of
безоши́бочный *прил* correct
безрабо́тиц|а (**-ы**) *ж* unemployment
безрабо́тн|ый *прил* unemployed ▷ (**-ого**) *м* unemployed person
безразли́чный *прил* indifferent
безразме́рн|ый *прил*: **безразме́рные носки́** one-size socks
безрука́в|ка (**-ки**; *gen pl* **-ок**) *ж* (*кофта*) sleeveless top; (*куртка*) sleeveless jacket
безу́мный *прил* mad; (*о чувстве*) wild
безуспе́шный *прил* unsuccessful
безуча́стный *прил* indifferent
безымя́нный *прил* (*герой, автор*) anonymous; **безымя́нный па́лец** ring finger
бей(ся) *несов см* **бить(ся)**
Белару́с|ь (**-и**) *ж* Belarus
белору́с (**-а**) *м* Belorussian
беле́|ть (**-ю**; *perf* **побеле́ть**) *несов* (*лицо*) to go *или* turn white; (*no perf*: *цветы*) to show white
бели́л|а (**-**) *мн* emulsion *ед*
бел|и́ть (**-ю́, -ишь**; *perf* **побели́ть**) *несов перех* to whitewash
бе́л|ка (**-ки**; *gen pl* **-ок**) *ж* squirrel
бел|о́к (**-ка́**) *м* protein; (*яйца*) (egg) white; (*Анат*) white (of the eye)
белокро́ви|е (**-я**) *ср* (*Мед*) leukaemia (*Brit*), leukemia (*US*)
белоку́рый *прил* (*человек*) fair(-haired); (*волосы*) fair
бе́лый *прил* white; **бе́лый медве́дь** polar bear
Бе́льги|я (**-и**) *ж* Belgium
бель|ё (**-я́**) *ср собир* linen; **ни́жнее бельё** underwear
бельэта́ж (**-а**) *м* (*Театр*) dress circle
бемо́л|ь (**-я**) *м* (*Муз*) flat
бензи́н (**-а**) *м* petrol (*Brit*), gas (*US*)
бензоба́к (**-а**) *м* petrol (*Brit*) *или* gas (*US*) tank
бензоколо́н|ка (**-ки**; *gen pl* **-ок**) *ж* petrol (*Brit*) *или* gas (*US*) pump
бенуа́р (**-а**) *м* (*Театр*) boxes *мн*
бе́рег (**-а**; *loc sg* **-у́**, *nom pl* **-а́**) *м* (*моря, озера*) shore; (*реки*) bank
бе́режный *прил* caring
берёз|а (**-ы**) *ж* birch (tree)
берём *несов см* **брать**
бере́мене|ть (**-ю**; *perf* **забере́менеть**) *несов* to get pregnant
бере́менн|ая *прил* pregnant ▷ (**-ой**) *ж* pregnant woman
бере́менност|ь (**-и**) *ж* pregnancy
берёт *etc несов см* **брать**
бер|е́чь (**-егу́, -ежёшь** *etc*, **-егу́т**; *pt* **-ёг, -егла́**) *несов перех* (*здоровье, детей*) to look after,

take care of; (*деньги*) to be careful with; (*время*) to make good use of; **бере́чься** (*perf* **побере́чься**) *несов возв*: **бере́чься** +*gen* to watch out for; **береги́тесь!** watch out!

Берли́н (**-а**) *м* Berlin

беру́(сь) *etc несов см* **брать(ся)**

бесе́д|а (**-ы**) *ж* conversation; (*популярный доклад*) talk

бесе́д|ка (**-ки**; *gen pl* **-ок**) *ж* pavilion

бесе́д|овать (**-ую**) *несов*: **бесе́довать (с** +*instr*) to talk (to)

бесконта́ктный *прил* contactless

бесперспекти́вный *прил* (*работа*) without prospects

беспе́чный *прил* carefree

беспла́тный *прил* free

бесподо́бный *прил* (*разг*) fantastic

беспоко́|ить (**-ю, -ишь**) *несов перех* (*perf* **побеспоко́ить**) (*мешать*) to disturb, trouble ▷ (*perf* **обеспоко́ить**) (*тревожить*) to worry; **беспоко́иться** *несов возв* (*утруждать себя*) to trouble o.s.; (*тревожиться*): **беспоко́иться о** +*prp или* **за** +*acc* to worry about

беспоко́йный *прил* anxious; (*ребёнок*) restless; (*время*) troubled

беспоко́йств|о (**-а**) *ср* anxiety; (*хлопоты*) trouble; **прости́те за беспоко́йство!** sorry to trouble you!

бесполе́зный *прил* useless

беспо́мощный *прил* helpless

беспоря́дк|и (**-ов**) *мн* disturbances

беспоря́д|ок (**-ка**) *м* disorder; **в беспоря́дке** (*комната, дела*) in a mess; *см также* **беспоря́дки**

беспо́шлинный *прил* duty-free

беспоща́дный *прил* merciless

бespра́вный *прил* without (civil) rights

беспрецеде́нтный *прил* unprecedented

беспризо́рный *прил* homeless

беспристра́стный *прил* unbias(s)ed

беспроводны́й *прил* wireless; **беспроводна́я связь** Wi-Fi (connection)

бессерде́чный *прил* heartless

бесси́льный *прил* feeble, weak; (*гнев*) impotent; (*президент*) powerless

бессме́ртный *прил* immortal

бессодержа́тельный *прил* (*речь*) empty

бессозна́тельн|ый *прил* (*действия*) instinctive; **быть** (*impf*) **в бессозна́тельном состоя́нии** to be unconscious

бессо́нниц|а (**-ы**) *ж* insomnia

бесстра́шный *прил* fearless

бессты́дный *прил* shameless

беста́ктный *прил* tactless

бестолко́вый *прил* stupid

бестсе́ллер (**-а**) *м* best seller

бесхозя́йственный *прил* (*руководитель*) inefficient

бесцве́тный *прил* colourless (*Brit*), colorless (*US*)

бесце́нный *прил* priceless

бесце́нок *м*: **за бесце́нок** dirt cheap, for next to nothing

бесчи́сленный *прил* countless

бето́н (**-а**) *м* concrete

бетони́р|овать (**-ую**; *perf* **забетони́ровать**) *несов перех* to concrete

бефстро́ганов *м нескл* boeuf *или* beef stroganoff

бе́шенств|о (**-а**) *ср* (*Мед*) rabies; (*раздражение*) rage

бе́шеный *прил* (*взгляд*) furious;

(*характер, ураган*) violent; (*разг*: *цены*) crazy
Би-би-си *ж сокр* (= *Брита́нская радиовеща́тельная корпора́ция*) BBC (= *British Broadcasting Corporation*)
библиоте́к|а (**-и**) *ж* library
библиоте́кар|ь (**-я**) *м* librarian
библиоте́чный *прил* library
Би́бли|я (**-и**) *ж* the Bible
бигуди́ *ср/мн нескл* curlers *мн*
бижуте́ри|я (**-и**) *ж* costume jewellery
би́знес (**-а**) *м* business; **бизнесме́н** (**-а**) *м* businessman (*мн* businessmen)
бики́ни *ср нескл* bikini
биле́т (**-а**) *м* ticket; (*членский*) (membership) card; **обра́тный биле́т** return (*Brit*) *или* roundtrip (*US*) ticket; **входно́й биле́т** entrance ticket (*for standing room*)
биллио́н (**-а**) *м* billion (*one thousand million*)
бино́кл|ь (**-я**) *м* binoculars *мн*
бинт (**-а́**) *м* bandage; **бинт|ова́ть** (**-у́ю**; *perf* **забинтова́ть**) *несов перех* to bandage
биогра́фи|я (**-и**) *ж* biography
биоло́ги|я (**-и**) *ж* biology
би́рж|а (**-и**) *ж* (*Комм*) exchange; **фо́ндовая би́ржа** stock exchange *или* market; **биржеви́к** (**-а́**) *м* stockbroker
би́р|ка (**-ки**; *gen pl* **-ок**) *ж* tag
бирюз|а́ (**-ы́**) *ж* turquoise
бис *межд*: **Бис!** encore!
би́сер (**-а**) *м собир* glass beads *мн*
бискви́т (**-а**) *м* sponge (cake)
бит (**-а**) *м* (*Комп*) byte
би́тв|а (**-ы**) *ж* battle
бить (**бью, бьёшь**; *imper* **бей(те)**, *perf* **поби́ть**) *несов перех* to beat; (*стёкла*) to break ▷ (*perf* **проби́ть**) *неперех* (*часы*) to strike; **бить** (*impf*) **в** *+acc* (*в дверь*) to bang at; (*дождь, ветер*) to beat against; (*орудие*) to hit; **его́ бьёт озно́б** he's got a fit of the shivers; **би́ться** *несов возв* (*сердце*) to beat; (*стекло*) to be breakable; (*сражаться*) to fight; **би́ться** (*impf*) **о** *+acc* to bang against; **би́ться** (*impf*) **над** *+instr* (*над задачей*) to struggle with
бифште́кс (**-а**) *м* steak
бла́г|а (-) *мн* rewards *мн*; **всех благ!** all the best!
бла́г|о (**-а**) *ср* benefit; *см также* **бла́га**
благови́дный *прил* plausible
благодар|и́ть (**-ю́, -и́шь**; *perf* **поблагодари́ть**) *несов перех* to thank
благода́рност|ь (**-и**) *ж* gratitude, thanks *мн*
благода́р|ный *прил* grateful; (*тема*) rewarding; **я Вам о́чень благода́рен** I am very grateful to you
благодаря́ *предл +dat* thanks to ▷ *союз*: **благодаря́ тому́, что** owing to the fact that
благ|о́й *прил*: **благи́е наме́рения** good intentions *мн*
благополу́чи|е (**-я**) *ср* (*в семье*) welfare; (*материальное*) prosperity
благополу́чный *прил* successful; **благополу́чная семья́** good family
благоприя́тный *прил* favourable (*Brit*), favorable (*US*)
благоразу́мный *прил* prudent
благоро́дный *прил* noble
благослов|и́ть (**-лю́, -и́шь**; *impf* **благословля́ть**) *сов перех* to bless
благотвори́тельност|ь (**-и**) *ж* charity; **благотвори́тельн|ый**

прил charitable; **благотвори́тельная организа́ция** charity (organization); **благотвори́тельный конце́рт** charity concert
благоустро́енный *прил* (*дом*) *with all modern conveniences*
блаже́нств|о (**-а**) *ср* bliss
бланк (**-а**) *м* form; (*организации*) headed notepaper
блат (**-а**) *м* (*разг*) connections *мн*; **по бла́ту** (*разг*) through (one's) connections
бледне́|ть (**-ю**; *perf* **побледне́ть**) *несов* to (grow) pale
бле́дный *прил* pale; (*перен*) dull
блесн|у́ть (**-у́, -ёшь**) *сов* to flash; (*на экзамене*) to do brilliantly
бле|сте́ть (**-щу́, -сти́шь** *или*, **-щешь**) *несов* (*звёзды, металл*) to shine; (*глаза*) to sparkle
ближа́йший *прил* (*город, дом*) the nearest; (*год*) the next; (*планы*) immediate; (*друг, участие*) closest; **ближа́йший ро́дственник** next of kin
бли́же *сравн прил от* **бли́зкий** ▷ *сравн нареч от* **бли́зко**
бли́жний *прил* (*город*) neighbouring; **бли́жнее зарубе́жье** former Soviet republics; **Бли́жний Восто́к** Middle East
бли́зк|ие (**-их**) *мн* relatives *мн*
бли́зкий *прил* close; (*конец*) imminent; **бли́зкий кому́-н** (*интересы, тема*) close to sb's heart; **бли́зкий по** +*dat* (*по содержанию, по цели*) similar *или* close in; **бли́зко** *нареч* near *или* close by ▷ *как сказ* not far off; **бли́зко от** +*gen* near, close to
близне́ц (**-а́**) *м* (*обычно мн*) twin; **бра́тья/сёстры-близнецы́** twin brothers/sisters
Близнец|ы́ (**-о́в**) *мн* Gemini *ед*
близору́кий *прил* short-sighted (*Brit*), nearsighted (*US*)
блин (**-а́**) *м* pancake
блог (**-а**) *ж* blog; **бло́гер** (**-а**) *м* blogger
блок (**-а**) *м* bloc; (*Тех*) unit
блока́д|а (**-ы**) *ж* (*Воен*) siege; (*экономическая*) blockade
блоки́р|овать (**-ую**) *(не)сов перех* to block; (*город*) to blockade
блонди́н (**-а**) *м*: **он — блонди́н** he is blond; **блонди́н|ка** (**-ки**; *gen pl* **-ок**) *ж* blonde
блох|а́ (**-и́**; *nom pl* **-и**) *ж* flea
блужда́|ть (**-ю**) *несов* to wander *или* roam (around)
блю́д|о (**-а**) *ср* dish
блю|сти́ (**-ду́, -дёшь**; *pt* **-л, -ла́, -ло́**, *perf* **соблюсти́**) *несов перех* (*интересы*) to guard; (*чистоту*) to maintain
боб (**-а́**) *м* (*обычно мн*) bean
бобр (**-а́**) *м* beaver
Бог (**-а**; *voc* **Бо́же**) *м* God; **не дай Бог!** God forbid!; **ра́ди Бо́га!** for God's sake!; **сла́ва Бо́гу** (*к счастью*) thank God
богате́|ть (**-ю**; *perf* **разбогате́ть**) *несов* to become rich
бога́тств|а (**-**) *мн* (*природные*) resources
бога́тств|о (**-а**) *ср* wealth, riches *мн*; *см также* **бога́тства**
бога́тый *прил* rich; **бога́тый урожа́й** bumper harvest
богаты́р|ь (**-я́**) *м* *warrior hero of Russian folk epics*; (*перен*) Hercules
бога́ч (**-а́**) *м* rich man (*мн* men)
боги́н|я (**-и**) *ж* goddess
Богоро́диц|а (**-ы**) *ж* the Virgin Mary

богосло́ви|е (**-я**) *ср* theology
богослуже́ни|е (**-я**) *ср* service
боготвор|и́ть (**-ю́, -и́шь**) *несов перех* to worship
бо́дрый *прил* energetic; (*настроение, музыка*) cheerful
боеви́к (**-а́**) *м* militant; (*фильм*) action movie
боево́й *прил* military; (*настроение, дух*) fighting
боеприпа́с|ы (**-ов**) *мн* ammunition *ед*
бо|е́ц (**-йца́**) *м* (*солдат*) soldier
Бо́же *сущ см* **Бог** ▷ *межд*: **Бо́же (ты мой)!** good Lord *или* God!; **Бо́же! кака́я красота́!** God, it's beautiful!; **Бо́же упаси́** (*разг*) God forbid; **боже́ственный** *прил* divine; **Бо́ж|ий** *прил* God's; **ка́ждый бо́жий день** (*разг*) every single day; **бо́жья коро́вка** ladybird
бо|й (**-я**; *loc sg* **-ю́**, *nom pl* **-и́**, *gen pl* **-ёв**) *м* battle; (*боксёров*) fight; (*барабанов*) beating; (*часов*) striking
бо́йкий *прил* (*речь, ответ*) quick; (*продавец*) smart; (*место*) busy
бойко́т (**-а**) *м* boycott
бойкоти́р|овать (**-ую**) *(не)сов перех* to boycott
бок (**-а**; *loc sg* **-у́**, *nom pl* **-а́**) *м* side
бо́ком *нареч* sideways
бокс (**-а**) *м* (*Спорт*) boxing; (*Мед*) isolation ward
боксёр (**-а**) *м* boxer
Болга́ри|я (**-и**) *ж* Bulgaria
бо́лее *нареч* more; **бо́лее или ме́нее** more or less; **бо́лее того́** what's more; **тем бо́лее** all the more so
боле́зненный *прил* sickly; (*укол*) painful; (*перен*: *подозрительность*) unhealthy; (*самолюбие*) unnatural
боле́зн|ь (**-и**) *ж* illness; (*заразная*) disease
боле́льщик (**-а**) *м* fan
бол|е́ть (**-е́ю**) *несов*: **боле́ть** (*+instr*) to be ill (with); (*Спорт*): **боле́ть за** *+acc* to be a fan of ▷ (*3sg* **-и́т**) (*руки итп*) to ache
болеутоля́ющ|ий *прил*: **болеутоля́ющее сре́дство** painkiller
боло́нь|я (**-и**) *ж* (*ткань*) *lightweight waterproof material*
боло́т|о (**-а**) *ср* marsh, bog
болт (**-а́**) *м* bolt
болта́|ть (**-ю**) *несов перех* (*разг*: *вздор*) to talk ▷ *неперех* (*разговаривать*) to chat; (: *много*) to chatter; **болта́ть** (*impf*) **нога́ми** to dangle one's legs
бол|ь (**-и**) *ж* pain; **зубна́я боль** toothache; **головна́я боль** headache
больни́ц|а (**-ы**) *ж* hospital
больни́чный *прил* hospital; **больни́чный лист** medical certificate
бо́льно *нареч* (*удариться, упасть*) badly, painfully; (*обидеть*) deeply; **бо́льно!** that hurts!; **мне бо́льно** I am in pain
больн|о́й *прил* (*рука итп*) sore; (*воображение*) morbid; (*нездоров*) ill, sick ▷ (**-о́го**) *м* (*болеющий*) sick person; (*пациент*) patient; **больно́й вопро́с** a sore point
бо́льше *сравн прил от* **большо́й** ▷ *сравн нареч от* **мно́го** ▷ *нареч* (*+gen*: *часа, килограмма итп*) more than; (*не хотеть, не жить*) anymore; **бо́льше не бу́ду** (*разг*) I won't do it again; **бо́льше так не де́лай** don't do that again
большинств|о́ (**-а́**) *ср* majority

больш|о́й *прил* big, large; (*радость*) great; (*дети*) grown-up; **бо́льшей ча́стью, по бо́льшей ча́сти** for the most part; **больша́я бу́ква** capital letter

боля́ч|ка (**-ки**; *gen pl* **-ек**) *ж* sore

бо́мб|а (**-ы**) *ж* bomb

бомбардиро́вщик (**-а**) *м* bomber

бомб|и́ть (**-лю́, -и́шь**) *несов перех* to bomb

бомбоубе́жищ|е (**-а**) *ср* bomb shelter

бомж (**-а́**) *м* homeless person

бордо́вый *прил* dark red, wine colour

бордю́р (**-а**) *м* (*тротуара*) kerb (*Brit*), curb (*US*); (*салфетки*) border

борм|ота́ть (**-очу́, -о́чешь**) *несов перех* to mutter

бор|ода́ (*acc sg* **-оду**, *gen sg* **-оды́**, *nom pl* **-оды**, *gen pl* **-о́д**, *dat pl* **-ода́м**) *ж* beard

борода́в|ка (**-ки**; *gen pl* **-ок**) *ж* wart

бор|о́ться (**-ю́сь, -ешься**) *несов возв* (*Спорт*) to wrestle; **боро́ться** (*impf*) (**с** *+instr*) to fight (with *или* against)

борт (**-а**; *acc sg* **за́ борт** *или* **за бо́рт**, *instr sg* **за бо́ртом** *или* **за борто́м**, *loc sg* **-у́**, *nom pl* **-а́**) *м* side; **на борту́** *или* **борт** on board, aboard; **челове́к за борто́м**! man overboard!

бортпроводни́к (**-а́**) *м* steward (*on plane*); **бортпроводни́ц|а** (**-ы**) *ж* air hostess, stewardess (*on plane*)

борщ (**-а́**) *м* borsch (*beetroot-based soup*)

борьб|а́ (**-ы́**) *ж* (*за мир*) fight, struggle; (*Спорт*) wrestling

босико́м *нареч* barefoot

бос́ой *прил* barefoot

боти́н|ок (**-ка**) *м* (*обычно мн*) ankle boot

бо́ч|ка (**-ки**; *gen pl* **-ек**) *ж* barrel

бо|я́ться (**-ю́сь, -и́шься**) *несов возв*: **боя́ться** (*+gen*) to be afraid (of) *+infin* to be afraid of doing *или* to do

бразды́ *мн*: **бразды́ правле́ния** the reins of power

брак (**-а**) *м* (*супружество*) marriage; (*продукция*) rejects *мн*; (*деффект*) flaw

брако́ванный *прил* reject

брак|ова́ть (**-у́ю**; *perf* **забракова́ть**) *несов перех* to reject

бракосочета́ни|е (**-я**) *ср* marriage ceremony

бран|и́ть (**-ю́, -и́шь**) *несов* to scold

брат (**-а**; *nom pl* **-ья**, *gen pl* **-ьев**) *м* brother; **двою́родный брат** cousin

бра|ть (**беру́, берёшь**; *pt* **-л, -ла́, -ло**, *perf* **взять**) *несов перех* to take; (*билет*) to get; (*работника*) to take on; (*барьер*) to clear; (*разг*: *арестовать*) to nick; **бра́ться** (*perf* **взя́ться**) *несов возв*: **бра́ться за** *+acc* (*хватать рукой*) to take hold of; (*за работу*) to get down to; (*за книгу*) to begin; (*за решение проблемы*) to take on; **бра́ться** (*perf* **взя́ться**) **за ум** to see sense

бра́тья *etc сущ см* **брат**

бревн|о́ (**-а́**; *nom pl* **брёвна**, *gen pl* **брёвен**) *ср* log; (*Спорт*) the beam

бре́|дить (**-жу, -дишь**) *несов* to be delirious; **бре́дить** (*impf*) **кем-н/чем-н** to be mad about sb/sth

бре́зг|овать (**-ую**; *perf* **побре́зговать**) *несов +instr* to be fastidious about

бре́м|я (**-ени**; *как* **вре́мя**; см *Table 4*) *ср* burden
бригади́р (**-а**) *м* team leader
бриллиа́нт (**-а**) *м* (cut) diamond
брита́н|ец (**-ца**) *м* Briton; **брита́нцы** the British
Брита́ни|я (**-и**) *ж* Britain
брита́нский *прил* British
бри́тв|а (**-ы**) *ж* razor; **безопа́сная бри́тва** safety razor
бр|ить (**-е́ю, -е́ешь**; *perf* **побри́ть**) *несов перех* (*человека*) to shave; (*бороду*) to shave off; **бри́ться** (*perf* **побри́ться**) *несов возв* to shave
бри́финг (**-а**) *м* briefing
бров|ь (**-и**; *gen pl* **-е́й**) *ж* eyebrow
бро|ди́ть (**-жу́, -дишь**) *несов* to wander
бродя́г|а (**-и**) *м/ж* tramp
бро́кер (**-а**) *м* broker
бронежиле́т (**-а**) *м* bullet-proof jacket
бронетранспортёр (**-а**) *м* armoured (*Brit*) *или* armored (*US*) personnel carrier
бро́нз|а (**-ы**) *ж* bronze
брони́р|овать (**-ую**; *perf* **заброни́ровать**) *(не)сов перех* to reserve
бронх (**-а**) *м* bronchial tube
бронхи́т (**-а**) *м* bronchitis
бро́н|я (**-и**) *ж* reservation
брон|я́ (**-и́**) *ж* armour (*Brit*) *или* armor (*US*) plating
броса́|ть (**-ю**) *несов от* **бро́сить**; **броса́ться** *несов от* **бро́ситься** ▷ *возв*: **броса́ться снежка́ми/камня́ми** to throw snowballs/stones at each other
бро́|сить (**-шу, -сишь**; *impf* **броса́ть**) *сов перех* (*камень, мяч итп*) to throw; (*якорь, сети*) to cast; (*семью, друга*) to abandon; (*войска*) to dispatch; (*спорт*) to give up; **меня́ бро́сило в жар** I broke out in a sweat; **броса́ть** (*perf* **бро́сить**) *+infin* to give up doing; **бро́ситься** (*impf* **броса́ться**) *сов возв*: **бро́ситься на** *+acc* (*на врага*) to throw o.s. at; **броса́ться** (*perf* **бро́ситься**) **в ата́ку** to rush to the attack
бро́ш|ка (**-ки**; *gen pl* **-ек**) *ж* brooch; **брош|ь** (**-и**) *ж* = **бро́шка**
брошю́р|а (**-ы**) *ж* (*книжка*) booklet
брус (**-а**; *nom pl* **-ья**, *gen pl* **-ьев**) *м* beam; *см также* **бру́сья**
бру́сь|я (**-ев**) *мн* parallel bars *мн*
бру́тто *прил неизм* gross
бры́з|гать (**-жу, -жешь**) *несов* to splash ▷ (**-гаю**) (*опрыскивать*): **бры́згать на** *+acc* to spray
бры́зг|и (-) *мн* splashes; (*мелкие*) spray *ед*
бры́нз|а (**-ы**) *ж* feta cheese
брю́кв|а (**-ы**) *ж* swede
брю́к|и (-) *мн* trousers, pants (*US*)
брюне́т (**-а**) *м*: **он брюне́т** he has dark hair; **брюне́т|ка** (**-ки**; *gen pl* **-ок**) *ж* brunette
Брюссе́л|ь (**-я**) *м* Brussels
БТР *сокр* = **бронетранспортёр**
бу́блик (**-а**) *м* ≈ bagel
бу́б|ны (**-ён**; *dat pl* **-нам**) *мн* (*Карты*) diamonds
буг|о́р (**-ра́**) *м* mound; (*на коже*) lump
Будапе́шт (**-а**) *м* Budapest
бу́дем *несов см* **быть**
бу́дет *несов см* **быть** ▷ *част* that's enough; **бу́дет тебе́!** that's enough from you!
бу́дешь *etc несов см* **быть**
буди́льник (**-а**) *м* alarm clock
бу|ди́ть (**-жу́, -дишь**; *perf* **разбуди́ть**) *несов перех* to wake (up), awaken
бу́д|ка (**-ки**; *gen pl* **-ок**) *ж*

б

(*сторожа*) hut; (*для собаки*) kennel; **телефо́нная бу́дка** telephone box

бу́дн|и (**-ей**) *мн* working *или* week days; (*перен*: *повседневность*) routine *ед*

бу́дто *союз* (*якобы*) supposedly; (*словно*): **(как) бу́дто (бы)** as if; **он уверя́ет, бу́дто сам её ви́дел** he claims to have seen her himself

бу́ду *etc несов см* **быть**

бу́дущ|ее (**-его**) *ср* the future; **в бу́дущем** in the future

бу́дущ|ий *прил* (*следующий*) next; (*предстоящий*) future; **бу́дущее вре́мя** future tense

бу́дь(те) *несов см* **быть** ▷ *союз*: **будь то** be it

буженин|а (**-ы**) *ж* *cold cooked and seasoned pork*

бу|й (**-я**; *nom pl* **-и́**) *м* buoy

бу́йвол (**-а**) *м* buffalo

бук (**-а**) *м* beech

бу́кв|а (**-ы**) *ж* letter

буква́льный *прил* literal

буква́р|ь (**-я́**) *м* first reading book

буке́т (**-а**) *м* bouquet

букинисти́ческий *прил*: **букинисти́ческий магази́н** second-hand bookshop

букле́т (**-а**) *м* booklet

була́в|ка (**-ки**; *gen pl* **-ок**) *ж* pin

бу́л|ка (**-ки**; *gen pl* **-ок**) *ж* roll; (*белый хлеб*) loaf; **бу́лоч|ка** (**-ки**; *gen pl* **-ек**) *ж* small roll

бу́лочн|ая (**-ой**) *ж* baker, baker's (shop)

булы́жн|ый *прил*: **булы́жная мостова́я** cobbled street

бульдо́зер (**-а**) *м* bulldozer

бульо́н (**-а**; *part gen* **-у**) *м* stock

бум (**-а**) *м* boom

бума́г|а (**-и**) *ж* paper; **це́нные бума́ги** securities

бума́ж|ка (**-ки**; *gen pl* **-ек**) *ж* piece of paper

бума́жник (**-а**) *м* wallet, pocketbook (*US*)

бума́жный *прил* paper

бу́нкер (**-а**) *м* bunker

бунт (**-а**) *м* (*мятеж*) riot; (*: на корабле*) mutiny

бунт|ова́ть (**-у́ю**) *несов* (*см сущ*) to riot; to mutiny

бура́в|ить (**-лю, -ишь**; *perf* **пробура́вить**) *несов перех* to drill

бур|и́ть (**-ю́, -и́шь**; *perf* **пробури́ть**) *несов перех* to bore, drill

бу́рный *прил* (*погода, океан*) stormy; (*чувство*) wild; (*рост*) rapid

бу́рый *прил* brown

бу́р|я (**-и**) *ж* storm

бу́с|ы (**-**) *мн* beads

бутафо́ри|я (**-и**) *ж* (*Театр*) props *мн* (= *properties*); (*перен*) sham

бутербро́д (**-а**) *м* sandwich

буто́н (**-а**) *м* bud

бу́тс|а (**-ы**) *ж* football boot

буты́л|ка (**-ки**; *gen pl* **-ок**) *ж* bottle

бу́фер (**-а**; *nom pl* **-а́**) *м* buffer

буфе́т (**-а**) *м* snack bar; (*шкаф*) sideboard

буфе́тчик (**-а**) *м* barman, barmen *мн*

буха́н|ка (**-ки**; *gen pl* **-ок**) *ж* loaf

Бухаре́ст (**-а**) *м* Bucharest

бу́хт|а (**-ы**) *ж* bay

буш|ева́ть (**-у́ю**) *несов* (*пожар, ураган*) to rage

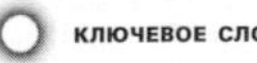

бы *част* **1** (*выражает возможность*): **купи́л бы, е́сли бы бы́ли де́ньги** I would buy it if I had the money; **я бы давно́ уже́ купи́л э́ту кни́гу, е́сли бы у меня́ бы́ли де́ньги** I would have bought this

book long ago if I had had the money
2 (*выражает пожелание*): **я бы хотéл поговори́ть с тобóй** I would like to speak to you
3 (*выражает совет*): **ты бы написáл ей** you should write to her
4 (*выражает опасение*): **не захвати́л бы нас дождь** I hope we don't get caught in the rain; **отдохну́ть/погуля́ть бы** it would be nice to have a rest/go for a walk

бывáло *част expresses repeated action in the past*; **бывáло сиди́м и разговáриваем** we used to *или* would sit and talk
бывá|ть (**-ю**) *несов* (*посещать*) to be; (*случаться*) to happen, take place; **он бывáет у нас чáсто** he often comes to see us; **как ни в чём не бывáло** (*разг*) as if nothing had happened
бы́вший *прил* former
бык (**-á**) *м* bull; (*рабочий*) ox
был *etc несов см* **быть**
были́н|а (**-ы**) *ж* heroic poem
был|ь (**-и**) *ж* true story
бы́стро *нареч* quickly
бы́стрый *прил* (*машина итп*) fast; (*руки, взгляд, речь*) quick
быт (**-а**; *loc sg* **-ý**) *м* life; (*повседневность*) everyday life; **слу́жба бы́та** consumer services
бытов|óй *прил* everyday; **бытовóе обслу́живание населéния** consumer services; **бытовáя тéхника** household electrical appliances

 **КЛЮЧЕВОЕ СЛОВО**

быть (см *Table 21*) *несов*
1 (*omitted in present tense*) to be; **кни́га на столé** the book is on the table; **зáвтра я бу́ду в шкóле** I will be at school tomorrow; **дом был на краю́ гóрода** the house was *или* stood on the edge of the town; **на ней краси́вое плáтье** she is wearing a beautiful dress; **вчерá был дождь** it rained yesterday
2 (*часть составного сказ*) to be; **я хочу́ быть учи́телем** I want to be a teacher; **я был рад ви́деть тебя́** I was happy to see you; **так и быть!** so be it!; **как быть?** what is to be done?; **э́того не мóжет быть** that's impossible; **кто/какóй бы то ни был** whoever/whatever it might be; **бу́дьте добры́!** excuse me!; **бу́дьте добры́, позови́те егó!** would you be so good *или* kind as to call him?; **бу́дьте здорóвы!** take care!
3 (*образует будущее время*) *+impf vb*; **вéчером я бу́ду писáть пи́сьма** I'll be writing letters this evening; **я бу́ду люби́ть тебя́ всегдá** I'll love you forever

бью(сь) *etc несов см* **бить(ся)**
бюджéт (**-а**) *м* budget; **дохóдный бюджéт** revenue; **расхóдный бюджéт** expenditure
бюджéтник (**-а**) *м person working in a state-funded institution*
бюллетéн|ь (**-я**) *м* bulletin; (*на выборах*) ballot paper; (*справка*) medical certificate
бюрó *ср нескл* office; **бюрó нахóдок** lost property office
бюрокрáт (**-а**) *м* bureaucrat
бюрокрáти|я (**-и**) *ж* bureaucracy
бюст (**-а**) *м* bust
бюстгáльтер (**-а**) *м* bra (= *brassiere*)

В

КЛЮЧЕВОЕ СЛОВО

в *предл +acc* **1** (*о месте направления*) in(to); **я положи́л кни́гу в портфе́ль** I put the book in(to) my briefcase; **я сел в маши́ну** I got in(to) the car
2 (*уехать, пойти*) to; **он уе́хал в Москву́** he went to Moscow
3 (*об изменении состояния*): **погружа́ться в рабо́ту** to be absorbed in one's work
4 (*об объекте физического действия*): **он постуча́л в дверь** he knocked on the door; **он посмотре́л мне в глаза́** he looked me in the eyes; **мать поцелова́ла меня́ в щёку** mother kissed me on the cheek
5 (*о времени совершения чего-н*): **он пришёл в понеде́льник** he came on Monday; **я ви́дел его́ в про́шлом году́** I saw him last year; **я встре́тил его́ в два часа́** I met him at two o'clock; **э́то случи́лось в ма́рте/в двадца́том ве́ке** it happened in March/in the twentieth century
6 (*о размере, количестве*): **ве́сом в 3 то́нны** 3 tons *или* tonnes in weight: *+prp*; **дра́ма в трёх частя́х** a drama in three acts; **в пяти́ ме́трах от доро́ги** five metres (*Brit*) *или* meters (*US*) from the road
7 (*о соотношении величин*): **в два раза́ бо́льше/длинне́е** twice as big/long; **во мно́го раз лу́чше/умне́е** much better/cleverer
8 (*обозначает форму, вид*): **брю́ки в клётку** checked trousers; **лека́рство в табле́тках** medicine in tablet form
9 (*+prp: о месте*) in; **ко́шка сиди́т в корзи́не** the cat is sitting in the basket; **я живу́ в дере́вне** I live in the country; **сын у́чится в шко́ле** my son is at school
10 (*о чём-н облегающем, покрывающем*): **ру́ки в кра́ске/са́же** hands covered in paint/soot; **това́р в упако́вке** packaged goods
11 (*об одежде*) in; **мужчи́на в очка́х/в ша́пке** a man in *или* wearing glasses/a hat
12 (*о состоянии*): **быть в у́жасе/негодова́нии** to be terrified/indignant

в. *сокр* (= *век*) c (= *century*); (= *восто́к*) E (= *East*)
ваго́н (**-а**) *м* (*пассажирский*) carriage (*Brit*), coach (*Brit*), car (*US*); (*товарный*) wagon (*Brit*), truck; **спа́льный ваго́н** couchette car; **мя́гкий ваго́н** ≈ sleeping car;

ваго́н-рестора́н dining (*Brit*) *или* club (*US*) car
ва́жный *прил* important
ва́з|а (**-ы**) *ж* vase
вазели́н (**-а**) *м* Vaseline
вака́нси|я (**-и**) *ж* vacancy
вака́нтн|ый *прил* vacant; **вака́нтная до́лжность** vacancy
ва́куум (**-а**) *м* vacuum
вакци́н|а (**-ы**) *ж* vaccine
вакцини́р|овать (**-ую**) *(не)сов перех* to vaccinate
ва́лен|ок (**-ка**) *м* felt boot
валериа́нк|а (**-и**) *ж* valerian drops *мн*
вале́т (**-а**) *м* (*Карты*) jack
вал|и́ть (**-ю́, -ишь**; *perf* **свали́ть** *или* **повали́ть**) *несов перех* (*заставить падать*) to knock over; (*рубить*) to fell ▷ (*perf* **свали́ть**) (*разг*: *бросать*) to dump ▷ *неперех* (*дым, пар*) to pour out; **вали́ть** (*perf* **свали́ть**) **вину́ на** *+acc* (*разг*) to point the finger at; **вали́ться** (*perf* **свали́ться** *или* **повали́ться**) *несов возв* (*падать*) to fall; **вали́ться** (*impf*) **с ног** (*разг*) to be dead on one's feet
валово́й *прил* (*доход*) gross
валу́н (**-а́**) *м* boulder
вальс (**-а**) *м* waltz
валю́т|а (**-ы**) *ж* currency ▷ *собир* foreign currency
валю́тный *прил* currency; **валю́тный курс** rate of exchange
валя́|ть (**-ю**) *несов перех* (*катать*) to roll ▷ (*perf* **сваля́ть**) (*скатывать*) to shape; **валя́ться** *несов возв* (*кататься*) to roll about; (*разг*: *человек, бумаги итп*) to lie about
вам *etc мест см* **вы**
вампи́р (**-а**) *м* vampire
вани́л|ь (**-и**) *ж* vanilla
ва́нн|а (**-ы**) *ж* bath; **ва́нн|ая** (**-ой**) *ж* bathroom
варёный *прил* boiled
варе́нь|е (**-я**) *ср* jam
вариа́нт (**-а**) *м* variant
вар|и́ть (**-ю́, -ишь**; *perf* **свари́ть**) *несов перех* (*обед*) to cook; (*суп, кофе*) to make; (*картофель*) to boil; (*Тех*) to weld; **вари́ться** (*perf* **свари́ться**) *несов возв* (*обед*) to be cooking
Варша́в|а (**-ы**) *ж* Warsaw
варьете́ *ср нескл* variety show
варьи́р|овать (**-ую**) *несов (не) перех* to vary
вас *мест см* **вы**
ва́т|а (**-ы**) *ж* cotton wool (*Brit*), (absorbent) cotton (*US*)
ва́тман (**-а**) *м* *heavy paper for drawing etc*
ва́тный *прил* cotton-wool (*Brit*), absorbent cotton (*US*)
ватру́ш|ка (**-ки**; *gen pl* **-ек**) *ж* curd tart
ватт (**-а**) *м* watt
ва́учер (**-а**) *м* voucher
ва́хт|а (**-ы**) *ж* watch; **стоя́ть** (*impf*) **на ва́хте** to keep watch
вахтёр (**-а**) *м* caretaker, janitor (*esp US, Scottish*)
ваш (**-его**; *f* **-а**, *nt* **-е**, *pl* **-и**; *как* **наш**; *см Table 9*) *притяж мест* your; **э́то ва́ше** this is yours
вбе|жа́ть (*как* **бежа́ть**; *см Table 20*; *impf* **вбега́ть**) *сов*: **вбежа́ть** (**в** *+acc*) to run in(to)
вбить (**вобью́, вобьёшь**; *impf* **вбива́ть**) *сов перех*: **вбить** (**в** *+acc*) to drive *или* hammer in(to)
вблизи́ *нареч* nearby ▷ *предл*: **вблизи́** *+gen или* **от** *+gen* near (to)
вбок *нареч* sideways
вбро́|сить (**-шу, -сишь**; *impf* **вбра́сывать**) *сов перех* to throw in
ввал|и́ться (**-ю́сь, -ишься**; *impf*

вва́ливаться) *сов возв* (*щеки, глаза*) to become sunken
введе́ни|е (**-я**) *ср* introduction
ввез|ти́ (**-у́, -ёшь**; *pt* **ввёз, -ла́, -ло́**, *impf* **ввози́ть**) *сов перех* (*в дом итп*) to take in; (*в страну*) to import
вверх *нареч* up ▷ *предл*: **вверх по** *+dat* up; **вверх по тече́нию** upstream; **в до́ме всё вверх дном** (*разг*) everything in the house is topsy-turvy; **вверх нога́ми** (*разг*) upside down
вверху́ *нареч* up ▷ *предл +gen* at the top of
вв|ести́ (**-еду́, -едёшь**; *pt* **-ёл, -ела́**, *impf* **вводи́ть**) *сов перех* to take in; (*лекарство*) to inject; (*в компьютер*) to enter; (*закон*) to introduce; (*сделать действующим*): **ввести́ что-н в** *+acc* to put sth into
ввиду́ *предл +gen* in view of ▷ *союз*: **ввиду́ того́, что** in view of the fact that
ввод (**-а**) *м* bringing in; (*данных*) input, feeding in
вво|ди́ть (**-жу́, -дишь**) *несов от* **ввести́**
вво|зи́ть (**-жу́, -зишь**) *несов от* **ввезти́**
вглубь *нареч* (down) into the depths ▷ *предл* (*+gen*: *вниз*) into the depths of; (*внутрь*) into the heart of
вда|ва́ться (**-ю́сь**) *несов от* **вда́ться**
вдав|и́ть (**-лю́, -ишь**; *impf* **вда́вливать**) *сов перех*: **вдави́ть** (**в** *+acc*) to press in(to)
вдалеке́ *нареч* in the distance; **вдалеке́ от** *+gen* a long way from
вдали́ *нареч* = **вдалеке́**
вдаль *нареч* into the distance
вда́ться (*как* **дать**; см *Table 16*; *impf* **вдава́ться**) *сов возв*: **вда́ться в** *+acc* to jut out into; (*перен*: *в рассуждения*) to get caught up in; **вдава́ться** (*perf* **вда́ться**) **в подро́бности** to go into details
вдво́е *нареч* (*сложить*) in two; **вдво́е сильне́е** twice as strong
вдвоём *нареч*: **они́ живу́т вдвоём** the two of them live together
вдвойне́ *нареч* double (the amount)
вде|ть (**-ну, -нешь**; *impf* **вдева́ть**) *сов перех* to put in
вдоба́вок *нареч* (*разг*) in addition ▷ *предл*: **вдоба́вок к** *+dat* in addition to
вдов|а́ (**-ы́**; *nom pl* **-ы**) *ж* widow
вдов|е́ц (**-ца́**) *м* widower
вдо́воль *нареч* to one's heart's content
вдоль *нареч* (*сломаться*) lengthways ▷ *предл +gen* along
вдохнове́ни|е (**-я**) *ср* inspiration
вдохнов|и́ть (**-лю́, -и́шь**; *impf* **вдохновля́ть**) *сов перех* to inspire
вдохн|у́ть (**-у́**; *impf* **вдыха́ть**) *сов перех* (*воздух*) to breathe in; (*дым, лекарство*) to inhale
вдре́безги *нареч* to smithereens
вдруг *нареч* suddenly; (*а если*) what if
вду́ма|ться (**-юсь**; *impf* **вду́мываться**) *сов возв*: **вду́маться в** *+acc* to think over
вдыха́|ть (**-ю**) *несов от* **вдохну́ть**
веб-а́дрес (**-а**; *nom pl* **-а́**) *м* web address
веб-ка́мер|а (**-ы**) *ж* webcam
вегетариа́н|ец (**-ца**) *м* vegetarian
вегетариа́нский *прил* vegetarian

В

ве́да|ть (**-ю**) *несов* (*+instr*: *управлять*) to be in charge of
ве́дени|е (**-я**) *ср* authority
ведёт(ся) *etc несов см* **вести́(сь)**
ве́дом|о *ср*: **с/без ве́дома кого́-н** (*согласие*) with/without sb's consent; (*уведомление*) with/without sb's knowledge
ве́домств|о (**-а**) *ср* department
ведр|о́ (**-а́**; *nom pl* **вёдра**, *gen pl* **вёдер**) *ср* bucket, pail
веду́щ|ий *прил* leading ▷ (**-его**) *м* presenter
ведь *нареч* (*в вопросе*): **ведь ты хо́чешь пое́хать?** you do want to go, don't you?; (*в утверждении*): **ведь она́ не спра́вится одна́!** she can't surely manage alone! ▷ *союз* (*о причине*) seeing as; **пое́шь, ведь ты го́лоден** you should eat, seeing as you're hungry
ве́дьм|а (**-ы**) *ж* witch
ве́ер (**-а**; *nom pl* **-а́**) *м* fan
ве́жливый *прил* polite
везде́ *нареч* everywhere; **везде́ и всю́ду** everywhere you go
вездехо́д (**-а**) *м* ≈ Landrover
везе́ни|е (**-я**) *ср* luck
вез|ти́ (**-у́, -ёшь**) *несов перех* to transport, take; (*сани*) to pull; (*тачку*) to push ▷ (*perf* **повезти́**) *безл* (*+dat*: *разг*) to be lucky
век (**-а**; *nom pl* **-а́**) *м* century; (*период*) age; **на века́, во ве́ки веко́в** forever
ве́к|о (**-а**) *ср* eyelid
векови́й *прил* ancient
ве́ксел|ь (**-я**; *nom pl* **-я́**) *м* promissory note
вел|е́ть (**-ю́, -и́шь**) *(не)сов +dat* to order
велика́н (**-а**) *м* giant
вели́к|ий *прил* great ▷ *как сказ*: **сапоги́ мне велики́** the boots are too big for me; **вели́кие держа́вы** the Great Powers
Великобрита́ни|я (**-и**) *ж* Great Britain
великоду́шный *прил* magnanimous, big-hearted
великору́сский *прил* Great Russian
великоле́пный *прил* magnificent
величин|а́ (**-ы́**) *ж* size; (*Мат*) quantity
велого́н|ка (**-ки**; *gen pl* **-ок**) *ж* cycle race
велосипе́д (**-а**) *м* bicycle
вельве́т (**-а**) *м* corduroy
Ве́н|а (**-ы**) *ж* Vienna
ве́н|а (**-ы**) *ж* vein
Ве́нгри|я (**-и**) *ж* Hungary
вен|о́к (**-ка́**) *м* wreath
вентиля́тор (**-а**) *м* (ventilator) fan
венча́|ть (**-ю**; *perf* **обвенча́ть** *или* **повенча́ть**) *несов перех* to marry (*in church*); **венча́ть** (*impf*) **на ца́рство кого́-н** to crown sb; **венча́ться** (*perf* **обвенча́ться**) *несов возв* to be married (*in church*)
ве́р|а (**-ы**) *ж* faith; (*в Бога*) belief
ве́рб|а (**-ы**) *ж* pussy willow
верблю́д (**-а**) *м* camel
ве́рбн|ый *прил*: **Ве́рбное воскресе́нье** ≈ Palm Sunday
верб|ова́ть (**-у́ю**; *perf* **завербова́ть**) *несов перех* to recruit
верёв|ка (**-ки**; *gen pl* **-ок**) *ж* (*толстая*) rope; (*тонкая*) string
ве́р|ить (**-ю, -ишь**; *perf* **пове́рить**) *несов +dat* to believe; (*доверять*) to trust; **ве́рить** (*perf* **пове́рить**) **в кого́-н/что-н** to believe in sb/sth; **ве́рить** (*perf* **пове́рить**) **на́ слово кому́-н** to take sb at his *итп* word; **ве́риться** *несов безл*: **не ве́рится, что э́то пра́вда** it's hard to believe it's true

верне́е *вводн сл* or rather; **верне́е всего́** most likely

ве́рно *нареч* (*преданно*) faithfully; (*правильно*) correctly ▷ *как сказ* that's right

верн|у́ть (**-у́, -ёшь**) *сов перех* to return, give back; (*долг*) to pay back; (*здоровье, надежду*) to restore; **верну́ться** *сов возв*: **верну́ться (к** *+dat*) to return (to)

ве́рный *прил* (*друг*) faithful; (*надёжный*) sure; (*правильный*) correct; **ве́рный сло́ву** true to one's word

ве́ровани|е (**-я**) *ср* (*обычн мн*) faith

вероисповеда́ни|е (**-я**) *ср* faith

вероя́тно *как сказ* it is probable ▷ *вводн сл* probably

вероя́тн|ый *прил* probable; **вероя́тнее всего́** most likely *или* probably

ве́рси|я (**-и**) *ж* version

верста́к (**-а́**) *м* (*Tex*) (work)bench

вертика́льный *прил* vertical

вертолёт (**-а**) *м* helicopter

верф|ь (**-и**) *ж* shipyard

верх (**-а**; *loc sg* **-у́**, *nom pl* **-и́**) *м* (*дома, стола*) top; (*обуви*) upper; **верх соверше́нства/глу́пости** the height of perfection/stupidity; *см также* **верхи́**

верх|и́ (**-о́в**) *мн*: **в верха́х** at the top; **встре́ча/перегово́ры в верха́х** summit meeting/talks

ве́рхн|ий *прил* top; **ве́рхняя оде́жда** outer clothing *или* garments; **Ве́рхняя пала́та** Upper Chamber

верхо́вный *прил* supreme; **Верхо́вный Суд** High Court (*Brit*), Supreme Court (*US*)

верхов|о́й *прил*: **верхова́я езда́** horse (*Brit*) *или* horseback (*US*) riding

верши́н|а (**-ы**) *ж* top; (*горы*) summit

вес (**-а**; *nom pl* **-а́**) *м* weight; (*перен*: *влияние*) authority

веселе́|ть (**-ю**; *perf* **повеселе́ть**) *несов* to cheer up

весел|и́ть (**-ю́, -и́шь**; *perf* **развесели́ть**) *несов перех* to amuse; **весели́ться** *несов возв* to have fun

ве́село *нареч* (*сказать*) cheerfully ▷ *как сказ*: **здесь ве́село** it's fun here; **мне ве́село** I'm having fun

весёлый *прил* cheerful

весе́нний *прил* spring

ве́|сить (**-шу, -сишь**) *несов* to weigh

ве́ский *прил* (*аргумент*) potent

весл|о́ (**-а́**; *nom pl* **вёсла**, *gen pl* **вёсел**) *ср* oar

весн|а́ (**-ы́**; *nom pl* **вёсны**, *gen pl* **вёсен**) *ж* spring

весно́й *нареч* in (the) spring

весну́ш|ка (**-ки**; *gen pl* **-ек**) *ж* freckle

весо́мый *прил* (*вклад*) substantial

ве|сти́ (**-ду́, -дёшь**; *pt* **вёл, -ла́, -ло́**) *несов перех* to take; (*машину*) to drive; (*корабль*) to navigate; (*отряд*) to lead; (*заседание*) to chair; (*работу*) to conduct; (*хозяйство*) to run; (*записи*) to keep ▷ (*perf* **привести́**) *неперех*: **вести́ к** *+dat* to lead to; **вести́** (*impf*) **себя́** to behave; **вести́сь** *несов возв* (*расследование*) to be carried out; (*переговоры*) to go on

вестибю́л|ь (**-я**) *м* lobby

вест|ь (**-и**) *ж* news; **пропада́ть** (*perf* **пропа́сть**) **бе́з вести** (*Воен*) to go missing; **бе́з вести пропа́вший** (*Воен*) missing feared dead; **Бог весть кто/что** (*разг*) God

knows who/what
вес|ы́ (**-о́в**) *мн* scales; (*созвездие*): **Весы́** Libra
весь (**всего́**; *f* **вся**, *nt* **всё**, *pl* **все**; см *Table 13*) *мест* all; **всего́ хоро́шего** *или* **до́брого**! all the best!
ветв|ь (**-и**; *gen pl* **-е́й**) *ж* branch; **ветвь диску́ссии** (*Комп*) thread
ве́т|ер (**-ра**) *м* wind
ветера́н (**-а**) *м* veteran
ветерина́р (**-а**) *м* vet (*Brit*), veterinarian (*US*)
ве́т|ка (**-ки**; *gen pl* **-ок**) *ж* branch; **ве́тка диску́ссии** (*Комп*) thread
ве́то *ср нескл* veto
ве́треный *прил* windy
ветров|о́й *прил*: **ветрово́е стекло́** windscreen (*Brit*), windshield (*US*)
ветря́н|ка (**-ки**) *ж* (*Мед*) chickenpox
ветрян|о́й *прил* wind-powered; **ветряна́я электроста́нция** wind farm; **ветряна́я о́спа** chickenpox
ве́тхий *прил* (*дом*) dilapidated; (*одежда*) shabby; **Ве́тхий Заве́т** the Old Testament
ветч|ина́ (**-ины́**; *nom pl* **-и́ны**) *ж* ham
ве́х|а (**-и**) *ж* landmark
ве́чер (**-а**; *nom pl* **-а́**) *м* evening; (*праздник*) party; **вече́рний** *прил* evening

Вече́рнее отделе́ние

A degree can be obtained by taking courses in the evening. People who do not want to give up their job may opt for this method. This course runs over 4 days a week with over 20 contact hours a week and is very much like the day-time course. The entire degree takes 6 years to complete. See also notes at **зао́чный** and **о́чный**.

ве́чером *нареч* in the evening
ве́чно *нареч* eternally
ве́чност|ь (**-и**) *ж* eternity
ве́чный *прил* eternal, everlasting
ве́шал|ка (**-ки**; *gen pl* **-ок**) *ж* (*планка*) rack; (*стойка*) hatstand; (*плечики*) coat hanger; (*гардероб*) cloakroom; (*петля*) loop
ве́ша|ть (**-ю**; *perf* **пове́сить**) *несов перех* to hang ▷ (*perf* **све́шать**) (*товар*) to weigh; **ве́шаться** (*perf* **пове́ситься**) *несов возв* to hang o.s.
веща́|ть (*3sg* **-ет**) *несов* to broadcast
веще́ственный *прил* material
веществ|о́ (**-а́**) *ср* substance
вещ|ь (**-и**; *gen pl* **-е́й**) *ж* thing; (*книга, фильм*) piece
ве́|ять (**-ю, -ешь**) *несов* (*ветер*) to blow lightly
взаи́мный *прил* mutual
взаимоде́йстви|е (**-я**) *ср* (*связь*) interaction
взаимоотноше́ни|е (**-я**) *ср* (inter)relationship
взаимопо́мощ|ь (**-и**) *ж* mutual assistance *или* aid
взаимопонима́ни|е (**-я**) *ср* mutual understanding
взаймы́ *нареч*: **дава́ть/брать де́ньги взаймы́** to lend/borrow money
взаме́н *нареч* in exchange ▷ *предл* (*+gen*: *вместо*) instead of; (*в обмен*) in exchange for
взаперти́ *нареч* under lock and key
взбить (**взобью́, взобьёшь**; *imper* **взбей(те)**, *impf* **взбива́ть**) *сов перех* (*яйца*) to beat; (*сливки*) to whip; (*волосы*) to fluff up; (*подушки*) to plump up
взвал|и́ть (**-ю́, -ишь**; *impf* **взва́ливать**) *сов перех*: **взвали́ть**

что-н на *+acc* to haul sth up onto
взве́|сить (**-шу, -сишь**; *impf* **взве́шивать**) *сов перех* (*товар*) to weigh; (*факты*) to weigh up
взве|сти́ (**-ду́, -дёшь**; *pt* **взвёл, -ла́**, *impf* **вводи́ть**) *сов перех*: **взвести́ куро́к** to cock a gun
взве́шива|ть (**-ю**) *несов от* **взве́сить**
взвин|ти́ть (**-чу́, -ти́шь**; *impf* **взви́нчивать**) *сов перех* (*разг*: *цены*) to jack up
взво|ди́ть (**-жу́, -дишь**) *несов от* **взвести́**
взволн|ова́ть(ся) (**-у́ю(сь)**) *сов от* **волнова́ть(ся)**
взв|ыть (**-о́ю, -о́ешь**) *сов* to howl; (*сирена*) to wail
взгляд (**-а**) *м* glance; (*выражение*) look; (*перен*: *мнение*) view; **на мой/твой взгляд** in my/your view
взглян|у́ть (**-у́, -ешь**) *сов*: **взгляну́ть на** *+acc* to look at
вздор (**-а**) *м* (*разг*) rubbish; **вздо́рный** *прил* (*нелепый*) absurd
вздох (**-а**) *м* sigh; (*ужаса*) gasp
вздохн|у́ть (**-у́, -ёшь**) *сов* to sigh
вздро́гн|уть (**-у**; *impf* **вздра́гивать**) *сов* to shudder
взду́ма|ть (**-ю**) *сов* (*разг*): **не взду́майте лгать!** don't even think of lying!
вздыха́|ть (**-ю**) *несов* to sigh
взима́|ть (**-ю**) *несов перех* (*налоги*) to collect
взлёт (**-а**) *м* (*самолёта*) takeoff
взле|те́ть (**-чу́, -ти́шь**; *impf* **взлета́ть**) *сов* (*птица*) to soar; (*самолёт*) to take off; **взлета́ть** (*perf* **взлете́ть**) **на во́здух** to explode
взлётн|ый *прил*: **взлётная полоса́** runway; airstrip
взлома́|ть (**-ю**; *impf* **взла́мывать**) *сов перех* to break open, force; (*Комп*) to hack into
взло́мщик (**-а**) *м* burglar
взмахн|у́ть (**-у́, -ёшь**; *impf* **взма́хивать**) *сов* (*+instr*: *рукой*) to wave; (*крылом*) to flap
взнос (**-а**) *м* payment; (*в фонд*) contribution; (*членский*) fee
взойти́ (*как* **идти́**; *см Table 18*; *impf* **всходи́ть** *или* **восходи́ть**) *сов* to rise; (*семена*) to come up; (*на трон*) to ascend
взорв|а́ть (**-у́, -ёшь**; *impf* **взрыва́ть**) *сов перех* (*бомбу*) to detonate; (*дом, мост*) to blow up; **взорва́ться** (*impf* **взрыва́ться**) *сов возв* (*бомба*) to explode; (*мост, дом*) to be blown up
взрев|е́ть (**-у́, -ёшь**) *сов* to roar
взросле́|ть (**-ю**; *perf* **повзросле́ть**) *несов* to grow up; (*духовно*) to mature
взро́сл|ый *прил* (*человек*) grown-up; (*фильм*) adult ▷ (**-ого**) *м* adult
взрыв (**-а**) *м* explosion; (*дома*) blowing up; (*+gen*: *возмущения*) outburst of
взрыва́|ть(ся) (**-ю(сь)**) *несов от* **взорва́ть(ся)**
взрывоопа́сный *прил* explosive
взрывча́т|ка (**-ки**; *gen pl* **-ок**) *ж* explosive (substance)
взы|ска́ть (**-щу́, -щешь**; *impf* **взы́скивать**) *сов перех* (*долг*) to recover; (*штраф*) to exact ▷ *неперех*: **взыска́ть с кого́-н** to call sb to account
взя́т|ка (**-ки**; *gen pl* **-ок**) *ж* bribe
взя|ть (**возьму́, возьмёшь**) *сов от* **брать** ▷ *перех*: **возьму́ (да) и откажу́сь** (*разг*) I could refuse just like that; **с чего́** *или* **отку́да ты взял?** (*разг*) whatever gave you

that idea?; **взяться** *сов от* **браться**

вид (**-а**; *part gen* **-у**, *loc sg* **-у́**) *м* (*внешность*) appearance; (*предмета, искусства*) form; (*панорама*) view; (*растений, животных*) species; (*спорта*) type; (*Линг*) aspect; **в ви́де** *+gen* in the form of; **на виду́ у** *+gen* in full view of; **под ви́дом** *+gen* in the guise of; **вид на о́зеро/го́ры** a view of the lake/hills; **име́ть** (*impf*) **в виду́** to mean; (*учитывать*) to bear in mind; **де́лать** (*perf* **сде́лать**) **вид** to pretend; **упуска́ть** (**упусти́ть** *perf*) **из ви́ду что-н** (*факт*) to lose sight of sth; **теря́ть** (*perf* **потеря́ть**) **кого́-н из ви́ду** to lose sight of sb; **вид на жи́тельство** residence permit

вида́|ть (*pt* **-л, -ла, -ло**, *perf* **повида́ть**) *несов перех* (*разг*) to see; (*испытать*) to know; **вида́ться** (*perf* **повида́ться**) *несов возв* (*разг*) to see each other

ви́део *ср нескл* video

видеобло́г (**-а**) *м* vlog; **видеобло́гер** (**-а**) *м* vlogger

видеоза́пис|ь (**-и**) *ж* video recording

видеоигр|а́ (**-ы́**; *nom pl* **-ы**) *ж* video game

видеока́мер|а (**-ы**) *ж* camcorder, videocamera

видеокассе́т|а (**-ы**) *ж* video cassette

видеомагнитофо́н (**-а**) *м* video (recorder)

ви́|деть (**-жу, -дишь**) *несов* to see ▷ (*perf* **уви́деть**) *перех* to see; (*испытать*) to know; **ви́дите ли** you see; **ви́деться** (*perf* **уви́деться**) *несов возв* to see each other

ви́димо *вводн сл* apparently

ви́димо-неви́димо *нареч* (*разг*): **наро́ду в го́роде ви́димо-неви́димо** there are masses of people in the city

ви́димост|ь (**-и**) *ж* visibility; (*подобие*) appearance; **по всей ви́димости** apparently

видне́|ться (*3sg* **-ется**) *несов возв* to be visible

ви́дно *как сказ* one can see; (*понятно*) clearly ▷ *вводн сл* probably; **тебе́ видне́е** you know best; **там ви́дно бу́дет** we'll see

ви́дный *прил* (*заметный*) visible; (*известный*) prominent

ви́жу(сь) *несов см* **ви́деть(ся)**

ви́з|а (**-ы**) *ж* visa

визажи́ст (**-а**) *м* make-up artist

визи́т (**-а**) *м* visit

визи́т|ка (**-ки**; *gen pl* **-ок**) *ж* business card

визи́тн|ый *прил*: **визи́тная ка́рточка** (business) card

виктори́н|а (**-ы**) *ж* quiz game

ви́л|ка (**-ки**; *gen pl* **-ок**) *ж* fork; (**ште́псельная**) **ви́лка** plug

ви́лл|а (**-ы**) *ж* villa

ви́л|ы (**-**) *мн* pitchfork *ед*

вин|а́ (**-ы́**) *м* blame; (*чувство*) guilt

винегре́т (**-а**) *м* beetroot salad

вини́тельный *прил*: **вини́тельный паде́ж** accusative (case)

вин|и́ть (**-ю́, -и́шь**) *несов перех*: **вини́ть кого́-н в** *+prp* to blame sb for; (*упрекать: за лень*): **вини́ть кого́-н за** *+acc* to accuse sb of

вин|о́ (**-а́**; *nom pl* **-а**) *ср* wine

винова́тый *прил* (*взгляд итп*) guilty; **винова́тый** (**в** *+prp*) (*в неудаче*) responsible *или* to blame (for); **винова́т!** sorry!, excuse me!

вино́вност|ь (**-и**) *ж* guilt

вино́вн|ый *прил* guilty ▷ (**-ого**)

м guilty party
виногра́д (**-а**) *м* (*растение*) (grape)vine; (*ягоды*) grapes *мн*; **виногра́дник** (**-а**) *м* vineyard
винт (**-а́**) *м* screw
винто́в|ка (**-ки**; *gen pl* **-ок**) *ж* rifle
виолонче́л|ь (**-и**) *ж* cello
вира́ж (**-а́**) *м* (*поворот*) turn
виртуа́льный *прил* virtual
ви́рус (**-а**) *м* virus
ви|се́ть (**-шу́, -си́шь**) *несов* to hang; (*Комп*) to freeze
ви́ски *ср нескл* whisky (*Brit*), whiskey (*US, Ireland*)
вис|о́к (**-ка́**) *м* (*Анат*) temple
високо́сный *прил*: **високо́сный год** leap year
витами́н (**-а**) *м* vitamin
вита́|ть (**-ю**) *несов* to hang in the air
вит|о́к (**-ка́**) *м* (*спирали*) twist
витра́ж (**-а́**) *м* stained-glass window
витри́н|а (**-ы**) *ж* (*в магазине*) shop window; (*в музее*) display case
ви|ть (**вью, вьёшь**; *imper* **вей(те)**, *perf* **свить**) *несов перех* (*венок*) to weave; (*гнездо*) to build; **ви́ться** *несов возв* (*растения*) to trail; (*волосы*) to curl
ви́це-президе́нт (**-а**) *м* vice president
ВИЧ *м сокр* (= *ви́рус иммунодефици́та челове́ка*) HIV (= *human immunodeficiency virus*); **ВИЧ-инфици́рованный** HIV-positive
ви́ш|ня (**-ни**; *gen pl* **-ен**) *ж* cherry
вка́лыва|ть (**-ю**) *несов от* **вколо́ть**
вка|ти́ть (**-чу́, -тишь**; *impf* **вка́тывать**) *сов перех* (*что-н на колёсах*) to wheel in; (*что-н круглое*) to roll in
вклад (**-а**) *м* (*в науку*) contribution; (*в банке*) deposit; **вкла́дчик** (**-а**) *м* investor
вкла́дыва|ть (**-ю**) *несов от* **вложи́ть**
включа́|ть (**-ю**) *несов от* **включи́ть** ▷ *перех*: **включа́ть (в себя́)** to include; **включа́ться** *несов от* **включи́ться**
включа́я *предл +acc* including
включи́тельно *нареч* inclusive
включ|и́ть (**-у́, -и́шь**; *impf* **включа́ть**) *сов перех* to turn *или* switch on; **включа́ть (***perf* **включи́ть) кого́-н/что-н во что-н** to include sb/sth in sth; **включи́ться** (*impf* **включа́ться**) *сов возв* to come on; (*в спор*): **включи́ться в** *+acc* to join in
вкол|о́ть (**-ю́, -ешь**; *impf* **вка́лывать**) *сов перех* to stick in
вкра́тце *нареч* briefly
вкривь *нареч*: **вкривь и вкось** (*разг*) all over the place
вкру|ти́ть (**-чу́, -тишь**; *impf* **вкру́чивать**) *сов перех* to screw in
вкруту́ю *нареч*: **яйцо́ вкруту́ю** hard-boiled egg
вкус (**-а**) *м* taste; **она́ оде́та со вку́сом** she is tastefully dressed
вку́сно *нареч* tastily ▷ *как сказ*: **о́чень вку́сно** it's delicious; **она́ вку́сно гото́вит** she is a good cook
вку́сный *прил* tasty; (*обед*) delicious
вла́г|а (**-и**) *ж* moisture
владе́л|ец (**-ьца**) *м* owner
владе́ни|е (**-я**) *ср* ownership; (*помещика*) estate
владе́|ть (**-ю**) *несов* (*+instr*: *обладать*) to own, possess; (*языком*) to be proficient in; (*оружием*) to handle proficiently;

владе́ть (*impf*) **собо́й** to control o.s.; **владе́ть** (*impf*) **рука́ми/нога́ми** to have the use of one's arms/legs
вла́жност|ь (**-и**) *ж* humidity
вла́жный *прил* damp; (*глаза, кожа*) moist
властв|овать (**-ую**) *несов*: **вла́ствовать над** *+instr* to rule; (*перен*) to hold sway over
вла́ст|и (**-е́й**) *мн* authorities
власт|ь (**-и**; *gen pl* **-е́й**) *ж* power; (*родительская*) authority; *см также* **вла́сти**
вле́во *нареч* (to the) left
влез|ть (**-у, -ешь**; *pt* **-, -ла**, *impf* **влеза́ть**) *сов*: **влезть на** *+acc* to climb (up); (*на крышу*) to climb onto; (*в дом*) to break in
вле|те́ть (**-чу́, -ти́шь**; *impf* **влета́ть**) *сов*: **влете́ть в** *+acc* to fly into
влече́ни|е (**-я**) *ср*: **влече́ние (к** *+dat*) attraction (to)
вле|чь (**-ку́, -чёшь** *etc*, **-ку́т**; *pt* **влёк, -кла́**, *perf* **повле́чь**) *несов перех*: **влечь за собо́й** to lead to; **его́ влечёт нау́ка** he is drawn to science
влива́ни|е (**-я**) *ср* (*денег*) injection
вли|ть (**волью́, вольёшь**; *pt* **-л, -ла́, -ло**, *imper* **вле́й(те)**, *impf* **влива́ть**) *сов перех* to pour in; (*деньги*) to inject
влия́ни|е (**-я**) *ср* influence
влия́тельный *прил* influential
влия́|ть (**-ю**) *несов*: **влия́ть на** *+acc* to influence; (*на организм*) to affect
влож|и́ть (**-у́, -ишь**; *impf* **вкла́дывать**) *сов перех* to insert; (*средства*) to invest
влюб|и́ться (**-лю́сь, -ишься**; *impf* **влюбля́ться**) *сов возв*: **влюби́ться в** *+acc* to fall in love with; **влюблённ|ый** *прил* in love; (*взгляд*) loving ▷ (**-ого**) *м*: **влюблённые** lovers
вме́сте *нареч* together; **вме́сте с тем** at the same time
вмести́тельный *прил* spacious
вме|сти́ть (**-щу́, -сти́шь**; *impf* **вмеща́ть**) *сов перех* (*о зале*) to hold; (*о гостинице*) to accommodate; **вмести́ться** (*impf* **вмеща́ться**) *несов возв* to fit in
вме́сто *предл* (*+gen*: *взамен*) instead of ▷ *союз*: **вме́сто того́ что́бы** instead of, rather than
вмеша́|ть (**-ю**; *impf* **вме́шивать**) *сов перех* (*добавить*) to mix in; (*перен*): **вмеша́ть кого́-н в** *+acc* to get sb mixed up in; **вмеша́ться** (*impf* **вме́шиваться**) *сов возв* to interfere; (*в переговоры итп*) to intervene
вмеща́|ть(ся) (**-ю(сь)**) *несов от* **вмести́ть(ся)**
вмиг *нареч* instantly
вмя́тин|а (**-ы**) *ж* dent
внаём *нареч*: **отдава́ть внаём** to let, rent out
внача́ле *нареч* at first
вне *предл* *+gen* outside; **вне о́череди** out of turn; **он был вне себя́** he was beside himself
внедоро́жник (**-а**) *м* four-wheel drive
внедре́ни|е (**-я**) *ср* introduction
внеза́пный *прил* sudden
внес|ти́ (**-у́, -ёшь**; *pt* **внёс, -ла́**, *impf* **вноси́ть**) *сов перех* (*вещи*) to carry *или* bring in; (*сумму*) to pay; (*законопроект*) to bring in; (*поправку*) to insert
вне́шн|ий *прил* (*стена*) exterior; (*спокойствие*) outward; (*связи*) external; **вне́шний мир** outside world; **вне́шний вид** appearance;

вне́шняя поли́тика/торго́вля foreign policy/trade; **вне́шност|ь** (**-и**) *ж* appearance
внешта́тный *прил* freelance
вниз *нареч*: **вниз (по** *+dat*) down; **вниз по тече́нию** downstream
внизу́ *нареч* below; (*в здании*) downstairs ▷ *предл*: **внизу́ страни́цы** at the foot *или* bottom of the page
вни́к|нуть (**-ну**; *pt* **-, -ла**, *impf* **вника́ть**) *сов*: **вни́кнуть во что-н** to understand sth well; (*изучать*) to scrutinize sth
внима́ни|е (**-я**) *ср* attention; **внима́тельный** *прил* attentive; (*работа*) careful; (*сын*) caring
вничью́ *нареч* (*Спорт*): **сыгра́ть вничью́** to draw
вновь *нареч* again
вно|си́ть (**-шу́, -сишь**) *несов от* **внести́**
вну|к (**-ка**; *nom pl* **-ки** *или* **-ча́та**) *м* grandson; *см также* **вну́ки**
вну́к|и (**-ов**) *мн* grandchildren
вну́тренн|ий *прил* interior; (*побуждение, голос*) inner; (*политика, рынок*) domestic; (*рана*) internal; **Министе́рство вну́тренних дел** ≈ the Home Office (*Brit*), ≈ the Department of the Interior (*US*)
внутри́ *нареч* inside ▷ *предл* (*+gen*: *дома*) inside; (*организации*) within
внутрь *нареч* inside ▷ *предл* *+gen* inside
вну́ч|ка (**-ки**; *gen pl* **-ек**) *ж* granddaughter
внуша́|ть (**-ю**) *несов от* **внуши́ть**
внуши́тельный *прил* imposing; (*сумма, успех*) impressive
внуш|и́ть (**-у́, -и́шь**; *impf* **внуша́ть**) *сов перех*: **внуши́ть что-н кому́-н** (*чувство*) to inspire sb with sth; (*идею*) to instil (*Brit*) *или* instill (*US*) sth in sb
вня́тный *прил* articulate, audible
во *предл* = **в**
вовл|е́чь (**-еку́, -ечёшь** *etc* **-еку́т**; *pt* **-ёк, -екла́**, *impf* **вовлека́ть**) *сов перех*: **вовле́чь кого́-н в** *+acc* to draw sb into
во́время *нареч* on time
во́все *нареч* (*разг*) completely; **во́все нет** not at all
во-вторы́х *вводн сл* secondly, in the second place
вод|а́ (*acc sg* **-у**, *gen sg* **-ы́**, *nom pl* **-ы**) *ж* water; *см также* **во́ды**
води́тел|ь (**-я**) *м* driver
води́тельск|ий *прил*: **води́тельские права́** driving licence (*Brit*), driver's license (*US*)
во|ди́ть (**-жу́, -дишь**) *несов перех* (*ребёнка*) to take; (*машину, поезд*) to drive; (*самолёт*) to fly; (*корабль*) to sail; **води́ться** *несов возв* (*рыба итп*) to be (found)
во́дк|а (**-и**) *ж* vodka
во́дный *прил* water
водоём (**-а**) *м* reservoir
водола́з (**-а**) *м* diver
Водоле́|й (**-я**) *м* Aquarius
водонепроница́емый *прил* waterproof
водопа́д (**-а**) *м* waterfall
водопрово́д (**-а**) *м* water supply system; **у них в до́ме есть водопрово́д** their house has running water; **водопрово́дный** *прил* (*труба, кран*) water; (*система*) plumbing; **водопрово́дчик** (**-а**) *м* plumber
водоро́д (**-а**) *м* hydrogen
водохрани́лищ|е (**-а**) *ср* reservoir
во́д|ы (**-**) *мн* (*государственные*) waters; (*минеральные*) spa *ед*
водяно́й *прил* water

во|ева́ть (**-ю́ю**) *несов* (*страна*) to be at war; (*человек*) to fight

военача́льник (**-а**) *м* (military) commander

военкома́т (**-а**) *м сокр* (= *вое́нный комиссариа́т*) *office for military registration and enlistment*

вое́нно-возду́шн|ый *прил*: **вое́нно-возду́шные си́лы** (the) air force

вое́нно-морско́й *прил*: **вое́нно-морско́й флот** (the) navy

военнообя́занн|ый (**-ого**) *м* *person eligible for compulsory military service*

военнопле́нн|ый (**-ого**) *м* prisoner of war

вое́нно-промы́шленный *прил*: **вое́нно-промы́шленный ко́мплекс** military-industrial complex

военнослу́жащ|ий (**-его**) *м* serviceman (*мн* servicemen)

вое́нн|ый *прил* military; (*врач*) army ▷ (**-ого**) *м* serviceman (*мн* servicemen); **вое́нное положе́ние** martial law

вожде́ни|е (**-я**) *ср* (*машины*) driving; (*судна*) steering

вожд|ь (**-я́**) *м* (*племени*) chief, chieftain; (*партии*) leader

вожж|а́ (**-и́**; *nom pl* **-и**, *gen pl* **-е́й**) *ж* rein

возб|уди́ть (**-ужу́, -у́дишь**; *impf* **возбужда́ть**) *сов перех* (*вызвать*) to arouse; (*взволновать*) to excite; **возбужда́ть** (*perf* **возбуди́ть**) **де́ло** *или* **проце́сс про́тив** *+gen* to bring a case *или* institute proceedings against; **возбуди́ться** *сов возв* (*человек*) to become excited

возве|сти́ (**-ду́, -дёшь**; *pt* **возвёл, -ла́**, *impf* **возводи́ть**) *сов перех* to erect

возвра́т (**-а**) *м* return; (*долга*) repayment; **без возвра́та** irrevocably

возвра|ти́ть (**-щу́, -ти́шь**; *impf* **возвраща́ть**) *сов перех* to return; (*долг*) to repay; (*здоровье, счастье*) to restore; **возврати́ться** (*impf* **возвраща́ться**) *сов возв*: **возврати́ться** (**к** *+dat*) to return *или* come back (to)

возвраще́ни|е (**-я**) *ср* return

возгла́в|ить (**-лю, -ишь**; *impf* **возглавля́ть**) *сов перех* to head

возда́ть (*как* **дать**; *см* *Table 16*; *impf* **воздава́ть**) *сов перех*: **возда́ть кому́-н по заслу́гам** (*в награду*) to reward sb for their services; (*в наказание*) to give sb what they deserve; **воздава́ть** (*perf* **возда́ть**) **до́лжное кому́-н** to give sb their due

воздви́г|нуть (**-ну**; *pt* **-, -ла**, *impf* **воздвига́ть**) *сов перех* to erect

возде́йстви|е (**-я**) *ср* effect; (*идеологическое*) influence

возде́йств|овать (**-ую**) *(не)сов*: **возде́йствовать на** *+acc* to have an effect on

возде́ла|ть (**-ю**; *impf* **возде́лывать**) *сов перех* (*поле*) to cultivate

возд|ержа́ться (**-ержу́сь, -е́ржишься**; *impf* **возде́рживаться**) *сов возв*: **воздержа́ться от** *+gen* to refrain from; (*от голосования*) to abstain from

во́здух (**-а**) *м* air; **на (откры́том) во́здухе** outside, outdoors; **возду́шный** *прил* air; (*десант*) airborne; **возду́шный флот** civil aviation; (*Воен*) air force

воззва́ни|е (**-я**) *ср* appeal

во|зи́ть (**-жу́, -зишь**) *несов перех* to take; **вози́ться** *несов возв* to potter about; **вози́ться** (*impf*) **с** *+instr* (*разг*: *с работой итп*) to dawdle over; (*с детьми итп*) to spend a lot of time with

во́зле *нареч* nearby ▷ *предл +gen* near

возлю́бленн|ый (**-ого**) *м* beloved

возме|сти́ть (**-щу́, -сти́шь**; *impf* **возмеща́ть**) *сов перех* (*убытки*) to compensate for; (*затраты*) to refund, reimburse

возмо́жно *как сказ* it is possible ▷ *вводн сл* (*может быть*) possibly; **возмо́жност|и** (**-ей**) *мн* (*творческие*) potential *ед*; **фина́нсовые возмо́жности** financial resources; **возмо́жност|ь** (**-и**) *ж* opportunity; (*вероятность*) possibility; **по (ме́ре) возмо́жности** as far as possible; *см также* **возмо́жности**; **возмо́жный** *прил* possible

возмужа́|ть (**-ю**) *сов от* **мужа́ть**

возмути́тельный *прил* appalling; **возму|ти́ть** (**-щу́, -ти́шь**; *impf* **возмуща́ть**) *сов перех* to appal (*Brit*), appall (*US*); **возмути́ться** (*impf* **возмуща́ться**) *сов возв* to be appalled

вознагра|ди́ть (**-жу́, -ди́шь**; *impf* **вознагражда́ть**) *сов перех* to reward

возни́к|нуть (**-ну**; *pt* **-, -ла**, *impf* **возника́ть**) *сов* to arise

возобнов|и́ть (**-лю́, -и́шь**; *impf* **возобновля́ть**) *сов перех* (*работу*) to resume; (*контракт*) to renew; **возобнови́ться** (*impf* **возобновля́ться**) *сов возв* to resume

возобновля́емый *прил* renewable

возраже́ни|е (**-я**) *ср* objection; **возра|зи́ть** (**-жу́, -зи́шь**; *impf* **возража́ть**) *сов*: **возрази́ть** (*+dat*) to object (to)

во́зраст (**-а**) *м* age; **он был уже́ в во́зрасте** he was getting on in years

возр|асти́ (*3sg* **-астёт**, *pt* **-о́с, -осла́**, *impf* **возраста́ть**) *сов* to grow

возро|ди́ть (**-жу́, -ди́шь**; *impf* **возрожда́ть**) *сов перех* to revive; **возроди́ться** (*impf* **возрожда́ться**) *сов возв* to revive

возрожде́ни|е (**-я**) *ср* revival; (*нации, веры*) rebirth; **Возрожде́ние** Renaissance

возьму́(сь) *etc сов см* **взя́ть(ся)**

во́инск|ий *прил* military; **во́инская обя́занность** conscription

во|й (**-я**) *м* howl

во́йлок (**-а**) *м* felt

войн|а́ (**-ы́**; *nom pl* **-ы**) *ж* war

во́йск|о (**-а**; *nom pl* **-а́**) *ср* (the) forces *мн*

войти́ (*как* **идти́**; см *Table 18*; *impf* **входи́ть**) *сов*: **войти́ (в** *+acc*) to enter, go in(to); (*в комитет*) to become a member (of); (*уместиться*) to fit in(to); (*Комп*) to log in; **па́пка "Входя́щие"** inbox

вока́льный *прил* vocal; (*конкурс*) singing

вокза́л (**-а**) *м* station

вокру́г *нареч* around, round ▷ *предл* (*+gen*: *кругом*) around, round; (*по поводу*) about, over; **ходи́ть** (*impf*) **вокру́г да о́коло** (*разг*) to beat about the bush

вол (**-а́**) *м* ox (*мн* oxen), bullock

волейбо́л (**-а**) *м* volleyball

волк (**-а**; *gen pl* **-о́в**) *м* wolf (*мн* wolves)

волн|а́ (**-ы́**; *nom pl* **во́лны**) *ж* wave

волне́ни|е (**-я**) *ср* (*радостное*) excitement; (*нервное*) agitation; (*обычно мн*: *в массах*) unrest

волни́стый *прил* (*волосы*) wavy

волн|ова́ть (**-у́ю**; *perf* **взволнова́ть**) *несов перех* to be concerned about; (*подлеж:музыка*) to excite; **волнова́ться** (*perf* **взволнова́ться**) *несов возв* (*море*) to be rough; (*человек*) to worry

вол|окно́ (**-окна́**; *nom pl* **-о́кна**, *gen pl* **-о́кон**) *ср* fibre (*Brit*), fiber (*US*)

во́лос (**-а**; *gen pl* **воло́с**, *dat pl* **-а́м**) *м* hair *только ед*

волос|о́к (**-ка́**) *м* hair; **быть** (*impf*) *или* **находи́ться** (*impf*) **на волосо́к** *или* **на волоске́ от** +*gen* to be within a hair's-breadth of

волоч|и́ть (**-у́**, **-и́шь**) *несов перех* to drag

во́лчий *прил* wolf

волше́бниц|а (**-ы**) *ж* (good *или* white) witch

волше́бный *прил* magic; (*музыка*) magical

во́льно *нареч* freely; **во́льно!** (*Воен*) at ease!; **во́л|ьный** *прил* (*свободный*) free ▷ *как сказ*: **во́лен** +*infin* he is free to do

во́л|я (**-и**) *ж* will; (*стремление*): **во́ля к побе́де** the will to win

вон *нареч* (*разг*: *прочь*) out; (: *там*) (over) there; **вон отсю́да!** get out of here!; **вон (оно́) что** so that's it!

вообра|зи́ть (**-жу́**, **-зи́шь**; *impf* **вообража́ть**) *сов перех* to imagine

вообще́ *нареч* (*в общем*) on the whole; (*совсем*) absolutely; (+*noun*: *без частностей*) in general; **вообще́ говоря́** generally speaking

воодушев|и́ть (**-лю́**, **-и́шь**; *impf* **воодушевля́ть**) *сов перех* to inspire; **воодушеви́ться** *сов возв*: **воодушеви́ться** +*instr* to be inspired by; **воодушевле́ни|е** (**-я**) *ср* inspiration

вооружа́|ть(ся) (**-ю(сь)**) *несов см* **вооружи́ть(ся)**

вооруже́ни|е (**-я**) *ср* (*процесс*) arming; (*оружие*) arms *мн*; **вооружённ|ый** *прил* armed; **вооружённые си́лы** (the) armed forces; **вооруж|и́ть** (**-у́**, **-и́шь**; *impf* **вооружа́ть**) *сов перех* to arm; (*перен*) to equip; **вооружи́ться** (*impf* **вооружа́ться**) *сов возв* to arm o.s.

во-пе́рвых *нареч* firstly, first of all

вопло|ти́ть (**-щу́**, **-ти́шь**; *impf* **воплоща́ть**) *сов перех* to embody; **воплоща́ть (***perf* **воплоти́ть) в жизнь** to realize; **воплоти́ться** (*impf* **воплоща́ться**) *сов возв*: **воплоти́ться в** +*prp* to be embodied in; **воплоща́ться (***perf* **воплоти́ться) в жизнь** to be realized

вопл|ь (**-я**) *м* scream

вопреки́ *предл* +*dat* contrary to

вопро́с (**-а**) *м* question; (*проблема*) issue; **задава́ть (***perf* **зада́ть) вопро́с** to ask a question; **вопроси́тельный** *прил* (*взгляд*) questioning; (*Линг*) interrogative; **вопроси́тельный знак** question mark

вор (**-а**; *gen pl* **-о́в**) *м* thief

ворв|а́ться (**-у́сь**, **-ёшься**; *impf* **врыва́ться**) *сов возв* to burst in

вороб|е́й (**-ья́**) *м* sparrow
вор|ова́ть (**-у́ю**) *несов перех* to steal; **воровств|о́** (**-а́**) *ср* theft
во́рон (**-а**) *м* raven
воро́н|а (**-ы**) *ж* crow
во́рот (**-а**) *м* neck (*of clothes*)
воро́т|а (-) *мн* gates; (*Спорт*) goal *ед*
воротни́к (**-а́**) *м* collar
воро́ча|ть (**-ю**) *несов перех* to shift ▷ *неперех* (*+instr*: *разг*: *деньгами*) to have control of; **воро́чаться** *несов возв* to toss and turn
ворс (**-а**) *м* (*на ткани*) nap
ворч|а́ть (**-у́, -и́шь**) *несов* (*зверь*) to growl; (*человек*) to grumble
восемна́дцатый *чис* eighteenth
восемна́дцат|ь (**-и**; *как* **пять**; см *Table 26*) *чис* eighteen
во́с|емь (**-ьми́**; *как* **пять**; см *Table 26*) *чис* eight; **во́с|емьдесят** (**-ьми́десяти**; *как* **пятьдеся́т**; см *Table 26*) *чис* eighty; **вос|емьсо́т** (**-ьмисо́т**; *как* **пятьсо́т**; см *Table 28*) *чис* eight hundred
воск (**-а**) *м* wax
восклица́тельный *прил* exclamatory; **восклица́тельный знак** exclamation mark (*Brit*) *или* point (*US*)
восково́й *прил* wax
воскреса́|ть (**-ю**) *несов от* **воскре́снуть**
воскресе́ни|е (**-я**) *ср* resurrection
воскресе́нь|е (**-я**) *ср* Sunday
воскре́с|нуть (**-ну**; *pt* **-, -ла**, *impf* **воскреса́ть**) *сов* to be resurrected; (*перен*) to be revived
воскре́сный *прил* Sunday
воспале́ни|е (**-я**) *ср* inflammation; **воспале́ние лёгких** pneumonia
воспал|и́ться (*3sg* **-и́тся**, *impf* **воспаля́ться**) *сов возв* to become inflamed
воспита́ни|е (**-я**) *ср* upbringing; (*граждан*) education; (*честности*) fostering; **воспита́тел|ь** (**-я**) *м* teacher; (*в лагере*) instructor;
воспита́|ть (**-ю**; *impf* **воспи́тывать**) *сов перех* (*ребёнка*) to bring up; (*трудолюбие*) to foster
воспо́льз|оваться (**-уюсь**) *сов от* **по́льзоваться**
воспомина́ни|е (**-я**) *ср* recollection; *см также* **воспомина́ния**
воспомина́ни|я (**-й**) *мн* memoirs *мн*, reminiscences *мн*
воспрепя́тств|овать (**-ую**) *сов от* **препя́тствовать**
воспреща́|ться (*3sg* **-ется**) *несов возв* to be forbidden
воспр|иня́ть (**-иму́, -и́мешь**; *impf* **воспринима́ть**) *сов перех* (*смысл*) to comprehend
воспроизв|ести́ (**-еду́, -едёшь**; *pt* **-ёл, -ела́, -ело́**, *impf* **воспроизводи́ть**) *сов перех* to reproduce
воспроти́в|иться (**-люсь, -ишься**) *сов от* **проти́виться**
восста|ва́ть (**-ю́, -ёшь**) *несов от* **восста́ть**
восста́ни|е (**-я**) *ср* uprising
восстан|ови́ть (**-овлю́, -о́вишь**; *impf* **восстана́вливать**) *сов перех* to restore
восста́|ть (**-ну, -нешь**; *impf* **восстава́ть**) *сов*: **восста́ть (про́тив** *+gen*) to rise up (against)
восто́к (**-а**) *м* east; **Восто́к** the East, the Orient
восторжеств|ова́ть (**-ую**) *сов от* **торжествова́ть**
восто́чный *прил* eastern; **восто́чный ве́тер** east wind

востре́бовани|е (**-я**) *ср* (*багажа*) claim; **письмо́ до востре́бования** a letter sent poste restante (*Brit*) *или* general delivery (*US*)

восхити́тельный *прил* delightful

восхи|ти́ть (**-щу́, -ти́шь**; *impf* **восхища́ть**) *сов перех*: **меня́ восхища́ет он/его́ хра́брость** I admire him/his courage; **восхити́ться** (*impf* **восхища́ться**) *сов возв*: **восхити́ться** *+instr* to admire

восхище́ни|е (**-я**) *ср* admiration

восхо́д (**-а**) *м*: **восхо́д со́лнца** sunrise

восх|оди́ть (**-ожу́, -о́дишь**) *несов от* **взойти́**

восьмёр|ка (**-ки**; *gen pl* **-ок**) *ж* (*разг*: *цифра*) eight

восьмидеся́тый *чис* eightieth

восьмо́й *чис* eighth

КЛЮЧЕВОЕ СЛОВО

вот *част* **1** (*о близком предмете*): **вот моя́ ма́ма** here is my mother; **вот мои́ де́ти** here are my children

2 (*выражает указание*) this; **вот в чём де́ло** this is what it's about; **вот где ну́жно иска́ть** this is where we need to look

3 (*при эмфатике*): **вот ты и сде́лай э́то** YOU do this; **вот негодя́й!** what a rascal!

4 (*во фразах*): **вот-во́т** (*разг*: *вот именно*) that's it; **он вот-во́т ля́жет спать** he is just about to go to bed; **вот ещё!** (*разг*) not likely!; **вот (оно́) как** *или* **что!** is that so *или* right?; **вот тебе́ и на** *или* **те раз!** (*разг*) well I never!

воткн|у́ть (**-у́, -ёшь**; *impf* **втыка́ть**) *сов перех* to stick in

во́тум (**-а**) *м*: **во́тум дове́рия/недове́рия** vote of confidence/no confidence

вошёл *etc сов см* **войти́**

вошь (**вши**; *instr sg* **во́шью**, *nom pl* **вши**) *ж* louse (*мн* lice)

впада́|ть (**-ю**) *несов от* **впасть** ▷ *неперех*: **впада́ть в** *+acc* to flow into

впа|сть (**-ду́, -дёшь**; *impf* **впада́ть**) *сов* (*щёки, глаза*) to become sunken; **впада́ть (***perf* **впасть) в** *+acc* (*в истерику*) to go into

впервы́е *нареч* for the first time

вперёд *нареч* (*идти*) ahead, forward; (*заплатить*) in advance

впереди́ *нареч* in front; (*в будущем*) ahead ▷ *предл +gen* in front of

впечатле́ни|е (**-я**) *ср* impression

впечатля́|ть (**-ю**) *несов* to be impressive

впи|са́ть (**-шу́, -шешь**; *impf* **впи́сывать**) *сов перех* to insert

впита́|ть (**-ю**; *impf* **впи́тывать**) *сов перех* to absorb; **впита́ться** *сов возв* to be absorbed

вплавь *нареч* by swimming

вплотну́ю *нареч* (*близко*) close (by) ▷ *предл*: **вплотну́ю к** *+dat* (*к городу*) right up close to; (*к стене*) right up against

вплоть *предл*: **вплоть до** *+gen* (*зимы*) right up till; (*включая*) right up to

вполго́лоса *нареч* softly

впо́ру *как сказ*: **пла́тье/шля́па мне впо́ру** the dress/hat fits me nicely

впосле́дствии *нареч* subsequently

впра́ве *как сказ* (*+infin*: *знать, требовать*) to have a right to do

впра́во *нареч* to the right

впредь *нареч* in future ▷ *предл*: **впредь до** *+gen* pending
впро́голодь *нареч*: **жить впро́голодь** to live from hand to mouth
впро́чем *союз* however, though ▷ *вводн сл* but then again
впу|сти́ть (**-щу́, -стишь**; *impf* **впуска́ть**) *сов перех* to let in
враг (**-а́**) *м* enemy
вражд|а́ (**-ы́**) *ж* enmity, hostility; **вражде́бный** *прил* hostile
вражд|ова́ть (**-у́ю**) *несов*: **враждова́ть** (**с** *+instr*) to be on hostile terms (with)
вразре́з *нареч*: **вразре́з с** *+instr* in contravention of
вран|ьё (**-я́**) *ср* (*разг*) lies *мн*
врата́р|ь (**-я́**) *м* goalkeeper
врач (**-а́**) *м* doctor; **враче́бный** *прил* medical
враща́|ть (**-ю**) *несов перех* (*колесо*) to turn; **враща́ться** *несов возв* to revolve, rotate
вред (**-а́**) *м* damage; (*человеку*) harm ▷ *предл*: **во вред** *+dat* to the detriment of; **вреди́тел|ь** (**-я**) *м* (*насекомое*) pest; **вре|ди́ть** (**-жу́, -ди́шь**; *perf* **навреди́ть**) *несов* *+dat* to harm; (*здоровью*) to damage; (*врагу*) to inflict damage on; **вре́дно** *нареч*: **вре́дно влия́ть на** *+acc* to have a harmful effect on ▷ *как сказ*: **кури́ть вре́дно** smoking is bad for you; **вре́дный** *прил* harmful; (*разг*: *человек*) nasty
вре́|заться (**-жусь, -жешься**; *impf* **вреза́ться**) *сов возв*: **вре́заться в** *+acc* (*верёвка*) to cut into; (*машина*) to plough (*Brit*) *или* plow (*US*) into; (*в память*) to engrave itself on
времена́ми *нареч* at times
вре́менный *прил* temporary
вре́м|я (**-ени**; см *Table 4*) *ср* time; (*Линг*) tense ▷ *предл*: **во вре́мя** *+gen* during ▷ *союз*: **в то вре́мя как** *или* **когда́** while; **(а) в то же вре́мя** (but) at the same time; **вре́мя от вре́мени** from time to time; **в после́днее вре́мя** recently; **в своё вре́мя** (*когда необходимо*) in due course; **в своё вре́мя она́ была́ краса́вицей** she was a real beauty in her day; **на вре́мя** for a while; **со вре́менем** with *или* in time; **тем вре́менем** meanwhile; **ско́лько вре́мени?** what time is it?; **хорошо́ проводи́ть** (*perf* **провести́**) **вре́мя** to have a good time; **вре́мя го́да** season
вро́вень *нареч*: **вро́вень с** *+instr* level with
вро́де *предл* *+gen* like ▷ *част* sort of
врозь *нареч* (*жить*) apart
вруч|и́ть (**-у́, -и́шь**; *impf* **вруча́ть**) *сов перех*: **вручи́ть что-н кому́-н** to hand sth (over) to sb
вручну́ю *нареч* (*разг*) by hand
врыва́|ться (**-юсь**) *несов от* **ворва́ться**
вряд *част*: **вряд ли** hardly; **вряд ли она́ придёт** she's unlikely to come
все *мест см* **весь**

КЛЮЧЕВОЕ СЛОВО

всё (**всего́**) *мест см* **весь** ▷ *ср* (*как сущ*: *без исключения*) everything; **вот и всё, э́то всё** that's all; **ча́ще всего́** most often; **лу́чше всего́ написа́ть ей письмо́** it would be best to write to her; **меня́ э́то волну́ет ме́ньше всего́** that is the least of my worries; **мне всё равно́** it's all the same to me;

Вы хоти́те чай или ко́фе? — всё равно́ do you want tea or coffee? — I don't mind; **я всё равно́ пойду́ туда́** I'll go there all the same
▷ *нареч* **1** (*разг*: *всё время*) all the time
2 (*только*) all; **э́то всё он винова́т** it's all his fault
3 (*о нарастании признака*): **шум всё уси́ливается** the noise is getting louder and louder
4 (*о постоянстве признака*): **всё так же** still the same; **всё там же** still there; **всё же** all the same; **всё ещё** still

всевозмо́жный *прил* all sorts of
всегда́ *нареч* always
всего́ *мест см* **весь**; **всё** ▷ *нареч* in all ▷ *част* only; **всего́ лишь** (*разг*) only; **всего́-на́всего** (*разг*) only, mere
вселе́нн|ая (**-ой**) *ж* the whole world; **Вселе́нная** universe
всел|и́ть (**-ю́, -и́шь**; *impf* **вселя́ть**) *сов перех* (*жильцов*) to install; **всели́ться** (*impf* **вселя́ться**) *сов возв* (*жильцы*) to move in
всем *мест см* **весь**; **всё**; **все**
всеме́рный *прил* all possible
всеми́р|ный *прил* worldwide; (*конгресс*) world; **всеми́рная паути́на** (*Комп*) World-Wide Web
всенаро́дный *прил* national
всео́бщ|ий *прил* universal; **всео́бщая забасто́вка** general strike
всеобъе́млющий *прил* comprehensive
всеросси́йский *прил* all-Russia
всерьёз *нареч* in earnest; **ты э́то говори́шь всерьёз?** are you serious?
всесторо́нний *прил* comprehensive
всё-таки *част* still, all the same ▷ *союз*: **а всё-таки** all the same, nevertheless
всеуслы́шание *ср*: **во всеуслы́шание** publicly
всех *мест см* **все**
вска́кива|ть (**-ю**) *несов от* **вскочи́ть**
вскачь *нареч* at a gallop
вски́н|уть (**-у**; *impf* **вски́дывать**) *сов перех* (*мешок, ружьё*) to shoulder; (*голову*) to jerk up
вскип|е́ть (**-лю́, -и́шь**; *impf* **кипе́ть**) *сов* to boil; (*перен*) to flare up
вскользь *нареч* in passing
вско́ре *нареч* soon ▷ *предл*: **вско́ре по́сле** +*gen* soon *или* shortly after
вскоч|и́ть (**-у́, -ишь**; *impf* **вска́кивать**) *сов*: **вскочи́ть в/на** +*acc* to leap up onto
вскри́кн|уть (**-у**; *impf* **вскри́кивать**) *сов* to cry out
вслед *нареч* (*бежать*) behind ▷ *предл*: **вслед (за** +*instr*) after; (+*dat*: *другу, поезду*) after
всле́дствие *предл* +*gen* as a result of, because of ▷ *союз*: **всле́дствие того́ что** because; **всле́дствие чего́** as a result of which
вслух *нареч* aloud
всмя́тку *нареч*: **яйцо́ всмя́тку** soft-boiled egg
всплеск (**-а**) *м* (*волны*) splash
всплесн|у́ть (**-у́, ёшь**; *impf* **всплёскивать**) *сов* (*рыба*) to splash; **всплесну́ть** (*perf*) **рука́ми** to throw up one's hands
всплы|ть (**-ву́, -вёшь**; *impf*

всплыва́ть) *сов* to surface

вспо́мн|ить (**-ю, -ишь**; *impf* **вспомина́ть**) *сов перех* to remember ▷ *неперех*: **вспо́мнить о** *+prp* to remember about

вспомога́тельный *прил* supplementary; (*судно, отряд*) auxiliary; **вспомога́тельный глаго́л** auxiliary verb

вспорхн|у́ть (**-у́, -ёшь**) *сов* to fly off

вспоте́|ть (**-ю**) *сов от* **поте́ть**

вспугн|у́ть (**-у́, ёшь**; *impf* **вспу́гивать**) *сов перех* to scare away *или* off

вспу́хн|уть (**-у**) *сов от* **пу́хнуть**

вспы́хн|уть (**-у**; *impf* **вспы́хивать**) *сов* (*зажечься*) to burst into flames; (*конфликт*) to flare up; (*покраснеть*) to blush

вспы́ш|ка (**-ки**; *gen pl* **-ек**) *ж* flash; (*гнева*) outburst; (*болезни*) outbreak

вста|ва́ть (**-ю́**; *imper* **-ва́й(те)**) *несов от* **встать**

вста́в|ить (**-лю, -ишь**; *impf* **вставля́ть**) *сов перех* to insert, put in

вста|ть (**-ну, -нешь**; *impf* **встава́ть**) *сов* (*на ноги*) to stand up; (*с постели*) to get up; (*солнце*) to rise; (*вопрос*) to arise

встрево́ж|ить(ся) (**-у(сь), -ишь(ся)**) *несов от* **трево́жить(ся)**

встре́|тить (**-чу, -тишь**; *impf* **встреча́ть**) *сов перех* to meet; (*факт*) to come across; (*оппозицию*) to encounter; (*праздник итп*) to celebrate; **встре́титься** (*impf* **встреча́ться**) *сов возв*: **встре́титься с** *+instr* to meet; **мне встре́тились интере́сные фа́кты** I came across some interesting facts

встре́ч|а (**-и**) *ж* meeting

встреча́|ть(ся) (**-ю(сь)**) *несов от* **встре́тить(ся)**

встре́чный *прил* (*машина*) oncoming; (*мера*) counter; **встре́чный ве́тер** head wind

встряхн|у́ть (**-у́, -ёшь**; *impf* **встря́хивать**) *сов перех* to shake (out)

вступи́тельный *прил* (*речь, статья*) introductory; **вступи́тельный экза́мен** entrance exam

вступ|и́ть (**-лю́, -ишь**; *impf* **вступа́ть**) *сов*: **вступи́ть в** *+acc* to enter; (*в партию*) to join; (*в переговоры*) to enter into; **вступи́ться** (*impf* **вступа́ться**) *сов возв*: **вступи́ться за** *+acc* to stand up for

вступле́ни|е (**-я**) *ср* entry; (*в партию*) joining; (*в книге*) introduction

всхли́пыва|ть (**-ю**) *несов* to sob

всхо|ди́ть (**-жу́, -дишь**) *несов от* **взойти́**

всхо́д|ы (**-ов**) *мн* shoots

всю́ду *нареч* everywhere

вс|я (**-ей**) *мест см* **весь**

вся́к|ий *мест* (*каждый*) every; (*разнообразный*) all kinds of; (*любой*) any ▷ (**-ого**) *м* (*любой*) anyone; (*каждый*) everyone

вся́ческий *мест* all possible; (*товары*) all kinds of

вся́чин|а (**-ы**) *ж* (*разг*): **вся́кая вся́чина** all sorts of things

втащ|и́ть (**-у́, -ишь**; *impf* **вта́скивать**) *сов перех*: **втащи́ть (в** *+acc*) to drag in(to)

втере́ть (**вотру́, вотрёшь**; *pt* **втёр, втёрла**, *impf* **втира́ть**) *сов перех*: **втере́ть (в** *+acc*) to rub in(to)

вти́сн|уть (**-у**; *impf* **вти́скивать**) *сов перех*: **вти́снуть (в** *+acc*) to cram in(to)
вто́ргн|уться (**-усь**; *impf* **вторга́ться**) *сов возв*: **вто́ргнуться в** *+acc* to invade
втори́чный *прил* (*повторный*) second; (*фактор*) secondary
вто́рник (**-а**) *м* Tuesday
втор|о́е (**-о́го**) *ср* main course
втор|о́й *прил* second; **сейча́с второ́й час** it's after one; **сейча́с полови́на второ́го** it's half past one
второпя́х *нареч* in a hurry
второстепе́нный *прил* secondary
в-тре́тьих *вводн сл* thirdly, in the third place
втроём *нареч* in a group of three
втройне́ *нареч* three times as much
втыка́|ть (**-ю**) *несов от* **воткну́ть**
втян|у́ть (**-у́**; *impf* **втя́гивать**) *сов перех* (*втащить*) to pull in; **втя́гивать (***perf* **втяну́ть) кого́-н в** *+acc* (*в дело*) to involve sb in
вуа́л|ь (**-и**) *ж* veil
вуз (**-а**) *м сокр* (= *вы́сшее учёбное заведе́ние*) higher education establishment
вулка́н (**-а**) *м* volcano
вульга́рный *прил* vulgar
вход (**-а**) *м* (*движение*) entry; (*место*) entrance; (*Тех*) inlet; (*Комп*) input
вхо|ди́ть (**-жу́, -дишь**) *несов от* **войти́**
входно́й *прил* (*дверь*) entrance; (*Комп*) input
вцеп|и́ться (**-лю́сь, -ишься**) *сов возв*: **вцепи́ться в** *+acc* to seize
вчера́ *нареч, м нескл* yesterday
вчера́шний *прил* yesterday's
вче́тверо *нареч* four times
вчетверо́м *нареч* in a group of four
вши *etc сущ см* **вошь**
вширь *нареч* in breadth
въезд (**-а**) *м* (*движение*) entry; (*место*) entrance; **въездно́й** *прил* entry
въе́|хать (*как* **е́хать**; см *Table 19*; *impf* **въезжа́ть**) *сов* to enter; (*в новый дом*) to move in; (*наверх*: *на машине*) to drive up; (: *на коне, велосипеде*) to ride up
Вы (**Вас**; см *Table 6b*) *мест* you (*formal*)
вы (**вас**; см *Table 6b*) *мест* you (*plural*)
вы́бе|жать (*как* **бежа́ть**; см *Table 20*; *impf* **выбега́ть**) *сов* to run out
выбива́|ть(ся) (**-ю(сь)**) *несов от* **вы́бить(ся)**
выбира́|ть (**-ю**) *несов от* **вы́брать**
вы́б|ить (**-ью, -ьешь**; *impf* **выбива́ть**) *сов перех* to knock out; (*противника*) to oust; (*ковёр*) to beat; (*надпись*) to carve; **выбива́ть (***perf* **вы́бить) чек** (*кассир*) to ring up the total; **вы́биться** (*impf* **выбива́ться**) *сов возв*: **вы́биться из** *+gen* (*освободиться*) to get out of
вы́бор (**-а**) *м* choice; *см также* **вы́боры**; **вы́борный** *прил* (*кампания*) election; (*пост, орган*) elective; **вы́борочн|ый** *прил* selective; **вы́борочная прове́рка** spot check; **вы́бор|ы** (**-ов**) *мн* election *ед*; *см также* **вы́бор**
выбра́сыва|ть(ся) (**-ю(сь)**) *несов от* **вы́бросить(ся)**
вы́б|рать (**-еру, -ерешь**; *impf* **выбира́ть**) *сов перех* to choose; (*голосованием*) to elect
вы́брос (**-а**) *м* (*газа*) emission;

(*отходов*) discharge; (*нефти*) spillage

вы́бро|сить (**-шу, -сишь**; *impf* **выбра́сывать**) *сов перех* to throw out; (*отходы*) to discharge; (*газы*) to emit; **вы́броситься** (*impf* **выбра́сываться**) *сов возв* to throw oneself out; **выбра́сываться** (*perf* **вы́броситься**) **с парашю́том** to bale out

вы́б|ыть (*как* **быть**; см *Table 21*; *impf* **выбыва́ть**) *сов*: **вы́быть из** +*gen* to leave

вы́вез|ти (**-у, -ешь**; *impf* **вывози́ть**) *сов перех* to take; (*товар*: *из страны*) to take out

вы́ве|сить (**-шу, -сишь**; *impf* **выве́шивать**) *сов перех* (*флаг*) to put up; (*бельё*) to hang out

вы́вес|ка (**-ки**; *gen pl* **-ок**) *ж* sign

вы́ве|сти (**-ду, -дешь**; *impf* **выводи́ть**) *сов перех* to take out; (*войска*: *из города*) to pull out, withdraw; (*формулу*) to deduce; (*птенцов*) to hatch; (*породу*) to breed; (*уничтожить*) to exterminate; (*исключить*): **вы́вести кого́-н из** +*gen* (*из партии*) to expel sb from; **выводи́ть** (*perf* **вы́вести**) **кого́-н из терпе́ния** to exasperate sb; **выводи́ть** (*perf* **вы́вести**) **кого́-н из себя́** to drive sb mad; **вы́вестись** (*impf* **выводи́ться**) *сов возв* (*цыплята*) to hatch (out); (*исчезнуть*) to be eradicated

выве́шива|ть (**-ю**) *несов от* **вы́весить**

вы́вод (**-а**) *м* (*войск*) withdrawal; (*умозаключение*) conclusion

вы|води́ть(ся) (**-вожу́(сь), -во́дишь(ся)**) *несов от* **вы́вести(сь)**

вы́воз (**-а**) *м* removal; (*товаров*) export

вы|вози́ть (**-вожу́, -во́зишь**) *несов от* **вы́везти**

вывора́чива|ть(ся) (**-ю(сь)**) *несов от* **вы́вернуть(ся)**

выгиба́|ть (**-ю**) *несов от* **вы́гнуть**

вы́гля|деть (**-жу, -дишь**) *несов* to look

вы́глян|уть (**-у**; *impf* **выгля́дывать**) *сов* to look out

вы́г|нать (**-оню, -онишь**; *impf* **выгоня́ть**) *сов перех* to throw out; (*стадо*) to drive out

вы́гн|уть (**-у**; *impf* **выгиба́ть**) *сов перех* to bend; (*спину*) to arch

вы́говор (**-а**) *м* (*произношение*) accent; (*наказание*) reprimand; **вы́говор|ить** (**-ю, -ишь**; *impf* **выгова́ривать**) *сов перех* (*произнести*) to pronounce

вы́год|а (**-ы**) *ж* advantage, benefit; (*прибыль*) profit

вы́годно *нареч* (*продать*) at a profit ▷ *как сказ* it is profitable; **мне э́то вы́годно** this is to my advantage; (*прибыльно*) this is profitable for me

выгоня́|ть (**-ю**) *несов от* **вы́гнать**

вы́гор|еть (*3sg* **-ит**, *impf* **выгора́ть**) *сов* (*сгореть*) to burn down; (*выцвести*) to fade

вы́гре|сти (**-бу, -бешь**; *pt* **-б, -бла, -бло**, *impf* **выгреба́ть**) *сов перех* to rake out

вы́гру|зить (**-жу, -зишь**; *impf* **выгружа́ть**) *сов перех* to unload; **вы́грузиться** (*impf* **выгружа́ться**) *сов возв* to unload

выда|ва́ть(ся) (**-ю́(сь)**) *несов от* **вы́дать(ся)**

вы́дав|ить (**-лю, -ишь**; *impf* **выда́вливать**) *сов перех* (*лимон*) to squeeze

вы́да|ть (*как* **дать**; см *Table 16*; *impf* **выдава́ть**) *сов перех* to give out; (*патент*) to issue; (*продукцию*) to produce; (*тайну*) to give away; **выдава́ть** (*perf* **вы́дать**) **кого́-н/что-н за** *+acc* to pass sb/sth off as; **выдава́ть** (*perf* **вы́дать**) **де́вушку за́муж** to marry a girl off; **вы́даться** (*impf* **выдава́ться**) *сов возв* (*берег*) to jut out

вы́дач|а (**-и**) *ж* (*справки*) issue; (*продукции*) output; (*заложников*) release

выдаю́щийся *прил* outstanding

выдвига́|ть(ся) (**-ю(сь)**) *несов от* **вы́двинуть(ся)**

выдвиже́ни|е (**-я**) *ср* (*кандидата*) nomination

вы́двин|уть (**-у**; *impf* **выдвига́ть**) *сов перех* to put forward; (*ящик*) to pull out; (*обвинение*) to level; **вы́двинуться** (*impf* **выдвига́ться**) *сов возв* to slide out; (*работник*) to advance

вы́дел|ить (**-ю, -ишь**; *impf* **выделя́ть**) *сов перех* to assign, allocate; (*отличить*) to pick out; (*газы*) to emit; **вы́делиться** (*impf* **выделя́ться**) *сов возв* (*пот*) to be secreted; (*газ*) to be emitted; **выделя́ться** (*perf* **вы́делиться**) **чем-н** to stand out by virtue of sth

выдёргива|ть (**-ю**) *несов от* **вы́дернуть**

вы́держ|ать (**-у, -ишь**; *impf* **выде́рживать**) *сов перех* (*давление*) to withstand; (*боль*) to bear; (*экзамен*) to get through ▷ *неперех* (*человек*) to hold out; (*мост*) to hold; **не вы́держать** (*perf*) (*человек*) to give in

вы́держ|ка (**-ки**; *gen pl* **-ек**) *ж* (*самообладание*) self-control; (*отрывок*) excerpt; (*Фото*) exposure

вы́дерн|уть (**-у**; *impf* **выдёргивать**) *сов перех* to pull out

вы́дума|ть (**-ю**; *impf* **выду́мывать**) *сов перех* (*историю*) to make up, invent; (*игру*) to invent

вы́дум|ка (**-ки**; *gen pl* **-ок**) *ж* invention

выдыха́|ть (**-ю**) *несов от* **вы́дохнуть**

вы́езд (**-а**) *м* (*отъезд*) departure; (*место*) way out; **игра́ на вы́езде** (*Спорт*) away game

выездно́й *прил* (*документ*) exit; **выездно́й спекта́кль** guest performance; **выездно́й матч** away match

вы́е|хать (*как* **е́хать**; см *Table 19*; *impf* **выезжа́ть**) *сов* (*уехать*) to leave; (*машина*) to drive out

вы́ж|ать (**-му, -мешь**; *impf* **выжима́ть**) *сов перех* (*лимон*) to squeeze; (*бельё*) to wring (out)

вы́ж|ечь (**-гу, -жешь** *итп* **-гут**; *pt* **-ег, -гла**, *impf* **выжига́ть**) *сов перех* to burn; (*подлеж: солнце*) to scorch

выжива́ни|е (**-я**) *ср* survival

выжива́|ть (**-ю**) *несов от* **вы́жить**

выжига́|ть (**-ю**) *несов от* **вы́жечь**

выжима́|ть (**-ю**) *несов от* **вы́жать**

вы́жи|ть (**-ву, -вешь**; *impf* **выжива́ть**) *сов* to survive ▷ *перех* (*разг*) to drive out

вы́з|вать (**-ову, -овешь**; *impf* **вызыва́ть**) *сов перех* to call; (*гнев, критику*) to provoke; (*восторг*) to arouse; (*пожар*) to cause; **вызыва́ть** (*perf* **вы́звать**) **кого́-н на что-н** to challenge sb to sth; **вы́зваться** (*impf* **вызыва́ться**) *сов возв*: **вы́зваться** *+infin* to volunteer to do

вы́здорове|ть (**-ю, -ешь**; *impf* **выздора́вливать**) *сов* to recover

вы́зов (**-а**) *м* call; (*в суд*) summons; (*+dat*: *обществу, родителям итп*) challenge to; **броса́ть** (*perf* **бро́сить**) **вы́зов кому́-н/чему́-н** to challenge sb/sth

вы́зубр|ить (**-ю, -ишь**) *сов от* **зубри́ть**

вызыва́|ть(ся) (**-ю(сь)**) *несов от* **вы́звать(ся)**

вызыва́ющий *прил* challenging

вы́игра|ть (**-ю**; *impf* **выи́грывать**) *сов перех* to win

вы́|йти (*как* **идти́**; *см Table 18*; *impf* **выходи́ть**) *сов* to leave; (*из игры*) to drop out; (*из автобуса*) to get off; (*книга*) to come out; (*случиться*) to ensue; (*оказаться*) *+instr* to come out; **выходи́ть** (*perf* **вы́йти**) **за́муж** (**за**) *+acc* to marry (*of woman*); **выходи́ть** (*perf* **вы́йти**) **из больни́цы** to leave hospital

выка́лыва|ть (**-ю**) *несов от* **вы́колоть**

выка́пыва|ть (**-ю**) *несов от* **вы́копать**

выка́рмлива|ть (**-ю**) *несов от* **вы́кормить**

вы́кача|ть (**-ю**; *impf* **выка́чивать**) *сов перех* to pump out

вы́кидыш (**-а**) *м* miscarriage

вы́кин|уть (**-у**; *impf* **выки́дывать**) *сов перех* to throw out; (*слово*) to omit

вы́кип|еть (*3sg* **-ит**, *impf* **выкипа́ть**) *сов* to boil away

выкла́дыва|ть (**-ю**) *несов от* **вы́ложить**

выключа́тел|ь (**-я**) *м* switch

вы́ключ|ить (**-у, -ишь**; *impf* **выключа́ть**) *сов перех* to turn off; **вы́ключиться** (*impf* **выключа́ться**) *сов возв* (*мотор*) to go off; (*свет*) to go out

вы́к|овать (**-ую**; *impf* **выко́вывать**) *сов перех* (*металл*) to forge

вы́кол|оть (**-ю, -ешь**; *impf* **выка́лывать**) *сов перех* to poke out

вы́копа|ть (**-ю**) *сов от* **копа́ть** ▷ (*impf* **выка́пывать**) *перех* (*яму*) to dig; (*овощи*) to dig up

вы́корм|ить (**-лю, -ишь**; *impf* **выка́рмливать**) *сов перех* to rear

вы́крик (**-а**) *м* shout

вы́крикн|уть (**-у**; *impf* **выкри́кивать**) *сов перех* to shout *или* cry out

вы́кро|йка (**-йки**; *gen pl* **-ек**) *ж* pattern

вы́купа|ть(ся) (**-ю(сь)**) *сов от* **купа́ть(ся)**

вы́куп|ить (**-лю, -ишь**; *impf* **выкупа́ть**) *сов перех* (*заложника*) to ransom; (*вещи*) to redeem

вылáвлива|ть (**-ю**) *несов от* **вы́ловить**

выла́мыва|ть (**-ю**) *несов от* **вы́ломать**

вы́лез|ти (**-у, -ешь**; *pt* **-, -ла**, *impf* **вылеза́ть**) *сов* (*волосы*) to fall out; **вылеза́ть** (*perf* **вы́лезти**) **из** *+gen* to climb out of

вы́леп|ить (**-лю, -ишь**) *сов от* **лепи́ть**

вы́лет (**-а**) *м* departure

вы́ле|теть (**-чу, -тишь**; *impf* **вылета́ть**) *сов* to fly out; **его́ и́мя вы́летело у меня́ из головы́** his name has slipped my mind

вы́леч|ить (**-у, -ишь**; *impf*

вылечивать) *сов перех* to cure; **вылечиться** *несов возв* to be cured

вы́л|ить (**-ью, -ьешь**; *impf* **вылива́ть**) *сов перех* to pour out ▷ (*impf* **лить**) (*деталь, статую*) to cast; **вы́литься** (*impf* **вылива́ться**) *сов возв* to pour out; **вылива́ться** (*perf* **вы́литься**) **в** *+acc* to turn into

вы́лов|ить (**-лю, -ишь**; *impf* **выла́вливать**) *сов перех* to catch

вы́лож|ить (**-у, -ишь**; *impf* **выкла́дывать**) *сов перех* to lay out; **выкла́дывать** (*perf* **вы́ложить**) **что-н чем-н** (*плиткой*) to face sth with sth

вы́лома|ть (**-ю**; *impf* **выла́мывать**) *сов перех* to break open

вы́луп|иться (*3sg* **-ится**, *impf* **вылу́пливаться**) *сов возв* (*птенцы*) to hatch (out)

выма́чива|ть (**-ю**) *несов от* **вы́мочить**

вы́м|ереть (*3sg* **-рет**, *impf* **вымира́ть**) *сов* (*динозавры*) to become extinct; (*город*) to be dead

вы́ме|сти (**-ту, -тешь**; *pt* **-л, -ла**, *impf* **вымета́ть**) *сов перех* to sweep out

вы́ме|стить (**-щу, -стишь**; *impf* **вымеща́ть**) *сов перех*: **вы́местить что-н на ком-н** to take sth out on sb

вымета́|ть (**-ю**) *несов от* **вы́мести**

вымира́|ть (*3sg* **-ет**) *несов от* **вы́мереть**

вы́мок|нуть (**-ну, -нешь**; *pt* **-, -ла**) *сов* to get soaked through

вы́моч|ить (**-у, -ишь**; *impf* **выма́чивать**) *сов перех* to soak

вы́м|ыть (**-ою, -оешь**) *сов от* **мыть**

вына́шива|ть (**-ю**) *несов перех* to nurture

вы́нес|ти (**-у, -ешь**; *pt* **-, -ла**, *impf* **выноси́ть**) *сов перех* to carry *или* take out; (*приговор*) to pass, pronounce; (*впечатления, знания*) to gain; (*боль, оскорбление*) to bear

вынима́|ть (**-ю**) *несов от* **вы́нуть**

вын|оси́ть (**-ошу́, -о́сишь**) *несов от* **вы́нести** ▷ *перех*: **я его́ не выношу́** I can't bear *или* stand him

вы́ну|дить (**-жу, -дишь**; *impf* **вынужда́ть**) *сов перех*: **вы́нудить кого́-н/что-н к чему́-н** to force sb/sth into sth

вы́нужденн|ый *прил* forced; **вы́нужденная поса́дка** emergency landing

вы́н|уть (**-у**; *impf* **вынима́ть**) *сов перех* to take out

вы́нырн|уть (**-у**) *сов* (*из воды*) to surface; (*разг*: *из-за угла*) to pop up

выпада́|ть (**-ю**) *несов от* **вы́пасть**

выпаде́ни|е (**-я**) *ср* (*осадков*) fall; (*зубов, волос*) falling out

вы́па|сть (**-ду, -дешь**; *impf* **выпада́ть**) *сов* to fall out; (*осадки*) to fall; (*задача итп*) *+dat* to fall to; **мне вы́пал слу́чай/ вы́пало сча́стье встре́тить его́** I chanced to/had the luck to meet him

вы́пивк|а (**-и**) *ж* booze

вы́пи|сать (**-шу, -шешь**; *impf* **выпи́сывать**) *сов перех* to copy *или* write out; (*пропуск, счёт, рецепт*) to make out; (*газету*) to subscribe to; (*пациента*) to discharge; **вы́писаться** (*impf*

выпи́сываться) *несов возв* (*из больницы*) to be discharged; (*с адреса*) to change one's residence permit
вы́пис|ка (**-ки**; *gen pl* **-ок**) *ж* (*цитата*) extract
вы́п|ить (**-ью, -ьешь**; *imper* **-ей(те)**) *сов от* **пить**
вы́плав|ить (**-лю, -ишь**; *impf* **выплавля́ть**) *сов перех* to smelt
вы́плат|а (**-ы**) *ж* payment
вы́пла|тить (**-чу, -тишь**; *impf* **выпла́чивать**) *сов перех* to pay; (*долг*) to pay off
вы́плесн|уть (**-у**; *impf* **выплёскивать**) *сов перех* to pour out
вы́плы|ть (**-ву, -вешь**; *impf* **выплыва́ть**) *сов* to swim out
вы́полз|ти (**-у**; *pt* **-, -ла, -ло**, *impf* **выполза́ть**) *сов* to crawl out
выполни́мый *прил* feasible
вы́полн|ить (**-ю, -ишь**; *impf* **выполня́ть**) *сов перех* (*задание, заказ*) to carry out; (*план, условие*) to fulfil (*Brit*), fulfill (*US*)
вы́потрош|ить (**-у, -ишь**) *сов от* **потроши́ть**
выпра́шива|ть (**-ю**) *несов перех* to beg for
вы́про|сить (**-шу, -сишь**) *сов перех*: **он вы́просил у отца́ маши́ну** he persuaded his father to give him the car
вы́прыгн|уть (**-у**; *impf* **выпры́гивать**) *сов* to jump out
вы́прям|ить (**-лю, -ишь**; *impf* **выпрямля́ть**) *сов перех* to straighten (out); **вы́прямиться** (*impf* **выпрямля́ться**) *несов возв* to straighten (up)
вы́пуск (**-а**) *м* (*продукции*) output; (*газа*) emission, release; (*книги*) publication; (*денег, акций*) issue; (*учащиеся*) school leavers *мн* (*Brit*), graduates *мн* (*US*)
выпуска́|ть (**-ю**) *несов от* **вы́пустить**
выпускни́к (**-а́**) *м* (*вуза*) graduate; **выпускни́к шко́лы** school-leaver
выпускно́й *прил* (*класс*) final-year; (*Тех*): **выпускно́й кла́пан** exhaust valve; **выпускно́й ве́чер** graduation; **выпускно́й экза́мен** final exam, finals *мн*
вы́пу|стить (**-щу, -стишь**; *impf* **выпуска́ть**) *сов перех* to let out; (*дым*) to exhale; (*заключённого*) to release; (*специалистов*) to turn out; (*продукцию*) to produce; (*книгу*) to publish; (*заём, марки*) to issue; (*акции*) to put into circulation; (*исключить: параграф*) to omit
вы́пью *etc сов см* **вы́пить**
вы́работа|ть (**-ю**; *impf* **выраба́тывать**) *сов перех* to produce; (*план*) to work out; (*привычку*) to develop
выра́внива|ть (**-ю**) *несов от* **вы́ровнять**
выража́|ть(ся) (**-ю(сь)**) *несов от* **вы́разить(ся)**
выраже́ни|е (**-я**) *ср* expression
вы́ра|зить (**-жу, -зишь**; *impf* **выража́ть**) *сов перех* to express; **вы́разиться** (*impf* **выража́ться**) *сов возв* (*чувство*) to manifest *или* express itself; (*человек*) to express o.s.
вы́р|асти (**-асту, -астешь**; *pt* **-ос, -осла, -осли**) *сов от* **расти́** ▷ (*impf* **выраста́ть**) *неперех* (*появиться*) to rise up; **выраста́ть** (*perf* **вы́расти**) **в** *+acc* to (grow to) become

вы́ра|стить (**-щу, -стишь**) *сов от* **расти́ть**
выра́щива|ть (**-ю**; *perf* **вы́растить**) *несов перех* = **расти́ть**
вы́рв|ать (**-у, -ешь**; *impf* **вырыва́ть**) *сов перех* to pull out; (*отнять*): **вы́рвать что-н у кого́-н** to snatch sth from sb ▷ (*impf* **рвать**) *безл* (*разг*): **её вы́рвало** she threw up; **ему́ вы́рвали зуб** he had his tooth taken out; **вы́рваться** (*impf* **вырыва́ться**) *сов возв* (*из тюрьмы*) to escape; (*перен*: *в театр*) to manage to get away; (*пламя*) to shoot out
вы́рез (**-а**) *м*: **пла́тье с больши́м вы́резом** a low-cut dress
вы́ре|зать (**-жу, -жешь**; *impf* **выреза́ть**) *сов перех* to cut out; (*опухоль, гнойник*) to remove; (*из дерева, из кости итп*) to carve; (*на камне, на металле итп*) to engrave; (*убить*) to slaughter
вы́рез|ка (**-ки**; *gen pl* **-ок**) *ж* (*газетная*) cutting, clipping; (*мясная*) fillet
вы́ровня|ть (**-ю**) *сов от* **ровня́ть** ▷ (*impf* **выра́внивать**) *перех* to level
вы́род|иться (*3sg* **-ится**, *impf* **вырожда́ться**) *сов возв* to degenerate
вы́рон|ить (**-ю, -ишь**) *сов перех* to drop
вы́рос *etc сов см* **вы́расти**
вы́руб|ить (**-лю, -ишь**; *impf* **выруба́ть**) *сов перех* (*деревья*) to cut down; (*свет*) to cut off
вы́руга|ть(ся) (**-ю(сь)**) *сов от* **руга́ть(ся)**
вы́руч|ить (**-у, -ишь**; *impf* **выруча́ть**) *сов перех* to help out; (*деньги*) to make
вы́ручк|а (**-и**) *ж* rescue; (*деньги*) takings *мн*
вырыва́|ть(ся) (**-ю(сь)**) *несов от* **вы́рвать(ся)**
вы́р|ыть (**-ою, -оешь**) *сов от* **рыть** ▷ (*impf* **вырыва́ть**) *перех* to dig up; (*яму*) to dig
вы́са|дить (**-жу, -дишь**; *impf* **выса́живать**) *сов перех* (*растение*) to plant out; (*пассажира*: *дать выйти*) to drop off; (: *силой*) to throw out; (*войска*) to land; **вы́садиться** (*impf* **выса́живаться**) *сов возв*: **вы́садиться (из +*gen*)** to get off; (*войска*) to land
выса́сыва|ть (**-ю**) *несов от* **вы́сосать**
вы́свобо|дить (**-жу, -дишь**; *impf* **высвобожда́ть**) *сов перех* (*ногу, руку*) to free; (*время*) to set aside
вы́си|деть (**-жу, -дишь**; *impf* **выси́живать**) *сов перех* to hatch; (*перен*: *лекцию*) to sit out
выс|иться (*3sg* **-ится**) *несов возв* to tower
вы́ска|зать (**-жу, -жешь**; *impf* **выска́зывать**) *сов перех* to express; **вы́сказаться** (*impf* **выска́зываться**) *сов возв* to speak one's mind; **выска́зываться** (*perf* **вы́сказаться**) **про́тив +*gen*/за +*acc*** to speak out against/in favour of
выска́зывани|е (**-я**) *ср* statement
выска́кива|ть (**-ю**) *несов от* **вы́скочить**
вы́скользн|уть (**-у**; *impf* **выска́льзывать**) *сов* to slip out
вы́скоч|ить (**-у, -ишь**; *impf* **выска́кивать**) *сов* to jump out; **его́ и́мя вы́скочило у меня́ из головы́** (*разг*) his name has slipped my mind

вы́|слать (**-шлю, -шлешь**; *impf* **высыла́ть**) *сов перех* to send off; (*изгнать*) to deport
вы́сле|дить (**-жу, -дишь**; *impf* **выле́живать**) *сов перех* to track down
вы́слуг|а (**-и**) *ж*: **за вы́слугу лет** for long service
вы́слуша|ть (**-ю**; *impf* **выслу́шивать**) *сов перех* to hear out
вы́сме|ять (**-ю**; *impf* **высме́ивать**) *сов перех* to ridicule
вы́сморка|ть(ся) (**-ю(сь)**) *сов от* **сморка́ть(ся)**
высо́выва|ть(ся) (**-ю(сь)**) *несов от* **вы́сунуть(ся)**
высо́кий *прил* high; (*человек*) tall; (*честь*) great; (*гость*) distinguished
высоко́ *нареч* high (up) ▷ *как сказ* it's high (up)
вы́сос|ать (**-у, -ешь**; *impf* **выса́сывать**) *сов перех* to suck out; (*насосом*) to pump out
выс|ота́ (**-оты́**; *nom pl* **-о́ты**) *ж* height; (*Гео*) altitude; (*звука*) pitch
высо́тный *прил* (*здание*) high-rise
вы́сох|нуть (**-ну**; *pt* **-, -ла, -ло**) *сов от* **со́хнуть**
высо́честв|о (**-а**) *ср*: **Ва́ше** *итп* **Высо́чество** Your *etc* Highness
вы́сп|аться (**-люсь, -ишься**; *impf* **высыпа́ться**) *сов возв* to sleep well
вы́став|ить (**-лю, -ишь**; *impf* **выставля́ть**) *сов перех* (*поставить наружу*) to put out; (*грудь*) to stick out; (*кандидатуру*) to put forward; (*товар*) to display; (*охрану*) to post; (*разг*: *выгнать*) to chuck out
вы́став|ка (**-ки**; *gen pl* **-ок**) *ж* exhibition
выставля́|ть (**-ю**) *несов от* **вы́ставить**
вы́стира|ть (**-ю**) *сов от* **стира́ть**
вы́стрел (**-а**) *м* shot
вы́стрел|ить (**-ю, -ишь**) *сов* to fire
вы́стро|ить(ся) (**-ю(сь), -ишь(ся)**) *сов от* **стро́ить(ся)**
вы́ступ (**-а**) *м* ledge
вы́ступ|ить (**-лю, -ишь**; *impf* **выступа́ть**) *сов* (*против, в защиту*) to come out; (*из толпы*) to step out; (*актёр*) to perform; (*пот, сыпь*) to break out; (*в поход, на поиски*) to set off *или* out
выступле́ни|е (**-я**) *ср* (*актёра*) performance; (*в печати*) article; (*речь*) speech
вы́сун|уть (**-у**; *impf* **высо́вывать**) *сов перех* to stick out; **вы́сунуться** (*impf* **высо́вываться**) *сов возв* (*из окна*) to lean out; (*рука, нога*) to stick out
вы́суш|ить(ся) (**-у(сь), -ишь(ся)**) *сов от* **суши́ть(ся)**
вы́счита|ть (**-ю**; *impf* **высчи́тывать**) *сов перех* to calculate
вы́сш|ий *прил* (*орган власти*) highest, supreme; **в вы́сшей сте́пени** extremely; **вы́сшая ме́ра наказа́ния** capital punishment; **вы́сшее образова́ние** higher education; **вы́сшее учёбное заведе́ние** = **вуз**
высыла́|ть (**-ю**) *несов от* **вы́слать**
вы́сып|ать (**-лю, -лешь**; *impf* **высыпа́ть**) *сов перех* to pour out; **вы́сыпаться** (*impf* **высыпа́ться**) *сов возв* to pour out
выта́лкива|ть (**-ю**) *несов от* **вы́толкнуть**

вы́тащ|ить (**-у, -ишь**) *сов от* **тащи́ть** ▷ (*impf* **вытáскивать**) *перех* (*мебель*) to drag out

вытекá|ть (*3sg* **-ет**) *несов от* **вы́течь** ▷ *неперех* (*вывод*) to follow; (*река*) to flow out

вы́т|ереть (**-ру, -решь**; *impf* **вытирáть**) *сов перех* to wipe up; (*посуду*) to dry (up); (*руки, глаза*) to wipe; **вы́тереться** (*impf* **вытирáться**) *сов возв* (*человек*) to dry o.s.

вы́те|чь (*3sg* **-чет**, *3pl* **-кут**, *pt* **-к, -кла**, *impf* **вытекáть**) *сов* to flow out

вытирá|ть(ся) (**-ю(сь)**) *несов от* **вы́тереть(ся)**

вы́толкн|уть (**-у**; *impf* **вытáлкивать**) *сов перех* to push out

вытрезви́тел|ь (**-я**) *м overnight police cell for drunks*

вы́тряхн|уть (**-у**; *impf* **вытря́хивать**) *сов перех* to shake out

выть (**вóю, вóешь**) *несов* (*зверь, ветер*) to howl; (*сирена*) to wail

вы́тян|уть (**-у**; *impf* **вытя́гивать**) *сов перех* to pull out; (*дым*) to extract; (*руки*) to stretch; **вы́тянуться** (*impf* **вытя́гиваться**) *сов возв* (*на диване, вдоль берега*) to stretch out; (*встать смирно*) to stand at attention

вы́у|дить (**-жу, -дишь**; *impf* **выу́живать**) *сов перех* (*рыбу*) to catch; (*разг: сведения*) to wheedle out

вы́уч|ить(ся) (**-у(сь), -ишь(ся)**) *сов от* **учи́ть(ся)**

выхáжива|ть (**-ю**) *несов от* **вы́ходить**

вы́хва|тить (**-чу, -тишь**; *impf* **выхвáтывать**) *сов перех* to snatch

выхлопн|óй *прил* exhaust; **выхлопны́е гáзы** exhaust fumes

вы́ход (**-а**) *м* (*войск*) withdrawal; (*из кризиса*) way out; (*на сцену*) appearance; (*в море*) sailing; (*книги*) publication; (*на экран*) showing; (*место*) exit

вы́хо|дить (**-жу, -дишь**; *impf* **выхáживать**) *сов перех* (*больного*) to nurse (back to health)

вых|оди́ть (**-ожу́, -óдишь**) *несов от* **вы́йти** ▷ *неперех*: **выходи́ть на** *+acc* (*юг, север*) to face; **окнó выхóдит в парк** the window looks out onto the park

выходн|óй *прил* exit; (*платье*) best ▷ (**-óго**) *м* (*также* **выходнóй день**) day off (work); **сегóдня выходнóй** (*разг*) today is a holiday; **выходны́е** weekend *ед*

вы́цве|сти (*3sg* **-тет**, *impf* **выцветáть**) *сов* to fade

вы́черкн|уть (**-у**; *impf* **вычёркивать**) *сов перех* to cross *или* score out

вы́чет (**-а**) *м* deduction ▷ *предл*: **за вы́четом** *+gen* minus

вычислéни|е (**-я**) *ср* calculation; **вычисли́тельн|ый** *прил* (*операция*) computing; **вычисли́тельная маши́на** computer; **вычисли́тельная тéхника** computers *мн*; **вычисли́тельный центр** computer centre (*Brit*) *или* center (*US*); **вы́числ|ить** (**-ю, -ишь**; *impf* **вычисля́ть**) *сов перех* to calculate

вычитá|ть (**-ю**) *несов от* **вы́честь**

вы́ше *сравн прил от* **высóкий** ▷ *сравн нареч от* **высокó** ▷ *нареч* higher; (*в тексте*) above

▷ *предл +gen* above
вышел *сов см* **выйти**
вышива́|ть (**-ю**) *несов от* **вышить**
вышив|ка (**-ки**; *gen pl* **-ок**) *ж* embroidery
выш|ка (**-ки**; *gen pl* **-ек**) *ж* (*строение*) tower; (*Спорт*) diving board
вышла *etc сов см* **выйти**
выяв|ить (**-лю, -ишь**; *impf* **выявля́ть**) *сов перех* (*талант*) to discover; (*недостатки*) to expose; **выявиться** (*impf* **выявля́ться**) *сов возв* to come to light, be revealed
выясн|ить (**-ю, -ишь**; *impf* **выясня́ть**) *сов перех* to find out; **выясниться** (*impf* **выясня́ться**) *сов возв* to become clear
Вьетна́м (**-а**) *м* Vietnam
вью́г|а (**-и**) *ж* snowstorm, blizzard
вяз (**-а**) *м* elm
вяза́ни|е (**-я**) *ср* knitting
вя|за́ть (**-жу́, -жешь**; *perf* **связа́ть**) *несов перех* to tie up; (*свитер*) to knit
вя́з|нуть (**-ну**; *pt* **-, -ла, -ло**, *perf* **завя́знуть** *или* **увя́знуть**) *несов*: **вя́знуть (в** *+prp*) to get stuck (in)
вя́н|уть (**-у**; *perf* **завя́нуть** *или* **увя́нуть**) *несов* (*цветы*) to wilt, wither; (*красота*) to fade

Г

г *сокр* (= *грамм*) g (= *gram(me)*)
г. *сокр* = **год; го́род**
Гаа́г|а (**-и**) *ж* The Hague
габари́т (**-а**) *м* (*Tex*) dimension
га́вань|ь (**-и**) *ж* harbour (*Brit*), harbor (*US*)
гада́|ть (**-ю**) *несов* (*предполагать*) to guess; **гада́ть (***perf* **погада́ть) кому́-н** to tell sb's fortune
га́дост|ь (**-и**) *ж* filth
га́ечный *прил*: **га́ечный ключ** spanner
газ (**-а**) *м* gas; *см также* **га́зы**
газе́т|а (**-ы**) *ж* newspaper
газиро́ванн|ый *прил*: **газиро́ванная вода́** carbonated water
га́зов|ый *прил* gas; **га́зовая плита́** gas cooker
газо́н (**-а**) *м* lawn
газопрово́д (**-а**) *м* gas pipeline
га́з|ы (**-ов**) *мн* (*Мед*) wind *ед*

ГАЙ *ж сокр* (= *Госуда́рственная автомоби́льная инспе́кция*) *state motor vehicle inspectorate*
га́|йка (**-йки**; *gen pl* **-ек**) *ж* nut
галантере́|я (**-и**) *ж* haberdashery (*Brit*), notions store (*US*)
галере́|я (**-и**) *ж* gallery
галло́н (**-а**) *м* gallon
галлюцина́ци|я (**-и**) *ж* hallucination
га́лоч|ка (**-ки**; *gen pl* **-ек**) *ж* (*в тексте*) tick, check (*US*)
га́лстук (**-а**) *м* tie, necktie (*US*)
га́льк|а (**-и**) *ж собир* pebbles *мн*
га́мбургер (**-а**) *м* hamburger
га́мм|а (**-ы**) *ж* (*Муз*) scale
га́нгстер (**-а**) *м* gangster
гара́ж (**-а́**) *м* garage
гаранти́йный *прил* guarantee
гаранти́р|овать (**-ую**) *(не)сов перех* to guarantee
гара́нти|я (**-и**) *ж* guarantee
гардеро́б (**-а**) *м* wardrobe; (*в общественном здании*) cloakroom
гармони́р|овать (**-ую**) *несов*: **гармони́ровать с** *+instr* (*со средой*) to be in harmony with; (*одежда*) to go with
гармони́ст (**-а**) *м* concertina player
гармо́ни|я (**-и**) *ж* harmony
гармо́ш|ка (**-ки**; *gen pl* **-ек**) *ж* (*разг*) ≈ squeeze-box
гарнизо́н (**-а**) *м* garrison
гарни́р (**-а**) *м* side dish
гарниту́р (**-а**) *м* (*мебель*) suite
гар|ь (**-и**) *ж* (*угля*) cinders *мн*
га|си́ть (**-шу́, -сишь**; *perf* **погаси́ть**) *несов перех* (*свет*) to turn off; (*пожар*) to extinguish, put out
га́с|нуть (**-ну**; *pt* — *или* **-нул, -ла**, *perf* **пога́снуть** *или* **уга́снуть**) *несов* (*огни*) to go out
гастро́л|и (**-ей**) *мн performances of touring company*; **е́здить/е́хать** (*perf* **пое́хать**) **на гастро́ли** to go on tour; **гастроли́р|овать** (**-ую**) *несов* to be on tour
гастроно́м (**-а**) *м* food store; **гастроно́ми|я** (**-и**) *ж* delicatessen
гаши́ш (**-а**) *м* cannabis
гва́рди|я (**-и**) *ж* (*Воен*) Guards *мн*
гвозди́к|а (**-и**) *ж* (*цветок*) carnation; (*пряность*) cloves *мн*
гвозд|ь (**-я́**) *м* nail
гг *сокр* = **го́ды**; **господа́**
где *нареч* where; (*разг*: *где-нибудь*) somewhere, anywhere ▷ *союз* where; **где Вы живёте?** where do you live?
где́-либо *нареч* = **где́-нибудь**
где́-нибудь *нареч* somewhere; (*в вопросе*) anywhere
где́-то *нареч* somewhere
геморро́|й (**-я**) *м* piles *мн*
гел|ь (**-я**) *м*: **гель для ду́ша** shower gel
ген (**-а**) *м* gene
генера́л (**-а**) *м* (*Воен*) general
генера́тор (**-а**) *м* generator
гене́тик|а (**-и**) *ж* genetics
гениа́льный *прил* great
ге́ни|й (**-я**) *м* genius
ге́нный *прил* (*терапия*) gene
геогра́фи|я (**-и**) *ж* geography
геоме́три|я (**-и**) *ж* geometry
гера́н|ь (**-и**) *ж* geranium
герб (**-а́**) *м* coat of arms; **госуда́рственный герб** national emblem
ге́рбов|ый *прил*: **ге́рбовая бума́га** stamped paper
геркуле́с (**-а**) *м* (*Кулин*) porridge oats *мн*
Герма́ни|я (**-и**) *ж* Germany; **герма́нский** *прил* German
герои́н|я (**-и**) *ж* heroine; **герои́ческий** *прил* heroic;
геро́|й (**-я**) *м* hero

г-жа *м сокр* = **госпожá**
гúбел|ь (**-и**) *ж* (*человека*) death; (*армии*) destruction; (*самолёта, надежды*) loss; (*карьеры*) ruin
гúбкий *прил* flexible
гúб|нуть (**-ну**; *pt* **-, ла**, *perf* **погúбнуть**) *несов* to perish; (*перен*) to come to nothing
гигáнт (**-а**) *м* giant; **гигáнтский** *прил* gigantic
гигиéн|а (**-ы**) *ж* hygiene; **гигиенúчный** *прил* hygienic
гид (**-а**) *м* guide
гидрометцéнтр (**-а**) *м сокр* (= *Гидрометеорологúческий центр*) meteorological office
гидроэлектростáнци|я (**-и**) *ж* hydroelectric power station
гимн (**-а**) *м*: **государственный гимн** national anthem
гимнáзи|я (**-и**) *ж* ≈ grammar school

ГимнÁзия

This institution of secondary education strives for higher academic standards than comprehensive schools. Pupils can study subjects which are not offered by mainstream education, e.g. classics and two modern languages.

гимнáстик|а (**-и**) *ж* exercises *мн*; **(спортúвная) гимнáстика** gymnastics; **худóжественная гимнáстика** modern rhythmic gymnastics
гинекóлог (**-а**) *м* gynaecologist (*Brit*), gynecologist (*US*)
гиперссы́л|ка (**-ки**; *gen pl* **-ок**) *ж* hyperlink
гипертонú|я (**-и**) *ж* high blood pressure
гипóтез|а (**-ы**) *ж* hypothesis
гипотонú|я (**-и**) *ж* low blood pressure
гиппопотáм (**-а**) *м* hippopotamus, hippo (*inf*)
гипс (**-а**) *м* (*Искусство*) plaster of Paris; (*Мед*) plaster
гитáр|а (**-ы**) *ж* guitar
глав|á (**-ы́**; *nom pl* **-ы**) *ж* (*книги*) chapter; (*здания*) dome ▷ *м* (*делегации*) head; **во главé с** *+instr* headed by; **во главé** *+gen* at the head of
главáр|ь (**-я́**) *м* (*банды*) leader
главнокомáндующ|ий (**-его**) *м* commander in chief
глáвн|ый *прил* main; (*старший по положению*) senior, head; **глáвным óбразом** chiefly, mainly
глагóл (**-а**) *м* verb
гладúльн|ый *прил*: **гладúльная доскá** ironing board
глá|дить (**-жу, -дишь**; *perf* **поглáдить**) *несов перех* to iron; (*волосы*) to stroke; **глáдкий** *прил* (*ровный*) smooth
глаз (**-а**; *loc sg* **-ý**, *nom pl* **-á**, *gen pl* **-**) *м* eye; **с глáзу нá глаз** tête `a tête; **на глаз** roughly
глазнóй *прил* eye
глазýнь|я (**-и**) *ж* fried egg
глáнд|а (**-ы**) *ж* (*обычно мн*) tonsil
глáсн|ый (**-ого**) *м* vowel; (*открытый*) open, public
глúн|а (**-ы**) *ж* clay; **глúняный** *прил* clay
глобáльный *прил* universal
глóбус (**-а**) *м* globe
глотá|ть (**-ю**; *perf* **проглотúть**) *несов перех* to swallow
глот|óк (**-кá**) *м* gulp, swallow; (*воды, чая*) drop
глóх|нуть (**-ну**; *pt* **-, -ла**, *perf* **оглóхнуть**) *несов* to grow deaf; (*мотор*) to stall

глу́бже *сравн прил от* **глубо́кий** ▷ *сравн нареч от* **глубоко́**
глуб|ина́ (**-ины́**; *nom pl* **-и́ны**) *ж* depth; (*леса*) heart; (*перен*): **в глубине́ души́** in one's heart of hearts
глубо́кий *прил* deep; (*провинция*) remote; (*мысль*) profound; **глубоко́** *нареч* deeply ▷ *как сказ*: **здесь глубоко́** it's deep here
глубокоуважа́емый *прил* dear
глупе́|ть (**-ю**; *perf* **поглупе́ть**) *несов* to grow stupid
глу́по *как сказ* it's stupid *или* silly; **глу́пост|ь** (**-и**) *ж* stupidity, silliness; (*поступок*) stupid *или* silly thing; (*слова*) nonsense; **глу́пый** *прил* stupid, silly
глухо́й *прил* deaf; (*звук*) muffled
глуш|ь (**-и́**; *instr sg* **-ью**, *loc sg* **-и́**) *ж* wilderness
глы́б|а (**-ы**) *ж* (*ледяная*) block
глюко́з|а (**-ы**) *ж* glucose
гля|де́ть (**-жу́, -ди́шь**; *perf* **погляде́ть**) *несов* to look
гля́нцевый *прил* glossy
гна|ть (**гоню́, го́нишь**; *pt* **-л, -ла́**) *несов перех* (*стадо*) to drive; (*человека*) to throw out; (*машину*) to drive fast; **гна́ться** *несов возв*: **гна́ться за** *+instr* to pursue
гнезд|о́ (**-а́**; *nom pl* **гнёзда**, *gen pl* **гнёзд**) *ср* (*птиц*) nest
гнету́щий *прил* depressing
гнило́й *прил* rotten
гнил|ь (**-и**) *ж* rotten stuff
гни|ть (**-ю́, -ёшь**; *perf* **сгнить**) *несов* to rot
гно|й (**-я**) *м* pus
ГНС *сокр* (= *Госуда́рственная нало́говая слу́жба*) ≈ Inland Revenue
гн|уть (**-у, -ёшь**; *perf* **согну́ть**) *несов перех* to bend; **гну́ться** *несов возв* (*ветка*) to bend
говор|и́ть (**-ю́, -и́шь**; *perf* **сказа́ть**) *несов перех* to say; (*правду*) to tell ▷ *неперех по perf* to speak, talk; (*обсуждать*): **говори́ть о** *+prp* to talk about; (*общаться*): **говори́ть с** *+instr* to talk to *или* with
говя́дин|а (**-ы**) *ж* beef
год (**-а**; *loc sg* **-у́**, *nom pl* **-ы**, *gen pl* **-о́в/лет**) *м* year; **прошло́ 3 го́да/5 лет** 3/5 years passed; **из го́да в год** year in year out; **кру́глый год** all year round
го|ди́ться (**-жу́сь, -ди́шься**) *несов возв +dat* to suit; **годи́ться** (*impf*) **для** *+gen* to be suitable for; **го́д|ный** *прил*: **го́дный к** *+dat* *или* **для** *+gen* fit *или* suitable for; **биле́т го́ден до ...** the ticket is valid until ...
годовщи́н|а (**-ы**) *ж* anniversary
гол (**-а**; *nom pl* **-ы́**) *м* goal
Голла́нди|я (**-и**) *ж* Holland
голла́ндский *прил* Dutch; **голла́ндский язы́к** Dutch
гол|ова́ (**-овы́**; *acc sg* **-ову**, *dat sg* **-ове́**, *nom pl* **-овы**, *gen pl* **-о́в**, *dat pl* **-ова́м**) *ж* head
головно́й *прил* (*офис*) main; (*боль*) head
го́лод (**-а**) *м* hunger; (*недоедание*) starvation; (*бедствие*) famine; **голода́|ть** (**-ю**) *несов* to starve; (*воздерживаться от пищи*) to fast; **голо́дный** *прил* hungry
голодо́в|ка (**-ки**; *gen pl* **-ок**) *ж* hunger strike
гололёд (**-а**) *м* black ice
го́лос (**-а**; *part gen* **-у**, *nom pl* **-а́**) *м* voice; (*Полит*) vote; **во весь го́лос** at the top of one's voice
голосова́ни|е (**-я**) *ср* ballot
голос|ова́ть (**-у́ю**; *perf*

проголосова́ть) *несов* to vote; (*разг*: *на дороге*) to hitch (a lift)
голуб|о́й *прил* light blue ▷ (**-ого**) *м* (*разг*) gay
го́луб|ь (**-я**; *gen pl* **-е́й**) *м* pigeon; dove
го́лый *прил* (*человек*) naked
гольф (**-а**) *м* golf; (*обычно мн*: *чулки*) knee sock
гомеопа́т (**-а**) *м* homoeopath (*Brit*), homeopath (*US*)
го́мик (**-а**) *м* (*разг*) homo(sexual)
гомосексуали́ст (**-а**) *м* homosexual
гоне́ни|е (**-я**) *ср* persecution
го́н|ка (**-ки**; *gen pl* **-ок**) *ж* (*разг*: *спешка*) rush; (*соревнования*) race; **го́нка вооруже́ний** arms race
гонора́р (**-а**) *м* fee; **а́вторский гонора́р** royalty
го́ночный *прил* racing
го́нщик (**-а**) *м* racing (*Brit*) *или* race car (*US*) driver; (*велосипедист*) racing cyclist
гоня́|ть (**-ю, -ешь**) *несов перех* (*ученика*) to grill ▷ *неперех* to race; **гоня́ться** *несов возв*: **гоня́ться за** *+instr* (*преследовать*) to chase (after); (*перен*) to pursue
гор. *сокр* = **го́род**
гор|а́ (*acc sg* **-у**, *gen sg* **-ы́**, *nom pl* **-ы**, *dat pl* **-а́м**) *ж* mountain; (*небольшая*) hill
гора́здо *нареч* much
горб (**-а́**; *loc sg* **-у́**) *м* hump
го́рб|ить (**-лю, -ишь**; *perf* **сго́рбить**) *несов перех*: **го́рбить спи́ну** to stoop; **го́рбиться** (*perf* **сго́рбиться**) *несов возв* to stoop
горбу́ш|ка (**-ки**; *gen pl* **-ек**) *ж* crust
гор|ди́ться (**-жу́сь, -ди́шься**) *несов возв +instr* to be proud of
го́рдост|ь (**-и**) *ж* pride; **го́рдый** *прил* proud
го́р|е (**-я**) *ср* (*скорбь*) grief; (*несчастье*) misfortune; **гор|ева́ть** (**-ю́ю**) *несов* to grieve
гор|е́ть (**-ю́, -и́шь**; *perf* **сгоре́ть**) *несов* to burn; (*по perf*: *дом*) to be on fire; (*больной*) to be burning hot; (*глаза*) to shine
горизо́нт (**-а**) *м* horizon; **горизонта́л|ь** (**-и**) *ж* horizontal; **горизонта́льный** *прил* horizontal
гори́лл|а (**-ы**) *ж* gorilla
гори́стый *прил* mountainous
го́р|ка (**-ки**; *gen pl* **-ок**) *ж* hill; (*кучка*) small pile
го́рл|о (**-а**) *ср* throat; **го́рлыш|ко** (**-ка**; *nom pl* **-ки**, *gen pl* **-ек**) *ср* (*бутылки*) neck
гормо́н (**-а**) *м* hormone
го́рный *прил* mountain; (*лыжи*) downhill; (*промышленность*) mining
го́род (**-а**; *nom pl* **-а́**) *м* (*большой*) city; (*небольшой*) town; **горожа́н|ин** (**-ина**; *nom pl* **-е**, *gen pl* **-**) *м* city dweller
гороско́п (**-а**) *м* horoscope
горо́х (**-а**) *м собир* peas *мн*; **горо́ш|ек** (**-ка**) *м собир* peas *мн*; (*на платье итп*) polka dots *мн*; **ткань в горо́шек** spotted material; **горо́шин|а** (**-ы**) *ж* pea
горст|ь (**-и**; *gen pl* **-е́й**) *ж* handful
горч|и́ть (*3sg* **-ит**) *несов* to taste bitter
горчи́ц|а (**-ы**) *ж* mustard
горш|о́к (**-ка́**) *м* pot
го́рький *прил* bitter
го́рько *нареч* (*плакать*) bitterly ▷ *как сказ*: **во рту го́рько** I have a bitter taste in my mouth
горю́ч|ее (**-его**) *ср* fuel
горя́ч|ий *прил* hot; (*перен*: *любовь*) passionate; (*: спор*)

heated; (: *желание*) burning; (: *человек*) hot-tempered; **горя́чая ли́ния** hot line

горячо́ *нареч* (*спорить, любить*) passionately ▷ *как сказ* it's hot

гос. *сокр* = **госуда́рственный**

Госба́нк (**-а**) *м сокр* (= *госуда́рственный банк*) state bank

госбезопа́сност|ь (**-и**) *ж сокр* (= *госуда́рственная безопа́сность*) national security

госбюдже́т (**-а**) *м сокр* (= *госуда́рственный бюдже́т*) state budget

го́спитал|ь (**-я**) *м* army hospital

господа́ *итп сущ см* **господи́н** ▷ *мн* (*при фамилии, при звании*) Messrs

го́споди *межд*: **Го́споди!** good Lord!

госп|оди́н (**-оди́на**; *nom pl* **-ода́**, *gen pl* **-о́д**) *м* gentleman (*мн* gentlemen); (*хозяин*) master; (*при обращении*) sir; (*при фамилии*) Mr (= *Mister*)

госпо́дств|овать (**-ую**) *несов* to rule; (*мнение*) to prevail

Госпо́дь (**Го́спода**; *voc* **Го́споди**) *м* (*также* **Госпо́дь Бог**) the Lord; **не дай Го́споди!** God forbid!; **сла́ва тебе́ Го́споди!** Glory be to God!; (*разг*) thank God!

госпож|а́ (**-и́**) *ж* lady; (*хозяйка*) mistress; (*при обращении, при звании*) Madam; (*при фамилии*: *замужняя*) Mrs; (: *незамужняя*) Miss; (: *замужняя или незамужняя*) Ms

госстра́х (**-а**) *м сокр* (= *госуда́рственное страхова́ние*) ≈ national insurance

гости́н|ая (**-ой**) *ж* living *или* sitting room, lounge (*Brit*)

гости́ниц|а (**-ы**) *ж* hotel

го|сти́ть (**-щу́, -сти́шь**) *несов* to stay

гост|ь (**-я**; *gen pl* **-е́й**) *м* guest; **идти́ (*perf* пойти́) в го́сти к кому́-н** to go to see sb; **быть** (*impf*) **в гостя́х у кого́-н** to be at sb's house

госуда́рственный *прил* state; **госуда́рств|о** (**-а**) *ср* state

гото́в|ить (**-лю, -ишь**; *perf* **пригото́вить**) *несов перех* to get ready; (*уроки*) to prepare; (*обед*) to prepare, make ▷ (*perf* **подгото́вить**) (*специалиста*) to train ▷ *неперех* to cook; **гото́виться** (*perf* **пригото́виться**) *несов возв*: **гото́виться к** *+dat* (*к отъезду*) to get ready for; **гото́виться (*perf* подгото́виться) к** *+dat* (*к экзамену*) to prepare for

гото́вност|ь (**-и**) *ж +infin* readiness *или* willingness to do

гото́во *как сказ* that's it; **гото́вый** *прил* (*изделие*) ready-made; **я/обе́д гото́в** I am/ dinner is ready; **гото́вый к** *+dat/ +infin* prepared for/to do

гр. *сокр* (= *граждани́н*) Mr (= *Mister*); (= *гражда́нка*) Mrs

граб|ёж (**-ежа́**) *м* robbery; (*дома*) burglary; **граби́тел|ь** (**-я**) *м* robber

гра́б|ить (**-лю, -ишь**; *perf* **огра́бить**) *несов перех* (*человека*) to rob; (*дом*) to burgle; (*город*) to pillage

гра́б|ли (**-ель** *или* **-лей**) *мн* rake *ед*

гра́ви|й (**-я**) *м* gravel

град (**-а**) *м* (*также перен*) hail

гра́дус (**-а**) *м* degree; **гра́дусник** (**-а**) *м* thermometer

граждани́н (**-а**; *nom pl* **гра́ждане**, *gen pl* **гра́ждан**) *м* citizen

граждáн|ка (**-ки**; *gen pl* **-ок**) *ж* citizen; **граждáнский** *прил* civil; (*долг*) civic; (*платье*) civilian

граждáнств|о (**-а**) *ср* citizenship

грамм (**-а**) *м* gram(me)

граммáтик|а (**-и**) *ж* grammar

грамматúческий *прил* grammatical; (*упражнение*) grammar

грáмот|а (**-ы**) *ж* (*документ*) certificate; **грáмотный** *прил* (*человек*) literate; (*текст*) correctly written; (*специалист, план*) competent

грампластúнк|а (**-и**) *ж* record

грандиóзный *прил* grand

гранúц|а (**-ы**) *ж* (*государства*) border; (*участка*) boundary; (*обычно мн*: *перен*) limit; **éхать** (*perf* **поéхать) за границу** to go abroad; **жить** (*impf*) **за гранúцей** to live abroad; **из-за границы** from abroad; **гранúч|ить** (**-у, -ишь**) *несов*: **гранúчить с** *+instr* to border on; (*перен*) to verge on

грант (**-а**) *м* grant

граф|á (**-ы́**) *ж* column

грáфик (**-а**) *м* (*Мат*) graph; (*план*) schedule, timetable

графúческий *прил* graphic

грáци|я (**-и**) *ж* grace

гребён|ка (**-ки**; *gen pl* **-ок**) *ж* comb

гребеш|óк (**-кá**) *м* comb

грéбл|я (**-и**) *ж* rowing

грéйпфрут (**-а**) *м* grapefruit

грек (**-а**) *м* Greek (man) (*мн* men)

грéл|ка (**-ки**; *gen pl* **-ок**) *ж* hot-water bottle

грем|éть (**-лю́, -úшь**; *perf* **прогремéть**) *несов* (*поезд*) to thunder by; (*гром*) to rumble; **гремéть** (*perf* **прогремéть**) *+instr* (*ведром*) to clatter

грéн|ка (**-ки**; *gen pl* **-ок**) *ж* toast

гре|стú (**-бу́, -бёшь**; *pt* **грёб, -блá**) *несов* to row; (*веслом, руками*) to paddle ▷ *перех* (*листья*) to rake

гре|ть (**-ю**) *несов перех* (*подлеж*: *солнце*) to heat, warm; (: *шуба*) to keep warm; (*воду*) to heat (up); (*руки*) to warm; **грéться** *несов возв* (*человек*) to warm o.s.; (*вода*) to warm *или* heat up

грех (**-á**) *м* sin

Грéци|я (**-и**) *ж* Greece

грéцкий *прил*: **грéцкий орéх** walnut

грéческий *прил* Greek; **грéческий язы́к** Greek

грéчк|а (**-и**) *ж* buckwheat; **грéчневый** *прил* buckwheat

греш|úть (**-у́, -úшь**; *perf* **согрешúть**) *несов* to sin

гриб (**-á**) *м* (*съедобный*) (edible) mushroom; **несъедóбный гриб** toadstool; **грибнóй** *прил* (*суп*) mushroom

гриб|óк (**-кá**) *м* (*на коже*) fungal infection; (*на дереве*) fungus

гримир|овáть (**-у́ю**; *perf* **загримировáть**) *несов перех*: **гримировáть когó-н** to make sb up

грипп (**-а**) *м* flu

грúфел|ь (**-я**) *м* (pencil) lead

гроб (**-а**; *loc sg* **-у́**, *nom pl* **-ы́**) *м* coffin

гр|озá (**-озы́**; *nom pl* **-óзы**) *ж* thunderstorm

гроздь|ь (**-и**; *gen pl* **-éй**) *ж* (*винограда*) bunch; (*сирени*) cluster

гро|зúть (**-жу́, -зúшь**) *несов*: **грозúть** (*perf* **пригрозúть**) **комý-н чем-н** to threaten sb with sth; (*+instr*: *катастрофой*) to threaten to become

грозов|óй *прил*: **грозовáя тýча** storm cloud

гром (**-а**; *gen pl* **-óв**) *м* thunder
громáдный *прил* enormous, huge
гром|ить (**-лю́, -и́шь**) *несов перех* to destroy
гро́мкий *прил* (*голос*) loud; (*скандал*) big; **гро́мко** *нареч* loudly
гро́мче *сравн прил от* **гро́мкий** ▷ *сравн нареч от* **гро́мко**
гро́хот (**-а**) *м* racket; **грох|отáть** (**-очу́, -о́чешь**; *perf* **прогрохотáть**) *несов* to rumble
грубé|ть (**-ю**; *perf* **огрубéть**) *несов* (*человек*) to become rude ▷ (*perf* **загрубéть**) (*кожа*) to become rough
груб|и́ть (**-лю́, -и́шь**; *perf* **нагруби́ть**) *несов +dat* to be rude to; **грубия́н** (**-а**) *м* rude person; **гру́бо** *нареч* (*отвечать*) rudely; (*подсчитать*) roughly; **гру́бо говоря́** roughly speaking; **гру́бост|ь** (**-и**) *ж* rudeness; **гру́бый** *прил* (*человек*) rude; (*ткань, пища*) coarse; (*кожа, подсчёт*) rough; (*ошибка, шутка*) crude; (*нарушение правил*) gross
гру́д|а (**-ы**) *ж* pile, heap
грудно́й *прил* (*молоко*) breast; (*кашель*) chest; **грудно́й ребёнок** baby; **гр|удь** (**-уди́**; *instr sg* **-у́дью**, *nom pl* **-у́ди**) *ж* (*Анат*) chest; (*: женщины*) breasts *мн*; **корми́ть** (*impf*) **гру́дью** to breast-feed
гружёный *прил* loaded
груз (**-а**) *м* (*тяжесть*) weight; (*товар*) cargo
грузи́н (**-а**) *м* Georgian
гр|узи́ть (**-ужу́, -у́зишь**; *perf* **загрузи́ть** *или* **нагрузи́ть**) *несов перех* (*корабль итп*) to load (up); **грузи́ть (***perf* **погрузи́ть) (в/на** *+acc*) (*товар*) to load (onto)
Гру́зи|я (**-и**) *ж* Georgia
грузови́к (**-á**) *м* lorry (*Brit*), truck (*US*)
грузов|о́й *прил* (*судно, самолёт*) cargo; **грузовáя маши́на** goods vehicle; **грузово́е такси́** removal (*Brit*) *или* moving (*US*) van
грузоподъёмност|ь (**и**) *ж* freight *или* cargo capacity
гру́зчик (**-а**) *м* porter; (*в магазине*) stockroom worker
гру́пп|а (**-ы**) *ж* group; **гру́ппа кро́ви** blood group
гру|сти́ть (**-щу́, -сти́шь**) *несов* to feel melancholy *или* very sad; **грусти́ть** (*impf*) **по** *+dat* *или* **о** *+prp* to pine for, miss; **гру́стно** *нареч* sadly ▷ *как сказ*: **мне гру́стно** I feel sad; **гру́стный** *прил* sad; **груст|ь** (**-и**) *ж* sadness
гру́ш|а (**-и**) *ж* pear
грыз|ть (**-у́, -ёшь**; *pt* **-, -ла**) *несов перех* (*яблоки*) to nibble (at) ▷ (*perf* **разгры́зть**) (*кость*) to gnaw (on)
гря́д|ка (**-ки**; *gen pl* **-ок**) *ж* row
гря́зно *как сказ безл*: **до́ма/на у́лице гря́зно** the street/house is filthy
гря́зный *прил* dirty; **гряз|ь** (**-и**; *loc sg* **-и́**) *ж* dirt; (*на дороге*) mud; (*перен*) filth
губ|á (**-ы́**; *nom pl* **-ы**, *dat pl* **-áм**) *ж* lip
губе́рни|я (**-и**) *ж* gubernia (*administrative region*)
губернáтор (**-а**) *м* governor
губ|и́ть (**-лю́, -ишь**; *perf* **погуби́ть**) *несов перех* to kill; (*здоровье*) to ruin
гу́б|ка (**-ки**; *gen pl* **-ок**) *ж* sponge
губн|о́й *прил*: **губнáя помáда** lipstick; **губнáя гармо́шка** harmonica
гу|дéть (**-жу́, -ди́шь**) *несов*

(*шмель, провода*) to hum; (*ветер*) to moan

гуля́|ть (**-ю**; *perf* **погуля́ть**) *несов* to stroll; (*быть на улице*) to be out; (*на свадьбе*) to have a good time, enjoy o.s.; **идти́ (***perf* **пойти́)** **гуля́ть** to go for a walk

гуманита́рный *прил* (*помощь*) humanitarian; (*образование*) arts

гума́нный *прил* humane

гуси́н|ый *прил* (*яйцо*) goose; **гуси́ная ко́жа** goose flesh, goose pimples (*Brit*) *или* bumps (*US*)

густе́|ть (*3sg* **-ет**, *perf* **погусте́ть**) *несов* (*туман*) to become denser ▷ (*perf* **загусте́ть**) (*каша*) to thicken; **густо́й** *прил* (*лес*) dense; (*брови*) bushy; (*облака, суп, волосы*) thick; (*цвет, бас*) rich

густонаселённый *прил* densely populated

гус|ь (**-я**; *gen pl* **-е́й**) *м* goose

гуся́тниц|а (**-ы**) *ж* casserole (dish)

ГЭС *ж сокр* = **гидроэлектроста́нция**

КЛЮЧЕВОЕ СЛОВО

да *част* **1** (*выражает согласие*) yes

2 (*не так ли*): **ты придёшь, да?** you're coming, aren't you?; **ты меня́ лю́бишь, да?** you love me, don't you?

3 (*пусть: в лозунгах, в призывах*): **да здра́вствует демокра́тия!** long live democracy!

4 (*во фразах*): **вот э́то да!** (*разг*) cool!; **ну да!** (*разг*) sure!; (*выражает недоверие*) I'll bet!; **да ну́!** (*разг*) no way!

▷ *союз* (*и*) and; **у неё то́лько одно́ пла́тье, да и то ста́рое** she only has one dress and even that's old

дава́й(те) *несов см* **дава́ть** ▷ *част* let's; **дава́й(те) пить чай**

let's have some tea; **дава́й-дава́й!** (*разг*) come on!, get on with it!
да|ва́ть (**-ю**; *imper* **дава́й(те)**) *несов от* **дать**
дав|и́ть (**-лю́, -ишь**) *несов перех* (*подлеж*: *обувь*) to pinch ▷ (*perf* **задави́ть**) (*калечить*) to crush, trample; (*подлеж*: *машина*) to run over ▷ (*perf* **раздави́ть**) (*насекомых*) to squash; **дави́ть** (*impf*) **на** *+acc* (*налегать*) to press *или* weigh down on; **дави́ться** *несов возв*: **дави́ться** (*perf* **подави́ться**) *+instr* (*костью*) to choke on
да́в|ка (**-ки**; *gen pl* **-ок**) *ж* crush
давле́ни|е (**-я**) *ср* pressure
да́вн|ий *прил*: **с да́вних пор** for a long time; **давно́** *нареч* (*случиться*) a long time ago; (*долго*) for a long time; **давно́ бы так!** about time too!; **давны́м-давно́** *нареч* (*разг*) ages ago
дади́м *etc сов см* **дать**
да́же *част* even
да́й(те) *сов см* **дать**
дал *etc сов см* **дать**
да́лее *нареч* further; **и так да́лее** and so on
далёкий *прил* distant, far-off
далеко́ *нареч* (*о расстоянии*) far away ▷ *как сказ* it's a long way away; **далеко́ за** *+acc* long after; **далеко́ не** by no means
дало́ *etc сов см* **дать**
дальне́йш|ий *прил* further; **в дальне́йшем** in the future
да́льний *прил* distant; (*поезд*) long-distance; **Да́льний Восто́к** the Far East
дальнозо́ркий *прил* long-sighted (*Brit*), far-sighted (*US*)
да́льше *сравн прил от* **далёкий** ▷ *сравн нареч от* **далеко́**
дам *сов см* **дать**
да́м|а (**-ы**) *ж* lady; (*Карты*) queen
да́мский *прил* (*одежда*) ladies'
Да́ни|я (**-и**) *ж* Denmark
да́нн|ые (**-ых**) *мн* (*сведения*) data *ед*; (*способности*) talent *ед*
да́нный *прил* this, the given
дан|ь (**-и**) *ж* tribute
дар (**-а**; *nom pl* **-ы́**) *м* gift
дар|и́ть (**-ю́, -ишь**; *perf* **подари́ть**) *несов перех* to give
да́ром *нареч* (*бесплатно*) free, for nothing; (*бесполезно*) in vain
даст *сов см* **дать**
да́т|а (**-ы**) *ж* date
да́тельный *прил*: **да́тельный паде́ж** the dative (case)
дати́р|овать (**-ую**) *(не)сов перех* to date
дать (*см Table 16*; *impf* **дава́ть**) *сов* to give; (*позволить*): **дать кому́-н** *+infin* to allow sb to do, let sb do; **я тебе́ дам!** (*угроза*) I'll show you!
да́ч|а (**-и**) *ж* (*дом*) dacha (*holiday cottage in the country*); (*показаний*) provision
дашь *сов см* **дать**
дв|а (**-ух**; см *Table 23*; *f* **две**, *nt* **два**) *м чис* two ▷ *м нескл* (*Просвещ*) ≈ poor (*school mark*)
двадца́тый *чис* twentieth
два́дцат|ь (**-и́**; *как* **пять**; см *Table 26*) *чис* twenty
два́жды *нареч* twice; **два́жды три — шесть** two times three is six
две *ж чис см* **два**
двена́дцатый *чис* twelfth
двена́дцат|ь (**-и**; *как* **пять**; см *Table 26*) *чис* twelve
двер|ь (**-и**; *loc sg* **-и́**, *gen pl* **-е́й**) *ж* door
дв|ести (**-ухсо́т**; см *Table 28*) *чис* two hundred
дви́гател|ь (**-я**) *м* engine, motor

дви́га|ть (**-ю**; *perf* **дви́нуть**) *несов перех* to move; (*no perf*: *механизм*) to drive; **дви́гаться** (*perf* **дви́нуться**) *несов возв* to move; (*отправляться*): **дви́гаться в/на** *+acc* to set off *или* start out for
движе́ни|е (**-я**) *ср* movement; (*дорожное*) traffic; (*души́*) impulse; **пра́вила доро́жного** *или* **у́личного движе́ния** ≈ the Highway Code
дви́н|уть(ся) (**-у(сь)**) *сов от* **дви́гать(ся)**
дво́|е (**-и́х**; см *Table 30a*) *м чис* two
двоето́чи|е (**-я**) *ср* (*Линг*) colon
дво́|йка (**-йки**; *gen pl* **-ек**) *ж* (*цифра, карта*) two; (*Просвещ*) ≈ fail, ≈ E (*school mark*)
двойно́й *прил* double
дво́|йня (**-йни**; *gen pl* **-ен**) *ж* twins *мн*
дво́йственный *прил* (*позиция*) ambiguous
двор (**-а́**) *м* yard; (*королевский*) court
двор|е́ц (**-ца́**) *м* palace
дво́рник (**-а**) *м* (*работник*) road sweeper; (*Авт*) windscreen (*Brit*) *или* windshield (*US*) wiper
дворня́ж|ка (**-ки**; *gen pl* **-ек**) *ж* mongrel
дворя́нств|о (**-а**) *ср* nobility
двою́родн|ый *прил*: **двою́родный брат** (first) cousin (*male*); **двою́родная сестра́** (first) cousin (*female*)
двум *etc чис см* **два**
двумста́м *etc чис см* **две́сти**
двусмы́сленный *прил* ambiguous
двуспа́льн|ый *прил*: **двуспа́льная крова́ть** double bed
двух *чис см* **два**
двухсо́т *чис см* **две́сти**
двухсо́тый *чис* two hundredth
двухста́х *чис см* **две́сти**
двуязы́чный *прил* bilingual
дебати́р|овать (**-ую**) *несов перех* to debate
деба́т|ы (**-ов**) *мн* debate *ед*
де́бет (**-а**) *м* debit
деби́л (**-а**) *м* mentally challenged person; (*разг*: *глупый*) idiot
деби́льный *прил* mentally challenged
де́в|а (**-ы**) *ж*: **ста́рая де́ва** spinster; (*созвездие*): **Де́ва** Virgo
дева́|ть(ся) (**-ю(сь)**) *несов от* **деть(ся)**
деви́з (**-а**) *м* motto
де́вич|ий *прил*: **де́вичья фами́лия** maiden name
де́воч|ка (**-ки**; *gen pl* **-ек**) *ж* (*ребёнок*) little girl
де́вуш|ка (**-ки**; *gen pl* **-ек**) *ж* girl
девяно́ст|о (**-а**; *как* **сто**; см *Table 27*) *чис* ninety
девяно́стый *чис* ninetieth
девя́т|ка (**-ки**; *gen pl* **-ок**) *ж* nine
девятна́дцатый *чис* nineteenth
девятна́дцат|ь (**-и**; *как* **пять**; см *Table 26*) *чис* nineteen
девя́тый *чис* ninth
де́вят|ь (**-и́**; *как* **пять**; см *Table 26*) *чис* nine
девят|ьсо́т (**-исот**; *как* **пятьсо́т**; см *Table 28*) *чис* nine hundred
дёг|оть (**-тя**) *м* tar
деградир|овать (**-ую**) *(не)сов* to degenerate
дед (**-а**) *м* grandfather; **Дед Моро́з** ≈ Father Christmas, ≈ Santa (Claus)
дедовщи́н|а (**-ы**) *ж* *mental and physical harassment in the army by older conscripts*
де́душ|ка (**-ки**; *gen pl* **-ек**) *м* grandad

Д

дежу́р|ить (**-ю, -ишь**) *несов* to be on duty
дежу́рн|ый *прил*: **дежу́рный врач** doctor on duty ▷ (**-ого**) *м* person on duty
дезодора́нт (**-а**) *м* antiperspirant, deodorant
де́йственный *прил* effective
де́йстви|е (**-я**) *ср* (*механизма*) functioning; (*романа итп*) action; (*часть пьесы*) act; (*лекарства*) effect; *см также* **де́йствия**
действи́тельно *нареч, вводн сл* really; **действи́тельност|ь** (**-и**) *ж* reality
действи́тельный *прил* real, actual; (*документ*) valid
де́йстви|я (**-й**) *мн* (*поступки*) actions *мн*
де́йств|овать (**-ую**) *несов* (*человек*) to act; (*механизмы, закон*) to operate ▷ (*perf* **поде́йствовать**) (*влиять*): **де́йствовать на** *+acc* to have an effect on
де́йствующ|ий *прил*: **де́йствующие ли́ца** (*персонажи*) characters *мн*; **де́йствующая а́рмия** standing army; **де́йствующий вулка́н** active volcano
дека́бр|ь (**-я́**) *м* December
дека́н (**-а**) *м* dean; **декана́т** (**-а**) *м* faculty office
деклара́ци|я (**-и**) *ж* declaration; **тамо́женная деклара́ция** customs declaration
декора́ци|я (**-и**) *ж* (*Театр*) set
декре́т (**-а**) *м* (*приказ*) decree; (*разг*: *отпуск*) maternity leave; **декре́тный** *прил*: **декре́тный о́тпуск** maternity leave
де́ла|ть (**-ю**; *perf* **сде́лать**) *сов перех* to make; (*упражнения, опыты итп*) to do; **де́лать не́чего** there is nothing to be done; **де́латься** (*perf* **сде́латься**) *несов возв*: **де́латься** *+instr* to become
делега́т (**-а**) *м* delegate
деле́ни|е (**-я**) *ср* division; (*на линейке, в термометре*) point
деликате́с (**-а**) *м* delicacy
дел|и́ть (**-ю́, -ишь**; *perf* **подели́ть** *или* **раздели́ть**) *несов перех* (*также Мат*) to divide; **дели́ть** (*perf* **раздели́ть**) **что-н на** *+acc* to divide sth by; **дели́ть** (*perf* **раздели́ть**) **что-н с** *+instr* to share sth with; **дели́ться** (*perf* **раздели́ться**) *несов возв*: **дели́ться (на** *+acc*) (*отряд*) to divide *или* split up (into); **дели́ться** (*perf* **подели́ться**) **чем-н с кем-н** to share sth with sb
де́л|о (**-а**; *nom pl* **-а́**) *ср* matter; (*надобность*: *также Комм*) business; (*положение*) situation; (*поступок*) act; (*Юр*) case; (*Админ*) file; **э́то моё де́ло** that's my business; **э́то не твоё де́ло** it's none of your business; **как дела́?** how are things?; **в чём де́ло?** what's wrong?; **де́ло в том, что ...** the thing is that ...; **на (са́мом) де́ле** in (actual) fact; **на де́ле** in practise; **то и де́ло** every now and then
делово́й *прил* business; (*дельный*) efficient; (*вид, тон*) businesslike
де́льный *прил* (*человек*) efficient; (*предложение*) sensible
дельфи́н (**-а**) *м* dolphin
демисезо́нн|ый *прил*: **демисезо́нное пальто́** *coat for spring and autumn wear*
демобилиз|ова́ться (**-у́юсь**) *(не)сов возв* to be demobilized
демокра́т (**-а**) *м* democrat;

демократи́ческий *прил* democratic; **демокра́ти|я** (**-и**) *ж* democracy
де́мон (**-а**) *м* demon
демонстра́ци|я (**-и**) *ж* demonstration; (*фильма*) showing
демонстри́р|овать (**-ую**) *(не)сов* (*Полит*) to demonstrate ▷ *несов перех* to show
демонти́р|овать (**-ую**) *(не)сов* to dismantle
де́нежный *прил* monetary; (*рынок*) money; **де́нежный знак** banknote
день (**дня**) *м* day; **на днях** (*скоро*) in the next few days; (*недавно*) the other day; **день рожде́ния** birthday
де́н|ьги (**-ег**; *dat pl* **-ьга́м**) *мн* money *ед*
депо́ *ср нескл* depot
депорти́р|овать (**-ую**) *(не)сов перех* to deport
депре́сси|я (**-и**) *ж* depression
депута́т (**-а**) *м* deputy (*Pol*)
дёрга|ть (**-ю**) *несов перех* to tug *или* pull (at) ▷ *неперех* (*+instr*: *плечом, головой*) to jerk; **дёргаться** *несов возв* (*машина, лошадь*) to jerk; (*лицо, губы*) to twitch
дереве́нский *прил* country, village; (*пейзаж*) rural
дере́в|ня (**-ни**; *gen pl* **-е́нь**, *dat* **-ня́м**) *ж* (*селение*) village; (*местность*) the country
де́р|ево (**-ева**; *nom pl* **-е́вья**, *gen pl* **-е́вьев**) *ср* tree; (*древесина*) wood
деревя́нный *прил* wooden
держа́в|а (**-ы**) *ж* power
держа́тел|ь (**-я**) *м* holder
держ|а́ть (**-у́, -ишь**) *сов перех* to keep; (*в руках, во рту, в зубах*) to hold; **держа́ть** (*impf*) **себя́ в рука́х** to keep one's head; **держа́ться** *несов возв* to stay; (*на колоннах, на сваях*) to be supported; (*иметь осанку*) to stand; (*вести себя*) to behave; **держа́ться** (*impf*) *+gen* (*берега, стены итп*) to keep to
дёрн (**-а**) *м* turf
дёрн|уть (**-у**) *несов перех* to tug (at) ▷ *неперех* (*+instr*: *плечом, головой*) to jerk; **дёрнуться** *несов возв* (*машина*) to start with a jerk; (*губы*) to twitch
деса́нт (**-а**) *м* landing troops *мн*
десе́рт (**-а**) *м* dessert
десн|а́ (**-ы́**; *nom pl* **дёсны**, *gen pl* **дёсен**) *ж* (*Анат*) gum
десятиле́ти|е (**-я**) *ср* (*срок*) decade
деся́тк|и (**-ов**) *мн*: **деся́тки люде́й/книг** scores of people/books
деся́т|ок (**-ка**) *м* ten
деся́тый *прил* tenth
де́сят|ь (**-и́**; *как* **пять**; см *Table 26*) *чис* ten
дета́л|ь (**-и**) *ж* detail; (*механизма*) component, part; **дета́льный** *прил* detailed
детдо́м (**-а**; *nom pl* **-а́**) *м сокр* = **де́тский дом**
детекти́в (**-а**) *м* (*фильм*) detective film; (*книга*) detective novel
детёныш (**-а**) *м* cub
де́т|и (**-е́й**; *dat pl* **-ям**, *instr pl* **-ьми́**, *prp pl* **-ях**, *nom sg* **ребёнок**) *мн* children *мн*
де́тск|ий *прил* (*годы, болезнь*) childhood; (*книга, игра*) children's; (*рассуждение*) childish; **де́тская площа́дка** playground; **де́тский дом** children's home; **де́тский сад** kindergarten

Д

Де́тский сад

Children go to kindergarten from around the age of three and stay there until they are six or seven. The kindergartens provide full-time childcare and pre-primary education five days a week.

де́тств|о (**-а**) *ср* childhood
де|ть (**-ну, -нешь**; *impf* **дева́ть**) *сов перех* (*разг*) to put; (*время, деньги*) to do with; **де́ться** (*impf* **дева́ться**) *сов возв* (*разг*) to get to
дефе́кт (**-а**) *м* defect
дефици́т (**-а**) *м* (*Экон*) deficit; (*нехватка*): **дефици́т** *+gen* *или* **в** *+prp* shortage of; **дефици́тный** *прил* in short supply
дециме́тр (**-а**) *м* decimetre (*Brit*), decimeter (*US*)
дешеве́|ть (*3sg* **-ет**, *perf* **подешеве́ть**) *несов* to go down in price
дешёвый *прил* cheap
де́ятел|ь (**-я**) *м*: **госуда́рственный де́ятель** statesman; **полити́ческий де́ятель** politician; **де́ятельност|ь** (**-и**) *ж* work; (*сердца, мозга*) activity; **де́ятельный** *прил* active
джаз (**-а**) *м* jazz
джем (**-а**) *м* jam
джи́нс|ы (**-ов**) *мн* jeans
джу́нгл|и (**-ей**) *мн* jungle *ед*
дзюдо́ *ср нескл* judo
диа́гноз (**-а**) *м* diagnosis
диагности́р|овать (**-ую**) *(не)сов перех* to diagnose
диагона́л|ь (**-и**) *ж* diagonal
диагра́мм|а (**-ы**) *ж* diagram
диале́кт (**-а**) *м* dialect
диало́г (**-а**) *м* dialogue
диа́метр (**-а**) *м* diameter
диапозити́в (**-а**) *м* (*Фото*) slide
дива́н (**-а**) *м* sofa
дива́н-крова́т|ь (**-и**) *ж* sofa bed
диве́рси|я (**-и**) *ж* sabotage
диви́зи|я (**-и**) *ж* division
ди́в|о (**-а**) *ср* wonder; **на ди́во** wonderfully
дие́з (**-а**) *м* (*Муз*) sharp
дие́т|а (**-ы**) *ж* diet
диза́йн (**-а**) *м* design; **диза́йнер** (**-а**) *м* designer
дика́р|ь (**-я́**) *м* savage
ди́кий *прил* wild; (*поступок*) absurd; (*нравы*) barbarous
дикта́тор (**-а**) *м* dictator
дикт|ова́ть (**-у́ю**; *perf* **продиктова́ть**) *несов перех* to dictate
ди́лер (**-а**) *м*: **ди́лер (по** *+prp*) dealer (in)
дина́мик (**-а**) *м* (loud)speaker
дина́мик|а (**-и**) *ж* dynamics *мн*
динами́чный *прил* dynamic
диноза́вр (**-а**) *м* dinosaur
дипло́м (**-а**) *м* (*университета*) degree certificate; (*училища*) diploma; (*работа*) dissertation (*for undergraduate degree*)
диплома́т (**-а**) *м* diplomat; (*разг*: *портфель*) briefcase
дире́ктор (**-а**; *nom pl* **-á**) *м* director; **дире́ктор шко́лы** headmaster; **дире́кци|я** (**-и**) *ж* (*завода*) management; (*школы*) senior management
дирижёр (**-а**) *м* (*Муз*) conductor; **дирижи́р|овать** (**-ую**) *несов +instr* to conduct
диск (**-а**) *м* (*также Комп*) disc, disk (*esp US*); (*Спорт*) discus; (*Муз*) record; **ги́бкий/жёсткий диск** floppy/hard disk
диске́т (**-а**) *м* diskette
дисково́д (**-а**) *м* (*Комп*) disc drive

дискримина́ци|я (**-и**) *ж* discrimination
диску́сси|я (**-и**) *ж* discussion
диспансе́р (**-а**) *м specialized health centre*
диссерта́ци|я (**-и**) *ж* ≈ PhD thesis
дистанцио́нн|ый *прил*: **дистанцио́нное управле́ние** remote control
диста́нци|я (**-и**) *ж* distance
дисципли́н|а (**-ы**) *ж* discipline
дич|ь (**-и**) *ж собир* game
длин|а́ (**-ы́**) *ж* length; **в длину́** lengthways
дли́нный *прил* long; (*разг*: *человек*) tall
дли́тельный *прил* lengthy
дл|и́ться (*3sg* **-и́тся**, *perf* **продли́ться**) *несов возв* (*урок, беседа*) to last
для *предл +gen* for; (*в отношении*): **для меня́ э́то о́чень ва́жно** this is very important to me; **для того́ что́бы** in order to; **крем для лица́** face cream; **альбо́м для рисова́ния** sketch pad
дневни́к (**-а́**) *м* diary; (*Просвещ*) register
дневн|о́й *прил* daily; **дневно́е вре́мя** daytime
днём *сущ см* **день** ▷ *нареч* in the daytime; (*после обеда*) in the afternoon
дни *etc сущ см* **день**
дн|о (**-а**) *ср* (*ямы*) bottom; (*моря, реки*) bottom, bed

КЛЮЧЕВОЕ СЛОВО

до *предл +gen* **1** (*о пределе движения*) as far as, to; **мы дое́хали до реки́** we went as far as *или* to the river; **я проводи́л его́ до ста́нции** I saw him off at the station
2 (*о расстоянии*) to; **до го́рода 3 киломе́тра** it is 3 kilometres (*Brit*) *или* kilometers (*US*) to the town
3 (*о временном пределе*) till, until; **я отложи́л заседа́ние до утра́** I postponed the meeting till *или* until morning; **до свида́ния!** goodbye!
4 (*перед*) before; **мы зако́нчили до переры́ва** we finished before the break
5 (*о пределе состояния*): **мне бы́ло оби́дно до слёз** I was so hurt I cried
6 (*полностью*): **я отда́л ей всё до копе́йки** I gave her everything down to my last kopeck; **он вы́пил буты́лку до дна́** he drank the bottle dry
7 (*направление действия*): **ребёнок дотро́нулся до игру́шки** the child touched the toy

доба́в|ить (**-лю, -ишь**; *impf* **добавля́ть**) *сов перех* to add
добавле́ни|е (**-я**) *ср* addition
добежа́ть (*как* **бежа́ть**; *см Table 20*; *impf* **добега́ть**) *сов*: **добежа́ть до** *+gen* to run to *или* as far as
доб|и́ться (**-ью́сь, -ьёшься**; *impf* **добива́ться**) *сов возв +gen* to achieve
доб|ра́ться (**-еру́сь, -ерёшься**; *impf* **добира́ться**) *сов возв*: **добра́ться до** *+gen* to get to, reach
добре́|ть (**-ю**; *perf* **подобре́ть**) *несов* to become kinder
добр|о́ (**-а́**) *ср* good; (*разг*: *имущество*) belongings *мн*, property; **добро́ пожа́ловать (в Москву́)!** welcome (to Moscow)!; **э́то не к добру́** this is a bad omen
доброво́л|ец (**-ьца**) *м* volunteer
доброво́льный *прил* voluntary
доброду́шный *прил* good-natured

Д

доброка́чественный *прил* quality; (*опухоль*) benign

добросо́вестный *прил* conscientious

доброт|а́ (**-ы́**) *ж* kindness

до́бр|ый *прил* kind; (*совет, имя*) good; **бу́дьте добры́!** excuse me!; **бу́дьте добры́, позвони́те нам за́втра!** would you be so good as to phone us tomorrow?; **всего́ до́брого!** all the best!; **до́брого здоро́вья!** take care!; **до́брый день/ве́чер!** good afternoon/ evening!; **до́брое у́тро!** good morning!

добы́ть (*как* **быть**; см *Table 21*; *impf* **добыва́ть**) *сов перех* to get; (*нефть*) to extract; (*руду*) to mine

довез|ти́ (**-у́**; *pt* **довёз, -ла́**, *impf* **довози́ть**) *сов перех*: **довезти́ кого́-н до** *+gen* to take sb to *или* as far as

дове́ренност|ь (**-и**) *ж* power of attorney

дове́ренн|ый (**-ого**) *м* (*также* **дове́ренное лицо́**) proxy

дове́ри|е (**-я**) *ср* confidence, trust; **телефо́н** *or* **Слу́жба дове́рия** help line

дове́р|ить (**-ю, -ишь**; *impf* **доверя́ть**) *сов перех*: **дове́рить что-н кому́-н** to entrust sb with sth

дове|сти́ (**-ду́, -дёшь**; *pt* **довёл, -ла́**, *impf* **доводи́ть**) *сов перех*: **довести́ кого́-н/что-н до** *+gen* to take sb/sth to *или* as far as; **доводи́ть** (*perf* **довести́**) **что-н до конца́** to see sth through to the end; **доводи́ть** (*perf* **довести́**) **что-н до све́дения кого́-н** to inform sb of sth

дов|оди́ться (**-ожу́сь, -о́дишься**) *несов +dat* to be related to

дов|ози́ть (**-ожу́, -о́зишь**) *несов от* **довезти́**

дово́льно *нареч* (*сильный*) quite ▷ *как сказ* (that is) enough

догада́|ться (**-юсь**; *impf* **дога́дываться**) *сов возв* to guess

дога́д|ка (**-ки**; *gen pl* **-ок**) *ж* guess

дог|на́ть (**-оню́, -о́нишь**; *impf* **догоня́ть**) *сов перех* to catch up with

догово́р (**-а**) *м* (*Полит*) treaty; (*Комм*) agreement

договорённост|ь (**-и**) *ж* agreement

договор|и́ть (**-ю́, -и́шь**; *impf* **догова́ривать**) *сов (не)перех* to finish

договор|и́ться (**-ю́сь, -и́шься**; *impf* **догова́риваться**) *сов возв*: **договори́ться с кем-н о чём-н** (*о встрече*) to arrange sth with sb; (*о цене*) to agree sth with sb

догола́ *нареч*: **разде́ться догола́** to strip bare *или* naked

догоня́|ть (**-ю**) *несов от* **догна́ть**

догор|е́ть (**-ю́, -и́шь**; *impf* **догора́ть**) *сов* to burn out

доде́ла|ть (**-ю**; *impf* **доде́лывать**) *сов перех* to finish

доду́ма|ться (**-юсь**; *impf* **доду́мываться**) *сов возв*: **доду́маться до** *+gen* to hit on; **как ты мог до тако́го доду́маться?** what on earth gave you that idea?

доеда́|ть (**-ю**) *несов от* **дое́сть**

дое́ду *etc сов см* **дое́хать**

доезжа́|ть (**-ю**) *несов от* **дое́хать**

дое́м *сов см* **дое́сть**

дое́сть (*как* **есть**; см *Table 15*; *impf* **доеда́ть**) *сов перех* to eat up

дое́хать (*как* **е́хать**; см *Table 19*; *impf* **доезжа́ть**) *сов*: **дое́хать до**

+gen to reach
дожд|а́ться (**-у́сь, -ёшься**; *imper* **-и́(те)сь**) *сов возв*: **дожда́ться кого́-н/чего́-н** to wait until sb/sth comes
дождли́вый *прил* rainy
дожд|ь (**-я́**) *м* rain; **дождь идёт** it's raining; **дождь пошёл** it has started to rain
дожида́|ться (**-юсь**) *несов возв* *+gen* to wait for
дожи́|ть (**-ву́, -вёшь**; *impf* **дожива́ть**) *сов неперех*: **дожи́ть до** *+gen* to live to
до́з|а (**-ы**) *ж* dose
дозвон|и́ться (**-ю́сь, -и́шься**; *impf* **дозва́ниваться**) *сов возв* to get through
доигра́|ть (**-ю**; *impf* **доигрывать**) *сов перех* to finish playing
доистори́ческий *прил* prehistoric
до|и́ть (**-ю́, -ишь**; *perf* **подои́ть**) *несов перех* to milk
дойти́ (*как* **идти́**; см *Table 18*; *impf* **доходи́ть**) *сов*: **дойти́ до** *+gen* to reach
док (**-а**) *м* dock
доказа́тельств|о (**-а**) *ср* proof, evidence
док|аза́ть (**-ажу́, -а́жешь**; *impf* **дока́зывать**) *сов перех* (*правду, виновность*) to prove
докла́д (**-а**) *м* (*на съезде итп*) paper; (*начальнику*) report; **докла́дчик** (**-а**) *м* speaker
докла́дыва|ть (**-ю**) *несов от* **доложи́ть**
до́ктор (**-а**; *nom pl* **-а́**) *м* doctor; **до́ктор нау́к** Doctor of Sciences (*postdoctoral research degree in Russia*)
до́кторский *прил* (*Мед*) doctor's; (*Просвещ*) postdoctoral
докуме́нт (**-а**) *м* document; **документа́льный** *прил* documentary; **документа́льный фильм** documentary; **документа́ци|я** (**-и**) *ж собир* documentation
долг (**-а**; *loc sg* **-у́**, *nom pl* **-и́**) *м* debt; **дава́ть** (*perf* **дать**)**/брать** (**взять** *perf*) **что-н в долг** to lend/borrow sth; **быть** (*impf*) **в долгу́ пе́ред кем-н** *или* **у кого́-н** to be indebted to sb
до́лгий *прил* long
до́лго *нареч* for a long time; **как до́лго ...?** how long ...?
долгоигра́ющ|ий *прил*: **долгоигра́ющая пласти́нка** LP (= *long-playing record*)
долгосро́чный *прил* long-term
долгот|а́ (**-ы́**) *ж* length; (*Гео*) longitude

КЛЮЧЕВОЕ СЛОВО

до́лж|ен (**-на́, -но́, -ны́**) *часть сказуемого +infin* **1** (*обязан*): **я до́лжен уйти́** I must go; **я до́лжен бу́ду уйти́** I will have to go; **она́ должна́ была́ уйти́** she had to go
2 (*выражает предположение*): **он до́лжен ско́ро прийти́** he should arrive soon
3 (*о долге*): **ты до́лжен мне 5 рубле́й** you owe me 5 roubles
4: должно́ быть (*вероятно*) probably; **должно́ быть, она́ о́чень уста́ла** she must have been very tired

должностн|о́й *прил* official; **должностно́е лицо́** official
до́лжност|ь (**-и**; *gen pl* **-е́й**) *ж* post
доли́н|а (**-ы**) *ж* valley
до́ллар (**-а**) *м* dollar

дол|ожи́ть (**-ожу́, -о́жишь**; *impf* **докла́дывать**) *сов перех* to report
дол|ото́ (**-ота́**; *nom pl* **-о́та**) *ср* chisel
до́льше *сравн прил от* **до́лгий** ▷ *сравн нареч от* **до́лго**
до́л|ька (**-ьки**; *gen pl* **-ек**) *ж* segment
до́л|я (**-и**; *gen pl* **-е́й**) *ж* share; (*пирога*) portion; (*судьба*) fate; **до́ля секу́нды** a fraction of a second
дом (**-а**; *nom pl* **-а́**) *м* house; (*своё жильё*) home; (*семья*) household; **дом моде́лей** fashion house; **дом о́тдыха** ≈ holiday centre (*Brit*) *или* center (*US*); **до́ма** *нареч* at home; **дома́шн|ий** *прил* (*адрес*) home; (*еда*) home-made; (*животное*) domestic; **дома́шняя хозя́йка** housewife; **дома́шнее зада́ние** homework
домини́р|овать (**-ую**) *несов* to dominate
домкра́т (**-а**) *м* (*Тех*) jack
домовладе́л|ец (**-ьца**) *м* home owner; **домовладе́ни|е** (**-я**) *ср* (*дом*) *house with grounds attached*
домово́дств|о (**-а**) *ср* home economics
домо́й *нареч* home
домоуправле́ни|е (**-я**) *ср* ≈ housing department
домохозя́|йка (**-йки**; *gen pl* **-ек**) *ж* = **дома́шняя хозя́йка**
домрабо́тниц|а (**-ы**) *ж* (= *дома́шняя рабо́тница*) domestic help (*Brit*), maid (*US*)
донесе́ни|е (**-я**) *ср* report
донес|ти́ (**-у́, -ёшь**; *pt* **донёс, -ла́**, *impf* **доноси́ть**) *сов перех* to carry ▷ *неперех*: **донести́ на** *+acc* to inform on; **донести́** (*perf*) **о** *+prp* to report on; **донести́сь** (*impf* **доноси́ться**) *сов возв*: **донести́сь до** *+gen* to reach
до́низу *нареч* to the bottom; **све́рху до́низу** from top to bottom
до́нор (**-а**) *м* (*Мед*) donor
доно́с (**-а**) *м*: **доно́с (на** *+acc*) denunciation (of)
дон|оси́ть (**-ошу́, -о́сишь**) *несов от* **донести́**
допива́|ть (**-ю**) *несов от* **допи́ть**
до́пинг (**-а**) *м* drugs *мн*
допи|са́ть (**-шу́, -шешь**; *impf* **допи́сывать**) *сов перех* to finish (writing)
допи́ть (**допью́, допьёшь**; *imper* **допе́й(те)**, *impf* **допива́ть**) *сов перех* to drink up
допла́т|а (**-ы**) *ж* surcharge; **допла́та за бага́ж** excess baggage (charge)
доплы́|ть (**-ву́, -вёшь**; *impf* **доплыва́ть**) *сов*: **доплы́ть до** *+gen* (*на корабле*) to sail to; (*вплавь*) to swim to
дополне́ни|е (**-я**) *ср* supplement; (*Линг*) object; **в дополне́ние (к** *+dat*) in addition (to)
дополни́тельный *прил* additional
допо́лн|ить (**-ю, -ишь**; *impf* **дополня́ть**) *сов перех* to supplement
допра́шива|ть (**-ю**) *несов от* **допроси́ть**
допро́с (**-а**) *м* interrogation
допуска́|ть (**-ю**; *perf* **допусти́ть**) *несов перех* to admit, allow in; (*предположить*) to assume
допу́стим *вводн сл* let us assume
допуще́ни|е (**-я**) *ср* assumption
дораст|и́ (**-у́, -ёшь**; *pt* **доро́с, доросла́, доросло́**, *impf* **дораста́ть**) *сов*: **дорасти́ до** *+gen* to grow to

дорóг|а (**-и**) *ж* road, way; **по дорóге** on the way
дóрого *нареч* (*купить, продать*) at a high price ▷ *как сказ* it's expensive
дорог|óй *прил* expensive; (*цена*) high; (*друг, мать*) dear; (*воспоминания, подарок*) cherished ▷ (**-óго**) *м* dear, darling
дорожá|ть (*3sg* **-ет**, *perf* **подорожáть**) *несов* to go up *или* rise in price
дорóже *сравн прил от* **дорогóй** ▷ *сравн нареч от* **дóрого**
дорож|и́ть (**-ý, -и́шь**) *несов* +*instr* to value
дорóжный *прил* road; (*костюм, расходы*) travelling (*Brit*), traveling (*US*); (*сумка*) travel
дос|кá (**-ки́**; *nom pl* **-ки**, *gen pl* **-ок**) *ж* board; (*деревянная*) plank; (*мраморная*) slab; (*чугунная*) plate; **доскá объявлéний** notice (*Brit*) *или* bulletin (*US*) board
досконáльный *прил* thorough
дослóвно *нареч* word for word
дослýша|ть (**-ю**; *impf* **дослýшивать**) *сов перех* to listen to
досмóтр (**-а**) *м*: **тамóженный досмóтр** customs examination
досм|отрéть (**-отрю́, -óтришь**; *impf* **досмáтривать**) *сов перех* to watch the end of; (*багаж*) to check
досрóчно *нареч* ahead of time
досрóчный *прил* early
доста|вáть(ся) (**-ю́(сь)**) *несов от* **достáть(ся)**
достáв|ить (**-лю, -ишь**; *impf* **доставля́ть**) *сов перех* (*груз*) to deliver; (*пассажиров*) to carry, transport; (*удовольствие, возможность*) to give
достáв|ка (**-ки**; *gen pl* **-ок**) *ж* delivery
достáт|ок (**-ка**) *м* prosperity
достáточно *нареч*: **достáточно хорошó/подрóбно** good/detailed enough ▷ *как сказ* that's enough
достá|ть (**-ну, -нешь**; *imper* **достáнь(те)**, *impf* **доставáть**) *сов перех* to take; (*раздобыть*) to get ▷ *неперех*: **достáть до** +*gen* to reach; **достáться** (*impf* **доставáться**) *сов возв* (*при разделе*): **мне достáлся дом** I got the house
достигá|ть (**-ю**) *несов от* **дости́чь**
достижéни|е (**-я**) *ср* achievement; (*предела, возраста*) reaching
дости́|чь (**-гну, -гнешь**; *pt* **-г, -гла**, *impf* **достигáть**) *сов* +*gen* to reach; (*результата, цели*) to achieve; (*положения*) to attain
достовéрный *прил* reliable
достóинств|о (**-а**) *ср* (*книги, плана*) merit; (*уважение к себе*) dignity; (*Комм*) value
достóйный *прил* (*награда, кара*) fitting; (*человек*) worthy
достопримечáтельност|ь (**-и**) *ж* sight; (*музея*) showpiece; **осмáтривать** (*perf* **осмотрéть**) **достопримечáтельности** to go sightseeing
достоя́ни|е (**-я**) *ср* property; **станови́ться** (*perf* **стать**) **достоя́нием общéственности** to become public knowledge
дóступ (**-а**) *м* access
досýг (**-а**) *м* leisure (time); **на досýге** in one's spare *или* free time
дотáци|я (**-и**) *ж* subsidy
дотлá *нареч*: **сгорéть дотлá** to burn down (to the ground)
дотрóн|уться (**-усь**; *impf* **дотрáгиваться**) *сов возв*: **дотрóнуться до** +*gen* to touch

дот|яну́ть (**-яну́, -я́нешь**; *impf* **дотя́гивать**) *сов перех*: **дотяну́ть что-н до** *+gen* to extend sth as far as; **дотяну́ться** (*impf* **дотя́гиваться**) *сов возв*: **дотяну́ться до** *+gen* to reach
до́хлый *прил* dead
до́х|нуть (**-ну**; *pt* **-, -ла**, *perf* **подо́хнуть**) *несов* (*животное*) to die
дохо́д (**-а**) *м* income, revenue; (*человека*) income
доходи́ть *несов от* **дойти́**
дохо́дчивый *прил* clear, easy to understand
доце́нт (**-а**) *м* ≈ reader (*Brit*), ≈ associate professor (*US*)
до́ч|ка (**-ки**; *gen pl* **-ек**) *ж* daughter
доч|ь (**-ери**; см *Table 2*) *ж* daughter
дошёл *сов см* **дойти́**
дошко́льник (**-а**) *м* preschool child
дошла́ *итп сов см* **дойти́**
ДПР *ж сокр* (= *Демократи́ческая Па́ртия Росси́и*) *см* **ЛДПР**
драгоце́нност|ь (**-и**) *ж* jewel
драгоце́нный *прил* precious
дразн|и́ть (**-ю́, -ишь**) *несов перех* to tease
дра́к|а (**-и**) *ж* fight
драко́н (**-а**) *м* dragon
дра́м|а (**-ы**) *ж* drama; **драмати́ческий** *прил* dramatic; (*актёр*) stage; **драмату́рг** (**-а**) *м* playwright
драматурги́|я (**-и**) *ж* drama ▷ *собир* plays *мн*
драпир|ова́ть (**-у́ю**; *perf* **задрапирова́ть**) *несов перех*: **драпирова́ть что-н** (**чем-н**) to drape sth (with sth)
драть (**деру́, дерёшь**; *perf* **разодра́ть**) *несов перех* (*бумагу, одежду*) to tear *или* rip up ▷ (*perf* **задра́ть**) (*подлеж*: *волк*) to tear to pieces ▷ (*perf* **содра́ть**) (*кору, обои*) to strip; **дра́ться** (*perf* **подра́ться**) *несов возв*: **подра́ться** (**с** *+instr*) to fight (with)
дре́безг *м*: **в дре́безги** to smithereens
древеси́н|а (**-ы**) *ж собир* timber
древе́сный *прил* wood; **древе́сный у́голь** charcoal
дре́вний *прил* ancient
дрейф|ова́ть (**-у́ю**) *несов* to drift
дрел|ь (**-и**) *ж* drill
дрессир|ова́ть (**-у́ю**; *perf* **вы́дрессировать**) *несов перех* to train
дроб|и́ть (**-лю́, -и́шь**; *perf* **раздроби́ть**) *несов перех* to crush; (*силы*) to split
дроб|ь (**-и**; *gen pl* **-е́й**) *ж* fraction; (*барабана*) beat
дров|а́ (**-**; *dat pl* **-а́м**) *мн* firewood *ед*
дро́гн|уть (**-у**) *сов* (*стёкла, руки*) to shake; (*голос, лицо*) to quiver
дрож|а́ть (**-у́, -и́шь**) *несов* to shake, tremble; (*лицо*) to quiver; **дрожа́ть** (*impf*) **за** *+acc или* **над** *+instr* (*разг*) to fuss over
дро́жж|и (**-е́й**) *мн* yeast *ед*
дрозд (**-а́**) *м* thrush; **чёрный дрозд** blackbird
дру|г (**-га**; *nom pl* **-зья́**, *gen pl* **-зе́й**) *м* friend; **друг друга́** each other, one another; **друг дру́гу** (*говорить*) to each other *или* one another; **друг за дру́гом** one after another; **друг о дру́ге** (*говорить*) about each other *или* one another
друг|о́й *прил* (*иной*) another; (*второй*) the other; (*не такой, как этот*) different ▷ (**-о́го**) *м* (*кто-то иной*) another (person); (*второй*) the other (one); **в друго́й раз**

another time; **и тот и друго́й** both
дру́жб|а (**-ы**) *ж* friendship
дружелю́бный *прил* friendly, amicable
дру́жеский *прил* friendly
дру́жественный *прил* friendly
друж|и́ть (**-у́, -ишь**) *несов*: **дружи́ть с** *+instr* to be friends with
друж|о́к (**-ка́**) *м* (*друг*) friend, pal (*inf*)
друзья́ *etc сущ см* **друг**
дрян|ь (**-и**) *ж* (*разг*) rubbish (*Brit*), trash (*US*)
дуб (**-а**; *nom pl* **-ы́**) *м* (*Бот*) oak (tree); (*древесина*) oak
дублён|ка (**-ки**; *gen pl* **-ок**) *ж* sheepskin coat
дублика́т (**-а**) *м* duplicate
дubли́р|овать (**-ую**) *несов перех* to duplicate; (*Кино*) to dub; (*Комп*) to back up
дуг|а́ (**-и́**; *nom pl* **-и**) *ж* (*Геом*) arc
ду́л|о (**-а**) *ср* muzzle; (*ствол*) barrel
ду́м|а (**-ы**) *ж* (*размышление*) thought; **Ду́ма** (*Полит*) the Duma (*lower house of Russian parliament*)
ду́ма|ть (**-ю**) *несов*: **ду́мать (о чём-н)** to think (about sth); **ду́мать** (*impf*) **над чем-н** to think sth over; **я ду́маю, что да/нет** I think/don't think so
дум|е́ц (**-ца́**) *м* (*разг*) member of the Duma
думск|о́й *прил*: **думско́е заседа́ние** meeting of the Duma
ду́н|уть (**-у**) *сов* to blow
дуп|ло́ (**-ла́**; *nom pl* **-ла**, *gen pl* **-ел**) *ср* (*дерева*) hollow
ду́р|а (**-ы**) *ж* (*разг*) fool
дура́к (**-а́**) *м* (*разг*) fool
дура́цкий *прил* (*разг*) foolish; (*шляпа*) silly
дура́ч|ить (**-у, -ишь**; *perf* **одура́чить**) *несов перех* (*разг*) to con; **дура́читься** *несов возв* (*разг*) to play the fool
дур|и́ть (**-ю, -ишь**; *perf* **обдури́ть**) *несов перех* to fool
ду́рно *нареч* badly
ду́роч|ка (**-ки**; *gen pl* **-ек**) *ж* (*разг*) silly girl
дуршла́г (**-а**) *м* colander
ду|ть (**-ю, -ешь**) *несов* to blow ▷ (*perf* **вы́дуть**) *перех* (*Тех*) to blow; **здесь ду́ет** it's draughty (*Brit*) *или* drafty (*US*) in here
дух (**-а**; *part gen* **-у**) *м* spirit; **быть** (*impf*) **в ду́хе/не в ду́хе** to be in high/low spirits
дух|и́ (**-о́в**) *мн* perfume *ед*, scent *ед*
духо́вк|а (**-и**) *ж* oven
духо́вный *прил* spiritual; (*религиозный*) sacred, church
духов|о́й *прил* (*Муз*) wind; **духовы́е инструме́нты** brass section (*in orchestra*); **духово́й орке́стр** brass band
душ (**-а**) *м* shower
душ|а́ (*acc sg* **-у**, *gen sg* **-и́**, *nom pl* **-и**) *ж* soul; **на ду́шу (населе́ния)** per head (of the population); **он в ней души́ не ча́ет** she's the apple of his eye; **говори́ть** (*impf*)/ **бесе́довать** (*impf*) **по душа́м** to have a heart-to-heart talk/chat; **в глубине́ души́** in one's heart of hearts
душевнобольн|о́й (**-о́го**) *м* mentally ill person
душе́вн|ый *прил* (*силы, подъём*) inner; (*разговор*) sincere; (*человек*) kindly; **душе́вное потрясе́ние** shock
душ|и́ть (**-у́, -ишь**; *perf* **задуши́ть** *или* **удуши́ть**) *несов перех* to strangle; (*свободу, прогресс*) to stifle ▷ (*perf* **надуши́ть**) (*платок*) to perfume, scent

ду́шно *как сказ* it's stuffy *или* close

ды́бом *нареч*: **встава́ть ды́бом** (*волосы, шерсть*) to stand on end

ды́бы *мн*: **станови́ться на ды́бы** (*лошадь*) to rear up

дым (**-а**; *loc sg* **-у́**) *м* smoke; **дым|и́ть** (**-лю́, -и́шь**; *perf* **надыми́ть**) *несов* (*печь, дрова*) to smoulder (*Brit*), smolder (*US*); **дыми́ться** *несов возв* (*труба*) to be smoking

ды́мк|а (**-и**) *ж* haze

ды́мчатый *прил* (*стёкла*) tinted

ды́н|я (**-и**) *ж* melon

дыр|а́ (**-ы́**; *nom pl* **-ы**) *ж* hole

ды́р|ка (**-ки**; *gen pl* **-ок**) *ж* hole

дыроко́л (**-а**) *м* punch

дыш|а́ть (**-у́, -ишь**) *несов* to breathe; (*+instr*: *ненавистью*) to exude; (*любовью*) to radiate

дья́вол (**-а**) *м* devil

дю́жин|а (**-ы**) *ж* dozen

дя́д|я (**-и**) *м* uncle; (*разг*) bloke

е

Ева́нгели|е (**-я**) *ср* the Gospels *мн*; (*одна из книг*) gospel

евре́|й (**-я**) *м* Jew

евре́йский *прил* (*народ, обычаи*) Jewish; **евре́йский язы́к** Hebrew

е́вро *м нескл* euro

Евро́п|а (**-ы**) *ж* Europe; **европе́|ец** (**-йца**) *м* European; **европе́йск|ий** *прил* European; **Европе́йский сове́т** Council of Europe; **Европе́йское соо́бщество** European Community

его́ *мест см* **он**; **оно́** ▷ *притяж мест* (*о мужчине*) his; (*о предмете*) its

ед|а́ (**-ы́**) *ж* (*пища*) food; (*процесс*): **за едо́й, во вре́мя еды́** at mealtimes

едва́ *нареч* (*с трудом*: *нашёл, достал, доехал итп*) only just;

(*только, немного*) barely, hardly; (*только что*) just ▷ *союз* (*как только*) as soon as; **едва́ ли** hardly
е́дем *etc сов см* **е́хать**
еди́м *несов см* **есть**
едини́ц|а (**-ы**) *ж* (*цифра*) one; (*измерения, часть целого*) unit; **де́нежная едини́ца** monetary unit
единобо́рств|о (**-а**) *ср* single combat
единовре́менн|ый *прил*: **единовре́менная су́мма** lump sum
единогла́сный *прил* unanimous
единоду́шный *прил* unanimous
еди́нственн|ый *прил* (the) only; **еди́нственное число́** (*Линг*) singular
еди́н|ый *прил* (*цельный*) united; (*общий*) common; **все до еди́ного** to a man; **еди́ный госуда́рственный экза́мен** *university entrance exam*; **еди́ный (проездно́й) биле́т** travel card (*for use on all forms of transport*)

Еди́ный госуда́рственный экза́мен

This exam is sat by school-leavers after completing 10 years of education. The mark obtained determines whether the student can be admitted to a higher education institue. See note at **проходно́й балл**.

Еди́ный проездно́й биле́т

This is a cheap and convenient way of city travel. It covers many types of transport including the trams, trolleybuses and buses.

еди́те *несов см* **есть**
е́ду *etc несов см* **е́хать**
едя́т *несов см* **есть**
её *мест см* **она́** ▷ *притяж мест* (*о женщине итп*) her; (*о предмете итп*) its
ёж (**-а́**) *м* hedgehog
ежего́дный *прил* annual
ежедне́вник (**-а**) *м* diary
ежедне́вный *прил* daily
ежеме́сячный *прил* monthly
еженеде́льный *прил* weekly
езд|а́ (**-ы́**) *ж* journey
е́з|дить (**-жу, -дишь**) *несов* to go; **е́здить** *impf* **на** (*+prp*) (*на лошади, на велосипеде*) to ride; (*на поезде, на автобусе итп*) to travel *или* go by
ей *мест см* **она́**
ел *etc несов см* **есть**
е́ле *нареч* (*с трудом*) only just; (*едва*) barely, hardly; **е́ле-е́ле** with great difficulty
ёл|ка (**-ки**; *gen pl* **-ок**) *ж* fir (tree); (*праздник*) *New Year party for children*; **(рожде́ственская** *или* **нового́дняя) ёлка** ≈ Christmas tree
ело́вый *прил* fir
ёлочн|ый *прил*: **ёлочные игру́шки** Christmas-tree decorations *мн*
ел|ь (**-и**) *ж* fir (tree)
ем *несов см* **есть**
ёмкост|ь (**-и**) *ж* (*объём*) capacity; (*вместилище сосуд*) container
ему́ *мест см* **он**; **оно́**
ерунд|а́ (**-ы́**) *ж* rubbish, nonsense
ЕС *сокр* EU

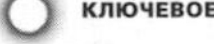

КЛЮЧЕВОЕ СЛОВО

е́сли *союз* **1** (*в том случае когда*) if; **е́сли она́ придёт, дай ей э́то письмо́** if she comes, give her this letter; **е́сли ..., то ...** (*если*) if ...,

then ...; **если он опоздает, то иди один** if he is late, (then) go alone
2 (*об условном действии*): **если бы(, то** *или* **тогда)** if; **если бы я мог, (то) помог бы тебе** if I could, I would help you
3 (*выражает сильное желание*): **(ах** *или* **о) если бы** if only; **ах если бы он пришёл!** oh, if only he would come!; **если уж на то пошло** if it comes to it; **что если...?** (*а вдруг*) what if...?

ест *несов см* **есть**
естественно *нареч* naturally ▷ *вводн сл* (*конечно*) of course;
естественный *прил* natural
есть[1] *несов* (*один предмет*) there is; (*много предметов*) there are; **у меня есть друг** I have a friend
есть[2] (см *Table 15*; *perf* **поесть** *или* **съесть**) *несов перех* (*питаться*) to eat; **мне хочется есть** I'm hungry
ехать (см *Table 19*) *несов* to go; (*поезд, автомобиль: приближаться*) to come; (: *двигаться*) to go; (*разг: скользить*) to slide; **ехать** *impf* **на (+***prp***)** (*на лошади, на велосипеде*) to ride; **ехать** (*impf*) *+instr или* **на** *+prp* (*на поезде, на автобусе*) to travel *или* go by
ехидный *прил* spiteful
ешь *несов см* **есть**
ещё *нареч* (*дополнительно*) more; **хочу ещё кофе** I want more coffee
ею *мест см* **она**

ж *союз, част см* **же**
жаб|а (**-ы**) *ж* (*Зоол*) toad
жаворон|ок (**-ка**) *м* (*Зоол*) lark
жадност|ь (**-и**) *ж*: **жадность (к** *+dat***)** (*к вещам, к деньгам*) greed (for)
жадный *прил* greedy
жажд|а (**-ы**) *ж* thirst
жакет (**-а**) *м* (woman's) jacket
жале|ть (**-ю**; *perf* **пожалеть**) *несов перех* to feel sorry for; (*скупиться*) to grudge ▷ *неперех*: **жалеть о** *+prp* to regret; **не жалея сил** sparing no effort
жал|ить (**-ю, -ишь**; *perf* **ужалить**) *несов перех* (*подлеж: оса*) to sting; (: *змея*) to bite
жалкий *прил* (*вид*) pitiful, pathetic
жалко *как сказ* = **жаль**
жал|о (**-а**) *ср* (*пчелы*) sting; (*змеи*) bite

жáлоб|а (**-ы**) *ж* complaint
жáлованье|е (**-я**) *ср* salary
жáл|оваться (**-уюсь**; *perf* **пожáловаться**) *несов возв*: **жáловаться на** *+acc* to complain about; (*ябедничать*) to tell on
жáлост|ь (**-и**) *ж*: **жáлость к** *+dat* sympathy for; **какáя жáлость!** what a shame!

КЛЮЧЕВОЕ СЛОВО

жаль *как сказ* **1** (*+acc*: *о сострадании*): **(мне) жаль дрýга** I am sorry for my friend
2 (*+acc или +gen*: *о сожалении, о досаде*): **(мне) жаль врéмени/ дéнег** I grudge the time/money
3 *+infin*; **жаль уезжáть** it's a pity *или* shame to leave

жар (**-а**) *м* heat; (*Мед*) fever
жар|á (**-ы́**) *ж* heat
жаргóн (**-а**) *м* slang; (*профессиональный*) jargon
жáреный *прил* (*на сковороде*) fried; (*в духовке*) roast
жáр|ить (**-ю, -ишь**; *perf* **зажáрить**) *несов перех* (*на сковороде*) to fry; (*в духовке*) to roast; **жáриться** (*perf* **зажáриться**) *несов возв* to fry
жáркий *прил* hot; (*спор*) heated
жáрко *нареч* (*спорить*) heatedly ▷ *как сказ* it's hot; **мнé жáрко** I'm hot
жáтв|а (**-ы**) *ж* harvest
жать[1] (**жму, жмёшь**) *несов перех* (*руку*) to shake; (*лимон, сок*) to squeeze; **сапоги́ мне жмут** my boots are pinching (my feet)
жать[2] (**жну, жнёшь**; *perf* **сжать**) *несов перех* to harvest
жвáч|ка (**-ки**; *gen pl* **-ек**) *ж* (*разг*: *резинка*) chewing gum

жд|ать (**-у, -ёшь**; *pt* **-ал, -алá, -áло**) *несов (не)перех* (*+acc или +gen*: *письмо, гостей*) to expect; (*поезда*) to wait for

КЛЮЧЕВОЕ СЛОВО

же *союз* **1** (*при противопоставлении*) but; **я не люблю математику, литератýру же обожáю** I don't like mathematics, but I love literature
2 (*вводит дополнительные сведения*) and; **успéх зави́сит от нали́чия ресýрсов, ресýрсов же мáло** success depends on the presence of resources, and the resources are insufficient
▷ *част* **1** (*ведь*): **вы́пей ещё чáю, хóчешь же!** have more tea, you want some, don't you?
2 (*именно*): **придý сейчáс же** I'll come right now
3 (*выражает сходство*): **такóй же** the same; **в э́том же годý** this very year

ж|евáть (**-ую́**) *несов перех* to chew
желáни|е (**-я**) *ср* (*просьба*) request; **желáние** *+gen/+infin* desire for/to do
желáтельный *прил* desirable
желá|ть (**-ю**; *perf* **пожелáть**) *несов +gen* to desire; **желáть (***perf* **пожелáть)** *+infin* to wish *или* want to do; **желáть (***perf* **пожелáть) комý-н счáстья/всегó хорóшего** to wish sb happiness/all the best
желáющ|ий (**-его**) *м*: **желáющие поéхать/порабóтать** those interested in going/working
желé *ср нескл* jelly (*Brit*), jello (*US*)
жел|езá (**-езы́**; *nom pl* **-езы**, *gen*

Ж

pl **-ёз**, *dat pl* **-еза́м**) *ж* gland
железнодоро́жный *прил* (*вокзал*) railway (*Brit*), railroad (*US*); (*транспорт*) rail
желе́зн|ый *прил* iron; **желе́зная доро́га** railway (*Brit*), railroad (*US*)
желе́з|о (**-а**) *ср* iron
жёлоб (**-а**; *nom pl* **-а́**) *м* gutter
желте́|ть (**-ю**; *perf* **пожелте́ть**) *несов* to turn yellow
желт|о́к (**-ка́**) *м* yolk
жёлтый *прил* yellow
желу́д|ок (**-ка**) *м* (*Анат*) stomach
желу́дочный *прил* (*боль*) stomach; (*сок*) gastric
жёлуд|ь (**-я**) *м* acorn
жёлчный *прил*: **жёлчный пузы́рь** gall bladder
же́мчуг (**-а**; *nom pl* **-а́**) *м* pearls *мн*
жемчу́жин|а (**-ы**) *ж* pearl
жен|а́ (**-ы́**; *nom pl* **жёны**, *gen pl* **жён**) *ж* wife
жена́т|ый *прил* married (*of man*); **он жена́т на** *+prp* he is married to; **они́ жена́ты** they are married
Жене́в|а (**-ы**) *ж* Geneva
жен|и́ть (**-ю́**, **-ишь**) *(не)сов перех* (*сына, внука*): **жени́ть кого́-н (на** *+prp*) to marry sb (off) (to); **жени́ться** *(не)сов возв*: **жени́ться на** *+prp* to marry (*of man*) ▷ (*perf* **пожени́ться**) (*разг*) to get hitched
жени́х (**-а́**) *м* (*до свадьбы*) fiancé; (*на свадьбе*) (bride)groom
же́нский *прил* women's; (*логика, органы*) female; **же́нский пол** the female sex; **же́нский род** feminine gender
же́нственный *прил* feminine
же́нщин|а (**-ы**) *ж* woman
жерд|ь (**-и**; *gen pl* **-е́й**) *ж* pole
жереб|ёнок (**-ёнка**; *nom pl* **-я́та**, *gen pl* **-я́т**) *м* foal
же́ртв|а (**-ы**) *ж* victim; (*Рел*) sacrifice; **челове́ческие же́ртвы** casualties
же́ртв|овать (**-ую**; *perf* **поже́ртвовать**) *несов* (*+instr*: *жизнью*) to sacrifice ▷ *перех* (*деньги*) to donate
жест (**-а**) *м* gesture
жёсткий *прил* (*кровать, человек*) hard; (*мясо*) tough; (*волосы*) coarse; (*условия*) strict; **жёсткий ваго́н** *railway carriage with hard seats*; **жёсткий диск** hard disk
жесто́кий *прил* cruel; (*мороз*) severe
жесто́кост|ь (**-и**) *ж* cruelty
жето́н (**-а**) *м* tag; (*в метро*) token
жечь (**жгу, жжёшь** *etc*, **жгут**; *pt* **жёг, жгла**, *perf* **сжечь**) *несов перех* to burn
жже́ни|е (**-я**) *ср* burning sensation
живо́й *прил* alive; (*организм*) living; (*животное*) live; (*человек*: *энергичный*) lively
живопи́сный *прил* picturesque
жи́вопис|ь (**-и**) *ж* painting
живо́т (**-а́**) *м* stomach; (*разг*) tummy
живо́тн|ое (**-ого**) *ср* animal
живо́тный *прил* animal
живу́ *etc несов см* **жить**
жи́дкий *прил* liquid
жи́дкост|ь (**-и**) *ж* liquid
жи́зненный *прил* (*вопрос, интересы*) vital; (*необходимость*) basic; **жи́зненный у́ровень** standard of living; **жи́зненный о́пыт** experience
жизнера́достный *прил* cheerful
жизнеспосо́бный *прил* viable
жизн|ь (**-и**) *ж* life

жил *etc несов см* **жить**
жилéт (**-а**) *м* waistcoat (*Brit*), vest (*US*)
жил|éц (**-ьцá**) *м* (*дома*) tenant
жилúщный *прил* housing
жил|óй *прил* (*дом, здание*) residential; **жилáя плóщадь** accommodation
жиль|ё (**-я́**) *ср* accommodation
жир (**-а**; *nom pl* **-ы́**) *м* fat; (*растительный*) oil
жирáф (**-а**) *м* giraffe
жи́рный *прил* (*пища*) fatty; (*человек*) fat; (*волосы*) greasy
жи́тел|ь (**-я**) *м* resident;
жи́тельств|о (**-а**) *ср* residence
жи|ть (**-вý, -вёшь**; *pt* **-л, -лá, -ло**) *несов* to live; **жил-был** there once was, once upon a time there was
жмýр|ить (**-ю, -ишь**; *perf* **зажмýрить**) *несов*: **жмýрить глазá** to screw up one's eyes;
жмýриться (*perf* **зажмýриться**) *несов возв* to squint
жокé|й (**-я**) *м* jockey
жонгли́р|овать (**-ую**) *несов +instr* to juggle (with)
жрéби|й (**-я**) *м*: **бросáть жрéбий** to cast lots
ЖСК *м сокр* (= *жилищно-строительный кооперати́в*) ≈ housing cooperative
жужж|áть (**-ý, -и́шь**) *несов* to buzz
жук (**-á**) *м* beetle
журнáл (**-а**) *м* magazine; (*классный*) register
журнали́ст (**-а**) *м* journalist;
журнали́стик|а (**-и**) *ж* journalism
жýткий *прил* terrible
ЖЭК (**-а**) *м сокр* (= *жи́лищно-эксплуатаци́онная контóра*) ≈ housing office
жюри́ *ср нескл* panel of judges

З

з. *сокр* (= *зáпад*) W (= *West*); (= *зáпадный*) W (= *West*)

 **КЛЮЧЕВОЕ СЛОВО**

за *предл +асс* **1** out (of); **выходи́ть** (*perf* **вы́йти**) **за дверь** to go out (of) the door
2 (*позади*) behind; **прятаться** (*perf* **спрятаться**) **за дéрево** to hide behind a tree
3 (*около*: *сесть, встать*) at; **сади́ться** (*perf* **сесть**) **за стол** to sit down at the table
4 (*свыше какого-н предела*) over; **емý за сóрок** he is over forty
5 (*при указании на расстояние, на время*): **за пять киломéтров отсю́да** five kilometres (*Brit*) *или* kilometers (*US*) from here; **за три чáса до начáла спектáкля** three hours before the beginning of the show

6 (*при указании объекта действия*): **держа́ться за** *+acc* to hold onto; **ухвати́ться** (*perf*) **за** *+acc* to take hold of; **брать** (*perf* **взять**) **кого́-н за́ руку** to take sb by the hand; **бра́ться** (*perf* **взя́ться**) **за рабо́ту** to start work
7 (*об объекте чувств*) for; **ра́доваться** (*impf*) **за сы́на** to be happy for one's son; **беспоко́иться** (*impf*) **за му́жа** to worry about one's husband
8 (*о цели*) for; **сража́ться** (*impf*) **за побе́ду** to fight for victory
9 (*в пользу*) for, in favour (*Brit*) *или* favor (*US*) of; **голосова́ть** (*perf* **проголосова́ть**) **за предложе́ние** to vote for *или* in favour of a proposal
10 (*по причине, в обмен*) for; **благодарю́ Вас за по́мощь** thank you for your help; **плати́ть** (*impf*) **за что-н** to pay for sth
11 (*вместо кого-н*) for; **рабо́тать** (*impf*) **за дру́га** to fill in for a friend
▷ *предл +instr* **1** (*по другую сторону*) on the other side of; **жить** (*impf*) **за реко́й** to live on the other side of the river
2 (*вне*) outside; **жить** (*impf*) **за́ городом** to live outside the town; **за грани́цей** abroad
3 (*позади*) behind; **стоя́ть** (*impf*) **за две́рью** to stand behind the door
4 (*около: стоять, сидеть*) at; **сиде́ть** (*impf*) **за столо́м** to sit at the table
5 (*о смене событий*) after; **год за го́дом** year after year
6 (*во время чего-н*) over; **за за́втраком** over breakfast
7 (*о объекте внимания*): **смотре́ть** *или* **уха́живать за** *+instr* to look after
8 (*с целью получить, достать что-н*) for; **я посла́л его́ за газе́той** I sent him out for a paper
9 (*по причине*) owing to
▷ *как сказ* (*согласен*) in favour; **кто за?** who is in favour?
▷ *ср нескл* pro; **взве́сить** (*perf*) **все за и про́тив** to weigh up all the pros and cons

забасто́в|ка (**-ки**; *gen pl* **-ок**) *ж* strike
забасто́вщик (**-а**) *м* striker
забе́г (**-а**) *м* (*Спорт*) race (*in running*); (*: отборочный*) heat
забежа́ть (*как* **бежа́ть**; *см Table 20*; *impf* **забега́ть**) *сов*: **забежа́ть** (**в** *+acc*) (*в дом, в деревню*) to run in(to); (*разг: на недолго*) to drop in(to); **забега́ть** (*perf* **забежа́ть**) **вперёд** to run ahead
забира́|ть(ся) (**-ю(сь)**) *несов от* **забра́ть(ся)**
заб|и́ть (**-ью́, -ьёшь**; *impf* **забива́ть**) *перех* (*гвоздь, сваю*) to drive in; (*Спорт: гол*) to score; (*наполнить*) to overfill; (*засорить*) to clog (up); (*скот, зверя*) to slaughter; **заби́ться** *сов возв* (*сердце*) to start beating ▷ (*impf* **забива́ться**) (*спрятаться*) to hide (away)
забл|уди́ться (**-ужу́сь, -у́дишься**) *сов возв* to get lost
заблужда́|ться (**-юсь**) *несов возв* to be mistaken; **заблужде́ни|е** (**-я**) *ср* misconception
заболева́ни|е (**-я**) *ср* illness
заболе́|ть (**-ю**; *impf* **заболева́ть**) *сов* (*нога, горло*) to begin to hurt; **заболева́ть** (*perf* **заболе́ть**) *+instr* (*гриппом*) to fall ill with
забо́р (**-а**) *м* fence
забо́т|а (**-ы**) *ж* (*беспокойство*)

worry; (*уход*) care; (*обычно мн*: *хлопоты*) trouble; **забо́|титься** (**-чусь, -тишься**; *perf* **позабо́титься**) *несов возв*: **забо́титься о** *+prp* to take care of; **забо́тливый** *прил* caring

забра́сыва|ть (**-ю**) *несов от* **заброса́ть**; **забро́сить**

заб|ра́ть (**-еру́, -ерёшь**; *impf* **забира́ть**) *сов перех* to take; **забра́ться** (*impf* **забира́ться**) *сов возв* (*влезть*): **забра́ться на** *+acc* to climb up; (*проникнуть*): **забра́ться в** *+acc* to get into

заброса́|ть (**-ю**; *impf* **забра́сывать**) *сов перех* (*+instr*: *канаву, яму*) to fill with; (*цветами*) to shower with

забро́|сить (**-шу, -сишь**; *impf* **забра́сывать**) *сов перех* (*мяч, камень*) to fling; (*десант*) to drop; (*учёбу*) to neglect

забры́зга|ть (**-ю**; *impf* **забры́згивать**) *сов перех* to splash

забы́ть (*как* **быть**; *см Table 21*; *impf* **забыва́ть**) *сов перех* to forget

зав. *сокр* = **заве́дующий**

зава́л (**-а**) *м* obstruction; **зав|али́ть** (**-алю́, -а́лишь**; *impf* **зава́ливать**) *сов перех* (*вход*) to block off; (*разг*: *экзамен*) to mess up; **зава́ливать** (*perf* **завали́ть**) *+instr* (*дорогу*: *снегом*) to cover with; (*яму*: *землёй*) to fill with; **завали́ться** (*impf* **зава́ливаться**) *сов возв* (*забор*) to collapse; (*разг*: *на экзамене*) to come a cropper

зав|ари́ть (**-арю́, -а́ришь**; *impf* **зава́ривать**) *сов перех* (*чай, кофе*) to brew; (*Тех*) to weld

заварно́й *прил*: **заварно́й крем** custard

заведе́ни|е (**-я**) *ср* establishment

заве́д|овать (**-ую**) *несов +instr* to be in charge of

заве́дующ|ий (**-его**) *м* manager; (*лабораторией, кафедрой*) head; **заве́дующий хозя́йством** (*в школе*) bursar; (*на заводе*) *person in charge of supplies*

заве́р|ить (**-ю, -ишь**; *impf* **заверя́ть**) *сов перех* (*копию, подпись*) to witness; **заверя́ть** (*perf* **заве́рить**) **кого́-н в чём-н** to assure sb of sth

заверн|у́ть (**-у́, -ёшь**; *impf* **завора́чивать**) *сов перех* (*рукав*) to roll up; (*гайку*) to tighten up; (*налево, направо, за угол*) to turn; **завора́чивать** (*perf* **заверну́ть**) (**в** *+acc*) (*посылку, книгу, ребёнка*) to wrap (in); **заверну́ться** (*impf* **завора́чиваться**) *сов возв*: **заверну́ться в** *+acc* (*в полотенце, в плед*) to wrap o.s. up in

заверша́|ть (**-ю**) *несов от* **заверши́ть**

заверша́ющий *прил* final

заверше́ни|е (**-я**) *ср* completion; (*разговора, лекции*) conclusion; **заверш|и́ть** (**-у́, -и́шь**; *impf* **заверша́ть**) *сов перех* to complete; (*разговор*) to end

заверя́|ть (**-ю**) *несов от* **заве́рить**

зав|ести́ (**-еду́, -едёшь**; *pt* **-ёл, -ела́, -ело́**, *impf* **заводи́ть**) *сов перех* to take; (*приобрести*) to get; (*установить*) to introduce; (*переписку, разговор*) to initiate; (*часы*) to wind up; (*машину*) to start; **завести́сь** (*impf* **заводи́ться**) *сов возв* (*появиться*) to appear; (*мотор, часы*) to start working

завеща́ни|е (**-я**) *ср* (*документ*) will, testament; **завеща́|ть** (**-ю**)

3

(не)сов перех: **завеща́ть что-н кому́-н** *(наследство)* to bequeath sth to sb

завива́|ть(ся) (**-ю(сь)**) *несов от* **зави́ть(ся)**

зави́дно *как сказ*: **ему́ зави́дно** he feels envious

зави́д|овать (**-ую**; *perf* **позави́довать**) *несов +dat* to envy, be jealous of

завин|ти́ть (**-чу́, -ти́шь**; *impf* **зави́нчивать**) *сов перех* to tighten (up)

зави́|сеть (**-шу, -сишь**) *несов*: **зави́сеть от** *+gen* to depend on; **зави́симост|ь** (**-и**) *ж* *(отношение)* correlation; **зави́симость (от** *+gen***)** dependence (on); **в зави́симости от** *+gen* depending on

зави́стливый *прил* envious, jealous; **за́вист|ь** (**-и**) *ж* envy, jealousy

завит|о́к (**-ка́**) *м* *(локон)* curl

зав|и́ть (**-ью, -ьёшь**; *impf* **завива́ть**) *сов перех* *(волосы)* to curl; **зави́ться** (*impf* **завива́ться**) *сов возв* *(волосы)* to curl; *(сделать завивку)* to curl one's hair

заво́д (**-а**) *м* factory; *(в часах, у игрушки)* clockwork

зав|оди́ть(ся) (**-ожу́(сь), -о́дишь(ся)**) *несов от* **завести́(сь)**

завоева́ни|е (**-я**) *ср* *(страны)* conquest; *(успех)* achievement; **завоева́тельный** *прил* aggressive; **заво|ева́ть** (**-ю́ю**; *impf* **завоёвывать**) *сов перех* to conquer

заворáчива|ть(ся) (**-ю(сь)**) *несов от* **заверну́ть(ся)**

за́втра *нареч, ср нескл* tomorrow; **до за́втра!** see you tomorrow!

за́втрак (**-а**) *м* breakfast; **за́втрака|ть** (**-ю**; *impf* **поза́втракать**) *несов* to have breakfast

за́втрашний *прил* tomorrow's; **за́втрашний день** tomorrow

за́вуч (**-а**) *м сокр* ≈ deputy head

завхо́з (**-а**) *м сокр* = **заве́дующий хозя́йством**

зав|яза́ть (**-яжу́, -я́жешь**; *impf* **завя́зывать**) *сов перех* *(верёвку)* to tie; *(руку, посылку)* to bind; *(разговор)* to start (up); *(дружбу)* to form; **завяза́ться** (*impf* **завя́зываться**) *сов возв* *(шнурки)* to be tied; *(разговор)* to start (up); *(дружба)* to form

загада́|ть (**-ю**; *impf* **зага́дывать**) *сов перех* *(загадку)* to set; *(желание)* to make

зага́д|ка (**-ки**; *gen pl* **-ок**) *ж* riddle; *(перен)* puzzle; **зага́дочный** *прил* puzzling

зага́р (**-а**) *м* (sun)tan

загиба́|ть(ся) (**-ю(сь)**) *несов от* **загну́ть(ся)**

загла́ви|е (**-я**) *ср* title; **загла́вн|ый** *прил*: **загла́вная бу́ква** capital letter; **загла́вная роль** title role

загла́|дить (**-жу, -дишь**; *impf* **загла́живать**) *сов перех* *(складки)* to iron

загло́хн|уть (**-у**) *сов от* **гло́хнуть**

заглуш|и́ть (**-у́, -и́шь**) *сов от* **глуши́ть**

загл|яну́ть (**-яну́, -я́нешь**; *impf* **загля́дывать**) *сов* *(в окно, в комнату)* to peep; *(в книгу, в словарь)* to glance; *(разг: посетить)* to pop in

заг|на́ть (**-оню́, -о́нишь**; *pt* **-на́л, -нала́, -на́ло**, *impf* **загоня́ть**) *сов перех* *(коров, детей)* to drive

загн|и́ть (**-ию́, -иёшь**; *impf* **загнива́ть**) *сов* to rot
загн|у́ть (**-у́, -ёшь**; *impf* **загиба́ть**) *сов перех* to bend; (*край*) to fold; **загну́ться** (*impf* **загиба́ться**) *сов возв* (*гвоздь*) to bend; (*край*) to fold
за́говор (**-а**) *м* conspiracy
заговор|и́ть (**-ю́, -и́шь**) *сов* to begin to speak
заголо́в|ок (**-ка**) *м* headline
заго́н (**-а**) *м* (*для коров*) enclosure; (*для овец*) pen
загоня́|ть (**-ю**) *несов от* **загна́ть**
загора́жива|ть (**-ю**) *несов от* **загороди́ть**
загора́|ть(ся) (**-ю(сь)**) *несов от* **загоре́ть(ся)**
загоре́лый *прил* tanned
загор|е́ть (**-ю́, -и́шь**; *impf* **загора́ть**) *сов* to go brown, get a tan; **загоре́ться** (*impf* **загора́ться**) *сов возв* (*дрова, костёр*) to light; (*здание итп*) to catch fire; (*лампочка, глаза*) to light up
за́город (**-а**) *м* (*разг*) the country
загор|оди́ть (**-ожу́, -о́дишь**; *impf* **загора́живать**) *сов перех* to block off; (*свет*) to block out
за́городный *прил* (*экскурсия*) out-of-town; (*дом*) country
загото́в|ить (**-лю, -ишь**; *impf* **загота́вливать**) *сов перех* to lay in; (*документы итп*) to prepare
загражде́ни|е (**-я**) *ср* barrier
грани́ц|а
загранíц|а (**-ы**) *ж* (*разг*) foreign countries *мн*
заграни́чный *прил* foreign, overseas; **заграни́чный па́спорт** passport (*for travel abroad*)
загрем|е́ть (**-лю́, -и́шь**) *сов* (*гром*) to crash
загро́бн|ый *прил*: **загро́бный мир** the next world; **загро́бная жизнь** the afterlife
загружа́емый *прил* downloadable
загр|узи́ть (**-ужу́, -у́зишь**) *сов от* **грузи́ть** ▷ (*impf* **загружа́ть**) *перех* (*машину*) to load up; (*Комп*) to boot up, to download, to upload
загру́з|ка (**-ки**; *gen pl* **-ок**) *ж* download
загрязне́ни|е (**-я**) *ср* pollution; **загрязне́ние окружа́ющей среды́** (environmental) pollution
загрязн|и́ть (**-ю́, -и́шь**; *impf* **загрязня́ть**) *сов перех* to pollute; **загрязни́ться** (*impf* **загрязня́ться**) *сов возв* to become polluted
ЗАГС (**-а**) *м сокр* (= *за́пись а́ктов гражда́нского состоя́ния*) ≈ registry office
зад (**-а**; *nom pl* **-ы́**, *gen pl* **-о́в**) *м* (*человека*) behind; (*животного*) rump; (*машины*) rear
зада|ва́ть(ся) (**-ю́(сь), -ёшь(ся)**) *несов от* **зада́ть(ся)**
зад|ави́ть (**-авлю́, -а́вишь**) *сов от* **дави́ть** ▷ *перех* to crush; **его́ задави́ла маши́на** he was run over by a car
зада́ни|е (**-я**) *ср* task; (*учебное*) exercise; (*Воен*) mission; **дома́шнее зада́ние** homework
зада́т|ок (**-ка**) *м* deposit
зада́ть (*как* **дать**; см *Table 16*; *impf* **задава́ть**) *сов перех* to set; **задава́ть** (*perf* **зада́ть**) **кому́-н вопро́с** to ask sb a question; **зада́ться** (*impf* **задава́ться**) *сов возв*: **зада́ться це́лью** *+infin* to set o.s. the task of doing
зада́ч|а (**-и**) *ж* task; (*Мат*) problem
задви́га|ть (**-ю**) *сов +instr* to begin to move; **задви́гаться** *сов*

возв to begin to move
задви́жк|а (**-и**) *ж* bolt
задви́н|уть (**-у**) *сов перех* to push; (*ящик, занавески*) to close
задева́|ть (**-ю**) *несов от* **заде́ть**
заде́ла|ть (**-ю**; *impf* **заде́лывать**) *сов перех* to seal up
задёргива|ть (**-ю**) *несов от* **задёрнуть**
зад|ержа́ть (**-ержу́, -е́ржишь**; *impf* **заде́рживать**) *сов перех* to delay, hold up; (*преступника*) to detain; **я не хочу́ Вас заде́рживать** I don't want to hold you back; **задержа́ться** (*impf* **заде́рживаться**) *сов возв* to be delayed *или* held up; (*ждать*) to pause
заде́рж|ка (**-ки**; *gen pl* **-ек**) *ж* delay, hold-up
задёрн|уть (**-у**; *impf* **задёргивать**) *сов перех* (*шторы*) to pull shut
заде́|ть (**-ну, -нешь**; *impf* **задева́ть**) *сов перех* (*перен*: *самолюбие*) to wound; **задева́ть** (*perf* **заде́ть**) **за** *+acc* (*за стол*) to brush against; (*кость*) to graze against
задира́|ть(ся) (**-ю**) *несов от* **задра́ть(ся)**
за́дн|ий *прил* back; **помеча́ть** (*perf* **поме́тить**) **за́дним число́м** to backdate; **опла́чивать** (*perf* **оплати́ть**) **за́дним число́м** to make a back payment
задо́лго *нареч*: **задо́лго до** *+gen* long before
задо́лженност|ь (**-и**) *ж* debts *мн*
за́дом *нареч* backwards (*Brit*), backward (*US*); **за́дом наперёд** back to front
задохн|у́ться (**-у́сь, -ёшься**; *impf* **задыха́ться**) *сов возв* (*в дыму*) to suffocate; (*от бега*) to be out of breath; (*от злости*) to choke
зад|ра́ть (**-еру́, -ерёшь**; *impf* **задира́ть**) *сов перех* (*платье*) to hitch *или* hike up; **задра́ться** (*impf* **задира́ться**) *сов возв* (*платье итп*) to ruck up
задр|ема́ть (**-емлю́, -е́млешь**) *сов* to doze off
задрож|а́ть (**-у́, -и́шь**) *сов* (*человек, голос*) to begin to tremble; (*здание*) to begin to shake
заду́ма|ть (**-ю**; *impf* **заду́мывать**) *сов перех* (*план*) to think up; (*карту, число*) to think of; **заду́мывать** (*perf* **заду́мать**) *+infin* (*уехать итп*) to think of doing; **заду́маться** *сов возв* (*impf* **заду́мываться**) to be deep in thought
заду́мыва|ть(ся) (**-ю(сь)**) *несов от* **заду́мать(ся)**
зад|уши́ть (**-ушу́, -у́шишь**) *сов от* **души́ть**
задыха́|ться (**-юсь**) *несов от* **задохну́ться**
заеда́|ть (**-ю**) *несов от* **зае́сть**
зае́зд (**-а**) *м* (*Спорт*) race (*in horse-racing, motor-racing*)
заезжа́|ть (**-ю**) *несов от* **зае́хать**
заём (**за́йма**) *м* loan
зае́|сть (*как* **есть**; см *Table 15*; *impf* **заеда́ть**) *сов перех* (*подлеж*: *комары*) to eat ▷ *безл* (*разг*: *ружьё*) to jam; **пласти́нку зае́ло** (*разг*) the record is stuck
зае́хать (*как* **е́хать**; см *Table 19*; *impf* **заезжа́ть**) *сов*: **зае́хать за кем-н** to go to fetch sb; **заезжа́ть** (*perf* **зае́хать**) **в** *+acc* (*в канаву, во двор*) to drive into; (*в Москву, в магазин итп*) to stop off at
заж|а́ть (**-му́, -мёшь**; *impf* **зажима́ть**) *сов перех* to squeeze; (*рот, уши*) to cover

заж|éчь (**-гý, -жёшь** *итп*, **-гýт**; *pt* **-ёг, -гла**, *impf* **зажигáть**) *сов перех* (*спичку*) to light; (*свет*) to turn on; **зажéчься** (*impf* **зажигáться**) *сов возв* (*спичка*) to light; (*свет*) to go on
зажива́|ть (**-ю**) *несов от* **зажи́ть**
зажигáл|ка (**-ки**; *gen pl* **-ок**) *ж* (cigarette) lighter; **зажигáни|е** (**-я**) *ср* (*Авт*) ignition
зажигá|ть(ся) (**-ю(сь)**) *несов от* **зажéчь(ся)**
зажимá|ть (**-ю**) *несов от* **зажáть**
заж|и́ть (**-ивý, -ивёшь**; *impf* **заживáть**) *сов* (*рана*) to heal (up)
заземлéни|е (**-я**) *ср* (*Элек*: *устройство*) earth (*Brit*), ground (*US*); **заземл|и́ть** (**-ю́, -и́шь**; *impf* **заземля́ть**) *сов перех* to earth (*Brit*), ground (*US*)
заигрá|ть (**-ю**) *сов (не)перех* to begin to play ▷ *неперех* (*музыка*) to begin
заи́грыва|ть (**-ю**) *несов*: **заи́грывать с** *+instr* (*разг*: *любезничать*) to flirt with; (: *заискивать*) to woo
заикá|ться (**-юсь**) *несов возв* to have a stutter; **заикáться** (*perf* **заикнýться**) **о** *+prp* (*упомянуть*) to mention
заи́мств|овать (**-ую**; *impf* **позаи́мствовать**) *(не)сов перех* to borrow; (*опыт*) to take on board
заинтересóванный *прил* interested; **я заинтересóван в э́том дéле** I have an interest in the matter
заинтерес|ова́ть (**-ýю**) *сов перех* to interest; **заинтересовáться** *сов возв*: **заинтересовáться** *+instr* to become interested in
заи́скива|ть (**-ю**) *несов*: **заи́скивать пéред** *+instr* to ingratiate o.s. with
зайти́ (*как* **идти́**; *см Table 18*; *impf* **заходи́ть**) *сов* (*солнце, луна*) to go down; (*спор, разговор*) to start up; (*посетить*): **зайти́ (в/на** *+acc*/**к** *+dat*) to call in (at); (*попасть*): **зайти́ в/на** *+acc* to stray into; **заходи́ть** (*perf* **зайти́**) **за кем-н** to go to fetch sb; **заходи́ть** (*perf* **зайти́**) **спрáва/слéва** to come in from the right/left
закавкáзский *прил* Transcaucasian
закáз (**-а**) *м* (*см глаг*) ordering; commissioning; (*заказанный предмет*) order; **по закáзу** to order; **зак|азáть** (**-ажý, -áжешь**; *impf* **закáзывать**) *сов перех* to order; to book; (*портрет*) to commission; **заказн|óй** *прил*: **заказнóе уби́йство** contract killing; **заказнóе письмó** registered letter; **закáзчик** (**-а**) *м* customer
закáлыва|ть (**-ю**) *несов от* **закoлóть**
закáнчива|ть(ся) (**-ю**) *несов от* **закóнчить(ся)**
закáпыва|ть (**-ю**) *несов от* **закáпать**; **закопáть**
закáт (**-а**) *м* (*перен*: *жизни*) twilight; **закáт (сóлнца)** sunset
закатá|ть (**-ю**; *impf* **закáтывать**) *сов перех* to roll up
зак|ати́ть (**-ачý, -áтишь**; *impf* **закáтывать**) *сов перех* (*что-н круглое*) to roll; (*что-н на колёсах*) to wheel; **закати́ться** (*impf* **закáтываться**) *сов возв* to roll
закидá|ть (**-ю**; *impf* **заки́дывать**) *сов* = **забросáть**
заки́н|уть (**-у**; *impf* **заки́дывать**) *сов перех* to throw
закип|éть (*3sg* **-и́т**, *impf* **закипáть**) *сов* to start to boil; (*перен*: *работа*) to intensify

заки́с|нуть (**-ну**; *pt* **-**, **-ла**, *impf* **закиса́ть**) *сов* to turn sour
закла́дк|а (**-и**) *ж* (*в книге*) bookmark
закладн|а́я (**-ой**) *ж* mortgage deed
закла́дыва|ть (**-ю**) *несов от* **заложи́ть**
закле́|ить (**-ю, -ишь**; *impf* **закле́ивать**) *сов перех* to seal (up)
заклина́|ть (**-ю**) *несов перех* (*духов, змея*) to charm; (*перен*: *умолять*) to plead with
закли́н|ить (**-ю, -ишь**; *impf* **закли́нивать**) *сов перех* to jam
заключа́|ть (**-ю**) *несов от* **заключи́ть**; **заключа́ться** *несов возв*: **заключа́ться в** *+prp* (*состоять в*) to lie in; (*содержаться в*) to be contained in; **пробле́ма заключа́ется в том, что ...** the problem is that ...
заключённ|ый (**-ого**) *м* prisoner
заключ|и́ть (**-у́, -и́шь**; *impf* **заключа́ть**) *сов перех* (*договор, сделку*) to conclude
зак|оло́ть (**-олю́, -о́лешь**) *сов от* **коло́ть** ▷ (*impf* **зака́лывать**) *перех* (*волосы*) to pin up
зако́н (**-а**) *м* law; **объявля́ть** (*perf* **объяви́ть**) **кого́-н вне зако́на** to outlaw sb; **зако́нный** *прил* legitimate, lawful; (*право*) legal; **законода́тельный** *прил* legislative; **законода́тельств|о** (**-а**) *ср* legislation
закономе́рный *прил* predictable; (*понятный*) legitimate
законопрое́кт (**-а**) *м* (*Полит*) bill
зако́нченный *прил* complete
зако́нч|ить (**-у, -ишь**; *impf* **зака́нчивать**) *сов перех* to finish; **зако́нчиться** (*impf* **зака́нчиваться**) *сов возв* to finish, end
закопа́|ть (**-ю**; *impf* **зака́пывать**) *сов перех* to bury; (*яму*) to fill in
закоп|ти́ть (**-чу́, -ти́шь**) *сов от* **копти́ть**; **закопти́ться** *сов возв* to be covered in smoke
закреп|и́ть (**-лю́, -и́шь**; *impf* **закрепля́ть**) *сов перех* to fasten; (*победу, позицию*) to consolidate; (*Фото*) to fix
закрич|а́ть (**-у́, -и́шь**) *сов* to start shouting
закругл|и́ть (**-ю́, -и́шь**; *impf* **закругля́ть**) *сов перех* (*край, беседу*) to round off
закр|ути́ть (**-учу́, -у́тишь**; *impf* **закру́чивать**) *сов перех* (*волосы*) to twist; (*гайку*) to screw in
закрыва́|ть(ся) (**-ю(сь)**) *несов от* **закры́ть(ся)**
закры́ти|е (**-я**) *ср* closing (time)
закры́т|ый *прил* closed, shut; (*терраса, машина*) enclosed; (*стадион*) indoor; (*собрание*) closed, private; (*рана*) internal; **в закры́том помеще́нии** indoors
закр|ы́ть (**-о́ю, -о́ешь**; *impf* **закрыва́ть**) *сов перех* to close, shut; (*заслонить, накрыть*) to cover (up); (*проход, границу*) to close (off); (*воду, газ итп*) to shut off; **закры́ться** (*impf* **закрыва́ться**) *сов возв* to close, shut; (*магазин*) to close *или* shut down; (*запереться*: *в доме итп*) to shut o.s. up
зак|ури́ть (**-урю́, -у́ришь**; *impf* **заку́ривать**) *сов перех* to light (up)
зак|уси́ть (**-ушу́, -у́сишь**; *impf* **заку́сывать**) *сов* (*поесть*) to have a bite to eat
заку́ск|а (**-и**) *ж* snack; (*обычно мн*: *для водки*) zakuska (*мн*

zakuski); nibbles *мн*; (*в начале обеда*) hors d'oeuvre;
заку́сочн|ая (**-ой**) *ж* snack bar
заку́та|ть(ся) (**-ю(сь)**) *сов от* **ку́тать(ся)**
зал (**-а**) *м* hall; (*в библиотеке*) room; **зал ожида́ния** waiting room
заледене́лый *прил* covered in ice; (*руки*) icy; **заледене́|ть** (**-ю**) *сов* (*дорога*) to ice over; (*перен*: *руки*) to freeze
зале́з|ть (**-у, -ешь**; *impf* **залеза́ть**) *сов*: **зале́зть на** +*acc* (*на крышу*) to climb onto; (*на дерево*) to climb (up); (*разг*): **зале́зть в** +*acc* (*в квартиру*) to break into; (*в долги*) to fall into
зале|те́ть (**-чу́, -ти́шь**; *impf* **залета́ть**) *сов*: **залете́ть (в** +*acc*) to fly in(to)
зал|ечи́ть (**-ечу́, -е́чишь**; *impf* **зале́чивать**) *сов перех* to heal
зали́в (**-а**) *м* bay; (*длинный*) gulf
зал|и́ть (**-ью́, -ьёшь**; *impf* **залива́ть**) *сов перех* to flood; (*костёр*) to extinguish; **залива́ть (***perf* **зали́ть) бензи́н в маши́ну** to fill a car with petrol; **зали́ться** (*impf* **залива́ться**) *сов возв* (*вода*) to seep; **залива́ться (***perf* **зали́ться) слеза́ми/сме́хом** to burst into tears/out laughing
зало́г (**-а**) *м* (*действие*: *вещей*) pawning; (: *квартиры*) mortgaging; (*заложенная вещь*) security; (*Линг*) voice
зал|ожи́ть (**-ожу́, -о́жишь**; *impf* **закла́дывать**) *сов перех* (*покрыть*) to clutter up; (*отметить*) to mark; (*кольцо, шубу*) to pawn; (*дом*) to mortgage; (*заполнить*) to block up; **у меня́ зало́жило нос/го́рло** (*разг*) my nose/throat is all bunged up
зало́жник (**-а**) *м* hostage
за́лпом *нареч* all in one go
зама́|зать (**-жу, -жешь**; *impf* **зама́зывать**) *сов перех* (*щели*) to fill with putty; (*запачкать*) to smear
зама́нчивый *прил* tempting
замахн|у́ться (**-у́сь, -ёшься**; *impf* **зама́хиваться**) *сов возв*: **замахну́ться на** +*acc* (*на ребёнка*) to raise one's hand to; (*перен*) to set one's sights on
зама́чива|ть (**-ю**) *несов от* **замочи́ть**
заме́дл|ить (**-ю, -ишь**; *impf* **замедля́ть**) *сов перех* to slow down; **заме́длиться** (*impf* **замедля́ться**) *сов возв* to slow down
заме́н|а (**-ы**) *ж* replacement; (*Спорт*) substitution; **зам|ени́ть** (**-еню́, -е́нишь**; *impf* **заменя́ть**) *сов перех* to replace
зам|ере́ть (**-ру́, -рёшь**; *pt* **-ер, -ерла́**, *impf* **замира́ть**) *сов* (*человек*) to stop dead; (*перен*: *сердце*) to stand still; (: *работа, страна*) to come to a standstill; (*звук*) to die away
замёрз|нуть (**-ну**; *pt* **-, -ла**, *impf* **замерза́ть**) *сов* to freeze; (*окно*) to ice up; **я замёрз** I'm freezing
замести́тел|ь (**-я**) *м* (*директора*) deputy
заме|сти́ть (**-щу́, -сти́шь**) *сов от* **замеща́ть**
заме́|тить (**-чу, -тишь**; *impf* **замеча́ть**) *сов перех* to notice; (*сказать*) to remark
заме́т|ка (**-ки**; *gen pl* **-ок**) *ж* note; (*в газете*) short piece *или* article
заме́тно *нареч* noticeably ▷ *как сказ* (*видно*) it's obvious; **заме́тный** *прил* noticeable;

З

(*личность*) prominent
замеча́ни|е (**-я**) *ср* comment, remark; (*выговор*) reprimand
замеча́тельно *нареч* (*красив, умён*) extremely; (*делать что-н*) wonderfully, brilliantly ▷ *как сказ*: **замеча́тельно!** that's wonderful *или* brilliant!; **замеча́тельный** *прил* wonderful, brilliant
замеча́|ть (**-ю**) *несов от* **заме́тить**
замеша́тельств|о (**-а**) *ср* confusion
заме́шива|ть (**-ю**) *несов от* **замеси́ть**
замеща́|ть (**-ю**) *несов перех* (*временно*) to stand in for ▷ (*perf* **замести́ть**) (*заменять*: *работника итп*) to replace; (: *игрока*) to substitute; (*вакансию*) to fill; **замеще́ни|е** (**-я**) *ср* (*работника*) replacement; (*игрока*) substitution
зами́н|ка (**-ки**; *gen pl* **-ок**) *ж* hitch
замира́|ть (**-ю**) *несов от* **замере́ть**
замкн|у́ть (**-у́, -ёшь**; *impf* **замыка́ть**) *сов перех* to close; **замкну́ться** (*impf* **замыка́ться**) *сов возв* to close; (*перен*: *обособиться*) to shut o.s. off
за́м|ок (**-ка**) *м* castle
зам|о́к (**-ка́**) *м* lock; (*также* **вися́чий замо́к**) padlock
замо́лк|нуть (**-ну**; *pt* **-, -ла**, *impf* **замолка́ть**) *сов* to fall silent
замолч|а́ть (**-у́, -и́шь**) *сов* (*человек*) to go quiet; **замолчи́!** be quiet!, shut up!
заморо́|зить (**-жу, -зишь**; *impf* **замора́живать**) *сов перех* to freeze
за́морозк|и (**-ов**) *мн* frosts
зам|очи́ть (**-очу́, -о́чишь**; *impf* **зама́чивать**) *сов перех* to soak
за́муж *нареч*: **выходи́ть за́муж** (**за** *+acc*) to get married (to), marry; **за́мужем** *нареч* married; **заму́жеств|о** (**-а**) *ср* marriage; **заму́жняя** *прил* married
заму́ч|ить (**-у, -ишь**) *сов от* **му́чить** ▷ *перех*: **заму́чить** (*perf*) **кого́-н до сме́рти** to torture sb to death; **заму́читься** *сов от* **му́читься**
за́мш|а (**-и**) *ж* suede
замыка́ни|е (**-я**) *ср* (*также* **коро́ткое замыка́ние**) short circuit
замыка́|ть(ся) (**-ю(сь)**) *несов от* **замкну́ть(ся)**
за́мыс|ел (**-ла**) *м* scheme; **замы́сл|ить** (**-ю, -ишь**; *impf* **замышля́ть**) *сов перех* to think up
за́навес (**-а**) *м* (*Театр*) curtain; **занаве́|сить** (**-шу, -сишь**; *impf* **занаве́шивать**) *сов перех* to hang a curtain over; **занаве́с|ка** (**-ки**; *gen pl* **-ок**) *ж* curtain
зан|ести́ (**-есу́, -есёшь**; *pt* **-ёс, -есла́**, *impf* **заноси́ть**) *сов перех* (*принести*) to bring; (*записать*) to take down; (*доставить*): **доро́гу занесло́ сне́гом** the road is covered (over) with snow
занима́|ть (**-ю**) *несов от* **заня́ть**; **занима́ться** *несов возв* (*на рояле итп*) to practise (*Brit*), practice (*US*); **занима́ться** (*impf*) *+instr* (*учиться*) to study; (*уборкой*) to do; **занима́ться** (*impf*) **спо́ртом/му́зыкой** to play sports/music; **чем ты сейча́с занима́ешься?** what are you doing at the moment?
за́ново *нареч* again
зано́з|а (**-ы**) *ж* splinter
зано́с (**-а**) *м* (*обычно мн*) drift
зан|оси́ть (**-ошу́, -о́сишь**) *несов от* **занести́**

зано́счивый *прил* arrogant
за́нят *прил* busy; **он был о́чень за́нят** he was very busy; **телефо́н за́нят** the phone *или* line is engaged
заня́ти|е (**-я**) *ср* occupation; (*в школе*) lesson, class; (*времяпрепровождение*) pastime
за́нятост|ь (**-и**) *ж* employment
заня́ть (**займу́, займёшь**; *impf* **занима́ть**) *сов перех* to occupy; (*позицию*) to take up; (*деньги*) to borrow; (*время*) to take; **заня́ть** (*perf*) **пе́рвое/второ́е ме́сто** to take first/second place; **заня́ться** *сов возв*: **заня́ться** *+instr* (*языком, спортом*) to take up; (*бизнесом*) to go into; **заня́ться** (*perf*) **собо́й/детьми́** to devote time to o.s./one's children
заодно́ *нареч* (*вместе*) as one
зао́чный *прил* part-time

Зао́чное отделе́ние

Part-time study is one of the ways of obtaining a degree. It is intended for people who do not want to give up their work. Most students work independently with regular postal communication with their tutors. Two exam sessions a year are preceded by a month of intensive series of lectures and tutorials which prepare students for the exams. See also notes at **о́чный** and **вече́рний**.

за́пад (**-а**) *м* west; **За́пад** (*Полит*) the West; **западноевропе́йский** *прил* West European; **за́падный** *прил* western; (*ветер*) westerly
западн|я́ (**-и́**) *ж* trap
запа́с (**-а**) *м* store; (*руды*) deposit; (*Воен*) the reserves *мн*
запаса́|ть(ся) (**-ю(сь)**) *несов от* **запасти́(сь)**
запасн|о́й *прил* spare ▷ (**-о́го**) *м* (*Спорт: также* **запасно́й игро́к**) substitute; **запасна́я часть** spare part
зап|асти́ (**-асу́, -асёшь**; *impf* **запаса́ть**) *сов перех* to lay in; **запасти́сь** (*impf* **запаса́ться**) *сов возв*: **запасти́сь** (*+instr*) to stock up (on)
за́пах (**-а**) *м* smell
запая́|ть (**-ю**) *сов перех* to solder
зап|ере́ть (**-ру́, -рёшь**; *impf* **запира́ть**) *сов перех* (*дверь*) to lock; (*дом, человека*) to lock up; **запере́ться** (*impf* **запира́ться**) *сов возв* (*дверь*) to lock; (*человек*) to lock o.s. up
зап|е́ть (**-ою́, -оёшь**) *сов (не) перех* to start singing
запеча́та|ть (**-ю**; *impf* **запеча́тывать**) *сов перех* to seal up
запира́|ть(ся) (**-ю(сь)**) *несов от* **запере́ть(ся)**
зап|иса́ть (**-ишу́, -и́шешь**; *impf* **запи́сывать**) *сов перех* to write down; (*концерт, пластинку*) to record; (*на курсы*) to enrol; **записа́ться** (*impf* **запи́сываться**) *сов возв* (*на курсы*) to enrol (o.s.); (*на плёнку*) to make a recording; **записа́ться** (*perf*) **(на приём) к врачу́** to make a doctor's appointment
запи́ск|а (**-и**) *ж* note; (*служебная*) memo
записн|о́й *прил*: **записна́я кни́жка** notebook
запи́сыва|ть(ся) (**-ю(сь)**) *несов от* **записа́ть(ся)**
за́пис|ь (**-и**) *ж* record; (*в дневнике*) entry; (*Муз*) recording;

(*на курсы*) enrolment (*Brit*), enrollment (*US*); (*на приём к врачу*) appointment
запла́|кать (**-чу, -чешь**) *сов* to start crying *или* to cry
запла́т|а (**-ы**) *ж* patch
запл|ати́ть (**-ачу́, -а́тишь**) *сов от* **плати́ть**
заплы́в (**-а**) *м* (*Спорт*) race (*in swimming*); (: *отборочный*) heat
запл|ы́ть (**-ыву́, -ывёшь**; *impf* **заплыва́ть**) *сов* (*человек*) to swim off; (*глаза*) to become swollen
запове́дник (**-а**) *м* (*природный*) nature reserve
заподо́зр|ить (**-ю, -ишь**) *сов перех* to suspect
запо́лн|ить (**-ю, -ишь**; *impf* **заполня́ть**) *сов перех* to fill; (*анкету, бланк*) to fill in *или* out; **запо́лниться** (*impf* **заполня́ться**) *сов возв* to fill up
заполя́рный *прил* polar
запо́мн|ить (**-ю, -ишь**; *impf* **запомина́ть**) *сов перех* to remember
за́понк|а (**-и**) *ж* cuff link
запо́р (**-а**) *м* (*Мед*) constipation; (*замок*) lock
запоте́|ть (**-ю**) *сов* to steam up
запра́в|ить (**-лю, -ишь**; *impf* **заправля́ть**) *сов перех* (*рубашку*) to tuck in; (*салат*) to dress; **заправля́ть** (*perf* **запра́вить**) **маши́ну** to fill up the car; **запра́виться** (*impf* **заправля́ться**) *сов возв* (*разг*: *горючим*) to tank up
запра́в|ка (**-ки**; *gen pl* **-ок**) *ж* (*машины, самолёта итп*) refuelling; (*разг*: *станция*) filling station; (*Кулин*) dressing
запра́вочн|ый *прил*: **запра́вочная ста́нция** filling station
запре́т (**-а**) *м*: **запре́т** (**на что-н**/*+infin*) ban (on sth/on doing);
запре|ти́ть (**-щу́, -ти́шь**; *impf* **запреща́ть**) *сов перех* to ban; **запреща́ть** (*perf* **запрети́ть**) **кому́-н** *+infin* to forbid sb to do;
запре́тный *прил* forbidden
запро́с (**-а**) *м* inquiry; (*обычно мн*: *требования*) expectation
запр|я́чь (**-ягу́, -яжёшь** *итп*, **-ягу́т**; *pt* **-я́г, -ягла́**, *impf* **запряга́ть**) *сов перех* (*лошадь*) to harness
запуга́|ть (**-ю**; *impf* **запу́гивать**) *сов перех* to intimidate
за́пуск (**-а**) *м* (*станка*) starting; (*ракеты*) launch
зап|усти́ть (**-ущу́, -у́стишь**; *impf* **запуска́ть**) *сов перех* (*бросить*) to hurl; (*станок*) to start (up); (*ракету*) to launch; (*хозяйство, болезнь*) to neglect ▷ *неперех*: **запусти́ть чем-н в кого́-н** to hurl sth at sb; **запуска́ть** (*perf* **запусти́ть**) **что-н в произво́дство** to launch (production of) sth
запу́танный *прил* (*нитки, волосы*) tangled; (*дело, вопрос*) confused
запу́та|ть (**-ю**) *сов от* **пу́тать**; **запу́таться** *сов от* **пу́таться** ▷ (*impf* **запу́тываться**) *возв* (*человек*) to get caught up; (*дело, вопрос*) to become confused
запча́ст|ь (**-и**) *ж сокр* = **запасна́я часть**
запя́ст|ье (**-ья**; *gen pl* **-ий**) *ср* wrist
запят|а́я (**-о́й**) *ж, decl like adj* comma
зарабо́та|ть (**-ю**; *impf* **зараба́тывать**) *сов перех* to earn ▷ *неперех* (*no impf*: *начать работать*) to start up

за́работн|ый *прил*: **за́работная пла́та** pay, wages *мн*
за́работ|ок (**-ка**) *м* earnings *мн*
заража́|ть(ся) (**-ю(сь)**) *несов от* **зарази́ть(ся)**
зара́з|а (**-ы**) *ж* infection
зара́зный *прил* infectious
зара́нее *нареч* in advance
зар|асти́ (**-асту́, -астёшь**; *pt* **-о́с, -осла́**, *impf* **зараста́ть**) *сов* (*зажить: рана*) to close up; **зараста́ть** (*perf* **зарасти́**) *+instr* (*травой*) to be overgrown with
заре́|зать (**-жу, -жешь**) *сов от* **ре́зать** ▷ *перех* (*человека*) to stab to death
зарекоменд|ова́ть (**-у́ю**) *сов*: **зарекомендова́ть себя́** *+instr* to prove oneself to be
зарод|и́ться (*3sg* **-и́тся**, *impf* **зарожда́ться**) *сов возв* (*явление*) to emerge; (*перен*: *чувство*) to arise
заро́дыш (**-а**) *м* (*Био*) embryo; (*растения, также перен*) germ
зарпла́т|а (**-ы**) *ж сокр* (= *за́работная пла́та*) pay
зарубе́жный *прил* foreign; **зарубе́жь|е** (**-я**) *ср* overseas; **бли́жнее зарубе́жье** former Soviet republics
зар|ы́ть (**-о́ю, -о́ешь**; *impf* **зарыва́ть**) *сов перех* to bury; **зары́ться** (*impf* **зарыва́ться**) *сов возв*: **зары́ться в** *+acc* to bury o.s. in
зар|я́ (**-и́**; *nom pl* **зо́ри**, *gen pl* **зорь**, *dat pl* **зо́рям**) *ж* dawn; (*вечерняя*) sunset; **ни свет ни заря́** at the crack of dawn
заря́д (**-а**) *м* (*Воен, Элек*) charge; (*перен*: *бодрости*) boost
заса́д|а (**-ы**) *ж* ambush; (*отряд*) ambush party
заса́сыва|ть (*3sg* **-ет**) *несов от* **засоса́ть**
засверка́|ть (**-ю**) *сов* to flash
засв|ети́ть (**-ечу́, -е́тишь**; *impf* **засве́чивать**) *сов перех* (*Фото*) to expose
засева́|ть (**-ю**) *несов от* **засе́ять**
заседа́ни|е (**-я**) *ср* meeting; (*парламента, суда*) session
заседа́тел|ь (**-я**) *м*: **прися́жный заседа́тель** member of the jury
заседа́|ть (**-ю**) *несов* (*на совещании*) to meet; (*в парламенте, в суде*) to sit; (*парламент, суд*) to be in session
засека́|ть (**-ю**) *несов от* **засе́чь**
засел|и́ть (**-ю́, -и́шь**; *impf* **заселя́ть**) *сов перех* (*земли*) to settle; (*дом*) to move into
зас|е́чь (**-еку́, -ечёшь** *etc*, **-еку́т**; *pt* **-ёк, -екла́, -екло́**, *impf* **засека́ть**) *сов перех* (*место*) to locate; **засека́ть** (*perf* **засе́чь**) **вре́мя** to record the time
засе́|ять (**-ю**; *impf* **засева́ть**) *сов перех* to sow
засло́н (**-а**) *м* shield; **заслон|и́ть** (**-ю́, -и́шь**; *impf* **заслоня́ть**) *сов перех* to shield
заслу́г|а (**-и**) *ж* (*обычно мн*) service; **награди́ть** (*perf*) **кого́-н по заслу́гам** to fully reward sb; **его́ наказа́ли по заслу́гам** he got what he deserved
засл|ужи́ть (**-ужу́, -у́жишь**; *impf* **заслу́живать**) *сов перех* to earn
заслу́ша|ть (**-ю**; *impf* **заслу́шивать**) *сов перех* to listen to
засме|я́ться (**-ю́сь, -ёшься**) *сов возв* to start laughing
засн|у́ть (**-у́, -ёшь**; *impf* **засыпа́ть**) *сов* to go to sleep, fall asleep
засо́в (**-а**) *м* bolt
засо́выва|ть (**-ю**) *несов от* **засу́нуть**

З

засоре́ни|е (**-я**) *ср* (*рек*) pollution; (*туалета*) blockage; **засор|и́ть** (**-ю́, -и́шь**; *impf* **засоря́ть**) *сов перех* (*туалет*) to clog up, block; **засори́ться** (*impf* **засоря́ться**) *сов возв* (*туалет*) to become clogged up *или* blocked
засос|а́ть (**-у́, -ёшь**; *impf* **заса́сывать**) *сов перех* to suck in
засо́хн|уть (**-у**; *impf* **засыха́ть**) *сов* (*грязь*) to dry up; (*растение*) to wither
заста́в|а (**-ы**) *ж* (*также* **пограни́чная заста́ва**) frontier post
заста|ва́ть (**-ю́, -ёшь**) *несов от* **заста́ть**
заста́в|ить (**-лю, -ишь**; *impf* **заставля́ть**) *сов перех* (*занять*) to clutter up; **заставля́ть** (*perf* **заста́вить**) **кого́-н** *+infin* to force sb to do, make sb do
заста́|ть (**-ну, -нешь**; *impf* **застава́ть**) *сов перех* to catch, find
застегн|у́ть (**-у́, -ёшь**; *impf* **застёгивать**) *сов перех* to do up; **застегну́ться** (*impf* **застёгиваться**) *сов возв* (*на пуговицы*) to button o.s. up; (*на молнию*) to zip o.s. up
застекл|и́ть (**-ю́, -и́шь**; *impf* **застекля́ть**) *сов перех* to glaze
застел|и́ть (**-ю́, -ишь**; *impf* **застила́ть**) *сов перех* (*кровать*) to make up
засте́нчивый *прил* shy
застига́|ть (**-ю**) *несов от* **засти́чь**
застила́|ть (**-ю**) *несов от* **застели́ть**
засти́|чь (**-гну, -гнешь**; *pt* **-г, -гла, -гло**, *impf* **застига́ть**) *сов перех* to catch
засто́йный *прил* stagnant
застра́ива|ть (**-ю**) *несов от* **застро́ить**
застрах|ова́ть(ся) (**-у́ю(сь)**) *сов от* **страхова́ть(ся)**
застрева́|ть (**-ю**) *несов от* **застря́ть**
застр|ели́ть (**-елю́, -е́лишь**) *сов перех* to gun down; **застрели́ться** *сов возв* to shoot o.s.
застро́|ить (**-ю, -ишь**; *impf* **застра́ивать**) *сов перех* to develop
застря́|ть (**-ну, -нешь**; *impf* **застрева́ть**) *сов* to get stuck
заст|упи́ться (**-уплю́сь, -у́пишься**; *impf* **заступа́ться**) *сов возв*: **заступи́ться за** *+acc* to stand up for
засты́|ть (**-ну, -нешь**; *impf* **застыва́ть**) *сов* to freeze; (*цемент*) to set
засу́н|уть (**-у**; *impf* **засо́вывать**) *сов перех*: **засу́нуть что-н в** *+acc* to thrust sth into
за́сух|а (**-и**) *ж* drought
зас|уши́ть (**-ушу́, -у́шишь**; *impf* **засу́шивать**) *сов перех* to dry up
засу́шливый *прил* dry
засчита́|ть (**-ю**; *impf* **засчи́тывать**) *сов перех* (*гол*) to allow (to stand)
засы́п|ать (**-лю, -лешь**; *impf* **засыпа́ть**) *сов перех* (*яму*) to fill (up); (*покрыть*) to cover; **засыпа́ть** (*perf* **засы́пать**) **кого́-н вопро́сами** to bombard sb with questions; **засыпа́ть** (*perf* **засы́пать**) **кого́-н пода́рками** to shower sb with gifts
засыпа́|ть (**-ю**) *несов от* **засну́ть**
засыха́|ть (**-ю**) *несов от* **засо́хнуть**
зата|и́ть (**-ю́, -и́шь**; *impf* **зата́ивать**) *сов перех* (*неприязнь*) to harbour (*Brit*),

harbor (*US*); **затаи́ть** (*perf*) **дыха́ние** to hold one's breath; **затаи́ться** *сов возв* to hide
зата́плива|ть (**-ю**) *несов от* **затопи́ть**
зат|ащи́ть (**-ащу́, -а́щишь**; *impf* **зата́скивать**) *сов перех* to drag
затво́р (**-а**) *м* shutter
затева́|ть (**-ю**) *несов от* **зате́ять**
затека́|ть (**-ю**) *несов от* **зате́чь**
зате́м *нареч* (*потом*) then; (*для того*) for that reason; **зате́м что́бы** in order to
зат|е́чь (*3sg* **-ечёт**, *pt* **-ёк, -екла́, -екло́**, *impf* **затека́ть**) *сов* (*опухнуть*) to swell up; (*онеметь*) to go numb; **затека́ть** (*perf* **зате́чь**) **за** *+acc*/**в** *+acc* (*вода*) to seep behind/into
зате́|я (**-и**) *ж* (*замысел*) idea, scheme
зате́|ять (**-ю**; *impf* **затева́ть**) *сов перех* (*разговор, игру*) to start (up)
зати́х|нуть (**-ну**; *pt* **-, -ла**, *impf* **затиха́ть**) *сов* to quieten (*Brit*) *или* quiet (*US*) down; (*буря*) to die down
зати́шь|е (**-я**) *ср* lull
заткн|у́ть (**-у́, -ёшь**; *impf* **затыка́ть**) *сов перех* to plug; **заткну́ть** (*perf*) **что-н за** *+acc*/**в** *+acc* to stuff sth behind/into; **затыка́ть** (*perf* **заткну́ть**) **кого́-н** *или* **рот кому́-н** (*разг*) to shut sb up; **заткну́ться** (*impf* **затыка́ться**) *сов возв* (*разг*: *замолчать*) to shut up; **заткни́сь!** (*разг*: *пренебр*) shut it!
затме́ни|е (**-я**) *ср* eclipse
зато́ *союз* (*также* **но зато́**) but then (again)
зат|ону́ть (**-ону́, -о́нешь**) *сов* to sink
зат|опи́ть (**-оплю́, -о́пишь**; *impf* **зата́пливать**) *сов перех* (*печь*) to light ▷ (*impf* **затопля́ть**) (*деревню*) to flood; (*судно*) to sink
зато́р (**-а**) *м* congestion; (*на улице*) traffic jam
затра́гива|ть (**-ю**) *несов от* **затро́нуть**
затра́т|а (**-ы**) *ж* expenditure
затро́н|уть (**-у**; *impf* **затра́гивать**) *сов перех* (*перен*: *тему*) to touch on; (: *человека*) to affect
затрудне́ни|е (**-я**) *ср* difficulty; **затрудни́тельный** *прил* difficult, awkward; **затрудн|и́ть** (**-ю́, -и́шь**; *impf* **затрудня́ть**) *сов перех*: **затрудни́ть что-н** to make sth difficult; **е́сли Вас не затрудни́т** if it isn't too much trouble; **затрудни́ться** (*impf* **затрудня́ться**) *сов возв*: **затрудни́ться** *+infin*/**с чем-н** to have difficulty doing/with sth
зат|упи́ть(ся) (**-уплю́, -у́пишь**) *сов от* **тупи́ть(ся)**
зат|уши́ть (**-ушу́, -у́шишь**) *сов от* **туши́ть**
затыка́|ть(ся) (**-ю(сь)**) *несов от* **заткну́ть(ся)**
заты́л|ок (**-ка**) *м* the back of the head
зат|яну́ть (**-яну́, -я́нешь**; *impf* **затя́гивать**) *сов перех* (*шнурки, гайку*) to tighten; (*дело*) to drag out; (*вовлечь*): **затяну́ть кого́-н в** *+acc* to drag sb into; **затяну́ться** (*impf* **затя́гиваться**) *сов возв* (*петля, узел*) to tighten; (*рана*) to close up; (*дело*) to overrun; (*при курении*) to inhale
зауря́дный *прил* mediocre
зау́трен|я (**-и**) *ж* (*Рел*) dawn mass
за|учи́ть (**-учу́, -у́чишь**; *impf* **зау́чивать**) *сов перех* to learn, memorize

3

захва́т (**-а**) *м* seizure, capture; (*Спорт*) hold; (*Тех*) clamp; **захв|ати́ть** (**-ачу́, -а́тишь**; *impf* **захва́тывать**) *сов перех* to seize, capture; (*взять с собой*) to take; (*подлеж: музыка*) to captivate; (*болезнь, пожар*) to catch (in time); **дух захва́тывает** it takes your breath away; **у меня́ дух захвати́ло от волне́ния** I was breathless with excitement; **захва́тнический** *прил* aggressive; **захва́тывающий** *прил* gripping; (*вид*) breathtaking

захлебн|у́ться (**-у́сь, -ёшься**; *impf* **захлёбываться**) *сов возв* to choke

захло́па|ть (**-ю**) *сов*: **захло́пать (в ладо́ши)** (*зрители*) to start clapping

захло́пн|уть (**-у**; *impf* **захло́пывать**) *сов перех* to slam (shut); **захло́пнуться** (*impf* **захло́пываться**) *сов возв* to slam (shut)

захо́д (**-а**) *м* (*также* **захо́д со́лнца**) sunset; (*в порт*) call; (*попытка*) go; **с пе́рвого/второ́го захо́да** at the first/second go

зах|оди́ть (**-ожу́, -о́дишь**) *несов от* **зайти́**

захор|они́ть (**-оню́, -о́нишь**) *сов перех* to bury

зах|оте́ть (*как* **хоте́ть**; см *Table 14*) *сов перех* to want; **захоте́ться** *сов безл*: **мне захоте́лось есть/пить** I started to feel hungry/thirsty

зац|епи́ть (**-еплю́, -е́пишь**; *impf* **зацепля́ть**) *сов перех* (*поддеть*) to hook up; (*разг: задеть*) to catch against; **зацепи́ться** *сов возв*: **зацепи́ться за** *+acc* (*задеть за*) to catch *или* get caught on; (*ухватиться за*) to grab hold of

зача́т|ок (**-ка**; *nom pl* **-ки**) *м* (*идеи итп*) beginning, germ

заче́м *нареч* why; **заче́м-то** *нареч* for some reason

зачеркн|у́ть (**-у́, -ёшь**; *impf* **зачёркивать**) *сов перех* to cross out

зачерпн|у́ть (**-у́, -ёшь**; *impf* **заче́рпывать**) *сов перех* to scoop up

зач|еса́ть (**-ешу́, -е́шешь**; *impf* **зачёсывать**) *сов перех* to comb

зачёт (**-а**) *м* (*Просвещ*) test; **сдава́ть** (*impf*)**/сдать** (*perf*) **зачёт по фи́зике** to sit (*Brit*) *или* take/pass a physics test; **зачётн|ый** *прил*: **зачётная рабо́та** assessed essay (*Brit*), term paper (*US*); **зачётная кни́жка** student's record book

Зачётная кни́жка

This is a special booklet into which all exam marks attained by the students are entered. It is the students' responsibility to look after their own record books.

зачисл|ить (**-ю, -ишь**; *impf* **зачисля́ть**) *сов перех* (*в институт*) to enrol; (*на работу*) to take on; (*на счёт*) to enter

зачита́|ть (**-ю**; *impf* **зачи́тывать**) *сов перех* to read out

зашёл *сов см* **зайти́**

заш|и́ть (**-ью́, -ьёшь**; *impf* **зашива́ть**) *сов перех* (*дырку*) to mend; (*шов, рану*) to stitch

зашла́ *etc сов см* **зайти́**

зашто́па|ть (**-ю**) *сов от* **што́пать**

защёлк|а (**-и**) *ж* (*на двери*) latch

защёлкн|уть (**-у**; *impf* **защёлкивать**) *сов перех* to shut

защи́т|а (**-ы**) *ж* (*также Юр, Спорт*)

defence (*Brit*), defense (*US*); (*от комаров, от пыли*) protection; (*диплома*) (public) viva;
защи|ти́ть (**-щу́, -ти́шь**; *impf* **защища́ть**) *сов перех* to defend; (*от солнца, от комаров итп*) to protect; **защити́ться** (*impf* **защища́ться**) *сов возв* to defend o.s.; (*студент*) to defend one's thesis; **защи́тник** (**-а**) *м* (*также Спорт*) defender; (*Юр*) defence counsel (*Brit*), defense attorney (*US*); **ле́вый/пра́вый защи́тник** (*футбол*) left/right back
защи́тный *прил* protective; **защи́тный цвет** khaki
защища́|ть (**-ю**) *несов от* **защити́ть** ▷ *перех* (*Юр*) to defend; **защища́ться** *несов от* **защити́ться**
за|яви́ть (**-явлю́, -я́вишь**; *impf* **заявля́ть**) *сов перех* (*протест*) to make ▷ *неперех*: **заяви́ть о** *+prp* to announce; **заявля́ть** (*perf* **заяви́ть**) **на кого́-н в мили́цию** to report sb to the police; **зая́в|ка** (**-ки**; *gen pl* **-ок**) *ж*: **зая́вка (на** *+acc*) application (for); **заявле́ни|е** (**-я**) *ср* (*правительства*) statement; (*просьба*): **заявле́ние (о** *+prp*) application (for)
заявля́|ть (**-ю**) *несов от* **заяви́ть**
за́|яц (**-йца**) *м* (*Зоол*) hare
зва́ни|е (**-я**) *ср* (*воинское*) rank; (*учёное, почётное*) title
звать (**зову́, зовёшь**; *perf* **позва́ть**) *несов перех* to call; (*приглашать*) to ask; (*no perf*: *называть*): **звать кого́-н кем-н** to call sb sth; **как Вас зову́т?** what is your name?; **меня́/его́ зову́т Алекса́ндр** my/his name is Alexander; **звать** (*perf* **позва́ть**) **кого́-н в го́сти/в кино́** to ask sb over/to the cinema
звезд|а́ (**-ы́**; *nom pl* **звёзды**) *ж* star
звен|о́ (**-а́**; *nom pl* **-ья**, *gen pl* **-ьев**) *ср* link; (*конструкции*) section
звери́ный *прил* (wild) animal
зве́рский *прил* (*поступок*) brutal; **зве́рств|овать** (**-ую**) *несов* to commit atrocities
звер|ь (**-я**; *gen pl* **-е́й**) *м* (wild) animal, beast
звон|и́ть (**-ю́, -и́шь**; *perf* **позвони́ть**) *несов* to ring; (*Тел*): **звони́ть кому́** to ring *или* phone *или* call (*US*) sb
звон|о́к (**-ка́**; *nom pl* **-ки́**) *м* bell; (*звук*) ring; (*по телефону*) (telephone) call
звук (**-а**) *м* sound
звуков|о́й *прил* sound, audio; **звукова́я доро́жка** track (*on audio tape*); **звукова́я аппарату́ра** hi-fi equipment
звукоза́пис|ь (**-и**) *ж* sound recording
звуч|а́ть (*3sg* **-и́т**) *несов* (*гитара*) to sound; (*гнев*) to be heard
зда́ни|е (**-я**) *ср* building
здесь *нареч* here
здоро́ва|ться (**-юсь**; *perf* **поздоро́ваться**) *несов возв*: **здоро́ваться с** *+instr* to say hello to
здо́рово *нареч* (*разг*: *отлично*) really well ▷ *как сказ* (*разг*) it's great
здоро́в|ый *прил* healthy; (*перен*: *идея*) sound; (*разг*: *большой*) hefty; **бу́дьте здоро́вы!** (*при прощании*) take care!; (*при чихании*) bless you!
здоро́вь|е (**-я**) *ср* health; **как Ва́ше здоро́вье?** how are you keeping?; **за Ва́ше здоро́вье!** (to)

your good health!; **на здоро́вье!** enjoy it!
здравомы́слящий *прил* sensible
здравоохране́ни|е (**-я**) *ср* health care; **министе́рство здравоохране́ния** ≈ Department of Health
здра́вств|овать (**-ую**) *несов* to thrive; **здра́вствуйте** hello; **да здра́вствует...!** long live ...!
здра́вый *прил* sound
зе́бр|а (**-ы**) *ж* zebra; (*переход*) zebra crossing (*Brit*), crosswalk (*US*)
зева́|ть (**-ю**) *несов* to yawn ▷ (*perf* **прозева́ть**) *перех* (*разг*) to miss out
зевн|у́ть (**-у́, -ёшь**) *сов* to yawn
зелене́|ть (**-ю**; *perf* **позелене́ть**) *несов* to go *или* turn green; **зелён|ый** *прил* green; **зе́лен|ь** (**-и**) *ж* (*цвет*) green ▷ *собир* (*растительность*) greenery; (*овощи и травы*) greens *мн*
земе́льный *прил* land; **земе́льный наде́л** *или* **уча́сток** plot of land
землевладе́л|ец (**-ьца**) *м* landowner
земледе́ли|е (**-я**) *ср* arable farming
земледе́льческий *прил* (*район*) agricultural; (*машины*) farming
землетрясе́ни|е (**-я**) *ср* earthquake
зем|ля́ (**-ли́**; *acc sg* **-лю**, *nom pl* **-ли**, *gen pl* **-е́ль**) *ж* land; (*поверхность*) ground; (*почва*) earth, soil; (*планета*): **Земля́** Earth
земляни́к|а (**-и**) *ж* (*растение*) wild strawberry (plant) ▷ *собир* (*ягоды*) wild strawberries *мн*
земно́й *прил* (*поверхность, кора*) earth's; (*перен*: *желания*) earthly; **земно́й шар** the globe
зе́рк|ало (**-ала**; *nom pl* **-ала́**, *gen pl* **-а́л**, *dat pl* **-ала́м**) *ср* mirror
зерн|о́ (**-а́**; *nom pl* **зёрна**, *gen pl* **зёрен**) *ср* (*пшеницы*) grain; (*кофе*) bean; (*мака*) seed ▷ *собир* (*семенное, на хлеб*) grain
зигза́г (**-а**) *м* zigzag
зим|а́ (**-ы́**; *acc sg* **-у**, *dat sg* **-е́**, *nom pl* **-ы**) *ж* winter; **зи́мний** *прил* (*день*) winter's; (*погода*) wintry; (*лес, одежда*) winter; **зим|ова́ть** (**-у́ю**; *perf* **прозимова́ть**) *несов* (*человек*) to spend the winter; (*птицы*) to winter; **зимо́й** *нареч* in the winter
зл|ить (**-ю, -ишь**; *perf* **разозли́ть**) *несов перех* to annoy; **зли́ться** (*perf* **разозли́ться**) *несов возв* to get angry
зл|о (**-а**; *gen pl* **зол**) *ср* evil; (*неприятность*) harm ▷ *нареч* (*посмотреть, сказать*) spitefully; **со зла** out of spite; **меня́ зло берёт** (*разг*) it makes me angry; **у меня́ на неё зла не хвата́ет** (*разг*) she annoys me no end
зло́бный *прил* mean; (*улыбка*) evil; (*голос*) nasty
злободне́вный *прил* topical
злове́щий *прил* sinister
злоде́|й (**-я**) *м* villain
злоде́йский *прил* wicked
злой *прил* evil; (*собака*) vicious; (*глаза, лицо*) mean; (*карикатура*) scathing; **я зол на тебя́** I'm angry with you
злока́чественный *прил* malignant
зло́стный *прил* malicious
злоупотреб|и́ть (**-лю́, -и́шь**; *impf* **злоупотребля́ть**) *сов +instr* to abuse; (*доверием*) to breach;

злоупотребле́ни|е (**-я**) *ср* (*обычно мн*: *преступление*) malpractice *ед*; **злоупотребле́ние нарко́тиками** drug abuse; **злоупотребле́ние дове́рием** breach of confidence

зме́йный *прил* (*кожа*) snake; **зме́йный яд** venom

зме|й (**-я**; *gen pl* **-ев**) *м* serpent; (*также* **возду́шный змей**) kite

зм|ея́ (**-еи́**; *nom pl* **-е́и**, *gen pl* **-е́й**) *ж* snake

знак (**-а**) *м* sign, symbol; (*Комп*) character; **в знак** *+gen* as a token of; **под зна́ком** *+gen* in an atmosphere of; **знак ра́венства** equals sign; **зна́ки зодиа́ка** signs of the Zodiac

знако́м|ить (**-лю, -ишь**; *perf* **познако́мить**) *несов перех*: **знако́мить кого́-н с** *+instr* to introduce sb to; **знако́миться** (*perf* **познако́миться**) *несов возв*: **знако́миться с** *+instr* (*с человеком*) to meet ▷ (*perf* **ознако́миться**) to study; **знако́мств|о** (**-а**) *ср* acquaintance; **знако́м|ый** *прил*: **знако́мый (с** *+instr*) familiar (with) ▷ (**-ого**) *м* acquaintance

знамена́тельный *прил* momentous

знамени́тый *прил* famous

зна́м|я (**-ени**; *как* **вре́мя**; *см Table 4*) *ср* banner

зна́ни|е (**-я**) *ср* knowledge *только ед*; **со зна́нием де́ла** expertly

зна́тный *прил* (*род, человек*) noble

зна|ть (**-ю**) *несов перех* to know; **как зна́ешь** as you wish; **ну, зна́ешь!** well I never!

значе́ни|е (**-я**) *ср* (*слова, взгляда*) meaning; (*победы*) importance

зна́чит *вводн сл* (*разг*) so ▷ *союз* (*следовательно*) that means

значи́тельный *прил* significant; (*вид, взгляд*) meaningful

зна́ч|ить (**-у, -ишь**) *несов (не) перех* to mean; **зна́читься** *несов возв* (*состоять*) to appear

знач|о́к (**-ка́**) *м* badge; (*пометка*) mark

зна́ющий *прил* knowledgeable

зноб|и́ть (*3sg* **-и́т**) *несов безл*: **его́ зноби́т** he's shivery

зно|й (**-я**) *м* intense heat

зов (**-а**) *м* call

зову́ *итп несов см* **звать**

зодиа́к (**-а**) *м* zodiac

зол|а́ (**-ы́**) *ж* cinders *мн*

золо́в|ка (**-ки**; *gen pl* **-ок**) *ж* sister-in-law, husband's sister

зо́лот|о (**-а**) *ср* gold; **золото́й** *прил* gold, golden; (*перен*: *человек, время*) wonderful

зо́н|а (**-ы**) *ж* zone; (*лесная*) area; (*для заключённых*) prison camp

зона́льный *прил* (*граница, деление*) zone; (*местный*) regional

зонд (**-а**) *м* probe

зонт (**-а́**) *м* (*от дождя*) umbrella; (*от солнца*) parasol

зо́нтик (**-а**) *м* = **зонт**

зооло́ги|я (**-и**) *ж* zoology

зоомагази́н (**-а**) *м* pet shop

зоопа́рк (**-а**) *м* zoo

зрач|о́к (**-ка́**) *м* (*Анат*) pupil

зре́лищ|е (**-а**) *ср* sight; (*представление*) show

зре́лый *прил* mature; (*плод*) ripe

зре́ни|е (**-я**) *ср* (eye)sight

зре|ть (**-ю**; *perf* **созре́ть**) *несов* to mature; (*плод*) to ripen

зри́мый *прил* visible

зри́тел|ь (**-я**) *м* (*в театре, в кино*) member of the audience; (*на стадионе*) spectator; (*наблюдатель*) onlooker;

зри́тельный *прил* (*память*) visual; **зри́тельный зал** auditorium

зря *нареч* (*разг: без пользы*) for nothing, in vain; **зря тра́тить** (*perf* **потра́тить**) **де́ньги/вре́мя** to waste money/time; **зря ты ему́ э́то сказа́л** you shouldn't have told him about it

зуб (**-а**; *nom pl* **-ы**, *gen pl* **-о́в**) *м* tooth ▷ (*мн* teeth, *nom pl* **-ья**, *gen pl* **-ьев**) (*пилы*) tooth (*мн* teeth); (*грабель, вилки*) prong

зубн|о́й *прил* dental; **зубна́я щётка** toothbrush; **зубно́й врач** dentist

зуд (**-а**) *м* itch

зы́бкий *прил* shaky

зыб|ь (**-и**) *ж* ripple

зят|ь (**-я**) *м* (*муж дочери*) son-in-law; (*муж сестры*) brother-in-law

КЛЮЧЕВОЕ СЛОВО

и *союз* **1** and; **я и мой друг** my friend and I; **и вот показа́лся лес** and then a forest came into sight
2 (*тоже*): **и он пошёл в теа́тр** he went to the theatre too; **и он не пришёл** he didn't come either
3 (*даже*) even; **и сам не рад** even he himself is not pleased
4 (*именно*): **о том и речь!** that's just it!
5 (*во фразах*): **ну и нагле́ц же ты!** what a cheek you have!; **туда́ и сюда́** here and there; **и ... и ...** both ... and ...

и́в|а (**-ы**) *ж* willow

иглоука́лывани|е (**-я**) *ср* acupuncture

иго́л|ка (**-ки**; *gen pl* **-ок**) *ж* = **игла́**

иго́рный *прил*: **иго́рный дом** gaming club

игр|а́ (**-ы́**; *nom pl* **-ы**) *ж* game; (*на скрипке итп*) playing; (*актёра*) performance; **игра́ слов** play on words; **игра́льн|ый** *прил*: **игра́льные ка́рты** playing cards *мн*; **игра́|ть** (**-ю**) *несов* to play ▷ (*perf* **сыгра́ть**) *перех* to play; (*пьесу*) to perform; **игра́ть** (*perf* **сыгра́ть**) **в** *+acc* (*Спорт*) to play

игри́стый *прил* sparkling

игро́к (**-а́**) *м* player

игру́шечный *прил* toy

игру́ш|ка (**-ки**; *gen pl* **-ек**) *ж* toy; **ёлочные игру́шки** Christmas tree decorations

идеа́льный *прил* ideal

идём *несов см* **идти́**

идеоло́ги|я (**-и**) *ж* ideology

идёшь *etc несов см* **идти́**

иде́|я (**-и**) *ж* idea; **по иде́е** (*разг*) supposedly

идио́м|а (**-ы**) *ж* idiom

идио́т (**-а**) *м* idiot

идти́ (см *Table 18*) *несов* to go; (*пешком*) to walk; (*годы*) to go by; (*фильм*) to be on; (*часы*) to work; (*подходить*: *одежда*): **идти́ к** *+dat* to go with; **иди́ сюда́!** come here!; **иду́!** (I'm) coming!; **идёт по́езд/авто́бус** the train/bus is coming; **идёт дождь/снег** it's raining/snowing; **дела́ иду́т хорошо́/пло́хо** things are going well/badly; **Вам идёт э́та шля́па** the hat suits you; **идти́** (*perf* **пойти́**) **пешко́м** to walk, go on foot

 **КЛЮЧЕВОЕ СЛОВО**

из *предл +gen* **1** (*о направлении*) out of; **он вы́шел из ко́мнаты** he went out of the room

2 (*об источнике*) from; **све́дения из кни́ги** information from a book; **я из Москвы́** I am from Moscow

3 (*при выделении части из целого*) of; **вот оди́н из приме́ров** here is one of the examples

4 (*о материале*) made of; **э́тот стол сде́лан из сосны́** this table is made of pine; **ва́за из стекла́** a glass vase; **варе́нье из я́блок** apple jam

5 (*о причине*) out of; **из осторо́жности/за́висти** out of wariness/envy; **из эконо́мии** in order to save money

6 (*во фразах*): **из го́да в год** year in, year out; **я бежа́л изо всех сил** I ran at top speed

изб|а́ (**-ы́**; *nom pl* **-ы**) *ж* hut

изба́в|ить (**-лю, -ишь**; *impf* **избавля́ть**) *сов перех*: **изба́вить кого́-н от** *+gen* (*от проблем*) to free sb from; (*от врагов*) to deliver sb from; **изба́виться** (*impf* **избавля́ться**) *сов возв*: **изба́виться от** *+gen* to get rid of; (*от страха*) to get over

избега́|ть (**-ю**) *несов от* **избежа́ть** ▷ *неперех*: **избега́ть чего́-н/** *+infin* to avoid sth/doing

избежа́ть (*как* **бежа́ть**; см *Table 20*; *impf* **избега́ть**) *сов +gen* to avoid

избива́|ть (**-ю**) *несов от* **изби́ть**

избира́тел|ь (**-я**) *м* voter; **избира́тельн|ый** *прил* (*система*) electoral; **избира́тельная кампа́ния** election campaign; **избира́тельный уча́сток** polling station; **избира́тельный бюллете́нь** ballot paper

избира́|ть (**-ю**) *несов от* **избра́ть**

из|би́ть (**-обью́, -обьёшь**; *impf* **избива́ть**) *сов перех* to beat up

и́збранный *прил* (*рассказы*)

selected; (*люди, круг*) select
изб|ра́ть (**-еру́, -ерёшь**; *pt* **-ра́л, -рала́, -ра́ло**, *impf* **избира́ть**) *сов перех* (*профессию*) to choose; (*президента*) to elect
избы́т|ок (**-ка**) *м* (*излишек*) surplus; (*обилие*) excess; **избы́точный** *прил* (*вес*) excess
изверже́ни|е (**-я**) *ср* eruption
изве́сти|е (**-я**) *ср* news; *см также* **изве́стия**
изве|сти́ть (**-щу́, -сти́шь**; *impf* **извеща́ть**) *сов перех*: **извести́ть кого́-н о** *+prp* to inform sb of
изве́сти|я (**-й**) *мн* (*издание*) bulletin *ед*
изве́стно *как сказ*: **изве́стно, что ...** it is well known that ...; **мне э́то изве́стно** I know about it; **наско́лько мне изве́стно** as far as I know; **как изве́стно** as is well known; **изве́стност|ь** (**-и**) *ж* fame; **ста́вить** (*perf* **поста́вить**) **кого́-н в изве́стность** to inform sb; **изве́стный** *прил* famous, well-known; (*разг*: *лентяй*) notorious; (*условия*) certain
и́звест|ь (**-и**) *ж* lime
извеща́|ть (**-ю**) *несов от* **извести́ть**
извива́|ться (**-юсь**) *несов возв* (*змея*) to slither; (*человек*) to writhe
извине́ни|е (**-я**) *ср* apology; (*оправдание*) excuse; **извин|и́ть** (**-ю́, -и́шь**; *impf* **извиня́ть**) *сов перех* (*простить*): **извини́ть что-н** (**кому́-н**) to excuse (sb for) sth; **извини́те!** excuse me!; **извини́те, Вы не ска́жете, где вокза́л?** excuse me, could you tell me where the station is?; **извини́ться** (*impf* **извиня́ться**) *сов возв*: **извини́ться** (**за** *+acc*) to apologize (for)
извл|е́чь (**-еку́, -ечёшь** *итп*, **-еку́т**; *pt* **-ёк, -екла́, -екло́**, *impf* **извлека́ть**) *сов перех* (*осколок*) to remove; (*перен*: *пользу*) to derive
изги́б (**-а**) *м* bend
изгиба́|ть(ся) (**-ю(сь)**) *несов от* **изогну́ть(ся)**
изгна́ни|е (**-я**) *ср* (*ссылка*) exile; **изг|на́ть** (**-оню́, -о́нишь**; *pt* **-на́л, -нала́, -на́ло**, *impf* **изгоня́ть**) *сов перех* to drive out; (*сослать*) to exile
и́згород|ь (**-и**) *ж* fence; **жива́я и́згородь** hedge
изгото́в|ить (**-лю, -ишь**; *impf* **изготовля́ть**) *сов перех* to manufacture
изда|ва́ть (**-ю́, -ёшь**) *несов от* **изда́ть**
издалека́ *нареч* from a long way off
и́здали *нареч* = **издалека́**
изда́ни|е (**-я**) *ср* publication; (*изданная вещь*) edition; **изда́тел|ь** (**-я**) *м* publisher; **изда́тельств|о** (**-а**) *ср* publisher, publishing house; **изда́ть** (*как* **дать**; см *Table 16*; *impf* **издава́ть**) *сов перех* (*книгу*) to publish; (*закон*) to issue; (*стон*) to let out
издева́тельств|о (**-а**) *ср* mockery; (*жестокое*) abuse; **издева́|ться** (**-юсь**) *несов возв*: **издева́ться над** *+instr* (*над подчинёнными*) to make a mockery of; (*над чьей-н одеждой*) to mock, ridicule
изде́ли|е (**-я**) *ср* (*товар*) product, article
изде́рж|ки (**-ек**) *мн* expenses; **суде́бные изде́ржки** legal costs
из-за *предл* (*+gen*: *занавески*) from behind; (*угла*) from around; (*по вине*) because of; **из-за того́**

что because
излага́|ть (**-ю**) *несов от* **изложи́ть**
излече́ни|е (**-я**) *ср* (*выздоровление*) recovery
изл|ечи́ться (**-ечу́сь, -е́чишься**; *impf* **изле́чиваться**) *сов возв*: **излечи́ться от** *+gen* to be cured of
изли́ш|ек (**-ка**) *м* (*остаток*) remainder; (*+gen*: *веса*) excess of
изли́шний *прил* unnecessary
изложе́ни|е (**-я**) *ср* presentation; **изл|ожи́ть** (**-ожу́, -о́жишь**; *impf* **излага́ть**) *сов перех* (*события*) to recount; (*просьбу*) to state
излуче́ни|е (**-я**) *ср* radiation
изме́н|а (**-ы**) *ж* (*родине*) treason; (*другу*) betrayal; **супру́жеская изме́на** adultery; **измене́ни|е** (**-я**) *ср* change; (*поправка*) alteration; **изм|ени́ть** (**-еню́, -е́нишь**; *impf* **изменя́ть**) *сов перех* to change ▷ *неперех* (*+dat*: *родине, другу*) to betray; (*супругу*) to be unfaithful to; (*память*) to fail; **измени́ться** (*impf* **изменя́ться**) *сов возв* to change; **изме́нник** (**-а**) *м* traitor
изме́р|ить (**-ю, -ишь**) *сов от* **ме́рить** ▷ (*impf* **измеря́ть**) *перех* to measure
изму́ч|ить (**-у, -ишь**) *сов от* **му́чить**
из|мя́ть (**-омну́, -омнёшь**) *сов от* **мять**
изна́нк|а (**-и**) *ж* (*одежды*) inside; (*ткани*) wrong side
изнаси́ловани|е (**-я**) *ср* rape
изнаси́л|овать (**-ую**) *сов от* **наси́ловать**
изна́шива|ть(ся) (**-ю(сь)**) *несов от* **износи́ть(ся)**
изнемога́|ть (**-ю**) *несов от* **изнемо́чь**
изнеможе́ни|е (**-я**) *ср* exhaustion
изнем|о́чь (**-огу́, -о́жешь** *итп*, **-о́гут**; *pt* **-о́г, -огла́, -огло́**, *impf* **изнемога́ть**) *сов* to be exhausted
изно́с (**-а**) *м* (*механизмов*) wear
изн|оси́ть (**-ошу́, -о́сишь**; *impf* **изна́шивать**) *сов перех* to wear out; **износи́ться** (*impf* **изна́шиваться**) *сов возв* to wear out
изнур|и́ть (**-ю́, -и́шь**; *impf* **изнуря́ть**) *сов перех* to exhaust
изнутри́ *нареч* from inside
изо *предл* = **из**
изобража́|ть (**-ю**) *несов от* **изобрази́ть**
изобрази́тельн|ый *прил* descriptive; **изобрази́тельное иску́сство** fine art
изобра|зи́ть (**-жу́, -зи́шь**; *impf* **изобража́ть**) *сов перех* to depict, portray
изобр|ести́ (**-ету́, -етёшь**; *pt* **-ёл, -ела́**, *impf* **изобрета́ть**) *сов перех* to invent; **изобрета́тел|ь** (**-я**) *м* inventor; **изобрете́ни|е** (**-я**) *ср* invention
изогн|у́ть (**-у́, -ёшь**; *impf* **изгиба́ть**) *сов перех* to bend; **изогну́ться** (*impf* **изгиба́ться**) *сов возв* to bend
изоля́ци|я (**-и**) *ж* (*см глаг*) isolation; cutting off; insulation
изощрённый *прил* sophisticated
из-под *предл +gen* from under(neath); (*около*) from outside; **ба́нка из-под варе́нья** jam jar
Изра́ил|ь (**-я**) *м* Israel
израильтя́н|ин (**-ина**; *nom pl* **-е**) *м* Israeli
изра́ильский *прил* Israeli
и́зредка *нареч* now and then
изрече́ни|е (**-я**) *ср* saying
изуве́ч|ить (**-у, -ишь**; *impf*

изуве́чивать) *сов перех* to maim
изуми́тельный *прил* marvellous (*Brit*), marvelous (*US*), wonderful
изум|и́ть (**-лю́, -и́шь**; *impf* **изумля́ть**) *сов перех* to amaze, astound; **изуми́ться** (*impf* **изумля́ться**) *сов возв* to be amazed *или* astounded; **изумле́ни|е** (**-я**) *ср* amazement
изумру́д (**-а**) *м* emerald
изуча́|ть (**-ю**) *несов от* **изучи́ть** ▷ *перех* (*о процессе*) to study
изуче́ни|е (**-я**) *ср* study
из|учи́ть (**-учу́, -у́чишь**; *impf* **изуча́ть**) *сов перех* (*язык, предмет*) to learn; (*понять*) to get to know; (*исследовать*) to study
изъ|яви́ть (**-явлю́, -я́вишь**; *impf* **изъявля́ть**) *сов перех* to indicate
изъя́н (**-а**) *м* defect
изъя́ть (**изыму́, изы́мешь**; *impf* **изыма́ть**) *сов перех* to withdraw
изы́сканный *прил* refined, sophisticated
изю́м (**-а**) *м собир* raisins *мн*
изя́щный *прил* elegant
ика́|ть (**-ю**) *несов* to hiccup
ико́н|а (**-ы**) *ж* (*Рел*) icon
икр|а́ (**-ы́**) *ж* (*чёрная, красная*) caviar(e) ▷ (*nom pl* **-ы**) (*Анат*) calf (*мн* calves)
ИЛ (**-а**) *м сокр самолёт конструкции С.В. Ильюшина*
и́ли *союз* or; **и́ли ... и́ли ...** either ... or ...
иллюстра́ци|я (**-и**) *ж* illustration
иллюстри́р|овать (**-ую**; *perf* **иллюстри́ровать** *или* **проиллюстри́ровать**) *несов перех* to illustrate
им *мест см* **он**; **оно́**; **они́**
им. *сокр* = **и́мени**
и́мени *etc сущ см* **и́мя**
име́ни|е (**-я**) *ср* estate
имени́нник (**-а**) *м person celebrating his name day or birthday*
имени́тельный *прил* (*Линг*): **имени́тельный паде́ж** the nominative (case)
и́менно *част* exactly, precisely ▷ *союз* (*перед перечислением*): **а и́менно** namely; **вот и́менно**! exactly!, precisely!
име́|ть (**-ю**) *несов перех* to have; **име́ть** (*impf*) **ме́сто** (*событие*) to take place; **име́ть** (*impf*) **де́ло с** *+instr* to deal with; **име́ть** (*impf*) **в виду́** to bear in mind; (*подразумевать*) to mean; **име́ться** *несов возв* (*сведения*) to be available
и́ми *мест см* **они́**
иммигра́нт (**-а**) *м* immigrant
иммиграцио́нный *прил* immigration
иммигра́ци|я (**-и**) *ж* immigration
иммигри́р|овать (**-ую**) *(не)сов* to immigrate
иммуните́т (**-а**) *м* (*Мед: перен*): **иммуните́т (к** *+dat*) immunity (to)
импера́тор (**-а**) *м* emperor
импе́ри|я (**-и**) *ж* empire
и́мпорт (**-а**) *м* (*ввоз*) importation; **импорти́р|овать** (**-ую**) *(не)сов перех* to import; **и́мпортный** *прил* imported
импровизи́р|овать (**-ую**; *perf* **импровизи́ровать** *или* **сымпровизи́ровать**) *(не)сов перех* to improvise
и́мпульс (**-а**) *м* impulse
иму́ществ|о (**-а**) *ср* property; (*принадлежности*) belongings *мн*
и́м|я (**-ени**; *как* **время́**; см *Table 4*) *ср* (*также перен*) name; (*также* **ли́чное и́мя**) first *или* Christian name; **во и́мя** *+gen* (*ради*) in the name of; **на и́мя** *+gen* (*письмо*) addressed to; **от и́мени** *+gen* on

behalf of; **имя по́льзователя** user name, login
ина́че *нареч* (*по-другому*) differently ▷ *союз* otherwise, or else
инвали́д (**-а**) *м* person with a disability; **инвали́дн|ый** *прил*: **инвали́дная коля́ска** wheelchair; **инвали́дный дом** home for people with disabilities; **инвали́дност|ь** (**-и**) *ж* disability; **получа́ть** (*perf* **получи́ть**) **инвали́дность** to be registered as having a disability
инвалю́т|а (**-ы**) *ж сокр* (= *иностра́нная валю́та*) foreign currency
инвести́р|овать (**-ую**) *(не)сов (не)перех* (*Экон*) to invest; **инвести́ци|я** (**-и**) *ж* investment
инде́|ец (**-йца**) *м* Native American, North American Indian
инде́|йка (**-йки**; *gen pl* **-ек**) *ж* turkey
и́ндекс (**-а**) *м* (*цен, книг*) index (*мн* indexes); (*также* **почто́вый и́ндекс**) post (*Brit*) *или* zip (*US*) code
индивидуа́льный *прил* individual
инди́|ец (**-йца**) *м* Indian
инди́йский *прил* Indian; **Инди́йский океа́н** the Indian Ocean
И́нди|я (**-и**) *ж* India
индустриа́льный *прил* industrial
индустри́|я (**-и**) *ж* industry
инжене́р (**-а**) *м* engineer
инициа́л|ы (**-ов**) *мн* initials
инициати́в|а (**-ы**) *ж* initiative
инициати́вн|ый *прил* enterprising; **инициати́вная гру́ппа** ≈ pressure group
инкасса́тор (**-а**) *м* security guard (*employed to collect and deliver money*)
иногда́ *нареч* sometimes
иногоро́дн|ий *прил* from another town ▷ (**-его**) *м person from another town*
ин|о́й *прил* different ▷ *мест* (*некоторый*) some (people); **ины́ми слова́ми** in other words; **не что ино́е, как ..., не кто ино́й, как ...** none other than ...
инома́р|ка (**-ки**; *gen pl* **-ок**) *ж* foreign car
инопланетя́н|ин (**-ина**; *nom pl* **-е**) *м* alien
иноро́дн|ый *прил* alien; **иноро́дное те́ло** (*Мед*) foreign body
иностра́н|ец (**-ца**) *м* foreigner; **иностра́нн|ый** *прил* foreign; **Министе́рство иностра́нных дел** Ministry of Foreign Affairs, ≈ Foreign Office (*Brit*), ≈ State Department (*US*)
инспекти́р|овать (**-ую**; *perf* **проинспекти́ровать**) *несов перех* to inspect
инспе́ктор (**-а**) *м* inspector
инспе́кци|я (**-и**) *ж* inspection
инста́нци|я (**-и**) *ж* authority
инсти́нкт (**-а**) *м* instinct
институ́т (**-а**) *м* institute
инструкти́р|овать (**-ую**; *perf* **проинструкти́ровать**) *(не)сов перех* to instruct
инстру́кци|я (**-и**) *ж* instructions *мн*; (*также* **инстру́кция по эксплуата́ции**) instructions (for use)
инструме́нт (**-а**) *м* instrument
инсули́н (**-а**) *м* insulin
инсу́льт (**-а**) *м* (*Мед*) stroke
инсцени́р|овать (**-ую**) *(не)сов перех* (*роман*) to adapt
интелле́кт (**-а**) *м* intellect
интеллектуа́л (**-а**) *м* intellectual
интеллектуа́льный *прил* intellectual

интеллиге́нт (**-а**) *м* member of the intelligentsia; **интеллиге́нтный** *прил* cultured and educated; **интеллиге́нци|я** (**-и**) *ж собир* the intelligentsia
интенси́вный *прил* intensive; (*окраска*) intense
интерва́л (**-а**) *м* interval
интервью́ *ср нескл* interview
интервьюи́р|овать (**-ую**; *perf* **проинтервьюи́ровать**) *(не)сов перех* to interview
интере́с (**-а**) *м*: **интере́с (к** *+dat*) interest (in)
интере́сно *нареч*: **он о́чень интере́сно расска́зывает** he is very interesting to listen to ▷ *как сказ*: **интере́сно(, что ...)** it's interesting (that ...); **мне э́то о́чень интере́сно** I find it very interesting; **интере́сно, где он э́то нашёл** I wonder where he found that
интере́сный *прил* interesting; (*внешность, женщина*) attractive
интерес|ова́ть (**-у́ю**) *несов перех* to interest; **интересова́ться** *несов возв*: **интересова́ться** *+instr* to be interested in; (*осведомляться*) to inquire after; **он интересова́лся, когда́ ты приезжа́ешь** he was asking when you would be arriving
интерна́т (**-а**) *м* boarding school
интернациона́льный *прил* international
Интерне́т (**-а**) *м* Internet
интерпрета́ци|я (**-и**) *ж* interpretation
интерье́р (**-а**) *м* (*здания*) interior
инти́мный *прил* intimate
интуи́ци|я (**-и**) *ж* intuition
Интури́ст (**-а**) *м сокр* (= *Гла́вное управле́ние по иностра́нному тури́зму*) *Russian tourist agency dealing with foreign tourism*
интури́ст (**-а**) *м сокр* = **иностра́нный тури́ст**
инфа́ркт (**-а**) *м* (*также* **инфа́ркт миока́рда**) heart attack
инфекцио́нный *прил* infectious
инфе́кци|я (**-и**) *ж* infection
инфинити́в (**-а**) *м* infinitive
информацио́нн|ый *прил* information; **информацио́нная програ́мма** news programme (*Brit*) *или* program (*US*)
информа́ци|я (**-и**) *ж* information
информи́р|овать (**-ую**; *perf* **информи́ровать** *или* **проинформи́ровать**) *несов перех* to inform
инфраструкту́р|а (**-ы**) *ж* infrastructure
инциде́нт (**-а**) *м* incident
инъе́кци|я (**-и**) *ж* injection
иня́з (**-а**) *м сокр* (= *факульте́т иностра́нных языко́в*) modern languages department
и.о. *сокр* (= *исполня́ющий обя́занности*) acting
Иорда́ни|я (**-и**) *ж* Jordan
ипоте́к|а (**-и**) *ж* (*Комм*) mortgage
ипоте́чн|ый *прил* mortgage; **ипоте́чная ссу́да** mortgage; **ипоте́чный банк** ≈ building society
ипподро́м (**-а**) *м* racecourse (*Brit*), racetrack (*US*)
Ира́к (**-а**) *м* Iraq
Ира́н (**-а**) *м* Iran
и́рис (**-а**) *м* (*Бот*) iris
ирла́нд|ец (**-ца**) *м* Irishman
Ирла́нди|я (**-и**) *ж* Ireland
ирла́нд|ка (**-ки**; *gen pl* **-ок**) *ж* Irishwoman
иронизи́р|овать (**-ую**) *несов*: **иронизи́ровать (над** *+instr*) to be ironic (about)
иро́ни|я (**-и**) *ж* irony
иск (**-а**) *м* lawsuit; **предъявля́ть** (*perf* **предъяви́ть) кому́-н иск** to

take legal action against sb
искажа́|ть(ся) (**-ю(сь)**) *несов от* **искази́ть(ся)**
иска́ть (**ищу́, и́щешь**) *несов перех* to look *или* search for
исключе́ни|е (**-я**) *ср* (*из списка*) exclusion; (*из института*) expulsion; (*отклонение*) exception; **за исключе́нием** *+gen* with the exception of; **де́лать** (*perf* **сде́лать**) **что-н в ви́де исключе́ния** to make an exception of sth
исключи́тельный *прил* exceptional
исключ|и́ть (**-у́, -и́шь**; *impf* **исключа́ть**) *сов перех* (*из списка*) to exclude; (*из института*) to expel; (*ошибку*) to exclude the possibility of; **э́то исключено́** that is out of the question
иско́нный *прил* (*население, язык*) native, original; (*право*) intrinsic
ископа́ем|ое (**-ого**) *ср* fossil; (*также* **поле́зное ископа́емое**) mineral
искорен|и́ть (**-ю́, -и́шь**; *impf* **искореня́ть**) *сов перех* to eradicate
и́скр|а (**-ы**) *ж* spark
и́скренне *нареч* sincerely; **и́скренне Ваш** Yours sincerely
и́скренний *прил* sincere
искрив|и́ть (**-лю́, -и́шь**; *impf* **искривля́ть**) *сов перех* to bend
искупа́|ть(ся) (**-ю(сь)**) *сов от* **купа́ть(ся)**
иск|упи́ть (**-уплю́, -у́пишь**; *impf* **искупа́ть**) *сов перех* to atone for
иску́сный *прил* (*работник*) skilful (*Brit*), skillful (*US*); (*работа*) fine
иску́сственный *прил* artificial; (*ткань*) synthetic; (*мех*) fake
иску́сств|о (**-а**) *ср* art
искуша́|ть (**-ю**) *несов перех* to tempt
искуше́ни|е (**-я**) *ср* temptation
исла́м (**-а**) *м* Islam; **исла́мский** *прил* Islamic
Исла́нди|я (**-и**) *ж* Iceland
испа́н|ец (**-ца**) *м* Spaniard
Испа́ни|я (**-и**) *ж* Spain
испа́чка|ть(ся) (**-ю(сь)**) *сов от* **па́чкать(ся)**
испове́д|овать (**-ую**) *несов перех* (*религию, идею*) to profess ▷ (*не*)*сов перех* (*Рел*): **испове́довать кого́-н** to hear sb's confession; **испове́доваться** (*не*)*сов возв*: **испове́доваться кому́-н** *или* **у кого́-н** to confess to sb
и́сповед|ь (**-и**) *ж* confession
исполко́м (**-а**) *м сокр* (= *исполни́тельный комите́т*) executive committee
исполне́ни|е (**-я**) *ср* (*приказа*) execution; (*обещания*) fulfilment (*Brit*), fulfillment (*US*); (*роли*) performance
исполни́тельный *прил* (*власть*) executive; (*работник*) efficient
испо́лн|ить (**-ю, -ишь**; *impf* **исполня́ть**) *сов перех* (*приказ*) to carry out; (*обещание*) to fulfil (*Brit*), fulfill (*US*); (*роль*) to perform; **испо́лниться** (*impf* **исполня́ться**) *сов возв* (*желание*) to be fulfilled; **ему́ испо́лнилось 10 лет** he is 10
испо́льзовани|е (**-я**) *ср* use
испо́льз|овать (**-ую**) (*не*)*сов перех* to use
испра́в|ить (**-лю, -ишь**; *impf* **исправля́ть**) *сов перех* (*повреждение*) to repair; (*ошибку*) to correct; (*характер*) to improve; **испра́виться** (*impf* **исправля́ться**) *сов возв* (*человек*) to change (for the better)

испра́вный *прил* (*механизм*) in good working order
испу́г (**-а**) *м* fright; **в испу́ге, с испу́гу** in *или* with fright
испу́ганный *прил* frightened
испуга́|ть(ся) (**-ю(сь)**) *сов от* **пуга́ть(ся)**
испыта́тельный *прил*: **испыта́тельный срок** trial period, probation
испыта́|ть (**-ю**; *impf* **испы́тывать**) *сов перех* (*механизм*) to test; (*нужду, радость*) to experience
иссле́довани|е (**-я**) *ср* (*см глаг*) research; examination; (*научный труд*) study; **иссле́довательск|ий** *прил*: **иссле́довательская рабо́та** research; **иссле́довательский институ́т** research institute; **иссле́д|овать** (**-ую**) *(не)сов перех* to research; (*больного*) to examine
исся́к|нуть (*3sg* **-нет**, *pt* **-, -ла**, *impf* **иссяка́ть**) *сов* (*запасы*) to run dry; (*перен*: *терпение*) to run out
истека́|ть (**-ю**) *несов от* **исте́чь**
исте́рик|а (**-и**) *ж* hysterics *мн*
ист|е́чь (*3sg* **-ечёт**, *pt* **-ёк, -екла́, -екло́**, *impf* **истека́ть**) *сов* (*срок*) to expire; (*время*) to run out
и́стинный *прил* true
исто́к (**-а**) *м* (*реки*) source
исто́рик (**-а**) *м* historian
истори́ческий *прил* historical; (*важный*) historic; **истори́ческий факульте́т** history department
исто́ри|я (**-и**) *ж* (*наука*) history; (*рассказ*) story
исто́чник (**-а**) *м* (*водный*) spring; (*сил*) source
истоще́ни|е (**-я**) *ср* exhaustion
истра́|тить (**-чу, -тишь**) *сов от* **тра́тить**
истреби́тел|ь (**-я**) *м* (*самолёт*) fighter (plane); (*лётчик*) fighter pilot
истреб|и́ть (**-лю́, -и́шь**; *impf* **истребля́ть**) *сов перех* to destroy; (*крыс*) to exterminate
исхо́д (**-а**) *м* outcome
исх|оди́ть (**-ожу́, -о́дишь**) *несов*: **исходи́ть из** *+gen* (*сведения*) to originate from; (*основываться*) to be based on; **исходя́ из** *+gen или* **от** *+gen* on the basis of
исхо́дный *прил* primary
исходя́щий *прил* outgoing; **исходя́щий но́мер** (*Админ*) reference number
исче́з|нуть (**-ну, -нешь**; *pt* **-, -ла**, *impf* **исчеза́ть**) *сов* to disappear
исче́рпа|ть (**-ю**; *impf* **исче́рпывать**) *сов перех* to exhaust
исчисля́|ться (*3pl* **-ются**) *несов возв +instr* to amount to
ита́к *союз* thus, hence
Ита́ли|я (**-и**) *ж* Italy
италья́н|ец (**-ца**) *м* Italian; **италья́нский** *прил* Italian; **италья́нский язы́к** Italian
и т.д. *сокр* (= *и так да́лее*) etc. (= *et cetera*)
ито́г (**-а**) *м* (*работы итп*) result; (*общая сумма*) total; **в ито́ге** (*при подсчёте*) in total; **в (коне́чном) ито́ге** in the end; **подводи́ть (***perf* **подвести́) ито́ги** to sum up
итого́ *нареч* in total, altogether
ито́говый *прил* (*сумма*) total
и т.п. *сокр* (= *и тому́ подо́бное*) etc. (= *et cetera*)
иудаи́зм (**-а**) *м* Judaism
их *мест см* **они́** ▷ *притяж мест* their

и́хн|ий *притяж мест* (*разг*) their;
по и́хнему (in) their way

ищу́ *итп* *несов см* **иска́ть**

ию́л|ь (**-я**) *м* July

ию́н|ь (**-я**) *м* June

йо́г|а (**-и**) *ж* yoga

йо́гурт (**-а**) *м* yoghurt

йод (**-а**) *м* iodine

 КЛЮЧЕВОЕ СЛОВО

к *предл +dat* **1** (*о направлении*) towards; **я пошёл к до́му** I went towards the house; **звать (***perf* **позва́ть) кого́-н к телефо́ну** to call sb to the phone; **мы пое́хали к друзья́м** we went to see friends; **поста́вь ле́стницу к стене́** put the ladder against the wall
2 (*о добавлении, включении*) to; **э́та ба́бочка отно́сится к о́чень ре́дкому ви́ду** this butterfly belongs to a very rare species
3 (*об отношении*) of; **любо́вь к му́зыке** love of music; **он привы́к к хоро́шей еде́** he is used to good food; **к моему́ удивле́нию** to my surprise
4 (*назначение*) with; **припра́вы к мя́су** seasonings for meat

каба́н (**-а́**) *м* (*дикий*) wild boar
кабач|о́к (**-ка́**) *м* marrow (*Brit*), squash (*US*)
ка́бел|ь (**-я**) *м* cable
каби́н|а (**-ы**) *ж* (*телефонная*) booth; (*грузовика*) cab; (*самолёта*) cockpit; (*лифта*) cage
кабине́т (**-а**) *м* (*в доме*) study; (*на работе*) office; (*школьный*) classroom; (*врача*) surgery (*Brit*), office (*US*); (*Полит*: *также* **кабине́т мини́стров**) cabinet
каблу́к (**-а́**) *м* heel
Кавка́з (**-а**) *м* Caucasus
кавка́з|ец (**-ца**) *м* Caucasian
кавы́ч|ки (**-ек**; *dat pl* **-ка́м**) *мн* inverted commas, quotation marks
кадр (**-а**) *м* (*Фото, Кино*) shot
ка́др|ы (**-ов**) *мн* (*работники*) personnel *ед*, staff *ед*
ка́ждый *прил* each, every
каз|а́к (**-ака́**; *nom pl* **-а́ки**) *м* Cossack
каза́рм|а (**-ы**) *ж* barracks *мн*
ка|за́ться (**-жу́сь, -жешься**; *perf* **показа́ться**) *несов возв +instr* to look, seem; **(мне) ка́жется, что ...** it seems (to me) that ...
каза́чий *прил* Cossack
казино́ *ср нескл* casino
казн|а́ (**-ы́**) *ж* treasury
казн|и́ть (**-ю́, -и́шь**) *(не)сов перех* to execute
казн|ь (**-и**) *ж* execution
ка|йма́ (**-ймы́**; *nom pl* **-ймы́**, *gen pl* **-ём**) *ж* hem

 КЛЮЧЕВОЕ СЛОВО

как *местоимённое нареч*
1 (*вопросительное*) how; **как Вы себя́ чу́вствуете?** how do you feel?; **как дела́?** how are things?; **как тебя́ зову́т?** what's your name?
2 (*относительное*): **я сде́лал, как**

ты проси́л I did as you asked; **я не зна́ю, как э́то могло́ случи́ться** I don't know how that could have happened
3 (*насколько*): **как бы́стро/давно́** how quickly/long ago
4 (*до какой степени*): **как краси́во!** how beautiful!; **как жаль!** what a pity *или* shame!
5 (*выражает возмущение*) what
▷ *союз* **1** (*подобно*) as; **мя́гкий, как ва́та** as soft as cotton wool; **как мо́жно скоре́е/гро́мче** as soon/loud as possible; **он оде́т, как бродя́га** he is dressed like a tramp
2 (*в качестве*) as
3 (*о временных отношениях: о будущем, об одновременности*) when; (: *о прошлом*) since; **как зако́нчишь, позвони́ мне** phone (*Brit*) *или* call (*US*) me when you finish; **прошло́ два го́да, как она́ исче́зла** two years have passed since she disappeared
4: как бу́дто, как бы as if; **он согласи́лся как бы не́хотя** he agreed as if unwillingly; **как же** of course; **как говоря́т** *или* **говори́тся** as it were; **как ни** however; **как ника́к** after all; **как раз во́время/то, что на́до** just in time/what we need; **э́то пла́тье/пальто́ мне как раз** this dress/coat is just my size; **как ..., так и ...** both ... and ...; **как то́лько** as soon as

кака́о *ср нескл* cocoa
ка́к-либо *нареч* = **ка́к-нибудь**
ка́к-нибудь *нареч* (*так или иначе*) somehow; (*когда-нибудь*) sometime

КЛЮЧЕВОЕ СЛОВО

как|о́й (**-а́я, -о́е, -и́е**) *мест*
1 (*вопросительное*) what; **како́й тебе́ нра́вится цвет?** what colour do you like?
2 (*относительное*) which; **скажи́, кака́я кни́га интере́снее** tell me which book is more interesting
3 (*выражает оценку*) what; **како́й подле́ц!** what a rascal!
4 (*разг: неопределённое*) any; **нет ли каки́х вопро́сов?** are there any questions?
5 (*во фразах*): **ни в каку́ю** not for anything; **каки́м о́бразом** in what way

како́й-либо *мест* = **како́й-нибудь**
как|о́й-нибудь *мест* (*тот или иной*) any; (*приблизительно*) some; **он и́щет како́й-нибудь рабо́ты** he's looking for any kind of work
как-ника́к *нареч* after all
как|о́й-то *мест*: **Вам како́е-то письмо́** there's a letter for you; (*напоминающий*): **она́ кака́я-то стра́нная сего́дня** she is acting kind of oddly today
ка́к-то *мест* (*каким-то образом*) somehow; (*в некоторой степени*) somewhat; (*разг*): **ка́к-то (раз)** once
ка́ктус (**-а**) *м* cactus (*мн* cacti)
кале́к|а (**-и**) *м/ж* person with a disability
календа́р|ь (**-я́**) *м* calendar
кале́ч|ить (**-у, -ишь**; *perf* **покале́чить** *или* **искале́чить**) *несов перех* to cripple; (*мина*) to maim
кали́бр (**-а**) *м* calibre (*Brit*), caliber (*US*)
кали́т|ка (**-ки**; *gen pl* **-ок**) *ж* gate
кало́ри|я (**-и**) *ж* calorie
калькуля́тор (**-а**) *м* calculator
ка́льци|й (**-я**) *м* calcium

К

камене́|ть (**-ю**) *несов от* **окамене́ть**
ка́менный *прил* stone
ка́м|ень (**-ня**; *gen pl* **-не́й**) *м* stone
ка́мер|а (**-ы**) *ж* (*тюремная*) cell; (*также* **телека́мера, кинока́мера**) camera; **ка́мера хране́ния** (*на вокзале*) left-luggage office (*Brit*), checkroom (*US*); (*в музее*) cloakroom
ка́мерн|ый *прил*: **ка́мерная му́зыка** chamber music
ками́н (**-а**) *м* fireplace
кампа́ни|я (**-и**) *ж* campaign
камы́ш (**-а́**) *м* rushes *мн*
кана́в|а (**-ы**) *ж* ditch
Кана́д|а (**-ы**) *ж* Canada
кана́л (**-а**) *м* canal; (*Связь, Тел*) channel
канализацио́нн|ый *прил*: **канализацио́нная труба́** sewer pipe
кана́т (**-а**) *м* cable; **кана́тн|ый** *прил*: **кана́тная доро́га** cable car
кандида́т (**-а**) *м* candidate; (*Просвещ*): **кандида́т нау́к** ≈ Doctor
кани́кул|ы (**-**) *мн* holidays *мн* (*Brit*), vacation *ед* (*US*)
кани́стр|а (**-ы**) *ж* jerry can
кано́э *ср нескл* canoe
кану́н (**-а**) *м* eve; **в кану́н** *+gen* on the eve of
канцеля́ри|я (**-и**) *ж* office; **канцеля́рский** *прил* office
ка́па|ть (**-ю**) *несов* (*вода*) to drip ▷ (*perf* **нака́пать**) *перех*: **ка́пать что-н** (*микстуру*) to pour sth out drop by drop
капе́лл|а (**-ы**) *ж* (*Муз*) choir
ка́пельниц|а (**-ы**) *ж* (*Мед*) drip
капита́л (**-а**) *м* (*Комм*) capital; **капитали́зм** (**-а**) *м* capitalism; **капиталисти́ческий** *прил* capitalist
капита́льный *прил* (*Экон, Комм*) capital; (*сооружение, труд*) main; (*ремонт, покупка*) major
капита́н (**-а**) *м* captain
капка́н (**-а**) *м* trap
ка́п|ля (**-ли**; *gen pl* **-ель**) *ж* (*также перен*) drop
капо́т (**-а**) *м* (*Авт*) bonnet (*Brit*), hood (*US*)
капри́знича|ть (**-ю**) *несов* to behave capriciously
капро́н (**-а**) *м* synthetic thread
ка́псул|а (**-ы**) *ж* capsule
капу́ст|а (**-ы**) *ж* cabbage; **цветна́я капу́ста** cauliflower
капюшо́н (**-а**) *м* hood
кара́бка|ться (**-юсь**; *perf* **вскара́бкаться**) *несов возв*: **кара́бкаться на** *+acc* (*человек*) to clamber up
караме́л|ь (**-и**) *ж собир* (*леденцы*) caramels *мн*
каранда́ш (**-а́**; *gen pl* **-е́й**) *м* pencil
каранти́н (**-а**) *м* quarantine
кара́|ть (**-ю**; *perf* **покара́ть**) *несов перех* to punish
карау́л (**-а**) *м* guard
карау́л|ить (**-ю, -ишь**) *несов перех* to guard
карбюра́тор (**-а**) *м* carburettor (*Brit*), carburetor (*US*)
ка́рий *прил* (*глаза*) hazel
карка́с (**-а**) *м* framework (*of building*)
ка́рлик (**-а**) *м* person of small stature
карма́н (**-а**) *м* pocket
карнава́л (**-а**) *м* carnival
карни́з (**-а**) *м* (*для штор*) curtain rail
ка́рт|а (**-ы**) *ж* (*Гео*) map; (*также* **игра́льная ка́рта**) (playing) card; **магни́тная ка́рта** (swipe)card;

ка́рта па́мяти memory card
карти́н|а **(-ы)** *ж* picture
карти́н|ка **(-ки**; *gen pl* **-ок)** *ж* (*иллюстрация*) picture (*in book etc*)
карто́н **(-а)** *м* (*бумага*) cardboard
картоте́к|а **(-и)** *ж* card index
карто́фелин|а **(-ы)** *ж* potato (*мн* potatoes); **карто́фел|ь** **(-я)** *м* (*плод*) potatoes *мн*; **карто́фельный** *прил* potato
ка́рточ|ка **(-ки**; *gen pl* **-ек)** *ж* card; (*также* **фотока́рточка**) photo
карто́ш|ка **(-ки**; *gen pl* **-ек)** *ж* (*разг*) = **карто́фелина**; **карто́фель**
ка́ртридж **(-а)** *м* (*Комп*) cartridge
карусе́л|ь **(-и)** *ж* merry-go-round (*Brit*), carousel (*US*)
карье́р|а **(-ы)** *ж* career
каса́|ться **(-юсь**; *perf* **косну́ться)** *несов возв* (*+gen*: *дотрагиваться*) to touch; (*затрагивать*) to touch on; (*иметь отношение*) to concern; **э́то тебя́ не каса́ется** it doesn't concern you; **что каса́ется Вас, то ...** as far as you are concerned ...
ка́с|ка **(-ки**; *gen pl* **-ок)** *ж* helmet
каспи́йск|ий *прил*: **Каспи́йское мо́ре** Caspian Sea
ка́сс|а **(-ы)** *ж* (*Театр, Кино*) box office; (*железнодорожная*) ticket office; (*в магазине*) cash desk
кассе́т|а **(-ы)** *ж* (*магнитофонная*) cassette; (*Фото*) cartridge
касси́р **(-а)** *м* cashier
кастрю́л|я **(-и)** *ж* saucepan
катало́г **(-а)** *м* catalogue (*Brit*), catalog (*US*)
ката́р **(-а)** *м* catarrh
катастро́ф|а **(-ы)** *ж* disaster
ката́|ть **(-ю)** *несов перех* (*что-н круглое*) to roll; (*что-н на колёсах*) to wheel; **ката́ть** (*impf*) **кого́-н на маши́не** to take sb for a drive; **ката́ться** *несов возв*: **ката́ться на маши́не/велосипе́де** to go for a drive/cycle; **ката́ться** (*impf*) **на конька́х/ло́шади** to go skating/horse (*Brit*) *или* horseback (*US*) riding
катего́ри|я **(-и)** *ж* category
ка́тер **(-а)** *м* boat
ка|ти́ть **(-чу́, -тишь)** *несов перех* (*что-н круглое*) to roll; (*что-н на колёсах*) to wheel; **кати́ться** *несов возв* to roll; (*капли*) to run
като́лик **(-а)** *м* Catholic; **католи́ческий** *прил* Catholic
кафе́ *ср нескл* café
ка́федр|а **(-ы)** *ж* (*Просвещ*) department; (*Рел*) pulpit; **заве́дующий ка́федрой** chair
ка́фел|ь **(-я)** *м собир* tiles *мн*
кафете́ри|й **(-я)** *м* cafeteria
кача́|ть **(-ю)** *несов перех* (*колыбель*) to rock; (*нефть*) to pump; **кача́ть** (*impf*) **голово́й** to shake one's head; **кача́ться** *несов возв* to swing; (*на волнах*) to rock, roll
каче́л|и **(-ей)** *мн* swing *ед*
ка́честв|о **(-а)** *ср* quality
▷ *предл*: **в ка́честве** *+gen* as; **в ка́честве приме́ра** by way of example
ка́ш|а **(-и)** *ж* ≈ porridge
ка́ш|ель **(-ля)** *м* cough
ка́шля|ть **(-ю)** *несов* to cough
кашта́н **(-а)** *м* chestnut
каю́т|а **(-ы)** *ж* (*Мор*) cabin
ка́|яться **(-юсь, -ешься**; *perf* **пока́яться)** *несов возв*: **ка́яться (в чём-н пе́ред кем-н)** to confess (sth to sb) ▷ (*perf* **раска́яться**) (*грешник*) to repent
кв. *сокр* (= *квадра́тный*) sq. (= *square*); (= *кварти́ра*) Apt. (= *apartment*)

квадра́т (**-а**) *м* square; **квадра́тный** *прил* square
квалифика́ци|я (**-и**) *ж* qualification; (*специальность*) profession
квалифици́рованный *прил* (*работник*) qualified; (*труд*) skilled
кварта́л (**-а**) *м* quarter
кварти́р|а (**-ы**) *ж* flat (*Brit*), apartment (*US*); (*снимаемое жильё*) lodgings *мн*; **квартира́нт** (**-а**) *м* lodger
квартпла́т|а (**-ы**) *ж сокр* (= *кварти́рная пла́та*) rent (*for a flat*)
квас (**-а**) *м* kvass (*malted drink*)
квита́нци|я (**-и**) *ж* receipt
кг *сокр* (= *килогра́мм*) kg (= *kilogram(me)*)
КГБ *м сокр* (*Ист*) (= *Комите́т госуда́рственной безопа́сности*) KGB
ке́д|ы (-) *мн* pumps *мн*
кекс (**-а**) *м* (fruit)cake
кем *мест см* **кто**
ке́мпинг (**-а**) *м* campsite
ке́п|ка (**-ки**; *gen pl* **-ок**) *ж* cap
кера́мик|а (**-и**) *ж собир* ceramics *мн*; **керами́ческий** *прил* ceramic
кефи́р (**-а**) *м* kefir (*yoghurt drink*)
кибербу́ллинг (**-а**) *м* cyberbullying
кива́|ть (**-ю**) *несов +dat* to nod to; **кивн|у́ть** (**-у́, -ёшь**) *сов*: **кивну́ть** (*+dat*) to nod (to)
кида́|ть (**-ю**) *несов от* **ки́нуть**; **кида́ться** *несов от* **ки́нуться** ▷ *возв*: **кида́ться камня́ми** to throw stones at each other
ки́ллер (**-а**) *м* hit man (*мн* hit men)
килогра́мм (**-а**) *м* kilogram(me)
киломе́тр (**-а**) *м* kilometre (*Brit*), kilometer (*US*)
кино́ *ср нескл* cinema; (*разг*: *фильм*) film, movie (*US*); **идти́** (*perf* **пойти́**) **в кино́** (*разг*) to go to the pictures (*Brit*) *или* movies (*US*); **киноактёр** (**-а**) *м* (film) actor; **киноактри́с|а** (**-ы**) *ж* (film) actress; **кинокарти́н|а** (**-ы**) *ж* film; **кинотеа́тр** (**-а**) *м* cinema; **кинофи́льм** (**-а**) *м* film
ки́н|уть (**-у**; *impf* **кида́ть**) *сов перех* (*камень*) to throw; (*взгляд*) to cast; (*друзей*) to desert; (*разг*: *обмануть*) to cheat; **ки́нуться** (*impf* **кида́ться**) *сов возв*: **ки́нуться на** *+acc* (*на врага*) to attack; (*на еду*) to fall upon
кио́ск (**-а**) *м* kiosk
ки́п|а (**-ы**) *ж* bundle
кипе́ни|е (**-я**) *ср* boiling; **кип|е́ть** (**-лю́, -и́шь**; *perf* **вскипе́ть**) *несов* (*вода*) to boil; (*страсти*) to run high
кипя|ти́ть (**-чу́, -ти́шь**; *perf* **вскипяти́ть**) *несов перех* to boil; **кипяти́ться** *несов возв* (*овощи*) to boil; **кипят|о́к** (**-ка́**) *м* boiling water; **кипячёный** *прил* boiled
кирпи́ч (**-а́**) *м* brick
кислоро́д (**-а**) *м* oxygen
кисл|ота́ (**-оты́**; *nom pl* **-о́ты**) *ж* acid
ки́сл|ый *прил* sour; **ки́слая капу́ста** sauerkraut
ки́с|нуть (**-ну**; *pt* **-, -ла**, *perf* **проки́снуть** *или* **ски́снуть**) *несов* to go off
кист|ь (**-и**) *ж* (*Анат*) hand; (*гроздь*: *рябины*) cluster; (: *винограда*) bunch; (*на скатерти итп*) tassel; (*художника, маляра*) (paint)brush
кит (**-а́**) *м* whale
кита́|ец (**-йца**) *м* Chinese; **Кита́|й** (**-я**) *м* China; **кита́йский** *прил* Chinese; **кита́йский язы́к** Chinese

кише́чник (**-а**) *м* intestines *мн*
клавиату́р|а (**-ы**) *ж* keyboard
кла́виш|а (**-и**) *ж* key
клад (**-а**) *м* treasure
кла́дбищ|е (**-а**) *ср* cemetery
кладу́ *etc несов см* **класть**
клад|ь (**-и**) *ж*: **ручна́я кладь** hand luggage
клал *etc несов см* **класть**
кла́ня|ться (**-юсь**; *perf* **поклони́ться**) *несов возв +dat* to bow to
кла́пан (**-а**) *м* valve
класс (**-а**) *м* class; (*комната*) classroom
кла́ссик|а (**-и**) *ж* classics *мн*; **класси́ческий** *прил* (*пример, работа*) classic; (*музыка, литература*) classical
кла́ссный *прил* (*Просвещ*) class; (*разг: хороший*) cool
кла|сть (**-ду́, -дёшь**; *pt* **-л, -ла**, *perf* **положи́ть**) *несов перех* to put ▷ (*perf* **сложи́ть**) (*фундамент*) to lay
кл|ева́ть (**-юю**) *несов перех* (*подлеж: птица*) to peck ▷ *неперех* (*рыба*) to bite
кле́|ить (**-ю, -ишь**; *perf* **скле́ить**) *несов перех* to glue; **кле́иться** *несов возв* to stick
кле|й (**-я**) *м* glue; **кле́йк|ий** *прил* sticky; **кле́йкая ле́нта** sticky tape
клейм|о́ (**-а́**; *nom pl* **-а**) *ср* stamp; (*на скоте, на осуждённом*) brand; **клеймо́ позо́ра** stigma
клён (**-а**) *м* maple (tree)
кле́т|ка (**-ки**; *gen pl* **-ок**) *ж* (*для птиц, животных*) cage; (*на ткани*) check; (*на бумаге*) square; (*Био*) cell; **ткань в кле́тку** checked material
кле́щ|и (**-е́й**) *мн* tongs
клие́нт (**-а**) *м* client
кли́макс (**-а**) *м* (*Био*) menopause
кли́мат (**-а**) *м* (*также перен*) climate; **измене́ние кли́мата** climate change
клин (**-а**; *nom pl* **-ья**, *gen pl* **-ьев**) *м* wedge
кли́ник|а (**-и**) *ж* clinic
кли́пс|ы (**-ов**) *мн* clip-on earrings
кли́ч|ка (**-ки**; *gen pl* **-ек**) *ж* (*кошки итп*) name; (*человека*) nickname
клише́ *ср нескл* (*перен*) cliché
клони́р|овать (**-ую**) *(не)сов перех* to clone
клон|и́ть (**-ю́, -ишь**) *несов*: **его́ клони́ло ко сну** he was drifting off (to sleep); **к чему́ ты кло́нишь?** what are you getting *или* driving at?
кло́ун (**-а**) *м* clown
клоч|о́к (**-ка́**) *м, уменьш от* **клок**; (*земли*) plot; (*бумаги*) scrap
клуб (**-а**) *м* club ▷ (*nom pl* **-ы́**) (*обычно мн: дыма, пыли*) cloud
клуб|и́ться (*3sg* **-и́тся**) *несов возв* to swirl
клубни́к|а (**-и**) *ж собир* (*ягоды*) strawberries *мн*
клуб|о́к (**-ка́**) *м* (*шерсти*) ball
клюв (**-а**) *м* beak
клю́кв|а (**-ы**) *ж собир* (*ягоды*) cranberries *мн*
клю́н|уть (**-у**) *сов перех* to peck
ключ (**-а́**) *м* (*также перен*) key; (*родник*) spring; (*Муз*): **басо́вый/скрипи́чный ключ** bass/treble clef; **га́ечный ключ** spanner; **ключево́й** *прил* (*главный*) key
клю́ш|ка (**-ки**; *gen pl* **-ек**) *ж* (*Хоккей*) hockey stick; (*Гольф*) club
кля́|сться (**-ну́сь, -нёшься**; *pt* **-лся, -ла́сь**, *perf* **покля́сться**) *несов возв* to swear; **кля́сться** (*perf* **покля́сться**) **в чём-н** to swear sth
кля́тв|а (**-ы**) *ж* oath
км. *сокр* (= *киломе́тр*) km

К

книг|а (**-и**) *ж* book
книж|ка (**-ки**; *gen pl* **-ек**) *ж*, *уменьш от* **книга**; (*разг*) book; **трудовая книжка** employment record book; **чековая книжка** chequebook (*Brit*), checkbook (*US*)
книжный *прил*: **книжный магазин** bookshop
книзу *нареч* downwards
кноп|ка (**-ки**; *gen pl* **-ок**) *ж* (*звонка*) button; (*канцелярская*) drawing pin (*Brit*), thumbtack (*US*); (*застёжка*) press stud, popper (*Brit*)
КНР *ж сокр* (= *Китайская Народная Республика*) PRC (= *People's Republic of China*)
княз|ь (**-я**; *nom pl* **-ья**, *gen pl* **-ей**) *м* prince (*in Russia*)
ко *предл* = **к**
кобыл|а (**-ы**) *ж* mare
коварный *прил* devious
ков|ёр (**-ра**) *м* carpet
коврик (**-а**) *м* rug; (*дверной*) mat; (*Комп*) mouse mat
ковш (**-а**) *м* ladle
ковыря|ть (**-ю**) *несов перех* to dig up; **ковырять** (*impf*) **в зубах/носу** to pick one's teeth/nose
когда *нареч* when; **когда как** it depends
когда-либо *нареч* = **когда-нибудь**
когда-нибудь *нареч* (*в вопросе*) ever; (*в утверждении*) some *или* one day; **Вы когда-нибудь там были?** have you ever been there?; **я когда-нибудь туда поеду** I'll go there some *или* one day
когда-то *нареч* once
кого *мест от* **кто**
ког|оть (**-тя**; *gen pl* **-тей**) *м* claw
код (**-а**) *м* code
кодекс (**-а**) *м* code
кое-где *нареч* here and there
кое-как *нареч* (*небрежно*) any old how; (*с трудом*) somehow
кое-какой (**кое-какого**) *мест* some
кое-кто (**кое-кого**) *мест* (*некоторые*) some (people)
кое-что (**кое-чего**) *мест* (*нечто*) something; (*немногое*) a little
кож|а (**-и**) *ж* skin; (*материал*) leather; **кожаный** *прил* leather
кожн|ый *прил*: **кожные болезни** skin diseases
кожур|а (**-ы**) *ж* (*апельсина итп*) peel
коз|а (**-ы**; *nom pl* **-ы**) *ж* (nanny) goat
коз|ёл (**-ла**) *м* (billy) goat
Козерог (**-а**) *м* (*созвездие*) Capricorn
ко|йка (**-йки**; *gen pl* **-ек**) *ж* (*в казарме*) bunk; (*в больнице*) bed
кокаин (**-а**) *м* cocaine
коклюш (**-а**) *м* whooping cough
коктейл|ь (**-я**) *м* cocktail
кол (**-а**; *nom pl* **-ья**) *м* stake
колбас|а (**-ы**) *ж* sausage
колгот|ки (**-ок**) *мн* tights *мн* (*Brit*), pantihose *мн* (*US*)
колд|овать (**-ую**) *несов* to practise (*Brit*) *или* practice (*US*) witchcraft
кол|ебать (**-еблю, -еблешь**) *несов перех* to rock, swing ▷ (*perf* **поколебать**) (*авторитет*) to shake; **колебаться** *несов возв* (*Физ*) to oscillate; (*пламя итп*) to flicker; (*цены*) to fluctuate; (*сомневаться*) to waver
колен|о (**-а**; *nom pl* **-и**, *gen pl* **-ей**) *ср* knee
кол|есо (**-еса**; *nom pl* **-ёса**) *ср* wheel
количеств|о (**-а**) *ср* quantity
колкост|ь (**-и**) *ж* (*насмешка*) biting remark
коллег|а (**-и**) *м/ж* colleague

колле́ги|я (**-и**) *ж*: **адвока́тская колле́гия** ≈ the Bar; **редакцио́нная колле́гия** editorial board
колле́дж (**-а**) *м* college
коллекти́в (**-а**) *м* collective
коллекти́вный *прил* collective
коллекциони́р|овать (**-ую**) *несов перех* to collect
колле́кци|я (**-и**) *ж* collection
коло́д|а (**-ы**) *ж* (*бревно*) block; (*карт*) pack, deck
коло́д|ец (**-ца**) *м* well; (*в шахте*) shaft
ко́локол (**-а**; *nom pl* **-а́**) *м* bell
колоко́льчик (**-а**) *м* bell; (*Бот*) bluebell
коло́ни|я (**-и**) *ж* colony; **исправи́тельно-трудова́я коло́ния** penal colony
коло́н|ка (**-ки**; *gen pl* **-ок**) *ж* column; (*газовая*) water heater; (*для воды, для бензина*) pump
коло́нн|а (**-ы**) *ж* (*Архит*) column
колори́т (**-а**) *м* (*перен*: *эпохи*) colour (*Brit*), color (*US*); **колори́тный** *прил* colourful (*Brit*), colorful (*US*)
ко́л|ос (**-оса**; *nom pl* **-о́сья**, *gen pl* **-о́сьев**) *м* ear (*of corn, wheat*)
кол|оти́ть (**-очу́, -о́тишь**) *несов*: **колоти́ть по столу́/в дверь** to thump the table/on the door; **колоти́ться** *несов возв* (*сердце*) to thump
кол|о́ть (**-ю́, -ешь**; *perf* **расколо́ть**) *несов перех* (*дрова*) to chop (up); (*орехи*) to crack ▷ (*perf* **заколо́ть**) (*штыком итп*) to spear ▷ (*perf* **уколо́ть**) (*иголкой*) to prick; (*разг*: *делать укол*): **коло́ть кого́-н** to give sb an injection; **коло́ть** (*impf*) **кому́-н что-н** (*разг*) to inject sb with sth; **у меня́ ко́лет в боку́** I've got a stitch; **коло́ться** *несов возв* (*ёж, шиповник*) to be prickly; (*наркоман*) to be on drugs
колыбе́льн|ая (**-ой**) *ж* (*также* **колыбе́льная пе́сня**) lullaby
кольцев|о́й *прил* round, circular; **кольцева́я доро́га** ring road; **кольцева́я ли́ния** (*в метро*) circle line
кол|ьцо́ (**-ьца́**; *nom pl* **-ьца**, *gen pl* **-е́ц**) *ср* ring; (*в маршруте*) circle
колю́ч|ий *прил* (*куст*) prickly; **колю́чая про́волока** barbed wire; **колю́ч|ка** (**-ки**; *gen pl* **-ек**) *ж* thorn
коля́с|ка (**-ки**; *gen pl* **-ок**) *ж*: (**де́тская**) **коля́ска** pram (*Brit*), baby carriage (*US*); **инвали́дная коля́ска** wheelchair
ком *мест см* **кто** ▷ (**-а**; *nom pl* **-ья**, *gen pl* **-ьев**) *м* lump
кома́нд|а (**-ы**) *ж* command; (*судна*) crew; (*Спорт*) team
командиро́в|ка (**-ки**; *gen pl* **-ок**) *ж* (*короткая*) business trip; (*длительная*) secondment (*Brit*), posting
кома́ндовани|е (**-я**) *ср*: **кома́ндование** (**+***instr*) (*судном, войском*) command (of) ▷ *собир* command
кома́нд|овать (**-ую**; *perf* **скома́ндовать**) *несов* to give orders; (**+***instr*: *армией*) to command; (*мужем*) to order around
кома́р (**-а́**) *м* mosquito (*мн* mosquitoes)
комба́йн (**-а**) *м* (*С.-х.*) combine (harvester); **ку́хонный комба́йн** food processor
комбина́т (**-а**) *м* plant
комбина́ци|я (**-и**) *ж* combination; (*женское бельё*) slip
комбинезо́н (**-а**) *м* overalls *мн*; (*детский*) dungarees *мн*

комбини́р|овать (**-ую**; *perf* **скомбини́ровать**) *несов перех* to combine
комеди́йный *прил* comic; (*актёр*) comedy
коме́ди|я (**-и**) *ж* comedy
коме́т|а (**-ы**) *ж* comet
ко́мик (**-а**) *м* comedian, comic
комиссио́нный *прил*: **комиссио́нный магази́н** *second-hand shop which sells goods on a commission basis*
коми́сси|я (**-и**) *ж* commission
комите́т (**-а**) *м* committee
коммента́ри|й (**-я**) *м* commentary; **коммента́тор** (**-а**) *м* commentator; **комменти́р|овать** (**-ую**) *(не)сов перех* (*текст*) to comment on; (*матч*) to commentate on
коммерса́нт (**-а**) *м* businessman (*мн* businessmen)
комме́рческий *прил* commercial; **комме́рческое at** at symbol, @; **комме́рческий магази́н** privately-run shop
коммуна́льн|ый *прил* communal; **коммуна́льные платежи́** bills; **коммуна́льные услу́ги** utilities

Коммуна́льные услу́ги

The communal services include water supply, hot water and heating, public radio, rubbish collection and street sweeping, and building maintenance. All these are paid for on a standing charge basis. Electricity and telephone are the two services which are metered and hence paid for separately.

коммуни́зм (**-а**) *м* communism
коммуника́ци|я (**-и**) *ж* communication
коммуни́ст (**-а**) *м* communist
ко́мнат|а (**-ы**) *ж* room; **ко́мнатн|ый** *прил* indoor; **ко́мнатная температу́ра** room temperature; **ко́мнатное расте́ние** house plant
компа́кт-диск (**-а**) *м* compact disc
компа́ктный *прил* compact
компа́ни|я (**-и**) *ж* (*Комм*) company; (*друзья*) group of friends
компаньо́н (**-а**) *м* (*Комм*) partner
компа́рти|я (**-и**) *ж сокр* (= *коммунисти́ческая па́ртия*) Communist Party
ко́мпас (**-а**) *м* compass
компенса́ци|я (**-и**) *ж* compensation; **компенси́р|овать** (**-ую**) *(не)сов перех*: **компенси́ровать (кому́-н)** to compensate (sb) for
компете́нтный *прил* (*человек*) competent; (*органы*) appropriate
ко́мплекс (**-а**) *м* complex; (*мер*) range
компле́кт (**-а**) *м* set; **комплект|ова́ть** (**-у́ю**; *perf* **укомплектова́ть**) *несов перех* to build up
комплиме́нт (**-а**) *м* compliment
компози́тор (**-а**) *м* composer
компоне́нт (**-а**) *м* component
компости́р|овать (**-ую**; *perf* **закомпости́ровать**) *сов перех* to punch *или* clip (*ticket*)
компромети́р|овать (**-ую**; *perf* **скомпромети́ровать**) *несов перех* to compromise
компроми́сс (**-а**) *м* compromise
компью́тер (**-а**) *м* computer
компью́терщик (**-а**) *м* (*разг*) computer specialist
кому́ *мест см* **кто**

комфóрт (**-а**) *м* comfort; **комфортáбельный** *прил* comfortable
конвéйер (**-а**) *м* conveyor (belt)
конвéрси|я (**-и**) *ж* conversion
конвéрт (**-а**) *м* envelope
конвертúр|овать (**-ую**) *(не)сов перех* (*деньги*) to convert
конвó|й (**-я**) *м* escort
конгрéсс (**-а**) *м* (*съезд*) congress
кондúтерский *прил* confectionery; **кондúтерский магазúн** confectioner's
кондиционéр (**-а**) *м* air conditioner
кон|ёк (**-ькá**) *м* (*обычно мн*: *Спорт*) skate; **катáться** (*impf*) **на конькáх** to skate; *см также* **конькú**
кон|éц (**-цá**) *м* end; **без концá** endlessly; **в концé концóв** in the end; **билéт в одúн конéц** single (*Brit*) *или* one-way ticket; **под конéц** towards the end
конéчно *вводн сл* of course, certainly
конéчност|ь (**-и**) *ж* (*Анат*) limb
конéчный *прил* (*цель, итог*) final; (*станция*) last
конкрéтно *нареч* (*говорить*) specifically; (*именно*) actually
конкрéтный *прил* (*реальный*) concrete; (*факт*) actual
конкурéнт (**-а**) *м* competitor; **конкурентоспосóбный** *прил* competitive; **конкурéнци|я** (**-и**) *ж* competition; **конкурúр|овать** (**-ую**) *несов*: **конкурúровать с** *+instr* to compete with
кóнкурс (**-а**) *м* competition
консéнсус (**-а**) *м* consensus
консервативный *прил* conservative
консервáтор (**-а**) *м* conservative
консерватóри|я (**-и**) *ж* (*Муз*) conservatoire (*Brit*), conservatory (*US*)
консервúр|овать (**-ую**) *(не)сов перех* to preserve; (*в жестяных банках*) to can
консéрвн|ый *прил*: **консéрвная бáнка** can
консéрв|ы (**-ов**) *мн* canned food *ед*
конспéкт (**-а**) *м* notes *мн*; **конспектúр|овать** (**-ую**; *perf* **законспектúровать**) *несов перех* to take notes on
конспирáци|я (**-и**) *ж* conspiracy
конститýци|я (**-и**) *ж* constitution
конструúр|овать (**-ую**; *perf* **сконструúровать**) *несов перех* to construct
конструктор (**-а**) *м* designer; (*детская игра*) construction set; **конструкторск|ий** *прил*: **конструкторское бюрó** design studio; **конструкци|я** (**-и**) *ж* construction
кóнсул (**-а**) *м* consul; **кóнсульств|о** (**-а**) *ср* consulate
консультáнт (**-а**) *м* consultant; **консультáци|я** (**-и**) *ж* (*у врача, у юриста*) consultation; (*учреждение*) consultancy; **консультúр|овать** (**-ую**; *perf* **проконсультúровать**) *несов перех* to give professional advice to; **консультúроваться** (*impf* **проконсультúроваться**) *несов возв*: **консультúроваться с кем-н** to consult sb
контáкт (**-а**) *м* contact; **контáктный** *прил* (*линзы*) contact; **контáктный телефóн** contact number
контéйнер (**-а**) *м* container
контéкст (**-а**) *м* context
континéнт (**-а**) *м* continent
контóр|а (**-ы**) *ж* office; **контóрский** *прил* office
контрабáс (**-а**) *м* double bass

контра́кт (**-а**) *м* contract
контра́ктный *прил* contractual
контра́ст (**-а**) *м* contrast
контрацепти́в (**-а**) *м* contraceptive
контролёр (**-а**) *м* (*в поезде*) (ticket) inspector; (*театральный*) ≈ usher; (*сберкассы*) cashier;
контроли́р|овать (**-ую**) *несов перех* to control
контро́л|ь (**-я**) *м* (*наблюдение*) monitoring; (*проверка*) testing, checking; (*в транспорте*) ticket inspection; (*в магазине*) checkout
контро́льн|ая (**-ой**) *ж* (*также* **контро́льная рабо́та**) class test
контро́льн|ый *прил*: **контро́льная коми́ссия** inspection team; **контро́льные ци́фры** control figures
контрразве́дк|а (**-и**) *ж* counterespionage
конур|а́ (**-ы́**) *ж* (*собачья*) kennel
ко́нус (**-а**) *м* cone
конфере́нц-за́л (**-а**) *м* conference room
конфере́нци|я (**-и**) *ж* conference
конфе́т|а (**-ы**) *ж* sweet
конфиденциа́льный *прил* confidential
конфли́кт (**-а**) *м* (*военный*) conflict; (*в семье, на работе*) tension; **конфликт|ова́ть** (**-у́ю**) *несов*: **конфликтова́ть с** *+instr* (*разг*) to be at loggerheads with
конфо́р|ка (**-ки**; *gen pl* **-ок**) *ж* ring (*on cooker*)
конфронта́ци|я (**-и**) *ж* confrontation
концентра́ци|я (**-и**) *ж* concentration
концентри́р|овать (**-ую**; *perf* **сконцентри́ровать**) *несов перех* to concentrate; **концентри́роваться** (*perf* **сконцентри́роваться**) *несов возв* (*капитал*) to be concentrated; (*ученик*) to concentrate
конце́пци|я (**-и**) *ж* concept
конце́рн (**-а**) *м* (*Экон*) concern
конце́рт (**-а**) *м* concert
концла́гер|ь (**-я**; *nom pl* **-я́**) (= *концентрацио́нный ла́герь*) concentration camp
конча́|ть(ся) (**-ю(сь)**) *несов от* **ко́нчить(ся)**
ко́нчик (**-а**) *м* tip (*of finger etc*)
ко́нч|ить (**-у, -ишь**; *impf* **конча́ть**) *сов перех* to end; (*университет, книгу, работу*) to finish; **ко́нчиться** (*impf* **конча́ться**) *сов возв* (*разговор, книга*) to end, finish; (*запасы*) to run out; (*лес итп*) to end
кон|ь (**-я́**; *nom pl* **-и**, *gen pl* **-е́й**) *м* (*лошадь*) horse; (*Шахматы*) knight
коньк|и́ (**-о́в**) *мн* skates *мн*
конья́к (**-а́**) *м* brandy, cognac
конъюнкту́р|а (**-ы**) *ж* (*Комм*) situation; **конъюнкту́ра ры́нка** market conditions
коопера́тор (**-а**) *м* *member of private enterprise*
коопера́ци|я (**-и**) *ж* cooperative enterprise
координа́т|а (**-ы**) *ж* (*Геом*: *обычно мн*) coordinate; (*разг*: *адрес*) number (and address)
координи́р|овать (**-ую**) *(не)сов перех* to coordinate
копа́|ть (**-ю**) *несов перех* (*землю*) to dig ▷ (*perf* **вы́копать**) (*колодец*) to sink; (*овощи*) to dig up; **копа́ться** *несов возв* (*в чужих вещах*) to snoop about; (*разг*: *возиться*) to dawdle
копе́|йка (**-йки**; *gen pl* **-ек**) *ж* kopeck
копирова́льн|ый *прил*: **копирова́льная маши́на**

photocopying machine, photocopier; **копирова́льная бума́га** carbon paper
копи́р|овать (**-ую**; *perf* **скопи́ровать**) *несов перех* to copy
коп|и́ть (**-лю́, -ишь**; *perf* **накопи́ть** *или* **скопи́ть**) *несов перех* to save; **копи́ться** (*perf* **накопи́ться** *или* **скопи́ться**) *несов возв* to accumulate
ко́пи|я (**-и**) *ж* copy; (*перен*: *о человеке*) spitting image
ко́пот|ь (**-и**) *ж* layer of soot
коп|ти́ть (**-чу́, -ти́шь**) *несов* (*лампа*) to give off soot ▷ (*perf* **закопти́ть**) *перех* (*мясо, рыбу*) to smoke
копчёный *прил* smoked
копы́т|о (**-а**) *ср* hoof (*мн* hooves)
коп|ьё (**-ья́**; *nom pl* **-ья**, *gen pl* **-ий**) *ср* spear; (*Спорт*) javelin
кор|а́ (**-ы́**) *ж* (*дерева*) bark; **земна́я кора́** the earth's crust
кораблекруше́ни|е (**-я**) *ср* shipwreck
кора́бл|ь (**-я́**) *м* ship
кора́лл (**-а**) *м* coral
кордебале́т (**-а**) *м* corps de ballet
коренн|о́й *прил* (*население*) indigenous; (*вопрос, реформы*) fundamental; **коренны́м о́бразом** fundamentally; **коренно́й зуб** molar
кореш|о́к (**-ка́**) *м* (*переплёта*) spine
Коре́|я (**-и**) *ж* Korea
корзи́н|а (**-ы**) *ж* basket
коридо́р (**-а**) *м* corridor
кори́ц|а (**-ы**) *ж* cinnamon
кори́чневый *прил* brown
ко́р|ка (**-ки**; *gen pl* **-ок**) *ж* (*апельсинная*) peel
корм (**-а**; *nom pl* **-а́**) *м* (*для скота*) fodder, feed; (*диких животных*) food
корм|а́ (**-ы́**) *ж* stern
корм|и́ть (**-лю́, -ишь**; *perf* **накорми́ть**) *несов перех*: **корми́ть кого́-н чем-н** to feed sb sth ▷ (*perf* **прокорми́ть**) (*содержать*) to feed, keep; **корми́ть** (*impf*) **гру́дью** to breast-feed; **корми́ться** (*perf* **прокорми́ться**) *несов возв* (*животное*) to feed; (*человек*): **корми́ться** *+instr* to survive
коро́б|ка (**-ки**; *gen pl* **-ок**) *ж* box; **коро́бка скоросте́й** gearbox
коро́в|а (**-ы**) *ж* cow
короле́в|а (**-ы**) *ж* queen
короле́вский *прил* royal
короле́вств|о (**-а**) *ср* kingdom
коро́л|ь (**-я́**) *м* king
коро́н|а (**-ы**) *ж* crown
коро́н|ка (**-ки**; *gen pl* **-ок**) *ж* (*на зубе*) crown
корон|ова́ть (**-у́ю**) *(не)сов перех* to crown
коро́тк|ий *прил* short; **коро́ткие во́лны** short wave; **коро́ткое замыка́ние** short circuit; **ко́ротко** *нареч* briefly; (*стричься*) short ▷ *как сказ*: **э́то пла́тье мне ко́ротко** this dress is too short for me
коро́че *сравн нареч*: **коро́че говоря́** to put it briefly, in short
корпора́ци|я (**-и**) *ж* corporation
корректи́в (**-а**) *м* amendment
корректи́р|овать (**-ую**; *perf* **откорректи́ровать**) *несов перех* (*ошибку*) to correct
корреспонде́нт (**-а**) *м* correspondent; **корреспонде́нци|я** (**-и**) *ж* correspondence
коррумпи́рованный *прил* corrupt

К

корру́пци|я (**-и**) *ж* corruption
корт (**-а**) *м* (tennis) court
ко́рточ|ки (**-ек**) *мн*: **присе́сть на ко́рточки** to squat down; **сиде́ть** (*impf*) **на ко́рточках** to squat
ко́рч|иться (**-усь, -ишься**; *perf* **скорчиться**) *несов возв* (*от боли*) to double up
кор|ь (**-и**) *ж* measles *мн*
коси́л|ка (**-ки**; *gen pl* **-ок**) *ж* mower (*machine*)
ко|си́ть (**-шу́, -сишь**; *perf* **скоси́ть**) *несов перех* (*газон, сено*) to mow; (*глаза*) to slant
косме́тик|а (**-и**) *ж* make-up ▷ *собир* cosmetics *мн*
космети́ческий *прил* cosmetic; **космети́ческий кабине́т** beauty salon
космети́ч|ка (**-ки**; *gen pl* **-ек**) *ж* (*специалистка*) beautician; (*сумочка*) make-up bag
косми́ческ|ий *прил* space; **косми́ческое простра́нство** (outer) space
космона́вт (**-а**) *м* cosmonaut; (*в США итп*) astronaut
ко́смос (**-а**) *м* the cosmos, space
косн|у́ться (**-у́сь, -ёшься**) *сов от* **каса́ться**
ко́стный *прил* (*Анат*): **ко́стный мозг** (bone) marrow
ко́сточ|ка (**-ки**; *gen pl* **-ек**) *ж* (*абрикосовая, вишнёвая*) stone; (*винограда*) seed; (*лимона*) pip
косты́л|ь (**-я́**) *м* (*инвалида*) crutch (*мн* crutches)
кост|ь (**-и**; *gen pl* **-е́й**) *ж* bone
костю́м (**-а**) *м* outfit; (*на сцене*) costume; (*пиджак и брюки/юбка*) suit
костя́ш|ка (**-ки**; *gen pl* **-ек**) *ж* (*пальцев*) knuckle
косы́н|ка (**-ки**; *gen pl* **-ок**) *ж* (triangular) scarf
кот (**-а́**) *м* cat
кот|ёл (**-ла́**) *м* (*паровой*) boiler
котел|о́к (**-ка́**) *м* (*кастрюля*) billy(can); (*шляпа*) bowler (hat) (*Brit*), derby (*US*)
коте́льн|ая (**-ой**) *ж* boiler house
кот|ёнок (**-ёнка**; *nom pl* **-я́та**, *gen pl* **-я́т**) *м* kitten
ко́тик (**-а**) *м* (*тюлень*) fur seal
коти́р|оваться (**-уюсь**) *несов возв* (*Комм*): **коти́роваться (в** *+acc*) to be quoted (at); (*также перен*) to be highly valued
котле́т|а (**-ы**) *ж* rissole; (*также* **отбивна́я котле́та**) chop

КЛЮЧЕВОЕ СЛОВО

кото́р|ый (**-ая, -ое, -ые**) *мест*
1 (*вопросительное*) which; **кото́рый час?** what time is it?
2 (*относительное*: *о предмете*) which; (: *о человеке*) who; **же́нщина, кото́рую я люблю́** the woman I love
3 (*не первый*): **кото́рый день/год мы не ви́делись** we haven't seen each other for many days/years

ко́фе *м нескл* coffee; **ко́фе в зёрнах** coffee beans
кофе́йник (**-а**) *м* coffeepot
кофе́йный *прил* coffee
кофемо́л|ка (**-ки**; *gen pl* **-ок**) *ж* coffee grinder
ко́фт|а (**-ы**) *ж* blouse; (*шерстяная*) cardigan
коча́н (**-а́**) *м*: **коча́н капу́сты** cabbage
кочене́|ть (**-ю**; *perf* **окочене́ть**) *несов* (*руки*) to go stiff; (*человек*) to get stiff
коша́чий *прил* (*мех, лапа*) cat's
кошел|ёк (**-ька́**) *м* purse
ко́ш|ка (**-ки**; *gen pl* **-ек**) *ж* cat

кошма́р (**-а**) *м* nightmare
кошма́рный *прил* nightmarish
краб (**-а**) *м* crab
краево́й *прил* regional
кра́ж|а (**-и**) *ж* theft; **кра́жа со взло́мом** burglary
кра|й (**-я**; *loc sg* **-ю́**, *nom pl* **-я́**, *gen pl* **-ёв**) *м* edge; (*чашки, коробки*) rim; (*местность*) land; (*Полит*) krai (*regional administrative unit*)
кра́йне *нареч* extremely
кра́йн|ий *прил* extreme; (*дом*) end; (*пункт маршрута*) last, final; **в кра́йнем слу́чае** as a last resort; **по кра́йней ме́ре** at least; **Кра́йний Се́вер** the Arctic; **кра́йний срок** (final) deadline
кран (**-а**) *м* tap, faucet (*US*); (*Строит*) crane
крапи́в|а (**-ы**) *ж* nettle
краси́вый *прил* beautiful; (*мужчина*) handsome; (*решение, фраза*) fine
краси́тел|ь (**-я**) *м* dye; **кра́|сить** (**-шу, -сишь**; *perf* **покра́сить**) *несов перех* to paint; (*волосы*) to dye ▷ (*perf* **накра́сить**) (*губы итп*) to make up; **кра́ситься** (*perf* **накра́ситься**) *несов возв* to wear make-up
кра́с|ка (**-ки**; *gen pl* **-ок**) *ж* paint; (*обычно мн*: *нежные, весенние итп*) colour (*Brit*), color (*US*)
красне́|ть (**-ю**; *perf* **покрасне́ть**) *несов* to turn red; (*от стыда*) to blush, flush; (*от гнева*) to go red
кра́сн|ый *прил* red; **кра́сная ры́ба** salmon; **кра́сная строка́** new paragraph
крас|ота́ (**-оты́**; *nom pl* **-о́ты**) *ж* beauty
кра́сочный *прил* colourful (*Brit*), colorful (*US*)
кра|сть (**-ду́, -дёшь**; *perf* **укра́сть**) *несов перех* to steal;
кра́сться *несов возв* (*человек*) to creep, steal
кра́тк|ий *прил* short; (*беседа*) brief; **кра́ткое прилага́тельное** short-form adjective
кратковре́менный *прил* short; **кратковре́менный дождь** shower
краткосро́чный *прил* short; (*заём, ссуда*) short-term
краудфа́ндинг (**-а**) *м* crowdfunding
крах (**-а**) *м* collapse
крахма́л (**-а**) *м* starch; **крахма́л|ить** (**-ю, -ишь**; *perf* **накрахма́лить**) *несов перех* to starch
креве́т|ка (**-ки**; *gen pl* **-ок**) *ж* shrimp
креди́т (**-а**) *м* credit; **креди́тн|ый** *прил* credit; **креди́тная ка́рточка** credit card; **креди́тный счёт** credit account; **кредитоспосо́бный** *прил* solvent
крем (**-а**) *м* cream; **сапо́жный крем** shoe polish
кремл|ь (**-я́**) *м* citadel; **Кремль** the Kremlin
кре́мовый *прил* cream
креп|и́ть (**-лю́, -и́шь**) *несов перех* to fix
кре́пкий *прил* strong; **кре́пко** *нареч* strongly; (*спать, любить*) deeply; (*завязать*) tightly
кре́п|нуть (**-ну**; *pt* **-, -ла**, *perf* **окре́пнуть**) *несов* to get stronger; (*уверенность*) to grow
кре́пост|ь (**-и**) *ж* (*Воен*) fortress
кре́с|ло (**-ла**; *gen pl* **-ел**) *ср* armchair; (*в театре*) seat
крест (**-а́**) *м* cross
кре|сти́ть (**-щу́, -сти́шь**; *perf* **окрести́ть**) *несов перех* to christen, baptize; **крести́ться** *(не) сов возв* to be christened *или*

baptized; **крёстн|ый** *прил*: **крёстная мать** godmother; **крёстный оте́ц** godfather
крестья́н|ин (**-ина**; *nom pl* **-е**, *gen pl* **-**) *м* peasant; **крестья́нский** *прил* peasant
креще́ни|е (**-я**) *ср* christening, baptism; (*праздник*): **Креще́ние** ≈ the Epiphany
крив|и́ть (**-лю́, -и́шь**; *perf* **скриви́ть** *или* **покриви́ть**) *несов перех* to curve; (*лицо, губы*) to twist
кри́зис (**-а**) *м* crisis
крик (**-а**; *part gen* **-у**) *м* cry
кри́кн|уть (**-у**) *сов* to shout
кримина́л (**-а**) *м* crime; **криминали́ст** (**-а**) *м* specialist in crime detection; **кримина́льный** *прил* (*случай*) criminal; (*история, хроника*) crime
криста́лл (**-а**) *м* crystal
крите́ри|й (**-я**) *м* criterion (*мн* criteria)
кри́тик (**-а**) *м* critic; **кри́тик|а** (**-и**) *ж* criticism; **критик|ова́ть** (**-у́ю**) *несов перех* to criticize; **крити́ческий** *прил* critical
крич|а́ть (**-у́, -и́шь**) *несов* (*человек: от боли, от гнева*) to cry (out); (: *говорить громко*) to shout; **крича́ть** (*impf*) **на** *+acc* (*бранить*) to shout at
крова́т|ь (**-и**) *ж* bed
кро́в|ля (**-ли**; *gen pl* **-ель**) *ж* roof
кро́вн|ый *прил* (*родство*) blood; **кро́вные интере́сы** vested interest *ед*; **кро́вный враг** deadly enemy
кровообраще́ни|е (**-я**) *ср* (*Мед*) circulation
кровопроли́тный *прил* bloody
кровоточ|и́ть (*3sg* **-и́т**) *несов* to bleed
кров|ь (**-и**; *loc sg* **-и́**) *ж* blood
кро|и́ть (**-ю́, -и́шь**) *несов перех* to cut out
крокоди́л (**-а**) *м* crocodile
кро́лик (**-а**) *м* rabbit; (*мех*) rabbit fur; **кро́личий** *прил* rabbit
кро́ме *предл* (*+gen*: *за исключением*) except; (*сверх чего-н*) as well as; **кро́ме того́** besides
кро́н|а (**-ы**) *ж* (*дерева*) crown
кронште́йн (**-а**) *м* (*балкона*) support; (*полки*) bracket
кропотли́вый *прил* painstaking
кроссво́рд (**-а**) *м* crossword
кроссо́в|ка (**-ки**; *gen pl* **-ок**) *ж* (*обычно мн*) trainer
кро́хотный *прил* tiny
крош|и́ть (**-у́, -ишь**) *несов перех* (*хлеб*) to crumble; **кроши́ться** *несов возв* (*хлеб, мел*) to crumble
кро́ш|ка (**-ки**; *gen pl* **-ек**) *ж* (*кусочек*) crumb; (*ребёнок*) little one
круг (**-а**; *nom pl* **-и́**) *м* circle; (*Спорт*) lap ▷ (*loc sg* **-у́**) (*перен*: *знакомых*) circle; (: *обязанностей, интересов*) range
круглосу́точный *прил* (*работа*) round-the-clock; (*магазин*) twenty-four-hour
кру́гл|ый *прил* round; (*дурак*) total; **кру́глый год** all year (round); **кру́глые су́тки** twenty-four hours
круговоро́т (**-а**) *м* cycle
кругозо́р (**-а**) *м*: **он челове́к широ́кого кругозо́ра** he is knowledgeable
круго́м *нареч* around
кругосве́тный *прил* round-the-world
кружевно́й *прил* lace; **кру́жев|о** (**-а**; *nom pl* **-а́**) *ср* lace
круж|и́ть (**-у́, -ишь**) *несов перех* to spin ▷ *неперех* (*птица*) to circle;

кружи́ться *несов возв* (*в танце*) to spin (around); **у меня́ голова́ кру́жится** my head's spinning
кру́ж|ка (**-ки**; *gen pl* **-ек**) *ж* mug
круж|о́к (**-ка́**) *м* circle; (*организация*) club
круи́з (**-а**) *м* cruise
круп|а́ (**-ы́**; *nom pl* **-ы**) *ж* grain
кру́пный *прил* (*размеры, фирма*) large; (*песок, соль*) coarse; (*учёный, дело*) prominent; (*событие, успех*) major; **кру́пный план** close-up
кру|ти́ть (**-чу́, -тишь**) *несов перех* (*руль*) to turn ▷ (*perf* **скрути́ть**) (*руки*) to twist; **крути́ться** *несов возв* (*вертеться*) to turn around; (: *колесо*) to spin; (: *дети*) to fidget
круто́й *прил* steep; (*перемены*) sharp; (*разг*: *хороший*) cool
крыжо́вник (**-а**) *м собир* (*ягоды*) gooseberries *мн*
крыл|о́ (**-а́**; *nom pl* **-ья**, *gen pl* **-ьев**) *ср* wing
крыльц|о́ (**-а́**) *ср* porch
Крым (**-а**; *loc sg* **-у́**) *м* Crimea
кры́с|а (**-ы**) *ж* rat
кр|ыть (**-о́ю, -о́ешь**; *perf* **покры́ть**) *несов перех* to cover
кры́ш|а (**-и**) *ж* roof; (*разг*: *перен*) protection; **кры́ш|ка** (**-ки**; *gen pl* **-ек**) *ж* (*ящика, чайника*) lid
крю|к (**-ка́**; *nom pl* **-чья**, *gen pl* **-чьев**) *м* hook
крюч|о́к (**-ка́**) *м* hook; **крючо́к для вяза́ния** crochet hook
крях|те́ть (**-чу́, -ти́шь**) *несов* to groan
ксероко́пи|я (**-и**) *ж* photocopy, Xerox; **ксе́рокс** (**-а**) *м* photocopier; (*копия*) photocopy, Xerox
кста́ти *вводн сл* (*между прочим*) incidentally, by the way; (*случайно*) by any chance ▷ *нареч* (*сказать, прийти*) at the right time

 **КЛЮЧЕВОЕ СЛОВО**

кто (**кого́**; см *Table 7*) *мест*
1 (*вопросительное, относительное*) who; **кто там?** who is there?
2 (*разг*: *кто-нибудь*) anyone; **е́сли кто позвони́т, позови́ меня́** if anyone phones, please call me
3: **ма́ло ли кто** many (people); **ма́ло кто** few (people); **ма́ло кто пошёл в кино́** only a few of us went to the cinema; **кто из вас ...** which of you ...; **кто (его́) зна́ет!** who knows!

кто́-либо (**кого́-либо**; *как* **кто**; см *Table 7*) *мест* = **кто́-нибудь**
кто́-нибудь (**кого́-нибудь**; *как* **кто**; см *Table 7*) *мест* (*в вопросе*) anybody, anyone; (*в утверждении*) somebody, someone
кто́-то (**кого́-то**; *как* **кто**; см *Table 7*) *мест* somebody, someone
куб (**-а**) *м* (*Геом, Мат*) cube
ку́бик (**-а**) *м* (*игрушка*) building brick *или* block
ку́б|ок (**-ка**) *м* (*Спорт*) cup
кубоме́тр (**-а**) *м* cubic metre (*Brit*) *или* meter (*US*)
кувши́н (**-а**) *м* jug (*Brit*), pitcher (*US*)
кувырка́|ться (**-юсь**) *несов возв* to somersault
куда́ *нареч* (*вопросительное, относительное*) where; **куда́ ты положи́л мою́ ру́чку?** where did you put my pen?; **скажи́, куда́ ты идёшь** tell me where you are going
куда́-либо *нареч* = **куда́-нибудь**
куда́-нибудь *нареч* (*в вопросе*) anywhere; (*в утверждении*) somewhere

К

куда́-то *нареч* somewhere
ку́др|и (**-е́й**) *мн* curls; **кудря́вый** *прил* (*волосы*) curly; (*человек*) curly-haired
кузне́чик (**-а**) *м* grasshopper
ку́зов (**-а**; *nom pl* **-а́**) *м* (*Авт*) back (*of van, lorry etc*)
кукаре́ка|ть (**-ю**) *несов* to crow
ку́к|ла (**-лы**; *gen pl* **-ол**) *ж* (*также перен*) doll; (*в театре*) puppet
ку́кольный *прил*: **ку́кольный теа́тр** puppet theatre (*Brit*) *или* theater (*US*)
кукуру́з|а (**-ы**) *ж* (*Бот*) maize; (*Кулин*) (sweet)corn
куку́ш|ка (**-ки**; *gen pl* **-ек**) *ж* cuckoo
кула́к (**-а́**) *м* fist
кул|ёк (**-ька́**) *м* paper bag
кулина́р (**-а**) *м* master chef
кулинари́|я (**-и**) *ж* cookery; (*магазин*) ≈ delicatessen
кули́с|а (**-ы**) *ж* (*Театр*) wing
кулуа́р|ы (**-ов**) *мн* (*Полит*) lobby *ед*
кульмина́ци|я (**-и**) *ж* (*перен*) high point, climax
культ (**-а**) *м* cult
культу́р|а (**-ы**) *ж* culture
культу́рный *прил* cultural; (*растение*) cultivated
куми́р (**-а**) *м* (*также перен*) idol
купа́льник (**-а**) *м* swimming *или* bathing costume (*Brit*), bathing suit (*US*); **купа́льный** *прил*: **купа́льный костю́м** swimming *или* bathing costume (*Brit*), bathing suit (*US*)
купа́|ть (**-ю**; *perf* **вы́купать** *или* **искупа́ть**) *несов перех* to bath; **купа́ться** (*perf* **вы́купаться** *или* **искупа́ться**) *несов возв* to bathe; (*плавать*) to swim; (*в ванне*) to have a bath
купе́ *ср нескл* compartment (*in railway carriage*); **купе́йный** *прил*: **купе́йный ваго́н** Pullman (car)
купи́рованный *прил* = **купе́йный**
куп|и́ть (**-лю́, -ишь**; *impf* **покупа́ть**) *сов перех* to buy
куплю́ *сов см* **купи́ть**
купо́н (**-а**) *м* (*ценных бумаг*) ticket; **пода́рочный купо́н** gift voucher
купю́р|а (**-ы**) *ж* (*Экон*) denomination; (*сокращение*) cut
куре́ни|е (**-я**) *ср* smoking; **кури́льщик** (**-а**) *м* smoker
кури́ный *прил* (*бульон*) chicken
кур|и́ть (**-ю́, -ишь**) *несов (не) перех* to smoke
ку́р|ица (**-ицы**; *nom pl* **ку́ры**) *ж* hen, chicken; (*мясо*) chicken
кур|о́к (**-ка́**) *м* hammer (*on gun*)
куро́рт (**-а**) *м* (holiday) resort
курс (**-а**) *м* course; (*Полит*) policy; (*Комм*) exchange rate; (*Просвещ*) year (*of university studies*); **быть** (*impf*) **в ку́рсе (де́ла)** to be well-informed; **входи́ть** (*perf* **войти́**) **в курс чего́-н** to bring o.s. up to date on sth; **вводи́ть** (*perf* **ввести́**) **кого́-н в курс (чего́-н)** to put sb in the picture (about sth)
курси́в (**-а**) *м* italics *мн*
курси́р|овать (**-ую**) *несов*: **курси́ровать ме́жду** *+instr* **...** **и** *+instr* **...** (*самолёт, автобус*) to shuttle between ... and ...; (*судно*) to sail between ... and ...
курсов|о́й *прил*: **курсова́я рабо́та** project; **курсова́я ра́зница** (*Комм*) difference in exchange rates
курсо́р (**-а**) *м* cursor
ку́рт|ка (**-ки**; *gen pl* **-ок**) *ж* jacket
ку́р|ы (**-**) *мн от* **ку́рица**
курье́р (**-а**) *м* messenger

курятин|а (**-ы**) *ж* chicken
куса́|ть (**-ю**) *несов перех* to bite; **куса́ться** *несов возв* (*животное*) to bite
кус|о́к (**-ка́**) *м* piece; **кусо́к са́хара** sugar lump; **кусо́к мы́ла** bar of soap
куст (**-а́**) *м* (*Бот*) bush
ку́та|ть (**-ю**; *perf* **заку́тать**) *несов перех* (*плечи*) to cover up; (*ребёнка*) to bundle up; **ку́таться** (*perf* **заку́таться**) *несов возв*: **ку́таться в** *+acc* to wrap o.s. up in
ку́х|ня (**-ни**; *gen pl* **-онь**) *ж* (*помещение*) kitchen; **ру́сская ку́хня** Russian cuisine; **ку́хонный** *прил* kitchen
ку́ч|а (**-и**) *ж* (*песка, листьев*) pile, heap; (*+gen*: *разг*: *денег, проблем*) heaps *или* loads of
ку́ша|ть (**-ю**; *perf* **поку́шать** *или* **ску́шать**) *несов перех* to eat
куше́т|ка (**-ки**; *gen pl* **-ок**) *ж* couch
кюве́т (**-а**) *м* ditch

Л

лабора́нт (**-а**) *м* lab(oratory) technician
лаборато́ри|я (**-и**) *ж* laboratory
ла́в|ка (**-ки**; *gen pl* **-ок**) *ж* (*скамья*) bench; (*магазин*) shop
лавро́вый *прил*: **лавро́вый лист** bay leaf
ла́гер|ь (**-я**) *м* camp
ла́дно *част* (*разг*) O.K., all right
ладо́н|ь (**-и**) *ж* palm
ла́зер (**-а**) *м* laser
ла́|зить (**-жу, -зишь**) *несов* to climb; (*под стол*) to crawl
ла́йнер (**-а**) *м* liner
лак (**-а**) *м* (*для ногтей, для пола*) varnish; **лак для во́лос** hairspray
ла́мп|а (**-ы**) *ж* lamp; (*Tex*) tube; **ла́мпа дневно́го све́та** fluorescent light
ла́мпоч|ка (**-ки**; *gen pl* **-ек**) *ж* lamp; (*для освещения*) light bulb
ла́ндыш (**-а**) *м* lily of the valley

ла́п|а (**-ы**) *ж* (*зверя*) paw; (*птицы*) foot
лапто́п (**-а**) *м* laptop
лар|ёк (**-ька́**) *м* stall
ла́сковый *прил* affectionate
ла́стик (**-а**) *м* (*разг*) rubber (*Brit*), eraser
ла́сточ|ка (**-ки**; *gen pl* **-ек**) *ж* swallow
Ла́тви|я (**-и**) *ж* Latvia
лату́н|ь (**-и**) *ж* brass
латы́н|ь (**-и**) *ж* Latin
лауреа́т (**-а**) *м* winner (*of award*)
ла́цкан (**-а**) *м* lapel
ла́|ять (**-ю**; *perf* **прола́ять**) *несов* to bark
лгать (**лгу, лжёшь** *итп*, **лгут**; *perf* **солга́ть**) *несов* to lie; **лгун** (**-а́**) *м* liar
ЛДПР *ж сокр* (= *Либера́льно-демократи́ческая Па́ртия Росси́и*) Liberal Democratic Party of Russia
ле́бед|ь (**-я**; *gen pl* **-е́й**) *м* swan
лев (**льва**) *м* lion; (*созвездие*): **Лев** Leo
левосторо́нний *прил* on the left
левш|а́ (**-и́**; *gen pl* **-е́й**) *м/ж* left-handed person
ле́вый *прил* left; (*Полит*) left-wing
лёг *итп сов см* **лечь**
леге́нд|а (**-ы**) *ж* legend
лёгк|ий *прил* (*груз*) light; (*задача*) easy; (*боль, насморк*) slight; (*характер, человек*) easy-going; **лёгкая атле́тика** athletics (*Brit*), track (*US*); **легко́** *нареч* easily ▷ *как сказ*: **э́то легко́** it's easy
легкоатле́т (**-а**) *м* athlete (*in track and field events*)
легков|о́й *прил*: **легкова́я маши́на, легково́й автомоби́ль** car, automobile (*US*)
лёгк|ое (**-ого**) *ср* (*обычно мн*) lung
легкомы́сленный *прил* frivolous, flippant; (*поступок*) thoughtless; **легкомы́сли|е** (**-я**) *ср* frivolity
лёгкост|ь (**-и**) *ж* (*задания*) simplicity, easiness
ле́гче *сравн прил от* **лёгкий** ▷ *сравн нареч от* **легко́** ▷ *как сказ*: **больно́му сего́дня ле́гче** the patient is feeling better today
лёд (**льда**; *loc sg* **льду**) *м* ice
леден|е́ц (**-ца́**) *м* fruit drop
ледяно́й *прил* (*покров*) ice; (*вода, взгляд*) icy
леж|а́ть (**-у́, -и́шь**) *несов* (*человек, животное*) to lie; (*предмет, вещи*) to be; **лежа́ть** (*impf*) **в больни́це** to be in hospital
лез *etc несов см* **лезть**
ле́зви|е (**-я**) *ср* blade
лез|ть (**-у, -ешь**; *pt* **-, -ла**) *несов* (*выпадать: волосы*) to fall out; (*проникать*): **лезть в** *+acc* to climb in; **лезть** (*impf*) **на** *+acc* to climb (up)
ле́|йка (**-йки**; *gen pl* **-ек**) *ж* watering can
лейкопла́стыр|ь (**-я**) *м* sticking plaster (*Brit*), adhesive tape (*US*)
лейтена́нт (**-а**) *м* lieutenant
лека́рств|о (**-а**) *ср* medicine; **лека́рство от** *+gen* medicine for; **лека́рство от ка́шля** cough medicine
ле́ктор (**-а**) *м* lecturer
ле́кци|я (**-и**) *ж* lecture
лени́вый *прил* lazy
лен|и́ться (**-ю́сь, -ишься**; *perf* **полени́ться**) *несов возв* to be lazy
ле́нт|а (**-ы**) *ж* ribbon; (*Тех*) tape; (*Комп*) feed
лепест|о́к (**-ка́**) *м* petal
леп|и́ть (**-лю́, -ишь**; *perf* **вы́лепить**) *несов перех* to model ▷ (*perf* **слепи́ть**) (*соты, гнёзда*) to build

лес (**-а**; *loc sg* **-у́**, *nom pl* **-а́**) *м* (*большой*) forest; (*небольшой*) wood ▷ *собир* (*материал*) timber (*Brit*), lumber (*US*)
лесбия́н|ка (**-ки**; *gen pl* **-ок**) *ж* lesbian
ле́ск|а (**-и**) *ж* fishing line
лесно́й *прил* forest
ле́стниц|а (**-ы**) *ж* staircase; (*ступени*) stairs *мн*; (*переносная*) ladder; (*стремянка*) stepladder
лета́ (**лет**) *мн см* **год**; (*возраст*): **ско́лько Вам лет?** how old are you?; **ему́ 16 лет** he is 16 (years old)
лета́|ть (**-ю**) *несов* to fly
ле|те́ть (**-чу́, -ти́шь**) *несов* to fly
ле́тний *прил* summer
ле́т|о (**-а**) *ср* summer; **ле́том** *нареч* in summer
летý́ч|ий *прил*: **лету́чая мышь** bat
лётчик (**-а**) *м* pilot
ле́чащий *прил*: **ле́чащий врач** ≈ consultant-in-charge (*Brit*), ≈ attending physician (*US*)
лече́бниц|а (**-ы**) *ж* clinic
лече́бный *прил* (*учреждение*) medical; (*трава*) medicinal
лече́ни|е (**-я**) *ср* (*больных*) treatment; (*от простуды*) cure; **леч|и́ть** (**-у́, -ишь**) *несов перех* to treat; (*больного*): **лечи́ть кого́-н от** *+gen* to treat sb for; **лечи́ться** *несов возв* to undergo treatment
лечу́ *несов см* **лете́ть**
ле|чь (**ля́гу, ля́жешь** *итп*, **ля́гут**; *pt* **лёг, -гла́**, *imper* **ля́г(те)**, *impf* **ложи́ться**) *сов* to lie down; (*перен*): **лечь на** *+acc* (*задача*) to fall on; **ложи́ться** (*perf* **лечь**) **в больни́цу** to go into hospital
лжец (**-а́**) *м* liar
лжи *сущ см* **ложь**
ли *част* (*в вопросе*): **зна́ешь ли ты, что ...** do you know that ...; (*в косвенном вопросе*): **спроси́, смо́жет ли он нам помо́чь** ask if he can help us; (*в разделительном вопросе*): **она́ краси́вая, не так ли?** she's beautiful, isn't she?
либера́льный *прил* liberal
ли́бо *союз* (*или*) or
ли́г|а (**-и**) *ж* (*Полит, Спорт*) league
ли́дер (**-а**) *м* leader; **лиди́р|овать** (**-ую**) *несов* to lead, be in the lead
ли|за́ть (**-жу́, -жешь**) *несов перех* (*тарелку, мороженое*) to lick
лизн|у́ть (**-у́, -ёшь**) *сов перех* to lick
ликёр (**-а**) *м* liqueur
ли́ли|я (**-и**) *ж* lily
лило́вый *прил* purple
лими́т (**-а**) *м* (*на бензин*) quota; (*цен*) limit; **лимити́р|овать** (**-ую**) *(не)сов перех* to limit; (*цены*) to cap
лимо́н (**-а**) *м* lemon; **лимона́д** (**-а**) *м* lemonade; **лимо́нн|ый** *прил* lemon; **лимо́нная кислота́** citric acid
лине́|йка (**-йки**; *gen pl* **-ек**) *ж* (*линия*) line; (*инструмент*) ruler; **тетра́дь в лине́йку** lined notebook
ли́нз|а (**-ы**) *ж* lens
ли́ни|я (**-и**) *ж* line; **по ли́нии** *+gen* in the line of; **железнодоро́жная ли́ния** railway (*Brit*) *или* railroad (*US*) track
линя́|ть (*3sg* **-ет**, *perf* **полиня́ть**) *несов* to run (*colour*) ▷ (*perf* **облиня́ть**) (*животные*) to moult (*Brit*), molt (*US*)
ли́пкий *прил* sticky
ли́п|нуть (**-ну**; *pt* **-, ла**, *perf* **прили́пнуть**) *несов* (*грязь, тесто*) to stick
липу́ч|ка (**-ки**; *gen pl* **-ек**) *ж*

Л

(*разг*: *застёжка*) Velcro fastening
ли́рик|а (**-и**) *ж* lyric poetry
лис|а́ (**-ы́**; *nom pl* **-ы**) *ж* fox
лист (**-а́**; *nom pl* **-ья**) *м* (*растения*) leaf ▷ (*nom pl* **-ы́**) (*бумаги, железа*) sheet
листа́|ть (**-ю**) *несов перех* (*страницы*) to turn
листв|а́ (**-ы́**) *ж собир* foliage, leaves *мн*
листо́в|ка (**-ки**; *gen pl* **-ок**) *ж* leaflet
лист|о́к (**-ка́**) *м* (*бумаги*) sheet
ли́стья *итп сущ см* **лист**
Литв|а́ (**-ы́**) *ж* Lithuania
литерату́р|а (**-ы**) *ж* literature; (*также* **худо́жественная литерату́ра**) fiction; **литерату́рный** *прил* literary
литр (**-а**) *м* litre (*Brit*), liter (*US*); **литро́вый** *прил* (*бутылка итп*) (one-)litre (*Brit*), (one-)liter (*US*)
ли|ть (**лью, льёшь**; *pt* **-л, -ла́**) *несов перех* (*воду*) to pour; (*слёзы*) to shed; (*Тех*: *детали, изделия*) to cast, mould (*Brit*), mold (*US*) ▷ *неперех* (*вода, дождь*) to pour; **ли́ться** *несов возв* (*вода*) to pour out
лифт (**-а**) *м* lift
ли́фчик (**-а**) *м* bra
лихора́дк|а (**-и**) *ж* fever; (*на губах*) cold sore
лицев|о́й *прил*: **лицева́я сторона́ мате́рии** the right side of the material
лице́|й (**-я**) *м* lycée, ≈ grammar school
лицеме́рный *прил* hypocritical
лице́нзи|я (**-и**) *ж* licence (*Brit*), license (*US*)
ли|цо́ (**-ца́**; *nom pl* **-ца**) *ср* face; (*перен*: *индивидуальность*) image; (*ткани итп*) right side; (*Линг*) person; **от лица́** *+gen* in the name of, on behalf of
ли́чно *нареч* (*знать*) personally; (*встретить*) in person
ли́чност|ь (**-и**) *ж* individual
ли́чный *прил* personal; (*частный*) private
лиша́|ть (**-ю**) *несов от* **лиши́ть**
лиш|и́ть (**-у́, -и́шь**; *impf* **лиша́ть**) *сов перех*: **лиши́ть кого́-н/что-н** *+gen* (*отнять*: *прав, привилегий*) to deprive sb/sth of; (*покоя, счастья*) to rob sb/sth of
ли́шний *прил* (*вес*) extra; (*деньги, билет*) spare; **ли́шний раз** once again *или* more
лишь *част* (*только*) only ▷ *союз* (*как только*) as soon as; **лишь бы она́ согласи́лась!** if only she would agree!
лоб (**лба**; *loc sg* **лбу**) *м* forehead
ло́бби *ср нескл* lobby
лобов|о́й *прил* frontal; **лобово́е стекло́** windscreen (*Brit*), windshield (*US*)
лов|и́ть (**-лю́, -ишь**; *perf* **пойма́ть**) *несов перех* to catch; (*момент*) to seize; **лови́ть** (*impf*) **ры́бу** to fish
лову́ш|ка (**-ки**; *gen pl* **-ек**) *ж* trap
ло́гик|а (**-и**) *ж* logic; **логи́чный** *прил* logical
логоти́п (**-а**) *м* logo
ло́д|ка (**-ки**; *gen pl* **-ок**) *ж* boat
лоды́ж|ка (**-ки**; *gen pl* **-ек**) *ж* ankle
ло́ж|а (**-и**) *ж* (*в театре, в зале*) box
лож|и́ться (**-у́сь, -и́шься**) *несов от* **лечь**
ло́ж|ка (**-ки**; *gen pl* **-ек**) *ж* spoon
ло́жный *прил* false; (*вывод*) wrong
ложь (**лжи**; *instr sg* **ло́жью**) *ж* lie
лоз|а́ (**-ы́**; *nom pl* **-ы**) *ж* vine

ло́зунг (**-а**) *м* (*призыв*) slogan; (*плакат*) banner
ло́к|оть (**-тя**; *gen pl* **-те́й**, *dat pl* **-тя́м**) *м* elbow
лома́|ть (**-ю**; *perf* **слома́ть**) *несов перех* to break; (*традиции*) to challenge; (*планы*) to frustrate ▷ (*perf* **слома́ть** *или* **полома́ть**) (*механизм*) to break; **лома́ть** (*impf*) **го́лову над чем-то** to rack one's brains over sth; **лома́ться** (*perf* **слома́ться**) *несов возв* to break
ло́мтик (**-а**) *м* slice
Ло́ндон (**-а**) *м* London
ло́паст|ь (**-и**; *gen pl* **-е́й**) *ж* blade
лопа́т|а (**-ы**) *ж* spade; **лопа́т|ка** (**-ки**; *gen pl* **-ок**) *ж, уменьш от* **лопа́та**; (*Анат*) shoulder blade
ло́пн|уть (**-у**; *perf* **ло́паться**) *сов* (*шар*) to burst; (*стекло*) to shatter; (*разг*: *банк*) to go bust
лоску́т (**-а́**) *м* (*материи*) scrap
лосо́с|ь (**-я**) *м* salmon
лосьо́н (**-а**) *м* lotion
лотере́|я (**-и**) *ж* lottery
лото́ *ср нескл* lotto
лот|о́к (**-ка́**) *м* (*прилавок*) stall
лохмо́ть|я (**-ев**) *мн* rags *мн*
ло́шад|ь (**-и**; *gen pl* **-е́й**) *ж* horse
луг (**-а**; *loc sg* **-у́**, *nom pl* **-а́**) *м* meadow
лу́ж|а (**-и**) *ж* (*на дороге*) puddle; (*на полу, на столе*) pool
лук (**-а**) *м собир* (*плоды*) onions *мн* ▷ *м* (*оружие*) bow; **зелёный лук** spring onion (*Brit*), scallion
лу́ковиц|а (**-ы**) *ж* bulb
лун|а́ (**-ы́**) *ж* moon
лу́н|ка (**-ки**; *gen pl* **-ок**) *ж* hole
лу́нный *прил*: **лу́нный свет** moonlight
лу́п|а (**-ы**) *ж* magnifying glass
луч (**-а́**) *м* ray; (*фонаря*) beam; **лучев|о́й** *прил*: **лучева́я боле́знь** radiation sickness
лу́чше *сравн прил от* **хоро́ший** ▷ *сравн нареч от* **хорошо́** ▷ *как сказ*: **так лу́чше** that's better ▷ *част*: **лу́чше не опра́вдывайся** don't try and justify yourself ▷ *вводн сл*: **лу́чше (всего́), позвони́ ве́чером** it would be better if you phone in the evening; **больно́му лу́чше** the patient is feeling better; **нам лу́чше, чем им** we're better off than them; **как нельзя́ лу́чше** couldn't be better
лу́чш|ий *прил* (*самый хороший*) best; **в лу́чшем слу́чае мы зако́нчим за́втра** the best-case scenario is that we'll finish tomorrow; **э́то (всё) к лу́чшему** it's (all) for the best
лы́ж|а (**-и**) *ж* (*обычно мн*) ski; *см также* **лы́жи**; **лы́ж|и** (**-**) *мн* (*спорт*) skiing *ед*; **во́дные лы́жи** water-skis; (*спорт*) water-skiing; **го́рные лы́жи** downhill skis; (*спорт*) downhill skiing; **лы́жник** (**-а**) *м* skier; **лы́жный** *прил* (*крепления, мазь итп*) ski; (*соревнования*) skiing; **лыжн|я́** (**-и́**) *ж* ski track
лысе́|ть (**-ю**; *perf* **облысе́ть** *или* **полысе́ть**) *несов* to go bald; **лы́син|а** (**-ы**) *ж* bald patch; **лы́сый** *прил* bald
ль *част* = **ли**
льго́т|а (**-ы**) *ж* benefit; (*предприятиям итп*) special term; **нало́говые льго́ты** tax relief; **льго́тный** *прил* (*тариф*) concessionary; (*условия*) privileged; (*заём*) special-rate; **льго́тный биле́т** concessionary ticket
льди́н|а (**-ы**) *ж* ice floe
льнян|о́й *прил* (*полотенце*) linen
любе́зност|ь (**-и**) *ж* (*одолжение*)

favour (*Brit*), favor (*US*)
любе́зн|ый *прил* polite; **бу́дьте любе́зны!** excuse me, please!; **бу́дьте любе́зны, принеси́те нам ко́фе!** could you be so kind as to bring us some coffee?
люби́м|ец (**-ца**) *м* favourite (*Brit*), favorite (*US*)
люби́мый *прил* (*женщина, брат*) beloved; (*писатель, занятие итп*) favourite (*Brit*), favorite (*US*)
люби́тел|ь (**-я**) *м* (*непрофессионал*) amateur; **люби́тель му́зыки/спо́рта** music-/ sports-lover; **люби́тельский** *прил* amateur
люб|и́ть (**-лю́, -ишь**) *несов перех* to love; (*музыку, спорт итп*) to like
люб|ова́ться (**-у́юсь**; *perf* **полюбова́ться**) *несов возв +instr* to admire
любо́вник (**-а**) *м* lover; **любо́вный** *прил* (*дела*) lover's; (*песня, письмо*) love; (*отношение, подход*) loving
люб|о́вь (**-ви́**; *instr sg* **-о́вью**) *ж* love; (*привязанность*): **любо́вь к** *+dat* (*к родине, к матери итп*) love for; (*к чтению, к искусству итп*) love of
люб|о́й *мест* (*всякий*) any ▷ (**-о́го**) *м* (*любой человек*) anyone
любопы́тный *прил* (*случай*) interesting; (*человек*) curious
любопы́тств|о (**-а**) *ср* curiosity
лю́бящий *прил* loving
лю́д|и (**-е́й**; *dat pl* **-ям**, *instr pl* **-ьми́**, *prp pl* **-ях**) *мн* people *мн*; (*кадры*) staff *ед*; **молоды́е лю́ди** young men; (*молодёжь*) young people; *см также* **челове́к**; **лю́дный** *прил* (*улица итп*) busy
людско́й *прил* human
люкс (**-а**) *м* (*о вагоне*) first-class carriage; (*о каюте*) first-class cabin ▷ *прил неизм* first-class
лю́стр|а (**-ы**) *ж* chandelier
ляга́|ть (**-ю**) *несов перех* (*подлеж*: *лошадь, корова*) to kick; **ляга́ться** *несов возв* (*лошадь, корова*) to kick
ля́гу *итп сов см* **лечь**
лягу́ш|ка (**-ки**; *gen pl* **-ек**) *ж* frog
ля́жешь *итп сов см* **лечь**
ля́ж|ка (**-ки**; *gen pl* **-ек**) *ж* thigh
ля́м|ка (**-ки**; *gen pl* **-ок**) *ж* strap

M

1 Мáя: Прáздник весны́ и трудá

Spring and Labour Day, formerly known as International Day of Workers' Solidarity, has been greatly depoliticized since the collapse of the Soviet Union. For most people it is simply an opportunity to celebrate the spring and to enjoy a short holiday.

М *сокр* = **метрó**
м *сокр* (= *метр*) m
мавзолé|й (**-я**) *м* mausoleum
магази́н (**-а**) *м* shop
маги́стр (**-а**) *м* master's degree
магистрáл|ь (**-и**) *ж* main line
маги́ческий *прил* magic
магни́т (**-а**) *м* magnet
магнитофóн (**-а**) *м* tape recorder
мá|зать (**-жу, -жешь**; *perf* **намáзать** *или* **помáзать**) *несов перех* to spread ▷ (*perf* **измáзать**) (*разг*: *пачкать*) to get dirty; **мáзаться** *несов возв* (*perf* **измáзаться**) (*разг*: *пачкаться*) to get dirty; **мáзаться** (*perf* **намáзаться**) **крéмом** to apply cream
маз|óк (**-кá**) *м* (*Мед*) smear
маз|ь (**-и**) *ж* (*Мед*) ointment; (*Тех*) grease
ма|й (**-я**) *м* May
мá|йка (**-йки**; *gen pl* **-ек**) *ж* vest (*Brit*), sleeveless undershirt (*US*)
майонéз (**-а**) *м* mayonnaise
майóр (**-а**) *м* (*Воен*) major
мак (**-а**) *м* poppy
макарóн|ы (**-**) *мн* pasta *ед*
макá|ть (**-ю**) *несов перех* to dip
макéт (**-а**) *м* model
мáклер (**-а**) *м* (*Комм*) broker
макн|ýть (**-ý, -ёшь**) *сов перех* to dip
максимáльный *прил* maximum
мáксимум (**-а**) *м* maximum
макулатýр|а (**-ы**) *ж собир* wastepaper (*for recycling*)
малéйший *прил* (*ошибка*) the slightest
мáленький *прил* small, little
мали́н|а (**-ы**) *ж* (*кустарник*) raspberry cane *или* bush; (*ягоды*) raspberries *мн*

 **ключевое слово**

мáло *чис* (*+gen*: *друзей, книг*) only a few; (*работы, денег*) not much, little; **нам дáли мáло книг** they only gave us a few books; **у меня́ мáло дéнег** I don't have much money; **мáло рáдости** little joy ▷ *нареч* not much; **онá мáло измени́лась** she hasn't changed much

▷ *как сказ*: **мне э́того ма́ло** this is not enough for me; **ма́ло ли что** so what?; **ма́ло ли кто/где/когда́** it doesn't matter who/where/when; **ма́ло того́** (and) what's more; **ма́ло того́ что** not only

маловероя́тный *прил* improbable
малоду́шный *прил* cowardly
малокро́ви|е (**-я**) *ср* (sickle-cell) anaemia (*Brit*) *или* anemia (*US*)
малоле́тний *прил* young
малочи́сленный *прил* small
ма́л|ый *прил* small, little; (*доход, скорость*) low ▷ *как сказ*: **пла́тье/пальто́ мне мало́** the dress/coat is too small for me; **са́мое ма́лое** at the very least
малы́ш (**-а́**) *м* little boy
малы́ш|ка (**-ки**; *gen pl* **-ек**) *ж* little girl
ма́льчик (**-а**) *м* boy
малю́т|ка (**-ки**; *gen pl* **-ок**) *м/ж* baby
маля́р (**-а́**) *м* painter (and decorator)
маляри́|я (**-и**) *ж* malaria
ма́м|а (**-ы**) *ж* mummy (*Brit*), mommy (*US*)
мама́ш|а (**-и**) *ж* mummy (*Brit*), mommy (*US*)
мандари́н (**-а**) *м* tangerine
манда́т (**-а**) *м* mandate
манёвр (**-а**) *м* manoevre (*Brit*), maneuver (*US*)
манеке́н (**-а**) *м* (*портного*) dummy; (*в витрине*) dummy, mannequin
манеке́нщиц|а (**-ы**) *ж* model
мане́р|а (**-ы**) *ж* manner; (*художника*) style
манже́т|а (**-ы**) *ж* cuff
маникю́р (**-а**) *м* manicure
манипули́р|овать (**-ую**) *несов* +*instr* to manipulate
манифе́ст (**-а**) *м* manifesto
манифеста́ци|я (**-и**) *ж* rally
ма́ни|я (**-и**) *ж* mania
ма́нн|ый *прил*: **ма́нная ка́ша, ма́нная крупа́** semolina
манья́к (**-а**) *м* maniac
мара́зм (**-а**) *м* (*Мед*) dementia; (*перен*: *разг*) idiocy; **ста́рческий мара́зм** senile dementia
марафо́н (**-а**) *м* marathon; **марафо́н|ец** (**-ца**) *м* marathon runner
маргари́н (**-а**) *м* margarine
маргари́т|ка (**-ки**; *gen pl* **-ок**) *ж* daisy
марин|ова́ть (**-у́ю**; *perf* **замаринова́ть**) *несов перех* (*овощи*) to pickle; (*мясо, рыбу*) to marinate, marinade
марионе́т|ка (**-ки**; *gen pl* **-ок**) *ж* puppet
ма́р|ка (**-ки**; *gen pl* **-ок**) *ж* (*почтовая*) stamp; (*сорт*) brand; (*качество*) grade; (*модель*) make; (*деньги*) mark; **торго́вая ма́рка** trademark
ма́ркетинг (**-а**) *м* marketing
маркси́зм (**-а**) *м* Marxism
мармела́д (**-а**) *м* fruit jellies *мн*
Марс (**-а**) *м* Mars
март (**-а**) *м* March

8 Ма́рта: Междунаро́дный же́нский день

International Women's Day. This is a celebration of women of all ages. Women receive gifts from men and mothers receive gifts and greetings from their children. Special variety shows are put on in major concert halls and broadcast on television.

марш (**-а**) *м* march

мáршал (**-а**) *м* marshal
марширова́ть (**-у́ю**; *perf* **промарширова́ть**) *несов* to march
маршру́т (**-а**) *м* route; **маршру́т|ный** *прил*: **маршру́тное такси́** fixed-route taxi
мáс|ка (**-ки**; *gen pl* **-ок**) *ж* mask; (*косметическая*) face pack
маскара́д (**-а**) *м* masked ball
маскир|ова́ть (**-у́ю**; *perf* **замаскирова́ть**) *несов перех* to camouflage; **маскирова́ться** (*perf* **замаскирова́ться**) *несов возв* to camouflage o.s.
мáслениц|а (**-ы**) *ж* ≈ Shrove Tuesday, Pancake Day
масли́н|а (**-ы**) *ж* (*дерево*) olive (tree); (*плод*) olive
мáс|ло (**-ла**; *nom pl* **-ла́**, *gen pl* **-ел**) *ср* oil; (*сливочное*) butter
мáсляный *прил* oil; (*пятно*) oily
масóн (**-а**) *м* (Free)mason
мáсс|а (**-ы**) *ж* (*также Физ*) mass; (*древесная*) pulp; (*много*) loads *мн*
масса́ж (**-а**) *м* massage; **массажи́ст** (**-а**) *м* masseur
масси́в (**-а**) *м* (*водный*) expanse; (*земельный*) tract; **гóрный масси́в** massif; **жилóй** *или* **жили́щный масси́в** housing estate (*Brit*) *или* project (*US*); **масси́вный** *прил* massive
мáссов|ый *прил* mass; **товáры мáссового спрóса** consumer goods
мáстер (**-а**; *nom pl* **-á**) *м* master; (*в цеху*) foreman (*мн* foremen)
мастерск|áя (**-óй**) *ж* workshop; (*художника*) studio
мастерств|ó (**-á**) *ср* skill
масти́к|а (**-и**) *ж* floor polish
маст|ь (**-и**; *gen pl* **-éй**) *ж* (*лошади*) colour (*Brit*), color (*US*); (*Карты*) suit
масшта́б (**-а**) *м* scale; **масшта́бный** *прил* scale; (*большой*) large-scale
мат (**-а**) *м* (*Шахматы*) checkmate; (*половик*: *также Спорт*) mat; (*ругательства*) bad language
матемáтик (**-а**) *м* mathematician; **матемáтик|а** (**-и**) *ж* mathematics
мáтери *etc сущ см* **мать**
материáл (**-а**) *м* material; (*обычно мн*: *следствия*) document
материáльный *прил* material; (*финансовый*) financial
матери́к (**-á**) *м* continent; (*суша*) mainland
матери́нский *прил* maternal
матери́нств|о (**-а**) *ср* motherhood
матéри|я (**-и**) *ж* matter; (*разг*: *ткань*) cloth
мáтер|ь (**-и**) *ж*: **Мáтерь Бóжья** Mother of God
мáтерью *etc сущ см* **мать**
мáтов|ый *прил* (*без блеска*) mat(t); **мáтовое стеклó** frosted glass
матрáс (**-а**) *м* mattress
матрёш|ка (**-ки**; *gen pl* **-ек**) *ж* Russian doll (*containing range of smaller dolls*)
мáтричный *прил*: **мáтричный при́нтер** (*Комп*) dot-matrix printer
матрóс (**-а**) *м* sailor
мáтуш|ка (**-ки**; *gen pl* **-ек**) *ж* (*мать*) mother
матч (**-а**) *м* match
мат|ь (**-ери**; *см Table 1*) *ж* mother; **мать-одинóчка** single mother
мафиóзный *прил* mafia
мáфи|я (**-и**) *ж* the Mafia
мах (**-а**) *м* (*крыла*) flap; (*рукой*) swing; **одни́м махом** in a stroke; **с мáху** straight away
ма|хáть (**-шу́, -шешь**) *несов* +*instr* to wave; (*крыльями*) to flap;

маха́ть (*impf*) **кому́-н руко́й** to wave to sb
махн|у́ть (**-у́, -ёшь**) *сов* to wave
махо́рк|а (**-и**) *ж* coarse tobacco
ма́чех|а (**-и**) *ж* stepmother
ма́чт|а (**-ы**) *ж* mast
маши́н|а (**-ы**) *ж* machine; (*автомобиль*) car
машина́льный *прил* mechanical
машини́ст (**-а**) *м* driver, operator; **машини́ст|ка** (**-ки**; *gen pl* **-ок**) *ж* typist
маши́н|ка (**-ки**; *gen pl* **-ок**) *ж* machine; **пи́шущая маши́нка** typewriter
маши́нн|ый *прил* machine; **маши́нное отделе́ние** engine room
машинострое́ни|е (**-я**) *ср* mechanical engineering
мая́к (**-а́**) *м* lighthouse
МВД *ср сокр* (= *Министе́рство вну́тренних дел*) ≈ the Home Office (*Brit*), ≈ the Department of the Interior (*US*)
мгл|а (**-ы**) *ж* haze; (*вечерняя*) gloom
мгнове́ни|е (**-я**) *ср* moment
мгнове́нный *прил* instant; (*злость*) momentary
МГУ *м сокр* (= *Моско́вский госуда́рственный университе́т*) Moscow State University
ме́бел|ь (**-и**) *ж собир* furniture
мёд (**-а**) *м* honey
меда́л|ь (**-и**) *ж* medal
медве́д|ь (**-я**) *м* bear; **медвеж|о́нок** (**-о́нка**; *nom pl* **-а́та**, *gen pl* **-а́т**) *м* bear cub
медикаме́нт (**-а**) *м* medicine
медици́н|а (**-ы**) *ж* medicine
ме́дленный *прил* slow
медли́тельный *прил* slow
ме́дл|ить (**-ю, -ишь**) *несов* to delay; **ме́длить** (*impf*) **с реше́нием** to be slow in deciding
ме́дный *прил* copper; (*Муз*) brass
медо́вый *прил* honey; **медо́вый ме́сяц** honeymoon
медпу́нкт (**-а**) *м сокр* (= *медици́нский пункт*) ≈ first-aid centre (*Brit*) *или* center (*US*)
медсестр|а́ (**-ы́**) *ж сокр* (= *медици́нская сестра́*) nurse
меду́з|а (**-ы**) *ж* jellyfish
мед|ь (**-и**) *ж* copper
ме́жду *предл +instr* between; (*+gen*: *в окружении*) amongst; **ме́жду про́чим** (*попутно*) in passing; (*кстати*) by the way; **ме́жду тем** meanwhile; **ме́жду тем как** while; **они́ договори́лись ме́жду собо́й** they agreed between them
междугоро́дный *прил* intercity
междунаро́дный *прил* international
мел (**-а**) *м* chalk
меле́|ть (*3sg* **-ет**, *perf* **обмеле́ть**) *несов* to become shallower
ме́лкий *прил* small; (*песок, дождь*) fine; (*интересы*) petty
мело́ди|я (**-и**) *ж* tune, melody; **мело́дия для моби́льного телефо́на** ringtone
ме́лочный *прил* petty
ме́лоч|ь (**-и**; *gen pl* **-е́й**) *ж* (*пустяк*) triviality; (*подробность*) detail ▷ *ж собир* little things *мн*; (*деньги*) small change
мел|ь (**-и**; *loc sg* **-и́**) *ж* shallows *мн*; **сади́ться** (*perf* **сесть**) **на мель** (*Мор*) to run aground
мелька́|ть (**-ю**) *несов* to flash past; **мелькн|у́ть** (**-у́, -ёшь**) *сов* to flash
ме́льком *нареч* in passing
ме́льниц|а (**-ы**) *ж* mill
мельхио́р (**-а**) *м* nickel silver

ме́льче *сравн прил от* **ме́лкий**
мельч|и́ть (**-у́, -и́шь**; *perf* **измельчи́ть** *или* **размельчи́ть**) *несов перех* (*ножом*) to cut up into small pieces; (*в ступке*) to crush
мем (**-а**) *м* meme
мемориа́л (**-а**) *м* memorial
мему́ар|ы (**-ов**) *мн* memoirs
ме́неджер (**-а**) *м* manager
менеджме́нт (**-а**) *м* management
ме́нее *сравн нареч от* **ма́ло** ▷ *нареч* (*опасный*) less; (*года*) less than; **тем не ме́нее** nevertheless
менинги́т (**-а**) *м* meningitis
менструа́ци|я (**-и**) *ж* menstruation
ме́ньше *сравн прил от* **ма́лый**; **ма́ленький** ▷ *сравн нареч от* **ма́ло** ▷ *нареч* less than; **ме́ньше всего́** least of all
ме́ньш|ий *сравн прил от* **ма́лый**; **ма́ленький** ▷ *прил*: **по ме́ньшей ме́ре** at least; **са́мое ме́ньшее** no less than
меньшинств|о́ (**-а́**) *ср собир* minority
меню́ *ср нескл* menu
меня́ *мест см* **я**
меня́|ть (**-ю**; *perf* **поменя́ть**) *несов перех* to change; **меня́ть** (*perf* **поменя́ть**) **что-н на** *+acc* to exchange sth for; **меня́ться** (*perf* **поменя́ться**) *несов возв* to change
ме́р|а (**-ы**) *ж* measure; (*предел*) limit; **в по́лной ме́ре** fully; **по ме́ре** *+gen* with; **по ме́ре того́ как** as
ме́рзкий *прил* disgusting; (*погода, настроение*) foul
мёрзлый *прил* (*земля*) frozen
мёрз|нуть (**-ну**; *pt* **-, -ла**, *perf* **замёрзнуть**) *несов* to freeze
ме́р|ить (**-ю, -ишь**; *perf* **сме́рить** *или* **изме́рить**) *несов перех* to measure ▷ (*perf* **поме́рить**) (*примерять*) to try on
ме́р|ка (**-ки**; *gen pl* **-ок**) *ж* measurements *мн*; (*перен*: *критерий*) standard
ме́рк|нуть (*3sg* **-нет**, *perf* **поме́ркнуть**) *несов* to fade
мероприя́ти|е (**-я**) *ср* measure; (*событие*) event
мертве́|ть (**-ю**; *perf* **омертве́ть**) *несов* (*от холода*) to go numb ▷ (*perf* **помертве́ть**) (*от страха, от горя*) to be numb
мертве́ц (**-а́**) *м* dead person
мёртвый *прил* dead
мерца́|ть (*3sg* **-ет**) *несов* to glimmer, flicker; (*звёзды*) to twinkle
ме|сти́ (**-ту́, -тёшь**; *pt* **мёл, -ла́**, *perf* **подмести́**) *несов перех* (*пол*) to sweep; (*мусор*) to sweep up
ме́стност|ь (**-и**) *ж* area
ме́стный *прил* local
ме́ст|о (**-а**; *nom pl* **-а́**) *ср* place; (*действия*) scene; (*в театре, в поезде итп*) seat; (*багажа*) item
местожи́тельств|о (**-а**) *ср* place of residence
местоиме́ни|е (**-я**) *ср* pronoun
местонахожде́ни|е (**-я**) *ср* location
месторожде́ни|е (**-я**) *ср* (*угля, нефти*) field
мест|ь (**-и**) *ж* revenge, vengeance
ме́сяц (**-а**; *nom pl* **-ы**) *м* month; (*часть луны*) crescent moon; (*диск луны*) moon
ме́сячный *прил* monthly
мета́лл (**-а**) *м* metal
металлоло́м (**-а**) *м* scrap metal
ме|та́ть (**-чу́, -чешь**) *несов перех* (*гранату, диск итп*) to throw

▷ (*perf* **намета́ть**) (*шов*) to tack (*Brit*), baste; **мета́ться** *несов возв* (*в постели*) to toss and turn; (*по комнате*) to rush about
мете́л|ь (**-и**) *ж* snowstorm, blizzard
метеоро́лог (**-а**) *м* meteorologist
метеосво́д|ка (**-ки**; *gen pl* **-ок**) *ж сокр* (= *метеорологи́ческая сво́дка*) weather forecast *или* report
метеоста́нци|я (**-и**) *ж сокр* (= *метеорологи́ческая ста́нция*) weather station
ме́|тить (**-чу, -тишь**; *perf* **поме́тить**) *несов перех* to mark ▷ *неперех*: **ме́тить в** *+acc* (*в цель*) to aim at; **ме́титься** (*perf* **наме́титься**) *несов возв*: **ме́титься в** *+acc* to aim at
ме́т|ка (**-ки**; *gen pl* **-ок**) *ж* mark
ме́ткий *прил* (*точный*) accurate; (*замечание*) apt
метн|у́ть (**-у́, -ёшь**) *сов перех* to throw; **метну́ться** *сов возв* to rush
ме́тод (**-а**) *м* method
метр (**-а**) *м* metre (*Brit*), meter (*US*); (*линейка*) measure
метрдоте́л|ь (**-я**) *м* head waiter
ме́трик|а (**-и**) *ж* birth certificate
метри́ческий *прил* metric
метро́ *ср нескл* metro, tube (*Brit*), subway (*US*)
мех (**-а**; *nom pl* **-а́**) *м* fur
мех|а́ (**-о́в**) *мн* (*кузнечный*) bellows *мн*
механи́зм (**-а**) *м* mechanism
меха́ник (**-а**) *м* mechanic
механи́ческий *прил* mechanical; (*цех*) machine
мехово́й *прил* fur
мецена́т (**-а**) *м* patron
меч (**-а́**) *м* sword
мече́т|ь (**-и**) *ж* mosque
мечт|а́ (**-ы́**; *gen pl* **-а́ний**) *ж* dream
мечта́|ть (**-ю**) *несов*: **мечта́ть (о** *+prp*) to dream (of)
меша́|ть (**-ю**; *perf* **помеша́ть**) *несов перех* (*суп, чай*) to stir ▷ (*perf* **смеша́ть**) (*напитки, краски*) to mix ▷ (*perf* **помеша́ть**) *неперех* (*+dat*: *быть помехой*) to disturb, bother; (*реформам*) to hinder; **меша́ть (*perf* помеша́ть) кому́-н** *+infin* (*препятствовать*) to make it difficult for sb to do; **меша́ться** (*perf* **смеша́ться**) *несов возв* (*путаться*) to get mixed up
меш|о́к (**-ка́**) *м* sack
мещ|ани́н (**-ани́на**; *nom pl* **-а́не**, *gen pl* **-а́н**) *м* petty bourgeois
миг (**-а**) *м* moment
мига́|ть (**-ю**) *несов* to wink; (*огни*) to twinkle
мигн|у́ть (**-у́, -ёшь**) *сов* to wink
ми́гом *нареч* (*разг*) in a jiffy
мигра́ци|я (**-и**) *ж* migration
МИД (**-а**) *м сокр* (= *Министе́рство иностра́нных дел*) ≈ the Foreign Office (*Brit*), ≈ the State Department (*US*)
ми́довский *прил* (*разг*) Foreign Office
ми́зерный *прил* meagre (*Brit*), meager (*US*)
мизи́н|ец (**-ца**) *м* (*на руке*) little finger; (*на ноге*) little toe
микроавто́бус (**-а**) *м* minibus
микрорайо́н (**-а**) *м* ≈ catchment area

Микрорайо́н

These are modern housing estates with densely built blocks of flats and are a feature of all big Russian cities. They have their own infrastructure of schools, health centres, cinemas, and shops.

микроско́п (**-а**) *м* microscope
микрофо́н (**-а**) *м* microphone
ми́ксер (**-а**) *м* mixer
микстýр|а (**-ы**) *ж* mixture
милиционе́р (**-а**) *м* policeman (*in Russia*) (*мн* policemen)
мили́ци|я (**-и**) *ж, собир* police (*in Russia*)
миллиа́рд (**-а**) *м* billion
миллигра́мм (**-а**) *м* milligram(me)
миллиме́тр (**-а**) *м* millimetre (*Brit*), millimeter (*US*)
миллио́н (**-а**) *м* million; **миллионе́р** (**-а**) *м* millionaire
ми́л|овать (**-ую**; *perf* **поми́ловать**) *несов перех* to have mercy on; (*преступника*) to pardon
милосе́рди|е (**-я**) *ср* compassion
ми́лостын|я (**-и**) *ж* alms *мн*
ми́лост|ь (**-и**) *ж* (*доброта*) kind-heartedness; **ми́лости про́сим!** welcome!
ми́лый *прил* (*симпатичный*) pleasant, nice; (*дорогой*) dear
ми́л|я (**-и**) *ж* mile
ми́мик|а (**-и**) *ж* expression
ми́мо *нареч* past ▷ *предл +gen* past
мимолётный *прил* fleeting
мимохо́дом *нареч* on the way; (*упомянуть*) in passing
ми́н|а (**-ы**) *ж* (*Воен*) mine
минда́лин|а (**-ы**) *ж* (*Мед*) tonsil
минда́л|ь (**-я́**) *м* almond
минера́л (**-а**) *м* mineral
минздра́в (**-а**) *м сокр* (= *министе́рство здравоохране́ния*) Ministry of Health
миниатю́р|а (**-ы**) *ж* miniature; (*Театр*) short play; **миниатю́рный** *прил* miniature
минима́льный *прил* minimum
ми́нимум (**-а**) *м* minimum ▷ *нареч* at least, minimum; **прожи́точный ми́нимум** minimum living wage
мини́р|овать (**-ую**; *perf* **замини́ровать**) *(не)сов перех* (*Воен*) to mine
министе́рств|о (**-а**) *ср* ministry; **мини́стр** (**-а**) *м* (*Полит*) minister
ми́нн|ый *прил* mine; **ми́нное по́ле** minefield
мин|ова́ть (**-ýю**) *(не)сов перех* to pass
минýвший *прил* past
ми́нус (**-а**) *м* minus
минýт|а (**-ы**) *ж* minute; **минýтный** *прил* (*стрелка*) minute; (*дело*) brief
ми́н|уть (*3sg* **-ет**) *сов* (*исполниться*): **ей/емý ми́нуло 16 лет** she/he has turned 16
минфи́н (**-а**) *м сокр* (*разг*) (= *Министе́рство фина́нсов*) Ministry of Finance
мир (**-а**; *nom pl* **-ы́**) *м* world; (*Вселенная*) universe ▷ (*loc sg* **-ý**) (*Рел*) (secular) world; (*состояние без войны*) peace
мир|и́ть (**-ю́, -и́шь**; *perf* **помири́ть** *или* **примири́ть**) *несов перех* to reconcile; **мири́ться** (*perf* **помири́ться**) *несов возв*: **мири́ться с** *+instr* to make up *или* be reconciled with ▷ (*perf* **примири́ться**) (*с недостатками*) to reconcile o.s. to, come to terms with
ми́рн|ый *прил* peaceful; **ми́рное вре́мя** peacetime; **ми́рное населе́ние** civilian population;

ми́рные перегово́ры peace talks *или* negotiations
мировоззре́ни|е (**-я**) *ср* philosophy of life
миров́ой *прил* world
миротво́р|ец (**-ца**) *м* peacemaker, peacekeeper
миротво́рческ|ий *прил* peacemaking; **миротво́рческие войска́** peacekeeping force
мирско́й *прил* secular, lay
ми́сси|я (**-и**) *ж* mission
ми́стер (**-а**) *м* Mr
ми́тинг (**-а**) *м* rally
митрополи́т (**-а**) *м* metropolitan
миф (**-а**) *м* myth
мише́н|ь (**-и**) *ж* target
младе́н|ец (**-ца**) *м* infant, baby
мла́дше *сравн прил от* **молодо́й**
мла́дший *прил* younger; (*сотрудник, класс*) junior
млекопита́ющ|ее (**-его**) *ср* mammal
мле́чный *прил*: **Мле́чный Путь** the Milky Way
мм *сокр* (= *миллиме́тр*) mm
мне *мест см* **я**
мне́ни|е (**-я**) *ср* opinion
мни́мый *прил* imaginary; (*ложный*) fake
мни́тельный *прил* suspicious
мно́г|ие *прил* many ▷ (**-их**) *мн* (*много людей*) many (people)
мно́го *чис* (*+gen*: *книг, друзей*) many, a lot of; (*работы*) much, a lot of ▷ *нареч* (*разговаривать, пить итп*) a lot; (*+comparative*: *гораздо*) much; **мно́го книг тебе́ да́ли?** did they give you many *или* a lot of books?; **мно́го рабо́ты тебе́ да́ли?** did they give you much *или* a lot of work?
многоде́тный *прил* with a lot of children
мно́г|ое (**-ого**) *ср* a great deal
многозначи́тельный *прил* significant
многоле́тний *прил* (*планы*) long-term; (*труд*) of many years; (*растения*) perennial
многолю́дный *прил* crowded
многонациона́льный *прил* multinational
многообеща́ющий *прил* promising
многообра́зи|е (**-я**) *ср* variety
многообра́зный *прил* varied
многосторо́нний *прил* (*переговоры*) multilateral; (*личность*) many-sided; (*интересы*) diverse
многоуважа́емый *прил* (*в обращении*) Dear
многочи́сленный *прил* numerous
многоэта́жный *прил* multistorey (*Brit*), multistory (*US*)
мно́жественн|ый *прил*: **мно́жественное число́** (*Линг*) the plural (number)
мно́жеств|о (**-а**) *ср +gen* a great number of
мно́жительн|ый *прил*: **мно́жительная те́хника** photocopying equipment
мно́ж|ить (**-у, -ишь**; *perf* **умно́жить**) *несов перех* to multiply
мной *мест см* **я**
мобилиз|ова́ть (**-у́ю**) *(не)сов перех* to mobilize
моби́льник (**-а**) *м* (*разг*) mobile
моби́льный *прил* mobile; **моби́льный телефо́н** mobile phone
мог *итп несов см* **мочь**
моги́л|а (**-ы**) *ж* grave
могу́ *etc несов см* **мочь**
могу́чий *прил* mighty
могу́честв|о (**-а**) *ср* power, might

мо́д|а (**-ы**) *ж* fashion; *см также* **мо́ды**
модели́р|овать (**-ую**) *(не)сов перех* (*одежду*) to design ▷ (*perf* **смоделúровать**) (*процесс, поведение*) to simulate
моде́л|ь (**-и**) *ж* model; **моделье́р** (**-а**) *м* fashion designer
моде́м (**-а**) *м* (*Комп*) modem
мо́дный *прил* fashionable
мо́д|ы (**-**) *мн* fashions; **журна́л мод** fashion magazine
мо́жет *несов см* **мочь** ▷ *вводн сл* (*также* **мо́жет быть**) maybe
мо́жно *как сказ* (*возможно*) *+infin* it is possible to do; **мо́жно (войти́)?** may I (come in)?; **как мо́жно лу́чше** as well as possible
мозг (**-а**; *loc sg* **-у́**, *nom sg* **-и́**) *м* brain; **спинно́й мозг** spinal cord
мой (**моего́**; см *Table 8*; *f* **моя́**, *nt* **моё**, *pl* **мои́**) *притяж мест* my; **по-мо́ему** my way; (*по моему мнению*) in my opinion
мо́к|нуть (**-ну**; *pt* **-**, **-ла**) *несов* to get wet; (*лежать в воде*) to be soaking
мо́крый *прил* wet
молв|а́ (**-ы́**) *ж* rumour (*Brit*), rumor (*US*)
мо́леб|ен (**-на**) *м* (*Рел*) service
моле́кул|а (**-ы**) *ж* molecule
моли́тв|а (**-ы**) *ж* prayer; **моли́твенник** (**-а**) *м* prayer book
мол|и́ться (**-ю́сь, -ишься**; *perf* **помоли́ться**) *несов возв +dat* to pray to
мо́лни|я (**-и**) *ж* lightning; (*застёжка*) zip (fastener) (*Brit*), zipper (*US*)
молодёжный *прил* youth; (*мода, газета*) for young people
молодёж|ь (**-и**) *ж собир* young people *мн*
молоде́|ть (**-ю**; *perf* **помолоде́ть**) *несов* to become younger
молод|е́ц (**-ца́**) *м* strong fellow; **молоде́ц!** (*разг*) well done!; **она́/он молоде́ц!** (*разг*) she/he has done well!
молодо́й *прил* young; (*картофель, листва*) new; **мо́лодост|ь** (**-и**) *ж* youth
моло́же *сравн прил от* **молодо́й**
молок|о́ (**-а́**) *ср* milk
мо́лот (**-а**) *м* hammer
молот|о́к (**-ка́**) *м* hammer
мо́лотый *прил* (*кофе, перец*) ground
моло́ть (**мелю́, ме́лешь**; *perf* **смоло́ть** *или* **помоло́ть**) *несов перех* to grind
моло́чник (**-а**) *м* (*посуда*) milk jug
моло́чный *прил* (*продукты, скот*) dairy; (*коктейль*) milk
мо́лча *нареч* silently
молча́ни|е (**-я**) *ср* silence; **молч|а́ть** (**-у́, -и́шь**) *несов* to be silent; **молча́ть** (*impf*) **о** *+prp* to keep silent *или* quiet about
мол|ь (**-и**) *ж* moth
моме́нт (**-а**) *м* moment; (*доклада*) point; **теку́щий моме́нт** the current situation; **момента́льный** *прил* instant
монасты́р|ь (**-я́**) *м* (*мужской*) monastery; (*женский*) convent
мона́х (**-а**) *м* monk; **мона́хин|я** (**-и**; *gen pl* **-ь**) *ж* nun
моне́т|а (**-ы**) *ж* coin; **моне́тный** *прил*: **моне́тный двор** mint
монито́р (**-а**) *м* monitor
моното́нный *прил* monotonous
монта́ж (**-а́**) *ж* (*сооружения*) building; (*механизма*) assembly; (*кадров*) editing
монти́р|овать (**-ую**; *perf* **смонти́ровать**) *несов перех*

М

(*оборудование*) to assemble; (*фильм*) to edit
монуме́нт (**-а**) *м* monument
мора́л|ь (**-и**) *ж* morals *мн*, ethics *мн*; (*басни, сказки*) moral
мора́льный *прил* moral
морг (**-а**) *м* morgue
морга́|ть (**-ю**) *несов* to blink; (*подмигивать*): **морга́ть** (**+*dat***) to wink (at)
моргн|у́ть (**-у́, -ёшь**) *сов* to blink; (*подмигнуть*): **моргну́ть** (**+*dat***) to wink (at)
мо́рд|а (**-ы**) *ж* (*животного*) muzzle; (*разг*: *человека*) mug
мо́р|е (**-я**; *nom pl* **-я́**, *gen pl* **-е́й**) *ср* sea
морехо́дный *прил* naval
морж (**-а́**) *м* walrus
морко́в|ь (**-и**) *ж* carrots *мн*
моро́жен|ое (**-ого**) *ср* ice cream
моро́женый *прил* frozen
моро́з (**-а**) *м* frost
мороз́ильник (**-а**) *м* freezer
моро́|зить (**-жу, -зишь**) *несов перех* to freeze
моро́зный *прил* frosty
морос|и́ть (*3sg* **-и́т**) *несов* to drizzle
моро́ч|ить (**-у, -ишь**; *perf* **заморо́чить**) *несов перех*: **моро́чить го́лову кому́-н** (*разг*) to pull sb's leg
морск|о́й *прил* sea; (*Био*) marine; (*курорт*) seaside; **морско́е пра́во** maritime law; **морска́я боле́знь** seasickness; **морска́я сви́нка** guinea pig
морщи́н|а (**-ы**) *ж* (*на лице*) wrinkle
мо́рщ|ить (**-у, -ишь**; *perf* **намо́рщить**) *несов перех* (*брови*) to knit ▷ (*perf* **смо́рщить**) (*нос, лоб*) to wrinkle; (*лицо*) to screw up; **мо́рщиться** (*perf* **смо́рщиться**) *несов возв*: **мо́рщиться от +*gen*** (*от старости*) to become wrinkled from; (*от боли*) to wince in
моря́к (**-а́**) *м* sailor
Москв|а́ (**-ы́**) *ж* Moscow
москви́ч (**-а́**) *м* Muscovite
мост (**-а́**; *loc sg* **-у́**) *м* bridge
мо́стик (**-а**) *м* bridge; **капита́нский мо́стик** bridge (*Naut*)
мо|сти́ть (**-щу́, -сти́шь**; *perf* **вы́мостить**) *несов перех* to pave
мостов|а́я (**-о́й**) *ж* road
мота́|ть (**-ю**; *perf* **намота́ть**) *несов перех* (*нитки*) to wind ▷ (*perf* **помота́ть**) *неперех* (*+instr*: *головой*) to shake; **мота́ться** *несов возв* to swing
моте́л|ь (**-я**) *м* motel
моти́в (**-а**) *м* (*преступления*) motive; (*мелодия*) motif
мотиви́р|овать (**-ую**) *(не)сов перех* to justify
мото́р (**-а**) *м* motor; (*автомобиля, лодки*) engine
моторо́ллер (**-а**) *м* (motor) scooter
мотоци́кл (**-а**) *м* motorcycle
мотыл|ёк (**-ька́**) *м* moth
мох (**мха**; *loc sg* **мху**, *nom pl* **мхи**) *м* moss
мохе́р (**-а**) *м* mohair
моч|а́ (**-и́**) *ж* urine
моча́л|ка (**-ки**; *gen pl* **-ок**) *ж* sponge
мочево́й *прил*: **мочево́й пузы́рь** bladder
моч|и́ть (**-у́, -ишь**; *perf* **намочи́ть**) *несов перех* to wet ▷ (*perf* **замочи́ть**) (*бельё*) to soak
мо|чь (**-гу́, -жешь** *etc*, **-гут**; *pt* **-г, -гла́, -гло́**, *perf* **смочь**) *несов +infin* can do, to be able to do; **я могу́ игра́ть на гита́ре/говори́ть по-англи́йски** I can play the guitar/

speak English; **он мóжет прийти́** he can *или* is able to come; **я сдéлаю всё, что могу́** I will do all I can; **зáвтра мóжешь не приходи́ть** you don't have to come tomorrow; **он мóжет оби́деться** he may well be offended; **не могу́ поня́ть э́того** I can't understand this; **мóжет быть** maybe; **не мóжет быть!** it's impossible!

мóш|ка (**-ки**; *gen pl* **-ек**) *ж* midge

мóщност|ь (**-и**) *ж* power

мóщный *прил* powerful

мощ|ь (**-и**) *ж* might, power

мо|я́ (**-éй**) *притяж мест см* **мой**

MP3-плéер (**-а**) *м* MP3 player

мрак (**-а**) *м* darkness

мрáмор (**-а**) *м* marble

мрáчный *прил* gloomy

мстить (**мщу, мсти́шь**; *perf* **отомсти́ть**) *несов*: **мстить комý-н** to take revenge on sb

МТС *ж сокр* (= *междугорóдная телефóнная стáнция*) ≈ intercity telephone exchange

му́дрост|ь (**-и**) *ж* wisdom

му́дрый *прил* wise

муж (**-а**; *nom pl* **-ья́**, *gen pl* **-éй**) *м* husband

мужá|ть (**-ю**; *perf* **возмужáть**) *несов* to mature; **мужáться** *несов возв* to take heart, have courage

му́жественный *прил* (*поступок*) courageous

му́жеств|о (**-а**) *ср* courage

мужскóй *прил* men's; (*характер*) masculine; (*органы, клетка*) male; **мужскóй род** masculine gender

мужчи́н|а (**-ы**) *м* man (*мн* men)

музé|й (**-я**) *м* museum

му́зык|а (**-и**) *ж* music

музыкáльн|ый *прил* musical; **музыкáльная шкóла** music school

музыкáнт (**-а**) *м* musician

му́к|а (**-и**) *ж* torment

мук|á (**-и́**) *ж* flour

му́льтик (**-а**) *м* (*разг*) cartoon

мультимеди́йный *прил* (*Комп*) multimedia

мультипликациóнный *прил*: **мультипликациóнный фильм** cartoon, animated film

мунди́р (**-а**) *м* uniform; **картóфель в мунди́ре** jacket potatoes

муниципалитéт (**-а**) *м* municipality, city council

мурав|éй (**-ья́**) *м* ant

мурáш|ки (**-ек**) *мн*: **у меня́ мурáшки по спинé бéгают** shivers are running down my spine

мурлы́|кать (**-чу, -чешь**) *несов* to purr

мускáт (**-а**) *м* (*орех*) nutmeg

му́скул (**-а**) *м* muscle

мускули́стый *прил* muscular

му́сор (**-а**) *м* rubbish (*Brit*), garbage (*US*); **му́сорн|ый** *прил* rubbish (*Brit*), garbage (*US*); **му́сорное ведрó** dustbin (*Brit*), trash can (*US*); **мусоропровóд** (**-а**) *м* refuse *или* garbage (*US*) chute

мусульмáнин (**-а**) *м* Muslim

му|ти́ть (**-чу́, -ти́шь**; *perf* **взмути́ть** *или* **замути́ть**) *несов перех* (*жидкость*) to cloud; **мути́ться** (*perf* **замути́ться**) *несов возв* (*вода, раствор*) to become cloudy

мутнé|ть (*3sg* **-ет**, *perf* **помутнéть**) *несов* (*жидкость*) to become cloudy; (*взор*) to grow dull

му́тный *прил* (*жидкость*) cloudy; (*стекло*) dull

му́х|а (**-и**) *ж* fly

мухомóр (**-а**) *м* (*Бот*) fly agaric

мучéни|е (**-я**) *ср* torment, torture

му́ченик (**-а**) *м* martyr
му́ч|ить (**-у, -ишь**; *perf* **заму́чить** *или* **изму́чить**) *несов перех* to torment; **му́читься** (*perf* **заму́читься**) *несов возв*: **му́читься** *+instr* (*сомнениями*) to be tormented by; **му́читься** (*impf*) **над** *+instr* to agonize over
мч|ать (**-у, -ишь**) *несов* (*машину*) to speed along; (*лошадь*) to race along; **мча́ться** *несов возв* (*поезд*) to speed along; (*лошадь*) to race along
мще́ни|е (**-я**) *ср* vengeance, revenge
мы (**нас**; см *Table 6b*) *мест* we; **мы с тобо́й/жено́й** you/my wife and I
мы́л|ить (**-ю, -ишь**; *perf* **намы́лить**) *несов перех* to soap; **мы́литься** (*perf* **намы́литься**) *несов возв* to soap o.s.
мы́л|о (**-а**) *ср* soap
мы́льниц|а (**-ы**) *ж* soap dish
мы́льн|ый *прил* (*пена*) soap; **мы́льная о́пера** soap (opera)
мыс (**-а**; *loc sg* **-у́**, *nom pl* **-ы**) *м* point
мы́сленный *прил* mental
мы́сл|ить (**-ю, -ишь**) *несов* to think ▷ *перех* to imagine
мысл|ь (**-и**) *ж* thought; (*идея*) idea; **за́дняя мысль** ulterior motive; **о́браз мы́слей** way of thinking
мыть (**мо́ю, мо́ешь**; *perf* **вы́мыть** *или* **помы́ть**) *несов перех* to wash; **мы́ться** (*perf* **вы́мыться** *или* **помы́ться**) *несов возв* to wash o.s.
мы́шечный *прил* muscular
мы́ш|ка (**-ки**; *gen pl* **-ек**) *ж* mouse; **под мы́шкой** under one's arm
мышле́ни|е (**-я**) *ср* (*способность*) reason; (*процесс*) thinking
мы́шц|а (**-ы**) *ж* muscle
мыш|ь (**-и**) *ж* (*Зоол, Комп*) mouse
мэр (**-а**) *м* mayor
мэ́ри|я (**-и**) *ж* city hall
мя́гкий *прил* soft; (*движения*) smooth; (*характер, климат*) mild; (*наказание*) lenient; **мя́гкий ваго́н** *railway carriage with soft seats*; **мя́гкий знак** soft sign (*Russian letter*)
мя́гко *нареч* gently; (*отругать*) mildly; **мя́гко говоря́** to put it mildly
мя́кот|ь (**-и**) *ж* flesh; (*мясо*) fillet
мя́мл|ить (**-ю, -ишь**; *perf* **промя́млить**) *несов перех* to mumble
мясни́к (**-а́**) *м* butcher
мясно́й *прил* (*котлета*) meat; **мясно́й магазин** the butcher's
мя́с|о (**-а**) *ср* meat
мя́т|а (**-ы**) *ж* mint
мяте́ж (**-а́**) *м* revolt
мя́тный *прил* mint
мять (**мну, мнёшь**; *perf* **измя́ть** *или* **смять**) *несов перех* (*одежду*) to crease; (*бумагу*) to crumple
мяч (**-а́**) *м* ball; **футбо́льный мяч** football

КЛЮЧЕВОЕ СЛОВО

на *предл +acc* **1** (*направление на поверхность*) on; **положи́ таре́лку на стол** put the plate on the table
2 (*направление в какое-нибудь место*) to; **сесть** (*perf*) **на по́езд** to get on(to) the train
3 (*об объекте воздействия*): **обрати́ внима́ние на э́того челове́ка** pay attention to this man; **нажми́ на педа́ль/кно́пку** press the pedal/button; **я люблю́ смотре́ть на дете́й/на звёзды** I love watching the children/the stars
4 (*о времени, сроке*) for; **он уе́хал на ме́сяц** he has gone away for a month
5 (*о цели, о назначении*) for; **де́ньги на кни́ги** money for books
6 (*о мере*) into; **дели́ть** (*impf*) **что-н на ча́сти** to divide sth into parts
7 (*при сравнении*): **я получа́ю на сто рубле́й ме́ньше** I get one hundred roubles less
8 (*об изменении состояния*) into; **на́до перевести́ текст на англи́йский** the text must be translated into English
▷ *предл +prp* **1** (*нахождение на поверхности*) on; **кни́га на по́лке** the book is on the shelf; **на де́вочке ша́пка/шу́ба** the girl has a hat/fur coat on
2 (*о пребывании где-нибудь*) in; **на Кавка́зе** in the Caucasus; **на у́лице** in the street; **быть** (*impf*) **на рабо́те/заседа́нии** to be at work/at a meeting
3 (*о времени осуществления чего-н*): **встре́тимся на сле́дующей неде́ле** let's meet next week
4 (*об объекте воздействия*) on; **сосредото́читься** (*perf*)**/ останови́ться** (*perf*) **на чём-н** to concentrate/dwell on sth
5 (*о средстве осуществления чего-н*): **е́здить на по́езде/ велосипе́де** to travel by train/ bicycle; **игра́ть** (*impf*) **на роя́ле/ скри́пке** to play the piano/violin; **ката́ться** (*impf*) **на лы́жах/ конька́х** to go skiing/skating; **говори́ть** (*impf*) **на ру́сском/ англи́йском языке́** to speak (in) English/Russian
6 (*о составной части предмета*): **ка́ша на воде́** porridge made with water

на (**на́те**) *част* (*разг*) here (you are)
набежа́ть (*как* **бежа́ть**; см *Table*

20; *impf* **набега́ть**) *сов* (*разг*: *тучи*) to gather; (*наскочить*): **набежа́ть на** *+acc* to run into; (*волны*: *на берег*) to lap against

на́бело *нареч*: **переписа́ть что-н на́бело** to write sth out neatly

на́бережн|ая (**-ой**) *ж* embankment

набива́|ть(ся) (**-ю(сь)**) *несов от* **наби́ть(ся)**

наби́вк|а (**-и**) *ж* stuffing

набира́|ть (**-ю**) *несов от* **набра́ть**

наб|и́ть (**-ью́, -ьёшь**; *impf* **набива́ть**) *сов перех*: **наби́ть** (*+instr*) to stuff (with); **набива́ть** (*perf* **наби́ть**) **це́ну** (*разг*) to talk up the price; **наби́ться** (*impf* **набива́ться**) *сов возв* (*разг*): **наби́ться в** *+acc* to be crammed into

наблюда́тел|ь (**-я**) *м* observer; **наблюда́тельный** *прил* (*человек*) observant; **наблюда́тельный пункт** observation point

наблюда́|ть (**-ю**) *несов перех* to observe ▷ *неперех*: **наблюда́ть за** *+instr* to monitor

на́бок *нареч* to one side

набра́сыва|ть (**-ю**) *несов от* **наброса́ть**; **набро́сить**; **набра́сываться** *несов от* **набро́ситься**

наб|ра́ть (**-еру́, -ерёшь**; *pt* **-ра́л, -рала́, -ра́ло**, *impf* **набира́ть**) *сов перех* (*+gen*: *цветы*) to pick; (*воду*) to fetch; (*студентов*) to take on; (*скорость, высоту, баллы*) to gain; (*код*) to dial; (*текст*) to typeset

наброса́|ть (**-ю**; *impf* **набра́сывать**) *сов перех* (*план, текст*) to sketch out ▷ *(не)перех* (*+acc или +gen*: *вещей, окурков*) to throw about

набро́|сить (**-шу, -сишь**; *impf* **набра́сывать**) *сов перех* (*пальто, платок*) to throw on; **набро́ситься** (*impf* **набра́сываться**) *сов возв*: **набро́ситься на** *+acc* (*на жертву*) to fall upon

набро́с|ок (**-ка**) *м* (*рисунок*) sketch; (*статьи*) draft

набу́х|нуть (*3sg* **-нет**, *pt* **-, -ла**, *impf* **набуха́ть**) *сов* to swell up

нав|али́ть (**-алю́, -а́лишь**; *impf* **нава́ливать**) *сов (не)перех* (*+acc или +gen*: *мусору*) to pile up; **навали́ться** (*impf* **нава́ливаться**) *сов возв*: **навали́ться на** *+acc* (*на дверь итп*) to lean into

нава́лом *как сказ* (*+gen*: *разг*) loads of; **у него́ де́нег нава́лом** he has loads of money

наведе́ни|е (**-я**) *ср* (*порядка*) establishment; (*справок*) making

наве́к(и) *нареч* (*навсегда*) forever

наве́рно(е) *вводн сл* probably

наверняка́ *вводн сл* (*конечно*) certainly ▷ *нареч* (*несомненно*) definitely, for sure

наве́рх *нареч* up; (*на верхний этаж*) upstairs; (*на поверхность*) to the top

наверху́ *нареч* at the top; (*на верхнем этаже*) upstairs

нав|ести́ (**-еду́, -едёшь**; *pt* **-ёл, -ела́, -ело́**, *impf* **наводи́ть**) *сов перех* (*ужас, грусть итп*) to cause; (*бинокль*) to focus; (*орудие*) to aim; (*порядок*) to establish; **наводи́ть** (*perf* **навести́**) **кого́-н на** *+acc* (*на место, на след*) to lead sb to; **наводи́ть** (*perf* **навести́**) **спра́вки** to make inquiries

наве|сти́ть (**-щу́, -сти́шь**; *impf* **навеща́ть**) *сов перех* to visit

на́взничь *нареч* on one's back

навига́ци|я (**-и**) *ж* navigation
нави́с|нуть (**-ну**; *pt* **-**, **-ла**, *impf* **нависа́ть**) *сов*: **нави́снуть на** *+acc* (*волосы*: *на лоб*) to hang down over
нав|оди́ть (**-ожу́**, **-о́дишь**) *несов от* **навести́**
наводне́ни|е (**-я**) *ср* flood
наво́з (**-а**) *м* manure
на́волоч|ка (**-ки**; *gen pl* **-ек**) *ж* pillowcase
навре|ди́ть (**-жу́**, **-ди́шь**) *сов от* **вреди́ть**
навсегда́ *нареч* forever; **раз и навсегда́** once and for all
навстре́чу *предл +dat* towards ▷ *нареч*: **идти́ навстре́чу кому́-н** (*перен*) to give sb a hand
на́вык (**-а**) *м* skill
навы́нос *нареч* to take away (*Brit*), to go (*US*)
навы́пуск *нареч* outside, over
нав|яза́ть (**-яжу́**, **-я́жешь**; *impf* **навя́зывать**) *сов перех*: **навяза́ть что-н кому́-н** to impose sth on sb; **навяза́ться** (*impf* **навя́зываться**) *сов возв* to impose o.s.
навя́зчивый *прил* persistent
нагиба́|ть(ся) (**-ю(сь)**) *несов от* **нагну́ть(ся)**
нагле́|ть (**-ю**; *perf* **обнагле́ть**) *несов* to get cheeky; **нагле́ц** (**-а́**) *м* impudent upstart
нагля́дный *прил* (*пример*, *случай*) clear; (*метод обучения*) visual
наг|на́ть (**-оню́**, **-о́нишь**; *impf* **нагоня́ть**) *сов перех* (*беглеца*) to catch up with; (*упущенное*) to make up for; **нагоня́ть** (*perf* **нагна́ть**) **страх на кого́-н** to strike fear into sb
нагнета́|ть (**-ю**) *несов перех* (*воздух*) to pump; (*перен*: *напряжение*) to heighten
нагн|у́ть (**-у́**, **-ёшь**; *impf* **нагиба́ть**) *сов перех* (*ветку*) to pull down; (*голову*) to bend; **нагну́ться** (*impf* **нагиба́ться**) *сов возв* to bend down
наго́й *прил* (*человек*) naked, nude
на́голо *нареч*: **остри́чься на́голо** to shave one's head
нагоня́|ть (**-ю**) *несов от* **нагна́ть**
наготове *нареч* at the ready
награ́д|а (**-ы**) *ж* reward, prize; (*Воен*) decoration; **награ|ди́ть** (**-жу́**, **-ди́шь**; *impf* **награжда́ть**) *сов перех*: **награди́ть кого́-н чем-н** (*орденом*) to award sb sth, award sth to sb; (*перен*: *талантом*) to endow sb with sth
нагрева́тельный *прил*: **нагрева́тельный прибо́р** heating appliance
нагре́|ть (**-ю**; *impf* **нагрева́ть**) *сов перех* to heat, warm; **нагре́ться** (*impf* **нагрева́ться**) *сов возв* to warm up
нагромożде́ни|е (**-я**) *ср* pile
нагруб|и́ть (**-лю́**, **-и́шь**) *сов от* **груби́ть**
нагру́дник (**-а**) *м* bib; **нагру́дный** *прил*: **нагру́дный карма́н** breast pocket
нагр|узи́ть (**-ужу́**, **-у́зишь**) *сов от* **грузи́ть** ▷ (*impf* **нагружа́ть**) *перех* to load up; **нагру́зк|а** (**-и**) *ж* load
над *предл +instr* above; **рабо́тать** (*impf*) **над** *+instr* to work on; **ду́мать** (*impf*) **над** *+instr* to think about; **смея́ться** (*impf*) **над** *+instr* to laugh at; **сиде́ть** (*impf*) **над кни́гой** to sit over a book
над|ави́ть (**-авлю́**, **-а́вишь**; *impf* **нада́вливать**) *сов*: **надави́ть на** *+acc* (*на дверь итп*) to lean against; (*на кнопку*) to press

Н

надви́н|уть (**-у**; *impf* **надвига́ть**) *сов перех*: **надви́нуть что-н (на** *+acc*) to pull sth down (over); **надви́нуться** (*impf* **надвига́ться**) *сов возв* (*опасность, старость*) to approach
на́двое *нареч* in half
надгро́би|е (**-я**) *ср* gravestone
надева́|ть (**-ю**) *несов от* **наде́ть**
наде́жд|а (**-ы**) *ж* hope
надёжный *прил* reliable; (*механизм*) secure
наде́ла|ть (**-ю**) *сов (не)перех* (*+acc или +gen*: *ошибок*) to make lots of; **что ты наде́лал?** what have you done?
надел|и́ть (**-ю́, -и́шь**; *impf* **наделя́ть**) *сов перех*: **надели́ть кого́-н чем-н** (*землёй*) to grant sb sth
наде́|ть (**-ну, -нешь**; *impf* **надева́ть**) *сов перех* to put on
наде́|яться (**-юсь**) *несов возв* *+infin* to hope to do; **наде́яться** (*perf* **понаде́яться) на** *+acc* (*на друга*) to rely on; (*на улучшение*) to hope for
надзира́тел|ь (**-я**) *м* guard
надзо́р (**-а**) *м* control; (*орган*) monitoring body
надл|оми́ть (**-омлю́, -о́мишь**; *impf* **надла́мывать**) *сов перех* to break; (*здоровье, психику*) to damage

КЛЮЧЕВОЕ СЛОВО

на́до[1] *как сказ* **1** (*следует*): **на́до ему́ помо́чь** it is necessary to help him; **на́до, что́бы он пришёл во́время** he must come on time; **на́до всегда́ говори́ть пра́вду** one must always speak the truth; **мне/ ему́ на́до зако́нчить рабо́ту** I/he must finish the job; **помо́чь тебе́? — не на́до!** can I help you? — there's no need!; **не на́до!** (*не делай этого*) don't!
2 (*о потребности*): **на́до мно́го лет** it takes many years; **им на́до 5 рубле́й** they need 5 roubles; **что тебе́ на́до?** what do you want?; **так ему́/ей и на́до** (*разг*) it serves him/ her right; **на́до же!** (*разг*) of all things!

на́до[2] *предл* = **над**
надое́|сть (*как* **есть**; см *Table 15*; *impf* **надоеда́ть**) *сов*: **надое́сть кому́-н (***+instr***)** (*разговорами, упрёками*) to bore sb (with); **мне надое́ло ждать** I'm tired of waiting; **он мне надое́л** I've had enough of him
надо́лго *нареч* for a long time
надорв|а́ть (**-у́, -ёшь**; *impf* **надрыва́ть**) *сов перех* (*перен*: *силы*) to tax; (: *здоровье*) to put a strain on; **надорва́ться** (*impf* **надрыва́ться**) *сов возв* to do o.s. an injury; (*перен*) to overexhaust o.s.
надсмо́трщик (**-а**) *м* (*тюремный*) warden
наду́|ть (**-ю, -ешь**; *impf* **надува́ть**) *сов перех* (*мяч, колесо*) to inflate, blow up; **наду́ться** (*impf* **надува́ться**) *сов возв* (*матрас, мяч*) to inflate; (*вены*) to swell; (*перен*: *от важности*) to swell up; (: *разг*: *обидеться*) to sulk
наеда́|ться (**-юсь**) *несов от* **нае́сться**
наедине́ *нареч*: **наедине́ (с** *+instr*) alone (with); **они́ оста́лись наедине́** they were left on their own
нае́здник (**-а**) *м* rider
наезжа́|ть (**-ю**) *несов от* **нае́хать**

наёмник (**-а**) *м* mercenary; (*работник*) casual worker
наёмный *прил* (*труд, работник*) hired; **наёмный уби́йца** hitman
нае́|сться (*как* **есть**; см *Table 15*; *impf* **наеда́ться**) *сов возв* (*+gen*: *сладкого*) to eat a lot of; **я нае́лся** I'm full
нае́хать (*как* **е́хать**; см *Table 19*; *impf* **наезжа́ть**) *сов* (*разг*: *гости*) to arrive in droves; **наезжа́ть** (*perf* **нае́хать**) **на** *+acc* to drive into
наж|а́ть (**-му́, -мёшь**; *impf* **нажима́ть**) *сов* (*перен*): **нажа́ть на** *+acc* (*на кнопку*) to press
нажда́чн|ый *прил*: **нажда́чная бума́га** emery paper
нажи́м (**-а**) *м* pressure
нажима́|ть (**-ю**) *несов от* **нажа́ть**
нажи́|ть (**-ву́, -вёшь**; *impf* **нажива́ть**) *сов перех* (*состояние*) to acquire; **нажи́ться** (*impf* **нажива́ться**) *сов возв*: **нажи́ться (на** *+prp*) to profiteer (from)
наза́д *нареч* back; (*нагнуться, катиться итп*) backwards; **(тому́) наза́д** ago; **де́сять лет/неде́лю (тому́) наза́д** ten years/one week ago
назва́ни|е (**-я**) *ср* name; **торго́вое назва́ние** trade name
наз|ва́ть (**-ову́, -овёшь**; *impf* **называ́ть**) *сов перех* (*дать имя*) to call; (*назначить*) to name
назе́мн|ый *прил* surface; **назе́мные войска́** ground troops
на́земь *нареч* to the ground
назло́ *нареч* out of spite; **назло́ кому́-н** to spite sb; **как назло́** to make things worse
назначе́ни|е (**-я**) *ср* (*цены итп*) setting; (*на работу*) appointment; (*функция*) function; **пункт** *или* **ме́сто назначе́ния** destination;
назна́ч|ить (**-у, -ишь**; *impf* **назнача́ть**) *сов перех* (*на работу*) to appoint; (*цену*) to set; (*встречу*) to arrange; (*лекарство*) to prescribe
назо́йливый *прил* persistent
назре́|ть (*3sg* **-ет**, *impf* **назрева́ть**) *сов* (*вопрос*) to become unavoidable
называ́емый *прил*: **так называ́емый** so-called
называ́|ть (**-ю**) *несов от* **назва́ть**; **называ́ться** *несов возв* (*носить название*) to be called
наибо́лее *нареч*: **наибо́лее интере́сный/краси́вый** the most interesting/beautiful
наибо́льший *прил* the greatest
наи́вный *прил* naive
наизна́нку *нареч* inside out
наизу́сть *нареч*: **знать/вы́учить наизу́сть** to know/learn by heart
наиме́нее *нареч*: **наиме́нее уда́чный/спосо́бный** the least successful/capable
наименова́ни|е (**-я**) *ср* name; (*книги*) title, name
наиме́ньший *прил* (*длина, вес*) the smallest; (*усилие*) the least
на|йти́ (**-йду́, -йдёшь**; *pt* **-шёл, -шла́, -шло́**, *impf* **находи́ть**) *сов перех* to find; **на меня́ нашёл смех** I couldn't help laughing; **найти́сь** (*impf* **находи́ться**) *сов возв* (*потерянное*) to turn up; (*добровольцы*) to come forward; (*не растеряться*) to regain control
наказа́ни|е (**-я**) *ср* punishment;
нак|аза́ть (**-ажу́, -а́жешь**; *impf* **нака́зывать**) *сов перех* to punish
нака́л (**-а**) *м* (*борьбы*) heat
накал|и́ть (**-ю́, -и́шь**; *impf* **накаля́ть**) *сов перех* to heat up; (*перен*: *обстановку*) to hot up; **накали́ться** (*impf* **накаля́ться**)

сов возв to heat; (*перен*: *обстановка*) to hot up

накану́не *нареч* the day before, the previous day ▷ *предл +gen* on the eve of

нака́плива|ть(ся) (**-ю(сь)**) *несов от* **накопи́ть(ся)**

нак|ати́ть (**-ачу́, -а́тишь**; *impf* **нака́тывать**) *сов*: **накати́ть (на** *+acc*) (*волна*) to roll up (onto)

накача́|ть (**-ю**; *impf* **нака́чивать**) *сов перех* (*камеру*) to pump up

наки́д|ка (**-ки**; *gen pl* **-ок**) *ж* (*одежда*) wrap; (*покрывало*) bedspread, throw

наки́н|уть (**-у**; *impf* **наки́дывать**) *сов перех* (*платок*) to throw on; **наки́нуться** (*impf* **наки́дываться**) *сов возв*: **наки́нуться на** *+acc* (*на человека*) to hurl o.s. at; (*разг*: *на еду, на книгу*) to get stuck into

на́кип|ь (**-и**) *ж* (*на бульоне*) scum; (*в чайнике*) fur (*Brit*), scale (*US*)

накладн|а́я (**-о́й**) *ж* (*Комм*) bill of lading (*Brit*), waybill (*US*); **грузова́я накладна́я** consignment note

накла́дыва|ть (**-ю**) *несов от* **наложи́ть**

накле́|ить (**-ю, -ишь**; *impf* **накле́ивать**) *сов перех* to stick on

накле́|йка (**-йка**; *gen pl* **-ек**) *ж* label

накло́н (**-а**) *м* incline, slope

накл|они́ть (**-оню́, -о́нишь**; *impf* **наклоня́ть**) *сов перех* to tilt; **наклони́ться** (*impf* **наклоня́ться**) *сов возв* to bend down

накло́нност|ь (**-и**) *ж*: **накло́нность к** *+dat* (*к музыке итп*) aptitude for; **дурны́е/хоро́шие накло́нности** bad/good habits

нак|оло́ть (**-олю́, -о́лешь**; *impf* **нака́лывать**) *сов перех* (*руку*) to prick; (*прикрепить*): **наколо́ть (на** *+acc*) (*на шляпу, на дверь*) to pin on(to)

наконе́ц *нареч* at last, finally ▷ *вводн сл* after all; **наконе́ц-то!** at long last!

наконе́чник (**-а**) *м* tip, end

накоп|и́ть (**-лю́, -ишь**) *сов от* **копи́ть** ▷ (*impf* **нака́пливать**) *перех* (*силы, информацию*) to store up; (*средства*) to accumulate; **накопи́ться** *сов от* **копи́ться** ▷ (*impf* **нака́пливаться**) *возв* (*силы*) to build up; (*средства*) to accumulate

нак|орми́ть (**-ормлю́, -о́рмишь**) *сов от* **корми́ть**

накрич|а́ть (**-у́, -и́шь**) *сов*: **накрича́ть на** *+acc* to shout at

накр|ути́ть (**-учу́, -у́тишь**; *impf* **накру́чивать**) *сов перех*: **накрути́ть (на** *+acc*) (*гайку*) to screw on(to); (*канат*) to wind (round)

накр|ы́ть (**-о́ю, -о́ешь**; *impf* **накрыва́ть**) *сов перех* to cover; **накрыва́ть (***perf* **накры́ть) (на) стол** to lay the table; **накры́ться** (*impf* **накрыва́ться**) *сов возв*: **накры́ться (***+instr*) (*одеялом*) to cover o.s. up (with)

налага́|ть (**-ю**) *несов от* **наложи́ть**

нала́|дить (**-жу, -дишь**; *impf* **нала́живать**) *сов перех* (*механизм*) to repair, fix; (*сотрудничество*) to initiate; (*хозяйство*) to sort out; **нала́диться** (*impf* **нала́живаться**) *сов возв* (*работа*) to go well; (*отношения, здоровье*) to improve

нале́во *нареч* (to the) left; (*разг*:

прода́ть) on the side

налегке́ *нареч* (*ехать*) without luggage

налёт (**-а**) *м* raid; (*пыли, плесени*) thin coating *или* layer; **нале|те́ть** (**-чу́, -ти́шь**; *impf* **налета́ть**) *сов* (*буря*) to spring up; **налета́ть** (*perf* **налете́ть**) **на** *+acc* (*натолкнуться*) to fly against; (*напасть*) to swoop down on

нал|и́ть (**-ью́, -ьёшь**; *impf* **налива́ть**) *сов перех* to pour (out)

налицо́ *как сказ*: **фа́кты налицо́** the facts are obvious; **доказа́тельство налицо́** there is proof

нали́чи|е (**-я**) *ср* presence

нали́чност|ь (**-и**) *ж* cash

нали́чн|ые (**-ых**) *мн* cash *ед*

нали́чн|ый *прил*: **нали́чные де́ньги** cash; **нали́чный расчёт** cash payment; **нали́чный счёт** cash account

нало́г (**-а**) *м* tax; **нало́г на ввоз** *+gen* import duty on; **нало́гов|ый** *прил* tax; **нало́говая деклара́ция** tax return; **налогоплате́льщик** (**-а**) *м* taxpayer

нал|ожи́ть (**-ожу́, -о́жишь**; *impf* **накла́дывать**) *сов перех* to put *или* place on; (*компресс, бинт, лак*) to apply ▷ (*impf* **налага́ть**) (*штраф*) to impose

нам *мест см* **мы**

нама́|зать (**-жу, -жешь**) *сов от* **ма́зать**

нама́тыва|ть (**-ю**) *несов от* **намота́ть**

намёк (**-а**) *м* hint

намека́|ть (**-ю**; *perf* **намекну́ть**) *несов*: **намека́ть на** *+acc* to hint at

намерева́|ться (**-юсь**) *несов возв +infin* to intend to do

наме́рен *как сказ*: **он наме́рен уе́хать** he intends to leave

наме́рени|е (**-я**) *ср* intention; **наме́ренный** *прил* deliberate

намета́|ть (**-ю**) *сов от* **мета́ть**

наме́|тить (**-чу, -тишь**; *impf* **намеча́ть**) *сов перех* to plan; (*план*) to project; **наме́титься** *сов от* **ме́титься** ▷ (*impf* **намеча́ться**) *возв* to begin to show; (*событие*) to be coming up

на́ми *мест см* **мы**

намно́го *нареч* much, far; **намно́го ху́же/интере́снее** much worse/more interesting

намо́кн|уть (**-у**; *impf* **намока́ть**) *сов* to get wet

намо́рдник (**-а**) *м* muzzle

намо́рщ|ить (**-у, -ишь**) *сов от* **мо́рщить**

намота́|ть (**-ю**) *сов от* **мота́ть**

нам|очи́ть (**-очу́, -о́чишь**) *сов от* **мочи́ть**

нан|ести́ (**-есу́, -есёшь**; *pt* **-ёс, -есла́, -есло́**, *impf* **наноси́ть**) *сов перех* (*мазь, краску*) to apply; (*рисунок*) to draw; (*на карту*) to plot; (*удар*) to deliver; (*урон*) to inflict; **нанести́** (*perf*) **кому́-н визи́т** to pay sb a visit

нани́зыва|ть (**-ю**) *несов перех* to string

на|ня́ть (**-йму, -ймёшь**; *impf* **нанима́ть**) *сов перех* (*работника*) to hire; (*лодку, машину*) to hire, rent; **наня́ться** (*impf* **нанима́ться**) *сов возв* to get a job

наоборо́т *нареч* (*делать*) the wrong way (round) ▷ *вводн сл, част* on the contrary

наобу́м *нареч* without thinking

напада́|ть (**-ю**) *несов от* **напа́сть**

напада́ющ|ий (**-его**) *м* (*Спорт*) forward

нападе́ни|е (**-я**) *ср* attack; (*Спорт*) forwards *мн*

напа́д|ки (**-ок**) *мн* attacks
нап|а́сть (**-аду́, -адёшь**; *impf* **напада́ть**) *сов*: **напа́сть на** *+acc* to attack; (*обнаружить*) to strike; (*тоска, страх*) to grip, seize
напе́в (**-а**) *м* tune, melody
напева́|ть (**-ю**) *несов от* **напе́ть** ▷ *перех* (*песенку*) to hum
наперебо́й *нареч* vying with each other
наперегонки́ *нареч* (*разг*) racing each other
напере́д *нареч* (*знать, угадать*) beforehand; **за́дом наперёд** back to front
напереко́р *предл +dat* in defiance of
нап|е́ть (**-ою́, -оёшь**; *impf* **напева́ть**) *сов перех* (*мотив, песню*) to sing
напива́|ться (**-юсь**) *несов от* **напи́ться**
напи́льник (**-а**) *м* file
напира́|ть (**-ю**) *несов*: **напира́ть на** *+acc* (*теснить*) to push against
написа́ни|е (**-я**) *ср* writing; (*слова*) spelling
нап|иса́ть (**-ишу́, -и́шешь**) *сов от* **писа́ть**
напи́т|ок (**-ка**) *м* drink
нап|и́ться (**-ью́сь, -ьёшься**; *impf* **напива́ться**) *сов возв*: **напи́ться** (*+gen*) to have a good drink (of); (*разг*: *опьянеть*) to get drunk
напл|ева́ть (**-юю́**) *сов от* **плева́ть**
наплы́в (**-а**) *м* (*туристов*) influx; (: *заявлений, чувств*) flood
наплы́|ть (**-ву́, -вёшь**; *impf* **наплыва́ть**) *сов* (*перен*: *воспоминания*) to come flooding back; **наплыва́ть** (*perf* **наплы́ть**) **на** *+acc* (*на мель, на камень*) to run against
напова́л *нареч* (*убить*) outright
нап|ои́ть (**-ою́, -о́ишь**) *сов от* **пои́ть**
напока́з *нареч* for show
напо́лн|ить (**-ю, -ишь**; *impf* **наполня́ть**) *сов перех +instr* to fill with; **напо́лниться** (*impf* **наполня́ться**) *сов возв*: **напо́лниться** *+instr* to fill with
наполови́ну *нареч* by half; (*наполнить*) half
напомина́|ть (**-ю**) *несов от* **напо́мнить** ▷ *перех* (*иметь сходство*) to resemble
напо́мн|ить (**-ю, -ишь**; *impf* **напомина́ть**) *сов (не)перех*: **напо́мнить кому́-н** *+acc или* **о** *+prp* to remind sb of
напо́р (**-а**) *м* pressure
напосле́док *нареч* finally
напра́в|ить (**-лю, -ишь**; *impf* **направля́ть**) *сов перех* to direct; (*к врачу*) to refer; (*послание*) to send; **напра́виться** (*impf* **направля́ться**) *сов возв*: **напра́виться в** *+acc*/**к** *+dat итп* to make for
направле́ни|е (**-я**) *ср* direction; (*деятельности*: *также Воен*) line; (*политики*) orientation; (*документ*: *в больницу*) referral; (: *на работу, на учёбу*) directive; **по направле́нию к** *+dat* towards
напра́во *нареч* (*идти*) (to the) right
напра́сно *нареч* in vain
напра́шива|ться (**-юсь**) *несов от* **напроси́ться**
наприме́р *вводн сл* for example *или* instance
напрока́т *нареч*: **взять напрока́т** to hire; **отдава́ть** (*perf* **отда́ть**) **напрока́т** to hire out
напролёт *нареч* without a break
напроло́м *нареч* stopping at nothing

напр|оси́ться (**-ошу́сь, -о́сишься**; *impf* **напра́шиваться**) *сов возв* (*разг*: *в гости*) to force o.s.; **напра́шиваться** (*perf* **напроси́ться**) **на** *+acc* (*на комплимент*) to invite

напро́тив *нареч* opposite
▷ *вводн сл* on the contrary
▷ *предл +gen* opposite

напряга́|ть(ся) (**-ю(сь)**) *несов от* **напря́чь(ся)**

напряже́ни|е (**-я**) *ср* tension; (*Физ*: *механическое*) strain, stress; (: *электрическое*) voltage

напряжённый *прил* tense; (*отношения, встреча*) strained

напрями́к *нареч* (*идти*) straight

напр|я́чь (**-ягу́, -яжёшь** *итп*, **-ягу́т**; *pt* **-я́г, -ягла́**, *impf* **напряга́ть**) *сов перех* to strain; **напря́чься** (*impf* **напряга́ться**) *сов возв* (*мускулы*) to become tense; (*человек*) to strain o.s.

напыл|и́ть (**-ю́, -и́шь**) *сов от* **пыли́ть**

напы́щенный *прил* pompous

наравне́ *нареч*: **наравне́ с** *+instr* (*по одной линии*) on a level with; (*на равных правах*) on an equal footing with

нарас|ти́ (*3sg* **-тёт**, *impf* **нараста́ть**) *сов* (*проценты*) to accumulate; (*волнение, сопротивление*) to grow

нарасхва́т *нареч* like hot cakes

нара́щива|ть (**-ю**) *несов перех* (*темпы, объём итп*) to increase

нарв|а́ть (**-у́, -ёшь**) *сов (не)перех* (*+acc или +gen*: *цветов, ягод*) to pick; **нарва́ться** (*impf* **нарыва́ться**) *сов возв* (*разг*): **нарва́ться на** *+acc* (*на хулигана*) to run up against; (*на неприятность*) to run into

наре́|зать (**-жу, -жешь**; *impf* **нареза́ть**) *сов перех* to cut

наре́чи|е (**-я**) *ср* (*Линг*: *часть речи*) adverb; (: *говоры*) dialect

нарис|ова́ть (**-у́ю**) *сов от* **рисова́ть**

наркоби́знес (**-а**) *м* drug trafficking

наркодел|е́ц (**-ьца́**) *м* drug dealer

нарко́з (**-а**) *м* (*Мед*) anaesthesia (*Brit*), anesthesia (*US*)

наркологи́ческий *прил*: **наркологи́ческий диспансе́р** drug-abuse clinic

наркома́н (**-а**) *м* drug addict *или* abuser; **наркома́ни|я** (**-и**) *ж* (*Мед*) drug addiction *или* abuse

нарко́тик (**-а**) *м* drug

наркоти́ческий *прил* (*средства*) drug

наро́д (**-а**; *part gen* **-у**) *м* people *мн*; **наро́дност|ь** (**-и**) *ж* nation

наро́дный *прил* national; (*фронт*) popular; (*искусство*) folk

нарочи́тый *прил* deliberate; **наро́чно** *нареч* purposely, on purpose; **как наро́чно** (*разг*) to make things worse

нар|уби́ть (**-ублю́, -у́бишь**; *impf* **наруба́ть**) *сов (не)перех +acc или +gen* to chop

нару́жност|ь (**-и**) *ж* appearance; **нару́жный** *прил* (*дверь, стена*) exterior; (*спокойствие*) outward; **нару́жу** *нареч* out

нару́чник (**-а**) *м* (*обычн мн*) handcuff

нару́чн|ый *прил*: **нару́чные часы́** (wrist)watch *ед*

наруша́|ть(ся) (**-ю(сь)**) *несов от* **нару́шить(ся)**

наруши́тел|ь (**-я**) *м* (*закона*) transgressor; (*Юр*: *порядка*) offender; **наруши́тель грани́цы**

Н

person who illegally crosses a border; **наруши́тель дисципли́ны** troublemaker

нару́ш|ить (**-у, -ишь**; *impf* **наруша́ть**) *сов перех* (*покой*) to disturb; (*связь*) to break; (*правила, договор*) to violate; (*дисциплину*) to breach; **наруша́ть** (*perf* **нару́шить**) **грани́цу** to illegally cross a border; **нару́шиться** (*impf* **наруша́ться**) *сов возв* to be broken *или* disturbed

нары́в (**-а**) *м* (*Мед*) abscess, boil

наря́д (**-а**) *м* (*одежда*) attire; (*красивый*) outfit; (*распоряжение*) directive; (*Комм*) order; **нар|яди́ть** (**-яжу́, -я́дишь**; *impf* **наряжа́ть**) *сов перех* (*одеть*) to dress; **наряжа́ть** (*perf* **наряди́ть**) **ёлку** ≈ to decorate (*Brit*) *или* trim (*US*) the Christmas tree; **наряди́ться** (*impf* **наряжа́ться**) *сов возв*: **наряди́ться** (**в** *+acc*) to dress o.s. (in); **наря́дный** *прил* (*человек*) well-dressed; (*комната, улица*) nicely decorated; (*шляпа, платье*) fancy

наряду́ *нареч*: **наряду́ с** *+instr* along with; (*наравне*) on an equal footing with

наряжа́|ть(ся) (**-ю(сь)**) *несов от* **наряди́ть(ся)**

нас *мест см* **мы**

насеко́м|ое (**-ого**) *ср* insect

населе́ни|е (**-я**) *ср* population

населённый *прил* (*район*) populated; **населённый пункт** locality

насел|и́ть (**-ю́, -и́шь**; *impf* **населя́ть**) *сов перех* (*регион*) to settle

населя́|ть (**-ю**) *несов от* **насели́ть** ▷ *перех* (*проживать*) to inhabit

насе́ч|ка (**-ки**; *gen pl* **-ек**) *ж* notch

наси́ли|е (**-я**) *ср* violence; **наси́л|овать** (**-ую**; *perf* **изнаси́ловать**) *несов перех* (*женщину*) to rape

наси́льственный *прил* violent

наска́кива|ть (**-ю**) *несов от* **наскочи́ть**

наскво́зь *нареч* through

наско́лько *нареч* so much

наск|очи́ть (**-очу́, -о́чишь**; *impf* **наска́кивать**) *сов*: **наскочи́ть на** *+acc* to run into

наску́ч|ить (**-у, -ишь**) *сов*: **наску́чить кому́-н** to bore sb

насла|ди́ться (**-жу́сь, -ди́шься**; *impf* **наслажда́ться**) *сов возв* *+instr* to relish

наслажде́ни|е (**-я**) *ср* enjoyment, relish

насле́ди|е (**-я**) *ср* (*культурное*) heritage; (*идеологическое*) legacy

насле́д|овать (**-ую**) *(не)сов перех* to inherit; (*престол*) to succeed to

насле́дств|о (**-а**) *ср* (*имущество*) inheritance; (*культурное*) heritage; (*идеологическое*) legacy

наслы́шан *как сказ*: **я наслы́шан об э́том** I have heard a lot about it

насма́рку *нареч* (*разг*): **идти́ насма́рку** to be wasted

на́смерть *нареч* (*сражаться*) to the death; (*ранить*) fatally

насмеха́|ться (**-юсь**) *несов возв*: **насмеха́ться над** *+instr* to taunt

насмеш|и́ть (**-у́, -и́шь**) *сов от* **смеши́ть**

насмея́|ться (**-юсь**) *сов возв*: **насмея́ться над** *+instr* to offend

на́сморк (**-а**) *м* runny nose

насовсе́м *нареч* (*разг*) for good

насор|и́ть (**-ю́, -и́шь**) *сов от* **сори́ть**

насо́с (**-а**) *м* pump

наста|ва́ть (*3sg* **-ёт**) *несов от*

настать
наста́ива|ть (**-ю**) *несов от* **настоя́ть**
наста́|ть (*3sg* **-нет**, *impf* **настава́ть**) *сов* to come; (*ночь*) to fall
на́стежь *нареч* (*открыть*) wide
насти́|чь (**-гну, -гнешь**; *pt* **-г, -гла**, *impf* **настига́ть**) *сов перех* to catch up with
насто́йчивый *прил* persistent; (*просьба*) insistent
насто́лько *нареч* so
насто́льный *прил* (*лампа, часы*) table; (*календарь*) desk
настороже́ *как сказ*: **он всегда́ настороже́** he is always on the alert
насторож|и́ть (**-у́, -и́шь**; *impf* **насторáживать**) *сов перех* to alert; **насторожи́ться** (*impf* **насторáживаться**) *сов возв* to become more alert
настоя́ни|е (**-я**) *ср*: **по настоя́нию кого́-н** on sb's insistence
настоя́тельный *прил* (*просьба*) persistent; (*задача*) urgent
настоя́щ|ий *прил* real; (*момент*) present; **по-настоя́щему** (*как надо*) properly; (*преданный*) really; **настоя́щее вре́мя** (*Линг*) the present tense
настра́ива|ть(ся) (**-ю(сь)**) *несов от* **настро́ить(ся)**
настрое́ни|е (**-я**) *ср* mood; (*антивоенное*) feeling; **не в настрое́нии** in a bad mood
настро́|ить (**-ю, -ишь**; *impf* **настра́ивать**) *сов перех* (*пианино итп*) to tune; (*механизм*) to adjust; **настра́ивать** (*perf* **настро́ить**) **кого́-н на** *+acc* to put sb in the right frame of mind for; **настра́ивать** (*perf* **настро́ить**) **кого́-н про́тив** *+gen* to incite sb against; **настро́иться** (*impf* **настра́иваться**) *сов возв*: **настро́иться** (*perf*) *+infin* to be disposed to do
настро́|й (**-я**) *м* mood
настро́йщик (**-а**) *м*: **настро́йщик роя́ля** piano tuner
наступа́|ть (**-ю**) *несов от* **наступи́ть** ▷ *неперех* (*Воен*) to go on the offensive
наст|упи́ть (**-уплю́, -у́пишь**; *impf* **наступа́ть**) *сов* to come; (*ночь*) to fall; **наступа́ть** (*perf* **наступи́ть**) **на** *+acc* (*на камень итп*) to step on
наступле́ни|е (**-я**) *ср* (*Воен*) offensive; (*весны, старости*) beginning; (*темноты*) fall
на́сухо *нареч*: **вы́тереть что-н на́сухо** to dry sth thoroughly
насу́щный *прил* vital
насчёт *предл +gen* regarding
насчита́|ть (**-ю**; *impf* **насчи́тывать**) *сов перех* to count
насчи́тыва|ть (**-ю**) *несов от* **насчита́ть** ▷ *неперех* to have
насы́п|ать (**-лю, -лешь**; *impf* **насыпа́ть**) *сов перех* to pour
на́сып|ь (**-и**) *ж* embankment
ната́лкива|ть(ся) (**-ю(сь)**) *несов от* **натолкну́ть(ся)**
натвор|и́ть (**-ю́, -и́шь**) *сов (не) перех* (*+acc или +gen*: *разг*) to get up to
нат|ере́ть (**-ру́, -рёшь**; *pt* **-ёр, -ёрла**, *impf* **натира́ть**) *сов перех* (*ботинки, полы*) to polish; (*морковь, сыр итп*) to grate; (*ногу*) to chafe
на́тиск (**-а**) *м* pressure
наткн|у́ться (**-у́сь, -ёшься**; *impf* **натыка́ться**) *сов возв*: **наткну́ться на** *+acc* to bump into
НАТО *ср сокр* NATO (= *North*

Atlantic Treaty Organization)
натолкн|у́ть (**-у́, -ёшь**; *impf* **ната́лкивать**) *сов перех*: **натолкну́ть кого́-н на** *+acc* (*на идею*) to lead sb to; **натолкну́ться** (*impf* **ната́лкиваться**) *сов возв*: **натолкну́ться на** *+acc* to bump into
натоща́к *нареч* on an empty stomach
на́три|й (**-я**) *м* sodium
нату́р|а (**-ы**) *ж* (*характер*) nature; (*натурщик*) model (*Art*); **нату́рой, в нату́ре** (*Экон*) in kind; **натура́льный** *прил* natural; (*мех, кожа*) real; **нату́рщик** (**-а**) *м* model (*Art*)
натыка́|ться (**-юсь**) *несов от* **наткну́ться**
натюрмо́рт (**-а**) *м* still life
натя́гива|ть(ся) (**-ю**) *несов от* **натяну́ть(ся)**
натя́нутый *прил* strained
нат|яну́ть (**-яну́, -я́нешь**; *impf* **натя́гивать**) *сов перех* to pull tight; (*перчатки*) to pull on; **натяну́ться** (*impf* **натя́гиваться**) *сов возв* to tighten
науга́д *нареч* at random
нау́к|а (**-и**) *ж* science; **есте́ственные нау́ки** science; **гуманита́рные нау́ки** arts
нау́тро *нареч* next morning
на|учи́ть(ся) (**-учу́(сь), -у́чишь(ся)**) *сов от* **учи́ть(ся)**
нау́чно-популя́рный *прил* science
нау́чно-техни́ческий *прил* scientific
нау́чный *прил* scientific
нау́шник (**-а**) *м* (*обычно мн*: *также* **магнитофо́нные нау́шники**) headphones
наха́л (**-а**) *м* (*разг*) cheeky beggar;
наха́льный *прил* cheeky
нахлы́н|уть (*3sg* **-ет**) *сов* to surge
нахму́р|ить(ся) (**-ю(сь), -ишь(ся)**) *несов от* **хму́рить(ся)**
нах|оди́ть (**-ожу́, -о́дишь**) *несов от* **найти́**; **находи́ться** *несов от* **найти́сь** ▷ *возв* (*дом, город*) to be situated; (*человек*) to be
нахо́д|ка (**-ки**; *gen pl* **-ок**) *ж* (*потерянного*) discovery; **он — нахо́дка для нас** he is a real find for us; **Бюро́ нахо́док** lost property office (*Brit*), lost and found (*US*)
нахо́дчивый *прил* resourceful
наце́л|ить (**-ю, -ишь**; *impf* **наце́ливать**) *сов перех*: **наце́лить кого́-н на** *+acc* to push sb towards; **наце́литься** *сов от* **це́литься**
наце́н|ка (**-ки**; *gen pl* **-ок**) *ж* (*на товар*) surcharge
национали́ст (**-а**) *м* nationalist
национа́льност|ь (**-и**) *ж* nationality; (*нация*) nation
национа́льный *прил* national
наци́ст (**-а**) *м* Nazi
на́ци|я (**-и**) *ж* nation; **Организа́ция Объединённых На́ций** United Nations Organization
нача|ди́ть (**-жу́, -ди́шь**) *сов от* **чади́ть**
нача́л|о (**-а**) *ср* beginning, start; **быть** (*impf*) **под нача́лом кого́-н** *или* **у кого́-н** to be under sb
нача́льник (**-а**) *м* (*руководитель*) boss; (*цеха*) floor manager; (*управления*) head
нача́льн|ый *прил* (*период*) initial; (*глава книги*) first; **нача́льная шко́ла** (*Просвещ*) primary (*Brit*) *или* elementary (*US*) school; **нача́льные кла́ссы** (*Просвещ*) *the first three classes of primary school*

Нача́льные кла́ссы

Children start school at the age of six or seven. There are no separate primary schools in Russia. The first three classes of the 10-year education system are referred to as **нача́льные кла́ссы**. The main emphasis is on reading, writing and arithmetic. Other subjects taught include drawing, PE and singing.

нача́льств|о (**-а**) *ср* (*власть*) authority ▷ *собир* (*руководители*) management
нач|а́ть (**-ну́, -нёшь**; *impf* **начина́ть**) *сов перех* to begin, start
начеку́ *нареч*: **быть начеку́** to be on one's guard
на́черно *нареч* roughly
нач|ерти́ть (**-ерчу́, -е́ртишь**) *сов от* **черти́ть**
начина́ни|е (**-я**) *ср* initiative
начина́|ть (**-ю**) *несов от* **нача́ть**
начина́ющ|ий *прил* (*писатель*) novice ▷ (**-его**) *м* beginner
начина́я *предл* (*+instr: включая*) including; **начина́я с** *+gen* from; (*при отсчёте*) starting from; **начина́я от** *+gen* (*включая*) including
начин|и́ть (**-ю́, -и́шь**; *impf* **начиня́ть**) *сов перех* (*пирог*) to fill
начи́н|ка (**-ки**; *gen pl* **-ок**) *ж* filling
начну́ *итп сов см* **нача́ть**
наш (**-его**; *см Table 9*; *f* **-а**, *nt* **-е**, *pl* **-и**) *притяж мест* our; **чей э́то дом? — наш** whose is this house? — ours; **чьи э́то кни́ги? — на́ши** whose are these books? — ours; **по-на́шему** our way; (*по нашему мнению*) in our opinion
наше́стви|е (**-я**) *ср* invasion
нащу́па|ть (**-ю**; *impf* **нащу́пывать**) *сов перех* to find
НДС *м сокр* (= *нало́г на доба́вленную сто́имость*) VAT (= *value-added tax*)
не *част* not; **не я написа́л э́то письмо́** I didn't write this letter; **я не рабо́таю** I don't work; **не пла́чьте/опозда́йте** don't cry/be late; **не могу́ не согласи́ться/не возрази́ть** I can't help agreeing/objecting; **не мне на́до помо́чь, а ему́** I am not the one who needs help, he is; **не до** *+gen* no time for; **мне не до тебя́** I have no time for you; **не без того́** (*разг*) that's about it; **не то** (*разг: в противном случае*) or else
небе́сный *прил* (*тела́*) celestial; (*перен*) heavenly; **небе́сный цвет** sky blue
неблагода́рный *прил* ungrateful; (*работа*) thankless
не́б|о (**-а**; *nom pl* **небеса́**, *gen pl* **небе́с**) *ср* sky; (*Рел*) heaven
небольшо́й *прил* small
небоскло́н (**-а**) *м* sky above the horizon
небоскрёб (**-а**) *м* skyscraper
небре́жный *прил* careless
небыва́лый *прил* unprecedented
нева́жно *нареч* (*делать что-н*) not very well ▷ *как сказ* it's not important
нева́жный *прил* unimportant; (*не очень хороший*) poor
неве́дени|е (**-я**) *ср* ignorance; **он пребыва́ет в по́лном неве́дении** he doesn't know anything (about it)
неве́жественный *прил* ignorant; **неве́жеств|о** (**-а**) *ср* ignorance
невезе́ни|е (**-я**) *ср* bad luck
неве́рный *прил* (*ошибочный*)

Н

incorrect; (*муж*) unfaithful
невероя́тный *прил* improbable; (*чрезвычайный*) incredible
неве́ст|а (**-ы**) *ж* (*после помолвки*) fiancée; (*на свадьбе*) bride
неве́ст|ка (**-ки**; *gen pl* **-ок**) *ж* (*жена сына*) daughter-in-law; (*жена брата*) sister-in-law
невзго́д|а (**-ы**) *ж* adversity *ед*
невзира́я *предл*: **невзира́я на** *+acc* in spite of
невзл|юби́ть (**-юблю́, -ю́бишь**) *сов перех* to take a dislike to
невзнача́й *нареч* (*разг*) by accident
неви́данный *прил* unprecedented
неви́димый *прил* invisible
неви́нный *прил* innocent
невино́вный *прил* innocent
невня́тный *прил* muffled
не́вод (**-а**) *м* fishing net
невозмо́жно *нареч* (*большой, трудный*) impossibly ▷ *как сказ* (*+infin*: *сделать, найти итп*) it is impossible to do; **(э́то) невозмо́жно** that's impossible; **невозмо́жный** *прил* impossible
нево́л|я (**-и**) *ж* captivity
невооружённ|ый *прил* unarmed; **невооружённым гла́зом** (*без приборов*) with the naked eye; **э́то ви́дно невооружённым гла́зом** (*перен*) it's plain for all to see
невпопа́д *нареч* (*разг*) out of turn
неврасте́ник (**-а**) *м* neurotic
неврастени́|я (**-и**) *ж* (*Мед*) nervous tension
невыноси́мый *прил* unbearable, intolerable
негати́в (**-а**) *м* (*Фото*) negative
негати́вный *прил* negative
не́где *как сказ*: **не́где отдохну́ть** *итп* there is nowhere to rest *итп*; **мне не́где жить** I have nowhere to live
негла́сный *прил* secret
него́ *мест от* **он**; **оно́**
него́дност|ь (**-и**) *ж*: **приходи́ть** (*perf* **прийти́**) **в него́дность** (*оборудование*) to become defunct
негод|ова́ть (**-у́ю**) *несов* to be indignant
негра́мотный *прил* illiterate; (*работа*) incompetent
негритя́нский *прил* African-American
неда́вн|ий *прил* recent; **до неда́внего вре́мени** until recently; **неда́вно** *нареч* recently
недалёк|ий *прил* (*перен*: *человек, ум*) limited; **в недалёком бу́дущем** in the near future; **недалеко́** *нареч* (*жить, быть*) nearby; (*идти, ехать*) not far ▷ *как сказ*: **недалеко́ (до** *+gen***)** it isn't far (to); **недалеко́ от** *+gen* not far from
неда́ром *нареч* (*не напрасно*) not in vain; (*не без цели*) for a reason
недви́жимост|ь (**-и**) *ж* property; **недви́жим|ый** *прил*: **недви́жимое иму́щество = недви́жимость**
неде́л|я (**-и**) *ж* week; **че́рез неде́лю** in a week('s time); **на про́шлой/э́той/сле́дующей неде́ле** last/this/next week
недове́ри|е (**-я**) *ср* mistrust, distrust
недово́льств|о (**-а**) *ср*: **недово́льство (***+instr***)** dissatisfaction (with)
недоговор|и́ть (**-ю́, -и́шь**; *impf* **недогова́ривать**) *сов перех* to leave unsaid; **он что́-то недогова́ривает** there is something that he's not saying

недоеда́|ть (-ю) *несов* to eat badly
недолю́блива|ть (-ю) *несов перех* to dislike
недомога́ни|е (-я) *ср*: **чу́вствовать** (*impf*) **недомога́ние** to feel unwell
недомога́|ть (-ю) *несов* to feel unwell
недоно́шенный *прил*: **недоно́шенный ребёнок** premature baby
недооц|ени́ть (-еню́, -е́нишь; *impf* **недооце́нивать**) *сов перех* to underestimate
недоразуме́ни|е (-я) *ср* misunderstanding
недосмо́тр (-а) *м* oversight
недоста|ва́ть (*3sg* **-ёт**) *несов безл*: **мне недостаёт сме́лости** I lack courage; **мне недостаёт де́нег** I need money
недоста́точно *нареч* insufficiently ▷ *как сказ*: **у нас недоста́точно еды́/де́нег** we don't have enough food/money; **я недоста́точно зна́ю об э́том** I don't know enough about it
недоста́точный *прил* insufficient
недоста́ч|а (-и) *ж* (*мало*) lack; (*при проверке*) shortfall
недостаю́щий *прил* missing
недосто́йный *прил*: **недосто́йный** (*+gen*) unworthy (of)
недоумева́|ть (-ю) *несов* to be perplexed *или* bewildered
недочёт (-а) *м* (*в подсчётах*) shortfall; (*в работе*) deficiency
не́др|а (-) *мн* depths *мн*; **в не́драх земли́** in the bowels of the earth
неё *мест см* **она́**
нежда́нный *прил* unexpected
не́ж|иться (-усь, -ишься) *несов возв* to laze about
не́жный *прил* tender, gentle; (*кожа, пух*) soft; (*запах*) subtle
незабыва́емый *прил* unforgettable
незави́симо *нареч* independently; **незави́симо от** *+gen* regardless of; **незави́симост|ь** (-и) *ж* independence
незави́симый *прил* independent
незадо́лго *нареч*: **незадо́лго до** *+gen или* **пе́ред** *+instr* shortly before
незаме́тно *нареч* (*изменяться*) imperceptibly ▷ *как сказ* it isn't noticeable; **он незаме́тно подошёл** he approached unnoticed; **незаме́тный** *прил* barely noticeable; (*перен*: *человек*) unremarkable
незауря́дный *прил* exceptional
не́зачем *как сказ* (*разг*): **не́зачем ходи́ть/э́то де́лать** there's no reason to go/do it
нездоро́в|иться (*3sg* **-ится**) *несов безл*: **мне нездоро́вится** I feel unwell, I don't feel well
незнако́м|ец (-ца) *м* stranger
незначи́тельный *прил* (*сумма*) insignificant; (*факт*) trivial
неизбе́жный *прил* inevitable
неизве́стн|ый *прил* unknown ▷ (-ого) *м* stranger
неиме́ни|е (-я) *ср*: **за неиме́нием** *+gen* for want of
неимове́рный *прил* extreme
неиму́щий *прил* deprived
не́истовый *прил* intense
ней *мест см* **она́**
нейло́н (-а) *м* nylon
нейтра́льный *прил* neutral
не́кем *мест см* **не́кого**
не́к|ий (-ого; *f* **-ая**, *nt* **-ое**, *pl* **-ие**) *мест* a certain
не́когда *как сказ* (*читать*) there is

no time; **ей не́когда** she is busy; **ей не́когда** *+infin* **...** she has no time to ...

не́к|ого (*как* **кто**; см *Table 7*) *мест*: **не́кого спроси́ть/позва́ть** there is nobody to ask/call

не́кому *мест см* **не́кого**

не́котор|ый (**-ого**; *f* **-ая**, *nt* **-ое**, *pl* **-ые**) *мест* some

некроло́г (**-а**) *м* obituary

некста́ти *нареч* at the wrong time ▷ *как сказ*: **э́то некста́ти** this is untimely

не́кто *мест* a certain person

не́куда *как сказ* (*идти*) there is nowhere; **да́льше** *или* **ху́же/лу́чше не́куда** (*разг*) it can't get any worse/better

нелегити́мный *прил* illegitimate

неле́пый *прил* stupid

нелётн|ый *прил*: **нелётная пого́да** poor weather for flying

нельзя́ *как сказ* (*невозможно*) it is impossible; (*не разрешается*) it is forbidden; **нельзя́ ли?** would it be possible?; **как нельзя́ лу́чше** as well as could be expected

нём *мест см* **он**; **оно́**

неме́дленно *нареч* immediately; **неме́дленный** *прил* immediate

неме́|ть (**-ю**; *perf* **онеме́ть**) *несов* (*от ужаса, от восторга*) to be struck dumb; (*нога, рука*) to go numb

не́м|ец (**-ца**) *м* German; **неме́цкий** *прил* German; **неме́цкий язы́к** German

немину́емый *прил* unavoidable

не́м|ка (**-ки**; *gen pl* **-ок**) *ж от* **не́мец**

немно́г|ие (**-их**) *мн* few

немно́го *нареч* (*отдохнуть, старше*) a little, a bit *+gen* a few; (*денег*) a bit

немно́жко *нареч* (*разг*) = **немно́го**

нем|о́й *прил* (*человек*) with a speech impairment; (*перен*: *вопрос*) implied; **немо́й фильм** silent film

нему́ *мест от* **он**; **оно́**

ненави́|деть (**-жу, -дишь**) *несов перех* to hate; **не́навист|ь** (**-и**) *ж* hatred

нена́стный *прил* wet and dismal

нена́сть|е (**-я**) *ср* awful weather

ненорма́льн|ый *прил* abnormal; (*разг*: *сумасшедший*) mad ▷ (**-ого**) *м* (*разг*) crackpot

необита́емый *прил* (*место*) uninhabited; **необита́емый о́стров** desert island

необозри́мый *прил* vast

необходи́мо *как сказ* it is necessary; **мне необходи́мо с Ва́ми поговори́ть** I really need to talk to you; **необходи́мост|ь** (**-и**) *ж* necessity; **необходи́мый** *прил* necessary

необъя́тный *прил* vast

необыкнове́нный *прил* exceptional

необыча́йный *прил* = **необыкнове́нный**

необы́чный *прил* unusual

неожи́данност|ь (**-и**) *ж* surprise

неожи́данный *прил* unexpected

неотврати́мый *прил* inevitable

неотдели́мый *прил*: **неотдели́мый (от** *+gen*) inseparable (from)

не́откуда *как сказ*: **мне не́откуда де́нег взять** I can't get money from anywhere

неотло́жн|ый *прил* urgent; **неотло́жная медици́нская по́мощь** emergency medical service

неотрази́мый *прил* irresistible; (*впечатление*) powerful

неохо́т|а (**-ы**) *ж* (*разг*:

нежелание) reluctance ▷ *как сказ*: **мне неохóта спóрить** I don't feel like arguing
неоценúмый *прил* invaluable
непереxóдный *прил*: **непереxóдный глагóл** (*Линг*) intransitive verb
неповторúмый *прил* unique
непогóд|а (**-ы**) *ж* bad weather
неподвúжный *прил* motionless; (*взгляд*) fixed
неподдéльный *прил* genuine
неполáд|ки (**-ок**) *мн* fault *ед*
неполноцéнный *прил* inadequate, insufficient
непонятно *нареч* incomprehensibly ▷ *как сказ* it is incomprehensible; **мне э́то непонятно** I cannot understand this
непосрéдственный *прил* (*начальник*) immediate; (*результат, участник*) direct
непочáтый *прил*: **непочáтый край** no end, a great deal
неправд|а (**-ы**) *ж* lie ▷ *как сказ* it's not true; **э́то неправда!** this is a lie!
неправильно *нареч* (*решить*) incorrectly, wrongly ▷ *как сказ*: **э́то неправильно** it's wrong; **неправильный** *прил* wrong; (*форма, глагол*) irregular
непредсказýемый *прил* unpredictable
непреклóнный *прил* firm
непремéнный *прил* necessary
непрерывный *прил* continuous
непривычно *как сказ*: **мне непривычно** *+infin* I'm not used to doing
неприличный *прил* indecent
непристóйный *прил* obscene
неприязн|ь (**-и**) *ж* hostility
неприятно *как сказ +infin* it's unpleasant to; **мне неприятно говорить об э́том** I don't enjoy talking about it; **неприятност|ь** (**-и**) *ж* (*обычно мн*: *на работе, в семье*) trouble; **неприятный** *прил* unpleasant
непромокáемый *прил* waterproof
нерáвенств|о (**-а**) *ср* inequality
неравноправи|е (**-я**) *ср* inequality (of rights)
нерáвный *прил* unequal
неразберúх|а (**-и**) *ж* (*разг*) muddle
неразýмный *прил* unreasonable
нерв (**-а**) *м* (*Анат*) nerve; **нéрвы** (*вся система*) nervous system
нéрвнича|ть (**-ю**) *несов* to fret
нéрвный *прил* nervous
нервóзный *прил* (*человек*) nervous, highly (*Brit*) *или* high (*US*) strung
неряшливый *прил* (*человек, одежда*) scruffy; (*работа*) careless
нёс *несов см* **нести́**
несварéни|е (**-я**) *ср*: **несварéние желýдка** indigestion
несгибáемый *прил* staunch
нéскольк|о (**-их**) *чис +gen* a few ▷ *нареч* (*обидеться*) somewhat
нескрóмный *прил* (*человек*) immodest; (*вопрос*) indelicate; (*жест, предложение*) indecent
неслыханный *прил* unheard of
неслышно *нареч* (*сделать*) quietly ▷ *как сказ*: **мне неслышно** I can't hear
несмотря́ *предл*: **несмотря́ на** *+acc* in spite of, despite; **несмотря́ на то что ...** in spite of *или* despite the fact that ...; **несмотря́ ни на что** no matter what
несовершеннолéтн|ий (**-его**) *м* minor ▷ *прил*: **несовершеннолéтний ребёнок** minor

Н

несовершéнный *прил* flawed; **несовершéнный вид** (*Линг*) imperfective (aspect)
несовместúмый *прил* incompatible
несомнéнно *нареч* (*правильный, хороший итп*) indisputably ▷ *вводн сл* without a doubt ▷ *как сказ*: **это несомнéнно** this is indisputable; **несомнéнно, что он придёт** there is no doubt that he will come
несправедлúвост|ь (**-и**) *ж* injustice
несправедлúвый *прил* (*человек, суд, упрёк*) unfair, unjust
непростá *нареч* (*разг*) for a reason
нес|тú (**-ý, -ёшь**; *pt* **нёс, -лá**) *несов от* **носúть** ▷ *перех* to carry; (*влечь: неприятности*) to bring ▷ (*perf* **понестú**) (*службу*) to carry out ▷ (*perf* **снестú**) (*яйцо*) to lay; **нестúсь** *несов возв* (*человек, машина*) to race ▷ (*perf* **снестúсь**) (*курица*) to lay eggs
несчáстный *прил* unhappy; (*разг: жалкий*) wretched; **несчáстный слýчай** accident
несчáсть|е (**-я**) *ср* misfortune; **к несчáстью** unfortunately

КЛЮЧЕВОЕ СЛОВО

нет *част* **1** (*при отрицании, несогласии*) no; **ты соглáсен? — нет** do you agree? — no; **тебé не нрáвится мой суп? — нет, нрáвится** don't you like my soup? — yes, I do
2 (*для привлечения внимания*): **нет, ты тóлько посмотрú на негó!** would you just look at him!
3 (*выражает недоверие*): **нет, ты действúтельно не сéрдишься?** so you are really not angry?
▷ *как сказ* (*+gen*: *не имеется*: *об одном предмете*) there is no; (: *о нескольких предметах*) there are no; **нет врéмени** there is no time; **нет билéтов** *или* **билéтов нет** there are no tickets; **у меня нет дéнег** I have no money; **его нет в гóроде** he is not in town
▷ *союз* (*во фразах*): **нет — так нет** it can't be helped; **чегó тóлько нет!** what don't they have!; **нет чтóбы извинúться** (*разг*) instead of saying sorry

нетерпéни|е (**-я**) *ср* impatience; **с нетерпéнием ждать** (*impf*)/ **слýшать** (*impf*) to wait/listen impatiently; **с нетерпéнием жду Вáшего отвéта** I look forward to hearing from you
нетрéзв|ый *прил* drunk; **в нетрéзвом состоя́нии** drunk
нетрудовóй *прил*: **нетрудовóй дохóд** unearned income
нетрудоспосóбност|ь (**-и**) *ж* disability; **посóбие по нетрудоспосóбности** disability living allowance
нетрудоспосóбный *прил* *unable to work through disability*
нéтто *прил неизм* (*о весе*) net
неудáч|а (**-и**) *ж* bad luck; (*в делах*) failure
неудáчный *прил* (*попытка*) unsuccessful; (*фильм, стихи*) bad
неудóбно *нареч* (*расположенный, сидеть*) uncomfortably ▷ *как сказ* it's uncomfortable; (*неприлично*) it's awkward; **мне неудóбно** I am uncomfortable; **неудóбно задавáть лю́дям такúе вопрóсы** it's awkward to ask people such questions; **(мне) неудóбно сказáть**

ему́ об э́том I feel uncomfortable telling him that
неудо́бный *прил* uncomfortable
неудовлетвори́тельный *прил* unsatisfactory
неудово́льстви|е (**-я**) *ср* dissatisfaction
неуже́ли *част* really
неузнава́емост|ь (**-и**) *ж*: **до неузнава́емости** beyond (all) recognition
неукло́нный *прил* steady
неуклю́жий *прил* clumsy
неуме́стный *прил* inappropriate
неурожа́йный *прил*: **неурожа́йный год** year with a poor harvest
неуря́диц|а (**-ы**) *ж* (*разг*: *обычно мн*: *ссоры*) squabble
нефо́рма́льный *прил* (*организация*) informal
нефтедобыва́ющий *прил* (*промышленность*) oil
нефтедобы́ч|а (**-и**) *ж* drilling for oil
нефтеперерабо́тк|а (**-и**) *ж* oil processing
нефтепрово́д (**-а**) *м* oil pipeline
нефт|ь (**-и**) *ж* oil, petroleum
нефтя́ник (**-а**) *м* *worker in the oil industry*
нефтяно́й *прил* oil
нехва́тк|а (**-и**) *ж* *+gen* shortage of
нехорошо́ *наречь* badly ▷ *как сказ* it's bad; **мне нехорошо́** I'm not well
нечаянный *прил* unintentional; (*неожиданный*) chance
не́чего *как сказ*: **не́чего расска́за́ть** there is nothing to tell; (*разг*: *не следует*) there's no need to do; **не́ за что!** (*в ответ на благодарность*) not at all!, you're welcome! (*US*); **де́лать не́чего** there's nothing else to be done
нечётный *прил* (*число*) odd
не́что *мест* something
нея́сно *нареч*: **он нея́сно объясни́л положе́ние** he didn't explain the situation clearly ▷ *как сказ* it's not clear; **мне нея́сно, почему́ он отказа́лся** I'm not clear *или* it's not clear to me why he refused
нея́сный *прил* (*очертания, звук*) indistinct; (*мысль, вопрос*) vague

 **КЛЮЧЕВОЕ СЛОВО**

ни *част* **1** (*усиливает отрицание*) not a; **ни оди́н** not one, not a single; **она́ не произнесла́ ни сло́ва** she didn't say a word; **она́ ни ра́зу не пришла́** she didn't come once; **у меня́ не оста́лось ни рубля́** I don't have a single rouble left
2: **кто/что/как ни** who-/what-/ however; **ско́лько ни** however much; **что ни говори́** whatever you say; **как ни стара́йся** however hard you try
▷ *союз* (*при перечислении*): **ни …, ни …** neither … nor …; **ни за что** no way

нигде́ *нареч* nowhere; **его́ нигде́ не́ было** he was nowhere to be found; **нигде́ нет моёй кни́ги** I can't find my book anywhere, my book is nowhere to be found; **я нигде́ не мог пое́сть** I couldn't find anywhere to get something to eat
ни́же *сравн прил от* **ни́зкий** ▷ *сравн нареч от* **ни́зко** ▷ *нареч* (*далее*) later on ▷ *предл +gen* below
ни́жн|ий *прил* (*ступенька, ящик*) bottom; **ни́жний эта́ж** ground (*Brit*) *или* first (*US*) floor; **ни́жнее бельё**

Н

underwear; **нижняя юбка** underskirt

низ (**-а**) *м* (*стола, ящика итп*) bottom

низкий *прил* low

низко *нареч* low

низший *сравн прил от* **низкий**; (*звание*) junior

НИИ *м сокр* (= *научно-исследовательский институт*) scientific research institute

никак *нареч* (*никаким образом*) no way; **никак не могу запомнить это слово** I can't remember this word at all; **дверь никак не открывалась** the door just wouldn't open

никак|ой *мест*: **нет никакого сомнения** there is no doubt at all; **никакие деньги не помогли** no amount of money would have helped

никел|ь (**-я**) *м* (*Хим*) nickel

никогда *нареч* never; **как никогда** as never before

никого *мест см* **никто**

ник|ой *нареч*: **никоим образом** not at all; **ни в коем случае** under no circumstances

ни|кто (**-кого**; *как* **кто**; см *Table 7*) *мест* nobody

никуда *нареч*: **я никуда не поеду** I'm not going anywhere; **никуда я не поеду** I'm going nowhere; **это никуда не годится** that just won't do

ниоткуда *нареч* from nowhere; **ниоткуда нет помощи** I get no help from anywhere

нисколько *нареч* not at all; (*не лучше*) no; (*не рад*) at all

нит|ка (**-ки**; *gen pl* **-ок**) *ж* (*обычно мн*: *для шитья*) thread; (: *для вязания*) yarn

нит|ь (**-и**) *ж* = **нитка**

них *мест см* **они**

ничего *мест см* **ничто** ▷ *нареч* fairly well; **(это) ничего, что ...** it's all right that ...; **извините, я Вас побеспокою — ничего!** sorry to disturb you — it's all right!; **как живёшь? — ничего** how are you? — all right; **ничего себе** (*сносно*) fairly well; **ничего себе!** (*удивление*) well, I never!

нич|ей (**-ьего**; *f* **-ья**, *nt* **-ьё**, *pl* **-ьи**; *как* **чей**; см *Table 5*) *мест* nobody's

ничейн|ый *прил*: **ничейный результат/ничейная партия** draw

ничком *нареч* face down

нич|то (**-его**; *как* **что**; см *Table 7*) *мест, ср* nothing; **ничего подобного не видел** I've never seen anything like it; **ничего подобного!** (*разг*: *совсем не так*) nothing like it!; **ни за что!** (*ни в коем случае*) no way!; **ни за что не соглашайся** whatever you do, don't agree; **я здесь ни при чём** it has nothing to do with me; **ничего не поделаешь** there's nothing to be done

ничуть *нареч* (*нисколько*) not at all; (*не лучше, не больше*) no; (*не испугался, не огорчился*) at all

ничь|я (**-ей**) *ж* (*Спорт*) draw; **сыграть** (*perf*) **в ничью** to draw (*Brit*), tie (*US*)

нищенск|ий *прил* (*зарплата*) meagre (*Brit*), meager (*US*); **нищенская жизнь** life of begging

нищет|а (**-ы**) *ж* poverty

но *союз* but ▷ *межд*: **но!** gee up!

новенький *прил* (*разг*) new

новизн|а (**-ы**) *ж* novelty

новин|ка (**-ки**; *gen pl* **-ок**) *ж* new product

нович|ок (**-ка**) *м* newcomer; (*в классе*) new pupil

новобра́н|ец (**-ца**) *м* new recruit
новогодн|ий *прил* New Year; **новогодняя ёлка** ≈ Christmas tree
новорождённ|ый *прил* newborn ▷ (**-ого**) *м* newborn boy
новосёл (**-а**) *м* (*дома*) new owner
новосе́л|ье (**-ья**; *gen pl* **-ий**) *ср* house-warming (party)
но́вост|ь (**-и**; *gen pl* **-е́й**) *ж* news
но́вшеств|о (**-а**) *ср* (*явление*) novelty; (*метод*) innovation
но́в|ый *прил* new; **но́вая исто́рия** modern history; **Но́вый Заве́т** the New Testament; **Но́вая Зела́ндия** New Zealand
ног|а́ (**-и́**; *acc sg* **-у**, *nom pl* **-и**, *gen pl* **-**, *dat pl* **-а́м**) *ж* (*ступня*) foot; (*выше ступни*) leg; **вверх нога́ми** upside down
но́г|оть (**-тя**; *gen pl* **-те́й**) *м* nail
нож (**-а́**) *м* knife
но́ж|ка (**-ки**; *gen pl* **-ек**) *ж, уменьш от* **нога́**; (*стула, стола итп*) leg; (*циркуля*) arm
но́жниц|ы (**-**) *мн* scissors
ножно́й *прил* foot
ноздр|я́ (**-и́**; *nom pl* **-и**, *gen pl* **-е́й**) *ж* (*обычно мн*) nostril
нол|ь (**-я́**) *м* (*Мат*) zero, nought; (*о температуре*) zero; (*перен*: *человек*) nothing; **ноль це́лых пять деся́тых, 0.5** zero *или* nought point five, 0.5; **в де́сять ноль-ноль** at exactly ten o'clock
номенклату́р|а (**-ы**) *ж* (*товаров*) list ▷ *собир* (*работники*) nomenklatura
но́мер (**-а**; *nom pl* **-а́**) *м* number; (*журнала*) issue; (*в гостинице*) room; **но́мер маши́ны** registration (number)
номерно́й *прил*; **номерно́й знак (автомоби́ля)** (car) number (*Brit*) *или* license (*US*) plate
номер|о́к (**-ка́**) *ж* (*для пальто*) ≈ ticket
Норве́ги|я (**-и**) *ж* Norway
но́рм|а (**-ы**) *ж* standard; (*выработки*) rate
норма́льно *нареч* normally ▷ *как сказ*: **э́то вполне норма́льно** this is quite normal; **как дела́? — норма́льно** how are things? — not bad; **у нас всё норма́льно** everything's fine with us
норма́льный *прил* normal
нос (**-а**; *loc sg* **-у́**, *nom pl* **-ы́**) *м* nose; (*корабля*) bow; (*птицы*) beak, bill; (*ботинка*) toe
носи́л|ки (**-ок**) *мн* stretcher *ед*
носи́льщик (**-а**) *м* porter
носи́тел|ь (**-я**) *м* (*инфекции*) carrier; **носи́тель языка́** native speaker
но|си́ть (**-шу́, -сишь**) *несов перех* to carry; (*платье, очки*) to wear; (*усы, причёску*) to sport; (*фамилию мужа*) to use; **носи́ться** *несов возв* (*человек*) to rush; (*слухи*) to spread; (*одежда*) to wear; (*разг*: *увлекаться*): **носи́ться с** *+instr* (*с идеей*) to be preoccupied with; (*с человеком*) to make a fuss of
носов|о́й *прил* (*звук*) nasal; **носова́я часть** bow; **носово́й плато́к** handkerchief
нос|о́к (**-ка́**; *gen pl* **-о́к**) *м* (*обычно мн*: *чулок*) sock ▷ (*gen pl* **-ко́в**) (*ботинка, чулка, ноги*) toe
носоро́г (**-а**) *м* rhinoceros, rhino
ностальги́|я (**-и**) *ж* nostalgia
но́т|а (**-ы**) *ж* note; *см также* **но́ты**
нота́риус (**-а**) *м* notary (public)
но́т|ы (**-**) *мн* (*Муз*) sheet music
но́утбук (**-а**) *м* (*Комп*) laptop (computer)

ноч|евать (**-ую**; *perf* **переночевать**) *несов* to spend the night
ночёв|ка (**-ки**; *gen pl* **-ок**) *ж*: **остановиться на ночёвку** to spend the night
ночлег (**-а**) *м* (*место*) somewhere to spend the night; **останавливаться** (*perf* **остановиться**) **на ночлег** to spend the night
ночн|ой *прил* (*час, холод*) night; **ночная рубашка** nightshirt
ноч|ь (**-и**; *loc sg* **-и**, *nom pl* **-и**, *gen pl* **-ей**) *ж* night; **на ночь** before bed; **спокойной ночи!** good night!
ночью *нареч* at night
ношеный *прил* second-hand
ношу(сь) *несов см* **носить(ся)**
ноябр|ь (**-я**) *м* November
нрав (**-а**) *м* (*человека*) temperament; *см также* **нравы**
нрав|иться (**-люсь, -ишься**; *perf* **понравиться**) *несов возв*: **мне/им нравится этот фильм** I/they like this film; **мне нравится читать/гулять** I like to read *или* reading/to go for a walk
нравственный *прил* moral
нрав|ы (**-ов**) *мн* morals
н.с. *сокр* (= *нового стиля*) NS, New Style
НТР *ж сокр* = **научно-техническая революция**

КЛЮЧЕВОЕ СЛОВО

ну *межд* **1** (*выражает побуждение*) come on; **ну, начинай!** come on, get started!
2 (*выражает восхищение*) what; **ну и сила!** what strength!
3 (*выражает иронию*) well (well)
▷ *част* **1** (*неужели*): **(да) ну?!** not really?!
2 (*усиливает выразительность*): **ну конечно!** why of course!; **ну, я тебе покажу!** why, I'll show you!
3 (*допустим*): **ты говоришь по-английски?- ну, говорю** do you speak English — what if I do
4 (*во фразах*): **ну и ну!** (*разг*) well well!; **ну-ка!** (*разг*) come on!; **ну тебя/его!** (*разг*) forget it!

нудный *прил* tedious
нужд|а (**-ы**; *nom pl* **-ы**) *ж* (*no pl*: *бедность*) poverty; (*потребность*): **нужда (в** *+prp*) need (for)
нужда|ться (**-юсь**) *несов возв* (*бедствовать*) to be needy; **нуждаться** (*impf*) **в** *+prp* to need, be in need of
нужно *как сказ* (*необходимо*): **нужно, чтобы им помогли, нужно им помочь** it is necessary to help them; **мне нужно идти** I have to go, I must go; **мне нужно 10 рублей** I need 10 roubles; **очень нужно!** (*разг*) my foot!
нужный *прил* necessary
нулев|ой *прил*: **нулевая температура** temperature of zero; **нулевая отметка** (mark of) zero
нул|ь (**-я**) *м* (*Мат*) zero, nought; (*о температуре*) zero; (*перен*: *человек*) nothing; **начинать** (*perf* **начать**) **с нуля** to start from scratch
нумер|овать (**-ую**; *perf* **пронумеровать**) *несов перех* to number
ныне *нареч* today
нынешний *прил* the present
нырн|уть (**-у, -ёшь**) *сов* to dive
ныря|ть (**-ю**) *несов* to dive
ныть (**ною, ноешь**) *несов* (*рана*) to ache; (*жаловаться*) to moan
Нью-Йорк (**-а**) *м* New York
н.э. *сокр* (= *нашей эры*) AD (= *anno Domini*)

нюх (**-а**) *м* (*собаки*) nose
ню́ха|ть (**-ю**; *perf* **понюхать**) *несов перех* (*цветы, воздух*) to smell
ня́неч|ка (**-ки**; *gen pl* **-ек**) *ж* (*разг*) = **ня́ня**
ня́нч|ить (**-у, -ишь**) *несов перех* to mind; **ня́нчиться** *несов возв*: **ня́нчиться с** *+instr* (*с младенцем*) to mind
ня́н|ька (**-ьки**; *gen pl* **-ек**) *ж* (*разг*: *ребёнка*) nanny
ня́н|я (**-и**; *gen pl* **-ь**) *ж* nanny; (*работающая на дому*) child minder; (*в больнице*) auxiliary nurse; (*в детском саду*) cleaner; **приходя́щая ня́ня** babysitter

о *межд* oh ▷ *предл +prp* about; (*+acc*: *опереться, удариться*) against; (*споткнуться*) over
об *предл* = **о**
о́б|а (**-о́их**; см *Table 25*; *f* **о́бе**, *nt* **о́ба**) *м чис* both
обанкро́|титься (**-чусь, -тишься**) *сов возв* to go bankrupt
обая́ни|е (**-я**) *ср* charm; **обая́тельный** *прил* charming
обва́л (**-а**) *м* (*снежный*) avalanche; (*здания, экономики*) collapse
обвал|и́ться (*3sg* **-ится**, *impf* **обва́ливаться**) *сов возв* to collapse
обв|ести́ (**-еду́, -едёшь**; *pt* **-ёл, -ела́**, *impf* **обводи́ть**) *сов перех* (*букву, чертёж*) to go over; **обводи́ть** (*perf* **обвести́**) **вокру́г** *+gen* to lead *или* take round
обвине́ни|е (**-я**) *ср*: **обвине́ние**

(**в** +*prp*) accusation (of); (*Юр*) charge (of) ▷ *собир* (*обвиняющая сторона*) the prosecution

обвин|и́ть (**-ю́, -и́шь**; *impf* **обвиня́ть**) *сов перех*: **обвини́ть кого́-н** (**в** +*prp*) to accuse sb (of); (*Юр*) to charge sb (with)

обвиня́ем|ый (**-ого**) *м* the accused, the defendant

обвиня́|ть (**-ю**) *несов от* **обвини́ть** ▷ *перех* (*Юр*) to prosecute

об|ви́ть (**-овью́, -овьёшь**; *impf* **обвива́ть**) *сов перех* (*подлеж*: *плющ*) to twine around; **обвива́ть** (*perf* **обви́ть**) **кого́-н/что-н чем-н** to wind sth round sb/sth

обв|оди́ть (**-ожу́, -о́дишь**) *несов от* **обвести́**

обв|яза́ть (**-яжу́, -я́жешь**; *impf* **обвя́зывать**) *сов перех*: **обвяза́ть кого́-н/что-н чем-н** to tie sth round sb/sth; **обвяза́ться** (*impf* **обвя́зываться**) *сов возв*: **обвяза́ться чем-н** to tie sth round o.s.

обгоня́|ть (**-ю**) *несов от* **обогна́ть**

обгор|е́ть (**-ю́, -и́шь**; *impf* **обгора́ть**) *сов* (*дом*) to be burnt; (*на солнце*) to get sunburnt

обдира́|ть (**-ю**) *несов от* **ободра́ть**

обду́ма|ть (**-ю**; *impf* **обду́мывать**) *сов перех* to consider, think over

о́б|е (**-е́их**) *ж чис см* **о́ба**

обега́|ть (**-ю**) *несов от* **обежа́ть**

обе́д (**-а**) *м* lunch, dinner; (*время*) lunch *или* dinner time; **по́сле обе́да** after lunch *или* dinner; (*после 12 часов дня*) in the afternoon

обе́да|ть (**-ю**; *perf* **пообе́дать**) *несов* to have lunch *или* dinner

обе́денный *прил* (*стол, сервиз*) dinner; (*время*) lunch, dinner

обедне́|ть (**-ю**) *сов от* **бедне́ть**

обежа́ть (*как* **бежа́ть**; *см Table 20*; *impf* **обега́ть**) *сов*: **обежа́ть вокру́г** +*gen* to run round

обезбо́ливающ|ее (**-его**) *ср* painkiller

обезбо́л|ить (**-ю, -ишь**; *impf* **обезбо́ливать**) *сов перех* to anaesthetize (*Brit*), anesthetize (*US*)

обезвре́|дить (**-жу, -дишь**; *impf* **обезвре́живать**) *сов перех* (*бомбу*) to defuse; (*преступника*) to disarm

обездо́ленный *прил* deprived

обезору́ж|ить (**-у, -ишь**; *impf* **обезору́живать**) *сов перех* to disarm

обезу́ме|ть (**-ю**) *сов*: **обезу́меть от** +*gen* to go out of one's mind with

обе́их *чис см* **о́бе**

оберега́|ть (**-ю**) *несов перех* (*человека*) to protect

оберн|у́ть (**-у́, -ёшь**; *impf* **обёртывать** *или* **обора́чивать**) *сов перех* to wrap (up); **оберну́ться** (*impf* **обора́чиваться**) *сов возв* (*повернуться назад*) to turn (round); **обора́чиваться** (*perf* **оберну́ться**) +*instr* (*неприятностями*) to turn out to be

обёрт|ка (**-ки**; *gen pl* **-ок**) *ж* (*конфетная*) wrapper

обёрточн|ый *прил*: **обёрточная бума́га** wrapping paper

обёртыва|ть (**-ю**) *несов от* **оберну́ть**

обеспе́чени|е (**-я**) *ср* (*мира, договора*) guarantee; (+*instr*: *сырьём*) provision of; **материа́льное обеспе́чение** financial security

обеспе́ченност|ь (**-и**) *ж* (material) comfort; **фина́нсовая обеспе́ченность** financial security
обеспе́ч|ить (**-у, -ишь**; *impf* **обеспе́чивать**) *сов перех* (*семью*) to provide for; (*мир, успех*) to guarantee; **обеспе́чивать** (*perf* **обеспе́чить**) **кого́-н/что-н чем-н** to provide *или* supply sb/sth with sth
обесси́ле|ть (**-ю**; *impf* **обесси́левать**) *сов* to become *или* grow weak
обесцве́|тить (**-чу, -тишь**; *impf* **обесцве́чивать**) *несов перех* to bleach
обеща́ни|е (**-я**) *ср* promise
обеща́|ть (**-ю**; *perf* **обеща́ть** *или* **пообеща́ть**) *несов (не)перех* to promise
обжа́ловани|е (**-я**) *ср* appeal; **обжа́л|овать** (**-ую**) *сов перех* to appeal against
об|же́чь (**-ожгу́, -ожжёшь** *etc*, **-ожгу́т**; *pt* **-жёг, -ожгла́, -ожгло́**, *impf* **обжига́ть**) *сов перех* to burn; (*кирпич итп*) to fire; (*подлеж*: *крапива*) to sting; **обже́чься** (*impf* **обжига́ться**) *сов возв* to burn o.s.
обзо́р (**-а**) *м* view; (*новостей*) review; **обзо́рный** *прил* general
обива́|ть (**-ю**) *несов от* **оби́ть**
оби́вк|а (**-и**) *ж* upholstery
оби́д|а (**-ы**) *ж* insult; (*горечь*) grievance; **кака́я оби́да!** what a pity!; **быть** (*impf*) **в оби́де на кого́-н** to be in a huff with sb
оби́|деть (**-жу, -дишь**; *impf* **обижа́ть**) *сов перех* to hurt, offend; **оби́деться** (*impf* **обижа́ться**) *сов возв*: **оби́деться** (**на** *+acc*) to be hurt *или* offended (by)
оби́дно *как сказ* (*см прил*) it's offensive; it's upsetting; **мне оби́дно слы́шать э́то** it hurts me to hear this
обижа́|ть(ся) (**-ю(сь)**) *несов от* **оби́деть(ся)**
оби́льный *прил* abundant
обита́|ть (**-ю**) *несов* to live
об|и́ть (**-обью́, -обьёшь**; *imper* **обе́й(те)**, *impf* **обива́ть**) *сов перех*: **оби́ть** (*+instr*) to cover (with)
обихо́д (**-а**) *м*: **быть в обихо́де** to be in use
обкле́|ить (**-ю, -ишь**; *impf* **обкле́ивать**) *сов перех* (*плакатами*) to cover; (*обоями*) to (wall)paper
обкра́дыва|ть (**-ю**) *несов от* **обокра́сть**
обл. *сокр* = **о́бласть**
обла́в|а (**-ы**) *ж* (*на преступников*) roundup
облага́|ть (**-ю**) *несов от* **обложи́ть**
облада́|ть (**-ю**) *несов +instr* to possess
о́блак|о (**-а**; *nom pl* **-а́**, *gen pl* **-о́в**) *ср* cloud
областно́й *прил* ≈ regional; **о́бласт|ь** (**-и**; *gen pl* **-е́й**) *ж* region; (*Админ*) ≈ region, oblast; (*науки, искусства*) field
о́блачный *прил* cloudy
облега́|ть (**-ю**) *несов от* **обле́чь** ▷ *перех* to fit
облегче́ни|е (**-я**) *ср* (*жизни*) improvement; (*успокоение*) relief
облегч|и́ть (**-у́, -и́шь**; *impf* **облегча́ть**) *сов перех* (*вес*) to lighten; (*жизнь*) to make easier; (*боль*) to ease
обле́з|ть (**-у, -ешь**; *impf* **облеза́ть**) *сов* (*разг*) to grow mangy; (*краска, обои*) to peel (off)
облека́|ть (**-ю**) *несов от* **обле́чь**

О

обле|те́ть (**-чу́, -ти́шь**; *impf* **облета́ть**) *сов перех* to fly round ▷ *неперех* (*листья*) to fall off

облива́|ть (**-ю**) *несов от* **обли́ть**; **облива́ться** *несов от* **обли́ться** ▷ *возв*: **облива́ться слеза́ми** to be in floods of tears

обл|иза́ть (**-ижу́, -и́жешь**; *impf* **обли́зывать**) *сов перех* to lick

о́блик (**-а**) *м* appearance

об|ли́ть (**-олью́, -ольёшь**; *impf* **облива́ть**) *сов перех*: **обли́ть кого́-н/что-н чем-н** (*намеренно*) to pour sth over sb/sth; (*случайно*) to spill sth over sb/sth; **обли́ться** (*impf* **облива́ться**) *сов возв*: **обли́ться чем-н** (*водой*) to sluice o.s. with sth

обл|ожи́ть (**-ожу́, -о́жишь**; *impf* **облага́ть**) *сов перех*: **обложи́ть нало́гом** to tax

обло́ж|ка (**-ки**; *gen pl* **-ек**) *ж* (*книги, тетради*) cover

облок|оти́ться (**-очу́сь, -о́тишься**) *сов возв*: **облокоти́ться на** *+acc* to lean one's elbows on

обло́м|ок (**-ка**) *м* fragment

облысе́|ть (**-ю**) *сов от* **лысе́ть**

обмакн|у́ть (**-у́, -ёшь**; *impf* **обма́кивать**) *сов перех*: **обмакну́ть что-н в** *+acc* to dip sth into

обма́н (**-а**) *м* deception

обм|ану́ть (**-ану́, -а́нешь**; *impf* **обма́нывать**) *сов перех* to deceive; (*поступить нечестно*) to cheat

обма́нчивый *прил* deceptive

обма́нывa|ть (**-ю**) *несов от* **обману́ть**

обма́тыва|ть (**-ю**) *несов от* **обмота́ть**

обме́н (**-а**) *м* exchange; (*документов*) renewal; (*также* **обме́н веще́ств**: *Био*) metabolism; (*также* **обме́н жилпло́щадью**) exchange (*of flats etc*)

обме́нный *прил* exchange

обменя́|ть (**-ю**; *impf* **обме́нивать**) *сов перех* (*вещи, билеты*) to change; **обменя́ться** (*impf* **обме́ниваться**) *сов возв*: **обменя́ться** *+instr* to exchange

обморо́|зить (**-жу, -зишь**; *impf* **обмора́живать**) *сов перех*: **обморо́зить но́гу** to get frostbite in one's foot

о́бморок (**-а**) *м* faint; **па́дать** (*perf* **упа́сть**) **в о́бморок** to faint

обмота́|ть (**-ю**; *impf* **обма́тывать**) *сов перех*: **обмота́ть кого́-н/что-н чем-н** to wrap sth round sb/sth

обм|ы́ть (**-о́ю, -о́ешь**; *impf* **обмыва́ть**) *сов перех* (*рану*) to bathe; (*разг*: *событие*) to celebrate (*by drinking*)

обнагле́|ть (**-ю**) *сов от* **нагле́ть**

обнадёж|ить (**-у, -ишь**; *impf* **обнадёживать**) *сов перех* to reassure

обнажённый *прил* bare

обнаж|и́ть (**-у́, -и́шь**; *impf* **обнажа́ть**) *сов перех* to expose; (*руки, ноги*) to bare; (*ветки*) to strip bare; **обнажи́ться** (*impf* **обнажа́ться**) *сов возв* to be exposed; (*человек*) to strip

обнару́ж|ить (**-у, -ишь**; *impf* **обнару́живать**) *сов перех* (*найти*) to find; (*проявить*) to show; **обнару́житься** (*impf* **обнару́живаться**) *сов возв* (*найтись*) to be found; (*стать явным*) to become evident

обн|ести́ (**-есу́, -есёшь**; *pt* **-ёс, -есла́, -есло́**, *impf* **обноси́ть**) *сов перех*: **обнести́ что-н/кого́-н**

вокру́г *+gen* to carry sth/sb round; (*огородить*): **обнести́ что-н чем-н** to surround sth with sth
обнима́|ть(ся) (**-ю(сь)**) *несов от* **обня́ть(ся)**
обни́мк|а *ж*: **в обни́мку** (*разг*) with their arms around each other
обнов|и́ть (**-лю́, -и́шь**; *impf* **обновля́ть**) *сов перех* (*оборудование, гардероб*) to replenish; (*репертуар*) to refresh; (*старую мебель*) to upcycle; **обнови́ться** (*impf* **обновля́ться**) *сов возв* (*репертуар*) to be refreshed; (*организм*) to be regenerated
обн|я́ть (**-иму́, -и́мешь**; *pt* **-ял, -яла́, -яло**, *impf* **обнима́ть**) *сов перех* to embrace; **обня́ться** (*impf* **обнима́ться**) *сов возв* to embrace (each other)
обо *предл* = **о**
обобщ|и́ть (**-у́, -и́шь**; *impf* **обобща́ть**) *сов перех* (*факты*) to generalize from; (*статью*) to summarize
обога|ти́ть (**-щу́, -ти́шь**; *impf* **обогаща́ть**) *сов перех* to enrich; **обогати́ться** (*impf* **обогаща́ться**) *сов возв* (*человек, страна*) to be enriched
обогре́|ть (**-ю**; *impf* **обогрева́ть**) *сов перех* (*помещение*) to heat; (*человека*) to warm
о́б|од (**-ода**; *nom pl* **-о́дья**, *gen pl* **-о́дьев**) *м* rim; (*ракетки*) frame
об|одра́ть (**-деру́, -дерёшь**; *impf* **обдира́ть**) *сов перех* (*кору, шкуру*) to strip; (*руки*) to scratch
ободр|и́ть (**-ю́, -и́шь**; *impf* **ободря́ть**) *сов перех* to encourage
обо́з (**-а**) *м* convoy
обознача́|ть (**-ю**) *несов от* **обозна́чить** ▷ *перех* to signify
обозна́ч|ить (**-у, -ишь**; *impf* **обознача́ть**) *сов перех* (*границу*) to mark; (*слово*) to mean
обозрева́тел|ь (**-я**) *м* (*событий*) observer; (*на радио итп*) editor
обозре́ни|е (**-я**) *ср* review
обо́|и (**-ев**) *мн* wallpaper *ед*
обо́их *чис см* **о́ба**
обойти́ (*как* **идти́**; *см Table 18*; *impf* **обходи́ть**) *сов перех* to go round; (*закон*) to get round; (*обогнать*) to pass; **обойти́сь** (*impf* **обходи́ться**) *сов возв* (*уладиться*) to turn out well; (*стоить*): **обойти́сь в** *+acc* to cost; **обходи́ться** (*perf* **обойти́сь**) **с кем-н/чем-н** to treat sb/sth; **обходи́ться** (*perf* **обойти́сь**) **без** *+gen* (*разг*) to get by without
об|окра́сть (**-краду́, -крадёшь**; *impf* **обкра́дывать**) *сов перех* to rob
обоня́ни|е (**-я**) *ср* sense of smell
обора́чива|ть(ся) (**-ю(сь)**) *несов от* **оберну́ть(ся)**
оборв|а́ть (**-у́, -ёшь**; *pt* **-а́л, -ала́, -а́ло**, *impf* **обрыва́ть**) *сов перех* (*верёвку*) to break; (*ягоды, цветы*) to pick; (*перен*: *разговор, дружбу*) to break off; (: *разг*: *говорящего*) to cut short; **оборва́ться** (*impf* **обрыва́ться**) *сов возв* (*верёвка*) to break; (*перен*: *жизнь, разговор*) to be cut short
оборо́н|а (**-ы**) *ж* defence (*Brit*), defense (*US*); **оборо́нный** *прил* defence (*Brit*), defense (*US*); **обороня́|ть** (**-ю**) *несов перех* to defend; **обороня́ться** *несов возв* (*защищаться*) to defend o.s.
оборо́т (**-а**) *м* (*полный круг*) revolution; (*Комм*) turnover; (*обратная сторона*) back; (*перен*: *поворот событий*) turn; (*Линг*) turn of phrase; (*употребление*) circulation

обору́довани|е (**-я**) *ср* equipment
обору́д|овать (**-ую**) *(не)сов перех* to equip
обосо́бленный *прил* (*дом*) detached; (*жизнь*) solitary
обостр|и́ть (**-ю́, -и́шь**; *impf* **обостря́ть**) *сов перех* to sharpen; (*желания, конфликт*) to intensify; **обостри́ться** (*impf* **обостря́ться**) *сов возв* (*см перех*) to sharpen; to intensify
обошёл(ся) *etc сов см* **обойти́(сь)**
обою́дный *прил* mutual
обрабо́та|ть (**-ю**; *impf* **обраба́тывать**) *сов перех* (*камень*) to cut; (*кожу*) to cure; (*деталь*) to turn; (*текст*) to polish up; (*землю*) to till; (*перен: разг: человека*) to work on
обра́д|овать(ся) (**-ую(сь)**) *сов от* **ра́довать(ся)**
о́браз (**-а**) *м* image; (*Литература*) figure; (*жизни*) way; (*икона*) icon; **каки́м о́бразом?** in what way?; **таки́м о́бразом** in this way; (*следовательно*) consequently; **гла́вным о́бразом** mainly; **не́которым о́бразом** to some extent; **образ|е́ц** (**-ца́**) *м* sample; (*скромности, мужества*) model
образова́ни|е (**-я**) *ср* formation; (*получение знаний*) education; **образо́ванный** *прил* educated; **образ|ова́ть** (**-у́ю**; *impf* **образова́ть**) *(не)сов перех* to form; **образова́ться** (*impf* **образова́ться**) *(не)сов возв* to form; (*группа, комиссия*) to be formed
обра|ти́ть (**-щу́, -ти́шь**; *impf* **обраща́ть**) *сов перех* (*взгляд, мысли*) to turn; **обраща́ть** (*perf* **обрати́ть**) **кого́-н/что-н в** *+acc* to turn sb/sth into; **обраща́ть** (*perf* **обрати́ть**) **внима́ние на** *+acc* to pay attention to; **обрати́ться** (*impf* **обраща́ться**) *сов возв* (*взгляд*) to turn; (*превратиться*): **обрати́ться в** *+acc* to turn into; **обраща́ться** (*perf* **обрати́ться**) **к** *+dat* (*к врачу итп*) to consult; (*к проблеме*) to address; **обраща́ться** (*perf* **обрати́ться**) **в суд** to go to court
обра́тно *нареч* back; **туда́ и обра́тно** there and back; **биле́т туда́ и обра́тно** return (*Brit*) *или* round-trip (*US*) ticket
обра́тн|ый *прил* reverse; (*дорога, путь*) return; **на обра́тном пути́** on the way back; **в обра́тную сто́рону** in the opposite direction; **обра́тная сторона́** reverse (side); **обра́тный а́дрес** return address
обраща́|ть (**-ю**) *несов от* **обрати́ть**; **обраща́ться** *несов от* **обрати́ться** ▷ *возв* (*деньги, товар*) to circulate; **обраща́ться** (*impf*) **с** *+instr* (*с машиной*) to handle; (*с человеком*) to treat
обраще́ни|е (**-я**) *ср* address; (*Экон*) circulation; **обраще́ние к** *+dat* (*к народу итп*) address to; **обраще́ние с** *+instr* (*с прибором*) handling of
обремен|и́ть (**-ю́, -и́шь**; *impf* **обременя́ть**) *сов перех*: **обремени́ть кого́-н чем-н** to load sb down with sth
о́бруч (**-а**) *м* hoop
обруча́льн|ый *прил*: **обруча́льное кольцо́** wedding ring
обру́ш|ить (**-у, -ишь**; *impf* **обру́шивать**) *сов перех* (*стену, крышу*) to bring down; **обру́шиться** (*impf* **обру́шиваться**) *сов возв*

(*крыша, здание*) to collapse; **обру́шиваться** (*perf* **обру́шиться**) **на** *+acc* (*на голову*) to crash down onto; (*на врага*) to fall upon
обрыва́|ть(ся) (**-ю(сь)**) *несов от* **оборва́ть(ся)**
обры́в|ок (**-ка**) *м* (*бумаги*) scrap; (*воспоминаний*) fragment
обры́зга|ть (**-ю**; *impf* **обры́згивать**) *сов перех*: **обры́згать кого́-н/что-н** *+instr* (*водой*) to splash sb/sth with; (*грязью*) to splatter sb/sth with; **обры́згаться** (*impf* **обры́згиваться**) *сов возв*: **обры́згаться** *+instr* (*см перех*) to get splashed with; to get splattered with
обря́д (**-а**) *м* ritual
обсле́д|овать (**-ую**) *(не)сов перех* to inspect; (*больного*) to examine
обслу́живани|е (**-я**) *ср* service
обсл|ужи́ть (**-ужу́, -у́жишь**; *impf* **обслу́живать**) *сов перех* (*клиентов*) to serve; (*подлеж: поликлиника*) to see to
обста́в|ить (**-лю, -ишь**; *impf* **обставля́ть**) *сов перех* (*квартиру*) to furnish
обстано́в|ка (**-ки**; *gen pl* **-ок**) *ж* situation; (*квартиры*) furnishings *мн*
обстоя́тельств|о (**-а**) *ср* circumstance; **смотря́ по обстоя́тельствам** depending on the circumstances; (*как ответ на вопрос*) it depends
обс|уди́ть (**-ужу́, -у́дишь**; *impf* **обсужда́ть**) *сов перех* to discuss
обсужде́ни|е (**-я**) *ср* discussion
обува́|ть(ся) (**-ю(сь)**) *несов от* **обу́ть(ся)**
обувно́й *прил* shoe; **о́був|ь** (**-и**) *ж* footwear
обусло́в|ить (**-лю, -ишь**; *impf* **обусла́вливать**) *сов перех* (*явиться причиной*) to lead to
обу́|ть (**-ю**; *impf* **обува́ть**) *сов перех* (*ребёнка*) to put shoes on; **обу́ться** (*impf* **обува́ться**) *сов возв* to put on one's shoes or boots
обуче́ни|е (**-я**) *ср* (*+dat*: *преподавание*) teaching of
обхв|ати́ть (**-ачу́, -а́тишь**; *impf* **обхва́тывать**) *сов перех*: **обхвати́ть что-н** (**рука́ми**) to put one's arms round sth
обхо́д (**-а**) *м* (*путь*) way round; (*в больнице*) round; **в обхо́д** *+gen* (*озера, закона*) bypassing
обх|оди́ть(ся) (**-ожу́(сь), -о́дишь(ся)**) *несов от* **обойти́(сь)**
обходно́й *прил* (*путь*) detour
обши́рный *прил* extensive
обща́|ться (**-юсь**) *несов возв*: **обща́ться с** *+instr* to mix with; (*с одним человеком*) to see; (*вести разговор*) to communicate with
общегосуда́рственный *прил* state
общедосту́пный *прил* (*способ*) available to everyone; (*цены*) affordable; (*лекция*) accessible
о́бщ|ее (**-его**) *ср* similarity; **в о́бщем** (*разг*) on the whole; **у них мно́го о́бщего** they have a lot in common
общежи́ти|е (**-я**) *ср* (*рабочее*) hostel; (*студенческое*) hall of residence (*Brit*), dormitory *или* hall (*US*)
общеизве́стный *прил* well-known
обще́ни|е (**-я**) *ср* communication
общеобразова́тельный *прил* comprehensive
общепри́знанный *прил* universally recognized

общепри́нятый *прил* generally accepted
обще́ственност|ь (**-и**) *ж собир* community; **обще́ственн|ый** *прил* social; (*не частный*) public; (*организация*) civic; **обще́ственное мне́ние** public opinion; **о́бществ|о** (**-а**) *ср* society
о́бщ|ий *прил* general; (*труд*) communal; (*дом*) shared; (*друзья*) mutual; (*интересы*) common; (*количество*) total; (*картина, описание*) general; **в о́бщей сло́жности** altogether
общи́тельный *прил* sociable
о́бщност|ь (**-и**) *ж* (*идей*) similarity; (*социальная*) community
объединённый *прил* joint
объедин|и́ть (**-ю́, -и́шь**; *impf* **объединя́ть**) *сов перех* to join, unite; (*ресурсы*) to pool; (*компании*) to amalgamate; **объедини́ться** (*impf* **объединя́ться**) *сов возв* to unite
объе́зд (**-а**) *м* detour; (*с целью осмотра*) tour
объезжа́|ть (**-ю**) *несов от* **объе́хать**
объе́кт (**-а**) *м* subject; (*Строит, Воен*) site
объекти́в (**-а**) *м* lens
объекти́вный *прил* objective
объём (**-а**) *м* volume
объе́хать (*как* **е́хать**; см *Table 19*; *impf* **объезжа́ть**) *сов перех* (*яму*) to go *или* drive round; (*друзей, страны*) to visit
объ|яви́ть (**-явлю́, -я́вишь**; *impf* **объявля́ть**) *сов перех* to announce; (*войну*) to declare ▷ *неперех*: **объяви́ть о** *+prp* to announce; **объявле́ни|е** (**-я**) *ср* announcement; (*войны*) declaration; (*реклама*) advertisement; (*извещение*) notice
объясне́ни|е (**-я**) *ср* explanation; **объясн|и́ть** (**-ю́, -и́шь**; *impf* **объясня́ть**) *сов перех* to explain; **объясни́ться** (*impf* **объясня́ться**) *сов возв*: **объясни́ться (с** *+instr*) to clear things up (with)
объясня́|ться (**-юсь**) *несов от* **объясни́ться** ▷ *возв* (*на английском языке*) to communicate; (*+instr*: *трудностями*) to be explained by
обыкнове́нный *прил* ordinary
о́быск (**-а**) *м* search; **об|ыска́ть** (**-ыщу́, -ы́щешь**; *impf* **обы́скивать**) *сов перех* to search
обы́ча|й (**-я**) *м* custom
обы́чно *нареч* usually; **обы́чный** *прил* usual; (*заурядный*) ordinary
обя́занност|и (**-ей**) *мн* duties, responsibilities; **исполня́ть** (*impf*) **обя́занности** *+gen* to act as; **обя́занност|ь** (**-и**) *ж* duty; *см также* **обя́занности**; **обя́занный** *прил* (*+infin*: *сделать итп*) obliged to do
обяза́тельно *нареч* definitely; **не обяза́тельно** not necessarily; **обяза́тельный** *прил* (*правило*) binding; (*исполнение, обучение*) compulsory, obligatory; (*работник*) reliable
обяза́тельств|о (**-а**) *ср* commitment; (*обычно мн*: *Комм*) liability
ова́л (**-а**) *м* oval
овдове́|ть (**-ю**) *сов* (*женщина*) to become a widow, be widowed; (*мужчина*) to become a widower, be widowed
Ов|е́н (**-на́**) *м* (*созвездие*) Aries
ов|ёс (**-са́**) *м собир* oats *мн*

ОВИР (**-а**) *м сокр* = **отде́л виз и регистра́ций**
овладе́|ть (**-ю, -ешь**; *impf* **овладева́ть**) *сов* (*+instr: городом, вниманием*) to capture; (*языком, профессией*) to master
о́вощ (**-а**) *м* vegetable
овощно́й *прил* (*суп, блюдо*) vegetable; **овощно́й магази́н** greengrocer's (*Brit*), fruit and vegetable shop
овра́г (**-а**) *м* ditch
овся́нк|а (**-и**) *ж собир* (*каша*) porridge (*Brit*), oatmeal (*US*); **овся́ный** *прил* oat
овча́р|ка (**-ки**; *gen pl* **-ок**) *ж* sheepdog
оглавле́ни|е (**-я**) *ср* (table of) contents
огло́хн|уть (**-у**) *сов от* **гло́хнуть**
огл|уши́ть (**-ушу́, -уши́шь**; *impf* **оглуша́ть**) *сов перех*: **оглуши́ть кого́-н чем-н** to deafen sb with sth
огля|де́ть (**-жу́, -ди́шь**; *impf* **огля́дывать**) *сов перех* to look round; **огляде́ться** (*impf* **огля́дываться**) *сов возв* to look around
огл|яну́ться (**-яну́сь, -я́нешься**; *impf* **огля́дываться**) *сов возв* to look back; **(я) не успе́л огляну́ться, как ...** before I knew it ...
огнеопа́сный *прил* (in) flammable
огнестре́льн|ый *прил*: **огнестре́льное ору́жие** firearms *мн*; **огнестре́льная ра́на** bullet wound
огнетуши́тел|ь (**-я**) *м* fire-extinguisher
ог|о́нь (**-ня́**) *м* fire; (*фонарей, в окне*) light
огоро́д (**-а**) *м* vegetable *или* kitchen garden
огорче́ни|е (**-я**) *ср* distress; **к моему́ огорче́нию** to my dismay
огорч|и́ть (**-у́, -и́шь**; *impf* **огорча́ть**) *сов перех* to distress; **огорчи́ться** (*impf* **огорча́ться**) *сов возв* to be distressed *или* upset
огра́б|ить (**-лю, -ишь**) *сов от* **гра́бить**
ограбле́ни|е (**-я**) *ср* robbery
огра́д|а (**-ы**) *ж* (*забор*) fence; (*решётка*) railings *мн*
огра|ди́ть (**-жу́, -ди́шь**; *impf* **огражда́ть**) *сов перех* (*сберечь*) to shelter, protect
огражде́ни|е (**-я**) *ср* = **огра́да**
ограниче́ни|е (**-я**) *ср* limitation; (*правило*) restriction
ограни́ч|ить (**-у, -ишь**; *impf* **ограни́чивать**) *сов перех* to limit, restrict; **ограни́читься** (*impf* **ограни́чиваться**) *сов возв*: **ограни́читься** *+instr* (*удовлетвориться*) to content o.s. with; (*свестись*) to become limited to
огро́мный *прил* enormous
огры́з|ок (**-ка**) *м* (*яблока*) half-eaten bit; (*карандаша*) stub
огур|е́ц (**-ца́**) *м* cucumber
ода́лжива|ть (**-ю**) *несов от* **одолжи́ть**
одарённый *прил* gifted
одева́|ть(ся) (**-ю(сь)**) *несов от* **оде́ть(ся)**
оде́жд|а (**-ы**) *ж* clothes *мн*
одеколо́н (**-а**) *м* eau de Cologne
оде́ну(сь) *etc сов см* **оде́ть(ся)**
од|ержа́ть (**-ержу́, -е́ржишь**; *impf* **оде́рживать**) *сов перех*: **одержа́ть побе́ду** to be victorious
оде́|ть (**-ну, -нешь**; *impf* **одева́ть**) *сов перех* to dress; **оде́ться** (*impf* **одева́ться**) *сов возв* to get dressed; (*тепло, красиво*) to dress

О

одея́л|о (**-а**) *ср* (*шерстяное*) blanket; (*стёганое*) quilt

 **КЛЮЧЕВОЕ СЛОВО**

од|и́н (**-ного́**; см *Table 22*; *f* **одна́**, *nt* **одно́**, *pl* **одни́**) *м чис* one; **одна́ кни́га** one book; **одни́ брю́ки** one pair of trousers
▷ *прил* alone; (*единственный, единый*) one; (*одинаковый, тот же самый*) the same; **он идёт в кино́ оди́н** he goes to the cinema alone; **есть то́лько оди́н вы́ход** there is only one way out; **у них одни́ взгля́ды** they hold similar views
▷ *мест* **1** (*какой-то*): **оди́н мой знако́мый** a friend of mine; **одни́ неприя́тности** nothing but problems
2 (*во фразах*): **оди́н из** *+gen pl* one of; **оди́н и то́т же** the same; **одно́ и то́ же** the same thing; **оди́н раз** once; **оди́н на оди́н** one to one; **все до одного́** all to a man; **ни оди́н** not one; **оди́н за други́м** one after the other; **по одному́** one by one; **оди́н-еди́нственный** only one

одина́ковый *прил* similar
оди́ннадцатый *чис* eleventh
оди́ннадцат|ь (**-и**; *как* **пять**; см *Table 26*) *чис* eleven
одино́кий *прил* (*жизнь, человек*) lonely; (*не семейный*) single;
одино́честв|о (**-а**) *ср* loneliness
одино́чный *прил* single
одн|а́ (**-о́й**) *ж чис см* **оди́н**
одна́жды *нареч* once
одна́ко *союз, вводн сл* however; **одна́ко!** well, I never!
одни́ (**-х**) *мн чис см* **оди́н**
одн|о́ (**-ого́**) *ср чис см* **оди́н**
одновреме́нно *нареч*: **одновреме́нно (с** *+instr*) at the same time (as)
одного́ *etc чис см* **оди́н**; **одно́**
одно-: **однообра́зный** *прил* monotonous; **однора́зовый** *прил* disposable; **одноро́дный** *прил* (*явления*) similar; (*масса*) homogeneous; **односторо́нний** *прил* unilateral; (*движение*) one-way; **одноцве́тный** *прил* plain; **одноэта́жный** *прил* single-storey (*Brit*), single-story (*US*), one-storey (*Brit*), one-story (*US*)
одобре́ни|е (**-я**) *ср* approval; **одобри́тельный** *прил* (*отзыв*) favourable (*Brit*), favorable (*US*); (*восклицание*) approving;
одо́бр|ить (**-ю, -ишь**; *impf* **одобря́ть**) *сов перех* to approve
одолже́ни|е (**-я**) *ср* favour (*Brit*), favor (*US*); **одолж|и́ть** (**-у́, -и́шь**; *impf* **ода́лживать**) *сов перех*: **одолжи́ть что-н кому́-н** to lend sth to sb; **ода́лживать (***perf* **одолжи́ть) что-н у кого́-н** (*разг*) to borrow sth from sb
одува́нчик (**-а**) *м* dandelion
ожере́л|ье (**-ья**; *gen pl* **-ий**) *ср* necklace
ожесточе́ни|е (**-я**) *ср* resentment
ожива́|ть (**-ю**) *несов от* **ожи́ть**
ожив|и́ть (**-лю́, -и́шь**; *impf* **оживля́ть**) *сов перех* to revive; (*глаза, лицо*) to light up; **оживи́ться** (*impf* **оживля́ться**) *сов возв* to liven up; (*лицо*) to brighten; **оживлённый** *прил* lively; (*беседа, спор*) animated
ожида́ни|е (**-я**) *ср* anticipation; (*обычно мн*: *надежды*) expectation; **ожида́|ть** (**-ю**) *несов перех* (*ждать*) to expect; (*+gen*: *надеяться*) to expect; **э́того мо́жно бы́ло ожида́ть** that was to

be expected; **ожида́ться** *несов возв* to be expected
ож|и́ть (**-иву́, -ивёшь**; *impf* **ожива́ть**) *сов* to come to life
ожо́г (**-а**) *м* burn
озабо́ченный *прил* worried
о́з|еро (**-ера**; *nom pl* **-ёра**) *ср* lake
озира́|ться (**-юсь**) *несов возв*: **озира́ться (по сторона́м)** to glance about *или* around
означа́|ть (**-ю**) *несов перех* to mean, signify
озо́н (**-а**) *м* ozone; **озо́нов|ый** *прил*: **озо́новый слой** ozone layer; **озо́новая дыра́** hole in the ozone layer
ой *межд*: **ой!** (*выражает испуг*) argh!; (*выражает боль*) ouch!, ow!
ок|аза́ть (**-ажу́, -а́жешь**; *impf* **ока́зывать**) *сов перех*: **оказа́ть по́мощь кому́-н** to provide help for sb; **ока́зывать (***perf* **оказа́ть) влия́ние/давле́ние на** *+acc* to exert influence/pressure on; **ока́зывать (***perf* **оказа́ть) внима́ние кому́-н** to pay attention to sb; **ока́зывать (***perf* **оказа́ть) сопротивле́ние (кому́-н)** to offer resistance (to sb); **ока́зывать (***perf* **оказа́ть) услу́гу кому́-н** to do sb a service; **оказа́ться** (*impf* **ока́зываться**) *сов возв* (*найтись*: *на столе итп*) to appear; (*очутиться*: *на острове итп*) to end up; **ока́зываться (***perf* **оказа́ться)** *+instr* (*вором, шпионом*) to turn out to be; **ока́зывается, она́ была́ права́** it turns out that she was right
окамене́|ть (*impf* **камене́ть**) *сов* (*перен*: *лицо*) to freeze; (*: сердце*) to turn to stone
ока́нчива|ть (**-ю**) *несов от* **око́нчить**; **ока́нчиваться** *несов от* **око́нчиться** ▷ *возв*: **ока́нчиваться на гла́сную/согла́сную** to end in a vowel/consonant
океа́н (**-а**) *м* ocean
оки́н|уть (**-у**; *impf* **оки́дывать**) *сов перех*: **оки́нуть кого́-н/что-н взгля́дом** to glance over at sb/sth
оккупи́р|овать (**-ую**) *(не)сов перех* to occupy
окла́д (**-а**) *м* (*зарплата*) salary
окле́|ить (**-ю, -ишь**; *impf* **окле́ивать**) *сов перех*: **окле́ить что-н чем-н** to cover sth with sth
ок|но́ (**-на́**; *nom pl* **-на**, *gen pl* **-он**) *ср* window
о́коло *нареч* nearby ▷ *предл* (*+gen*: *рядом с*) near; (*приблизительно*) about, around
околозе́мный *прил* around the earth
око́нча́ни|е (**-я**) *ср* end; (*Линг*) ending; **оконча́тельно** *нареч* (*ответить*) definitely; (*победить*) completely; (*отредактировать*) finally; **оконча́тельный** *прил* final; (*победа, свержение*) complete
око́нч|ить (**-у, -ишь**; *impf* **ока́нчивать**) *сов перех* to finish; (*вуз*) to graduate from; **око́нчиться** (*impf* **ока́нчиваться**) *сов возв* to finish; **око́нчиться** (*perf*) *+instr* (*скандалом*) to result in
око́п (**-а**) *м* trench
о́корок (**-а**; *nom pl* **-а́**) *м* gammon
окочене́|ть (**-ю**) *сов от* **кочене́ть**
окра́ин|а (**-ы**) *ж* (*города*) outskirts *мн*; (*страны*) remote parts *мн*
окра́с|ка (**-ки**; *gen pl* **-ок**) *ж* (*стены*) painting; (*животного*) colouring (*Brit*), coloring (*US*)

О

окре́пн|уть (**-у**) *сов от* **кре́пнуть**
окре́стност|ь (**-и**) *ж* (*обычн мн*) environs *мн*; **окре́стный** *прил* (*деревни*) neighbouring (*Brit*), neighboring (*US*)
о́крик (**-а**) *м* shout; **окри́кн|уть** (**-у**; *impf* **окри́кивать**) *сов перех*: **окри́кнуть кого́-н** to shout to sb
о́круг (**-а**) *м* (*административный*) district; (*избирательный*) ward; (*национальный*) territory; (*города*) borough
округл|и́ть (**-ю́, -и́шь**; *impf* **округля́ть**) *сов перех* (*форму*) to round off; (*цифру*) to round up *или* down
окружа́|ть (**-ю**) *несов от* **окружи́ть** ▷ *перех* to surround
окружа́ющ|ее (**-его**) *ср* environment; **окружа́ющ|ие** (**-их**) *мн* (*также* **окружа́ющие лю́ди**) *the people around one*; **окружа́ющий** *прил* surrounding
окруже́ни|е (**-я**) *ср* (*среда*) environment; (*компания*) circles *мн*; (*Воен*) encirclement; **в окруже́нии** *+gen* (*среди*) surrounded by; **окруж|и́ть** (**-у́, -и́шь**; *impf* **окружа́ть**) *сов перех* to surround
окружн|о́й *прил* regional; **окружна́я доро́га** bypass
окру́жност|ь (**-и**) *ж* circle
октя́бр|ь (**-я́**) *м* October
окун|у́ть (**-у́, -ёшь**; *impf* **окуна́ть**) *сов перех* to dip
ок|упи́ть (**-уплю́, -у́пишь**; *impf* **окупа́ть**) *сов перех* (*расходы*) to cover; (*поездку, проект*) to cover the cost of
оку́р|ок (**-ка**; *nom pl* **-ки**) *м* stub, butt
ола́д|ья (**-ьи**; *gen pl* **-ий**) *ж* ≈ drop scone, ≈ (Scotch) pancake
оле́н|ь (**-я**) *м* deer (*мн* deer)
оли́вк|а (**-и**) *ж* olive
олимпиа́д|а (**-ы**) *ж* (*Спорт*) the Olympics *мн*; (*по физике итп*) Olympiad; **олимпи́йск|ий** *прил* Olympic; **олимпи́йские и́гры** the Olympic Games
о́лов|о (**-а**) *ср* (*Хим*) tin
омерзи́тельный *прил* disgusting
омле́т (**-а**) *м* omelet(te)
ОМО́Н *м сокр* (= *отря́д мили́ции осо́бого назначе́ния*) *special police force*
омо́ним (**-а**) *м* homonym
омо́нов|ец (**-ца**) *м* *member of the special police force*
он (**его́**; *см* *Table 6a*) *мест* (*человек*) he; (*животное, предмет*) it
она́ (**её**; *см* *Table 6a*) *мест* (*человек*) she; (*животное, предмет*) it
они́ (**их**; *см* *Table 6b*) *мест* they
онла́йновый *прил* (*Комп*) on-line
оно́ (**его́**; *см* *Table 6a*) *мест* it; **оно́ и ви́дно!** (*разг*) sure! (*used ironically*); **вот оно́ что** *или* **как!** (*разг*) so that's what it is!
ОО́Н *ж сокр* (= *Организа́ция Объединённых На́ций*) UN(O) (= *United Nations (Organization)*)
опа́здыва|ть (**-ю**) *несов от* **опозда́ть**
опаса́|ться (**-юсь**) *несов возв* *+gen* to be afraid of; **опаса́ться** (*impf*) **за** *+acc* to be worried about
опа́сност|ь (**-и**) *ж* danger
опа́сный *прил* dangerous
опека́|ть (**-ю**) *несов перех* to take care of; (*сироту*) to be guardian to
о́пер|а (**-ы**) *ж* opera
операти́вн|ый *прил* (*меры*) efficient; (*хирургический*) surgical; **операти́вная гру́ппа** ≈ task force;

операти́вное запомина́ющее устро́йство RAM
опера́тор (**-а**) *м* operator
опера́ци|я (**-и**) *ж* operation
опер|е́ться (**обопру́сь, обопрёшься**; *pt* **опёрся, -ла́сь**, *impf* **опира́ться**) *сов*: **опере́ться на** *+acc* to lean on
опери́р|овать (**-ую**; *perf* **опери́ровать** *или* **прооопери́ровать**) *несов перех* (*больного*) to operate on ▷ *неперех* (*no perf*: *Воен*) to operate; (*+instr*: *акциями*) to deal in; (*перен*: *цифрами, фактами*) to use
о́перный *прил* operatic; (*певец*) opera
опеча́та|ть (**-ю**; *impf* **опеча́тывать**) *сов перех* to seal
опеча́т|ка (**-ки**; *gen pl* **-ок**) *ж* misprint
опи́л|ки (**-ок**) *мн* (*древесные*) sawdust *ед*; (*металлические*) filings *мн*
опира́|ться (**-юсь**) *несов от* **опере́ться**
описа́ни|е (**-я**) *ср* description
оп|иса́ть (**-ишу́, -и́шешь**; *impf* **опи́сывать**) *сов перех* to describe
опла́т|а (**-ы**) *ж* payment;
опл|ати́ть (**-ачу́, -а́тишь**; *impf* **опла́чивать**) *сов перех* (*работу, труд*) to pay for; (*счёт*) to pay
опове|сти́ть (**-щу́, -сти́шь**; *impf* **оповеща́ть**) *сов перех* to notify
опозда́ни|е (**-я**) *ср* lateness; (*поезда, самолёта*) late arrival;
опозда́|ть (**-ю**; *impf* **опа́здывать**) *сов*: **опозда́ть (в/на** *+acc*) (*в школу, на работу итп*) to be late (for)
опозна́|ть (**-ю**; *impf* **опознава́ть**) *сов перех* to identify
опозо́р|ить(ся) (**-ю(сь)**) *сов от* **позо́рить(ся)**
опо́мн|иться (**-юсь, -ишься**) *сов возв* (*прийти в сознание*) to come round; (*одуматься*) to come to one's senses
опо́р|а (**-ы**) *ж* support
опо́рный *прил* supporting; **опо́рный прыжо́к** vault; **опо́рный пункт** base
оппозицио́нный *прил* opposition
оппози́ци|я (**-и**) *ж* opposition
оппоне́нт (**-а**) *м* (*в споре*) opponent; (*диссертации*) external examiner
опра́в|а (**-ы**) *ж* frame
оправда́ни|е (**-я**) *ср* justification; (*Юр*) acquittal; (*извинение*) excuse
оправда́|ть (**-ю**; *impf* **опра́вдывать**) *сов перех* to justify; (*надежды*) to live up to; (*Юр*) to acquit; **оправда́ться** (*impf* **опра́вдываться**) *сов возв* to justify o.s.; (*расходы*) to be justified
опра́в|ить (**-лю, -ишь**; *impf* **оправля́ть**) *сов перех* (*платье, постель*) to straighten; (*линзы*) to frame; **опра́виться** (*impf* **оправля́ться**) *сов возв*: **опра́виться от** *+gen* to recover from
опра́шива|ть (**-ю**) *несов от* **опроси́ть**
определе́ни|е (**-я**) *ср* determination; (*Линг*) attribute
определённый *прил* (*установленный*) definite; (*некоторый*) certain
определ|и́ть (**-ю́, -и́шь**; *impf* **определя́ть**) *сов перех* to determine; (*понятие*) to define
оприхо́д|овать (**-ую**) *сов от* **прихо́довать**

опрове́ргн|уть (-у; *impf* **опроверга́ть**) *сов перех* to refute
опроки́н|уть (-у; *impf* **опроки́дывать**) *сов перех* (*стакан*) to knock over; **опроки́нуться** (*impf* **опроки́дываться**) *сов возв* (*стакан, стул, человек*) to fall over; (*лодка*) to capsize
опро́с (-а) *м* (*свидетелей*) questioning; (*населения*) survey; **опро́с обще́ственного мне́ния** opinion poll
опр|оси́ть (-ошу́, -о́сишь; *impf* **опра́шивать**) *сов перех* (*свидетелей*) to question; (*население*) to survey
опро́сный *прил*: **опро́сный лист** questionnaire
опротест|ова́ть (-у́ю) *сов перех* (*Юр*) to appeal against
опря́тный *прил* neat, tidy
оптима́льный *прил* optimum
оптими́зм (-а) *м* optimism
оптимисти́чный *прил* optimistic
опто́в|ый *прил* wholesale; **опто́вые заку́пки** (*Комм*) bulk buying; **о́птом** *нареч*: **купи́ть/прода́ть о́птом** to buy/sell wholesale
опуска́|ть(ся) (-ю(сь)) *несов от* **опусти́ть(ся)**
опусте́|ть (*3sg* -ет) *сов от* **пусте́ть**
оп|усти́ть (-ущу́, -у́стишь; *impf* **опуска́ть**) *сов перех* to lower; (*пропустить*) to miss out; **опуска́ть** (*perf* **опусти́ть**) **в** *+acc* (*в ящик*) to drop *или* put in(to); **опусти́ться** (*impf* **опуска́ться**) *сов возв* (*человек: на диван, на землю*) to sit (down); (*солнце*) to sink; (*мост, шлагбаум*) to be lowered; (*перен: человек*) to let o.s. go

опу́хн|уть (-у) *сов от* **пу́хнуть** ▷ (*impf* **опуха́ть**) *неперех* to swell (up); **о́пухол|ь** (-и) *ж* (*рана*) swelling; (*внутренняя*) tumour (*Brit*), tumor (*US*); **опу́хший** *прил* swollen
о́пыт (-а) *м* experience; (*эксперимент*) experiment
о́пытный *прил* (*рабочий*) experienced; (*лаборатория*) experimental
опьяне́|ть (-ю) *сов от* **пьяне́ть**
опя́ть *нареч* again; **опя́ть же** (*разг*) at that
ора́нжевый *прил* orange
орби́т|а (-ы) *ж* orbit
о́рган (-а) *м* (*также Анат*) organ; (*власти*) body; (*орудие: +gen: пропаганды*) vehicle for; **ме́стные о́рганы вла́сти** local authorities (*Brit*) *или* government (*US*); **половы́е о́рганы** genitals
орга́н (-а) *м* (*Муз*) organ
организа́тор (-а) *м* organizer
организа́ци|я (-и) *ж* organization; (*устройство*) system
органи́зм (-а) *м* organism
организ|ова́ть (-у́ю) *(не)сов перех* (*создать*) to organize
органи́ческий *прил* organic
оргкомите́т (-а) *м сокр* (= *организацио́нный комите́т*) organizational committee
оргте́хник|а (-и) *ж* office automation equipment
о́рден (-а; *nom pl* -а́) *м* order
орёл (**орла́**; *nom pl* **орлы́**) *м* eagle
оре́х (-а) *м* nut
оригина́л (-а) *м* original; **оригина́льный** *прил* original
ориенти́р (-а) *м* landmark
орке́стр (-а) *м* orchestra
орна́мент (-а) *м* (decorative) pattern

оробé|ть (**-ю**) *сов от* **робéть**
оросúтельный *прил* irrigation; **орошéни|е** (**-я**) *ср* irrigation
ортодоксáльный *прил* orthodox
ортопéд (**-а**) *м* orthopaedic (*Brit*) *или* orthopedic (*US*) surgeon; **ортопедúческий** *прил* orthopaedic (*Brit*), orthopedic (*US*)
орýди|е (**-я**) *ср* tool; (*Воен*) gun (*used of artillery*)
орýжи|е (**-я**) *ж* weapon
орфогрáфи|я (**-и**) *ж* spelling
ОС *ж нескл сокр* (*Комп*) (= *операциóнная систéма*) operating system
ос|á (**-ы́**; *nom pl* **óсы**) *ж* wasp
осáд|а (**-ы**) *ж* siege
осáд|ки (**-ков**) *мн* precipitation *ед*
осваúва|ть(ся) (**-ю(сь)**) *несов от* **освóить(ся)**
освéдом|ить (**-лю, -ишь**; *impf* **осведомля́ть**) *сов перех* to inform; **освéдомиться** (*impf* **осведомля́ться**) *сов возв*: **освéдомиться о** *+prp* to inquire about
освеж|úть (**-ý, -úшь**; *impf* **освежáть**) *сов перех* (*знания*) to refresh; **освежúться** (*impf* **освежáться**) *сов возв* (*воздух*) to freshen; (*человек*) to freshen up
осветúтельный *прил*: **осветúтельный прибóр** light
осве|тúть (**-щý, -тúшь**; *impf* **освещáть**) *сов перех* to light up; (*проблему*) to cover; **осветúться** (*impf* **освещáться**) *сов возв* to be lit up
освещéни|е (**-я**) *ср* lighting; (*проблемы, дела*) coverage
освобо|дúть (**-жý, -дúшь**; *impf* **освобождáть**) *сов перех* (*из тюрьмы*) to release; (*город*) to liberate; (*дом*) to vacate; (*время*) to free up; **освободúть** (*perf*) **когó-н от дóлжности** to dismiss sb; **освободúться** (*impf* **освобождáться**) *сов возв* (*из тюрьмы*) to be released; (*дом*) to be vacated; **освобождéни|е** (**-я**) *ср* release; (*города*) liberation; **освобождéние от дóлжности** dismissal
освó|ить (**-ю, -ишь**; *impf* **осваúвать**) *сов перех* (*технику, язык*) to master; (*земли*) to cultivate; **освóиться** (*impf* **осваúваться**) *сов возв* (*на новой работе*) to find one's feet
освя|тúть (**-щý, -тúшь**; *impf* **освящáть**) *сов перех* (*Рел*) to bless
оседá|ть (**-ю**) *несов от* **осéсть**
ос|ёл (**-лá**) *м* donkey
осéнний *прил* autumn, fall (*US*)
óсен|ь (**-и**) *ж* autumn, fall (*US*)
óсенью *нареч* in autumn *или* the fall (*US*)
ос|éсть (**-я́ду, -я́дешь**; *impf* **оседáть**) *сов* (*пыль, осадок*) to settle
ос|ётр (**-етрá**) *м* sturgeon (*Zool*); **осетрúн|а** (**-ы**) *ж* sturgeon (*Culin*)
осúн|ый *прил*: **осúное гнездó** (*перен*) hornet's nest
оскóл|ок (**-ка**) *м* (*стекла*) piece; (*снаряда*) shrapnel *ед*
оскорбúтельный *прил* offensive
оскорб|úть (**-лю́, -úшь**; *impf* **оскорбля́ть**) *сов перех* to insult; **оскорбúться** (*impf* **оскорбля́ться**) *сов возв* to be offended, take offence *или* offense (*US*); **оскорблéни|е** (**-я**) *ср* insult
ослáб|ить (**-лю, -ишь**; *impf* **ослабля́ть**) *сов перех* to weaken;

О

(*дисциплину*) to relax
ослеп|и́ть (**-лю́, -и́шь**; *impf* **ослепля́ть**) *сов перех* to blind; (*подлеж*: *красота*) to dazzle
осле́п|нуть (**-ну**; *pt* **-, -ла**) *сов от* **сле́пнуть**
осложне́ни|е (**-я**) *ср* complication
осложн|и́ть (**-ю́, -и́шь**; *impf* **осложня́ть**) *сов перех* to complicate; **осложни́ться** (*impf* **осложня́ться**) *сов возв* to become complicated
осма́трива|ть(ся) (**-ю(сь)**) *несов от* **осмотре́ть(ся)**
осмеле́|ть (**-ю**) *несов от* **смеле́ть**
осме́л|иться (**-юсь, -ишься**; *impf* **осме́ливаться**) *сов возв* to dare
осмо́тр (**-а**) *м* inspection; (*больного*) examination; (*музея*) visit; **осм|отре́ть** (**-отрю́, -о́тришь**; *impf* **осма́тривать**) *сов перех* (*см сущ*) to inspect; to examine; to visit; **осмотре́ться** (*impf* **осма́триваться**) *сов возв* (*по сторонам*) to look around; (*перен*: *на новом месте*) to settle in
осмотри́тельный *прил* cautious
осна|сти́ть (**-щу́, -сти́шь**; *impf* **оснаща́ть**) *сов перех* to equip; **оснаще́ни|е** (**-я**) *ср* equipment
осно́в|а (**-ы**) *ж* basis; (*сооружения*) foundations *мн*; **на осно́ве** *+gen* on the basis of; *см также* **осно́вы**
основа́ни|е (**-я**) *ср* base; (*теории*) basis; (*поступка*) grounds *мн*; **без вся́ких основа́ний** without any reason; **до основа́ния** completely; **на основа́нии** *+gen* on the grounds of; **на како́м основа́нии?** on what grounds?
основа́тел|ь (**-я**) *м* founder
основа́тельный *прил* (*анализ*) thorough
основа́|ть (*pt* **-л, -ла, -ло**, *impf* **осно́вывать**) *сов перех* to found; **осно́вывать** (*perf* **основа́ть**) **что-н на** *+prp* to base sth on *или* upon; **основа́ться** (*impf* **осно́вываться**) *сов возв* (*компания*) to be founded
основн|о́й *прил* main; (*закон*) fundamental; **в основно́м** on the whole
осно́выва|ть(ся) (**-ю(сь)**) *несов от* **основа́ть(ся)**
осно́в|ы (**-**) *мн* (*физики*) basics
осо́бенно *нареч* particularly; (*хорошо*) especially, particularly
осо́бенный *прил* special, particular
особня́к (**-а**) *м* mansion
осо́бый *прил* (*вид, случай*) special, particular; (*помещение*) separate
осозна́|ть (**-ю**; *impf* **осознава́ть**) *сов перех* to realize
оспа́рива|ть (**-ю**) *несов от* **оспо́рить** ▷ *перех* (*первенство*) to contend *или* compete for
оспо́р|ить (**-ю, -ишь**; *impf* **оспа́ривать**) *сов перех* to question
оста|ва́ться (**-ю́сь, -ёшься**) *несов от* **оста́ться**
оста́в|ить (**-лю, -ишь**; *impf* **оставля́ть**) *сов перех* to leave; (*сохранить*) to keep; (*прекратить*) to stop; (*перен*: *надежды*) to give up; **оста́вь!** stop it!
остальн|о́е (**-о́го**) *ср* the rest *мн*; **в остально́м** in other respects; **остально́й** *прил* (*часть*) the remaining; **остальн|ы́е** (**-ы́х**) *мн* the others
остан|ови́ть (**-овлю́, -о́вишь**;

impf **остана́вливать**) *сов перех* to stop; **останови́ться** (*impf* **остана́вливаться**) *сов возв* to stop; (*в гостинице, у друзей*) to stay; **останови́ться** (*perf*) **на** +*prp* (*на вопросе*) to dwell on; (*на решении*) to come to; (*взгляд*) to rest on

остано́вк|а (**-и**) *ж* stop; (*мотора*) stopping; (*в работе*) pause

оста́т|ок (**-ка**) *м* (*пищи, дня*) the remainder, the rest; **оста́тки** (*дома*) remains; (*еды*) leftovers

оста́|ться (**-нусь**; *impf* **остава́ться**) *сов возв* (*не уйти*) to stay; (*сохраниться*) to remain; (*оказаться*) to be left

остекл|и́ть (**-ю́, -и́шь**) *сов от* **стекли́ть**

осторо́жно *нареч* (*взять*) carefully; (*ходить, говорить*) cautiously; **осторо́жно!** look out!; **осторо́жност|ь** (**-и**) *ж* care; (*поступка, поведения*) caution; **осторо́жный** *прил* careful

остри|ё (**-я́**) *ср* point; (*ножа*) edge

остр|и́ть (**-ю́, -и́шь**; *perf* **сострить**) *несов* to make witty remarks

о́стров (**-а**; *nom pl* **-а́**) *м* island

остросюже́тный *прил* (*пьеса*) gripping; **остросюже́тный фильм, остросюже́тный рома́н** thriller

остроу́мный *прил* witty

о́стрый *прил* (*нож, память, вкус*) sharp; (*борода, нос*) pointed; (*зрение, слух*) keen; (*шутка, слово*) witty; (*еда*) spicy; (*желание*) burning; (*боль, болезнь*) acute; (*ситуация*) critical

ост|уди́ть (**-ужу́, -у́дишь**; *impf* **остужа́ть**) *сов перех* to cool

осты́|ть (**-ну, -нешь**) *сов от* **стыть** ▷ (*impf* **остыва́ть**) *неперех* to cool down

ос|уди́ть (**-ужу́, -у́дишь**; *impf* **осужда́ть**) *сов перех* to condemn; (*приговорить*) to convict

осуждённ|ый (**-ого**) *м* convict

ос|уши́ть (**-ушу́, -у́шишь**; *impf* **осуша́ть**) *сов перех* to drain

осуществ|и́ть (**-лю́, -и́шь**; *impf* **осуществля́ть**) *сов перех* (*мечту, идею*) to realize; (*план*) to implement; **осуществи́ться** (*impf* **осуществля́ться**) *сов возв* (*мечты, идея*) to be realized

осчастли́в|ить (**-лю, -ишь**) *сов перех* to make happy

осы́п|ать (**-лю, -лешь**; *impf* **осыпа́ть**) *сов перех*: **осыпа́ть** (*perf* **осы́пать**) **кого́-н/что-н чем-н** to scatter sth over sb/sth; (*перен*: *подарками*) to shower sb/sth with sth; **осы́паться** (*impf* **осыпа́ться**) *сов возв* (*насыпь*) to subside; (*штукатурка*) to crumble; (*листья*) to fall

осьмино́г (**-а**) *м* octopus (*мн* octopuses)

КЛЮЧЕВОЕ СЛОВО

от *предл* +*gen* **1** from; **он отошёл от стола́** he moved away from the table; **он узна́л об э́том от дру́га** he found out about it from a friend
2 (*указывает на причину*): **бума́га размо́кла от дождя́** the paper got wet with rain; **от зло́сти** with anger; **от ра́дости** for joy; **от удивле́ния** in surprise; **от разочарова́ния/стра́ха** out of disappointment/fear
3 (*указывает на что-н, против чего направлено действие*) for; **лека́рство от ка́шля** medicine for a cough, cough medicine
4 (*о части целого*): **ру́чка/ключ от две́ри** door handle/key; **я потеря́л**

пу́говицу от пальтó I lost the button off my coat
5 (*в датах*): **письмó от пéрвого февраля́** a letter of *или* dated the first of February
6 (*о временной последовательности*): **год от гóда** from year to year; **врéмя от врéмени** from time to time

отáплива|ть (**-ю**) *несов перех* to heat; **отáпливаться** *несов возв* to be heated
отбежáть (*как* **бежáть**; см *Table 20*; *impf* **отбегáть**) *сов* to run off
отб|ели́ть (**-елю́, -éлишь**; *impf* **отбéливать**) *сов перех* to bleach
отбивн|áя (**-óй**) *ж* tenderized steak; (*также* **отбивнáя котлéта**) chop
отбирá|ть (**-ю**) *несов от* **отобрáть**
от|би́ть (**-обью́, -обьёшь**; *impf* **отбивáть**) *сов перех* (*отколоть*) to break off; (*мяч, удар*) to fend off; (*атаку*) to repulse; **отби́ться** (*impf* **отбивáться**) *сов возв*: **отби́ться** (*perf*) **(от** *+gen*) (*от нападающих*) to defend o.s. (against); (*отстать*) to fall behind
отблагодар|и́ть (**-ю́, -и́шь**) *сов перех* to show one's gratitude to
отбóр (**-а**) *м* selection
отбрó|сить (**-шу, -сишь**; *impf* **отбрáсывать**) *сов перех* to throw aside; (*сомнения*) to cast aside; (*тень*) to cast
отбрóс|ы (**-ов**) *мн* (*производства*) waste *ед*; (*пищевые*) scraps *мн*
отб|ы́ть (*как* **быть**; см *Table 21*; *impf* **отбывáть**) *сов*: **отбы́ть (из** *+gen*/**в** *+acc*) to depart (from/for) ▷ (*pt* **-ы́л, -ылá, -ы́ло**) *перех*: **отбы́ть наказáние** to serve a sentence

отвáжный *прил* brave
отвáр (**-а**) *м* (*мясной*) broth
отв|ари́ть (**-арю́, -áришь**; *impf* **отвáривать**) *сов перех* to boil
отв|езти́ (**-езу́, -езёшь**; *pt* **-ёз, -езлá**, *impf* **отвози́ть**) *сов перех* (*увезти*) to take away; **отвози́ть** (*perf* **отвезти́**) **когó-н/что-н в гóрод/на дáчу** to take sb/sth off to town/the dacha
отвéргн|уть (**-у**; *impf* **отвергáть**) *сов перех* to reject
отверн|у́ть (**-у́, -ёшь**; *impf* **отвёртывать**) *сов перех* (*гайку*) to unscrew ▷ (*impf* **отворáчивать**) (*лицо, голову*) to turn away; **отверну́ться** (*impf* **отворáчиваться**) *сов возв* (*человек*) to turn away
отвéрсти|е (**-я**) *ср* opening
отвёрт|ка (**-ки**; *gen pl* **-ок**) *ж* screwdriver
отв|ести́ (**-еду́, -едёшь**; *pt* **-ёл, -елá**, *impf* **отводи́ть**) *сов перех* (*человека*: *домой, к врачу*) to take (off); (: *от окна*) to lead away; (*глаза*) to avert; (*кандидатуру*) to reject; (*участок*) to allot; (*средства*) to allocate
отвéт (**-а**) *м* (*на вопрос*) answer; (*реакция*) response; (*на письмо, на приглашение*) reply; **в отвéт (на** *+acc*) in response (to); **быть** (*impf*) **в отвéте за** *+acc* to be answerable for
ответвлéни|е (**-я**) *ср* branch
отвé|тить (**-чу, -тишь**; *impf* **отвечáть**) *сов*: **отвéтить (на** *+acc*) to answer, reply (to); **отвéтить** (*perf*) **за** *+acc* (*за преступление*) to answer for
отвéтственност|ь (**-и**) *ж* (*за поступки*) responsibility; (*задания*) importance; **нести́ (***perf* **понести́) отвéтственность за** *+acc* to be

responsible for; **привлека́ть** (*perf* **привле́чь**) **кого́-н к отве́тственности** to call sb to account

отве́тственный *прил*: **отве́тственный** (**за** *+acc*) responsible (for); (*важный*) important; **отве́тственный рабо́тник** executive

отвеча́|ть (**-ю**) *несов от* **отве́тить** ▷ *неперех* (*+dat*: *требованиям*) to meet; (*описанию*) to answer; **отвеча́ть** (*impf*) **за кого́-н/что-н** to be responsible for sb/sth

отвл|е́чь (**-еку́, -ечёшь** *итп*, **-еку́т**; *pt* **-ёк, -екла́**, *impf* **отвлека́ть**) *сов перех*: **отвле́чь** (**от** *+gen*) (*от дел*) to distract (from); (*противника*) to divert (from); **отвле́чься** (*impf* **отвлека́ться**) *сов возв*: **отвле́чься** (**от** *+gen*) to be distracted (from); (*от темы*) to digress (from)

отв|оди́ть (**-ожу́, -о́дишь**) *несов от* **отвести́**

отво|ева́ть (**-ю́ю**; *impf* **отвоёвывать**) *сов перех* to win back

отв|ози́ть (**-ожу́, -о́зишь**) *несов от* **отвезти́**

отвора́чива|ть(ся) (**-ю(сь)**) *несов от* **отверну́ть(ся)**

отврати́тельный *прил* disgusting

отвраще́ни|е (**-я**) *ср* disgust

отвы́к|нуть (**-ну**; *pt* **-, -ла**, *impf* **отвыка́ть**) *сов*: **отвы́кнуть от** *+gen* (*от людей, от работы*) to become unaccustomed to; (*от наркотиков*) to give up

отв|яза́ть (**-яжу́, -я́жешь**; *impf* **отвя́зывать**) *сов перех* (*верёвку*) to untie; **отвяза́ться** (*impf* **отвя́зываться**) *сов возв* (*разг*): **отвяза́ться от** *+gen* (*отделаться*) to get rid of

отгада́|ть (**-ю**; *impf* **отга́дывать**) *сов перех* to guess

отговор|и́ть (**-ю́, -и́шь**; *impf* **отгова́ривать**) *сов перех*: **отговори́ть кого́-н от чего́-н/***+infin* to dissuade sb from sth/from doing; **отгово́р|ка** (**-ки**; *gen pl* **-ок**) *ж* excuse

отгоня́|ть (**-ю**) *несов от* **отогна́ть**

отгу́л (**-а**) *м* day off

отда|ва́ть (**-ю́, -ёшь**) *несов от* **отда́ть**

отдалённый *прил* distant; (*место, сходство*) remote

отда́ть (*как* **дать**; см *Table 16*; *impf* **отдава́ть**) *сов перех* (*возвратить*) to return; (*дать*) to give; (*ребёнка*: *в школу*) to send; **отдава́ть** (*perf* **отда́ть**) **кого́-н под суд** to prosecute sb; **отдава́ть** (*perf* **отда́ть**) **кому́-н честь** to salute sb; **отдава́ть** (*perf* **отда́ть**) **себе́ отчёт в** *+prep* to realize

отде́л (**-а**) *м* (*учреждения*) department; (*газеты*) section; (*истории, науки*) branch; **отде́л ка́дров** personnel department

отде́ла|ть (**-ю**; *impf* **отде́лывать**) *сов перех* (*квартиру*) to do up; **отде́лывать** (*perf* **отде́лать**) **что-н чем-н** (*пальто*: *мехом*) to trim sth with sth; **отде́латься** (*impf* **отде́лываться**) *сов возв*: **отде́латься от** *+gen* (*разг*) to get rid of; **отде́латься** (*perf*) *+instr* (*разг*: *испугом*) to get away with

отделе́ни|е (**-я**) *ср* section; (*учреждения*) department; (*филиал*) branch; (*концерта*) part; **отделе́ние свя́зи** post office; **отделе́ние мили́ции** police station

отд|ели́ть (**-елю́, -е́лишь**; *impf* **отделя́ть**) *сов перех* to separate; **отдели́ться** (*impf* **отделя́ться**) *сов возв*: **отдели́ться (от** *+gen*) to separate (from)

отде́л|ка (**-ки**; *gen pl* **-ок**) *ж* decoration; (*на платье*) trimmings *мн*

отде́лыва|ть(ся) (**-ю(сь)**) *несов от* **отде́лать(ся)**

отде́льный *прил* separate

отдохн|у́ть (**-у́, -ёшь**; *impf* **отдыха́ть**) *сов* to (have a) rest; (*на море*) to have a holiday, take a vacation (*US*)

о́тдых (**-а**) *м* rest; (*отпуск*) holiday, vacation (*US*); **на о́тдыхе** (*в отпуске*) on holiday; **дом о́тдыха** holiday centre (*Brit*) *или* center (*US*)

отдыха́|ть (**-ю**) *несов от* **отдохну́ть**

отдыха́ющ|ий (**-его**) *м* holidaymaker (*Brit*), vacationer (*US*)

отёк (**-а**) *м* swelling; **отека́|ть** (**-ю**) *несов от* **оте́чь**

оте́л|ь (**-я**) *м* hotel

от|е́ц (**-ца́**) *м* father

оте́чественн|ый *прил* (*промышленность*) domestic; **Оте́чественная Война́** patriotic war (*fought in defence of one's country*)

оте́честв|о (**-а**) *ср* fatherland

от|е́чь (**-еку́, -ечёшь** *итп*, **-еку́т**; *pt* **отёк, -екла́, -екло́**, *impf* **отека́ть**) *сов* to swell up

о́тзвук (**-а**) *м* echo

о́тзыв (**-а**) *м* (*рецензия*) review

отзыва́|ть(ся) (**-ю(сь)**) *несов от* **отозва́ть(ся)**

отзы́вчивый *прил* ready to help

отка́з (**-а**) *м* refusal; (*от решения*) rejection; (*механизма*) failure; **закру́чивать** (*perf* **закрути́ть**) **что-н до отка́за** to turn sth full on; **набива́ть** (*perf* **наби́ть**) **до отка́за** to cram

отк|аза́ть (**-ажу́, -а́жешь**; *impf* **отка́зывать**) *сов* (*мотор, нервы*) to fail; **отка́зывать** (*perf* **отказа́ть**) **кому́-н в чём-н** to refuse sb sth; (*в помощи*) to deny sb sth; **отказа́ться** (*impf* **отка́зываться**) *сов возв*: **отказа́ться (от** *+gen*) to refuse; (*от отдыха, от мысли*) to give up; **отка́зываться** (*perf* **отказа́ться**) **от свои́х слов** to retract one's words

отка́лыва|ть(ся) (**-ю(сь)**) *несов от* **отколо́ть(ся)**

открача́|ть (**-ю**; *impf* **отка́чивать**) *сов перех* to pump (out)

отки́н|уть (**-у**; *impf* **отки́дывать**) *сов перех* to throw; (*верх, сидение*) to open; (*волосы, голову*) to toss back; **отки́нуться** (*impf* **отки́дываться**) *сов возв*: **отки́нуться на** *+acc* to lean back against

откла́дыва|ть (**-ю**) *несов от* **отложи́ть**

отключ|и́ть (**-у́, -и́шь**; *impf* **отключа́ть**) *сов перех* to switch off; (*телефон*) to cut off; **отключи́ться** (*impf* **отключа́ться**) *сов возв* to switch off

откорректи́р|овать (**-ую**) *сов от* **корректи́ровать**

открове́нно *нареч* frankly

открове́нный *прил* frank; (*обман*) blatant

откро́ю(сь) *etc сов см* **откры́ть(ся)**

открыва́л|ка (**-ки**; *gen pl* **-ок**) *ж* (*разг: для консервов*) tin-opener; (*для бутылок*) bottle-opener

открыва́|ть(ся) (**-ю(сь)**) *несов от*

откры́ть(ся)
откры́ти|е (**-я**) *ср* discovery; (*сезона, выставки*) opening
откры́т|ка (**-ки**; *gen pl* **-ок**) *ж* postcard
откры́тый *прил* open; (*голова, шея*) bare; (*взгляд, человек*) frank
откр|ы́ть (**-о́ю, -о́ешь**; *impf* **открыва́ть**) *сов перех* to open; (*намерения, правду итп*) to reveal; (*воду, кран*) to turn on; (*возможность, путь*) to open up; (*закон*) to discover; **откры́ться** (*impf* **открыва́ться**) *сов возв* to open; (*возможность, путь*) to open up
отку́да *нареч* where from ▷ *союз* from where; **Вы отку́да?** where are you from?; **отку́да Вы прие́хали?** where have you come from?; **отку́да ты э́то зна́ешь?** how do you know about that?; **отку́да-нибудь** *нареч* from somewhere (or other); **отку́да-то** *нареч* from somewhere
отк|уси́ть (**-ушу́, -у́сишь**; *impf* **отку́сывать**) *сов перех* to bite off
отла́|дить (**-жу, дишь**) *сов перех от* **отла́живать**
отла́жива|ть (**-ю**; *perf* **отла́дить**) *+gen несоб перех* (*Комп*) to debug
отлага́тельств|о (**-а**) *ср* delay
отла́мыва|ть(ся) (**-ю**) *несов от* **отломи́ть(ся)**
отле|те́ть (**-чу́, -ти́шь**; *impf* **отлета́ть**) *сов* to fly off; (*мяч*) to fly back
отлича́|ть (**-ю**) *несов от* **отличи́ть**; **отлича́ться** *возв* (*быть другим*): **отлича́ться (от** *+gen*) to be different (from)
отли́чи|е (**-я**) *ср* distinction; **в отли́чие от** *+gen* unlike
отлич|и́ть (**-у́, -и́шь**; *impf* **отлича́ть**) *сов перех* (*наградить*) to honour (*Brit*), honor (*US*); **отлича́ть** (*perf* **отличи́ть) кого́-н/что-н от** *+gen* to tell sb/sth from
отли́чник (**-а**) *м* 'A'grade pupil
отли́чно *нареч* extremely well ▷ *как сказ* it's excellent *или* great ▷ *ср нескл* (*Просвещ*) excellent *или* outstanding (*school mark*); **он отли́чно зна́ет, что он винова́т** he knows perfectly well that he's wrong; **учи́ться** (*impf*) **на отли́чно** to get top marks
отли́чный *прил* excellent; (*иной*): **отли́чный от** *+gen* distinct from
отл|ожи́ть (**-ожу́, -о́жишь**; *impf* **откла́дывать**) *сов перех* (*деньги*) to put aside; (*собрание*) to postpone
отл|оми́ть (**-омлю́, -о́мишь**; *impf* **отла́мывать**) *сов перех* to break off; **отломи́ться** (*impf* **отла́мываться**) *сов возв* to break off
отмахн|у́ться (**-у́сь, -ёшься**; *impf* **отма́хиваться**) *сов возв*: **отмахну́ться от** *+gen* (*от мухи*) to brush away; (*от предложения*) to brush *или* wave aside
отме́н|а (**-ы**) *ж* (*см глаг*) repeal; reversal; abolition; cancellation; **отм|ени́ть** (**-еню́, -е́нишь**; *impf* **отменя́ть**) *сов перех* (*решение, приговор*) to reverse; (*налог*) to abolish; (*лекцию*) to cancel; (*закон*) to repeal
отме́|тить (**-чу, -тишь**; *impf* **отмеча́ть**) *сов перех* (*на карте, в книге*) to mark; (*указать*) to note; (*юбилей*) to celebrate; **отме́титься** (*impf* **отмеча́ться**) *сов возв* to register
отме́т|ка (**-ки**; *gen pl* **-ок**) *ж* mark; (*в документе*) note

Отме́тка

The Russian scale of marking is from 1 to 5, with 5 being the highest mark.

отмеча́|ть(ся) (**-ю(сь)**) *несов от* **отме́тить(ся)**

отморо́|зить (**-жу, -зишь**; *impf* **отмора́живать**) *сов перех*: **отморо́зить ру́ки/но́ги** to get frostbite in one's hands/feet

отм|ы́ть (**-о́ю, -о́ешь**; *impf* **отмыва́ть**) *сов перех*: **отмы́ть что-н** to get sth clean; (*грязь*) to wash sth out; (*деньги*) to launder sth

отн|ести́ (**-есу́, -есёшь**; *pt* **-ёс, -есла́**, *impf* **относи́ть**) *сов перех* to take (off); (*подлеж*: *течение*) to carry off; (*причислить к*): **отнести́ что-н к** *+dat* (*к периоду, к году*) to date sth back to; (*к число группе*) to categorize sth as; (*к категории*) to put sth into; **относи́ть** (*perf* **отнести́**) **что-н за** *или* **на счёт** *+gen* to put sth down to; **отнести́сь** (*impf* **относи́ться**) *сов возв*: **отнести́сь к** *+dat* (*к человеку*) to treat; (*к предложению, к событию*) to take

отнима́|ть (**-ю**) *несов от* **отня́ть**

относи́тельно *нареч* relatively ▷ *предл* (*+gen*: *в отношении*) regarding, with regard to

относи́тельный *прил* relative

отн|оси́ть (**-ошу́, -о́сишь**) *несов от* **отнести́**; **относи́ться** *несов от* **отнести́сь** ▷ *возв*: **относи́ться к** *+dat* to relate to; (*к классу*) to belong to; (*к году*) to date from; **он к ней хорошо́ отно́сится** he likes her; **как ты отно́сишься к нему́?** what do you think about him?; **э́то к нам не отно́сится** it has nothing to do with us

отноше́ни|е (**-я**) *ср* (*Мат*) ratio; **отноше́ние (к** *+dat*) attitude (to); (*связь*) relation (to); **в отноше́нии** *+gen* with regard to; **по отноше́нию к** *+dat* towards; **в э́том отноше́нии** in this respect *или* regard; **в не́котором отноше́нии** in certain respects; **име́ть** (*impf*) **отноше́ние к** *+dat* to be connected with; **не име́ть** (*impf*) **отноше́ния к** *+dat* to have nothing to do with

отню́дь *нареч*: **отню́дь не** by no means, far from; **отню́дь нет** absolutely not

отн|я́ть (**-иму́, -и́мешь**; *impf* **отнима́ть**) *сов перех* to take away; (*силы, время*) to take up

ото *предл* = **от**

от|обра́ть (**-беру́, -берёшь**; *pt* **-обра́л, -обрала́**, *impf* **отбира́ть**) *сов перех* (*отнять*) to take away; (*выбрать*) to select

отовсю́ду *нареч* from all around

от|огна́ть (**-гоню́, -го́нишь**; *impf* **отгоня́ть**) *сов перех* to chase away

отодви́н|уть (**-у**; *impf* **отодвига́ть**) *сов перех* (*шкаф*) to move; (*засов*) to slide back; (*срок, экзамен*) to put back; **отодви́нуться** (*impf* **отодвига́ться**) *сов возв* (*человек*) to move

от|озва́ть (**-зову́, -зовёшь**; *impf* **отзыва́ть**) *сов перех* to call back; (*посла, документы*) to recall; **отзыва́ть** (*perf* **отозва́ть**) **кого́-н в сто́рону** to take sb aside; **отозва́ться** (*impf* **отзыва́ться**) *сов возв*: **отозва́ться (на** *+acc*) to respond (to); **хорошо́/пло́хо отозва́ться** (*perf*) **о** *+prp* to speak well/badly of

отойти́ (*как* **идти**; см *Table 18*;

impf **отходи́ть**) *сов* (*поезд, автобус*) to leave; (*пятно*) to come out; (*отлучиться*) to go off; **отходи́ть (***perf* **отойти́) от** *+gen* to move away from; (*перен*: *от друзей, от взглядов*) to distance o.s. from; (*от темы*) to depart from
отом|сти́ть (**-щу́, -сти́шь**) *сов от* **мстить**
отопи́тельный *прил* (*прибор*) heating; **отопи́тельный сезо́н** the cold season

Отопи́тельный сезо́н

The heating comes on around the middle of October and goes off around the middle of May. The central heating is controlled centrally and individual home owners do not have any say over it.

отопле́ни|е (**-я**) *ср* heating
оторв|а́ть (**-у́, -ёшь**; *impf* **отрыва́ть**) *сов перех* to tear off; **отрыва́ть (***perf* **оторва́ть) (от** *+gen*) to tear away (from); **оторва́ться** (*impf* **отрыва́ться**) *сов возв* (*пуговица*) to come off; **отрыва́ться (***perf* **оторва́ться) (от** *+gen*) (*от работы*) to tear o.s. away (from); (*убежать*) to break away (from); (*от семьи*) to lose touch (with); **отрыва́ться (***perf* **оторва́ться) от земли́** (*самолёт*) to take off
отпева́ни|е (**-я**) *ср* funeral service; **отпева́|ть** (**-ю**) *несов от* **отпе́ть**
отп|е́ть (**-ою́, -оёшь**; *impf* **отпева́ть**) *сов перех* (*Рел*) to conduct a funeral service for
отпеча́та|ть (**-ю**; *impf* **отпеча́тывать**) *сов перех* to print; **отпеча́таться** (*impf* **отпеча́тываться**) *сов возв* (*на земле*) to leave a print; (*перен*: *в памяти*) to imprint itself
отпеча́т|ок (**-ка**) *м* imprint; **отпеча́тки па́льцев** fingerprints
отпира́|ть (**-ю**) *несов от* **отпере́ть**
отпл|ати́ть (**-ачу́, -а́тишь**; *impf* **отпла́чивать**) *сов* (*+dat*: *наградить*) to repay; (*отомстить*) to pay back
отплы́|ть (**-ву́, -вёшь**; *impf* **отплыва́ть**) *сов* (*человек*) to swim off; (*корабль*) to set sail
отполз|ти́ (**-у́, -ёшь**; *impf* **отполза́ть**) *сов* to crawl away
отправи́тел|ь (**-я**) *м* sender
отпра́в|ить (**-лю, -ишь**; *impf* **отправля́ть**) *сов перех* to send; **отпра́виться** (*impf* **отправля́ться**) *сов возв* (*человек*) to set off
отпра́в|ка (**-ки**; *gen pl* **-ок**) *ж* (*письма*) posting; (*груза*) dispatch
отправле́ни|е (**-я**) *ср* (*письма*) dispatch; (*почтовое*) item
отправн|о́й *прил*: **отправно́й пункт** point of departure; **отправна́я то́чка** (*перен*) starting point
отпр|оси́ться (**-ошу́сь, -о́сишься**; *impf* **отпра́шиваться**) *сов перех* to ask permission to leave
о́тпуск (**-а**) *м* holiday (*Brit*), vacation (*US*); **быть** (*impf*) **в о́тпуске** to be on holiday
отп|усти́ть (**-ущу́, -у́стишь**; *impf* **отпуска́ть**) *сов перех* to let out; (*из рук*) to let go of; (*товар*) to sell; (*деньги*) to release; (*бороду*) to grow
отрабо́та|ть (**-ю**; *impf* **отраба́тывать**) *сов перех*

(*какое-то время*) to work; (*освоить*) to perfect, polish ▷ *неперех* (*кончить работать*) to finish work

отр|авить (**-авлю́, -а́вишь**; *impf* **отравля́ть**) *сов перех* to poison; (*перен*: *праздник*) to spoil; **отрави́ться** (*impf* **отравля́ться**) *сов возв* to poison o.s.; (*едой*) to get food-poisoning

отраже́ни|е (**-я**) *ср* (*см глаг*) reflection; deflection

отра|зи́ть (**-жу́, -зи́шь**; *impf* **отража́ть**) *сов перех* to reflect; (*удар*) to deflect; **отрази́ться** (*impf* **отража́ться**) *сов возв*: **отрази́ться в** *+prp* to be reflected; **отража́ться** (*perf* **отрази́ться**) (*в зеркале*) to be reflected in; **отража́ться** (*perf* **отрази́ться**) **на** *+prp* (*на здоровье*) to have an effect on

о́трасл|ь (**-и**) *ж* branch (*of industry*)

отр|асти́ (*3sg* **-астёт**, *pt* **-о́с, -осла́**, *impf* **отраста́ть**) *сов* to grow

отра|сти́ть (**-щу́, -сти́шь**; *impf* **отра́щивать**) *сов перех* to grow

отре́з (**-а**) *м* piece of fabric

отре́|зать (**-жу, -жешь**; *impf* **отреза́ть**) *сов перех* to cut off

отре́з|ок (**-ка**) *м* (*ткани*) piece; (*пути*) section; (*времени*) period

отрица́ни|е (**-я**) *ср* denial; (*Линг*) negation; **отрица́тельный** *прил* negative

отрица́|ть (**-ю**) *несов перех* to deny; (*моду итп*) to reject

отро́ст|ок (**-ка**) *м* (*побег*) shoot

отр|уби́ть (**-ублю́, -у́бишь**; *impf* **отруба́ть**) *сов перех* to chop off

отруга́|ть (**-ю**) *сов от* **руга́ть**

отры́в (**-а**) *м*: **отры́в от** *+gen* (*от семьи*) separation from; **ли́ния отры́ва** perforated line; **быть** (*impf*) **в отры́ве от** *+gen* to be cut off from

отрыва́|ть(ся) (**-ю(сь)**) *несов от* **оторва́ть(ся)**

отря́д (**-а**) *м* party, group; (*Воен*) detachment

отряхн|у́ть (**-у́, -ёшь**; *impf* **отря́хивать**) *сов перех* (*снег, пыль*) to shake off; (*пальто*) to shake down

отсе́к (**-а**) *м* compartment

отс|е́чь (**-еку́, -ечёшь** *etc*, **-ку́т**; *pt* **-ёк, -екла́**, *impf* **отсека́ть**) *сов перех* to cut off

отск|очи́ть (**-очу́, -о́чишь**; *impf* **отска́кивать**) *сов* (*в сторону, назад*) to jump; (*разг*: *пуговица, кнопка*) to come off; **отска́кивать** (*perf* **отскочи́ть**) **от** *+gen* (*мяч*) to bounce off; (*человек*) to jump off

отсро́ч|ить (**-у, -ишь**; *impf* **отсро́чивать**) *сов перех* to defer

отста|ва́ть (**-ю́, -ёшь**) *несов от* **отста́ть**

отста́в|ка (**-ки**; *gen pl* **-ок**) *ж* retirement; (*кабинета*) resignation; **подава́ть** (*perf* **пода́ть**) **в отста́вку** to offer one's resignation

отста́ива|ть(ся) (**-ю**) *несов от* **отстоя́ть(ся)**

отста́лый *прил* backward

отста́|ть (**-ну, -нешь**; *impf* **отстава́ть**) *сов* (*перен*: *в учёбе, в работе*) to fall behind; (*часы*) to be slow; **отстава́ть** (*perf* **отста́ть**) (**от** *+gen*) (*от группы*) to fall behind; (*от поезда, от автобуса*) to be left behind; **отста́нь от меня́!** stop pestering me!

отсто|я́ть (**-ю́, -и́шь**; *impf* **отста́ивать**) *сов перех* (*город, своё мнение*) to defend; (*раствор*) to allow to stand; (*два часа итп*) to wait; **отстоя́ться** (*impf*

отстáиваться) *сов возв* to settle
отстран|и́ть (**-ю́, -и́шь**; *impf* **отстраня́ть**) *сов перех* (*отодвинуть*) to push away; (*уволить*): **отстрани́ть от** *+gen* to remove, dismiss; **отстрани́ться** (*impf* **отстраня́ться**) *сов возв*: **отстрани́ться от** *+gen* (*от должности*) to relinquish; (*отодвинуться*) to draw back
отст|упи́ть (**-уплю́, -ýпишь**; *impf* **отступáть**) *сов* to step back; (*Воен*) to retreat; (*перен*: *перед трудностями*) to give up
отступлéни|е (**-я**) *ср* retreat; (*от темы*) digression
отсýтстви|е (**-я**) *ср* (*человека*) absence; (*денег, вкуса*) lack
отсýтств|овать (**-ую**) *несов* (*в классе итп*) to be absent; (*желание*) to be lacking
отсýтствующ|ий *прил* (*взгляд, вид*) absent ▷ (**-его**) *м* absentee
отсчёт (**-а**) *м* (*минут*) calculation; **тóчка отсчёта** point of reference
отсчитá|ть (**-ю**; *impf* **отсчи́тывать**) *сов перех* (*деньги*) to count out
отсю́да *нареч* from here
оттáива|ть (**-ю**) *несов от* **оттáять**
оттáлкива|ть(ся) (**-ю(сь)**) *несов от* **оттолкнýть(ся)**
отт|ащи́ть (**-ащý, -áщишь**; *impf* **оттáскивать**) *сов перех* to drag
оттá|ять (**-ю**; *impf* **оттáивать**) *сов* (*земля*) to thaw; (*мясо*) to thaw out
оттéн|ок (**-ка**) *м* shade
óттепел|ь (**-и**) *ж* thaw
óттиск (**-а**) *м* (*ступни*) impression; (*рисунка*) print
оттогó *нареч* for this reason; **оттогó что** because
оттолкн|ýть (**-ý, -ёшь**; *impf* **оттáлкивать**) *сов перех* to push away; **оттолкнýться** (*impf* **оттáлкиваться**) *сов возв*: **оттолкнýться от чегó-н** (*от берега*) to push o.s. away *или* back from sth; (*перен*: *от данных*) to take sth as one's starting point
оттýда *нареч* from there
отт|янýть (**-янý, -я́нешь**; *impf* **оття́гивать**) *сов перех* to pull back; (*карман*) to stretch; (*разг*: *выполнение*) to delay; **оття́гивать** (**оттянýть** *impf*) **врéмя** to play for time
от|учи́ть (**-учý, -ýчишь**; *impf* **отучáть**) *сов перех*: **отучи́ть когó-н от** *+gen* (*от курения*) to wean sb off; **отучáть** (*perf* **отучи́ть**) **когó-н** *+infin* (*врать*) to teach sb not to do; **отучи́ться** (*impf* **отучáться**) *сов возв*: **отучи́ться** *+infin* to get out of the habit of doing
отхлы́н|уть (*3sg* **-ет**) *сов* (*волны*) to roll back
отхóд (**-а**) *м* departure; (*Воен*) withdrawal; *см также* **отхóды**
отх|оди́ть (**-ожý, -óдишь**) *несов от* **отойти́**
отхóд|ы (**-ов**) *мн* waste *ед*
отцá *etc сущ см* **отéц**
отцóвский *прил* father's; (*чувства, права*) paternal
отчáива|ться (**-юсь**) *несов от* **отчáяться**
отчáл|ить (**-ю, -ишь**; *impf* **отчáливать**) *сов* to set sail
отчáяни|е (**-я**) *ср* despair; **отчáянный** *прил* desperate; (*смелый*) daring; **отчá|яться** (**-юсь**; *impf* **отчáиваться**) *сов возв*: **отчáяться** (*+infin*) to despair (of doing)
отчегó *нареч* (*почему*) why ▷ *союз* (*вследствие чего*) which is why; **отчегó-нибудь** *нареч* for

any reason; **отчего́-то** *нареч* for some reason
о́тчеств|о (**-а**) *ср* patronymic

О́тчество

The full name of a Russian person must include his or her patronymic. Besides being the formal way of addressing people, the use of the patronymic also shows your respect for that person. Patronymics are not as officious as they sound to some foreign ears. In fact, quite often the patronymic replaces the first name and is used as an affectionate way of addressing people you know well.

отчёт (**-а**) *м* account; **фина́нсовый отчёт** financial report; (*выписка*) statement; **отдава́ть** (*perf* **отда́ть**) **себе́ отчёт в чём-н** to realize sth
отчётливый *прил* distinct; (*объяснение*) clear
отчи́зн|а (**-ы**) *ж* mother country
о́тчим (**-а**) *м* stepfather
отчисле́ни|е (**-я**) *ср* (*работника*) dismissal; (*студента*) expulsion; (*обычно мн*: *на строительство*) allocation; (: *денежные*: *удержание*) deduction: (: *выделение*) assignment
отчита́|ть (**-ю**; *impf* **отчи́тывать**) *сов перех* (*ребёнка*) to tell off; **отчита́ться** (*impf* **отчи́тываться**) *сов возв* to report
отъе́зд (**-а**) *м* departure; **быть** (*impf*) **в отъе́зде** to be away
отъе́хать (*как* **е́хать**; см *Table 19*; *impf* **отъезжа́ть**) *сов* to travel; **отъезжа́ть** (*perf* **отъе́хать**) **от** *+gen* to move away from
отъя́вленный *прил* utter
отыгра́|ть (**-ю**; *impf* **оты́грывать**) *сов перех* to win back; **отыгра́ться** (*impf* **оты́грываться**) *сов возв* (*в карты, в шахматы*) to win again; (*перен*) to get one's own back
от|ыска́ть (**-ыщу́, -ы́щешь**; *impf* **оты́скивать**) *сов перех* to hunt out; (*Комп*) to retrieve
о́фис (**-а**) *м* office
офице́р (**-а**) *м* (*Воен*) officer; (*разг*: *Шахматы*) bishop
официа́льн|ый *прил* official; **официа́льное лицо́** official
официа́нт (**-а**) *м* waiter
офла́йный *прил* off-line
оформи́тел|ь (**-я**) *м*: **оформи́тель спекта́кля** set designer; **оформи́тель витри́н** window dresser
офо́рм|ить (**-лю, -ишь**; *impf* **оформля́ть**) *сов перех* (*документы, договор*) to draw up; (*книгу*) to design the layout of; (*витрину*) to dress; (*спектакль*) to design the sets for; **оформля́ть** (*perf* **офо́рмить**) **кого́-н на рабо́ту** (*+instr*) to take sb on (as); **офо́рмиться** (*impf* **оформля́ться**) *сов возв* (*взгляды*) to form; **оформля́ться** (*perf* **офо́рмиться**) **на рабо́ту** (*+instr*) to be taken on (as)
оформле́ни|е (**-я**) *ср* design; (*документов, договора*) drawing up; **музыка́льное оформле́ние** music
оформля́|ть(ся) (**-ю(сь)**) *несов от* **офо́рмить**
оффшо́рный *прил* (*Комм*) offshore
охладе́|ть (**-ю**; *impf* **охладева́ть**) *сов* (*отношения*) to cool; **охладева́ть** (*perf* **охладе́ть**) **к**

+*dat* (*к мужу*) to grow cool towards
охла|ди́ть (**-жу́, -ди́шь**; *impf* **охлажда́ть**) *сов перех* (*воду, чувства*) to cool; **охлади́ться** (*impf* **охлажда́ться**) *сов возв* (*печка, вода*) to cool down
охо́т|а (**-ы**) *ж* hunt; (*разг*: *желание*) desire; **охо́|титься** (**-чусь, -тишься**) *несов возв*: **охо́титься на** +*acc* to hunt (*to kill*); **охо́титься** (*impf*) **за** +*instr* to hunt (*to catch*); (*перен*: *разг*) to hunt for; **охо́тник** (**-а**) *м* hunter; **охо́тничий** *прил* hunting
охо́тно *нареч* willingly
охра́н|а (**-ы**) *ж* (*защита*) security; (*группа людей*) bodyguard; (*растений, животных*) protection; (*здоровья*) care; **охра́на труда́** health and safety regulations
охра́нник (**-а**) *м* guard
охраня́|ть (**-ю**) *несов перех* to guard; (*природу*) to protect
оц|ени́ть (**-еню́, -е́нишь**; *impf* **оце́нивать**) *сов перех* (*вещь*) to value; (*знания*) to assess; (*признать достоинства*) to appreciate; **оце́н|ка** (**-ки**; *gen pl* **-ок**) *ж* (*вещи*) valuation; (*работника, поступка*) assessment; (*отметка*) mark
оц|епи́ть (**-еплю́, -е́пишь**; *impf* **оцепля́ть**) *сов перех* to cordon off
оча́г (**-а́**) *м* hearth; (*перен*: *заболевания*) source
очарова́ни|е (**-я**) *ср* charm
очарова́тельный *прил* charming
очар|ова́ть (**-у́ю**; *impf* **очаро́вывать**) *сов перех* to charm
очеви́дно *нареч, част* obviously ▷ *как сказ*: **очеви́дно, что он винова́т** it's obvious that he is guilty ▷ *вводн сл*: **очеви́дно, он не придёт** apparently he's not coming; **очеви́дный** *прил* (*факт*) plain; (*желание*) obvious
о́чень *нареч* +*adv*, +*adj* very +*vb* very much
очередно́й *прил* next; (*ближайший*: *задача*) immediate; (: *номер газеты*) latest; (*повторяющийся*) another
о́черед|ь (**-и**) *ж* (*порядок*) order; (*место в порядке*) turn; (*группа людей*) queue (*Brit*), line (*US*); (*в строительстве*) section; **в пе́рвую о́чередь** in the first instance; **в поря́дке о́череди** when one's turn comes; **в свою́ о́чередь** in turn; **по о́череди** in turn
о́черк (**-а**) *м* (*литературный*) essay; (*газетный*) sketch
очерта́ни|е (**-я**) *ср* outline
оче́чник (**-а**) *м* spectacle case
очи́|стить (**-щу, -стишь**; *impf* **очища́ть**) *сов перех* to clean; (*газ, воду*) to purify; (*город, квартиру*) to clear; **очи́ститься** (*impf* **очища́ться**) *сов возв* (*газ, вода*) to be purified
очистн|о́й *прил*: **очистны́е сооруже́ния** purification plant *ед*
очища́|ть(ся) (**-ю**) *несов от* **очи́стить(ся)**
очк|и́ (**-ов**) *мн* (*для чтения*) glasses, spectacles; (*для плавания*) goggles; **защи́тные очки́** safety specs
очк|о́ (**-а́**) *ср* (*Спорт*) point; (*Карты*) pip
очн|у́ться (**-у́сь, -ёшься**) *сов возв* (*после сна*) to wake up; (*после обморока*) to come round
о́чн|ый *прил* (*обучение, институт итп*) *with direct contact between students and teachers*; **о́чная ста́вка** (*Юр*) confrontation

О

О́чное отделе́ние

This is one of the ways of obtaining a degree. Most students choose this method. It is full time course with over 30 contact hours a week and two exam sessions. See also notes at **зао́чный** and **вече́рный**.

оч|ути́ться (*2sg* **-у́тишься**) *сов возв* to end up
оше́йник (**-а**) *м* collar
ош|иби́ться (**-ибу́сь, -ибёшься**; *pt* **-и́бся, -и́блась**, *impf* **ошиба́ться**) *сов возв* to make a mistake; **ошиба́ться** (*perf* **ошиби́ться**) **в ком-н** to misjudge sb; **оши́б|ка** (**-ки**; *gen pl* **-ок**) *ж* mistake, error; **по оши́бке** by mistake; **оши́бочный** *прил* (*мнение*) mistaken, erroneous; (*суждение, вывод*) wrong
ощу́па|ть (**-ю**; *impf* **ощу́пывать**) *сов перех* to feel; **о́щуп|ь** (**-и**) *ж*: **на о́щупь** by touch; **пробира́ться** (*impf*) **на о́щупь** to grope one's way through
ощу|ти́ть (**-щу́, -ти́шь**; *impf* **ощуща́ть**) *сов перех* (*желание, боль*) to feel
ощуще́ни|е (**-я**) *ср* sense; (*радости, боли*) feeling

павильо́н (**-а**) *м* pavilion
павли́н (**-а**) *м* peacock
па́да|ть (**-ю**; *perf* **упа́сть** *или* **пасть**) *несов* to fall; (*настроение*) to sink; (*дисциплина, нравы*) to decline
паде́ж (**-а́**) *м* (*Линг*) case
паде́ни|е (**-я**) *ср* fall; (*нравов, дисциплины*) decline
па́йщик (**-а**) *м* shareholder
паке́т (**-а**) *м* package; (*мешок*) (paper *или* plastic) bag
пак|ова́ть (**-у́ю**; *perf* **запакова́ть** *или* **упакова́ть**) *несов перех* to pack
пала́т|а (**-ы**) *ж* (*в больнице*) ward; (*Полит*) chamber, house
пала́т|ка (**-ки**; *gen pl* **-ок**) *ж* tent
па́л|ец (**-ьца**) *м* (*руки*) finger; (*ноги*) toe; **большо́й па́лец** (*руки*) thumb; (*ноги*) big toe
па́л|ка (**-ки**; *gen pl* **-ок**) *ж* stick

пало́мничеств|о (**-а**) *ср* pilgrimage
па́лоч|ка (**-ки**; *gen pl* **-ек**) *ж* (*Муз*): **дирижёрская па́лочка** (conductor's) baton; **волше́бная па́лочка** magic wand
па́луб|а (**-ы**) *ж* (*Мор*) deck
па́льм|а (**-ы**) *ж* palm (tree)
пальто́ *ср нескл* overcoat
па́мятник (**-а**) *м* monument; (*на могиле*) tombstone
па́мят|ь (**-и**) *ж* memory; (*воспоминание*) memories *мн*
пана́м|а (**-ы**) *ж* Panama (hat)
пане́л|ь (**-и**) *ж* (*Строит*) panel
па́ник|а (**-и**) *ж* panic; **паник|ова́ть** (**-у́ю**) *несов* (*разг*) to panic
панихи́д|а (**-ы**) *ж* (*Рел*) funeral service; **гражда́нская панихи́да** civil funeral
панора́м|а (**-ы**) *ж* panorama
пансиона́т (**-а**) *м* boarding house
па́п|а (**-ы**) *м* dad; (*также* **Ри́мский па́па**) the Pope
папиро́с|а (**-ы**) *ж* *type of cigarette*
папиро́сн|ый *прил*: **папиро́сная бума́га** (*тонкая бумага*) tissue paper
па́п|ка (**-ки**; *gen pl* **-ок**) *ж* folder (*Brit*), file (*US*)
пар (**-а**; *nom pl* **-ы́**) *м* steam; *см также* **пары́**
па́р|а (**-ы**) *ж* (*туфель итп*) pair; (*супружеская*) couple
пара́граф (**-а**) *м* paragraph
пара́д (**-а**) *м* parade
пара́дн|ое (**-ого**) *ср* entrance
пара́дный *прил* (*вход, лестница*) front, main
парадо́кс (**-а**) *м* paradox
парази́т (**-а**) *м* parasite
парали́ч (**-а́**) *м* paralysis
паралле́л|ь (**-и**) *ж* parallel
парашю́т (**-а**) *м* parachute
па́рен|ь (**-я**) *м* (*разг*) guy
пари́ *ср нескл* bet
Пари́ж (**-а**) *м* Paris
пари́к (**-а́**) *м* wig
парикма́хер (**-а**) *м* hairdresser; **парикма́херск|ая** (**-ой**) *ж* hairdresser's (*Brit*), beauty salon (*US*)
па́р|иться (**-юсь, -ишься**) *несов возв* (*в бане*) to have a sauna
пар|и́ть (**-ю́, -и́шь**) *несов* to glide
парк (**-а**) *м* park
парк|ова́ть (**-у́ю**) *несов перех* to park
парла́мент (**-а**) *м* parliament
парла́ментский *прил* parliamentary
парни́к (**-а́**) *м* greenhouse
парнико́вый *прил*: **парнико́вый эффе́кт** greenhouse effect
парово́з (**-а**) *м* steam engine
паров|о́й *прил* steam; **парово́е отопле́ние** central heating
паро́ди|я (**-и**) *ж*: **паро́дия (на** *+acc*) parody (of)
паро́л|ь (**-я**) *м* password
паро́м (**-а**) *м* ferry
па́рт|а (**-ы**) *ж* desk (*in schools*)
парте́р (**-а**) *м* the stalls *мн*
парти́йный *прил* party
па́рти|я (**-и**) *ж* (*Полит*) party; (*Муз*) part; (*груза*) consignment; (*изделий: в производстве*) batch; (*Спорт*): **па́ртия в ша́хматы/волейбо́л** a game of chess/volleyball
партнёр (**-а**) *м* partner; **партнёрств|о** (**-а**) *ср* partnership
па́рус (**-а**; *nom pl* **-а́**) *м* sail
парфюме́ри|я (**-и**) *ж собир* *perfume and cosmetic goods*
пар|ы́ (**-о́в**) *мн* vapour *ед* (*Brit*), vapor *ед* (*US*)
пас (**-а**) *м* (*Спорт*) pass

па́смурный *прил* overcast, dull
па́спорт (**-а**; *nom pl* **-á**) *м* passport; (*автомобиля, станка*) registration document

Па́спорт

Russian citizens are required by law to have a passport at the age of 14. This is then renewed at the ages of 20 and 45. The passport serves as an essential identification document and has to be produced on various occasions ranging from applying for a job to collecting a parcel from the post office. Those who travel abroad have to get a separate passport for foreign travel.

пассажи́р (**-а**) *м* passenger
пасси́вный *прил* passive
па́ст|а (**-ы**) *ж* paste; (*томатная*) purée; **зубна́я па́ста** toothpaste
пас|ти́ (**-у́, -ёшь**; *pt* **-, -ла́**) *несов перех* (*скот*) to graze; **пасти́сь** *несов возв* to graze
паст|ила́ (**-илы́**; *nom pl* **-и́лы**) *ж* ≈ marshmallow
па|сть (**-ду́, -дёшь**; *pt* **-л, -ла, -ло**) *сов от* **па́дать** ▷ (**-сти**) *ж* (*зверя*) mouth
Па́сх|а (**-и**) *ж* (*в иудаизме*) Passover; (*в христианстве*) ≈ Easter
пате́нт (**-а**) *м* patent; **патент|ова́ть** (**-у́ю**; *perf* **запатентова́ть**) *несов перех* to patent
патриа́рх (**-а**) *м* patriarch
патро́н (**-а**) *м* (*Воен*) cartridge; (*лампы*) socket
патрули́р|овать (**-ую**) *несов (не) перех* to patrol
патру́л|ь (**-я́**) *м* patrol
па́уз|а (**-ы**) *ж* (*также Муз*) pause
пау́к (**-á**) *м* spider
паути́н|а (**-ы**) *ж* spider's web, spiderweb (*US*); (*в помещении*) cobweb; (*перен*) web
пах (**-а**; *loc sg* **-у́**) *м* groin
па|ха́ть (**-шу́, -шешь**; *perf* **вспаха́ть**) *несов перех* to plough (*Brit*), plow (*US*)
па́х|нуть (**-ну**; *pt* **-, -ла**) *несов*: **па́хнуть** (**+*instr***) to smell (of)
пацие́нт (**-а**) *м* patient
па́ч|ка (**-ки**; *gen pl* **-ек**) *ж* (*бумаг*) bundle; (*чая, сигарет итп*) packet
па́чка|ть (**-ю**; *perf* **запа́чкать** *или* **испа́чкать**) *несов перех*: **па́чкать что-н** to get sth dirty; **па́чкаться** (*perf* **запа́чкаться** *или* **испа́чкаться**) *несов возв* to get dirty
паште́т (**-а**) *м* pâté
working|ть (**-ю**) *несов перех* to solder
пев|е́ц (**-цá**) *м* singer; **певи́ц|а** (**-ы**) *ж от* **пев́ец**
педаго́г (**-а**) *м* teacher; **педагоги́ческий** *прил* (*коллектив*) teaching; **педагоги́ческий институ́т** teacher-training (*Brit*) *или* teachers' (*US*) college; **педагоги́ческий сове́т** staff meeting
педа́л|ь (**-и**) *ж* pedal
педиа́тр (**-а**) *м* paediatrician (*Brit*), pediatrician (*US*)
пей *несов см* **пить**
пе́йджер (**-а**) *м* pager
пейза́ж (**-а**) *м* landscape
пе́йте *несов см* **пить**
пека́р|ня (**-ни**; *gen pl* **-ен**) *ж* bakery
пелён|ка (**-ки**; *gen pl* **-ок**) *ж* swaddling clothes *мн*
пельме́н|ь (**-я**; *nom pl* **-и**) *м* (*обычно мн*) ≈ ravioli *ед*

пе́н|а (**-ы**) *ж* (*мыльная*) suds *мн*; (*морская*) foam; (*бульонная*) froth
пена́л (**-а**) *м* pencil case
пе́ни|е (**-я**) *ср* singing
пе́н|иться (*3sg* **-ится**, *perf* **вспе́ниться**) *несов возв* to foam, froth
пеницилли́н (**-а**) *м* penicillin
пе́нк|а (**-и**) *ж* (*на молоке*) skin
пенсионе́р (**-а**) *м* pensioner
пенсио́нный *прил* (*фонд*) pension
пе́нси|я (**-и**) *ж* pension; **выходи́ть** (*perf* **вы́йти**) **на пе́нсию** to retire
пень (**пня**) *м* (tree) stump
пе́п|ел (**-ла**) *м* ash; **пе́пельниц|а** (**-ы**) *ж* ashtray
пе́рвенств|о (**-а**) *ср* championship; (*место*) first place
пе́рв|ое (**-ого**) *ср* first course
первокла́ссник (**-а**) *м* *pupil in first year at school*
первонача́льный *прил* (*исходный*) original, initial
пе́рв|ый *чис* first; (*по времени*) first, earliest; **пе́рвый эта́ж** ground (*Brit*) *или* first (*US*) floor; **пе́рвое вре́мя** at first; **в пе́рвую о́чередь** in the first place *или* instance; **пе́рвый час дня/но́чи** after midday/midnight; **това́р пе́рвого со́рта** top grade product (*on a scale of 1-3*); **пе́рвая по́мощь** first aid
перебежа́ть (*как* **бежа́ть**; см *Table 20*; *impf* **перебега́ть**) *сов*: **перебежа́ть (че́рез** *+acc*) to run across
перебива́|ть (**-ю**) *несов от* **переби́ть**
перебира́|ть(ся) (**-ю(сь)**) *несов от* **перебра́ть(ся)**
переб|и́ть (**-ью́, -ьёшь**; *impf* **перебива́ть**) *сов перех* to interrupt; (*разбить*) to break
переболе́|ть (**-ю**) *сов +instr* to recover from
переб|оро́ть (**-орю́, -о́решь**) *сов перех* to overcome
перебра́сыва|ть (**-ю**) *несов от* **перебро́сить**
переб|ра́ть (**-еру́, -ерёшь**; *impf* **перебира́ть**) *сов перех* (*бумаги*) to sort out; (*крупу, ягоды*) to sort; (*события*) to go over *или* through (in one's mind); **перебра́ться** (*impf* **перебира́ться**) *сов возв* (*через реку*) to manage to get across
перебро́|сить (**-шу, -сишь**; *impf* **перебра́сывать**) *сов перех* (*мяч*) to throw; (*войска*) to transfer
перева́л (**-а**) *м* (*в горах*) pass
перева́лочный *прил*: **перева́лочный пункт/ла́герь** transit area/camp
перев|ари́ть (**-арю́, -а́ришь**; *impf* **перева́ривать**) *сов перех* to overcook (*by boiling*); (*пищу, информацию*) to digest; **перевари́ться** (*impf* **перева́риваться**) *сов возв* to be overcooked *или* overdone; (*пища*) to be digested
перев|езти́ (**-езу́, -езёшь**; *pt* **-ёз, -езла́**, *impf* **перевози́ть**) *сов перех* to take *или* transport across
переверн|у́ть (**-у́, -ёшь**; *impf* **перевора́чивать**) *сов перех* to turn over; (*изменить*) to change (completely); (*no impf*: *комнату*) to turn upside down; **переверну́ться** (*impf* **перевора́чиваться**) *сов возв* (*человек*) to turn over; (*лодка, машина*) to overturn
переве́с (**-а**) *м* (*преимущество*) advantage
перев|ести́ (**-еду́, -едёшь**; *pt* **-ёл, -ела́**, *impf* **переводи́ть**) *сов*

П

перех (*помочь перейти*) to take across; (*текст*) to translate; (: *устно*) to interpret; (*часы*) to reset; (*учреждение, сотрудника*) to transfer, move; (*переслать: деньги*) to transfer; (*доллары, метры итп*) to convert; **перевести́сь** (*impf* **переводи́ться**) *сов возв* to move
перево́д (**-а**) *м* transfer; (*стрелки часов*) resetting; (*текст*) translation; (*деньги*) remittance
перев|оди́ть(ся) (**-ожу́(сь), -о́дишь(ся)**) *несов от* **перевести́(сь)**
перево́дчик (**-а**) *м* translator; (*устный*) interpreter
перев|ози́ть (**-ожу́, -о́зишь**) *несов от* **перевезти́**
перевора́чива|ть(ся) (**-ю(сь)**) *несов от* **переверну́ться(ся)**
переворо́т (**-а**) *м* (*Полит*) coup (d'état); (*в судьбе*) turning point
перев|яза́ть (**-яжу́, -я́жешь**; *impf* **перевя́зывать**) *сов перех* (*руку, раненого*) to bandage; (*рану*) to dress, bandage; (*коробку*) to tie up
перег|на́ть (**-оню́, -о́нишь**; *pt* **-на́л, -нала́, -на́ло**, *impf* **перегоня́ть**) *сов перех* (*обогнать*) to overtake; (*нефть*) to refine; (*спирт*) to distil (*Brit*), distill (*US*)
перегова́рива|ться (**-юсь**) *несов возв*: **перегова́риваться (с +*instr*)** to exchange remarks (with)
перегово́рный *прил*: **перегово́рный пункт** telephone office (*for long-distance calls*)
перегово́р|ы (**-ов**) *мн* negotiations, talks; (*по телефону*) call *ед*
перегоня́|ть (**-ю**) *несов от* **перегна́ть**
перегор|е́ть (*3sg* **-и́т**, *impf* **перегора́ть**) *сов* (*лампочка*) to fuse; (*двигатель*) to burn out
перегоро|ди́ть (**-жу́, -ди́шь**; *impf* **перегора́живать**) *сов перех* (*комнату*) to partition (off); (*дорогу*) to block
перегр|узи́ть (**-ужу́, -у́зишь**; *impf* **перегружа́ть**) *сов перех* to overload
перегру́з|ка (**-ки**; *gen pl* **-ок**) *ж* overload; (*обычно мн*: *нервные*) strain

КЛЮЧЕВОЕ СЛОВО

пе́ред *предл +instr*
1 (*о положении, в присутствии*) in front of
2 (*раньше чего-н*) before
3 (*об объекте воздействия*): **пе́ред тру́дностями** in the face of difficulties; **извиня́ться (*perf* извини́ться) пе́ред кем-н** to apologize to sb; **отчи́тываться (*perf* отчита́ться) пе́ред +*instr*** to report to
4 (*по сравнению*) compared to
5 (*как союз*): **пе́ред тем как** before; **пе́ред тем как зако́нчить** before finishing

переда|ва́ть (**-ю́**; *imper* **передава́й(те)**) *несов от* **переда́ть**
переда́м *etc сов см* **переда́ть**
переда́тчик (**-а**) *м* transmitter
переда́|ть (*как* **дать**; см *Table 16*; *impf* **передава́ть**) *сов перех*: **переда́ть что-н (кому́-н)** (*письмо, подарок*) to pass *или* hand sth (over) (to sb); (*известие, интерес*) to pass sth on (to sb); **переда́йте ему́ (мой) приве́т** give him my regards; **переда́йте ей, что я не**

приду́ tell her I am not coming; **передава́ть (*perf* переда́ть) что-н по телеви́дению/ра́дио** to televise/broadcast sth
переда́ч|а (**-и**) *ж* (*денег, письма*) handing over; (*матча*) transmission; (*Тел, Радио*) programme (*Brit*), program (*US*); **програ́мма переда́ч** television and radio guide
переда́шь *сов см* **переда́ть**
передвига́|ть(ся) (**-ю(сь)**) *несов от* **передви́нуть(ся)**
передвиже́ни|е (**-я**) *ср* movement; **сре́дства передвиже́ния** means of transport
передви́н|уть (**-у**; *impf* **передвига́ть**) *сов перех* to move; **передви́нуться** (*impf* **передвига́ться**) *сов возв* to move
переде́ла|ть (**-ю**; *impf* **переде́лывать**) *сов перех* (*работу*) to redo; (*характер*) to change
пере́дний *прил* front
пере́дн|яя (**-ей**) *ж* (entrance) hall
пе́редо *предл* = **пе́ред**
передов|а́я (**-о́й**) *ж* (*также* **передова́я статья́**) editorial; (*также* **передова́я пози́ция**: *Воен*) vanguard
передово́й *прил* (*технология*) advanced; (*писатель, взгляды*) progressive
передр|азни́ть (**-азню́, -а́знишь**; *impf* **передра́знивать**) *сов перех* to mimic
перее́зд (**-а**) *м* (*в новый дом*) move
перее́хать (*как* **е́хать**; см *Table 19*; *impf* **переезжа́ть**) *сов* (*переселиться*) to move; **переезжа́ть (*perf* перее́хать) (че́рез *+acc*)** to cross
пережива́ни|е (**-я**) *ср* feeling
пережива́|ть (**-ю**) *несов от* **пережи́ть** ▷ *неперех*: **пережива́ть (за *+acc*)** (*разг*) to worry (about)
пережи́|ть (**-ву́, -вёшь**; *impf* **пережива́ть**) *сов перех* (*вытерпеть*) to suffer
перезвон|и́ть (**-ю́, -и́шь**; *impf* **перезва́нивать**) *сов* to phone (*Brit*) *или* call (*US*) back
пере|йти́ (*как* **идти́**; см *Table 18*; *impf* **переходи́ть**) *сов (не)перех*: **перейти́ (че́рез *+acc*)** to cross ▷ *неперех*: **перейти́ в/на *+acc*** (*поменять место*) to go (over) to; (*на другую работу*) to move to; **переходи́ть (*perf* перейти́) к *+dat*** (*к сыну итп*) to pass to; (*к делу, к обсуждению*) to turn to; **переходи́ть (*perf* перейти́) на *+acc*** to switch to
переки́н|уть (**-у**; *impf* **переки́дывать**) *сов перех* to throw
перекла́дыва|ть (**-ю**) *несов от* **переложи́ть**
переключа́тел|ь (**-я**) *м* switch
переключ|и́ть (**-у́, -и́шь**; *impf* **переключа́ть**) *сов перех* to switch; **переключи́ться** (*impf* **переключа́ться**) *сов возв*: **переключи́ться (на *+acc*)** (*внимание*) to shift (to)
перекопа́|ть (**-ю**) *сов перех* (*огород*) to dig up; (*разг*: *шкаф*) to rummage through
перекр|ести́ть (**-ещу́, -е́стишь**) *сов от* **крести́ть**; **перекрести́ться** *сов от* **крести́ться** ▷ (*impf* **перекре́щиваться**) *возв* (*дороги, интересы*) to cross
перекрёст|ок (**-ка**) *м* crossroads
перекр|ы́ть (**-о́ю, -о́ешь**; *impf*

П

перекрыва́ть) *сов перех* (*реку*) to dam; (*воду, газ*) to cut off
перек|упи́ть (**-уплю́, -у́пишь**; *impf* **перекупа́ть**) *сов перех* to buy
перек|уси́ть (**-ушу́, -у́сишь**) *сов* (*разг*) to have a snack
переле́з|ть (**-у, -ешь**; *pt* **-, -ла**, *impf* **перелеза́ть**) *сов (не)перех*: **переле́зть (че́рез +***acc***)** (*забор, канаву*) to climb (over)
перелёт (**-а**) *м* flight; (*птиц*) migration; **переле|те́ть** (**-чу́, -ти́шь**; *impf* **перелета́ть**) *сов (не)перех*: **перелете́ть (че́рез +***acc***)** to fly over
перелива́ни|е (**-я**) *ср*: **перелива́ние кро́ви** blood transfusion
перелива́|ть (**-ю**) *несов от* **перели́ть**
перелиста́|ть (**-ю**; *impf* **перели́стывать**) *сов перех* (*просмотреть*) to leaf through
перел|и́ть (**-ью́, -ьёшь**; *impf* **перелива́ть**) *сов перех* to pour (*from one container to another*); **перелива́ть (***perf* **перели́ть) кровь кому́-н** to give sb a blood transfusion
перел|ожи́ть (**-ожу́, -о́жишь**; *impf* **перекла́дывать**) *сов перех* to move; **перекла́дывать (***perf* **переложи́ть) что-н на кого́-н** (*задачу*) to pass sth onto sb
перело́м (**-а**) *м* (*Мед*) fracture; (*перен*) turning point
перело́мный *прил* critical
перема́тыва|ть (**-ю**) *несов от* **перемота́ть**
переме́н|а (**-ы**) *ж* change; (*в школе*) break (*Brit*), recess (*US*); **переме́нный** *прил* (*успех, ветер*) variable; **переме́нный ток** alternating current
переме|сти́ть (**-щу́, -сти́шь**; *impf* **перемеща́ть**) *сов перех* (*предмет*) to move; (*людей*) to transfer; **перемести́ться** (*impf* **перемеща́ться**) *сов возв* to move
перемеша́|ть (**-ю**; *impf* **переме́шивать**) *сов перех* (*кашу*) to stir; (*угли, дрова*) to poke; (*вещи, бумаги*) to mix up
перемеща́|ть(ся) (**-ю(сь)**) *несов от* **перемести́ть(ся)**
перемеще́ни|е (**-я**) *ср* transfer
переми́ри|е (**-я**) *ср* truce
перемота́|ть (**-ю**; *impf* **перема́тывать**) *сов перех* (*нитку*) to wind; (*плёнку*) to rewind
перенапряга́|ть (**-ю**) *несов от* **перенапря́чь**
перенаселённый *прил* overpopulated
перен|ести́ (**-есу́, -есёшь**; *pt* **-ёс, -есла́, -есло́**, *impf* **переноси́ть**) *сов перех*: **перенести́ что-н че́рез** *+acc* to carry sth over *или* across; (*поменять место*) to move; (*встречу, заседание*) to reschedule; (*болезнь*) to suffer from; (*голод, холод итп*) to endure
перенима́|ть (**-ю**) *несов от* **переня́ть**
перен|оси́ть (**-ошу́, -о́сишь**) *несов от* **перенести́** ▷ *перех*: **не переноси́ть антибио́тиков/ самолёта** to react badly to antibiotics/flying
перено́сиц|а (**-ы**) *ж* bridge of the nose
переносно́й *прил* portable
перено́сный *прил* (*значение*) figurative
перено́счик (**-а**) *м* (*Мед*) carrier
переноч|ева́ть (**-у́ю**) *сов от* **ночева́ть**

переоде́|ть (**-ну, -нешь**; *impf* **переодева́ть**) *сов перех* (*одежду*) to change (out of); **переодева́ть** (*perf* **переоде́ть**) **кого́-н** to change sb *или* sb's clothes; **переоде́ться** (*impf* **переодева́ться**) *сов возв* to change, get changed

перепа́д (**-а**) *м* +*gen* fluctuation in

переп|иса́ть (**-ишу́, -и́шешь**; *impf* **перепи́сывать**) *сов перех* (*написать заново*) to rewrite; (*скопировать*) to copy

перепи́сыва|ть (**-ю**) *несов от* **переписа́ть**; **перепи́сываться** *несов возв*: **перепи́сываться (с** +*instr*) to correspond (with)

пе́репис|ь (**-и**) *ж* (*населения*) census; (*имущества*) inventory

перепл|ести́ (**-ету́, -етёшь**; *pt* **-ёл, -ела́**, *impf* **переплета́ть**) *сов перех* (*книгу*) to bind

переплы́|ть (**-ву́, -вёшь**; *pt* **-л, -ла́**, *impf* **переплыва́ть**) *сов (не) перех*: **переплы́ть (че́рез** +*acc*) (*вплавь*) to swim (across); (*на лодке, на корабле*) to sail (across)

переполз|ти́ (**-у́, -ёшь**; *pt* **-, -ла́, -ло́**, *impf* **переполза́ть**) *сов (не) перех*: **переползти́ (че́рез** +*acc*) to crawl across

перепра́в|а (**-ы**) *ж* crossing

перепра́в|ить (**-лю, -ишь**; *impf* **переправля́ть**) *сов перех*: **перепра́вить кого́-н/что-н че́рез** +*acc* to take across; **перепра́виться** (*impf* **переправля́ться**) *сов возв*: **перепра́виться че́рез** +*acc* to cross

перепры́гн|уть (**-у**; *impf* **перепры́гивать**) *сов (не)перех*: **перепры́гнуть (че́рез** +*acc*) to jump (over)

перепуга́|ть (**-ю**) *сов перех*: **перепуга́ть кого́-н** to scare the life out of sb

перепу́та|ть (**-ю**) *сов от* **пу́тать**

перере́|зать (**-жу, -жешь**; *impf* **перереза́ть**) *сов перех* (*провод*) to cut in two; (*путь*) to cut off

переры́в (**-а**) *м* break; **де́лать** (*perf* **сде́лать**) **переры́в** to take a break

перес|ади́ть (**-ажу́, -а́дишь**; *impf* **переса́живать**) *сов перех* to move; (*дерево, цветок, сердце*) to transplant

переса́д|ка (**-ки**; *gen pl* **-ок**) *ж* (*на поезд итп*) change; (*Мед*: *сердца*) transplant; (: *кожи*) graft

переса́жива|ть (**-ю**) *несов от* **пересади́ть**; **переса́живаться** *несов от* **пересе́сть**

пересека́|ть(ся) (**-ю(сь)**) *несов от* **пересе́чь(ся)**

пересел|и́ть (**-ю́, -и́шь**; *impf* **переселя́ть**) *сов перех* (*на новые земли*) to settle; (*в новую квартиру*) to move; **пересели́ться** (*impf* **переселя́ться**) *сов возв* (*в новый дом*) to move

перес|е́сть (**-я́ду, -я́дешь**; *impf* **переса́живаться**) *сов* (*на другое место*) to move; **переса́живаться** (*perf* **пересе́сть**) **на друго́й по́езд/самолёт** to change trains/planes

пересече́ни|е (**-я**) *ср* (*действие*) crossing; (*место*) intersection

переск|аза́ть (**-ажу́, -а́жешь**; *impf* **переска́зывать**) *сов перех* to tell

пере|сла́ть (**-шлю́, -шлёшь**; *impf* **пересыла́ть**) *сов перех* (*отослать*) to send; (*по другому адресу*) to forward

пересм|отре́ть (**-отрю́, -о́тришь**; *impf*

П

пересма́тривать) *сов перех* (*решение, вопрос*) to reconsider

пересн|я́ть (**-иму́, -и́мешь**; *pt* **-я́л, -яла́**, *impf* **переснима́ть**) *сов перех* (*документ*) to make a copy of

перес|оли́ть (**-олю́, -о́лишь**; *impf* **переса́ливать**) *сов перех*: **пересоли́ть что-н** to put too much salt in sth

пересо́х|нуть (*3sg* **-нет**, *pt* **-, -ла**, *impf* **пересыха́ть**) *сов* (*почва, бельё*) to dry out; (*река*) to dry up

пересп|р|оси́ть (**-ошу́, -о́сишь**; *impf* **переспра́шивать**) *сов перех* to ask again

переста|ва́ть (**-ю́**) *несов от* **переста́ть**

переста́в|ить (**-лю, -ишь**; *impf* **переставля́ть**) *сов перех* to move; (*изменить порядок*) to rearrange

перестара́|ться (**-юсь**) *сов возв* to overdo it

переста́|ть (**-ну, -нешь**; *impf* **переставáть**) *сов* to stop; **перестава́ть** (*perf* **переста́ть**) *+infin* to stop doing

перестра́ива|ть (**-ю**) *несов от* **перестро́ить**

перестре́л|ка (**-ки**; *gen pl* **-ок**) *ж* exchange of fire

перестро́|йка (**-йки**; *gen pl* **-ек**) *ж* (*дома*) rebuilding; (*экономики*) reorganization; (*Ист*) perestroika

пересчита́|ть (**-ю**; *impf* **пересчи́тывать**) *сов перех* to count; (*повторно*) to re-count, count again; (*в других единицах*) to convert

пересыла́|ть (**-ю**) *несов от* **пересла́ть**

пересы́п|ать (**-лю, -лешь**; *impf* **пересыпа́ть**) *сов перех* (*насыпать*) to pour

пересыха́|ть (*3sg* **-ет**) *несов от* **пересо́хнуть**

перет|ащи́ть (**-ащу́, -а́щишь**; *impf* **перета́скивать**) *сов перех* (*предмет*) to drag over

перетр|уди́ться (**-ужу́сь, -у́дишься**; *impf* **перетружда́ться**) *сов возв* (*разг*) to be overworked

перет|яну́ть (**-яну́, -я́нешь**; *impf* **перетя́гивать**) *сов перех* (*передвинуть*) to pull, tow; (*быть тяжелее*) to outweigh

переубе|ди́ть (**-жу́, -ди́шь**; *impf* **переубежда́ть**) *сов перех*: **переубеди́ть кого́-н** to make sb change his *итп* mind

переу́л|ок (**-ка**) *м* lane, alley

переутом|и́ться (**-лю́сь, -и́шься**; *impf* **переутомля́ться**) *сов возв* to tire o.s. out; **переутомле́ни|е** (**-я**) *ср* exhaustion

перехитр|и́ть (**-ю́, -и́шь**) *сов перех* to outwit

перехо́д (**-а**) *м* crossing; (*к другой системе*) transition; (*подземный, в здании*) passage

перех|оди́ть (**-ожу́, -о́дишь**) *несов от* **перейти́**

перехо́дный *прил* (*промежуточный*) transitional; **перехо́дный глаго́л** transitive verb

пе́р|ец (**-ца**) *м* pepper

пе́реч|ень (**-ня**) *м* list

перечеркн|у́ть (**-у́, -ёшь**; *impf* **перечёркивать**) *сов перех* to cross out

перечи́сл|ить (**-ю, -ишь**; *impf* **перечисля́ть**) *сов перех* (*упомянуть*) to list; (*Комм*) to transfer

перечита́|ть (**ю**; *impf* **перечи́тывать**) *сов перех*

(*книгу*) to reread, read again
перешагн|у́ть (**-у́, -ёшь**; *impf* **переша́гивать**) *сов (не)перех*: **перешагну́ть (че́рез** *+acc*) to step over
перешёл *итп сов см* **перейти́**
переш|и́ть (**-ью́, -ьёшь**; *impf* **перешива́ть**) *сов перех* (*платье*) to alter; (*пуговицу*) to move (*by sewing on somewhere else*)
пери́л|а (-) *мн* railing *ед*; (*лестницы*) ban(n)isters *мн*
пери́метр (**-а**) *м* perimeter
пери́од (**-а**) *м* period; **пе́рвый/второ́й пери́од игры́** (*Спорт*) first/second half (of the game); **периоди́ческий** *прил* periodical
перифери́|я (**-и**) *ж* the provinces *мн*
перло́вый *прил* barley
пер|о́ (**-а́**; *nom pl* **-ья**, *gen pl* **-ьев**) *ср* (*птицы*) feather; (*для письма*) nib
перочи́нный *прил*: **перочи́нный нож** penknife (*мн* penknives)
перро́н (**-а**) *м* platform (*Rail*)
пе́рсик (**-а**) *м* peach
персона́ж (**-а**) *м* character
персона́л (**-а**) *м* (*Админ*) personnel, staff; **персона́льный** *прил* personal; **персона́льный компью́тер** PC (= *personal computer*)
перспекти́в|а (**-ы**) *ж* (*Геом*) perspective; (*вид*) view; (*обычн мн*: *планы*) prospects; **в перспекти́ве** (*в будущем*) in store
перспекти́вный *прил* (*изображение*) in perspective; (*планирование*) long-term; (*ученик*) promising
пе́рст|ень (**-ня**) *м* ring
перча́т|ка (**-ки**; *gen pl* **-ок**) *ж* glove
пе́рч|ить (**-у, -ишь**; *perf* **напе́рчить**) *сов перех* to pepper
перш|и́ть (*3sg* **-и́т**) *несов безл* (*разг*): **у меня́ перши́т в го́рле** I've got a frog in my throat
пе́рья *etc сущ см* **перо́**
пёс (**пса**) *м* dog
пес|е́ц (**-ца́**) *м* arctic fox
пе́с|ня (**-ни**; *gen pl* **-ен**) *ж* song
пес|о́к (**-ка́**; *part gen* **-ку́**) *м* sand; **песо́чный** *прил* sandy; (*печенье*) short
пессимисти́чный *прил* pessimistic
пёстрый *прил* (*ткань*) multi-coloured (*Brit*), multi-colored (*US*)
песча́ный *прил* sandy
петру́шк|а (**-и**) *ж* parsley
пету́х (**-а́**) *м* cock, rooster (*US*)
петь (**пою́, поёшь**; *imper* **по́й(те)**, *perf* **спеть**) *несов перех* to sing
пехо́т|а (**-ы**) *ж* infantry
печа́л|ь (**-и**) *ж* (*грусть*) sadness, sorrow
печа́льный *прил* sad; (*ошибка, судьба*) unhappy
печа́та|ть (**-ю**; *perf* **напеча́тать**) *несов перех* (*также Фото*) to print; (*публиковать*) to publish; (*на компьютере*) to type
печён|ка (**-ки**; *gen pl* **-ок**) *ж* liver
печёный *прил* baked
пе́чен|ь (**-и**) *ж* (*Анат*) liver
пече́нь|е (**-я**) *ср* biscuit (*Brit*), cookie (*US*)
пе́ч|ка (**-ки**; *gen pl* **-ек**) *ж* stove
пе|чь (**-чи**; *loc sg* **-чи́**, *gen pl* **-е́й**) *ж* stove; (*Tex*) furnace ▷ (**-ку́, -чёшь** *etc*, **-ку́т**; *pt* **пёк, -кла́**, *perf* **испе́чь**) *несов перех* to bake; **микроволно́вая печь** microwave oven; **пе́чься** (*perf* **испе́чься**) *несов возв* to bake
пешехо́д (**-а**) *м* pedestrian;

П

пешехо́дный *прил* pedestrian
пе́ш|ка (**-ки**; *gen pl* **-ек**) *ж* pawn
пешко́м *нареч* on foot
пеще́р|а (**-ы**) *ж* cave
пиани́но *ср нескл* (upright) piano; **пиани́ст** (**-а**) *м* pianist
пивн|а́я (**-о́й**) *ж* ≈ bar, ≈ pub (*Brit*)
пивно́й *прил* (*бар, бочка*) beer
пи́в|о (**-а**) *ср* beer
пиджа́к (**-а́**) *м* jacket
пижа́м|а (**-ы**) *ж* pyjamas *мн*
пик (**-а**) *м* peak ▷ *прил неизм* (*часы, период, время*) peak; **часы́ пик** rush hour
пи́к|и (-) *мн* (*в картах*) spades; **пи́ковый** *прил* (*в картах*) of spades
пил|а́ (**-ы́**; *nom pl* **-ы**) *ж* saw
пил|и́ть (**-ю́, -ишь**) *несов перех* to saw; (*перен: разг*) to nag
пи́л|ка (**-ки**; *gen pl* **-ок**) *ж* nail file
пило́т (**-а**) *м* pilot
пило́тный *прил* (*пробный*) pilot, trial
пина́|ть (**-ю**) *несов перех* to kick
пингви́н (**-а**) *м* penguin
пин|о́к (**-ка́**) *м* kick
пинце́т (**-а**) *м* (*Мед*) tweezers *мн*
пионе́р (**-а**) *м* pioneer; (*в СССР*) *member of Communist Youth organization*
пир (**-а**; *nom pl* **-ы́**) *м* feast
пирами́д|а (**-ы**) *ж* pyramid
пира́т (**-а**) *м* pirate
пиро́г (**-а́**) *м* pie
пиро́жн|ое (**-ого**) *ср* cake
пирож|о́к (**-ка́**) *м* (*с мясом*) pie; (*с вареньем*) tart
писа́ни|е (**-я**) *ср*: **Свяще́нное Писа́ние** Holy Scripture
писа́тел|ь (**-я**) *м* writer
пи|са́ть (**-шу́, -шешь**; *perf* **написа́ть**) *несов перех* to write; (*картину*) to paint ▷ *неперех* (*no perf: ребёнок*) to be able to write; (*ручка*) to write; **писа́ться** *несов возв* (*слово*) to be spelt *или* spelled
пистоле́т (**-а**) *м* pistol
пи́сьменно *нареч* in writing; **пи́сьменн|ый** *прил* (*просьба, экзамен*) written; (*стол, прибор*) writing; **в пи́сьменной фо́рме** in writing
пис|ьмо́ (**-ьма́**; *nom pl* **-ьма**, *gen pl* **-ем**) *ср* letter; (*no pl: алфавитное*) script
пита́ни|е (**-я**) *ср* (*ребёнка*) feeding; (*Тех*) supply; (*вегетарианское*) diet; **обще́ственное пита́ние** public catering
пита́|ть (**-ю**) *несов перех* (*перен: любовь*) to feel; **пита́ться** *несов возв*: **пита́ться** +*instr* (*человек, растение*) to live on; (*животное*) to feed on
пито́мник (**-а**) *м* (*Бот*) nursery
пи|ть (**пью, пьёшь**; *pt* **-л, -ла́**, *imper* **пе́й(те)**, *perf* **вы́пить**) *несов перех* to drink ▷ *неперех*: **пить за кого́-н/что-н** to drink to sb/sth
питьев|о́й *прил*: **питьева́я вода́** drinking water
пи́цц|а (**-ы**) *ж* pizza
пи́чка|ть (**-ю**; *perf* **напи́чкать**) *несов перех* to stuff
пишу́ *etc несов см* **писа́ть(ся)**
пи́щ|а (**-и**) *ж* food
пищеваре́ни|е (**-я**) *ср* digestion
пищев|о́й *прил* food; (*соль*) edible; **пищева́я со́да** baking soda
ПК *м сокр* = **персона́льный компью́тер**
пл. *сокр* (= *пло́щадь*) Sq. (= *Square*)
пла́вани|е (**-я**) *ср* swimming; (*на судне*) sailing; (*рейс*) voyage

пла́вательный *прил*: **пла́вательный бассе́йн** swimming pool
пла́ва|ть (**-ю**) *несов* to swim; (*корабль*) to sail; (*в воздухе*) to float
пла́в|ить (**-лю, -ишь**; *perf* **распла́вить**) *несов перех* to smelt; **пла́виться** (*perf* **распла́виться**) *несов возв* to melt
пла́в|ки (**-ок**) *мн* swimming trunks
пла́вленый *прил*: **пла́вленый сыр** processed cheese
плавни́к (**-а́**) *м* (*у рыб*) fin
пла́вный *прил* smooth
плака́т (**-а**) *м* poster
пла́|кать (**-чу, -чешь**) *несов* to cry, weep; **пла́кать** (*impf*) **от** *+gen* (*от боли итп*) to cry from; (*от радости*) to cry with
пла́м|я (**-ени**; *как* **вре́мя**; см *Table 4*) *ср* flame
план (**-а**) *м* plan; (*чертёж*) plan, map; **пере́дний план** foreground; **за́дний план** background
планёр (**-а**) *м* glider
плане́т|а (**-ы**) *ж* planet
плани́р|овать (**-ую**) *несов перех* to plan ▷ (*perf* **заплани́ровать**) (*намереваться*) to plan
планиро́вк|а (**-и**) *ж* layout
планоме́рный *прил* systematic
планше́т (**-а**) *м* (*Комп*) tablet
пла́стик (**-а**) *м* = **пластма́сса**
пласти́н|а (**-ы**) *ж* plate; **пласти́н|ка** (**-ки**; *gen pl* **-ок**) *ж*, *уменьш от* **пласти́на**; (*Муз*) record
пласти́ческий *прил* plastic
пласти́чный *прил* (*жесты, движения*) graceful; (*материалы, вещества*) plastic
пластма́сс|а (**-ы**) *ж сокр* (= *пласти́ческая ма́сса*) plastic
пла́стыр|ь (**-я**) *м* (*Мед*) plaster
пла́т|а (**-ы**) *ж* (*за труд, за услуги*) pay; (*за квартиру*) payment; (*за проезд*) fee; (*перен*: *награда*) reward
плат|ёж (**-ежа́**) *м* payment; **платёжеспосо́бный** *прил* (*Комм*) solvent
пла|ти́ть (**-чу́, -тишь**; *perf* **заплати́ть** *или* **уплати́ть**) *несов перех* to pay
пла́тный *прил* (*вход, стоянка*) chargeable; (*школа*) fee-paying; (*больница*) private
плат|о́к (**-ка́**) *м* (*головной*) headscarf (*мн* headscarves); (*наплечный*) shawl; (*также* **носово́й плато́к**) handkerchief
платфо́рм|а (**-ы**) *ж* platform; (*станция*) halt; (*основание*) foundation
пла́ть|е (**-я**; *gen pl* **-ев**) *ср* dress ▷ *собир* (*одежда*) clothing, clothes *мн*
плафо́н (**-а**) *м* (*абажур*) shade (*for ceiling light*)
плацка́ртный *прил*: **плацка́ртный ваго́н** *railway car with open berths instead of compartments*
пла́чу *etc несов см* **пла́кать**
плачу́ *несов см* **плати́ть**
плащ (**-а́**) *м* raincoat
пл|ева́ть (**-юю́**) *несов* to spit ▷ (*perf* **наплева́ть**) (*перен*): **плева́ть на** *+acc* (*разг*: *на правила, на мнение других*) to not give a damn about; **плева́ться** *несов возв* to spit
плед (**-а**) *м* (tartan) rug
пле́йер (**-а**) *м* Walkman
пле́м|я (**-ени**; *как* **вре́мя**; см *Table 4*) *ср* (*также перен*) tribe
племя́нник (**-а**) *м* nephew;

племя́нниц|а (**-ы**) *ж* niece
плен (**-а**; *loc sg* **-у́**) *м* captivity; **бра́ть** (*perf* **взя́ть**) **кого́-н в плен** to take sb prisoner; **попада́ть** (*perf* **попа́сть**) **в плен** to be taken prisoner
плён|ка (**-ки**; *gen pl* **-ок**) *ж* film; (*кожица*) membrane; (*магнитофонная*) tape
пле́нн|ый (**-ого**) *м* prisoner
пле́сен|ь (**-и**) *ж* mould (*Brit*), mold (*US*)
плеск (**-а**) *м* splash
пле|ска́ться (**-щу́сь, -ещешься**) *несов возв* to splash
пле́сневе|ть (*3sg* **-ет**, *perf* **запле́сневеть**) *несов* to go mouldy (*Brit*) *или* moldy (*US*)
плёт|ка (**-ки**; *gen pl* **-ок**) *ж* whip
пле́чик|и (**-ов**) *мн* (*вешалка*) coat hangers; (*подкладки*) shoulder pads
плеч|о́ (**-а́**; *nom pl* **-и**) *ср* shoulder
пли́нтус (**-а**) *м* skirting board (*Brit*), baseboard (*US*)
плиссе́ *прил неизм*: **ю́бка/пла́тье плиссе́** pleated skirt/dress
плит|а́ (**-ы́**; *nom pl* **-ы**) *ж* (*каменная*) slab; (*металлическая*) plate; (*печь*) cooker, stove
пли́т|ка (**-ки**; *gen pl* **-ок**) *ж* (*керамическая*) tile; (*шоколада*) bar; (*электрическая*) hot plate; (*газовая*) camping stove
плов|е́ц (**-ца́**) *м* swimmer
плод (**-а́**) *м* (*Бот*) fruit; (*Био*) foetus (*Brit*), fetus (*US*); (*+gen*: *перен*: *усилий*) fruits of
плод|и́ться (*3sg* **-и́тся**, *perf* **расплоди́ться**) *несов возв* to multiply
плодоро́дный *прил* fertile
пло́мб|а (**-ы**) *ж* (*в зубе*) filling; (*на дверях, на сейфе*) seal
пломби́р (**-а**) *м* *rich creamy ice-cream*
пломбир|ова́ть (**-у́ю**; *perf* **запломбирова́ть**) *несов перех* (*зуб*) to fill ▷ (*perf* **опломбирова́ть**) (*дверь, сейф*) to seal
пло́ский *прил* flat
плоскогу́бц|ы (**-ев**) *мн* pliers
пло́скост|ь (**-и**; *gen pl* **-е́й**) *ж* plane
плот (**-а́**; *loc sg* **-у́**) *м* raft
плоти́н|а (**-ы**) *ж* dam
пло́тник (**-а**) *м* carpenter
пло́тный *прил* (*туман*) dense, thick; (*толпа*) dense; (*бумага, кожа*) thick; (*обед*) substantial
пло́хо *нареч* (*учиться, работать*) badly ▷ *как сказ* it's bad; **мне пло́хо** I feel bad; **у меня́ пло́хо с деньга́ми** I am short of money
плохо́й *прил* bad
площа́д|ка (**-ки**; *gen pl* **-ок**) *ж* (*детская*) playground; (*спортивная*) ground; (*строительная*) site; (*часть вагона*) corridor; **ле́стничная площа́дка** landing; **поса́дочная площа́дка** landing pad
пло́щад|ь (**-и**; *gen pl* **-е́й**) *ж* (*место*) square; (*пространство*: *также Мат*) area; (*также* **жила́я пло́щадь**) living space
плуг (**-а**; *nom pl* **-и́**) *м* plough (*Brit*), plow (*US*)
плы|ть (**-ву́, -вёшь**; *pt* **-л, -ла́**) *несов* to swim; (*судно*) to sail; (*облако*) to float
плю́н|уть (**-у**) *сов* to spit; **плюнь!** (*разг*) forget it!
плюс *м нескл, союз* plus
пляж (**-а**) *м* beach
пневмони́|я (**-и**) *ж* pneumonia
ПО *ср нескл сокр* (= *програ́ммное обеспе́чение*) software; (*Комм*) (= *произво́дственное объедине́ние*) ≈ large industrial company

КЛЮЧЕВОЕ СЛОВО

по *предл +dat* **1** (*о месте действия, вдоль*) along; **ло́дка плывёт по реке́** the boat is sailing on the river; **спуска́ться** (*perf* **спусти́ться) по ле́стнице** to go down the stairs
2 (*при глаголах движения*) round; **ходи́ть** (*impf*) **по ко́мнате/са́ду** to walk round the room/garden; **плыть** (*impf*) **по тече́нию** to go downstream
3 (*об объекте воздействия*) on; **уда́рить** (*impf*) **по врагу́** to deal a blow to the enemy
4 (*в соответствии с*): **де́йствовать по зако́ну/пра́вилам** to act in accordance with the law/the rules; **по расписа́нию/пла́ну** according to schedule/plan
5 (*об основании*): **суди́ть по вне́шности** to judge by appearances; **жени́ться** (*impf/perf*) **по любви́** to marry for love
6 (*вследствие*) due to; **по необходи́мости** out of necessity
7 (*посредством*): **говори́ть по телефо́ну** to speak on the phone; **отправля́ть** (*perf* **отпра́вить) что-н по по́чте** to send sth by post; **передава́ть** (*perf* **переда́ть) что-н по ра́дио/по телеви́дению** to broadcast/televise sth
8 (*с целью, для*): **орга́ны по борьбе́ с престу́пностью** organizations in the fight against crime; **я позва́л тебя́ по де́лу** I called on you on business
9 (*о какой-н характеристике объекта*) in; **по профе́ссии** by profession; **дед по ма́тери** maternal grandfather; **това́рищ по шко́ле** school friend
10 (*о сфере деятельности*) in
11 (*о мере времени*): **по вечера́м/утра́м** in the evenings/mornings; **по воскресе́ньям/пя́тницам** on Sundays/Fridays; **я рабо́таю по це́лым дням** I work all day long; **рабо́та расчи́тана по мину́там** the work is planned by the minute
12 (*о единичности предметов*): **ма́ма дала́ всем по я́блоку** Mum gave them each an apple; **мы купи́ли по одно́й кни́ге** we bought a book each
▷ *предл +acc* **1** (*вплоть до*) up to; **с пе́рвой по пя́тую главу́** from the first to (*Brit*) *или* through (*US*) the fifth chapter; **я за́нят по го́рло** (*разг*: *перен*) I am up to my eyes in work; **он по́ уши в неё влюблён** he is head over heels in love with her
2 (*при обозначении цены*): **по два/три рубля́ за шту́ку** two/three roubles each
3 (*при обозначении количества*): **по два/три челове́ка** in twos/threes
▷ *предл* (*+prp*: *после*) on; **по прие́зде** on arrival

п/о *сокр* (= *почто́вое отделе́ние*) post office
по-англи́йски *нареч* in English
побегу́ *etc сов см* **побежа́ть**
побе́д|а **(-ы)** *ж* victory; **победи́тел|ь** **(-я)** *м* (*в войне*) victor; (*в состязании*) winner; **побед|и́ть** (*2sg* **-и́шь**, *3sg* **-и́т**, *impf* **побежда́ть**) *сов перех* to defeat ▷ *неперех* to win
победоно́сный *прил* victorious
побежа́ть (*как* **бежа́ть**; *см Table 20*) *сов* (*человек, животное*) to start running; (*дни, годы*) to start to fly by; (*ручьи, слёзы*) to begin to flow

п

побежда́|ть (**-ю**) *несов от* **победи́ть**
побеле́|ть (**-ю**) *сов от* **беле́ть**
побел|и́ть (**-ю́, -ишь**) *сов от* **бели́ть**
побере́ж|ье (**-ья**; *gen pl* **-ий**) *ср* coast
побеспоко́|ить (**-ю, -ишь**) *сов от* **беспоко́ить**
поб|и́ть (**-ью́, -ьёшь**) *сов от* **бить** ▷ *перех* (*повредить*) to destroy; (*разбить*) to break
побли́зости *нареч* nearby ▷ *предл*: **побли́зости от** *+gen* near (to), close to
побо́рник (**-а**) *м* champion (*of cause*)
поб|оро́ть (**-орю́, -о́решь**) *сов перех* (*также перен*) to overcome
побо́чный *прил* (*продукт, реакция*) secondary; **побо́чный эффе́кт** side effect
побу|ди́ть (**-жу́, -ди́шь**) *сов перех*: **побуди́ть кого́-н к чему́-н/** *+infin* to prompt sb into sth/to do
побужде́ни|е (**-я**) *ср* (*к действию*) motive
побыва́|ть (**-ю**) *сов*: **побыва́ть в А́фрике/у роди́телей** to visit Africa/one's parents
поб|ы́ть (*как* **быть**; см *Table 21*) *сов* to stay
пов|али́ть(ся) (**-алю́(сь), -а́лишь(ся)**) *сов от* **вали́ть(ся)**
по́вар (**-а**; *nom pl* **-а́**) *м* cook; **пова́ренн|ый** *прил*: **пова́ренная кни́га** cookery (*Brit*) *или* cook (*US*) book; **пова́ренная соль** table salt
поведе́ни|е (**-я**) *ср* behaviour (*Brit*), behavior (*US*)
повез|ти́ (**-у́, -ёшь**; *pt* **-ёз, -езла́**) *сов от* **везти́** ▷ *перех* to take
пове́ренн|ый (**-ого**) *м*: **пове́ренный в дела́х** chargé d'affaires
пове́р|ить (**-ю, -ишь**) *сов от* **ве́рить**
поверн|у́ть (**-у́, -ёшь**; *impf* **повора́чивать**) *сов (не)перех* to turn; **поверну́ться** (*impf* **повора́чиваться**) *сов возв* to turn
пове́рх *предл +gen* over
пове́рхностный *прил* surface; (*перен*) superficial; **пове́рхност|ь** (**-и**) *ж* surface
пове́р|ье (**-ья**; *gen pl* **-ий**) *ср* (popular) belief
пове́|сить(ся) (**-шу(сь), -сишь(ся)**) *сов от* **ве́шать(ся)**
повествова́ни|е (**-я**) *ср* narrative
пов|ести́ (**-еду́, -едёшь**; *pt* **-ёл, -ла́**) *сов перех* (*начать вести*: *ребёнка*) to take; (: *войска*) to lead; (*машину, поезд*) to drive; (*войну, следствие итп*) to begin ▷ (*impf* **поводи́ть**) *неперех* (*+instr*: *бровью*) to raise; (*плечом*) to shrug; **повести́** (*perf*) **себя́** to start behaving
по́вест|ь (**-и**) *ж* story
по-ви́димому *вводн сл* apparently
пови́дл|о (**-а**) *ср* jam (*Brit*), jelly (*US*)
повин|ова́ться (**-у́юсь**) *сов возв +dat* to obey
повинове́ни|е (**-я**) *ср* obedience
пови́с|нуть (**-ну**; *pt* **-, -ла**, *impf* **повиса́ть**) *сов* to hang; (*тучи*) to hang motionless
повл|е́чь (**-еку́, -ечёшь** *итп*, **-еку́т**; *pt* **-ёк, -екла́, -екло́**) *сов от* **влечь**
по́в|од (**-ода**; *loc sg* **-оду́**, *nom pl* **-о́дья**, *gen pl* **-ьев**) *м* (*лошади*) rein ▷ (*nom pl* **-оды**) (*причина*) reason ▷ *предл*: **по по́воду** *+gen* regarding, concerning

пово|ди́ть (**-ожу́, -о́дишь**) *несов от* **повести́**
повод|о́к (**-ка́**) *м* lead, leash
пово́з|ка (**-ки**; *gen pl* **-ок**) *ж* cart
повора́чива|ть(ся) (**-ю(сь)**) *несов от* **поверну́ть(ся)**
поворо́т (**-а**) *м* (*действие*) turning; (*место*) bend; (*перен*) turning point
повре|ди́ть (**-жу́, -ди́шь**; *impf* **поврежда́ть**) *сов перех* (*поранить*) to injure; (*поломать*) to damage
поврежде́ни|е (**-я**) *ср* (*см глаг*) injury; damage
повседне́вный *прил* everyday, routine; (*занятия, встречи*) daily
повсеме́стный *прил* widespread
повсю́ду *нареч* everywhere
по-вся́кому *нареч* in different ways
повторе́ни|е (**-я**) *ср* repetition; (*урока*) revision
повтор|и́ть (**-ю́, -и́шь**; *impf* **повторя́ть**) *сов перех* to repeat; **повтори́ться** (*impf* **повторя́ться**) *сов возв* (*ситуация*) to repeat itself; (*болезнь*) to recur
повы́|сить (**-шу, -сишь**; *impf* **повыша́ть**) *сов перех* to increase; (*интерес*) to heighten; (*качество, культуру*) to improve; (*работника*) to promote; **повыша́ть** (*perf* **повы́сить**) **го́лос** to raise one's voice; **повы́ситься** (*impf* **повыша́ться**) *сов возв* to increase; (*интерес*) to heighten; (*качество, культура*) to improve
пов|яза́ть (**-яжу́, -я́жешь**; *impf* **повя́зывать**) *сов перех* to tie; **повя́з|ка** (**-ки**; *gen pl* **-ок**) *ж* bandage
пога́н|ка (**-ки**; *gen pl* **-ок**) *ж* toadstool
пог|аси́ть (**-ашу́, -а́сишь**) *сов от* **гаси́ть** ▷ (*impf* **погаша́ть**) *перех* (*заплатить*) to pay (off)
пога́с|нуть (**-ну**; *pt* **-, -ла**) *сов от* **га́снуть**
погаша́|ть (**-ю**) *несов от* **погаси́ть**
поги́б|нуть (**-ну**; *pt* **-, -ла**) *сов от* **ги́бнуть**
поги́бш|ий (**-его**) *м* casualty (*dead*)
погл|оти́ть (**-ощу́, -о́тишь**; *impf* **поглоща́ть**) *сов перех* to absorb; (*время*) to take up; (*фирму*) to take over
пог|на́ться (**-оню́сь, -о́нишься**) *сов возв*: **погна́ться за кем-н/чем-н** to set off in pursuit of sb/sth
погово́р|ка (**-ки**; *gen pl* **-ок**) *ж* saying
пого́д|а (**-ы**) *ж* weather; **пого́дный** *прил* weather
поголо́вь|е (**-я**) *ср* (*скота*) total number
пого́н (**-а**) *м* (*обычно мн*) (shoulder) stripe
пого́н|я (**-и**) *ж*: **пого́ня за** *+instr* pursuit of
пограни́чник (**-а**) *м* frontier *или* border guard; **пограни́чный** *прил* border
по́греб (**-а**; *nom pl* **-а́**) *м* cellar
погреба́льный *прил* funeral
погрему́ш|ка (**-ки**; *gen pl* **-ек**) *ж* rattle
погре́|ть (**-ю**) *сов перех* to warm up; **погре́ться** *сов возв* to warm up
погр|узи́ть (**-ужу́, -у́зишь**) *сов перех от* **грузи́ть** ▷ (**-ужу́, -узи́шь**; *impf* **погружа́ть**) *перех*: **погрузи́ть что-н в** *+acc* to immerse sth in; **погрузи́ться** (*impf* **погружа́ться**) *сов возв*: **погрузи́ться в** *+acc* (*человек*) to

П

immerse o.s. in; (*предмет*) to sink into

погря́зн|уть (-у; *impf* **погряза́ть**) *сов*: **погря́знуть в** *+prp* (*в долгах, во лжи*) to sink into

 **КЛЮЧЕВОЕ СЛОВО**

под *предл +acc* **1** (*ниже*) under; **идти́** (*impf*) **по́д гору** to go downhill
2 (*поддерживая снизу*) by
3 (*указывает на положение, состояние*) under; **отдава́ть** (*perf* **отда́ть**) **кого́-н под суд** to prosecute sb; **попада́ть** (*perf* **попа́сть**) **под дождь** to be caught in the rain
4 (*близко к*): **под у́тро/ве́чер** towards morning/evening; **под ста́рость** approaching old age
5 (*указывает на функцию*) as; **мы приспосо́били помеще́ние под магази́н** we fitted out the premises as a shop
6 (*в виде чего-н*): **сте́ны под мра́мор** marble-effect walls
7 (*в обмен на*) on; **брать** (*perf* **взять**) **что-н под зало́г/че́стное сло́во** to take sth on security/trust
8 (*в сопровождении*): **под роя́ль/скри́пку** to the piano/violin; **мне э́то не под си́лу** that is beyond my powers
▷ *предл +instr* **1** (*ниже чего-н*) under
2 (*около*) near; **под но́сом у кого́-н** under sb's nose; **под руко́й** to hand, at hand
3 (*об условиях существования объекта*) under; **быть** (*impf*) **под наблюде́нием/аре́стом** to be under observation/arrest; **под назва́нием, под и́менем** under the name of
4 (*вследствие*) under; **под влия́нием/тя́жестью чего́-н** under the influence/weight of sth; **понима́ть** (*impf*)/**подразумева́ть** (*impf*) **под чем-н** to understand/imply by sth

пода|ва́ть (-ю́) *несов от* **пода́ть**

под|ави́ть (-авлю́, -а́вишь; *impf* **подавля́ть**) *сов перех* to suppress; **подави́ться** *сов от* **дави́ться**

пода́вленный *прил* (*настроение, человек*) depressed

подавля́|ть (-ю) *несов от* **подави́ть**

подавля́ющий *прил* (*большинство*) overwhelming

под|ари́ть (-арю́, -а́ришь) *сов от* **дари́ть**

пода́р|ок (-ка) *м* present, gift; **пода́рочный** *прил* gift

пода́ть (*как* **дать**; *см Table 16*; *impf* **подава́ть**) *сов перех* to give; (*еду*) to serve up; (*поезд, такси итп*) to bring; (*заявление, жалобу итп*) to submit; (*Спорт*: *в теннисе*) to serve; (: *в футболе*) to pass; **подава́ть** (*perf* **пода́ть**) **го́лос за** *+acc* to cast a vote for; **подава́ть** (*perf* **пода́ть**) **в отста́вку** to hand in *или* submit one's resignation; **подава́ть** (*perf* **пода́ть**) **на кого́-н в суд** to take sb to court; **подава́ть** (*perf* **пода́ть**) **кому́-н ру́ку** (*при встрече*) to give sb one's hand

пода́ч|а (-и) *ж* (*действие*: *заявления*) submission; (*Спорт*: *в теннисе*) serve; (: *в футболе*) pass

подбежа́ть (*как* **бежа́ть**; *см Table 20*; *impf* **подбега́ть**) *сов* to run up

подбива́|ть (-ю) *несов от* **подби́ть**

подбира́|ть (-ю) *несов от*

подобра́ть

под|би́ть (**-обью́, -обьёшь**; *impf* **подбива́ть**) *сов перех* (*птицу, самолёт*) to shoot down; (*глаз, крыло*) to injure

подбо́р (**-а**) *м* selection

подборо́д|ок (**-ка**) *м* chin

подбро́|сить (**-шу, -сишь**; *impf* **подбра́сывать**) *сов перех* (*мяч, камень*) to toss; (*наркотик*) to plant; (*разг*: *подвезти*) to give a lift

подва́л (**-а**) *м* cellar; (*для жилья*) basement; **подва́льный** *прил* (*помещение*) basement

подв|езти́ (**-езу́, -езёшь**; *pt* **-ёз, -езла́**, *impf* **подвози́ть**) *сов перех* (*машину, товар*) to take up; (*человека*) to give a lift

подве́рг|нуть (**-ну**; *pt* **-, -ла**, *impf* **подверга́ть**) *сов перех*: **подве́ргнуть кого́-н/что-н чему́-н** to subject sb/sth to sth; **подверга́ть** (*perf* **подве́ргнуть**) **кого́-н ри́ску/опа́сности** to put sb at risk/in danger; **подве́ргнуться** (*impf* **подверга́ться**) *сов возв*: **подве́ргнуться** *+dat* to be subjected to

подве́рженный *прил* (*+dat*: *дурному влиянию*) subject to; (*простуде*) susceptible to

подверн|у́ть (**-у́, -ёшь**; *impf* **подвора́чивать**) *сов перех* (*сделать короче*) to turn up; **подвора́чивать** (*perf* **подверну́ть**) **но́гу** to turn *или* twist one's ankle; **подверну́ться** (*impf* **подвора́чиваться**) *сов возв* (*разг*: *попасться*) to turn up

подве́|сить (**-шу, -сишь**; *impf* **подве́шивать**) *сов перех* to hang up

подв|ести́ (**-еду́, -едёшь**; *pt* **-ёл, -ела́**, *impf* **подводи́ть**) *сов перех* (*разочаровать*) to let down; **подводи́ть** (*perf* **подвести́**) **к** *+dat* (*человека*) to bring up to; (*машину*) to drive up to; (*поезд*) to bring into; (*корабль*) to sail up to; (*электричество*) to bring to; **подводи́ть** (*perf* **подвести́**) **глаза́/гу́бы** to put eyeliner/lipstick on; **подводи́ть** (*perf* **подвести́**) **ито́ги** to sum up

подве́шива|ть (**-ю**) *несов от* **подве́сить**

по́двиг (**-а**) *м* exploit

подвига́|ть(ся) (**-ю(сь)**) *несов от* **подви́нуть(ся)**

подви́н|уть (**-у**; *impf* **подвига́ть**) *сов перех* (*передвинуть*) to move; **подви́нуться** (*impf* **подвига́ться**) *сов возв* (*человек*) to move

подвла́стный *прил* (*+dat*: *закону*) subject to; (*президенту*) under the control of

подв|оди́ть (**-ожу́, -о́дишь**) *несов от* **подвести́**

подво́дн|ый *прил* (*растение, работы*) underwater; **подво́дная ло́дка** submarine

подв|ози́ть (**-ожу́, -о́зишь**) *несов от* **подвезти́**

подвора́чива|ть (**-ю**) *несов от* **подверну́ть**

подгиба́|ть(ся) (**-ю(сь)**) *несов от* **подогну́ть(ся)**

подгля|де́ть (**-жу́, -ди́шь**; *impf* **подгля́дывать**) *сов перех* to peep through

подгор|е́ть (*3sg* **-и́т**, *impf* **подгора́ть**) *сов* to burn slightly

подгото́в|ить (**-лю, -ишь**; *impf* **подгота́вливать**) *сов перех* to prepare; **подгото́виться** (*impf* **подгота́вливаться**) *сов возв* to prepare (o.s.)

подгото́вк|а (**-и**) *ж* preparation; (*запас знаний*) training

подгу́зник (**-а**) *м* nappy (*Brit*), diaper (*US*)
подда|ва́ться (**-ю́сь**) *несов от* **подда́ться** ▷ *возв*: **не поддава́ться сравне́нию/описа́нию** to be beyond comparison/words
по́дданн|ый (**-ого**) *м* subject
по́дданств|о (**-а**) *ср* nationality
подда́ться (*как* **дать**; *см Table 16*; *impf* **поддава́ться**) *сов возв* (*дверь итп*) to give way; **поддава́ться** (*perf* **подда́ться**) *+dat* (*влиянию, соблазну*) to give in to
подде́ла|ть (**-ю**; *impf* **подде́лывать**) *сов перех* to forge; **подде́л|ка** (**-ки**; *gen pl* **-ок**) *ж* forgery
подд|ержа́ть (**-ержу́, -е́ржишь**; *impf* **подде́рживать**) *сов перех* to support; (*падающего*) to hold on to; (*предложение итп*) to second; (*беседу*) to keep up
подде́ржива|ть (**-ю**) *несов от* **поддержа́ть** ▷ *перех* (*переписку*) to keep up; (*порядок, отношения*) to maintain
подде́ржк|а (**-и**) *ж* support
поде́ла|ть (**-ю**) *сов перех* (*разг*) to do; **что поде́лаешь** (*разг*) it can't be helped
под|ели́ть(ся) (**-елю́(сь), -е́лишь(ся)**) *сов от* **дели́ть(ся)**
поде́ржанный *прил* (*одежда, мебель итп*) second-hand
под|же́чь (**-ожгу́, -ожжёшь** *etc*, **-ожгу́т**; *impf* **поджига́ть**) *сов перех* to set fire to
подзаты́льник (**-а**) *м* (*разг*) clip round the ear
подзе́мный *прил* underground
подзо́рн|ый *прил*: **подзо́рная труба́** telescope
подкаст (**-а**) *м* podcast
подк|ати́ть (**-ачу́, -а́тишь**; *impf* **подка́тывать**) *сов перех* (*что-н круглое*) to roll; (*что-н на колёсах*) to wheel
подка́шива|ть(ся) (**-ю(сь)**) *несов от* **подкоси́ть(ся)**
подки́н|уть (**-у**; *impf* **подки́дывать**) *сов* = **подбро́сить**
подкла́д|ка (**-ки**; *gen pl* **-ок**) *ж* lining
подкла́дыва|ть (**-ю**) *несов от* **подложи́ть**
подключ|и́ть (**-у́, -и́шь**; *impf* **подключа́ть**) *сов перех* (*телефон*) to connect; (*лампу*) to plug in; (*специалистов*) to involve
подко́в|а (**-ы**) *ж* (*лошади итп*) shoe
подк|ова́ть (**-ую́**; *impf* **подко́вывать**) *сов перех* to shoe
подкр|а́сться (**-аду́сь, -адёшься**; *impf* **подкра́дываться**) *сов возв* to sneak *или* steal up
подкреп|и́ть (**-лю́, -и́шь**; *impf* **подкрепля́ть**) *сов перех* to support, back up
по́дкуп (**-а**) *м* bribery; **подк|упи́ть** (**-уплю́, -у́пишь**; *impf* **подкупа́ть**) *сов перех* to bribe
подлеж|а́ть (*3sg* **-и́т**) *несов* (*+dat*: *проверке, обложению налогом*) to be subject to; **э́то не подлежи́т сомне́нию** there can be no doubt about that
подлежа́щ|ее (**-его**) *ср* (*Линг*) subject
подли́в|ка (**-ки**; *gen pl* **-ок**) *ж* (*Кулин*) sauce
по́длинник (**-а**) *м* original; **по́длинный** *прил* original; (*документ*) authentic; (*чувство*) genuine; (*друг*) true
подло́г (**-а**) *м* forgery

подл|ожи́ть (**-ожу́, -о́жишь**; *impf* **подкла́дывать**) *сов перех* (*бомбу*) to plant; (*добавить*) to put; (*дров, сахара*) to add
подлоко́тник (**-а**) *м* arm(rest)
по́длый *прил* base
подмен|и́ть (**-ю́, -и́шь**; *impf* **подме́нивать**) *сов перех* to substitute; (*коллегу*) to stand in for
подм|ести́ (**-ету́, -етёшь**; *pt* **-ёл, -ела́**) *сов от* **мести́** ▷ (*impf* **подмета́ть**) *перех* (*пол*) to sweep; (*мусор*) to sweep up
подмётк|а (**-и**) *ж* (*подошва*) sole
подмигн|у́ть (**-у́, -ёшь**; *impf* **подми́гивать**) *сов*: **подмигну́ть кому́-н** to wink at sb
поднес|ти́ (**-у́, -ёшь**; *impf* **подноси́ть**) *сов перех*: **поднести́ что-н к чему́-н** to bring sth up to sth
поднима́|ть(ся) (**-ю(сь)**) *несов от* **подня́ть(ся)**
подно́жи|е (**-я**) *ср* (*горы*) foot
подно́ж|ка (**-ки**; *gen pl* **-ек**) *ж* (*автобуса итп*) step; **поста́вить** (*perf*) **подно́жку кому́-н** to trip sb up
подно́с (**-а**) *м* tray
подн|оси́ть (**-ошу́, -о́сишь**) *несов от* **поднести́**
подн|я́ть (**-иму́, -и́мешь**; *impf* **поднима́ть**) *сов перех* to raise; (*что-н лёгкое*) to pick up; (*что-н тяжёлое*) to lift (up); (*флаг*) to hoist; (*спящего*) to rouse; (*панику, восстание*) to start; (*экономику, дисциплину*) to improve; (*архивы, документацию итп*) to unearth; **поднима́ть** (*perf* **подня́ть**) **крик** *или* **шум** to make a fuss; **подня́ться** (*impf* **поднима́ться**) *сов возв* to rise; (*на этаж, на сцену*) to go up; (*с постели, со стула*) to get up; (*паника, метель, драка*) to break out; **поднима́ться** (*perf* **подня́ться**) **на́ гору** to climb a hill; **подня́лся крик** there was an uproar
подо *предл* = **под**
подоба́ющий *прил* appropriate
подо́бно *предл +dat* like, similar to
подо́бн|ый *прил* (*+dat*: *сходный с*) like, similar to; **и тому́ подо́бное** et cetera, and so on; **ничего́ подо́бного** (*разг*) nothing of the sort
под|обра́ть (**-беру́, -берёшь**; *impf* **подбира́ть**) *сов перех* to pick up; (*приподнять*) to gather (up); (*выбрать*) to pick, select
подобре́|ть (**-ю**) *сов от* **добре́ть**
подогн|у́ть (**-у́, -ёшь**; *impf* **подгиба́ть**) *сов перех* (*рукава*) to turn up; **подогну́ться** (*impf* **подгиба́ться**) *сов возв* to curl under
подогре́|ть (**-ю**; *impf* **подогрева́ть**) *сов перех* to warm up
пододви́н|уть (**-у**; *impf* **пододвига́ть**) *сов перех* to move closer
пододея́льник (**-а**) *м* ≈ duvet cover
подожд|а́ть (**-у́, -ёшь**; *pt* **-а́л, -ала́**) *сов перех* to wait for; **подожда́ть** (*perf*) **с чем-н** to put sth off
подозрева́|ть (**-ю**) *несов перех* to suspect; **подозрева́ть** (*impf*) **кого́-н в чём-н** to suspect sb of sth; **подозрева́ть** (*impf*) **(о чём-н)** to have an idea (about sth)
подозре́ни|е (**-я**) *ср* suspicion
подозри́тельный *прил* suspicious
подо|и́ть (**-ю́, -ишь**) *сов от* **дои́ть**

П

подойти́ (*как* **идти́**; см *Table 18*; *impf* **подходи́ть**) *сов*: **подойти́ к** *+dat* to approach; (*соответствовать*): **подойти́ к** *+dat* (*юбка*) to go (well) with; **э́то мне подхо́дит** this suits me
подоко́нник (**-а**) *м* windowsill
подо́лгу *нареч* for a long time
подо́пытный *прил*: **подо́пытный кро́лик** (*перен*) guinea pig
подорв|а́ть (**-у́, -ёшь**; *pt* **-а́л, -ала́**, *impf* **подрыва́ть**) *сов перех* to blow up; (*перен*: *авторитет*) to undermine; (: *здоровье*) to destroy
подохо́дный *прил*: **подохо́дный нало́г** income tax
подо́шв|а (**-ы**) *ж* (*обуви*) sole
подошёл *etc сов см* **подойти́**
под|пере́ть (**-опру́, -опрёшь**; *pt* **-пёр, -пёрла**, *impf* **подпира́ть**) *сов перех*: **подпере́ть что-н чем-н** to prop sth up with sth
подп|иса́ть (**-ишу́, -и́шешь**; *impf* **подпи́сывать**) *сов перех* to sign; **подписа́ться** (*impf* **подпи́сываться**) *сов возв*: **подписа́ться под** *+instr* to sign; **подпи́сываться** (*perf* **подписа́ться**) **на** *+acc* (*на газету*) to subscribe to; (*аккаунт в социальной сети*) to follow
подпи́с|ка (**-ки**; *gen pl* **-ок**) *ж* subscription; (*о невыезде*) signed statement
по́дпис|ь (**-и**) *ж* signature
подплы́|ть (**-ву́, -вёшь**; *pt* **-л, -ла́**, *impf* **подплыва́ть**) *сов* (*лодка*) to sail (up); (*пловец, рыба*) to swim (up)
подполко́вник (**-а**) *м* lieutenant colonel
подпо́льный *прил* underground
подпо́р|ка (**-ки**; *gen pl* **-ок**) *ж* prop, support
подпры́гн|уть (**-у**; *impf* **подпры́гивать**) *сов* to jump
подп|усти́ть (**-ущу́, -у́стишь**; *impf* **подпуска́ть**) *сов перех* to allow to approach
подрабо́та|ть (**-ю**) *сов (не)перех +acc или +gen* to earn extra
подра́внива|ть (**-ю**) *несов от* **подровня́ть**
подража́ни|е (**-я**) *ср* imitation; **подража́|ть** (**-ю**) *несов +dat* to imitate
подразделя́|ться (*3sg* **-ется**) *несов возв* to be subdivided
подразумева́|ть (**-ю**) *несов перех* to imply; **подразумева́ться** *несов возв* to be implied
подр|асти́ (**-асту́, -астёшь**; *pt* **-о́с, -осла́**, *impf* **подраста́ть**) *сов* to grow
под|ра́ться (**-еру́сь, -ерёшься**) *сов от* **дра́ться**
подре́|зать (**-жу, -жешь**; *impf* **подреза́ть**) *сов перех* (*волосы*) to cut
подро́бност|ь (**-и**) *ж* detail; **подро́бный** *прил* detailed
подровня́|ть (**-ю**; *impf* **подра́внивать**) *сов перех* to trim
подро́ст|ок (**-ка**) *м* teenager, adolescent
подру́г|а (**-и**) *ж* (girl)friend
по-друго́му *нареч* (*иначе*) differently
подр|ужи́ться (**-ужу́сь, -у́жишься**) *сов возв*: **подружи́ться с** *+instr* to make friends with
подру́чный *прил*: **подру́чный материа́л** the material to hand
подрыва́|ть (**-ю**) *несов от* **подорва́ть**
подря́д *нареч* in succession ▷ (**-а**) *м* (*рабочий договор*) contract; **все/всё подря́д** everyone/

everything without exception; **подря́дный** *прил* contract; **подря́дчик** (**-а**) *м* contractor

подса́жива|ться (**-юсь**) *несов от* **подсе́сть**

подсве́чник (**-а**) *м* candlestick

подс|е́сть (**-я́ду, -я́дешь**; *impf* **подса́живаться**) *сов*: **подсе́сть к** *+dat* to sit down beside

подск|аза́ть (**-ажу́, -а́жешь**; *impf* **подска́зывать**) *сов перех* (*перен*: *идею*) to suggest; (*разг*: *адрес*) to give out; **подска́зывать** (*perf* **подсказа́ть**) **что-н кому́-н** to prompt sb with sth

подска́з|ка (**-ки**; *gen pl* **-ок**) *ж* prompt

подслу́ша|ть (**-ю**; *impf* **подслу́шивать**) *сов перех* to eavesdrop on

подсм|отре́ть (**-отрю́, -о́тришь**; *impf* **подсма́тривать**) *сов перех* (*увидеть*) to spy on

подсо́бный *прил* subsidiary

подсо́выва|ть (**-ю**) *несов от* **подсу́нуть**

подсозна́ни|е (**-я**) *ср* the subconscious

подсозна́тельный *прил* subconscious

подсо́лнечн|ый *прил*: **подсо́лнечное ма́сло** sunflower oil

подсо́лнух (**-а**) *м* (*разг*) sunflower

подста́в|ить (**-лю, -ишь**; *impf* **подставля́ть**) *сов перех*: **подста́вить под** *+acc* to put under

подста́в|ка (**-ки**; *gen pl* **-ок**) *ж* stand

подставля́|ть (**-ю**) *несов от* **подста́вить**

подстере́|чь (**-гу́, -жёшь** *итп*, **-гу́т**; *impf* **подстерега́ть**) *сов перех* to lie in wait for

подстра́ива|ть (**-ю**) *несов от* **подстро́ить**

подстр|ели́ть (**-елю́, -е́лишь**; *impf* **подстре́ливать**) *сов перех* to wound

подстри́|чь (**-гу́, -жёшь** *итп*, **-гу́т**; *pt* **-г, -ла**, *impf* **подстрига́ть**) *сов перех* to trim; (*для укорачивания*) to cut; **подстри́чься** (*impf* **подстрига́ться**) *сов возв* to have one's hair cut

подстро́|ить (**-ю, -ишь**; *impf* **подстра́ивать**) *сов перех* to fix

по́дступ (**-а**) *м* (*обычно мн*) approach

подст|упи́ть (**-уплю́, -у́пишь**; *impf* **подступа́ть**) *сов* (*слёзы*) to well up; (*рыдания*) to rise; **подступа́ть** (*perf* **подступи́ть**) **к** *+dat* (*к городу, к теме*) to approach

подсуди́м|ый (**-ого**) *м* (*Юр*) the accused, the defendant

подсу́дный *прил* (*Юр*) sub judice

подсу́н|уть (**-у**; *impf* **подсо́вывать**) *сов перех* to shove

подсчита́|ть (**-ю**; *impf* **подсчи́тывать**) *сов перех* to count (up)

подта́лкива|ть (**-ю**) *несов от* **подтолкну́ть**

подтвер|ди́ть (**-жу́, -ди́шь**; *impf* **подтвержда́ть**) *сов перех* to confirm; (*фактами*) to back up; **подтверди́ться** (*impf* **подтвержда́ться**) *сов* to be confirmed

подтвержде́ни|е (**-я**) *ср* confirmation

подтолкн|у́ть (**-у́, -ёшь**; *impf* **подта́лкивать**) *сов перех* to nudge; (*побудить*) to urge on

подтя́гива|ть(ся) (**-ю(сь)**) *несов от* **подтяну́ть(ся)**

подтя́ж|ки (**-ек**) *мн* (*для брюк*) braces (*Brit*), suspenders (*US*)
подтя́нутый *прил* smart
подт|яну́ть (**-яну́, -я́нешь**; *impf* **подтя́гивать**) *сов перех* (*тяжёлый предмет*) to haul up; (*гайку*) to tighten; (*войска*) to bring up; **подтяну́ться** (*impf* **подтя́гиваться**) *сов возв* (*на брусьях*) to pull o.s. up; (*войска*) to move up
поду́ма|ть (**-ю**) *сов*: **поду́мать (о +prp)** to think (about); **поду́мать** (*perf*) **над** *+instr или* **о** *+prp* to think about; **поду́мать** (*perf*), **что...** to think that ...; **кто бы мог поду́мать!** who would have thought it!
поду́|ть (**-ю**) *сов* to blow; (*ветер*) to begin to blow
под|уши́ть (**-ушу́, -у́шишь**) *сов перех* to spray lightly with perfume
поду́ш|ка (**-ки**; *gen pl* **-ек**) *ж* (*для сидения*) cushion; (*под голову*) pillow
подхв|ати́ть (**-ачу́, -а́тишь**; *impf* **подхва́тывать**) *сов перех* (*падающее*) to catch; (*подлеж: течение, толпа*) to carry away; (*идею, болезнь*) to pick up
подхо́д (**-а**) *м* approach
подх|оди́ть (**-ожу́, -о́дишь**) *несов от* **подойти́**
подходя́щий *прил* (*дом*) suitable; (*момент, слова*) appropriate
подчеркн|у́ть (**-у́, -ёшь**; *impf* **подчёркивать**) *сов перех* (*в тексте*) to underline; (*в речи*) to emphasize
подчине́ни|е (**-я**) *ср* obedience; **подчинённ|ый** *прил* subordinate ▷ (**-ого**) *м* subordinate
подше́фный *прил*: **подше́фный де́тский дом** children's home under patronage
подшива́|ть (**-ю**) *несов от* **подши́ть**
подши́в|ка (**-ки**; *gen pl* **-ок**) *ж* (*газет, документов*) file
подши́пник (**-а**) *м* (*Тех*) bearing
под|ши́ть (**-ошью́, -ошьёшь**; *imper* **-ше́й(те)**, *impf* **подшива́ть**) *сов перех* (*рукав*) to hem; (*подол*) to take up
подш|ути́ть (**-учу́, -у́тишь**; *impf* **подшу́чивать**) *сов*: **подшути́ть над** *+instr* to make fun of
подъе́ду *etc сов см* **подъе́хать**
подъе́зд (**-а**) *м* (*к городу, к дому*) approach; (*в здании*) entrance
подъезжа́|ть (**-ю**) *несов от* **подъе́хать**
подъём (**-а**) *м* (*груза*) lifting; (*флага*) raising; (*на гору*) ascent; (*промышленный*) revival; **подъёмник** (**-а**) *м* lift (*Brit*), elevator (*US*)
подъе́хать (*как* **е́хать**; см *Table 19*; *impf* **подъезжа́ть**) *сов* (*на автомобиле*) to drive up; (*на коне*) to ride up
под|ыша́ть (**-ышу́, -ы́шешь**) *сов* to breathe
пое́дешь *etc сов см* **пое́хать**
поеди́м *итп сов см* **пое́сть**
поеди́те *сов см* **пое́сть**
пое́ду *etc сов см* **пое́хать**
поедя́т *сов см* **пое́сть**
по́езд (**-а**; *nom pl* **-а́**) *м* train
пое́зд|ка (**-ки**; *gen pl* **-ок**) *ж* trip
поезжа́й(те) *сов см* **пое́хать**
пое́сть (*как* **есть**; см *Table 15*) *сов от* **есть** ▷ *перех*: **пое́сть чего́-н** to eat a little bit of sth
пое́хать (*как* **е́хать**; см *Table 19*) *сов* to set off
пое́шь *сов см* **пое́сть**
пожале́|ть (**-ю**) *сов от* **жале́ть**

пожа́л|овать (**-ую**) *сов*: **добро́ пожа́ловать** welcome; **пожа́ловаться** *сов от* **жа́ловаться**

пожа́луйста *част* please; (*в ответ на благодарность*) don't mention it (*Brit*), you're welcome (*US*); **пожа́луйста, помоги́те мне** please help me; **скажи́те, пожа́луйста, где вокза́л!** could you please tell me where the station is; **мо́жно здесь сесть? — пожа́луйста!** may I sit here? — please do!

пожа́р (**-а**) *м* fire; **пожа́рник** (**-а**) *м* (*разг*) fireman (*мн* firemen); **пожа́рн|ый** (**-ого**) *м* fireman (*мн* firemen) *прил*: **пожа́рная кома́нда** fire brigade (*Brit*) *или* department (*US*); **пожа́рная маши́на** fire engine

пож|а́ть (**-му́, -мёшь**; *impf* **пожима́ть**) *сов перех* to squeeze; **он пожа́л мне ру́ку** he shook my hand; **пожима́ть** (*perf* **пожа́ть**) **плеча́ми** to shrug one's shoulders

пожела́ни|е (**-я**) *ср* wish; **прими́те мои́ наилу́чшие пожела́ния** please accept my best wishes

пожела́|ть (**-ю**) *сов от* **жела́ть**

пож|ени́ться (**-еню́сь, -е́нишься**) *сов возв* to marry, get married

поже́ртвовани|е (**-я**) *ср* donation

пожива́|ть (**-ю**) *несов* (*разг*): **как ты пожива́ешь?** how are you?

пожило́й *прил* elderly

пожима́|ть (**-ю**) *несов от* **пожа́ть**

пож|и́ть (**-иву́, -ивёшь**; *pt* **-и́л, -ила́**) *сов* (*пробыть*) to live for a while

по́з|а (**-ы**) *ж* posture; (*перен*: *поведение*) pose

позавчера́ *нареч* the day before yesterday

позади́ *нареч* (*сзади*) behind; (*в прошлом*) in the past ▷ *предл* +*gen* behind

позаимств|овать (**-ую**) *сов от* **заимствовать**

позапро́шлый *прил* before last

поз|ва́ть (**-ову́, -овёшь**) *сов от* **звать**

позво́л|ить (**-ю, -ишь**; *impf* **позволя́ть**) *сов* to permit ▷ *перех*: **позво́лить что-н кому́-н** to allow sb sth; **позволя́ть** (*perf* **позво́лить**) **себе́ что-н** (*покупку*) to be able to afford sth

позвон|и́ть (**-ю́, -и́шь**) *сов от* **звони́ть**

позвоно́чник (**-а**) *м* spine, spinal column

поздне́е *сравн нареч от* **по́здно** ▷ *нареч* later ▷ *предл* +*gen* after; **(не) поздне́е** +*gen* (no) later than

по́здн|ий *прил* late; **са́мое по́зднее** (*разг*) at the latest

по́здно *нареч* late ▷ *как сказ* it's late

поздоро́ва|ться (**-юсь**) *сов от* **здоро́ваться**

поздра́в|ить (**-лю, -ишь**; *impf* **поздравля́ть**) *сов перех*: **поздра́вить кого́-н с** +*instr* to congratulate sb on; **поздравля́ть** (*perf* **поздра́вить**) **кого́-н с днём рожде́ния** to wish sb a happy birthday; **поздравле́ни|е** (**-я**) *ср* congratulations *мн*; (*с днём рождения*) greetings *мн*

по́зже *нареч* = **поздне́е**

позити́вный *прил* positive

пози́ци|я (**-и**) *ж* position

познако́м|ить(ся) (**-лю(сь), -ишь(ся)**) *сов от* **знако́мить(ся)**

позна́ни|я (**-й**) *мн* knowledge *ед*

позову́ *итп сов см* **позва́ть**

позо́р (**-а**) *м* disgrace; **позо́р|ить** (**-ю, -ишь**; *perf* **опозо́рить**) *несов перех* to disgrace; **позо́риться** (*perf* **опозо́риться**) *несов возв* to disgrace o.s.

позо́рный *прил* disgraceful

пойм|ка (**-ки**; *gen pl* **-ок**) *ж* capture

поинтерес|ова́ться (**-у́юсь**) *сов возв +instr* to take an interest in

по́иск (**-а**) *м* search; (*научный*) quest; *см также* **по́иски**

по|иска́ть (**-ищу́, -и́щешь**) *сов перех* to have a look for

по́иск|и (**-ов**) *мн*: **по́иски** (*+gen*) search *ед* (for); **в по́исках** *+gen* in search of

по|и́ть (**-ю́, -ишь**; *imper* **пои́(те)**, *perf* **напои́ть**) *несов перех*: **пои́ть кого́-н чем-н** to give sb sth to drink

пойду́ *etc сов см* **пойти́**

пойма́|ть (**-ю**) *сов от* **лови́ть** ▷ *перех* to catch

пойму́ *etc сов см* **поня́ть**

пойти́ (*как* **идти́**; см *Table 18*) *сов* to set off; (*по пути реформ*) to start off; (*о механизмах, к цели*) to start working; (*дождь, снег*) to begin to fall; (*дым, пар*) to begin to rise; (*кровь*) to start flowing; (*фильм итп*) to start showing; (*подойти*): **пойти́** *+dat или* **к** *+dat* (*шляпа, поведение*) to suit

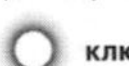

КЛЮЧЕВОЕ СЛОВО

пока́ *нареч* **1** (*некоторое время*) for a while
2 (*тем временем*) in the meantime
▷ *союз* **1** (*в то время как*) while
2 (*до того времени как*): **пока́ не** until; **пока́!** so long!; **пока́ что** for the moment

покажу́(сь) *etc сов см* **показа́ть(ся)**

пока́з (**-а**) *м* (*фильма*) showing; (*опыта*) demonstration; **показа́ни|е** (**-я**) *ср* (*Юр*: *обычно мн*) evidence; (*на счётчике итп*) reading; **показа́тел|ь** (**-я**) *м* indicator; (*Мат, Экон*) index (*мн* indices); **показа́тельный** *прил* (*пример*) revealing

пока|за́ть (**-жу́, -жешь**; *impf* **пока́зывать**) *сов перех* to show ▷ *неперех* (*на суде*) to testify; **пока́зывать** (*perf* **показа́ть**) **приме́р** to set an example; **показа́ться** *сов от* **каза́ться** ▷ (*impf* **пока́зываться**) *возв* to appear; **пока́зываться** (*perf* **показа́ться**) **врачу́** to see a doctor

поката́|ть (**-ю**) *сов перех*: **поката́ть кого́-н на маши́не** to take sb for a drive; **поката́ться** *сов возв* to go for a ride

пок|ати́ть (**-ачу́, -а́тишь**) *сов перех* (*что-н круглое*) to roll; (*что-н на колёсах*) to wheel; **покати́ться** *сов возв* to start rolling *или* to roll

покача́|ть (**-ю**) *сов перех* to rock ▷ *неперех*: **покача́ть голово́й** to shake one's head; **покача́ться** *сов возв* (*на качелях*) to swing

пока́чива|ться (**-юсь**) *несов возв* to rock

поки́н|уть (**-у**; *impf* **покида́ть**) *сов перех* to abandon

покло́н (**-а**) *м* (*жест*) bow; (*приветствие*) greeting

покл|они́ться (**-оню́сь, -о́нишься**) *сов от* **кла́няться**

покло́нник (**-а**) *м* admirer

покланя́|ться (**-юсь**) *несов возв +dat* to worship

поко́|иться (*3sg* **-ится**) *несов возв*: **поко́иться на** *+prp* to rest on

поко́|й (**-я**) *м* peace; **оставля́ть** (*perf* **оста́вить**) **кого́-н в поко́е** to leave sb in peace
поко́йн|ый *прил* the late
▷ (**-ого**) *м* the deceased
поколе́ни|е (**-я**) *ср* generation
поко́нч|ить (**-у, -ишь**) *сов*: **поко́нчить с** *+instr* (*с делами*) to be finished with; (*с бедностью, с проблемой*) to put an end to; **поко́нчить** (*perf*) **с собо́й** to kill o.s., commit suicide
покор|и́ть (**-ю́, -и́шь**; *impf* **покоря́ть**) *сов перех* (*страну, народ*) to conquer; **покоря́ть** (*perf* **покори́ть**) **кого́-н** (*заставить любить*) to win sb's heart; **покори́ться** (*impf* **покоря́ться**) *сов возв*: **покори́ться** (*+dat*) to submit (to)
покрови́тельств|о (**-а**) *ср* protection
покро́|й (**-я**) *ср* cut (*of clothing*)
покрыва́л|о (**-а**) *ср* bedspread
покр|ы́ть (**-о́ю, -о́ешь**) *сов от* **крыть** ▷ (*impf* **покрыва́ть**) *перех* (*звуки*) to cover up; (*расходы, расстояние*) to cover; **покры́ться** (*impf* **покрыва́ться**) *сов возв*: **покры́ться** *+instr* (*одеялом*) to cover o.s. with; (*снегом итп*) to be covered in
покры́ш|ка (**-ки**; *gen pl* **-ек**) *ж* (*Авт*) tyre (*Brit*), tire (*US*)
покупа́тел|ь (**-я**) *м* buyer; (*в магазине*) customer; **покупа́тельский** *прил* (*спрос, интересы*) consumer
покупа́|ть (**-ю**) *несов от* **купи́ть**
поку́п|ка (**-ки**; *gen pl* **-ок**) *ж* purchase; **де́лать** (*perf* **сде́лать**) **поку́пки** to go shopping
покуша́|ться (**-юсь**) *несов возв*: **покуша́ться на** *+acc* to attempt to take; **покуше́ни|е** (**-я**) *ср*: **покуше́ние** (**на** *+acc*) (*на свободу, на права*) infringement (of); (*на жизнь*) attempt (on)
пол (**-а**; *loc sg* **-у́**, *nom pl* **-ы́**) *м* floor ▷ (*nom pl* **-ы**, *gen pl* **-о́в**, *dat pl* **-а́м**) sex
полага́|ть (**-ю**) *несов* (*думать*) to suppose; **на́до полага́ть** supposedly
пол|го́да (**-уго́да**) *ср/мн* half a year
по́лдень (**полу́дня** *или* **по́лдня**) *м* midday, noon; **2 часа́ по́сле полу́дня** 2 p.m
по́л|е (**-я**; *nom pl* **-я́**, *gen pl* **-е́й**) *ср* field; **по́ле де́ятельности** sphere of activity; **по́ле зре́ния** field of vision
поле́зн|ый *прил* useful; (*пища*) healthy; **поле́зные ископа́емые** minerals
поле́з|ть (**-у, -ешь**) *сов*: **поле́зть на** *+acc* (*на гору*) to start climbing *или* to climb; **поле́зть** (*perf*) **в** *+acc* (*в драку, в спор*) to get involved in; **поле́зть** (*perf*) **в карма́н** to put one's hand in(to) one's pocket
поле́н|о (**-а**; *nom pl* **-ья**, *gen pl* **-ьев**) *ср* log
полёт (**-а**) *м* flight
поле|те́ть (**-чу́, -ти́шь**) *сов* (*птица, самолёт*) to fly off; (*время*) to start to fly by
по́лза|ть (**-ю**) *несов* to crawl
полз|ти́ (**-у́, -ёшь**; *pt* **-, -ла́**) *несов* to crawl
ползунк|и́ (**-о́в**) *мн* rompers
полива́|ть (**-ю**) *несов от* **poли́ть**
поливитами́н|ы (**-ов**) *мн* multivitamins
полиго́н (**-а**) *м* (*для учений*) shooting range; (*для испытания оружия*) test(ing) site
поликли́ник|а (**-и**) *ж* health centre (*Brit*) *или* center (*US*)

П

Поликлиника

These centres are staffed by a range of specialist doctors: surgeons, eye doctors, dermatologists etc. Patients can make an appointment with a number of doctors at any time.

полир|ова́ть (**-у́ю**; *perf* **отполирова́ть**) *несов перех* to polish

по́лис (**-а**) *м*: **страхово́й по́лис** insurance policy

поли́тик (**-а**) *м* politician; **поли́тик|а** (**-и**) *ж* (*курс*) policy; (*события, наука*) politics; **полити́ческий** *прил* political

пол|и́ть (**-ью́, -ьёшь**; *pt* **-и́л, -ила́**, *impf* **полива́ть**) *сов* (*дождь*) to start pouring *или* to pour down ▷ *перех*: **поли́ть что-н чем-н** (*соусом*) to pour sth over sth; **полива́ть** (*perf* **поли́ть**) **цветы́** to water the flowers

полице́йск|ий *прил* police ▷ (**-ого**) *м* policeman (*мн* policemen); **полице́йский уча́сток** police station

поли́ци|я (**-и**) *ж* the police

поли́чн|ое (**-ого**) *ср*: **пойма́ть кого́-н с поли́чным** to catch sb at the scene of a crime; (*перен*) to catch sb red-handed *или* in the act

полиэтиле́н (**-а**) *м* polythene

полк (**-а́**; *loc sg* **-у́**) *м* regiment

по́л|ка (**-ки**; *gen pl* **-ок**) *ж* shelf; (*в поезде*: *для багажа*) luggage rack; (: *для лежания*) berth; **кни́жная по́лка** bookshelf

полко́вник (**-а**) *м* colonel

полне́|ть (**-ю**; *perf* **пополне́ть**) *несов* to put on weight

полномо́чи|е (**-я**) *ср* authority; (*обычно мн*: *право*) power; **полномо́чный** *прил* fully authorized

полнопра́вный *прил* (*гражданин*) fully fledged; (*наследник*) rightful

по́лностью *нареч* fully, completely

полноце́нный *прил* proper

по́л|ночь (**-у́ночи**) *ж* midnight

по́лный *прил* full; (*победа, счастье итп*) complete, total; (*толстый*) stout; **по́лный** *+gen или +instr* full of; (*тревоги, любви итп*) filled with

полови́к (**-а́**) *м* mat

полови́н|а (**-ы**) *ж* half; **на полови́не доро́ги** halfway; **сейча́с полови́на пе́рвого/второ́го** it's (now) half past twelve/one

поло́вник (**-а**) *м* ladle

полово́дь|е (**-я**) *ср* high water

полово́й *прил* (*тряпка, мастика*) floor; (*Био*) sexual

положе́ни|е (**-я**) *ср* situation; (*географическое*) location, position; (*тела, головы итп*) position; (*социальное, семейное итп*) status; (*правила*) regulations *мн*; (*обычно мн*: *тезис*) point; **она́ в положе́нии** (*разг*) she's expecting; **положе́ние дел** the state of affairs

поло́женный *прил* due

положи́тельный *прил* positive

пол|ожи́ть (**-ожу́, -о́жишь**) *сов от* **класть**

поло́м|ка (**-ки**; *gen pl* **-ок**) *ж* breakdown

полос|а́ (**-ы́**; *nom pl* **по́лосы**, *gen pl* **поло́с**, *dat pl* **по́лосам**) *ж* (*ткани, металла*) strip; (*на ткани, на рисунке итп*) stripe; **полоса́тый** *прил* striped, stripy; **поло́с|ка** (**-ки**; *gen pl* **-ок**) *ж* (*ткани, бумаги*) (thin) strip; (*на* *ткани*) (thin) stripe; **в поло́ску** striped

пол|оска́ть (**-ощу́, -о́щешь**; *perf* **прополоска́ть**) *несов перех* (*бельё, посуду*) to rinse; (*рот*) to rinse out

по́лост|ь (**-и**; *gen pl* **-е́й**) *ж* (*Анат*) cavity

полоте́н|це (**-ца**; *gen pl* **-ец**) *ср* towel

пол|отно́ (**-отна́**; *nom pl* **-о́тна**, *gen pl* **-о́тен**) *ср* (*ткань*) sheet; (*картина*) canvas

пол|о́ть (**-ю́, -ешь**; *perf* **прополо́ть**) *несов перех* to weed

полпути́ *м нескл* half (*of journey*); **на полпути́** halfway

пол|тора́ (**-у́тора**; *f* **полторы́**) *м/ср чис* one and a half

полботи́н|ок (**-ка**) *м* ankle boot

полуго́ди|е (**-я**) *ср* (*Просвещ*) semester; (*Экон*) half (*of the year*)

полукру́г (**-а**) *м* semicircle

полупальто́ *ср нескл* jacket, short coat

полуфабрика́т (**-а**) *м* (*Кулин*) *partially prepared food*

полуфина́л (**-а**) *м* semifinal

получа́тел|ь (**-я**) *м* recipient

получа́|ть(ся) (**-ю(сь)**) *несов от* **получи́ть(ся)**

пол|учи́ть (**-учу́, -у́чишь**; *impf* **получа́ть**) *сов перех* to receive, get; (*урожай, насморк, удовольствие*) to get; (*известность*) to gain ▷ *неперех* (*разг: быть наказанным*) to get it in the neck; **получи́ться** (*impf* **получа́ться**) *сов возв* to turn out; (*удасться*) to work; (*фотография*) to come out; **из него́ полу́чится хоро́ший учи́тель** he'll make a good teacher; **у меня́ э́то не получа́ется** I can't do it

полу́ч|ка (**-ки**; *gen pl* **-ек**) *ж* (*разг*) pay

пол|часа́ (**-уча́са**) *м* half an hour

по́лый *прил* hollow

по́льз|а (**-ы**) *ж* benefit; **в по́льзу** *+gen* in favour (*Brit*) *или* favor (*US*) of

по́льзовани|е (**-я**) *ср*: **по́льзование** (*+instr*) use (of);

по́льз|оваться (**-уюсь**; *perf* **воспо́льзоваться**) *несов возв +instr* to use; (*no perf: авторитетом, успехом итп*) to enjoy

по́льский *прил* Polish; **по́льский язы́к** Polish

По́льш|а (**-и**) *ж* Poland

пол|юби́ть (**-юблю́, -ю́бишь**) *сов перех* (*человека*) to come to love; **полюби́ть** (*perf*) **что-н/**+*infin* to develop a love for sth/doing

по́люс (**-а**; *nom pl* **-а́**) *м* pole

пол|я́ (**-е́й**) *мн* (*шляпы*) brim *ед*; (*на странице*) margin *ед*

поля́рный *прил* (*Гео*) polar; (*разные*) diametrically opposed

пома́д|а (**-ы**) *ж* (*также* **губна́я пома́да**) lipstick

пом|аха́ть (**-ашу́, -а́шешь**) *сов* *+instr* to wave

поме́дл|ить (**-ю, -ишь**) *сов*: **поме́длить с** *+instr/+infin* to linger over sth/doing

поменя́|ть(ся) (**-ю(сь)**) *сов от* **меня́ть(ся)**

поме́р|ить (**-ю, -ишь**) *сов от* **ме́рить**

поме|сти́ть (**-щу́, -сти́шь**; *impf* **помеща́ть**) *сов перех* to put; **помести́ться** (*impf* **помеща́ться**) *сов возв* (*уместиться*) to fit

помёт (**-а**) *м* dung; (*птиц*) droppings *мн*; (*детёныши*) litter

поме́т|а (**-ы**) *ж* note

поме́|тить (**-чу, -тишь**) *сов от*

ме́тить ▷ (*impf* **помеча́ть**) *перех* to note
поме́т|ка (**-ки**; *gen pl* **-ок**) *ж* note
поме́х|а (**-и**) *ж* hindrance; (*Связь: обычно мн*) interference
помеча́|ть (**-ю**) *несов от* **поме́тить**
помеша́|ть (**-ю**) *сов от* **меша́ть**
помеща́|ть(ся) (**-ю(сь)**) *несов от* **помести́ть(ся)**
помеще́ни|е (**-я**) *ср* room; (*под офис*) premises *мн*; **жило́е помеще́ние** living space
помидо́р (**-а**) *м* tomato (*мн* tomatoes)
поми́л|овать (**-ую**) *сов от* **ми́ловать**
поми́мо *предл +gen* besides; **поми́мо того́/всего́ про́чего** apart from that/anything else
поми́н|ки (**-ок**) *мн* wake *ед*
помину́тный *прил* at one-minute intervals; (*очень частый*) constant
помир|и́ть(ся) (**-ю́(сь), -и́шь(ся)**) *сов от* **мири́ть(ся)**
по́мн|ить (**-ю, -ишь**) *несов (не) перех*: **по́мнить (о** *+prp или* **про** *+acc*) to remember
помо́г *итп сов см* **помо́чь**
помога́|ть (**-ю**) *несов от* **помо́чь**
по-мо́ему *нареч* my way ▷ *вводн сл* in my opinion
помо́|и (**-ев**) *мн* dishwater *ед*; (*отходы*) slops *мн*
помолч|а́ть (**-у́, -и́шь**) *сов* to pause
помо́рщ|иться (**-усь, -ишься**) *сов возв* to screw up one's face
помо́ст (**-а**) *м* (*для обозрения*) platform; (*для выступлений*) rostrum
пом|о́чь (**-огу́, -о́жешь** *итп*, **-о́гут**; *pt* **-о́г, -огла́**, *impf* **помога́ть**) *сов +dat* to help; (*другой стране*) to aid
помо́щник (**-а**) *м* helper; (*должность*) assistant
по́мощ|ь (**-и**) *ж* help, assistance
пом|ы́ть(ся) (**-о́ю(сь), -о́ешь(ся)**) *сов от* **мы́ть(ся)**
пона́доб|иться (**-люсь, -ишься**) *сов возв* to be needed
по-настоя́щему *нареч* properly
по-на́шему *нареч* in our opinion, our way
понеде́льник (**-а**) *м* Monday
понемно́гу *нареч* a little; (*постепенно*) little by little
пон|ести́ (**-есу́, -есёшь**; *pt* **-ёс, -есла́**) *сов от* **нести́**; **понести́сь** *сов возв* (*человек*) to tear off; (*лошадь*) to charge off; (*машина*) to speed off
по́ни *м нескл* pony
понижа́|ть(ся) (**-ю(сь)**) *несов от* **пони́зить(ся)**
пони́|зить (**-жу, -зишь**; *impf* **понижа́ть**) *сов перех* to reduce; (*в должности*) to demote; (*голос*) to lower; **пони́зиться** (*impf* **понижа́ться**) *сов возв* to be reduced
понима́|ть (**-ю**) *несов от* **поня́ть** ▷ *перех* to understand ▷ *неперех*: **понима́ть в** *+prp* to know about; **понима́ете** you see
поно́с (**-а**) *м* diarrhoea (*Brit*), diarrhea (*US*)
пон|оси́ть (**-ошу́, -о́сишь**) *сов перех* to carry for a while; (*одежду*) to wear
поно́шенный *прил* (*одежда*) worn
понра́в|иться (**-люсь, -ишься**) *сов от* **нра́виться**
по́нчик (**-а**) *м* doughnut (*Brit*), donut (*US*)
поня́ти|е (**-я**) *ср* notion; (*знание*)

idea; **поня́тия не име́ю** (*разг*) I've no idea; **поня́тно** *нареч* intelligibly ▷ *как сказ*: **мне поня́тно** I understand; **поня́тно!** I see!; **поня́тно?** got it?; **поня́тный** *прил* intelligible; (*ясный*) clear; (*оправданный*) understandable

по|ня́ть (**-йму́, -ймёшь**; *pt* **-нял, -няла́**, *impf* **понима́ть**) *сов перех* to understand

поощре́ни|е (**-я**) *ср* encouragement

поощр|и́ть (**-ю́, -и́шь**; *impf* **поощря́ть**) *сов перех* to encourage

поп (**-а́**) *м* (*разг*) priest

попада́ни|е (**-я**) *ср* hit

попада́|ть(ся) (**-ю(сь)**) *несов от* **попа́сть(ся)**

попа́рно *нареч* in pairs

попа́|сть (**-ду́, -дёшь**; *impf* **попада́ть**) *сов*: **попа́сть в** *+acc* (*в цель*) to hit; (*в ворота*) to end up in; (*в чужой город*) to find o.s. in; (*в беду*) to land in; **мы́ло попа́ло мне в глаза́** the soap got in my eyes; **попада́ть** (*perf* **попа́сть**) **в ава́рию** to have an accident; **попада́ть** (*perf* **попа́сть**) **в плен** to be taken prisoner; **попада́ть** (*perf* **попа́сть**) **под дождь** to be caught in the rain; **ему́ попа́ло** (*разг*) he got a hiding; **(Вы) не туда́ попа́ли** you've got the wrong number; **попа́сться** (*impf* **попада́ться**) *сов возв* (*преступник*) to be caught; **мне попа́лась интере́сная кни́га** I came across an interesting book; **попада́ться** (*perf* **попа́сться**) **кому́-н на глаза́** to catch sb's eye

попе́й(те) *сов см* **попи́ть**

попере́к *нареч* crossways ▷ *предл +gen* across

попере́чный *прил* horizontal

поперхн|у́ться (**-у́сь, -ёшься**) *сов возв* to choke

попе́рч|ить (**-у, -ишь**) *сов от* **пе́рчить**

попече́ни|е (**-я**) *ср* (*о детях*) care; (*о делах, о доме*) charge

поп|и́ть (**-ью́, -ьёшь**; *pt* **-и́л, -ила́**, *imper* **-е́й(те)**) *сов перех* to have a drink of

поплы́|ть (**-ву́, -вёшь**; *pt* **-л, -ла́**) *сов* to start swimming; (*судно*) to set sail

попола́м *нареч* in half; **попола́м с** *+instr* mixed with

попо́лн|ить (**-ю, -ишь**; *impf* **пополня́ть**) *сов перех*: **попо́лнить что-н** *+instr* (*запасы*) to replenish sth with; (*коллекцию*) to expand sth with; (*коллектив*) to reinforce sth with; **попо́лниться** (*impf* **пополня́ться**) *сов возв* (*запасы*) to be replenished; (*коллекция*) to be expanded

попра́в|ить (**-лю, -ишь**; *impf* **поправля́ть**) *сов перех* to correct; (*галстук, платье*) to straighten; (*причёску*) to tidy; (*здоровье, дела*) to improve; **попра́виться** (*impf* **поправля́ться**) *сов возв* to improve; (*пополнеть*) to put on weight

попра́в|ка (**-ки**; *gen pl* **-ок**) *ж* (*ошибки*) correction; (*в решение, в закон*) amendment

по-пре́жнему *нареч* as before; (*всё ещё*) still

попро́б|овать (**-ую**) *сов от* **про́бовать**

попр|оси́ть(ся) (**-ошу́(сь), -о́сишь(ся)**) *сов от* **проси́ть(ся)**

попроща́|ться (**-юсь**) *сов возв*: **попроща́ться с** *+instr* to say goodbye to

попуга́|й (**-я**) *м* parrot

популя́рност|ь (**-и**) *ж* popularity

популя́рный *прил* popular; (*понятный*) accessible
попу́тный *прил* (*замечание*) accompanying; (*машина*) passing; (*ветер*) favourable (*Brit*), favorable (*US*)
попу́тчик (**-а**) *м* travelling (*Brit*) *или* traveling (*US*) companion
попы́т|ка (**-ки**; *gen pl* **-ок**) *ж* attempt
попью́ *итп сов см* **попи́ть**
попя́|титься (**-чусь, -тишься**) *сов возв* to take a few steps backwards (*Brit*) *или* backward (*US*)
по́р|а (**-ы**) *ж* pore
пор|а́ (**-ы́**; *acc sg* **-у**, *dat sg* **-é**, *nom pl* **-ы**) *ж* time ▷ *как сказ* it's time; **до каки́х пор?** until when?; **до сих пор** (*раньше*) up till now; (*всё ещё*) still; **до тех пор** until then; **до тех пор, пока́** until; **с каки́х пор?** since when?
поравня́|ться (**-юсь**) *сов возв*: **поравня́ться с** *+instr* (*человек*) to draw level with; (*машина*) to come alongside
пораже́ни|е (**-я**) *ср* (*цели*) hitting; (*Мед*) damage; (*проигрыш*) defeat; **наноси́ть (*perf* нанести́) кому́-н пораже́ние** to defeat sb; **терпе́ть (*perf* потерпе́ть) пораже́ние** to be defeated
порази́тельный *прил* striking; (*о неприятном*) astonishing
пора́н|ить (**-ю, -ишь**) *сов перех* to hurt
порв|а́ть(ся) (**-у́, -ёшь**) *сов от* **рва́ть(ся)**
поре́з (**-а**) *м* cut; **поре́|зать** (**-жу, -жешь**) *сов перех* to cut; **поре́заться** *сов возв* to cut o.s.
порногра́фи|я (**-и**) *ж* pornography
по́ровну *нареч* equally
поро́г (**-а**) *м* (*также перен*) threshold
поро́д|а (**-ы**) *ж* (*животных*) breed; **поро́дистый** *прил* pedigree
поро́й *нареч* from time to time
пороло́н (**-а**) *м* foam rubber
порош|о́к (**-ка́**) *м* powder
порт (**-а**; *loc sg* **-у́**, *nom pl* **-ы**, *gen pl* **-о́в**) *м* port
портати́вный *прил* portable; **портат"ивный компь"ютер** laptop (computer)
портве́йн (**-а**) *м* port (*wine*)
по́р|тить (**-чу, -тишь**; *perf* **испо́ртить**) *несов перех* to damage; (*настроение, праздник, ребёнка*) to spoil; **по́ртиться** (*perf* **испо́ртиться**) *сов возв* (*механизм*) to be damaged; (*здоровье, погода*) to deteriorate; (*настроение*) to be spoiled; (*молоко*) to go off; (*мясо, овощи*) to go bad
портре́т (**-а**) *м* portrait
Португа́ли|я (**-и**) *ж* Portugal
португа́льский *прил* Portuguese; **португа́льский язы́к** Portuguese
портфе́л|ь (**-я**) *м* briefcase; (*Полит, Комм*) portfolio
портье́р|а (**-ы**) *ж* curtain
поруга́|ться (**-юсь**) *сов от* **руга́ться** ▷ *возв* (*разг*): **поруга́ться (с** *+instr*) to fall out (with)
пору́к|а (**-и**) *ж*: **брать кого́-н на пору́ки** to take sb on probation; (*Юр*) to stand bail for sb
по-ру́сски *нареч* (*говорить, писать*) in Russian; **говори́ть** (*impf*)**/понима́ть** (*impf*) **по-ру́сски** to speak/understand Russian
поруча́|ть (**-ю**) *несов от* **поручи́ть**
поруче́ни|е (**-я**) *ср* (*задание*)

errand; (: *важное*) mission
поручи́тельств|о (**-а**) *ср* guarantee
пор|учи́ть (**-учу́, -у́чишь**; *impf* **поруча́ть**) *сов*: **поручи́ть кому́-н что-н** to entrust sb with sth; **поруча́ть** (*perf* **поручи́ть**) **кому́-н** *+infin* to instruct sb to do; **поруча́ть** (*perf* **поручи́ть**) **кому́-н кого́-н/что-н** (*отдать на попечение*) to leave sb/sth in sb's care; **поручи́ться** *сов от* **руча́ться**
по́рци|я (**-и**) *ж* portion
поры́в (**-а**) *м* (*ветра*) gust
поря́д|ок (**-ка**) *м* order; (*правила*) procedure; **в поря́дке** *+gen* (*в качестве*) as; **в поря́дке** in order; **всё в поря́дке** everything's O.K.; **поря́док дня** agenda
поря́дочный *прил* (*честный*) decent; (*значительный*) fair
пос|ади́ть (**-ажу́, -а́дишь**) *сов от* **сажа́ть**
поса́д|ка (**-ки**; *gen pl* **-ок**) *ж* (*овощей*) planting; (*пассажиров*) boarding; (*самолёта итп*) landing; **поса́дочный** *прил* (*талон*) boarding; (*площадка*) landing
по-сво́ему *нареч* his *итп* way; **он по-сво́ему прав** in his own way, he is right
посвя|ти́ть (**-щу́, -ти́шь**; *impf* **посвяща́ть**) *сов перех*: **посвяти́ть что-н** *+dat* to devote sth to; (*книгу*) to dedicate sth to
посе́в|ы (**-ов**) *мн* crops
поселе́ни|е (**-я**) *ср* settlement
пос|ели́ть(ся) (**-елю́(сь), -е́лишь(ся)**) *сов от* **сели́ть(ся)**
посёл|ок (**-ка**) *м* village; **да́чный посёлок** *village made up of dachas*
посереди́не *нареч* in the middle ▷ *предл +gen* in the middle of
посети́тел|ь (**-я**) *м* visitor
посе|ти́ть (**-щу́, -ти́шь**; *impf* **посеща́ть**) *сов перех* to visit
посеще́ни|е (**-я**) *ср* visit
посе́|ять (**-ю, -ишь**) *сов от* **се́ять**
поси|де́ть (**-жу́, -ди́шь**) *сов* to sit for a while
поскользн|у́ться (**-у́сь, -ёшься**) *сов возв* to slip
поско́льку *союз* as
посла́ни|е (**-я**) *ср* message; **посла́нник** (**-а**) *м* envoy
по|сла́ть (**-шлю́, -шлёшь**; *impf* **посыла́ть**) *сов перех* to send
по́сле *нареч* (*потом*) afterwards (*Brit*), afterward (*US*) ▷ *предл +gen* after ▷ *союз*: **по́сле того́ как** after
после́дн|ий *прил* last; (*новости, мода*) latest; **за** *или* **в после́днее вре́мя** recently
после́дователь|ь (**-я**) *м* follower
после́довательност|ь (**-и**) *ж* sequence; (*политики*) consistency
после́довательный *прил* (*один за другим*) consecutive; (*логический*) consistent
после́д|овать (**-ую**) *сов от* **сле́довать**
после́дстви|е (**-я**) *ср* consequence
послеза́втра *нареч* the day after tomorrow
посло́виц|а (**-ы**) *ж* proverb, saying
послу́ша|ть (**-ю**) *сов от* **слу́шать** ▷ *перех*: **послу́шать что-н** to listen to sth for a while; **послу́шаться** *сов от* **слу́шаться**
послу́шный *прил* obedient
посме́|ть (**-ю**) *сов от* **сметь**
посм|отре́ть (**-отрю́, -о́тришь**) *сов от* **смотре́ть** ▷ *неперех*: **посмо́трим** (*разг*) we'll see; **посмотре́ться** *сов от* **смотре́ться**

П

посо́би|е (**-я**) *ср* (*помощь*) benefit; (*Просвещ*: *учебник*) textbook; (: *наглядное*) visual aids *мн*; **посо́бие по безрабо́тице** unemployment benefit; **посо́бие по инвали́дности** disability living allowance

пос|о́л (**-ла́**) *м* ambassador

пос|оли́ть (**-олю́, -о́лишь**) *сов от* **соли́ть**

посо́льств|о (**-а**) *ср* embassy

посп|е́ть (*3sg* **-е́ет**) *сов от* **спеть**

поспеш|и́ть (**-у́, -и́шь**) *сов от* **спеши́ть**

поспо́р|ить (**-ю, -ишь**) *сов от* **спо́рить**

посреди́ *нареч* in the middle ▷ *предл +gen* in the middle of

посреди́не *нареч* in the middle ▷ *предл +gen* in the middle of

посре́дник (**-а**) *м* intermediary; (*при конфликте*) mediator; **торго́вый посре́дник** middleman (*мн* middlemen); **посре́днический** *прил* (*Комм*) intermediary; (*услуги*) agent's; **посре́дничеств|о** (**-а**) *ср* mediation

посре́дственно *нареч* (*учиться, писать*) so-so ▷ *ср нескл* (*Просвещ*) ≈ satisfactory (*school mark*); **посре́дственный** *прил* mediocre

посре́дством *предл +gen* by means of; (*человека*) through

поссо́р|ить(ся) (**-ю(сь), -ишь(ся)**) *сов от* **ссо́рить(ся)**

пост (**-а́**; *loc sg* **-у́**) *м* (*люди*) guard; (*место*) lookout post; (*должность*) post; (*Рел*) fast; (*Комп*) blogpost

поста́в|ить (**-лю, -ишь**) *сов от* **ста́вить** ▷ (*impf* **поставля́ть**) *перех* (*товар*) to supply; **поста́в|ка** (**-ки**; *gen pl* **-ок**) *ж* (*снабжение*) supply; **поставщи́к** (**-а́**) *м* supplier

постаме́нт (**-а**) *м* pedestal

постан|ови́ть (**-овлю́, -о́вишь**; *impf* **постановля́ть**) *сов +infin* to resolve to do

постано́в|ка (**-ки**; *gen pl* **-ок**) *ж* (*Театр*) production; **постано́вка вопро́са** the formulation of the question

постановле́ни|е (**-я**) *ср* (*решение*) resolution; (*распоряжение*) decree

постано́вщик (**-а**) *м* producer

постара́|ться (**-юсь**) *сов от* **стара́ться**

пост|ели́ть (**-елю́, -е́лишь**) *сов от* **стели́ть**

посте́л|ь (**-и**) *ж* bed

посте́льн|ый *прил*: **посте́льное бельё** bedclothes *мн*

постепе́нно *нареч* gradually

постепе́нный *прил* gradual

постира́|ть (**-ю**) *сов от* **стира́ть**

по|сти́ться (**-щу́сь, -сти́шься**) *несов возв* (*Рел*) to fast

по́стн|ый *прил* (*суп*) vegetarian; **по́стное ма́сло** vegetable oil

посто́льку *союз*: **посто́льку ... поско́льку** insofar as ...

посторо́нн|ий *прил* (*чужой*) strange; (*помощь, влияние*) outside; (*вопрос*) irrelevant ▷ (**-его**) *м* stranger, outsider; **посторо́нним вход воспрещён** authorized entry only

постоя́нн|ый *прил* (*работа, адрес*) permanent; (*шум*) constant; **постоя́нное запомина́ющее устро́йство** ROM

посто|я́ть (**-ю́, -и́шь**) *сов от* **стоя́ть** ▷ *неперех* (*стоять недолго*) to stand for a while

постри́|чь(ся) (**-гу́(сь), -жёшь(ся)** *итп*, **-гу́т(ся)**; *pt*

-г(ся), -гла(сь)) *сов от* **стричь(ся)**
постро́|ить (**-ю, -ишь**) *сов от* **стро́ить**
постро́|йка (**-йки**; *gen pl* **-ек**) *ж* construction; (*здание*) building
пост|упи́ть (**-уплю́, -у́пишь**; *impf* **поступа́ть**) *сов* (*человек*) to act; (*товар, известия*) to come in; (*жалоба*) to be received; **поступа́ть** (*perf* **поступи́ть**) **в/на** *+acc* (*в университет, на работу*) to start
поступле́ни|е (**-я**) *ср* (*действие*: *в университет, на работу*) starting; (*обычно мн*: *бюджетное*) revenue *ед*; (*в библиотеке*) acquisition
посту́п|ок (**-ка**) *м* deed
постуч|а́ть(ся) (**-у́(сь), -и́шь(ся)**) *сов от* **стуча́ть(ся)**
посу́д|а (**-ы**) *ж собир* crockery; **ку́хонная посу́да** kitchenware; **стекля́нная посу́да** glassware; **мыть** (*perf* **помы́ть**) **посу́ду** to wash the dishes, wash up
посчита́|ть (**-ю**) *сов от* **счита́ть**
посыла́|ть (**-ю**) *несов от* **посла́ть**
посы́л|ка (**-ки**; *gen pl* **-ок**) *ж* (*действие*: *книг, денег*) sending; (*посланное*) parcel
посы́п|ать (**-лю, -лешь**) *сов перех* to sprinkle; **посы́паться** *сов от* **сы́паться**
пот (**-а**; *loc sg* **-у́**) *м* sweat
по-тво́ему *нареч* your way
потенциа́л (**-а**) *м* potential
потенциа́льный *прил* potential
потепле́ни|е (**-я**) *ср* warmer spell
пот|ере́ть (**-ру́, -рёшь**; *pt* **-ёр, -ёрла**) *сов перех* (*ушиб*) to rub; (*морковь*) to grate
потерпе́вш|ий (**-его**) *м* (*Юр*) victim
пот|ерпе́ть (**-ерплю́, -е́рпишь**) *сов от* **терпе́ть**
поте́р|я (**-и**) *ж* loss
потеря́|ть(ся) (**-ю(сь)**) *сов от* **теря́ть(ся)**
поте́|ть (**-ю**; *impf* **вспоте́ть**) *несов* to sweat
по́тный *прил* sweaty
пото́к (**-а**) *м* stream
потол|о́к (**-ка́**) *м* ceiling
пото́м *нареч* (*через некоторое время*) later; (*после*) then ▷ *союз*: **а/и пото́м** and then, anyhow; **на пото́м** for later
пото́мк|и (**-ов**) *мн* descendants
пото́мств|о (**-а**) *ср собир* descendants *мн*; (*дети*) offspring *мн*
потому́ *нареч*: **потому́ (и)** that's why; **потому́ что** because
пото́п (**-а**) *м* flood
потороп|и́ть(ся) (**-лю́(сь), -ишь(ся)**) *сов от* **торопи́ть(ся)**
пото́чн|ый *прил* (*производство*) mass; **пото́чная ли́ния** production line
потра́|тить (**-чу, -тишь**) *сов от* **тра́тить**
потреби́тел|ь (**-я**) *м* consumer; **потреби́тельский** *прил* (*спрос*) consumer
потреб|и́ть (**-лю́, -и́шь**) *сов от* **потребля́ть**; **потребле́ни|е** (**-я**) *ср* (*действие*) consumption; **това́ры широ́кого потребле́ния** consumer goods; **потребля́|ть** (**-ю**; *perf* **потреби́ть**) *несов перех* to consume; **потре́бност|ь** (**-и**) *ж* need
потре́б|овать(ся) (**-ую(сь)**) *сов от* **тре́бовать(ся)**
потрох|а́ (**-о́в**) *мн* (*птицы*) giblets *мн*
потрош|и́ть (**-у́, -и́шь**; *perf* **вы́потрошить**) *несов перех* (*курицу, рыбу*) to gut
потру|ди́ться (**-жу́сь, -ди́шься**) *сов возв* to work *+infin* to take the trouble to do

П

потряса́ющий *прил* (*музыка, стихи*) fantastic; (*красота*) stunning
потрясе́ни|е (**-я**) *ср* (*нервное*) breakdown; (*социальное*) upheaval; (*впечатление*) shock
потряс|ти́ (**-у́, -ёшь**; *pt* **-, -ла́**) *сов перех* to shake; (*взволновать*) to stun
поту́хн|уть (*3sg* **-ет**, *impf* **потуха́ть**) *сов* (*лампа, свет*) to go out
пот|уши́ть (**-ушу́, -у́шишь**) *сов от* **туши́ть**
пот|яну́ться (**-яну́сь, -я́нешься**; *impf* **потя́гиваться**) *сов возв* (*в постели, в кресле*) to stretch out
поу́жина|ть (**-ю**) *сов от* **у́жинать**
поумне́|ть (**-ю**) *сов от* **умне́ть**
похвал|а́ (**-ы́**) *ж* praise
похва́ста|ться (**-юсь**) *сов от* **хва́статься**
похити́тел|ь (**-я**) *м* (*см глаг*) thief; abductor; kidnapper
похи́|тить (**-щу, -тишь**; *impf* **похища́ть**) *сов перех* (*предмет*) to steal; (*человека*) to abduct; (: *для выкупа*) to kidnap
похище́ни|е (**-я**) *ср* (*см глаг*) theft; abduction; kidnap(ping)
похло́па|ть (**-ю**) *сов перех* to pat
похме́ль|е (**-я**) *ср* hangover
похо́д (**-а**) *м* (*военный*) campaign; (*туристический*) hike (*walking and camping expedition*)
пох|оди́ть (**-ожу́, -о́дишь**) *несов*: **походи́ть на кого́-н/что-н** to resemble sb/sth ▷ *сов* to walk
похо́ж|ий *прил*: **похо́жий (на** *+acc или* **с** *+instr*) similar (to); **он похо́ж на бра́та, они́ с бра́том похо́жи** he looks like his brother; **они́ похо́жи** they look alike; **похо́же на то, что ...** it looks as if ...; **э́то на него́ (не) похо́же** it's (not) like him
похолода́ни|е (**-я**) *ср* cold spell
похолода́|ть (*3sg* **-ет**) *сов от* **холода́ть**
похор|они́ть (**-оню́, -о́нишь**) *сов от* **хорони́ть**
похоро́нн|ый *прил* funeral; **похоро́нное бюро́** undertaker's
по́хор|оны (**-о́н**; *dat pl* **-она́м**) *мн* funeral *ед*
поцел|ова́ть(ся) (**-у́ю(сь)**) *сов от* **целова́ть(ся)**
поцелу́|й (**-я**) *м* kiss
почасово́й *прил* (*оплата*) hourly
по́чв|а (**-ы**) *ж* soil; (*перен*) basis; **на по́чве** *+gen* arising from
почём *нареч* (*разг*) how much?
почему́ *нареч* why; **вот почему́** that is why
почему́-либо *нареч* for some reason or other
почему́-нибудь *нареч* = **почему́-либо**
почему́-то *нареч* for some reason
по́черк (**-а**) *м* handwriting
почерне́|ть (**-ю**) *сов от* **черне́ть**
поче|са́ть(ся) (**-шу́(сь), -шешь(ся)**) *сов от* **чеса́ть(ся)**
почёт (**-а**) *м* honour (*Brit*), honor (*US*)
почётный *прил* (*гость*) honoured (*Brit*), honored (*US*); (*член*) honorary; (*обязанность*) honourable (*Brit*), honorable (*US*); **почётный карау́л** guard of honour (*Brit*) *или* honor (*US*)
поч|ини́ть (**-иню́, -и́нишь**) *сов от* **чини́ть**
почи́н|ка (**-ки**; *gen pl* **-ок**) *ж* repair
почи́|стить (**-щу, -стишь**) *сов от* **чи́стить**
почита́тел|ь (**-я**) *м* admirer
почита́|ть (**-ю**) *сов перех* (*книгу*) to read ▷ *несов перех* to admire

по́ч|ка (**-ки**; *gen pl* **-ек**) *ж* (*Бот*) bud; (*Анат*) kidney
по́чт|а (**-ы**) *ж* (*учреждение*) post office; (*письма*) post, mail; **почтальо́н** (**-а**) *м* postman (*Brit*) (*мн* postmen), mailman (*US*) (*мн* mailmen); **почта́мт** (**-а**) *м* main post office
почти́ *нареч* almost, nearly; **почти́ что** (*разг*) almost
почти́тельный *прил* respectful
почти́ть (*как* **чтить**; см *Table 17*) *сов перех* (*память*) to pay homage to
почто́в|ый *прил* postal; (*марка*) postage; **почто́вая откры́тка** postcard; **почто́вый и́ндекс** postcode (*Brit*), zip code (*US*); **почто́вый перево́д** (*деньги*) postal order; **почто́вый я́щик** postbox
почу́вств|овать (**-ую**) *сов от* **чу́вствовать**
пошатн|у́ть (**-у́, -ёшь**) *сов перех* (*веру*) to shake; (*здоровье*) to damage; **пошатну́ться** *сов возв* to sway; (*авторитет*) to be undermined
пошёл *сов см* **пойти́**
пошла́ *etc сов см* **пойти́**
по́шлин|а (**-ы**) *ж* duty
пошло́ *сов см* **пойти́**
пошлю́ *итп сов см* **посла́ть**
пош|ути́ть (**-учу́, -у́тишь**) *сов от* **шути́ть**
поща́д|а (**-ы**) *ж* mercy
поща|ди́ть (**-жу́, -ди́шь**) *сов от* **щади́ть**
пощёчин|а (**-ы**) *ж* slap across the face
поэ́зи|я (**-и**) *ж* poetry
поэ́м|а (**-ы**) *ж* poem
поэ́т (**-а**) *м* poet; **поэте́сс|а** (**-ы**) *ж от* **поэ́т**; **поэти́ческий** *прил* poetic
поэ́тому *нареч* therefore
пою́ *итп несов см* **петь**
по|яви́ться (**-явлю́сь, -я́вишься**; *impf* **появля́ться**) *сов возв* to appear; **у него́ появи́лись иде́и/сомне́ния** he has had an idea/begun to have doubts
появле́ни|е (**-я**) *ср* appearance
появля́|ться (**-юсь**) *несов от* **появи́ться**
по́яс (**-а**; *nom pl* **-а́**) *м* (*ремень*) belt; (*талия*) waist; (*Гео*) zone
поясне́ни|е (**-я**) *ср* explanation; (*к схеме*) explanatory note
поясн|и́ть (**-ю́, -и́шь**; *impf* **поясня́ть**) *сов перех* to explain
поясни́ц|а (**-ы**) *ж* small of the back
пр. *сокр* = **прое́зд**; **проспе́кт**
праба́буш|ка (**-ки**; *gen pl* **-ек**) *ж* great-grandmother
прав|а́ (**-**) *мн* (*также* **води́тельские права́**) driving licence *ед* (*Brit*), driver's license *ед* (*US*); *см также* **пра́во**
пра́вд|а (**-ы**) *ж* truth ▷ *нареч* really ▷ *вводн сл* true ▷ *как сказ* it's true; **пра́вду** *или* **по пра́вде говоря́** *или* **сказа́ть** to tell the truth
правди́вый *прил* truthful
правдоподо́бный *прил* plausible
пра́вил|о (**-а**) *ср* rule; **э́то не в мои́х пра́вилах** that's not my way; **как пра́вило** as a rule; **по всем пра́вилам** by the rules; **пра́вила доро́жного движе́ния** rules of the road, ≈ Highway Code
пра́вильно *нареч* correctly ▷ *как сказ* that's correct *или* right; **пра́вильный** *прил* correct; (*вывод, ответ*) right
прави́тел|ь (**-я**) *м* ruler; **прави́тельственный** *прил* government; **прави́тельств|о** (**-а**) *ср* government

пра́в|ить (**-лю, -ишь**) *несов перех* (*исправлять*) to correct ▷ *неперех* (*+instr*: *страной*) to rule, govern; (*машиной*) to drive; **правле́ни|е** (**-я**) *ср* government; (*орган*) board

пра́в|о (**-а**; *nom pl* **-а́**) *ср* (*свобода*) right; (*нормы, наука*) law; **име́ть** (*impf*) **пра́во на что-н/***+infin* to be entitled *или* have the right to sth/to do; **на ра́вных права́х с** *+instr* on equal terms with; **права́ челове́ка** human rights

пра́во-: **правонаруше́ни|е** (**-я**) *ср* offence; **правонаруши́тел|ь** (**-я**) *м* offender; **правописа́ни|е** (**-я**) *ср* spelling; **правопоря́д|ок** (**-ка**) *м* law and order

правосла́ви|е (**-я**) *ср* orthodoxy; **правосла́вн|ый** *прил* (*церковь, обряд*) orthodox ▷ (**-ого**) *м* *member of the Orthodox Church*

правосу́ди|е (**-я**) *ср* justice

пра́вый *прил* right; (*Полит*) right-wing; **он прав** he is right

пра́вящий *прил* ruling

Пра́г|а (**-и**) *ж* Prague

праде́душ|ка (**-ки**; *gen pl* **-ек**) *м* great-grandfather

пра́зднеств|о (**-а**) *ср* festival

пра́здник (**-а**) *м* public holiday; (*религиозный*) festival; (*нерабочий день*) holiday; (*радость, торжество*) celebration; **с пра́здником!** best wishes!; **пра́здничный** *прил* (*салют, обед*) celebratory; (*одежда, настроение*) festive; **пра́здничный день** holiday; **пра́здн|овать** (**-ую**) *несов перех* to celebrate

пра́ктик|а (**-и**) *ж* practice; (*часть учёбы*) practical experience *или* work; **на пра́ктике** in practice; **практика́нт** (**-а**) *м* trainee (*on placement*); **практик|ова́ть** (**-у́ю**) *несов перех* to practise (*Brit*), practice (*US*); **практикова́ться** *несов возв* (*обучаться*): **практикова́ться в чём-н** to practise sth

практи́чески *нареч* (*на деле*) in practice; (*по сути дела*) practically

практи́чный *прил* practical

прах (**-а**) *м* (*умершего*) ashes *мн*

пра́чечн|ая (**-ой**) *ж* laundry

пребыва́ни|е (**-я**) *ср* stay

пребыва́|ть (**-ю**) *несов* to be

превзойти́ (*как* **идти́**; см *Table 18*; *impf* **превосходи́ть**) *сов перех* (*врага, соперника*) to beat; (*результаты, ожидания*) to surpass; (*доходы, скорость*) to exceed

превосхо|ди́ть (**-жу́, -дишь**) *несов от* **превзойти́**

превосхо́дно *нареч* superbly ▷ *как сказ* it's superb; *част* **превосхо́дно!** (*хорошо*) excellent!

превосхо́дн|ый *прил* superb; **превосхо́дная сте́пень** (*Линг*) superlative degree

превра|ти́ть (**-щу́, -ти́шь**; *impf* **превраща́ть**) *сов перех*: **преврати́ть что-н/кого́-н в** *+acc* to turn *или* transform sth/sb into; **преврати́ться** (*impf* **превраща́ться**) *сов возв*: **преврати́ться (в** *+acc*) to turn (into)

превраще́ни|е (**-я**) *ср* transformation

превы́|сить (**-шу́, -сишь**; *impf* **превыша́ть**) *сов перех* to exceed

прегра́д|а (**-ы**) *ж* barrier

прегра|ди́ть (**-жу́, -ди́шь**; *impf* **прегражда́ть**) *сов перех*: **прегради́ть кому́-н доро́гу/вход** to block *или* bar sb's way/entrance

преда|ва́ть (**-ю́**) *несов от* **преда́ть**

пре́данный *прил* devoted

преда́тел|ь (**-я**) *м* traitor
преда́ть (*как* **дать**; см *Table 16*; *impf* **предава́ть**) *сов перех* to betray; **предава́ть** (*perf* **преда́ть**) **что-н гла́сности** to make sth public
предвари́тельный *прил* preliminary; (*продажа*) advance
предви́|деть (**-жу, -дишь**) *сов перех* to predict
предводи́тел|ь (**-я**) *м* leader
преде́л (**-а**) *м* (*обычно мн*: *города, страны*) boundary; (*перен*: *приличия*) bound; (: *терпения*) limit; (*подлости, совершенства*) height; (*мечтаний*) pinnacle; **на преде́ле** at breaking point; **в преде́лах** *+gen* (*закона, года*) within; (*приличия*) within the bounds of; **за преде́лами** *+gen* (*страны, города*) outside
преде́льный *прил* maximum; (*восторг, важность*) utmost; **преде́льный срок** deadline
предисло́ви|е (**-я**) *ср* foreword, preface
предлага́|ть (**-ю**) *несов от* **предложи́ть**
предло́г (**-а**) *м* pretext; (*Линг*) preposition; **под предло́гом** *+gen* on the pretext of
предложе́ни|е (**-я**) *ср* suggestion, proposal; (*замужества*) proposal; (*Комм*) offer; (*Линг*) sentence; **де́лать** (*perf* **сде́лать**) **предложе́ние кому́-н** (*девушке*) to propose to sb; (*Комм*) to make sb an offer; **вноси́ть** (*perf* **внести́**) **предложе́ние** (*на собрании*) to propose a motion
предл|ожи́ть (**-ожу́, -о́жишь**; *impf* **предлага́ть**) *сов перех* to offer; (*план, кандидатуру*) to propose ▷ *неперех* to suggest, propose
предло́жный *прил* (*Линг*) prepositional
предме́т (**-а**) *м* object; (*обсуждения, изучения*) subject
пре́д|ок (**-ка**) *м* ancestor
предоста́в|ить (**-лю, -ишь**) *сов перех*: **предоста́вить что-н кому́-н** to give sb sth ▷ *неперех*: **предоста́вить кому́-н** *+infin* (*выбирать, решать*) to let sb do
предостереже́ни|е (**-я**) *ср* warning
предостер|е́чь (**-егу́, -ежёшь** *etc*, **-егу́т**; *pt* **-ёг, -егла́**, *impf* **предостерега́ть**) *сов перех*: **предостере́чь кого́-н** (**от** *+gen*) to warn sb (against)
предотвра|ти́ть (**-щу́, -ти́шь**; *impf* **предотвраща́ть**) *сов перех* to prevent; (*войну, кризис*) to avert
предохрани́тел|ь (**-я**) *м* safety device; (*Элек*) fuse (*Brit*), fuze (*US*)
предохран|и́ть (**-ю́, -и́шь**; *impf* **предохраня́ть**) *сов перех* to protect
предположи́тельно *нареч* supposedly
предпол|ожи́ть (**-ожу́, -о́жишь**; *impf* **предполага́ть**) *сов перех* (*допустить возможность*) to assume, suppose; **предполо́жим** (*возможно*) let's assume *or* suppose
предпосле́дний *прил* (*номер, серия*) penultimate; (*в очереди*) last but one
предприи́мчивый *прил* enterprising
предпринима́тел|ь (**-я**) *м* entrepreneur, businessman (*мн* businessmen); **предпринима́тельств|о** (**-а**) *ср* enterprise
предпр|иня́ть (**-иму́, -и́мешь**; *pt* **-и́нял, -иняла́**, *impf*

предпринима́ть) *сов перех* to undertake
предприя́ти|е (**-я**) *ср* plant; (*Комм*) enterprise, business
предрассу́д|ок (**-ка**) *м* prejudice
председа́тел|ь (**-я**) *м* chairman (*мн* chairmen)
предсказа́ни|е (**-я**) *ср* prediction; **предск|аза́ть** (**-ажу́, -а́жешь**; *impf* **предска́зывать**) *сов перех* to predict
предсме́ртный *прил* (*агония*) death; (*воля*) last
представи́тел|ь (**-я**) *м* representative; **представи́тельный** *прил* representative; **представи́тельств|о** (**-а**) *ср* (*Полит*) representation; **дипломати́ческое представи́тельство** diplomatic corps
предста́в|ить (**-лю, -ишь**; *impf* **представля́ть**) *сов перех* to present; **представля́ть** (*perf* **предста́вить**) **кого́-н кому́-н** (*познакомить*) to introduce sb to sb; **представля́ть** (*perf* **предста́вить**) (**себе́**) to imagine; **предста́виться** (*impf* **представля́ться**) *несов возв* (*при знакомстве*) to introduce o.s.; (*возможность*) to present itself
представле́ни|е (**-я**) *ср* presentation; (*Театр*) performance; (*знание*) idea; **не име́ть** (*impf*) (**никако́го**) **представле́ния о** *+prp* to have no idea about
представля́|ть (**-ю**) *несов от* **предста́вить** ▷ *перех* (*организацию, страну*) to represent; **представля́ть** (*impf*) (**себе́**) **что-н** (*понимать*) to understand sth; **представля́ться** *несов от* **предста́виться**
предсто|я́ть (*3sg* **-и́т**) *несов* to lie ahead
предубежде́ни|е (**-я**) *ср* prejudice
предупре|ди́ть (**-жу́, -ди́шь**; *impf* **предупрежда́ть**) *сов перех* to warn; (*остановить*) to prevent
предупрежде́ни|е (**-я**) *ср* warning; (*аварии, заболевания*) prevention
предусм|отре́ть (**-отрю́, -о́тришь**; *impf* **предусма́тривать**) *сов перех* (*учесть*) to foresee; (*приготовиться*) to provide for; **предусмотри́тельный** *прил* prudent
предчу́встви|е (**-я**) *ср* premonition
предше́ствующий *прил* previous
предъ|яви́ть (**-явлю́, -я́вишь**; *impf* **предъявля́ть**) *сов перех* (*паспорт, билет итп*) to show; (*доказательства*) to produce; (*требования, претензии*) to make; (*иск*) to bring; **предъявля́ть** (*perf* **предъяви́ть**) **права́ на что-н** to lay claim to sth
предыду́щий *прил* previous
предысто́ри|я (**-и**) *ж* background
прее́мник (**-а**) *м* successor
пре́жде *нареч* (*в прошлом*) formerly; (*сначала*) first ▷ *предл +gen* before; **пре́жде всего́** first of all; **пре́жде чем** before
преждевре́менный *прил* premature
пре́жний *прил* former
презента́ци|я (**-и**) *ж* presentation
презервати́в (**-а**) *м* condom
президе́нт (**-а**) *м* president
презира́|ть (**-ю**) *несов перех* to despise

презрéни|е (**-я**) *ср* contempt
преимýществ|о (**-а**) *ср* advantage
прейскурáнт (**-а**) *м* price list
преклонéни|е (**-я**) *ср*: **преклонéние (пéред** *+instr*) admiration (for)
преклоня́|ться (**-юсь**) *несов возв*: **преклоня́ться пéред** *+instr* to admire
прекрáсно *нареч* (*сделать*) brilliantly; **част прекрáсно!** excellent!; **ты прекрáсно знáешь, что ты не прав** you know perfectly well that you are wrong
прекрáсный *прил* beautiful; (*врач, результат*) excellent
прекра|ти́ть (**-щý, -ти́шь**; *impf* **прекращáть**) *сов перех* to stop ▷ *неперех +infin* to stop doing; **прекрати́ться** (*impf* **прекращáться**) *сов возв* (*дождь, занятия*) to stop; (*отношения*) to end
прелéстный *прил* charming
прéлест|ь (**-и**) *ж* charm
прелю́ди|я (**-и**) *ж* prelude
прéми|я (**-и**) *ж* (*работнику*) bonus; (*победителю*) prize; (*Комм*) premium
премьéр (**-а**) *м* premier
премьéр|а (**-ы**) *ж* première
премьéр-министр (**-а**) *м* prime minister, premier
пренебрегá|ть (**-ю**) *несов от* **пренебрéчь**
пренебрежéни|е (**-я**) *ср* (*законами итп*) disregard; (: *обязанностями*) neglect; (*высокомерие*) contempt
пренебр|éчь (**-егý, -ежёшь** *etc*, **-гýт**; *pt* **-ёг, -eглá**, *impf* **пренебрегáть**) *сов* (*+instr*: *опасностью*) to disregard; (*богатством, правилами*) to scorn; (*советом, просьбой*) to ignore
прéни|я (**-й**) *мн* debate *ед*
преобладá|ть (*3sg* **-ет**) *несов*: **преобладáть (над** *+instr*) to predominate (over)
преобразовáни|е (**-я**) *ср* transformation; **преобраз|овáть** (**-ýю**; *impf* **преобразóвывать**) *сов перех* to transform
преодолé|ть (**-ю**; *impf* **преодолевáть**) *сов перех* to overcome; (*барьер*) to clear
препарáт (**-а**) *м* (*Мед*: *также* **медици́нский препарáт**) drug
препинáни|е (**-я**) *ср*: **знáки препинáния** punctuation marks
преподавáтел|ь (**-я**) *м* (*школы, курсов*) teacher; (*вуза*) lecturer
препода|вáть (**-ю́, -ёшь**) *несов перех* to teach
преподн|ести́ (**-есý, -есёшь**; *pt* **-ёс, -еслá**, *impf* **преподноси́ть**) *сов перех*: **преподнести́ что-н комý-н** to present sb with sth
препя́тстви|е (**-я**) *ср* obstacle
препя́тств|овать (**ую**; *perf* **воспрепя́тствовать**) *несов +dat* to impede
прерв|áть (**-ý, -ёшь**; *impf* **прерывáть**) *сов перех* (*разговор, работу итп*) to cut short; (*отношения*) to break off; (*говорящего*) to interrupt; **прервáться** (*impf* **прерывáться**) *сов возв* (*разговор, игра*) to be cut short; (*отношения*) to be broken off
прес|éчь (**-екý, -ечёшь** *etc*, **-екýт**; *pt* **-ёк, -еклá**, *impf* **пресекáть**) *сов перех* to suppress
преслéдовани|е (**-я**) *ср* pursuit; (*сексуальное*) harassment; (*инакомыслия*) persecution; **преслéд|овать** (**-ую**) *несов*

перех to pursue; (*инакомыслящих*) to persecute; (*насмешками*) to harass
пресловутый *прил* notorious
пресмыкающ|ееся (**-егося**) *ср* reptile
пресноводный *прил* freshwater
пресный *прил* (*вода*) fresh; (*пища*) bland
пресс (**-а**) *м* (*Tex*) press
пресс|а (**-ы**) *ж собир* the press
пресс-конференци|я (**-и**) *ж* press conference
пресс-релиз (**-а**) *м* press release
пресс-секретар|ь (**-я**) *м* press secretary
пресс-центр (**-а**) *м* press office
престарел|ый *прил* aged; **дом (для) престарелых** old people's home
престиж (**-а**) *м* prestige; **престижный** *прил* prestigious
преступлени|е (**-я**) *ср* crime; **преступник** (**-а**) *м* criminal; **преступност|ь** (**-и**) *ж* (*количество*) crime; **преступный** *прил* criminal
претенд|овать (**-ую**) *несов*: **претендовать на** *+acc* (*стремиться*) to aspire to; (*заявлять права*) to lay claim to
претензи|я (**-и**) *ж* (*обычно мн*: *на наследство*) claim; (: *на ум, на красоту итп*) pretension; (*жалоба*) complaint
преткновени|е (**-я**) *ср*: **камень преткновения** stumbling block
преувелич|ить (**-у, -ишь**; *impf* **преувеличивать**) *сов перех* to exaggerate
преуменьш|ить (**-у, -ишь**; *impf* **преуменьшать**) *сов перех* to underestimate
преуспе|ть (**-ю**; *impf* **преуспевать**) *сов* (*в учёбе*) to be successful; (*в жизни*) to prosper, thrive
прецедент (**-а**) *м* precedent
при *предл* (*+prp*: *возле*) by, near; (*о части*) at; (*в присутствии*) in front of; (*о времени*) under; (*о наличии чего-н у кого-н*) on; **он всегда при деньгах** he always has money on him; **я здесь ни при чём** it has nothing to do with me
прибав|ить (**-лю, -ишь**; *impf* **прибавлять**) *сов перех* to add; (*увеличить*) to increase; **прибавиться** (*impf* **прибавляться**) *сов возв* (*проблемы, работа итп*) to mount up ▷ *безл* (*воды в реке*) to rise
прибежать (*как* **бежать**; *см* *Table 20*) *сов* to come running
приб|ить (**-ью, -ьёшь**; *imper* **-ей(те)**, *impf* **прибивать**) *сов перех* (*гвоздями*) to nail
приближа|ть(ся) (**-ю(сь)**) *несов от* **приблизить(ся)**
приближени|е (**-я**) *ср* approach
приблизительный *прил* approximate
прибли|зить (**-жу, -зишь**; *impf* **приближать**) *сов перех* (*придвинуть*) to move nearer; (*ускорить*) to bring nearer; **приблизиться** (*impf* **приближаться**) *сов возв* to approach
прибо|й (**-я**) *м* breakers *мн*
прибор (**-а**) *м* (*измерительный*) device; (*оптический*) instrument; (*нагревательный*) appliance; (*бритвенный*) set; **столовый прибор** setting
прибыва|ть (**-ю**) *несов от* **прибыть**
прибыл|ь (**-и**) *ж* profit; **прибыльный** *прил* profitable
прибыти|е (**-я**) *ср* arrival;

прибы́ть (*как* **быть**; см *Table 21*; *impf* **прибыва́ть**) *сов* to arrive

приватизи́р|овать (**-ую**) *(не)сов перех* to privatize

прив|езти́ (**-езу́, -езёшь**; *pt* **-ёз, -езла́**, *impf* **привози́ть**) *сов перех* to bring

прив|ести́ (**-еду́, -едёшь**; *pt* **-ёл, -ела́**) *сов от* **вести** ▷ (*impf* **приводи́ть**) *перех* (*сопроводить*) to bring; (*подлеж*: *дорога*: *к дому*) to take; (*пример*) to give; **привести́** (*perf*) **в у́жас** to horrify; **приводи́ть** (*perf* **привести́**) **в восто́рг** to delight; **приводи́ть** (*perf* **привести́**) **в изумле́ние** to astonish; **приводи́ть** (*perf* **привести́**) **в исполне́ние** to put into effect; **приводи́ть** (*perf* **привести́**) **в поря́док** to put in order

приве́т (**-а**) *м* regards *мн*; (*разг*: *при встрече*) hi; (: *при расставании*) bye; **передава́ть** (*perf* **переда́ть**) **кому́-н приве́т** to give sb one's regards; **приве́тливый** *прил* friendly; **приве́тстви|е** (**-я**) *ср* (*при встрече*) greeting; (*делегации*) welcome; **приве́тств|овать** (**-ую**; *perf* **поприве́тствовать**) *несов перех* to welcome

приви́в|ка (**-ки**; *gen pl* **-ок**) *ж* (*Мед*) vaccination

привиде́ни|е (**-я**) *ср* ghost

привиле́ги|я (**-и**) *ж* privilege

привин|ти́ть (**-чу́, -ти́шь**; *impf* **приви́нчивать**) *сов перех* to screw on

при́вкус (**-а**) *м* flavour (*Brit*), flavor (*US*)

привлека́тельный *прил* attractive

привлека́|ть (**-ю**) *несов от* **привле́чь**

привлече́ни|е (**-я**) *ср* (*покупателей, внимания*) attraction; (*ресурсов*) use

привл|е́чь (**-еку́, -ечёшь** *etc*, **-еку́т**; *pt* **-ёк, -екла́**, *impf* **привлека́ть**) *сов перех* to attract; (*ресурсы*) to use; **привлека́ть** (*perf* **привле́чь**) **кого́-н к** *+dat* (*к работе, к участию*) to involve sb in; (*к суду*) to take sb to; **привлека́ть** (*perf* **привле́чь**) **кого́-н к отве́тственности** to call sb to account

прив|оди́ть (**-ожу́, -о́дишь**) *несов от* **привести́**

прив|ози́ть (**-ожу́, -о́зишь**) *несов от* **привезти́**

привы́к|нуть (**-ну**; *pt* **-, -ла**, *impf* **привыка́ть**) *сов +infin* to get into the habit of doing; **привыка́ть** (*perf* **привы́кнуть**) **к** *+dat* (*к новому*) to get used to

привы́ч|ка (**-ки**; *gen pl* **-ек**) *ж* habit; **привы́чный** *прил* familiar

привя́занност|ь (**-и**) *ж* attachment

прив|яза́ть (**-яжу́, -я́жешь**; *impf* **привя́зывать**) *сов перех*: **привяза́ть что-н/кого́-н к** *+dat* to tie sth/sb to; **привяза́ться** (*impf* **привя́зываться**) *сов возв*: **привяза́ться к** *+dat* (*к сиденью*) to fasten o.s. to; (*полюбить*) to become attached to

пригласи́тельный *прил*: **пригласи́тельный биле́т** invitation

пригла|си́ть (**-шу́, -си́шь**; *impf* **приглаша́ть**) *сов перех* to invite

приглаше́ни|е (**-я**) *ср* invitation

приговор|и́ть (**-ю́, -и́шь**; *impf* **пригова́ривать**) *сов перех*: **приговори́ть кого́-н к** *+dat* to sentence sb to

приго|ди́ться (**-жу́сь, -ди́шься**) *сов возв +dat* to be useful to; **приго́дный** *прил* suitable

П

пригор|е́ть (*3sg* **-и́т**, *impf* **пригора́ть**) *сов* to burn
при́город (**-а**) *м* suburb; **при́городный** *прил* suburban; (*поезд*) commuter
пригото́в|ить (**-лю, -ишь**) *сов от* **гото́вить** ▷ (*impf* **приготовля́ть**) *перех* to prepare; (*постель*) to make; **пригото́виться** *сов от* **гото́виться** ▷ *возв*: **пригото́виться (к** *+dat*) (*к путешествию*) to get ready (for); (*к уроку*) to prepare (o.s.) (for)
приготовле́ни|е (**-я**) *ср* preparation
пригро|зи́ть (**-жу́, -зи́шь**) *сов от* **грози́ть**
прида|ва́ть (**-ю́, -ёшь**) *несов от* **прида́ть**
прида́ть (*как* **дать**; *см Table 16*; *impf* **придава́ть**) *сов*: **прида́ть чего́-н кому́-н** (*уверенности*) to instil (*Brit*) *или* instill (*US*) sth in sb ▷ *перех*: **прида́ть что-н чему́-н** (*вид, форму*) to give sth to sth; (*важность*) to attach sth to sth
прида́ч|а (**-и**) *ж*: **в прида́чу** in addition
придви́н|уть (**-у**; *impf* **придвига́ть**) *сов перех*: **придви́нуть (к** *+dat*) to move over *или* up (to)
приде́ла|ть (**-ю**; *impf* **приде́лывать**) *сов перех*: **приде́лать что-н к** *+dat* to attach sth to
прид|ержа́ть (**-ержу́, -е́ржишь**; *impf* **приде́рживать**) *сов перех* (*дверь*) to hold (steady); (*лошадь*) to restrain
приде́ржива|ться (**-юсь**) *несов возв* (*+gen*: *взглядов*) to hold
придира́|ться (**-юсь**) *несов от* **придра́ться**
приди́рчивый *прил* (*человек*) fussy; (*замечание, взгляд*) critical
прид|ра́ться (**-еру́сь, -ерёшься**; *impf* **придира́ться**) *сов возв*: **придра́ться к** *+dat* to find fault with
приду́ *etc* *сов см* **прийти́**
приду́ма|ть (**-ю**; *impf* **приду́мывать**) *сов перех* (*отговорку, причину*) to think of *или* up; (*новый прибор*) to devise; (*песню, стихотворение*) to make up
прие́ду *etc* *сов см* **прие́хать**
прие́зд (**-а**) *м* arrival
приезжа́|ть (**-ю**) *несов от* **прие́хать**
приём (**-а**) *м* reception; (*у врача*) surgery (*Brit*), office (*US*); (*Спорт*) technique; (*наказания, воздействия*) means; **в два/в три приёма** in two/three attempts; **запи́сываться (***perf* **записа́ться) на приём к** *+dat* to make an appointment with
приёмн|ая (**-ой**) *ж* (*также* **приёмная ко́мната**) reception
приёмник (**-а**) *м* receiver; (*радио*) radio
приёмный *прил* (*часы*) reception; (*день*) visiting; (*экзамены*) entrance; (*комиссия*) selection; (*родители, дети*) adoptive
прие́хать (*как* **е́хать**; *см Table 19*; *impf* **приезжа́ть**) *сов* to arrive *или* come (*by transport*)
приж|а́ть (**-му́, -мёшь**; *impf* **прижима́ть**) *сов перех*: **прижа́ть что-н/кого́-н к** *+dat* to press sth/sb to *или* against; **прижа́ться** (*impf* **прижима́ться**) *сов возв*: **прижа́ться к** *+dat* to press o.s. against; (*к груди*) to snuggle up to
приз (**-а**; *nom pl* **-ы́**) *м* prize

призва́ни|е (**-я**) *ср* (*к науке итп*) vocation

приз|ва́ть (**-ову́, -овёшь**; *pt* **-ва́л, -вала́**, *impf* **призыва́ть**) *сов перех* (*к борьбе, к защите*) to call; **призыва́ть** (*perf* **призва́ть**) **к ми́ру** to call for peace; **призыва́ть** (*perf* **призва́ть**) **кого́-н к поря́дку** to call sb to order; **призыва́ть** (*perf* **призва́ть**) **в а́рмию** to call up (to join the army)

приземл|и́ть (**-ю́, -и́шь**; *impf* **приземля́ть**) *сов перех* to land; **приземли́ться** (*impf* **приземля́ться**) *сов возв* to land

призна|ва́ть(ся) (**-ю́(сь), -ёшь(ся)**) *несов от* **призна́ть(ся)**

при́знак (**-а**) *м* (*кризиса, успеха*) sign; (*отравления*) symptom

призна́ни|е (**-я**) *ср* recognition; (*согласие*) acknowledgment; (*в любви*) declaration; (*в преступлении*) confession

призна́тельност|ь (**-и**) *ж* gratitude; **призна́тельный** *прил* grateful

призна́|ть (**-ю**; *impf* **признава́ть**) *сов перех* to recognize; (*счесть*): **призна́ть что-н/кого́-н** *+instr* to recognize sth/sb as; **призна́ться** (*impf* **признава́ться**) *сов возв*: **призна́ться кому́-н в чём-н** (*в преступлении*) to confess sth to sb; **признава́ться** (*perf* **призна́ться**) **кому́-н в любви́** to make a declaration of love to sb

при́зрак (**-а**) *м* ghost

призы́в (**-а**) *м* call; (*в армию*) conscription, draft (*US*); (*лозунг*) slogan

призыва́|ть (**-ю**) *несов от* **призва́ть**

призывни́к (**-а́**) *м* conscript

прийти́ (*как* **идти́**; см *Table 18*; *impf* **приходи́ть**) *сов* (*идя, достичь*) to come (*on foot*); (*телеграмма, письмо*) to arrive; (*весна, час свободы*) to come; (*достигнуть*): **прийти́ к** *+dat* (*к власти, к выводу*) to come to; (*к демократии*) to achieve; **приходи́ть** (*perf* **прийти́**) **в у́жас/недоуме́ние** to be horrified/bewildered; **приходи́ть** (*perf* **прийти́**) **в восто́рг** to go into raptures; **приходи́ть** (*perf* **прийти́**) **кому́-н в го́лову** *или* **на ум** to occur to sb; **приходи́ть** (*perf* **прийти́**) **в себя́** (*после обморока*) to come to *или* round; (*успокоиться*) to come to one's senses; **прийти́сь** (*impf* **приходи́ться**) *сов возв*: **прийти́сь на** *+acc* to fall on; **(нам) придётся согласи́ться** we'll have to agree

прика́з (**-а**) *м* order; **приказа́ни|е** (**-я**) *ср* = **прика́з**; **прик|аза́ть** (**-ажу́, -а́жешь**; *impf* **прика́зывать**) *сов*: **приказа́ть кому́-н** *+infin* to order sb to do

прика́лыва|ть (**-ю**) *несов от* **приколо́ть**

прикаса́|ться (**-юсь**) *несов от* **прикосну́ться**

прикла́д (**-а**) *м* (*ружья*) butt

прикла́дыва|ть (**-ю**) *несов от* **приложи́ть**

прикле́|ить (**-ю, -ишь**; *impf* **прикле́ивать**) *сов перех* to glue, stick; **прикле́иться** (*impf* **прикле́иваться**) *сов возв* to stick

приключе́ни|е (**-я**) *ср* adventure

прик|оло́ть (**-олю́, -о́лешь**; *impf* **прика́лывать**) *сов перех* to fasten

прикосн|у́ться (**-у́сь, -ёшься**;

impf **прикаса́ться**) *сов возв*: **прикосну́ться к** *+dat* to touch lightly

прикреп|и́ть (**-лю́, -и́шь**; *impf* **прикрепля́ть**) *сов перех*: **прикрепи́ть что-н/кого́-н к** *+dat* to attach sth/sb to

прикр|ы́ть (**-о́ю, -о́ешь**; *impf* **прикрыва́ть**) *сов перех* to cover; (*закрыть*) to close (over)

прик|ури́ть (**-урю́, -у́ришь**; *impf* **прику́ривать**) *сов* to get a light (*from a lit cigarette*)

прила́в|ок (**-ка**) *м* (*в магазине*) counter; (*на рынке*) stall

прилага́тельн|ое (**-ого**) *ср* (*Линг*: *также* **имя прилага́тельное**) adjective

прилага́|ть (**-ю**) *несов от* **приложи́ть**

прилега́|ть (*3sg* **-ет**) *несов*: **прилега́ть к чему́-н** (*одежда*) to fit sth tightly

приле|те́ть (**-чу́, -ти́шь**; *impf* **прилета́ть**) *сов* to arrive (*by air*), fly in

прил|е́чь (**-я́гу, -я́жешь** *etc*, **-я́гут**; *pt* **-ёг, -егла́**) *сов* to lie down for a while

прили́в (**-а**) *м* (*в море*) tide

прили́п|нуть (**-ну**; *pt* **-, -ла**, *impf* **прилипа́ть** *или* **ли́пнуть**) *сов*: **прили́пнуть к** *+dat* to stick to

прили́чный *прил* (*человек*) decent; (*сумма, результат*) fair, decent

приложе́ни|е (**-я**) *ср* (*знаний, энергии*) application; (*к журналу*) supplement; (*к документу*) addendum (*мн* addenda); (Комп) app

прил|ожи́ть (**-ожу́, -о́жишь**; *impf* **прилага́ть**) *сов перех* (*присоединить*) to attach; (*силу, знания*) to apply; **прикла́дывать** (*perf* **приложи́ть**) **что-н к** *+dat* (*руку*: *ко лбу*) to put sth to; **ума́ не приложу́** (*разг*) I don't have a clue

примене́ни|е (**-я**) *ср* (*оружия, машин*) use; (*лекарств*) application; (*мер, метода*) adoption

прим|ени́ть (**-еню́, -е́нишь**; *impf* **применя́ть**) *сов перех* (*меры*) to implement; (*силу*) to use, apply; **применя́ть** (*perf* **примени́ть**) **что-н** (**к** *+dat*) (*метод, теорию*) to apply sth (to)

применя́|ться (*3sg* **-ется**) *несов* (*использоваться*) to be used

приме́р (**-а**) *м* example

приме́р|ка (**-ки**; *gen pl* **-ок**) *ж* trying on

приме́рно *нареч* (*см прил*) in an exemplary fashion; (*около*) approximately

при́мес|ь (**-и**) *ж* dash

приме́т|а (**-ы**) *ж* (*признак*) sign; (*суеверная*) omen

примета́|ть (**-ю**; *impf* **примётывать**) *сов перех* to stitch on

примеча́ни|е (**-я**) *ср* note

примити́вный *прил* primitive

примо́рский *прил* seaside

принадлеж|а́ть (**-у́, -и́шь**) *несов* *+dat* to belong to; (*заслуга*) to go to

принадле́жност|ь (**-и**) *ж* characteristic; (*обычно мн*: *комплект*) tackle; (: *письменные*) accessories *мн*

прин|ести́ (**-есу́, -есёшь**; *pt* **-ёс, -есла́**, *impf* **приноси́ть**) *сов перех* to bring; (*извинения, благодарность*) to express; (*присягу*) to take; **приноси́ть** (*perf* **принести́**) **по́льзу** *+dat* to be of use to; **приноси́ть** (*perf* **принести́**) **вред** *+dat* to harm

принима́|ть(ся) (**-ю(сь)**) *несов от* **приня́ть(ся)**

прин|оси́ть (**-ошу́, -о́сишь**) *несов от* **принести́**
при́нтер (**-а**) *м* (*Комп*) printer
принуди́тельный *прил* forced
прину́|дить (**-жу, -дишь**; *impf* **принужда́ть**) *сов перех*: **прину́дить кого́-н/что-н к чему́-н/**+*infin* to force sb/sth into sth/to do
принц (**-а**) *м* prince; **принце́сс|а** (**-ы**) *ж* princess
при́нцип (**-а**) *м* principle
при|ня́ть (**-му́, -мешь**; *pt* **-нял, -няла́**, *impf* **принима́ть**) *сов перех* to take; (*подарок, условия*) to accept; (*пост*) to take up; (*гостей, телеграмму*) to receive; (*закон, резолюцию*) to pass; (*отношение, вид*) to take on; (*христианство итп*) to adopt; **принима́ть** (*perf* **приня́ть**) **в/на** +*acc* (*в университет, на работу*) to accept for; **принима́ть** (*perf* **приня́ть**) **что-н/кого́-н за** +*acc* to mistake sth/sb for; (*счесть*) to take sth/sb as; **приня́ться** (*impf* **принима́ться**) *сов возв*: **приня́ться** +*infin* (*приступить*) to get down to doing; **принима́ться** (*perf* **приня́ться**) **за** +*acc* (*приступить*) to get down to
приобр|ести́ (**-ету́, -етёшь**; *pt* **-ёл, -ела́**, *impf* **приобрета́ть**) *сов перех* to acquire, obtain; (*друзей, врагов*) to make
приорите́т (**-а**) *м* priority
приостан|ови́ть (**-овлю́, -о́вишь**; *impf* **приостана́вливать**) *сов перех* to suspend
припа́д|ок (**-ка**) *м* (*Мед*) attack
припа́с|ы (**-ов**) *мн* supplies; (*Воен*) ammunition *ед*
припе́в (**-а**) *м* (*песни*) chorus, refrain
прип|иса́ть (**-ишу́, -и́шешь**; *impf* **припи́сывать**) *сов перех* to add; **припи́сывать** (*perf* **приписа́ть**) **что-н кому́-н** to attribute sth to sb
припол з|ти́ (**-у́, -ёшь**; *impf* **приполза́ть**) *сов перех* to crawl in
припо́мн|ить (**-ю, -ишь**; *impf* **припомина́ть**) *сов перех* to remember
припра́в|а (**-ы**) *ж* seasoning
приравня́|ть (**-ю**; *impf* **прира́внивать**) *сов перех*: **приравня́ть кого́-н/что-н к** +*dat* to equate sb/sth with
приро́д|а (**-ы**) *ж* nature; (*места вне города*) countryside; **приро́дный** *прил* natural
приро́ст (**-а**) *м* (*населения*) growth; (*доходов, урожая*) increase
прируч|и́ть (**-у́, -и́шь**; *impf* **прируча́ть**) *сов перех* to tame
приса́жива|ться (**-юсь**) *несов от* **присе́сть**
присво́|ить (**-ю, -ишь**; *impf* **присва́ивать**) *сов перех* (*чужое*) to appropriate; (*дать*): **присво́ить что-н кому́-н** (*звание*) to confer sth on sb
приседа́ни|е (**-я**) *ср* squatting (*physical exercise*)
прис|е́сть (**-я́ду, -я́дешь**; *impf* **приседа́ть**) *сов* to squat ▷ (*impf* **приса́живаться**) (*на стул*) to sit down (*for a short while*)
приск|ака́ть (**-ачу́, -а́чешь**; *impf* **приска́кивать**) *сов* to gallop *или* come galloping up
при|сла́ть (**-шлю́, -шлёшь**; *impf* **присыла́ть**) *сов перех* to send
прислон|и́ть (**-ю́, -и́шь**; *impf* **прислоня́ть**) *сов перех*: **прислони́ть что-н к** +*dat* to lean

П

sth against; **прислони́ться** (*impf* **прислоня́ться**) *сов возв*: **прислони́ться к** + *dat* to lean against

прислу́жива|ть (**-ю**) *несов* (*+dat*: *официант*) to wait on

прислу́ша|ться (**-юсь**; *impf* **прислу́шиваться**) *сов возв*: **прислу́шаться к** *+dat* (*к звуку*) to listen to

присмо́тр (**-а**) *м* care

присм|отре́ть (**-отрю́, -о́тришь**; *impf* **присма́тривать**) *сов*: **присмотре́ть за** *+instr* to look after; (*найти*) to spot

присн|и́ться (*3sg* **-и́тся**) *сов от* **сни́ться**

присоедине́ни|е (**-я**) *ср* attachment; (*провода*) connection; (*территории*) annexation

присоедин|и́ть (**-ю́, -и́шь**; *impf* **присоединя́ть**) *сов перех*: **присоедини́ть что-н к** *+dat* to attach sth to; (*провод*) to connect sth to; (*территорию*) to annex sth to; **присоедини́ться** (*impf* **присоединя́ться**) *сов возв*: **присоедини́ться к** *+dat* to join; (*к мнению*) to support

приспосо́б|ить (**-лю, -ишь**; *impf* **приспоса́бливать**) *сов перех* to adapt; **приспосо́биться** (*impf* **приспоса́бливаться**) *сов возв* (*делать что-н*) to learn how; (*к условиям*) to adapt (o.s.)

приста|ва́ть (**-ю́, -ёшь**) *несов от* **приста́ть**

приста́в|ить (**-лю, -ишь**; *impf* **приставля́ть**) *сов перех*: **приста́вить что-н к** *+dat* to put sth against

приста́в|ка (**-ки**; *gen pl* **-ок**) *ж* (*Линг*) prefix; (*Тех*) attachment

приставля́|ть (**-ю**) *несов от* **приста́вить**

при́стальный *прил* (*взгляд, внимание*) fixed; (*интерес, наблюдение*) intent

при́стан|ь (**-и**) *ж* pier

приста́|ть (**-ну, -нешь**; *impf* **пристава́ть**) *сов*: **приста́ть к** *+dat* (*прилипнуть*) to stick to; (*присоединиться*) to join; (*разг*: *с вопросами*) to pester; (*причалить*) to moor

пристегн|у́ть (**-у́, -ёшь**; *impf* **пристёгивать**) *сов перех* to fasten; **пристегну́ться** (*impf* **пристёгиваться**) *сов возв* (*в самолёте итп*) to fasten one's seat belt

пристра́ива|ть (**-ю**) *несов от* **пристро́ить**

пристр|ели́ть (**-елю́, -е́лишь**; *impf* **пристре́ливать**) *сов перех* (*животное*) to put down

пристро́|ить (**-ю, -ишь**; *impf* **пристра́ивать**) *сов перех* (*комнату*) to build on; **пристро́|йка** (**-йки**; *gen pl* **-ек**) *ж* extension

при́ступ (**-а**) *м* (*атака, сердечный*) attack; (*смеха, гнева, кашля*) fit; **прист|упи́ть** (**-уплю́, -у́пишь**; *impf* **приступа́ть**) *сов*: **приступи́ть к** *+dat* (*начать*) to commence

прис|уди́ть (**-ужу́, -у́дишь**; *impf* **присужда́ть**) *сов перех*: **присуди́ть что-н кому́-н** to award sth to sb; (*учёную степень*) to confer sth on sb

прису́тстви|е (**-я**) *ср* presence; **прису́тств|овать** (**-ую**) *несов* to be present

прису́тствующ|ие (**-их**) *мн* those present *мн*

присыла́|ть (**-ю**) *несов от* **присла́ть**

прися́г|а (**-и**) *ж* oath
прит|ащи́ть (**-ащу́, -а́щишь**; *impf* **прита́скивать**) *сов перех* to drag
притвор|и́ться (**-ю́сь, -и́шься**; *impf* **притворя́ться**) *сов возв* +*instr* to pretend to be
прити́х|нуть (**-ну, -нешь**; *pt* **-, -ла**, *impf* **притиха́ть**) *сов* to grow quiet
прито́к (**-а**) *м* (*река*) tributary; (+*gen*: *энергии, средств*) supply of; (*населения*) influx of
прито́м *союз* and what's more
прито́н (**-а**) *м* den
при́торный *прил* sickly sweet
прит|упи́ться (*3sg* **-у́пится**, *impf* **притупля́ться**) *сов возв* (*нож*) to go blunt; (*перен*: *внимание итп*) to diminish; (: *чувства*) to fade; (: *слух*) to fail
притяза́ни|е (**-я**) *ср*: **притяза́ние на** +*acc* claim to
приуро́ч|ить (**-у, -ишь**) *сов перех*: **приуро́чить что-н к** +*dat* to time sth to coincide with
при|учи́ть (**-учу́, -у́чишь**; *impf* **приу́чивать**) *сов перех*: **приучи́ть кого́-н к** +*dat*/ +*infin* to train sb for/to do; **приучи́ться** (*impf* **приу́чиваться**) *сов возв*: **приучи́ться к** +*dat*/ +*infin* to train for/to do
прихв|ати́ть (**-ачу́, -а́тишь**) *сов перех* (*разг*: *взять*) to take
прихо́д (**-а**) *м* arrival; (*Комм*) receipts *мн*; (*Рел*) parish; **прихо́д и расхо́д** (*Комм*) credit and debit
прих|оди́ть (**-ожу́, -о́дишь**) *несов от* **прийти́**; **приходи́ться** *несов от* **прийти́сь** ▷ *возв*: **приходи́ться кому́-н ро́дственником** to be sb's relative
прихо́д|овать (**-ую**; *perf* **оприхо́довать**) *несов перех* (*Комм*: *сумму*) to enter (*in receipt book*)
приходя́щ|ий *прил* nonresident; **приходя́щая ня́ня** babysitter
прихо́ж|ая (**-ей**) *ж* entrance hall
прихожу́(сь) *несов см* **приходи́ть(ся)**
при́хот|ь (**-и**) *ж* whim
прице́л (**-а**) *м* (*ружья, пушки*) sight
прице́л|иться (**-юсь, -ишься**; *impf* **прице́ливаться**) *сов возв* to take aim
прице́п (**-а**) *м* trailer; **прицеп|и́ть** (**-еплю́, -е́пишь**; *impf* **прицепля́ть**) *сов перех* (*вагон*) to couple
прича́л (**-а**) *м* mooring; (*пассажирский*) quay; (*грузовой, ремонтный*) dock; **прича́л|ить** (**-ю, -ишь**; *impf* **прича́ливать**) *сов (не)перех* to moor
прича́сти|е (**-я**) *ср* (*Линг*) participle; (*Рел*) communion
прича|сти́ть (**-щу́, -сти́шь**; *impf* **причаща́ть**) *сов перех* (*Рел*) to give communion to; **причасти́ться** (*impf* **причаща́ться**) *сов возв* (*Рел*) to receive communion
прича́стный *прил* (*связанный*): **прича́стный к** +*dat* connected with
причаща́|ть(ся) (**-ю(сь)**) *несов от* **причасти́ть(ся)**
причём *союз* moreover
прич|еса́ть (**-ешу́, -е́шешь**; *impf* **причёсывать**) *сов перех* (*расчёской*) to comb; (*щёткой*) to brush; **причёсывать** (*perf* **причеса́ть**) **кого́-н** to comb/brush sb's hair; **причеса́ться** (*impf* **причёсываться**) *сов возв* (*см перех*) to comb one's hair; to brush one's hair

причёс|ка (**-ки**; *gen pl* **-ок**) *ж* hairstyle
причи́н|а (**-ы**) *ж* (*то, что вызывает*) cause; (*обоснование*) reason; **по причи́не** *+gen* on account of
причин|и́ть (**-ю́, -и́шь**; *impf* **причиня́ть**) *сов перех* to cause
причу́д|а (**-ы**) *ж* whim
пришёл(ся) *сов см* **прийти́(сь)**
приш|и́ть (**-ью́, -ьёшь**; *imper* **-е́й(те)**, *impf* **пришива́ть**) *сов перех* to sew on
пришла́ *etc сов см* **прийти́**
прищем|и́ть (**-лю́, -и́шь**; *impf* **прищемля́ть**) *сов перех* to catch
прищу́р|ить (**-ю, -ишь**; *impf* **прищу́ривать**) *сов перех* (*глаза*) to screw up; **прищу́риться** (*impf* **прищу́риваться**) *сов возв* to screw up one's eyes
приют|и́ть (**-чу́, -ти́шь**) *сов перех* to shelter; **приюти́ться** *сов возв* to take shelter
прия́тел|ь (**-я**) *м* friend
прия́тно *нареч* (*удивлён*) pleasantly ▷ *как сказ* it's nice *или* pleasant; **мне прия́тно э́то слы́шать** I'm glad to hear that; **о́чень прия́тно** (*при знакомстве*) pleased to meet you; **прия́тный** *прил* pleasant
про *предл +acc* about
про́б|а (**-ы**) *ж* (*испытание*) test; (*образец*) sample; (*золота*) standard (*of quality*); (*клеймо*) hallmark
пробе́г (**-а**) *м* (*Спорт*) race; (: *лыжный*) run; (*Авт*) mileage
пробежа́ть (*как* **бежа́ть**; см *Table 20*; *impf* **пробега́ть**) *сов перех* (*текст*) to skim; (*5 километров*) to cover ▷ *неперех* (*время*) to pass; (*миновать бегом*): **пробежа́ть ми́мо** *+gen* to run past; (*появиться и исчезнуть*): **пробежа́ть по** *+dat* (*шум, дрожь*) to run through; **пробежа́ться** *сов возв* to run
пробе́л (**-а**) *м* (*также перен*) gap
пробива́|ть(ся) (**-ю(сь)**) *несов от* **проби́ть(ся)**
пробира́|ться (**-юсь**) *несов от* **пробра́ться**
проб|и́ть (**-ью́, -ьёшь**) *сов от* **бить** ▷ (*impf* **пробива́ть**) *перех* (*дыру*) to knock; (*крышу, стену*) to make a hole in; **проби́ться** (*impf* **пробива́ться**) *сов возв* (*прорваться*) to fight one's way through; (*растения*) to push through *или* up
про́б|ка (**-ки**; *gen pl* **-ок**) *ж* cork; (*перен: на дороге*) jam; (*Элек*) fuse (*Brit*), fuze (*US*)
пробле́м|а (**-ы**) *ж* problem
проблемати́чный *прил* problematic(al)
про́бный *прил* trial
про́б|овать (**-ую**; *perf* **попро́бовать**) *несов перех* (*пирог, вино*) to taste; (*пытаться*) *+infin* to try to do
пробо́ин|а (**-ы**) *ж* hole
пробо́р (**-а**) *м* parting (*of hair*)
проб|ра́ться (**-еру́сь, -ерёшься**; *impf* **пробира́ться**) *сов возв* (*с трудом пройти*) to fight one's way through; (*тихо пройти*) to steal past *или* through
пробы́ть (*как* **быть**; см *Table 21*) *сов* (*прожить*) to stay, remain
прова́л (**-а**) *м* (*в почве, в стене*) hole; (*перен: неудача*) flop; (: *памяти*) failure
пров|али́ть (**-алю́, -а́лишь**; *impf* **прова́ливать**) *сов перех* (*крышу, пол*) to cause to collapse; (*разг: перен: дело, затею*) to botch up; (: *студента*) to fail; **провали́ться**

(*impf* **прова́ливаться**) *сов возв* (*человек*) to fall; (*крыша*) to collapse; (*разг: перен: студент, попытка*) to fail; **как сквозь зе́млю провали́лся** he disappeared into thin air

проведу́ *etc сов см* **провести́**

пров|езти́ (**-езу́, -езёшь**; *pt* **-ёз, -езла́**, *impf* **провози́ть**) *сов перех* (*незаконно*) to smuggle; (*везя, доставить*): **провезти́ по** *+dat*/**ми́мо** *+gen*/**че́рез** *+acc* to take along/past/across

прове́р|ить (**-ю, -ишь**; *impf* **проверя́ть**) *сов перех* to check; (*знание, двигатель*) to test; **прове́риться** (*impf* **проверя́ться**) *сов возв* (*у врача*) to get a check up

прове́р|ка (**-ки**; *gen pl* **-ок**) *ж* (*см глаг*) check-up; test

пров|ести́ (**-еду́, -едёшь**; *pt* **-ёл, -ела́**, *impf* **проводи́ть**) *сов перех* (*черту, границу*) to draw; (*дорогу*) to build; (*план, реформу*) to implement; (*урок, репетицию*) to hold; (*операцию*) to carry out; (*детство, день*) to spend; **проводи́ть** (*perf* **провести́**) **ми́мо** *+gen*/**че́рез** *+acc* (*людей*) to take past/across

прове́тр|ить (**-ю, -ишь**; *impf* **прове́тривать**) *сов перех* to air; **прове́триться** (*impf* **прове́триваться**) *сов возв* (*комната, одежда*) to have an airing

провин|и́ться (**-ю́сь, -и́шься**) *сов возв*: **провини́ться** (**в** *+prp*) to be guilty (of)

провинциа́льный *прил* provincial

прови́нци|я (**-и**) *ж* province

про́вод (**-а**; *nom pl* **-а́**) *м* cable

пров|оди́ть (**-ожу́, -о́дишь**) *несов от* **провести́** ▷ (*impf* **провожа́ть**) *сов перех* to see off; **провожа́ть** (*perf* **проводи́ть**) **глаза́ми/взгля́дом кого́-н** to follow sb with one's eyes/gaze

прово́д|ка (**-ки**; *gen pl* **-ок**) *ж* (*Элек*) wiring

проводни́к (**-а́**) *м* (*в горах*) guide; (*в поезде*) steward (*Brit*), porter (*US*)

про́вод|ы (**-ов**) *мн* (*прощание*) send-off *ед*

провожа́|ть (**-ю**) *несов от* **проводи́ть**

провожу́ (*не*)*сов см* **проводи́ть**

прово́з (**-а**) *м* (*багажа*) transport; (*незаконный*) smuggling

провозгла|си́ть (**-шу́, -си́шь**; *impf* **провозглаша́ть**) *сов перех* to proclaim

пров|ози́ть (**-ожу́, -о́зишь**) *несов от* **провезти́**

провокацио́нный *прил* provocative

про́волок|а (**-и**) *ж* wire

провоци́р|овать (**-ую**; *perf* **спровоци́ровать**) *несов перех* to provoke

прогиба́|ть(ся) (**-ю(сь)**) *несов от* **прогну́ть(ся)**

прогл|оти́ть (**-очу́, -о́тишь**; *impf* **прогла́тывать** *или* **глота́ть**) *сов перех* (*также перен*) to swallow

прог|на́ть (**-оню́, -о́нишь**; *pt* **-на́л, -нала́**, *impf* **прогоня́ть**) *сов перех* (*заставить уйти*) to turn out

прогно́з (**-а**) *м* forecast

прогоня́|ть (**-ю**) *несов от* **прогна́ть**

програ́мм|а (**-ы**) *ж* programme (*Brit*), program (*US*); (*Полит*) manifesto; (*также* **веща́тельная програ́мма**) channel; (*Просвещ*) curriculum; (*Комп*) program

программи́р|овать (**-ую**; *perf*

запрограмми́ровать) *несов перех* (*Комп*) to program
программи́ст (**-а**) *м* (*Комп*) programmer
програ́ммн|ый *прил* programmed (*Brit*), programed (*US*); (*экзамен, зачёт*) set; **програ́ммное обеспе́чение** (*Комп*) software
прогре́сс (**-а**) *м* progress; **прогресси́вный** *прил* progressive
прогу́л (**-а**) *м* (*на работе*) absence; (*в школе*) truancy
прогу́лива|ть (**-ю**) *несов от* **прогуля́ть**
прогу́л|ка (**-ки**; *gen pl* **-ок**) *ж* walk; (*недалёкая поездка*) trip
прогу́льщик (**-а**) *м* (*об ученике*) truant
прогуля́|ть (**-ю**; *impf* **прогу́ливать**) *сов перех* (*работу*) to be absent from; (*уроки*) to miss; (*гулять*) to walk
прода|ва́ть (**-ю́**) *несов от* **прода́ть**
продав|е́ц (**-ца́**) *м* seller; (*в магазине*) (shop-)assistant; **продавщи́ц|а** (**-ы**) *ж от* **продаве́ц**
прода́ж|а (**-и**) *ж* (*дома, товара*) sale; (*торговля*) trade
прода́ть (*как* **дать**; см *Table 16*; *impf* **продава́ть**) *сов перех* to sell; (*перен*: *друга*) to betray
продвига́|ть(ся) (**-ю(сь)**) *несов от* **продви́нуть(ся)**
продвиже́ни|е (**-я**) *ср* (*войск*) advance; (*по службе*) promotion
продви́н|уть (**-у**; *impf* **продвига́ть**) *сов перех* to move; (*перен*: *работника*) to promote; **продви́нуться** (*impf* **продвига́ться**) *сов возв* to move; (*войска*) to advance; (*перен*: *работник*) to be promoted; (: *работа*) to progress
продева́|ть (**-ю**) *несов от* **проде́ть**
проде́ла|ть (**-ю**; *impf* **проде́лывать**) *сов перех* (*отверстие*) to make; (*работу*) to do
проде́|ть (**-ну, -нешь**; *impf* **продева́ть**) *сов перех* to thread
продлева́|ть (**-ю**) *несов от* **продли́ть**
продле́ни|е (**-я**) *ср* (*см глаг*) extension; prolongation
продл|и́ть (**-ю́, -и́шь**; *impf* **продлева́ть**) *сов перех* to extend; (*жизнь*) to prolong
продл|и́ться (*3sg* **-и́тся**) *сов от* **дли́ться**
продово́льственный *прил* food; **продово́льственный магази́н** grocer's (shop) (*Brit*), grocery (*US*)
продово́льстви|е (**-я**) *ср* provisions *мн*
продолжа́|ть (**-ю**; *perf* **продо́лжить**) *несов перех* to continue; **продолжа́ть** (*perf* **продо́лжить**) +*impf infin* to continue *или* carry on doing; **продолжа́ться** (*perf* **продо́лжиться**) *несов возв* to continue, carry on;
продолже́ни|е (**-я**) *ср* (*борьбы, лекции*) continuation; (*романа*) sequel; **в продолже́ние** +*gen* for the duration of;
продолжи́тельност|ь (**-и**) *ж* duration; **(сре́дняя) продолжи́тельность жи́зни** (average) life expectancy
продо́лж|ить(ся) (**-у(сь), -ишь(ся)**) *сов от* **продолжа́ть(ся)**
проду́кт (**-а**) *м* product; *см также*

проду́кты; **продукти́вност|ь** (**-и**) *ж* productivity; **продукти́вный** *прил* productive; **продукто́вый** *прил* food; **проду́кт|ы** (**-ов**) *мн* (*также* **проду́кты пита́ния**) foodstuffs

проду́кци|я (**-и**) *ж* produce

проду́манный *прил* well thought-out

проду́ма|ть (**-ю**; *impf* **проду́мывать**) *сов перех* (*действия*) to think out

прое́зд (**-а**) *м* (*в транспорте*) journey; (*место*) passage; **проездно́й** *прил* (*документ*) travel; **проездно́й биле́т** travel card; **прое́здом** *нареч* en route

проезжа́|ть (**-ю**) *несов от* **прое́хать**

прое́зж|ий *прил* (*люди*) passing through; **прое́зжая часть (у́лицы)** road

прое́кт (**-а**) *м* project; (*дома*) design; (*закона, договора*) draft; **проекти́р|овать** (**-ую**; *perf* **спроекти́ровать**) *несов перех* (*дом*) to design; (*дороги*) to plan ▷ (*perf* **запроекти́ровать**) (*наметить*) to plan

прое́ктор (**-а**) *м* (*Оптика*) projector

прое́хать (*как* **е́хать**; см *Table 19*) *сов перех* (*миновать*) to pass; (*пропустить*) to miss ▷ (*impf* **проезжа́ть**) *неперех*: **прое́хать ми́мо** *+gen*/**по** *+dat*/**че́рез** *+acc* *итп* to drive past/along/across *итп*; **прое́хаться** *сов возв* (*на машине*) to go for a drive

прож|е́чь (**-гу́, -жёшь** *итп*, **-гу́т**; *pt* **-ёг, -гла́**, *impf* **прожига́ть**) *сов перех* to burn a hole in

прожива́ни|е (**-я**) *ср* stay

прожива́|ть (**-ю**) *несов от* **прожи́ть** ▷ *неперех* to live

прожига́|ть (**-ю**) *несов от* **проже́чь**

прожи́|ть (**-ву́, -вёшь**) *сов* (*пробыть живым*) to live; (*жить*) to spend

про́з|а (**-ы**) *ж* prose

про́звищ|е (**-а**) *ср* nickname

прозева́|ть (**-ю**) *сов от* **зева́ть**

прозра́чный *прил* transparent; (*ткань*) see-through

проигра́|ть (**-ю**; *impf* **прои́грывать**) *сов перех* to lose; (*играть*) to play

прои́грывател|ь (**-я**) *м* record player

про́игрыш (**-а**) *м* loss

произведе́ни|е (**-я**) *ср* work

произв|ести́ (**-еду́, -едёшь**; *pt* **-ёл, -ела́**, *impf* **производи́ть**) *сов перех* (*операцию*) to carry out; (*впечатление, суматоху*) to create

производи́тел|ь (**-я**) *м* producer; **производи́тельност|ь** (**-и**) *ж* productivity; **производи́тельный** *прил* (*продуктивный*) productive

произв|оди́ть (**-ожу́, -о́дишь**) *несов от* **произвести́** ▷ *перех* (*изготовлять*) to produce, manufacture

произво́дственный *прил* (*процесс, план*) production; **произво́дственное объедине́ние** large industrial company

произво́дств|о (**-а**) *ср* (*товаров*) production, manufacture; (*отрасль*) industry; (*завод, фабрика*) factory; **промы́шленное произво́дство** industrial output; (*отрасль*) industry

произво́льный *прил* (*свободный*) free; (*Спорт*) freestyle; (*вывод*) arbitrary

произн|ести́ (**-есу́, -есёшь**; *pt* **-ёс, -есла́**, *impf* **произноси́ть**) *сов перех* (*слово*) to pronounce; (*речь*) to make

произн|оси́ть (**-ошу́, -о́сишь**) *несов от* **произнести́**

произноше́ни|е (**-я**) *ср* pronunciation

произойти́ (*как* **идти́**; см *Table 18*; *impf* **происходи́ть**) *сов* to occur

происх|оди́ть (**-ожу́, -о́дишь**) *несов от* **произойти́** ▷ *неперех*: **происходи́ть от/из** *+gen* to come from

происхожде́ни|е (**-я**) *ср* origin

происше́стви|е (**-я**) *ср* event; **доро́жное происше́ствие** road accident

пройти́ (*как* **идти́**; см *Table 18*; *impf* **проходи́ть**) *сов* to pass; (*расстояние*) to cover; (*слух*) to spread; (*дорога, канал итп*) to stretch; (*дождь, снег*) to fall; (*операция, переговоры итп*) to go ▷ *перех* (*практику, службу итп*) to complete; (*изучить: тему итп*) to do; **пройти́** (*impf* **проходи́ть**) **в** *+acc* (*в институт итп*) to get into; **пройти́сь** (*impf* **проха́живаться**) *сов возв* (*по комнате*) to pace; (*по парку*) to stroll

прока́лыва|ть (**-ю**) *несов от* **проколо́ть**

прока́т (**-а**) *м* (*телевизора*) hire; (*также* **кинопрока́т**) film distribution; **брать** (*perf* **взять**) **что-н на прока́т** to hire sth

прок|ати́ть (**-ачу́, -а́тишь**) *сов перех*: **прокати́ть кого́-н** (*на машине итп*) to take sb for a ride; **прокати́ться** *сов возв* (*на машине*) to go for a ride

прокис|нуть (*3sg* **-нет**, *pt* **-, -ла**) *сов от* **ки́снуть**

прокла́д|ка (**-ки**; *gen pl* **-ок**) *ж* (*действие: труб*) laying out; (: *провода*) laying; (*защитная*) padding

прокла́дыва|ть (**-ю**) *несов от* **проложи́ть**

прокл|я́сть (**-яну́, -янёшь**; *pt* **-ял, -яла́, -я́ло**, *impf* **проклина́ть**) *сов перех* to curse

проко́л (**-а**) *м* (*см глаг*) puncturing; lancing; piercing; (*отверстие: в шине*) puncture

прокр|а́сться (**-аду́сь, -адёшься**; *impf* **прокра́дываться**) *сов возв*: **прокра́сться в** *+acc*/**ми́мо** *+gen*/**че́рез** *+acc итп* to creep (*Brit*) *или* sneak (*US*) in(to)/past/through *итп*

прокрич|а́ть (**-у́, -и́шь**) *сов перех* (*выкрикнуть*) to shout out

прокр|ути́ть (**-учу́, -у́тишь**; *impf* **прокру́чивать**) *сов перех* (*провернуть*) to turn; (*мясо*) to mince; (*разг: деньги*) to invest illegally

пролага́|ть (**-ю**) *несов от* **проложи́ть**

прола́мыва|ть (**-ю**) *несов от* **проломи́ть**

прола́|ять (**-ю**) *сов от* **ла́ять**

пролеж|а́ть (**-у́, -и́шь**) *сов* to lie

проле́з|ть (**-у, -ешь**; *impf* **пролеза́ть**) *сов* to get through

проле|те́ть (**-чу́, -ти́шь**; *impf* **пролета́ть**) *сов* to fly; (*человек, поезд*) to fly past; (*лето, отпуск*) to fly by

проли́в (**-а**) *м* strait(s) (*мн*)

пролива́|ть(ся) (**-ю(сь)**) *несов от* **проли́ть(ся)**

прол|и́ть (**-ью, -ьёшь**; *pt* **-и́л, -ила́**, *impf* **пролива́ть**) *сов перех* to spill; **проли́ться** (*impf* **пролива́ться**) *сов возв* to spill

прол|ожи́ть (**-ожу́, -о́жишь**;

impf **прокла́дывать**) *сов перех* to lay

прол|оми́ть (**-омлю́, -о́мишь**; *impf* **прола́мывать**) *сов перех* (*лёд*) to break; (*череп*) to fracture

про́мах (**-а**) *м* miss; (*перен*) blunder

промахн|у́ться (**-у́сь, -ёшься**; *impf* **прома́хиватся**) *сов возв* to miss

прома́чива|ть (**-ю**) *несов от* **промочи́ть**

промедле́ни|е (**-я**) *ср* delay

промéдл|ить (**-ю, -ишь**) *сов*: **промéдлить с** *+instr* to delay

промежу́т|ок (**-ка**) *м* gap

промелькн|у́ть (**-у́, -ёшь**) *сов* to flash past; **промелькну́ть** (*perf*) **в** *+prp* (*в голове*) to flash through; (*перед глазами*) to flash past

промока́|ть (**-ю**) *несов от* **промо́кнуть**; **промокну́ть** ▷ *неперех* to let water through

промока́ш|ка (**-ки**; *gen pl* **-ек**) *ж* (*разг*) blotting paper

промо́кн|уть (**-у**; *impf* **промока́ть**) *сов* to get soaked

промокн|у́ть (**-у́, -ёшь**; *impf* **промока́ть**) *сов перех* to blot

промолч|а́ть (**-у́, -и́шь**) *сов* to say nothing

пром|очи́ть (**-очу́, -о́чишь**; *impf* **прома́чивать**) *сов перех* to get wet

промтова́рный *прил*: **промтова́рный магази́н** small department store

промтова́р|ы (**-ов**) *мн* = **промы́шленные това́ры**

промч|а́ться (**-у́сь, -и́шься**) *сов возв* (*год, лето, жизнь*) to fly by; **промча́ться** (*perf*) **ми́мо** *+gen/* **че́рез** *+acc* (*поезд, человек*) to fly past/through

пром|ы́ть (**-о́ю, -о́ешь**; *impf* **промыва́ть**) *сов перех* (*желудок*) to pump; (*рану, глаз*) to bathe

промы́шленност|ь (**-и**) *ж* industry

промы́шленн|ый *прил* industrial; **промы́шленные това́ры** manufactured goods

прон|ести́ (**-есу́, -есёшь**; *pt* **-ёс, -есла́**, *impf* **проноси́ть**) *сов перех* to carry; (*секретно*) to sneak in; **пронести́сь** (*impf* **проноси́ться**) *сов возв* (*машина, пуля, бегун*) to shoot by; (*время*) to fly by; (*буря*) to whirl past

прони́к|нуть (**-ну**; *pt* **-, -ла**, *impf* **проника́ть**) *сов перех*: **прони́кнуть в** *+acc* to penetrate; (*залезть*) to break into; **прони́кнуться** (*impf* **проника́ться**) *сов возв*: **прони́кнуться** *+instr* to be filled with

прон|оси́ть(ся) (**-ошу́(сь), -о́сишь(ся)**) *несов от* **пронести́(сь)**

пропага́нд|а (**-ы**) *ж* propaganda; (*спорта*) promotion; **пропаганди́р|овать** (**-ую**) *несов перех* (*политику*) to spread propaganda about; (*знания, спорт*) to promote

пропада́|ть (**-ю**) *несов от* **пропа́сть**

пропа́ж|а (**-и**) *ж* (*денег, документов*) loss

проп|а́сть (**-аду́, -адёшь**; *impf* **пропада́ть**) *сов* to disappear; (*деньги, письмо*) to go missing; (*аппетит, голос, слух*) to go; (*усилия, билет в театр*) to be wasted; **пропада́ть** (*perf* **пропа́сть**) **бе́з вести** (*человек*) to go missing

пропе́ллер (**-а**) *м* (*Авиа*) propeller

проп|е́ть (**-ою́, -оёшь**) *сов от* **петь**

проп|иса́ть (**-ишу́, -и́шешь**; *impf* **пропи́сывать**) *сов перех* (*человека*) to register; (*лекарство*) to prescribe; **прописа́ться** *сов возв* to register

пропи́с|ка (**-ки**) *ж* registration

Пропи́ска

By law every Russian citizen is required to register at his or her place of residence. A stamp confirming the registration is displayed in the passport. This registration stamp is as essential as having the passport itself. See also note at **па́спорт**.

прописн|о́й *прил*: **прописна́я бу́ква** capital letter

пропи́сыва|ть (**-ю**) *несов от* **прописа́ть**

пропита́ни|е (**-я**) *ср* food

пропл|ы́ть (**-ыву́, -ывёшь**; *impf* **проплыва́ть**) *сов* (*человек*) to swim; (: *миновать*) to swim past; (*судно*) to sail; (: *миновать*) to sail past

пропове́дник (**-а**) *м* (*Рел*) preacher; (*перен*: *теории*) advocate

пропове́д|овать (**-ую**) *несов перех* (*Рел*) to preach; (*теорию*) to advocate

прополз|ти́ (**-у́, -ёшь**; *pt* **-, -ла́**) *сов*: **проползти́ по** *+dat*/**в** *+acc итп* (*насекомое, человек*) to crawl along/in(to) *итп*; (*змея*) to slither along/in(to) *итп*

прополоска́|ть (**-ю**) *сов от* **полоска́ть**

проп|оло́ть (**-олю́, -о́лешь**) *сов от* **поло́ть**

пропо́рци|я (**-и**) *ж* proportion

про́пуск (**-а**) *м* (*действие*: *в зал, через границу итп*) admission; (*в тексте, в изложении*) gap; (*неявка*: *на работу, в школу*) absence ▷ (*nom pl* **-а́**) (*документ*) pass

пропуска́|ть (**-ю**) *несов от* **пропусти́ть** ▷ *перех* (*свет итп*) to let through; (*воду, холод*) to let in

проп|усти́ть (**-ущу́, -у́стишь**; *impf* **пропуска́ть**) *сов перех* to miss; (*разрешить*) to allow; **пропуска́ть** (*perf* **пропусти́ть**) **кого́-н вперёд** to let sb by

прорабо́та|ть (**-ю**; *impf* **прораба́тывать**) *сов* to work

прорв|а́ть (**-у́, -ёшь**; *pt* **-а́л, -ала́**, *impf* **прорыва́ть**) *сов перех* (*плотину*) to burst; (*оборону, фронт*) to break through; **прорва́ться** (*impf* **прорыва́ться**) *сов возв* (*плотина, шарик*) to burst; **прорыва́ться** (*perf* **прорва́ться**) **в** *+acc* to burst in(to)

проре́|зать (**-жу, -жешь**; *impf* **проре́зывать**) *сов перех* to cut through; **проре́заться** *сов от* **ре́заться**

прор́ектор (**-а**) *м* vice-principal

проро́ч|ить (**-у, -ишь**; *perf* **напроро́чить**) *несов перех* to predict

прор|уби́ть (**-ублю́, -у́бишь**; *impf* **проруба́ть**) *сов перех* to make a hole in

про́руб|ь (**-и**) *ж* ice-hole

прорыва́|ть(ся) (**-ю(сь)**) *несов от* **прорва́ть(ся)**

прор|ы́ть (**-о́ю, -о́ешь**; *impf* **прорыва́ть**) *сов перех* to dig

проса́чива|ться (*3sg* **-ется**) *несов от* **просочи́ться**

просверл|и́ть (**-ю́, -и́шь**; *impf* **просве́рливать** *или* **сверли́ть**) *сов перех* to bore, drill

просве́т (**-а**) *м* (*в тучах*) break; (*перен*: *в кризисе*) light at the end of the tunnel

просве́чива|ть (**-ю**) *несов от* **просвети́ть** ▷ *неперех* (*солнце, луна*) to shine through; (*ткань*) to let light through

просвеща́|ть (**-ю**) *несов от* **просвети́ть**

просвеще́ни|е (**-я**) *ср* education

просви|сте́ть (**-щу́, -сти́шь**) *сов от* **свисте́ть** ▷ *неперех* (*пуля*) to whistle past

просе́|ять (**-ю**; *impf* **просе́ивать**) *сов перех* (*муку, песок*) to sift

проси|де́ть (**-жу́, -ди́шь**; *impf* **проси́живать**) *сов* (*сидеть*) to sit; (*пробыть*) to stay

про|си́ть (**-шу́, -сишь**; *perf* **попроси́ть**) *несов перех* to ask; **прошу́ Вас!** if you please!; **проси́ть** (*perf* **попроси́ть**) **кого́-н о чём-н**/*+infin* to ask sb for sth/to do; **проси́ть** (*perf* **попроси́ть**) **кого́-н за кого́-н** to ask sb a favour (*Brit*) *или* favor (*US*) on behalf of sb; **проси́ться** (*perf* **попроси́ться**) *несов возв* (*просьбе*) to ask permission

проск|ака́ть (**-ачу́, -а́чешь**) *сов*: **проскака́ть че́рез/сквозь** *+acc* (*лошадь*) to gallop across/through

проскользн|у́ть (**-у́, -ёшь**; *impf* **проска́льзывать**) *сов* (*монета*) to slide in; (*человек*) to slip in; (*перен*: *сомнение*) to creep in

просла́вленный *прил* renowned

просле|ди́ть (**-жу́, -ди́шь**; *impf* **просле́живать**) *сов перех* (*глазами*) to follow; (*исследовать*) to trace ▷ *неперех*: **проследи́ть за** *+instr* to follow; (*контролировать*) to monitor

просмо́тр (**-а**) *м* (*фильма*) viewing; (*документов*) inspection

просм|отре́ть (**-отрю́, -о́тришь**; *impf* **просма́тривать**) *сов перех* (*ознакомиться*: *читая*) to look through; (: *смотря*) to view; (*пропустить*) to overlook

просн|у́ться (**-у́сь, -ёшься**; *impf* **просыпа́ться**) *сов возв* to wake up; (*перен*: *любовь, страх итп*) to be awakened

просоч|и́ться (*3sg* **-и́тся**, *impf* **проса́чиваться**) *сов возв* (*также перен*) to filter through

просп|а́ть (**-лю́, -и́шь**; *pt* **-а́л, -ала́**) *сов* (*спать*) to sleep ▷ (*impf* **просыпа́ть**) (*встать поздно*) to oversleep, sleep in

проспе́кт (**-а**) *м* (*в городе*) avenue; (*издание*) brochure

просро́ч|ить (**-у, -ишь**; *impf* **просро́чивать**) *сов перех* (*платёж*) to be late with; (*паспорт, билет*) to let expire

проста́ива|ть (**-ю**) *несов от* **простоя́ть**

простира́|ться (**-юсь**; *perf* **простере́ться**) *несов возв* to extend

проститу́т|ка (**-ки**; *gen pl* **-ок**) *ж* prostitute

прости́|ть (**прощу́, прости́шь**; *impf* **проща́ть**) *сов перех* to forgive; **проща́ть** (*perf* **прости́ть**) **что-н кому́-н** to excuse *или* forgive sb (for) sth; **прости́те, как пройти́ на ста́нцию?** excuse me, how do I get to the station?; **прости́ться** (*impf* **проща́ться**) *сов возв*: **прости́ться с** *+instr* to say goodbye to

про́сто *нареч* (*делать*) easily; (*объяснять*) simply ▷ *част* just; **всё э́то про́сто недоразуме́ние** all this is just a misunderstanding;

просто (так) for no particular reason

прост|ой *прил* simple; (*одежда*) plain; (*задача*) easy, simple; (*человек, манеры*) unaffected; (*обыкновенный*) ordinary ▷ (**-оя**) *м* downtime; (*рабочих*) stoppage; **простой карандаш** lead pencil

прост|онать (**-ону, -онешь**) *сов* *(не)перех* to groan

просторный *прил* spacious

простот|а (**-ы**) *ж* (*см прил*) simplicity

просто|ять (**-ю, -ишь**; *impf* **простаивать**) *сов* to stand; (*бездействуя*) to stand idle

простр|елить (**-елю, -елишь**; *impf* **простреливать**) *сов перех* to shoot through

простуд|а (**-ы**) *ж* (*Мед*) cold

прост|удить (**-ужу, -удишь**; *impf* **простужать**) *сов перех*: **простудить кого-н** to give sb a cold; **простудиться** (*impf* **простужаться**) *сов возв* to catch a cold

простуженный *прил*: **ребёнок простужен** the child has got a cold

прост|упить (*3sg* **-упит**, *impf* **проступать**) *сов* (*пот, пятна*) to come through; (*очертания*) to appear

проступ|ок (**-ка**) *м* misconduct

простын|я (**-и**; *nom pl* **простыни**, *gen pl* **простынь**, *dat pl* **-ям**) *ж* sheet

просун|уть (**-у, -ешь**; *impf* **просовывать**) *сов перех*: **просунуть в** *+acc* to push in

просчёт (**-а**) *м* (*счёт*) counting; (*ошибка*: *в подсчёте*) error; (: *в действиях*) miscalculation

просчита|ть (**-ю**; *impf* **просчитывать**) *сов перех* (*считать*) to count; (*ошибиться*) to miscount; **просчитаться** (*impf* **просчитываться**) *сов возв* (*при счёте*) to miscount; (*в планах*) to miscalculate

просып|ать (**-лю, -лешь**; *impf* **просыпать**) *сов перех* to spill; **просыпаться** (*impf* **просыпаться**) *сов возв* to spill

просыпа|ть (**-ю**) *несов от* **проспать**; **просыпать**; **просыпаться** *несов от* **проснуться**; **просыпаться**

просьб|а (**-ы**) *ж* request

проталкива|ть (**-ю**) *несов от* **протолкнуть**

прот|ащить (**-ащу, -ащишь**; *impf* **протаскивать**) *сов перех* to drag

протека|ть (*3sg* **-ет**) *несов от* **протечь** ▷ *неперех* (*вода*) to flow; (*болезнь, явление*) to progress

прот|ереть (**-ру, -рёшь**; *pt* **-ёр, -ёрла**, *impf* **протирать**) *сов перех* (*износить*) to wear a hole in; (*очистить*) to wipe; **протереться** (*impf* **протираться**) *сов возв* (*износиться*) to wear through

протест (**-а**) *м* protest; (*Юр*) objection

протестант (**-а**) *м* Protestant; **протестантский** *прил* Protestant

протест|овать (**-ую**) *несов*: **протестовать (против** *+gen***)** to protest (against)

протеч|ка (**-ки**; *gen pl* **-ек**) *ж* leak

против *предл +gen* against; (*прямо перед*) opposite ▷ *как сказ*: **я против этого** I am against this

против|ень (**-ня**) *м* baking tray

против|иться (**-люсь, -ишься**;

perf **воспроти́виться**) *несов возв +dat* to oppose
проти́вник (**-а**) *м* opponent ▷ *собир* (*Воен*) the enemy
проти́вно *нареч* offensively ▷ *как сказ безл* it's disgusting
проти́вный *прил* (*мнение*) opposite; (*неприятный*) disgusting
противоде́йств|овать (**-ую**) *несов +dat* to oppose
противозако́нный *прил* unlawful
противозача́точн|ый *прил* contraceptive; **противозача́точное сре́дство** contraceptive
противопоста́в|ить (**-лю, -ишь**; *impf* **противопоставля́ть**) *сов перех*: **противопоста́вить кого́-н/что-н** *+dat* to contrast sb/sth with
противоре́чи|е (**-я**) *ср* contradiction; (*классовое*) conflict
противоре́ч|ить (**-у, -ишь**) *несов* (*+dat*: *человеку*) to contradict; (*логике, закону итп*) to defy
противосто|я́ть (**-ю́, -и́шь**) *несов* (*+dat*: *ветру*) to withstand; (*уговорам*) to resist
противоя́ди|е (**-я**) *ср* antidote
протира́|ть(ся) (**-ю(сь)**) *несов от* **протере́ть(ся)**
протокн|у́ть (**-у́, -ёшь**; *impf* **протыка́ть**) *сов перех* to pierce
прото́к (**-а**) *м* (*рукав реки*) tributary; (*соединяющая река*) channel
протоко́л (**-а**) *м* (*собрания*) minutes *мн*; (*допроса*) transcript; (*соглашение*) protocol
протолкн|у́ть (**-у́, -ёшь**; *impf* **прота́лкивать**) *сов перех* to push through
прото́чный *прил* (*вода*) running
проту́хн|уть (*3sg* **-ет**, *impf* **протуха́ть** *или* **ту́хнуть**) *сов* to go bad *или* off
протыка́|ть (**-ю**) *несов от* **проткну́ть**
протя́гива|ть(ся) (**-ю(сь)**) *несов от* **протяну́ть(ся)**
протяже́ни|е (**-я**) *ср*: **на протяже́нии двух неде́ль/ме́сяцев** over a period of two weeks/months; **протяжённост|ь** (**-и**) *ж* length
протян|у́ть (**-у́, -ешь**) *сов от* **тяну́ть** ▷ (*impf* **протя́гивать**) *перех* (*верёвку*) to stretch; (*провод*) to extend; (*руки, ноги*) to stretch (out); (*предмет*) to hold out; **протяну́ться** (*impf* **протя́гиваться**) *сов возв* (*дорога*) to stretch; (*провод*) to extend; (*рука*) to stretch out
про|учи́ть (**-учу́, -у́чишь**; *impf* **проу́чивать**) *сов перех* (*разг*: *наказать*) to teach a lesson; **проучи́ться** *сов возв* to study
профессиона́л (**-а**) *м* professional; **профессиона́льный** *прил* professional; (*болезнь, привычка, обучение*) occupational; (*обучение*) vocational; **профессиона́льный сою́з** trade (*Brit*) *или* labor (*US*) union
профе́сси|я (**-и**) *ж* profession
профе́ссор (**-а**; *ном pl* **-а́**) *м* professor
профила́ктик|а (**-и**) *ж* prevention
про́фил|ь (**-я**) *м* profile
профсою́з (**-а**) *м сокр* = **профессиона́льный сою́з**
профсою́зный *прил* trade union
прoха́жива|ться (**-юсь**) *несов от* **пройти́сь**
прохла́д|а (**-ы**) *ж* cool

прохлади́тельный *прил*: **прохлади́тельный напи́ток** cool soft drink
прохла́дно *нареч* (*встретить*) coolly ▷ *как сказ* it's cool
прохла́дный *прил* cool
прохо́д (**-а**) *м* passage
прох|оди́ть (**-ожу́, -о́дишь**) *несов от* **пройти́**
проходн|а́я (**-о́й**) *ж* checkpoint (*at entrance to factory etc*)
проходно́й *прил*: **проходно́й балл** pass mark

Проходно́й балл

This is the score which the student has to achieve to be admitted into a higher education institution. It consists of a mark out of 100, obtained in the **ЕГЭ**. Each university and department sets its own pass mark.

прохо́ж|ий (**-его**) *м* passer-by
процвета́|ть (**-ю**) *несов* (*фирма, бизнесмен*) to prosper; (*театр, наука*) to flourish; (*хорошо жить*) to thrive
проц|еди́ть (**-ежу́, -е́дишь**) *сов от* **цеди́ть** ▷ (*impf* **проце́живать**) *перех* (*бульон, сок*) to strain
процеду́р|а (**-ы**) *ж* procedure; (*Мед*: *обычно мн*) course of treatment
проце́жива|ть (**-ю**) *несов от* **процеди́ть**
проце́нт (**-а**) *м* percentage; **в разме́ре 5 проце́нтов годовы́х** at a yearly rate of 5 percent; *см также* **проце́нты**; **проце́нтный** *прил* percentage; **проце́нтная ста́вка** interest rate
проце́нт|ы (**-ов**) *мн* (*Комм*) interest *ед*; (*плата*) commission *ед*
проце́сс (**-а**) *м* process; (*Юр*: *порядок*) proceedings *мн*; (: *также* **суде́бный проце́сс**) trial; **воспали́тельный проце́сс** inflammation; **в проце́ссе** *+gen* in the course of
проце́ссор (**-а**) *м* (*Комп*) processor
прочёл *сов см* **проче́сть**
проч|е́сть (**-ту́, -тёшь**; *pt* **-ёл, -ла́**) *сов от* **чита́ть**
про́ч|ий *прил* other; **поми́мо всего́ про́чего** apart from anything else
прочита́|ть (**-ю**) *сов от* **чита́ть**
прочла́ *etc сов см* **проче́сть**
про́чно *нареч* (*закрепить*) firmly
про́чный *прил* (*материал итп*) durable; (*постройка*) solid; (*знания*) sound; (*отношение, семья*) stable; (*мир, счастье*) lasting
прочту́ *etc сов см* **проче́сть**
прочь *нареч* (*в сторону*) away; **ру́ки прочь!** hands off!
проше́дш|ий *прил* (*прошлый*) past; **проше́дшее вре́мя** past tense
прошёл(ся) *сов см* **пройти́(сь)**
проше́ни|е (**-я**) *ср* plea; (*ходатайство*) petition
прош|епта́ть (**-епчу́, -е́пчешь**) *сов перех* to whisper
прошла́ *итп сов см* **пройти́**
прошлого́дний *прил* last year's
про́шл|ое (**-ого**) *ср* the past
про́шл|ый *прил* last; (*прежний*) past; **в про́шлый раз** last time; **на про́шлой неде́ле** last week; **в про́шлом ме́сяце/году́** last month/year
прошу́(сь) *несов см* **проси́ть(ся)**
проща́йте *част* goodbye
проща́льный *прил* parting;

(*вечер*) farewell
прощани|е (**-я**) *ср* (*действие*) parting; **на прощание** on parting
проща|ть(ся) (**-ю(сь)**) *несов от* **простить(ся)**
проще *сравн нареч от* **просто** ▷ *сравн прил от* **простой**
прощени|е (**-я**) *ср* (*ребёнка, друга итп*) forgiveness; (*преступника*) pardon; **просить** (*perf* **попросить**) **прощения** to say sorry; **прошу прощения!** (I'm) sorry!
проявител|ь (**-я**) *м* (*Фото*) developer
про|явить (**-явлю, -явишь**; *impf* **проявлять**) *сов перех* to display; (*Фото*) to develop; **проявиться** (*impf* **проявляться**) *сов возв* (*талант, потенциал итп*) to reveal itself; (*Фото*) to be developed
проявлени|е (**-я**) *ср* display
проявля|ть(ся) (**-ю(сь)**) *несов от* **проявить(ся)**
проясн|ить (**-ю, -ишь**; *impf* **прояснять**) *сов перех* (*обстановку*) to clarify; **проясниться** (*impf* **проясняться**) *сов возв* (*погода, небо*) to brighten *или* clear up; (*обстановка*) to be clarified; (*мысли*) to become lucid
пруд (**-а**; *loc sg* **-у**) *м* pond
пружин|а (**-ы**) *ж* (*Tex*) spring
прут (**-а**; *nom pl* **-ья**) *м* twig
прыгал|ка (**-ки**; *gen pl* **-ок**) *ж* skipping-rope (*Brit*), skip rope (*US*)
прыга|ть (**-ю**) *несов* to jump; (*мяч*) to bounce
прыгн|уть (**-у**) *сов* to jump; (*мяч*) to bounce
прыгун (**-а**) *м* (*Спорт*) jumper
прыж|ок (**-ка**) *м* jump; (*в воду*) dive; **прыжки в высоту/длину** high/long jump
прыщ (**-а**) *м* spot
пряд|ь (**-и**) *ж* lock (*of hair*)
пряж|ка (**-ки**; *gen pl* **-ек**) *ж* (*на ремне*) buckle; (*на юбке*) clasp
прям|ая (**-ой**) *ж* straight line
прямо *нареч* (*о направлении*) straight ahead; (*ровно*) upright; (*непосредственно*) straight; (*откровенно*) directly ▷ *част* (*действительно*) really
прям|ой *прил* straight; (*путь, слова, человек*) direct; (*ответ, политика*) open; (*вызов, обман*) obvious; (*улики*) hard; (*сообщение, обязанность итп*) direct; (*выгода, смысл*) real; (*значение слова*) literal; **прямая трансляция** live broadcast; **прямое дополнение** direct object
прямоугольник (**-а**) *м* rectangle
пряник (**-а**) *м* ≈ gingerbread
пряност|ь (**-и**) *ж* spice; **пряный** *прил* spicy
пря|тать (**-чу, -чешь**; *perf* **спрятать**) *несов перех* to hide; **прятаться** (*perf* **спрятаться**) *несов возв* to hide; (*человек: от холода*) to shelter
прят|ки (**-ок**) *мн* hide-and-seek *ед* (*Brit*), hide-and-go-seek *ед* (*US*)
псевдоним (**-а**) *м* pseudonym
псих (**-а**) *м* (*разг*) nut
психиатр (**-а**) *м* psychiatrist
психиатрический *прил* psychiatric
психический *прил* (*заболевание*) mental
психолог (**-а**) *м* psychologist; **психологический** *прил* psychological; **психологи|я** (**-и**) *ж* psychology
птен|ец (**-ца**) *м* chick
птиц|а (**-ы**) *ж* bird ▷ *собир*: (**домашняя**) **птица** poultry

п

пти́чий *прил* (*корм, клетка*) bird
пу́блик|а (**-и**) *ж собир* audience; (*общество*) public
публика́ци|я (**-и**) *ж* publication
публик|ова́ть (**-у́ю**; *perf* **опубликова́ть**) *несов перех* to publish
публици́ст (**-а**) *м* *social commentator*; **публици́стик|а** (**-и**) *ж собир* sociopolitical journalism
публи́чный *прил* public; **публи́чный дом** brothel
пу́гал|о (**-а**) *ср* scarecrow; (*перен*: *о человеке*) fright
пуга́|ть (**-ю**; *perf* **испуга́ть** *или* **напуга́ть**) *несов перех* to frighten, scare; **пуга́ться** (*perf* **испуга́ться** *или* **напуга́ться**) *несов возв* to be frightened *или* scared
пу́говиц|а (**-ы**) *ж* button
пу́дел|ь (**-я**) *м* poodle
пу́динг (**-а**) *м* ≈ pudding
пу́др|а (**-ы**) *ж* powder; **са́харная пу́дра** icing sugar
пу́дрениц|а (**-ы**) *ж* powder compact
пу́др|ить (**-ю, -ишь**; *perf* **напу́дрить**) *несов перех* to powder; **пу́дриться** (*perf* **напу́дриться**) *несов возв* to powder one's face
пузы́р|ь (**-я́**) *м* (*мыльный*) bubble; (*на коже*) blister
пулемёт (**-а**) *м* machine gun
пуло́вер (**-а**) *м* pullover
пульс (**-а**) *м* (*Мед*: *перен*) pulse
пульт (**-а**) *м* panel
пу́л|я (**-и**) *ж* bullet
пункт (**-а**) *м* point; (*документа*) clause; (*медицинский*) centre (*Brit*), center (*US*); (*наблюдательный, командный*) post; **населённый пункт** small settlement
пункти́р (**-а**) *м* dotted line
пунктуа́льный *прил* (*человек*) punctual
пунктуа́ци|я (**-и**) *ж* punctuation
пуп|о́к (**-ка́**) *м* (*Анат*) navel
пург|а́ (**-и́**) *ж* snowstorm
пуск (**-а**) *м* (*завода итп*) launch
пуска́|ть(ся) (**-ю(сь)**) *несов от* **пусти́ть(ся)**
пусте́|ть (*3sg* **-ет**, *perf* **опусте́ть**) *несов* to become empty; (*улицы*) to become deserted
пу|сти́ть (**-щу́, -стишь**; *impf* **пуска́ть**) *сов перех* (*руку, человека*) to let go of; (*лошадь, санки итп*) to send off; (*станок*) to start; (*в вагон, в зал*) to let in; (*пар, дым*) to give off; (*камень, снаряд*) to throw; (*корни*) to put out; **пуска́ть** (*perf* **пусти́ть**) **что-н на** *+acc*/**под** *+acc* (*использовать*) to use sth as/for; **пуска́ть** (*perf* **пусти́ть**) **кого́-н куда́-нибудь** to let sb go somewhere; **пусти́ться** (*impf* **пуска́ться**) *сов возв*: **пусти́ться в** *+acc* (*в объяснения*) to go into; **пуска́ться** (*perf* **пусти́ться**) **в путь** to set off
пу́сто *нареч* empty ▷ *как сказ* (*ничего нет*) it's empty; (*никого нет*) there's no-one there
пусто́й *прил* empty
пуст|ота́ (**-оты́**; *nom pl* **-о́ты**) *ж* emptiness; (*полое место*) cavity
пусты́н|я (**-и**; *gen pl* **-ь**) *ж* desert
пусты́ш|ка (**-ки**; *gen pl* **-ек**) *ж* (*разг*: *соска*) dummy (*Brit*), pacifier (*US*)

 **КЛЮЧЕВОЕ СЛОВО**

пусть *част +3sg/pl* **1** (*выражает приказ, угрозу*): **пусть он придёт у́тром** let him come in the

morning; **пусть она́ то́лько попро́бует отказа́ться** let her just try to refuse
2 (*выражает согласие*): **пусть бу́дет так** so be it; **пусть бу́дет по-тво́ему** have it your way
3 (*всё равно*) O.K., all right

пустя́к (**-а́**) *м* trifle; (*неценный предмет*) trinket ▷ *как сказ*: **э́то пустя́к** it's nothing
пу́таниц|а (**-ы**) *ж* muddle
пу́та|ть (**-ю**; *perf* **запу́тать** *или* **спу́тать**) *несов перех* (*нитки, волосы*) to tangle; (*сбить с толку*) to confuse ▷ (*perf* **спу́тать** *или* **перепу́тать**) (*бумаги, факты итп*) to mix up ▷ (*perf* **впу́тать**) (*разг*): **пу́тать кого́-н в** *+acc* to get sb mixed up in; **я его́ с кем-то пу́таю** I'm confusing him with somebody else; **он всегда́ пу́тал на́ши имена́** he always got our names mixed up; **пу́таться** (*perf* **запу́таться** *или* **спу́таться**) *несов возв* to get tangled; (*в рассказе, в объяснении*) to get mixed up
путёв|ка (**-ки**; *gen pl* **-ок**) *ж* holiday voucher; (*водителя*) manifest (*of cargo drivers*)
путеводи́тел|ь (**-я**) *м* guidebook
путём *предл +gen* by means of
путеше́ственник (**-а**) *м* traveller (*Brit*), traveler (*US*)
путеше́стви|е (**-я**) *ср* journey, trip; (*морское*) voyage
путеше́ств|овать (**-ую**) *несов* to travel
пу́тник (**-а**) *м* traveller (*Brit*), traveler (*US*)
пут|ь (**-и́**; см *Table 3*) *м* (*также перен*) way; (*платформа*) platform; (*рельсы*) track; (*путешествие*) journey; **во́дные пути́** waterways; **возду́шные пути́** air lanes; **нам с Ва́ми не по пути́** we're not going the same way; **счастли́вого пути́**! have a good trip!; **пути́ сообще́ния** transport network
пух (**-а**; *loc sg* **-у́**) *м* (*у животных*) fluff; (*у птиц, у человека*) down; **ни пу́ха ни пера́!** good luck!
пу́х|нуть (**-ну**; *pt* **-, -ла**, *perf* **вспу́хнуть** *или* **опу́хнуть**) *несов* to swell (up)
пуч|о́к (**-ка́**) *м* bunch; (*света*) beam
пуши́стый *прил* (*мех, ковёр итп*) fluffy; (*волосы*) fuzzy; (*кот*) furry
пу́ш|ка (**-ки**; *gen pl* **-ек**) *ж* cannon; (*на танке*) artillery gun
пчел|а́ (**-ы́**; *nom pl* **пчёлы**) *ж* bee
пшени́ц|а (**-ы**) *ж* wheat; **пшени́чный** *прил* wheat
пшённ|ый *прил*: **пшённая ка́ша** millet porridge
пыла́|ть (**-ю**) *несов* (*костёр*) to blaze; (*перен*: *лицо*) to burn
пылесо́с (**-а**) *м* vacuum cleaner, hoover; **пылесо́с|ить** (**-ишь**; *perf* **пропылесо́сить**) *сов перех* to vacuum, hoover
пыли́н|ка (**-ки**; *gen pl* **-ок**) *ж* speck of dust
пыл|и́ть (**-ю́, -и́шь**; *perf* **напыли́ть**) *несов* to raise dust; **пыли́ться** (*perf* **запыли́ться**) *несов возв* to get dusty
пыл|ь (**-и**; *loc sg* **-и́**) *ж* dust; **вытира́ть** (*perf* **вы́тереть**) **пыль** to dust; **пы́льный** *прил* dusty
пыльц|а́ (**-ы́**) *ж* pollen
пыта́|ть (**-ю**) *несов перех* to torture; **пыта́ться** (*perf* **попыта́ться**) *несов возв*: **пыта́ться** *+infin* to try to do
пы́т|ка (**-ки**; *gen pl* **-ок**) *ж* torture
пьедеста́л (**-а**) *м* (*основание*) pedestal; (*для победителей*) rostrum

пье́с|а (**-ы**) *ж* (*Литература*) play; (*Муз*) piece
пью *etc несов см* **пить**
пью́щ|ий (**-его**) *м* heavy drinker
пьяне́|ть (**-ю**; *perf* **опьяне́ть**) *несов* to get drunk
пья́ниц|а (**-ы**) *м/ж* drunk(ard)
пья́нств|о (**-а**) *ср* heavy drinking; **пья́нств|овать** (**-ую**) *несов* to drink heavily
пья́н|ый *прил* (*человек*) drunk; (*крики, песни итп*) drunken ▷ (**-ого**) *м* drunk
пюре́ *ср нескл* (*фруктовое*) purée; **карто́фельное пюре́** mashed potato
пя́т|ая (**-ой**) *ж*: **одна́ пя́тая** one fifth
пятёр|ка (**-ки**; *gen pl* **-ок**) *ж* (*цифра, карта*) five; (*Просвещ*) ≈ A (*school mark*); (*группа из пяти*) group of five
пя́тер|о (**-ы́х**; *как* **че́тверо**; см *Table 30b*) *чис* five
пяти́десяти *чис см* **пятьдеся́т**
пятидесятиле́ти|е (**-я**) *ср* fifty years *мн*; (*годовщина*) fiftieth anniversary
пятидеся́тый *чис* fiftieth
пя́|титься (**-чусь, -тишься**; *perf* **попя́титься**) *несов возв* to move backwards
пятиуго́льник (**-а**) *м* pentagon
пятиэта́жный *прил* five-storey (*Brit*), five-story (*US*)
пя́т|ка (**-ки**; *gen pl* **-ок**) *ж* heel
пятна́дцатый *чис* fifteenth
пятна́дцат|ь (**-и**; *как* **пять**; см *Table 26*) *чис* fifteen
пя́тниц|а (**-ы**) *ж* Friday
пят|но́ (**-на́**; *nom pl* **пя́тна**, *gen pl* **-ен**) *ср* (*также перен*) stain; (*другого цвета*) spot
пя́тый *чис* fifth
пят|ь (**-и́**; см *Table 26*) *чис* five; (*Просвещ*) ≈ A (*school mark*)
пят|ьдеся́т (**-и́десяти**; см *Table 26*) *чис* fifty
пят|ьсо́т (**-исо́т**; см *Table 28*) *чис* five hundred

Р

р. *сокр* (= *река́*) R., r. (= *river*); (= *роди́лся*) b. (= *born*); (= *рубль*) R., r. (= *rouble*)
раб (**-а́**) *м* slave
рабо́т|а (**-ы**) *ж* work; (*источник заработка*) job; **сме́нная рабо́та** shiftwork
рабо́та|ть (**-ю**) *несов* to work; (*магазин*) to be open; **рабо́тать** (*impf*) **на кого́-н/что-н** to work for sb/sth; **кем Вы рабо́таете?** what do you do for a living?
рабо́тник (**-а**) *м* worker; (*учреждения*) employee
работода́тел|ь (**-я**) *м* employer
работоспосо́бный *прил* (*человек*) able to work hard
рабо́ч|ий *прил* worker's; (*человек, одежда*) working ▷ (**-его**) *м* worker; **рабо́чая си́ла** workforce; **рабо́чий день** working day (*Brit*), workday (*US*)
ра́бств|о (**-а**) *ср* slavery;
рабы́н|я (**-и**) *ж* slave
равви́н (**-а**) *м* rabbi
ра́венств|о (**-а**) *ср* equality; **знак ра́венства** (*Мат*) equals sign
равни́н|а (**-ы**) *ж* plain
равно́ *нареч* equally ▷ *союз*: **равно́ (как) и** as well as ▷ *как сказ*: **э́то всё равно́** it doesn't make any difference; **мне всё равно́** I don't mind; **я всё равно́ приду́** I'll come anyway
равноду́шный *прил*: **равноду́шный (к** *+dat*) indifferent (to)
равноме́рный *прил* even
равнопра́ви|е (**-я**) *ср* equality
равноси́льн|ый *прил* *+dat* equal to; **э́то равноси́льно отка́зу** this amounts to a refusal
равноце́нный *прил* of equal value *или* worth
ра́вн|ый *прил* equal; **ра́вным о́бразом** equally
равня́|ть (**-ю**; *perf* **сравня́ть**) *несов перех*: **равня́ть (с** *+instr*) (*делать равным*) to make equal (with); **равня́ться** *несов возв*: **равня́ться по** *+dat* to draw level with; (*считать себя равным*): **равня́ться с** *+instr* to compare o.s. with; (*быть равносильным*): **равня́ться** *+dat* to be equal to
рад *как сказ*: **рад (**+*dat*) glad (of) *+infin* glad *или* pleased to do; **рад познако́миться с Ва́ми** pleased to meet you
ра́ди *предл* *+gen* for the sake of; **ра́ди Бо́га!** (*разг*) for God's sake!
радиа́ци|я (**-и**) *ж* radiation
радика́льный *прил* radical
радикули́т (**-а**) *м* lower back pain
ра́дио *ср нескл* radio
радиоакти́вный *прил* radioactive

радиовеща́ни|е (**-я**) *ср* (radio) broadcasting
радиопереда́ч|а (**-и**) *ж* radio programme (*Brit*) *или* program (*US*)
радиоприёмник (**-а**) *м* radio (set)
радиослу́шател|ь (**-я**) *м* (radio) listener
радиоста́нци|я (**-и**) *ж* radio station
ра́д|овать (**-ую**; *perf* **обра́довать**) *несов перех*: **ра́довать кого́-н** to make sb happy, please sb; **ра́доваться** *несов возв* (*перен*: *душа*) to rejoice; **ра́доваться** (*perf* **обра́доваться**) *+dat* (*успехам*) to take pleasure in; **он всегда́ ра́дуется гостя́м** he is always happy to have visitors
ра́дост|ь (**-и**) *ж* joy; **с ра́достью** gladly
ра́дуг|а (**-и**) *ж* rainbow
ра́дужн|ый *прил* (*перен*: *приятный*) bright; **ра́дужная оболо́чка** (*Анат*) iris
раду́шный *прил* warm
раз (**-а**; *nom pl* **-ы́**, *gen pl* -) *м* time ▷ *нескл* (*один*) one ▷ *нареч* (*разг*: *однажды*) once ▷ *союз* (*разг*: *если*) if; **в тот/про́шлый раз** that/last time; **на э́тот раз** this time; **ещё раз** (once) again; **раз и навсегда́** once and for all; **ни ра́зу** not once; **(оди́н) раз в день** once a day; **раз … то …** (*разг*) if … then …
разба́в|ить (**-лю, -ишь**; *impf* **разбавля́ть**) *сов перех* to dilute
разбежа́ться (*как* **бежа́ть**; см *Table 20*; *impf* **разбега́ться**) *сов возв* to run off, scatter; (*перед прыжком*) to take a run-up; **у меня́ глаза́ разбега́ются** (*разг*) I'm spoilt for choice
разбива́|ть(ся) (**-ю(сь)**) *несов от* **разби́ть(ся)**
разбира́|ть (**-ю**) *несов от* **разобра́ть**; **разбира́ться** *несов от* **разобра́ться** ▷ *возв* (*разг*: *понимать*): **разбира́ться в** *+prp* to be an expert in
раз|би́ть (**-обью́, -обьёшь**; *imper* **-бе́й(те)**, *impf* **разбива́ть**) *сов перех* to break; (*машину*) to smash up; (*армию*) to crush; (*аллею*) to lay; **разби́ться** (*impf* **разбива́ться**) *сов возв* to break, smash; (*в аварии*) to be badly hurt; (*на группы, на участки*) to break up
разбогате́|ть (**-ю**) *сов от* **богате́ть**
разбо́|й (**-я**) *м* robbery; **разбо́йник** (**-а**) *м* robber
разбра́сыва|ть (**-ю**) *несов от* **разброса́ть**; **разбра́сываться** *несов возв*: **разбра́сываться** (*impf*) *+instr* (*деньгами*) to waste; (*друзьями*) to underrate
разброса́|ть (**-ю**; *impf* **разбра́сывать**) *сов перех* to scatter
разб|уди́ть (**-ужу́, -у́дишь**) *сов от* **буди́ть**
разва́л (**-а**) *м* chaos
разва́лин|а (**-ы**) *ж* ruins *мн*
разв|али́ть (**-алю́, -а́лишь**; *impf* **разва́ливать**) *сов перех* to ruin; **развали́ться** (*impf* **разва́ливаться**) *сов возв* to collapse
разв|ари́ться (*3sg* **-а́рится**, *impf* **разва́риваться**) *сов возв* to be overcooked
ра́зве *част* really; **ра́зве он согласи́лся/не знал?** did he really agree/not know?; **ра́зве то́лько** *или* **что** except that
развева́|ться (*3sg* **-ется**) *несов возв* (*флаг*) to flutter
разведённый *прил* (*в разводе*) divorced

разве́д|ка (**-ки**; *gen pl* **-ок**) *ж* (*Гео*) prospecting; (*шпионаж*) intelligence; (*Воен*) reconnaissance; **разве́дчик** (**-а**) *м* (*Гео*) prospector; (*шпион*) intelligence agent; (*Воен*) scout

разв|езти́ (**-езу́, -езёшь**; *pt* **-ёз, -езла́, -езло́**, *impf* **развози́ть**) *сов перех* (*товар*) to take

разверн|у́ть (**-у́, -ёшь**; *impf* **развёртывать** *или* **развора́чивать**) *сов перех* (*бумагу*) to unfold; (*торговлю итп*) to launch; (*корабль, самолёт*) to turn around; (*батальон*) to deploy; **развернуться** (*impf* **развёртываться** *или* **развора́чиваться**) *сов возв* (*кампания, работа*) to get under way; (*автомобиль*) to turn around; (*вид*) to open up

развесел|и́ть (**-ю́, -и́шь**) *сов от* **весели́ть**

разве́|сить (**-шу, -сишь**; *impf* **разве́шивать**) *сов перех* to hang

разв|ести́ (**-еду́, -едёшь**; *pt* **-ёл, -ела́**, *impf* **разводи́ть**) *сов перех* (*доставить*) to take; (*порошок*) to dissolve; (*сок*) to dilute; (*животных*) to breed; (*цветы, сад*) to grow; (*мост*) to raise; **развести́сь** (*impf* **разводи́ться**) *сов возв*: **развести́сь (с** *+instr*) to divorce, get divorced (from)

разветвле́ни|е (**-я**) *ср* (*дороги*) fork

разве́|ять (**-ю**; *impf* **разве́ивать**) *сов перех* (*облака*) to disperse; (*сомнения, грусть*) to dispel; **разве́яться** (*impf* **разве́иваться**) *сов возв* (*облака*) to disperse; (*человек*) to relax

развива́|ть(ся) (**-ю(сь)**) *несов от* **разви́ть(ся)**

развива́ющ|ийся *прил*: **развива́ющаяся страна́** developing country

разви́л|ка (**-ки**; *gen pl* **-ок**) *ж* fork (*in road*)

разви́ти|е (**-я**) *ср* development

раз|ви́ть (**-овью́, -овьёшь**; *imper* **-ве́й(те)**, *impf* **развива́ть**) *сов перех* to develop; **разви́ться** (*impf* **развива́ться**) *сов возв* to develop

развлека́тельный *прил* entertaining

развлече́ни|е (**-я**) *ср* entertaining

развл|е́чь (**-еку́, -ечёшь** *etc*, **-еку́т**; *pt* **-ёк, -екла́**, *impf* **развлека́ть**) *сов перех* to entertain; **развле́чься** (*impf* **развлека́ться**) *сов возв* to have fun

разво́д (**-а**) *м* (*супругов*) divorce

разв|оди́ть(ся) (**-ожу́(сь), -о́дишь(ся)**) *несов от* **развести́(сь)**

развора́чива|ть(ся) (**-ю(сь)**) *несов от* **разверну́ть(ся)**

разворо́т (**-а**) *м* (*машины*) U-turn; (*в книге*) double page

развя́з|ка (**-ки**; *gen pl* **-ок**) *ж* (*конец*) finale; (*Авт*) junction

разгада́|ть (**-ю**; *impf* **разга́дывать**) *сов перех* (*загадку*) to solve; (*замыслы, тайну*) to guess

разга́р (**-а**) *м*: **в разга́ре** *+gen* (*сезона*) at the height of; (*боя*) in the heart of; **кани́кулы в (по́лном) разга́ре** the holidays are in full swing

разгиба́|ть(ся) (**-ю(сь)**) *несов от* **разогну́ть(ся)**

разгла́|дить (**-жу, -дишь**; *impf* **разгла́живать**) *сов перех* to smooth out

разгла|си́ть (**-шу́, -си́шь**; *impf*

Р

разглаша́ть) *сов перех* to divulge, disclose
разгова́рива|ть (**-ю**) *несов*: **разгова́ривать** (**с** *+instr*) to talk (to)
разгово́р (**-а**) *м* conversation; **разгово́рник** (**-а**) *м* phrase book; **разгово́рный** *прил* colloquial
разго́н (**-а**) *м* (*демонстрации*) breaking up; (*автомобиля*) acceleration
разгоня́|ть(ся) (**-ю(сь)**) *несов от* **разогна́ть(ся)**
разгор|е́ться (*3sg* **-и́тся**, *impf* **разгора́ться**) *сов возв* to flare up
разгоряч|и́ться (**-у́сь, -и́шься**) *сов возв* (*от волнения*) to get het up; (*от бега*) to be hot
разгром|и́ть (**-лю́, -и́шь**) *сов перех* (*врага*) to crush; (*книгу*) to slam
разгр|узи́ть (**-ужу́, -у́зишь**; *impf* **разгружа́ть**) *сов перех* to unload
разгры́з|ть (**-у, -ёшь**) *сов от* **грызть**
разда|ва́ть(ся) (**-ю́, -ёшь(ся)**) *несов от* **разда́ть(ся)**
разд|ави́ть (**-авлю́, -а́вишь**) *сов от* **дави́ть**
разда́ть (*как* **дать**; см *Table 16*; *impf* **раздава́ть**) *сов перех* to give out, distribute; **разда́ться** (*impf* **раздава́ться**) *сов возв* (*звук*) to be heard
раздва́ива|ться (**-юсь**) *несов от* **раздвои́ться**
раздви́н|уть (**-у**; *impf* **раздвига́ть**) *сов перех* to move apart
раздво|и́ться (**-ю́сь, -и́шься**; *impf* **раздва́иваться**) *сов возв* (*дорога, река*) to divide into two; (*перен: мнение*) to be divided
раздева́л|ка (**-ки**; *gen pl* **-ок**) *ж* changing room
раздева́|ть(ся) (**-ю(сь)**) *несов от* **разде́ть(ся)**
разде́л (**-а**) *м* (*имущества*) division; (*часть*) section
разде́ла|ть (**-ю**; *impf* **разде́лывать**) *сов перех* (*тушу*) to cut up; **разде́латься** (*impf* **разде́лываться**) *сов возв* (*разг*): **разде́латься с** *+instr* (*с делами*) to finish; (*с долгами*) to settle
разд|ели́ть (**-елю́, -е́лишь**) *сов от* **дели́ть** ▷ (*impf* **разделя́ть**) *перех* (*мнение*) to share; **раздели́ться** *сов от* **дели́ться** ▷ (*impf* **разделя́ться**) *возв* (*мнения, общество*) to become divided
разде́|ть (**-ну, -нешь**; *impf* **раздева́ть**) *сов перех* to undress; **разде́ться** (*impf* **раздева́ться**) *сов возв* to get undressed
раздира́|ть (**-ю**) *несов перех* (*душу, общество*) to tear apart
раздраже́ни|е (**-я**) *ср* irritation; **раздражи́тельный** *прил* irritable; **раздраж|и́ть** (**-у́, -и́шь**; *impf* **раздража́ть**) *сов перех* to irritate, annoy; (*нервы*) to agitate; **раздражи́ться** (*impf* **раздража́ться**) *сов возв* (*кожа, глаза*) to become irritated; (*человек*): **раздражи́ться** (*+instr*) to be irritated (by)
раздува́|ть(ся) (**-ю(сь)**) *несов от* **разду́ть(ся)**
разду́ма|ть (**-ю**; *impf* **разду́мывать**) *сов +infin* to decide not to do
разду́мыва|ть (**-ю**) *несов от* **разду́мать** ▷ *неперех*: **разду́мывать** (**о** *+prp*) (*долго думать*) to contemplate
разд|у́ть (**-у́ю**; *impf* **раздува́ть**) *сов перех* (*огонь*) to fan; **у неё разду́ло щёку** her cheek has

swollen up; **раздуться** (*impf* **раздуваться**) *сов возв* (*щека*) to swell up

раз|жать (**-ожму, -ожмёшь**; *impf* **разжимать**) *сов перех* (*пальцы, губы*) to relax; **разжаться** (*impf* **разжиматься**) *сов возв* to relax

разж|евать (**-ую**; *impf* **разжёвывать**) *сов перех* to chew

разлага|ть(ся) (**-ю**) *несов от* **разложить(ся)**

разламыва|ть (**-ю**) *несов от* **разломать**; **разломить**

разле|теться (**-чусь, -тишься**; *impf* **разлетаться**) *сов возв* to fly off (*in different directions*)

разлив (**-а**) *м* flooding

раз|лить (**-олью, -ольёшь**; *impf* **разливать**) *сов перех* (*пролить*) to spill; **разлиться** (*impf* **разливаться**) *сов возв* (*пролиться*) to spill; (*река*) to overflow

различа|ть (**-ю**) *несов от* **различить**; **различаться** *несов возв*: **различаться по** *+dat* to differ in

различи|е (**-я**) *ср* difference

различ|ить (**-у, -ишь**; *impf* **различать**) *сов перех* (*увидеть, услышать*) to make out; (*отличить*): **различить (по** *+dat*) to distinguish (by)

различный *прил* different

разл|ожить (**-ожу, -ожишь**; *impf* **раскладывать**) *сов перех* (*карты*) to arrange; (*диван*) to open out ▷ (*impf* **разлагать**) (*Хим, Био*) to decompose; **разложиться** *сов возв* (*impf* **разлагаться**) (*Хим, Био*) to decompose; (*общество*) to disintegrate

разл|омить (**-омлю, -омишь**; *impf* **разламывать**) *сов перех* (*на части*) to break up

разлук|а (**-и**) *ж* separation

разлуч|ить (**-у, -ишь**; *impf* **разлучать**) *сов перех*: **разлучить кого-н с** *+instr* to separate sb from; **разлучиться** (*impf* **разлучаться**) *сов возв*: **разлучиться (с** *+instr*) to be separated (from)

разл|юбить (**-юблю, -юбишь**) *сов перех* (*+infin*: *читать, гулять итп*) to lose one's enthusiasm for doing; **он меня разлюбил** he doesn't love me any more

разма|зать (**-жу, -жешь**; *impf* **размазывать**) *сов перех* to smear

разматыва|ть (**-ю**) *несов от* **размотать**

размах (**-а**) *м* (*рук*) span; (*перен*: *деятельности*) scope; (: *проекта*) scale; **размах крыльев** wingspan

размахн|уться (**-усь, -ёшься**; *impf* **размахиваться**) *сов возв* to bring one's arm back; (*перен*: *разг*: *в делах итп*) to go to town

размен (**-а**) *м* (*денег, пленных*) exchange; **размен квартиры** flat swap (*of one large flat for two smaller ones*)

разменн|ый *прил*: **разменный автомат** change machine; **разменная монета** (small) change

разменя|ть (**-ю**; *impf* **разменивать**) *сов перех* (*деньги*) to change; (*квартиру*) to exchange; **разменяться** (*impf* **размениваться**) *сов возв* (*перен*: *разг*: *обменять жилплощадь*) to do a flat swap (*of one large flat for two smaller ones*)

размер (**-а**) *м* size

разме|стить (**-щу, -стишь**; *impf*

размеща́ть) *сов перех* (*в отеле*) to place; (*на столе*) to arrange; **размести́ться** (*impf* **размеща́ться**) *сов возв* (*по комнатам*) to settle o.s.

разме́|тить (**-чу, -тишь**; *impf* **размеча́ть**) *сов перех* to mark out

размеша́|ть (**-ю**; *impf* **разме́шивать**) *сов перех* to stir

размеща́|ть(ся) (**-ю(сь)**) *несов от* **размести́ть(ся)**

размина́|ть(ся) (**-ю(сь)**) *несов от* **размя́ть(ся)**

размини́р|овать (**-ую**) *(не)сов перех*: **размини́ровать по́ле** to clear a field of mines

размин|у́ться (**-у́сь, -ёшься**) *сов возв* (*не встретиться*) to miss each other; (*дать пройти*) to pass

размно́ж|ить (**-у, -ишь**; *impf* **размножа́ть**) *сов перех* to make (multiple) copies of; **размно́житься** (*perf* **размножа́ться**) *сов возв* (*Био*) to reproduce

размо́к|нуть (**-ну**; *pt* **-, -ла**, *impf* **размока́ть**) *сов* (*хлеб, картон*) to go soggy; (*почва*) to become sodden

размо́лв|ка (**-ки**) *ж* quarrel

размота́|ть (**-ю**; *impf* **разма́тывать**) *сов перех* to unwind

разм|ы́ть (*3sg* **-о́ет**, *impf* **размыва́ть**) *сов перех* to wash away

размышля́|ть (**-ю**) *несов*: **размышля́ть (о** *+prp*) to contemplate, reflect (on)

раз|мя́ть (**-омну́, -омнёшь**; *impf* **размина́ть**) *сов перех* to loosen up; **размя́ться** (*impf* **размина́ться**) *сов возв* to warm up

разна́шива|ть(ся) (**-ю**) *несов от* **разноси́ть(ся)**

разн|ести́ (**-есу́, -есёшь**; *pt* **-ёс, -есла́**, *impf* **разноси́ть**) *сов перех* (*письма*) to deliver; (*тарелки*) to put out; (*тучи*) to disperse; (*заразу, слухи*) to spread; (*раскритиковать*) to slam; **разнести́сь** (*impf* **разноси́ться**) *сов возв* (*слух, запах*) to spread; (*звук*) to resound

разнима́|ть (**-ю**) *несов от* **разня́ть**

ра́зниц|а (**-ы**) *ж* difference; **кака́я ра́зница?** what difference does it make?

разнови́дност|ь (**-и**) *ж* (*Био*) variety; (*людей*) type, kind

разногла́си|е (**-я**) *ср* disagreement

разнообра́зи|е (**-я**) *ср* variety

разнообра́зный *прил* various

разн|оси́ть (**-ошу́, -о́сишь**) *несов от* **разнести́** ▷ (*impf* **разна́шивать**) *сов перех* (*обувь*) to break in; **разноси́ться** *несов от* **разнести́сь** ▷ (*impf* **разна́шиваться**) *сов возв* (*обувь*) to be broken in

разносторо́нний *прил* (*деятельность*) wide-ranging; (*ум, личность*) multifaceted

ра́зност|ь (**-и**) *ж* difference

разноцве́тный *прил* multicoloured (*Brit*), multicolored (*US*)

ра́зный *прил* different

разоблач|и́ть (**-у́, -и́шь**; *impf* **разоблача́ть**) *сов перех* to expose

раз|обра́ть (**-беру́, -берёшь**; *impf* **разбира́ть**) *сов перех* (*бумаги*) to sort out; (*текст*) to analyse (*Brit*), analyze (*US*); (*вкус, подпись итп*) to make out;

разбира́ть (*perf* **разобра́ть**) **(на ча́сти)** to take apart; **разобра́ться** (*impf* **разбира́ться**) *сов возв*: **разобра́ться в** +*prp* (*в вопросе, в деле*) to sort out

ра́зовый *прил*: **ра́зовый биле́т** single (*Brit*) *или* one-way ticket

раз|огна́ть (**-гоню́, -го́нишь**; *impf* **разгоня́ть**) *сов перех* (*толпу*) to break up; (*тучи*) to disperse; (*машину*) to increase the speed of; **разогна́ться** (*impf* **разгоня́ться**) *сов возв* to build up speed, accelerate

разогн|у́ть (**-у́, -ёшь**; *impf* **разгиба́ть**) *сов перех* (*проволоку*) to straighten out; **разогну́ться** (*impf* **разгиба́ться**) *сов возв* to straighten up

разогре́|ть (**-ю**; *impf* **разогрева́ть**) *сов перех* (*чайник, суп*) to heat; **разогре́ться** (*impf* **разогрева́ться**) *сов возв* (*суп*) to heat up

разозл|и́ть(ся) (**-ю́(сь), -и́шь(ся)**) *сов от* **зли́ть(ся)**

разойти́сь (*как* **идти́**; см *Table 18*; *impf* **расходи́ться**) *сов возв* (*гости*) to leave; (*толпа*) to disperse; (*тираж*) to sell out; (*не встретиться*) to miss each other; (*супруги*) to split up; (*шов, крепления*) to come apart; (*перен*: *мнения*) to diverge; (*разг*: *дать волю себе*) to get going

ра́зом *нареч* (*разг*: *все вместе*) all at once; (: *в один приём*) all in one go

разорв|а́ть (**-у́, -ёшь**) *сов от* **рвать** ▷ (*impf* **разрыва́ть**) *перех* to tear *или* rip up; (*перен*: *связь*) to sever; (: *договор*) to break; **разорва́ться** *сов от* **рва́ться** ▷ (*impf* **разрыва́ться**) *возв* (*одежда*) to tear, rip; (*верёвка, цепь*) to break; (*связь*) to be severed; (*снаряд*) to explode

разор|и́ть (**-ю́, -и́шь**; *impf* **разоря́ть**) *сов перех* (*деревню, гнездо*) to plunder; (*население*) to impoverish; (: *компанию, страну*) to ruin; **разори́ться** (*impf* **разоря́ться**) *сов возв* (*человек*) to become impoverished; (*компания*) to go bust *или* bankrupt

разоруж|и́ть (**-у́, -и́шь**; *impf* **разоружа́ть**) *сов перех* to disarm; **разоружи́ться** (*impf* **разоружа́ться**) *сов возв* to disarm

разоря́|ть(ся) (**-ю(сь)**) *несов от* **разори́ть(ся)**

разо|сла́ть (**-шлю́, -шлёшь**; *impf* **рассыла́ть**) *сов перех* to send out

разостла́ть (**расстелю́, рассте́лешь**) *несов* = **расстели́ть**

разочарова́ни|е (**-я**) *ср* disappointment; (*потеря веры*): **разочарова́ние в** +*prp* (*в идее*) disenchantment with

разочаро́ванный *прил* disappointed; **разочаро́ванный в** +*prp* (*в идее*) disenchanted with

разочар|ова́ть (**-у́ю**; *impf* **разочаро́вывать**) *сов перех* to disappoint; **разочарова́ться** (*impf* **разочаро́вываться**) *сов возв*: **разочарова́ться в** +*prp* to become disenchanted with

разрабо́та|ть (**-ю**; *impf* **разраба́тывать**) *сов перех* to develop

разрабо́т|ка (**-ки**) *ж* development; **га́зовые разрабо́тки** gas fields *мн*; **нефтяны́е разрабо́тки** oilfields *мн*

Р

разра|зи́ться (**-жу́сь, -зи́шься**; *impf* **разража́ться**) *сов возв* to break out

разр|асти́сь (*3sg* **-астётся**, *pt* **-о́сся, -осла́сь**, *impf* **разраста́ться**) *сов возв* (*лес*) to spread

разре́з (**-а**) *м* (*на юбке*) slit; (*Геом*) section

разре́|зать (**-жу, -жешь**) *сов от* **ре́зать**

разреша́|ть (**-ю**) *несов от* **разреши́ть**; **разреша́ться** *несов от* **разреши́ться** ▷ *неперех* (*допускаться*) to be allowed *или* permitted

разреше́ни|е (**-я**) *ср* (*действие*) authorization; (*родителей*) permission; (*проблемы*) resolution; (*документ*) permit

разреш|и́ть (**-у́, -и́шь**; *impf* **разреша́ть**) *сов перех* (*решить*) to resolve; (*позволить*): **разреши́ть кому́-н** *+infin* to allow *или* permit sb to do; **разреши́те?** may I come in?; **разреши́те пройти́** may I pass; **разреши́ться** (*impf* **разреша́ться**) *сов возв* to be resolved

разровня́|ть (**-ю**) *сов от* **ровня́ть**

разр|уби́ть (**-ублю́, -у́бишь**; *impf* **разруба́ть**) *сов перех* to chop in two

разруши́тельный *прил* (*война*) devastating; (*действие*) destructive

разру́ш|ить (**-у, -ишь**; *impf* **разруша́ть**) *сов перех* to destroy; **разру́шиться** (*impf* **разруша́ться**) *сов возв* to be destroyed

разры́в (**-а**) *м* (*во времени, в цифрах*) gap; (*отношений*) severance; (*снаряда*) explosion

разрыва́|ть(ся) (**-ю(сь)**) *несов от* **разорва́ть(ся)**

разря́д (**-а**) *м* (*тип*) category; (*квалификация*) grade

разря|ди́ть (**-жу́, -ди́шь**; *impf* **разряжа́ть**) *сов перех* (*ружьё*) to discharge; **разряжа́ть** (*perf* **разряди́ть**) **обстано́вку** to diffuse the situation

разря́д|ка (**-ки**; *gen pl* **-ок**) *ж* escape; (*в тексте*) spacing; **разря́дка (междунаро́дной напряжённости)** détente

разряжа́|ть (**-ю**) *несов от* **разряди́ть**

разубе|ди́ть (**-жу́, -ди́шь**; *impf* **разубежда́ть**) *сов перех*: **разубеди́ть кого́-н (в** *+prp*) to dissuade sb (from)

разува́|ть(ся) (**-ю(сь)**) *несов от* **разу́ть(ся)**

ра́зум (**-а**) *м* reason; **разуме́|ться** (*3sg* **-ется**) *сов возв*: **под э́тим разуме́ется, что ...** by this is meant that ...; **(само́ собо́й) разуме́ется** that goes without saying ▷ *вводн сл*: **он, разуме́ется, не знал об э́том** naturally, he knew nothing about it; **разу́мный** *прил* (*существо*) intelligent; (*поступок, решение*) reasonable

разу́тый *прил* (*без обуви*) barefoot

раз|у́ть (**-у́ю**; *impf* **разува́ть**) *сов перех*: **разу́ть кого́-н** to take sb's shoes off; **разу́ться** (*impf* **разува́ться**) *сов возв* to take one's shoes off

раз|учи́ть (**-учу́, -у́чишь**; *impf* **разу́чивать**) *сов перех* to learn; **разучи́ться** (*impf* **разу́чиваться**) *сов возв*: **разучи́ться** *+infin* to forget how to do

разъеда́|ть (*3sg* **-ет**) *несов от* **разъе́сть**

разъезжá|ть (**-ю**) *несов* (*по делам*) to travel; (*кататься*) to ride about; **разъезжáться** *несов от* **разъéхаться**

разъéхаться (*как* **éхать**; см *Table 19*; *impf* **разъезжáться**) *сов возв* (*гости*) to leave

разъярённый *прил* furious

разъясн|и́ть (**-ю́, -и́шь**; *impf* **разъясня́ть**) *сов перех* to clarify

разыгрá|ть (**-ю**; *impf* **разы́грывать**) *сов перех* (*Муз, Спорт*) to play; (*сцену*) to act out; (*в лотерею*) to raffle; (*разг*: *подшутить*) to play a joke *или* trick on

раз|ыскáть (**-ыщу́, -ы́щешь**; *impf* **разы́скивать**) *сов перех* to find

РАИС *ср сокр* (= *Росси́йское аге́нтство интеллектуа́льной со́бственности*) copyright protection agency

ра|й (**-я**; *loc sg* **-ю́**) *м* paradise

райóн (**-а**) *м* (*страны*) region; (*города*) district

райóнный *прил* district

рáйский *прил* heavenly

рак (**-а**) *м* (*Зоол*: *речной*) crayfish (*мн* crayfish); (: *морской*) crab; (*Мед*) cancer; (*созвездие*): **Рак** Cancer

ракéт|а (**-ы**) *ж* rocket; (*Воен*) missile; (*судно*) hydrofoil

ракéт|ка (**-ки**; *gen pl* **-ок**) *ж* (*Спорт*) racket

рáковин|а (**-ы**) *ж* (*Зоол*) shell; (*для умывания*) sink

рáковый *прил* (*Зоол, Кулин*) crab; (*Мед*) cancer

рáм|ка (**-ки**; *gen pl* **-ок**) *ж* frame; *см также* **рáмки**

рáм|ки (**-ок**) *мн* (*+gen*: *рассказа, обязанностей*) framework *ед* of; (*закона*) limits *мн* of; **в рáмках** *+gen* (*закона, приличия*) within the bounds of; (*переговоров*) within the framework of; **за рáмками** *+gen* beyond the bounds of

РАН *м сокр* (= *Росси́йская акаде́мия нау́к*) Russian Academy of Sciences

рáн|а (**-ы**) *ж* wound

рáненый *прил* injured; (*Воен*) wounded

рáн|ить (**-ю, -ишь**) *(не)сов перех* to wound

рáнний *прил* early

рáно *нареч* early ▷ *как сказ* it's early; **рáно и́ли пóздно** sooner or later

рáньше *сравн нареч от* **рáно** ▷ *нареч* (*прежде*) before ▷ *предл +gen* before; **рáньше врéмени** (*радоваться итп*) too soon

рáпорт (**-а**) *м* report

рапорт|овáть (**-у́ю**) *(не)сов*: **рапортовáть (кому́-н о чём-н)** to report back (to sb on sth)

рáс|а (**-ы**) *ж* race; **раси́зм** (**-а**) *м* racism; **раси́ст** (**-а**) *м* racist

раскáива|ться (**-юсь**) *несов от* **раскáяться**

раскал|и́ть (**-ю́, -и́шь**; *impf* **раскаля́ть**) *сов перех* to bring to a high temperature; **раскали́ться** (*impf* **раскаля́ться**) *сов возв* to get very hot

раскáлыва|ть(ся) (**-ю(сь)**) *несов от* **расколóть(ся)**

раскáпыва|ть (**-ю**) *несов от* **раскопáть**

раскá|яться (**-юсь**; *impf* **раскáиваться**) *сов возв*: **раскáяться (в** *+prp*) to repent (of)

раскидá|ть (**-ю**; *impf* **раски́дывать**) *сов перех* to scatter

раски́н|уть (**-у**; *impf*

раски́дывать) *сов перех* (*руки*) to throw open; (*сети*) to spread out; (*лагерь*) to set up; **раски́нуться** (*impf* **раски́дываться**) *сов возв* to stretch out

раскладно́й *прил* folding

раскладу́ш|ка (**-ки**; *gen pl* **-ек**) *ж* (*разг*) camp bed (*Brit*), cot (*US*)

раскла́дыва|ть (**-ю**) *несов от* **разложи́ть**

раско́ванный *прил* relaxed

раск|оло́ть (**-олю́, -о́лешь**; *impf* **раска́лывать**) *сов перех* to split; (*лёд, орех*) to crack; **расколо́ться** (*impf* **раска́лываться**) *сов возв* (*полено, орех*) to split open; (*перен*: *организация*) to be split

раскопа́|ть (**-ю**; *impf* **раска́пывать**) *сов перех* to dig up

раско́п|ки (**-ок**) *мн* (*работы*) excavations; (*место*) (archaeological) dig *ед*

раскра́|сить (**-шу, -сишь**; *impf* **раскра́шивать**) *сов перех* to colour (*Brit*) *или* color (*US*) (in)

раскро|и́ть (**-ю́, -и́шь**) *сов перех* to cut

раскру́т|ка (**-ки**; *gen pl* **-ок**) *ж* (*разг*) hyping up

раскр|ы́ть (**-о́ю, -о́ешь**; *impf* **раскрыва́ть**) *сов перех* to open; (*перен*: *чью-нибудь тайну, план*) to discover; (: *свою тайну, план*) to disclose; **раскры́ться** (*impf* **раскрыва́ться**) *сов возв* to open

раск|упи́ть (**-уплю́, -у́пишь**; *impf* **раскупа́ть**) *сов перех* to buy up

ра́совый *прил* racial

распада́|ться (*3sg* **-ется**) *несов от* **распа́сться** ▷ *возв* (*состоять из частей*): **распада́ться на** *+acc* to be divided into

распахн|у́ть (**-у́, -ёшь**; *impf* **распа́хивать**) *сов перех* to throw open; **распахну́ться** (*impf* **распа́хиваться**) *сов возв* to fly open

распашо́н|ка (**-ки**; *gen pl* **-ок**) *ж* *cotton baby top without buttons*

распеча́та|ть (**-ю**; *impf* **распеча́тывать**) *сов перех* (*письмо, пакет*) to open; (*размножить*) to print off

распеча́т|ка (**-ки**; *gen pl* **-ок**) *ж* (*доклада*) print-out

распина́|ть (**-ю**) *несов от* **распя́ть**

расписа́ни|е (**-я**) *ср* timetable, schedule

расп|иса́ть (**-ишу́, -и́шешь**; *impf* **распи́сывать**) *сов перех* (*дела*) to arrange; (*стены, шкатулку*) to paint; (*разг*: *женить*) to marry (*in registry office*); **расписа́ться** (*impf* **распи́сываться**) *сов возв* (*поставить подпись*) to sign one's name; **распи́сываться** (*perf* **расписа́ться**) **с** *+instr* to get married to (*in registry office*)

распи́с|ка (**-ки**; *gen pl* **-ок**) *ж* (*о получении денег*) receipt; (*о невыезде*) warrant

распла́т|а (**-ы**) *ж* payment; (*перен*: *за преступление*) retribution; **распл|ати́ться** (**-ачу́сь, -а́тишься**; *impf* **распла́чиваться**) *сов возв*: **расплати́ться** (**с** *+instr*) to pay; (*перен*: *с предателем*) to revenge o.s. on

распл|еска́ть (**-ещу́, -е́щешь**; *impf* **расплёскивать**) *сов перех* to spill; **расплеска́ться** (*impf* **расплёскиваться**) *сов возв* to spill

расплы́вчатый *прил* (*рисунок,*

очертания) blurred; (*перен*: *ответ, намёк*) vague

расплы́|ться (**-ву́сь, -вёшься**; *impf* **расплыва́ться**) *сов возв* (*краски*) to run; (*перен*: *фигуры*) to be blurred

распого́д|иться (*3sg* **-ится**) *сов возв* (*о погоде*) to clear up

распозна́|ть (**-ю**; *impf* **распознава́ть**) *сов перех* to identify

располага́|ть (**-ю**) *несов от* **расположи́ть** ▷ *неперех* (*+instr*: *временем*) to have available; **располага́ться** *несов от* **расположи́ться** ▷ *возв* (*находиться*) to be situated *или* located

расположе́ни|е (**-я**) *ср* (*место*: *лагеря*) location; (*комнат*) layout; (*симпатия*) disposition

располо́женный *прил*: **располо́женный к** *+dat* (*к человеку*) well-disposed towards; (*к болезни*) susceptible to

распол|ожи́ть (**-ожу́, -о́жишь**; *impf* **располага́ть**) *сов перех* (*мебель, вещи итп*) to arrange; (*отряд*) to station; **располага́ть** (*perf* **расположи́ть**) **кого́-н к себе́** to win sb over; **расположи́ться** (*impf* **располага́ться**) *сов возв* (*человек*) to settle down; (*отряд*) to position itself

распоряди́тел|ь (**-я**) *м* (*Комм*) manager; **распоряди́тельный** *прил*: **распоряди́тельный дире́ктор** managing director

распоря|ди́ться (**-жу́сь, -ди́шься**; *impf* **распоряжа́ться**) *сов возв* to give out instructions

распоря́д|ок (**-ка**) *м* routine

распоряжа́|ться (**-юсь**) *несов от* **распоряди́ться** ▷ *возв*: **распоряжа́ться** (*+instr*) to be in charge (of)

распоряже́ни|е (**-я**) *ср* (*управление*) management; **ба́нковское распоряже́ние** banker's order; **в распоряже́ние кого́-н/чего́-н** at sb's/sth's disposal

распра́в|ить (**-лю, -ишь**; *impf* **расправля́ть**) *сов перех* to straighten out; (*крылья*) to spread; **распра́виться** (*impf* **расправля́ться**) *сов возв* (*см перех*) to be straightened out; to spread

распределе́ни|е (**-я**) *ср* distribution; (*после института*) work placement

распредел|и́ть (**-ю́, -и́шь**; *impf* **распределя́ть**) *сов перех* to distribute; **распредели́ться** (*impf* **распределя́ться**) *сов возв*: **распредели́ться (по** *+dat*) (*по группам, по бригадам*) to divide up (into)

распрода́ж|а (**-и**) *ж* sale

распрода́ть (*как* **дать**; *см Table 16*; *impf* **распродава́ть**) *сов перех* to sell off; (*билеты*) to sell out of

распростране́ни|е (**-я**) *ср* spreading; (*оружия*) proliferation; (*приказа*) application

распространённый *прил* widespread

распростран|и́ть (**-ю́, -и́шь**; *impf* **распространя́ть**) *сов перех* to spread; (*правило, приказ*) to apply; (*газеты*) to distribute; (*запах*) to emit; **распространи́ться** (*impf* **распространя́ться**) *сов возв* to spread; **распространи́ться** (*perf*) **на** *+acc* to extend to; (*приказ*) to apply to

распрям|и́ть (**-лю́, -и́шь**; *impf* **распрямля́ть**) *сов перех*

(*проволоку*) to straighten (out); (*плечи*) to straighten
расп|усти́ть (**-ущу́, -у́стишь**; *impf* **распуска́ть**) *сов перех* (*армию*) to disband; (*волосы*) to let down; (*парламент*) to dissolve; (*слухи*) to spread; (*перен*: *ребёнка итп*) to spoil; **распусти́ться** (*impf* **распуска́ться**) *сов возв* (*цветы, почки*) to open out; (*дети, люди*) to get out of hand
распу́хн|уть (**-у**; *impf* **распуха́ть**) *сов* to swell up
распыл|и́ть (**-ю́, -и́шь**; *impf* **распыля́ть**) *сов перех* to spray
расса́д|а (**-ы**) *ж собир* (*Бот*) seedlings *мн*
расс|ади́ть (**-ажу́, -а́дишь**; *impf* **расса́живать**) *сов перех* (*гостей, публику*) to seat; (*цветы*) to thin out
рассве|сти́ (*3sg* **-тёт**, *pt* **-ло́**, *impf* **рассвета́ть**) *сов безл*: **рассвело́** dawn was breaking
рассве́т (**-а**) *м* daybreak
рассе́ива|ть(ся) (**-ю(сь)**) *несов от* **рассе́ять(ся)**
рассека́|ть (**-ю**) *несов от* **рассе́чь**
расс|ели́ть (**-елю́, -е́лишь**; *impf* **расселя́ть**) *сов перех* (*по комнатам*) to accommodate
расс|ерди́ть(ся) (**-ержу́(сь), -е́рдишь(ся)**) *сов от* **серди́ть(ся)**
расс|е́сться (**-я́дусь, -я́дешься**; *pt* **-е́лся, -е́лась**) *сов возв* (*по столам, в зале*) to take one's seat
расс|е́чь (**-еку́, -ечёшь** *etc*, **-еку́т**; *pt* **-ёк, -екла́**, *impf* **рассека́ть**) *сов перех* to cut in two; (*губу, лоб*) to cut
рассе́|ять (**-ю**; *impf* **рассе́ивать**) *сов перех* (*семена, людей*) to scatter; (*перен*: *сомнения*) to dispel; **рассе́яться** (*impf* **рассе́иваться**) *сов возв* (*люди*) to be scattered; (*тучи, дым*) to disperse
расска́з (**-а**) *м* story; (*свидетеля*) account; **расск|аза́ть** (**-ажу́, -а́жешь**; *impf* **расска́зывать**) *сов перех* to tell; **расска́зчик** (**-а**) *м* storyteller; (*автор*) narrator
рассла́б|ить (**-лю, -ишь**; *impf* **расслабля́ть**) *сов перех* to relax; **рассла́биться** (*impf* **расслабля́ться**) *сов возв* to relax
рассле́д|овать (**-ую**) *(не)сов перех* to investigate
рассма́трива|ть (**-ю**) *несов от* **рассмотре́ть** ▷ *перех*: **рассма́тривать что-н как** to regard sth as
рассмеш|и́ть (**-у́, -и́шь**) *сов от* **смеши́ть**
рассме|я́ться (**-ю́сь, -ёшься**) *сов возв* to start laughing
рассм|отре́ть (**-отрю́, -о́тришь**; *impf* **рассма́тривать**) *сов перех* (*изучить*) to examine; (*различить*) to discern
расспр|оси́ть (**-ошу́, -о́сишь**; *impf* **расспра́шивать**) *сов перех*: **расспроси́ть (о** *+prp*) to question (about)
рассро́ч|ка (**-ки**; *gen pl* **-ек**) *ж* installment (*Brit*), instalment (*US*); **в рассро́чку** on hire purchase (*Brit*), on the installment plan (*US*)
расстава́ни|е (**-я**) *ср* parting
расста|ва́ться (**-ю́сь, -ёшься**) *сов от* **расста́ться**
расста́в|ить (**-лю, -ишь**; *impf* **расставля́ть**) *сов перех* to arrange
расстано́в|ка (**-ки**; *gen pl* **-ок**) *ж* (*мебели, книг*) arrangement
расста́|ться (**-нусь, -нешься**; *impf* **расстава́ться**) *сов возв*:

расстáться с *+instr* to part with
расстегн|ýть (**-ý, -ёшь**; *impf* **расстёгивать**) *сов перех* to undo; **расстегнýться** (*impf* **расстёгиваться**) *сов возв* (*человек*) to unbutton o.s.; (*рубашка, пуговица*) to come undone
расст|ели́ть (**-елю́, -éлешь**; *impf* **расстилáть**) *сов перех* to spread out
расстоя́ни|е (**-я**) *ср* distance
расстрáива|ть(ся) (**-ю(сь)**) *несов от* **расстрóить(ся)**
расстрéл (**-а**) *м* *+gen* shooting *или* firing at; (*казнь*) execution (*by firing squad*)
расстреля́|ть (**-ю**; *impf* **расстрéливать**) *сов перех* (*демонстрацию*) to open fire on; (*казнить*) to shoot
расстрóенный *прил* (*здоровье, нервы*) weak; (*человек, вид*) upset; (*рояль*) out of tune
расстрó|ить (**-ю, -ишь**; *impf* **расстрáивать**) *сов перех* (*планы*) to disrupt; (*человека, желудок*) to upset; (*здоровье*) to damage; (*Муз*) to put out of tune; **расстрóиться** (*impf* **расстрáиваться**) *сов возв* (*планы*) to fall through; (*человек*) to get upset; (*нервы*) to weaken; (*здоровье*) to be damaged; (*Муз*) to go out of tune
расстрóйств|о (**-а**) *ср* (*огорчение*) upset; (*речи*) dysfunction; **расстрóйство желýдка** stomach upset
расст|упи́ться (*3sg* **-ýпится**, *impf* **расступáться**) *сов возв* (*толпа*) to make way
расс|уди́ть (**-ужý, -ýдишь**) *сов*: **онá рассуди́ла прáвильно** her judgement was correct
рассýд|ок (**-ка**) *м* reason
рассуждá|ть (**-ю**) *несов* to reason; **рассуждáть** (*impf*) **о** *+prp* to debate
рассуждéни|е (**-я**) *ср* judg(e)ment
рассчитá|ть (**-ю**; *impf* **рассчи́тывать**) *сов перех* to calculate; **рассчитáться** (*impf* **рассчи́тываться**) *сов возв*: **рассчитáться (с** *+instr*) (*с продавцом*) to settle up (with)
рассчи́тыва|ть (**-ю**) *несов от* **рассчитáть** ▷ *неперех*: **рассчи́тывать на** *+acc* (*надеяться*) to count *или* rely on; **рассчи́тываться** *несов от* **рассчитáться**
рассылá|ть (**-ю**) *несов от* **разослáть**
рассы́п|ать (**-лю, -лешь**; *impf* **рассыпáть**) *сов перех* to spill; **рассы́паться** (*impf* **рассыпáться**) *сов возв* (*сахар, бусы*) to spill; (*толпа*) to scatter
растáплива|ть (**-ю**) *несов от* **растопи́ть**
растáптыва|ть (**-ю**) *несов от* **растоптáть**
растá|ять (**-ю**) *сов от* **тáять**
раствóр (**-а**) *м* (*Хим*) solution; (*строительный*) mortar
раствори́мый *прил* soluble; **раствори́мый кóфе** instant coffee
раствори́тел|ь (**-я**) *м* solvent
раствор|и́ть (**-ю́, -и́шь**; *impf* **растворя́ть**) *сов перех* (*порошок*) to dissolve; (*окно, дверь*) to open; **раствори́ться** (*impf* **растворя́ться**) *сов возв* (*см перех*) to dissolve; to open
растéни|е (**-я**) *ср* plant
раст|ерéть (**разотрý, разотрёшь**; *pt* **-ёр, -ёрла**, *impf*

Р

растирáть) *сов перех* (*рану, тело*) to massage
растéрянный *прил* confused
растеря́|ться (**-юсь**) *сов возв* (*человек*) to be at a loss, be confused; (*письма*) to disappear
раст|éчься (*3sg* **-ечётся**, *pt* **-ёкся, -еклáсь**, *impf* **растекáться**) *сов возв* (*вода*) to spill
раст|и́ (**-ý, -ёшь**; *pt* **рос, рослá, рослó**, *perf* **вы́расти**) *несов* to grow
растирá|ть (**-ю**) *несов от* **растерéть**
расти́тельн|ый *прил* (*Бот*) plant; **расти́тельное мáсло** vegetable oil
ра|сти́ть (**-щý, -сти́шь**; *perf* **вы́растить**) *несов перех* (*детей*) to raise; (*цветы*) to grow
раст|опи́ть (**-оплю́, -óпишь**; *impf* **растáпливать**) *сов перех* (*печку*) to light; (*воск, жир, лёд*) to melt; **растопи́ться** *сов от* **топи́ться**
раст|оптáть (**-опчý, -óпчешь**; *impf* **растáптывать**) *сов перех* to trample on
растрáт|а (**-ы**) *ж* (*времени, денег*) waste; (*хищение*) embezzlement
растрóга|ть (**-ю**) *сов перех*: **растрóгать когó-н** (*+instr*) to touch *или* move sb (by); **растрóгаться** *сов возв* to be touched *или* moved
раст|янýть (**-янý, -я́нешь**; *impf* **растя́гивать**) *сов перех* to stretch; (*связки*) to strain; **растянýться** (*impf* **растя́гиваться**) *сов возв* to stretch; (*человек, обоз*) to stretch out; (*связки*) to be strained
расхватá|ть (**-ю**; *impf* **расхвáтывать**) *сов перех* (*разг*) to snatch up
расхóд (**-а**) *м* (*энергии*) consumption; (*обычно мн*: *затраты*) expense; (: *Комм*: *в бухгалтерии*) expenditure
расх|оди́ться (**-ожýсь, -óдишься**) *несов от* **разойти́сь**
расхóд|овать (**-ую**; *perf* **израсхóдовать**) *несов перех* (*деньги*) to spend; (*материалы*) to use up
расхождéни|е (**-я**) *ср* discrepancy; (*во взглядах*) divergence
расхотéть (*как* **хотéть**; см *Table 14*) *сов* (*+infin*: *спать, гулять итп*) to no longer want to do; **расхотéться** *сов безл*: **(мне) расхотéлось спать** I don't feel sleepy any more
расцв|ести́ (**-етý, -етёшь**; *pt* **-ёл, -елá, -елó**, *impf* **расцветáть**) *сов* to blossom
расцвéт (**-а**) *м* (*науки*) heyday; (*таланта*) height; **он в расцвéте сил** he is in the prime of life
расцвéт|ка (**-ки**; *gen pl* **-ок**) *ж* colour (*Brit*) *или* color (*US*) scheme
расцéнива|ться (*3sg* **-ется**) *несов*: **расцéниваться как** to be regarded as
расц|ени́ть (**-еню́, -éнишь**; *impf* **расцéнивать**) *сов перех* to judge
расцéн|ка (**-ки**; *gen pl* **-ок**) *ж* (*работы*) rate; (*цена*) tariff
расч|есáть (**-ешý, -éшешь**; *impf* **расчёсывать**) *сов перех* (*волосы*) to comb; **расчёсывать** (*perf* **расчесáть**) **когó-н** to comb sb's hair
расчёс|ка (**-ки**; *gen pl* **-ок**) *ж* comb
расчёт (**-а**) *м* (*стоимости*) calculation; (*выгода*) advantage; (*бережливость*) economy; **из**

расчёта *+gen* on the basis of; **брать** (*perf* **взять**) *или* **принимáть (принять** *perf*) **что-н в расчёт** to take sth into account; **я с Вáми в расчёте** we are all even

расчи́|стить (**-щу, -стишь**; *impf* **расчищáть**) *сов перех* to clear

расшатá|ть (**-ю**; *impf* **расшáтывать**) *сов перех* (*стул*) to make wobbly; (*здоровье*) to damage; **расшатáться** (*impf* **расшáтываться**) *сов возв* (*стул*) to become wobbly; (*здоровье*) to be damaged

расширéни|е (**-я**) *ср* widening; (*связей, дела*) expansion; (*знаний*) broadening

расши́р|ить (**-ю, -ишь**; *impf* **расширя́ть**) *сов перех* to widen; (*дело*) to expand; **расши́риться** (*impf* **расширя́ться**) *сов возв* (*см перех*) to widen; to expand

ратифици́р|овать (**-ую**) *(не)сов перех* to ratify

рáунд (**-а**) *м* (*Спорт, Полит*) round

рафинáд (**-а**) *м* sugar cubes *мн*

рациóн (**-а**) *м* ration

рационáльн|ый *прил* rational; **рационáльное питáние** well-balanced diet

рвáный *прил* torn; (*ботинки*) worn

рв|ать (**-у, -ёшь**; *perf* **порвáть** *или* **разорвáть**) *несов перех* to tear, rip; (*перен*: *дружбу*) to break off ▷ (*perf* **вы́рвать**) (*предмет из рук*) to snatch ▷ (*perf* **сорвáть**) (*цветы, траву*) to pick ▷ (*perf* **вы́рвать**) *безл*: **егó рвёт** he is vomiting *или* being sick; **рвáться** (*perf* **порвáться** *или* **разорвáться**) *несов возв* to tear, rip; (*обувь*) to become worn ▷ (*perf* **разорвáться**) (*снаряд*) to explode; **рвáться** (*impf*) **к влáсти** to be hungry for power

рвéни|е (**-я**) *ср* enthusiasm

рвóт|а (**-ы**) *ж* vomiting

реаги́р|овать (**-ую**) *несов*: **реаги́ровать (на** *+acc*) (*на свет*) to react (to) ▷ (*perf* **отреаги́ровать** *или* **прореаги́ровать**) (*на критику, на слова*) to react *или* respond (to)

реакти́вный *прил*: **реакти́вный дви́гатель** jet engine; **реакти́вный самолёт** jet (plane)

реáктор (**-а**) *м* reactor

реáкци|я (**-и**) *ж* reaction

реализáци|я (**-и**) *ж* (*см глаг*) implementation; disposal

реализ|овáть (**-ýю**) *(не)сов перех* to implement; (*товар*) to sell

реáльност|ь (**-и**) *ж* reality; (*плана*) feasibility

реáльный *прил* real; (*политика*) realistic; (*план*) feasible

реанимáци|я (**-и**) *ж* resuscitation; **отделéние реанимáции** intensive care unit

ребён|ок (**-ка**; *nom pl* **дéти** *или* **ребя́та**) *м* child (*мн* children); (*грудной*) baby

ребр|ó (**-á**; *nom pl* **рёбра**) *ср* (*Анат*) rib; (*кубика итп*) edge

ребя́т|а (**-**) *мн от* **ребёнок**; (*разг*: *парни*) guys *мн*

рёв (**-а**) *м* roar

ревáнш (**-а**) *м* revenge

ревéн|ь (**-я́**) *м* rhubarb

рев|éть (**-ý, -ёшь**) *несов* to roar

ревизиóнн|ый *прил*: **ревизиóнная коми́ссия** audit commission

реви́зи|я (**-и**) *ж* (*Комм*) audit; (*теории*) revision; **ревиз|овáть** (**-ýю**) *(не)сов перех* (*Комм*) to audit; **ревизóр** (**-а**) *м* (*Комм*) auditor

р

ревмати́зм (**-а**) *м* rheumatism
ревни́вый *прил* jealous
ревн|ова́ть (**-у́ю**) *несов перех*: **ревнова́ть (кого́-н)** to be jealous (of sb)
ре́вност|ь (**-и**) *ж* jealousy
революционе́р (**-а**) *м* revolutionary
револю́ци|я (**-и**) *ж* revolution
ре́гби *ср нескл* rugby; **регби́ст** (**-а**) *м* rugby player
регио́н (**-а**) *м* region; **региона́льный** *прил* regional
реги́стр (**-а**) *м* register; (*на пишущей машинке*): **ве́рхний/ни́жний реги́стр** upper/lower case
регистра́тор (**-а**) *м* receptionist; **регистрату́р|а** (**-ы**) *ж* reception
регистри́р|овать (**-ую**; *perf* **зарегистри́ровать**) *несов перех* to register; **регистри́роваться** (*perf* **зарегистри́роваться**) *несов возв* to register; (*оформлять брак*) to get married (*at a registry office*)
регла́мент (**-а**) *м* (*порядок*) order of business; (*время*) speaking time
регули́р|овать (**-ую**) *несов перех* to regulate ▷ (*perf* **отрегули́ровать**) (*мотор*) to adjust
регулиро́вщик (**-а**) *м*: **регулиро́вщик у́личного движе́ния** traffic policeman
регуля́рный *прил* regular
редакти́р|овать (**-ую**; *perf* **отредакти́ровать**) *несов перех* to edit
реда́ктор (**-а**) *м* editor; (*Комп*) spellchecker; **редакцио́нн|ый** *прил* editorial; **редакцио́нная колле́гия** editorial board; **редакцио́нная статья́** editorial; **реда́кци|я** (**-и**) *ж* (*действие: текста*) editing; (*формулировка: статьи закона*) wording; (*учреждение*) editorial offices *мн*; (*на радио*) desk; (*на телевидении*) division; **под реда́кцией** *+gen* edited by
реде́|ть (*3sg* **-ет**, *perf* **пореде́ть**) *несов* to thin out
реди́с (**-а**) *м* radish
ре́дкий *прил* rare; (*волосы*) thin; **ре́дко** *нареч* rarely, seldom
редколле́ги|я (**-и**) *ж сокр* = **редакцио́нная колле́гия**
режи́м (**-а**) *ж* regime; (*больничный*) routine; (*Комп*) mode
режиссёр (**-а**) *м* director (*of film, play etc*); **режиссёр-постано́вщик** (stage) director
ре́|зать (**-жу, -жешь**; *perf* **разре́зать**) *несов перех* (*металл, кожу*) to cut; (*хлеб*) to slice ▷ (*perf* **заре́зать**) (*разг: свинью*) to slaughter; (*no perf: фигурки итп*) to carve; **ре́заться** (*perf* **проре́заться**) *несов возв* (*зубы, рога*) to come through
резе́рв (**-а**) *м* reserve
резиде́нци|я (**-и**) *ж* residence
рези́н|а (**-ы**) *ж* rubber; **рези́н|ка** (**-ки**; *gen pl* **-ок**) *ж* (*ластик*) rubber (*Brit*), eraser (*esp US*); (*тесёмка*) elastic; **рези́новый** *прил* rubber
ре́зкий *прил* sharp; (*свет, голос*) harsh; (*запах*) pungent; **ре́зко** *нареч* sharply
резн|я́ (**-и́**) *ж* slaughter
резолю́ци|я (**-и**) *ж* (*съезда*) resolution; (*распоряжение*) directive
результа́т (**-а**) *м* result
результати́вный *прил* productive
резьб|а́ (**-ы́**) *ж* carving; (*винта*) thread

резюме́ *ср нескл* résumé, summary
рейс (**-а**) *м* (*самолёта*) flight; (*автобуса*) run; (*парохода*) sailing
ре́йсовый *прил* regular
ре́йтинг (**-а**) *м* popularity rating
рейту́з|ы (-) *мн* long johns, thermal pants (*US*)
рек|а́ (**-и́**; *acc sg* **-у**, *dat sg* **-е́**, *nom pl* **-и**) *ж* river
рекла́м|а (**-ы**) *ж* (*действие*: *торговая*) advertising; (*средство*) advert (*Brit*), advertisement; **реклами́р|овать** (**-ую**) *(не)сов перех* to advertise; **рекла́мный** *прил* (*отдел, колонка*) advertising; (*статья, фильм*) publicity; **рекла́мный ро́лик** advertisement; (*фильма*) trailer; **рекламода́тел|ь** (**-я**) *м* advertiser
рекоменда́тельн|ый *прил*: **рекоменда́тельное письмо́** letter of recommendation
рекоменд|ова́ть (**-у́ю**) *(не)сов перех* to recommend
реконструи́р|овать (**-ую**) *(не)сов перех* to rebuild; (*здание*) to reconstruct
реко́рд (**-а**) *м* record; **реко́рдный** *прил* record(-breaking); **рекордсме́н** (**-а**) *м* record holder
ре́ктор (**-а**) *м* ≈ principal; **ректора́т** (**-а**) *м* principal's office
религио́зный *прил* religious
рели́ги|я (**-и**) *ж* religion
рельс (**-а**) *м* (*обычно мн*) rail
рем|е́нь (**-ня́**) *м* belt; (*сумки*) strap; **привязны́е ремни́** seat belt
ремесл|о́ (**-а́**; *nom pl* **ремёсла**, *gen pl* **ремёсел**) *ср* trade
ремеш|о́к (**-ка́**) *м* strap
ремо́нт (**-а**) *м* repair; (*здания*: *крупный*) refurbishment; (: *мелкий*) redecoration; **теку́щий ремо́нт** maintenance; **ремонти́р|овать** (**-ую**; *perf* **отремонти́ровать**) *несов перех* to repair; (*здание*) to renovate; **ремо́нтн|ый** *прил*: **ремо́нтные рабо́ты** repairs *мн*; **ремо́нтная мастерска́я** repair workshop
рента́бельный *прил* profitable
рентге́н (**-а**) *м* (*Мед*) X-ray
репети́р|овать (**-ую**; *perf* **отрепети́ровать**) *несов (не) перех* to rehearse; **репети́тор** (**-а**) *м* private tutor; **репети́ци|я** (**-и**) *ж* rehearsal
ре́плик|а (**-и**) *ж* remark
репорта́ж (**-а**) *м* report; **репортёр** (**-а**) *м* reporter
репре́сси|я (**-и**) *ж* repression
репроду́ктор (**-а**) *м* loudspeaker
репроду́кци|я (**-и**) *ж* reproduction (*of painting etc*)
репута́ци|я (**-и**) *ж* reputation
ресни́ц|а (**-ы**) *ж* (*обычно мн*) eyelash
респу́блик|а (**-и**) *ж* republic
ессо́р|а (**-ы**) *ж* spring
реставра́ци|я (**-и**) *ж* restoration
реставри́р|овать (**-ую**; *perf* **реставри́ровать** *или* **отреставри́ровать**) *несов перех* to restore
ресторա́н (**-а**) *м* restaurant
ресу́рс (**-а**) *м* (*обычно мн*) resource
рефле́кс (**-а**) *м* reflex
рефо́рм|а (**-ы**) *ж* reform
рецензи́р|овать (**-ую**; *perf* **прорецензи́ровать**) *несов перех* to review
реце́нзи|я (**-и**) *ж*: **реце́нзия (на** *+acc*) review (of)
реце́пт (**-а**) *м* (*Мед*) prescription; (*Кулин*: *перен*) recipe
речево́й *прил* speech

речно́й *прил* river
реч|ь (**-и**) *ж* speech; (*разговорная итп*) language; **речь идёт о том, как/где/кто …** the matter in question is how/where/who …; **об э́том не мо́жет быть и ре́чи** there can be absolutely no question of this; **о чём речь!** (*разг*) sure!, of course!
реша́|ть(ся) (**-ю(сь)**) *несов от* **реши́ть(ся)**
реше́ни|е (**-я**) *ср* decision; (*проблемы*) solution
реши́мост|ь (**-и**) *ж* resolve
реши́тельно *нареч* resolutely; (*действовать*) decisively
реш|и́ть (**-у́, -и́шь**; *impf* **реша́ть**) *сов перех* to decide; (*проблему*) to solve; **реши́ться** (*impf* **реша́ться**) *сов возв* (*вопрос, судьба*) to be decided; **реша́ться** (*perf* **реши́ться**) *+infin* to resolve to do; **реша́ться** (*perf* **реши́ться**) **на** *+acc* to decide on
ре́шк|а (**-и**) *ж* (*на монете*) tails; **орёл или ре́шка?** heads or tails?
ре́|ять (*3sg* **-ет**) *сов* (*флаг*) to fly
ржа́ве|ть (*3sg* **-ет**, *perf* **заржа́веть**) *несов* to rust
ржа́вчин|а (**-ы**) *ж* rust
ржа́вый *прил* rusty
ржано́й *прил* rye
рж|ать (**-у, -ёшь**) *несов* to neigh
ржи *итп сущ см* **рожь**
РИА *ср сокр* (= *Росси́йское информацио́нное аге́нтство*) Russian News Agency
Рим (**-а**) *м* Rome
ринг (**-а**) *м* (boxing) ring
ри́н|уться (**-усь**) *сов возв* to charge
рис (**-а**) *м* rice
риск (**-а**) *по pl м* risk; **риско́ванный** *прил* risky; **риск|ова́ть** (**-у́ю**; *perf* **рискну́ть**) *несов* to take risks; **рискова́ть** (*perf* **рискну́ть**) *+instr* (*жизнью, работой*) to risk
рисова́ни|е (**-я**) *ср* (*карандашом*) drawing; (*красками*) painting;
рис|ова́ть (**-у́ю**; *perf* **нарисова́ть**) *несов перех* (*карандашом*) to draw; (*красками*) to paint
ри́совый *прил* rice
рису́н|ок (**-ка**) *м* drawing; (*на ткани*) pattern
ритм (**-а**) *м* rhythm; **ритми́ческий** *прил* rhythmic(al)
ритуа́л (**-а**) *м* ritual
риф (**-а**) *м* reef
ри́фм|а (**-ы**) *ж* rhyme
р-н *сокр* = **райо́н**
робе́|ть (**-ю**; *perf* **оробе́ть**) *несов* to go shy; **ро́бкий** *прил* shy
ро́бот (**-а**) *м* robot
р|ов (**-ва**; *loc sg* **-ву**) *м* ditch
рове́сник (**-а**) *м*: **он мой рове́сник** he is the same age as me
ро́вно *нареч* (*писать*) evenly; (*чертить*) straight; (*через год*) exactly; **ро́вно в два часа́** at two o'clock sharp
ро́вный *прил* even; (*линия*) straight; **ровня́|ть** (**-ю**; *perf* **сровня́ть** *или* **вы́ровнять**) *несов перех* (*строй*) to straighten ▷ (*perf* **разровня́ть** *или* **сровня́ть**) (*дорожку*) to level
род (**-а**; *loc sg* **-у́**, *nom pl* **-ы́**) *м* (*о семье*) clan, family; (*вид*) type; (*Линг*) gender; **своего́ ро́да** a kind of; **в не́котором ро́де** to some extent; **что-то в э́том** *или* **тако́м ро́де** something like that
род. *сокр* (= *родился*) b. (= *born*)
роддо́м (**-а**) *м сокр* = **роди́льный дом**
роди́льный *прил*: **роди́льный дом** maternity hospital

роди́м|ый *прил*: **роди́мое пятно́** birthmark
ро́дин|а (**-ы**) *ж* homeland
роди́тел|и (**-ей**) *мн* parents
роди́тельный *прил*: **роди́тельный паде́ж** the genitive (case)
роди́тельск|ий *прил* parental; **роди́тельское собра́ние** parents' meeting
ро|ди́ть (**-жу́, -ди́шь**; *impf* **рожа́ть** *или* **рожда́ть**) *(не)сов перех* to give birth to; **роди́ться** (*impf* **рожда́ться**) *(не)сов возв* to be born
родни́к (**-а́**) *м* spring (*water*)
родно́й *прил* (*брат, мать итп*) natural; (*город, страна*) native; (*в обращении*) dear; **родно́й язы́к** mother tongue; *см также* **родны́е**
родны́|е (**-х**) *мн* relatives
родово́й *прил* (*понятие, признак*) generic; (*Линг*) gender; (*имение*) family; (*Мед*: *судороги, травма*) birth
родосло́вн|ый *прил*: **родосло́вное де́рево** family tree
ро́дственник (**-а**) *м* relation, relative
ро́дственный *прил* family; (*языки, науки*) related
родств|о́ (**-а́**) *ср* relationship; (*душ, идей*) affinity
ро́д|ы (**-ов**) *мн* labour *ед* (*Brit*), labor *ед* (*US*); **принима́ть** (*perf* **приня́ть**) **ро́ды** to deliver a baby
рожа́|ть (**-ю**) *несов от* **роди́ть**
рожда́емост|ь (**-и**) *ж* birth rate
рожда́|ть(ся) (**-ю(сь)**) *несов от* **роди́ть(ся)**
рожде́ни|е (**-я**) *ср* birth; **день рожде́ния** birthday
рожде́ственский *прил* Christmas
Рождеств|о́ (**-а́**) *ср* (*Рел*) Nativity; (*праздник*) Christmas; **С Рождество́м!** Happy *или* Merry Christmas!
рожь (**ржи**) *ж* rye
ро́з|а (**-ы**) *ж* (*растение*) rose(bush); (*цветок*) rose
розе́т|ка (**-ки**; *gen pl* **-ок**) *ж* power point
ро́зниц|а (**-ы**) *ж* retail goods *мн*; **продава́ть** (*perf* **прода́ть**) **в ро́зницу** to retail; **ро́зничный** *прил* retail
ро́зовый *прил* rose; (*цвет*) pink; (*мечты*) rosy
ро́зыск (**-а**) *м* search; **Уголо́вный ро́зыск** Criminal Investigation Department (*Brit*), Federal Bureau of Investigation (*US*)
ро|й (**-я**; *nom pl* **-и́**) *м* (*пчёл*) swarm
рок (**-а**) *м* (*судьба*) fate; (*также* **рок-му́зыка**) rock
роково́й *прил* fatal
рол|ь (**-и**; *gen pl* **-е́й**) *ж* role
ром (**-а**) *м* rum
рома́н (**-а**) *м* novel; (*любовная связь*) affair
романи́ст (**-а**) *м* novelist
рома́нс (**-а**) *м* (*Муз*) romance
роня́|ть (**-ю**; *perf* **урони́ть**) *несов перех* to drop; (*авторитет*) to lose
рос *итп несов см* **расти́**
рос|а́ (**-ы́**; *nom pl* **-ы**) *ж* dew
роско́шный *прил* luxurious, glamorous
ро́скош|ь (**-и**) *ж* luxury
ро́спис|ь (**-и**) *ж* (*узор*: *на шкатулке*) design; (: *на стенах*) mural; (*подпись*) signature
росси́йск|ий *прил* Russian; **Росси́йская Федера́ция** the Russian Federation
Росси́|я (**-и**) *ж* Russia
россия́н|ин (**-ина**; *nom pl* **-е**, *gen pl* **-**) *м* Russian

Р

рост (**-а**) *м* growth; (*увеличение*) increase; (*размер*: *человека*) height ▷ (*nom pl* **-á**) (*длина*: *пальто, платья*) length
рóстбиф (**-а**) *м* roast beef
рост|óк (**-ка́**) *м* (*Бот*) shoot
рот (**рта**; *loc sg* **рту́**) *м* mouth
рóт|а (**-ы**) *ж* (*Воен*) company
роя́л|ь (**-я**) *м* grand piano
РПЦ *ж сокр* (= *Ру́сская правосла́вная це́рковь*) Russian Orthodox Church
р/с *сокр* = **расчётный счёт**
рта *etc сущ см* **рот**
ртут|ь (**-и**) *ж* mercury
руб. *сокр* = **рубль** R., r. (= *rouble*)
руба́ш|ка (**-ки**; *gen pl* **-ек**) *ж* (*мужская*) shirt; **ни́жняя руба́шка** (*женская*) slip; **ночна́я руба́шка** nightshirt
рубе́ж (**-á**) *м* (*государства*) border; (: *водный, лесной*) boundary; **он живёт за рубежóм** he lives abroad
руби́н (**-а**) *м* ruby
руб|и́ть (**-лю́, -ишь**; *perf* **сруби́ть**) *сов перех* (*дерево*) to fell; (*ветку*) to chop off
рубл|ь (**-я́**) *м* rouble
ру́брик|а (**-и**) *ж* (*раздел*) column; (*заголовок*) heading
руга́|ть (**-ю**; *perf* **вы́ругать** *или* **отруга́ть**) *несов перех* to scold; **руга́ться** *несов возв* (*бранить*): **руга́ться с** *+instr* to scold ▷ (*perf* **вы́ругаться**) to swear; **руга́ться** (*perf* **поруга́ться**) **с** *+instr* (*с мужем, с другом*) to fall out with
руд|á (**-ы́**; *nom pl* **-ы**) *ж* ore; **рудни́к** (**-á**) *м* mine
руж|ьё (**-ья́**; *nom pl* **-ья**, *gen pl* **-ей**) *ср* rifle
рук|á (*acc sg* **-у**, *gen sg* **-и́**, *nom pl* **-и**, *gen pl* **-**, *dat pl* **-áм**) *ж* hand; (*верхняя конечность*) arm; **из пéрвых рук** first hand; **под рукóй, под рукáми** to hand, handy; **отсю́да до гóрода рукóй подáть** it's a stone's throw from here to the town; **э́то емý нá руку** that suits him
рукáв (**-á**) *м* (*одежды*) sleeve
руководи́тел|ь (**-я**) *м* leader; (*кафедры, предприятия*) head; **руково|ди́ть** (**-жý, -ди́шь**) *несов +instr* to lead; (*учреждением*) to be in charge of; (*страной*) to govern; (*аспирантами*) to supervise; **руковóдств|о** (**-а**) *м* leadership; (*заводом, институтом*) management; (*пособие*) manual; (*по эксплуатации, по уходу*) instructions *мн*
рýкопис|ь (**-и**) *ж* manuscript
рукоя́т|ка (**-ки**; *gen pl* **-ок**) *ж* handle
рулев|óй *прил*: **рулевóе колесó** steering wheel
рулéт (**-а**) *м* (*с джемом*) ≈ swiss roll
рул|и́ть (**-ю́, -и́шь**) *несов перех* to steer
рулóн (**-а**) *м* roll
рул|ь (**-я́**) *м* steering wheel
румя́н|а (**-**) *мн* blusher *ед*; **румя́н|ец** (**-ца**) *м* glow; **румя́н|ить** (**-ю, -ишь**; *perf* **нарумя́нить**) *несов перех* (*щёки*) to apply blusher to; **румя́ниться** (*perf* **разрумя́ниться**) *несов возв* to flush ▷ (*perf* **нарумя́ниться**) (*женщина*) to apply blusher ▷ (*perf* **подрумя́ниться**) (*пирог*) to brown
РУО́П (**-а**) *ср сокр* (= *Региона́льное управле́ние по борьбе́ с организо́ванной престу́пностью*) *department fighting organised crime*
руóпов|ец (**-ца**) *м* member of the

department fighting organized crime
ру́с|ло (**-ла**; *gen pl* **-ел**) *ср* bed (*of river*); (*перен*: *направление*) course
ру́сск|ий *прил* Russian ▷ (**-ого**) *м* Russian; **ру́сский язы́к** Russian
ру́сый *прил* (*волосы*) light brown
ру́хн|уть (**-у**) *сов* to collapse
руча́тельств|о (**-а**) *ср* guarantee
руча́|ться (**-юсь**; *perf* **поручи́ться**) *несов возв*: **руча́ться за** *+acc* to guarantee
руч|е́й (**-ья́**) *м* stream
ру́ч|ка (**-ки**; *gen pl* **-ек**) *ж*, *уменьш от* **рука́**; (*двери, чемодана итп*) handle; (*кресла, дивана*) arm; (*для письма*) pen
ручн|о́й *прил* hand; (*животное*) tame; **ручна́я кладь, ручно́й бага́ж** hand luggage; **ручны́е часы́** (wrist)watch
РФ *ж сокр* = **Росси́йская Федера́ция**
ры́б|а (**-ы**) *ж* fish; **ни ры́ба ни мя́со** neither here nor there; **рыба́к** (**-а́**) *м* fisherman (*мн* fishermen); **рыба́л|ка** (**-ки**; *gen pl* **-ок**) *ж* fishing; **рыба́цкий** *прил* fishing; **ры́бий** *прил* fish; **ры́бий жир** cod-liver oil; **ры́бный** *прил* (*магазин*) fish; (*промышленность*) fishing; **рыболо́в** (**-а**) *м* angler, fisherman (*мн* fishermen)
Ры́б|ы (-) *мн* (*созвездие*) Pisces *ед*
рыв|о́к (**-ка́**) *м* jerk; (*в работе*) push
рыда́|ть (**-ю**) *несов* to sob
ры́жий *прил* (*волосы*) ginger; (*человек*) red-haired
ры́н|ок (**-ка**) *м* market; **ры́ночный** *прил* (*Комм*) market
рысц|а́ (**-ы́**) *ж* jog trot
ры́цар|ь (**-я**) *м* knight
рыча́г (**-а́**) *м* (*управления*) lever; (*перен*: *реформ*) instrument
рыч|а́ть (**-у́, -и́шь**) *несов* to growl
рэ́кет (**-а**) *м* racket
рюкза́к (**-а́**) *м* rucksack
рю́м|ка (**-ки**; *gen pl* **-ок**) *ж* ≈ liqueur glass
ряд (**-а**; *loc sg* **-у́**, *nom pl* **-ы́**) *м* row; (*явлений*) sequence ▷ (*prp sg* **-е**) (*+gen*: *несколько*: *вопросов, причин*) a number of; **из ря́да вон выходя́щий** extraordinary; *см также* **ряды́**; **рядов|о́й** *прил* (*обычный*) ordinary; (*член партии*) rank-and-file ▷ (**-о́го**) *м* (*Воен*) private
ря́дом *нареч* side by side; (*близко*) nearby; **ря́дом с** *+instr* next to; **э́то совсе́м ря́дом** it's really near
ряд|ы́ (**-о́в**) *мн* (*армии*) ranks
ря́женк|а (**-и**) *ж* *natural set yoghurt*

С

с[1] *сокр* (= *се́вер*) N (= *North*); (= *секу́нда*) s (= *second*)

КЛЮЧЕВОЕ СЛОВО

с[2] *предл +instr* **1** (*указывает на объект, от которого что-н отделяется*) off; **лист упа́л с де́рева** a leaf fell off the tree; **с рабо́ты/ле́кции** from work/a lecture
2 (*следуя чему-н*) from; **перево́д с ру́сского** a translation from Russian
3 (*об источнике*) from; **де́ньги с зака́зчика** money from a customer
4 (*начиная с*) since; **жду тебя́ с утра́** I've been waiting for you since morning; **с января́ по май** from January to May
5 (*на основании чего-н*) with; **с одобре́ния парла́мента** with the approval of parliament
6 (*по причине*): **с го́лоду/хо́лода/го́ря** of hunger/cold/grief; **я уста́л с доро́ги** I was tired from the journey
▷ *предл* (*+acc*: *приблизительно*) about; **с киломе́тр/то́нну** about a kilometre (*Brit*) *или* kilometer (*US*)/ton(ne)
▷ *предл +instr* **1** (*совместно*) with; **я иду́ гуля́ть с дру́гом** I am going for a walk with a friend; **он познако́мился с де́вушкой** he has met a girl; **мы с ним** he and I
2 (*о наличии чего-н в чём-н*): **пиро́г с мя́сом** a meat pie; **хлеб с ма́слом** bread and butter; **челове́к с ю́мором** a man with a sense of humour (*BRIT*) *или* humor (*US*)
3 (*при указании на образ действия*) with; **слу́шать** (*impf*) **с удивле́нием** to listen with *или* in surprise; **ждём с нетерпе́нием встре́чи с Ва́ми** we look forward to meeting you
4 (*при посредстве*): **с курье́ром** by courier
5 (*при наступлении чего-н*): **с во́зрастом** with age; **мы вы́ехали с рассве́том** we left at dawn
6 (*об объекте воздействия*) with; **поко́нчить** (*perf*) **с несправедли́востью** to do away with injustice; **спеши́ть** (*perf* **поспеши́ть**) **с вы́водами** to draw hasty conclusions; **что с тобо́й?** what's the matter with you?

с. *сокр* (= *страни́ца*) p. (= *page*); = **село́**

са́б|ля (**-ли**; *gen pl* **-ель**) *ж* sabre (*Brit*), saber (*US*)

сад (**-а**; *loc sg* **-у́**, *nom pl* **-ы́**) *м* garden; (*фруктовый*) orchard; (*также* **де́тский сад**) nursery

(school) (*Brit*), kindergarten
са|ди́ться (**-жу́сь, -ди́шься**) *несов от* **сесть**
садо́вник (**-а**) *м* (professional) gardener
садо́вый *прил* garden
сажа́|ть (**-ю**; *perf* **посади́ть**) *несов перех* to seat; (*дерево*) to plant; (*самолёт*) to land; **сажа́ть** (*perf* **посади́ть**) **кого́-н в тюрьму́** to put sb in prison
сайт (**-а**) *м* (*Комп*) site
саксофо́н (**-а**) *м* saxophone
сала́т (**-а**) *м* (*Кулин*) salad; **сала́тниц|а** (**-ы**) *ж* salad bowl
са́л|о (**-а**) *ср* (*животного*) fat; (*Кулин*) lard
сало́н (**-а**) *м* salon; (*автобуса, самолёта итп*) passenger section
салфе́т|ка (**-ки**; *gen pl* **-ок**) *ж* napkin
са́льто *ср нескл* mid-air somersault
салю́т (**-а**) *м* salute
сам (**-ого́**; *f* **сама́**, *nt* **само́**, *pl* **са́ми**) *мест* (*я*) myself; (*ты*) yourself; (*он*) himself; (*как таковой*) itself; **сам по себе́** (*отдельно*) by itself
сам|а́ (**-о́й**) *мест* (*я*) myself; (*ты*) yourself; (*она*) herself; *см также* **сам**
сам|е́ц (**-ца́**) *м* male (*Zool*)
са́м|и (**-и́х**) *мест* (*мы*) ourselves; (*они*) themselves; *см также* **сам**
са́м|ка (**-ки**; *gen pl* **-ок**) *ж* female (*Zool*)
са́ммит (**-а**) *м* summit
сам|о́ (**-ого́**) *мест* itself; **само́ собо́й (разуме́ется)** it goes without saying; *см также* **сам**
самова́р (**-а**) *м* samovar
самоде́льный *прил* home-made
самоде́ятельност|ь (**-и**) *ж* initiative; (*также* **худо́жественная самоде́ятельность**) amateur art and performance; **самоде́ятельный** *прил* (*театр*) amateur
самока́т (**-а**) *м* scooter
самолёт (**-а**) *м* (aero)plane (*Brit*), (air)plane (*US*)
самостоя́тельный *прил* independent
самоуби́йств|о (**-а**) *ср* suicide; **поко́нчить** (*perf*) **жизнь самоуби́йством** to commit suicide; **самоуби́йц|а** (**-ы**) *м/ж* suicide (victim)
самоуве́ренный *прил* self-confident, self-assured
самоучи́тел|ь (**-я**) *м* teach-yourself book
самочу́встви|е (**-я**) *ср*: **как Ва́ше самочу́вствие?** how are you feeling?
са́м|ый *мест +n* the very; (*+adj*: *вкусный, красивый итп*) the most; **в са́мом нача́ле/конце́** right at the beginning/end; **в са́мом де́ле** really; **на са́мом де́ле** in actual fact
санато́ри|й (**-я**) *м* sanatorium (*Brit*), sanitarium (*US*) (*мн* sanatoriums *или* sanatoria)
санда́ли|я (**-и**) *ж* (*обычно мн*) sandal
са́н|и (**-е́й**) *мн* sledge *ед* (*Brit*), sled *ед* (*US*); (*спортивные*) toboggan *ед*
санита́р|ка (**-ки**; *gen pl* **-ок**) *ж* nursing auxiliary
санита́рн|ый *прил* sanitary; (*Воен*) medical; **санита́рная те́хника** *collective term for plumbing equipment and bathroom accessories*
са́н|ки (**-ок**) *мн* sledge *ед* (*Brit*), sled *ед* (*US*)
санкциони́р|овать (**-ую**) *(не) сов перех* to sanction

са́нкци|я (**-и**) *ж* sanction
санте́хник (**-а**) *м сокр* (= *санита́рный те́хник*) plumber; **санте́хник|а** (**-и**) *ж сокр* = **санита́рная те́хника**
сантиме́тр (**-а**) *м* centimetre (*Brit*), centimeter (*US*); (*линейка*) tape measure
сапо́г (**-а́**; *nom pl* **-и́**, *gen pl* **-**) *м* boot
сапфи́р (**-а**) *м* sapphire
сара́|й (**-я**) *м* shed; (*для сена*) barn
сарафа́н (**-а**) *м* (*платье*) pinafore (dress) (*Brit*), jumper (*US*)
сати́р|а (**-ы**) *ж* satire
сау́довск|ий *прил*: **Сау́довская Ара́вия** Saudi Arabia
са́ун|а (**-ы**) *ж* sauna
са́хар (**-а**; *part gen* **-у**) *м* sugar; **са́харниц|а** (**-ы**) *ж* sugar bowl; **са́харный** *прил* sugary; **са́харный диабе́т** diabetes; **са́харный песо́к** granulated sugar
сач|о́к (**-ка́**) *м* (*для ловли рыб*) landing net; (*для бабочек*) butterfly net
сба́в|ить (**-лю, -ишь**; *impf* **сбавля́ть**) *сов перех* to reduce
сбе́га|ть (**-ю**) *сов* (*разг*): **сбе́гать в магази́н** to run to the shop
сбежа́ть (*как* **бежа́ть**; см *Table 20*; *impf* **сбега́ть**) *сов* (*убежать*) to run away; **сбега́ть** (*perf* **сбежа́ть**) **с** *+gen* (*с горы итп*) to run down; **сбежа́ться** (*impf* **сбега́ться**) *сов возв* to come running
сберба́нк (**-а**) *м сокр* (= *сберега́тельный банк*) savings bank
сберега́тельн|ый *прил*: **сберега́тельный банк** savings bank; **сберега́тельная ка́сса** savings bank; **сберега́тельная кни́жка** savings book
сберега́|ть (**-ю**) *несов от* **сбере́чь**
сбереже́ни|е (**-я**) *ср* (*действие*) saving; **сбереже́ния** savings *мн*
сбер|е́чь (**-егу́, -ежёшь** *итп*, **-егу́т**; *pt* **-ёг, -егла́**, *impf* **сберега́ть**) *сов перех* (*здоровье, любовь, отношение*) to preserve; (*деньги*) to save (up)
сберка́сс|а (**-ы**) *ж сокр* = **сберега́тельная ка́сса**
сберкни́ж|ка (**-ки**; *gen pl* **-ек**) *ж сокр* = **сберега́тельная кни́жка**
сбить (**собью́, собьёшь**; *imper* **сбе́й(те)**, *impf* **сбива́ть**) *сов перех* to knock down; (*птицу, самолёт*) to shoot down; (*сливки, яйца*) to beat; **сби́ться** (*impf* **сбива́ться**) *сов возв* (*шапка, повязка итп*) to slip; **сбива́ться** (*perf* **сби́ться**) **с пути́** (*также перен*) to lose one's way
сбли́|зить (**-жу, -зишь**; *impf* **сближа́ть**) *сов перех* to bring closer together; **сбли́зиться** (*impf* **сближа́ться**) *сов возв* (*люди, государства*) to become closer
сбо́ку *нареч* at the side
сбор (**-а**) *м* (*урожая, данных*) gathering; (*налогов*) collection; (*плата*: *страховой итп*) fee; (*прибыль*) takings *мн*, receipts *мн*; (*собрание*) assembly, gathering; **тамо́женный/ге́рбовый сбор** customs/stamp duty; **все в сбо́ре** everyone is present
сбо́р|ка (**-ки**; *gen pl* **-ок**) *ж* (*изделия*) assembly
сбо́рн|ая (**-ой**) *ж* (*разг*) = **сбо́рная кома́нда**
сбо́рник (**-а**) *м* collection (*of stories, articles*)

сбо́рн|ый *прил*: **сбо́рный пункт** assembly point; **сбо́рная ме́бель** kit furniture; **сбо́рная кома́нда (страны́)** national team

сбо́рочный *прил* assembly

сбра́сыва|ть(ся) (**-ю(сь)**) *несов от* **сбро́сить(ся)**

сбр|ить (**-е́ю, -е́ешь**; *impf* **сбрива́ть**) *сов перех* to shave off

сбро́|сить (**-шу, -сишь**; *impf* **сбра́сывать**) *сов перех* (*предмет*) to throw down; (*свергнуть*) to overthrow; (*скорость, давление*) to reduce; **сбро́ситься** (*impf* **сбра́сываться**) *сов возв*: **сбра́сываться** (*perf* **сбро́ситься**) **с** +*gen* to throw o.s. from

сбру́|я (**-и**) *ж* harness

сбыт (**-а**) *м* sale

сбыть (*как* **быть**; см *Table 21*; *impf* **сбыва́ть**) *сов перех* (*товар*) to sell; **сбы́ться** (*impf* **сбыва́ться**) *сов возв* (*надежды*) to come true

св. *сокр* (= *свято́й*) St (= *Saint*)

сва́д|ьба (**-ьбы**; *gen pl* **-еб**) *ж* wedding

св|али́ть (**-алю́, -а́лишь**) *сов от* **вали́ть** ▷ (*impf* **сва́ливать**) *перех* to throw down; **свали́ться** *сов от* **вали́ться**

сва́л|ка (**-ки**; *gen pl* **-ок**) *ж* (*место*) rubbish dump

сваля́|ть (**-ю**) *сов от* **валя́ть**

св|ари́ть(ся) (**-арю́(сь), -а́ришь(ся)**) *сов от* **вари́ть(ся)**

сва́та|ть (**-ю**; *perf* **посва́тать** *или* **сосва́тать**) *несов перех*: **сва́тать кого́-н** (**за** +*acc*) to try to marry sb off (to); **сва́таться** (*perf* **посва́таться**) *несов возв*: **сва́таться к** +*dat или* **за** +*acc* to court

сва́|я (**-и**) *ж* (*Строит*) pile

све́дени|е (**-я**) *ср* information *только ед*; **доводи́ть** (*perf* **довести́**) **что-н до све́дения кого́-н** to bring sth to sb's attention

сведе́ни|е (**-я**) *ср* (*пятна́*) removal; (*в таблицу, в график итп*) arrangement

све́жий *прил* fresh; (*журнал*) recent

свёкл|а (**-ы**) *ж* beetroot

свёк|ор (**-ра**) *м* father-in-law, husband's father

свекро́в|ь (**-и**) *ж* mother-in-law, husband's mother

све́ргн|уть (**-у**; *impf* **сверга́ть**) *сов перех* to overthrow; **сверже́ни|е** (**-я**) *ср* overthrow

све́р|ить (**-ю, -ишь**; *impf* **сверя́ть**) *сов перех*: **све́рить** (**с** +*instr*) to check (against)

сверка́|ть (**-ю**) *несов* (*звезда, глаза*) to twinkle; (*огни*) to flicker; **сверка́ть** (*impf*) **умо́м/красото́й** to sparkle with intelligence/beauty

сверкн|у́ть (**-у́, -ёшь**) *сов* to flash

сверл|и́ть (**-ю́, -и́шь**; *perf* **просверли́ть**) *несов перех* to drill, bore

св|ерло́ (**-ерла́**; *nom pl* **свёрла**) *ср* drill

све́рстник (**-а**) *м* peer; **мы с ней све́рстники** she and I are the same age

свёрт|ок (**-ка**) *м* package

сверх *предл* (+*gen*: *нормы*) over and above

све́рху *нареч* (*о направлении*) from the top; (*в верхней части*) on the surface

сверхуро́чн|ые (**-ых**) *мн* (*плата*) overtime pay *ед*

сверхуро́чн|ый *прил*: **сверхуро́чная рабо́та** overtime

сверхъесте́ственный *прил* supernatural
сверч|о́к (**-ка́**) *м* (*Зоол*) cricket
сверя́|ть (**-ю**) *несов от* **све́рить**
св|ести́ (**-еду́, -едёшь**; *pt* **-ёл, -ела́**, *impf* **своди́ть**) *сов перех*: **свести́ с** *+gen* to lead down; (*пятно*) to shift; (*собрать*) to arrange; **своди́ть** (*perf* **свести́**) **кого́-н с ума́** to drive sb mad; **свести́сь** (*impf* **своди́ться**) *сов возв*: **свести́сь к** *+dat* to be reduced to
свет (**-а**) *м* light; (*Земля*) the world; **ни свет ни заря́** at the crack of dawn; **выходи́ть** (*perf* **вы́йти**) **в свет** (*книга*) to be published; **ни за что на све́те не сде́лал бы э́того** (*разг*) I wouldn't do it for the world
света́|ть (*3sg* **-ет**) *несов безл* to get *или* grow light
свети́льник (**-а**) *м* lamp
св|ети́ть (**-ечу́, -е́тишь**) *несов* to shine; **свети́ть** (*perf* **посвети́ть**) **кому́-н** (*фонарём итп*) to light the way for sb; **свети́ться** *несов возв* to shine
све́тлый *прил* light; (*комната, день*) bright; (*ум*) lucid
светофо́р (**-а**) *м* traffic light
свеч|а́ (**-и́**; *nom pl* **-и**, *gen pl* **-е́й**) *ж* candle; (*Мед*) suppository; (*Тех*) spark(ing) plug; (*Спорт*) lob
све́ч|ка (**-ки**; *gen pl* **-ек**) *ж* candle
све́ша|ть (**-ю**) *сов от* **ве́шать**
све́шива|ться (**-юсь**) *несов от* **све́ситься**
свива́|ть (**-ю**; *perf* **свить**) *несов перех* to weave
свида́ни|е (**-я**) *ср* rendezvous; (*деловое*) appointment; (*с заключённым, с больным*) visit; (*влюблённых*) date; **до свида́ния** goodbye; **до ско́рого свида́ния** see you soon
свиде́тел|ь (**-я**) *м* witness; **свиде́тельств|о** (**-а**) *ср* evidence; (*документ*) certificate; **свиде́тельство о бра́ке/ рожде́нии** marriage/birth certificate; **свиде́тельств|овать** (**-ую**) *несов*: **свиде́тельствовать о** *+prp* to testify to
свин|е́ц (**-ца́**) *м* lead (*metal*)
свини́н|а (**-ы**) *ж* pork
сви́нк|а (**-и**) *ж* (*Мед*) mumps
свино́й *прил* (*сало, корм*) pig; (*из свинины*) pork
свин|ья́ (**-ьи́**; *nom pl* **-ьи**, *gen pl* **-е́й**) *ж* pig
свиса́|ть (*3sg* **-ет**) *несов* to hang
свист (**-а**) *м* whistle; **сви|сте́ть** (**-щу́, -сти́шь**; *perf* **просвисте́ть**) *несов* to whistle; **сви́стн|уть** (**-у**) *сов* to give a whistle
свист|о́к (**-ка́**) *м* whistle
сви́тер (**-а**) *м* sweater
свить (**совью́, совьёшь**) *сов от* **вить**; **свива́ть**
свобо́д|а (**-ы**) *ж* freedom; **лише́ние свобо́ды** imprisonment
свобо́дный *прил* free; (*незанятый: место*) vacant; (*движение, речь*) fluent; **вход свобо́дный** free admission; **свобо́дный уда́р** (*в футболе*) free kick
св|оди́ть(ся) (**-ожу́(сь), -о́дишь(ся)**) *несов от* **свести́(сь)**
сво́д|ка (**-ки**; *gen pl* **-ок**) *ж*: **сво́дка пого́ды/новосте́й** weather/ news summary
сво́дн|ый *прил* (*таблица*) summary; **сво́дный брат** stepbrother; **сво́дная сестра́** stepsister
сво|ё (**-его́**) *мест см* **свой**
своевре́менный *прил* timely
своеобра́зный *прил* original; (*необычный*) peculiar

КЛЮЧЕВОЕ СЛОВО

сво|й (**-его́**; *f* **своя́**, *nt* **своё**, *pl* **свои́**; *как* **мой**; см *Table 8*) *мест*
1 (*я*) my; (*ты*) your; (*он*) his; (*она*) her; (*оно*) its; (*мы*) our; (*вы*) your; (*они*) their; **я люблю́ свою́ рабо́ту** I love my work; **мы собра́ли свои́ ве́щи** we collected our things
2 (*собственный*) one's own; **у неё свой компью́тер** she has her own computer
3 (*своеобразный*) its; **э́тот план име́ет свои́ недоста́тки** this plan has its shortcomings
4 (*близкий*): **свой челове́к** one of us

сво́йственный *прил +dat* characteristic of
сво́йств|о (**-а**) *ср* characteristic, feature
свора́чива|ть(ся) (**-ю(сь)**) *несов от* **сверну́ть(ся)**
сво|я́ (**-е́й**) *мест см* **свой**
свы́ше *предл* (*+gen*: *выше*) beyond; (*больше*) over, more than
свя́занный *прил*: **свя́занный (с** *+instr*) connected (to *или* with); (*имеющий связи*): **свя́занный с** *+instr* (*с деловыми кругами*) associated with; (*несвободный*) restricted
свя|за́ть (**-жу́, -жешь**) *сов от* **вяза́ть** ▷ (*impf* **свя́зывать**) *перех* (*верёвку итп*) to tie; (*вещи, человека*) to tie up; (*установить сообщение, зависимость*): **связа́ть что-н с** *+instr* to connect *или* link sth to; **связа́ться** (*impf* **свя́зываться**) *сов возв*: **связа́ться с** *+instr* to contact; (*разг*: *с невыгодным делом*) to get (o.s.) caught up in
свя́з|ка (**-ки**; *gen pl* **-ок**) *ж* (*ключей*) bunch; (*бумаг, дров*) bundle; (*Анат*) ligament; (*Линг*) copula
связ|ь (**-и**) *ж* tie; (*причинная*) connection, link; (*почтовая итп*) communications *мн*; **в свя́зи с** *+instr* (*вследствие*) due to; (*по поводу*) in connection with; **свя́зи с обще́ственностью** public relations
свят|о́й *прил* holy; (*дело, истина*) sacred ▷ (**-о́го**) *м* (*Рел*) saint
свяще́нник (**-а**) *м* priest
свяще́нный *прил* holy, sacred; (*долг*) sacred
с.г. *сокр* = **сего́ го́да**
сгиб (**-а**) *м* bend; **сгиба́|ть** (**-ю**; *perf* **согну́ть**) *несов перех* to bend; **сгиба́ться** (*perf* **согну́ться**) *несов возв* to bend down
сгни|ть (**-ю, -ёшь**) *сов от* **гнить**
сгно|и́ть (**-ю́, -и́шь**) *сов от* **гнои́ть**
сгора́|ть (**-ю**) *несов от* **сгоре́ть** ▷ *неперех*: **сгора́ть от любопы́тства** to be burning with curiosity
сгор|е́ть (**-ю́, -и́шь**; *impf* **сгора́ть** *или* **горе́ть**) *сов* to burn ▷ (*impf* **сгора́ть**) (*Элек*) to fuse; (*на солнце*) to get burnt
сгр|ести́ (**-ебу́, -ебёшь**; *pt* **-ёб, -ебла́**, *impf* **сгреба́ть**) *сов перех* (*собрать*) to rake up
сгр|узи́ть (**-ужу́, -у́зишь**; *impf* **сгружа́ть**) *сов перех*: **сгрузи́ть (с** *+gen*) to unload (from)
сгусти́ться (*impf* **сгуща́ться**) *сов возв* to thicken
сгущённ|ый *прил*: **сгущённое молоко́** condensed milk
сда|ва́ть (**-ю́, -ёшь**; *imper* **-ва́й(те)**) *несов от* **сдать** ▷ *перех*: **сдава́ть экза́мен** to sit an exam;

сдава́ться *несов от* **сда́ться** ▷ *возв* (*помещение*) to be leased out; **"сдаётся внаём"** "to let"

сд|ави́ть (**-авлю́, -а́вишь**; *impf* **сда́вливать**) *сов перех* to squeeze

сда́ть (*как* **дать**; см *Table 16*; *impf* **сдава́ть**) *сов перех* (*пальто, багаж, работу*) to hand in; (*дом, комнату итп*) to rent out, let; (*город, позицию*) to surrender; (*no impf*: *экзамен, зачёт итп*) to pass; **сда́ться** (*impf* **сдава́ться**) *сов возв* to give up; (*солдат, город*) to surrender

сдвиг (**-а**) *м* (*в работе*) progress

сдви́н|уть (**-у**; *impf* **сдвига́ть**) *сов перех* (*переместить*) to move; (*сблизить*) to move together; **сдви́нуться** (*impf* **сдвига́ться**) *сов возв*: **сдви́нуться (с места́)** to move

сде́ла|ть(ся) (**-ю(сь)**) *сов от* **де́лать(ся)**

сде́л|ка (**-ки**; *gen pl* **-ок**) *ж* deal

сде́ржанный *прил* (*человек*) reserved

сд|ержа́ть (**-ержу́, -е́ржишь**; *impf* **сде́рживать**) *сов перех* to contain, hold back; **сде́рживать** (*perf* **сдержа́ть**) **сло́во/обеща́ние** to keep one's word/promise; **сдержа́ться** (*impf* **сде́рживаться**) *сов возв* to restrain o.s.

сдёрн|уть (**-у**; *impf* **сдёргивать**) *сов перех* to pull off

сдира́|ть (**-ю**) *несов от* **содра́ть**

сдо́бный *прил* (*тесто*) rich

сду|ть (**-ю**; *impf* **сдува́ть**) *сов перех* to blow away

сеа́нс (**-а**) *м* (*Кино*) show; (*терапии*) session

себе́ *мест см* **себя́** ▷ *част* (*разг*): **так себе́** so-so; **ничего́ себе́** (*сносно*) not bad; (*ирония*) well, I never!

себесто́имост|ь (**-и**) *ж* cost price

КЛЮЧЕВОЕ СЛОВО

себя́ *мест* (*я*) myself; (*ты*) yourself; (*он*) himself; (*она*) herself; (*оно*) itself; (*мы*) ourselves; (*вы*) yourselves; (*они*) themselves; **он тре́бователен к себе́** he asks a lot of himself; **она́ вини́т себя́** she blames herself; **к себе́** (*домой*) home; (*в свою комнату*) to one's room; **"к себе́"** (*на двери*) "pull"; **"от себя́"** (*на двери*) "push"; **по себе́** (*по своим вкусам*) to one's taste; **говори́ть** (*impf*)**/чита́ть** (*impf*) **про себя́** to talk/read to o.s.; **она́ себе́ на уме́** (*разг*) she is secretive; **он у себя́** (*в своём доме*) he is at home; (*в своём кабинете*) he is in the office

се́вер (**-а**) *м* north; **Се́вер** (*Арктика*) the Arctic North; **се́верн|ый** *прил* north; (*ветер, направление*) northerly; (*климат, полушарие*) northern; **Се́верный Ледови́тый океа́н** Arctic Ocean; **се́верное сия́ние** the northern lights *мн*

се́веро-восто́к (**-а**) *м* northeast

се́веро-за́пад (**-а**) *м* northwest

сего́ *мест см* **сей**

сего́дня *нареч, сущ нескл* today; **сего́дня у́тром/днём/ве́чером** this morning/afternoon/evening

седе́|ть (**-ю**; *perf* **поседе́ть**) *несов* to go grey (*Brit*) *или* gray (*US*)

сед|ина́ (**-ины́**; *nom pl* **-и́ны**) *ж* grey (*Brit*) *или* gray (*US*) hair

седл|о́ (**-а́**) *ср* saddle

седо́й *прил* (*волосы*) grey (*Brit*), gray (*US*)
седьмо́й *чис* seventh; **сейча́с седьмо́й час** it's after six
сезо́н (**-а**) *м* season
сезо́нный *прил* seasonal
сей (**сего́**; см *Table 12*) *мест* this
сейф (**-а**) *м* (*ящик*) safe
сейча́с *нареч* (*теперь*) now; (*скоро*) just now; **сейча́с же!** right now!
секре́т (**-а**) *м* secret
секрета́рш|а (**-и**) *ж* (*разг*) secretary
секрета́р|ь (**-я́**) *м* secretary; **секрета́рь-машини́стка** secretary
секре́тный *прил* secret
секс (**-а**) *м* sex
сексуа́льн|ый *прил* sexual; (*жизнь, образование*) sex; **сексуа́льное пресле́дование** *or* **домога́тельство** sexual harassment
се́кт|а (**-ы**) *ж* sect
секта́нт (**-а**) *м* sect member
се́ктор (**-а**) *м* sector
секу́нд|а (**-ы**) *ж* second
се́кци|я (**-и**) *ж* section
сел *итп сов см* **сесть**
селёд|ка (**-ки**; *gen pl* **-ок**) *ж* herring
селе́ктор (**-а**) *м* (*Тел*) intercom
селе́кци|я (**-и**) *ж* (*Био*) selective breeding
селе́ни|е (**-я**) *ср* village
сел|и́ть (**-ю́, -ишь**; *perf* **посели́ть**) *несов перех* (*в местности*) to settle; (*в доме*) to house; **сели́ться** (*perf* **посели́ться**) *несов возв* to settle
сел|о́ (**-а́**; *nom pl* **сёла**) *ср* village
се́лфи *ср нескл* selfie
сельдере́|й (**-я**) *м* celery
сельд|ь (**-и**; *gen pl* **-е́й**) *ж* herring
се́льск|ий *прил* (*см сущ*) village; country, rural; **се́льское хозя́йство** agriculture
сельскохозя́йственный *прил* agricultural
сёмг|а (**-и**) *ж* salmon
семе́йный *прил* family
семе́йств|о (**-а**) *ср* family
семёр|ка (**-ки**; *gen pl* **-ок**) *ж* (*цифра, карта*) seven
се́мер|о (**-ы́х**; *как* **че́тверо**; см *Table 30b*) *чис* seven
семе́стр (**-а**) *м* term (*Brit*), semester (*US*)
се́меч|ко (**-ка**; *gen pl* **-ек**) *ср* seed; **се́мечки** sunflower seeds
семидеся́тый *чис* seventieth
семина́р (**-а**) *м* seminar
семна́дцатый *чис* seventeenth
семна́дцат|ь (**-и**; *как* **пять**; см *Table 26*) *чис* seventeen
сем|ь (**-и́**; *как* **пять**; см *Table 26*) *чис* seven
се́м|ьдесят (**-и́десяти**; *как* **пятьдеся́т**; см *Table 26*) *чис* seventy
сем|ьсо́т (**-исо́т**; *как* **пятьсо́т**; см *Table 28*) *чис* seven hundred
семь|я́ (**-и́**; *nom pl* **-и**) *ж* family
се́м|я (**-ени**; *как* **вре́мя**; см *Table 4*) *ср* seed; (*no pl*: *Био*) semen
сена́тор (**-а**) *м* senator
сенн|о́й *прил*: **сенна́я лихора́дка** hay fever
се́н|о (**-а**) *м* hay
сенса́ци|я (**-и**) *ж* sensation
сентимента́льный *прил* sentimental
сентя́бр|ь (**-я́**) *м* September
се́р|а (**-ы**) *ж* sulphur (*Brit*), sulfur (*US*); (*в ушах*) (ear)wax
серва́нт (**-а**) *м* buffet unit
се́рвер (**-а**) *м* (*Комп*) server
серви́з (**-а**) *м*: **столо́вый/ча́йный серви́з** dinner/tea service
се́рвис (**-а**) *м* service (*in shop etc*)

серде́чный *прил* heart, cardiac; (*человек*) warm-hearted; (*приём, разговор*) cordial; **серде́чный при́ступ** heart attack

серди́тый *прил* angry

сер|ди́ть (**-жу́, -дишь**; *perf* **рассерди́ть**) *несов перех* to anger, make angry; **серди́ться** (*perf* **рассерди́ться**) *несов возв*: **серди́ться (на кого́-н/что-н)** to be angry (with sb/about sth)

се́рд|це (**-ца**; *nom pl* **-ца́**) *ср* heart; **в глубине́ се́рдца** in one's heart of hearts; **от всего́ се́рдца** from the bottom of one's heart

сердцебие́ни|е (**-я**) *ср* heartbeat

серебр|о́ (**-а́**) *ср, собир* silver; **серéбряный** *прил* silver

середи́н|а (**-ы**) *ж* middle

серёж|ка (**-ки**; *gen pl* **-ек**) *ж, уменьш от* **серьга́**

сержа́нт (**-а**) *м* sergeant

сериа́л (**-а**) *м* (*Тел*) series

се́ри|я (**-и**) *ж* series; (*кинофильма*) part

се́рн|ый *прил*: **се́рная кислота́** sulphuric (*Brit*) *или* sulfuric (*US*) acid

сертифика́т (**-а**) *м* certificate; (*товара*) guarantee (certificate)

серф|ить (**-лю, -ишь**) *несов перех* (*Комп*) to surf

се́рый *прил* grey (*Brit*), gray (*US*); **се́рый хлеб** brown bread

сер|ьга́ (**-ьги́**; *nom pl* **-ьги**, *gen pl* **-ёг**, *dat pl* **-ьга́м**) *ж* earring

серьёзно *нареч, вводн сл* seriously

серьёзный *прил* serious

се́сси|я (**-и**) *ж* (*суда, парламента*) session; (*также* **экзаменацио́нная се́ссия**) examinations *мн*

сестр|а́ (**-ы́**; *nom pl* **сёстры**, *gen pl* **сестёр**) *ж* sister; (*также* **медици́нская сестра́**) nurse

сесть (**ся́ду, ся́дешь**; *pt* **сел, се́ла**, *impf* **сади́ться**) *сов* to sit down; (*птица, самолёт*) to land; (*солнце, луна*) to go down; (*одежда*) to shrink; (*батарейка*) to run down; **сади́ться** (*perf* **сесть**) **в по́езд/на самолёт** to get on a train/plane; **сади́ться** (*perf* **сесть**) **в тюрьму́** to go to prison

сетево́й *прил* (*Комп*) net; (*магазин*) chain

се́т|ка (**-ки**; *gen pl* **-ок**) *ж* net; (*сумка*) net bag

сет|ь (**-и**; *prp sg* **-и́**, *gen pl* **-е́й**) *ж* (*для ловли рыб итп*) net; (*дорог*) network; (*магазинов*) chain; (*Комп*) the Net; **социа́льные се́ти** social media

сече́ни|е (**-я**) *ср* section; **ке́сарево сече́ние** Caesarean (*Brit*) *или* Cesarean (*US*) (section)

сечь (**секу́, сечёшь** *итп*, **секу́т**; *pt* **сёк, секла́**) *несов перех* (*рубить*) to cut up

се́|ять (**-ю**; *perf* **посе́ять**) *несов перех* to sow

сжа́л|иться (**-юсь, -ишься**) *сов возв*: **сжа́литься (над** *+instr*) to take pity (on)

сжать (**сожму́, сожмёшь**; *impf* **сжима́ть**) *сов перех* to squeeze; (*воздух, газ*) to compress; **сжа́ться** (*impf* **сжима́ться**) *сов возв* (*пружина*) to contract; (*человек: от боли, от испуга*) to tense up; (*перен: сердце*) to seize up

сжечь (**сожгу́, сожжёшь** *итп*, **сожгу́т**; *pt* **сжёг, сожгла́**, *impf* **сжига́ть** *или* **жечь**) *сов перех* to burn

сжима́|ть(ся) (**-ю(сь)**) *несов от* **сжа́ть(ся)**

сза́ди *нареч* (*подойти*) from behind; (*находиться*) behind

▷ *предл +gen* behind
сзывá|ть (**-ю**) *несов от* **созвáть**
сибúрский *прил* Siberian
Сибúр|ь (**-и**) *ж* Siberia
сибиря́к (**-á**) *м* Siberian
сигарéт|а (**-ы**) *ж* cigarette
сигнáл (**-а**) *м* signal; **сигнализáци|я** (**-и**) *ж* (*в квартире*) burglar alarm
сидéнь|е (**-я**) *ср* seat
си|дéть (**-жý, -дúшь**) *несов* to sit; (*одежда*) to fit
сúдя *нареч*: **рабóтать/есть сúдя** to work/eat sitting down
сидя́ч|ий *прил* (*положение*) sitting; **сидя́чие местá** seats *мн*
сúл|а (**-ы**) *ж* strength; (*тока, ветра, закона*) force; (*воли, слова*) power; (*обычно мн*: *душевные, творческие*) energy; **в сúлу тогó что ...** owing to the fact that ...; **от сúлы** (*разг*) at (the) most; **вступáть** (*perf* **вступúть**) *или* **входúть** (**войтú** *perf*) **в сúлу** to come into *или* take effect; *см также* **сúлы**
сúлой *нареч* by force
силуэ́т (**-а**) *м* (*контур*) silhouette
сúл|ы (**-**) *мн* forces; **сúлами когó-н** through the efforts of sb; **своúми сúлами** by oneself
сúльно *нареч* strongly; (*ударить*) hard; (*хотеть, понравиться итп*) very much
сúльный *прил* strong; (*мороз*) hard; (*впечатление*) powerful; (*дождь*) heavy
СИМ-кáрт|а (**-ы**) *ж* SIM card
сúмвол (**-а**) *м* symbol; (*Комп*) character
симметрúческий *прил* symmetrical
симметрú|я (**-и**) *ж* symmetry
симпатизúр|овать (**-ую**) *несов*: **симпатизúровать комý-н** to like *или* be fond of sb
симпатúчный *прил* nice, pleasant
симпáти|я (**-и**) *ж* liking, fondness
симптóм (**-а**) *м* symptom
симфóни|я (**-и**) *ж* (*Муз*) symphony
синагóг|а (**-и**) *ж* synagogue
синдрóм (**-а**) *м* (*Мед*) syndrome
синé|ть (**-ю**; *perf* **посинéть**) *несов* to turn blue
сúний *прил* blue
синúц|а (**-ы**) *ж* tit (*Zool*)
синóним (**-а**) *м* synonym
синóптик (**-а**) *м* weather forecaster
синтетúческий *прил* synthetic
синя́к (**-á**) *м* bruise
сирéн|а (**-ы**) *ж* (*гудок*) siren
сирéневый *прил* lilac
сирéн|ь (**-и**) *ж* (*кустарник*) lilac bush ▷ *собир* (*цветы*) lilac
сирóп (**-а**) *м* syrup
сир|отá (**-оты́**; *nom pl* **-óты**) *м/ж* orphan
систéм|а (**-ы**) *ж* system
систематúческий *прил* regular
сúт|ец (**-ца**) *м* cotton
сúтеч|ко (**-ка**; *gen pl* **-ек**) *ср* (*для чая*) (tea) strainer
сúт|о (**-а**) *ср* sieve
ситуáци|я (**-и**) *ж* situation
сúтцевый *прил* (*ткань*) cotton
сия́|ть (**-ю**) *несов* (*солнце, звезда*) to shine; (*огонь*) to glow
ск|азáть (**-ажý, -áжешь**) *сов от* **говорúть** ▷ *перех*: **скáжем** (*разг*) let's say; **скажúте!** (*разг*) I say!; **так сказáть** so to speak; **сказáться** (*impf* **скáзываться**) *сов возв* (*ум, опыт итп*) to show; (*отразиться*): **сказáться на** *+prp* to take its toll on
скáз|ка (**-ки**; *gen pl* **-ок**) *ж* fairy tale
скáзочный *прил* fairy-tale

сказу́ем|ое (**-ого**) *ср* (*Линг*) predicate
ск|ака́ть (**-ачу́, -а́чешь**) *несов* (*человек*) to skip; (*мяч*) to bounce; (*лошадь, всадник*) to gallop
скаков|о́й *прил*: **скакова́я ло́шадь** racehorse
скаку́н (**-а́**) *м* racehorse
ск|ала́ (**-алы́**; *nom pl* **-а́лы**) *ж* cliff
скали́стый *прил* rocky
скаме́|йка (**-йки**; *gen pl* **-ек**) *ж* bench
скам|ья́ (**-ьи́**; *gen pl* **-е́й**) *ж* bench; **скамья́ подсуди́мых** (*Юр*) the dock
сканда́л (**-а**) *м* scandal; (*ссора*) quarrel
сканда́л|ить (**-ю, -ишь**; *perf* **поскандáлить**) *несов* to quarrel
ска́нер (**-а**) *м* (*Комп*) scanner
ска́плива|ться (**-юсь**) *несов от* **скопи́ться**
скарлати́н|а (**-ы**) *ж* scarlet fever
скат (**-а**) *м* slope; (*Авт*: *колесо*) wheel
ската́|ть (**-ю**; *impf* **ска́тывать**) *сов перех* to roll up
ска́терт|ь (**-и**) *ж* tablecloth
ск|ати́ть (**-ачу́, -а́тишь**; *impf* **ска́тывать**) *сов перех* to roll down; **скати́ться** (*impf* **ска́тываться**) *сов возв* (*слеза*) to roll down; (*перен*): **скати́ться к** *+dat*/**на** *+acc* to slide towards/into
ска́ч|ки (**-ек**) *мн* the races
скач|о́к (**-ка́**) *м* leap
скв *ж сокр* (= *свобо́дно конверти́руемая валю́та*) convertible currency
сквер (**-а**) *м* *small public garden*
скве́рный *прил* foul
скво́з|ить (*3sg* **-и́т**) *несов безл*: **здесь сквози́т** it's draughty here
сквозня́к (**-а́**) *м* (*в комнате*) draught (*Brit*), draft (*US*)
сквозь *предл +acc* through
скворе́чник (**-а**) *м* nesting box
скеле́т (**-а**) *м* skeleton
скепти́ческий *прил* sceptical
ски́д|ка (**-ки**; *gen pl* **-ок**) *ж* (*с цены*) discount, reduction
ски́н|уть (**-у**; *impf* **ски́дывать**) *сов перех* (*сбросить*) to throw down
ски́с|нуть (**-ну, -нешь**; *pt* **-, -ла, -ло**, *impf* **скиса́ть**) *сов* (*молоко*) to turn sour
склад (**-а**) *м* (*товарный*) store; (*оружия итп*) cache; (*образ*: *мыслей*) way
скла́д|ка (**-ки**; *gen pl* **-ок**) *ж* (*на одежде*) pleat
складно́й *прил* folding
скла́дыва|ть(ся) (**-ю(сь)**) *несов от* **сложи́ть(ся)**
скле́|ить (**-ю, -ишь**) *сов от* **кле́ить** ▷ (*impf* **скле́ивать**) *перех* to glue together
склон (**-а**) *м* slope
склоне́ни|е (**-я**) *ср* (*Линг*) declension
скл|они́ть (**-оню́, -о́нишь**; *impf* **склоня́ть**) *сов перех* (*опустить*) to lower; **склоня́ть** (*perf* **склони́ть**) **кого́-н к побе́гу/на преступле́ние** to persuade sb to escape/commit a crime; **склони́ться** (*impf* **склоня́ться**) *сов возв* (*нагнуться*) to bend; (*перен*): **склони́ться к** *+dat* to come round to
скло́нност|ь (**-и**) *ж*: **скло́нность к** *+dat* (*к музыке*) aptitude for; (*к меланхолии, к полноте*) tendency to
скло́нный *прил*: **скло́нный к** *+dat* (*к простудам*) prone *или* susceptible to; (*+infin*: *помириться*) inclined to do

склоня́емый *прил* declinable
склоня́|ть (**-ю**) *несов от* **склони́ть** ▷ (*perf* **просклоня́ть**) *перех* (*Линг*) to decline; **склоня́ться** *несов от* **склони́ться** ▷ *возв* (*Линг*) to decline
ск|оба́ (**-обы́**; *nom pl* **-óбы**) *ж* (*для опоры*) clamp; (*для крепления*) staple
скóб|ка (**-ки**; *gen pl* **-ок**) *ж*, *уменьш от* **скоба́**; (*обычно мн*: *в тексте*) bracket, parentheses *мн*
ск|ова́ть (**-ую́**; *impf* **скóвывать**) *сов перех* (*человека*) to paralyse
сковород|а́ (**-ы́**; *nom pl* **скóвороды**) *ж* frying-pan (*Brit*), skillet (*US*)
сколь *нареч* (*как*) how; (*возможно*) as much as; **сколь … столь (же) …** as much … as …
сколь|зи́ть (**-жу́, -зи́шь**) *несов* to glide; (*падая*) to slide
скóльзкий *прил* slippery; (*ситуация, вопрос*) sensitive
скользн|у́ть (**-у́, -ёшь**) *сов* to glide; (*быстро пройти*) to slip

КЛЮЧЕВОЕ СЛОВО

скóльк|о (**-их**) *местоимённое нареч* **1** (*+gen*: *книг, часов, дней итп*) how many; (*сахара, сил, работы итп*) how much; **скóлько людéй пришлó?** how many people came?; **скóлько дéнег тебé нáдо?** how much money do you need?; **скóлько э́то стóит?** how much is it?; **скóлько тебé лет?** how old are you?
2 (*относительное*) as much; **бери́, скóлько хóчешь** take as much as you want; **скóлько угóдно** as much as you like
▷ *нареч* **1** (*насколько*) as far as; **скóлько пóмню, он всегдá был агресси́вный** as far as I remember, he was always aggressive
2 (*много*): **скóлько людéй!** what a lot of people!; **не стóлько … скóлько …** not so much … as …

скóмка|ть (**-ю**) *сов от* **кóмкать**
скончá|ться (**-юсь**) *сов возв* to pass away
скоп|и́ть (**-лю́, -ишь**) *сов от* **копи́ть**; **скопи́ться** *сов от* **копи́ться** ▷ (*impf* **скáпливаться**) *возв* (*люди*) to gather; (*работа*) to mount up
скóр|ая (**-ой**) *ж* (*разг*: *также* **скóрая пóмощь**) ambulance
скорб|ь (**-и**; *gen pl* **-éй**) *ж* grief
скорéе *сравн прил от* **скóрый** ▷ *сравн нареч от* **скóро** ▷ *част* rather; **скорéе…чем** *или* **нежéли** (*в большей степени*) more likely … than; (*лучше, охотнее*) rather … than; **скорée всегó они́ дóма** it's most likely they'll be (at) home; **скорéе бы он верну́лся** I wish he would come back soon
скорл|упа́ (**-упы́**; *nom pl* **-у́пы**) *ж* shell
скóро *нареч* soon ▷ *как сказ* it's soon; **скóро зимá** it will soon be winter
скоропости́жн|ый *прил*: **скоропости́жная смерть** sudden death
скóрост|ь (**-и**; *gen pl* **-éй**) *ж* speed
скоросшивáтел|ь (**-я**) *м* (loose-leaf) binder
скорпиóн (**-а**) *м* scorpion; (*созвездие*): **Скорпиóн** Scorpio
скóр|ый *прил* (*движение*) fast; (*разлука, визит*) impending; **в скóром врéмени** shortly; **скóрая пóмощь** (*учреждение*) ambulance

service; (*автомашина*) ambulance; **ско́рый по́езд** express (train)
скот (**-а́**) *м собир* livestock; **моло́чный/мясно́й скот** dairy/beef cattle
скреп|и́ть (**-лю́, -и́шь**; *impf* **скрепля́ть**) *сов перех* (*соединить*) to fasten together
скре́п|ка (**-ки**; *gen pl* **-ок**) *ж* paperclip
скре|сти́ть (**-щу́, -сти́шь**; *impf* **скре́щивать**) *сов перех* to cross; (*животных*) to cross-breed; **скрести́ться** (*impf* **скре́щиваться**) *сов возв* to cross
скри́п|ка (**-ки**; *gen pl* **-ок**) *ж* violin
скро́мност|ь (**-и**) *ж* modesty
скро́мный *прил* modest; (*служащий, должность*) humble
скр|ути́ть (**-учу́, -у́тишь**) *сов от* **крути́ть** ▷ (*impf* **скру́чивать**) *перех* (*провода, волосы*) to twist together; **скрути́ться** *сов возв* to twist together
скрыва́|ть (**-ю**) *несов от* **скрыть**; **скрыва́ться** *несов от* **скры́ться** ▷ *возв* (*от полиции*) to hide
скры́тный *прил* secretive
скры́тый *прил* (*тайный*) hidden, secret
скр|ыть (**-о́ю, -о́ешь**; *impf* **скрыва́ть**) *сов перех* (*спрятать*) to hide; (*факты*) to conceal; **скры́ться** (*impf* **скрыва́ться**) *сов возв* (*от дождя, от погони*) to take cover; (*стать невидным*) to disappear
ску́дный *прил* (*запасы*) meagre (*Brit*), meager (*US*)
ску́к|а (**-и**) *ж* boredom
скул|и́ть (**-ю́, -и́шь**) *несов* to whine
ску́льптор (**-а**) *м* sculptor; **скульпту́р|а** (**-ы**) *ж* sculpture
ску́мбри|я (**-и**) *ж* mackerel
ск|упи́ть (**-уплю́, -у́пишь**; *impf* **скупа́ть**) *сов перех* to buy up
скупо́й *прил* mean
скуча́|ть (**-ю**) *несов* to be bored; (*тосковать*): **скуча́ть по** *+dat или* **о** *+prp* to miss
ску́чно *нареч* (*жить, рассказывать итп*) boringly ▷ *как сказ*: **здесь ску́чно** it's boring here; **мне ску́чно** I'm bored
ску́чный *прил* boring, dreary
слабе́|ть (**-ю**; *perf* **ослабе́ть**) *несов* to grow weak; (*дисциплина*) to slacken
слаби́тельн|ое (**-ого**) *ср* laxative
сла́бо *нареч* (*вскрикнуть*) weakly; (*нажать*) lightly; (*знать*) badly
сла́бост|ь (**-и**) *ж* weakness
сла́бый *прил* weak; (*ветер*) light; (*знания, доказательство итп*) poor; (*дисциплина итп*) slack
сла́в|а (**-ы**) *ж* (*героя*) glory; (*писателя, актёра итп*) fame; **сла́ва Бо́гу!** thank God!
слав|яни́н (**-яни́на**; *nom pl* **-я́не**, *gen pl* **-я́н**) *м* Slav; **славя́нский** *прил* Slavonic
слага́|ть (**-ю**) *несов от* **сложи́ть**
сла́дкий *прил* sweet
сла́дко *нареч* (*пахнуть*) sweet; (*спать*) deeply
сла́дк|ое (**-ого**) *ср* sweet things *мн*; (*разг*: *десерт*) afters (*Brit*), dessert (*US*)
слайд (**-а**) *м* (*Фото*) slide
слать (**шлю́, шлёшь**) *несов перех* to send
сла́ще *сравн прил от* **сла́дкий** ▷ *сравн нареч от* **сла́дко**
сле́ва *нареч* on the left
слегка́ *нареч* slightly
след (**-а**; *nom pl* **-ы́**) *м* trace; (*ноги*) footprint
сле|ди́ть (**-жу́, -ди́шь**) *несов*:

следи́ть за *+instr* to follow; (*заботиться*) to take care of; (*за шпионом*) to watch
сле́довани|е (**-я**) *ср* (*моде*) following; **по́езд/авто́бус да́льнего сле́дования** long-distance train/bus
сле́довател|ь (**-я**) *м* detective
сле́довательно *вводн сл* consequently ▷ *союз* therefore
сле́д|овать (**-ую**; *perf* **после́довать**) *несов* (*вывод, неприятность*) to follow ▷ *безл*: **Вам сле́дует поду́мать об э́том** you should think about it; **как сле́дует** properly
сле́дом *предл*: **сле́дом за** *+instr* following
сле́дстви|е (**-я**) *ср* (*последствие*) consequence; (*Юр*) investigation
сле́дующий *прил* next ▷ *мест* following; **на сле́дующий день** the next day
сл|еза́ (**-езы́**; *nom pl* **-ёзы**, *dat pl* **-еза́м**) *ж* tear
слеза́|ть (**-ю**) *несов от* **слезть**
слез|и́ться (*3sg* **-и́тся**) *несов возв* (*глаза*) to water
слезоточи́вый *прил*: **слезоточи́вый газ** tear gas
слез|ть (**-у, -ешь**; *pt* **-, ла**, *impf* **слеза́ть**) *сов* (*кожа, краска*) to peel off; **слеза́ть** (*perf* **слезть**) (**с** *+gen*) (*с дерева*) to climb down
слеп|и́ть (*3sg* **-и́т**) *сов перех*: **слепи́ть глаза́ кому́-н** to blind sb
сл|епи́ть (**-еплю́, -е́пишь**) *сов от* **лепи́ть**
сле́пн|уть (**-у**; *perf* **осле́пнуть**) *несов* to go blind
слеп|о́й *прил* blind ▷ (**-о́го**) *м* blind person (*мн* people)
сле́сар|ь (**-я**; *nom pl* **-я́**, *gen pl* **-е́й**) *м* maintenance man
сле|те́ть (**-чу́, -ти́шь**; *impf* **слета́ть**) *сов*: **слете́ть** (**с** *+gen*) (*птица*) to fly down (from); **слете́ться** (*impf* **слета́ться**) *сов возв* (*птицы*) to flock
сли́в|а (**-ы**) *ж* (*дерево*) plum (tree); (*плод*) plum
слива́|ть(ся) (**-ю(сь)**) *несов от* **сли́ть(ся)**
сли́в|ки (**-ок**) *мн* cream *ед*
сли́вочн|ый *прил* made with cream; **сли́вочное ма́сло** butter
слизист|ый *прил*: **сли́зистая оболо́чка** mucous membrane
сли́п|нуться (*3sg* **-нется**, *pt* **-ся, -лась**, *impf* **слипа́ться**) *сов возв* to stick together
сли|ть (**солью́, сольёшь**; *pt* **-л, -ла́**, *imper* **сле́й(те)**, *impf* **слива́ть**) *сов перех* to pour; (*перен*: *соединить*) to merge; **сли́ться** (*impf* **слива́ться**) *сов возв* to merge
сли́шком *нареч* too; **э́то уже́ сли́шком** (*разг*) that's just too much
слова́рный *прил* (*работа, статья*) dictionary, lexicographic(al); **слова́рный запа́с** vocabulary
слова́р|ь (**-я́**) *м* (*книга*) dictionary; (*запас слов*) vocabulary
слове́сный *прил* oral; (*протест*) verbal
сло́вно *союз* (*как*) like; (*как будто*) as if
сло́в|о (**-а**; *nom pl* **-а́**) *ср* word
сло́вом *вводн сл* in a word
словосочета́ни|е (**-я**) *ср* word combination
слог (**-а**; *nom pl* **-и**, *gen pl* **-о́в**) *м* syllable
слоён|ый *прил*: **слоёное те́сто** puff pastry
сложе́ни|е (**-я**) *ср* (*в математике*) addition; (*фигура*) build

сл|ожи́ть (**-ожу́, -о́жишь**; *impf* **скла́дывать**) *сов перех* (*вещи*) to put; (*чемодан итп*) to pack; (*придавая форму*) to fold (up) ▷ (*impf* **скла́дывать** *или* **слага́ть**) (*числа*) to add (up); (*песню, стихи*) to make up; **сиде́ть** (*impf*) **сложа́ ру́ки** to sit back and do nothing; **сложи́ться** (*impf* **скла́дываться**) *сов возв* (*ситуация*) to arise; (*характер*) to form; (*зонт, палатка*) to fold up; (*впечатление*) to be formed

сло́жно *нареч* (*делать*) in a complicated way ▷ *как сказ* it's difficult

сло́жност|ь (**-и**) *ж* (*многообразие*) complexity; (*обычно мн*: *трудность*) difficulty; **в о́бщей сло́жности** all in all

сло́жный *прил* complex; (*узор*) intricate; (*трудный*) difficult

сло|й (**-я**; *nom pl* **-и́**) *м* layer

слома́|ть(ся) (**-ю(сь)**) *сов от* **лома́ть(ся)**

слом|и́ть (**-лю́, -ишь**) *сов перех* to break; **сломя́ го́лову** (*разг*) at breakneck speed; **сломи́ться** *сов возв* (*перен*: *человек*) to crack

слон (**-а́**) *м* elephant; (*Шахматы*) bishop; **слон|ёнок** (**-ёнка**; *nom pl* **-я́та**, *gen pl* **-я́т**) *м* elephant calf (*мн* calves); **слони́х|а** (**-и**) *ж* cow (*elephant*); **слоно́в|ый** *прил* elephant; **слоно́вая кость** ivory

слуг|а́ (**-и́**; *nom pl* **-и**) *м* servant; **служа́н|ка** (**-ки**; *gen pl* **-ок**) *ж* maid

слу́жащ|ий (**-его**) *м* white collar worker; **госуда́рственный слу́жащий** civil servant; **конто́рский слу́жащий** clerk

слу́жб|а (**-ы**) *ж* service; (*работа*) work; (*орган*) agency; **срок слу́жбы** durability; **Слу́жба бы́та** consumer services; **Слу́жба за́нятости** ≈ Employment Agency

служе́бный *прил* (*дела итп*) official

служи́тел|ь (**-я**) *м* (*в музее, на автозаправке*) attendant; (*в зоопарке*) keeper; **служи́тель це́ркви** clergyman (*мн* clergymen)

сл|ужи́ть (**-ужу́, -у́жишь**) *несов* to serve; (*в банке*) to work; **чем могу́ служи́ть?** what can I do for you?

слух (**-а**) *м* hearing; (*музыкальный*) ear; (*известие*) rumour (*Brit*), rumor (*US*)

слухово́й *прил* (*нерв, орган*) auditory; **слухово́й аппара́т** hearing aid

слу́ча|й (**-я**) *м* occasion; (*случайность*) chance; **в слу́чае** *+gen* in the event of; **во вся́ком слу́чае** in any case; **на вся́кий слу́чай** just in case

случа́йно *нареч* by chance ▷ *вводн сл* by any chance

случа́йност|ь (**-и**) *ж* chance

случа́йный *прил* (*встреча*) chance

случ|и́ться (**-у́сь, -и́шься**; *impf* **случа́ться**) *сов возв* to happen

слу́шани|я (**-й**) *мн* hearing *ед*

слу́шател|ь (**-я**) *м* listener; (*Просвещ*) student

слу́ша|ть (**-ю**) *несов перех* (*музыку, речь*) to listen to; (*Юр*) to hear ▷ (*perf* **послу́шать**) (*совет*) to listen to; **слу́шаться** (*perf* **послу́шаться**) *несов возв*: **слу́шаться** *+gen* to obey; (*совета*) to follow

слы́ш|ать (**-у, -ишь**) *несов* to hear ▷ (*perf* **услы́шать**) *перех* to hear; **слы́шать** (*impf*) **о** *+prp* to hear about; **он пло́хо слы́шит** he's hard of hearing; **слы́шаться** *несов возв* to be heard

слы́шно *как сказ* it can be heard; **мне ничего́ не слы́шно** I can't hear a thing; **о ней ничего́ не слы́шно** there's no news of her

слы́шный *прил* audible

слюн|а́ (**-ы́**) *ж* saliva

слю́н|ки (**-ок**) *мн*: **у меня́ слю́нки теку́т** my mouth's watering

см *сокр* (= *сантиме́тр*) cm (= *centimetre* (*Brit*), centimeter (*US*))

смайл (**-а**) *м* (*Комп*) emoticon

смартфо́н (**-а**) *м* smart phone

сма́тыва|ть (**-ю**) *несов от* **смота́ть**

смахн|у́ть (**-у́, -ёшь**; *impf* **сма́хивать**) *сов перех* to brush off

сме́жный *прил* (*комната*) adjoining, adjacent; (*предприятие*) affiliated

смеле́|ть (**-ю**; *perf* **осмеле́ть**) *несов* to grow bolder

сме́лост|ь (**-и**) *ж* (*храбрость*) courage, bravery

сме́лый *прил* courageous, brave; (*идея, проект*) ambitious

сме́н|а (**-ы**) *ж* (*руководства*) change; (*на производстве*) shift

см|ени́ть (**-еню́, -е́нишь**; *impf* **сменя́ть**) *сов перех* to change; (*коллегу*) to relieve; **смени́ться** (*impf* **сменя́ться**) *сов возв* (*руководство*) to change

смерте́льный *прил* mortal; (*скука*) deadly; **смерте́льный слу́чай** fatality

сме́ртн|ый *прил* mortal; (*разг*: *скука*) deadly; **сме́ртный пригово́р** death sentence; **сме́ртная казнь** the death penalty, capital punishment

смерт|ь (**-и**) *ж* death; **я уста́л до́ сме́рти** I am dead tired

смеси́тел|ь (**-я**) *м* mixer

сме|си́ть (**-шу́, -сишь**) *сов от* **меси́ть**

см|ести́ (**-ету́, -етёшь**; *pt* **-ёл, -ела́, -ело́**, *impf* **смета́ть**) *сов перех* to sweep

сме|сти́ть (**-щу́, -сти́шь**; *impf* **смеща́ть**) *сов перех* (*уволить*) to remove; **смести́ться** (*impf* **смеща́ться**) *сов возв* to shift

смес|ь (**-и**) *ж* mixture; **моло́чная смесь** powdered baby milk

сме́т|а (**-ы**) *ж* (*Экон*) estimate

смета́н|а (**-ы**) *ж* sour cream

смета́|ть (**-ю**) *несов от* **смести́**

сме|ть (**-ю**; *perf* **посме́ть**) *несов +infin* to dare to do

смех (**-а**) *м* laughter

смехотво́рный *прил* ludicrous

смеша́|ть (**-ю**) *сов от* **меша́ть** ▷ (*impf* **сме́шивать**) *перех* (*спутать*) to mix up; **смеша́ться** *сов от* **меша́ться** ▷ (*impf* **сме́шиваться**) *возв* (*слиться*) to mingle; (*краски, цвета*) to blend

смеш|и́ть (**-у́, -и́шь**; *perf* **насмеши́ть** *или* **рассмеши́ть**) *несов перех*: **смеши́ть кого́-н** to make sb laugh

смешно́ *нареч* (*смотреться*) funny ▷ *как сказ* it's funny; (*глупо*) it's ludicrous

смешно́й *прил* funny

смеща́|ть(ся) (**-ю(сь)**) *несов от* **смести́ть(ся)**

смеще́ни|е (**-я**) *ср* (*руководства*) removal; (*понятий, критериев*) shift

сме|я́ться (**-ю́сь**) *несов возв* to laugh

СМИ *сокр* (= *сре́дства ма́ссовой информа́ции*) mass media

смир|и́ть (**-ю́, -и́шь**; *impf* **смиря́ть**) *сов перех* to suppress;

смири́ться (*impf* **смиря́ться**) *сов возв* (*покориться*) to submit; (*примириться*): **смири́ться с** *+instr* to resign o.s. to
сми́рно *нареч* (*сидеть, вести себя*) quietly; (*Воен*): **сми́рно!** attention!
смог *etc сов см* **смочь**
смо́жешь *etc сов см* **смочь**
смол|а́ (**-ы́**; *nom pl* **-ы**) *ж* (*дерево*) resin; (*дёготь*) tar
смо́лк|нуть (**-ну**; *pt* **-, -ла**, *impf* **смолка́ть**) *сов* to fade away
сморка́|ть (**-ю**; *perf* **вы́сморкать**) *несов перех*: **сморка́ть нос** to blow one's nose; **сморка́ться** (*perf* **вы́сморкаться**) *несов возв* to blow one's nose
сморо́дин|а (**-ы**) *ж*: **кра́сная сморо́дина** (*ягоды*) redcurrants *мн*; **чёрная сморо́дина** (*ягоды*) blackcurrants *мн*
смо́рщ|ить(ся) (**-у(сь), -ишь(ся)**) *сов от* **мо́рщить(ся)**
смота́|ть (**-ю**; *impf* **сма́тывать**) *сов перех* to wind
смотр (**-а**) *м* presentation; (*музыкальный*) festival
см|отре́ть (**-отрю́, -о́тришь**; *perf* **посмотре́ть**) *несов* to look ▷ *перех* (*фильм, игру*) to watch; (*картину*) to look at; (*музей, выставку*) to look round; (*следить*): **смотре́ть за** *+instr* to look after; **смотре́ть** (*impf*) **в/на** *+acc* to look onto; **смотря́ по** *+dat* depending on; **смотре́ться** (*perf* **посмотре́ться**) *несов возв*: **смотре́ться в** *+acc* (*в зеркало*) to look at o.s. in
смотри́тел|ь (**-я**) *м* attendant
смо|чь (**-гу́, -жешь** *etc*, **-гут**; *pt* **-г, -гла́, -гло́**) *сов от* **мочь**
SMS *ср нескл* text (message)
смýзи *м нескл* smoothie
сму́т|а (**-ы**) *ж* unrest
сму|ти́ть (**-щу́, -ти́шь**; *impf* **смуща́ть**) *сов перех* to embarrass; **смути́ться** (*impf* **смуща́ться**) *сов возв* to get embarrassed
сму́тный *прил* vague; (*время*) troubled
смуще́ни|е (**-я**) *ср* embarrassment; **смущённый** *прил* embarrassed
смысл (**-а**) *м* sense; (*назначение*) point
см|ыть (**-о́ю, -о́ешь**; *impf* **смыва́ть**) *сов перех* to wash off; (*подлеж*: *волна*) to wash away; **смы́ться** (*impf* **смыва́ться**) *сов возв* to wash off
смыч|о́к (**-ка́**) *м* (*Муз*) bow
смягч|и́ть (**-у́, -и́шь**; *impf* **смягча́ть**) *сов перех* (*кожу, удар*) to soften; (*боль*) to ease; (*наказание*) to mitigate; (*человека*) to appease; **смягчи́ться** (*impf* **смягча́ться**) *сов возв* to soften
смя́ть(ся) (**сомну́(сь), сомнёшь(ся)**) *сов от* **мя́ть(ся)**
сна *etc сущ см* **сон**
снаб|ди́ть (**-жу́, -ди́шь**; *impf* **снабжа́ть**) *сов перех*: **снабди́ть кого́-н/что-н чем-н** to supply sb/sth with sth
снабже́ни|е (**-я**) *ср* supply
сна́йпер (**-а**) *м* sniper
снару́жи *нареч* on the outside; (*закрыть*) from the outside
снаря́д (**-а**) *м* (*Воен*) shell; (*Спорт*) apparatus
снаря|ди́ть (**-жу́, -ди́шь**; *impf* **снаряжа́ть**) *сов перех* to equip; **снаряже́ни|е** (**-я**) *ср* equipment
снача́ла *нареч* at first; (*ещё раз*) all over again
СНГ *м сокр* (= *Содру́жество*

Незави́симых Госуда́рств) CIS (= *Commonwealth of Independent States*)

снег (**-а**; *loc sg* **-у́**, *nom pl* **-а́**) *м* snow; **идёт снег** it's snowing

снегови́к (**-а́**) *м* snowman (*мн* snowmen)

Снегу́роч|ка (**-ки**; *gen pl* **-ек**) *ж* Snow Maiden

Снегу́рочка

The Snow Maiden accompanies Father Christmas on his visits to children's New Year parties, where she organizes games and helps with the important task of giving out the presents.

сне́жный *прил* snow; (*зима*) snowy

снеж|о́к (**-ка́**) *м* snowball

сн|ести́ (**-есу́, -есёшь**; *pt* **-ёс, -есла́, -есло́**, *impf* **сноси́ть**) *сов перех* (*отнести*) to take; (*подлеж*: *буря*) to tear down; (*перен*: *вытерпеть*) to take; (*дом*) to demolish

снижа́|ть(ся) (**-ю(сь)**) *несов от* **сни́зить(ся)**

сниже́ни|е (**-я**) *ср* (*цен итп*) lowering; (*самолёта*) descent; (*выдачи*) reduction

сни́|зить (**-жу, -зишь**; *impf* **снижа́ть**) *сов перех* (*цены, давление итп*) to lower; (*скорость*) to reduce; **сни́зиться** (*impf* **снижа́ться**) *сов возв* to fall; (*самолёт*) to descend

сни́зу *нареч* (*внизу*) at the bottom; (*о направлении*) from the bottom

снима́|ть(ся) (**-ю(сь)**) *несов от* **снять(ся)**

сни́м|ок (**-ка**) *м* (*Фото*) snap(shot)

сн|и́ться (**-юсь, -и́шься**; *perf* **присни́ться**) *несов безл*: **мне сни́лся стра́шный сон** I was having a terrible dream; **мне сни́лось, что я в гора́х** I dreamt I was in the mountains; **ты ча́сто сни́шься мне** I often dream of you

сно́ва *нареч* again

снос (**-а**) *м* demolition

сно́с|ка (**-ки**; *gen pl* **-ок**) *ж* footnote

снотво́рн|ое (**-ого**) *ср* sleeping pill

снох|а́ (**-и́**) *ж* daughter-in-law (*of husband's father*)

сн|ять (**-иму́, -и́мешь**; *impf* **снима́ть**) *сов перех* to take down; (*плод*) to pick; (*одежду*) to take off; (*запрет, ответственность*) to remove; (*фотографировать*) to photograph; (*копию*) to make; (*нанять*) to rent; (*уволить*) to dismiss; **снима́ть** (*perf* **снять**) **фотогра́фию** to take a picture; **снима́ть** (*perf* **снять**) **фильм** to shoot a film; **сня́ться** (*impf* **снима́ться**) *сов возв* (*сфотографироваться*) to have one's photograph taken; (*в фильме*) to appear

со *предл* = **с**

соба́к|а (**-и**) *ж* dog

собе́с (**-а**) *м* social security; (*орган*) social security department

собесе́дник (**-а**) *м*: **мой собесе́дник замолча́л** the person I was talking to fell silent

собесе́довани|е (**-я**) *ср* interview

собира́тел|ь (**-я**) *м* collector

собира́|ть (**-ю**) *несов от* **собра́ть**; **собира́ться** *несов от* **собра́ться** ▷ *возв*: **я собира́юсь пойти́ туда́** I'm going to go there

соблазн|и́ть (**-ю́, -и́шь**; *impf*

С

соблазня́ть) *сов перех* to seduce; (*прельстить*): **соблазни́ть кого́-н чем-н** to tempt sb with sth; **соблазни́ться** (*impf* **соблазня́ться**) *сов возв*: **соблазни́ться** *+instr/+infin* to be tempted by/to do

соблюда́|ть (**-ю**) *несов от* **соблюсти́** ▷ *перех* (*дисциплину, порядок*) to maintain

соблю|сти́ (**-ду́, -дёшь**) *сов от* **блюсти́** ▷ (*impf* **соблюда́ть**) *перех* (*закон, правила*) to observe

соболе́зновани|е (**-я**) *ср* condolences *мн*

собо́р (**-а**) *м* cathedral

СОБР (**-а**) *м сокр* (= *Сво́дный отря́д бы́строго реаги́рования*) flying squad

собра́ни|е (**-я**) *ср* meeting; (*Полит*) assembly; (*картин итп*) collection; **собра́ние сочине́ний** collected works

соб|ра́ть (**-еру́, -ерёшь**; *pt* **-ра́л, -рала́, -ра́ло**, *impf* **собира́ть**) *сов перех* to gather (together); (*ягоды, грибы*) to pick; (*механизм*) to assemble; (*налоги, подписи*) to collect; **собра́ться** (*impf* **собира́ться**) *сов возв* (*гости*) to assemble, gather; (*приготовиться*): **собра́ться** *+infin* to get ready to do; **собира́ться** (*perf* **собра́ться**) **с** *+instr* (*с силами, с мыслями*) to gather

собро́в|ец (**-ца**) *м* member of the flying squad

со́бственник (**-а**) *м* owner

со́бственно *част* actually ▷ *вводн сл*: **со́бственно (говоря́)** as a matter of fact

со́бственност|ь (**-и**) *ж* property; **со́бственный** *прил* (one's) own

собы́ти|е (**-я**) *ср* event

сов|а́ (**-ы́**; *nom pl* **-ы**) *ж* owl

соверша́|ть(ся) (**-ю**) *несов от* **соверши́ть(ся)**

соверше́ни|е (**-я**) *ср* (*сделки*) conclusion; (*преступления*) committing

соверше́нно *нареч* (*очень хорошо*) perfectly; (*совсем*) absolutely, completely

совершенноле́тн|ий *прил*: **стать совершенноле́тним** to come of age

соверше́нный *прил* (*хороший*) perfect; (*абсолютный*) absolute, complete; **соверше́нный вид** (*Линг*) perfective (aspect); **соверше́нств|о** (**-а**) *ср* perfection; **соверше́нств|овать** (**-ую**; *perf* **усоверше́нствовать**) *несов перех* to perfect; **соверше́нствоваться** (*perf* **усоверше́нствоваться**) *несов возв*: **соверше́нствоваться в** *+prp* to perfect

соверш|и́ть (**-у́, -и́шь**; *impf* **соверша́ть**) *сов перех* to make; (*сделку*) to conclude; (*преступление*) to commit; (*обряд, подвиг*) to perform; **соверши́ться** (*impf* **соверша́ться**) *сов возв* (*событие*) to take place

со́вест|ь (**-и**) *ж* conscience; **на со́весть** (*сделанный*) very well

сове́т (**-а**) *м* advice *только ед*; (*военный*) council; **сове́тник** (**-а**) *м* (*юстиции итп*) councillor; (*президента*) adviser

сове́т|овать (**-ую**; *perf* **посове́товать**) *несов*: **сове́товать кому́-н** *+infin* to advise sb to do; **сове́товаться** (*perf* **посове́товаться**) *несов возв*: **сове́товаться с кем-н** (*с другом*) to ask sb's advice; (*с юристом*) to consult sb

сове́тский *прил* Soviet
совеща́ни|е (**-я**) *ср* (*собрание*) meeting; (*конгресс*) conference
совеща́|ться (**-юсь**) *несов возв* to deliberate
совмести́мый *прил* compatible
совме|сти́ть (**-щу́, -сти́шь**; *impf* **совмеща́ть**) *сов перех* to combine
совме́стн|ый *прил* (*общий*) joint
сов|о́к (**-ка́**) *м* (*для мусора*) dustpan; (*для муки*) scoop
совоку́пност|ь (**-и**) *ж* combination; **в совоку́пности** in total
совоку́пный *прил* (*усилия*) joint
совпа́|сть (*3sg* **-дёт**, *impf* **совпада́ть**) *сов* (*события*) to coincide; (*данные, цифры итп*) to tally; (*интересы, мнения*) to meet
совр|а́ть (**-у́, -ёшь**) *сов от* **врать**
совреме́нник (**-а**) *м* contemporary
совреме́нност|ь (**-и**) *ж* the present day; (*идей*) modernity
совреме́нный *прил* contemporary; (*техника*) up-to-date; (*человек, идеи*) modern
совсе́м *нареч* (*новый*) completely; (*молодой*) very; (*нисколько: не пригодный, не нужный*) totally; **не совсе́м** not quite
согла́си|е (**-я**) *ср* consent; (*в семье*) harmony, accord
согла|си́ться (**-шу́сь, -си́шься**; *impf* **соглаша́ться**) *сов возв* to agree
согла́сно *предл*: **согла́сно** *+dat* *или* **с** *+instr* in accordance with
согла́сн|ый (**-ого**) *м* (*также* **согла́сный звук**) consonant ▷ *прил*: **согла́сный на** *+acc* (*на условия*) agreeable to; **Вы согла́сны (со мной)?** do you agree (with me)?
соглас|ова́ть (**-у́ю**; *impf* **согласо́вывать**) *сов перех* (*действия*) to coordinate; (*обговорить*): **согласова́ть что-н с** *+instr* (*план, цену*) to agree sth with; **согласова́ться** *(не)сов возв*: **согласова́ться с** *+instr* to correspond with
соглаша́|ться (**-юсь**) *несов от* **согласи́ться**
соглаше́ни|е (**-я**) *ср* agreement
согн|у́ть (**-у́, -ёшь**) *сов от* **гнуть**; **сгиба́ть**
согре́|ть (**-ю**; *impf* **согрева́ть**) *сов перех* (*воду*) to heat up; (*ноги, руки*) to warm up; **согре́ться** (*impf* **согрева́ться**) *сов возв* to warm up; (*вода*) to heat up
со́д|а (**-ы**) *ж* soda
соде́йстви|е (**-я**) *ср* assistance
соде́йств|овать (**-ую**) *(не)сов* *+dat* to assist
содержа́ни|е (**-я**) *ср* (*семьи, детей*) upkeep; (*магазина, фермы*) keeping; (*книги*) contents *мн*; (*сахара, витаминов*) content; (*оглавление*) (table of) contents *мн*
содержа́тельный *прил* (*статья, доклад*) informative
сод|ержа́ть (**-ержу́, -е́ржишь**) *несов перех* (*детей, родителей, магазин*) to keep; (*ресторан*) to own; (*сахар, ошибки, информацию итп*) to contain; **содержа́ться** *несов возв* (*под арестом*) to be held
содр|а́ть (**сдеру́, сдерёшь**; *pt* **-а́л, -ала́**, *impf* **сдира́ть**) *сов перех* (*слой, одежду*) to tear off
содру́жеств|о (**-а**) *ср* (*дружба*) cooperation; (*союз*) commonwealth; **Содру́жество**

Незави́симых Госуда́рств the Commonwealth of Independent States
со́евый *прил* soya
соедин|и́ть (**-ю́, -и́шь**; *impf* **соединя́ть**) *сов перех* (*силы, детали*) to join; (*людей*) to unite; (*провода, трубы, по телефону*) to connect; (*города*) to link; **соедини́ться** (*impf* **соединя́ться**) *сов возв* (*люди, отряды*) to join together
сожале́ни|е (**-я**) *ср* (*сострадание*) pity; **сожале́ние (о +prp)** (*о прошлом, о потере*) regret (about); **к сожале́нию** unfortunately
сожале́|ть (**-ю**) *несов*: **сожале́ть о чём-н/, что** to regret sth/that
созвон|и́ться (**-ю́сь, -и́шься**; *impf* **созва́ниваться**) *сов возв*: **созвони́ться с** *+instr* to phone (*Brit*) *или* call (*US*)
созда|ва́ть(ся) (**-ю́, -ёшь**) *несов от* **созда́ть(ся)**
созда́ни|е (**-я**) *ср* creation; (*существо*) creature; **созда́тел|ь** (**-я**) *м* creator
созда́ть (*как* **дать**; см *Table 16*; *impf* **создава́ть**) *сов перех* to create; **созда́ться** (*impf* **создава́ться**) *сов возв* (*обстановка*) to emerge; (*впечатление*) to be created
созна|ва́ть (**-ю́, -ёшь**) *несов от* **созна́ть** ▷ *перех* to be aware of; **сознава́ться** *несов от* **созна́ться**
созна́ни|е (**-я**) *ср* consciousness; (*вины, долга*) awareness; **приходи́ть** (*perf* **прийти́**) **в созна́ние** to come round
созна́тельност|ь (**-и**) *ж* awareness; **созна́тельный** *прил* (*человек, возраст*) mature; (*жизнь*) adult; (*обман, поступок*) intentional
созна́|ть (**-ю**; *impf* **сознава́ть**) *сов перех* (*вину, долг*) to realize; **созна́ться** (*impf* **сознава́ться**) *сов возв*: **созна́ться (в** *+prp*) (*в ошибке*) to admit (to); (*в преступлении*) to confess (to)
созре́|ть (**-ю**) *сов от* **зреть**
созыва́|ть (**-ю**) *несов от* **созва́ть**
сойти́ (*как* **идти́**; см *Table 18*; *impf* **сходи́ть**) *сов* (*с горы, с лестницы*) to go down; (*с дороги*) to leave; (*разг*): **сойти́ с** *+instr* (*с поезда, с автобуса*) to get off; **сходи́ть** (*perf* **сойти́**) **с ума́** to go mad; **сойти́сь** (*impf* **сходи́ться**) *сов возв* (*собраться*) to gather; (*цифры, показания*) to tally
сок (**-а**) *м* juice
сокра|ти́ть (**-щу́, -ти́шь**; *impf* **сокраща́ть**) *сов перех* to shorten; (*расходы*) to reduce; **сократи́ться** (*impf* **сокраща́ться**) *сов возв* (*расстояние, сроки*) to be shortened; (*расходы, снабжение*) to be reduced; **сокраще́ни|е** (**-я**) *ср* (*см глаг*) shortening; reduction; (*сокращённое название*) abbreviation; (*также* **сокраще́ние шта́тов**) staff reduction
сокро́вищ|е (**-а**) *ср* treasure
соку́рсник (**-а**) *м*: **он мой соку́рсник** he is in my year
сол|га́ть (**-гу́, -жёшь** *etc*, **-гу́т**) *сов от* **лгать**
солда́т (**-а**; *gen pl* **-**) *м* soldier; **солда́тик** (**-а**) *м* (*игрушка*) toy soldier
солёный *прил* (*пища*) salty; (*овощи*) pickled in brine; (*вода*) salt
соли́дный *прил* (*постройка*) solid; (*фирма*) established
соли́ст (**-а**) *м* soloist

сол|и́ть (**-ю́, -ишь**; *perf* **посоли́ть**) *несов перех* to salt; (*засаливать*) to preserve in brine
со́лнечн|ый *прил* solar; (*день, погода*) sunny; **со́лнечный уда́р** sunstroke; **со́лнечные очки́** sunglasses
со́лнц|е (**-а**) *ср* sun
со́ло *ср нескл, нареч* solo
соло́м|а (**-ы**) *ж* straw; **соло́менный** *прил* (*шляпа*) straw
соло́н|ка (**-ки**; *gen pl* **-ок**) *ж* saltcellar
сол|ь (**-и**) *ж* salt
со́льный *прил* solo
сомнева́|ться (**-юсь**) *несов возв*: **сомнева́ться в чём-н/, что** to doubt sth/that
сомне́ни|е (**-я**) *ср* doubt; **сомни́тельный** *прил* (*дело, личность*) shady; (*предложение, знакомство*) dubious
сон (**сна**) *м* sleep; (*сновидение*) dream; **со́нный** *прил* (*заспанный*) sleepy
соображá|ть (**-ю**) *несов от* **сообрази́ть**
соображе́ни|е (**-я**) *ср* (*мысль*) idea; (*обычно мн*: *мотивы*) reasoning
сообрази́тельный *прил* smart
сообра|зи́ть (**-жу́, -зи́шь**; *impf* **соображáть**) *сов* to work out
сообща́ *нареч* together
сообща́|ть (**-ю**) *несов от* **сообщи́ть**
сообще́ни|е (**-я**) *ср* (*информация*) report; (*правительственное*) announcement; (*связь*) communications *мн*
soо́бществ|о (**-а**) *ср* association; **мирово́е** *или* **междунаро́дное соо́бщество** international community
сообщ|и́ть (**-у́, -и́шь**; *impf* **сообща́ть**) *сов*: **сообщи́ть кому́-н о** *+prp* to inform sb of ▷ *перех* (*новости, тайну*) to tell
соо́бщник (**-а**) *м* accomplice
соотве́тственно *предл* (*+dat*: *обстановке*) according to; **соотве́тственный** *прил* (*оплата*) appropriate; (*результаты*) fitting
соотве́тстви|е (**-я**) *ср* (*интересов, стилей итп*) correspondence; **в соотве́тствии с** *+instr* in accordance with; **соотве́тств|овать** (**-ую**) *несов +dat* to correspond to; (*требованиям*) to meet
соотве́тствующий *прил* appropriate
соотноше́ни|е (**-я**) *ср* correlation
сопе́рник (**-а**) *м* rival; (*в спорте*) competitor
сопе́рнича|ть (**-ю**) *несов*: **сопе́рничать с кем-н в чём-н** to rival sb in sth
сопра́но *ср нескл* soprano
сопровожда́|ть (**-ю**; *perf* **сопроводи́ть**) *несов перех* to accompany; **сопровожде́ни|е** (**-я**) *ср*: **в сопровожде́нии** *+gen* accompanied by
сопротивле́ни|е (**-я**) *ср* resistance
сопротивля́|ться (**-юсь**) *несов возв +dat* to resist
сор (**-а**) *м* rubbish
сорв|а́ть (**-у́, -ёшь**; *impf* **срыва́ть**) *сов перех* (*цветок, яблоко*) to pick; (*дверь, крышу, одежду*) to tear off; (*лекцию, переговоры*) to sabotage; (*планы*) to frustrate; **сорва́ться** (*impf* **срыва́ться**) *сов возв* (*человек*) to lose one's temper; (*планы*) to be

С

frustrated; **срыва́ться** (*perf* **сорва́ться**) **с** *+gen* (*с петель*) to come away from

соревнова́ни|е (**-я**) *ср* competition

соревн|ова́ться (**-у́юсь**) *несов возв* to compete

сор|и́ть (**-ю́, -и́шь**; *perf* **насори́ть**) *несов* to make a mess

сорня́к (**-а́**) *м* weed

со́рок (**-а́**; см *Table 27*) *чис* forty

сороково́й *чис* fortieth

сорт (**-а**; *nom pl* **-а́**) *м* sort; (*пшеницы*) grade; **сортир|ова́ть** (**-у́ю**; *perf* **рассортирова́ть**) *несов перех* to sort; (*по качеству*) to grade

сос|а́ть (**-у́, -ёшь**) *несов перех* to suck

сосе́д (**-а**; *nom pl* **-и**, *gen pl* **-ей**) *м* neighbour (*Brit*), neighbor (*US*); **сосе́дний** *прил* neighbouring (*Brit*), neighboring (*US*); **сосе́дств|о** (**-а**) *ср*: **жить по сосе́дству** to live nearby; **в сосе́дстве с** *+instr* near

соси́с|ка (**-ки**; *gen pl* **-ок**) *ж* sausage

соск|очи́ть (**-очу́, -о́чишь**; *impf* **соска́кивать**) *сов* to jump off

соску́ч|иться (**-усь, -ишься**) *сов возв* to be bored; **соску́читься** (*perf*) **по** *+dat* (*по детям*) to miss

сослага́тельн|ый *прил*: **сослага́тельное наклоне́ние** subjunctive mood

со|сла́ть (**-шлю́, -шлёшь**; *impf* **ссыла́ть**) *сов перех* to exile; **сосла́ться** (*impf* **ссыла́ться**) *сов возв*: **сосла́ться на** *+acc* to refer to

сослужи́в|ец (**-ца**) *м* colleague

сос|на́ (**-ны́**; *nom pl* **-ны**, *gen pl* **-ен**) *ж* pine (tree); **сосно́вый** *прил* pine

сос|о́к (**-ка́**) *м* nipple

сосредото́ч|ить (**-у, -ишь**; *impf* **сосредота́чивать**) *сов перех* to concentrate; **сосредото́читься** (*impf* **сосредота́чиваться**) *сов возв* (*войска*) to be concentrated; (*внимание*): **сосредото́читься на** *+acc* to focus on

соста́в (**-а**) *м* (*классовый*) structure; (*+gen*: *комитета*) members *мн* of; (*вещества*) composition of

соста́в|ить (**-лю, -ишь**; *impf* **составля́ть**) *сов перех* (*словарь, список*) to compile; (*план*) to draw up; (*сумму*) to constitute; (*команду*) to put together; **соста́виться** (*impf* **составля́ться**) *сов возв* to be formed

составн|о́й *прил*: **составна́я часть** component

соста́р|ить (**-ю, -ишь**) *сов от* **ста́рить**; **соста́риться** *сов возв* (*человек*) to grow old

состоя́ни|е (**-я**) *ср* state; (*больного*) condition; (*собственность*) fortune; **быть** (*impf*) **в состоя́нии** *+infin* to be able to do

состоя́тельный *прил* (*богатый*) well-off

состо|я́ть (**-ю́, -и́шь**) *несов*: **состоя́ть из** *+gen* (*книга*) to consist of; (*заключаться*): **состоя́ть в** *+prp* to be; (*в партии*) to be a member of; (*+instr*: *директором итп*) to be; **состоя́ться** *несов возв* (*собрание*) to take place

сострада́ни|е (**-я**) *ср* compassion

состяза́ни|е (**-я**) *ср* contest

состяза́|ться (**-юсь**) *несов возв* to compete

сосу́д (**-а**) *м* vessel

сот *чис см* **сто**
сотворе́ни|е (**-я**) *ср*: **сотворе́ние ми́ра** Creation
со́т|ня (**-ни**; *gen pl* **-ен**) *ж* (*сто*) a hundred
со́тов|ый *прил*: **со́товый телефо́н** mobile phone; **со́товая связь** network
сотру́дник (**-а**) *м* (*служащий*) employee; **нау́чный сотру́дник** research worker; **сотру́днича|ть** (**-ю**) *несов* to cooperate; (*работать*) to work; **сотру́дничеств|о** (**-а**) *ср* (*см глаг*) cooperation; work
сотряс|ти́ (**-у́, -ёшь**; *impf* **сотряса́ть**) *сов перех* to shake; **сотрясти́сь** (*impf* **сотряса́ться**) *сов возв* to shake
со́т|ы (**-ов**) *мн*: (**пчели́ные) со́ты** honeycomb *ед*
со́тый *чис* hundredth
со́ус (**-а**) *м* sauce
соуча́стник (**-а**) *м* accomplice
соф|а́ (**-ы́**; *nom pl* **-ы**) *ж* sofa
со́х|нуть (**-ну**; *pt* **-, -ла**, *perf* **вы́сохнуть**) *несов* to dry; (*растения*) to wither
сохран|и́ть (**-ю́, -и́шь**; *impf* **сохраня́ть**) *сов перех* to preserve; (*Комп*) to save; **сохрани́ться** (*impf* **сохраня́ться**) *сов возв* to be preserved
сохра́нност|ь (**-и**) *ж* (*вкладов, документов*) security; **в (по́лной) сохра́нности** (fully) intact
социа́л-демокра́т (**-а**) *м* social democrat
социали́зм (**-а**) *м* socialism; **социалисти́ческий** *прил* socialist
социа́льн|ый *прил* social; **социа́льная защищённость** social security
социоло́ги|я (**-и**) *ж* sociology
соцсе́т|ь (**-и**) *ж* social networking site
сочета́ни|е (**-я**) *ср* combination
сочета́|ть (**-ю**) *(не)сов перех* to combine; **сочета́ться** *(не)сов возв* (*соединиться*) to combine; (*гармонировать*) to match
сочине́ни|е (**-я**) *ср* (*литературное*) work; (*музыкальное*) composition; (*Просвещ*) essay
сочин|и́ть (**-ю́, -и́шь**; *impf* **сочиня́ть**) *сов перех* (*музыку*) to compose; (*стихи, песню*) to write
со́чный *прил* (*плод*) juicy; (*трава*) lush; (*краски*) vibrant
сочу́встви|е (**-я**) *ср* sympathy
сочу́вств|овать (**-ую**) *несов +dat* to sympathize with
сошёл(ся) *etc сов см* **сойти́(сь)**
сошью́ *итп сов см* **сшить**
сою́з (**-а**) *м* union; (*военный*) alliance; (*Линг*) conjunction; **сою́зник** (**-а**) *м* ally; **сою́зный** *прил* (*армия*) allied
со́|я (**-и**) *ж собир* soya beans *мн*
спад (**-а**) *м* drop; **экономи́ческий спад** recession
спада́|ть (*3sg* **-ет**) *несов от* **спасть**
спазм (**-а**) *м* spasm
спа́льный *прил* (*место*) sleeping; **спа́льный ваго́н** sleeping car; **спа́льный мешо́к** sleeping bag
спа́л|ьня (**-ьни**; *gen pl* **-ен**) *ж* (*комната*) bedroom; (*мебель*) bedroom suite
Спас (**-а**) *м* (*Рел*) the Day of the Saviour (*in Orthodox Church*)
спаса́тельн|ый *прил* (*станция*) rescue; **спаса́тельная ло́дка** lifeboat; **спаса́тельный жиле́т** life jacket; **спаса́тельный по́яс** life belt
спаса́|ть(ся) (**-ю(сь)**) *несов от* **спасти́(сь)**

спасе́ни|е (**-я**) *ср* rescue; (*Рел*) Salvation
спаси́бо *част*: **спаси́бо (Вам)** thank you; **большо́е спаси́бо!** thank you very much!; **спаси́бо за по́мощь** thanks for the help
спас|ти́ (**-у́, -ёшь**; *impf* **спаса́ть**) *сов перех* to save; **спасти́сь** (*impf* **спаса́ться**) *сов возв*: **спасти́сь (от** *+gen*) to escape
спа|сть (*3sg* **-дёт**, *impf* **спада́ть**) *сов* (*вода*) to drop
сп|ать (**-лю, -ишь**) *несов* to sleep; **ложи́ться** (*perf* **лечь**) **спать** to go to bed; **спа́ться** *несов возв*: **мне не спи́тся** I can't (get to) sleep
СПБ *сокр* (= *Санкт-Петербу́рг*) St Petersburg
спекта́кл|ь (**-я**) *м* performance
спектр (**-а**) *м* spectrum
спе́лый *прил* ripe
спе́реди *нареч* in front
спе́рм|а (**-ы**) *ж* sperm
сп|еть (*3sg* **-е́ет**, *perf* **поспе́ть**) *несов* (*фрукты, овощи*) to ripen ▷ (**-ою́, -оёшь**) *сов от* **петь**
спех (**-а**) *м*: **мне не к спе́ху** (*разг*) I'm in no hurry
специализи́р|оваться (**-уюсь**) *(не)сов возв*: **специализи́роваться в** *+prp или* **по** *+dat* to specialize in
специали́ст (**-а**) *м* specialist
специа́льност|ь (**-и**) *ж* (*профессия*) profession
специа́льный *прил* special
специ́фик|а (**-и**) *ж* specific nature
специфи́ческий *прил* specific
спе́ци|я (**-и**) *ж* spice
спецко́р (**-а**) *м сокр* (= *специа́льный корреспонде́нт*) special correspondent
спецку́рс (**-а**) *м сокр* (*в вузе*) (= *специа́льный курс*) *course of lectures in a specialist field*
спецна́з (**-а**) *м* special task force
спецна́зов|ец (**-ца**) *м* member of the special task force
спецоде́жд|а (**-ы**) *ж сокр* (= *специа́льная оде́жда*) work clothes *мн*
спецслу́жб|а (**-ы**) *ж сокр* (*обычно мн*) (= *специа́лньная слу́жба*) special service
спеш|и́ть (**-у́, -и́шь**) *несов* (*часы*) to be fast; (*человек*) to be in a rush; **спеши́ть** (*perf* **поспеши́ть**) *+infin*/**c** *+instr* to be in a hurry to do/with; **спеши́ть** (*impf*) **на по́езд** to rush for the train
спе́шк|а (**-и**) *ж* (*разг*) hurry, rush
спе́шный *прил* urgent
СПИД (**-а**) *м сокр* (= *синдро́м приобретённого иммунодефици́та*) AIDS (= *acquired immune deficiency syndrome*)
спидо́метр (**-а**) *м* speedometer
спи́кер (**-а**) *м* speaker
спин|а́ (**-ы́**; *acc sg* **-у**, *dat sg* **-е́**, *nom pl* **-ы**) *ж* (*человека, животного*) back
спи́н|ка (**-ки**; *gen pl* **-ок**) *ж*, *уменьш от* **спина́**; (*дивана, стула итп*) back; (*кровати*: *верхняя*) headboard; (: *нижняя*) foot
спинно́й *прил* (*позвонок*) spinal; **спинно́й мозг** spinal cord
спира́л|ь (**-и**) *ж* (*линия*) spiral; (*также* **внутрима́точная спира́ль**) coil (*contraceptive*)
спирт (**-а**) *м* (*Хим*) spirit
спиртн|о́е (**-о́го**) *ср* alcohol
спиртно́й *прил*: **спиртно́й напи́ток** alcoholic drink
сп|иса́ть (**-ишу́, -и́шешь**; *impf* **спи́сывать**) *сов перех* to copy; (*Комм*) to write off
спи́с|ок (**-ка**) *м* list

спи́ц|а (**-ы**) *ж* (*для вязания*) knitting needle; (*колеса*) spoke
спи́ч|ка (**-ки**; *gen pl* **-ек**) *ж* match
спла́чива|ть(ся) (**-ю**) *несов от* **сплоти́ть(ся)**
спле́тнича|ть (**-ю**) *несов* to gossip
спле́т|ня (**-ни**; *gen pl* **-ен**) *ж* gossip
спло|ти́ть (**-чу́, -ти́шь**; *impf* **спла́чивать**) *сов перех* to unite; **сплоти́ться** (*impf* **спла́чиваться**) *сов возв* to unite
сплошно́й *прил* (*степь*) continuous; (*перепись*) universal; (*разг*: *неудачи*) utter
сплошь *нареч* (*по всей поверхности*) all over; (*без исключения*) completely; **сплошь и ря́дом** (*разг*) everywhere
сплю *несов см* **спать**
споко́йный *прил* (*улица, жизнь*) quiet; (*море, взгляд*) calm
сполз|ти́ (**-у́, -ёшь**; *pt* **-, -ла́**, *impf* **сполза́ть**) *сов* to climb down
спонси́р|овать (**-ую**) *(не)сов* to sponsor
спо́нсор (**-а**) *м* sponsor
спор (**-а**) *м* debate; (*Юр*) dispute; **на́ спор** (*разг*) as a bet
спо́р|ить (**-ю, -ишь**; *perf* **поспо́рить**) *несов* (*вести спор*) to argue; (*держать пари*) to bet; **спо́рить** (*impf*) **с кем-н о чём-н** *или* **за что-н** (*о наследстве*) to dispute sth with sb
спо́рный *прил* (*дело*) disputed; (*победа*) doubtful; **спо́рный вопро́с** moot point
спорт (**-а**) *м* sport
спортза́л (**-а**) *м сокр* (= *спорти́вный зал*) sports hall
спортсме́н (**-а**) *м* sportsman (*мн* sportsmen)
спо́соб (**-а**) *м* way
спосо́бност|ь (**-и**) *ж* ability
спосо́бный *прил* capable; (*талантливый*) able
спосо́бств|овать (**-ую**) *сов* (*+dat*: *успеху, развитию*) to encourage
спотк|ну́ться (**-у́сь, -ёшься**; *impf* **спотыка́ться**) *сов возв* to trip
спою́ *итп несов см* **спеть**
спра́ва *нареч* to the right; **спра́ва от** *+gen* to the right of
справедли́вост|ь (**-и**) *ж* justice
справедли́вый *прил* fair, just; (*вывод*) correct
спра́виться (*impf* **справля́ться**) *сов возв*: **спра́виться с** *+instr* (*с работой*) to cope with, manage; (*с противником*) to deal with; (*узнавать*): **спра́виться о** *+prp* to enquire *или* ask about
спра́в|ка (**-ки**; *gen pl* **-ок**) *ж* (*сведения*) information; (*документ*) certificate
спра́вочник (**-а**) *м* directory; (*грамматический*) reference book
спра́вочн|ый *прил* (*литература*) reference; **спра́вочное бюро́** information office *или* bureau
спра́шива|ть(ся) (**-ю(сь)**) *несов от* **спроси́ть(ся)**
спрос (**-а**) *м*: **спрос на** *+acc* (*на товары*) demand for; (*требование*): **спрос с** *+gen* (*с родителей*) demands *мн* on; **без спро́са** *или* **спро́су** without permission
спр|оси́ть (**-ошу́, -о́сишь**; *impf* **спра́шивать**) *сов перех* (*дорогу, время*) to ask; (*совета, денег*) to ask for; (*взыскать*): **спроси́ть что-н с** *+gen* to call sb to account for sth; (*осведомиться*): **спроси́ть кого́-н о чём-н** to ask sb about sth; **спра́шивать** (*perf* **спроси́ть**)

ученика́ to question *или* test a pupil; **спроси́ться** (*impf* **спра́шиваться**) *сов возв*: **спроси́ться** *+gen или* **у** *+gen* (*у учителя итп*) to ask permission of

спры́г|нуть (**-ну**; *impf* **спры́гивать**) *сов*: **спры́гнуть с** *+gen* to jump off

спряже́ни|е (**-я**) *ср* (*Линг*) conjugation

спря́|тать(ся) (**-чу(сь), -чешь(ся)**) *сов от* **пря́тать(ся)**

спуска́|ть (**-ю**) *несов от* **спусти́ть** ▷ *перех*: **я не спуска́л глаз с неё** I didn't take my eyes off her; **спуска́ться** *несов от* **спусти́ться**

спу|сти́ть (**-щу́, -стишь**; *impf* **спуска́ть**) *сов перех* to lower; (*собаку*) to let loose; (*газ, воду*) to drain; **спусти́ться** (*impf* **спуска́ться**) *сов возв* to go down

спустя́ *нареч*: **спустя́ три дня/год** three days/a year later

спу́та|ть(ся) (**-ю(сь)**) *сов от* **пу́тать(ся)**

спу́тник (**-а**) *м* (*в пути*) travelling (*Brit*) *или* traveling (*US*) companion; (*Астрономия*) satellite; (*Космос*: *также* **иску́сственный спу́тник**) sputnik, satellite

сравне́ни|е (**-я**) *ср* comparison; **в сравне́нии** *или* **по сравне́нию с** *+instr* compared with

сра́внива|ть (**-ю**) *несов от* **сравни́ть; сравня́ть**

сравни́тельный *прил* comparative

сравн|и́ть (**-ю́, -и́шь**; *impf* **сра́внивать**) *сов перех*: **сравни́ть что-н/кого́-н** (**с** *+instr*) to compare sth/sb (with); **сравни́ться** *сов возв*: **сравни́ться с** *+instr* to compare with

сраже́ни|е (**-я**) *ср* battle

сра́зу *нареч* (*немедленно*) straight away; (*в один приём*) (all) at once

сраст|и́сь (*3sg* **-ётся**, *impf* **сраста́ться**) *сов возв* (*кости*) to knit (together)

сред|а́ (**-ы́**; *nom pl* **-ы**) *ж* medium; (*no pl*: *природная, социальная*) environment ▷ (*acc sg* **-у**) (*день недели*) Wednesday; **окружа́ющая среда́** environment; **охра́на окружа́ющей среды́** conservation

среди́ *предл +gen* in the middle of; (*в числе*) among

средизе́мн|ый *прил*: **Средизе́мное мо́ре** the Mediterranean (Sea)

среднеазиа́тский *прил* Central Asian

средневеко́вый *прил* medieval

среднегодово́й *прил* average annual

сре́дний *прил* average; (*размер*) medium; (*в середине*) middle; (*школа*) secondary

Сре́дняя шко́ла

Children in Russia start school at the age of six or seven. They stay in the same school throughout their education. They can leave school after eight years if they plan to continue into further education. Those who stay on study for a further two or three years before sitting their final exams. On completing the final exams they receive the Certificate of Secondary Education. See also note at **ЕГЭ**.

сре́дств|о (**-а**) *ср* means *мн*; (*лекарство*) remedy

срез (**-а**) *м* (*место*) cut; (*тонкий слой*) section
сре́|зать (**-жу, -жешь**; *impf* **среза́ть**) *сов перех* to cut
срок (**-а**) *м* (*длительность*) time, period; (*дата*) date; **в срок** (*во время*) in time; **после́дний** *или* **преде́льный срок** deadline; **срок го́дности** (*товара*) sell-by date; **срок де́йствия** period of validity
сро́чный *прил* urgent
срыв (**-а**) *м* disruption; (*на экзамене итп*) failure
срыва́|ть(ся) (**-ю(сь)**) *несов от* **сорва́ть(ся)**
сса́дин|а (**-ы**) *ж* scratch
ссо́р|а (**-ы**) *ж* quarrel
ссо́р|ить (**-ю, -ишь**; *perf* **поссо́рить**) *несов перех* (*друзей*) to cause to quarrel; **ссо́риться** (*perf* **поссо́риться**) *несов возв* to quarrel
СССР *м сокр* (*Ист*) (= *Сою́з Сове́тских Социалисти́ческих Респу́блик*) USSR (= *Union of Soviet Socialist Republics*)
ссу́д|а (**-ы**) *ж* loan
ссу|ди́ть (**-жу́, -дишь**; *impf* **ссужа́ть**) *сов перех* (*деньги*) to lend
ссыла́|ть (**-ю**) *несов от* **сосла́ть**; **ссыла́ться** *несов от* **сосла́ться** ▷ *возв*: **ссыла́ясь на** *+acc* with reference to
ссы́л|ка (**-ки**; *gen pl* **-ок**) *ж* exile; (*цитата*) quotation
ст. *сокр* = **ста́нция**
ста *чис см* **сто**
стабилизи́р|овать (**-ую**) *(не)сов перех* to stabilize
стаби́льный *прил* stable
ста́в|ить (**-лю, -ишь**; *perf* **поста́вить**) *несов перех* to put; (*назначать: министром*) to appoint; (*оперу*) to stage; **ста́вить** (*perf* **поста́вить**) **часы́** to set a clock
ста́в|ка (**-ки**; *gen pl* **-ок**) *ж* (*также Комм*) rate; (*Воен*) headquarters *мн*; (*в картах*) stake; (*перен*): **ста́вка на** *+acc* (*расчёт*) reliance on
стадио́н (**-а**) *м* stadium (*мн* stadia)
ста́ди|я (**-и**) *ж* stage
ста́д|о (**-а**; *nom pl* **-а́**) *ср* (*коров*) herd; (*овец*) flock
стаж (**-а**) *м* (*рабочий*) experience
стажир|ова́ться (**-у́юсь**) *несов возв* to work on probation
стажиро́в|ка (**-ки**; *gen pl* **-ок**) *ж* probationary period
стака́н (**-а**) *м* glass; **бума́жный стака́н** paper cup
стал *сов от* **стать**
ста́лкива|ть(ся) (**-ю(сь)**) *несов от* **столкну́ть(ся)**
стал|ь (**-и**) *ж* steel
стам *итп чис см* **сто**
станда́рт (**-а**) *м* standard
стан|ови́ться (**-овлю́сь, -о́вишься**) *несов от* **стать**
становле́ни|е (**-я**) *ср* formation
стан|о́к (**-ка́**) *м* machine (tool)
ста́ну *итп сов см* **стать**
ста́нци|я (**-и**) *ж* station; **телефо́нная ста́нция** telephone exchange
стара́ни|е (**-я**) *ср* effort
стара́|ться (**-юсь**; *perf* **постара́ться**) *несов возв +infin* to try to do
старе́|ть (**-ю**; *perf* **постаре́ть**) *несов* (*человек*) to grow old(er), age ▷ (*perf* **устаре́ть**) (*оборудование*) to become out of date
стари́к (**-а́**) *м* old man
стари́нный *прил* ancient
ста́р|ить (**-ю, -ишь**; *perf* **соста́рить**) *несов перех* to age

старомо́дный *прил* old-fashioned

ста́рост|а (**-ы**) *м* (*курса*) senior student; (*класса*: *мальчик*) head boy; (: *девочка*) head girl; (*клуба*) head, president

ста́рост|ь (**-и**) *ж* old age

старт (**-а**) *м* (*Спорт*) start; (*ракеты*) takeoff; (*место*) takeoff point

старт|ова́ть (**-у́ю**) *(не)сов* (*Спорт*) to start; (*ракета*) to take off

стару́х|а (**-и**) *ж* old woman (*мн* women)

стару́ш|ка (**-ки**; *gen pl* **-ек**) *ж* = **стару́ха**

ста́рше *сравн прил от* **ста́рый** ▷ *как сказ*: **я ста́рше сестры́ на́ год** I am a year older than my sister

старшекла́ссник (**-а**) *м* senior pupil

старшеку́рсник (**-а**) *м* senior student

ста́рший *прил* senior; (*сестра, брат*) elder

ста́рый *прил* old

стати́стик|а (**-и**) *ж* statistics

ста́тус (**-а**) *м* status

ста́ту|я (**-и**) *ж* statue

ста|ть (**-ти**) *ж*: **под стать кому́-н/чему́-н** like sb/sth ▷ (**-ну, -нешь**; *impf* **станови́ться**) *сов* to stand; (*по impf*: *остановиться*) to stop; (*+infin*: *начать*) to begin *или* start doing ▷ *безл* (*наличествовать*): **нас ста́ло бо́льше/тро́е** there are more/three of us; **с како́й ста́ти?** (*разг*) why?; **станови́ться** (*perf* **стать**) *+instr* (*учителем*) to become; **не ста́ло де́нег/сил** I have no more money/energy left; **ста́ло быть** (*значит*) so; **во что бы то ни ста́ло** no matter what

стат|ья́ (**-ьи́**; *gen pl* **-е́й**) *ж* (*в газете*) article; (*в законе, в договоре*) paragraph, clause

ствол (**-а́**) *м* (*дерева*) trunk; (*ружья, пушки*) barrel

сте́б|ель (**-ля**) *м* (*цветка*) stem

стега́|ть (**-ю**; *perf* **простега́ть**) *несов перех* (*одеяло*) to quilt; (*no perf*: *хлыстом*) to lash

стеж|о́к (**-ка́**) *м* stitch

стека́|ть(ся) (*3sg* **-ет(ся)**) *несов от* **сте́чь(ся)**

стекл|и́ть (**-ю́, -и́шь**; *perf* **остекли́ть**) *несов перех* (*окно*) to glaze

стекл|о́ (**-а́**; *nom pl* **стёкла**, *gen pl* **стёкол**) *ср* glass; (*также* **око́нное стекло́**) (window) pane; (*для очков*) lenses *мн* ▷ *собир* (*изделия*) glassware

стёклыш|ко (**-ка**; *gen pl* **-ек**) *ср* (*осколок*) piece of glass

стекля́нный *прил* glass

стел|и́ть (**-ю́, -ишь**; *perf* **постели́ть**) *несов перех* (*скатерть, подстилку*) to spread out ▷ (*perf* **настели́ть**) (*паркет*) to lay; **стели́ть** (*perf* **постели́ть**) **посте́ль** to make up a bed

стемне́|ть (*3sg* **-ет**) *сов от* **темне́ть**

стен|а́ (**-ы́**; *acc sg* **-у**, *dat sg* **-е́**, *nom pl* **-ы**, *dat pl* **-а́м**) *ж* wall

сте́н|ка (**-ки**; *gen pl* **-ок**) *ж*, *уменьш от* **стена́**; (*желудка*: *также Футбол*) wall; (*разг*: *мебель*) wall unit

стенн|о́й *прил* wall; **стенна́я ро́спись** mural

стенографи́р|овать (**-ую**; *perf* **застенографи́ровать**) *несов перех*: **стенографи́ровать что-н** to take sth down in shorthand (*Brit*) *или* stenography (*US*)

стенографи́ст (**-а**) *м* shorthand typist (*Brit*), stenographer (*US*)

сте́пен|ь (**-и**; *gen pl* **-е́й**) *ж*

(*также Просвещ*) degree; (*Мат*) power
степ|ь (**-и**; *gen pl* **-е́й**) *ж* the steppe
стереосисте́м|а (**-ы**) *ж* stereo
стереоти́п (**-а**) *м* stereotype
стере́ть (**сотру́, сотрёшь**; *pt* **стёр, стёрла**, *impf* **стира́ть**) *сов перех* to wipe off; **стере́ться** (*impf* **стира́ться**) *сов возв* (*надпись, краска*) to be worn away; (*подошвы*) to wear down
стер|е́чь (**-егу́, -ежёшь** *итп*, **-егу́т**; *pt* **-ёг, -егла́**) *несов перех* to watch over
стéрж|ень (**-ня**) *м* rod; (*шариковой ручки*) (ink) cartridge
стерилиз|ова́ть (**-у́ю**) *(не)сов перех* to sterilize
стéрлинг (**-а**) *м* (*Экон*) sterling; **10 фу́нтов стéрлингов** 10 pounds sterling
стесни́тельный *прил* shy
стесня́|ться (**-юсь**; *perf* **постесня́ться**) *несов возв*: **стесня́ться** (*+gen*) to be shy (of)
стече́ни|е (**-я**) *ср* (*народа*) gathering; (*случайностей*) combination
стил|ь (**-я**) *м* style
сти́мул (**-а**) *м* incentive, stimulus (*мн* stimuli)
стимули́р|овать (**-ую**) *(не)сов перех* to stimulate; (*работу, прогресс*) to encourage
стипе́нди|я (**-и**) *ж* grant
стира́льный *прил* washing
стира́|ть (**-ю**) *несов от* **стере́ть** ▷ (*perf* **вы́стирать** *или* **постира́ть**) *перех* to wash; **стира́ться** *несов от* **стере́ться**
сти́р|ка (**-ки**) *ж* washing
стиха́|ть (**-ю**) *несов от* **сти́хнуть**
стих|и́ (**-ов**) *мн* (*поэзия*) poetry *ед*
стихи́|я (**-и**) *ж* (*вода, огонь итп*) element; (*рынка*) natural force
сти́х|нуть (**-ну**; *pt* **-, -ла**, *impf* **стиха́ть**) *сов* to die down
стихотворе́ни|е (**-я**) *ср* poem
сто (**ста**; *см Table 27*) *чис* one hundred
стог (**-а**; *nom pl* **-а́**) *м*: **стог се́на** haystack
сто́имост|ь (**-и**) *ж* (*затраты*) cost; (*ценность*) value
сто́|ить (**-ю, -ишь**) *несов (не) перех* (*+acc или +gen*: *денег*) to cost ▷ *неперех* (*+gen*: *внимания, любви*) to be worth ▷ *безл +infin* to be worth doing; **мне ничего́ не сто́ит сде́лать э́то** it's no trouble for me to do it; **спаси́бо! — не сто́ит** thank you! — don't mention it; **сто́ит (то́лько) захоте́ть** you only have to wish
сто́|йка (**-йки**; *gen pl* **-ек**) *ж* (*положение тела*) stance; (*прилавок*) counter
стол (**-а́**) *м* table; (*письменный*) desk
столб (**-а́**) *м* (*пограничный*) post; (*телеграфный*) pole; (*перен*: *пыли*) cloud
сто́лбик (**-а**) *м, уменьш от* **столб**; (*цифр*) column
столе́ти|е (**-я**) *ср* (*срок*) century; (*+gen*: *годовщина*) centenary of
сто́лик (**-а**) *м, уменьш от* **стол**
столи́ц|а (**-ы**) *ж* capital (city)
столкнове́ни|е (**-я**) *ср* clash; (*машин*) collision
столкн|у́ть (**-у́, -ёшь**; *impf* **ста́лкивать**) *сов перех*: **столкну́ть (с +gen)** to push off; (*подлеж*: *случай*) to bring together; **столкну́ться** (*impf* **ста́лкиваться**) *сов возв* (*машины*) to collide; (*интересы, характеры*) to clash; (*встретиться*): **столкну́ться с** *+instr* to come into

С

contact with; (*случайно*) to bump *или* run into; (*с трудностями*) to encounter

столо́в|ая (**-ой**) *ж* (*заведение*) canteen; (*комната*) dining room

столо́в|ый *прил* (*мебель*) dining-room; **столо́вая ло́жка** tablespoon; **столо́вая соль** table salt; **столо́вый серви́з** dinner service

столп|и́ться (*3sg* **-и́тся**) *сов возв* to crowd

столь *нареч* so; **столь же ... ско́лько ...** as ... as ...

сто́льк|о *нареч* (*книг*) so many; (*сахара*) so much ▷ (**-их**) *мест* (*см нареч*) this many; this much

сто́лько-то *нареч* (*книг*) X number of; (*сахара*) X amount of

столя́р (**-а́**) *м* joiner

стомато́лог (**-а**) *м* dental surgeon

стоматологи́ческий *прил* dental

стометро́в|ый *прил*: **стометро́вая диста́нция** one hundred metres (*Brit*) *или* meters (*US*)

стон (**-а**) *м* groan

стон|а́ть (**-у́, -ешь**) *несов* to groan

стоп *межд* stop

стоп|а́ (**-ы́**; *nom pl* **-ы́**) *ж* (*Анат*) sole

сто́п|ка (**-ки**; *gen pl* **-ок**) *ж* (*бумаг*) pile

стоп-кра́н (**-а**) *м* emergency handle (*on train*)

сто́пор (**-а**) *м* (*Тех*) lock

стоп|та́ть (**-чу́, -чешь**; *impf* **ста́птывать**) *сов перех* to wear out; **стопта́ться** (*impf* **ста́птываться**) *сов возв* to wear out

сторож|и́ть (**-у́, -и́шь**) *несов перех* = **стере́чь**

стор|она́ (**-оны́**; *acc sg* **-ону**, *dat sg* **-оне́**, *nom pl* **-оны**, *gen pl* **-о́н**, *dat pl* **-она́м**) *ж* side; (*направление*): **ле́вая/пра́вая сторона́** the left/right; **в стороне́** a little way off; **в сто́рону** *+gen* towards; **э́то о́чень любе́зно с Ва́шей стороны́** that is very kind of you; **с одно́й стороны́ ... с друго́й стороны́ ...** on the one hand ... on the other hand ...

сторо́нник (**-а**) *м* supporter

сто́я *нареч* standing up

стоя́н|ка (**-ки**; *gen pl* **-ок**) *ж* (*остановка*) stop; (*автомобилей*) car park (*Brit*), parking lot (*US*); (*геологов*) camp; **стоя́нка такси́** taxi rank

сто|я́ть (**-ю́, -и́шь**; *imper* **сто́й(те)**) *несов* to stand; (*бездействовать*) to stand idle ▷ (*perf* **постоя́ть**) (*защищать*): **стоя́ть за** *+acc* to stand up for

сто́ящий *прил* (*дело*) worthwhile; (*человек*) worthy

страда́ни|е (**-я**) *ср* suffering

страда́тельный *прил* (*Линг*): **страда́тельный зало́г** passive voice

страда́|ть (**-ю**) *несов* to suffer

стра́ж|а (**-и**) *ж собир* guard; **под стра́жей** in custody

стран|а́ (**-ы́**; *nom pl* **-ы**) *ж* country

страни́ц|а (**-ы**) *ж* page

стра́нно *нареч* strangely ▷ *как сказ* that is strange *или* odd; **мне стра́нно, что ...** I find it strange that ...

стра́нный *прил* strange

стра́стный *прил* passionate

страст|ь (**-и**) *ж* passion

страте́ги|я (**-и**) *ж* strategy

страх (**-а**) *м* fear

страхова́ни|е (**-я**) *ср* insurance; **госуда́рственное страхова́ние** national insurance (*Brit*); **страхова́ние жи́зни** life insurance

страхова́тел|ь (**-я**) *м* *person taking out insurance*

страх|ова́ть (**-у́ю**; *perf* **застрахова́ть**) *несов перех*: **страхова́ть от** *+gen* (*имущество*) to insure (against); (*принимать меры*) to protect (against); **страхова́ться** (*perf* **застрахова́ться**) *несов возв*: **страхова́ться (от** *+gen*) to insure o.s. (against); (*принимать меры*) to protect o.s. (from)

страхо́в|ка (**-ки**; *gen pl* **-ок**) *ж* insurance

страхов|о́й *прил* (*фирма, агент*) insurance; **страхово́й взнос** *или* **страхова́я пре́мия** insurance premium

стра́шно *нареч* (*кричать*) in a frightening way; (*разг*: *усталый, довольный*) terribly ▷ *как сказ* it's frightening; **мне стра́шно** I'm frightened *или* scared

стра́шн|ый *прил* (*фильм, сон*) terrifying; (*холод итп*) terrible, awful; **ничего́ стра́шного** it doesn't matter

стрек|оза́ (**-озы́**; *nom pl* **-о́зы**) *ж* dragonfly (*мн* dragonflies)

стрел|а́ (**-ы́**; *nom pl* **-ы**) *ж* (*для стрельбы*) arrow; (*поезд*) express (train)

стрел|е́ц (**-ьца́**) *м* (*созвездие*): **Стреле́ц** Sagittarius

стре́л|ка (**-ки**; *gen pl* **-ок**) *ж*, *уменьш от* **стрела́**; (*часов*) hand; (*компаса*) needle; (*знак*) arrow

стреля́|ть (**-ю**) *несов*: **стреля́ть (в** *+acc*) to shoot (at) ▷ *перех* (*убивать*) to shoot; **стреля́ться** *несов возв* to shoot o.s.

стреми́тельный *прил* (*движение, атака*) swift; (*изменения*) rapid

стрем|и́ться (**-лю́сь, -и́шься**) *несов возв*: **стреми́ться в/на** *+acc* (*в университет*) to aspire to go to; (*на родину*) to long to go to; (*добиваться*): **стреми́ться к** *+dat* (*к славе*) to strive for

стремле́ни|е (**-я**) *ср*: **стремле́ние (к** *+dat*) striving (for), aspiration (to)

стремя́н|ка (**-ки**; *gen pl* **-ок**) *ж* stepladder

стресс (**-а**) *м* stress

стриж (**-а́**) *м* swift

стри́ж|ка (**-ки**; *gen pl* **-ек**) *ж* (*см глаг*) cutting; mowing; pruning; (*причёска*) haircut

стри|чь (**-гу́, -жёшь** *итп*, **-гу́т**; *pt* **-г, -гла**, *perf* **постри́чь**) *несов перех* (*волосы, траву*) to cut; (*газон*) to mow; (*кусты*) to prune; **стричь (***perf* **постри́чь) кого́-н** to cut sb's hair; **стри́чься** (*perf* **постри́чься**) *несов возв* (*в парикмахерской*) to have one's hair cut

стро́гий *прил* strict; (*причёска, наказание*) severe

строе́ни|е (**-я**) *ср* (*здание*) building; (*организации, вещества*) structure

стро́же *сравн прил от* **стро́гий** ▷ *сравн нареч от* **стро́го**

строи́тел|ь (**-я**) *м* builder

строи́тельный *прил* building, construction

строи́тельств|о (**-а**) *ср* (*зданий*) building, construction

стро́|ить (**-ю, -ишь**; *perf* **вы́строить** *или* **постро́ить**) *несов перех* to build, construct ▷ (*perf* **постро́ить**) (*общество,*

с

семью) to create; (*план*) to make; (*отряд*) to draw up; **строиться** (*perf* **выстроиться**) *несов возв* (*солдаты*) to form up
стро|й (**-я**) *м* (*социальный*) system; (*языка*) structure ▷ (*loc sg* **-ю**) (*Воен*: *шеренга*) line
стро́|йка (**-йки**; *gen pl* **-ек**) *ж* (*место*) building *или* construction site
стро́йный *прил* (*фигура*) shapely; (*человек*) well-built
строк|а́ (**-и́**; *nom pl* **-и**, *dat pl* **-а́м**) *ж* (*в тексте*) line
стро́ч|ка (**-ки**; *gen pl* **-ек**) *ж*, *уменьш от* **строка́**; (*шов*) stitch
строчн|о́й *прил*: **строчна́я бу́ква** lower case *или* small letter
структу́р|а (**-ы**) *ж* structure
струн|а́ (**-ы́**; *nom pl* **-ы**) *ж* string
стручко́в|ый *прил*: **стручко́вый пе́рец** chilli; **стручко́вая фасо́ль** runner beans *мн*
стру|я́ (**-и́**; *nom pl* **-и**) *ж* stream
стряхн|у́ть (**-у́, -ёшь**; *impf* **стря́хивать**) *сов перех* to shake off
студе́нт (**-а**) *м* student
студе́нческий *прил* student; **студе́нческий биле́т** student card
сту́д|ень (**-ня**) *м* jellied meat
сту́ди|я (**-и**) *ж* studio; (*школа*) school (*for actors, dancers, artists etc*); (*мастерская*) workshop
сту́ж|а (**-и**) *ж* severe cold
стук (**-а**) *м* (*в дверь*) knock; (*сердца*) thump; (*падающего предмета*) thud
сту́кн|уть (**-у**) *сов* (*в дверь, в окно*) to knock; (*по столу*) to bang; **сту́кнуться** (*impf* **сту́каться**) *сов возв* to bang o.s.
стул (**-а**; *nom pl* **-ья**, *gen pl* **-ьев**) *м* chair
ступе́н|ь (**-и**) *ж* step ▷ (*gen pl* **-е́й**) (*процесса*) stage
ступе́н|ька (**-ьки**; *gen pl* **-ек**) *ж* step
сту́п|ка (**-ки**; *gen pl* **-ок**) *ж* mortar
ступн|я́ (**-и́**) *ж* (*стопа*) foot (*мн* feet)
стуч|а́ть (**-у́, -и́шь**; *perf* **постуча́ть**) *несов* (*в дверь, в окно*) to knock; (*по столу*) to bang; (*сердце*) to thump; (*зубы*) to chatter; **стуча́ться** (*perf* **постуча́ться**) *несов возв*: **стуча́ться (в** *+acc*) to knock (at); **стуча́ться** (*perf* **постуча́ться**) **к кому́-н** to knock at sb's door
стыд (**-а́**) *м* shame
сты|ди́ть (**-жу́, -ди́шь**; *perf* **пристыди́ть**) *несов перех* to (put to) shame; **стыди́ться** (*perf* **постыди́ться**) *несов возв*: **стыди́ться** *+gen/+infin* to be ashamed of/to do
сты́дно *как сказ* it's a shame; **мне сты́дно** I am ashamed; **как тебе́ не сты́дно!** you ought to be ashamed of yourself!
сты|ть (**-ну, -нешь**; *perf* **осты́ть**) *несов* to go cold ▷ (*perf* **просты́ть**) (*мёрзнуть*) to freeze
стюарде́сс|а (**-ы**) *ж* air hostess
стян|у́ть (**-у́, -ешь**; *impf* **стя́гивать**) *сов перех* (*пояс, шнуровку*) to tighten; (*войска*) to round up
суббо́т|а (**-ы**) *ж* Saturday
субси́ди|я (**-и**) *ж* subsidy
субти́тр (**-а**) *м* subtitle
субъекти́вный *прил* subjective
суве́ни́р (**-а**) *м* souvenir
сувере́нный *прил* sovereign
сугро́б (**-а**) *м* snowdrift
суд (**-а́**) *м* (*орган*) court; (*заседание*) court session; (*процесс*) trial; (*мнение*)

judgement, verdict; **отдава́ть (***perf* **отда́ть) кого́-н под суд** to prosecute sb; **подава́ть (***perf* **пода́ть) на кого́-н в суд** to take sb to court

судебн|ый *прил* (*заседание, органы*) court; (*издержки, практика*) legal; **суде́бное реше́ние** adjudication; **суде́бное де́ло** court case

су|ди́ть (**-жу́, -дишь**) *несов перех* (*преступника*) to try; (*матч*) to referee; (*укорять*) to judge; **су́дя по** *+dat* judging by; **суди́ться** *несов возв*: **суди́ться с кем-н** to be involved in a legal wrangle with sb

су́д|но (**-на**; *nom pl* **-а́**, *gen pl* **-о́в**) *ср* vessel

судове́рф|ь (**-и**) *ж сокр* (*= судостройтельная верфь*) shipyard

судов|о́й *прил*: **судова́я кома́нда** ship's crew; **судово́й журна́л** ship's log

судо́ку *ср нескл* sudoku

судопроизво́дств|о (**-а**) *ср* legal proceedings *мн*

су́дорог|а (**-и**) *ж* (*от боли*) spasm

судострое́ни|е (**-я**) *ср* ship building

судохо́дств|о (**-а**) *ср* navigation

суд|ьба́ (**-ьбы́**; *nom pl* **-ьбы**, *gen pl* **-еб**) *ж* fate; (*будущее*) destiny; **каки́ми судьба́ми!** what brought you here?

суд|ья́ (**-ьи́**; *nom pl* **-ьи**, *gen pl* **-е́й**) *ж* judge; (*Спорт*) referee

суеве́ри|е (**-я**) *ср* superstition

суеве́рный *прил* superstitious

суе|ти́ться (**-чу́сь, -ти́шься**) *несов возв* to fuss (about)

суетли́вый *прил* fussy; (*жизнь, работа*) busy

су́етный *прил* futile; (*хлопотный*) busy; (*человек*) vain

сужа́|ть (**-ю**) *несов от* **су́зить**

сужде́ни|е (**-я**) *ср* (*мнение*) opinion

суждено́ *как сказ*: **(нам) не суждено́ бы́ло встре́титься** we weren't fated to meet

су́|зить (**-жу, -зишь**; *impf* **сужа́ть**) *сов перех* to narrow

су́к|а (**-и**) *ж* bitch (*also !*); **су́кин сын** (*разг*) son of a bitch (*!*)

сумасше́дш|ий *прил* mad; (*разг: успех*) amazing ▷ (**-его**) *м* madman (*мн* madmen)

сумасше́стви|е (**-я**) *ср* madness, lunacy

сумато́х|а (**-и**) *ж* chaos

су́мер|ки (**-ек**) *мн* twilight *ед*, dusk *ед*

суме́|ть (**-ю**) *сов +infin* to manage to do

су́м|ка (**-ки**; *gen pl* **-ок**) *ж* bag

су́мм|а (**-ы**) *ж* sum

сумми́р|овать (**-ую**) *(не)сов перех* (*затраты итп*) to add up; (*информацию*) to summarize

су́моч|ка (**-ки**; *gen pl* **-ек**) *ж, уменьш от* **су́мка**; (*дамская, вечерняя*) handbag

су́мрак (**-а**) *м* gloom

сунду́к (**-а́**) *м* trunk, chest

суп (**-а**; *nom pl* **-ы́**) *м* soup

суперма́ркет (**-а**) *м* supermarket

суперобло́ж|ка (**-ки**; *gen pl* **-ек**) *ж* (dust) jacket

супру́г (**-а**; *nom pl* **-и**) *м* spouse; **супру́ги** husband and wife

супру́г|а (**-и**) *ж* spouse

супру́жеский *прил* marital

сургу́ч (**-а́**) *м* sealing wax

суро́вый *прил* harsh

су́слик (**-а**) *м* ground squirrel (*Brit*), gopher (*US*)

суста́в (**-а**) *м* (*Анат*) joint

су́т|ки (**-ок**) *мн* twenty four hours; **кру́глые су́тки** round the clock

сýточный *прил* twenty-four-hour
сутýл|ить (**-ю, -ишь**; *perf* **ссутýлить**) *несов перех* to hunch; **сутýлиться** (*perf* **ссутýлиться**) *несов возв* to stoop
сут|ь (**-и**) *ж* essence; **суть дéла** the crux of the matter; **по сýти (дéла)** as a matter of fact
сýффикс (**-а**) *м* suffix
сухожи́ли|е (**-я**) *ср* tendon
сухóй *прил* dry; (*засушенный*) dried; **сухóй закóн** prohibition
сухопýтн|ый *прил* land; **сухопýтные войскá** ground forces *мн*
сухофрýкт|ы (**-ов**) *мн* dried fruit *ед*
сýш|а (**-и**) *ж* (dry) land
сýше *сравн прил от* **сухóй**
сушёный *прил* dried
суш|и́ть (**-ý, -ишь**; *perf* **вы́сушить**) *несов перех* to dry; **суши́ться** (*perf* **вы́сушиться**) *несов возв* to dry
сущéственный *прил* essential; (*изменения*) substantial
существи́тельн|ое (**-ого**) *ср* (*также* **и́мя существи́тельное**) noun
существ|ó (**-á**) *ср* (*вопроса, дела итп*) essence ▷ (*nom pl* **-á**) (*животное*) creature; **по существý** (*говорить*) to the point; (*вводн сл*) essentially
существовáни|е (**-я**) *ср* existence; **срéдства к существовáнию** livelihood
существ|овáть (**-ýю**) *несов* to exist
сýщност|ь (**-и**) *ж* essence
СФ *м сокр* (= *Совéт Федерáций*) *upper chamber of Russian parliament*
сфéр|а (**-ы**) *ж* sphere; (*производства, науки*) area; **в сфéре** *+gen* in the field of; **сфéра обслýживания** *или* **услýг** service industry
схва|ти́ть (**-чý, -тишь**) *сов от* **хватáть** ▷ (*impf* **схвáтывать**) *перех* (*мысль, смысл*) to grasp; **схвати́ться** *сов от* **хватáться**
схвáт|ка (**-ки**; *gen pl* **-ок**) *ж* fight; *см также* **схвáтки**
схвáт|ки (**-ок**) *мн* (*Мед*) contractions
схéм|а (**-ы**) *ж* (*метро, улиц*) plan; (*Элек*: *радио итп*) circuit board
схо|ди́ть (**-жý, -дишь**) *сов* (*разг*: *в театр, на прогулку*) to go ▷ *несов от* **сойти́**; **сходи́ться** *несов от* **сойти́сь**
схóдный *прил* similar
схóдств|о (**-а**) *ср* similarity
сцéн|а (**-ы**) *ж* (*подмостки*) stage; (*в пьесе, на улице*) scene
сценáри|й (**-я**) *м* (*фильма*) script
счáстливо *нареч* (*жить, рассмеяться*) happily; **счáстливо отдéлаться** (*perf*) to have a lucky escape
счастли́во *нареч*: **счастли́во!** all the best!; **счастли́во оставáться!** good luck!
счастли́в|ый *прил* happy; (*удачный*) lucky; **счастли́вого пути́!** have a good journey!
счáсть|е (**-я**) *ср* happiness; (*удача*) luck; **к счáстью** luckily, fortunately; **на нáше счáстье** luckily for us
счесть (**сочтý, сочтёшь**; *pt* **счёл, сочлá**) *сов от* **считáть**
счёт (**-а**; *loc sg* **-ý**, *nom pl* **-á**) *м* (*действие*) counting; (*Комм*: *в банке*) account; (: *накладная*) invoice; (*ресторанный, телефонный*) bill; (*no pl*: *Спорт*) score; **в счёт** *+gen* in lieu of; **за счёт** *+gen* (*фирмы*) at the expense

of; (*внедрений итп*) due to; **на счёт кого́-н** at sb's expense; **на э́тот счёт** in this respect; **э́то не в счёт** that doesn't count

счётн|ый *прил*: **счётная маши́на** calculator

счётчик (**-а**) *м* meter

счёт|ы (**-ов**) *мн* (*приспособление*) abacus *ед*; (*деловые*) dealings

счи́танн|ый *прил*: **счи́танные дни/мину́ты** only a few days/ minutes; **счи́танное коли́чество** very few

счита́|ть (**-ю**) *несов* to count ▷ (*perf* **посчита́ть** *или* **сосчита́ть**) *перех* (*деньги итп*) to count ▷ (*perf* **посчита́ть** *или* **счесть**); **счита́ть кого́-н/что-н** *+instr* to regard sb/sth as; **я счита́ю, что ...** I believe *или* think that ...; **счита́ться** *несов возв*: **счита́ться** *+instr* to be considered to be; (*уважать*): **счита́ться с** *+instr* to respect

США *мн сокр* (= *Соединённые Шта́ты Аме́рики*) USA (= *United States of America*)

сшить (**сошью́, сошьёшь**; *imper* **сше́й(те)**) *сов от* **шить** ▷ (*impf* **сшива́ть**) *перех* (*соединить шитьём*) to sew together

съеда́|ть (**-ю**) *несов от* **съесть**

съедо́бный *прил* edible

съезд (**-а**) *м* (*партийный*) congress

съе́з|дить (**-жу, -дишь**) *сов* **to go**

съезжа́|ть(ся) (**-ю(сь)**) *несов от* **съе́хать(ся)**

съем *сов см* **съесть**

съём|ка (**-ки**; *gen pl* **-ок**) *ж* (*обычно мн*: *фильма*) shooting

съёмочн|ый *прил*: **съёмочная площа́дка** film set; **съёмочная гру́ппа** film crew

съёмщик (**-а**) *м* tenant

съесть (*как* **есть**; *см* *Table 15*; *impf* **есть** *или* **съеда́ть**) *сов перех* (*хлеб, кашу*) to eat; (*подлеж*: *моль, тоска*) to eat away at

съе́хать (*как* **е́хать**; *см* *Table 19*; *impf* **съезжа́ть**) *сов*: **съе́хать (с** *+gen*) (*спуститься*) to go down; **съезжа́ть (***perf* **съе́хать) (с кварти́ры)** to move out (of one's flat); **съе́хаться** (*impf* **съезжа́ться**) *сов возв* (*делегаты*) to gather

съешь *сов см* **съесть**

сыгра́|ть (**-ю**) *сов от* **игра́ть**

сын (**-а**; *nom pl* **-овья́**, *gen pl* **-ове́й**, *dat pl* **-овья́м**) *м* son

сы́п|ать (**-лю, -лешь**; *imper* **сы́пь(те)**) *несов перех* to pour; **сы́паться** (*perf* **посы́паться**) *несов возв* to pour

сып|ь (**-и**) *ж* rash

сыр (**-а**; *nom pl* **-ы́**) *м* cheese

сыре́|ть (*3sg* **-ет**) *несов* to get damp

сыро́й *прил* damp; (*мясо, овощи*) raw

сыр|о́к (**-ка́**) *м*: **творо́жный сыро́к** sweet curd cheese; **пла́вленный сыро́к** processed cheese

сырь|ё (**-я́**) *ср собир* raw materials *мн*

сыск (**-а**) *м* criminal detection

сы́тный *прил* filling

сы́тый *прил* (*не голодный*) full

сэконо́м|ить (**-лю, -ишь**) *сов от* **эконо́мить**

сы́щик (**-а**) *м* detective

сюда́ *нареч* here

сюже́т (**-а**) *м* plot

сюрпри́з (**-а**) *м* surprise

ся́ду *итп сов см* **сесть**

Т

та (**той**) *мест см* **тот**
таба́к (**-а́**) *м* tobacco
та́бел|ь (**-я**) *м* (*Просвещ*) school report (*Brit*), report card (*US, Scottish*); (*график*) chart
табле́т|ка (**-ки**; *gen pl* **-ок**) *ж* tablet
табли́ц|а (**-ы**) *ж* table; (*Спорт*) (league) table; **табли́ца умноже́ния** multiplication table
табло́ *ср нескл* (information) board; (*на стадионе*) scoreboard
табу́н (**-а́**) *м* herd
таз (**-а**; *nom pl* **-ы́**) *м* (*сосуд*) basin; (*Анат*) pelvis
таинственный *прил* mysterious
та|и́ть (**-ю́, -и́шь**) *несов перех* to conceal; **таиться** *несов возв* (*скрываться*) to hide; (*опасность*) to lurk
тайг|а́ (**-и́**) *ж* the taiga
тайм (**-а**) *м* (*Спорт*) period; **пе́рвый/второ́й тайм** (*Футбол*) the first/second half
та́йн|а (**-ы**) *ж* (*личная*) secret; (*события*) mystery
тайни́к (**-а́**) *м* hiding place
та́йный *прил* secret

 **КЛЮЧЕВОЕ СЛОВО**

так *нареч* **1** (*указательное*: *таким образом*) like this, this way; **пусть бу́дет так** so be it
2 (*настолько*) so
3 (*разг*: *без какого-н намерения*) for no (special) reason; **почему́ ты пла́чешь? — да так** why are you crying? — for no reason
▷ *част* **1** (*разг*: *ничего*) nothing; **что с тобо́й? — так** what's wrong? — nothing
2 (*разг*: *приблизительно*) about; **дня так че́рез два** in about two days
3 (*например*) for example
4 (*да*) O.K.; **так, всё хорошо́** O.K. that's fine
▷ *союз* **1** (*в таком случае*) then; **е́хать, так е́хать** if we are going, (then) let's go
2 (*таким образом*) so; **так ты пое́дешь?** so, you are going?
3 (*в разделительных вопросах*): **э́то поле́зная кни́га, не так ли?** it's a useful book, isn't it?; **он хоро́ший челове́к, не так ли?** he's a good person, isn't he?
4 (*во фразах*): **и так** (*и без того уже*) anyway; **е́сли** *или* **раз так** in that case; **так и быть!** so be it!; **так и есть** (*разг*) sure enough; **так ему́!** serves him right!; **та́к себе** (*разг*) so-so; **так как** since; **так что** so; **так что́бы** so that

та́кже *союз, нареч* also; **С Но́вым**

Го́дом! — И Вас та́кже Happy New Year! — the same to you
тако́в (**-а́, -о́, -ы́**) *как сказ* such
таково́й *мест*: **как таково́й** as such
так|о́е (**-о́го**) *ср* (*о чём-н интересном, важном итп*) something; **что тут тако́го?** what is so special about that?
так|о́й *мест* such; **что тако́е?** what is it?
та́кс|а (**-ы**) *ж* (*Комм*) (fixed) rate
такси́ *ср нескл* taxi
такси́ст (**-а**) *м* taxi driver
таксопа́рк (**-а**) *м сокр* (= *таксомото́рный парк*) taxi depot
такт (**-а**) *м* (*тактичность*) tact; (*Муз*) bar (*Brit*), measure (*US*)
такти́чный *прил* tactful
тала́нт (**-а**) *м* talent; **тала́нтливый** *прил* talented
та́ли|я (**-и**) *ж* waist
тало́н (**-а**) *м* ticket; (*на продукты итп*) coupon
там *нареч* there; **там посмо́трим** (*разг*) we'll see
тамо́женник (**-а**) *м* customs officer
тамо́женн|ый *прил* (*досмотр*) customs; **тамо́женная по́шлина** customs (duty)
тамо́ж|ня (**-ни**; *gen pl* **-ен**) *ж* customs
тампо́н (**-а**) *м* tampon
та́н|ец (**-ца**) *м* dance
танк (**-а**) *м* tank
та́нкер (**-а**) *м* tanker (*ship*)
танц|ева́ть (**-у́ю**) *несов* (*не*)*перех* to dance
танцо́вщик (**-а**) *м* dancer
танцо́р (**-а**) *м* dancer
та́поч|ка (**-ки**; *gen pl* **-ек**) *ж* (*обычно мн*: *домашняя*) slipper; (: *спортивная*) plimsoll (*Brit*), sneaker (*US*)
та́р|а (**-ы**) *ж собир* containers *мн*
тарака́н (**-а**) *м* cockroach
таре́л|ка (**-ки**; *gen pl* **-ок**) *ж* plate; **я здесь не в свое́й таре́лке** (*разг*) I feel out of place here
тари́ф (**-а**) *м* tariff
тас|ова́ть (**-у́ю**; *perf* **стасова́ть**) *несов перех* to shuffle
ТАСС *м сокр* (= *Телегра́фное аге́нтство Сове́тского Сою́за*) Tass
татуиро́в|ка (**-ки**; *gen pl* **-ок**) *ж* tattoo
та́ч|ка (**-ки**; *gen pl* **-ек**) *ж* wheelbarrow
тащ|и́ть (**-у́, -ишь**) *несов перех* to drag; (*тянуть*) to pull; (*нести*) to haul ▷ (*perf* **вы́тащить**) (*перен*: *в театр, на прогулку*) to drag out; **тащи́ться** *несов возв* (*медленно ехать*) to trundle along
та́|ять (**-ю**; *perf* **раста́ять**) *несов* to melt
ТВ *м сокр* (= *телеви́дение*) TV (= *television*)
тверде́|ть (*3sg* **-ет**, *perf* **затверде́ть**) *несов* to harden
твёрдо *нареч* (*верить, сказать*) firmly; (*запомнить*) properly; **я твёрдо зна́ю, что ...** I know for sure that ...
твёрдый *прил* (*Физ*) solid; (*земля, предмет*) hard; (*решение, сторонник, тон*) firm; (*цены, ставки*) stable; (*знания*) solid; (*характер*) tough; **твёрдый знак** (*Линг*) hard sign
твёрже *сравн прил от* **твёрдый** ▷ *сравн нареч от* **твёрдо**
твит (**-а**) *м* tweet
тво|й (**-его́**; *f* **-я́**, *nt* **-ё**, *pl* **-и́**; *как* **мой**; см *Table 8*) *притяж мест* your; **как по-тво́ему?** what is your opinion?; **дава́й сде́лаем по-тво́ему** let's do it your way
творе́ни|е (**-я**) *ср* creation

твори́тельный *прил*: **твори́тельный паде́ж** (*Линг*) the instrumental (case)
твор|и́ть (**-ю́, -и́шь**) *несов* to create ▷ (*perf* **сотвори́ть**) *перех* to create ▷ (*perf* **натвори́ть**) (*разг*) to get up to; **твори́ться** *несов возв*: **что тут твори́тся?** what's going on here?
творо́г (**-а́**) *м* ≈ curd cheese
тво́рческий *прил* creative
тво́рчеств|о (**-а**) *ср* creative work; (*писателя*) work
тво|я́ (**-е́й**) *притяж мест см* **твой**
те (**тех**) *мест см* **тот**
т.е. *сокр* (= *то есть*) i.e. (= *id est*)
теа́тр (**-а**) *м* theatre (*Brit*), theater (*US*); **театра́льный** *прил* (*афиша, сезон*) theatre (*Brit*), theater (*US*); (*деятельность*) theatrical; **театра́льный институ́т** drama school
тебя́ *итп мест см* **ты**
текст (**-а**) *м* text; (*песни*) words *мн*, lyrics *мн*
теку́чий *прил* fluid
теку́щий *прил* (*год*) current; **теку́щий счёт** (*Комм*) current (*Brit*) *или* checking (*US*) account
тел. *сокр* (= *телефо́н*) tel. (= *telephone*)
телеви́дени|е (**-я**) *ср* television
телевизио́нный *прил* television; **телевизио́нный фильм** television drama
телеви́зор (**-а**) *м* television (set)
телегра́мм|а (**-ы**) *ж* telegram
телеграфи́р|овать (**-ую**) *(не)сов перех* to wire
теле́ж|ка (**-ки**; *gen pl* **-ек**) *ж* (*для багажа, в супермаркете*) trolley
телезри́тел|ь (**-я**) *м* viewer
телека́мер|а (**-ы**) *ж* television camera
тел|ёнок (**-ёнка**; *nom pl* **-я́та**) *м* calf (*мн* calves)
телепереда́ч|а (**-и**) *ж* TV programme (*Brit*) *или* program (*US*)
телеско́п (**-а**) *м* telescope
телесту́ди|я (**-и**) *ж* television studio
телета́йп (**-а**) *м* teleprinter (*Brit*), teletypewriter (*US*), Teletype
телефо́н (**-а**) *м* telephone; **телефо́нн|ый** *прил* telephone; **телефо́нная кни́га** telephone book *или* directory
Тел|е́ц (**-ьца́**) *м* (*созвездие*) Taurus
телеце́нтр (**-а**) *м* television centre (*Brit*) *или* center (*US*)
те́л|о (**-а**; *nom pl* **-а́**) *ср* body
телогре́|йка (**-йки**; *gen pl* **-ек**) *ж* body warmer
телохрани́тел|ь (**-я**) *м* bodyguard
теля́тин|а (**-ы**) *ж* veal
тем *мест см* **тот**; **то** ▷ *союз +comparative*; **чем бо́льше, тем лу́чше** the more the better; **тем бо́лее!** all the more so!; **тем бо́лее что ...** especially as ...; **тем не ме́нее** nevertheless; **тем са́мым** thus
те́м|а (**-ы**) *ж* topic; (*Муз, Литература*) theme
те́ми *мест см* **тот**; **то**
темне́|ть (*3sg* **-ет**, *perf* **потемне́ть**) *несов* to darken ▷ (*perf* **стемне́ть**) *безл* to get dark
темно́ *как сказ*: **на у́лице темно́** it's dark outside
темнот|а́ (**-ы́**) *ж* darkness
тёмный *прил* dark
темп (**-а**) *м* speed; **в те́мпе** (*разг*) quickly
темпера́мент (**-а**) *м* temperament

температу́р|а (**-ы**) *ж* temperature
тенде́нци|я (**-и**) *ж* tendency; (*предвзятость*) bias
те́н|и (**-е́й**) *мн* (*также* **те́ни для век**) eye shadow *ед*
те́ннис (**-а**) *м* tennis; **тенниси́ст** (**-а**) *м* tennis player
тен|ь (**-и**; *prp sg* **-и́**, *gen pl* **-е́й**) *ж* (*место*) shade; (*предмета, человека*) shadow; (*перен*: *+gen*: *волнения, печали*) flicker of; *см также* **те́ни**
теóри|я (**-и**) *ж* theory
тепе́рь *нареч* now
тепле́|ть (*3sg* **-ет**, *perf* **потепле́ть**) *несов* to get warmer
тепл|о́ *нареч* warmly ▷ (**-а́**) *ср* (*также перен*) warmth ▷ *как сказ* it's warm; **мне тепло́** I'm warm
теплово́й *прил* thermal
теплохо́д (**-а**) *м* motor ship *или* vessel
тепло(электро)центра́л|ь (**-и**) *ж* generator plant (*supplying central heating systems*)
тёплый *прил* warm
терапе́вт (**-а**) *м* ≈ general practitioner
тера́кт (**-а**) *м сокр* (= *террористи́ческий акт*) terrorist attack
терапи́|я (**-и**) *ж* (*Мед*: *наука*) (internal) medicine; (*лечение*) therapy
тере́ть (**тру, трёшь**; *pt* **тёр, тёрла, тёрло**) *несов перех* to rub; (*овощи*) to grate
терза́|ть (**-ю**; *perf* **растерза́ть**) *несов перех* (*добычу*) to savage ▷ (*perf* **истерза́ть**) (*перен*: *упрёками, ревностью*) to torment; **терза́ться** *несов возв*: **терза́ться** *+instr* (*сомнениями*) to be racked by
тёр|ка (**-ки**; *gen pl* **-ок**) *ж* grater
те́рмин (**-а**) *м* term
термина́л (**-а**) *м* terminal
термо́метр (**-а**) *м* thermometer
те́рмос (**-а**) *м* Thermos
терпели́вый *прил* patient
терпе́ни|е (**-я**) *ср* patience
терп|е́ть (**-лю́, -ишь**) *несов перех* (*боль, холод*) to suffer, endure ▷ (*perf* **потерпе́ть**) (*неудачу*) to suffer; (*грубость*) to tolerate; **терпе́ть** (*perf* **потерпе́ть**) **круше́ние** (*корабль*) to be wrecked; (*поезд*) to crash; **терпе́ть не могу́ таки́х люде́й** (*разг*) I can't stand people like that; **терпе́ть не могу́ спо́рить** (*разг*) I hate arguing; **терпе́ться** *несов безл*: **мне не те́рпится** *+infin* I can't wait to do
терпи́мост|ь (**-и**) *ж*: **терпи́мость** (**к** *+dat*) tolerance (of)
терпи́мый *прил* tolerant
терра́с|а (**-ы**) *ж* terrace
террито́ри|я (**-и**) *ж* territory
терроризи́р|овать (**-ую**) *(не)сов перех* to terrorize
террори́зм (**-а**) *м* terrorism
террори́ст (**-а**) *м* terrorist
террористи́ческий *прил* terrorist
теря́|ть (**-ю**; *perf* **потеря́ть**) *несов перех* to lose; **теря́ться** (*perf* **потеря́ться**) *несов возв* to get lost; (*робеть*) to lose one's nerve
тесн|и́ть (**-ю́, -и́шь**; *perf* **потесни́ть**) *несов перех* (*в толпе*) to squeeze; (*к стене*) to press
те́сно *нареч* (*располагать(ся)*) close together; (*сотрудничать*) closely ▷ *как сказ*: **в кварти́ре о́чень те́сно** the flat is very cramped; **мы с ним те́сно знако́мы** he and I know each other very well

T

те́сный *прил* (*проход*) narrow; (*помещение*) cramped; (*одежда*) tight; (*дружба*) close; **мир те́сен** it's a small world

тест (**-а**) *м* test

тести́р|овать (**-ую**) *(не)сов* to test

те́ст|о (**-а**) *ср* (*дрожжевое*) dough; (*слоёное, песочное*) pastry (*Brit*), paste (*US*)

тест|ь (**-я**) *м* father-in-law, wife's father

тесьм|а́ (**-ы́**) *ж* tape

тёт|ка (**-ки**; *gen pl* **-ок**) *ж* auntie

тетра́д|ь (**-и**) *ж* exercise book

тёт|я (**-и**; *gen pl* **-ь**) *ж* aunt; (*разг*: *женщина*) lady

те́фтел|и (**-ей**) *мн* meatballs

тех *мест см* **те**

те́хник|а (**-и**) *ж* technology; (*приёмы*) technique ▷ *собир* (*машины*) machinery; (*разг*: *Муз*) hi-fi; **те́хника безопа́сности** industrial health and safety

те́хникум (**-а**) *м* technical college

техни́ческ|ий *прил* technical; **техни́ческий осмо́тр** (*Авт*) ≈ MOT (*Brit*) (*annual roadworthiness check*); **техни́ческое обслу́живание** maintenance, servicing

технологи́ческий *прил* technical

техноло́ги|я (**-и**) *ж* technology

тече́ни|е (**-я**) *ср* (*поток*) current; (*в искусстве*) trend; **в тече́ние** *+gen* during

те|чь (*3sg* **-чёт**, *pt* **тёк, текла́**) *несов* to flow; (*крыша, лодка итп*) to leak ▷ (**-чи**) *ж* leak

тёщ|а (**-и**) *ж* mother-in-law, wife's mother

тигр (**-а**) *м* tiger

ти́ка|ть (*3sg* **-ет**) *несов* to tick

тип (**-а**) *м* type; **ти́па** *+gen* (*разг*) sort of

типи́чный *прил*: **типи́чный (для** *+gen***)** typical (of)

типогра́фи|я (**-и**) *ж* press, printing house

тир (**-а**) *м* shooting gallery

тире́ *ср нескл* dash

тиск|и́ (**-о́в**) *мн*: **в тиска́х** *+gen* (*перен*) in the grip of

титр (**-а**) *м* (*обычно мн*) credit (*of film*)

ти́тул (**-а**) *м* title

ти́тульный *прил*: **ти́тульный лист** title page

ти́хий *прил* quiet; **ти́хий у́жас!** (*разг*) what a nightmare!; **Ти́хий океа́н** the Pacific (Ocean)

ти́хо *нареч* (*говорить, жить*) quietly ▷ *как сказ*: **в до́ме ти́хо** the house is quiet; **ти́хо!** (be) quiet!

ти́ше *сравн прил от* **ти́хий** ▷ *сравн нареч от* **ти́хо** ▷ *как сказ*: **ти́ше!** quiet!, hush!

тишин|а́ (**-ы́**) *ж* quiet

т.к. *сокр* = **так как**

ткан|ь (**-и**) *ж* fabric, material; (*Анат*) tissue

тк|ать (**-у, -ёшь**; *perf* **сотка́ть**) *несов перех* to weave

тле|ть (*3sg* **-ет**) *несов* (*дрова, угли*) to smoulder (*Brit*), smolder (*US*)

тмин (**-а**) *м* (*Кулин*) caraway seeds *мн*

т.н. *сокр* = **так называ́емый**

то[1] *союз* (*условный*): **е́сли … то …** if … then …; (*разделительный*): **то … то …** sometimes … sometimes …; **и то** even; **то есть** that is

то[2] (**того́**) *мест см* **тот**

т.о. *сокр* = **таки́м о́бразом**

-то *част* (*для выделения*): **письмо́-то ты получи́л?** did you (at least) receive the letter?

тобо́й *мест см* **ты**

това́р (**-а**) *м* product; (*Экон*) commodity

това́рищ (**-а**) *м* (*приятель*) friend; (*по партии*) comrade;
това́рищеский *прил* comradely; **това́рищеский матч** (*Спорт*) friendly (match)

това́риществ|о (**-а**) *ср* (*Комм*) partnership

това́рн|ый *прил* (*производство*) goods; (*рынок*) commodity; **това́рная би́ржа** commodity exchange; **това́рный знак** trademark

товарооборо́т (**-а**) *м* turnover

тогда́ *нареч* then; **тогда́ как** (*хотя*) while; (*при противопоставлении*) whereas

того́ *мест см* **тот**; **то**

то́же *нареч* (*также*) too, as well, also

той *мест см* **та**

ток (**-а**) *м* (*Элек*) current

толк (**-а**) *м* (*в рассуждениях*) sense; (*разг*: *польза*) use; **сбива́ть** (*perf* **сбить**) **кого́-н с то́лку** to confuse sb

толка́|ть (**-ю**; *perf* **толкну́ть**) *несов перех* to push; (*перен*): **толка́ть кого́-н на** *+acc* to force sb into; **толка́ться** *несов возв* (*в толпе*) to push (one's way)

толк|ова́ть (**-у́ю**) *несов перех* to interpret

толко́вый *прил* intelligent

толп|а́ (**-ы́**; *nom pl* **-ы**) *ж* crowd

толп|и́ться (*3sg* **-и́тся**) *несов возв* to crowd around

толсте́|ть (**-ю**; *perf* **потолсте́ть**) *несов* to get fatter

то́лстый *прил* thick; (*человек*) fat

толч|о́к (**-ка́**) *м* (*в спину*) shove; (*при торможении*) jolt; (*при землетрясении*) tremor; (*перен*: *к работе*) incentive

то́лще *сравн прил от* **то́лстый**

толщин|а́ (**-ы́**) *ж* thickness

КЛЮЧЕВОЕ СЛОВО

то́лько *част* **1** only
2 (*+pron/+adv*: *усиливает выразительность*): **попро́буй то́лько отказа́ться!** just try to refuse!; **поду́мать то́лько!** imagine that!
▷ *союз* **1** (*сразу после*) as soon as
2 (*однако, но*) only; **позвони́, то́лько разгова́ривай недо́лго** phone (*Brit*) *или* call (*US*), only don't talk for long
▷ *нареч* **1** (*недавно*) (only) just; **ты давно́ здесь?- нет, то́лько вошла́** have you been here long? — no, I've (only) just come in
2 (*во фразах*): **то́лько лишь** (*разг*) only; **то́лько и всего́** (*разг*) that's all; **как** *или* **лишь** *или* **едва́ то́лько** as soon as; **не то́лько ..., но и ...** not only ... but also ...; **то́лько бы** if only; **то́лько что** only just

том *мест см* **тот**; **то** ▷ (**-а**; *nom pl* **-а́**) *м* volume

тома́тный *прил*: **тома́тный сок** tomato juice

тому́ *мест см* **тот**; **то**

тон (**-а**) *м* tone

тонзилли́т (**-а**) *м* tonsillitis

тонизи́рующ|ий *прил* (*напиток*) refreshing; **тонизи́рующее сре́дство** tonic

то́нкий *прил* thin; (*фигура*) slender; (*черты лица, работа, ум*) fine; (*различия, намёк*) subtle

тонне́л|ь (**-я**) *м* tunnel

тон|у́ть (**-у́, -ешь**; *perf* **утону́ть**) *несов* (*человек*) to drown ▷ (*perf* **затону́ть**) (*корабль*) to sink

то́ньше *сравн прил от* **то́нкий**
то́па|ть (**-ю**) *несов*: **то́пать нога́ми** to stamp one's feet
топ|и́ть (**-лю́, -ишь**) *несов перех* (*печь*) to stoke (up); (*масло, воск*) to melt ▷ (*perf* **утопи́ть** *или* **потопи́ть**) (*корабль*) to sink; (*человека*) to drown; **топи́ться** *несов возв* (*печь*) to burn ▷ (*perf* **утопи́ться**) (*человек*) to drown o.s.
то́плив|о (**-а**) *ср* fuel
то́пол|ь (**-я**) *м* poplar
топо́р (**-а́**) *м* axe (*Brit*), ax (*US*)
то́пот (**-а**) *м* clatter
топ|та́ть (**-чу́, -чешь**; *perf* **потопта́ть**) *несов перех* (*траву*) to trample; **топта́ться** *несов возв* to shift from one foot to the other
торг|и́ (**-о́в**) *мн* (*аукцион*) auction *ед*; (*состязание*) tender *ед*
торг|ова́ть (**-у́ю**) *несов* (*магазин*) to trade; **торгова́ть** (*impf*) *+instr* (*мясом, мебелью*) to trade in; **торгова́ться** (*perf* **сторгова́ться**) *несов возв* to haggle
торго́в|ец (**-ца**) *м* merchant; (*мелкий*) trader
торго́вл|я (**-и**) *ж* trade
торго́в|ый *прил* trade; (*судно, флот*) merchant; **торго́вая сеть** retail network; **торго́вая то́чка** retail outlet; **торго́вое представи́тельство** trade mission; **торго́вый центр** shopping centre (*Brit*), mall (*US*)
торгпре́д (**-а**) *м сокр* (= *торго́вый представи́тель*) head of the trade mission
торгпре́дств|о (**-а**) *ср сокр* = **торго́вое представи́тельство**
торже́ственный *прил* (*день, случай*) special; (*собрание*) celebratory; (*вид, обстановка*) festive; (*обещание*) solemn
торжеств|о́ (**-а́**) *ср* celebration; (*в голосе, в словах*) triumph; **торжеств|ова́ть** (**-у́ю**; *perf* **восторжествова́ть**) *несов*: **торжествова́ть (над** *+instr*) to triumph (over)
то́рмоз (**-а**; *nom pl* **-а́**) *м* brake
тормо|зи́ть (**-жу́, -зи́шь**; *perf* **затормози́ть**) *несов перех* (*машину*) to slow down ▷ *неперех* (*машина*) to brake; **тормози́ться** (*perf* **затормози́ться**) *несов возв* (*работа итп*) to be hindered
тор|опи́ть (**-оплю́, -о́пишь**; *perf* **поторопи́ть**) *несов перех* to hurry; **торопи́ться** (*perf* **поторопи́ться**) *несов возв* to hurry
тороплИ́вый *прил* (*человек*) hasty
торпе́д|а (**-ы**) *ж* torpedo (*мн* torpedoes)
торт (**-а**) *м* cake
торф (**-а**) *м* peat
торч|а́ть (**-у́, -и́шь**) *несов* (*вверх*) to stick up; (*в стороны*) to stick out; (*разг*: *на улице*) to hang around
торше́р (**-а**) *м* standard lamp
тоск|а́ (**-и́**) *ж* (*на сердце*) anguish; (*скука*) boredom; **тоска́ по ро́дине** homesickness; **тосклИ́вый** *прил* gloomy; **тоск|ова́ть** (**-у́ю**) *несов* to pine away; **тоскова́ть** (*impf*) **по** *+dat или* **о** *+prp* to miss
тост (**-а**) *м* toast

КЛЮЧЕВОЕ СЛОВО

то|т (**-го́**; *f* **та**, *nt* **то**, *pl* **те**; *см Table 11*) *мест* **1** that; **тот дом** that house
2 (*о ранее упомянутом*) that; **в тот раз/день** that time/day
3 (*в главных предложениях*): **э́то тот челове́к, кото́рый приходи́л**

вчерá it's the man who came yesterday
4 (*о последнем из названных лиц*): **я посмотрéл на дрýга, тот стоя́л мóлча** I looked at my friend, who stood silently
5 (*обычно с отрицанием*): **зашёл не в тот дом** I called at the wrong house
6 (*об одном из перечисляемых предметов*): **ни тот ни другóй** neither one nor the other; **тем или ины́м спóсобом** by some means or other; **тот же** the same
7 (*во фразах*): **до тогó** so; **мне не до тогó** I have no time for that; **к томý же** moreover; **ни с тогó ни с сегó** (*разг*) out of the blue; **томý назáд** ago; **и томý подóбное** et cetera, and so on

тоталитáрный *прил* totalitarian
тотáльный *прил* total; (*война*) all-out
то-то *част* (*разг: вот именно*) exactly, that's just it; (*вот почему*) that's why; (*выражает удовлетворение*): **то-то же** pleased to hear it; **то-то он удиви́тся!** he WILL be surprised!
тóтчас *нареч* immediately
точи́л|ка (**-ки**; *gen pl* **-ок**) *ж* pencil sharpener
точ|и́ть (**-ý, -ишь**; *perf* **наточи́ть**) *несов перех* to sharpen; (*no perf: подлеж: червь, ржавчина*) to eat away at
тóч|ка (**-ки**; *gen pl* **-ек**) *ж* point; (*пятнышко*) dot; (*Линг*) full stop (*Brit*), period (*esp US*); **тóчка зрéния** point of view; **тóчка с запятóй** semicolon
точнée *вводн сл* to be exact *или* precise
тóчно *нареч* exactly; (*объяснить*) precisely; (*подсчитать, перевести*) accurately ▷ *част* (*разг: действительно*) exactly, precisely
тóчност|ь (**-и**) *ж* accuracy
тóчный *прил* exact; (*часы, перевод, попадание*) accurate
точь-в-точь *нареч* (*разг*) just like
тошн|и́ть (*3sg* **-и́т**, *perf* **стошни́ть**) *несов безл*: **меня́ тошни́т** I feel sick
тошнот|á (**-ы́**) *ж* (*чувство*) nausea
тóщий *прил* (*человек*) skinny
т.п. *сокр* (= *томý подóбное*) etc. (= *et cetera*)
трав|á (**-ы́**; *nom pl* **-ы**) *ж* grass; (*лекарственная*) herb
трав|и́ть (**-лю́, -ишь**) *несов перех* (*также перен*) to poison ▷ (*perf* **затрави́ть**) (*дичь*) to hunt; (*перен: разг: притеснять*) to harass, hound; **трави́ть в Интернéте** to bully online, cyberbully; **трави́ться** (*perf* **отрави́ться**) *несов возв* to poison o.s.
трáвм|а (**-ы**) *ж* (*физическая*) injury; (*психическая*) trauma
травматóлог (**-а**) *м* *doctor working in a casualty department*
травматологи́ческий *прил*: **травматологи́ческий отдéл** casualty; **травматологи́ческий пункт** first-aid room
травми́р|овать (**-ую**) *(не)сов перех* to injure; (*перен: психически*) to traumatize
трагéди|я (**-и**) *ж* tragedy
траги́ческий *прил* tragic
традициóнный *прил* traditional
тради́ци|я (**-и**) *ж* tradition
трáктор (**-а**) *м* tractor; **трактори́ст** (**-а**) *м* tractor driver
трамвá|й (**-я**) *м* tram (*Brit*), streetcar (*US*)
транзи́стор (**-а**) *м* (*приёмник*) transistor (radio)

транзи́т (**-а**) *м* transit
транс (**-а**) *м* transport document
трансге́нный *прил* (*овощи*) genetically modified
трансли́р|овать (**-ую**) *(не)сов перех* to broadcast; **трансли́ровать в режи́ме онла́йн** to stream
трансля́ци|я (**-и**) *ж* (*передача*) broadcast
транспара́нт (**-а**) *м* banner
транспланта́ци|я (**-и**) *ж* transplant
тра́нспорт (**-а**) *м* transport
транспортёр (**-а**) *м* (*конвейер*) conveyor belt; (*Воен*) army personnel carrier
транспорти́р|овать (**-ую**) *(не)сов перех* to transport
тра́нспортный *прил* transport
транше́|я (**-и**) *ж* trench
тра́сс|а (**-ы**) *ж* (*лыжная*) run; (*трубопровода*) line; **автомоби́льная тра́сса** motorway (*Brit*), expressway (*US*)
тра́|тить (**-чу, -тишь**; *perf* **истра́тить** *или* **потра́тить**) *несов перех* to spend
тра́ур (**-а**) *м* mourning
тре́бовани|е (**-я**) *ср* demand; (*правило*) requirement
тре́бовательный *прил* demanding
тре́б|овать (**-ую**; *perf* **потре́бовать**) *несов перех*: **тре́бовать что-н/**+*infin* to demand sth/to do; **тре́боваться** (*perf* **потре́боваться**) *несов возв* to be needed *или* required
трево́г|а (**-и**) *ж* (*волнение*) anxiety; **возду́шная трево́га** air-raid warning
трево́ж|ить (**-у, -ишь**; *perf* **встрево́жить**) *несов перех* to alarm ▷ (*perf* **потрево́жить**) (*мешать*) to disturb;
трево́житься (*perf* **встрево́житься**) *несов возв* (*за детей*) to be concerned
трево́жный *прил* (*голос, взгляд*) anxious; (*сведения*) alarming
трезве́|ть (**-ю**; *perf* **отрезве́ть**) *несов* to sober up
тре́звый *прил* (*человек*) sober; (*перен*: *идея*) sensible
трём *etc чис см* **три**
трёмста́м *etc чис см* **три́ста**
тренажёр (**-а**) *м equipment used for physical training*
тре́нер (**-а**) *м* coach
тре́ни|е (**-я**) *ср* friction
тренир|ова́ть (**-у́ю**; *perf* **натренирова́ть**) *несов перех* to train; (*спортсменов*) to coach; **тренирова́ться** (*perf* **натренирова́ться**) *несов возв* (*спортсмен*) to train
трениро́в|ка (**-ки**; *gen pl* **-ок**) *ж* training; (*отдельное занятие*) training (session)
трениро́вочный *прил* training; **трениро́вочный костю́м** tracksuit
треп|а́ть (**-лю́, -лешь**; *perf* **потрепа́ть**) *несов перех* (*подлеж*: *ветер*) to blow about; (*человека*: *по плечу*) to pat ▷ (*perf* **истрепа́ть** *или* **потрепа́ть**) (*разг*: *обувь, книги*) to wear out; **трепа́ться** (*perf* **истрепа́ться** *или* **потрепа́ться**) *несов возв* (*одежда*) to wear out
треп|ета́ть (**-ещу́, -е́щешь**) *несов* (*флаги*) to quiver; (*от ужаса*) to quake, tremble
треск|а́ (**-и́**) *ж* cod
тре́ска|ться (*3sg* **-ется**, *perf* **потре́скаться**) *несов возв* to crack
тре́сн|уть (*3sg* **-ет**) *сов* (*ветка*) to snap; (*стакан, кожа*) to crack

трест (**-а**) *м* (*Экон*) trust
тре́т|ий *чис* third; **тре́тье лицо́** (*Линг*) the third person
трет|ь (**-и**; *nom pl* **-и**, *gen pl* **-е́й**) *ж* third
тре́ть|е (**-его**) *ср* (*Кулин*) sweet (*Brit*), dessert
треуго́льник (**-а**) *м* triangle
треуго́льный *прил* triangular
тре́ф|ы (**-**) *мн* (*Карты*) clubs
трёх *чис см* **три**
трёхме́рный *прил* 3-D, three-dimensional
трёхсо́т *чис см* **три́ста**
трёхсо́тый *чис* three hundredth
трещ|а́ть (**-у́, -и́шь**) *несов* (*лёд, доски*) to crack; (*кузнечики*) to chip
тре́щин|а (**-ы**) *ж* crack
тр|и (**-ёх**; см *Table 24*) *чис* three ▷ *нескл* (*Просвещ*) ≈ C (*school mark*)
трибу́н|а (**-ы**) *ж* platform; (*стадиона*) stand
трибуна́л (**-а**) *м* tribunal; **вое́нный трибуна́л** military court
тридца́тый *чис* thirtieth
три́дцат|ь (**-и́**; *как* **пять**; см *Table 26*) *чис* thirty
три́жды *нареч* three times
трико́ *ср нескл* leotard
трина́дцатый *чис* thirteenth
трина́дцат|ь (**-и**; *как* **пять**; см *Table 26*) *чис* thirteen
три́ста (**трёхсо́т**; *как* **сто**; см *Table 28*) *чис* three hundred
триу́мф (**-а**) *м* triumph
тро́гательный *прил* touching
тро́га|ть (**-ю**; *perf* **тро́нуть**) *несов перех* to touch; (*подлеж: рассказ, событие*) to move; **тро́гаться** (*perf* **тро́нуться**) *несов возв* (*поезд*) to move off
тр|о́е (**-ои́х**; см *Table 30a*) *чис* three
тро́иц|а (**-ы**) *ж* (*также* **Свята́я тро́ица**) the Holy Trinity; (*праздник*) ≈ Trinity Sunday
Тро́ицын *прил*: **Тро́ицын день** ≈ Trinity Sunday
тро́|йка (**-йки**; *gen pl* **-ек**) *ж* (*цифра, карта*) three; (*Просвещ*) ≈ C (*school mark*); (*лошадей*) troika; (*костюм*) three-piece suit
тройни́к (**-а́**) *м* (*Элек*) (three-way) adaptor
тройно́й *прил* triple
тролле́йбус (**-а**) *м* trolleybus
тромбо́н (**-а**) *м* trombone
трон (**-а**) *м* throne
тро́н|уть(ся) (**-у(сь)**) *сов от* **тро́гать(ся)**
тро́пик (**-а**) *м*: **се́верный/ю́жный тро́пик** the tropic of Cancer/ Capricorn
тропи́н|ка (**-ки**; *gen pl* **-ок**) *ж* footpath
тропи́ческий *прил* tropical
трос (**-а**) *м* cable
тростни́к (**-а́**) *м* reed; **са́харный тростни́к** sugar cane
трост|ь (**-и**) *ж* walking stick
тротуа́р (**-а**) *м* pavement (*Brit*), sidewalk (*US*)
трофе́|й (**-я**) *м* trophy
трою́родн|ый *прил*: **трою́родный брат** second cousin (*male*); **трою́родная сестра́** second cousin (*female*)
троя́кий *прил* triple
труб|а́ (**-ы́**; *nom pl* **-ы**) *ж* pipe; (*дымовая*) chimney; (*Муз*) trumpet
труб|и́ть (**-лю́, -и́шь**; *perf* **протруби́ть**) *несов* (*труба*) to sound; (*Муз*): **труби́ть в** *+acc* to blow
тру́б|ка (**-ки**; *gen pl* **-ок**) *ж* tube; (*курительная*) pipe; (*телефона*) receiver
труд (**-а́**) *м* work; (*Экон*) labour (*Brit*), labor (*US*); **без труда́**

without any difficulty; **с (больши́м) трудо́м** with (great) difficulty;
тру|ди́ться (**-жу́сь, -ди́шься**) *несов возв* to work hard
тру́дно *как сказ* it's hard *или* difficult; **у меня́ тру́дно с деньга́ми** I've got money problems; **мне тру́дно поня́ть э́то** I find it hard to understand; **(мне) тру́дно бе́гать/стоя́ть** I have trouble running/standing up; **тру́дно сказа́ть** it's hard to say
тру́дност|ь (**-и**) *ж* difficulty
тру́дный *прил* difficult
трудово́й *прил* working; **трудова́я кни́жка** *employment record book*

Трудова́я кни́жка

This is a booklet in which all employment details are recorded e.g. employment dates, position and any merits or reprimands received in the course of service. This is an extremely important document, the absence of which can make employment almost impossible.

трудоёмкий *прил* labour-intensive (*Brit*), labor-intensive (*US*)
трудолюби́вый *прил* hard-working, industrious
труп (**-а**) *м* corpse
тру́пп|а (**-ы**) *ж* (*Театр*) company
трус (**-а**) *м* coward
тру́сик|и (**-ов**) *мн* (*детские*) knickers (*Brit*), panties (*US*)
тру́|сить (**-шу, -сишь**; *perf* **стру́сить**) *несов* to get scared
трусли́вый *прил* cowardly
трус|ы́ (**-о́в**) *мн* (*бельё: обычно мужские*) (under)pants; (*спортивные*) shorts
трущо́б|а (**-ы**) *ж* slum
трюм (**-а**) *м* hold (*of ship*)
трюмо́ *ср нескл* (*мебель*) dresser
тря́п|ка (**-ки**; *gen pl* **-ок**) *ж* (*половая*) cloth; (*лоскут*) rag; **тря́пки** (*разг*) clothes *мн*
тряс|ти́ (**-у́, -ёшь**) *несов перех* to shake; **трясти́сь** *несов возв*: **трясти́сь пе́ред** *+instr* (*перед начальством*) to tremble before; **трясти́сь** (*impf*) **над** *+instr* (*разг*: *над ребёнком*) to fret over *или* about
тряхн|у́ть (**-у́, -ёшь**) *сов перех* to shake
ТУ *м сокр самолёт констру́кции А.Н.Ту́полева*
туале́т (**-а**) *м* toilet; (*одежда*) outfit; **туале́тн|ый** *прил*: **туале́тная бума́га** toilet paper; **туале́тное мы́ло** toilet soap; **туале́тные принадле́жности** toiletries; **туале́тный сто́лик** dressing table
туго́й *прил* (*струна, пружина*) taut; (*узел, одежда*) tight; **он туг на́ ухо** (*разг*) he's a bit hard of hearing
туда́ *нареч* there; **туда́ и обра́тно** there and back; **биле́т туда́ и обра́тно** return (*Brit*) *или* round-trip (*US*) ticket
туда́-сюда́ *нареч* all over the place; (*раскачиваться*) backwards and forwards
ту́же *сравн прил от* **туго́й**
туз (**-а́**) *м* (*Карты*) ace
тузе́м|ец (**-ца**) *м* native
тума́н (**-а**) *м* mist
тума́нный *прил* misty; (*идеи*) nebulous
ту́мбоч|ка (**-ки**; *gen pl* **-ек**) *ж*, *уменьш от* **ту́мба**; (*мебель*) bedside cabinet
тун|е́ц (**-ца́**) *м* tuna (fish)
тунея́д|ец (**-ца**) *м* parasite (*fig*)

тунне́л|ь (**-я**) *м* = **тонне́ль**
тупи́к (**-а́**) *м* (*улица*) dead end, cul-de-sac; (*для поездов*) siding; (*перен: в переговорах итп*) deadlock
туп|и́ть (**-лю́, -ишь**; *perf* **затупи́ть**) *несов перех* to blunt; **тупи́ться** (*perf* **затупи́ться**) *несов возв* to become blunt
тупо́й *прил* (*нож, карандаш*) blunt; (*человек*) stupid; (*боль, ум*) dull; (*покорность*) blind
тур (**-а**) *м* (*этап*) round; (*в танце*) turn
тури́зм (**-а**) *м* tourism; **тури́ст** (**-а**) *м* tourist; (*в походе*) hiker; **туристи́ческий** *прил* tourist
турне́ *ср нескл* (*Театр, Спорт*) tour
турни́р (**-а**) *м* tournament
Ту́рци|я (**-и**) *ж* Turkey
ту́склый *прил* (*стекло*) opaque; (*краска*) mat(t); (*свет, взгляд*) dull
тус|ова́ться (**-у́юсь**; *perf* **потусова́ться**) *несов* (*разг*) to hang out
тусо́вк|а (**-и**) *ж* (*разг: на улице*) hanging about; (*вечеринка*) party
тут *нареч* here; **и всё тут** (*разг*) and that's that; **не тут-то бы́ло** (*разг*) it wasn't to be
ту́ф|ля (**-ли**; *gen pl* **-ель**) *ж* shoe
ту́х|нуть (*3sg* **-нет**, *pt* **-, -ла,**, *perf* **поту́хнуть**) *несов* (*костёр, свет*) to go out ▷ (*perf* **проту́хнуть**) (*мясо*) to go off
ту́ч|а (**-и**) *ж* rain cloud
тушён|ка (**-ки**; *gen pl* **-ок**) *ж* (*разг*) tinned (*Brit*) *или* canned meat
туш|ь (**-и**) *ж* (*для ресниц*) mascara
т/ф *м сокр* = **телевизио́нный фильм**
ТЦ *м сокр* (= *телеизио́нный центр*) television centre (*Brit*) *или* center (*US*)

тща́тельный *прил* thorough
тщесла́ви|е (**-я**) *ср* vanity; **тщесла́вный** *прил* vain
ты (**тебя́**; см *Table 6a*) *мест* you; **быть** (*impf*) **с кем-н на ты** to be on familiar terms with sb
ты́|кать (**-чу, -чешь**; *perf* **ткнуть**) *несов перех* (*разг: ударять*): **ты́кать что-н/кого-н чем-н** to poke sth/sb with sth
ты́кв|а (**-ы**) *ж* pumpkin
тыл (**-а**; *loc sg* **-у́**, *nom pl* **-ы́**) *м* (*Воен: территория*) the rear; **ты́льный** *прил* back
тыс. *сокр* = **ты́сяча**
ты́сяч|а (**-и**; см *Table 29*) *ж чис* thousand
ты́сячный *чис* thousandth; (*толпа, армия*) of thousands
тьм|а (**-ы**) *ж* (*мрак*) darkness, gloom
ТЭЦ *ж сокр* = **тепло(электро) центра́ль**
тю́бик (**-а**) *м* tube
ТЮЗ (**-а**) *м сокр* (= *теа́тр ю́ного зри́теля*) children's theatre (*Brit*) *или* theater (*US*)
тюле́н|ь (**-я**) *м* (*Зоол*) seal
тюльпа́н (**-а**) *м* tulip
тюре́мн|ый *прил* prison; **тюре́мное заключе́ние** imprisonment
тюрьм|а́ (**-ы́**) *ж* prison
тя́г|а (**-и**) *ж* (*в печи*) draught (*Brit*), draft (*US*); (*насоса, пылесоса*) suction; **тя́га к** *+dat* (*перен*) attraction to
тяготе́ни|е (**-я**) *ср* (*Физ*) gravity
тя́гот|ы (**-**) *мн* hardships
тя́жб|а (**-ы**) *ж* dispute
тяжеле́|ть (**-ю**; *perf* **отяжеле́ть** *или* **потяжеле́ть**) *несов* to get heavier
тяжело́ *нареч* heavily; (*больной*) seriously ▷ *как сказ* (*нести*) it's

heavy; (*понять*) it's hard; **мне тяжело́ здесь** I find it hard here; **больно́му тяжело́** the patient is suffering

тяжёл|ый *прил* heavy; (*труд, день*) hard; (*сон*) restless; (*запах*) strong; (*воздух*) stale; (*преступление, болезнь, рана*) serious; (*зрелище, мысли, настроение*) grim; (*трудный: человек, характер*) difficult; **тяжёлая атле́тика** weightlifting; **тяжёлая промы́шленность** heavy industry

тя́жкий *прил* (*труд*) arduous; (*преступление*) grave

тян|у́ть (**-у́, -ешь**) *несов перех* (*канат, сеть итп*) to pull; (*шею, руку*) to stretch out; (*дело*) to drag out ▷ (*perf* **протяну́ть**) (*кабель*) to lay ▷ (*perf* **вы́тянуть**) (*жребий*) to draw ▷ *неперех*: **тяну́ть с** *+instr* (*с ответом, с решением*) to delay; **меня́ тя́нет в Петербу́рг** I want to go to Petersburg; **тяну́ться** *несов возв* to stretch; (*дело, время*) to drag on; (*дым, запах*) to waft; **тяну́ться** (*impf*) **к** *+dat* to be attracted *или* drawn to

КЛЮЧЕВОЕ СЛОВО

у *предл +gen* **1** (*около*) by; **у окна́** by the window

2 (*обозначает обладателя чего-н*): **у меня́ есть дом/де́ти** I have a house/children

3 (*обозначает объект, с которым соотносится действие*): **я живу́ у друзе́й** I live with friends; **я учи́лся у него́** I was taught by him

4 (*указывает на источник получения чего-н*) from; **я попроси́л у дру́га де́нег** I asked for money from a friend

▷ *межд* (*выражает испуг, восторг*) oh

убега́|ть (**-ю**) *несов от* **убежа́ть**

убеди́тельный *прил* (*пример*) convincing; (*просьба*) urgent

убед|и́ть (*2sg* **-и́шь**, *3sg* **-и́т**, *impf* **убежда́ть**) *сов перех*: **убеди́ть кого́-н** *+infin* to persuade sb to do; **убежда́ть** (*perf* **убеди́ть**) **кого́-н в чём-н** to convince sb of sth; **убеди́ться** (*impf* **убежда́ться**) *сов возв*: **убеди́ться в чём-н** to be convinced of sth

убежа́|ть (*как* **бежа́ть**; *см Table 20*; *impf* **убега́ть**) *сов* to run away

убежде́ни|е (**-я**) *ср* (*взгляд*) conviction

убе́жищ|е (**-а**) *ср* (*от дождя, от бомб*) shelter; **полити́ческое убе́жище** political asylum

убер|е́чь (**-егу́, -ежёшь** *итп*, **-егу́т**; *pt* **-ёг, -егла́**, *impf* **уберега́ть**) *сов перех* to protect; **убере́чься** (*impf* **уберега́ться**) *сов возв* (*от опасности итп*) to protect o.s.

убива́|ть (**-ю**) *несов от* **уби́ть**

уби́йств|о (**-а**) *ср* murder

уби́йц|а (**-ы**) *м/ж* murderer

убира́|ть (**-ю**) *несов от* **убра́ть**

уби́т|ый (**-ого**) *м* dead man (*мн* men)

уб|и́ть (**-ью́, -ьёшь**; *impf* **убива́ть**) *сов перех* to kill; (*о преступлении*) to murder

убо́гий *прил* wretched

убо́|й (**-я**) *м* slaughter

убо́р (**-а**) *м*: **головно́й убо́р** hat

убо́рк|а (**-и**) *ж* (*помещения*) cleaning; **убо́рка урожа́я** harvest

убо́рн|ая (**-ой**) *ж* (*артиста*) dressing room; (*туалет*) lavatory

убо́рщиц|а (**-ы**) *ж* cleaner

убр|а́ть (**уберу́, уберёшь**; *impf* **убира́ть**) *сов перех* (*унести: вещи*) to take away; (*комнату*) to tidy; (*урожай*) to gather (in); **убира́ть** (*perf* **убра́ть**) **со стола́** to clear the table

у́был|ь (**-и**) *ж* decrease; **идти́** (*impf*) **на у́быль** to decrease

убы́т|ок (**-ка**) *м* loss

убью́ *итп сов см* **уби́ть**

уважа́ем|ый *прил* respected, esteemed; **уважа́емый господи́н** Dear Sir; **уважа́емая госпожа́** Dear Madam

уважа́|ть (**-ю**) *несов перех* to respect

уваже́ни|е (**-я**) *ср* respect

УВД *ср сокр* (= *Управле́ние вну́тренних дел*) *administration of internal affairs within a town/region*

уве́дом|ить (**-лю, -ишь**; *impf* **уведомля́ть**) *сов перех* to notify

уведомле́ни|е (**-я**) *ср* notification

увез|ти́ (**-у́, -ёшь**; *pt* **увёз, -ла́**, *impf* **увози́ть**) *сов перех* to take away

увеличи́тельн|ый *прил*: **увеличи́тельное стекло́** magnifying glass

увели́ч|ить (**-у, -ишь**; *impf* **увели́чивать**) *сов перех* to increase; (*фотографию*) to enlarge; **увели́читься** (*impf* **увели́чиваться**) *сов возв* to increase

уве́ренност|ь (**-и**) *ж* confidence

уве́ренный *прил* confident

уверя́|ть (**-ю**) *несов перех*: **уверя́ть кого́-н/что-н (в чём-н)** to assure sb/sth (of sth)

ув|ести́ (**-еду́, -едёшь**; *pt* **-ёл, -ела́**, *impf* **уводи́ть**) *сов перех* to lead off

уви́|деть(ся) (**-жу(сь), -дишь(ся)**) *сов от* **ви́деть(ся)**

увлека́тельный *прил* (*рассказ*) absorbing; (*поездка*) entertaining

увлече́ни|е (**-я**) *ср* passion

увл|е́чь (**-еку́, -ечёшь** *итп*, **-еку́т**; *pt* **-ёк, -екла́**, *impf* **увлека́ть**) *сов перех* to lead

away; (*перен: захватить*) to captivate; **увле́чься** (*impf* **увлека́ться**) *сов возв*: **увле́чься** *+instr* to get carried away with; (*влюбиться*) to fall for; (*шахматами итп*) to become keen on
ув|оди́ть (**-ожу́, -о́дишь**) *несов от* **увести́**
ув|ози́ть (**-ожу́, -о́зишь**) *несов от* **увезти́**
уво́л|ить (**-ю, -ишь**; *impf* **увольня́ть**) *сов перех* (*с работы*) to dismiss, sack; **уво́литься** (*impf* **увольня́ться**) *сов возв*: **уво́литься (с рабо́ты)** to leave one's job
увольне́ни|е (**-я**) *ср* (*со службы*) dismissal; (*Воен*) leave
увя́н|уть (**-у**) *сов от* **вя́нуть**
угада́|ть (**-ю**; *impf* **уга́дывать**) *сов перех* to guess
уга́рный *прил*: **уга́рный газ** carbon monoxide
угаса́|ть (**-ю**; *perf* **уга́снуть**) *несов* (*огонь*) to die down
угла́ *итп сущ см* **у́гол**
углево́д (**-а**) *м* carbohydrate
углеки́слый *прил*: **углеки́слый газ** carbon dioxide
углеро́д (**-а**) *м* (*Хим*) carbon
углово́й *прил* corner; (*также* **углово́й уда́р**: *Спорт*) corner
углуб|и́ть (**-лю́, -и́шь**; *impf* **углубля́ть**) *сов перех* to deepen; **углуби́ться** (*impf* **углубля́ться**) *сов возв* to deepen
угля́ *итп сущ см* **у́голь**
угн|а́ть (**угоню́, уго́нишь**; *impf* **угоня́ть**) *сов перех* to drive off; (*самолёт*) to hijack
угнета́|ть (**-ю**) *несов перех* to oppress; (*тяготить*) to depress
уговор|и́ть (**-ю́, -и́шь**; *impf* **угова́ривать**) *сов перех* to persuade
уго|ди́ть (**-жу́, -ди́шь**; *impf* **угожда́ть**) *сов* (*попасть*) to end up; **угожда́ть** (*perf* **угоди́ть**) *+dat* to please
уго́дно *част*: **что уго́дно** whatever you like ▷ *как сказ*: **что Вам уго́дно?** what can I do for you?; **кто уго́дно** anyone; **когда́/како́й уго́дно** whenever/whichever you like; **от них мо́жно ожида́ть чего́ уго́дно** they might do anything
уго́дный *прил +dat* pleasing to
угожда́|ть (**-ю**) *несов от* **угоди́ть**
у́г|ол (**-ла́**; *loc sg* **-лу́**) *м* corner; (*Геом*) angle; **у́гол зре́ния** perspective
уголо́вник (**-а**) *м* criminal
уголо́вн|ый *прил* criminal; **уголо́вное преступле́ние** felony; **уголо́вный престу́пник** criminal; **уголо́вный ро́зыск** Criminal Investigation Department
у́г|оль (**-ля́**) *м* coal
угоня́|ть (**-ю**) *несов от* **угна́ть**
уго|сти́ть (**-щу́, -сти́шь**; *impf* **угоща́ть**) *сов перех*: **угости́ть кого́-н чем-н** (*пирогом, вином*) to offer sb sth
угоща́|ться (**-юсь**) *несов возв*: **угоща́йтесь!** help yourself!
угрожа́|ть (**-ю**) *несов*: **угрожа́ть кому́-н (чем-н)** to threaten sb (with sth)
угро́з|а (**-ы**) *ж* (*обычно мн*) threat
угрызе́ни|е (**-я**) *ср*: **угрызе́ния со́вести** pangs *мн* of conscience
уда|ва́ться (*3sg* **-ётся**) *несов от* **уда́ться**
удал|и́ть (**-ю́, -и́шь**; *impf* **удаля́ть**) *сов перех* (*отослать*) to send away; (*игрока*) to send off; (*пятно, занозу, орган*) to remove
уда́р (**-а**) *м* blow; (*ногой*) kick; (*инсульт*) stroke; (*сердца*) beat

ударе́ни|е (**-я**) *ср* stress
уда́р|ить (**-ю, -ишь**; *impf* **ударя́ть**) *сов перех* to hit; (*ногой*) to kick; (*подлеж*: *часы*) to strike; **уда́риться** (*impf* **ударя́ться**) *сов возв*: **уда́риться о** *+acc* to bang (o.s.) against
уда́рный *прил* (*инструмент*) percussion; (*слог*) stressed
уда́ться (*как* **дать**; см *Table 16*; *impf* **удава́ться**) *сов возв* (*опыт, дело*) to be successful, work; (*пирог*) to turn out well; **нам удало́сь поговори́ть/зако́нчить рабо́ту** we managed to talk to each other/finish the work
уда́ч|а (**-и**) *ж* (good) luck; **жела́ю уда́чи!** good luck!
уда́чный *прил* successful; (*слова*) apt
удво́|ить (**-ю, -ишь**; *impf* **удва́ивать**) *сов перех* to double
удел|и́ть (**-ю́, -и́шь**; *impf* **уделя́ть**) *сов перех*: **удели́ть что-н кому́-н/чему́-н** to devote sth to sb/sth
уд|ержа́ть (**-ержу́, -е́ржишь**; *impf* **уде́рживать**) *сов перех* to restrain; (*деньги*) to deduct; **уде́рживать** (*perf* **удержа́ть**) **(за собо́й)** to retain; **уде́рживать** (*perf* **удержа́ть**) **кого́-н от пое́здки** to keep sb from going on a journey; **удержа́ться** (*impf* **уде́рживаться**) *сов возв* to stop *или* restrain o.s.
удиви́тельный *прил* amazing
удив|и́ть (**-лю́, -и́шь**; *impf* **удивля́ть**) *сов перех* to surprise; **удиви́ться** (*impf* **удивля́ться**) *сов возв*: **удиви́ться** *+dat* to be surprised at *или* by
удивле́ни|е (**-я**) *ср* surprise
уди́ть (**ужу́, у́дишь**) *несов* to angle
удо́бно *нареч* (*сесть*) comfortably ▷ *как сказ* it's comfortable; (*прилично*) it's proper; **не удо́бно так говори́ть/де́лать** it is not proper to say so/do so; **мне не удо́бно** I feel awkward; **мне здесь удо́бно** I'm comfortable here; **мне удо́бно прийти́ ве́чером** it's convenient for me to come in the evening
удо́бный *прил* comfortable; (*время, место*) convenient
удобре́ни|е (**-я**) *ср* fertilizer
удо́бств|о (**-а**) *ср* comfort; **кварти́ра со все́ми удо́бствами** a flat with all (modern) conveniences
удовлетвори́тельный *прил* satisfactory
удовлетвор|и́ть (**-ю́, -и́шь**; *impf* **удовлетворя́ть**) *сов перех* to satisfy; (*потребности, просьбу*) to meet; (*жалобу*) to respond to; **удовлетвори́ться** (*impf* **удовлетворя́ться**) *сов возв*: **удовлетвори́ться** *+instr* to be satisfied with
удово́льстви|е (**-я**) *ср* pleasure
удостовере́ни|е (**-я**) *ср* identification (card); **удостовере́ние ли́чности** identity card
удочер|и́ть (**-ю́, -и́шь**; *impf* **удочеря́ть**) *сов перех* to adopt (*daughter*)
у́доч|ка (**-ки**; *gen pl* **-ек**) *ж* (fishing-)rod
уе́хать (*как* **е́хать**; см *Table 19*; *impf* **уезжа́ть**) *сов* to leave, go away
уж (**-а́**) *част* (*при усилении*): **здесь не так уж пло́хо** it's not as bad as all that here
ужа́л|ить (**-ю, -ишь**) *сов от* **жа́лить**
у́жас (**-а**) *м* horror; (*страх*) terror

▷ *как сказ* (*разг*): **(э́то) у́жас!** it's awful *или* terrible!; **ти́хий у́жас!** (*разг*) what a nightmare!; **до у́жаса** (*разг*) terribly

ужа́сно *нареч* (*разг: очень*) awfully, terribly ▷ *как сказ*: **э́то ужа́сно** it's awful *или* terrible

ужа́сный *прил* terrible, horrible, awful

у́же *сравн прил от* **у́зкий**

уже́ *нареч, част* already; **ты же уже́ не ма́ленький** you're not a child any more

ужива́|ться (**-юсь**) *несов от* **ужи́ться**

у́жин (**-а**) *м* supper

у́жина|ть (**-ю**; *perf* **поу́жинать**) *несов* to have supper

ужи́|ться (**-ву́сь, -вёшься**; *impf* **ужива́ться**) *сов возв*: **ужи́ться с кем-н** to get on with sb

узако́н|ить (**-ю, -ишь**; *impf* **узако́нивать**) *сов перех* to legalize

у́з|ел (**-ла́**) *м* knot; (*мешок*) bundle; **телефо́нный у́зел** telephone exchange; **железнодоро́жный у́зел** railway junction; **санита́рный у́зел** bathroom and toilet

у́зкий *прил* narrow; (*тесный*) tight; (*перен: человек*) narrow-minded

узна́|ть (**-ю**; *impf* **узнава́ть**) *сов перех* to recognize; (*новости*) to learn

у́зок *прил см* **у́зкий**

узо́р (**-а**) *м* pattern

уйти́ (*как* **идти́**; см *Table 18*; *impf* **уходи́ть**) *сов* (*человек*) to go away, leave; (*автобус, поезд*) to go, leave; (*избежать*): **уйти́ от** *+gen* (*от опасности итп*) to get away from; (*потребоваться*): **уйти́ на** *+acc* (*деньги, время*) to be spent on

ука́з (**-а**) *м* (*президента*) decree

указа́ни|е (**-я**) *ср* indication; (*разъяснение*) instruction; (*приказ*) directive

указа́тел|ь (**-я**) *м* (*дорожный*) sign; (*книга*) guide; (*список в книге*) index; (*прибор*) indicator

указа́тельн|ый *прил*; **указа́тельное местоиме́ние** demonstrative pronoun; **указа́тельный па́лец** index finger

ук|аза́ть (**-ажу́, -а́жешь**; *impf* **ука́зывать**) *сов перех* to point out; (*сообщить*) to indicate

укача́|ть (**-ю**; *impf* **ука́чивать**) *сов перех* (*усыпить*) to rock to sleep; **его́ укача́ло (в маши́не/на парохо́де)** he got (car-/sea-)sick

укла́дыва|ть (**-ю**) *несов от* **уложи́ть**; **укла́дываться** *несов от* **уложи́ться** ▷ *возв*: **э́то не укла́дывается в обы́чные ра́мки** this is out of the ordinary; **э́то не укла́дывается в голове́** *или* **в созна́нии** it's beyond me

укло́н (**-а**) *м* slant; **под укло́н** downhill

уко́л (**-а**) *м* prick; (*Мед*) injection

ук|оло́ть (**-олю́, -о́лешь**) *сов от* **коло́ть**

укра́|сить (**-шу, -сишь**; *impf* **украша́ть**) *сов перех* to decorate; (*жизнь итп*) to brighten (up)

укра́|сть (**-ду́, -дёшь**) *сов от* **красть**

украша́|ть (**-ю**) *несов от* **укра́сить**

украше́ни|е (**-я**) *ср* decoration; (*коллекции*) jewel; (*также* **ювели́рное украше́ние**) jewellery (*Brit*), jewelry (*US*)

укреп|и́ть (**-лю́, -и́шь**; *impf*

укреплять) *сов перех* to strengthen; (*стену*) to reinforce; **укрепиться** (*impf* **укрепляться**) *сов возв* to become stronger
укро|тить (**-щу́, -ти́шь**; *impf* **укроща́ть**) *сов перех* to tame
укры́ти|е (**-я**) *ср* shelter
укр|ы́ть (**-о́ю, -о́ешь**; *impf* **укрыва́ть**) *сов перех* (*закрыть*) to cover; (*беженца*) to shelter; **укры́ться** (*impf* **укрыва́ться**) *сов возв* to cover o.s.; (*от дождя*) to take cover
у́ксус (**-а**) *м* vinegar
уку́с (**-а**) *м* bite
ук|уси́ть (**-ушу́, -у́сишь**) *сов перех* to bite
уку́та|ть (**-ю**; *impf* **уку́тывать**) *сов перех* to wrap up; **уку́таться** (*impf* **уку́тываться**) *сов возв* to wrap o.s. up
ул. *сокр* (= *у́лица*) St (= *street*)
ула́влива|ть (**-ю**) *несов от* **улови́ть**
ула́|дить (**-жу, -дишь**; *impf* **ула́живать**) *сов перех* to settle
у́л|ей (**-ья**) *м* (bee-)hive
уле|те́ть (**-чу́, -ти́шь**; *impf* **улета́ть**) *сов* (*птица*) to fly away; (*самолёт*) to leave
ули́к|а (**-и**) *ж* (piece of) evidence (*мн* evidence)
ули́т|ка (**-ки**; *gen pl* **-ок**) *ж* snail
у́лиц|а (**-ы**) *ж* street; **на у́лице** outside
у́личн|ый *прил* street; **у́личное движе́ние** traffic
уло́в (**-а**) *м* catch (*of fish*)
улови́мый *прил*: **едва́** *или* **чуть** *или* **е́ле улови́мый** barely perceptible
ул|ови́ть (**-овлю́, -о́вишь**; *impf* **ула́вливать**) *сов перех* to detect; (*мысль, связь*) to grasp
ул|ожи́ть (**-ожу́, -о́жишь**; *impf* **укла́дывать**) *сов перех* (*ребёнка*) to put to bed; (*вещи, чемодан*) to pack; **уложи́ться** (*impf* **укла́дываться**) *сов возв* (*сложить вещи*) to pack; **укла́дываться** (*perf* **уложи́ться**) **в сро́ки** to keep to the time limit
улу́чш|ить (**-у, -ишь**; *impf* **улучша́ть**) *сов перех* to improve
улыба́|ться (**-юсь**; *perf* **улыбну́ться**) *несов возв*: **улыба́ться** (**+*dat***) to smile (at)
улы́б|ка (**-ки**; *gen pl* **-ок**) *ж* smile
ультрафиоле́тов|ый *прил*: **ультрафиоле́товые лучи́** ultraviolet rays *мн*
ум (**-а́**) *м* mind; **быть** (*impf*) **без ума́ от кого́-н/чего́-н** to be wild about sb/sth; **в уме́** (*считать*) in one's head; **бра́ться** (*perf* **взя́ться**) **за ум** to see sense; **сходи́ть** (*perf* **сойти́**) **с ума́** to go mad; **своди́ть** (*perf* **свести́**) **кого́-н с ума́** to drive sb mad; (*перен*: *увлечь*) to drive sb wild; **ума́ не приложу́, куда́/ ско́лько/кто ...** I can't think where/ how much/who ...
ума́лчива|ть (**-ю**) *несов от* **умолча́ть**
уме́лый *прил* skilful (*Brit*), skillful (*US*)
уме́ни|е (**-я**) *ср* ability, skill
уме́ньш|ить (**-у, -ишь**; *impf* **уменьша́ть**) *сов перех* to reduce; **уме́ньшиться** (*impf* **уменьша́ться**) *сов возв* to diminish
ум|ере́ть (**-ру́, -рёшь**; *impf* **умира́ть**) *сов* to die
уме́р|ить (**-ю, -ишь**; *impf* **умеря́ть**) *сов перех* to moderate
уме|сти́ть (**-щу́, -сти́шь**; *impf* **умеща́ть**) *сов перех* to fit; **умести́ться** (*impf* **умеща́ться**) *сов возв* to fit

уме́|ть (**-ю**) *несов* can, to be able to; (*иметь способность*) to know how to; **он уме́ет пла́вать/чита́ть** he can swim/read
умеща́|ть(ся) (**-ю(сь)**) *несов от* **умести́ть(ся)**
умира́|ть (**-ю**) *несов от* **умере́ть** ▷ *неперех* (*перен*): **умира́ю, как хочу́ есть/спать** I'm dying for something to eat/to go to sleep; **я умира́ю от ску́ки** I'm bored to death
умне́|ть (**-ю**; *perf* **поумне́ть**) *несов* (*человек*) to grow wiser
у́мниц|а (**-ы**) *м/ж*: **он/она́ у́мница** he's/she's a clever one; (*разг*): **вот у́мница!** good for you!, well done!
у́мно *нареч* (*сделанный*) cleverly; (*вести себя*) sensibly; (*говорить*) intelligently
умножа́|ть (**-ю**) *несов от* **умно́жить**
умноже́ни|е (**-я**) *ср* (*см глаг*) multiplication; increase
умно́ж|ить (**-у, -ишь**; *impf* **мно́жить** *или* **умножа́ть**) *сов перех* (*Мат*) to multiply
у́мный *прил* clever, intelligent
умозаключе́ни|е (**-я**) *ср* (*вывод*) deduction
умол|и́ть (**-ю́, -и́шь**; *impf* **умоля́ть**) *сов перех*: **умоли́ть кого́-н** (*+infin*) to prevail upon sb (to do)
умо́лкн|уть (**-у**; *impf* **умолка́ть**) *сов* to fall silent
умолч|а́ть (**-у́, -и́шь**; *impf* **ума́лчивать**) *сов*: **умолча́ть о чём-н** to keep quiet about sth
умоля́|ть (**-ю**) *несов от* **умоли́ть** ▷ *перех* to implore
умру́ *итп сов см* **умере́ть**
умо́ю(сь) *сов см* **умы́ть(ся)**
у́мственно *нареч*: **у́мственно отста́лый** with learning difficulties
у́мственный *прил* (*способности*) mental; **у́мственный труд** intellectual work
умудр|и́ться (**-ю́сь, -и́шься**; *impf* **умудря́ться**) *сов возв* to manage
умч|а́ть (**-у́, -и́шь**) *сов перех* to whisk off *или* away; **умча́ться** *сов возв* to dash off
умы́ть (**умо́ю, умо́ешь**; *impf* **умыва́ть**) *сов перех* to wash; **умы́ться** (*impf* **умыва́ться**) *сов возв* to wash
ун|ести́ (**-есу́, -есёшь**; *pt* **-ёс, -есла́**, *impf* **уноси́ть**) *сов перех* to take away; **унести́сь** (*impf* **уноси́ться**) *сов возв* to speed off
универма́г (**-а**) *м* = **универса́льный магази́н**
универса́льный *прил* universal; (*образование*) all-round; (*человек, машина*) versatile; **универса́льный магази́н** department store
универса́м (**-а**) *м* supermarket
университе́т (**-а**) *м* university
унижа́|ть(ся) (**-ю(сь)**) *несов от* **уни́зить(ся)**
униже́ни|е (**-я**) *ср* humiliation
уни́|зить (**-жу, -зишь**; *impf* **унижа́ть**) *сов перех* to humiliate; **унижа́ть** (*perf* **уни́зить**) **себя́** to abase o.s.; **уни́зиться** (*impf* **унижа́ться**) *сов возв*: **уни́зиться** (**пе́ред** *+instr*) to abase o.s. (before)
уника́льный *прил* unique
унита́з (**-а**) *м* toilet
уничто́ж|ить (**-у, -ишь**; *impf* **уничтожа́ть**) *сов перех* to destroy
ун|оси́ть(ся) (**-ошу́(сь), -о́сишь(ся)**) *несов от* **унести́(сь)**
уныва́|ть (**-ю**) *несов* (*человек*) to be downcast *или* despondent
уня́|ть (**-уйму́, уймёшь**; *pt* **-л,**

-ла́, -ло, *impf* **унима́ть**) *сов перех* (*волнение*) to suppress
упа́д|ок (**-ка**) *м* decline
упак|ова́ть (**-у́ю**) *сов от* **пакова́ть**
упако́вк|а (**-и**) *ж* packing; (*материал*) packaging
упасти́ *сов перех*: **упаси́ Бог** *или* **Бо́же** *или* **Го́споди!** God forbid!
упа́|сть (**-ду́, -дёшь**) *сов от* **па́дать**
упере́ть (**упру́, упрёшь**; *pt* **упёр, упёрла, упёрло**, *impf* **упира́ть**) *сов перех*: **упере́ть что-н в** *+acc* (*в стену итп*) to prop sth against; **упере́ться** (*impf* **упира́ться**) *сов возв*: **упере́ться чем-н в** *+acc* (*в землю*) to dig sth into; (*натолкнуться*): **упере́ться в** *+acc* (*в стену*) to come up against
упива́|ться (**-юсь**) *несов возв* (*+instr*: *перен*: *счастьем*) to be intoxicated by
упира́|ть (**-ю**) *несов от* **упере́ть**; **упира́ться** *несов от* **упере́ться** ▷ *возв* (*иметь причиной*): **упира́ться в** *+prp* to be down to
упла́т|а (**-ы**) *ж* payment
упл|ати́ть (**-ачу́, -а́тишь**) *сов от* **плати́ть**
уплы́|ть (**-ву́, -вёшь**; *impf* **уплыва́ть**) *сов* (*человек, рыба итп*) to swim away *или* off; (*корабль*) to sail away *или* off
уподо́б|ить (**-лю, -ишь**; *impf* **уподобля́ть**) *сов перех*: **уподо́бить что-н/кого́-н** *+dat* to compare sth/sb to; **уподо́биться** (*impf* **уподобля́ться**) *сов возв*: **уподо́биться** *+dat* to become like
уполз|ти́ (**-у́, -ёшь**; *pt* **-, -ла́**) *сов* (*змея*) to slither away
уполномо́чи|е (**-я**) *ср*: **по уполномо́чию** *+gen* on behalf of
уполномо́ч|ить (**-у, -ишь**; *impf* **уполномо́чивать**) *сов перех*: **уполномо́чить кого́-н** *+infin* to authorize sb to do
упом|яну́ть (**-яну́, -я́нешь**; *impf* **упомина́ть**) *сов (не)перех* (*назвать*): **упомяну́ть** *+acc или* (**о** *+prp*) to mention
упо́р (**-а**) *м* (*для ног*) rest; **в упо́р** (*стрелять*) point-blank; (*смотреть*) intently; **де́лать** (*perf* **сде́лать**) **упо́р на** *+prp* to put emphasis on
упо́рный *прил* persistent
употреби́тельный *прил* frequently used
употреб|и́ть (**-лю́, -и́шь**; *impf* **употребля́ть**) *сов перех* to use
употребле́ни|е (**-я**) *ср* (*слова*) usage; (*лекарства*) taking; (*алкоголя, пищи*) consumption
управле́ни|е (**-я**) *ср* (*делами*) administration; (*фирмой*) management; (*учреждение*) office; (*система приборов*) controls *мн*
управля́|ть (**-ю**) *несов* (*+instr*: *автомобилем*) to drive; (*судном*) to navigate; (*государством*) to govern; (*учреждением, фирмой*) to manage; (*оркестром*) to conduct
управля́ющ|ий (**-его**) *м* (*хозяйством*) manager; (*имением*) bailiff
упражне́ни|е (**-я**) *ср* exercise
упражня́|ть (**-ю**) *несов перех* to exercise; **упражня́ться** *несов возв* to practise
упраздн|и́ть (**-ю́, -и́шь**; *impf* **упраздня́ть**) *сов перех* to abolish
упра́шива|ть (**-ю**) *несов от* **упроси́ть**
упрека́|ть (**-ю**; *perf* **упрекну́ть**) *несов перех*: **упрека́ть кого́-н** (**в** *+prp*) to reproach sb (for)
упр|оси́ть (**-ошу́, -о́сишь**; *impf* **упра́шивать**) *сов перех*:

упросить кого-н *+infin* to persuade sb to do

упро|стить (**-щу́, -сти́шь**; *impf* **упроща́ть**) *сов перех* to simplify

упро́ч|ить (**-у, -ишь**; *impf* **упро́чивать**) *сов перех* to consolidate; **упро́читься** (*impf* **упро́чиваться**) *сов возв* (*положение, позиции*) to be consolidated

упроща́|ть (**-ю**) *несов от* **упрости́ть**

упря́ж|ка (**-ки**; *gen pl* **-ек**) *ж* team (*of horses, dogs etc*); (*упряжь*) harness

у́пряж|ь (**-и**) *ж по pl* harness

упря́мый *прил* obstinate, stubborn

упуска́|ть (**-ю**; *perf* **упусти́ть**) *несов перех* (*мяч*) to let go of; (*момент*) to miss; **упуска́ть** (*perf* **упусти́ть**) **из ви́ду** to overlook

упуще́ни|е (**-я**) *ср* error, mistake

ура́ *межд* hooray, hurrah

уравне́ни|е (**-я**) *ср* (*Мат*) equation

ура́внива|ть (**-ю**) *несов от* **уравня́ть**

уравнове́|сить (**-шу, -сишь**; *impf* **уравнове́шивать**) *сов перех* to balance; **уравнове́ситься** (*impf* **уравнове́шиваться**) *сов возв* (*силы*) to be counterbalanced

уравнове́шенный *прил* balanced

уравня́|ть (**-ю**; *impf* **ура́внивать**) *сов перех* to make equal

урага́н (**-а**) *м* hurricane

урага́нный *прил*: **урага́нный ве́тер** gale

ура́н (**-а**) *м* uranium

урегули́р|овать (**-ую**) *сов перех* to settle

у́рн|а (**-ы**) *ж* (*погребальная*) urn; (*для мусора*) bin; **избира́тельная у́рна** ballot box

у́ров|ень (**-ня**) *м* level; (*техники*) standard; (*зарплаты*) rate; **встре́ча на вы́сшем у́ровне** summit meeting; **у́ровень жи́зни** standard of living

уро́д (**-а**) *м* *person with a deformity*

урожа́|й (**-я**) *м* harvest

уро́к (**-а**) *м* lesson; (*задание*) task; (*обычно мн*: *домашняя работа*) homework; **де́лать** (*perf* **сде́лать**) **уро́ки** to do one's homework

ур|они́ть (**-оню́, -о́нишь**) *сов от* **роня́ть**

ус|ади́ть (**-ажу́, -а́дишь**; *impf* **уса́живать**) *сов перех* (*заставить делать*): **усади́ть кого́-н за что-н**/*+infin* to sit sb down to sth/to do

уса́жива|ть (**-ю**) *несов от* **усади́ть**; **уса́живаться** *несов от* **усе́сться**

уса́тый *прил*: **уса́тый мужчи́на** man with a moustache (*Brit*) *или* mustache (*US*)

ус|е́сться (**-я́дусь, -я́дешься**; *pt* **-е́лся, -е́лась**, *impf* **уса́живаться**) *сов возв* to settle down; **уса́живаться** (*perf* **усе́сться**) **за** *+acc* (*за работу*) to sit down to

уси́лива|ть (**-ю**) *несов от* **уси́лить**

уси́ли|е (**-я**) *ср* effort

уси́л|ить (**-ю, -ишь**; *impf* **уси́ливать**) *сов перех* to intensify; (*охрану*) to heighten; (*внимание*) to increase; **уси́литься** (*impf* **уси́ливаться**) *сов возв* (*ветер*) to get stronger; (*волнение*) to increase

ускользн|у́ть (**-у́, -ёшь**; *impf* **ускольза́ть**) *сов* to slip away

усло́ви|е (**-я**) *ср* condition; (*договора*) term; (*обычно мн*: *правила*) requirement; *см также* **усло́вия**

усло́в|иться (**-люсь, -ишься**; *impf* **усла́вливаться**) *сов возв*: **усло́виться о** *+prp* (*договориться*) to agree on

усло́ви|я (**-й**) *мн* (*природные*) conditions *мн*; (*задачи*) factors *мн*; **жили́щные усло́вия** housing; **усло́вия труда́** working conditions; **в усло́виях** *+gen* in an atmosphere of; **по усло́виям догово́ра** on the terms of the agreement; **на льго́тных усло́виях** on special terms

усло́вный *прил* conditional; (*сигнал*) code

усложн|и́ть (**-ю́, -и́шь**; *impf* **усложня́ть**) *сов перех* to complicate; **усложни́ться** (*impf* **усложня́ться**) *сов возв* to get more complicated

услу́г|а (**-и**) *ж* (*одолжение*) favour (*Brit*), favor (*US*); (*обычно мн*: *облуживание*) service; **к Ва́шим услу́гам!** at your service!

услы́ш|ать (**-у, -ишь**) *сов от* **слы́шать**

усма́трива|ть (**-ю**) *несов от* **усмотре́ть**

усмехн|у́ться (**-у́сь, -ёшься**; *impf* **усмеха́ться**) *сов возв* to smile slightly

усме́шк|а (**-и**) *ж* slight smile; **зла́я усме́шка** sneer

усмир|и́ть (**-ю́, -и́шь**; *impf* **усмиря́ть**) *сов перех* (*зверя*) to tame

усмотре́ни|е (**-я**) *ср* discretion

усм|отре́ть (**-отрю́, -о́тришь**; *impf* **усма́тривать**) *сов перех* (*счесть*): **усмотре́ть что-н в** *+prp* to see sth in

усн|у́ть (**-у́, -ёшь**) *сов* to fall asleep, go to sleep

усоверше́нствовани|е (**-я**) *ср* improvement

усомн|и́ться (**-ю́сь, -и́шься**) *сов возв*: **усомни́ться в** *+prp* to doubt

успева́емост|ь (**-и**) *ж* performance (*in studies*)

успе́|ть (**-ю**; *impf* **успева́ть**) *сов* (*о работе*) to manage; (*прийти вовремя*) to be *или* make it in time

успе́х (**-а**) *м* success; (*обычно мн*: *в спорте, в учёбе*) achievement; **как Ва́ши успе́хи?** how are you getting on?

успе́шный *прил* successful

успоко́|ить (**-ю, -ишь**; *impf* **успока́ивать**) *сов перех* to calm (down); **успоко́иться** (*impf* **успока́иваться**) *сов возв* (*человек*) to calm down

уста́в (**-а**) *м* (*партийный*) rules *мн*; (*воинский*) regulations *мн*; (*фирмы*) statute

уста|ва́ть (**-ю́, -ёшь**) *несов от* **уста́ть**

уста́в|ить (**-лю, -ишь**; *impf* **уставля́ть**) *сов перех* (*занять*): **уста́вить что-н чем-н** to cover sth with sth; (*разг*: *устремить*): **уста́вить что-н в** *+acc* to fix sth on; **уста́виться** (*impf* **уставля́ться**) *сов возв* (*разг*): **уста́виться на/в** *+acc* to stare at

уста́лост|ь (**-и**) *ж* tiredness, fatigue

уста́лый *прил* tired

устан|ови́ть (**-овлю́, -о́вишь**; *impf* **устана́вливать**) *сов перех* to establish; (*сроки*) to set; (*прибор*) to install; **установи́ться** (*impf* **устана́вливаться**) *сов возв* to be established

устано́вк|а (**-и**) *ж* installation

устаре́|ть (**-ю**) *сов от* **старе́ть**

▷ (*impf* **устарева́ть**) *неперех* (*оборудование*) to become obsolete
уста́|ть (**-ну, -нешь**; *impf* **устава́ть**) *сов* to get tired
у́стн|ый *прил* (*экзамен*) oral; (*обещание, приказ*) verbal; **у́стная речь** spoken language
усто́йчив|ый *прил* stable; **усто́йчивое (сло́во)сочета́ние** set phrase
усто|я́ть (**-ю́, -и́шь**) *сов* (*не упасть*) to remain standing; (*в борьбе итп*) to stand one's ground; (*перед соблазном*) to resist
устра́ива|ть(ся) (**-ю(сь)**) *несов от* **устро́ить(ся)**
устран|и́ть (**-ю́, -и́шь**; *impf* **устраня́ть**) *сов перех* to remove
устрем|и́ть (**-лю́, -и́шь**; *impf* **устремля́ть**) *сов перех* to direct; **устреми́ться** (*impf* **устремля́ться**) *сов возв*: **устреми́ться на** *+acc* (*толпа*) to charge at
у́стриц|а (**-ы**) *ж* oyster
устро́|ить (**-ю, -ишь**; *impf* **устра́ивать**) *сов перех* to organize; (*подлеж*: *цена*) to suit; **э́то меня́ устро́ит** that suits me; **устро́иться** (*impf* **устра́иваться**) *сов возв* (*расположиться*) to settle down; (*прийти в порядок*) to work out; **устра́иваться** (*perf* **устро́иться**) **на рабо́ту** to get a job
устро́йств|о (**-а**) *ср* (*прибора*) construction; (*техническое*) device, mechanism
усту́п (**-а**) *м* foothold
уст|упи́ть (**-уплю́, -у́пишь**; *impf* **уступа́ть**) *сов перех*: **уступи́ть что-н кому́-н** to give sth up for sb; (*победу*) to concede sth to sb ▷ *неперех*: **уступи́ть кому́-н/чему́-н** (*силе, желанию*) to yield to sb/sth; **уступа́ть** (*perf* **уступи́ть**) **в** *+prp* (*в силе, в уме*) to be inferior in
усту́п|ка (**-ки**; *gen pl* **-ок**) *ж* conciliation; (*скидка*) discount; **пойти́** (*perf*) **на усту́пку** to compromise
у́сть|е (**-я**) *ср* (*реки*) mouth
ус|ы́ (**-о́в**) *мн* (*у человека*) moustache *ед* (*Brit*), mustache *ед* (*US*); (*у животных*) whiskers
усынов|и́ть (**-лю́, -и́шь**; *impf* **усыновля́ть**) *сов перех* to adopt (*son*)
усып|и́ть (**-лю́, -и́шь**; *impf* **усыпля́ть**) *сов перех* (*больного*) to anaesthetize (*Brit*), anesthetize (*US*); (*ребёнка*) to lull to sleep
ут|ащи́ть (**-ащу́, -а́щишь**; *impf* **ута́скивать**) *сов перех* (*унести*) to drag away *или* off
утвер|ди́ть (**-жу́, -ди́шь**; *impf* **утвержда́ть**) *сов перех* (*закон*) to pass; (*договор*) to ratify; (*план*) to approve; (*порядок*) to establish; **утверди́ться** (*impf* **утвержда́ться**) *сов возв* to be established
утвержда́|ть (**-ю**) *несов от* **утверди́ть** ▷ *перех* (*настаивать*) to maintain; **утвержда́ться** *несов от* **утверди́ться**
утвержде́ни|е (**-я**) *ср* (*см глаг*) passing; ratification; approval; establishment; (*мысль*) statement
утёс (**-а**) *м* cliff
уте́чк|а (**-и**) *ж* (*также перен*) leak; (*кадров*) turnover; **уте́чка мозго́в** brain drain
ут|е́чь (*3sg* **-ечёт**, *pt* **-ёк, -екла́, -екло́**, *impf* **утека́ть**) *сов* (*вода*) to leak out
уте́ш|ить (**-у, -ишь**; *impf* **утеша́ть**) *сов перех* to comfort, console

ути́хн|уть (**-у**; *impf* **утиха́ть**) *сов* (*спор*) to calm down; (*звук*) to die away; (*вьюга*) to die down
у́т|ка (**-ки**; *gen pl* **-ок**) *ж* duck
уткн|у́ть (**-у́, -ёшь**) *сов перех* (*разг*: *лицо*) to bury; **уткну́ться** *сов возв* (*разг*): **уткну́ться в** *+acc* (*в книгу*) to bury one's nose in
утол|и́ть (**-ю́, -и́шь**; *impf* **утоля́ть**) *сов перех* to satisfy; (*жажду*) to quench
утоми́тельный *прил* tiring
утом|и́ть (**-лю́, -и́шь**; *impf* **утомля́ть**) *сов перех* to tire; **утоми́ться** (*impf* **утомля́ться**) *сов возв* to get tired
ут|ону́ть (**-ону́, -о́нешь**) *сов от* **тону́ть**
утопа́|ть (**-ю**) *несов* (*тонуть*) to drown
ут|опи́ть(ся) (**-оплю́(сь), -о́пишь(ся)**) *сов от* **топи́ть(ся)**
уточн|и́ть (**-ю́, -и́шь**; *impf* **уточня́ть**) *сов перех* to clarify
утра́т|а (**-ы**) *ж* loss
утра́|тить (**-чу, -тишь**; *impf* **утра́чивать**) *сов перех* (*потерять*) to lose; **утра́чивать** (*perf* **утра́тить**) **си́лу** (*документ*) to become invalid
у́тренний *прил* morning; (*событие*) this morning's
у́тренник (**-а**) *м* matinée; (*для детей*) children's party
у́тр|о (**-а́**; *nom pl* **-а**, *gen pl* **-**, *dat pl* **-ам**) *ср* morning; **до́брое у́тро!, с до́брым у́тром!** good morning!; **на у́тро** next morning; **под у́тро, к утру́** in the early hours of the morning
утро́б|а (**-ы**) *ж* (*матери*) womb
утро́|ить (**-ю, -ишь**) *сов перех* to treble, triple; **утро́иться** *сов возв* to treble, triple
у́тром *нареч* in the morning
утружда́|ть (**-ю**) *несов перех*: **утружда́ть кого́-н чем-н** to trouble sb with sth; **утружда́ться** *несов возв* to trouble o.s.
утю́г (**-а́**) *м* iron (*appliance*)
утю́ж|ить (**-у, -ишь**; *perf* **вы́утюжить** *или* **отутю́жить**) *несов перех* to iron
уф *межд*: **уф!** phew!
ух *межд*: **ух!** ooh!
ух|а́ (**-и́**) *ж* fish broth
уха́жива|ть (**-ю**) *несов*: **уха́живать за** *+instr* (*за больным*) to nurse; (*за садом*) to tend; (*за женщиной*) to court
ухв|ати́ть (**-ачу́, -а́тишь**; *impf* **ухва́тывать**) *сов перех* (*человека*: *за руку*) to get hold of; (*перен*: *идею, смысл*) to grasp; **ухвати́ться** (*impf* **ухва́тываться**) *сов возв*: **ухвати́ться за** *+acc* to grab hold of; (*за идею*) to jump at
у́х|о (**-а**; *nom pl* **у́ши**, *gen pl* **уше́й**) *ср* ear; (*у шапки*) flap
ухо́д (**-а**) *м* departure; (*из семьи*) desertion; (*со сцены*) exit; (*за больным, за ребёнком*) care; **ухо́д в отста́вку** resignation; **ухо́д на пе́нсию** retirement
ух|оди́ть (**-ожу́, -о́дишь**) *несов от* **уйти́**
уху́дш|ить (**-у, -ишь**; *impf* **ухудша́ть**) *сов перех* to make worse; **уху́дшиться** (*impf* **ухудша́ться**) *сов возв* to deteriorate
уцеле́|ть (**-ю**) *сов* to survive
уцен|и́ть (**-ю́, -ишь**; *impf* **уце́нивать**) *сов перех* to reduce (the price of)
уце́н|ка (**-ки**; *gen pl* **-ок**) *ж* reduction
уча́ств|овать (**-ую**) *сов*: **уча́ствовать в** *+prp* to take part in

участко́в|ый *прил* local ▷ **(-ого)** *м* (*разг*: *также* **участко́вый инспе́ктор**) local policeman; (: *также* **участко́вый врач**) local GP *или* doctor
уча́стник **(-а)** *м* participant; (*экспедиции*) member
уча́ст|ок **(-ка)** *м* (*земли, кожи итп*) area; (*реки, фронта*) stretch; (*врачебный*) catchment area; (*земельный*) plot; (*строительный*) site; (*работы*) field; **садо́вый уча́сток** allotment
у́част|ь **(-и)** *ж* lot
учаща́|ть(ся) **(-ю)** *несов от* **участи́ть(ся)**
уча́щ|ийся **(-егося)** *м* (*школы*) pupil; (*училища*) student
учёб|а **(-ы)** *ж* studies *мн*
уче́бник **(-а)** *м* textbook
уче́бн|ый *прил* (*работа*) academic; (*фильм*) educational; (*бой*) mock; (*судно*) training; (*методы*) teaching; **уче́бная програ́мма** curriculum; **уче́бное заведе́ние** educational establishment; **уче́бный год** academic year
уче́ни|е **(-я)** *ср* (*теория*) teachings *мн*; *см также* **уче́ния**
учени́к **(-а́)** *м* (*школы*) pupil; (*училища*) student; (*мастера*) apprentice
учени́ческий *прил* (*тетради*) school
уче́ни|я **(-й)** *мн* exercises *мн*
учён|ый *прил* academic; (*труды*) scholarly; (*человек*) learned, scholarly ▷ **(-ого)** *м* academic, scholar; (*в области точных и естественных наук*) scientist
уч|е́сть **(-ту́, -тёшь**; *pt* **-ёл, -ла́**, *impf* **учи́тывать**) *сов перех* to take into account; **учти́те, что ...** bear in mind that ...
учёт **(-а)** *м* (*факторов*) consideration; (*военный, медицинский*) registration; (*затрат*) record; **брать** (*perf* **взять**) **на учёт** to register; **вести́** (*impf*) **учёт** to keep a record
учётн|ый *прил*: **учётная ка́рточка** registration form
учи́лищ|е **(-а)** *ср* college
учи́тел|ь **(-я**; *nom pl* **-я́**) *м* teacher
учи́тельск|ая **(-ой)** *ж* staffroom
учи́тыва|ть **(-ю)** *несов от* **уче́сть**
уч|и́ть **(-у́, -ишь**; *perf* **вы́учить**) *несов перех* (*урок, роль*) to learn ▷ (*perf* **научи́ть** *или* **обучи́ть**); **учи́ть кого́-н чему́-н/**+*infin* to teach sb sth/to do; **учи́ться** *несов возв* (*в школе, в училище*) to study ▷ (*perf* **вы́учиться** *или* **научи́ться**): **учи́ться чему́-н/**+*infin* to learn sth/to do
учреди́тел|ь **(-я)** *м* founder
учреди́тельн|ый *прил*: **учреди́тельное собра́ние** inaugural meeting
учре|ди́ть **(-жу́, -ди́шь**; *impf* **учрежда́ть**) *сов перех* (*организацию*) to set up; (*контроль, порядок*) to introduce
учрежде́ни|е **(-я)** *ср* (*организации итп*) setting up; (*научное*) establishment; (*финансовое, общественное*) institution
уша́н|ка **(-ки**; *gen pl* **-ок**) *ж* cap with ear-flaps
ушёл *сов см* **уйти́**
у́ши *etc сущ см* **у́хо**
ушиб **(-а)** *м* bruise
ушиб|и́ть **(-у́, -ёшь**; *pt* **-, -ла**, *impf* **ушиба́ть**) *сов перех* to bang; **ушиби́ться** *сов возв* to bruise
уш|и́ть **(-ью́, -ьёшь**; *impf*

ушивать) *сов перех* (*одежду*) to take in
ýш|ко (**-ка**; *nom pl* **-ки**, *gen pl* **-ек**) *ср, уменьш от* **ýхо**; (*иголки*) eye
ушлá *etc сов см* **уйти́**
ушн|óй *прил* ear; **ушнáя боль** earache
ущéл|ье (**-ья**; *gen pl* **-ий**) *ср* gorge, ravine
ущем|и́ть (**-лю́, -и́шь**; *impf* **ущемля́ть**) *сов перех* (*палец*) to trap; (*права*) to limit
ущипн|ýть (**-ý, -ёшь**) *сов перех* to nip, pinch
ую́тно *нареч* (*расположиться*) comfortably ▷ *как сказ*: **здесь ую́тно** it's cosy here; **мне здесь ую́тно** I feel comfortable here
ую́тный *прил* cosy
уязви́мый *прил* vulnerable
уязв|и́ть (**-лю́, -и́шь**) *сов перех* to wound, hurt
уясн|и́ть (**-ю́, -и́шь**; *impf* **уясня́ть**) *сов перех* (*значение*) to comprehend

фáбрик|а (**-и**) *ж* factory; (*ткацкая, бумажная*) mill
фабри́чный *прил* factory
фáз|а (**-ы**) *ж* phase
фазáн (**-а**) *м* pheasant
файл (**-а**) *м* (*Комп*) file
фáкел (**-а**) *м* torch
факс (**-а**) *м* fax
факт (**-а**) *м* fact
факти́чески *нареч* actually, in fact
факти́ческий *прил* factual
фáктор (**-а**) *м* factor
фактýр|а (**-ы**) *ж* texture; (*Комм*) invoice
факультати́вный *прил* optional
факультéт (**-а**) *м* faculty
фами́ли|я (**-и**) *ж* surname; **дéвичья фами́лия** maiden name
фан (**-а**) *м* fan
фанáтик (**-а**) *м* fanatic
фантази́р|овать (**-ую**) *несов*

(*мечтать*) to dream; (*выдумывать*) to make up stories
фантáст (**-а**) *м* writer of fantasy; (*научный*) science-fiction writer
фантáстик|а (**-и**) *ж, собир* (*Литература*) fantasy; **наýчная фантáстика** science fiction
фантастúческий *прил* fantastic
фáр|а (**-ы**) *ж* (*Авт, Авиа*) light
фармацéвт (**-а**) *м* chemist, pharmacist
фáртук (**-а**) *м* apron
фарширова́ть (**-ýю**; *perf* **зафаршировáть**) *несов перех* to stuff
фасáд (**-а**) *м* (*передняя сторона*) facade, front; **зáдний фасáд** back
фасóл|ь (**-и**) *ж* (*растение*) bean plant ▷ *собир* (*семена*) beans *мн*
фасóн (**-а**) *м* style
фат|á (**-ы́**) *ж* veil
ФБР *ср сокр* (= *Федерáльное бюрó расслéдований (США)*) FBI (= *Federal Bureau of Investigation*)
феврáл|ь (**-я́**) *м* February

23 Февраля́: День защи́тника Оте́чества

This is an official celebration of the Russian army, though various sections of the armed forces have their own special holidays. Men of all ages and walks of life receive gifts and greetings, mainly from women.

федерáльный *прил* federal
федератúвный *прил* federal
федерáци|я (**-и**) *ж* federation
фéльдшер (**-а**) *м* (*в поликлинике*) ≈ practice nurse; **фéльдшер скóрой пóмощи** ≈ paramedic
фельетóн (**-а**) *м* satirical article
феминúст|ка (**-ки**; *gen pl* **-ок**) *ж* feminist
фен (**-а**) *м* hairdryer
ферз|ь (**-я́**) *м* (*Шахматы*) queen
фéрм|а (**-ы**) *ж* farm
фéрмер (**-а**) *м* farmer
фéрмерск|ий *прил*: **фéрмерское хозя́йство** farm
фестивáл|ь (**-я**) *м* festival
фетр (**-а**) *м* felt
фехтовáни|е (**-я**) *ср* (*Спорт*) fencing
фé|я (**-и**) *ж* fairy
фиáл|ка (**-ки**; *gen pl* **-ок**) *ж* violet
фиáско *ср нескл* fiasco
фúг|а (**-и**) *ж* (*Бот*) fig; (*разг*) fig (*gesture of refusal*); **идú нá фиг!** get lost!; **ни фигá** nothing at all
фигýр|а (**-ы**) *ж* figure; (*Шахматы*) (chess)piece
фигурúр|овать (**-ую**) *несов* to be present; (*имя, тема*) to feature
фигурúст (**-а**) *м* figure skater
фúзик (**-а**) *м* physicist
фúзик|а (**-и**) *ж* physics
физиотерапú|я (**-и**) *ж* physiotherapy
физúческ|ий *прил* physical; (*труд*) manual; **физúческая культýра** physical education
физкультýр|а (**-ы**) *ж сокр* (= *физúческая культýра*) PE (= *physical education*)
фиксúр|овать (**-ую**; *perf* **зафиксúровать**) *несов перех* to fix; (*отмечать*) to record
филармóни|я (**-и**) *ж* (*зал*) concert hall; (*организация*) philharmonic society
филé *ср нескл* fillet
филóлог (**-а**) *м* specialist in language and literature
филолóги|я (**-и**) *ж* language and literature
филологúческий *прил*

philological; **филологи́ческий факульте́т** department of language and literature
фило́соф (**-а**) *м* philosopher
филосо́фи|я (**-и**) *ж* philosophy
фильм (**-а**) *м* film
фильтр (**-а**) *м* filter
фильтр|ова́ть (**-у́ю**; *perf* **профильтрова́ть**) *несов перех* to filter
фина́л (**-а**) *м* finale; (*Спорт*) final
фина́льный *прил* final
финанси́р|овать (**-ую**) *несов перех* to finance
фина́нсовый *прил* financial; (*год*) fiscal; (*отдел, инспектор*) finance
фина́нс|ы (**-ов**) *мн* finances; **Министе́рство фина́нсов** ≈ the Treasury (*Brit*), ≈ the Department of the Treasury (*US*)
фи́ник (**-а**) *м* (*плод*) date
фи́ниш (**-а**) *м* (*Спорт*) finish
финиши́р|овать (**-ую**) *(не)сов* to finish
Финля́нди|я (**-и**) *ж* Finland
финн (**-а**) *м* Finn
фи́нский *прил* Finnish; **фи́нский язы́к** Finnish; **фи́нский зали́в** Gulf of Finland
Ф.И.О. *сокр* (= *фами́лия, и́мя, о́тчество*) *surname, first name, patronymic*
фиоле́товый *прил* purple
фи́рм|а (**-ы**) *ж* firm
фи́рменный *прил* (*магазин*) chain; (*разг: товар*) quality; **фи́рменный знак** brand name
фи́ш|ка (**-ки**; *gen pl* **-ек**) *ж* counter, chip
флаг (**-а**) *м* flag
флако́н (**-а**) *м* bottle
фланг (**-а**) *м* flank
флане́л|ь (**-и**) *ж* flannel
фле́йт|а (**-ы**) *ж* flute
фле́ш|ка (**-ки**; *gen pl* **-ек**) *ж* (*разг*) USB stick; **флеш-накопи́тел|ь** (**-я**) *м* USB stick
фли́гел|ь (**-я**) *м* (*Архит*) wing
флома́стер (**-а**) *м* felt-tip (pen)
флот (**-а**) *м* (*Воен*) navy; (*Мор*) fleet; **возду́шный флот** air force
фойе́ *ср нескл* foyer
фо́кус (**-а**) *м* trick; (*Тех: перен*) focus
фольг|а́ (**-и́**) *ж* foil
фолькло́р (**-а**) *м* folklore
фон (**-а**) *м* background
фона́р|ь (**-я́**) *м* (*уличный*) lamp; (*карманный*) torch
фо́ндов|ый *прил*: **фо́ндовая би́ржа** stock exchange
фоне́тик|а (**-и**) *ж* phonetics
фоноте́к|а (**-и**) *ж* music collection
фонта́н (**-а**) *м* fountain
форе́л|ь (**-и**) *ж* trout
фо́рм|а (**-ы**) *ж* form; (*одежда*) uniform; (*Тех*) mould (*Brit*), mold (*US*); (*Кулин*) (cake) tin
форма́льност|ь (**-и**) *ж* formality
форма́т (**-а**) *м* format
форма́ци|я (**-и**) *ж* (*общественная*) system
фо́рменн|ый *прил*: **фо́рменный бланк** standard form; **фо́рменная оде́жда** uniform
формирова́ни|е (**-я**) *ср* formation; **вое́нное формирова́ние** military unit
формир|ова́ть (**-у́ю**; *perf* **сформирова́ть**) *несов перех* to form; **формирова́ться** (*perf* **сформирова́ться**) *несов возв* to form
фо́рмул|а (**-ы**) *ж* formula
формули́р|овать (**-ую**; *perf* **сформули́ровать**) *несов перех* to formulate
формулиро́в|ка (**-ки**; *gen pl* **-ок**) *ж* (*определение*) definition
фортепья́но *ср нескл* (grand) piano

фóрточ|ка (**-ки**; *gen pl* **-ек**) *ж* *hinged, upper pane in window for ventilation*
фóрум (**-а**) *м* forum
фóто-: **фотоаппарáт** (**-а**) *м* camera; **фотóграф** (**-а**) *м* photographer; **фотографи́р|овать** (**-ую**; *perf* **сфотографи́ровать**) *несов перех* to photograph; **фотографи́роваться** (*perf* **сфотографи́роваться**) *несов возв* to have one's photo(graph) taken; **фотогрáфи|я** (**-и**) *ж* photography; (*снимок*) photograph; **фотокáрточ|ка** (**-ки**; *gen pl* **-ек**) *ж* photo
фрáз|а (**-ы**) *ж* phrase
фрак (**-а**) *м* tail coat, tails *мн*
фрáкци|я (**-и**) *ж* faction
Фрáнци|я (**-и**) *ж* France
францу́жен|ка (**-ки**) *ж* Frenchwoman (*мн* Frenchwomen)
францу́з (**-а**) *м* Frenchman (*мн* Frenchmen)
францу́зский *прил* French; **францу́зский язы́к** French
фрахт (**-а**) *м* freight
фрахт|овáть (**-у́ю**; *perf* **зафрахтовáть**) *несов перех* to charter
фрикаде́л|ька (**-ьки**; *gen pl* **-ек**) *ж* meatball
фронт (**-а**; *nom pl* **-ы́**) *м* front
фронтови́к (**-á**) *м* front line soldier; (*ветеран*) war veteran
фрукт (**-а**) *м* (*Бот*) fruit; **фруктóвый** *прил* fruit
ФСБ *ж нескл сокр* (= *Федерáльная слу́жба безопáсности*) *Department of State Security*
ФСК *ж нескл сокр* (= *Федерáльная слу́жба контрразве́дки*) *counterespionage intelligence service*
фтор (**-а**) *м* fluorin(e)
фу *межд*: **фу!** ugh!
фундáмент (**-а**) *м* (*Строит*) foundations *мн*, base; (*перен*: *семьи, науки*) foundation, basis
фундаментáльный *прил* (*здание*) sound, solid; (*перен*: *знания*) profound
функционе́р (**-а**) *м* official
функциони́р|овать (**-ую**) *несов* to function
фу́нкци|я (**-и**) *ж* function
фунт (**-а**) *м* pound
фурáж|ка (**-ки**; *gen pl* **-ек**) *ж* cap; (*Воен*) forage cap
фургóн (**-а**) *м* (*Авт*) van; (*повозка*) (covered) wagon
фуру́нкул (**-а**) *м* boil
футбóл (**-а**) *м* football (*Brit*), soccer; **футболи́ст** (**-а**) *м* football (*Brit*) *или* soccer player; **футбóл|ка** (**-ки**; *gen pl* **-ок**) *ж* T-shirt, tee shirt; **футбóльный** *прил* football (*Brit*), soccer; **футбóльный мяч** football
футля́р (**-а**) *м* case
фы́ркн|уть (**-у**) *сов* (*животное*) to give a snort

ха́кер (**-а**) *м* (*Комп*) hacker
хала́т (**-а**) *м* (*домашний*) dressing gown; (*врача*) gown
ха́мств|о (**-а**) *ср* rudeness
ха́ос (**-а**) *м* chaos
хаоти́чный *прил* chaotic
хара́ктер (**-а**) *м* character, nature; (*человека*) personality; **характериз|ова́ть** (**-у́ю**) *несов перех* to be typical of ▷ (*perf* **охарактеризова́ть**) (*человека, ситуацию*) to characterize; **характери́стик|а** (**-и**) *ж* (*документ*) (character) reference; (*описание*) description; **характе́рный** *прил* (*свойственный*): **характе́рный (для** *+gen*) characteristic (of); (*случай*) typical
хвале́бный *прил* complimentary
хвал|и́ть (**-ю́, -ишь**; *perf* **похвали́ть**) *несов перех* to praise
хва́ста|ться (**-юсь**; *perf* **похва́статься**) *несов возв*: **хва́статься** (*+instr*) to boast (about)
хвата́|ть (**-ю**; *perf* **схвати́ть**) *несов перех* to grab (hold of), snatch; (*преступника*) to arrest ▷ (*perf* **хвати́ть**) *безл* (*+gen*: *денег, времени*) to have enough; **мне хвата́ет де́нег на еду́** I've got enough to buy food; **э́того ещё не хвата́ло!** (*разг*) I'm not having this!; **не хвата́ет то́лько, что́бы он отказа́лся** (*разг*) now all we need is for him to refuse; **хвата́ться** (*perf* **схвати́ться**) *несов возв*: **хвата́ться за** *+acc* (*за ручку, за оружие*) to grab
хва|ти́ть (**-чу́, -тишь**) *сов от* **хвата́ть** ▷ *безл* (*разг*): **хва́тит!** that's enough!; **с меня́ хва́тит!** I've had enough!
хва́т|ка (**-ки**; *gen pl* **-ок**) *ж* grip; **делова́я хва́тка** business acumen
хво́рост (**-а**) *м собир* firewood
хвост (**-а́**) *м* tail; (*поезда*) tail end; (*причёска*) ponytail
хво́стик (**-а**) *м* (*мыши, редиски*) tail; (*причёска*) pigtail
хек (**-а**) *м* whiting
хе́рес (**-а**) *м* sherry
хи́жин|а (**-ы**) *ж* hut
хи́лый *прил* sickly
хи́мик (**-а**) *м* chemist; **химика́т** (**-а**) *м* chemical; **хими́ческ|ий** *прил* chemical; (*факультет, кабинет*) chemistry; **хими́ческая чи́стка** (*процесс*) dry-cleaning; (*пункт приёма*) dry-cleaner's
хи́ми|я (**-и**) *ж* chemistry
химчи́ст|ка (**-ки**; *gen pl* **-ок**) *ж* *сокр* = **хими́ческая чи́стка**
хиру́рг (**-а**) *м* surgeon; **хирурги́|я** (**-и**) *ж* surgery
хитр|и́ть (**-ю́, -и́шь**; *perf* **схитри́ть**) *несов* to act slyly;

хи́трост|ь (**-и**) *ж* cunning; **хи́трый** *прил* cunning
хихи́ка|ть (**-ю**) *несов* (*разг*) to giggle
хи́щник (**-а**) *м* predator
хлам (**-а**) *м собир* junk
хлеб (**-а**) *м* bread; (*зерно*) grain
хле́бниц|а (**-ы**) *ж* bread basket; (*для хранения*) breadbin (*Brit*), breadbox (*US*)
хлебн|у́ть (**-у́, -ёшь**) *сов перех* (*разг*: *чай итп*) to take a gulp of
хлебозаво́д (**-а**) *м* bakery
хлестн|у́ть (**-у́, -ёшь**) *сов перех* to whip; (*по щеке*) to slap
хло́па|ть (**-ю**) *несов перех* (*ладонью*) to slap ▷ *неперех* (*+instr*: *дверью, крышкой*) to slam; (*+dat*: *артисту*) to clap
хло́пковый *прил* cotton
хло́пн|уть (**-у**) *сов перех* (*по спине*) to slap ▷ *неперех* (*в ладони*) to clap; (*дверь*) to slam shut
хло́п|ок (**-ка**) *м* cotton
хлоп|о́к (**-ка́**) *м* (*удар в ладоши*) clap
хлоп|ота́ть (**-очу́, -о́чешь**) *несов* (*по дому*) to busy o.s.; **хлопота́ть** (*impf*) **о** *+prp* (*о разрешении*) to request
хлопотли́вый *прил* (*человек*) busy; (*работа*) troublesome
хло́п|оты (**-о́т**; *dat pl* **-отам**) *мн* (*по дому итп*) chores; (*прося чего-н*) efforts
хлопу́ш|ка (**-ки**; *gen pl* **-ек**) *ж* (*игрушка*) (Christmas) cracker
хлопчатобума́жный *прил* cotton
хло́пь|я (**-ев**) *мн* (*снега, мыла*) flakes *мн*; **кукуру́зные хло́пья** cornflakes
хлор (**-а**) *м* chlorine; **хло́рк|а** (**-и**) *ж* (*разг*) bleaching powder; **хло́рн|ый** *прил*: **хло́рная и́звесть** bleaching powder
хлы́н|уть (*3sg* **-ет**) *сов* to flood
хмеле́|ть (**-ю**; *perf* **захмеле́ть**) *несов* to be drunk
хны́ка|ть (**-ю**) *несов* (*разг*: *плакать*) to whimper
хо́бби *ср нескл* hobby
хо́бот (**-а**) *м* (*слона*) trunk
ход (**-а**; *part gen* **-у**, *loc sg* **-у́**) *м* (*машины, поршня*) movement; (*событий, дела*) course; (*часов, двигателя*) working; (*Карты*) go; (*маневр*: *также Шахматы*) move; (*возможность*) chance; (*вход*) entrance; **в хо́де** *+gen* in the course of; **ход мы́слей** train of thought; **идти́** (*perf* **пойти́**) **в ход** to come into use; **быть** (*impf*) **в (большо́м) ходу́** to be (very) popular; **на ходу́** (*есть, разговаривать*) on the move; (*пошутить*) in passing; **с хо́ду** straight off; **дава́ть** (*perf* **дать**) **ход де́лу** to set things in motion
хода́тайств|о (**-а**) *ср* petition; **хода́тайств|овать** (**-ую**; *perf* **похода́тайствовать**) *несов*: **хода́тайствовать о чём-н/за кого́-н** to petition for sth/on sb's behalf
хо|ди́ть (**-жу́, -дишь**) *несов* to walk; (*по магазинам, в гости*) to go (*on foot*); (*поезд, автобус итп*) to go; (*слухи*) to go round; (*часы*) to work; (*носить*): **ходи́ть в** *+prp* (*в пальто, в сапогах итп*) to wear; (*+instr*: *тузом итп*) to play; (*конём, пешкой итп*) to move
хожу́ *несов см* **ходи́ть**
хоздогово́р (**-а**) *м сокр* (= *хозя́йственный догово́р*) business deal (*between companies*)
хозрасчёт (**-а**) *м* (= *хозя́йственный расчёт*) system

of management based on self-financing and self-governing principles

хозрасчётн|ый *прил*: **хозрасчётное предприя́тие** self-financing, self-governing enterprise

хозя́|ин (**-ина**; *nom pl* **-ева**, *gen pl* **-ев**) *м* (*владелец*) owner; (*сдающий жильё*) landlord; (*принимающий гостей*) host; (*перен*: *распорядитель*) master; **хозя́|йка** (**-йки**; *gen pl* **-ек**) *ж* (*владелица*) owner; (*сдающая жильё*) landlady; (*принимающая гостей*) hostess; (*в доме*) housewife; **хозя́йнича|ть** (**-ю**) *несов* (*в доме, на кухне*) to be in charge; (*командовать*) to be bossy

хозя́йственн|ый *прил* (*деятельность*) economic; (*постройка, инвентарь*) domestic; (*человек*) thrifty; **хозя́йственные това́ры** hardware; **хозя́йственный магази́н** hardware shop

хозя́йств|о (**-а**) *ср* (*Экон*) economy; (*фермерское*) enterprise; (*предметы быта*) household goods *мн*; (**дома́шнее**) **хозя́йство** housekeeping; **хозя́йств|овать** (**-ую**) *несов*: **хозя́йствовать на предприя́тии** to manage a business

хоккеист (**-а**) *м* hockey player

хокке́|й (**-я**) *м* hockey

холл (**-а**) *м* (*театра, гостиницы*) lobby; (*в квартире, в доме*) hall

холм (**-а́**) *м* hill; **холми́стый** *прил* hilly

хо́лод (**-а**; *nom pl* **-а́**) *м* cold; (*погода*) cold weather; **холода́|ть** (*3sg* **-ет**, *perf* **похолода́ть**) *несов безл* to turn cold; **холоде́|ть** (**-ю**; *perf* **похолоде́ть**) *несов* to get cold; (*от страха*) to go cold

холоди́льник (**-а**) *м* (*домашний*) fridge; (*промышленный*) refrigerator

хо́лодно *нареч* coldly ▷ *как сказ* it's cold; **мне/ей хо́лодно** I'm/she's cold

холо́дный *прил* cold

холосто́й *прил* (*мужчина*) single, unmarried; (*выстрел, патрон*) blank; **холостя́к** (**-а́**) *м* bachelor

холст (**-а́**) *м* canvas

хомя́к (**-а́**) *м* hamster

хор (**-а**) *м* choir; (*насмешек*) chorus

Хорва́ти|я (**-и**) *ж* Croatia

хо́ром *нареч* in unison

хор|они́ть (**-оню́, -о́нишь**; *perf* **похорони́ть**) *несов перех* to bury

хоро́шенький *прил* (*лицо*) cute

хороше́нько *нареч* (*разг*) properly

хороше́|ть (**-ю**; *perf* **похороше́ть**) *несов* to become more attractive

хоро́ш|ий *прил* good; **он хоро́ш (собо́ю)** he's good-looking; **всего́ хоро́шего!** all the best!

хорошо́ *нареч* well ▷ *как сказ* it's good; **мне хорошо́** I feel good ▷ *част, вводн сл* O.K., all right ▷ *ср нескл* (*Просвещ*) ≈ good (*school mark*); **мне здесь хорошо́** I like it here; **ну, хорошо́!** (*разг*: *угроза*) right then!; **хорошо́ бы пое́сть/поспа́ть** (*разг*) I wouldn't mind a bite to eat/getting some sleep

хо|те́ть (см *Table 14*) *несов перех +infin* to want to do; **как хоти́те** (*как вам угодно*) as you wish; (*а всё-таки*) no matter what you say; **хо́чешь не хо́чешь** whether you like it or not; **хоте́ть** (*impf*) **есть/**

Х

пить to be hungry/thirsty; **хотéться** *несов безл*: **мне хóчется плáкать/есть** I feel like crying/something to eat

хóт-спóт (**-а**) *м* (wireless) hotspot

 **КЛЮЧЕВОЕ СЛОВО**

хоть *союз* **1** (*несмотря на то, что*) (al)though; **хоть я и обúжен, я помогý тебé** although I am hurt, I will help you
2 (*до такой степени, что*) even if; **не соглашáется, хоть до утрá просú** he won't agree, even if you ask all night; **хоть убéй, не могý пойтú на э́то** I couldn't do that to save my life; **хоть..., хоть...** either..., or...; **езжáй хоть сегóдня, хоть чéрез мéсяц** go either today, or in a month's time
▷ *част* **1** (*служит для усиления*) at least; **подвезú егó хоть до стáнции** take him to the station at least; **поймú хоть ты** you of all people should understand
2 (*во фразах*): **хоть бы** at least; **хоть бы ты емý позвонúл** you could at least phone him!; **хоть бы закóнчить сегóдня!** if only we could get finished today!; **хоть кто** anyone; **хоть какóй** any; **емý хоть бы что** it doesn't bother him; **хоть кудá!** (*разг*) excellent!; **хоть бы и так!** so what!

хотя́ *союз* although; **хотя́ и** even though; **хотя́ бы** at least

хóхот (**-а**) *м* loud laughter

хох|отáть (**-очý, -óчешь**) *несов* to guffaw; **хохотáть** (*impf*) (**над** *+instr*) to laugh (at)

хочý *etc несов см* **хотéть**

хрáброст|ь (**-и**) *ж* courage, bravery

хрáбрый *прил* courageous, brave

храм (**-а**) *м* (*Рел*) temple

хранéни|е (**-я**) *ср* (*денег*) keeping; **хранéние орýжия** possession of firearms; **кáмера хранéния** (*на вокзале*) left-luggage office (*Brit*) *или* checkroom (*US*)

хранúлищ|е (**-а**) *ср* store

хран|úть (**-ю́, -úшь**) *несов перех* to keep; (*достоинство*) to protect; (*традиции*) to preserve; **хранúться** *несов возв* to be kept

храп|éть (**-лю́, -úшь**) *несов* to snore

хреб|éт (**-тá**) *м* (*Анат*) spine; (*Гео*) ridge; **гóрный хребéт** mountain range

хрен (**-а**) *м* horseradish

хрип|éть (**-лю́, -úшь**) *несов* to wheeze

хрúплый *прил* (*голос*) hoarse

хрúпн|уть (**-у**; *perf* **охрúпнуть**) *несов* to become *или* grow hoarse

христи|анúн (**-анúна**; *nom pl* **-áне**, *gen pl* **-áн**) *м* Christian; **христиáнский** *прил* Christian; **христиáнств|о** (**-а**) *ср* Christianity

Христ|óс (**-á**) *м* Christ

хром (**-а**) *м* (*Хим*) chrome

хромá|ть (**-ю**) *несов* to limp

хромóй *прил* lame

хрóник|а (**-и**) *ж* chronicle; (*в газеты*) news items

хронúческий *прил* chronic

хрýпкий *прил* fragile; (*печенье, кости*) brittle; (*перен*: *фигура*) delicate; (: *здоровье, организм*) frail

хруст (**-а**) *м* crunch

хрустáлик (**-а**) *м* (*Анат*) lens

хрустáл|ь (**-я́**) *м, собир* crystal

хрустáльный *прил* crystal

хру|стéть (**-щý, -стúшь**) *несов* to crunch; **хрустя́щий** *прил*

crunchy, crisp
хрю́ка|ть (**-ю**) *несов* to grunt
худе́|ть (**-ю**) *несов* to grow thin; (*быть на диете*) to slim
худо́жественн|ый *прил* artistic; (*школа, выставка*) art; **худо́жественная литерату́ра** fiction; **худо́жественная самоде́ятельность** *amateur performing arts*; **худо́жественный сало́н** (*выставка*) art exhibition; (*магазин*) art gallery and craft shop; **худо́жественный фильм** feature film
худо́жник (**-а**) *м* artist
худо́й *прил* thin
ху́дший *превос прил* the worst
ху́же *сравн прил, нареч* worse
хулига́н (**-а**) *м* hooligan; **хулига́н|ить** (**-ю, -ишь**; *perf* **нахулига́нить**) *несов* to act like a hooligan

цара́па|ть (**-ю**; *perf* **оцара́пать**) *несов перех* (*руку*) to scratch; **цара́паться** (*perf* **оцара́паться**) *несов возв* to scratch
цара́пин|а (**-ы**) *ж* scratch
цари́ц|а (**-ы**) *ж* tsarina (*wife of tsar*)
ца́рский *прил* tsar's, royal; (*режим, правительство*) tsarist
ца́рств|о (**-а**) *ср* reign
ца́рств|овать (**-ую**) *несов* to reign
цар|ь (**-я́**) *м* tsar
цве|сти́ (**-ту́, -тёшь**) *несов* (*Бот*) to blossom, flower
цвет (**-а**; *nom pl* **-а́**) *м* (*окраска*) colour (*Brit*), color (*US*) ▷ (*prep sg* **-у́**) (*Бот*) blossom
цветно́й *прил* (*карандаш*) coloured (*Brit*), colored (*US*); (*фото, фильм*) colour (*Brit*), color (*US*)

цвет|о́к (**-ка́**; *nom pl* **-ы́**) *м* flower (*bloom*); (*комнатный*) plant
цвето́чный *прил* flower
це|ди́ть (**-жу́, -дишь**; *perf* **процеди́ть**) *несов перех* (*жидкость*) to strain; (*перен*: *слова*) to force out
це́др|а (**-ы**) *ж* (dried) peel *ед*
целе́бный *прил* medicinal; (*воздух*) healthy
целенапра́вленный *прил* single-minded; (*политика*) consistent
целико́м *нареч* (*без ограничений*) wholly, entirely; (*сварить*) whole
це́л|иться (**-юсь, -ишься**; *perf* **наце́литься**) *несов возв*: **це́литься в** *+acc* to (take) aim at
целлофа́н (**-а**) *м* cellophane
цел|ова́ть (**-у́ю**; *perf* **поцелова́ть**) *несов перех* to kiss; **целова́ться** (*perf* **поцелова́ться**) *несов возв* to kiss (each other)
це́л|ое (**-ого**) *ср* whole
це́л|ый *прил* whole, entire; (*неповреждённый*) intact; **в це́лом** (*полностью*) as a whole; (*в общем*) on the whole
цел|ь (**-и**) *ж* (*при стрельбе*) target; (*перен*) aim, goal; **с це́лью** *+infin* with the object *или* aim of doing; **с це́лью** *+gen* for; **в це́лях** *+gen* for the purpose of
це́льный *прил* (*кусок*) solid; (*характер*) complete
цеме́нт (**-а**) *м* cement; **цементи́р|овать** (**-ую**; *perf* **зацементи́ровать**) *несов перех* to cement
цен|а́ (**-ы́**; *acc sg* **-у**, *dat sg* **-е́**, *nom pl* **-ы**) *ж* price; (*перен*: *человека*) value; **цено́ю** *+gen* at the expense of
цензу́р|а (**-ы**) *ж* censorship
цен|и́ть (**-ю́, -ишь**) *несов перех* (*вещь*) to value; (*помощь*) to appreciate
це́нност|ь (**-и**) *ж* value; **це́нности** valuables; **материа́льные це́нности** commodities
це́нн|ый *прил* valuable; (*письмо*) registered
це́нтнер (**-а**) *м* centner (*100kg*)
центр (**-а**) *м* centre (*Brit*), center (*US*); **в це́нтре внима́ния** in the limelight; **торго́вый центр** shopping centre (*Brit*) *или* mall (*US*)
центра́льный *прил* central

Центра́льное отопле́ние

The vast majority of Russians live in flats for which hot water and central heating are provided by huge communal boiler systems. Each city borough has a boiler system of its own. These systems distribute hot water for domestic use all year round and radiators are heated during the cold months. The heating is controlled centrally and individual home owners do not have any say over it. See also note at **отопи́тельный сезо́н**.

Центроба́нк *м сокр* = **Центра́льный банк (Росси́и)**
цепля́|ться (**-юсь**) *несов возв*: **цепля́ться за** *+acc* to cling *или* hang on to
цепно́й *прил* chain
цепо́ч|ка (**-ки**; *gen pl* **-ек**) *ж* (*тонкая цепь*) chain; (*машин, людей*) line
цеп|ь (**-и**; *loc sg* **-и́**) *ж* chain; (*Элек*) circuit; **го́рная цепь**

mountain range
церемо́ни|я (**-и**) *ж* ceremony
церко́вный *прил* church
це́рк|овь (**-ви**; *instr sg* **-овью**, *nom pl* **-ви**, *gen pl* **-ве́й**) *ж* church
цех (**-а**; *loc sg* **-у́**, *nom pl* **-а́**) *м* (work)shop (*in factory*)
цивилиза́ци|я (**-и**) *ж* civilization; **цивилизо́ванный** *прил* civilized
цикл (**-а**) *м* cycle; (*лекций*) series
цикл|ева́ть (**-ю́ю**; *perf* **отциклева́ть**) *несов перех* to sand
цикло́н (**-а**) *м* cyclone
цили́ндр (**-а**) *м* cylinder; (*шляпа*) top hat
цини́чный *прил* cynical
цирк (**-а**) *м* circus
циркули́р|овать (*3sg* **-ует**) *несов* to circulate
ци́ркул|ь (**-я**) *м* (a pair of) compasses *мн*
циркуля́р (**-а**) *м* decree
цита́т|а (**-ы**) *ж* quote, quotation; **цити́р|овать** (**-ую**; *perf* **процити́ровать**) *несов перех* to quote
цифербла́т (**-а**) *м* dial; (*на часах*) face
ци́фр|а (**-ы**) *ж* number; (*арабские, римские*) numeral; (*обычно мн*: *расчёт*) figure
ЦРУ *ср сокр* (= *Центра́льное разве́дывательное управле́ние (США)*) CIA (= *Central Intelligence Agency*)
ЦСУ *ср сокр* = **Центра́льное статисти́ческое управле́ние**
ЦТ *ср сокр* = **Центра́льное телеви́дение**
цыга́н (**-а**; *nom pl* **-е**) *м* gypsy
цыпл|ёнок (**-ёнка**; *nom pl* **-я́та**, *gen pl* **-я́т**) *м* chick
цы́поч|ки (**-ек**) *мн*: **на цы́почках** on tiptoe

Ч

ча|ди́ть (**-жу́, -ди́шь**; *perf* **начади́ть**) *несов* to give off fumes
чаев|ы́е (**-ы́х**) *мн* tip *ед*
ча|й (**-я**; *part gen* **-ю**, *nom pl* **-и́**) *м* tea; **зава́ривать (***perf* **завари́ть) чай** to make tea; **дава́ть (***perf* **дать) кому́-н на чай** to give sb a tip
ча́|йка (**-йки**, *gen pl* **-ек**) *ж* (sea) gull
ча́йник (**-а**) *м* kettle; (*для заварки*) teapot
ча́йн|ый *прил*: **ча́йная ло́жка** teaspoon
час (**-а**; *nom pl* **-ы́**) *м* hour; **академи́ческий час** (*Просвещ*) ≈ period; **кото́рый час?** what time is it?; **сейча́с 3 часа́ но́чи/дня** it's 3 o'clock in the morning/afternoon; *см также* **часы́**
часо́в|ня (**-ни**; *gen pl* **-ен**) *ж* chapel

часов|о́й *прил* (*лекция*) one-hour; (*механизм*: *ручных часов*) watch; (: *стенных часов*) clock ▷ (**-о́го**) *м* sentry; **часова́я стре́лка** the small hand; **часово́й по́яс** time zone

части́ц|а (**-ы**) *ж* (*стекла*) fragment; (*желания*) bit; (*количества*) fraction; (*Физ, Линг*) particle

части́чный *прил* partial

ча́стник (**-а**) *м* (*собственник*) (private) owner

ча́стност|ь (**-и**) *ж* (*деталь*) detail; (*подробность*) particular; **в ча́стности** for instance

ча́стн|ый *прил* private; (*случай*) isolated; **ча́стная со́бственность** private property

ча́сто *нареч* (*много раз*) often; (*тесно*) close together

част|ота́ (**-оты́**; *nom pl* **-о́ты**) *ж* (*Тех*) frequency

ча́стый *прил* frequent

част|ь (**-и**; *gen pl* **-е́й**) *ж* part; (*отдел*) department; (*симфонии*) movement; (*Воен*) unit; **часть ре́чи** part of speech; **часть све́та** continent

час|ы́ (**-о́в**) *мн* (*карманные*) watch *ед*; (*стенные*) clock *ед*

чат (**-а**) *м* (*Интернет*) chat; **ча́т-ко́мнат|а** (**-ы**) *ж* chat room

ча́ш|ка (**-ки**; *gen pl* **-ек**) *ж* cup

ча́ще *сравн прил от* **ча́стый** ▷ *сравн нареч от* **ча́сто**

чего́ *мест см* **что**

чей (**чьего́**; см *Table 5*; *f* **чья**, *nt* **чьё**, *pl* **чьи**) *мест* whose; **чей бы то ни́ был** no matter whose it is

че́й-либо (**чьего́-либо**; *как* **чей**; см *Table 5*; *f* **чья́-либо**, *nt* **чьё-либо**, *pl* **чьи́-либо**) *мест* = **че́й-нибудь**

че́й-нибудь (**чьего́-нибудь**; *как* **чей**; см *Table 5*; *f* **чья́-нибудь**, *nt* **чьё-нибудь**, *pl* **чьи́-нибудь**) *мест* anyone's

че́й-то (**чьего́-то**; *как* **чей**; см *Table 5*; *f* **чья́-то**, *nt* **чьё-то**, *pl* **чьи́-то**) *мест* someone's, somebody's

чек (**-а**) *м* (*банковский*) cheque (*Brit*), check (*US*); (*товарный, кассовый*) receipt

че́ковый *прил* cheque (*Brit*), check (*US*)

чёл|ка (**-ки**; *gen pl* **-ок**) *ж* (*человека*) fringe (*Brit*), bangs *мн* (*US*)

челн|о́к (**-ка́**) *м* shuttle; (*торговец*) *small trader buying goods abroad and selling them on local markets*

челове́к (**-а**; *nom pl* **лю́ди**, *gen pl* **люде́й**) *м* human (being); (*некто, личность*) person (*мн* people)

челове́ческий *прил* human; (*человечный*) humane

челове́честв|о (**-а**) *ср* humanity, mankind

челове́чный *прил* humane

че́люст|ь (**-и**) *ж* (*Анат*) jaw

чем *мест см* **что** ▷ *союз* than; (*разг*: *вместо того чтобы*) instead of; **чем бо́льше/ра́ньше, тем лу́чше** the bigger/earlier, the better

чемода́н (**-а**) *м* suitcase

чемпио́н (**-а**) *м* champion; **чемпиона́т** (**-а**) *м* championship

чему́ *мест см* **что**

чепух|а́ (**-и́**) *ж* nonsense

че́рв|и (**-е́й**) *мн* (*Карты*) hearts *мн*

черв|ь (**-я́**; *nom pl* **-и**, *gen pl* **-е́й**) *м* worm; (*личинка*) maggot

червя́к (**-а́**) *м* worm

черда́к (**-а́**) *м* attic, loft

черед|ова́ть (**-у́ю**) *несов перех*: **чередова́ть что-н с** *+instr* to alternate sth with

КЛЮЧЕВОЕ СЛОВО

че́рез *предл +acc* **1** (*поперёк*) across, over; **переходи́ть** (*perf* **перейти́**) **че́рез доро́гу** to cross the road
2 (*сквозь*) through; **че́рез окно́** through the window
3 (*поверх*) over; **че́рез забо́р** over the fence
4 (*спустя*) in; **че́рез час** in an hour('s time)
5 (*минуя какое-н пространство*): **че́рез три кварта́ла — ста́нция** the station is three blocks away
6 (*при помощи*) via; **он переда́л письмо́ че́рез знако́мого** he sent the letter via a friend
7 (*при повторении действия*) every; **принима́йте табле́тки че́рез ка́ждый час** take the tablets every hour

че́реп (**-а**) *м* skull
черепа́х|а (**-и**) *ж* tortoise; (*морская*) turtle
черепи́ц|а (**-ы**) *ж собир* tiles *мн*
чере́ш|ня (**-ни**; *gen pl* **-ен**) *ж* cherry
черне́|ть (**-ю**; *perf* **почерне́ть**) *несов* (*становиться чёрным*) to turn black
черни́л|а (-) *мн* ink *ед*
чернови́к (**-а́**) *м* draft
чёрный (**-ен, -на́, -но́**) *прил* black; (*ход*) back
че́рпа|ть (**-ю**) *несов перех* (*жидкость*) to ladle
черстве́|ть (**-ю**; *perf* **зачерстве́ть**) *несов* (*хлеб*) to go stale
чёрствый *прил* (*хлеб*) stale; (*человек*) callous
чёрт (**-а**; *nom pl* **че́рти**, *gen pl* **черте́й**) *м* (*дьявол*) devil; **иди́ к чёрту!** (*разг*) go to hell!
черт|а́ (**-ы́**) *ж* (*линия*) line; (*признак*) trait; **в о́бщих черта́х** in general terms; *см также* **черты́**
чертёж (**-а́**) *м* draft
чер|ти́ть (**-чу́, -тишь**; *perf* **начерти́ть**) *несов перех* (*линию*) to draw; (*график*) to draw up
черт|ы́ (-) *мн* (*также* **черты́ лица́**) features
че|са́ть (**-шу́, -шешь**; *perf* **почеса́ть**) *несов перех* (*спину*) to scratch; **чеса́ться** (*perf* **почеса́ться**) *несов возв* to scratch o.s.; (*no perf*: *зудеть*) to itch
чесно́к (**-а́**) *м* garlic
че́стно *нареч* (*сказать*) honestly; (*решить*) fairly ▷ *как сказ*: **так бу́дет че́стно** that'll be fair
че́стност|ь (**-и**) *ж* honesty;
че́стн|ый *прил* honest; **че́стное сло́во** honestly
честолюби́вый *прил* ambitious
чест|ь (**-и**) *ж* honour (*Brit*), honor (*US*) ▷ (*loc sg* **-и́**) (*почёт*) glory; **к че́сти кого́-н** to sb's credit; **отдава́ть** (*perf* **отда́ть**) **кому́-н честь** to salute sb
четве́рг (**-а́**) *м* Thursday
четвере́н|ьки (**-ек**) *мн*: **на четвере́ньках** on all fours
четвёр|ка (**-ки**; *gen pl* **-ок**) *ж* (*цифра, карта*) four; (*Просвещ*) ≈ B (*school mark*)
че́твер|о (*см Table 30a*; **-ы́х**) *чис* four
четвёртый *чис* fourth; **сейча́с четвёртый час** it's after three
че́тверт|ь (**-и**) *ж* quarter; (*Просвещ*) term
четвертьфина́л (**-а**) *м* (*Спорт*) quarter final
чёткий *прил* clear; (*движения*) precise

Ч

чётный *прил* (*число*) even
четы́р|е (**-ёх**; *instr sg* **-ьмя́**; см *Table 24*) *чис* (*цифра, число*) four; (*Просвещ*) ≈ B (*school mark*)
четы́р|еста (**-ёхсо́т**; см *Table 28*) *чис* four hundred
четы́рнадцатый *чис* fourteenth
четы́рнадцат|ь (**-и**; *как* **пять**; см *Table 26*) *чис* fourteen
Че́хи|я (**-и**) *ж* the Czech Republic
чех|о́л (**-ла́**) *м* (*для мебели*) cover; (*для гитары, для оружия*) case
чешу|я́ (**-и́**) *ж собир* scales *мн*
чин (**-а**; *nom pl* **-ы́**) *м* rank
чин|и́ть (**-ю́, -ишь**; *perf* **почини́ть**) *несов перех* to mend, repair ▷ (*perf* **очини́ть**) (*карандаш*) to sharpen
чино́вник (**-а**) *м* (*служащий*) official
чи́пс|ы (**-ов**) *мн* crisps
чи́сленност|ь (**-и**) *ж* (*армии*) numbers *мн*; (*учащихся*) number; **чи́сленность населе́ния** population
чис|ло́ (**-ла́**; *nom pl* **-ла**, *gen pl* **-ел**) *ср* number; (*день месяца*) date; **быть** (*impf*) **в числе́** +*gen* to be among(st)
чи́|стить (**-щу, -стишь**; *perf* **вы́чистить** *или* **почи́стить**) *несов перех* to clean; (*зубы*) to brush, clean ▷ (*perf* **почи́стить**) (*яблоко, картошку*) to peel; (*рыбу*) to scale
чи́сто *нареч* (*только*) purely; (*убранный, сделанный*) neatly ▷ *как сказ*: **в до́ме чи́сто** the house is clean
чистови́к (**-а́**) *м* fair copy
чистосерде́чный *прил* sincere
чистот|а́ (**-ы́**) *ж* purity; **у него́ в до́ме всегда́ чистота́** his house is always clean
чи́стый *прил* (*одежда, комната*) clean; (*совесть, небо*) clear; (*золото, спирт, случайность*) pure; (*прибыль, вес*) net; **экологи́чески чи́стый** organic
чита́льный *прил*: **чита́льный зал** reading room
чита́тел|ь (**-я**) *м* reader
чита́|ть (**-ю**; *perf* **проче́сть** *или* **прочита́ть**) *несов перех* to read; (*лекцию*) to give; (*в Твиттере*) to follow
чиха́|ть (**-ю**; *perf* **чихну́ть**) *несов* to sneeze
член (**-а**) *м* member; (*обычно мн*: *конечности*) limb; **полово́й член** penis; **член предложе́ния** part of a sentence
чо́ка|ться (**-юсь**; *perf* **чо́кнуться**) *несов возв* to clink glasses (*during toast*)
чрева́тый *прил* +*instr* fraught with
чрезвыча́йно *нареч* extremely
чрезвыча́йн|ый *прил* (*исключительный*) extraordinary; (*экстренный*) emergency; **чрезвыча́йное положе́ние** state of emergency
чрезме́рный *прил* excessive
чте́ни|е (**-я**) *ср* reading

 **КЛЮЧЕВОЕ СЛОВО**

что (**чего́**; см *Table 7*) *мест*
1 (*вопросительное*) what; **что ты сказа́л?** what did you say?; **что Вы говори́те!** you don't say!
2 (*относительное*) which; **она́ не поздоро́валась, что мне бы́ло неприя́тно** she did not say hello, which was unpleasant for me; **что ни говори́ ...** whatever you say ...
3 (*столько сколько*): **она́ закрича́ла что бы́ло сил** she shouted with her all might
4 (*разг*: *что-нибудь*) anything;

е́сли что случи́тся if anything happens, should anything happen; **в слу́чае чего́** if anything happens; **чуть что — сра́зу скажи́ мне** get in touch at the slightest thing
▷ *нареч* (*почему*) why; **что ты грусти́шь?** why are you sad?
▷ *союз* **1** (*при сообщении, высказывании*): **я зна́ю, что на́до де́лать** I know what must be done; **я зна́ю, что он прие́дет** I know that he will come
2 (*во фразах*): **а что?** (*разг*) why (do you ask)?; **к чему́** (*зачем*) why; **не́ за что!** not at all! (*Brit*), you're welcome! (*US*); **ни за что!** (*разг*) no way!; **ни за что ни про что** (*разг*) for no (good) reason at all; **что ты!** (*при возражении*) what!; **я здесь ни при чём** it has nothing to do with me; **что к чему́** (*разг*) what's what

чтоб *союз* = **что́бы**

 **КЛЮЧЕВОЕ СЛОВО**

что́бы *союз* (*+infin*: *выражает цель*) in order *или* so as to do
▷ *союз +pt* **1** (*выражает цель*) so that
2 (*выражает желательность*): **я хочу́, что́бы она́ пришла́** I want her to come
3 (*выражает возможность*): **не мо́жет быть, что́бы он так поступи́л** it can't be possible that he could have acted like that
▷ *част* **1** (*выражает пожелание*): **что́бы она́ заболе́ла!** I hope she gets ill!
2 (*выражает требование*): **что́бы я его́ здесь бо́льше не ви́дел!** I hope (that) I never see him here again!

что́-либо (**чего́-либо**; *как* **что**; *см Table 7*) *мест* = **что́-нибудь**
что́-нибудь (**чего́-нибудь**; *как* **что**; *см Table 7*) *мест* (*в утверждении*) something; (*в вопросе*) anything
что́-то (**чего́-то**; *как* **что**; *см Table 7*) *мест* something; (*приблизительно*) something like ▷ *нареч* (*разг*: *почему-то*) somehow
чувстви́тельный *прил* sensitive
чу́вств|о (**-а**) *ср* feeling; (*+gen*: *юмора, долга*) sense of
чу́вств|овать (**-ую**; *perf* **почу́вствовать**) *несов перех* to feel; (*присутствие, опасность*) to sense; **чу́вствовать** (*impf*) **себя́ хорошо́/нело́вко** to feel good/ awkward; **чу́вствоваться** *несов возв* (*жара, усталость*) to be felt
чугу́н (**-а́**) *м* cast iron
чуда́к (**-а́**) *м* eccentric
чудеса́ *итп сущ см* **чу́до**
чуде́сный *прил* (*очень хороший*) marvellous (*Brit*), marvelous (*US*), wonderful; (*необычный*) miraculous
чу́д|о (**-а**; *nom pl* **-еса́**, *gen pl* **-е́с**, *dat pl* **-еса́м**) *ср* miracle
чудо́вищ|е (**-а**) *ср* monster
чу́дом *нареч* by a miracle
чу́ждый *прил* alien
чужо́й *прил* (*вещь*) someone *или* somebody else's; (*речь, обычай*) foreign; (*человек*) strange
чул|о́к (**-ка́**; *gen pl* **-о́к**, *dat pl* **-ка́м**) *м* (*обычно мн*) stocking
чум|а́ (**-ы́**) *ж* plague
чу́ткий *прил* sensitive; (*добрый*) sympathetic
чу́точку *нареч* (*разг*) a tiny bit
чуть *нареч* (*разг*: *едва*) hardly; (*немного*) a little ▷ *союз* (*как только*) as soon as; **чуть (бы́ло) не**

almost, nearly; **чуть что** (*разг*) at the slightest thing
чуть-чуть *нареч* (*разг*) a little
чу́чел|о (**-а**) *ср* scarecrow
чуш|ь (**-и**) *ж* (*разг*) rubbish (*Brit*), garbage (*US*), nonsense
чу́|ять (**-ю**) *несов перех* (*собака*) to scent; (*предвидеть*) to sense
чьё (**чьего́**) *мест см* **чей**
чьи (**чьих**) *мест см* **чей**
чья (**чьей**) *мест см* **чей**

шаг (**-а**; *nom pl* **-и́**) *м* step
шага́|ть (**-ю**) *несов* to march
шагн|у́ть (**-у́, -ёшь**) *сов* to step, take a step
ша́|йка (**-йки**; *gen pl* **-ек**) *ж* gang
шал|ь (**-и**) *ж* shawl
шампа́нск|ое (**-ого**) *ср* champagne
шампиньо́н (**-а**) *м* (*Бот*) (field) mushroom
шампу́н|ь (**-я**) *м* shampoo
шанс (**-а**) *м* chance
шанта́ж (**-а́**) *м* blackmail
шантажи́р|овать (**-ую**) *несов перех* to blackmail
ша́п|ка (**-ки**; *gen pl* **-ок**) *ж* hat
шар (**-а**; *nom pl* **-ы́**) *м* (*Геом*) sphere ▷ (*gen sg* **-а́**) (*бильярдный итп*) ball; **возду́шный шар** balloon
ша́рик (**-а**) *м* (*детский*) balloon
ша́риков|ый *прил*: **ша́риковая ру́чка** ballpoint pen

ша́рка|ть (**-ю**) *несов +instr* to shuffle

шарф (**-а**) *м* scarf

шата́|ть (**-ю**) *несов перех* (*раскачивать*) to rock; **шата́ться** *несов возв* (*зуб*) to be loose *или* wobbly; (*стол*) to be wobbly; (*от ветра*) to shake; (*от усталости*) to reel; (*по улицам*) to hang around

шах (**-а**) *м* (*в шахматах*) check

ша́хматный *прил* chess

ша́хмат|ы (-) *мн* (*игра*) chess *ед*; (*фигуры*) chessmen

ша́хт|а (**-ы**) *ж* mine; (*лифта*) shaft

шахтёр (**-а**) *м* miner

ша́ш|ки (**-ек**) *мн* (*игра*) draughts *ед* (*Brit*), checkers *ед* (*US*)

шашлы́к (**-а́**) *м* shashlik, kebab

шва́бр|а (**-ы**) *ж* mop

шварт|ова́ть (**-у́ю**; *perf* **пришвартова́ть**) *несов перех* to moor

швед (**-а**) *м* Swede

шве́дский *прил* Swedish

шве́йный *прил* sewing

швейца́р|ец (**-ца**) *м* Swiss

Швейца́ри|я (**-и**) *ж* Switzerland

швейца́рский *прил* Swiss

Шве́ци|я (**-и**) *ж* Sweden

шевел|и́ть (**-ю́, -и́шь**; *perf* **пошевели́ть**) *несов перех* (*сено*) to turn over; (*подлеж*: **ветер**) to stir ▷ *неперех* (*+instr*: *пальцами, губами*) to move; **шевели́ться** (*perf* **пошевели́ться**) *несов возв* to stir

шеде́вр (**-а**) *м* masterpiece

шёл *несов см* **идти́**

шёлк (**-а**; *nom pl* **-а́**) *м* silk

шёлковый *прил* silk

шелуш|и́ться (**-у́сь, -и́шься**) *несов возв* to peel

шепн|у́ть (**-у́, -ёшь**) *сов перех* to whisper

шёпот (**-а**) *м* whisper

шёпотом *нареч* in a whisper

шеп|та́ть (**-чу́, -чешь**) *несов перех* to whisper; **шепта́ться** *несов возв* to whisper to each other

шере́нг|а (**-и**) *ж* (*солдат*) rank

шерст|ь (**-и**) *ж* (*животного*) hair; (*пряжа, ткань*) wool

шерстяно́й *прил* (*пряжа, ткань*) woollen (*Brit*), woolen (*US*)

шерша́вый *прил* rough

ше́стер|о (**-ы́х**; см *Table 30b*) *чис* six

шестидеся́тый *чис* sixtieth

шестна́дцатый *чис* sixteenth

шестна́дцат|ь (**-и**; *как* **пять**; см *Table 26*) *чис* sixteen

шесто́й *чис* sixth

шест|ь (**-и́**; *как* **пять**; см *Table 26*) *чис* six

шест|ьдеся́т (**-и́десяти**; *как* **пятьдеся́т**; см *Table 26*) *чис* sixty

шест|ьсо́т (**-исо́т**; *как* **пятьсо́т**; см *Table 28*) *чис* six hundred

шеф (**-а**) *м* (*полиции*) chief; (*разг*: *начальник*) boss; (*благотворитель*: *лицо*) patron; (*организация*) sponsor

ше́фств|о (**-а**) *ср*: **ше́фство над** *+instr* (*лица*) patronage of; (*организация*) sponsorship of

ше́фств|овать (**-ую**) *несов*: **ше́фствовать над** *+instr* (*лицо*) to be patron of; (*организация*) to sponsor

ше́|я (**-и**) *ж* (*Анат*) neck

ши́ворот (**-а**) *м* (*разг*): **за ши́ворот** by the collar

шизофре́ник (**-а**) *м* schizophrenic

шика́рный *прил* (*разг*) glamorous, chic

шимпанзе́ *м нескл* chimpanzee

ши́н|а (**-ы**) *ж* (*Авт*) tyre (*Brit*), tire (*US*)

шине́л|ь (**-и**) *ж* overcoat
шинк|ова́ть (**-у́ю**; *perf* **нашинкова́ть**) *несов перех* (*овощи*) to shred
шип (**-а́**) *м* (*растения*) thorn; (*на колесе*) stud; (*на ботинке*) spike
шипу́чий *прил* fizzy
ши́ре *сравн прил от* **широ́кий** ▷ *сравн нареч от* **широко́**
ширин|а́ (**-ы́**) *ж* width; **доро́жка метр ширино́й** *или* **в ширину́** a path a metre (*Brit*) *или* meter (*US*) wide
ши́рм|а (**-ы**) *ж* screen
широ́к|ий *прил* wide; (*степи, планы*) extensive; (*перен*: *общественность*) general; (*: смысл*) broad; (*: натура, жест*) generous; **това́ры широ́кого потребле́ния** (*Экон*) consumer goods
широко́ *нареч* (*раскинуться*) widely; (*улыбаться*) broadly
широкополо́сный *прил* broadband; **широкополо́сная связь** broadband connection; **широкополо́сный доступ** broadband access
широкоэкра́нный *прил* (*фильм*) widescreen
шир|ота́ (**-оты́**) *ж* breadth ▷ (*nom pl* **-о́ты**) (*Гео*) latitude
ширпотре́б (**-а**) *м сокр* (= *широ́кое потребле́ние*) (*разг*: *о товарах*) consumer goods *мн*; (*: о плохом товаре*) shoddy goods *мн*
шить (**шью, шьёшь**; *perf* **сшить**) *несов перех* (*платье итп*) to sew
ши́фер (**-а**) *м* slate
шиш (**-а́**) *м* (*разг*) *gesture of refusal*; **(ни) шиша́** (*разг*: *ничего*) nothing at all
ши́ш|ка (**-ки**; *gen pl* **-ек**) *ж* (*Бот*) cone; (*на лбу*) bump, lump
шкал|а́ (**-ы́**; *nom pl* **-ы**) *ж* scale
шкаф (**-а**; *loc sg* **-у́**, *nom pl* **-ы́**) *м* (*для одежды*) wardrobe; (*для посуды*) cupboard; **кни́жный шкаф** bookcase
шки́пер (**-а**) *м* (*Мор*) skipper
шко́л|а (**-ы**) *ж* school; (*милиции*) academy; **сре́дняя шко́ла** secondary (*Brit*) *или* high (*US*) school
шко́л|а-интерна́т (**-ы, -а**) *м* boarding school
шко́льник (**-а**) *м* schoolboy; **шко́льниц|а** (**-ы**) *ж* schoolgirl
шко́льный *прил* (*здание*) school
шку́р|а (**-ы**) *ж* (*животного*) fur; (*убитого животного*) skin; (*: обработанная*) hide
шла *несов см* **идти́**
шлагба́ум (**-а**) *м* barrier
шланг (**-а**) *м* hose
шлем (**-а**) *м* helmet
шли *несов см* **идти́**
шлиф|ова́ть (**-у́ю**; *perf* **отшлифова́ть**) *несов перех* (*Тех*) to grind
шло *несов см* **идти́**
шлю́п|ка (**-ки**; *gen pl* **-ок**) *ж* (*Мор*) dinghy; **спаса́тельная шлю́пка** lifeboat
шля́п|а (**-ы**) *ж* hat
шля́п|ка (**-ки**; *gen pl* **-ок**) *ж* hat; (*гвоздя*) head; (*гриба*) cap
шмел|ь (**-я́**) *м* bumblebee
шмы́га|ть (**-ю**) *несов*: **шмы́гать но́сом** to sniff
шнур (**-а́**) *м* (*верёвка*) cord; (*телефонный, лампы*) cable
шнур|ова́ть (**-у́ю**; *perf* **зашнурова́ть**) *несов перех* (*ботинки*) to lace up
шнур|о́к (**-ка́**) *м* (*ботинка*) lace
шок (**-а**) *м* (*Мед*: *перен*) shock
шоки́р|овать (**-ую**) *(не)сов перех* to shock

шокола́д (**-а**) *м* chocolate
шокола́дный *прил* chocolate
шо́рт|ы (-) *мн* shorts
шоссе́ *ср нескл* highway
шотла́нд|ец (**-ца**) *м* Scotsman (*мн* Scotsmen)
Шотла́нди|я (**-и**) *ж* Scotland
шотла́ндский *прил* Scottish, Scots
шо́у *ср нескл* (*также перен*) show
шофёр (**-а**) *м* driver
шпа́г|а (**-и**) *ж* sword
шпага́т (**-а**) *м* (*бечёвка*) string
шпакл|ева́ть (**-ю́ю**; *perf* **зашпаклева́ть**) *несов перех* to fill
шпа́л|а (**-ы**) *ж* sleeper (*Rail*)
шпил|ь (**-я**) *м* spire
шпи́л|ька (**-ьки**; *gen pl* **-ек**) *ж* (*для волос*) hairpin; (*каблук*) stiletto (heel)
шпина́т (**-а**) *м* spinach
шпингале́т (**-а**) *м* (*на окне*) catch
шпио́н (**-а**) *м* spy
шпиона́ж (**-а**) *м* espionage
шпио́н|ить (**-ю, -ишь**) *несов* (*разг*) to spy
шприц (**-а**) *м* syringe
шпро́т|ы (**-ов**) *мн* sprats
шрам (**-а**) *м* (*на теле*) scar
шрифт (**-а**; *nom pl* **-ы́**) *м* type
штаб (**-а**) *м* headquarters *мн*
штамп (**-а**) *м* (*печать*) stamp
штамп|ова́ть (**-у́ю**; *perf* **проштампова́ть**) *несов перех* (*документы*) to stamp ▷ (*perf* **отштампова́ть**) (*детали*) to punch, press
шта́нг|а (**-и**) *ж* (*Спорт: в тяжёлой атлетике*) weight; (*: ворот*) post
штан|ы́ (**-о́в**) *мн* trousers
штат (**-а**) *м* (*государства*) state; (*работники*) staff
шта́тный *прил* (*сотрудник*) permanent
шта́тск|ий *прил* (*одежда*) civilian ▷ (**-ого**) *м* civilian
ште́псел|ь (**-я**) *м* (*Элек*) plug
што́пор (**-а**) *м* corkscrew
шторм (**-а**) *м* gale
штормов|о́й *прил* stormy; **штормово́е предупрежде́ние** storm warning
штраф (**-а**) *м* (*денежный*) fine; (*Спорт*) punishment; **штрафн|о́й** *прил* penal ▷ (**-о́го**) *м* (*Спорт: также* **штрафно́й уда́р**) penalty (kick)
штраф|ова́ть (**-у́ю**; *perf* **оштрафова́ть**) *несов перех* to fine; (*Спорт*) to penalize
штрих (**-а́**) *м* (*черта*) stroke
штрихово́й *прил*: **штрихово́й код** bar code
шту́к|а (**-и**) *ж* (*предмет*) item
штукату́р|ить (**-ю, -ишь**; *perf* **отштукату́рить** *или* **оштукату́рить**) *несов перех* to plaster
штукату́рк|а (**-и**) *ж* plaster
штурм (**-а**) *м* (*Воен*) storm
штурм|ова́ть (**-у́ю**) *несов перех* (*Воен*) to storm
шу́б|а (**-ы**) *ж* (*меховая*) fur coat
шум (**-а**; *part gen* **-у**) *м* (*звук*) noise
шум|е́ть (**-лю́, -и́шь**) *несов* to make a noise
шу́мный *прил* noisy; (*разговор, компания*) loud; (*оживлённый: улица*) bustling
шу́рин (**-а**) *м* brother-in-law (*wife's brother*)
шуру́п (**-а**) *м* (*Тех*) screw
шу|ти́ть (**-чу́, -тишь**; *perf* **пошути́ть**) *несов* to joke; (*смеяться*): **шути́ть над** *+instr* to make fun of; (*no perf, +instr: пренебрегать: здоровьем*) to disregard

шу́т|ка (**-ки**; *gen pl* **-ок**) *ж* joke; **без шу́ток** joking apart, seriously
шутли́вый *прил* humourous (*Brit*), humorous (*US*)
шу́точный *прил* (*рассказ*) comic, funny
шучу́ *несов см* **шути́ть**
шью *итп несов см* **шить**

щаве́л|ь (**-я́**) *м* sorrel
ща|ди́ть (**-жу́, -ди́шь**; *perf* **пощади́ть**) *несов перех* to spare
ще́дрост|ь (**-и**) *ж* generosity
ще́дрый *прил* generous
щека́ (**щеки́**; *nom pl* **щёки**, *gen pl* **щёк**, *dat pl* **щека́м**) *ж* cheek
щек|ота́ть (**-очу́, -о́чешь**; *perf* **пощекота́ть**) *несов перех* to tickle
щекотли́вый *прил* (*вопрос итп*) delicate
щёлк|а (**-и**) *ж* small hole
щёлка|ть (**-ю**) *несов* (*+instr*: *языком*) to click; (*кнутом*) to crack
щёлкн|уть (**-у**) *сов от* **щёлкать**
щёлоч|ь (**-и**) *ж* alkali
щелч|о́к (**-ка́**) *м* flick; (*звук*) click
щел|ь (**-и**; *loc sg* **-и́**, *gen pl* **-е́й**) *ж* (*в полу*) crack; **смотрова́я щель** peephole
щен|о́к (**-ка́**; *nom pl* **-я́та**, *gen pl*

-я́т) *м* (*собаки*) pup; (*лисы, волчицы*) cub
щепети́льный *прил* scrupulous
ще́п|ка (**-ки**; *gen pl* **-ок**) *ж* splinter; (*для растопки*): **ще́пки** chippings
щепо́т|ка (**-ки**; *gen pl* **-ок**) *ж* pinch
щети́н|а (**-ы**) *ж* (*животных, щётки*) bristle; (*у мужчины*) stubble
щёт|ка (**-ки**; *gen pl* **-ок**) *ж* brush; **щётка для воло́с** hairbrush
щи (**щей**; *dat pl* **щам**) *мн* cabbage soup *ед*
щи́колот|ка (**-ки**; *gen pl* **-ок**) *ж* ankle
щип|а́ть (**-лю́, -лешь**) *несов перех* (*до боли*) to nip, pinch; (*no perf*: *подлеж*: *мороз*) to bite ▷ (*perf* **ощипа́ть**) (*волосы, курицу*) to pluck; **щипа́ться** *несов возв* (*разг*) to nip, pinch
щипц|ы́ (**-о́в**) *мн*: **хирурги́ческие щипцы́** forceps; **щипцы́ для са́хара** sugar-tongs
щи́пчик|и (**-ов**) *мн* (*для ногтей*) tweezers
щит (**-а́**) *м* shield; (*рекламный, баскетбольный*) board; (*Tex*) panel
щитови́дн|ый *прил*: **щитови́дная железа́** thyroid gland
щу́к|а (**-и**) *ж* pike (*мн* pike)
щу́пал|ьце (**-ьца**; *nom pl* **-ьца**, *gen pl* **-ец**) *ср* (*осьминога*) tentacle; (*насекомых*) feeler
щу́па|ть (**-ю**; *perf* **пощу́пать**) *несов перех* to feel for
щу́р|ить (**-ю, -ишь**; *perf* **сощу́рить**) *несов перех*: **щу́рить глаза́** to screw up one's eyes; **щу́риться** (*perf* **сощу́риться**) *несов возв* (*от солнца*) to squint

Э

эвакуа́ци|я (**-и**) *ж* evacuation
эвакуи́р|овать (**-ую**) *(не)сов перех* to evacuate
ЭВМ *ж сокр* (= *электро́нная вычисли́тельная маши́на*) computer
эволю́ци|я (**-и**) *ж* evolution
эгои́ст (**-а**) *м* egoist
эгоисти́чный *прил* egotistic(al)
эква́тор (**-а**) *м* equator
эквивале́нт (**-а**) *м* equivalent
экза́мен (**-а**) *м*: **экза́мен (по** *+dat*) (*по истории*) exam(ination) (in); **выпускны́е экза́мены** Finals; **сдава́ть** (*impf*) **экза́мен** to sit (*Brit*) *или* take an exam(ination); **сдать** (*perf*) **экза́мен** to pass an exam(ination); **экзамена́тор** (**-а**) *м* examiner; **экзаменацио́нный** *прил* examination; (*вопрос*) exam
экземпля́р (**-а**) *м* copy
экзоти́ческий *прил* exotic

экипа́ж (**-а**) *м* crew
экологи́ческий *прил* ecological
эколо́ги|я (**-и**) *ж* ecology
эконо́мик|а (**-и**) *ж* economy; (*наука*) economics
экономи́ст (**-а**) *м* economist
эконо́м|ить (**-лю, -ишь**; *perf* **сэконо́мить**) *несов перех* (*энергию, деньги*) to save; (*выгадывать*): **эконо́мить на** *+prp* to economize *или* save on
экономи́ческий *прил* economic
эконо́ми|я (**-и**) *ж* economy
эконо́мный *прил* (*хозяин*) thrifty; (*метод*) economical
экра́н (**-а**) *м* screen
экскава́тор (**-а**) *м* excavator, digger
экску́рси|я (**-и**) *ж* excursion
экскурсово́д (**-а**) *м* guide
экспеди́ци|я (**-и**) *ж* (*научная*) field work; (*группа людей*) expedition
экспериме́нт (**-а**) *м* experiment
эксперименти́р|овать (**-ую**) *несов*: **эксперименти́ровать (над** *или* **с** *+instr*) to experiment (on *или* with)
экспе́рт (**-а**) *м* expert
эксплуата́ци|я (**-и**) *ж* exploitation; (*машин*) utilization
эксплуати́р|овать (**-ую**) *несов перех* to exploit; (*машины*) to use
экспона́т (**-а**) *м* exhibit
э́кспорт (**-а**) *м* export; **экспортёр** (**-а**) *м* exporter; **экспорти́р|овать** (**-ую**) *несов перех* to export
экстрема́льный *прил* extreme
э́кстренный *прил* urgent; (*заседание*) emergency
ЭКЮ́ *сокр* ECU (= *European Currency Unit*)
эласти́чный *прил* stretchy
элева́тор (**-а**) *м* (*С.-х.*) grain store *или* elevator (*US*)
элега́нтный *прил* elegant
эле́ктрик (**-а**) *м* electrician
электри́ческий *прил* electric
электри́честв|о (**-а**) *ср* electricity
электри́ч|ка (**-ки**; *gen pl* **-ек**) *ж* (*разг*) electric train
электробытов|о́й *прил*: **электробытовы́е прибо́ры** electrical appliances *мн*
эле́ктрогита́р|а (**-ы**) *ж* electric guitar
электромонтёр (**-а**) *м* electrician
электро́н (**-а**) *м* electron
электро́ник|а (**-и**) *ж* electronics
электро́нн|ый *прил* electronic; **электро́нный микроско́п** electron microscope; **электро́нная по́чта** (*Комп*) email, electronic mail; **электро́нный а́дрес** email address; **электро́нная страни́ца** webpage
электропереда́ч|а (**-и**) *ж* power transmission; **ли́ния электропереда́чи** power line
электропо́езд (**-а**) *м* electric train
электроприбо́р (**-а**) *м* electrical device
электропрово́дк|а (**-и**) *ж* (electrical) wiring
электроста́нци|я (**-и**) *ж* (electric) power station
электроте́хник (**-а**) *м* electrical engineer
электроэне́рги|я (**-и**) *ж* electric power
элеме́нт (**-а**) *м* element; **элемента́рный** *прил* elementary; (*правила*) basic
эли́т|а (**-ы**) *ж собир* élite
эли́тный *прил* (*лучший*) élite; (*дом, школа*) exclusive

эма́левый *прил* enamel
эмалиро́ванный *прил* enamelled
эма́л|ь (**-и**) *ж* enamel
эмба́рго *ср нескл* embargo
эмбле́м|а (**-ы**) *ж* emblem
эмбрио́н (**-а**) *м* embryo
эмигра́нт (**-а**) *м* emigrant
эмиграцио́нный *прил* emigration
эмигра́ци|я (**-и**) *ж* emigration
эмигри́р|овать (**-ую**) *(не)сов* to emigrate
эмоциона́льный *прил* emotional
эмо́ци|я (**-и**) *ж* emotion
эму́льси|я (**-и**) *ж* emulsion
энерге́тик|а (**-и**) *ж* power industry; **энергети́ческий** *прил* energy
энерги́чный *прил* energetic
эне́рги|я (**-и**) *ж* energy
э́нн|ый *прил*: **э́нное число́/коли́чество** X number/amount; **в э́нный раз** yet again
энтузиа́зм (**-а**) *м* enthusiasm
энциклопе́ди|я (**-и**) *ж* encyclopaedia (*Brit*), encyclopedia (*US*)
эпи́граф (**-а**) *м* epigraph
эпиде́ми|я (**-и**) *ж* epidemic
эпизо́д (**-а**) *м* episode
эпизоди́ческий *прил* (*явление*) random
эпиле́пси|я (**-и**) *ж* epilepsy
эпило́г (**-а**) *м* epilogue (*Brit*), epilog (*US*)
эпице́нтр (**-а**) *м* epicentre (*Brit*), epicenter (*US*)
эпопе́|я (**-и**) *ж* epic
э́пос (**-а**) *м* epic literature
эпо́х|а (**-и**) *ж* epoch
э́р|а (**-ы**) *ж* era; **пе́рвый век на́шей э́ры/до на́шей э́ры** the first century AD/BC
эро́зи|я (**-и**) *ж* erosion
эроти́ческий *прил* erotic
эскала́тор (**-а**) *м* escalator
эскала́ци|я (**-и**) *ж* escalation
эски́з (**-а**) *м* (*к картине*) sketch; (*к проекту*) draft
эскимо́ *ср нескл* choc-ice, Eskimo (*US*)
эско́рт (**-а**) *м* escort
эссе́нци|я (**-и**) *ж* (*Кулин*) essence
эстака́д|а (**-ы**) *ж* (*на дороге*) flyover (*Brit*), overpass
эстафе́т|а (**-ы**) *ж* (*Спорт*) relay (race)
эсте́тик|а (**-и**) *ж* aesthetics (*Brit*), esthetics (*US*); **эстети́ческий** *прил* aesthetic (*Brit*), esthetic (*US*)
эсто́н|ец (**-ца**) *м* Estonian
Эсто́ни|я (**-и**) *ж* Estonia
эстра́д|а (**-ы**) *ж* (*для оркестра*) platform; (*вид искусства*) variety; **эстра́дный** *прил*: **эстра́дный конце́рт** variety show
э́т|а (**-ой**) *мест см* **э́тот**
эта́ж (**-а́**) *м* floor, storey (*Brit*), story (*US*); **пе́рвый/второ́й/тре́тий эта́ж** ground/first/second floor (*Brit*), first/second/third floor (*US*)
этаже́р|ка (**-ки**; *gen pl* **-ок**) *ж* stack of shelves
этало́н (**-а**) *м* (*меры*) standard; (*перен*: *красоты*) model
эта́п (**-а**) *м* (*работы*) stage; (*гонки*) lap
э́т|и (**-их**) *мест см* **э́тот**
э́тик|а (**-и**) *ж* ethics
этике́т (**-а**) *м* etiquette
этике́т|ка (**-ки**; *gen pl* **-ок**) *ж* label
э́тим *мест см* **э́тот**
э́тими *мест см* **э́ти**
этимоло́ги|я (**-и**) *ж* etymology
эти́чный *прил* ethical

КЛЮЧЕВОЕ СЛОВО

э́т|о (**-ого**; см *Table 10*) *мест*
1 (*указательное*) this; **э́то бу́дет тру́дно** this will be difficult; **он на всё соглаша́ется — э́то о́чень стра́нно** he is agreeing to everything, this is most strange
2 (*связка в сказуемом*): **любо́вь — э́то проще́ние** love is forgiveness
3 (*как подлежащее*): **с кем ты разгова́ривал? — э́то была́ моя́ сестра́** who were you talking to? — that was my sister; **как э́то произошло́?** how did it happen?
4 (*для усиления*): **э́то он во всём винова́т** he is the one who is to blame for everything
▷ *част* **1** (*служит для усиления*): **кто э́то звони́л?** who was it who phoned (*Brit*) *или* called (*US*)?

КЛЮЧЕВОЕ СЛОВО

э́т|от (**-ого**; *f* **э́та**, *nt* **э́то**, *pl* **э́ти**; см *Table 10*) *мест*
1 (*указательное*: *о близком предмете*) this; (: *о близких предметах*) these; **э́тот дом** this house; **э́ти кни́ги** these books
2 (*о данном времени*) this; **э́тот год осо́бенно тру́дный** this year is particularly hard; **в э́ти дни я при́нял реше́ние** in the last few days I have come to a decision; **э́тот са́мый** that very
3 (*о чём-то только что упомянутом*) this; **он ложи́лся в 10 часо́в ве́чера — э́та привы́чка меня́ всегда́ удивля́ла** he used to go to bed at 10 p.m., this habit always amazed me
▷ *ср* (*как сущ*: *об одном предмете*) this one; (: *о многих предметах*) these ones; **дай мне вот э́ти** give me these ones; **э́тот на всё спосо́бен** this one is capable of anything; **при э́том** at that

этю́д (**-а**) *м* sketch
эфи́р (**-а**) *м* (*Хим*) ether; (*воздушное пространство*) air; **выходи́ть** (*perf* **вы́йти**) **в эфи́р** to go on the air; **прямо́й эфи́р** live broadcast
эффе́кт (**-а**) *м* effect
эффекти́вный *прил* effective
эффе́ктный *прил* (*одежда*) striking; (*речь*) impressive
э́х|о (**-а**) *ср* echo (*мн* echoes)
эшело́н (**-а**) *м* echelon; (*поезд*) special train

ю. *сокр* (= *юг*) S (= *South*); (= *ю́жный*) S (= *South*)

ю́б|ка (**-ки**; *gen pl* **-ок**) *ж* skirt

ювели́р (**-а**) *м* jeweller (*Brit*), jeweler (*US*); **ювели́рный** *прил* jewellery (*Brit*), jewelery (*US*)

юг (**-а**) *м* south

южа́нин (**-а**) *м* southerner

ю́жный *прил* southern

ю́мор (**-а**) *м* humour (*Brit*), humor (*US*)

юмори́ст (**-а**) *м* comedian; **юмористи́ческий** *прил* humorous

ЮНЕ́СКО *ср сокр* UNESCO (= *United Nations Educational Scientific and Cultural Organization*)

юнио́р (**-а**) *м* (*Спорт*) junior

ю́ност|ь (**-и**) *ж* youth

ю́нош|а (**-и**; *nom pl* **-и**, *gen pl* **-ей**) *м* young man; **ю́ношеский** *прил* youthful; (*организация*) youth

ю́ный *прил* (*молодой*) young

юриди́ческ|ий *прил* (*сила*) juridical; (*образование*) legal; **юриди́ческий факульте́т** law faculty; **юриди́ческая консульта́ция** ≈ legal advice office

юрисди́кци|я (**-и**) *ж* jurisdiction

юриско́нсульт (**-а**) *м* ≈ solicitor, ≈ lawyer

юри́ст (**-а**) *м* lawyer

я (**меня́**; см *Table 6a*) *мест* I ▷ *сущ нескл* (*личность*) the self, the ego

я́бед|а (**-ы**) *м/ж* sneak; **я́бednича|ть** (**-ю**; *perf* **ная́бедничать**) *несов*: **я́бедничать на** *+acc* (*разг*) to tell tales about

я́блок|о (**-а**; *nom pl* **-и**) *ср* apple; **я́блон|я** (**-и**) *ж* apple tree; **я́блочный** *прил* apple

яв|и́ться (**-лю́сь, -ишься**; *impf* **явля́ться**) *сов возв* to appear; (*домой, в гости*) to arrive; **явля́ться** (*perf* **яви́ться**) *+instr* (*причиной*) to be

я́в|ка (**-ки**; *gen pl* **-ок**) *ж* appearance

явле́ни|е (**-я**) *ср* phenomenon (*мн* phenomena); (*Рел*) manifestation

явля́|ться (**-юсь**) *несов от* **яви́ться** ▷ *возв +instr* to be

я́вно *нареч* (*очевидно*) obviously

я́вный *прил* (*вражда*) overt; (*ложь*) obvious

яв|ь (**-и**) *ж* reality

ягн|ёнок (**-ёнка**; *nom pl* **-я́та**, *gen pl* **-я́т**) *м* lamb

я́год|а (**-ы**) *ж* berry

ягоди́ц|а (**-ы**) *ж* (*обычно мн*) buttock

яд (**-а**) *м* poison

я́дерный *прил* nuclear

ядови́тый *прил* poisonous

яд|ро́ (**-ра́**; *nom pl* **-ра**, *gen pl* **-ер**) *ср* nucleus; (*Земли, древесины*) core; (*Спорт*) shot

я́зв|а (**-ы**) *ж* (*Мед*) ulcer

язв|и́ть (**-лю́, -и́шь**; *perf* **съязви́ть**) *несов +dat* to sneer at

язы́к (**-а́**) *м* tongue; (*русский, разговорный*) language; **владе́ть** (*impf*) **языко́м** to speak a language

языково́й *прил* language

язы́ч|о́к (**-ка́**) *м* (*ботинка*) tongue

яи́чниц|а (**-ы**) *ж* fried eggs *мн*

яи́чн|ый *прил*: **яи́чный бело́к** egg white; **яи́чная скорлупа́** eggshell

яйц|о́ (**яйца́**; *nom pl* **я́йца**, *gen pl* **яи́ц**, *dat pl* **я́йцам**) *ср* egg; **яйцо́ всмя́тку/вкруту́ю** soft-boiled/ hard-boiled egg

ЯК (**-а**) *м сокр* *самолёт конструкции А.С. Я́ковлева*

я́кобы *союз* (*будто бы*) that ▷ *част* supposedly

я́кор|ь (**-я**; *nom pl* **-я́**) *м* (*Мор*) anchor

я́м|а (**-ы**) *ж* (*в земле*) pit

я́моч|ка (**-ки**; *gen pl* **-ек**) *ж* dimple

янва́р|ь (**-я́**) *м* January

янта́р|ь (**-я́**) *м* amber

Япо́ни|я (**-и**) *ж* Japan

я́ркий *прил* bright; (*перен*:

человек, речь) brilliant
ярлы́к (**-á**) *м* label
я́рмар|ка (**-ки**; *gen pl* **-ок**) *ж* fair; **междунаро́дная я́рмарка** international trade fair
я́ростный *прил* (*взгляд, слова*) furious; (*атака, критика*) fierce
я́рост|ь (**-и**) *ж* fury
я́рус (**-а**) *м* (*в театре*) circle
я́сл|и (**-ей**) *мн* (*также* **де́тские я́сли**) crèche *ед*, day nursery *ед* (*Brit*)
я́сно *нареч* clearly ▷ *как сказ* (*о погоде*) it's fine; (*понятно*) it's clear
я́сност|ь (**-и**) *ж* clarity
я́сный *прил* clear
я́стреб (**-а**) *м* hawk
я́хт|а (**-ы**) *ж* yacht
яхтсме́н (**-а**) *м* yachtsman (*мн* yachtsmen)
ячме́нный *прил* barley
ячме́н|ь (**-я́**) *м* barley
я́щериц|а (**-ы**) *ж* lizard
я́щик (**-а**) *м* (*вместилище: большой*) chest; (*: маленький*) box; (*в письменном столе итп*) drawer; **му́сорный я́щик** dustbin (*Brit*), garbage can (*US*); **почто́вый я́щик** (*на улице*) postbox; (*дома*) letter box
я́щур (**-а**) *м* foot-and-mouth disease

A [eɪ] *n* (*Mus*) ля *nt ind*

KEYWORD

a [ə] (*before vowel or silent h:* **an**) *indef art* **1: a book** кни́га; **an apple** я́блоко; **she's a student** она́ студе́нтка
2 (*instead of the number "one"*): **a week ago** неде́лю наза́д; **a hundred pounds** сто фу́нтов
3 (*in expressing time*) в *+acc*; **3 a day** 3 в день; **10 km an hour** 10 км в час
4 (*in expressing prices*): **30p a kilo** 30 пе́нсов килогра́мм; **£5 a person** £5 с ка́ждого

AA *n abbr* (*Brit*) (= *Automobile Association*) автомоби́льная ассоциа́ция
AAA *n abbr* (= *American Automobile Association*) америка́нская автомоби́льная ассоциа́ция
aback [əˈbæk] *adv*: **I was taken aback** я был поражён
abandon [əˈbændən] *vt* (*person*) покида́ть (*perf* поки́нуть); (*search*) прекраща́ть (*perf* прекрати́ть); (*hope*) оставля́ть (*perf* оста́вить); (*idea*) отка́зываться (*perf* отказа́ться) от *+gen*
abbey [ˈæbɪ] *n* абба́тство
abbreviation [əbriːvɪˈeɪʃən] *n* сокраще́ние
abdomen [ˈæbdəmɛn] *n* брюшна́я по́лость *f*, живо́т
abide [əˈbaɪd] *vt*: **I can't abide it/him** я э́того/его́ не выношу́; **abide by** *vt fus* соблюда́ть (*perf* соблюсти́)
ability [əˈbɪlɪtɪ] *n* (*capacity*) спосо́бность *f*; (*talent, skill*) спосо́бности *fpl*
able [ˈeɪbl] *adj* (*capable*) спосо́бный; (*skilled*) уме́лый; **he is able to …** он спосо́бен *+infin …*
abnormal [æbˈnɔːml] *adj* ненорма́льный
aboard [əˈbɔːd] *prep* (*position*: *Naut, Aviat*) на борту́ *+gen*; (: *train, bus*) в *+prp*; (*motion*: *Naut, Aviat*) на борт *+gen*; (: *train, bus*) в *+acc* ▷ *adv*: **to climb aboard** (*train*) сади́ться (*perf* сесть) в по́езд
abolish [əˈbɔlɪʃ] *vt* отменя́ть (*perf* отмени́ть)
abolition [æbəˈlɪʃən] *n* отме́на
abortion [əˈbɔːʃən] *n* або́рт; **to have an abortion** де́лать (*perf* сде́лать) або́рт

KEYWORD

about [əˈbaut] *adv*
1 (*approximately*: *referring to time, price etc*) о́коло *+gen*,

примéрно *+acc*; **at about two (o'clock)** примéрно в два (часá), óколо двух (часóв); **I've just about finished** я почтú закóнчил
2 (*approximately*: *referring to height, size etc*) óколо *+gen*, примéрно *+nom*; **the room is about 10 metres wide** кóмната примéрно 10 мéтров в ширинý; **she is about your age** онá примéрно Вáшего вóзраста
3 (*referring to place*) повсю́ду; **to leave things lying about** разбрáсывать (*perf* разбросáть) вéщи повсю́ду; **to run/walk about** бéгать (*impf*)/ходúть (*impf*) вокрýг
4: to be about to do собирáться (*perf* собрáться) *+infin*; **he was about to go to bed** он собрáлся лечь спать
▷ *prep* **1** (*relating to*) о(б) *+prp*; **a book about London** кнúга о Лóндоне; **what is it about?** о чём э́то?; **what** *or* **how about doing ...?** как насчёт тогó, чтóбы *+infin* ...?
2 (*referring to place*) по *+dat*; **to walk about the town** ходúть (*impf*) по гóроду; **her clothes were scattered about the room** её одéжда былá разбрóсана по кóмнате

above [əˈbʌv] *adv* (*higher up*) наверхý ▷ *prep* (*higher than*) над *+instr*; (: *in rank etc*) вы́ше *+gen*; **from above** свéрху; **mentioned above** вышеупомя́нутый; **above all** прéжде всегó
abroad [əˈbrɔːd] *adv* (*to be*) за гранúцей *or* рубежóм; (*to go*) за гранúцу *or* рубéж; (*to come from*) из-за гранúцы *or* рубежá
abrupt [əˈbrʌpt] *adj* (*action, ending*) внезáпный; (*person, manner*) рéзкий
absence [ˈæbsəns] *n* отсýтствие
absent [ˈæbsənt] *adj* отсýтствующий
absolute [ˈæbsəluːt] *adj* абсолю́тный; **absolutely** [æbsəˈluːtlɪ] *adv* абсолю́тно, совершéнно; (*certainly*) безуслóвно
absorb [əbˈzɔːb] *vt* (*liquid, information*) впúтывать (*perf* впитáть); (*light, firm*) поглощáть (*perf* поглотúть); **he is absorbed in a book** он поглощён кнúгой; **absorbent cotton** *n* (*US*) гигроскопúческая вáта; **absorbing** *adj* увлекáтельный
abstract [ˈæbstrækt] *adj* абстрáктный
absurd [əbˈsəːd] *adj* абсýрдный, нелéпый
abundant [əˈbʌndənt] *adj* обúльный
abuse [*n* əˈbjuːs, *vb* əˈbjuːz] *n* (*insults*) брань *f*; (*ill-treatment*) жестóкое обращéние; (*misuse*) злоупотреблéние ▷ *vt* (*see n*) оскорбля́ть (*perf* оскорбúть); жестóко обращáться (*impf*) с *+instr*; злоупотребля́ть (*perf* злоупотребúть) *+instr*
abusive [əˈbjuːsɪv] *adj* (*person*) грýбый, жестóкий
academic [ækəˈdɛmɪk] *adj* (*system*) академúческий; (*qualifications*) учёный; (*work, books*) наýчный; (*person*) интеллектуáльный ▷ *n* учёный(-ая) *m(f) adj*
academy [əˈkædəmɪ] *n* (*learned body*) акадéмия; (*college*) учúлище; (*in Scotland*) срéдняя шкóла; **academy of music** консерватóрия
accelerate [ækˈsɛləreɪt] *vi* (*Aut*)

разгоня́ться (*perf* разогна́ться)
acceleration [æksɛlə'reɪʃən] *n* (*Aut*) разго́н
accelerator [æk'sɛləreɪtə^r] *n* акселера́тор
accent ['æksɛnt] *n* акце́нт; (*stress mark*) знак ударе́ния
accept [ək'sɛpt] *vt* принима́ть (*perf* приня́ть); (*fact, situation*) мири́ться (*perf* примири́ться) с *+instr*; (*responsibility, blame*) принима́ть (*perf* приня́ть) на себя́; **acceptable** *adj* прие́млемый; **acceptance** *n* приня́тие; (*of fact*) прия́тие
access ['æksɛs] *n* до́ступ; **accessible** [æk'sɛsəbl] *adj* досту́пный
accessory [æk'sɛsərɪ] *n* принадле́жность *f*; **accessories** *npl* (*Dress*) аксессуа́ры *mpl*
accident ['æksɪdənt] *n* (*disaster*) несча́стный слу́чай; (*in car etc*) ава́рия; **by accident** случа́йно; **accidental** [æksɪ'dɛntl] *adj* случа́йный; **accidentally** [æksɪ'dɛntəlɪ] *adv* случа́йно
acclaim [ə'kleɪm] *n* призна́ние
accommodate [ə'kɔmədeɪt] *vt* (*subj*: *person*) предоставля́ть (*perf* предоста́вить) жильё *+dat*; (: *car, hotel etc*) вмеща́ть (*perf* вмести́ть)
accommodation [əkɔmə'deɪʃən] *n* (*to live in*) жильё; (*to work in*) помеще́ние; **accommodations** *npl* (*US*: *lodgings*) жильё *ntsg*
accompaniment [ə'kʌmpənɪmənt] *n* сопровожде́ние; (*Mus*) аккомпанеме́нт
accompany [ə'kʌmpənɪ] *vt* сопровожда́ть (*perf* сопроводи́ть); (*Mus*) аккомпани́ровать (*impf*) *+dat*
accomplice [ə'kʌmplɪs] *n* соо́бщник(-ица)
accomplish [ə'kʌmplɪʃ] *vt* (*task*) заверша́ть (*perf* заверши́ть); (*goal*) достига́ть (дости́гнуть *or* дости́чь *perf*) *+gen*
accord [ə'kɔ:d] *n*: **of his own accord** по со́бственному жела́нию; **of its own accord** сам по себе́; **accordance** *n*: **in accordance with** в согла́сии *or* соотве́тствии с *+instr*; **according** *prep*: **according to** согла́сно *+dat*; **accordingly** *adv* соотве́тствующим о́бразом; (*as a result*) соотве́тственно
account [ə'kaunt] *n* (*bill*) счёт; (*in bank*) (расчётный) счёт; (*report*) отчёт; **accounts** *npl* (*Comm*) счета́ *mpl*; (*books*) бухга́лтерские кни́ги *fpl*; **to keep an account of** вести́ (*impf*) счёт *+gen or +dat*; **to bring sb to account for sth** призыва́ть (*perf* призва́ть) кого́-н к отве́ту за что-н; **by all accounts** по всем све́дениям; **it is of no account** э́то не ва́жно; **on account** в креди́т; **on no account** ни в ко́ем слу́чае; **on account of** по причи́не *+gen*; **to take into account, take account of** принима́ть (*perf* приня́ть) в расчёт; **account for** *vt fus* (*expenses*) отчи́тываться (*perf* отчита́ться) за *+acc*; (*absence, failure*) объясня́ть (*perf* объясни́ть); **accountable** *adj* отчётный; **to be accountable to sb for sth** отвеча́ть (*impf*) за что-н пе́ред кем-н; **accountancy** *n* бухгалте́рия, бухга́лтерское де́ло; **accountant** *n* бухга́лтер
accumulate [ə'kju:mjuleɪt] *vt* нака́пливать (*perf* накопи́ть) ▷ *vi* нака́пливаться (*perf* накопи́ться)
accuracy ['ækjurəsɪ] *n* то́чность *f*

accurate ['ækjurɪt] *adj* то́чный; (*person, device*) аккура́тный; **accurately** *adv* то́чно

accusation [ækju'zeɪʃən] *n* обвине́ние

accuse [ə'kju:z] *vt*: **to accuse sb (of sth)** обвиня́ть (*perf* обвини́ть) кого́-н (в чём-н); **accused** *n* (*Law*): **the accused** обвиня́емый(-ая) *m(f) adj*

accustomed [ə'kʌstəmd] *adj*: **I'm accustomed to working late/to the heat** я привы́к рабо́тать по́здно/к жаре́

ace [eɪs] *n* (*Cards*) туз; (*Tennis*) вы́игрыш с пода́чи, эйс

ache [eɪk] *n* боль *f* ▷ *vi* боле́ть (*impf*); **my head aches** у меня́ боли́т голова́

achieve [ə'tʃi:v] *vt* (*result*) достига́ть (дости́гнуть *or* дости́чь *perf*) +*gen*; (*success*) добива́ться (*perf* доби́ться) +*gen*; **achievement** *n* достиже́ние

acid ['æsɪd] *adj* (*Chem*) кисло́тный; (*taste*) ки́слый ▷ *n* (*Chem*) кислота́

acknowledge [ək'nɔlɪdʒ] *vt* (*letter etc*: *also* **acknowledge receipt of**) подтвержда́ть (*perf* подтверди́ть) получе́ние +*gen*; (*fact*) признава́ть (*perf* призна́ть); **acknowledgement** *n* (*of letter etc*) подтвержде́ние получе́ния

acne ['æknɪ] *n* угри́ *mpl*, прыщи́ *mpl*

acorn ['eɪkɔ:n] *n* жёлудь *m*

acquaintance *n* знако́мый(-ая) *m(f) adj*

acquire [ə'kwaɪə^r] *vt* приобрета́ть (*perf* приобрести́)

acquisition [ækwɪ'zɪʃən] *n* приобрете́ние

acre ['eɪkə^r] *n* акр

across [ə'krɔs] *prep* (*over*) че́рез +*acc*; (*on the other side of*) на друго́й стороне́ +*gen*, по ту сто́рону +*gen*; (*crosswise over*) че́рез +*acc*, попере́к +*gen* ▷ *adv* на ту́ *or* другу́ю сто́рону; (*measurement*: *width*) шириной́; **to walk across the road** переходи́ть (*perf* перейти́) доро́гу; **to take sb across the road** переводи́ть (*perf* перевести́) кого́-н че́рез доро́гу; **the lake is 12 km across** ширина́ о́зера — 12 км; **across from** напро́тив +*gen*

act [ækt] *n* (*also Law*) акт; (*deed*) посту́пок; (*of play*) де́йствие, акт ▷ *vi* (*do sth*) поступа́ть (*perf* поступи́ть), де́йствовать (*impf*); (*behave*) вести́ (*perf* повести́) себя́; (*have effect*) де́йствовать (*perf* поде́йствовать); (*Theat*) игра́ть (*perf* сыгра́ть); **in the act of** в проце́ссе +*gen*; **to act as** де́йствовать (*impf*) в ка́честве +*gen*; **acting** *adj*: **acting director** исполня́ющий обя́занности дире́ктора ▷ *n* (*profession*) актёрская профе́ссия

action ['ækʃən] *n* (*deed*) посту́пок, де́йствие; (*motion*) движе́ние; (*Mil*) вое́нные де́йствия *ntpl*; (*Law*) иск; **the machine was out of action** маши́на вы́шла из строя́; **to take action** принима́ть (*perf* приня́ть) ме́ры

active ['æktɪv] *adj* акти́вный; (*volcano*) де́йствующий; **actively** *adv* (*participate*) акти́вно; (*discourage, dislike*) си́льно

activist ['æktɪvɪst] *n* активи́ст(ка)

activity [æk'tɪvɪtɪ] *n* (*being active*) акти́вность *f*; (*action*) де́ятельность *f*; (*pastime*) заня́тие

actor ['æktə^r] *n* актёр

actress ['æktrɪs] *n* актри́са

actual ['æktjuəl] *adj* (*real*)

действи́тельный; **the actual work hasn't begun yet** сама́ рабо́та ещё не начала́сь; **actually** *adv* (*really*) действи́тельно; (*in fact*) на са́мом де́ле, факти́чески; (*even*) да́же

acupuncture ['ækjupʌŋktʃəʳ] *n* иглоука́лывание, акупункту́ра

acute [ə'kju:t] *adj* о́стрый; (*anxiety*) си́льный; **acute accent** аку́т

AD *adv abbr* (= *Anno Domini*) н.э. (= *на́шей э́ры*)

ad [æd] *n abbr* (*inf*) = **advertisement**

adamant ['ædəmənt] *adj* непреклóнный

adapt [ə'dæpt] *vt* (*alter*) приспоса́бливать (*perf* приспосо́бить) ▷ *vi*: **to adapt (to)** приспоса́бливаться (*perf* приспосо́биться) (к +*dat*), адапти́роваться (*impf/perf*) (к +*dat*)

add [æd] *vt* (*to collection etc*) прибавля́ть (*perf* приба́вить); (*comment*) добавля́ть (*perf* доба́вить); (*figures*: *also* **add up**) скла́дывать (*perf* сложи́ть) ▷ *vi*: **to add to** (*workload*) увели́чивать (*perf* увели́чить); (*problems*) усугубля́ть (*perf* усугуби́ть)

addict ['ædɪkt] *n* (*also* **drug addict**) наркома́н; **addicted** [ə'dɪktɪd] *adj*: **to be addicted to** (*drugs etc*) пристрасти́ться (*perf*) к +*dat*; (*fig*): **he's addicted to football** он зая́длый люби́тель футбо́ла; **addiction** [ə'dɪkʃən] *n* пристра́стие; **drug addiction** наркома́ния; **addictive** [ə'dɪktɪv] *adj* (*drug*) вызыва́ющий привыка́ние

addition [ə'dɪʃən] *n* (*sum*) сложе́ние; (*thing added*) добавле́ние; (*to collection*) пополне́ние; **in addition** вдоба́вок, дополни́тельно; **in addition to** в дополне́ние к +*dat*; **additional** *adj* дополни́тельный

address [ə'drɛs] *n* а́дрес; (*speech*) речь *f* ▷ *vt* адресова́ть (*impf/perf*); (*person*) обраща́ться (*perf* обрати́ться) к +*dat*; (*problem*) занима́ться (*perf* заня́ться) +*instr*; **address book** *n* записна́я кни́жка

adequate ['ædɪkwɪt] *adj* (*sufficient*) доста́точный; (*satisfactory*) адеква́тный

adhere [əd'hɪəʳ] *vi*: **to adhere to** (*fig*) приде́рживаться (*impf*) +*gen*

adhesive [əd'hi:zɪv] *adj* кле́йкий ▷ *n* клей

adjacent [ə'dʒeɪsənt] *adj*: **adjacent (to)** сме́жный (с +*instr*)

adjective ['ædʒɛktɪv] *n* прилага́тельное *nt adj*

adjust [ə'dʒʌst] *vt* (*plans, views*) приспоса́бливать (*perf* приспосо́бить); (*clothing*) поправля́ть (*perf* попра́вить); (*mechanism*) регули́ровать (*perf* отрегули́ровать) ▷ *vi*: **to adjust (to)** приспоса́бливаться (*perf* приспосо́биться) (к +*dat*); **adjustable** *adj* регули́руемый; **adjustment** *n* (*to surroundings*) адапта́ция; (*of prices, wages*) регули́рование; **to make adjustments to** вноси́ть (*perf* внести́) измене́ния в +*acc*

administer [əd'mɪnɪstəʳ] *vt* (*country, department*) управля́ть (*impf*) +*instr*, руководи́ть (*impf*) +*instr*; (*justice*) отправля́ть (*impf*); (*test*) проводи́ть (*perf* провести́)

administration [ədmɪnɪs'treɪʃən] *n* (*management*) администра́ция

administrative [əd'mɪnɪstrətɪv]

adj администрати́вный
admiration [ædmə'reɪʃən] *n* восхище́ние
admire [əd'maɪə^r] *vt* восхища́ться (*perf* восхити́ться) *+instr*; (*gaze at*) любова́ться (*impf*) *+instr*; **admirer** *n* покло́нник(-ица)
admission [əd'mɪʃən] *n* (*admittance*) до́пуск; (*entry fee*) входна́я пла́та; **"admission free", "free admission"** "вход свобо́дный"
admit [əd'mɪt] *vt* (*confess, accept*) признава́ть (*perf* призна́ть); (*permit to enter*) впуска́ть (*perf* впусти́ть); (*to hospital*) госпитализи́ровать (*impf/perf*); **admit to** *vt fus* (*crime*) сознава́ться (*perf* созна́ться) в *+prp*; **admittedly** [əd'mɪtɪdlɪ] *adv*: **admittedly it is not easy** призна́ться, э́то не легко́
adolescent [ædəu'lɛsnt] *adj* подро́стковый ▷ *n* подро́сток
adopt [ə'dɔpt] *vt* (*son*) усыновля́ть (*perf* усынови́ть); (*daughter*) удочеря́ть (*perf* удочери́ть); (*policy*) принима́ть (*perf* приня́ть); **adopted** *adj* (*child*) приёмный; **adoption** [ə'dɔpʃən] *n* (*see vt*) усыновле́ние; удочере́ние; приня́тие
adore [ə'dɔː^r] *vt* обожа́ть (*impf*)
Adriatic [eɪdrɪ'ætɪk] *n*: **the Adriatic** Адриа́тика
ADSL *abbr* (= *Asymmetric Digital Subscriber Line*) АЦАЛ *f* (= *асимметри́чная цифрова́я абоне́нтская ли́ния*)
adult ['ædʌlt] *n* взро́слый(-ая) *m(f) adj* ▷ *adj* (*grown-up*) взро́слый; **adult film** фильм для взро́слых
adultery [ə'dʌltərɪ] *n* супру́жеская неве́рность *f*
advance [əd'vɑːns] *n* (*progress*) успе́х; (*Mil*) наступле́ние; (*money*) ава́нс ▷ *adj* (*booking*) предвари́тельный ▷ *vt* (*theory, idea*) выдвига́ть (*perf* вы́двинуть) ▷ *vi* продвига́ться (*perf* продви́нуться) вперёд; (*Mil*) наступа́ть (*impf*); **in advance** зара́нее, предвари́тельно; **to advance sb money** плати́ть (*perf* заплати́ть) кому́-н ава́нсом; **advanced** *adj* (*studies*) для продви́нутого у́ровня; (*course*) продви́нутый; (*child, country*) развито́й; **advanced maths** вы́сшая матема́тика
advantage [əd'vɑːntɪdʒ] *n* преиму́щество; **to take advantage of** (*person*) испо́льзовать (*perf*); **to our advantage** в на́ших интере́сах
adventure [əd'vɛntʃə^r] *n* приключе́ние
adventurous [əd'vɛntʃərəs] *adj* (*person*) сме́лый
adverb ['ædvəːb] *n* наре́чие
adversary ['ædvəsərɪ] *n* проти́вник(-ница)
adverse ['ædvəːs] *adj* неблагоприя́тный
advert ['ædvəːt] *n abbr* (*Brit*) = **advertisement**
advertise ['ædvətaɪz] *vt, vi* реклами́ровать (*impf*); **to advertise on television/in a newspaper** дава́ть (*perf* дать) объявле́ние по телеви́дению/в газе́ту; **to advertise a job** объявля́ть (*perf* объяви́ть) ко́нкурс на ме́сто; **to advertise for staff** дава́ть (*perf* дать) объявле́ние, что тре́буются рабо́тники; **advertisement** [əd'vəːtɪsmənt] *n* рекла́ма;

(*classified*) объявле́ние
advice [əd'vaɪs] *n* сове́т; **a piece of advice** сове́т; **to take legal advice** обраща́ться (*perf* обрати́ться) (за сове́том) к юри́сту
advisable [əd'vaɪzəbl] *adj* целесообра́зный
advise [əd'vaɪz] *vt* сове́товать (*perf* посове́товать) *+dat*; (*professionally*) консульти́ровать (*perf* проконсульти́ровать) *+gen*; **to advise sb of sth** извеща́ть (*perf* извести́ть) кого́-н о чём-н; **to advise (sb) against doing** отсове́товать (*perf*) (кому́-н) *+impf infin*; **adviser** (*US* **advisor**) *n* сове́тник, консульта́нт; **legal adviser** юриско́нсульт
advisory [əd'vaɪzərɪ] *adj* консультати́вный
advocate [*vb* 'ædvəkeɪt, *n* 'ædvəkɪt] *vt* выступа́ть (*perf* вы́ступить) за *+acc* ▷ *n* (*Law*) защи́тник, адвока́т; (*supporter*): **advocate of** сторо́нник(-ица) *+gen*
Aegean [iː'dʒiːən] *n*: **the Aegean** Эге́йское мо́ре
aerial ['ɛərɪəl] *n* анте́нна ▷ *adj* возду́шный; **aerial photography** аэрофотосъёмка
aerobics [ɛə'rəubɪks] *n* аэро́бика
aeroplane ['ɛərəpleɪn] *n* (*Brit*) самолёт
aerosol ['ɛərəsɔl] *n* аэрозо́ль *m*
affair [ə'fɛə^r] *n* (*matter*) де́ло; (*also* **love affair**) рома́н
affect [ə'fɛkt] *vt* (*influence*) де́йствовать (*perf* поде́йствовать) *or* влия́ть (*perf* повлия́ть) на *+acc*; (*afflict*) поража́ть (*perf* порази́ть); (*move deeply*) тро́гать (*perf* тро́нуть)
affection [ə'fɛkʃən] *n* привя́занность *f*; **affectionate** *adj* не́жный
affluent ['æfluənt] *adj* благополу́чный
afford [ə'fɔːd] *vt* позволя́ть (*perf* позво́лить) себе́; **I can't afford it** мне э́то не по карма́ну; **I can't afford the time** мне вре́мя не позволя́ет; **affordable** *adj* досту́пный
Afghanistan [æf'gænɪstæn] *n* Афганиста́н
afraid [ə'freɪd] *adj* испу́ганный; **to be afraid of sth/sb/of doing** боя́ться (*impf*) чего́-н/кого́-н/*+infin*; **to be afraid to** боя́ться (*perf* побоя́ться) *+infin*; **I am afraid that** (*apology*) бою́сь, что; **I am afraid so/not** бою́сь, что да/нет
Africa ['æfrɪkə] *n* А́фрика; **African** *adj* африка́нский
after ['ɑːftə^r] *prep* (*time*) по́сле *+gen*, спустя́ *+acc*, че́рез *+acc*; (*place, order*) за *+instr* ▷ *adv* пото́м, по́сле ▷ *conj* по́сле того́ как; **after three years they divorced** спустя́ *or* че́рез три го́да они́ развели́сь; **who are you after?** кто Вам ну́жен?; **to name sb after sb** называ́ть (*perf* назва́ть) кого́-н в честь кого́-н; **it's twenty after eight** (*US*) сейча́с два́дцать мину́т девя́того; **to ask after sb** справля́ться (*perf* спра́виться) о ком-н; **after all** в конце́ концо́в; **after he left** по́сле того́ как он ушёл; **after having done this** сде́лав э́то; **aftermath** *n* после́дствия *ntpl*; **afternoon** *n* втора́я полови́на дня; **in the afternoon** днём; **after-shave (lotion)** *n* одеколо́н по́сле бритья́; **afterwards** (*US* **afterward**) *adv* впосле́дствии, пото́м
again [ə'gɛn] *adv* (*once more*)

ещё раз, снóва; (*repeatedly*) опя́ть; **I won't go there again** я бóльше не пойдý тудá; **again and again** снóва и снóва

against [ə'gɛnst] *prep* (*lean*) к +*dat*; (*hit, rub*) о +*acc*; (*stand*) у +*gen*; (*in opposition to*) прóтив +*gen*; (*at odds with*) вопреки́ +*dat*; (*compared to*) по сравнéнию с +*instr*

age [eɪdʒ] *n* вóзраст; (*period in history*) век; **aged** ['eɪdʒd] *adj*: **a boy aged ten** мáльчик десяти́ лет

agency ['eɪdʒənsɪ] *n* (*Comm*) бюрó *nt ind*, агéнтство; (*Pol*) управлéние

agenda [ə'dʒɛndə] *n* (*of meeting*) повéстка (дня)

agent ['eɪdʒənt] *n* агéнт; (*Comm*) посрéдник; (*Chem*) реакти́в

aggression [ə'grɛʃən] *n* агрéссия

aggressive [ə'grɛsɪv] *adj* (*belligerent*) агресси́вный

AGM *n abbr* = **annual general meeting**

ago [ə'gəu] *adv*: **two days ago** два дня назáд; **not long ago** недáвно; **how long ago?** как давнó?

agony ['ægənɪ] *n* мучи́тельная боль *f*; **to be in agony** мýчиться (*impf*) от бóли

agree [ə'gri:] *vt* согласóвывать (*perf* согласовáть) ▷ *vi*: **to agree with** (*have same opinion*) соглашáться (*perf* согласи́ться) с +*instr*; (*correspond*) согласовáться (*impf/perf*) с +*instr*; **to agree that** соглашáться (*perf* согласи́ться), что; **garlic doesn't agree with me** я не переношý чеснокá; **to agree to sth/to do** соглашáться (*perf* согласи́ться) на что-н/+*infin*; **agreeable** *adj* (*pleasant*) прия́тный; (*willing*): **I am agreeable** я соглáсен; **agreement** *n* (*consent*) соглáсие; (*arrangement*) соглашéние, договóр; **in agreement with** в соглáсии с +*instr*; **we are in complete agreement** мéжду нáми пóлное соглáсие

agricultural [ægrɪ'kʌltʃərəl] *adj* сельскохозя́йственный; **agricultural land** земéльные угóдья

agriculture ['ægrɪkʌltʃə[r]] *n* сéльское хозя́йство

ahead [ə'hɛd] *adv* впереди́; (*direction*) вперёд; **ahead of** впереди́ +*gen*; (*earlier than*) рáньше +*gen*; **ahead of time** *or* **schedule** досрóчно; **go right** *or* **straight ahead** иди́те вперёд *or* пря́мо; **go ahead!** (*giving permission*) приступáйте!, давáйте!

aid [eɪd] *n* (*assistance*) пóмощь *f*; (*device*) приспособлéние ▷ *vt* помогáть (*perf* помóчь) +*dat*; **in aid of** в пóмощь +*dat*; *see also* **hearing**

aide [eɪd] *n* помóщник

AIDS [eɪdz] *n abbr* (= *acquired immune deficiency syndrome*) СПИД (= *синдрóм приобретённого иммýнодефици́та*)

aim [eɪm] *n* (*objective*) цель *f* ▷ *vi* (*also* **take aim**) цéлиться (*perf* нацéлиться) ▷ *vt*: **to aim (at)** (*gun, camera*) наводи́ть (*perf* навести́) (на +*acc*); (*missile, blow*) цéлить (*perf* нацели́ть) (на +*acc*); (*remark*) направля́ть (*perf* напрáвить) (на +*acc*); **to aim to do** стáвить (*perf* постáвить) своéй цéлью +*infin*; **he has a good aim** он мéткий стрелóк

ain't [eɪnt] (*inf*) = **am not**; **are not**; **is not**

air [ɛə^r] *n* во́здух; (*appearance*) вид ▷ *vt* (*room, bedclothes*) прове́тривать (*perf* прове́трить); (*views*) обнаро́довать (*perf*) ▷ *cpd* возду́шный; **by air** по во́здуху; **on the air** (*be*) в эфи́ре; (*go*) в эфи́р; **airborne** *adj* (*attack*) возду́шный; **air conditioning** *n* кондициони́рование; **aircraft** *n inv* самолёт; **Air Force** *n* Вое́нно-Возду́шные Си́лы *fpl*; **air hostess** *n* (*Brit*) бортпроводни́ца, стюарде́сса; **airline** *n* авиакомпа́ния; **airmail** *n*: **by airmail** авиапо́чтой; **airplane** *n* (*US*) самолёт; **airport** *n* аэропо́рт; **air raid** *n* возду́шный налёт

airy ['ɛərɪ] *adj* (*room*) просто́рный

aisle [aɪl] *n* прохо́д

alarm [ə'lɑːm] *n* (*anxiety*) трево́га; (*device*) сигнализа́ция ▷ *vt* трево́жить (*perf* встрево́жить); **alarm clock** *n* буди́льник

Albania [æl'beɪnɪə] *n* Алба́ния

album ['ælbəm] *n* альбо́м

alcohol ['ælkəhɔl] *n* алкого́ль *m*; **alcoholic** [ælkə'hɔlɪk] *adj* алкого́льный ▷ *n* алкого́лик(-и́чка)

alcove ['ælkəuv] *n* алько́в

alert [ə'ləːt] *adj* внима́тельный; (*to danger*) бди́тельный ▷ *vt* (*police etc*) предупрежда́ть (*perf* предупреди́ть); **to be on the alert** (*also Mil*) быть (*impf*) начеку́

A LEVELS

A levels — квалификацио́нные экза́мены. Шко́льники сдаю́т их в во́зрасте 17-18 лет. Полу́ченные результа́ты определя́ют приём в университе́т. Экза́мены сдаю́тся по трём предме́там. Вы́бор предме́тов дикту́ется специа́льностью, кото́рую выпускники́ плани́руют изуча́ть в университе́те.

Algeria [æl'dʒɪərɪə] *n* Алжи́р

alias ['eɪlɪəs] *n* вы́мышленное и́мя *nt* ▷ *adv*: **alias John** он же Джон

alibi ['ælɪbaɪ] *n* а́либи *nt ind*

alien ['eɪlɪən] *n* (*extraterrestrial*) инопланетя́нин(-я́нка) ▷ *adj*: **alien (to)** чу́ждый (+*dat*); **alienate** ['eɪlɪəneɪt] *vt* отчужда́ть (*impf*), отта́лкивать (*perf* оттолкну́ть)

alight [ə'laɪt] *adj*: **to be alight** горе́ть (*impf*); (*eyes, face*) сия́ть (*impf*)

alike [ə'laɪk] *adj* одина́ковый ▷ *adv* одина́ково; **they look alike** они́ похо́жи друг на дру́га

alive [ə'laɪv] *adj* (*place*) оживлённый; **he is alive** он жив

 **KEYWORD**

all [ɔːl] *adj* весь (*f* вся, *nt* всё, *pl* все); **all day** весь день; **all night** всю ночь; **all five stayed** все пя́теро оста́лись; **all the books** все кни́ги; **all the time** всё вре́мя
▷ *pron* **1** всё; **I ate it all, I ate all of it** я всё съел; **all of us stayed** мы все оста́лись; **we all sat down** мы все се́ли; **is that all?** э́то всё?
2 (*in phrases*): **above all** пре́жде всего́; **after all** в конце́ концо́в; **all in all** в це́лом *or* о́бщем; **not at all** (*in answer to question*) совсе́м *or* во́все нет; (*in answer to thanks*) не́ за что; **I'm not at all tired** я совсе́м не уста́л
▷ *adv* совсе́м; **I am all alone** я

совсе́м оди́н; **I did it all by myself** я всё сде́лал сам; **it's not as hard as all that** э́то во́все не так уж тру́дно; **all the more/better** тем бо́лее/лу́чше; **I have all but finished** я почти́ (что) зако́нчил; **the score is two all** счёт 2:2

allegation [ælɪ'geɪʃən] *n* обвине́ние
allegedly [ə'lɛdʒɪdlɪ] *adv* я́кобы
allegiance [ə'li:dʒəns] *n* ве́рность *f*; (*to idea*) приве́рженность *f*
allergic [ə'lə:dʒɪk] *adj*: **he is allergic to ...** у него́ аллерги́я на *+acc ...*
allergy ['ælədʒɪ] *n* (*Med*) аллерги́я
alleviate [ə'li:vɪeɪt] *vt* облегча́ть (*perf* облегчи́ть)
alley ['ælɪ] *n* переу́лок
alliance [ə'laɪəns] *n* сою́з; (*Pol*) алья́нс
allied ['ælaɪd] *adj* сою́зный
alligator ['ælɪgeɪtə^r] *n* аллига́тор
all-in ['ɔ:lɪn] *adj* (*Brit*): **it cost me £100 all-in** в о́бщей сло́жности мне э́то сто́ило £100
allocate ['æləkeɪt] *vt* выделя́ть (*perf* вы́делить); (*tasks*) поруча́ть (*perf* поручи́ть)
all-out ['ɔ:laut] *adj* (*effort*) максима́льный; (*attack*) масси́рованный
allow [ə'lau] *vt* (*permit*) разреша́ть (*perf* разреши́ть); (: *claim, goal*) признава́ть (*perf* призна́ть) действи́тельным; (*set aside*: *sum*) выделя́ть (*perf* вы́делить); (*concede*): **to allow that** допуска́ть (*perf* допусти́ть), что; **to allow sb to do** разреша́ть (*perf* разреши́ть) *or* позволя́ть (*perf* позво́лить) кому́-н *+infin*;
allow for *vt fus* учи́тывать (*perf* уче́сть), принима́ть (*perf* приня́ть) в расчёт; **allowance** *n* (*Comm*) де́ньги *pl* на расхо́ды; (*pocket money*) карма́нные де́ньги; (*welfare payment*) посо́бие; **to make allowances for** де́лать (*perf* сде́лать) ски́дку для *+gen*
all right *adv* хорошо́, норма́льно; (*positive response*) хорошо́, ла́дно ▷ *adj* неплохо́й, норма́льный; **is everything all right?** всё норма́льно *or* в поря́дке?; **are you all right?** как ты?, ты в поря́дке? (*разг*); **do you like him? — he's all right** он Вам нра́вится? — ничего́
ally ['ælaɪ] *n* сою́зник
almighty [ɔ:l'maɪtɪ] *adj* (*tremendous*) колосса́льный
almond ['ɑ:mənd] *n* минда́ль *m*
almost ['ɔ:lməust] *adv* почти́; (*all but*) чуть *or* едва́ не
alone [ə'ləun] *adj, adv* оди́н (*f* одна́); **to leave sb/sth alone** оставля́ть (*perf* оста́вить) кого́-н/что-н в поко́е; **let alone ...** не говоря́ уже́ о *+prp ...*
along [ə'lɔŋ] *prep* (*motion*) по *+dat*, вдоль *+gen*; (*position*) вдоль *+gen* ▷ *adv*: **is he coming along (with us)?** он идёт с на́ми?; **he was limping along** он шёл хрома́я; **along with** вме́сте с *+instr*; **all along** с са́мого нача́ла; **alongside** *prep* (*position*) ря́дом с *+instr*, вдоль *+gen*; (*motion*) к *+dat* ▷ *adv* ря́дом
aloud [ə'laud] *adv* (*read, speak*) вслух
alphabet ['ælfəbɛt] *n* алфави́т
Alps [ælps] *npl*: **the Alps** А́льпы *pl*
already [ɔ:l'rɛdɪ] *adv* уже́
alright ['ɔ:l'raɪt] *adv* (*Brit*) = **all right**

also ['ɔ:lsəu] *adv* (*about subject*) та́кже, то́же; (*about object*) та́кже; (*moreover*) кро́ме того́, к тому́ же; **he also likes apples** он та́кже *or* то́же лю́бит я́блоки; **he likes apples also** он лю́бит та́кже я́блоки
altar ['ɔltəʳ] *n* алта́рь *m*
alter ['ɔltəʳ] *vt* изменя́ть (*perf* измени́ть) ▷ *vi* изменя́ться (*perf* измени́ться); **alteration** [ɔltə'reɪʃən] *n* измене́ние
alternate [*adj* ɔl'tə:nɪt, *vb* 'ɔltə:neɪt] *adj* чередý ющийся; (*US*: *alternative*) альтернати́вный ▷ *vi*: **to alternate (with)** чередова́ться (*impf*) (с *+instr*); **on alternate days** че́рез день
alternative [ɔl'tə:nətɪv] *adj* альтернати́вный ▷ *n* альтернати́ва; **alternatively** *adv*: **alternatively one could ...** кро́ме того́ мо́жно ...
although [ɔ:l'ðəu] *conj* хотя́
altitude ['æltɪtju:d] *n* (*of plane*) высота́; (*of place*) высота́ над у́ровнем мо́ря
altogether [ɔ:ltə'gɛðəʳ] *adv* (*completely*) соверше́нно; (*in all*) в о́бщем, в о́бщей сло́жности
aluminium [ælju'mɪnɪəm] (*US* **aluminum**) [ə'lu:mɪnəm] *n* алюми́ний
always ['ɔ:lweɪz] *adv* всегда́
am [æm] *vb see* **be**
a.m. *adv abbr* (= *ante meridiem*) до полу́дня
amateur ['æmətəʳ] *n* люби́тель *m*; **amateur dramatics** люби́тельский теа́тр; **amateur photographer** фотóграф-люби́тель *m*
amazement [ə'meɪzmənt] *n* изумле́ние
amazing [ə'meɪzɪŋ] *adj* (*surprising*) порази́тельный; (*fantastic*) изуми́тельный, замеча́тельный
ambassador [æm'bæsədəʳ] *n* посо́л
ambiguous [æm'bɪgjuəs] *adj* нея́сный, двусмы́сленный
ambition [æm'bɪʃən] *n* (*see adj*) честолю́бие; амби́ция; (*aim*) цель *f*
ambitious [æm'bɪʃəs] *adj* (*positive*) честолюби́вый; (*negative*) амбицио́зный
ambulance ['æmbjuləns] *n* ско́рая по́мощь *f*
ambush ['æmbuʃ] *n* заса́да ▷ *vt* устра́ивать (*perf* устро́ить) заса́ду *+dat*
amend [ə'mɛnd] *vt* (*law, text*) пересма́тривать (*perf* пересмотре́ть) ▷ *n*: **to make amends** загла́живать (*perf* загла́дить) (свою́) вину́; **amendment** *n* попра́вка
amenities [ə'mi:nɪtɪz] *npl* удо́бства *ntpl*
America [ə'mɛrɪkə] *n* Аме́рика; **American** *adj* америка́нский ▷ *n* америка́нец(-нка)
amicable ['æmɪkəbl] *adj* (*relationship*) дру́жеский
amid(st) [ə'mɪd(st)] *prep* посреди́ *+gen*
ammunition [æmju'nɪʃən] *n* (*for gun*) патро́ны *mpl*
amnesty ['æmnɪstɪ] *n* амни́стия
among(st) [ə'mʌŋ(st)] *prep* среди́ *+gen*
amount [ə'maunt] *n* коли́чество ▷ *vi*: **to amount to** (*total*) составля́ть (*perf* соста́вить)
amp(ère) ['æmp(ɛəʳ)] *n* ампе́р
ample ['æmpl] *adj* (*large*) соли́дный; (*abundant*) оби́льный; (*enough*) доста́точный; **to have**

ample time/room име́ть (*impf*) доста́точно вре́мени/ме́ста

amuse [ə'mju:z] *vt* развлека́ть (*perf* развле́чь); **amusement** *n* (*mirth*) удово́льствие; (*pastime*) развлече́ние; **amusement arcade** *n* павильо́н с игровы́ми аппара́тами

an [æn] *indef art see* **a**

anaemia [ə'ni:mɪə] (*US* **anemia**) *n* анеми́я, малокро́вие

anaesthetic [ænɪs'θɛtɪk] (*US* **anesthetic**) *n* нарко́з

analyse ['ænəlaɪz] (*US* **analyze**) *vt* анализи́ровать (*perf* проанализи́ровать)

analysis [ə'nælәsɪs] (*pl* **analyses**) *n* ана́лиз

analyst ['ænəlɪst] *n* (*political*) анали́тик, коммента́тор; (*financial, economic*) экспе́рт; (*US: psychiatrist*) психиа́тр

analyze ['ænəlaɪz] *vt* (*US*) = **analyse**

anarchy ['ænəkɪ] *n* ана́рхия

anatomy [ə'nætəmɪ] *n* анато́мия; (*body*) органи́зм

ancestor ['ænsɪstə^r] *n* пре́док

anchor ['æŋkə^r] *n* я́корь *m*

anchovy ['æntʃəvɪ] *n* анчо́ус

ancient ['eɪnʃənt] *adj* (*civilization, person*) дре́вний; (*monument*) стари́нный

and [ænd] *conj* и; **my father and I** я и мой оте́ц, мы с отцо́м; **bread and butter** хлеб с ма́слом; **and so on** и так да́лее; **try and come** постара́йтесь прийти́; **he talked and talked** он всё говори́л и говори́л

anemia [ə'ni:mɪə] *n* (*US*) = **anaemia**

anesthetic [ænɪs'θɛtɪk] *n* (*US*) = **anaesthetic**

angel ['eɪndʒəl] *n* а́нгел

anger ['æŋgə^r] *n* гнев, возмуще́ние

angle ['æŋgl] *n* (*corner*) у́гол

angler ['æŋglə^r] *n* рыболо́в

Anglican ['æŋglɪkən] *adj* англика́нский ▷ *n* англика́нец(-а́нка)

angling ['æŋglɪŋ] *n* ры́бная ло́вля

angrily ['æŋgrɪlɪ] *adv* серди́то, гне́вно

angry ['æŋgrɪ] *adj* серди́тый, гне́вный; (*wound*) воспалённый; **to be angry with sb/at sth** серди́ться (*impf*) на кого́-н/что-н; **to get angry** серди́ться (*perf* рассерди́ться)

anguish ['æŋgwɪʃ] *n* му́ка

animal ['ænɪməl] *n* живо́тное *nt adj*; (*wild animal*) зверь *m*; (*pej: person*) зверь, живо́тное ▷ *adj* живо́тный

animated *adj* оживлённый, живо́й; (*film*) мультипликацио́нный

animation [ænɪ'meɪʃən] *n* (*enthusiasm*) оживле́ние

ankle ['æŋkl] *n* лоды́жка

anniversary [ænɪ'vә:sərɪ] *n* годовщи́на

announce [ə'nauns] *vt* (*engagement, decision*) объявля́ть (*perf* объяви́ть) (о +*prp*); (*birth, death*) извеща́ть (*perf* извести́ть) о +*prp*; **announcement** *n* объявле́ние; (*in newspaper etc*) сообще́ние

annoy [ə'nɔɪ] *vt* раздража́ть (*perf* раздражи́ть); **annoying** *adj* (*noise*) раздража́ющий; (*mistake, event*) доса́дный

annual ['ænjuəl] *adj* (*meeting*) ежего́дный; (*income*) годово́й; **annually** *adv* ежего́дно

annum ['ænəm] *n see* **per**

anonymous [ə'nɔnɪməs] *adj* анони́мный
anorak ['ænəræk] *n* ку́ртка
anorexia [ænə'rɛksɪə] *n* аноре́ксия
another [ə'nʌðə^r] *pron* друго́й ▷ *adj*: **another book** (*additional*) ещё одна́ кни́га; (*different*) друга́я кни́га; *see also* **one**
answer ['ɑːnsə^r] *n* отве́т; (*to problem*) реше́ние ▷ *vi* отвеча́ть (*perf* отве́тить) ▷ *vt* (*letter, question*) отвеча́ть (*perf* отве́тить) на *+acc*; (*person*) отвеча́ть (*perf* отве́тить) *+dat*; **in answer to your letter** в отве́т на Ва́ше письмо́; **to answer the phone** подходи́ть (*perf* подойти́) к телефо́ну; **to answer the bell** *or* **the door** открыва́ть (*perf* откры́ть) дверь; **answering machine** *n* автоотве́тчик
ant [ænt] *n* муравéй
Antarctic [ænt'ɑːktɪk] *n*: **the Antarctic** Анта́рктика
antelope ['æntɪləup] *n* антило́па
anthem ['ænθəm] *n*: **national anthem** госуда́рственный гимн
antibiotic ['æntɪbaɪ'ɔtɪk] *n* антибио́тик
antibody ['æntɪbɔdɪ] *n* антите́ло
anticipate [æn'tɪsɪpeɪt] *vt* (*expect*) ожида́ть (*impf*) *+gen*; (*foresee*) предуга́дывать (*perf* преугада́ть); (*forestall*) предвосхища́ть (*perf* предвосхи́тить)
anticipation [æntɪsɪ'peɪʃən] *n* (*expectation*) ожида́ние; (*eagerness*) предвкуше́ние
antics ['æntɪks] *npl* (*of child*) ша́лости *fpl*
antidote ['æntɪdəut] *n* противоя́дие
antifreeze ['æntɪfriːz] *n* антифри́з
antique [æn'tiːk] *n* антиква́рная вещь *f*, предме́т старины́ ▷ *adj* антиква́рный
antiseptic [æntɪ'sɛptɪk] *n* антисе́птик
antivirus [æntɪ'vaɪrəs] *adj* (*Comput*) антиви́русный; **antivirus software** антиви́русное програ́ммное обеспече́ние
anxiety [æŋ'zaɪətɪ] *n* трево́га
anxious ['æŋkʃəs] *adj* (*person, look*) беспоко́йный, озабо́ченный; (*time*) трево́жный; **she is anxious to do** она́ о́чень хо́чет *+infin*; **to be anxious about** беспоко́иться (*impf*) о *+prp*

KEYWORD

any ['ɛnɪ] *adj* **1** (*in questions etc*): **have you any butter/children?** у Вас есть ма́сло/де́ти?; **do you have any questions?** у Вас есть каки́е-нибу́дь вопро́сы?; **if there are any tickets left** е́сли ещё оста́лись биле́ты
2 (*with negative*): **I haven't any bread/books** у меня́ нет хле́ба/книг; **I didn't buy any newspapers** я не купи́л газе́т
3 (*no matter which*) любо́й; **any colour will do** любо́й цвет подойдёт
4 (*in phrases*): **in any case** в любо́м слу́чае; **any day now** в любо́й день; **at any moment** в любо́й моме́нт; **at any rate** во вся́ком слу́чае; (*anyhow*) так и́ли ина́че; **any time** (*at any moment*) в любо́й моме́нт; (*whenever*) в любо́е вре́мя; (*as response*) не́ за что
▷ *pron* **1** (*in questions etc*): **I need some money, have you got any?** мне нужны́ де́ньги, у Вас есть?;

can any of you sing? кто́-нибудь из вас уме́ет петь?
2 (*with negative*) ни оди́н (*f* одна́, *nt* одно́, *pl* одни́); **I haven't any (of those)** у меня́ таки́х нет
3 (*no matter which one(s)*) любо́й; **take any you like** возьми́те то, что Вам нра́вится
▷ *adv* **1** (*in questions etc*): **do you want any more soup?** хоти́те ещё су́пу?; **are you feeling any better?** Вам лу́чше?
2 (*with negative*): **I can't hear him any more** я бо́льше его́ не слы́шу; **don't wait any longer** не жди́те бо́льше; **he isn't any better** ему́ не лу́чше

anybody ['ɛnɪbɔdɪ] *pron* = **anyone**

anyhow ['ɛnɪhau] *adv* (*at any rate*) так и́ли ина́че; **the work is done anyhow** (*haphazardly*) рабо́та сде́лана ко́е-как; **I shall go anyhow** я так и́ли ина́че пойду́

anyone ['ɛnɪwʌn] *pron* (*in questions etc*) кто́-нибудь; (*with negative*) никто́; (*no matter who*) любо́й, вся́кий; **can you see anyone?** Вы ви́дите кого́-нибудь?; **I can't see anyone** я никого́ не ви́жу; **anyone could do it** любо́й *or* вся́кий мо́жет э́то сде́лать; **you can invite anyone** Вы мо́жете пригласи́ть кого́ уго́дно

anything ['ɛnɪθɪŋ] *pron* (*in questions etc*) что́-нибудь; (*with negative*) ничего́; (*no matter what*) (всё,) что уго́дно; **can you see anything?** Вы ви́дите что́-нибудь?; **I can't see anything** я ничего́ не ви́жу; **anything (at all) will do** всё, что уго́дно подойдёт

anyway ['ɛnɪweɪ] *adv* всё равно́; (*in brief*): **anyway, I didn't want to go** в о́бщем, я не хоте́л идти́; **I will be there anyway** я всё равно́ там бу́ду; **anyway, I couldn't stay even if I wanted to** в любо́м слу́чае, я не мог оста́ться, да́же е́сли бы я хоте́л; **why are you phoning, anyway?** а всё-таки, почему́ Вы звони́те?

 **KEYWORD**

anywhere ['ɛnɪwɛəʳ] *adv* **1** (*in questions etc: position*) где́-нибудь; (*: motion*) куда́-нибудь; **can you see him anywhere?** Вы его́ где́-нибудь ви́дите?; **did you go anywhere yesterday?** Вы вчера́ куда́-нибудь ходи́ли?
2 (*with negative: position*) нигде́; (*: motion*) никуда́; **I can't see him anywhere** я нигде́ его́ не ви́жу; **I'm not going anywhere today** сего́дня я никуда́ не иду́
3 (*no matter where: position*) где уго́дно; (*: motion*) куда́ уго́дно; **anywhere in the world** где уго́дно в ми́ре; **put the books down anywhere** положи́те кни́ги куда́ уго́дно

apart [ə'pɑ:t] *adv* (*position*) в стороне́; (*motion*) в сто́рону; (*separately*) разде́льно, врозь; **they are ten miles apart** они́ нахо́дятся на расстоя́нии десяти́ миль друг от дру́га; **to take apart** разбира́ть (*perf* разобра́ть) (на ча́сти); **apart from** кро́ме *+gen*

apartment [ə'pɑ:tmənt] *n* (*US*) кварти́ра; (*room*) ко́мната

apathy ['æpəθɪ] *n* апа́тия

ape [eɪp] *n* человекообра́зная обезья́на ▷ *vt* копи́ровать (*perf* скопи́ровать)

aperitif [ə'pɛrɪti:f] *n* аперити́в
apologize [ə'pɔlədʒaɪz] *vi*: **to apologize (for sth to sb)** извиня́ться (*perf* извини́ться) (за что-н пе́ред кем-н)
apology [ə'pɔlədʒɪ] *n* извине́ние
app [æp] *n* приложе́ние
appalling [ə'pɔ:lɪŋ] *adj* (*awful*) ужа́сный; (*shocking*) возмути́тельный
apparatus [æpə'reɪtəs] *n* аппарату́ра; (*in gym*) (гимнасти́ческий) снаря́д; (*of organization*) аппара́т
apparent [ə'pærənt] *adj* (*seeming*) ви́димый; (*obvious*) очеви́дный; **apparently** *adv* по всей ви́димости
appeal [ə'pi:l] *vi* (*Law*) апелли́ровать (*impf/perf*), подава́ть (*perf* пода́ть) апелля́цию ▷ *n* (*attraction*) привлека́тельность *f*; (*plea*) призы́в; (*Law*) апелля́ция, обжа́лование; **to appeal (to sb) for** (*help, funds*) обраща́ться (*perf* обрати́ться) (к кому́-н) за *+instr*; (*calm, order*) призыва́ть (*perf* призва́ть) (кого́-н) к *+dat*; **to appeal to** (*attract*) привлека́ть (*perf* привле́чь), нра́виться (*perf* понра́виться) *+dat*; **appealing** *adj* привлека́тельный
appear [ə'pɪə^r] *vi* появля́ться (*perf* появи́ться); (*seem*) каза́ться (*perf* показа́ться); **to appear in court** представа́ть (*perf* предста́ть) пе́ред судо́м; **to appear on TV** выступа́ть (*perf* вы́ступить) по телеви́дению; **it would appear that ...** похо́же (на то), что ...; **appearance** *n* (*arrival*) появле́ние; (*look, aspect*) вне́шность *f*; (*in public, on TV*) выступле́ние
appendices [ə'pɛndɪsi:z] *npl of* **appendix**
appendicitis [əpɛndɪ'saɪtɪs] *n* аппендици́т
appendix [ə'pɛndɪks] (*pl* **appendices**) *n* приложе́ние; (*Anat*) аппе́ндикс
appetite ['æpɪtaɪt] *n* аппети́т
applaud [ə'plɔ:d] *vi* аплоди́ровать (*impf*), рукоплеска́ть (*impf*) ▷ *vt* аплоди́ровать (*impf*) *+dat*, рукоплеска́ть (*impf*) *+dat*; (*praise*) одобря́ть (*perf* одо́брить)
applause [ə'plɔ:z] *n* аплодисме́нты *pl*
apple ['æpl] *n* я́блоко
applicable [ə'plɪkəbl] *adj*: **applicable (to)** примени́мый (к *+dat*)
applicant ['æplɪkənt] *n* (*for job, scholarship*) кандида́т; (*for college*) абитурие́нт
application [æplɪ'keɪʃən] *n* (*for job, grant etc*) заявле́ние; **application form** *n* заявле́ние-анке́та
apply [ə'plaɪ] *vt* (*paint, make-up*) наноси́ть (*perf* нанести́) ▷ *vi*: **to apply to** применя́ться (*impf*) к *+dat*; (*ask*) обраща́ться (*perf* обрати́ться) (с про́сьбой) к *+dat*; **to apply o.s. to** сосредота́чиваться (*perf* сосредото́читься) на *+prp*; **to apply for a grant/job** подава́ть (*perf* пода́ть) заявле́ние на стипе́ндию/о приёме на рабо́ту
appoint [ə'pɔɪnt] *vt* назнача́ть (*perf* назна́чить); **appointment** *n* (*of person*) назначе́ние; (*post*) до́лжность *f*; (*arranged meeting*) приём; **to make an appointment (with sb)** назнача́ть (*perf* назна́чить) (кому́-н) встре́чу; **I have an appointment with the**

doctor я записа́лся (на приём) к врачу́
appraisal [ə'preɪzl] *n* оце́нка
appreciate [ə'pri:ʃɪeɪt] *vt* (*value*) цени́ть (*impf*); (*understand*) оце́нивать (*perf* оцени́ть) ▷ *vi* (*Comm*) повыша́ться (*perf* повы́ситься) в цене́
appreciation [əpri:ʃɪ'eɪʃən] *n* (*understanding*) понима́ние; (*gratitude*) призна́тельность *f*
apprehensive [æprɪ'hɛnsɪv] *adj* (*glance etc*) опа́сливый
apprentice [ə'prɛntɪs] *n* учени́к, подмасте́рье
approach [ə'prəutʃ] *vi* приближа́ться (*perf* прибли́зиться) ▷ *vt* (*ask, apply to*) обраща́ться (*perf* обрати́ться) к +*dat*; (*come to*) приближа́ться (*perf* прибли́зиться) к +*dat*; (*consider*) подходи́ть (*perf* подойти́) к +*dat* ▷ *n* подхо́д; (*advance*: *also fig*) приближе́ние
appropriate [ə'prəuprɪeɪt] *adj* (*behaviour*) подоба́ющий; (*remarks*) уме́стный; (*tools*) подходя́щий
approval [ə'pru:vəl] *n* одобре́ние; (*permission*) согла́сие; **on approval** (*Comm*) на про́бу
approve [ə'pru:v] *vt* (*motion, decision*) одобря́ть (*perf* одо́брить); (*product, publication*) утвержда́ть (*perf* утверди́ть); **approve of** *vt fus* одобря́ть (*perf* одо́брить)
approximate [ə'prɔksɪmɪt] *adj* приблизи́тельный; **approximately** *adv* приблизи́тельно
apricot ['eɪprɪkɔt] *n* абрико́с
April ['eɪprəl] *n* апре́ль *m*
apron ['eɪprən] *n* фа́ртук
apt [æpt] *adj* уда́чный, уме́стный; **apt to do** скло́нный +*infin*
aquarium [ə'kwɛərɪəm] *n* аква́риум
Aquarius [ə'kwɛərɪəs] *n* Водоле́й
Arab ['ærəb] *adj* ара́бский ▷ *n* ара́б(ка); **Arabian** [ə'reɪbɪən] *adj* ара́бский; **Arabic** *adj* ара́бский
arbitrary ['ɑ:bɪtrərɪ] *adj* произво́льный
arbitration [ɑ:bɪ'treɪʃən] *n* трете́йский суд; (*Industry*) арбитра́ж; **the dispute went to arbitration** спо́р пе́редан в арбитра́ж
arc [ɑ:k] *n* (*also Math*) дуга́
arch [ɑ:tʃ] *n* а́рка, свод; (*of foot*) свод ▷ *vt* (*back*) выгиба́ть (*perf* вы́гнуть)
archaeology [ɑ:kɪ'ɔlədʒɪ] (*US* **archeology**) *n* археоло́гия
archbishop [ɑ:tʃ'bɪʃəp] *n* архиепи́скоп
archeology [ɑ:kɪ'ɔlədʒɪ] *n* (*US*) = **archaeology**
architect ['ɑ:kɪtɛkt] *n* (*of building*) архите́ктор; **architecture** *n* архитекту́ра
archive ['ɑ:kaɪv] *n* архи́в; **archives** *npl* (*documents*) архи́в *msg*
Arctic ['ɑ:ktɪk] *adj* аркти́ческий ▷ *n*: **the Arctic** А́рктика
are [ɑ:ʳ] *vb see* **be**
area ['ɛərɪə] *n* о́бласть *f*; (*part*: *of place*) уча́сток; (: *of room*) часть *f*
arena [ə'ri:nə] *n* (*also fig*) аре́на
aren't [ɑ:nt] = **are not**
Argentina [ɑ:dʒən'ti:nə] *n* Аргенти́на
arguably ['ɑ:gjuəblɪ] *adv* возмо́жно
argue ['ɑ:gju:] *vi* (*quarrel*) ссо́риться (*perf* поссо́риться); (*reason*) дока́зывать (*perf* доказа́ть)

argument ['ɑːgjumənt] *n* (*quarrel*) ссо́ра; (*reasons*) аргуме́нт, до́вод

Aries ['ɛərɪz] *n* Ове́н

arise [ə'raɪz] (*pt* **arose**, *pp* **arisen**) *vi* (*occur*) возника́ть (*perf* возни́кнуть)

arithmetic [ə'rɪθmətɪk] *n* (*Math*) арифме́тика; (*calculation*) подсчёт

arm [ɑːm] *n* рука́; (*of chair*) ру́чка; (*of clothing*) рука́в ▷ *vt* вооружа́ть (*perf* вооружи́ть); **arms** *npl* (*Mil*) вооруже́ние *ntsg*; (*Heraldry*) герб; **arm in arm** по́д руку; **armchair** *n* кре́сло; **armed** *adj* вооружённый

armour ['ɑːmə^r] (*US* **armor**) *n* (*also* **suit of armour**) доспе́хи *mpl*

army ['ɑːmɪ] *n* (*also fig*) а́рмия

aroma [ə'rəumə] *n* арома́т; **aromatherapy** [ərəumə'θɛrəpɪ] *n* ароматерапи́я

arose [ə'rəuz] *pt of* **arise**

around [ə'raund] *adv* вокру́г ▷ *prep* (*encircling*) вокру́г *+gen*; (*near, about*) о́коло *+gen*

arouse [ə'rauz] *vt* (*interest, passions*) возбужда́ть (*perf* возбуди́ть)

arrange [ə'reɪndʒ] *vt* (*organize*) устра́ивать (*perf* устро́ить); (*put in order*) расставля́ть (*perf* расста́вить) ▷ *vi*: **we have arranged for a car to pick you up** мы договори́лись, что́бы за Ва́ми зае́хала маши́на; **to arrange to do** догова́риваться (*perf* договори́ться) *+infin*; **arrangement** *n* (*agreement*) договорённость *f*; (*order, layout*) расположе́ние; **arrangements** *npl* (*plans*) приготовле́ния *ntpl*

array [ə'reɪ] *n*: **array of** ряд *+gen*

arrears [ə'rɪəz] *npl* задо́лженность *fsg*; **to be in arrears with one's rent** име́ть (*impf*) задо́лженность по квартпла́те

arrest [ə'rɛst] *vt* (*Law*) аресто́вывать (*perf* арестова́ть) ▷ *n* аре́ст; **under arrest** под аре́стом

arrival [ə'raɪvl] *n* (*of person, vehicle*) прибы́тие; **new arrival** новичо́к; (*baby*) новорождённый(-ая) *m(f) adj*

arrive [ə'raɪv] *vi* (*traveller*) прибыва́ть (*perf* прибы́ть); (*letter, news*) приходи́ть (*perf* прийти́); (*baby*) рожда́ться (*perf* роди́ться)

arrogance ['ærəgəns] *n* высокоме́рие

arrogant ['ærəgənt] *adj* высокоме́рный

arrow ['ærəu] *n* (*weapon*) стрела́; (*sign*) стре́лка

arse [ɑːs] *n* (*Brit: inf!*) жо́па (*!*)

arson ['ɑːsn] *n* поджо́г

art [ɑːt] *n* иску́сство; **Arts** *npl* (*Scol*) гуманита́рные нау́ки *fpl*

artery ['ɑːtərɪ] *n* (*also fig*) арте́рия

art gallery *n* (*national*) карти́нная галере́я; (*private*) (арт-) галере́я

arthritis [ɑː'θraɪtɪs] *n* артри́т

artichoke ['ɑːtɪtʃəuk] *n* (*also* **globe artichoke**) артишо́к; (*also* **Jerusalem artichoke**) земляна́я гру́ша

article ['ɑːtɪkl] *n* (*object*) предме́т; (*Ling*) арти́кль *m*; (*in newspaper, document*) статья́

articulate [*vb* ɑː'tɪkjuleɪt, *adj* ɑː'tɪkjulɪt] *vt* (*ideas*) выража́ть (*perf* вы́разить) ▷ *adj*: **she is very articulate** она́ чётко выража́ет свои́ мы́сли

artificial [ɑːtɪ'fɪʃəl] *adj*

искýсственный; (*affected*) неестéственный

artist ['ɑːtɪst] *n* худóжник(-ица); (*performer*) артúст(ка); **artistic** [ɑː'tɪstɪk] *adj* худóжественный

 **KEYWORD**

as [æz, əz] *conj* **1** (*referring to time*) когдá; **he came in as I was leaving** он вошёл, когдá я уходúл; **as the years went by** с годáми; **as from tomorrow** с зáвтрашнего дня
2 (*in comparisons*): **as big as** такóй же большóй, как; **twice as big as** в два рáза бóльше, чем; **as white as snow** бéлый, как снег; **as much money/many books as** стóлько же дéнег/книг, скóлько; **as soon as** как тóлько; **as soon as possible** как мóжно скорéе
3 (*since, because*) поскóльку, так как
4 (*referring to manner, way*) как; **do as you wish** дéлайте, как хотúте; **as she said** как онá сказáла
5 (*concerning*): **as for** *or* **to** что касáется *+gen*
6: as if *or* **though** как бýдто; **he looked as if he had been ill** он вы́глядел так, как бýдто он был бóлен
▷ *prep* (*in the capacity of*): **he works as a waiter** он рабóтает официáнтом; **as chairman of the company, he …** как главá компáнии он …; *see also* **long**; **same**; **such**; **well**

a.s.a.p. *adv abbr* = **as soon as possible**
ascent [ə'sɛnt] *n* (*slope*) подъём; (*climb*) восхождéние
ash [æʃ] *n* (*of fire*) золá, пéпел; (*of cigarette*) пéпел; (*wood, tree*) я́сень *m*
ashamed [ə'ʃeɪmd] *adj*: **to be ashamed (of)** стыдúться (*impf*) (*+gen*); **I'm ashamed of …** мне сты́дно за *+acc* …
ashore [ə'ʃɔː[r]] *adv* (*be*) на берегý; (*swim, go*) на бéрег
ashtray ['æʃtreɪ] *n* пéпельница
Asia ['eɪʃə] *n* Áзия; **Asian** *adj* азиáтский ▷ *n* азиáт(ка)
aside [ə'saɪd] *adv* в стóрону ▷ *n* рéплика
ask [ɑːsk] *vt* (*inquire*) спрáшивать (*perf* спросúть); (*invite*) звать (*perf* позвáть); **to ask sb for sth/sb to do** просúть (*perf* попросúть) что-н у когó-н/когó-н *+infin*; **to ask sb about** спрáшивать (*perf* спросúть) когó-н о *+prp*; **to ask (sb) a question** задавáть (*perf* задáть) (комý-н) вопрóс; **to ask sb out to dinner** приглашáть (*perf* пригласúть) когó-н в ресторáн;
ask for *vt fus* просúть (*perf* попросúть); (*trouble*) напрáшиваться (*perf* напросúться) на *+acc*
asleep [ə'sliːp] *adj*: **to be asleep** спать (*impf*); **to fall asleep** засыпáть (*perf* заснýть)
asparagus [əs'pærəgəs] *n* спáржа
aspect ['æspɛkt] *n* (*element*) аспéкт, сторонá; (*quality, air*) вид
aspirin ['æsprɪn] *n* аспирúн
ass [æs] *n* (*also fig*) осёл; (*US: inf!*) жóпа (*!*)
assassin [ə'sæsɪn] *n* (политúческий) убúйца *m/f*
assault [ə'sɔːlt] *n* нападéние; (*Mil, fig*) атáка ▷ *vt* нападáть (*perf* напáсть) на *+acc*; (*sexually*) насúловать (*perf* изнасúловать)
assemble [ə'sɛmbl] *vt* собирáть

(*perf* собрáть) ▷ *vi* собирáться (*perf* собрáться)
assembly [ə'sɛmblɪ] *n* (*meeting*) собрáние; (*institution*) ассамблéя, законодáтельное собрáние; (*construction*) сбóрка
assert [ə'sə:t] *vt* (*opinion, authority*) утверждáть (*perf* утвердить); (*rights, innocence*) отстáивать (*perf* отстоять); **assertion** [ə'sə:ʃən] *n* (*claim*) утверждéние
assess [ə'sɛs] *vt* оцéнивать (*perf* оценить); **assessment** *n*: **assessment (of)** оцéнка (+*gen*)
asset ['æsɛt] *n* (*quality*) достóинство; **assets** *npl* (*property, funds*) активы *mpl*; (*Comm*) актив *msg* балáнса
assignment [ə'saɪnmənt] *n* задáние
assist [ə'sɪst] *vt* помогáть (*perf* помóчь) +*dat*; (*financially*) содéйствовать (*perf* посодéйствовать) +*dat*; **assistance** *n* (*see vt*) пóмощь *f*; содéйствие; **assistant** *n* помóщник(-ица); (*in office etc*) ассистéнт(ка); (*Brit*: *also* **shop assistant**) продавéц(-вщица)
associate [*n* ə'səuʃɪɪt, *vb* ə'səuʃɪeɪt] *n* (*colleague*) коллéга *m/f* ▷ *adj* (*member, professor*) ассоциированный ▷ *vt* (*mentally*) ассоциировать (*impf/perf*); **to associate with sb** общáться (*impf*) с кем-н
association [əsəusɪ'eɪʃən] *n* ассоциáция; (*involvement*) связь *f*
assorted [ə'sɔ:tɪd] *adj* разнообрáзный
assortment [ə'sɔ:tmənt] *n* (*of clothes, colours*) ассортимéнт; (*of books, people*) подбóр
assume [ə'sju:m] *vt* (*suppose*) предполагáть (*perf* предположить), допускáть (*perf* допустить); (*responsibility*) принимáть (*perf* принять) (на себя); (*air*) напускáть (*perf* напустить) на себя; (*power*) брать (*perf* взять)
assumption [ə'sʌmpʃən] *n* предположéние; (*of responsibility*) принятие на себя; **assumption of power** прихóд к влáсти
assurance [ə'ʃuərəns] *n* (*promise*) заверéние; (*confidence*) увéренность *f*; (*insurance*) страховáние
assure [ə'ʃuə^r] *vt* (*reassure*) заверять (*perf* завéрить); (*guarantee*) обеспéчивать (*perf* обеспéчить)
asthma ['æsmə] *n* áстма
astonishment [ə'stɔnɪʃmənt] *n* изумлéние
astrology [əs'trɔlədʒɪ] *n* астролóгия
astronomical [æstrə'nɔmɪkl] *adj* (*also fig*) астрономический
astronomy [əs'trɔnəmɪ] *n* астронóмия
astute [əs'tju:t] *adj* (*person*) проницáтельный

KEYWORD

at [æt] *prep* **1** (*referring to position*) в/на +*prp*; **at school** в шкóле; **at the theatre** в теáтре; **at a concert** на концéрте; **at the station** на стáнции; **at the top** наверхý; **at home** дóма; **they are sitting at the table** они сидят за столóм; **at my friend's (house)** у моегó дрýга; **at the doctor's** у врачá
2 (*referring to direction*) в/на +*acc*; **to look at** смотрéть (*perf*

посмотре́ть) на *+acc*; **to throw sth at sb** (*stone*) броса́ть (*perf* бро́сить) что-н *or* чем-н в кого́-н
3 (*referring to time*): **at four o'clock** в четы́ре часа́; **at half past two** в полови́не тре́тьего; **at a quarter to two** без чётверти два; **at a quarter past two** в чётверть тре́тьего; **at dawn** на заре́; **at night** но́чью; **at Christmas** на Рождество́; **at lunch** за обе́дом; **at times** времена́ми
4 (*referring to rates*): **at one pound a kilo** по фу́нту за килогра́мм; **two at a time** по́ двое; **at fifty km/h** со ско́ростью пятьдеся́т км/ч; **at full speed** на по́лной ско́рости
5 (*referring to manner*): **at a stroke** одни́м ма́хом; **at peace** в ми́ре
6 (*referring to activity*): **to be at home/work** быть (*impf*) до́ма/на рабо́те; **to play at cowboys** игра́ть (*impf*) в ковбо́и; **to be good at doing** хорошо́ уме́ть (*impf*) *+infin*
7 (*referring to cause*): **he is surprised/annoyed at sth** он удивлён/раздражён чем-н; **I am surprised at you** Вы меня́ удивля́ете; **I stayed at his suggestion** я оста́лся по его́ предложе́нию
8 (*@ symbol*) комме́рческое at *nt ind*

ate [eɪt] *pt of* **eat**
atheist ['eɪθɪɪst] *n* атеи́ст(ка)
Athens ['æθɪnz] *n* Афи́ны *pl*
athlete ['æθliːt] *n* спортсме́н(ка)
athletic [æθ'lɛtɪk] *adj* спорти́вный; **athletics** [æθ'lɛtɪks] *n* лёгкая атле́тика
Atlantic [ət'læntɪk] *n*: **the Atlantic (Ocean)** Атланти́ческий океа́н
atlas ['ætləs] *n* а́тлас
atmosphere ['ætməsfɪə[r]] *n* атмосфе́ра
atom ['ætəm] *n* а́том; **atomic** [ə'tɔmɪk] *adj* а́томный
attach [ə'tætʃ] *vt* прикрепля́ть (*perf* прикрепи́ть); (*document, letter*) прилага́ть (*perf* приложи́ть); **he is attached to** (*fond of*) он привя́зан к *+dat*; **to attach importance to** придава́ть (*perf* прида́ть) значе́ние *+dat*; **attachment** *n* (*device*) приспособле́ние, наса́дка; **attachment (to sb)** (*love*) привя́занность *f* (к кому́-н)
attack [ə'tæk] *vt* (*Mil, fig*) атакова́ть (*impf/perf*); (*assault*) напада́ть (*perf* напа́сть) на *+acc* ▷ *n* (*Mil, fig*) ата́ка; (*assault*) нападе́ние; (*of illness*) при́ступ; **attacker** *n*: **his/her attacker** напа́вший(-ая) *m(f) adj* на него́/неё
attain [ə'teɪn] *vt* (*happiness, success*) достига́ть (дости́гнуть *or* дости́чь *perf*) *+gen*, добива́ться (*perf* доби́ться) *+gen*
attempt [ə'tɛmpt] *n* попы́тка ▷ *vt*: **to attempt to do** пыта́ться (*perf* попыта́ться) *+infin*; **to make an attempt on sb's life** соверша́ть (*perf* соверши́ть) покуше́ние на кого́-н
attend [ə'tɛnd] *vt* (*school, church*) посеща́ть (*impf*); **attend to** *vt fus* (*needs, patient*) занима́ться (*perf* заня́ться) *+instr*; (*customer*) обслу́живать (*perf* обслужи́ть); **attendance** *n* прису́тствие; (*Scol*) посеща́емость *f*; **attendant** *n* сопровожда́ющий(-ая) *m(f) adj*; (*in garage*) служи́тель(ница) *m(f)*
attention [ə'tɛnʃən] *n* внима́ние; (*care*) ухо́д; **for the attention of ...** (*Admin*) к све́дению *+gen* ...

attic ['ætɪk] *n* (*living space*) манса́рда; (*storage space*) черда́к
attitude ['ætɪtjuːd] *n*: **attitude (to** *or* **towards)** отноше́ние (к *+dat*)
attorney [ə'təːnɪ] *n* (*US: lawyer*) юри́ст; **Attorney General** *n* (*Brit*) мини́стр юсти́ции; (*US*) Генера́льный прокуро́р
attract [ə'trækt] *vt* привлека́ть (*perf* привле́чь); **attraction** [ə'trækʃən] *n* (*appeal*) привлека́тельность *f*; **attractive** *adj* привлека́тельный
attribute [*n* 'ætrɪbjuːt, *vb* ə'trɪbjuːt] *n* при́знак, атрибу́т ▷ *vt*: **to attribute sth to** (*cause*) относи́ть (*perf* отнести́) что-н за счёт *+gen*; (*painting, quality*) припи́сывать (*perf* приписа́ть) что-н *+dat*
aubergine ['əubəʒiːn] *n* баклажа́н
auction ['ɔːkʃən] *n* (*also* **sale by auction**) аукцио́н ▷ *vt* продава́ть (*perf* прода́ть) на аукцио́не
audible ['ɔːdɪbl] *adj* слы́шный
audience ['ɔːdɪəns] *n* аудито́рия, пу́блика
audit ['ɔːdɪt] *vt* (*Comm*) проводи́ть (*perf* провести́) реви́зию *+gen*
audition [ɔː'dɪʃən] *n* прослу́шивание
auditor ['ɔːdɪtə^r] *n* реви́зия, ауди́тор
auditorium [ɔːdɪ'tɔːrɪəm] *n* зал
August ['ɔːgəst] *n* а́вгуст
aunt [ɑːnt] *n* тётя; **auntie** ['ɑːntɪ] *n dimin of* **aunt**
au pair ['əu'pɛə^r] *n* (*also* **au pair girl**) *молода́я ня́ня-иностра́нка, живу́щая в семье́*
aura ['ɔːrə] *n* (*fig: air*) орео́л
Australia [ɔs'treɪlɪə] *n* Австра́лия
Austria ['ɔstrɪə] *n* А́встрия
authentic [ɔː'θɛntɪk] *adj* по́длинный
author ['ɔːθə^r] *n* (*of text, plan*) а́втор; (*profession*) писа́тель(ница) *m(f)*
authority [ɔː'θɔrɪtɪ] *n* (*power*) власть *f*; (*Pol*) управле́ние; (*expert*) авторите́т; (*official permission*) полномо́чие; **authorities** *npl* (*ruling body*) вла́сти *fpl*
autobiography [ɔːtəbaɪ'ɔgrəfɪ] *n* автобиогра́фия
autograph ['ɔːtəgrɑːf] *n* авто́граф ▷ *vt* надпи́сывать (*perf* надписа́ть)
automatic [ɔːtə'mætɪk] *adj* автомати́ческий ▷ *n* (*US: gun*) (самозаря́дный) пистоле́т; (*car*) автомоби́ль *m* с автомати́ческим переключе́нием скоросте́й; **automatically** *adv* автомати́чески
automobile ['ɔːtəməbiːl] *n* (*US*) автомоби́ль *m*
autonomous [ɔː'tɔnəməs] *adj* (*region*) автоно́мный; (*person, organization*) самостоя́тельный
autonomy [ɔː'tɔnəmɪ] *n* автоно́мия, самостоя́тельность *f*
autumn ['ɔːtəm] *n* о́сень *f*; **in autumn** о́сенью
auxiliary [ɔːg'zɪlɪərɪ] *adj* вспомога́тельный ▷ *n* помо́щник
avail [ə'veɪl] *n*: **to no avail** напра́сно
availability [əveɪlə'bɪlɪtɪ] *n* нали́чие
available [ə'veɪləbl] *adj* досту́пный; (*person*) свобо́дный
avalanche ['ævəlɑːnʃ] *n* лави́на
avenue ['ævənjuː] *n* (*street*) у́лица; (*drive*) алле́я
average ['ævərɪdʒ] *n* сре́днее *nt*

adj ▷ *adj* сре́дний ▷ *vt* достига́ть (*perf* дости́чь) в сре́днем *+gen*; (*sum*) составля́ть (*perf* соста́вить) в сре́днем; **on average** в сре́днем

avert [ə'və:t] *vt* предотвраща́ть (*perf* предотврати́ть); (*blow, eyes*) отводи́ть (*perf* отвести́)

avid ['ævɪd] *adj* (*keen*) стра́стный

avocado [ævə'kɑ:dəu] *n* авока́до *nt ind*

avoid [ə'vɔɪd] *vt* избега́ть (*perf* избежа́ть)

await [ə'weɪt] *vt* ожида́ть (*impf*) *+gen*

awake [ə'weɪk] (*pt* **awoke**, *pp* **awoken** *or* **awaked**) *adj*: **he is awake** он просну́лся; **he was still awake** он ещё не спал

award [ə'wɔ:d] *n* награ́да ▷ *vt* награжда́ть (*perf* награди́ть); (*Law*) присужда́ть (*perf* присуди́ть)

aware [ə'wɛə^r] *adj*: **to be aware (of)** (*realize*) сознава́ть (*impf*) (*+acc*); **to become aware of sth/ that** осознава́ть (*perf* осозна́ть) что-н/, что; **awareness** *n* осозна́ние

away [ə'weɪ] *adv* (*movement*) в сто́рону; (*position*) в стороне́; (*far away*) далеко́; **the holidays are two weeks away** до кани́кул (оста́лось) две неде́ли; **away from** (*movement*) от *+gen*; (*position*) в стороне́ от *+gen*; **two kilometres away from the town** в двух киломе́трах от го́рода; **two hours away by car** в двух часа́х езды́ на маши́не; **he's away for a week** он в отъе́зде на неде́лю; **to take away (from)** (*remove*) забира́ть (*perf* забра́ть) (у *+gen*); (*subtract*) отнима́ть (*perf* отня́ть) (от *+gen*); **he is working away** (*continuously*) он продолжа́ет рабо́тать

awe [ɔ:] *n* благогове́ние

awful ['ɔ:fəl] *adj* ужа́сный; **an awful lot (of)** ужа́сно мно́го (*+gen*); **awfully** *adv* ужа́сно

awkward ['ɔ:kwəd] *adj* (*clumsy*) неуклю́жий; (*inconvenient*) неудо́бный; (*embarrassing*) нело́вкий

awoke [ə'wəuk] *pt of* **awake**; **awoken** *pp of* **awake**

axe [æks] (*US* **ax**) *n* топо́р ▷ *vt* (*project*) отменя́ть (*perf* отмени́ть); (*jobs*) сокраща́ть (*perf* сократи́ть)

b

B [biː] *n* (*Mus*) си *nt ind*

BA *n abbr* = **Bachelor of Arts**

baby [ˈbeɪbɪ] *n* ребёнок; (*newborn*) младе́нец; **baby carriage** *n* (*US*) коля́ска; **baby-sit** *vi* смотре́ть (*impf*) за детьми́; **baby-sitter** *n* приходя́щая ня́ня

bachelor [ˈbætʃələʳ] *n* холостя́к; **Bachelor of Arts/Science** ≈ бакала́вр гуманита́рных/есте́ственных нау́к

KEYWORD

back [bæk] *n* **1** (*of person, animal*) спина́; **the back of the hand** ты́льная сторона́ ладо́ни

2 (*of house, car etc*) за́дняя часть *f*; (*of chair*) спи́нка; (*of page, book*) оборо́т

3 (*Football*) защи́тник

▷ *vt* **1** (*candidate*: *also* **back up**) подде́рживать (*perf* поддержа́ть)

2 (*financially*: *horse*) ста́вить (*perf* поста́вить) на +*acc*; (: *person*) финанси́ровать (*impf*)

3: he backed the car into the garage он дал за́дний ход и поста́вил маши́ну в гара́ж

▷ *vi* (*car etc*: *also* **back up**) дава́ть (*perf* дать) за́дний ход

▷ *adv* **1** (*not forward*) обра́тно, наза́д; **he ran back** он побежа́л обра́тно *or* наза́д

2 (*returned*): **he's back** он верну́лся

3 (*restitution*): **to throw the ball back** кида́ть (*perf* ки́нуть) мяч обра́тно

4 (*again*): **to call back** (*visit again*) заходи́ть (*perf* зайти́) ещё раз; (*Tel*) перезва́нивать (*perf* перезвони́ть)

▷ *cpd* **1** (*payment*) за́дним число́м

2 (*Aut*: *seat, wheels*) за́дний

back down *vi* отступа́ть (*perf* отступи́ть)

back out *vi* (*of promise*) отступа́ться (*perf* отступи́ться)

back up *vt* (*person, theory etc*) подде́рживать (*perf* поддержа́ть)

back: **backache** *n* простре́л, боль *f* в поясни́це; **backbencher** *n* (*Brit*) заднескаме́ечник; **backbone** *n* позвоно́чник; **he's the backbone of the organization** на нём де́ржится вся организа́ция; **background** *n* (*of picture*) за́дний план; (*of events*) предысто́рия; (*experience*) о́пыт; **he's from a working class background** он из рабо́чей семьи́; **against a background of ...** на фо́не +*gen* ...; **backing** *n* (*support*) поддéржка; **backlog** *n*: **backlog of work** невы́полненная рабóта; **backpack** *n* рюкзáк; **backstage** *adv* за кули́сами; **backward** *adj* (*movement*) обрáтный; (*person, country*) отстáлый; **backwards** *adv* назáд; (*list*) наоборóт; (*fall*) нáвзничь; **to walk backwards** пя́титься (*perf* попя́титься); **backyard** *n* (*of house*) зáдний двор

bacon [ˈbeɪkən] *n* бекóн

bacteria [bækˈtɪərɪə] *npl* бактéрии *fpl*

bad [bæd] *adj* плохóй; (*mistake*) серьёзный; (*injury, crash*) тяжёлый; (*food*) тýхлый; **his bad leg** егó больнáя ногá; **to go bad** (*food*) тýхнуть (*perf* протýхнуть), пóртиться (*perf* испóртиться)

badge [bædʒ] *n* значóк

badger [ˈbædʒə[r]] *n* барсýк

badly [ˈbædlɪ] *adv* плóхо; **badly wounded** тяжелó рáненый; **he needs it badly** он си́льно в э́том нуждáется; **to be badly off (for money)** нуждáться (*impf*) (в деньгáх)

badminton [ˈbædmɪntən] *n* бадминтóн

bag [bæg] *n* сýмка; (*paper, plastic*) пакéт; (*handbag*) сýмочка; (*satchel*) рáнец; (*case*) портфéль *m*; **bags of** (*inf*) ýйма *+gen*

baggage [ˈbægɪdʒ] *n* (*US*) багáж

baggy [ˈbægɪ] *adj* мешковáтый

bail [beɪl] *n* (*money*) залóг ▷ *vt* (*also* **to grant bail to**) выпускáть (*perf* вы́пустить) под залóг; **he was released on bail** он был вы́пущен под залóг; **bail out** *vt* (*Law*) плати́ть (*perf* заплати́ть) залóговую сýмму за *+acc*; (*boat*) вычéрпывать (*perf* вы́черпать) вóду из *+gen*

bait [beɪt] *n* (*for fish*) нажи́вка; (*for animal, criminal*) примáнка ▷ *vt* (*hook, trap*) наживля́ть (*perf* наживи́ть)

bake [beɪk] *vt* печь (*perf* испéчь) ▷ *vi* (*bread etc*) пéчься (*perf* испéчься); (*make cakes etc*) печь (*impf*); **baked beans** *npl* консерви́рованная фасóль *fsg* (*в томáте*); **baker** *n* пéкарь *m*; (*also* **the baker's**) бýлочная *f adj*; **bakery** *n* пекáрня; (*shop*) бýлочная *f adj*

baking [ˈbeɪkɪŋ] *n* вы́печка; **she does her baking once a week** онá печёт раз в недéлю; **baking powder** *n* разрыхли́тель *m*

balance [ˈbæləns] *n* (*equilibrium*) равновéсие; (*Comm*: *in account*) балáнс; (: *remainder*) остáток; (*scales*) весы́ *pl* ▷ *vt* (*budget, account*) баланси́ровать (*perf* сбаланси́ровать); (*make equal*) уравновéшивать (*perf* уравновéсить); **balance of payments/trade** платёжный/торгóвый балáнс; **balanced** *adj* (*diet*) сбаланси́рованный

balcony [ˈbælkənɪ] *n* балкóн

bald [bɔːld] *adj* (*head*) лы́сый; (*tyre*) стёртый

ball [bɔːl] *n* (*for football, tennis*) мяч; (*for golf*) мя́чик; (*of wool, string*) клубóк; (*dance*) бал

ballerina [bæləˈriːnə] *n* балери́на

ballet [ˈbæleɪ] *n* балéт

balloon [bəˈluːn] *n* воздýшный шар; (*also* **hot air balloon**) аэростáт

ballot [ˈbælət] *n* голосовáние, баллотирóвка

ballroom [ˈbɔːlrum] *n* бáльный зал

Baltic [ˈbɔːltɪk] *n*: **the Baltic**

Балти́йское мо́ре ▷ *adj*: **the Baltic States** стра́ны *fpl* Ба́лтии, прибалти́йские госуда́рства *ntpl*

bamboo [bæm'bu:] *n* бамбу́к

ban [bæn] *vt* (*prohibit*) запреща́ть (*perf* запрети́ть); (*suspend, exclude*) отстраня́ть (*perf* отстрани́ть) ▷ *n* (*prohibition*) запре́т

banana [bə'nɑ:nə] *n* бана́н

band [bænd] *n* (*group*: *of people, rock musicians*) гру́ппа; (: *of jazz, military musicians*) орке́стр

bandage ['bændɪdʒ] *n* повя́зка ▷ *vt* бинтова́ть (*perf* забинтова́ть)

B & B *n abbr* = **bed and breakfast**

bang [bæŋ] *n* стук; (*explosion*) вы́стрел; (*blow*) уда́р ▷ *excl* бах ▷ *vt* (*door*) хло́пать (*perf* хло́пнуть) *+instr*; (*head etc*) ударя́ть (*perf* уда́рить) ▷ *vi* (*door*) захло́пываться (*perf* захло́пнуться)

bangs [bæŋz] *npl* (*US*) чёлка *fsg*

banish ['bænɪʃ] *vt* высыла́ть (*perf* вы́слать)

bank [bæŋk] *n* банк; (*of river, lake*) бе́рег; (*of earth*) на́сыпь *f*; **bank on** *vt fus* полага́ться (*perf* положи́ться) на *+acc*; **bank account** *n* ба́нковский счёт; **bank card** *n* ба́нковская ка́рточка; **bank holiday** *n* (*Brit*) нерабо́чий день *m* (*обы́чно понеде́льник*); **banknote** *n* банкно́т

bankrupt ['bæŋkrʌpt] *adj* обанкро́тившийся; **to go bankrupt** обанкро́титься (*perf*); **I am bankrupt** я — банкро́т, я обанкро́тился; **bankruptcy** *n* банкро́тство, несостоя́тельность *f*

banner ['bænə^r] *n* транспара́нт

bannister ['bænɪstə^r] *n* (*usu pl*) пери́ла *pl*

banquet ['bæŋkwɪt] *n* банке́т

baptism ['bæptɪzəm] *n* креще́ние

bar [bɑ:^r] *n* (*pub*) бар; (*counter*) сто́йка; (*rod*) прут; (*of soap*) брусо́к; (*of chocolate*) пли́тка; (*Mus*) такт ▷ *vt* (*door, way*) загора́живать (*perf* загороди́ть); (*person*) не допуска́ть (*perf* допусти́ть); **bars** *npl* (*on window*) решётка *fsg*; **behind bars** за решёткой; **the Bar** адвокату́ра; **bar none** без исключе́ния

barbaric [bɑ:'bærɪk] *adj* ва́рварский

barbecue ['bɑ:bɪkju:] *n* барбекю́ *nt ind*

barbed wire ['bɑ:bd-] *n* колю́чая про́волока

barber ['bɑ:bə^r] *n* парикма́хер

bare [bɛə^r] *adj* (*body*) го́лый, обнажённый; (*trees*) оголённый ▷ *vt* (*one's body*) оголи́ть (*perf* оголя́ть), обнажа́ть (*perf* обнажи́ть); (*teeth*) ска́лить (*perf* оска́лить); **in** *or* **with bare feet** босико́м; **barefoot** *adj* босо́й ▷ *adv* босико́м; **barely** *adv* едва́

bargain ['bɑ:gɪn] *n* сде́лка; (*good buy*) вы́годная поку́пка

barge [bɑ:dʒ] *n* ба́ржа

bark [bɑ:k] *n* (*of tree*) кора́ ▷ *vi* (*dog*) ла́ять (*impf*)

barley ['bɑ:lɪ] *n* ячме́нь *m*

barman ['bɑ:mən] *irreg n* ба́рмен

barn [bɑ:n] *n* амба́р

barometer [bə'rɔmɪtə^r] *n* баро́метр

baron ['bærən] *n* баро́н; (*of press, industry*) магна́т

barracks ['bærəks] *npl* каза́рма *fsg*

barrage ['bærɑ:ʒ] *n* (*fig*) лави́на

barrel ['bærəl] *n* (*of wine, beer*)

бо́чка; (*of oil*) барре́ль *m*; (*of gun*) ствол
barren [ˈbærən] *adj* (*land*) беспло́дный
barricade [bærɪˈkeɪd] *n* баррика́да ▷ *vt* баррикади́ровать (*perf* забаррикади́ровать); **to barricade o.s. in** баррикади́роваться (*perf* забаррикади́роваться)
barrier [ˈbærɪəʳ] *n* (*at entrance*) барье́р; (*at frontier*) шлагба́ум; (*fig*: *to progress*) препя́тствие
barring [ˈbɑːrɪŋ] *prep* за исключе́нием *+gen*
barrister [ˈbærɪstəʳ] *n* (*Brit*) адвока́т
barrow [ˈbærəu] *n* (*also* **wheelbarrow**) та́чка
base [beɪs] *n* основа́ние; (*of monument etc*) ба́за, постаме́нт; (*Mil*) ба́за; (*for organization*) местонахожде́ние ▷ *adj* ни́зкий ▷ *vt*: **to base sth on** (*opinion*) осно́вывать (*impf*) что-н на *+prp*; **baseball** *n* бейсбо́л; **basement** *n* подва́л
basic [ˈbeɪsɪk] *adj* (*fundamental*) фундамента́льный; (*elementary*) нача́льный; (*primitive*) элемента́рный; **basically** *adv* по существу́; (*on the whole*) в основно́м; **basics** *npl*: **the basics** осно́вы *fpl*
basil [ˈbæzl] *n* базили́к
basin [ˈbeɪsn] *n* (*also* **washbasin**) ра́ковина; (*Geo*) бассе́йн
basis [ˈbeɪsɪs] (*pl* **bases**) *n* основа́ние; **on a part-time basis** на непо́лной ста́вке; **on a trial basis** на испыта́тельный срок
basket [ˈbɑːskɪt] *n* корзи́на; **basketball** *n* баскетбо́л
bass [beɪs] *n* бас ▷ *adj* бассо́вый
bastard [ˈbɑːstəd] *n* внебра́чный ребёнок; (*inf!*) ублю́док (*!*)
bat [bæt] *n* (*Zool*) лету́чая мышь *f*; (*Sport*) бита́; (*Brit*: *Table Tennis*) раке́тка
batch [bætʃ] *n* (*of bread*) вы́печка; (*of papers*) па́чка
bath [bɑːθ] *n* ва́нна ▷ *vt* купа́ть (*perf* вы́купать); **to have a bath** принима́ть (*perf* приня́ть) ва́нну; **bathe** [beɪð] *vi* (*swim*) купа́ться (*impf*); (*US*: *have a bath*) принима́ть (*perf* приня́ть) ва́нну ▷ *vt* (*wound*) промыва́ть (*perf* промы́ть); **bathroom** [ˈbɑːθrum] *n* ва́нная *f adj*; **baths** [bɑːðz] *npl* (*also* **swimming baths**) пла́вательный бассе́йн *msg*; **bath towel** *n* ба́нное полоте́нце
baton [ˈbætən] *n* (*Mus*) дирижёрская па́лочка; (*Police*) дуби́нка; (*Sport*) эстафе́тная па́лочка
batter [ˈbætəʳ] *vt* (*person*) бить (*perf* изби́ть); (*subj*: *wind, rain*) бить (*perf* поби́ть) ▷ *n* (*Culin*) жи́дкое те́сто
battery [ˈbætərɪ] *n* (*of torch etc*) батаре́йка; (*Aut*) аккумуля́тор
battle [ˈbætl] *n* би́тва, бой
bay [beɪ] *n* зали́в; (*smaller*) бу́хта; **loading bay** погру́зочная площа́дка; **to hold sb at bay** держа́ть (*impf*) кого́-н на расстоя́нии
bazaar [bəˈzɑːʳ] *n* база́р, ры́нок; (*fete*) благотвори́тельный база́р
BBC *n abbr* (= *British Broadcasting Corporation*) Би-Би-Си *nt ind*
BC *adv abbr* (= *before Christ*) до рождества́ Христо́ва

KEYWORD

be [biː] (*pt* **was, were**, *pp* **been**) *aux vb* **1** (*with present participle*: *forming continuous tenses*): **what**

are you doing? что Вы де́лаете?; **it is raining** идёт дождь; **they're working tomorrow** они́ рабо́тают за́втра; **the house is being built** дом стро́ится; **I've been waiting for you for ages** я жду Вас уже́ це́лую ве́чность
2 (*with pp*: *forming passives*): **he was killed** он был уби́т; **the box had been opened** я́щик откры́ли; **the thief was nowhere to be seen** во́ра нигде́ не́ было ви́дно
3 (*in tag questions*) не так *or* пра́вда ли, да; **she's back again, is she?** она́ верну́лась, да *or* не так *or* пра́вда ли?; **she is pretty, isn't she?** она́ хоро́шенькая, не пра́вда ли *or* да?
4 (*to +infin*): **the house is to be sold** дом должны́ прода́ть; **you're to be congratulated for all your work** Вас сле́дует поздра́вить за всю Ва́шу рабо́ту; **he's not to open it** он не до́лжен открыва́ть э́то
▷ *vb* **1** (*+ complement*: *in present tense*): **he is English** он англича́нин; (*in past/future tense*) быть (*impf*) *+instr*; **he was a doctor** он был врачо́м; **she is going to be very tall** она́ бу́дет о́чень высо́кой; **I'm tired** я уста́л; **I was hot/cold** мне бы́ло жа́рко/хо́лодно; **two and two are four** два́жды два — четы́ре; **she's tall** она́ высо́кая; **be careful!** бу́дьте осторо́жны!; **be quiet!** ти́хо!, ти́ше!
2 (*of health*): **how are you feeling?** как Вы себя́ чу́вствуете?; **he's very ill** он о́чень бо́лен; **I'm better now** мне сейча́с лу́чше
3 (*of age*): **how old are you?** ско́лько Вам лет?; **I'm sixteen (years old)** мне шестна́дцать (лет)
4 (*cost*): **how much is the wine?** ско́лько сто́ит вино́?; **that'll be £5.75, please** с Вас £5,75, пожа́луйста
▷ *vi* **1** (*exist*) быть (*impf*); **there are people who ...** есть лю́ди, кото́рые ...; **there is one drug that ...** есть одно́ лека́рство, кото́рое ...; **is there a God?** Бог есть?
2 (*occur*) быва́ть (*impf*); **there are frequent accidents on this road** на э́той доро́ге ча́сто быва́ют ава́рии; **be that as it may** как бы то ни́ было; **so be it** так и быть, быть по сему́
3 (*referring to place*): **I won't be here tomorrow** меня́ здесь за́втра не бу́дет; **the book is on the table** кни́га на столе́; **there are pictures on the wall** на стене́ карти́ны; **Edinburgh is in Scotland** Эдинбу́рг нахо́дится в Шотла́ндии; **there is someone in the house** в до́ме кто-то есть; **we've been here for ages** мы здесь уже́ це́лую ве́чность
4 (*referring to movement*) быть (*impf*); **where have you been?** где Вы бы́ли?; **I've been to the post office** я был на по́чте
▷ *impers vb* **1** (*referring to time*): **it's five o'clock (now)** сейча́с пять часо́в; **it's the 28th of April (today)** сего́дня 28-ое апре́ля
2 (*referring to distance, weather*: *in present tense*): **it's 10 km to the village** до дере́вни 10 км; (: *in past/future tense*) быть (*impf*); **it's hot/cold (today)** сего́дня жа́рко/хо́лодно; **it was very windy yesterday** вчера́ бы́ло о́чень ве́трено; **it will be sunny tomorrow** за́втра бу́дет со́лнечно
3 (*emphatic*): **it's (only) me/the postman** э́то я/почтальо́н; **it was Maria who paid the bill** и́менно Мари́я оплати́ла счёт

beach [biːtʃ] *n* пляж
beacon [ˈbiːkən] *n* (*marker*) сигна́льный ого́нь *m*
bead [biːd] *n* бу́сина; (*of sweat*) ка́пля
beak [biːk] *n* клюв
beam [biːm] *n* (*Archit*) ба́лка, стропи́ло; (*of light*) луч
bean [biːn] *n* боб; **French bean** фасо́ль *f no pl*; **runner bean** фасо́ль о́гненная; **coffee bean** кофе́йное зерно́
bear [bɛəʳ] (*pt* **bore**, *pp* **borne**) *n* медве́дь(-е́дица) *m(f)* ▷ *vt* (*cost, responsibility*) нести́ (*perf* понести́); (*weight*) нести́ (*impf*) ▷ *vi*: **to bear right/left** (*Aut*) держа́ться (*impf*) пра́вого/ле́вого поворо́та; **bear out** *vt* подде́рживать (*perf* поддержа́ть)
beard [bɪəd] *n* борода́
bearing [ˈbɛərɪŋ] *n* (*connection*) отноше́ние; **bearings** *npl* (*also* **ball bearings**) ша́рики *mpl* подши́пника; **to take a bearing** ориенти́роваться (*impf/perf*)
beast [biːst] *n* (*also inf*) зверь *m*
beat [biːt] (*pt* **beat**, *pp* **beaten**) *n* (*of heart*) бие́ние; (*Mus*: *rhythm*) ритм; (*Police*) уча́сток ▷ *vt* (*wife, child*) бить (*perf* поби́ть); (*eggs etc*) взбива́ть (*perf* взбить); (*opponent, record*) побива́ть (*perf* поби́ть); (*drum*) бить (*impf*) в *+acc* ▷ *vi* (*heart*) би́ться (*impf*); (*rain, wind*) стуча́ть (*impf*); **beat it!** (*inf*) кати́сь!; **off the beaten track** по непроторённому пути́; **beat up** *vt* (*person*) избива́ть (*perf* изби́ть); **beating** *n* избие́ние; (*thrashing*) по́рка
beautiful [ˈbjuːtɪful] *adj* краси́вый; (*day, experience*) прекра́сный; **beautifully** [ˈbjuːtɪflɪ] *adv* (*play, sing etc*) краси́во, прекра́сно
beauty [ˈbjuːtɪ] *n* красота́; (*woman*) краса́вица
beaver [ˈbiːvəʳ] *n* (*Zool*) бобр
became [bɪˈkeɪm] *pt of* **become**
because [bɪˈkɔz] *conj* потому́ что; (*since*) так как; **because of** из-за *+gen*
become [bɪˈkʌm] (*irreg like* **come**) *vi* станови́ться (*perf* стать) *+instr*; **to become fat** толсте́ть (*perf* потолсте́ть); **to become thin** худе́ть (*perf* похуде́ть)
bed [bɛd] *n* крова́ть *f*; (*of river, sea*) дно; (*of flowers*) клу́мба; **to go to bed** ложи́ться (*perf* лечь) спать; **bed and breakfast** *n* *ма́ленькая ча́стная гости́ница с за́втраком*; (*terms*) ночлёг и за́втрак; **bedclothes** *npl* посте́льное бельё *ntsg*; **bedding** *n* посте́льные принадле́жности *fpl*; **bedroom** *n* спа́льня; **bedside** *n*: **at sb's bedside** у посте́ли кого́-н; **bedspread** *n* покрыва́ло; **bedtime** *n* вре́мя *nt* ложи́ться спать
bee [biː] *n* пчела́
beech [biːtʃ] *n* бук
beef [biːf] *n* говя́дина; **roast beef** ро́стбиф
been [biːn] *pp of* **be**
beer [bɪəʳ] *n* пи́во
beet [biːt] *n* (*vegetable*) кормова́я свёкла; (*US*: *also* **red beet**) свёкла
beetle [ˈbiːtl] *n* жук
beetroot [ˈbiːtruːt] *n* (*Brit*) свёкла
before [bɪˈfɔːʳ] *prep* пе́ред *+instr*, до *+gen* ▷ *conj* до того́ *or* пе́ред тем, как ▷ *adv* (*time*) ра́ньше, пре́жде; **the day before yesterday** позавчера́; **do this before you forget** сде́лайте э́то, пока́ Вы не забы́ли; **before going** пе́ред

ухо́дом; **before she goes** до того *or* пе́ред тем, как она́ уйдёт; **the week before** неде́лю наза́д, на про́шлой неде́ле; **I've never seen it before** я никогда́ э́того ра́ньше не ви́дел; **beforehand** *adv* зара́нее

beg [bɛg] *vi* попроша́йничать (*impf*), ни́щенствовать (*impf*) ▷ *vt* (*also* **beg for**: *food, money*) проси́ть (*impf*); (: *mercy, forgiveness*) умоля́ть (*perf* умоли́ть) о +*prp*; **to beg sb to do** умоля́ть (*perf* умоли́ть) кого́-н +*infin*

began [bɪ'gæn] *pt of* **begin**

beggar ['bɛgəʳ] *n* попроша́йка, ни́щий(-ая) *m(f) adj*

begin [bɪ'gɪn] (*pt* **began**, *pp* **begun**) *vt* начина́ть (*perf* нача́ть) ▷ *vi* начина́ться (*perf* нача́ться); **to begin doing** *or* **to do** начина́ть (*perf* нача́ть) +*impf infin*; **beginner** *n* начина́ющий(-ая) *m(f) adj*; **beginning** *n* нача́ло

begun [bɪ'gʌn] *pp of* **begin**

behalf [bɪ'hɑ:f] *n*: **on** *or (US)* **in behalf of** от и́мени +*gen*; (*for benefit of*) в по́льзу +*gen*, в интере́сах +*gen*; **on my/his behalf** от моего́/его́ и́мени

behave [bɪ'heɪv] *vi* вести́ (*impf*) себя́; (*also* **behave o.s.**) вести́ (*impf*) себя́ хорошо́

behaviour [bɪ'heɪvjəʳ] (*US* **behavior**) *n* поведе́ние

behind [bɪ'haɪnd] *prep* (*at the back of*) за +*instr*, позади́ +*gen*; (*supporting*) за +*instr*; (*lower in rank etc*) ни́же +*gen* ▷ *adv* сза́ди, позади́ ▷ *n* (*buttocks*) зад; **to be behind schedule** отстава́ть (*perf* отста́ть) от гра́фика

beige [beɪʒ] *adj* бе́жевый

Beijing ['beɪ'dʒɪŋ] *n* Пеки́н

Belarus [bɛlə'rus] *n* Белору́сь *f*

belated [bɪ'leɪtɪd] *adj* запозда́лый

Belgian ['bɛldʒən] *n* бельги́ец(-и́йка)

Belgium ['bɛldʒəm] *n* Бе́льгия

belief [bɪ'li:f] *n* (*conviction*) убежде́ние; (*trust, faith*) ве́ра; **it's beyond belief** э́то невероя́тно; **in the belief that** полага́я, что

believe [bɪ'li:v] *vt* ве́рить (*perf* пове́рить) +*dat or* в +*acc* ▷ *vi* ве́рить (*impf*); **to believe in** ве́рить (*perf* пове́рить) в +*acc*

bell [bɛl] *n* ко́локол; (*small*) колоко́льчик; (*on door*) звоно́к

belly ['bɛlɪ] *n* (*of animal*) брю́хо; (*of person*) живо́т

belong [bɪ'lɔŋ] *vi*: **to belong to** принадлежа́ть (*impf*) +*dat*; (*club*) состоя́ть (*impf*) в +*prp*; **this book belongs here** ме́сто э́той кни́ги здесь; **belongings** *npl* ве́щи *fpl*

beloved [bɪ'lʌvɪd] *adj* люби́мый

below [bɪ'ləu] *prep* (*position*) под +*instr*; (*motion*) под +*acc*; (*less than*) ни́же +*gen* ▷ *adv* (*position*) внизу́; (*motion*) вниз; **see below** смотри́ ни́же

belt [bɛlt] *n* (*leather*) реме́нь *m*; (*cloth*) по́яс; (*of land*) по́яс, зо́на; (*Tech*) приводно́й реме́нь

bemused [bɪ'mju:zd] *adj* озада́ченный

bench [bɛntʃ] *n* скамья́; (*Brit*: *Pol*) места́ *ntpl* па́ртий в парла́менте; (*in workshop*) верста́к; (*in laboratory*) лаборато́рный стол; **the Bench** (*Law*) суде́йская колле́гия

bend [bɛnd] (*pt, pp* **bent**) *vt* гнуть (*perf* согну́ть), сгиба́ть (*impf*) ▷ *vi* (*person*) гну́ться (*perf* согну́ться) ▷ *n* (*Brit*: *in road*) поворо́т; (*in pipe*) изги́б; (*in river*) излу́чина;

bend down *vi* наклоня́ться (*perf* наклони́ться), нагиба́ться (*perf* нагну́ться)
beneath [bɪ'ni:θ] *prep* (*position*) под *+instr*; (*motion*) под *+acc*; (*unworthy of*) ни́же *+gen* ▷ *adv* внизу́
beneficial [bɛnɪ'fɪʃəl] *adj*: **beneficial (to)** благотво́рный (для *+gen*)
benefit ['bɛnɪfɪt] *n* (*advantage*) вы́года; (*money*) посо́бие ▷ *vt* приноси́ть (*perf* принести́) по́льзу *+dat* ▷ *vi*: **he'll benefit from it** он полу́чит от э́того вы́году
benign [bɪ'naɪn] *adj* добросерде́чный; (*Med*) доброка́чественный
bent [bɛnt] *pt, pp of* **bend** ▷ *adj* (*wire, pipe*) по́гнутый; **he is bent on doing** он настро́ился *+infin*
bereaved [bɪ'ri:vd] *adj* понёсший тяжёлую утра́ту ▷ *n*: **the bereaved** друзья́ *mpl* и ро́дственники *mpl* поко́йного
Berlin [bə:'lɪn] *n* Берли́н
Bermuda [bə:'mju:də] *n* Берму́дские острова́ *mpl*
berry ['bɛrɪ] *n* я́года
berth [bə:θ] *n* (*in caravan, on ship*) ко́йка; (*on train*) по́лка; (*mooring*) прича́л
beside [bɪ'saɪd] *prep* ря́дом с *+instr*, о́коло *+gen*, у *+gen*; **to be beside o.s. (with)** быть (*impf*) вне себя́ (от *+gen*); **that's beside the point** э́то к де́лу не отно́сится
besides [bɪ'saɪdz] *adv* кро́ме того́ ▷ *prep* кро́ме *+gen*, поми́мо *+gen*
best [bɛst] *adj* лу́чший ▷ *adv* лу́чше всего́; **the best part of** (*quantity*) бо́льшая часть *+gen*; **at best** в лу́чшем слу́чае; **to make the best of sth** испо́льзовать (*impf*) что-н наилу́чшим о́бразом; **to do one's best** де́лать (*perf* сде́лать) всё возмо́жное; **to the best of my knowledge** наско́лько мне изве́стно; **to the best of my ability** в ме́ру мои́х спосо́бностей; **best man** *n* ша́фер; **bestseller** *n* бестсе́ллер
bet [bɛt] (*pt, pp* **bet** *or* **betted**) *n* (*wager*) пари́ *nt ind*; (*in gambling*) ста́вка ▷ *vi* (*wager*) держа́ть (*impf*) пари́; (*expect, guess*) би́ться (*impf*) об закла́д ▷ *vt*: **to bet sb sth** спо́рить (*perf* поспо́рить) с кем-н на что-н; **to bet money on sth** ста́вить (*perf* поста́вить) де́ньги на что-н
betray [bɪ'treɪ] *vt* (*friends*) предава́ть (*perf* преда́ть); (*trust*) обма́нывать (*perf* обману́ть)
better ['bɛtə[r]] *adj* лу́чший ▷ *adv* лу́чше ▷ *vt* (*score*) улучша́ть (*perf* улу́чшить) ▷ *n*: **to get the better of** бра́ть (*perf* взя́ть) верх над *+instr*; **I feel better** я чу́вствую себя́ лу́чше; **to get better** (*Med*) поправля́ться (*perf* попра́виться); **I had better go** мне лу́чше уйти́; **he thought better of it** он переду́мал
betting ['bɛtɪŋ] *n* пари́ *nt ind*
between [bɪ'twi:n] *prep* ме́жду *+instr* ▷ *adv*: **in between** ме́жду тем
beware [bɪ'wɛə[r]] *vi*: **to beware (of)** остерега́ться (*perf* остере́чься) (*+gen*)
bewildered [bɪ'wɪldəd] *adj* изумлённый
beyond [bɪ'jɔnd] *prep* (*position*) за *+instr*; (*motion*) за *+acc*; (*understanding*) вы́ше *+gen*; (*expectations*) сверх *+gen*; (*doubt*) вне *+gen*; (*age*) бо́льше *+gen*; (*date*) по́сле *+gen* ▷ *adv* (*position*) вдали́; (*motion*) вдаль; **it's beyond**

repair это невозмо́жно почини́ть
bias ['baɪəs] *n* (*against*) предубежде́ние; (*towards*) пристра́стие
bib [bɪb] *n* (*child's*) нагру́дник
Bible ['baɪbl] *n* Би́блия
bicycle ['baɪsɪkl] *n* велосипе́д
bid [bɪd] (*pt* **bade** *or* **bid**, *pp* **bid(den)**) *n* (*at auction*) предложе́ние цены́; (*attempt*) попы́тка ▷ *vt* (*offer*) предлага́ть (*perf* предложи́ть) ▷ *vi*: **to bid for** (*at auction*) предлага́ть (*perf* предложи́ть) це́ну за *+acc*; **bidder** *n*: **the highest bidder** лицо́, предлага́ющее наивы́сшую це́ну
big [bɪg] *adj* большо́й; (*important*) ва́жный; (*bulky*) кру́пный; (*older*: *brother, sister*) ста́рший
bike [baɪk] *n* (*inf*: *bicycle*) ве́лик
bikini [bɪ'ki:nɪ] *n* бики́ни *nt ind*
bilateral [baɪ'lætərl] *adj* двусторо́нний
bilingual [baɪ'lɪŋgwəl] *adj* двуязы́чный
bill [bɪl] *n* (*invoice*) счёт; (*Pol*) законопрое́кт; (*US*: *banknote*) казначе́йский биле́т, банкно́т; (*beak*) клюв; **billboard** *n* доска́ объявле́ний
billion ['bɪljən] *n* (*Brit*) биллио́н; (*US*) миллиа́рд
bin [bɪn] *n* (*Brit*: *also* **rubbish bin**) му́сорное ведро́; (*container*) я́щик
bind [baɪnd] (*pt, pp* **bound**) *vt* (*tie*) привя́зывать (*perf* привяза́ть); (*hands, feet*) свя́зывать (*perf* связа́ть); (*oblige*) обя́зывать (*perf* обяза́ть); (*book*) переплета́ть (*perf* переплести́)
bingo ['bɪŋgəu] *n* лото́ *nt ind*
binoculars [bɪ'nɔkjuləz] *npl* бино́кль *msg*
biography [baɪ'ɔgrəfɪ] *n* биогра́фия
biological [baɪə'lɔdʒɪkl] *adj* (*science*) биологи́ческий; (*warfare*) бактериологи́ческий; (*washing powder*) содержа́щий биопрепара́ты
biology [baɪ'ɔlədʒɪ] *n* биоло́гия
birch [bə:tʃ] *n* берёза
bird [bə:d] *n* пти́ца
Biro ['baɪərəu] *n* ша́риковая ру́чка
birth [bə:θ] *n* рожде́ние; **to give birth to** рожа́ть (*perf* роди́ть); **birth certificate** *n* свиде́тельство о рожде́нии; **birth control** *n* (*policy*) контро́ль *m* рожда́емости; (*methods*) противозача́точные ме́ры *fpl*; **birthday** *n* день *m* рожде́ния ▷ *cpd*: **birthday card** откры́тка ко дню рожде́ния; *see also* **happy**; **birthplace** *n* ро́дина
biscuit ['bɪskɪt] *n* (*Brit*) пече́нье; (*US*) ≈ кекс
bishop ['bɪʃəp] *n* (*Rel*) епи́скоп; (*Chess*) слон
bit [bɪt] *pt of* **bite** ▷ *n* (*piece*) кусо́к, кусо́чек; (*Comput*) бит; **a bit of** немно́го *+gen*; **a bit dangerous** слегка́ опа́сный; **bit by bit** ма́ло-пома́лу, понемно́гу
bitch [bɪtʃ] *n* (*also inf!*) су́ка (*also !*)
bite [baɪt] (*pt* **bit**, *pp* **bitten**) *vt* куса́ть (*perf* укуси́ть) ▷ *vi* куса́ться (*impf*) ▷ *n* (*insect bite*) уку́с; **to bite one's nails** куса́ть (*impf*) но́гти; **let's have a bite (to eat)** (*inf*) дава́йте переку́сим; **he had a bite of cake** он откуси́л кусо́к пирога́
bitter ['bɪtə^r] *adj* го́рький; (*wind*) прони́зывающий; (*struggle*) ожесточённый

bizarre [bɪˈzɑːʳ] *adj* стра́нный, причу́дливый
black [blæk] *adj* чёрный; (*tea*) без молока́; (*person*) чернокóжий ▷ *n* (*colour*) чёрный цвет, чёрное *nt adj*; **black and blue** в синяка́х; **to be in the black** име́ть (*impf*) де́ньги в ба́нке; **blackberry** *n* ежеви́ка *f no pl*; **blackbird** *n* (чёрный) дрозд; **blackboard** *n* кла́ссная доска́; **black coffee** *n* чёрный ко́фе *m ind*; **blackcurrant** *n* чёрная сморо́дина; **blackmail** *n* шанта́ж ▷ *vt* шантажи́ровать (*impf*); **black market** *n* чёрный ры́нок; **blackout** *n* (*Elec*) обесто́чка; (*TV, Radio*) приостановле́ние переда́ч; (*Med*) о́бморок; **black pepper** *n* чёрный пе́рец; **Black Sea** *n*: **the Black Sea** Чёрное мо́ре
bladder [ˈblædəʳ] *n* мочево́й пузы́рь *m*
blade [bleɪd] *n* ле́звие; (*of propeller, oar*) ло́пасть *f*; **a blade of grass** трави́нка
blame [bleɪm] *n* вина́ ▷ *vt*: **to blame sb for sth** вини́ть (*impf*) кого́-н в чём-н; **he is to blame (for sth)** он винова́т (в чём-н)
bland [blænd] *adj* (*food*) пре́сный
blank [blæŋk] *adj* (*paper*) чи́стый; (*look*) пусто́й ▷ *n* (*of memory*) прова́л; (*on form*) про́пуск; (*for gun*) холосто́й патро́н
blanket [ˈblæŋkɪt] *n* одея́ло; (*of snow*) покро́в; (*of fog*) пелена́
blast [blɑːst] *n* (*explosion*) взрыв ▷ *vt* (*blow up*) взрыва́ть (*perf* взорва́ть)
blatant [ˈbleɪtənt] *adj* (*obvious*) я́вный
blaze [bleɪz] *n* (*fire*) пла́мя *nt*; (*of colour*) полыха́ние
blazer [ˈbleɪzəʳ] *n* фо́рменный пиджа́к
bleach [bliːtʃ] *n* (*also* **household bleach**) отбе́ливатель *m* ▷ *vt* (*fabric*) отбе́ливать (*perf* отбели́ть)
bleak [bliːk] *adj* (*day, face*) уны́лый; (*prospect*) мра́чный
bleed [bliːd] (*pt, pp* **bled**) *vi* кровото́чить (*impf*); **my nose is bleeding** у меня́ из но́са идёт кровь
blend [blɛnd] *n* (*of tea, whisky*) буке́т ▷ *vt* (*Culin*) сме́шивать (*perf* смеша́ть) ▷ *vi* (*also* **blend in**) сочета́ться (*impf*)
bless [blɛs] (*pt, pp* **blessed** *or* **blest**) *vt* благословля́ть (*perf* благослови́ть); **bless you!** бу́дьте здоро́вы!; **blessing** *n* благослове́ние; (*godsend*) Бо́жий дар
blew [bluː] *pt of* **blow**
blind [blaɪnd] *adj* слепо́й ▷ *n* што́ра; (*also* **Venetian blind**) жалюзи́ *pl ind* ▷ *vt* ослепля́ть (*perf* ослепи́ть); **to be blind (to)** (*fig*) не ви́деть (*impf*) (*+acc*)
blink [blɪŋk] *vi* морга́ть (*impf*); (*light*) мига́ть (*impf*)
bliss [blɪs] *n* блаже́нство
blizzard [ˈblɪzəd] *n* вью́га
bloated [ˈbləutɪd] *adj* (*face, stomach*) взду́тый; **I feel bloated** я весь разду́лся
blob [blɔb] *n* (*of glue, paint*) сгу́сток; (*shape*) сму́тное очерта́ние
bloc [blɔk] *n* блок
block [blɔk] *n* (*of buildings*) кварта́л; (*of stone etc*) плита́ ▷ *vt* (*barricade*) блоки́ровать (*perf* заблоки́ровать), загора́живать (*perf* загороди́ть); (*progress*)

препя́тствовать (*impf*); **block of flats** (*Brit*) многокварти́рный дом; **mental block** прова́л па́мяти; **blockade** [blɔ'keɪd] *n* блока́да; **blockage** ['blɔkɪdʒ] *n* блоки́рование

blog [blɔg] *n* блог *f* ▷ *vi* писа́ть (*perf* написа́ть) в блог; **blogger** *n* бло́гер; **blogpost** *n* пост, статья́

bloke [bləuk] *n* (*Brit*: *inf*) па́рень *m*

blond(e) [blɔnd] *adj* белоку́рый ▷ *n*: **blonde** (*woman*) блонди́нка

blood [blʌd] *n* кровь *f*; **blood donor** *n* до́нор; **blood pressure** *n* кровяно́е давле́ние; **bloodshed** *n* кровопроли́тие; **bloodstream** *n* кровообраще́ние; **bloody** *adj* (*battle*) крова́вый; (*Brit*: *inf!*): **this bloody weather** э́та прокля́тая пого́да

blossom ['blɔsəm] *n* цвет, цвете́ние

blot [blɔt] *n* (*on text*) кля́кса

blow [bləu] (*pt* **blew**, *pp* **blown**) *n* уда́р ▷ *vi* (*wind, person*) дуть (*perf* поду́ть); (*fuse*) перегора́ть (*perf* перегоре́ть) ▷ *vt* (*subj*: *wind*) гнать (*impf*); (*instrument*) дуть (*impf*) в *+acc*; **to blow one's nose** сморка́ться (*perf* вы́сморкаться); **blow away** *vt* сдува́ть (*perf* сдуть); **blow up** *vi* (*storm, crisis*) разража́ться (*perf* разрази́ться) ▷ *vt* (*bridge*) взрыва́ть (*perf* взорва́ть); (*tyre*) надува́ть (*perf* наду́ть)

blue [blu:] *adj* (*colour*: *light*) голубо́й; (: *dark*) си́ний; (*unhappy*) гру́стный; **blues** *npl* (*Mus*) блюз *msg*; **out of the blue** (*fig*) как гром среди́ я́сного не́ба; **bluebell** *n* колоко́льчик

bluff [blʌf] *n*: **to call sb's bluff** заставля́ть (*perf* заста́вить) кого́-н раскры́ть ка́рты

blunder ['blʌndəʳ] *n* гру́бая оши́бка

blunt [blʌnt] *adj* тупо́й; (*person*) прямолине́йный

blur [bləːʳ] *n* (*shape*) сму́тное очерта́ние ▷ *vt* (*vision*) затума́нивать (*perf* затума́нить); (*distinction*) стира́ть (*perf* стере́ть)

blush [blʌʃ] *vi* красне́ть (*perf* покрасне́ть)

board [bɔ:d] *n* доска́; (*card*) карто́н; (*committee*) комите́т; (*in firm*) правле́ние ▷ *vt* (*ship, train*) сади́ться (*perf* сесть) на *+acc*; **on board** (*Naut, Aviat*) на борту́; **full board** (*Brit*) по́лный пансио́н; **half board** (*Brit*) пансио́н с за́втраком и у́жином; **board and lodging** прожива́ние и пита́ние; **boarding card** *n* (*Aviat, Naut*) поса́дочный тало́н; **boarding school** *n* шко́ла-интерна́т

boast [bəust] *vi*: **to boast (about or of)** хва́статься (*perf* похва́статься) (*+instr*)

boat [bəut] *n* (*small*) ло́дка; (*large*) кора́бль *m*

bob [bɔb] *vi* (*boat*: *also* **bob up and down**) пока́чиваться (*impf*)

body ['bɔdɪ] *n* те́ло; (*of car*) ко́рпус; (*torso*) ту́ловище; (*fig*: *group*) гру́ппа; (: *organization*) о́рган; **bodyguard** *n* телохрани́тель *m*; **bodywork** *n* ко́рпус

bog [bɔg] *n* (*Geo*) боло́то, тряси́на

bogus ['bəugəs] *adj* (*claim*) фикти́вный

boil [bɔɪl] *vt* (*water*) кипяти́ть (*perf* вскипяти́ть); (*eggs, potatoes*) вари́ть (*perf* свари́ть) ▷ *vi* кипе́ть (*perf* вскипе́ть) ▷ *n* фуру́нкул; **to**

come to the (*Brit*) *or* **a** (*US*) **boil** вскипе́ть (*perf*); **boiled egg** *n* варёное яйцо́; **boiler** *n* (*device*) парово́й котёл, бо́йлер

bold [bəuld] *adj* (*brave*) сме́лый; (*pej*: *cheeky*) на́глый; (*pattern, colours*) бро́ский

bolt [bəult] *n* (*lock*) засо́в; (*with nut*) болт ▷ *adv*: **bolt upright** вы́тянувшись в стру́нку

bomb [bɔm] *n* бо́мба ▷ *vt* бомби́ть (*impf*)

bomber ['bɔmər] *n* (*Aviat*) бомбардиро́вщик

bond [bɔnd] *n* у́зы *pl*; (*Finance*) облига́ция

bone [bəun] *n* кость *f* ▷ *vt* отделя́ть (*perf* отдели́ть) от косте́й

bonfire ['bɔnfaɪər] *n* костёр

bonnet ['bɔnɪt] *n* (*hat*) ка́пор; (*Brit*: *of car*) капо́т

bonus ['bəunəs] *n* (*payment*) пре́мия; (*fig*) дополни́тельное преиму́щество

boo [bu:] *excl* фу ▷ *vt* осви́стывать (*perf* освиста́ть)

book [buk] *n* кни́га; (*of stamps, tickets*) кни́жечка ▷ *vt* (*ticket, table*) зака́зывать (*perf* заказа́ть); (*seat, room*) брони́ровать (*perf* заброни́ровать); (*subj*: *policeman, referee*) штрафова́ть (*perf* оштрафова́ть); **books** *npl* (*accounts*) бухга́лтерские кни́ги *fpl*; **bookcase** *n* кни́жный шкаф; **booklet** *n* брошю́ра; **bookmark** *n* закла́дка; **bookshop** *n* кни́жный магази́н

boom [bu:m] *n* (*noise*) ро́кот; (*growth*) бум

boost [bu:st] *n* (*to confidence*) сти́мул ▷ *vt* стимули́ровать (*impf*)

boot [bu:t] *n* (*for winter*) сапо́г; (*for football*) бу́тса; (*for walking*) боти́нок; (*Brit*: *of car*) бага́жник

booth [bu:ð] *n* (*at fair*) ларёк; (*Tel, for voting*) бу́дка

booze [bu:z] (*inf*) *n* вы́пивка

border ['bɔ:dər] *n* (*of country*) грани́ца; (*for flowers*) бордю́р; (*on cloth etc*) кайма́ ▷ *vt* (*road, river etc*) окаймля́ть (*perf* окайми́ть); (*country*: *also* **border on**) грани́чить (*impf*) с +*instr*; **borderline** *n*: **on the borderline** на гра́ни

bore [bɔ:r] *pt of* **bear** ▷ *vt* (*hole*) сверли́ть (*perf* просверли́ть); (*person*) наску́чить (*perf*) +*dat* ▷ *n* (*person*) зану́да *m/f*; **to be bored** скуча́ть (*impf*); **boredom** *n* (*condition*) ску́ка; (*boring quality*) зану́дство

boring ['bɔ:rɪŋ] *adj* ску́чный

born [bɔ:n] *adj* рождённый; **to be born** рожда́ться (*perf* роди́ться)

borne [bɔ:n] *pp of* **bear**

borough ['bʌrə] *n* администрати́вный о́круг

borrow ['bɔrəu] *vt*: **to borrow sth from sb** занима́ть (*perf* заня́ть) что-н у кого́-н

Bosnia ['bɔznɪə] *n* Бо́сния; **Bosnia-Herzegovina** [-hɜ:tsəgəu'vi:nə] *n* Бо́сния-Герцегови́на

bosom ['buzəm] *n* (*Anat*) грудь *f*

boss [bɔs] *n* (*employer*) хозя́ин(-я́йка), босс ▷ *vt* (*also* **boss around, boss about**) распоряжа́ться (*impf*), кома́ндовать (*impf*) +*instr*; **bossy** *adj* вла́стный

both [bəuθ] *adj, pron* о́ба (*f* о́бе) *adv*: **both A and B** и А, и Б; **both of us went, we both went** мы о́ба пошли́

bother ['bɔðər] *vt* (*worry*)

беспоко́ить (*perf* обеспоко́ить); (*disturb*) беспоко́ить (*perf* побеспоко́ить) ▷ *vi* (*also* **bother o.s.**) беспоко́иться (*impf*) ▷ *n* (*trouble*) беспоко́йство; (*nuisance*) хло́поты *pl*; **to bother doing** брать (*perf* взять) на себя́ труд +*infin*

bottle [ˈbɔtl] *n* буты́лка; **bottle-opener** *n* што́пор

bottom [ˈbɔtəm] *n* (*of container, sea*) дно; (*Anat*) зад; (*of page, list*) низ; (*of class*) отстаю́щий(-ая) *m(f) adj* ▷ *adj* (*lowest*) ни́жний; (*last*) после́дний

bought [bɔːt] *pt, pp of* **buy**

boulder [ˈbəuldəʳ] *n* валу́н

bounce [bauns] *vi* (*ball*) отска́кивать (*perf* отскочи́ть); (*cheque*) верну́ться (*perf*) (*ввиду́ отсу́тствия де́нег на счету́*) ▷ *vt* (*ball*) ударя́ть (*perf* уда́рить); **bouncer** *n* (*inf*) вышиба́ла *m*

bound [baund] *pt, pp of* **bind** ▷ *vi* (*leap*) пры́гать (*perf* пры́гнуть) ▷ *adj*: **he is bound by law to ...** его́ обя́зывает зако́н +*infin* ... ▷ *npl*: **bounds** (*limits*) преде́лы *mpl*

boundary [ˈbaundrɪ] *n* грани́ца

bouquet [ˈbukeɪ] *n* буке́т

bout [baut] *n* (*of illness*) при́ступ; (*of activity*) всплеск

boutique [buːˈtiːk] *n* ла́вка

bow[1] [bəu] *n* (*knot*) бант; (*weapon*) лук; (*Mus*) смычо́к

bow[2] [bau] *n* (*of head, body*) покло́н; (*Naut*: *also* **bows**) нос ▷ *vi* (*with head, body*) кла́няться (*perf* поклони́ться); (*yield*): **to bow to** *or* **before** поддава́ться (*perf* подда́ться) +*dat or* на +*acc*

bowels [ˈbauəlz] *npl* кише́чник *msg*

bowl [bəul] *n* (*plate, food*) ми́ска, ча́ша; (*ball*) шар

bowling [ˈbəulɪŋ] *n* (*game*) кегельба́н

bowls [bəulz] *n* (*game*) игра́ в шары́

box [bɔks] *n* я́щик, коро́бка; (*also* **cardboard box**) карто́нная коро́бка; (*Theat*) ло́жа; (*inf*: *TV*) я́щик; **boxer** *n* боксёр; **boxing** *n* бокс; **Boxing Day** *n* (*Brit*) *день по́сле Рождества́*

Boxing Day

Boxing Day — пе́рвый день по́сле Рождества́. Буква́льно "День коро́бок". Э́тот день явля́ется пра́здничным. Его́ назва́ние свя́зано с обы́чаем де́лать пода́рки, упако́ванные в рожде́ственские коро́бки, почтальо́нам, разно́счикам газе́т и други́м рабо́тникам, ока́зывающим услу́ги на дому́.

box office *n* театра́льная ка́сса

boy [bɔɪ] *n* ма́льчик; (*son*) сыно́к

boycott [ˈbɔɪkɔt] *n* бойко́т ▷ *vt* бойкоти́ровать (*impf/perf*)

boyfriend [ˈbɔɪfrɛnd] *n* друг

bra [brɑː] *n* ли́фчик

brace [breɪs] *n* (*on leg*) ши́на; (*on teeth*) пласти́нка ▷ *vt* (*knees, shoulders*) напряга́ть (*perf* напря́чь); **braces** *npl* (*Brit*: *for trousers*) подтя́жки *pl*; **to brace o.s.** (*for shock*) собира́ться (*perf* собра́ться) с ду́хом

bracelet [ˈbreɪslɪt] *n* брасле́т

bracket [ˈbrækɪt] *n* (*Tech*) кронште́йн; (*group, range*) катего́рия; (*also* **brace bracket**) ско́бка; (*also* **round bracket**) кру́глая ско́бка; (*also* **square bracket**) квадра́тная ско́бка ▷ *vt* (*word, phrase*) заключа́ть (*perf* заключи́ть) в ско́бки

brain [breɪn] *n* мозг; **brains** *npl*

(*also Culin*) мозги́ *mpl*
brake [breɪk] *n* то́рмоз ▷ *vi* тормози́ть (*perf* затормози́ть)
bran [bræn] *n* о́труби *pl*
branch [brɑːntʃ] *n* (*of tree*) ве́тка, ветвь *f*; (*of bank, firm etc*) филиа́л
brand [brænd] *n* (*also* **brand name**) фи́рменная ма́рка ▷ *vt* (*cattle*) клейми́ть (*perf* заклейми́ть)
brand-new ['brænd'njuː] *adj* соверше́нно но́вый
brandy ['brændɪ] *n* бре́нди *nt ind*, конья́к
brash [bræʃ] *adj* наха́льный
brass [brɑːs] *n* (*metal*) лату́нь *f*; **the brass** (*Mus*) духовы́е инструме́нты *mpl*
brat [bræt] *n* (*pej*) озорни́к
brave [breɪv] *adj* сме́лый, хра́брый ▷ *vt* сме́ло *or* хра́бро встреча́ть (*perf* встре́тить); **bravery** ['breɪvərɪ] *n* сме́лость *f*, хра́брость *f*
brawl [brɔːl] *n* дра́ка
Brazil [brə'zɪl] *n* Брази́лия
breach [briːtʃ] *vt* (*defence, wall*) пробива́ть (*perf* проби́ть) ▷ *n* (*gap*) брешь *f*; **breach of contract/ of the peace** наруше́ние догово́ра/ обще́ственного поря́дка
bread [brɛd] *n* (*food*) хлеб; **breadbin** *n* (*Brit*) хле́бница; **breadbox** *n* (*US*) = **breadbin**; **breadcrumbs** *npl* (*Culin*) паниро́вочные сухари́ *mpl*
breadth [brɛtθ] *n* ширина́; (*fig*: *of knowledge, subject*) широта́
break [breɪk] (*pt* **broke**, *pp* **broken**) *vt* (*crockery*) разбива́ть (*perf* разби́ть); (*leg, arm*) лома́ть (*perf* слома́ть); (*law, promise*) наруша́ть (*perf* нару́шить); (*record*) побива́ть (*perf* поби́ть) ▷ *vi* (*crockery*) разбива́ться (*perf* разби́ться); (*storm*) разража́ться (*perf* разрази́ться); (*weather*) по́ртиться (*perf* испо́ртиться); (*dawn*) бре́зжить (*perf* забре́зжить); (*story, news*) сообща́ть (*perf* сообщи́ть) ▷ *n* (*gap*) пробе́л; (*chance*) шанс; (*fracture*) перело́м; (*playtime*) переме́на; **to break even** (*Comm*) зака́нчивать (*perf* зако́нчить) без убы́тка; **to break free** *or* **loose** вырыва́ться (*perf* вы́рваться) на свобо́ду; **break down** *vt* (*figures etc*) разбива́ть (*perf* разби́ть) по статья́м ▷ *vi* (*machine, car*) лома́ться (*perf* слома́ться); (*person*) сломи́ться (*perf*); (*talks*) срыва́ться (*perf* сорва́ться); **break in** *vi* (*burglar*) вла́мываться (*perf* вломи́ться); (*interrupt*) вме́шиваться (*perf* вмеша́ться); **break into** *vt fus* (*house*) вла́мываться (*perf* вломи́ться) в *+acc*; **break off** *vi* (*branch*) отла́мываться (*perf* отломи́ться); (*speaker*) прерыва́ть (*perf* прерва́ть) речь ▷ *vt* (*engagement*) расторга́ть (*perf* расто́ргнуть); **break out** *vi* (*begin*) разража́ться (*perf* разрази́ться); (*escape*) сбега́ть (*perf* сбежа́ть); **to break out in spots/a rash** покрыва́ться (*perf* покры́ться) прыща́ми/сы́пью; **break up** *vi* (*ship*) разбива́ться (*perf* разби́ться); (*crowd, meeting*) расходи́ться (*perf* разойти́сь); (*marriage, partnership*) распада́ться (*perf* распа́сться); (*Scol*) закрыва́ться (*perf* закры́ться) на кани́кулы ▷ *vt* разла́мывать (*perf* разломи́ть); (*journey*) прерыва́ть (*perf* прерва́ть); (*fight*) прекраща́ть (*perf* прекрати́ть); **breakdown** *n*

(*in communications*) нарушéние, срыв; (*of marriage*) распáд; (*also* **nervous breakdown**) нéрвный срыв

breakfast ['brɛkfəst] *n* зáвтрак

breakthrough ['breɪkθru:] *n* (*in technology*) перелóмное открытие

breast [brɛst] *n* грудь *f*; (*of meat*) грудúнка; (*of poultry*) бéлое мя́со; **breast-feed** (*irreg like* **feed**) *vt* кормúть (*perf* покормúть) грýдью ▷ *vi* кормúть (*impf*) (грýдью)

breath [brɛθ] *n* вдох; (*breathing*) дыхáние; **to be out of breath** запыхиваться (*perf* запыхáться); **breathe** [bri:ð] *vi* дышáть (*impf*); **breathe in** *vt* вдыхáть (*perf* вдохнýть) ▷ *vi* дéлать (*perf* сдéлать) вдох; **breathe out** *vi* дéлать (*perf* сдéлать) вы́дох; **breathing** ['bri:ðɪŋ] *n* дыхáние; **breathless** ['brɛθlɪs] *adj* (*from exertion*) запыхáвшийся; **breathtaking** ['brɛθteɪkɪŋ] *adj* захвáтывающий дух

bred [brɛd] *pt, pp of* **breed**

breed [bri:d] (*pt, pp* **bred**) *vt* (*animals, plants*) разводúть (*perf* развестú) ▷ *vi* размножáться (*impf*) ▷ *n* (*Zool*) порóда

breeze [bri:z] *n* бриз

breezy ['bri:zɪ] *adj* (*manner, tone*) оживлённый; (*weather*) прохлáдный

brew [bru:] *vt* (*tea*) завáривать (*perf* заварúть); (*beer*) варúть (*perf* сварúть) ▷ *vi* (*storm*) надвигáться (*perf* надвúнуться); (*fig*: *trouble*) назревáть (*perf* назрéть); **brewery** *n* пивовáренный завóд

bribe [braɪb] *n* взя́тка, пóдкуп ▷ *vt* (*person*) подкупáть (*perf* подкупúть), давáть (*perf* дать) взя́тку; **bribery** ['braɪbərɪ] *n* пóдкуп

brick [brɪk] *n* (*for building*) кирпúч

bride [braɪd] *n* невéста; **bridegroom** *n* женúх; **bridesmaid** *n* подрýжка невéсты

bridge [brɪdʒ] *n* мост; (*Naut*) капитáнский мóстик; (*Cards*) бридж; (*of nose*) перенóсица ▷ *vt* (*fig*: *gap*) преодолевáть (*perf* преодолéть)

bridle ['braɪdl] *n* уздéчка, уздá

brief [bri:f] *adj* (*period of time*) корóткий; (*description*) крáткий ▷ *n* (*task*) задáние ▷ *vt* знакóмить (*perf* ознакóмить) с +*instr*; **briefs** *npl* (*for men*) трусы́ *pl*; (*for women*) трýсики *pl*; **briefcase** *n* портфéль *m*; (*attaché case*) дипломáт; **briefing** *n* инструктáж; (*Press*) брúфинг; **briefly** *adv* (*glance, smile*) бéгло; (*explain*) вкрáтце

bright [braɪt] *adj* (*light, colour*) я́ркий; (*room, future*) свéтлый; (*clever*: *person, idea*) блестя́щий; (*lively*: *person*) живóй, весёлый

brilliant ['brɪljənt] *adj* блестя́щий; (*sunshine*) я́ркий; (*inf*: *holiday etc*) великолéпный

brim [brɪm] *n* (*of cup*) край; (*of hat*) поля́ *pl*

bring [brɪŋ] (*pt, pp* **brought**) *vt* (*thing*) приносúть (*perf* принестú); (*person*: *on foot*) приводúть (*perf* привестú); (: *by transport*) привозúть (*perf* привезтú); (*satisfaction, trouble*) доставля́ть (*perf* достáвить); **bring about** *vt* (*cause*: *unintentionally*) вызывáть (*perf* вы́звать); (: *intentionally*) осуществля́ть (*perf* осуществúть); **bring back** *vt* (*restore*) возрождáть (*perf* возродúть); (*return*) возвращáть (*perf* возвратúть), вернýть (*perf*);

bring down *vt* (*government*) свергáть (*perf* свéргнуть); (*plane*) сбивáть (*perf* сбить); (*price*) снижáть (*perf* сни́зить); **bring forward** *vt* (*meeting*) переноси́ть (*perf* перенести́) на бóлее рáнний срок; **bring out** *vt* вынимáть (*perf* вы́нуть); (*publish*) выпускáть (*perf* вы́пустить); **bring up** *vt* (*carry up*) приноси́ть (*perf* принести́) навéрх; (*child*) воспи́тывать (*perf* воспитáть); (*subject*) поднимáть (*perf* поднять); **he brought up his food** егó стошни́ло

brink [brɪŋk] *n*: **on the brink of** (*fig*) на грáни *+gen*

brisk [brɪsk] *adj* (*tone*) отры́вистый; (*person, trade*) оживлённый; **business is brisk** делá идýт пóлным хóдом

Britain ['brɪtən] *n* (*also* **Great Britain**) Бритáния

British ['brɪtɪʃ] *adj* бритáнский; *npl*: **the British** бритáнцы *mpl*; **British Isles** *npl*: **the British Isles** Бритáнские островá *mpl*

Briton ['brɪtən] *n* бритáнец(-нка)

brittle ['brɪtl] *adj* хрýпкий, лóмкий

broad [brɔːd] *adj* (*wide, general*) ширóкий; (*strong*) си́льный; **in broad daylight** средь бéла дня; **broadband** ['brəːdb[ae]nd] *adj* широкополóсный; **broadband connection** широкополóсная связь; **broadband access** широкополóсный дóступ; **broadcast** (*pt, pp* **broadcast**) *n* (рáдио)передáча; (*TV*) (теле)передáча ▷ *vt* трансли́ровать (*impf*) ▷ *vi* вещáть (*impf*); **broaden** *vt* расширя́ть (*perf* расши́рить) ▷ *vi* расширя́ться (*perf* расши́риться); **broadly** *adv* вообщé

broccoli ['brɔkəlɪ] *n* брóкколи *nt ind*

brochure ['brəuʃjuə^r] *n* брошю́ра

broke [brəuk] *pt of* **break** ▷ *adj*: **I am broke** (*inf*) я на мели́; **broken** *pp of* **break** ▷ *adj* (*window, cup etc*) разби́тый; (*machine, leg*) слóманный; **in broken Russian** на лóманом рýсском

broker ['brəukə^r] *n* (*in shares*) брóкер; (*in insurance*) страховóй агéнт

bronchitis [brɔŋ'kaɪtɪs] *n* бронхи́т

bronze [brɔnz] *n* (*metal*) брóнза; (*sculpture*) брóнзовая скульптýра

brooch [brəutʃ] *n* брошь *f*

Bros. *abbr* (*Comm*) (= *brothers*) брáтья *mpl*

broth [brɔθ] *n* похлёбка

brothel ['brɔθl] *n* публи́чный дом, бордéль *m*

brother ['brʌðə^r] *n* брат; **brother-in-law** *n* (*sister's husband*) зять *m*; (*wife's brother*) шýрин; (*husband's brother*) дéверь *m*

brought [brɔːt] *pt, pp of* **bring**

brow [brau] *n* лоб, челó; (*also* **eyebrow**) бровь *f*; (*of hill*) грéбень *m*

brown [braun] *adj* кори́чневый; (*hair*) тёмно-рýсый; (*eyes*) кáрий; (*tanned*) загорéлый ▷ *n* (*colour*) кори́чневый цвет ▷ *vt* (*Culin*) подрумя́нивать (*perf* подрумя́нить); **brown bread** *n* чёрный хлеб; **brown sugar** *n* неочи́щенный сáхар

browse [brauz] *vi* осмáтриваться (*perf* осмотрéться); **to browse through a book** пролистывать (*perf* пролистáть) кни́гу; **browser**

n (*Comput*) бра́узер

bruise [bru:z] *n* (*on face etc*) синя́к ▷ *vt* ушиба́ть (*perf* ушиби́ть)

brunette [bru:ˈnɛt] *n* брюне́тка

brush [brʌʃ] *n* (*for cleaning*) щётка; (*for painting*) кисть *f*; (*for shaving*) помазо́к ▷ *vt* (*sweep*) подмета́ть (*perf* подмести́); (*groom*) чи́стить (*perf* почи́стить) щёткой; (*also* **brush against**) задева́ть (*perf* заде́ть)

Brussels [ˈbrʌslz] *n* Брюссе́ль *m*; **Brussels sprout** *n* брюссе́льская капу́ста

brutal [ˈbru:tl] *adj* (*person, action*) жесто́кий, зве́рский; (*honesty*) жёсткий

bubble [ˈbʌbl] *n* пузы́рь *m*; **bubble bath** *n* пе́нистая ва́нна

bucket [ˈbʌkɪt] *n* ведро́

buckle [ˈbʌkl] *n* пря́жка

bud [bʌd] *n* (*of tree*) по́чка; (*of flower*) буто́н

Buddhism [ˈbudɪzəm] *n* будди́зм

buddy [ˈbʌdɪ] *n* (*US*) приятель *m*, дружо́к

budge [bʌdʒ] *vt* (*fig: person*) заставля́ть (*perf* заста́вить) уступи́ть ▷ *vi* сдвига́ться (*perf* сдви́нуться) (с ме́ста)

budgerigar [ˈbʌdʒərɪgɑ:ʳ] *n* волни́стый попуга́йчик

budget [ˈbʌdʒɪt] *n* бюдже́т

budgie [ˈbʌdʒɪ] *n* = **budgerigar**

buff [bʌf] *adj* кори́чневый ▷ *n* (*inf: enthusiast*) спец, знато́к

buffalo [ˈbʌfələu] (*pl* **buffalo** *or* **buffaloes**) *n* (*Brit*) бу́йвол; (*US: bison*) бизо́н

buffer [ˈbʌfəʳ] *n* бу́фер

buffet [ˈbufeɪ] *n* (*Brit: in station*) буфе́т; (*food*) шве́дский стол

bug [bʌg] *n* (*insect*) насеко́мое *nt adj*; (*Comput: glitch*) оши́бка; (*virus*) ви́рус; (*fig: germ*) ви́рус; (*hidden microphone*) подслу́шивающее устро́йство ▷ *vt* (*room etc*) прослу́шивать (*impf*); (*inf: annoy*): **to bug sb** де́йствовать (*impf*) кому́-н на не́рвы

buggy [ˈbʌgɪ] *n* (*also* **baby buggy**) складна́я (де́тская) коля́ска

build [bɪld] (*pt, pp* **built**) *n* (*of person*) (тело)сложе́ние ▷ *vt* стро́ить (*perf* постро́ить); **build up** *vt* (*forces, production*) нара́щивать (*impf*); (*stocks*) нака́пливать (*perf* накопи́ть); **builder** *n* строи́тель *m*; **building** *n* строе́ние; **building society** *n* (*Brit*) ≈ "строи́тельное о́бщество"

BUILDING SOCIETY

Building society — строи́тельные о́бщества или ипоте́чные ба́нки. Они́ бы́ли со́зданы для предоставле́ния ипоте́чного жили́щного кредитова́ния. Одновре́ме́нно строи́тельные о́бщества функциони́ровали как сберега́тельные ба́нки. В после́дние го́ды они ста́ли предоставля́ть бо́лее широ́кий объём ба́нковских услу́г.

built [bɪlt] *pt, pp of* **build** ▷ *adj*: **built-in** встро́енный

bulb [bʌlb] *n* (*Bot*) лу́ковица; (*Elec*) ла́мпа, ла́мпочка

Bulgaria [bʌlˈgɛərɪə] *n* Болга́рия

bulimia [bəˈlɪmɪə] *n* булими́я

bulk [bʌlk] *n* грома́да; **in bulk** о́птом; **the bulk of** бо́льшая часть *+gen*; **bulky** *adj* громо́здкий

bull [bul] *n* (*Zool*) бык

bulldozer [ˈbuldəuzəʳ] *n* бульдо́зер
bullet [ˈbulɪt] *n* пу́ля
bulletin [ˈbulɪtɪn] *n* (*journal*) бюллете́нь *m*; **news bulletin** сво́дка новосте́й; **bulletin board** *n* (*Comput*) доска́ объявле́ний
bully [ˈbulɪ] *n* задира *m/f*, пресле́дователь *m* ▷ *vt* трави́ть (*perf* затрави́ть)
bum [bʌm] *n* (*inf*: *backside*) за́дница; (*esp US*: *tramp*) бродя́га *m/f*; (: *good-for-nothing*) безде́льник
bumblebee [ˈbʌmblbiː] *n* шмель *m*
bump [bʌmp] *n* (*minor accident*) столкнове́ние; (*jolt*) толчо́к; (*swelling*) ши́шка ▷ *vt* (*strike*) ударя́ть (*perf* уда́рить); **bump into** *vt fus* ната́лкиваться (*perf* натолкну́ться) на *+acc*; **bumper** *n* (*Aut*) ба́мпер ▷ *adj*: **bumper crop** *or* **harvest** небыва́лый урожа́й; **bumpy** *adj* (*road*) уха́бистый
bun [bʌn] *n* (*Culin*) сдо́бная бу́лка; (*of hair*) у́зел
bunch [bʌntʃ] *n* (*of flowers*) буке́т; (*of keys*) свя́зка; (*of bananas*) гроздь *f*; (*of people*) компа́ния; **bunches** *npl* (*in hair*) хво́стики *mpl*
bundle [ˈbʌndl] *n* (*of clothes*) у́зел; (*of sticks*) вяза́нка; (*of papers*) па́чка ▷ *vt* (*also* **bundle up**) свя́зывать (*perf* связа́ть) в у́зел; **to bundle sth/sb into** зата́лкивать (*perf* затолкну́ть) что-н/кого́-н в *+acc*
bungalow [ˈbʌŋgələu] *n* бунга́ло *nt ind*
bunk [bʌŋk] *n* (*bed*) ко́йка; **bunk beds** *npl* двухъя́русная крова́ть *fsg*
bunker [ˈbʌŋkəʳ] *n* бу́нкер
bunny [ˈbʌnɪ] *n* (*also* **bunny rabbit**) за́йчик
buoy [bɔɪ] *n* буй, ба́кен
buoyant [ˈbɔɪənt] *adj* (*fig*: *economy, market*) оживлённый; (: *person*) жизнера́достный
burden [ˈbəːdn] *n* (*responsibility*) бре́мя *nt*; (*load*) но́ша ▷ *vt*: **to burden sb with** обременя́ть (*perf* обремени́ть) кого́-н *+instr*
bureau [ˈbjuərəu] (*pl* **bureaux**) *n* (*Brit*) бюро́ *nt ind*; (*US*) комо́д
bureaucracy [bjuəˈrɔkrəsɪ] *n* (*Pol, Comm*) бюрокра́тия; (*system*) бюрократи́зм
bureaucrat [ˈbjuərəkræt] *n* бюрокра́т
bureaux [ˈbjuərəuz] *npl of* **bureau**
burger [ˈbəːgəʳ] *n* бу́ргер
burglar [ˈbəːgləʳ] *n* взло́мщик; **burglar alarm** *n* сигнализа́ция; **burglary** *n* (*crime*) кра́жа со взло́мом, кварти́рный разбо́й
burial [ˈbɛrɪəl] *n* погребе́ние, по́хороны *pl*
burn [bəːn] (*pt, pp* **burned** *or* **burnt**) *vt* жечь (*perf* сжечь), сжига́ть (*perf* сжечь); (*intentionally*) поджига́ть (*perf* подже́чь) ▷ *vi* (*house, wood*) горе́ть (*perf* сгоре́ть), сгора́ть (*perf* сгоре́ть); (*cakes*) подгора́ть (*perf* подгоре́ть) ▷ *n* ожо́г; **burning** *adj* (*building, forest*) горя́щий; (*issue, ambition*) жгу́чий
burst [bəːst] (*pt, pp* **burst**) *vt* (*bag etc*) разрыва́ть (*perf* разорва́ть) ▷ *vi* (*tyre, balloon, pipe*) ло́паться (*perf* ло́пнуть) ▷ *n* (*of gunfire*) залп; (*of energy*) прили́в; (*also* **burst pipe**) проры́в; **to burst into flames** вспы́хивать (*perf* вспы́хнуть); **to burst into tears** распла́каться (*perf*); **to burst out laughing** расхохота́ться (*perf*); **to be bursting with** (*pride, anger*)

раздува́ться (*perf* разду́ться) от *+gen*; **burst into** *vt fus* (*room*) врыва́ться (*perf* ворва́ться)

bury ['bɛrɪ] *vt* (*object*) зарыва́ть (*perf* зары́ть), зака́пывать (*perf* закопа́ть); (*person*) хорони́ть (*perf* похорони́ть); **many people were buried in the rubble** мно́го люде́й бы́ло погребено́ под обло́мками

bus [bʌs] *n* авто́бус; (*double decker*) (двухэта́жный) авто́бус

bush [buʃ] *n* куст; **to beat about the bush** ходи́ть (*impf*) вокру́г да о́коло

business ['bɪznɪs] *n* (*matter*) де́ло; (*trading*) би́знес, де́ло; (*firm*) предприя́тие; (*occupation*) заня́тие; **to be away on business** быть (*impf*) в командиро́вке; **it's none of my business** э́то не моё де́ло; **he means business** он настро́ен серьёзно; **businesslike** *adj* делови́тый; **businessman** *irreg n* бизнесме́н; **businesswoman** *irreg n* бизнесме́нка

bus-stop ['bʌsstɔp] *n* авто́бусная остано́вка

bust [bʌst] *n* бюст, грудь *f*; (*measurement*) объём груди́; (*sculpture*) бюст ▷ *adj*: **to go bust** (*firm*) прогора́ть (*perf* прогоре́ть)

bustling ['bʌslɪŋ] *adj* оживлённый, шу́мный

busy ['bɪzɪ] *adj* (*person*) заня́той; (*street*) оживлённый, шу́мный; (*Tel*): **the line is busy** ли́ния занята́ ▷ *vt*: **to busy o.s. with** занима́ться (*perf* заня́ться) *+instr*

 **KEYWORD**

but [bʌt] *conj* **1** (*yet*) но; (: *in contrast*) а; **he's not very bright, but he's hard-working** он не о́чень умён, но усе́рден; **I'm tired but Paul isn't** я уста́л, а Па́вел нет

2 (*however*) но; **I'd love to come, but I'm busy** я бы с удово́льствием пришёл, но я за́нят

3 (*showing disagreement, surprise etc*) но; **but that's fantastic!** но э́то же потряса́юще!

▷ *prep* (*apart from, except*): **no-one but him can do it** никто́, кро́ме него́, не мо́жет э́то сде́лать; **nothing but trouble** сплошны́е *or* одни́ неприя́тности; **but for you/your help** е́сли бы не Вы/Ва́ша по́мощь; **I'll do anything but that** я сде́лаю всё, что уго́дно, но то́лько не э́то

▷ *adv* (*just, only*): **she's but a child** она́ всего́ лишь ребёнок; **had I but known** е́сли бы то́лько я знал; **I can but try** коне́чно, я могу́ попро́бовать; **the work is all but finished** рабо́та почти́ зако́нчена

butcher ['butʃəʳ] *n* мясни́к; (*also* **butcher's (shop)**) мясно́й магази́н

butt [bʌt] *n* (*large barrel*) бо́чка; (*of rifle*) прикла́д; (*of pistol*) рукоя́тка; (*of cigarette*) оку́рок; (*Brit*: *of teasing*) предме́т

butter ['bʌtəʳ] *n* (сли́вочное) ма́сло ▷ *vt* нама́зывать (*perf* нама́зать) (сли́вочным) ма́слом; **buttercup** *n* лю́тик

butterfly ['bʌtəflaɪ] *n* ба́бочка; (*also* **butterfly stroke**) баттерфля́й

buttocks ['bʌtəks] *npl* я́годицы *fpl*

button ['bʌtn] *n* (*on clothes*) пу́говица; (*on machine*) кно́пка; (*US*: *badge*) значо́к ▷ *vt* (*also* **button up**) застёгивать (*perf* застегну́ть)

buy [baɪ] (*pt, pp* **bought**) *vt* покупа́ть (*perf* купи́ть) ▷ *n* поку́пка; **to buy sb sth/sth from sb** покупа́ть (*perf* купи́ть) кому́-н что-н/что-н у кого́-н; **to buy sb a drink** покупа́ть (*perf* купи́ть) кому́-н вы́пить; **buyer** *n* покупа́тель(ница)

buzz [bʌz] *n* жужжа́ние; **buzzer** *n* зу́ммер, звоно́к

 **KEYWORD**

by [baɪ] *prep* **1** (*referring to cause, agent*): **he was killed by lightning** его́ уби́ло мо́лнией; **a painting by Van Gogh** карти́на Ван Го́га; **it's by Shakespeare** э́то Шекспи́р
2 (*referring to manner, means*): **by bus/train** авто́бусом/по́ездом; **by car** на маши́не; **by phone** по телефо́ну; **to pay by cheque** плати́ть (*perf* заплати́ть) че́ком; **by moonlight** при све́те луны́; **by candlelight** при свеча́х; **by working constantly, he ...** благодаря́ тому́, что он рабо́тал без остано́вки, он ...
3 (*via, through*) че́рез *+acc*; **by the back door** че́рез за́днюю дверь; **by land/sea** по су́ше/мо́рю
4 (*close to*) у *+gen*, о́коло *+gen*; **the house is by the river** дом нахо́дится у *or* о́коло реки́; **a holiday by the sea** о́тпуск на мо́ре
5 (*past*) ми́мо *+gen*; **she rushed by me** она́ пронесла́сь ми́мо меня́
6 (*not later than*) к *+dat*; **by four o'clock** к четырём часа́м; **by the time I got here ...** к тому́ вре́мени, когда́ я добра́лся сюда́ ...
7 (*during*): **by day** днём; **by night** но́чью
8 (*amount*): **to sell by the metre/kilo** продава́ть (*perf* прода́ть) ме́трами/килогра́ммами; **she is paid by the hour** у неё почасова́я опла́та
9 (*Math, measure*) на *+acc*; **to multiply/divide by three** умножа́ть (*perf* умно́жить)/дели́ть (*perf* раздели́ть) на три; **a room three metres by four** ко́мната разме́ром три ме́тра на четы́ре
10 (*according to*) по *+dat*; **to play by the rules** игра́ть (*impf*) по пра́вилам; **it's all right by me** я не возража́ю; **by law** по зако́ну
11: **(all) by oneself** (*alone*) (соверше́нно) оди́н (*f* одна́, *pl* одни́) (*unaided*) сам (*f* сама́, *pl* са́ми); **I did it all by myself** я сде́лал всё оди́н *or* сам; **he was standing by himself** он стоя́л оди́н
12: **by the way** кста́ти, ме́жду про́чим
▷ *adv* **1** *see* **pass** *etc*
2: **by and by** вско́ре; **by and large** в це́лом

bye(-bye) [ˈbaɪ(ˈbaɪ)] *excl* пока́

bypass [ˈbaɪpɑːs] *n* (*Aut*) объе́зд, окружна́я доро́га; (*Med*) обходно́е шунти́рование ▷ *vt* (*town*) объезжа́ть (*perf* объе́хать)

by-product [ˈbaɪprɔdʌkt] *n* (*Industry*) побо́чный проду́кт

byte [baɪt] *n* (*Comput*) байт

C

C [siː] *n* (*Mus*) до *nt ind*
C *abbr* = **Celsius**; **centigrade**
cab [kæb] *n* такси́ *nt ind*; (*of truck etc*) каби́на
cabaret ['kæbəreɪ] *n* кабаре́ *nt ind*
cabbage ['kæbɪdʒ] *n* капу́ста
cabin ['kæbɪn] *n* (*on ship*) каю́та; (*on plane*) каби́на
cabinet ['kæbɪnɪt] *n* шкаф; (*also* **display cabinet**) го́рка; (*Pol*) кабине́т (мини́стров)
cable ['keɪbl] *n* ка́бель *m*; (*rope*) кана́т; (*metal*) трос ▷ *vt* (*message*) телеграфи́ровать (*impf/perf*); **cable television** *n* ка́бельное телеви́дение
cactus ['kæktəs] (*pl* **cacti**) *n* ка́ктус
café ['kæfeɪ] *n* кафе́ *nt ind*
caffein(e) ['kæfiːn] *n* кофеи́н
cage [keɪdʒ] *n* (*for animal*) кле́тка
cagoule [kə'guːl] *n* дождеви́к
cake [keɪk] *n* (*large*) торт; (*small*) пиро́жное *nt adj*
calcium ['kælsɪəm] *n* ка́льций
calculate ['kælkjuleɪt] *vt* (*figures, cost*) подсчи́тывать (*perf* подсчита́ть); (*distance*) вычисля́ть (*perf* вы́числить); (*estimate*) рассчи́тывать (*perf* рассчита́ть)
calculation [kælkju'leɪʃən] *n* (*see vb*) подсчёт; вычисле́ние; расчёт
calculator ['kælkjuleɪtə^r] *n* калькуля́тор
calendar ['kæləndə^r] *n* календа́рь *m*
calf [kɑːf] (*pl* **calves**) *n* (*of cow*) телёнок; (*Anat*) икра́
calibre ['kælɪbə^r] (*US* **caliber**) *n* кали́бр
call [kɔːl] *vt* называ́ть (*perf* назва́ть); (*Tel*) звони́ть (*perf* позвони́ть) *+dat*; (*summon*) вызыва́ть (*perf* вы́звать); (*arrange*) созыва́ть (*perf* созва́ть) ▷ *vi* (*shout*) крича́ть (*perf* кри́кнуть); (*Tel*) звони́ть (*perf* позвони́ть); (*visit*: *also* **call in, call round**) заходи́ть (*perf* зайти́) ▷ *n* (*shout*) крик; (*Tel*) звоно́к; **she is called Suzanne** её зову́т Сюза́нна; **the mountain is called Ben Nevis** гора́ называ́ется Бен Не́вис; **to be on call** дежу́рить (*impf*); **call back** *vi* (*return*) заходи́ть (*perf* зайти́) опя́ть; (*Tel*) перезва́нивать (*perf* перезвони́ть) ▷ *vt* (*Tel*) перезва́нивать (*perf* перезвони́ть) *+dat*; **call for** *vt fus* (*demand*) призыва́ть (*perf* призва́ть) к *+dat*; (*fetch*) заходи́ть (*perf* зайти́) за *+instr*; **call off** *vt* отменя́ть (*perf* отмени́ть); **call on** *vt fus* (*visit*) заходи́ть (*perf* зайти́) к *+dat*; (*appeal to*) призыва́ть (*perf*

C

призва́ть) к *+dat*; **call out** *vi* крича́ть (*perf* кри́кнуть); **call centre** *n центр приёма комме́рческих итп звонко́в в большо́м объёме*

callous ['kæləs] *adj* безду́шный

calm [kɑːm] *adj* споко́йный; (*place*) ти́хий; (*weather*) безве́тренный ▷ *n* тишина́, поко́й ▷ *vt* успока́ивать (*perf* успоко́ить); **calm down** *vt* успока́ивать (*perf* успоко́ить) ▷ *vi* успока́иваться (*perf* успоко́иться)

calorie ['kælərɪ] *n* кало́рия

calves [kɑːvz] *npl of* **calf**

Cambodia [kæm'bəudɪə] *n* Камбо́джа

camcorder ['kæmkɔːdə[r]] *n* видеока́мера

came [keɪm] *pt of* **come**

camel ['kæməl] *n* верблю́д

camera ['kæmərə] *n* фотоаппара́т; (*also* **cine camera, movie camera**) кинока́мера; (*TV*) телека́мера; **cameraman** *irreg n* (*Cinema*) (кино)опера́тор; (*TV*) (теле)опера́тор; **camera phone** *n* камерафо́н *m* (*моби́льный телефо́н со встро́енной фотовидеока́мерой*)

camouflage ['kæməflɑːʒ] *n* (*Mil*) камуфля́ж, маскиро́вка ▷ *vt* маскирова́ть (*perf* замаскирова́ть)

camp [kæmp] *n* ла́герь *m*; (*Mil*) вое́нный городо́к ▷ *vi* разбива́ть (*perf* разби́ть) ла́герь; (*go camping*) жить (*impf*) в пала́тках

campaign [kæm'peɪn] *n* кампа́ния ▷ *vi*: **to campaign (for/against)** вести́ (*impf*) кампа́нию (за *+acc*/про́тив *+gen*)

camping ['kæmpɪŋ] *n* ке́мпинг; **to go camping** отправля́ться (*perf* отпра́виться) в похо́д

camp site *n* ке́мпинг

campus ['kæmpəs] *n* студе́нческий городо́к

can[1] [kæn] *n* (*for food*) консе́рвная ба́нка ▷ *vt* консерви́ровать (*perf* законсерви́ровать)

 **KEYWORD**

can[2] [kæn] (*negative* **cannot, can't**, *conditional, pt* **could**) *aux vb* **1** (*be able to*) мочь (*perf* смочь); **you can do it** Вы смо́жете э́то сде́лать; **I'll help you all I can** я помогу́ Вам всем, чем смогу́; **I can't go on any longer** я бо́льше не могу́; **I can't see you** я не ви́жу Вас; **she couldn't sleep that night** в ту ночь она́ не могла́ спать

2 (*know how to*) уме́ть (*impf*); **I can swim** я уме́ю пла́вать; **can you speak Russian?** Вы уме́ете говори́ть по-ру́сски?

3 (*may*) мо́жно; **can I use your phone?** мо́жно от Вас позвони́ть?; **could I have a word with you?** мо́жно с Ва́ми поговори́ть?; **you can smoke if you like** Вы мо́жете кури́ть, е́сли хоти́те; **can I help you with that?** я могу́ Вам в э́том помо́чь?

4 (*expressing disbelief, puzzlement*): **it can't be true!** (э́того) не мо́жет быть!; **what CAN he want?** что же ему́ ну́жно?

5 (*expressing possibility, suggestion*): **he could be in the library** он, мо́жет быть *or* возмо́жно, в библиоте́ке; **she could have been delayed** возмо́жно, что её задержа́ли

Canada ['kænədə] *n* Кана́да

canal [kə'næl] *n* кана́л

canary [kə'nɛərɪ] *n* канаре́йка

cancel ['kænsəl] *vt* отменя́ть (*perf* отмени́ть); (*contract, cheque, visa*) аннули́ровать (*impf/perf*); **cancellation** [kænsə'leɪʃən] *n* (*see vb*) отме́на; аннули́рование
cancer ['kænsə^r] *n* (*Med*) рак; **Cancer** Рак
candidate ['kændɪdeɪt] *n* претенде́нт; (*in exam*) экзамену́емый(-ая) *m(f) adj*; (*Pol*) кандида́т
candle ['kændl] *n* свеча́; **candlestick** *n* подсве́чник
candy ['kændɪ] *n* (*US*) конфе́та
cane [keɪn] *n* (*Bot*) тростни́к; (*stick*) ро́зга ▷ *vt* (*Brit*) нака́зывать (*perf* наказа́ть) ро́згами
cannabis ['kænəbɪs] *n* (*drug*) гаши́ш
canned [kænd] *adj* (*fruit etc*) консерви́рованный
cannon ['kænən] (*pl* **cannon** *or* **cannons**) *n* пу́шка
cannot ['kænɔt] = **can not** *see* **can²**
canoe [kə'nu:] *n* кано́э *nt ind*
canon ['kænən] *n* (*Rel*) кано́ник
can't [kænt] = **can not**
canteen [kæn'ti:n] *n* (*in school etc*) столо́вая *f adj*
canter ['kæntə^r] *vi* галопи́ровать (*impf*)
canvas ['kænvəs] *n* (*also Art*) холст; (*for tents*) брезе́нт; (*Naut*) паруси́на ▷ *adj* паруси́новый
canyon ['kænjən] *n* каньо́н
cap [kæp] *n* ке́пка; (*of uniform*) фура́жка; (*of pen*) колпачо́к; (*of bottle*) кры́шка ▷ *vt* (*outdo*) превосходи́ть (*perf* превзойти́)
capability [keɪpə'bɪlɪtɪ] *n* спосо́бность *f*
capable ['keɪpəbl] *adj* (*person*) спосо́бный; **capable of sth/doing** спосо́бный на что-н/+*infin*
capacity [kə'pæsɪtɪ] *n* ёмкость *f*; (*of ship, theatre etc*) вмести́тельность *f*; (*of person: capability*) спосо́бность *f*; (*: role*) роль *f*
cape [keɪp] *n* (*Geo*) мыс; (*cloak*) плащ
capital ['kæpɪtl] *n* (*also* **capital city**) столи́ца; (*money*) капита́л; (*also* **capital letter**) загла́вная бу́ква; **capitalism** *n* капитали́зм; **capitalist** *adj* капиталисти́ческий ▷ *n* капитали́ст; **capital punishment** *n* сме́ртная казнь *f*
Capricorn ['kæprɪkɔ:n] *n* Козеро́г
capsule ['kæpsju:l] *n* ка́псула
captain ['kæptɪn] *n* команди́р; (*of team, in army*) капита́н
caption ['kæpʃən] *n* по́дпись *f*
captivity [kæp'tɪvɪtɪ] *n* плен
capture ['kæptʃə^r] *vt* захва́тывать (*perf* захвати́ть); (*animal*) лови́ть (*perf* пойма́ть); (*attention*) прико́вывать (*perf* прикова́ть) ▷ *n* (*of person, town*) захва́т; (*of animal*) по́имка
car [kɑ:^r] *n* автомоби́ль *m*, маши́на; (*Rail*) ваго́н
caramel ['kærəməl] *n* (*sweet*) караме́ль *f*
carat ['kærət] *n* кара́т
caravan ['kærəvæn] *n* (*Brit*) жило́й автоприце́п; **caravan site** *n* (*Brit*) *площа́дка для стоя́нки жилы́х автоприце́пов*
carbohydrate [kɑ:bəu'haɪdreɪt] *n* углево́д
carbon ['kɑ:bən] *n* углеро́д; **carbon footprint** *показа́тель эми́ссии парнико́вых га́зов*; **carbon dioxide** [-daɪ'ɔksaɪd] *n* двуо́кись *f* углеро́да

CAR BOOT SALE

Car boot sale — буква́льно "прода́жа с бага́жника". Э́тим поня́тием обознача́ется прода́жа подéржанных веще́й. Това́ры выставля́ются в бага́жниках маши́н и́ли на стола́х. Прода́жи прово́дятся на автостоя́нках, в поля́х и́ли любы́х други́х откры́тых простра́нствах.

card [kɑ:d] *n* карто́н; (*also* **playing card**) игра́льная) ка́рта; (*also* **greetings card**) откры́тка; (*also* **visiting card, business card**) визи́тная ка́рточка; **cardboard** *n* карто́н
cardigan ['kɑ:dɪgən] *n* жаке́т (*вя́заный*)
cardinal ['kɑ:dɪnl] *adj* (*importance, principle*) кардина́льный; (*number*) коли́чественный ▷ *n* кардина́л
care [kɛəʳ] *n* (*worry*) забо́та; (*of patient*) ухо́д; (*attention*) внима́ние ▷ *vi*: **to care about** люби́ть (*impf*); **in sb's care** на чьём-н попече́нии; **to take care (to do)** позабо́титься (*perf*) (*+infin*); **to take care of** забо́титься (*perf* позабо́титься) о *+prp*; (*problem*) занима́ться (*perf* заня́ться) *+instr*; **care of** для переда́чи *+dat*; **I don't care** мне всё равно́; **I couldn't care less** мне наплева́ть; **care for** *vt fus* забо́титься (*perf* позабо́титься) о *+prp*; **he cares for her** (*like*) он неравноду́шен к ней
career [kə'rɪəʳ] *n* карье́ра
carefree ['kɛəfri:] *adj* беззабо́тный
careful ['kɛəful] *adj* осторо́жный; (*thorough*) тща́тельный; **(be) careful!** осторо́жно!, береги́сь!; **carefully** ['kɛəfəlɪ] *adv* (*see adj*) осторо́жно; тща́тельно
careless ['kɛəlɪs] *adj* невнима́тельный; (*casual*) небре́жный; (*untroubled*) беззабо́тный
caretaker ['kɛəteɪkəʳ] *n* завхо́з
cargo ['kɑ:gəu] (*pl* **cargoes**) *n* груз
car hire *n* (*Brit*) прока́т автомоби́лей
Caribbean [kærɪ'bi:ən] *n*: **the Caribbean (Sea)** Кари́бское мо́ре
caring ['kɛərɪŋ] *adj* забо́тливый
carnation [kɑ:'neɪʃən] *n* гвозди́ка
carnival ['kɑ:nɪvl] *n* карнава́л; (*US*: *funfair*) аттракцио́нный городо́к
carol ['kærəl] *n* (*also* **Christmas carol**) рожде́ственский гимн
car park *n* (*Brit*) автостоя́нка
carpenter ['kɑ:pɪntəʳ] *n* пло́тник
carpet ['kɑ:pɪt] *n* ковёр ▷ *vt* устила́ть (*perf* устла́ть) ковра́ми
carriage ['kærɪdʒ] *n* (*Brit*: *Rail*) (пассажи́рский) ваго́н; (*horse-drawn*) экипа́ж; (*costs*) сто́имость *f* перево́зки; **carriageway** *n* (*Brit*) прое́зжая часть *f* доро́ги
carrier ['kærɪəʳ] *n* (*Med*) носи́тель *m*; (*Comm*) транспортиро́вщик; **carrier bag** *n* (*Brit*) паке́т (*для поку́пок*)
carrot ['kærət] *n* (*Bot*) морко́вь *f*
carry ['kærɪ] *vt* (*take*) носи́ть/нести́ (*impf*); (*transport*) вози́ть/везти́ (*impf*); (*involve*) влечь (*perf* повле́чь) (за собо́й); (*Med*) переноси́ть (*impf*) ▷ *vi* (*sound*) передава́ться (*impf*); **to get carried away (by)** (*fig*) увлека́ться (*perf* увле́чься) (*+instr*); **carry on**

vi продолжа́ться (*perf* продо́лжиться) ▷ *vt* продолжа́ть (*perf* продо́лжить); **carry out** *vt* (*orders*) выполня́ть (*perf* вы́полнить); (*investigation*) проводи́ть (*perf* провести́)

cart [kɑ:t] *n* теле́га, пово́зка ▷ *vt* (*inf*) таска́ть/тащи́ть (*impf*)

carton ['kɑ:tən] *n* карто́нная коро́бка; (*container*) паке́т

cartoon [kɑ:'tu:n] *n* (*drawing*) карикату́ра; (*Brit*: *comic strip*) ко́микс; (*TV*) мультфи́льм

cartridge ['kɑ:trɪdʒ] *n* (*in gun*) ги́льза; (*of pen*) (черни́льный) балло́нчик

carve [kɑ:v] *vt* (*meat*) нареза́ть (*perf* наре́зать); (*wood, stone*) ре́зать (*impf*) по *+dat*

carving ['kɑ:vɪŋ] *n* резно́е изде́лие

car wash *n* мо́йка автомоби́лей

case [keɪs] *n* слу́чай; (*Med*: *patient*) больно́й(-а́я) *m(f) adj*; (*Law*) (суде́бное) де́ло; (*investigation*) рассле́дование; (*for spectacles*) футля́р; (*Brit*: *also* **suitcase**) чемода́н; (*of wine*) я́щик (*содержа́щий 12 буты́лок*); **in case (of)** в слу́чае (*+gen*); **in any case** во вся́ком слу́чае; **just in case** на во́лкий слу́чай

cash [kæʃ] *n* нали́чные *pl adj* (де́ньги) ▷ *vt*: **to cash a cheque** обнали́чивать (*perf* обнали́чить); **to pay (in) cash** плати́ть (*perf* заплати́ть) нали́чными; **cash on delivery** нало́женный платёж; **cash card** *n* банкома́тная ка́рточка; **cash desk** *n* (*Brit*) ка́сса; **cash dispenser** *n* (*Brit*) банкома́т; **cashier** [kæ'ʃɪə^r] *n* касси́р

cashmere ['kæʃmɪə^r] *n* кашеми́р

casino [kə'si:nəu] *n* казино́ *nt ind*

casserole ['kæsərəul] *n* рагу́ *nt ind*; (*also* **casserole dish**) ла́тка

cassette [kæ'sɛt] *n* кассе́та

cast [kɑ:st] (*pt, pp* **cast**) *vt* (*light, shadow, glance*) броса́ть (*perf* бро́сить); (*Fishing*) забра́сывать (*perf* забро́сить); (*doubts*) се́ять (*perf* посе́ять) ▷ *n* (*Theat*) соста́в (исполни́телей); (*Med*: *also* **plaster cast**) гипс; **to cast one's vote** отдава́ть (*perf* отда́ть) свой го́лос

caster sugar ['kɑ:stə-] *n* (*Brit*) са́харная пу́дра

castle ['kɑ:sl] *n* за́мок; (*fortified*) кре́пость *f*; (*Chess*) ладья́, тура́

casual ['kæʒjul] *adj* (*meeting*) случа́йный; (*attitude*) небре́жный; (*clothes*) повседне́вный

casualty ['kæʒjultɪ] *n* (*sb injured*) пострада́вший(-ая) *m(f) adj*; (*sb killed*) же́ртва; (*department*) травматоло́гия

cat [kæt] *n* (*pet*) ко́шка; (*tomcat*) кот; **big cats** (*Zool*) коша́чьи *pl adj*

catalogue ['kætəlɔg] (*US* **catalog**) *n* катало́г

catarrh [kə'tɑ:^r] *n* ката́р

catastrophe [kə'tæstrəfɪ] *n* катастро́фа

catch [kætʃ] (*pt, pp* **caught**) *vt* лови́ть (*perf* пойма́ть); (*bus etc*) сади́ться (*perf* сесть) на *+acc*; (*breath*: *in shock*) зата́ивать (*perf* затаи́ть); (: *after running*) передохну́ть (*perf*); (*attention*) привлека́ть (*perf* привле́чь); (*hear*) улáвливать (*perf* улови́ть); (*illness*) подхва́тывать (*perf* подхвати́ть) ▷ *vi* (*become trapped*) застрева́ть (*perf* застря́ть) ▷ *n* (*of fish*) уло́в; (*of ball*) захва́т; (*hidden problem*) подво́х; (*of lock*) защёлка; **to catch sight of** уви́деть (*perf*); **to catch fire** загора́ться (*perf* загоре́ться);

catch on *vi* приживáться (*perf* прижи́ться); **catch up** *vi* (*fig*) нагоня́ть (*perf* нагнáть) ▷ *vt* (*also* **catch up with**) догоня́ть (*perf* догнáть); **catching** *adj* (*Med*) зарáзный

category ['kætɪgərɪ] *n* категóрия

cater ['keɪtə[r]] *vi*: **to cater (for)** организовáть (*impf/perf*) питáние (для *+gen*); **cater for** *vt fus* (*Brit*: *needs, tastes*) удовлетворя́ть (*perf* удовлетвори́ть); (: *readers etc*) обслу́живать (*perf* обслужи́ть)

cathedral [kə'θi:drəl] *n* собóр

Catholic ['kæθəlɪk] *adj* католи́ческий ▷ *n* катóлик(-и́чка)

cattle ['kætl] *npl* скот *msg*

catwalk ['kætwɔ:k] *n* помóст (*для покáза мод*)

caught [kɔ:t] *pt, pp of* **catch**

cauliflower ['kɔlɪflauə[r]] *n* цветнáя капу́ста

cause [kɔ:z] *n* (*reason*) причи́на; (*aim*) дéло ▷ *vt* явля́ться (*perf* яви́ться) причи́ной *+gen*

caution ['kɔ:ʃən] *n* осторóжность *f*; (*warning*) предупреждéние, предостережéние ▷ *vt* предупреждáть (*perf* предупреди́ть)

cautious ['kɔ:ʃəs] *adj* осторóжный

cave [keɪv] *n* пещéра; **cave in** *vi* (*roof*) обвáливаться (*perf* обвали́ться)

caviar(e) ['kævɪɑ:[r]] *n* икрá

cavity ['kævɪtɪ] *n* (*in tooth*) дуплó

cc *abbr* (= *cubic centimetre*) куби́ческий сантимéтр

CCTV *n abbr* (= *closed-circuit television*) зáмкнутая телевизиóнная систéма

CD *n abbr* = **compact disc**; **CD player** проигрывáтель *m* для компáкт-ди́сков; **CD-ROM** *n* компáкт-диск ПЗУ

cease [si:s] *vi* прекращáться (*perf* прекрати́ться); **cease-fire** *n* прекращéние огня́

cedar ['si:də[r]] *n* кедр

ceiling ['si:lɪŋ] *n* (*also fig*) потолóк

celebrate ['sɛlɪbreɪt] *vt* прáздновать (*perf* отпрáздновать) ▷ *vi* весели́ться (*perf* повесели́ться); **to celebrate Mass** совершáть (*perf* соверши́ть) причáстие

celebration [sɛlɪ'breɪʃən] *n* (*event*) прáздник; (*of anniversary etc*) прáзднование

celebrity [sɪ'lɛbrɪtɪ] *n* знамени́тость *f*

celery ['sɛlərɪ] *n* сельдерéй

cell [sɛl] *n* (*in prison*) кáмера; (*Bio*) клéтка

cellar ['sɛlə[r]] *n* подвáл; (*also* **wine cellar**) ви́нный пóгреб

cello ['tʃɛləu] *n* виолончéль *f*

cellphone ['sɛlfəun] *n* моби́льный телефóн

Celsius ['sɛlsɪəs] *adj*: **30 degrees Celsius** 30 грáдусов по Цéльсию

Celtic ['kɛltɪk] *adj* кéльтский

cement [sə'mɛnt] *n* цемéнт

cemetery ['sɛmɪtrɪ] *n* клáдбище

censor ['sɛnsə[r]] *n* цéнзор ▷ *vt* подвергáть (*perf* подвéргнуть) цензу́ре; **censorship** *n* цензу́ра

census ['sɛnsəs] *n* пéрепись *f*

cent [sɛnt] *n* цент; *see also* **per cent**

centenary [sɛn'ti:nərɪ] *n* столéтие

center ['sɛntə[r]] *n, vb* (*US*) *see* **centre**

centigrade ['sɛntɪgreɪd] *adj*: **30 degrees centigrade** 30 грáдусов по Цéльсию

centimetre ['sɛntɪmi:tə[r]] (*US*

centimeter) *n* сантиме́тр
centipede ['sɛntɪpi:d] *n* многоно́жка
central ['sɛntrəl] *adj* центра́льный; **this flat is very central** э́та кварти́ра располо́жена бли́зко к це́нтру; **Central America** *n* Центра́льная Аме́рика; **central heating** *n* центра́льное отопле́ние
centre ['sɛntə^r] (*US* **center**) *n* центр ▷ *vt* (*Phot, Typ*) центри́ровать (*impf/perf*)
century ['sɛntjurɪ] *n* век
ceramic [sɪ'ræmɪk] *adj* керами́ческий
cereal ['si:rɪəl] *n*: **cereals** зерновы́е *pl adj*; (*also* **breakfast cereal**) хло́пья *pl* к за́втраку
ceremony ['sɛrɪmənɪ] *n* церемо́ния; (*behaviour*) церемо́нии *fpl*; **with ceremony** со все́ми форма́льностями
certain ['sə:tən] *adj* определённый; **I'm certain (that)** я уве́рен(, что); **certain days** определённые дни; **a certain pleasure** не́которое удово́льствие; **it's certain (that)** несомне́нно(, что); **in certain circumstances** при определённых обстоя́тельствах; **a certain Mr Smith** не́кий Ми́стер Смит; **for certain** наверняка́; **certainly** *adv* (*undoubtedly*) несомне́нно; (*of course*) коне́чно; **certainty** *n* (*assurance*) уве́ренность *f*; (*inevitability*) несомне́нность *f*
certificate [sə'tɪfɪkɪt] *n* свиде́тельство; (*doctor's etc*) спра́вка; (*diploma*) дипло́м
cf. *abbr* = **compare**
CFC *n abbr* (= *chlorofluorocarbon*) хлорфтороуглеро́д
chain [tʃeɪn] *n* цепь *f*; (*decorative, on bicycle*) цепо́чка; (*of shops, hotels*) сеть *f*; (*of events, ideas*) верени́ца ▷ *vt* (*also* **chain up**: *person*) прико́вывать (*perf* прикова́ть); (: *dog*) сажа́ть (*perf* посади́ть) на цепь; **a chain of mountains** го́рная цепь
chair [tʃɛə^r] *n* стул; (*also* **armchair**) кре́сло; (*of university*) ка́федра; (*also* **chairperson**) председа́тель *m* ▷ *vt* председа́тельствовать (*impf*) на +*prp*; **chairlift** *n* кана́тный подъёмник; **chairman** *irreg n* председа́тель *m*; (*Brit: Comm*) президе́нт
chalet ['ʃæleɪ] *n* шале́ *m ind*
chalk [tʃɔ:k] *n* мел
challenge ['tʃælɪndʒ] *n* вы́зов; (*task*) испыта́ние ▷ *vt* (*also Sport*) броса́ть (*perf* бро́сить) вы́зов +*dat*; (*authority, right etc*) оспа́ривать (*perf* оспо́рить); **to challenge sb to** вызыва́ть (*perf* вы́звать) кого́-н на +*acc*
challenging ['tʃælɪndʒɪŋ] *adj* (*tone, look*) вызыва́ющий; (*task*) тру́дный
chamber ['tʃeɪmbə^r] *n* ка́мера; (*Pol*) пала́та; **chamber of commerce** Торго́вая Пала́та
champagne [ʃæm'peɪn] *n* шампа́нское *nt adj*
champion ['tʃæmpɪən] *n* чемпио́н; (*of cause*) побо́рник(-ица); (*of person*) защи́тник(-ица); **championship** *n* (*contest*) чемпиона́т; (*title*) зва́ние чемпио́на
chance [tʃɑ:ns] *n* шанс; (*opportunity*) возмо́жность *f*; (*risk*) риск ▷ *vt* рискова́ть (*impf*) +*instr* ▷ *adj* случа́йный; **to take a chance** рискну́ть (*perf*); **by chance** случа́йно; **to leave to chance**

оставля́ть (*perf* оста́вить) на во́лю слу́чая

chancellor ['tʃɑ:nsələʳ] *n* (*Pol*) ка́нцлер; **Chancellor of the Exchequer** *n* (*Brit*) Ка́нцлер казначе́йства

Chancellor of the Exchequer

Chancellor of the Exchequer — ка́нцлер казначе́йства. В Великобрита́нии он выполня́ет фу́нкции мини́стра фина́нсов.

chandelier [ʃændə'lɪəʳ] *n* лю́стра

change [tʃeɪndʒ] *vt* меня́ть (*perf* поменя́ть); (*money*: *to other currency*) обме́нивать (*perf* обменя́ть); (: *for smaller currency*) разме́нивать (*perf* разменя́ть) ▷ *vi* (*alter*) меня́ться (*impf*), изменя́ться (*perf* измени́ться); (*one's clothes*) переодева́ться (*perf* переоде́ться); (*change trains etc*) де́лать (*perf* сде́лать) переса́дку ▷ *n* (*alteration*) измене́ние; (*difference*) переме́на; (*replacement*) сме́на; (*also* **small** *or* **loose change**) ме́лочь *f*; (*money returned*) сда́ча; **to change sb into** превраща́ть (*perf* преврати́ть) кого́-н в *+acc*; **to change one's mind** переду́мывать (*perf* переду́мать); **to change gear** переключа́ть (*perf* переключи́ть) ско́рость; **for a change** для разнообра́зия

channel ['tʃænl] *n* кана́л; (*Naut*) тра́сса ▷ *vt*: **to channel into** направля́ть (*perf* напра́вить) на *+acc* ▷ *adj*: **the Channel Islands** Норма́ндские острова́ *mpl*; **the (English) Channel** Ла-Ма́нш; **the Channel Tunnel** тунне́ль *m* под Ла-Ма́ншем

chant [tʃɑ:nt] *n* сканди́рование; (*Rel*) пе́ние

chaos ['keɪɔs] *n* ха́ос

chaotic [keɪ'ɔtɪk] *adj* хаоти́чный

chap [tʃæp] *n* (*Brit*: *inf*) па́рень *m*

chapel ['tʃæpl] *n* (*in church*) приде́л; (*in prison etc*) часо́вня; (*Brit*: *also* **non-conformist chapel**) протеста́нтская нонконформи́стская це́рковь

chapter ['tʃæptəʳ] *n* глава́; (*in life, history*) страни́ца

character ['kærɪktəʳ] *n* (*personality*) ли́чность *f*; (*nature*) хара́ктер; (*in novel, film*) персона́ж; (*letter, symbol*) знак; **characteristic** ['kærɪktə'rɪstɪk] *n* характе́рная черта́ ▷ *adj*: **characteristic (of)** характе́рный (для *+gen*)

charcoal ['tʃɑ:kəul] *n* (*fuel*) древе́сный у́голь *m*

charge [tʃɑ:dʒ] *n* (*fee*) пла́та; (*Law*) обвине́ние; (*responsibility*) отве́тственность *f*; (*Mil*) ата́ка ▷ *vi* атакова́ть (*impf/perf*) ▷ *vt* (*battery, gun*) заряжа́ть (*perf* заряди́ть); (*Law*): **to charge sb with** предъявля́ть (*perf* предъяви́ть) кому́-н обвине́ние в *+prp*; **charges** *npl* (*Comm*) де́нежный сбор *msg*; (*Tel*) телефо́нный тари́ф *msg*; **to reverse the charges** звони́ть (*perf* позвони́ть) по колле́кту; **to take charge of** (*child*) брать (*perf* взять) на попече́ние; (*company*) брать (*perf* взять) на себя́ руково́дство *+instr*; **to be in charge of** отвеча́ть (*impf*) за *+acc*; **who's in charge here?** кто здесь гла́вный?; **to charge (sb) (for)** проси́ть (*perf* попроси́ть) (у кого́-н) пла́ту (за *+acc*); **how much do you charge for**

...? ско́лько Вы про́сите за *+acc*?; **charge card** *n* креди́тная ка́рточка (*определённого магази́на*)

charity ['tʃærɪtɪ] *n* благотвори́тельная организа́ция; (*kindness*) милосе́рдие; (*money, gifts*) ми́лостыня

CHARITY SHOP

Charity shop — благотвори́тельный магази́н. В э́тих магази́нах рабо́тают волонтёры, продаю́щие поде́ржанную оде́жду, ста́рые кни́ги, предме́ты дома́шнего обихо́да. Получа́емая при́быль направля́ется в благотвори́тельные о́бщества, кото́рые э́ти магази́ны подде́рживают.

charm [tʃɑ:m] *n* очарова́ние, обая́ние; (*on bracelet etc*) брело́к ▷ *vt* очаро́вывать (*perf* очарова́ть); **charming** *adj* очарова́тельный

chart [tʃɑ:t] *n* гра́фик; (*of sea*) навигацио́нная ка́рта; (*of stars*) ка́рта звёздного не́ба ▷ *vt* наноси́ть (*perf* нанести́) на ка́рту; (*progress*) следи́ть (*impf*) за *+instr*; **charts** *npl* (*Mus*) хит-пара́д *msg*

charter ['tʃɑ:təʳ] *vt* фрахтова́ть (*perf* зафрахтова́ть) ▷ *n* ха́ртия; (*Comm*) уста́в; **chartered accountant** *n* (*Brit*) бухга́лтер вы́сшей квалифика́ции; **charter flight** *n* ча́ртерный рейс

chase [tʃeɪs] *vt* гоня́ться (*impf*) *or* гна́ться *impf* за (*+instr*) ▷ *n* пого́ня; **to chase away** *or* **off** прогоня́ть (*perf* прогна́ть)

chat [tʃæt] *vi* болта́ть (*perf* поболта́ть); (*Comput*) обща́ться (*perf* пообща́ться) в ча́те, писа́ть (*perf* написа́ть) в ча́те ▷ *n* бесе́да; (*Comput*) чат; **chat room** *n* (*Internet*) ча́т-ко́мната; **chat show** *n* (*Brit*) *шо́у с уча́стием знамени́тостей*

chatter ['tʃætəʳ] *n* (*gossip*) болтовня́

chauffeur ['ʃəufəʳ] *n* (персона́льный) шофёр

cheap [tʃi:p] *adj* дешёвый ▷ *adv* дёшево; **cheaply** *adv* дёшево

cheat [tʃi:t] *vi* (*at cards*) жу́льничать (*impf*); (*in exam*) спи́сывать (*perf* списа́ть) ▷ *vt*: **to cheat sb (out of £10)** надува́ть (*perf* наду́ть) кого́-н (на £10) ▷ *n* жу́лик

check [tʃɛk] *vt* проверя́ть (*perf* прове́рить); (*halt*) уде́рживать (*perf* удержа́ть); (*curb*) сде́рживать (*perf* сдержа́ть); (*US: items*) отмеча́ть (*perf* отме́тить) ▷ *n* (*inspection*) прове́рка; (*US: bill*) счёт; (: *Comm*) = **cheque**; (*pattern*) кле́тка ▷ *adj* кле́тчатый; **check in** *vi* регистри́роваться (*perf* зарегистри́роваться) ▷ *vt* (*luggage*) сдава́ть (*perf* сдать); **check out** *vi* выпи́сываться (*perf* выписаться); **check up** *vi*: **to check up on** наводи́ть (*perf* навести́) спра́вки о *+prp*; **checking account** *n* (*US*) теку́щий счёт; **checkout** *n* контро́ль *m*, ка́сса; **checkroom** *n* (*US*) ка́мера хране́ния; **checkup** *n* осмо́тр

cheek [tʃi:k] *n* щека́; (*impudence*) на́глость *f*; (*nerve*) де́рзость *f*; **cheeky** *adj* наха́льный, на́глый

cheer [tʃɪəʳ] *vt* приве́тствовать (*perf* поприве́тствовать) ▷ *vi* одобри́тельно восклица́ть (*impf*);

cheers *npl* (*of welcome*) привéтственные вóзгласы *mpl*; (*of approval*) одобри́тельные вóзгласы *mpl*; **cheers!** (за) Вáше здорóвье!; **cheer up** *vi* развесели́ться (*perf*), повеселéть (*perf*) ▷ *vt* развесели́ть (*perf*); **cheer up!** не грусти́те!; **cheerful** *adj* весёлый

cheese [tʃi:z] *n* сыр

chef [ʃɛf] *n* шеф-пóвар

chemical ['kɛmɪkl] *adj* хими́ческий ▷ *n* химикáт; (*in laboratory*) реакти́в

chemist ['kɛmɪst] *n* (*Brit*: *pharmacist*) фармацéвт; (*scientist*) хи́мик; **chemistry** *n* хи́мия

cheque [tʃɛk] *n* (*Brit*) чек; **chequebook** *n* (*Brit*) чéковая кни́жка; **cheque card** *n* (*Brit*) *кáрточка, подтверждáющая платёжеспосóбность владéльца*

cherry ['tʃɛrɪ] *n* черéшня; (*sour variety*) ви́шня

chess [tʃɛs] *n* шáхматы *pl*

chest [tʃɛst] *n* грудь *f*; (*box*) сундýк

chestnut ['tʃɛsnʌt] *n* каштáн

chest of drawers *n* комóд

chew [tʃu:] *vt* жевáть (*impf*); **chewing gum** *n* жевáтельная рези́нка

chic [ʃi:k] *adj* шикáрный, элегáнтный

chick [tʃɪk] *n* цыплёнок; (*of wild bird*) птенéц

chicken ['tʃɪkɪn] *n* кýрица; (*inf*: *coward*) труси́шка *m/f*; **chickenpox** *n* ветрянка

chief [tʃi:f] *n* (*of organization etc*) начáльник ▷ *adj* глáвный, основнóй; **chief executive** (*US* **chief executive officer**) *n* глáвный исполни́тельный дирéктор; **chiefly** *adv* глáвным óбразом

child [tʃaɪld] (*pl* **children**) *n* ребёнок; **do you have any children?** у Вас есть дéти?; **childbirth** *n* рóды *pl*; **childhood** *n* дéтство; **childish** *adj* (*games, attitude*) ребя́ческий; (*person*) ребя́чливый; **child minder** *n* (*Brit*) ня́ня; **children** ['tʃɪldrən] *npl of* **child**

Chile ['tʃɪlɪ] *n* Чи́ли *ind*

chill [tʃɪl] *n* (*Med*) простýда ▷ *vt* охлаждáть (*perf* охлади́ть); **to catch a chill** простужáться (*perf* простуди́ться)

chil(l)i ['tʃɪlɪ] (*US* **chili**) *n* крáсный стручкóвый пéрец

chilly ['tʃɪlɪ] *adj* холóдный

chimney ['tʃɪmnɪ] *n* (дымовáя) трубá

chimpanzee [tʃɪmpæn'zi:] *n* шимпанзé *m ind*

chin [tʃɪn] *n* подборóдок

China ['tʃaɪnə] *n* Китáй

china ['tʃaɪnə] *n* фарфóр

Chinese [tʃaɪ'ni:z] *adj* китáйский ▷ *n inv* китáец(-аянка)

chip [tʃɪp] *n* (*of wood*) щéпка; (*of stone*) оскóлок; (*also* **microchip**) микросхéма, чип ▷ *vt* отбивáть (*perf* отби́ть); **chips** *npl* (*Brit*) картóфель *msg* фри; (*US*: *also* **potato chips**) чи́псы *mpl*

chiropodist [kɪ'rɔpədɪst] *n* (*Brit*) мозóльный оперáтор *m/f*

chisel ['tʃɪzl] *n* (*for wood*) долотó; (*for stone*) зуби́ло

chives [tʃaɪvz] *npl* лук-рéзанец *msg*

chlorine ['klɔ:ri:n] *n* хлор

chocolate ['tʃɔklɪt] *n* шоколáд; (*sweet*) шоколáдная конфéта

choice [tʃɔɪs] *n* вы́бор

choir ['kwaɪə^r] *n* хор; (*area*) хóры *pl*

choke [tʃəuk] *vi* дави́ться (*perf* подави́ться); (*with smoke, anger*) задыха́ться (*perf* задохну́ться) ▷ *vt* (*strangle*) души́ть (задуши́ть *or* удуши́ть *perf*)
cholesterol [kəˈlɛstərɔl] *n* холестери́н; **high cholesterol** с высо́ким содержа́нием холестери́на
choose [tʃuːz] (*pt* **chose**, *pp* **chosen**) *vt* выбира́ть (*perf* вы́брать); **to choose to do** реша́ть (*perf* реши́ть) *+infin*
chop [tʃɔp] *vt* (*wood*) руби́ть (*perf* наруби́ть); (*also* **chop up**: *vegetables, meat*) ре́зать (наре́зать *or* поре́зать *perf*) ▷ *n* (*Culin*) ≈ отбивна́я (котле́та)
chord [kɔːd] *n* (*Mus*) акко́рд
chore [tʃɔːʳ] *n* (*burden*) повседне́вная обя́занность *f*; **household chores** дома́шние хло́поты
chorus [ˈkɔːrəs] *n* хор; (*refrain*) припе́в
chose [tʃəuz] *pt of* **choose**;
chosen [ˈtʃəuzn] *pp of* **choose**
Christ [kraɪst] *n* Христо́с
Christian [ˈkrɪstɪən] *adj* христиа́нский ▷ *n* христиани́н(-а́нка); **Christianity** [krɪstɪˈænɪtɪ] *n* христиа́нство; **Christian name** *n* и́мя *nt*
Christmas [ˈkrɪsməs] *n* Рождество́; **Happy** *or* **Merry Christmas!** Счастли́вого Рождества́!; **Christmas card** *n* рожде́ственская откры́тка

CHRISTMAS CRACKER

Christmas cracker — рожде́ственская хлопу́шка. В отли́чие от обы́чной хлопу́шки в неё завора́чиваются бума́жная коро́на, шу́тка и ма́ленький пода́рок. Механи́зм хлопу́шки приво́дится в де́йствие, е́сли дёрнуть за о́ба её конца́ одновреме́нно. Раздаётся хлопо́к и пода́рок выпада́ет.

Christmas Day *n* день *m* Рождества́
Christmas Eve *n* Соче́льник

CHRISTMAS PUDDING

Christmas pudding — рожде́ственский пу́динг. Кекс, пригото́вленный на пару́ и содержа́щий большо́е коли́чество сушёных фру́ктов.

Christmas tree *n* (рожде́ственская) ёлка
chrome [krəum] *n* хром
chronic [ˈkrɔnɪk] *adj* хрони́ческий
chubby [ˈtʃʌbɪ] *adj* пу́хлый
chuck [tʃʌk] *vt* (*inf*) швыря́ть (*perf* швырну́ть)
chuckle [ˈtʃʌkl] *vi* посме́иваться (*impf*)
chunk [tʃʌŋk] *n* (*of meat*) кусо́к
church [tʃəːtʃ] *n* це́рковь *f*; **churchyard** *n* пого́ст
CIA *n abbr* (*US*) (= *Central Intelligence Agency*) ЦРУ
CID *n abbr* (*Brit*) (= *Criminal Investigation Department*) уголо́вный ро́зыск
cider [ˈsaɪdəʳ] *n* сидр
cigar [sɪˈgɑːʳ] *n* сига́ра
cigarette [sɪgəˈrɛt] *n* сигаре́та
cinema [ˈsɪnəmə] *n* кинотеа́тр
cinnamon [ˈsɪnəmən] *n* кори́ца
circle [ˈsəːkl] *n* круг; (*Theat*) балко́н

circuit ['sə:kɪt] *n* (*Elec*) цепь *f*; (*tour*) турне́ *nt ind*; (*track*) трек
circular ['sə:kjulə[r]] *adj* (*plate, pond etc*) кру́глый ▷ *n* циркуля́р
circulate ['sə:kjuleɪt] *vi* циркули́ровать (*impf*) ▷ *vt* передава́ть (*perf* переда́ть)
circulation [sə:kju'leɪʃən] *n* (*Press*) тира́ж; (*Med*) кровообраще́ние; (*Comm*) обраще́ние; (*of air, traffic*) циркуля́ция
circumstances ['sə:kəmstənsɪz] *npl* обстоя́тельства *ntpl*
circus ['sə:kəs] *n* (*show*) цирк
cite [saɪt] *vt* цити́ровать (*perf* процити́ровать); (*Law*) вызыва́ть (*perf* вы́звать) в суд
citizen ['sɪtɪzn] *n* (*of country*) граждани́н(-а́нка); (*of town*) жи́тель(ница) *m(f)*; **citizenship** *n* гражда́нство
city ['sɪtɪ] *n* го́род; **the City** Си́ти *nt ind*

City

Э́тот райо́н Ло́ндона явля́ется его́ фина́нсовым це́нтром.

civic ['sɪvɪk] *adj* муниципа́льный; (*duties, pride*) гражда́нский
civil ['sɪvɪl] *adj* гражда́нский; (*authorities*) госуда́рственный; (*polite*) учти́вый; **civilian** [sɪ'vɪlɪən] *adj* (*life*) обще́ственный ▷ *n* ми́рный(-ая) жи́тель(ница) *m(f)*; **civilian casualties** же́ртвы среди́ ми́рного населе́ния
civilization [sɪvɪlaɪ'zeɪʃən] *n* цивилиза́ция
civilized ['sɪvɪlaɪzd] *adj* культу́рный; (*society*) цивилизо́ванный
civil: **civil servant** *n* госуда́рственный слу́жащий *m adj*; **Civil Service** *n* госуда́рственная слу́жба; **civil war** *n* гражда́нская война́
claim [kleɪm] *vt* (*responsibility*) брать (*perf* взять) на себя́; (*credit*) припи́сывать (*perf* приписа́ть) себе́; (*rights, inheritance*) претендова́ть (*impf*) *or* притяза́ть *impf* на (+*acc*) ▷ *vi* (*for insurance*) де́лать (*perf* сде́лать) страхову́ю зая́вку ▷ *n* (*assertion*) утвержде́ние; (*for compensation, pension*) зая́вка; (*to inheritance, land*) прете́нзия, притяза́ние; **to claim (that)** *or* **to be** утвержда́ть (*impf*), что
clamp [klæmp] *n* зажи́м ▷ *vt* зажима́ть (*perf* зажа́ть)
clan [klæn] *n* клан
clap [klæp] *vi* хло́пать (*impf*)
claret ['klærət] *n* бордо́ *nt ind*
clarify ['klærɪfaɪ] *vt* (*fig*) разъясня́ть (*perf* разъясни́ть)
clarinet [klærɪ'nɛt] *n* кларне́т
clarity ['klærɪtɪ] *n* (*fig*) я́сность *f*
clash [klæʃ] *n* столкнове́ние; (*of events etc*) совпаде́ние; (*of metal objects*) звя́канье ▷ *vi* ста́лкиваться (*perf* столкну́ться); (*colours*) не совмеща́ться (*impf*); (*events etc*) совпада́ть (*perf* совпа́сть) (по вре́мени); (*metal objects*) звя́кать (*impf*)
class [klɑ:s] *n* класс; (*lesson*) уро́к; (*of goods: type*) разря́д; (*: quality*) сорт ▷ *vt* классифици́ровать (*impf/perf*)
classic ['klæsɪk] *adj* класси́ческий ▷ *n* класси́ческое произведе́ние; **classical** *adj* класси́ческий
classification [klæsɪfɪ'keɪʃən] *n* классифика́ция; (*category*) разря́д
classroom ['klɑ:srum] *n* класс

clatter ['klætəʳ] *n* звя́канье; (*of hooves*) цо́канье
clause [klɔːz] *n* (*Law*) пункт
claustrophobic [klɔːstrə'fəubɪk] *adj*: **she is claustrophobic** она́ страда́ет клаустрофо́бией
claw [klɔː] *n* ко́готь *m*; (*of lobster*) клешня́
clay [kleɪ] *n* гли́на
clean [kliːn] *adj* чи́стый; (*edge, fracture*) ро́вный ▷ *vt* (*hands, face*) мыть (*perf* вы́мыть); (*car, cooker*) чи́стить (*perf* почи́стить); **clean out** *vt* (*tidy*) вычища́ть (*perf* вы́чистить); **clean up** *vt* (*room*) убира́ть (*perf* убра́ть); (*child*) мыть (*perf* помы́ть); **cleaner** *n* убо́рщик(-ица); (*substance*) мо́ющее сре́дство
cleanser [klɛnzəʳ] *n* очища́ющий лосьо́н
clear [klɪəʳ] *adj* я́сный; (*footprint, writing*) чёткий; (*glass, water*) прозра́чный; (*road*) свобо́дный; (*conscience, profit*) чи́стый ▷ *vt* (*space, room*) освобожда́ть (*perf* освободи́ть); (*suspect*) опра́вдывать (*perf* оправда́ть); (*fence etc*) брать (*perf* взять) ▷ *vi* (*sky*) проясня́ться (*perf* проясни́ться); (*fog, smoke*) рассе́иваться (*perf* рассе́яться) ▷ *adv*: **clear of** пода́льше от *+gen*; **to make it clear to sb that …** дава́ть (*perf* дать) кому́-н поня́ть, что …; **to clear the table** убира́ть (*perf* убра́ть) со стола́; **clear up** *vt* убира́ть (*perf* убра́ть); (*mystery, problem*) разреша́ть (*perf* разреши́ть); **clearance** *n* расчи́стка; (*permission*) разреше́ние; **clearing** *n* поля́на; **clearly** *adv* я́сно; (*obviously*) я́вно, очеви́дно
clergy ['kləːdʒɪ] *n* духове́нство
clerk [klɑːk, (*US*) kləːrk] *n* (*Brit*) клерк, делопроизводи́тель(ница) *m(f)*; (*US*: *sales person*) продаве́ц(-вщи́ца)
clever ['klɛvəʳ] *adj* у́мный
cliché ['kliːʃeɪ] *n* клише́ *nt ind*, штамп
click [klɪk] *vt* (*tongue, heels*) щёлкать (*perf* щёлкнуть) *+instr* ▷ *vi* (*device, switch*) щёлкать (*perf* щёлкнуть); **click on** *vi* (*Comput*) щёлкать (*perf* щёлкнуть)
client ['klaɪənt] *n* клие́нт
cliff [klɪf] *n* скала́, утёс
climate ['klaɪmɪt] *n* кли́мат; **climate change** *n* измене́ние кли́мата
climax ['klaɪmæks] *n* кульмина́ция
climb [klaɪm] *vi* поднима́ться (*perf* подня́ться); (*plant*) ползти́ (*impf*); (*plane*) набира́ть (*perf* набра́ть) высоту́ ▷ *vt* (*stairs*) взбира́ться (*perf* взобра́ться) по *+prp*; (*tree, hill*) взбира́ться (*perf* взобра́ться) *+acc* ▷ *n* подъём; **to climb over a wall** перелеза́ть (*perf* переле́зть) че́рез сте́ну; **climber** *n* альпини́ст(ка)
clinch [klɪntʃ] *vt* (*deal*) заключа́ть (*perf* заключи́ть); (*argument*) разреша́ть (*perf* разреши́ть)
cling [klɪŋ] (*pt, pp* **clung**) *vi* (*clothes*) прилега́ть (*impf*); **to cling to** вцепля́ться (*perf* вцепи́ться) в *+acc*; (*fig*) цепля́ться (*impf*) за *+acc*
clinic ['klɪnɪk] *n* кли́ника
clip [klɪp] *n* (*also* **paper clip**) скре́пка; (*for hair*) зако́лка; (*TV, Cinema*) клип ▷ *vt* (*fasten*) прикрепля́ть (*perf* прикрепи́ть); (*cut*) подстрига́ть (*perf* подстри́чь); **clipping** *n* (*Press*) вы́резка

cloak [kləuk] *n* (*cape*) плащ; **cloakroom** *n* гардероб; (*Brit*: *WC*) уборная *f adj*
clock [klɔk] *n* (*timepiece*) часы́ *pl*; **clockwise** *adv* по часово́й стре́лке; **clockwork** *adj* (*toy*) заводно́й
clone [kləun] *n* (*Bio*) клон
close[1] [kləus] *adj* бли́зкий; (*writing*) убо́ристый; (*contact, ties*) те́сный; (*watch, attention*) при́стальный; (*weather, room*) ду́шный ▷ *adv* бли́зко; **close to** (*near*) бли́зкий к +*dat*; **close to** *or* **on** (*almost*) бли́зко к +*dat*; **close by** *or* **at hand** ря́дом
close[2] [kləuz] *vt* закрыва́ть (*perf* закры́ть); (*finalize*) заключа́ть (*perf* заключи́ть); (*end*) заверша́ть (*perf* заверши́ть) ▷ *vi* закрыва́ться (*perf* закры́ться); (*end*) заверша́ться (*perf* заверши́ться) ▷ *n* коне́ц; **close down** *vt* закрыва́ть (*perf* закры́ть) ▷ *vi* закрыва́ться (*perf* закры́ться); **closed** *adj* закры́тый
closely ['kləuslɪ] *adv* при́стально; (*connected, related*) те́сно
closet ['klɔzɪt] *n* (*cupboard*) шкаф
closure ['kləuʒə^r] *n* (*of factory, road*) закры́тие
clot [klɔt] *n* сгу́сток; (*in vein*) тромб
cloth [klɔθ] *n* ткань *f*; (*for cleaning etc*) тря́пка
clothes [kləuðz] *npl* оде́жда *fsg*; **clothes peg** (*US* **clothes pin**) *n* прище́пка
clothing ['kləuðɪŋ] *n* = **clothes**
cloud [klaud] *n* о́блако; **cloudy** *adj* (*sky*) о́блачный; (*liquid*) му́тный
clove [kləuv] *n* гвозди́ка; **clove of garlic** до́лька чеснока́
clown [klaun] *n* кло́ун
club [klʌb] *n* клуб; (*weapon*) дуби́нка; (*also* **golf club**) клю́шка; **clubs** *npl* (*Cards*) тре́фы *fpl*
clue [klu:] *n* ключ; (*for police*) ули́ка; **I haven't a clue** (я) поня́тия не име́ю
clump [klʌmp] *n* за́росли *fpl*
clumsy ['klʌmzɪ] *adj* неуклю́жий; (*object*) неудо́бный
clung [klʌŋ] *pt, pp of* **cling**
cluster ['klʌstə^r] *n* скопле́ние
clutch [klʌtʃ] *n* хва́тка; (*Aut*) сцепле́ние ▷ *vt* сжима́ть (*perf* сжать)
cm *abbr* (= *centimetre*) см (= *сантиме́тр*)
Co *abbr* = **company**; **county**
coach [kəutʃ] *n* (*bus*) авто́бус; (*horse-drawn*) экипа́ж; (*of train*) ваго́н; (*Sport*) тре́нер; (*Scol*) репети́тор ▷ *vt* (*Sport*) тренирова́ть (*perf* натренирова́ть); (*Scol*): **to coach sb for** гото́вить (*perf* подгото́вить) кого́-н к +*dat*
coal [kəul] *n* у́голь *m*
coalition [kəuə'lɪʃən] *n* коали́ция
coarse [kɔ:s] *adj* гру́бый
coast [kəust] *n* бе́рег; (*area*) побере́жье; **coastal** *adj* прибре́жный; **coastguard** *n* офице́р берегово́й слу́жбы; **coastline** *n* берегова́я ли́ния
coat [kəut] *n* пальто́ *nt ind*; (*on animal*: *fur*) мех; (: *wool*) шерсть *f*; (*of paint*) слой ▷ *vt* покрыва́ть (*perf* покры́ть); **coat hanger** *n* ве́шалка
cobweb ['kɔbwɛb] *n* паути́на
cocaine [kə'keɪn] *n* кокаи́н
cock [kɔk] *n* пету́х ▷ *vt* (*gun*) взводи́ть (*perf* взвести́); **cockerel** ['kɔkərl] *n* пету́х

Cockney ['kɔknɪ] *n* кóкни

> **COCKNEY**
>
> Так назывáют вы́ходцев из востóчного райóна Лóндона. Они́ говоря́т на осóбом диалéкте англи́йского языкá. Кóкни тáкже обозначáет э́тот диалéкт.

cockpit ['kɔkpɪt] *n* каби́на
cockroach ['kɔkrəutʃ] *n* таракáн
cocktail ['kɔkteɪl] *n* коктéйль *m*; (*with fruit, prawns*) салáт
cocoa ['kəukəu] *n* какáо *nt ind*
coconut ['kəukənʌt] *n* кокóсовый орéх; (*flesh*) кокóс
COD *abbr* = **cash on delivery**; (*US*) (= *collect on delivery*) налóженный платёж
cod [kɔd] *n* трескá *f no pl*
code [kəud] *n* код; (*of behaviour*) кóдекс; **post code** почтóвый и́ндекс
coffee ['kɔfɪ] *n* кóфе *m ind*; **coffee table** *n* кофéйный стóлик
coffin ['kɔfɪn] *n* гроб
cognac ['kɔnjæk] *n* конья́к
coherent [kəu'hɪərənt] *adj* свя́зный, стрóйный; **she was very coherent** её речь былá óчень свя́зной
coil [kɔɪl] *n* motóк ▷ *vt* смáтывать (*perf* смотáть)
coin [kɔɪn] *n* монéта ▷ *vt* приду́мывать (*perf* приду́мать)
coincide [kəuɪn'saɪd] *vi* совпадáть (*perf* совпáсть); **coincidence** [kəu'ɪnsɪdəns] *n* совпадéние
coke [kəuk] *n* кокс
colander ['kɔləndə^r] *n* дуршлáг
cold [kəuld] *adj* холóдный ▷ *n* хóлод; (*Med*) простýда; **it's cold** хóлодно; **I am** *or* **feel cold** мне хóлодно; **to catch cold** *or* **a cold** простужáться (*perf* простуди́ться); **in cold blood** хладнокрóвно; **cold sore** *n* лихорáдка (*на губé и́ли носý*)
colic ['kɔlɪk] *n* кóлики *pl*
collapse [kə'læps] *vi* (*building, system, plans*) рýшиться (*perf* рýхнуть); (*table etc*) склáдываться (*perf* сложи́ться); (*company*) разоря́ться (*perf* разори́ться); (*government*) развáливаться (*perf* развали́ться); (*Med: person*) свали́ться (*perf*) ▷ *n* (*of building*) обвáл; (*of system, plans*) крушéние; (*of company*) разорéние; (*of government*) падéние; (*Med*) упáдок сил, коллáпс
collar ['kɔlə^r] *n* воротни́к; (*for dog etc*) ошéйник; **collarbone** *n* ключи́ца
colleague ['kɔli:g] *n* коллéга *m/f*
collect [kə'lɛkt] *vt* собирáть (*perf* собрáть); (*stamps etc*) коллекциони́ровать (*impf*); (*Brit: fetch*) забирáть (*perf* забрáть); (*debts etc*) взы́скивать (*perf* взыскáть) ▷ *vi* (*crowd*) собирáться (*perf* собрáться); **to call collect** (*US*) звони́ть (*impf*) по коллéкту; **collection** [kə'lɛkʃən] *n* (*of stamps etc*) коллéкция; (*for charity, also Rel*) пожéртвования *ntpl*; (*of mail*) вы́емка; **collective** *adj* коллекти́вный; **collector** *n* (*of stamps etc*) коллекционéр; (*of taxes etc*) сбóрщик
college ['kɔlɪdʒ] *n* учи́лище; (*of university*) кóлледж; (*of technology etc*) институ́т
collision [kə'lɪʒən] *n* столкновéние
colon ['kəulən] *n* (*Ling*)

двоето́чие; (*Anat*) пряма́я кишка́
colonel ['kə:nl] *n* полко́вник
colony ['kɔlənɪ] *n* коло́ния
colour ['kʌlə^r] (*US* **color**) *n* цвет ▷ *vt* раскра́шивать (*perf* раскра́сить); (*dye*) кра́сить (*perf* покра́сить); (*fig*: *opinion*) окра́шивать (*perf* окра́сить) ▷ *vi* красне́ть (*perf* покрасне́ть); **skin colour** цвет ко́жи; **in colour** в цве́те; **colour in** *vt* раскра́шивать (*perf* раскра́сить); **coloured** *adj* цветно́й; **colour film** *n* цветна́я плёнка; **colourful** *adj* кра́сочный; (*character*) я́ркий; **colouring** *n* (*of skin*) цвет лица́; (*in food*) краси́тель *m*; **colour television** *n* цветно́й телеви́зор
column ['kɔləm] *n* коло́нна; (*of smoke*) столб; (*Press*) ру́брика
coma ['kəumə] *n*: **to be in a coma** находи́ться (*impf*) в ко́ме
comb [kəum] *n* расчёска; (*ornamental*) гре́бень *m* ▷ *vt* расчёсывать (*perf* расчеса́ть); (*fig*) прочёсывать (*perf* прочеса́ть)
combat [kɔm'bæt] *n* бой; (*battle*) би́тва ▷ *vt* боро́ться (*impf*) про́тив *+gen*
combination [kɔmbɪ'neɪʃən] *n* сочета́ние, комбина́ция; (*code*) код
combine [kəm'baɪn] *vt* комбини́ровать (*perf* скомбини́ровать) ▷ *vi* (*groups*) объединя́ться (*perf* объедини́ться)

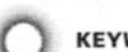 **KEYWORD**

come [kʌm] (*pt* **came**, *pp* **come**) *vi* **1** (*move towards*: *on foot*) подходи́ть (*perf* подойти́); (: *by transport*) подъезжа́ть (*perf* подъе́хать); **to come running** подбега́ть (*perf* подбежа́ть)
2 (*arrive*: *on foot*) приходи́ть (*perf* прийти́); (: *by transport*) приезжа́ть (*perf* прие́хать); **he came running to tell us** он прибежа́л, сказа́ть нам; **are you coming to my party?** Вы придёте ко мне на вечери́нку?; **I've only come for an hour** я зашёл то́лько на час
3 (*reach*) доходи́ть (*perf* дойти́) до *+gen*; **to come to** (*power, decision*) приходи́ть (*perf* прийти́) к *+dat*
4 (*occur*): **an idea came to me** мне в го́лову пришла́ иде́я
5 (*be, become*): **to come into being** возника́ть (*perf* возни́кнуть); **to come loose** отходи́ть (*perf* отойти́); **I've come to like him** он стал мне нра́виться
come about *vi*: **how did it come about?** каки́м о́бразом э́то произошло́?, как э́то получи́лось?; **it came about through ...** э́то получи́лось из-за *+gen* ...
come across *vt fus* ната́лкиваться (*perf* натолкну́ться) на *+acc*
come away *vi* уходи́ть (*perf* уйти́); (*come off*) отходи́ть (*perf* отойти́)
come back *vi* возвраща́ться (*perf* возврати́ться), верну́ться (*perf*)
come by *vt fus* достава́ть (*perf* доста́ть)
come down *vi* (*price*) понижа́ться (*perf* пони́зиться); **the tree came down in the storm** де́рево снесло́ бу́рей; **the building will have to come down soon** зда́ние должны́ ско́ро снести́
come forward *vi* (*volunteer*)

вызыва́ться (*perf* вы́зваться)
come from *vt fus*: **she comes from India** она́ из И́ндии
come in *vi* (*person*) входи́ть (*perf* войти́); **to come in on** (*deal*) вступа́ть (*perf* вступи́ть) в *+acc*; **where does he come in?** в чём его́ роль?
come in for *vt fus* подверга́ться (*perf* подве́ргнуться) *+dat*
come into *vt fus* (*fashion*) входи́ть (*perf* войти́) в *+acc*; (*money*) насле́довать (*perf* унасле́довать)
come off *vi* (*button*) отрыва́ться (*perf* оторва́ться); (*handle*) отла́мываться (*perf* отлома́ться); (*can be removed*) снима́ться (*impf*); (*attempt*) удава́ться (*perf* уда́ться)
come on *vi* (*pupil*) де́лать (*perf* сде́лать) успе́хи; (*work*) продвига́ться (*perf* продви́нуться); (*lights etc*) включа́ться (*perf* включи́ться); **come on!** ну!, дава́йте!
come out *vi* выходи́ть (*perf* вы́йти); (*stain*) сходи́ть (*perf* сойти́)
come round *vi* очну́ться (*perf*), приходи́ть (*perf* прийти́) в себя́
come to *vi* = **come round**
come up *vi* (*sun*) всходи́ть (*perf* взойти́); (*event*) приближа́ться (*perf* прибли́зиться); (*questions*) возника́ть (*perf* возни́кнуть); **something important has come up** случи́лось что-то ва́жное
come up against *vt fus* ста́лкиваться (*perf* столкну́ться) с *+instr*
come up with *vt fus* (*idea, solution*) предлага́ть (*perf* предложи́ть)
come upon *vt fus*ната́лкиваться (*perf* натолкну́ться) на *+acc*

comeback ['kʌmbæk] *n*: **to make a comeback** (*actor etc*) обрета́ть (*perf* обрести́) но́вую популя́рность
comedian [kə'mi:dɪən] *n* ко́мик
comedy ['kɔmɪdɪ] *n* коме́дия
comet ['kɔmɪt] *n* коме́та
comfort ['kʌmfət] *n* комфо́рт; (*relief*) утеше́ние ▷ *vt* утеша́ть (*perf* уте́шить); **comforts** *npl* (*luxuries*) удо́бства *ntpl*; **comfortable** *adj* комфорта́бельный, удо́бный; **to be comfortable** (*physically*) чу́вствовать (*impf*) себя́ удо́бно; (*financially*) жить (*impf*) в доста́тке; (*patient*) чу́вствовать (*impf*) себя́ норма́льно
comic ['kɔmɪk] *adj* коми́ческий, смешно́й ▷ *n* (*comedian*) ко́мик; (*Brit*: *magazine*) ко́микс
comma ['kɔmə] *n* запята́я *f adj*
command [kə'mɑ:nd] *n* кома́нда; (*control*) контро́ль *m*; (*mastery*) владе́ние ▷ *vt* (*Mil*) кома́ндовать (*impf*) *+instr*
commemorate [kə'mɛməreɪt] *vt* (*with statue etc*) увекове́чивать (*perf* увекове́чить); (*with event etc*) отмеча́ть (*perf* отме́тить)
commence [kə'mɛns] *vt* приступа́ть (*perf* приступи́ть) к *+dat* ▷ *vi* начина́ться (*perf* нача́ться)
commend [kə'mɛnd] *vt* хвали́ть (*perf* похвали́ть); (*recommend*): **to commend sth to sb** рекомендова́ть (*perf* порекомендова́ть) что-н кому́-н
comment ['kɔmɛnt] *n* замеча́ние ▷ *vi*: **to comment (on)** комменти́ровать (*perf* прокомменти́ровать); **"no comment"** "возде́рживаюсь от коммента́риев"; **commentary**

['kɔməntərɪ] *n* (*Sport*) репорта́ж; **commentator** ['kɔmənteɪtə^r] *n* коммента́тор
commerce ['kɔmə:s] *n* комме́рция
commercial [kə'mə:ʃəl] *adj* комме́рческий ▷ *n* рекла́ма
commission [kə'mɪʃən] *n* зака́з; (*Comm*) комиссио́нные *pl adj*; (*committee*) коми́ссия ▷ *vt* зака́зывать (*perf* заказа́ть); **out of commission** неиспра́вный
commit [kə'mɪt] *vt* (*crime*) соверша́ть (*perf* соверши́ть); (*money*) выделя́ть (*perf* вы́делить); (*entrust*) вверя́ть (*perf* вве́рить); **to commit o.s.** принима́ть (*perf* приня́ть) на себя́ обяза́тельства; **to commit suicide** поко́нчить (*perf*) жизнь самоуби́йством; **commitment** *n* (*belief*) пре́данность *f*; (*obligation*) обяза́тельство
committee [kə'mɪtɪ] *n* комите́т
commodity [kə'mɔdɪtɪ] *n* това́р
common ['kɔmən] *adj* о́бщий; (*usual*) обы́чный; (*vulgar*) вульга́рный ▷ *npl*: **the Commons** (*also* **the House of Commons**: *Brit*) Пала́та *fsg* о́бщин; **to have sth in common (with sb)** име́ть (*impf*) что-н о́бщее (с кем-н); **it's common knowledge that** общеизве́стно, что; **to** *or* **for the common good** для всео́бщего бла́га; **commonly** *adv* обы́чно; **commonplace** *adj* обы́чный, обы́денный

Commons

House of Commons — Пала́та о́бщин. Одна́ из пала́т брита́нского парла́мента. В ней заседа́ет 650 вы́борных чле́нов парла́мента.

Commonwealth *n* (*Brit*): **the Commonwealth** Содру́жество
communal ['kɔmju:nl] *adj* (*shared*) о́бщий; (*flat*) коммуна́льный
commune ['kɔmju:n] *n* комму́на
communicate [kə'mju:nɪkeɪt] *vt* передава́ть (*perf* переда́ть) ▷ *vi*: **to communicate (with)** обща́ться (*impf*) (с +*instr*)
communication [kəmju:nɪ'keɪʃən] *n* коммуника́ция
communion [kə'mju:nɪən] *n* (*also* **Holy Communion**) Свято́е Прича́стие
communism ['kɔmjunɪzəm] *n* коммуни́зм
communist ['kɔmjunɪst] *adj* коммунисти́ческий ▷ *n* коммуни́ст(ка)
community [kə'mju:nɪtɪ] *n* обще́ственность *f*; (*within larger group*) о́бщина; **the business community** делов́ые круги́; **community centre** *n* ≈ обще́ственный центр

COMMUNITY SERVICE

Community service — трудова́я пови́нность. Для не́которых наруши́телей зако́на така́я фо́рма наказа́ния заменя́ет тюре́мное заключе́ние.

commuter [kə'mju:tə^r] *n* *челове́к, кото́рый е́здит на рабо́ту из при́города в го́род*
compact [kəm'pækt] *adj* компа́ктный; **compact disc** *n* компа́кт-диск
companion [kəm'pænjən] *n* спу́тник(-ица)

company ['kʌmpənɪ] *n* компа́ния; (*Theat*) тру́ппа; (*companionship*) компа́ния, о́бщество; **to keep sb company** составля́ть (*perf* соста́вить) кому́-н компа́нию

comparable ['kɔmpərəbl] *adj* (*size*) сопостави́мый

comparative [kəm'pærətɪv] *adj* (*also Ling*) сравни́тельный; **comparatively** *adv* сравни́тельно

compare [kəm'pɛəʳ] *vt*: **to compare sb/sth with** *or* **to** сра́внивать (*perf* сравни́ть) кого́-н/что-н с *+instr*; (*set side by side*) сопоставля́ть (*perf* сопоста́вить) кого́-н/что-н с *+instr* ▷ *vi*: **to compare (with)** соотноси́ться (*impf*) (с *+instr*)

comparison [kəm'pærɪsn] *n* (*see vt*) сравне́ние; сопоставле́ние; **in comparison (with)** по сравне́нию *or* в сравне́нии (с *+instr*)

compartment [kəm'pɑ:tmənt] *n* купе́ *nt ind*; (*section*) отделе́ние

compass ['kʌmpəs] *n* ко́мпас; **compasses** *npl* (*also* **pair of compasses**) ци́ркуль *msg*

compassion [kəm'pæʃən] *n* сострада́ние

compatible [kəm'pætɪbl] *adj* совмести́мый

compel [kəm'pɛl] *vt* вынужда́ть (*perf* вы́нудить); **compelling** *adj* (*argument*) убеди́тельный; (*reason*) настоя́тельный

compensate ['kɔmpənseɪt] *vt*: **to compensate sb for sth** компенси́ровать (*impf/perf*) кому́-н что-н ▷ *vi*: **to compensate for** (*distress, loss*) компенси́ровать (*impf/perf*)

compensation [kɔmpən'seɪʃən] *n* компенса́ция

compete [kəm'pi:t] *vi* (*in contest etc*) соревнова́ться (*impf*); **to compete (with)** (*companies*) конкури́ровать (*impf*) (с *+instr*); (*rivals*) сопе́рничать (*impf*) (с *+instr*)

competent ['kɔmpɪtənt] *adj* (*person*) компете́нтный

competition [kɔmpɪ'tɪʃən] *n* соревнова́ние; (*between firms*) конкуре́нция; (*between rivals*) сопе́рничество

competitive [kəm'pɛtɪtɪv] *adj* (*person*) честолюби́вый; (*price*) конкурентноспосо́бный

competitor [kəm'pɛtɪtəʳ] *n* (*rival*) сопе́рник, конкуре́нт; (*participant*) уча́стник(-ица) соревнова́ния

complacent [kəm'pleɪsnt] *adj* безразли́чие

complain [kəm'pleɪn] *vi*: **to complain (about)** жа́ловаться (*perf* пожа́ловаться) (на *+acc*); **complaint** *n* жа́лоба; **to make a complaint against** подава́ть (*perf* пода́ть) жа́лобу на *+acc*

complement ['kɔmplɪmənt] *vt* дополня́ть (*perf* допо́лнить)

complete [kəm'pli:t] *adj* по́лный; (*finished*) завершённый ▷ *vt* (*building, task*) заверша́ть (*perf* заверши́ть); (*set*) комплектова́ть (*perf* укомплектова́ть); (*form*) заполня́ть (*perf* запо́лнить); **completely** *adv* по́лностью, соверше́нно

completion [kəm'pli:ʃən] *n* (*of building, task*) заверше́ние

complex ['kɔmplɛks] *adj* сло́жный ▷ *n* ко́мплекс

complexion [kəm'plɛkʃən] *n* (*of face*) цвет лица́

compliance [kəm'plaɪəns] *n*

(*submission*) послуша́ние; **compliance with** сле́дование *+dat*
complicate [ˈkɔmplɪkeɪt] *vt* усложня́ть (*perf* усложни́ть); **complicated** *adj* сло́жный
complication [kɔmplɪˈkeɪʃən] *n* осложне́ние
compliment [*n* ˈkɔmplɪmənt, *vb* ˈkɔmplɪmɛnt] *n* компли́ме́нт, хвала́ ▷ *vt* хвали́ть (*perf* похвали́ть); **compliments** *npl* (*regards*) наилу́чшие пожела́ния *ntpl*; **to compliment sb, pay sb a compliment** де́лать (*perf* сде́лать) кому́-н компли́ме́нт; **complimentary** [kɔmplɪˈmɛntərɪ] *adj* (*remark*) ле́стный; (*ticket etc*) да́рственный
comply [kəmˈplaɪ] *vi*: **to comply (with)** подчиня́ться (*perf* подчини́ться) (*+dat*)
component [kəmˈpəunənt] *adj* составно́й ▷ *n* компоне́нт
compose [kəmˈpəuz] *vt* сочиня́ть (*perf* сочини́ть); **to be composed of** состоя́ть (*impf*) из *+gen*; **to compose o.s.** успока́иваться (*perf* успоко́иться); **composer** *n* компози́тор
composition [kɔmpəˈzɪʃən] *n* (*structure*) соста́в; (*essay*) сочине́ние; (*Mus*) компози́ция
composure [kəmˈpəuʒəʳ] *n* самооблада́ние
compound [ˈkɔmpaund] *n* (*Chem*) соедине́ние; (*Ling*) сло́жное сло́во; (*enclosure*) ко́мплекс
comprehension [kɔmprɪˈhɛnʃən] *n* понима́ние
comprehensive [kɔmprɪˈhɛnsɪv] *adj* исче́рпывающий ▷ *n* (*Brit*: *also* **comprehensive school**) общеобразова́тельная шко́ла

COMPREHENSIVE SCHOOL

Comprehensive school — общеобразова́тельная шко́ла. В Великобрита́нии э́то госуда́рственная шко́ла для дете́й в во́зрасте 11-18 лет.

comprise [kəmˈpraɪz] *vt* (*also* **be comprised of**) включа́ть (*impf*) в себя́, состоя́ть (*impf*) из *+gen*; (*constitute*) составля́ть (*perf* соста́вить)
compromise [ˈkɔmprəmaɪz] *n* компроми́сс ▷ *vt* компромети́ровать (*perf* скомпромети́ровать) ▷ *vi* идти́ (*perf* пойти́) на компроми́сс
compulsive [kəmˈpʌlsɪv] *adj* патологи́ческий; (*reading etc*) захва́тывающий
compulsory [kəmˈpʌlsərɪ] *adj* (*attendance*) обяза́тельный; (*redundancy*) принуди́тельный
computer [kəmˈpjuːtəʳ] *n* компью́тер; **computer game** *n* компью́терная игра́
computing [kəmˈpjuːtɪŋ] *n* (*as subject*) компью́терное де́ло
comrade [ˈkɔmrɪd] *n* това́рищ
con [kɔn] *vt* надува́ть (*perf* наду́ть) ▷ *n* (*trick*) обма́н, надува́тельство
conceal [kənˈsiːl] *vt* укрыва́ть (*perf* укры́ть); (*keep back*) скрыва́ть (*perf* скрыть)
concede [kənˈsiːd] *vt* признава́ть (*perf* призна́ть)
conceited [kənˈsiːtɪd] *adj* высокоме́рный
conceive [kənˈsiːv] *vt* (*idea*) заду́мывать (*perf* заду́мать) ▷ *vi* забере́менеть (*perf*)
concentrate [ˈkɔnsəntreɪt] *vi* сосредото́чиваться (*perf*

сосредото́читься), концентри́роваться (*perf* сконцентри́роваться) ▷ *vt*: **to concentrate (on)** (*energies*) сосредото́чивать (*perf* сосредото́чить) *or* концентри́ровать (сконцентри́ровать *perf*) (*+prp* на)

concentration [kɔnsən'treɪʃən] *n* сосредото́чение, концентра́ция; (*attention*) сосредото́ченность *f*; (*Chem*) концентра́ция

concept ['kɔnsɛpt] *n* поня́тие

concern [kən'sə:n] *n* (*affair*) де́ло; (*worry*) трево́га, озабо́ченность *f*; (*care*) уча́стие; (*Comm*) предприя́тие ▷ *vt* (*worry*) беспоко́ить (*impf*), трево́жить (*impf*); (*involve*) вовлека́ть (*perf* вовле́чь); **to be concerned (about)** беспоко́иться (*impf*) (о *+prp*); **concerning** *prep* относи́тельно *+gen*

concert ['kɔnsət] *n* конце́рт

concession [kən'sɛʃən] *n* (*compromise*) усту́пка; (*right*) конце́ссия; (*reduction*) льго́та

concise [kən'saɪs] *adj* кра́ткий

conclude [kən'klu:d] *vt* зака́нчивать (*perf* зако́нчить); (*treaty, deal etc*) заключа́ть (*perf* заключи́ть); (*decide*) приходи́ть (*perf* прийти́) к заключе́нию *or* вы́воду

conclusion [kən'klu:ʒən] *n* заключе́ние; (*of speech*) оконча́ние; (*of events*) заверше́ние

concrete ['kɔŋkri:t] *n* бето́н ▷ *adj* бето́нный; (*fig*) конкре́тный

concussion [kən'kʌʃən] *n* сотрясе́ние мо́зга

condemn [kən'dɛm] *vt* осужда́ть (*perf* осуди́ть); (*building*) бракова́ть (*perf* забракова́ть)

condensation [kɔndɛn'seɪʃən] *n* конденса́ция

condition [kən'dɪʃən] *n* состоя́ние; (*requirement*) усло́вие ▷ *vt* формирова́ть (*perf* сформирова́ть); (*hair, skin*) обраба́тывать (*perf* обрабо́тать); **conditions** *npl* (*circumstances*) усло́вия *ntpl*; **on condition that** при усло́вии, что; **conditional** *adj* усло́вный; **conditioner** *n* (*for hair*) бальза́м; (*for fabrics*) смягча́ющий раство́р

condom ['kɔndəm] *n* презервати́в

condone [kən'dəun] *vt* потво́рствовать (*impf*) *+dat*

conduct [*n* 'kɔndʌkt, *vb* kən'dʌkt] *n* (*of person*) поведе́ние ▷ *vt* (*survey etc*) проводи́ть (*perf* провести́); (*Mus*) дирижи́ровать (*impf*); (*Phys*) проводи́ть (*impf*); **to conduct o.s.** вести́ (*perf* повести́) себя́; **conductor** [kən'dʌktə[r]] *n* (*Mus*) дирижёр; (*US: Rail*) контролёр; (*on bus*) конду́ктор

cone [kəun] *n* ко́нус; (*also* **traffic cone**) *конусообра́зное доро́жное загражде́ние*; (*Bot*) ши́шка; (*ice-cream*) моро́женое *nt adj* (*тру́бочка*)

confectionery [kən'fɛkʃənə[r]] *n* конди́терские изде́лия *ntpl*

confer [kən'fə:[r]] *vi* совеща́ться (*impf*) ▷ *vt*: **to confer sth (on sb)** (*honour*) ока́зывать (*perf* оказа́ть) что-н (кому́-н); (*degree*) присужда́ть (*perf* присуди́ть) что-н (кому́-н)

conference ['kɔnfərəns] *n* конфере́нция

confess [kən'fɛs] *vt* (*guilt, ignorance*) признава́ть (*perf* призна́ть); (*sin*) испове́доваться (*perf* испове́даться) в *+prp* ▷ *vi* (*to crime*) признава́ться (*perf* призна́ться); **confession** [kən'fɛʃən] *n* призна́ние; (*Rel*) и́споведь *f*

confide [kən'faɪd] *vi*: **to confide in** доверя́ться (*perf* дове́риться) *+dat*

confidence ['kɔnfɪdns] *n* уве́ренность *f*; (*in self*) уве́ренность в себе́; **in confidence** конфиденциа́льно

confident ['kɔnfɪdənt] *adj* (*see n*) уве́ренный; уве́ренный в себе́

confidential [kɔnfɪ'dɛnʃəl] *adj* конфиденциа́льный; (*tone*) довери́тельный

confine [kən'faɪn] *vt* (*lock up*) запира́ть (*perf* запере́ть); (*limit*): **to confine (to)** ограни́чивать (*perf* ограни́чить) (*+instr*); **confined** *adj* закры́тый

confirm [kən'fə:m] *vt* подтвержда́ть (*perf* подтверди́ть); **confirmation** [kɔnfə'meɪʃən] *n* подтвержде́ние

conflict ['kɔnflɪkt] *n* конфли́кт; (*of interests*) столкнове́ние

conform [kən'fɔ:m] *vi*: **to conform (to)** подчиня́ться (*perf* подчини́ться) (*+dat*)

confront [kən'frʌnt] *vt* (*problems*) ста́лкиваться (*perf* столкну́ться) с *+instr*; (*enemy*) противостоя́ть (*impf*) *+dat*; **confrontation** [kɔnfrən'teɪʃən] *n* конфронта́ция

confuse [kən'fju:z] *vt* запу́тывать (*perf* запу́тать); (*mix up*) пу́тать (*perf* спу́тать); **confused** *adj* (*person*) озада́ченный

confusing [kən'fju:zɪŋ] *adj* запу́танный

confusion [kən'fju:ʒən] *n* (*perplexity*) замеша́тельство; (*mix-up*) пу́таница; (*disorder*) беспоря́док

congestion [kən'dʒɛstʃən] *n* (*on road*) перегру́женность *f*; (*in area*) перенаселённость *f*

congratulate [kən'grætjuleɪt] *vt*: **to congratulate sb (on)** поздравля́ть (*perf* поздра́вить) кого́-н (с *+instr*)

congratulations [kəngrætju'leɪʃənz] *npl* поздравле́ния *ntpl*; **congratulations (on)** (*from one person*) поздравля́ю (с *+instr*); (*from several people*) поздравля́ем (с *+instr*)

congregation [kɔŋgrɪ'geɪʃən] *n* прихожа́не *mpl*, прихо́д

congress ['kɔŋgrɛs] *n* конгре́сс; (*US*): **Congress** конгре́сс США; **congressman** *irreg n* (*US*) конгрессме́н

conjunction [kən'dʒʌŋkʃən] *n* (*Ling*) сою́з

conjure ['kʌndʒə^r] *vt* (*fig*) сообража́ть (*perf* сообрази́ть); **conjure up** *vt* (*memories*) пробужда́ть (*perf* пробуди́ть)

connect [kə'nɛkt] *vt* (*Elec*) подсоединя́ть (*perf* подсоедини́ть), подключа́ть (*perf* подключи́ть); (*fig*: *associate*) свя́зывать (*perf* связа́ть) ▷ *vi*: **to connect with** согласо́вываться (*perf* согласова́ться) по расписа́нию с *+instr*; **to connect sb/sth (to)** соединя́ть (*perf* соедини́ть) кого́-н/что-н (с *+instr*); **he is connected with ...** он свя́зан с *+instr ...*; **I am trying to connect you** (*Tel*) я пыта́юсь подключи́ть Вас; **connection** [kə'nɛkʃən] *n* связь *f*; (*train etc*) переса́дка

conquer ['kɔŋkə^r] *vt* (*Mil*) завоёвывать (*perf* завоева́ть);

(*overcome*) поборо́ть (*perf*)
conquest ['kɔŋkwɛst] *n* (*Mil*) завоева́ние
cons [kɔnz] *npl see* **convenience**; **pro**
conscience ['kɔnʃəns] *n* со́весть *f*
conscientious [kɔnʃɪ'ɛnʃəs] *adj* добросо́вестный
conscious ['kɔnʃəs] *adj* (*deliberate*) созна́тельный; (*aware*): **to be conscious of sth/that** сознава́ть (*impf*) что-н/, что; **the patient was conscious** пацие́нт находи́лся в созна́нии; **consciousness** *n* созна́ние; (*of group*) самосозна́ние
consecutive [kən'sɛkjutɪv] *adj*: **on three consecutive occasions** в трёх слу́чаях подря́д; **on three consecutive days** три дня подря́д
consensus [kən'sɛnsəs] *n* еди́ное мне́ние; **consensus (of opinion)** консе́нсус
consent [kən'sɛnt] *n* согла́сие
consequence ['kɔnsɪkwəns] *n* сле́дствие; **of consequence** (*significant*) значи́тельный; **it's of little consequence** э́то не име́ет большо́го значе́ния; **in consequence** (*consequently*) сле́довательно, вследствие э́того
consequently ['kɔnsɪkwəntlɪ] *adv* сле́довательно
conservation [kɔnsə'veɪʃən] *n* (*also* **nature conservation**) охра́на приро́ды, природоохра́на
conservative [kən'sə:vətɪv] *adj* консервати́вный; (*estimate*) скро́мный; (*Brit*: *Pol*): **Conservative** консервати́вный ▷ *n* (*Brit*): **Conservative** консерва́тор
conservatory [kən'sə:vətrɪ] *n* застеклённая вера́нда
conserve [kən'sə:v] *vt* сохраня́ть (*perf* сохрани́ть); (*energy*) сберега́ть (*perf* сбере́чь) ▷ *n* варе́нье
consider [kən'sɪdə^r] *vt* (*believe*) счита́ть (*perf* посчита́ть); (*study*) рассма́тривать (*perf* рассмотре́ть); (*take into account*) учи́тывать (*perf* уче́сть); (*regard*): **to consider that ...** полага́ть (*impf*) *or* счита́ть (*impf*), что ...; **to consider sth** (*think about*) ду́мать (*impf*) о чём-н; **considerable** *adj* значи́тельный; **considerably** *adv* значи́тельно; **considerate** *adj* (*person*) забо́тливый; (*action*) внима́тельный; **consideration** [kənsɪdə'reɪʃən] *n* рассмотре́ние, обду́мывание; (*factor*) соображе́ние; (*thoughtfulness*) внима́ние; **considering** *prep* учи́тывая *+acc*
consignment [kən'saɪnmənt] *n* (*Comm*) па́ртия
consist [kən'sɪst] *vi*: **to consist of** состоя́ть (*impf*) из *+gen*
consistency [kən'sɪstənsɪ] *n* после́довательность *f*; (*of yoghurt etc*) консисте́нция
consistent [kən'sɪstənt] *adj* после́довательный
consolation [kɔnsə'leɪʃən] *n* утеше́ние
console [kən'səul] *vt* утеша́ть (*perf* уте́шить)
consonant ['kɔnsənənt] *n* согла́сный *m adj*
conspicuous [kən'spɪkjuəs] *adj* заме́тный
conspiracy [kən'spɪrəsɪ] *n* за́говор
constable ['kʌnstəbl] (*Brit*: *also* **police constable**) *n* (участко́вый) полице́йский *m adj*
constant ['kɔnstənt] *adj* постоя́нный; (*fixed*) неизме́нный;

constantly *adv* постоя́нно
constipation [kɔnstɪ'peɪʃən] *n* запо́р
constituency [kən'stɪtjuənsɪ] *n* (*area*) избира́тельный о́круг
constitute ['kɔnstɪtju:t] *vt* (*represent*) явля́ться (*perf* яви́ться) *+instr*; (*make up*) составля́ть (*perf* соста́вить)
constitution [kɔnstɪ'tju:ʃən] *n* (*of country, person*) конститу́ция; (*of organization*) уста́в
constraint [kən'streɪnt] *n* (*restriction*) ограниче́ние
construct [kən'strʌkt] *vt* сооружа́ть (*perf* сооруди́ть); **construction** [kən'strʌkʃən] *n* (*of building etc*) сооруже́ние; (*structure*) констру́кция; **constructive** *adj* конструкти́вный
consul ['kɔnsl] *n* ко́нсул; **consulate** ['kɔnsjulɪt] *n* ко́нсульство
consult [kən'sʌlt] *vt* (*friend*) сове́товаться (*perf* посове́товаться) с *+instr*; (*book, map*) справля́ться (*perf* спра́виться) в *+prp*; **to consult sb (about)** (*expert*) консульти́роваться (*perf* проконсульти́роваться) с кем-н (о *+prp*); **consultant** *n* консульта́нт; (*Med*) врач-консульта́нт; **consultation** [kɔnsəl'teɪʃən] *n* (*Med*) консульта́ция; (*discussion*) совеща́ние
consume [kən'sju:m] *vt* потребля́ть (*perf* потреби́ть); **consumer** *n* потреби́тель *m*
consumption [kən'sʌmpʃən] *n* потребле́ние; (*amount*) расхо́д
cont. *abbr* (= *continued*); **cont. on** продолже́ние на *+prp*
contact ['kɔntækt] *n* (*communication*) конта́кт; (*touch*) соприкоснове́ние; (*person*) делово́й(-а́я) знако́мый(-ая) *m(f) adj* ▷ *vt* свя́зываться (*perf* связа́ться) с *+instr*; **contact lenses** *npl* конта́ктные ли́нзы *fpl*; **contactless** *adj* бесконта́ктный
contagious [kən'teɪdʒəs] *adj* зара́зный; (*fig*) зарази́тельный
contain [kən'teɪn] *vt* (*hold*) вмеща́ть (*perf* вмести́ть); (*include*) содержа́ть (*impf*); (*curb*) сде́рживать (*perf* сдержа́ть); **to contain o.s.** сде́рживаться (*perf* сдержа́ться); **container** *n* конте́йнер
contemplate ['kɔntəmpleɪt] *vt* (*consider*) размышля́ть (*impf*) о *+prp*; (*look at*) созерца́ть (*impf*)
contemporary [kən'tɛmpərərɪ] *adj* совреме́нный ▷ *n* совреме́нник(-ица)
contempt [kən'tɛmpt] *n* презре́ние; **contempt of court** оскорбле́ние суда́
contend [kən'tɛnd] *vt*: **to contend that** утвержда́ть (*impf*), что ▷ *vi*: **to contend with** (*problem etc*) боро́ться (*impf*) с *+instr*
content [*n* 'kɔntɛnt, *adj, vb* kən'tɛnt] *n* содержа́ние ▷ *adj* дово́льный ▷ *vt* (*satisfy*) удовлетворя́ть (*perf* удовлетвори́ть); **contents** *npl* (*of bottle etc*) содержи́мое *ntsg adj*; (*of book*) содержа́ние *ntsg*; **(table of) contents** оглавле́ние; **contented** *adj* дово́льный
contest [*n* 'kɔntɛst, *vb* kən'tɛst] *n* (*sport*) соревнова́ние; (*beauty*) ко́нкурс; (*for power etc*) борьба́ ▷ *vt* оспа́ривать (*perf* оспо́рить); (*election, competition*) боро́ться

(*impf*) на *+prp*; **contestant** [kən'tɛstənt] *n* участник(-ница)
context ['kɔntɛkst] *n* контекст
continent ['kɔntınənt] *n* континент, материк; **the Continent** (*Brit*) Европа (*кроме британских островов*)
continental [kɔntı'nɛntl] *adj* (*Brit*) европейский

- **CONTINENTAL BREAKFAST**
-
- **Continental breakfast** —
- европейский завтрак. В
- европейский завтрак входит
- хлеб, масло и джем. Его подают
- в гостиницах вместо
- традиционного завтрака из
- бекона и яичницы.

continental quilt *n* (*Brit*) стёганое одеяло
continual [kən'tınjuəl] *adj* непрерывный, постоянный; **continually** *adv* непрерывно, постоянно
continue [kən'tınju:] *vi* (*carry on*) продолжаться (*impf*); (*after interruption: talk*) продолжаться (*perf* продолжиться); (: *person*) продолжать (*perf* продолжить) ▷ *vt* продолжать (*perf* продолжить)
continuity [kɔntı'nju:ıtı] *n* преемственность *f*
continuous [kən'tınjuəs] *adj* непрерывный; (*line*) сплошной
contraception [kɔntrə'sɛpʃən] *n* предупреждение беременности
contraceptive [kɔntrə'sɛptıv] *n* противозачаточное средство, контрацептив
contract [*n* 'kɔntrækt, *vb* kən'trækt] *n* договор, контракт ▷ *vi* сжиматься (*perf* сжаться) ▷ *vt* (*Med*) заболевать (*perf* заболеть) *+instr*; **contractor** [kən'træktə[r]] *n* подрядчик
contradict [kɔntrə'dıkt] *vt* (*person*) возражать (*perf* возразить) *+dat*; (*statement*) возражать (*perf* возразить) на *+acc*; **contradiction** [kɔntrə'dıkʃən] *n* противоречие
contrary ['kɔntrərı] *adj* противоположный ▷ *n* противоположность *f*; **on the contrary** напротив, наоборот; **unless you hear to the contrary** если не будет других инструкций
contrast [*n* 'kɔntra:st, *vb* kən'tra:st] *n* контраст ▷ *vt* сопоставлять (*perf* сопоставить); **in contrast to** *or* **with** по контрасту с *+instr*
contribute [kən'trıbju:t] *vi* (*give*) делать (*perf* сделать) вклад ▷ *vt* (*money, an article*) вносить (*perf* внести); **to contribute to** (*to charity*) жертвовать (*perf* пожертвовать) на *+acc or* для *+gen*; (*to paper*) писать (*perf* написать) для *+gen*; (*to discussion*) вносить (*perf* внести) вклад в *+prp*; (*to problem*) усугублять (*perf* усугубить)
contribution [kɔntrı'bju:ʃən] *n* (*donation*) пожертвование, вклад; (*to debate, campaign*) вклад; (*to journal*) публикация
contributor [kən'trıbjutə[r]] *n* (*to appeal*) жертвователь *m*; (*to newspaper*) автор
control [kən'trəul] *vt* контролировать (*impf*) ▷ *n* (*of country, organization*) контроль *m*; (*of o.s.*) самообладание; **controls** *npl* (*of vehicle*) управление; (*on radio etc*) ручки *fpl* настройки; **to control o.s.** сохранять (*perf*

сохранить) самообладание; **to be in control of** контролировать (*impf*); **everything is under control** всё под контролем; **out of control** неуправляемый

controversial [kɔntrəˈvəːʃl] *adj* спорный; (*person, writer*) неоднозначный

controversy [ˈkɔntrəvəːsɪ] *n* дискуссия, спор

convenience [kənˈviːnɪəns] *n* удобство; **at your convenience** когда Вам будет удобно; **a flat with all modern conveniences** *or* (*Brit*) **all mod cons** квартира со всеми удобствами

convenient [kənˈviːnɪənt] *adj* удобный

convent [ˈkɔnvənt] *n* (*Rel*) (женский) монастырь *m*

convention [kənˈvɛnʃən] *n* (*custom*) условность *f*; (*conference*) конференция; (*agreement*) конвенция; **conventional** *adj* традиционный; (*methods, weapons*) обычный

conversation [kɔnvəˈseɪʃən] *n* беседа, разговор; **to have a conversation with sb** разговаривать (*impf*) *or* беседовать (побеседовать *perf*) с кем-н

conversely [kɔnˈvəːslɪ] *adv* наоборот

conversion [kənˈvəːʃən] *n* обращение; (*of weights*) перевод; (*of substances*) превращение

convert [*vb* kənˈvəːt, *n* ˈkɔnvəːt] *vt* (*person*) обращать (*perf* обратить) ▷ *n* новообращённый(-ая)*m(f) adj*; **to convert sth into** превращать (*perf* превратить) что-н в *+acc*

convey [kənˈveɪ] *vt* передавать (*perf* передать); (*cargo, person*) перевозить (*perf* перевезти)

convict [*vb* kənˈvɪkt, *n* ˈkɔnvɪkt] *vt* осуждать (*perf* осудить) ▷ *n* каторжник; **conviction** [kənˈvɪkʃən] *n* (*belief*) убеждение; (*certainty*) убеждённость *f*; (*Law*) осуждение; (*: previous*) судимость *f*

convince [kənˈvɪns] *vt* (*assure*) уверять (*perf* уверить); (*persuade*) убеждать (*perf* убедить); **convinced** *adj*: **convinced of/that** убеждённый в *+prp*/, что

convincing [kənˈvɪnsɪŋ] *adj* убедительный

convoy [ˈkɔnvɔɪ] *n* (*of trucks*) колонна; (*of ships*) конвой

cook [kuk] *vt* готовить (*perf* приготовить) ▷ *vi* (*person*) готовить (*impf*); (*food*) готовиться (*impf*) ▷ *n* повар; **cooker** *n* плита; **cookery** *n* кулинария; **cookery book** *n* (*Brit*) поваренная *or* кулинарная книга; **cookie** *n* (*esp US*) печенье; **cooking** *n* готовка; **I like cooking** я люблю готовить

cool [kuːl] *adj* прохладный; (*dress, clothes*) лёгкий; (*person*: *calm*) невозмутимый; (*: hostile*) холодный; (*inf*: *great*) крутой ▷ *vi* (*water, air*) остывать (*perf* остыть); **cool!** (*inf*) здорово!

cooperate [kəuˈɔpəreɪt] *vi* (*collaborate*) сотрудничать (*impf*); (*assist*) содействовать (*impf*)

cooperation [kəuɔpəˈreɪʃən] *n* (*see vi*) кооперация, сотрудничество; содействие

cop [kɔp] *n* (*Brit*: *inf*) мент

cope [kəup] *vi*: **to cope with** справляться (*perf* справиться) с *+instr*

copper [ˈkɔpəʳ] *n* (*metal*) медь *f*

copy ['kɔpɪ] *n* (*duplicate*) ко́пия; (*of book etc*) экземпля́р ▷ *vt* копи́ровать (*perf* скопи́ровать); **copyright** *n* а́вторское пра́во, копира́йт
coral ['kɔrəl] *n* кора́лл
cord [kɔːd] *n* (*string*) верёвка; (*Elec*) шнур; (*fabric*) вельве́т
corduroy ['kɔːdərɔɪ] *n* вельве́т
core [kɔːʳ] *n* сердцеви́на; (*of problem*) суть *f* ▷ *vt* выреза́ть (*perf* вы́резать) сердцеви́ну *+gen*
coriander [kɔrɪ'ændəʳ] *n* (*spice*) ки́нза, кориа́ндр
cork [kɔːk] *n* про́бка; **corkscrew** *n* што́пор
corn [kɔːn] *n* (*Brit*) зерно́; (*US*: *maize*) кукуру́за; (*on foot*) мозо́ль *f*; **corn on the cob** поча́ток кукуру́зы
corner ['kɔːnəʳ] *n* у́гол; (*Sport*: *also* **corner kick**) углово́й *m adj* (уда́р)
cornflour ['kɔːnflauəʳ] *n* (*Brit*) кукуру́зная мука́
coronary ['kɔrənərɪ] *n* (*also* **coronary thrombosis**) корона́рный тромбо́з
coronation [kɔrə'neɪʃən] *n* corона́ция
coroner ['kɔrənəʳ] *n* (*Law*) ко́ронер (*судья́, рассле́дующий причи́ны сме́рти, происше́дшей при подозри́тельных обстоя́тельствах*)
corporal ['kɔːpərl] *adj*: **corporal punishment** теле́сное наказа́ние
corporate ['kɔːpərɪt] *adj* корпорацио́нный; (*ownership*) о́бщий; (*identity*) корпорати́вный
corporation [kɔːpə'reɪʃən] *n* (*Comm*) корпора́ция
corps [kɔːʳ] (*pl* **corps**) *n* (*also Mil*) ко́рпус
corpse [kɔːps] *n* труп
correct [kə'rɛkt] *adj* пра́вильный; (*proper*) соотве́тствующий ▷ *vt* исправля́ть (*perf* испра́вить); (*exam*) проверя́ть (*perf* прове́рить); **correction** [kə'rɛkʃən] *n* исправле́ние; (*mistake corrected*) попра́вка
correspond [kɔrɪs'pɔnd] *vi*: **to correspond (with)** (*write*) перепи́сываться (*impf*) (с *+instr*); (*tally*) согласо́вываться (*impf*) (с *+instr*); (*equate*): **to correspond (to)** соотве́тствовать (*impf*) (*+dat*); **correspondence** *n* (*letters*) перепи́ска; (: *in business*) корреспонде́нция; (*relationship*) соотноше́ние; **correspondent** *n* (*Press*) корреспонде́нт(ка)
corridor ['kɔrɪdɔːʳ] *n* коридо́р; (*in train*) прохо́д
corrupt [kə'rʌpt] *adj* прода́жный, коррумпи́рованный ▷ *vt* развраща́ть (*perf* разврати́ть); **corruption** [kə'rʌpʃən] *n* корру́пция, прода́жность *f*
cosmetic [kɔz'mɛtɪk] *n* (*usu pl*) косме́тика
cosmopolitan [kɔzmə'pɔlɪtn] *adj* (*place*) космополити́ческий
cost [kɔst] (*pt, pp* **cost**) *n* (*price*) сто́имость *f* ▷ *vt* сто́ить (*impf*) ▷ (*pt, pp* **costed**) (*find out cost of*) расчи́тывать (*perf* расчита́ть) сто́имость *+gen*; **costs** *npl* (*Comm*) расхо́ды *mpl*; (*Law*) суде́бные изде́ржки *fpl*; **how much does it cost?** ско́лько э́то сто́ит?; **to cost sb sth** (*time, job*) сто́ить (*impf*) кому́-н чего́-н; **at all costs** любо́й цено́й; **costly** *adj* (*expensive*) дорогостоя́щий; **cost of living** *n* сто́имость *f* жи́зни
costume ['kɔstjuːm] *n* костю́м; (*Brit*: *also* **swimming costume**)

купа́льник, купа́льный костю́м
cosy ['kəuzɪ] (*US* **cozy**) *adj* (*room, atmosphere*) ую́тный
cot [kɔt] *n* (*Brit*) де́тская крова́тка; (*US*: *camp bed*) ко́йка
cottage ['kɔtɪdʒ] *n* котте́дж
cotton ['kɔtn] *n* (*fabric*) хло́пок, хлопчатобума́жная ткань *f*; (*thread*) (шве́йная) ни́тка; **cotton wool** *n* (*Brit*) ва́та
couch [kautʃ] *n* тахта́, дива́н
cough [kɔf] *vi* ка́шлять (*impf*) ▷ *n* ка́шель *m*
could [kud] *pt of* **can²**; **couldn't** ['kudnt] = **could not**
council ['kaunsl] *n* сове́т; **city** *or* **town council** муниципалите́т, городско́й сове́т; **council house** *n* (*Brit*) *дом, принадлежа́щий муниципалите́ту*; **councillor** *n* член муниципалите́та; **council tax** *n* (*Brit*) муниципа́льный нало́г

COUNCIL ESTATE

Council estate — муниципа́льный жило́й микрорайо́н. Дома́ в таки́х райо́нах стро́ятся на сре́дства муниципалите́та. Типовы́е постро́йки включа́ют многоэта́жные дома́ и́ли ряд однoти́пных примыка́ющих друг к дру́гу домо́в с сада́ми.

counsel ['kaunsl] *n* (*advice*) сове́т; (*lawyer*) адвока́т ▷ *vt*: **to counsel sth/sb to do** сове́товать (*perf* посове́товать) что-н/кому́-н *+infin*; **counsellor** *n* (*advisor*) сове́тник; (*US*: *lawyer*) адвока́т
count [kaunt] *vt* счита́ть (*perf* посчита́ть); (*include*) счита́ть (*impf*) ▷ *vi* счита́ть (*perf* сосчита́ть); (*qualify*) счита́ться (*impf*); (*matter*) име́ть (*impf*) значе́ние ▷ *n* подсчёт; (*level*) у́ровень *m*; **count on** *vt fus* рассчи́тывать (*impf*) на *+acc*; **countdown** *n* обра́тный счёт
counter ['kauntə^r] *n* (*in shop, café*) прила́вок; (*in bank, post office*) сто́йка; (*in game*) фи́шка ▷ *vt* (*oppose*) опроверга́ть (*perf* опрове́ргнуть) ▷ *adv*: **counter to** в противове́с *+dat*
counterpart ['kauntəpɑːt] *n* (*of person*) колле́га *m/f*
countless ['kauntlɪs] *adj* несчётный, бесчи́сленный
country ['kʌntrɪ] *n* страна́; (*native land*) ро́дина; (*rural area*) дере́вня; **countryside** *n* дере́вня, се́льская ме́стность *f*
county ['kauntɪ] *n* гра́фство

COUNTY

В Великобрита́нии, Ирла́ндии и США **county** — администрати́вно-территориа́льная едини́ца эквивале́нтная о́бласти и управля́емая ме́стным прави́тельством.

coup [kuː] (*pl* **coups**) *n* (*also* **coup d'état**) госуда́рственный переворо́т
couple ['kʌpl] *n* (*married couple*) (супру́жеская) па́ра; (*of people, things*) па́ра; **a couple of** (*some*) па́ра *+gen*
coupon ['kuːpɔn] *n* (*voucher*) купо́н; (*form*) тало́н
courage ['kʌrɪdʒ] *n* сме́лость *f*, хра́брость *f*; **courageous** [kə'reɪdʒəs] *adj* сме́лый, хра́брый
courgette [kuə'ʒɛt] *n* (*Brit*)

молодо́й кабачо́к

courier ['kurɪəʳ] *n* курье́р; (*for tourists*) руководи́тель *m* гру́ппы

course [kɔːs] *n* курс; (*of events, time*) ход; (*of action*) направле́ние; (*of river*) тече́ние; **first/last course** пе́рвое/сла́дкое блю́до; **of course** коне́чно

court [kɔːt] *n* (*Law*) суд; (*Sport*) корт; (*royal*) двор; **to take sb to court** подава́ть (*perf* пода́ть) на кого́-н в суд

courtesy ['kəːtəsɪ] *n* ве́жливость *f*; **(by) courtesy of** благодаря́ любе́зности *+gen*

courtroom ['kɔːtrum] *n* зал суда́

courtyard ['kɔːtjɑːd] *n* вну́тренний двор

cousin ['kʌzn] *n* (*also* **first cousin**: *male*) двоюродный брат; (: *female*) двою́родная сестра́

cover ['kʌvəʳ] *vt* закрыва́ть (*perf* закры́ть); (*with cloth*) укрыва́ть (*perf* укры́ть); (*distance*) покрыва́ть (*perf* покры́ть); (*topic*) рассма́тривать (*perf* рассмотре́ть); (*include*) охва́тывать (*perf* охвати́ть); (*Press*) освеща́ть (*perf* освети́ть) ▷ *n* (*for furniture, machinery*) чехо́л; (*of book etc*) обло́жка; (*shelter*) укры́тие; **covers** *npl* (*for bed*) посте́льное бельё *ntsg*; **he was covered in** *or* **with** (*mud*) он был покры́т *+instr*; **to take cover** укрыва́ться (*perf* укры́ться); **under cover** в укры́тии; **under cover of darkness** под покро́вом темноты́; **cover up** *vt* закрыва́ть (*perf* закры́ть) ▷ *vi* (*fig*): **to cover up for sb** покрыва́ть (*perf* покры́ть) кого́-н; **coverage** *n* освеще́ние

cow [kau] *n* (*also inf!*) коро́ва (*also !*)

coward ['kauəd] *n* трус(и́ха); **cowardly** *adj* трусли́вый

cowboy ['kaubɔɪ] *n* ковбо́й

cozy ['kəuzɪ] *adj* (*US*) = **cosy**

crab [kræb] *n* краб

crack [kræk] *n* (*noise*) треск; (*gap*) щель *f*; (*in dish, wall*) тре́щина ▷ *vt* (*whip, twig*) щёлкать (*perf* щёлкнуть) *+instr*; (*dish etc*) раска́лывать (*perf* расколо́ть); (*nut*) коло́ть (*perf* расколо́ть); (*problem*) реша́ть (*perf* реши́ть); (*code*) разга́дывать (*perf* разгада́ть); (*joke*) отпуска́ть (*perf* отпусти́ть)

crackle ['krækl] *vi* потре́скивать (*impf*)

cradle ['kreɪdl] *n* (*crib*) колыбе́ль *f*

craft [krɑːft] *n* (*trade*) ремесло́; (*boat*: *pl inv*) кора́бль *f*; **craftsman** *irreg n* реме́сленник; **craftsmanship** *n* (*quality*) вы́делка; (*skill*) мастерство́

cram [kræm] *vt*: **to cram sth with** набива́ть (*perf* наби́ть) что-н *+instr*; **to cram sth into** вти́скивать (*perf* вти́снуть) что-н в *+acc*

cramp [kræmp] *n* су́дорога; **cramped** *adj* те́сный

crane [kreɪn] *n* (*Tech*) (подъёмный) кран

crash [kræʃ] *n* (*noise*) гро́хот; (*of car*) ава́рия; (*of plane, train*) круше́ние ▷ *vt* разбива́ть (*perf* разби́ть) ▷ *vi* разбива́ться (*perf* разби́ться); (*two cars*) ста́лкиваться (*perf* столкну́ться); **crash course** *n* интенси́вный курс; **crash helmet** *n* защи́тный шлем

crate [kreɪt] *n* деревя́нный я́щик; (*for bottles*) упако́вочный я́щик

crave [kreɪv] *vt, vi*: **to crave sth** *or* **for sth** жа́ждать (*impf*) чего́-н

crawl [krɔːl] *vi* (*move*) по́лзать/

ползти́ (*impf*) ▷ *n* (*Sport*) кроль *f*
craze [kreɪz] *n* пова́льное увлече́ние
crazy ['kreɪzɪ] *adj* сумасше́дший; **he's crazy about skiing** (*inf*) он поме́шан на лы́жах; **to go crazy** помеша́ться (*perf*)
cream [kri:m] *n* сли́вки *pl*; (*cosmetic*) крем ▷ *adj* (*colour*) кре́мовый; **creamy** *adj* (*taste*) сли́вочный
crease [kri:s] *n* (*fold*) скла́дка; (: *in trousers*) стре́лка; (*in dress, on brow*) морщи́на
create [kri:'eɪt] *vt* (*impression*) создава́ть (созда́ть *perf*); (*invent*) твори́ть (*impf*), создава́ть (*perf* созда́ть)
creation [kri:'eɪʃən] *n* созда́ние; (*Rel*) сотворе́ние
creative [kri:'eɪtɪv] *adj* тво́рческий
creature ['kri:tʃə^r] *n* (*animal*) существо́; (*person*) созда́ние
crèche [krɛʃ] *n* (де́тские) я́сли *pl*
credentials [krɪ'dɛnʃlz] *npl* (*references*) квалифика́ция *fsg*; (*for identity*) рекоменда́тельное письмо́ *ntsg*, рекоменда́ция *fsg*
credibility [krɛdɪ'bɪlɪtɪ] *n* (*see adj*) правдоподо́бность *f*; авторите́т
credible ['krɛdɪbl] *adj* вероя́тный, правдоподо́бный; (*person*) авторите́тный
credit ['krɛdɪt] *n* (*Comm*) креди́т; (*recognition*) до́лжное *nt adj* ▷ *vt* (*Comm*) кредитова́ть (*impf/perf*); **to credit sb with sth** (*sense etc*) припи́сывать (*perf* приписа́ть) кому́-н что-н; **credits** *npl* (*Cinema, TV*) ти́тры *mpl*; **credit card** *n* креди́тная ка́рточка; **credit crunch** *n* креди́тный кри́зис
creek [kri:k] *n* у́зкий зали́в; (*US: stream*) руче́й
creep [kri:p] (*pt, pp* **crept**) *vi* (*person, animal*) кра́сться (*impf*) ▷ *n* (*inf*) подхали́м(ка)
crept [krɛpt] *pt, pp of* **creep**
crescent ['krɛsnt] *n* полуме́сяц
cress [krɛs] *n* кресс-сала́т
crest [krɛst] *n* (*of hill*) гре́бень *m*; (*of bird*) хохоло́к, гребешо́к; (*coat of arms*) герб
crew [kru:] *n* экипа́ж; (*TV, Cinema*) съёмочная гру́ппа
cricket ['krɪkɪt] *n* (*game*) кри́кет; (*insect*) сверчо́к
crime [kraɪm] *n* преступле́ние; (*illegal activity*) престу́пность *f*
criminal ['krɪmɪnl] *n* престу́пник(-ица) ▷ *adj* (*illegal*) престу́пный
crimson ['krɪmzn] *adj* мали́новый, тёмно-кра́сный
cripple ['krɪpl] *n* (*inf!*) кале́ка *m/f* ▷ *vt* (*person*) кале́чить (*perf* искале́чить)
crisis ['kraɪsɪs] (*pl* **crises**) *n* кри́зис
crisp [krɪsp] *adj* (*food*) хрустя́щий; (*weather*) све́жий; (*reply*) чёткий; **crisps** *npl* (*Brit*) чи́псы *pl*
criterion [kraɪ'tɪərɪən] (*pl* **criteria**) *n* крите́рий
critic ['krɪtɪk] *n* кри́тик; **critical** *adj* крити́ческий; (*person, opinion*) крити́чный; **he is critical** (*Med*) он в крити́ческом состоя́нии; **criticism** ['krɪtɪsɪzəm] *n* кри́тика; (*of book, play*) крити́ческий разбо́р; **criticize** ['krɪtɪsaɪz] *vt* критикова́ть (*impf*)
Croatia [krəu'eɪʃə] *n* Хорва́тия
crockery ['krɔkərɪ] *n* посу́да
crocodile ['krɔkədaɪl] *n* крокоди́л

crocus ['krəukəs] *n* шафра́н
crook [kruk] *n* (*criminal*) жу́лик; **crooked** ['krukɪd] *adj* криво́й; (*dishonest*) жулнова́тый; (*business*) жу́льнический
crop [krɔp] *n* (сельскохозя́йственная) культу́ра; (*harvest*) урожа́й; (*also* **riding crop**) плеть *f*
cross [krɔs] *n* крест; (*mark*) кре́стик; (*Bio*) по́месь *f* ▷ *vt* пересека́ть (*perf* пересе́чь), переходи́ть (*perf* перейти́); (*cheque*) кросси́ровать (*impf/perf*); (*arms etc*) скре́щивать (*perf* скрести́ть) ▷ *adj* серди́тый; **cross out** *vt* вычёркивать (*perf* вы́черкнуть); **crossing** *n* перепра́ва; (*also* **pedestrian crossing**) перехо́д; **crossroads** *n* перекрёсток; **crossword** *n* кроссво́рд
crotch [krɔtʃ] *n* промéжность *f*; **the trousers are tight in the crotch** брю́ки жмут в шагу́
crouch [krautʃ] *vi* приседа́ть (*perf* присе́сть)
crow [krəu] *n* (*bird*) воро́на
crowd [kraud] *n* толпа́; **crowded** *adj* (*area*) перенаселённый; **the room was crowded** ко́мната была́ полна́ люде́й; **crowdfunding** *n* краудфа́ндинг
crown [kraun] *n* коро́на; (*of head*) маку́шка; (*of hill*) верши́на; (*of tooth*) коро́нка ▷ *vt* короно́вать (*impf/perf*); **the Crown** (Брита́нская) Коро́на
crucial ['kru:ʃl] *adj* реша́ющий; (*work*) ва́жный
crude [kru:d] *adj* (*materials*) сыро́й; (*fig*: *basic*) примити́вный; (: *vulgar*) гру́бый
cruel ['kruəl] *adj* жесто́кий; **cruelty** *n* жесто́кость *f*
cruise [kru:z] *n* круи́з ▷ *vi* крейси́ровать (*impf*)
crumb [krʌm] *n* (*of cake etc*) кро́шка
crumble ['krʌmbl] *vt* кроши́ть (*perf* раскроши́ть) ▷ *vi* осыпа́ться (*perf* осы́паться); (*fig*) ру́шиться (*perf* ру́хнуть)
crunch [krʌntʃ] *vt* (*food etc*) грызть (*perf* разгры́зть) ▷ *n* (*fig*): **the crunch** крити́ческий *or* реша́ющий моме́нт; **crunchy** *adj* хрустя́щий
crush [krʌʃ] *vt* (*squash*) выжима́ть (*perf* вы́жать); (*crumple*) мять (*perf* смять); (*defeat*) сокруша́ть (*perf* сокруши́ть); (*upset*) уничтожа́ть (*perf* уничто́жить) ▷ *n* (*crowd*) да́вка; **to have a crush on sb** сходи́ть (*impf*) с ума́ по кому́-н
crust [krʌst] *n* ко́рка; (*of earth*) кора́
crutch [krʌtʃ] *n* (*Med*) косты́ль *m*
cry [kraɪ] *vi* пла́кать (*impf*); (*also* **cry out**) крича́ть (*perf* кри́кнуть) ▷ *n* крик
crystal ['krɪstl] *n* (*glass*) хруста́ль; (*Chem*) криста́лл
cub [kʌb] *n* детёныш
Cuba ['kju:bə] *n* Ку́ба
cube [kju:b] *n* (*also Math*) куб ▷ *vt* возводи́ть (*perf* возвести́) в куб
cubicle ['kju:bɪkl] *n* (*at pool*) каби́нка
cuckoo ['kuku:] *n* куку́шка
cucumber ['kju:kʌmbə[r]] *n* огуре́ц
cuddle ['kʌdl] *vt* обнима́ть (*perf* обня́ть) ▷ *vi* обнима́ться (*perf* обня́ться) ▷ *n* ла́ска
cue [kju:] *n* кий; (*Theat*) ре́плика
cuff [kʌf] *n* (*of sleeve*) манже́та; (*US*: *of trousers*) отворо́т; (*blow*)

шлепо́к; **off the cuff** экспро́мтом
cuisine [kwɪ'zi:n] *n* ку́хня (*ку́шанья*)
cul-de-sac ['kʌldəsæk] *n* тупи́к
culprit ['kʌlprɪt] *n* (*person*) вино́вник(-вница)
cult [kʌlt] *n* (*also Rel*) культ
cultivate ['kʌltɪveɪt] *vt* (*crop, feeling*) культиви́ровать (*impf*); (*land*) возде́лывать (*impf*)
cultural ['kʌltʃərəl] *adj* культу́рный
culture ['kʌltʃə^r] *n* культу́ра
cunning ['kʌnɪŋ] *n* хи́трость *f* ▷ *adj* (*crafty*) хи́трый
cup [kʌp] *n* ча́шка; (*as prize*) ку́бок; (*of bra*) ча́шечка
cupboard ['kʌbəd] *n* шкаф
curator [kjuə'reɪtə^r] *n* храни́тель *m*
curb [kə:b] *vt* (*powers etc*) обу́здывать (*perf* обузда́ть) ▷ *n* (*US*: *kerb*) бордю́р
cure [kjuə^r] *vt* выле́чивать (*perf* вы́лечить); (*Culin*) обраба́тывать (*perf* обрабо́тать) ▷ *n* лека́рство; (*solution*) сре́дство
curfew ['kə:fju:] *n* коменда́нтский час
curiosity [kjuərɪ'ɔsɪtɪ] *n* (*see adj*) любопы́тство; любозна́тельность *f*
curious ['kjuərɪəs] *adj* любопы́тный; (*interested*) любозна́тельный
curl [kə:l] *n* (*of hair*) ло́кон, завито́к ▷ *vt* (*hair*) завива́ть (*perf* зави́ть); (*: tightly*) закру́чивать (*perf* закрути́ть) ▷ *vi* (*hair*) ви́ться (*impf*); **curly** *adj* вью́щийся
currant ['kʌrnt] *n* (*dried grape*) изю́минка; **currants** (*dried grapes*) кишми́ш
currency ['kʌrnsɪ] *n* валю́та
current ['kʌrnt] *n* (*of air, water*) пото́к; (*Elec*) ток ▷ *adj* (*present*) теку́щий, совреме́нный; (*accepted*) общепри́нятый; **current account** *n* (*Brit*) теку́щий счёт; **current affairs** *npl* теку́щие собы́тия *ntpl*; **currently** *adv* в да́нный *or* настоя́щий моме́нт
curriculum [kə'rɪkjuləm] (*pl* **curriculums** *or* **curricula**) *n* (*Scol*) (учёбная) ппрогра́мма; **curriculum vitae** [kərɪkjuləm'vi:taɪ] *n* автобиогра́фия
curry ['kʌrɪ] *n* *блю́до с ка́рри*
curse [kə:s] *n* прокля́тие; (*swearword*) руга́тельство
curt [kə:t] *adj* ре́зкий
curtain ['kə:tn] *n* за́навес; (*light*) занаве́ска
curve [kə:v] *n* изги́б
cushion ['kuʃən] *n* поду́шка ▷ *vt* смягча́ть (*perf* смягчи́ть)
custard ['kʌstəd] *n* заварно́й крем
custody ['kʌstədɪ] *n* опе́ка; **to take into custody** брать (*perf* взять) под стра́жу
custom ['kʌstəm] *n* (*traditional*) тради́ция; (*convention*) обы́чай; (*habit*) привы́чка
customer ['kʌstəmə^r] *n* (*of shop*) покупа́тель(ница) *m(f)*; (*of business*) клие́нт, зака́зчик
customs ['kʌstəmz] *npl* тамо́жня *fsg*
cut [kʌt] (*pt, pp* **cut**) *vt* (*bread, meat*) ре́зать (*perf* разре́зать); (*hand, knee*) ре́зать (*perf* поре́зать); (*grass, hair*) стричь (*perf* постри́чь); (*text*) сокраща́ть (*perf* сократи́ть); (*spending, supply*) уре́зывать (*perf* уре́зать); (*prices*) снижа́ть (*perf* сни́зить) ▷ *vi* ре́зать (*impf*) ▷ *n* (*in skin*) поре́з; (*in salary, spending*)

crocus ['krəukəs] *n* шафра́н
crook [kruk] *n* (*criminal*) жу́лик; **crooked** ['krukɪd] *adj* криво́й; (*dishonest*) жуликова́тый; (*business*) жу́льнический
crop [krɔp] *n* (сельскохозя́йственная) культу́ра; (*harvest*) урожа́й; (*also* **riding crop**) плеть *f*
cross [krɔs] *n* крест; (*mark*) кре́стик; (*Bio*) по́месь *f* ▷ *vt* пересека́ть (*perf* пересе́чь), переходи́ть (*perf* перейти́); (*cheque*) кросси́ровать (*impf/perf*); (*arms etc*) скре́щивать (*perf* скрести́ть) ▷ *adj* серди́тый; **cross out** *vt* вычёркивать (*perf* вы́черкнуть); **crossing** *n* перепра́ва; (*also* **pedestrian crossing**) перехо́д; **crossroads** *n* перекрёсток; **crossword** *n* кроссво́рд
crotch [krɔtʃ] *n* проме́жность *f*; **the trousers are tight in the crotch** брю́ки жмут в шагу́
crouch [krautʃ] *vi* приседа́ть (*perf* присе́сть)
crow [krəu] *n* (*bird*) воро́на
crowd [kraud] *n* толпа́; **crowded** *adj* (*area*) перенаселённый; **the room was crowded** ко́мната была́ полна́ люде́й; **crowdfunding** *n* краудфа́ндинг
crown [kraun] *n* коро́на; (*of head*) маку́шка; (*of hill*) верши́на; (*of tooth*) коро́нка ▷ *vt* коронова́ть (*impf/perf*); **the Crown** (Брита́нская) Коро́на
crucial ['kru:ʃl] *adj* реша́ющий; (*work*) ва́жный
crude [kru:d] *adj* (*materials*) сыро́й; (*fig: basic*) примити́вный; (*: vulgar*) гру́бый
cruel ['kruəl] *adj* жесто́кий; **cruelty** *n* жесто́кость *f*
cruise [kru:z] *n* круи́з ▷ *vi* крейси́ровать (*impf*)
crumb [krʌm] *n* (*of cake etc*) кро́шка
crumble ['krʌmbl] *vt* кроши́ть (*perf* раскроши́ть) ▷ *vi* осыпа́ться (*perf* осы́паться); (*fig*) ру́шиться (*perf* ру́хнуть)
crunch [krʌntʃ] *vt* (*food etc*) грызть (*perf* разгры́зть) ▷ *n* (*fig*): **the crunch** крити́ческий *or* реша́ющий моме́нт; **crunchy** *adj* хрустя́щий
crush [krʌʃ] *vt* (*squash*) выжима́ть (*perf* вы́жать); (*crumple*) мять (*perf* смять); (*defeat*) сокруша́ть (*perf* сокруши́ть); (*upset*) уничтожа́ть (*perf* уничто́жить) ▷ *n* (*crowd*) да́вка; **to have a crush on sb** сходи́ть (*impf*) с ума́ по кому́-н
crust [krʌst] *n* ко́рка; (*of earth*) кора́
crutch [krʌtʃ] *n* (*Med*) косты́ль *m*
cry [kraɪ] *vi* пла́кать (*impf*); (*also* **cry out**) крича́ть (*perf* кри́кнуть) ▷ *n* крик
crystal ['krɪstl] *n* (*glass*) хруста́ль; (*Chem*) криста́лл
cub [kʌb] *n* детёныш
Cuba ['kju:bə] *n* Ку́ба
cube [kju:b] *n* (*also Math*) куб ▷ *vt* возводи́ть (*perf* возвести́) в куб
cubicle ['kju:bɪkl] *n* (*at pool*) каби́нка
cuckoo ['kuku:] *n* куку́шка
cucumber ['kju:kʌmbə[r]] *n* огуре́ц
cuddle ['kʌdl] *vt* обнима́ть (*perf* обня́ть) ▷ *vi* обнима́ться (*perf* обня́ться) ▷ *n* ла́ска
cue [kju:] *n* кий; (*Theat*) ре́плика
cuff [kʌf] *n* (*of sleeve*) манже́та; (*US: of trousers*) отворо́т; (*blow*)

шлепóк; **off the cuff** экспрóмтом
cuisine [kwɪ'zi:n] *n* кýхня (*кýшанья*)
cul-de-sac ['kʌldəsæk] *n* тупи́к
culprit ['kʌlprɪt] *n* (*person*) винóвник(-вница)
cult [kʌlt] *n* (*also Rel*) культ
cultivate ['kʌltɪveɪt] *vt* (*crop, feeling*) культиви́ровать (*impf*); (*land*) возде́лывать (*impf*)
cultural ['kʌltʃərəl] *adj* культýрный
culture ['kʌltʃə^r] *n* культýра
cunning ['kʌnɪŋ] *n* хи́трость *f* ▷ *adj* (*crafty*) хи́трый
cup [kʌp] *n* чáшка; (*as prize*) кýбок; (*of bra*) чáшечка
cupboard ['kʌbəd] *n* шкаф
curator [kjuə'reɪtə^r] *n* храни́тель *m*
curb [kə:b] *vt* (*powers etc*) обýздывать (*perf* обуздáть) ▷ *n* (*US*: *kerb*) бордю́р
cure [kjuə^r] *vt* вылéчивать (*perf* вы́лечить); (*Culin*) обрабáтывать (*perf* обрабóтать) ▷ *n* лекáрство; (*solution*) срéдство
curfew ['kə:fju:] *n* комендáнтский час
curiosity [kjuərɪ'ɔsɪtɪ] *n* (*see adj*) любопы́тство; любознáтельность *f*
curious ['kjuərɪəs] *adj* любопы́тный; (*interested*) любознáтельный
curl [kə:l] *n* (*of hair*) лóкон, завитóк ▷ *vt* (*hair*) завивáть (*perf* зави́ть); (: *tightly*) закрýчивать (*perf* закрути́ть) ▷ *vi* (*hair*) ви́ться (*impf*); **curly** *adj* вью́щийся
currant ['kʌrnt] *n* (*dried grape*) изю́минка; **currants** (*dried grapes*) кишми́ш
currency ['kʌrnsɪ] *n* валю́та
current ['kʌrnt] *n* (*of air, water*) потóк; (*Elec*) ток ▷ *adj* (*present*) текýщий, совремéнный; (*accepted*) общепри́нятый; **current account** *n* (*Brit*) текýщий счёт; **current affairs** *npl* текýщие собы́тия *ntpl*; **currently** *adv* в дáнный *or* настоя́щий момéнт
curriculum [kə'rɪkjuləm] (*pl* **curriculums** *or* **curricula**) *n* (*Scol*) (учéбная) ппрогрáмма; **curriculum vitae** [kərɪkjuləm'vi:taɪ] *n* автобиогрáфия
curry ['kʌrɪ] *n* *блю́до с кэ́рри*
curse [kə:s] *n* прокля́тие; (*swearword*) ругáтельство
curt [kə:t] *adj* рéзкий
curtain ['kə:tn] *n* зáнавес; (*light*) занавéска
curve [kə:v] *n* изги́б
cushion ['kuʃən] *n* подýшка ▷ *vt* смягчáть (*perf* смягчи́ть)
custard ['kʌstəd] *n* заварнóй крем
custody ['kʌstədɪ] *n* опéка; **to take into custody** брать (*perf* взять) под стрáжу
custom ['kʌstəm] *n* (*traditional*) трáди́ция; (*convention*) обы́чай; (*habit*) привы́чка
customer ['kʌstəmə^r] *n* (*of shop*) покупáтель(ница) *m(f)*; (*of business*) клиéнт, закáзчик
customs ['kʌstəmz] *npl* тамóжня *fsg*
cut [kʌt] (*pt, pp* **cut**) *vt* (*bread, meat*) рéзать (*perf* разрéзать); (*hand, knee*) рéзать (*perf* порéзать); (*grass, hair*) стричь (*perf* постри́чь); (*text*) сокращáть (*perf* сократи́ть); (*spending, supply*) урéзывать (*perf* урéзать); (*prices*) снижáть (*perf* сни́зить) ▷ *vi* рéзать (*impf*) ▷ *n* (*in skin*) порéз; (*in salary, spending*)

снижéние; (*of meat*) кусóк; **cut down** *vt* (*tree*) срубáть (*perf* сруби́ть); (*consumption*) сокращáть (*perf* сократи́ть); **cut off** *vt* отрезáть (*perf* отрéзать); (*electricity, water*) отключáть (*perf* отключи́ть); (*Tel*) разъединя́ть (*perf* разъедини́ть); **cut out** *vt* (*remove*) вырезáть (*perf* вы́резать); (*stop*) прекращáть (*perf* прекрати́ть); **cut up** *vt* разрезáть (*perf* разрéзать)

cute [kju:t] *adj* (*sweet*) ми́лый, прелéстный

cutlery ['kʌtlərɪ] *n* столóвый прибóр

cut-price (*US* **cut-rate**) *adj* по сни́женной ценé

cut-rate *adj* (*US*) = **cut-price**

cutting ['kʌtɪŋ] *adj* (*edge*) óстрый; (*remark etc*) язви́тельный ▷ *n* (*Brit: Press*) вы́резка; (*from plant*) черенóк

CV *n abbr* = **curriculum vitae**

cyberbullying ['saɪbəbulɪɪŋ] *n* трáвля в Интернéте, кибербу́ллинг

cyberspace ['saɪbəspeɪs] *n* киберпрострáнство

cycle ['saɪkl] *n* цикл; (*bicycle*) велосипéд

cyclone ['saɪkləun] *n* циклóн

cylinder ['sɪlɪndə^r] *n* цили́ндр; (*of gas*) баллóн

cymbals ['sɪmblz] *npl* тарéлки *fpl*

cynical ['sɪnɪkl] *adj* цини́чный

Cyprus ['saɪprəs] *n* Кипр

cystitis [sɪs'taɪtɪs] *n* цисти́т

Czech [tʃɛk] *adj* чéшский ▷ *n* чех (чéшка); **Czech Republic** *n*: **the Czech Republic** Чéшская Респу́блика

d

D [di:] *n* (*Mus*) ре

dab [dæb] *vt* (*eyes, wound*) промокну́ть (*perf*); (*paint, cream*) наноси́ть (*perf* нанести́)

dad [dæd] *n* (*inf*) пáпа *m*, пáпочка *m*; **daddy** *n* (*inf*) = **dad**

daffodil ['dæfədɪl] *n* нарци́сс

daft [dɑ:ft] *adj* (*ideas*) дурáцкий; (*person*) чóкнутый

dagger ['dægə^r] *n* кинжáл

daily ['deɪlɪ] *adj* (*dose*) су́точный; (*routine*) повседнéвный; (*wages*) дневнóй ▷ *n* (*also* **daily paper**) ежеднéвная газéта ▷ *adv* ежеднéвно

dairy ['dɛərɪ] *n* (*Brit: shop*) молóчный магази́н; (*for making butter*) маслодéльня; (*for making cheese*) сыровáрня; **dairy farm** молóчная фéрма; **dairy products** молóчные продýкты *mpl*

daisy ['deɪzɪ] *n* маргари́тка

dam [dæm] *n* да́мба ▷ *vt* перекрыва́ть (*perf* перекры́ть) да́мбой
damage ['dæmɪdʒ] *n* (*harm*) уще́рб; (*dents etc*) поврежде́ние; (*fig*) вред ▷ *vt* поврежда́ть (*perf* поврди́ть); (*fig*) вреди́ть (*perf* повреди́ть) *+dat*; **damages** *npl* (*Law*) компенса́ция *fsg*
damn [dæm] *vt* осужда́ть (*perf* осуди́ть) ▷ *adj* (*inf*: *also* **damned**) проклятый ▷ *n* (*inf*): **I don't give a damn** мне плева́ть; **damn (it)!** чёрт возьми́ *or* побери́!
damp [dæmp] *adj* (*building, wall*) сыро́й; (*cloth*) вла́жный ▷ *n* сы́рость *f* ▷ *vt* (*also* **dampen**) смачивать (*perf* смочи́ть); (: *fig*) охлажда́ть (*perf* охлади́ть)
dance [dɑ:ns] *n* та́нец; (*social event*) та́нцы *mpl* ▷ *vi* танцева́ть (*impf*); **dancer** *n* танцо́вщик(-ица); (*for fun*) танцо́р
dandelion ['dændɪlaɪən] *n* одува́нчик
danger ['deɪndʒə^r] *n* опа́сность *f*; **"danger!"** "опа́сно!"; **he is in danger of losing his job** ему́ грози́т поте́ря рабо́ты; **dangerous** *adj* опа́сный
Danish ['deɪnɪʃ] *adj* да́тский ▷ *npl*: **the Danish** датча́не
dare [dɛə^r] *vt*: **to dare sb to do** вызыва́ть (*perf* вы́звать) кого́-н *+infin* ▷ *vi*: **to dare (to) do** сметь (*perf* посме́ть) *+infin*; **I dare say** сме́ю заме́тить
daring ['dɛərɪŋ] *adj* (*audacious*) де́рзкий; (*bold*) сме́лый
dark [dɑ:k] *adj* тёмный; (*complexion*) сму́глый ▷ *n*: **in the dark** в темноте́; **dark blue** *etc* тёмно-си́ний *etc*; **after dark** по́сле наступле́ния темноты́; **darkness** *n* темнота́; **darkroom** *n* тёмная ко́мната, проявительная лаборато́рия
darling ['dɑ:lɪŋ] *adj* дорого́й(-а́я) *m(f) adj*
dart [dɑ:t] *n* (*in game*) дро́тик (*для игры́ в дарт*); (*in sewing*) вы́тачка; **darts** *n* дарт
dash [dæʃ] *n* (*drop*) ка́пелька; (*sign*) тире́ *nt ind* ▷ *vt* (*throw*) швыря́ть (*perf* швырну́ть); (*shatter*: *hopes*) разруша́ть (*perf* разру́шить), разбива́ть (*perf* разби́ть) ▷ *vi*: **to dash towards** рвану́ться (*perf*) к *+dat*
dashboard ['dæʃbɔ:d] *n* (*Aut*) прибо́рная пане́ль *f*
dashcam ['dæʃkæm] *n* автомоби́льный видеорегистра́тор, видеорегистра́тор
data ['deɪtə] *npl* да́нные *pl adj*; **database** *n* ба́за да́нных
date [deɪt] *n* (*day*) число́, да́та; (*with friend*) свида́ние; (*fruit*) фи́ник ▷ *vt* дати́ровать (*impf/perf*); (*person*) встреча́ться (*impf*) с *+instr*; **date of birth** да́та рожде́ния; **to date** на сего́дняшний день; **out of date** устаре́лый; (*expired*) просро́ченный; **up to date** совреме́нный; **dated** *adj* устаре́лый
daughter ['dɔ:tə^r] *n* дочь *f*; **daughter-in-law** *n* сноха́
daunting ['dɔ:ntɪŋ] *adj* устраша́ющий
dawn [dɔ:n] *n* (*of day*) рассве́т
day [deɪ] *n* (*period*) су́тки *pl*, день *m*; (*daylight*) день; (*heyday*) вре́мя *nt*; **the day before** накану́не; **the day after** на сле́дующий день; **the day after tomorrow** послеза́втра; **the day before yesterday** позавчера́; **the following day** на сле́дующий день; **by day** днём; **daylight** *n* дневно́й свет; **day**

return *n* (*Brit*) обра́тный биле́т (*действи́тельный в тече́ние одного́ дня*); **daytime** *n* день *m*

dazzle ['dæzl] *vt* (*blind*) ослепля́ть (*perf* ослепи́ть)

DC *abbr* (= *direct current*) постоя́нный ток

dead [dɛd] *adj* мёртвый; (*arm, leg*) онеме́лый ▷ *adv* (*inf*: *completely*) абсолю́тно; (*inf*: *directly*) пря́мо ▷ *npl*: **the dead** мёртвые *pl adj*; (*in accident, war*) поги́бшие *pl adj*; **the battery is dead** батаре́йка се́ла; **the telephone is dead** телефо́н отключи́лся; **to shoot sb dead** застрели́ть (*perf*) кого́-н; **dead tired** смерте́льно уста́лый *or* уста́вший; **dead end** *n* тупи́к; **deadline** *n* после́дний *or* преде́льный срок; **deadly** *adj* (*lethal*) смертоно́сный; **Dead Sea** *n*: **the Dead Sea** Мёртвое мо́ре

deaf [dɛf] *adj* (*totally*) глухо́й

deal [di:l] (*pt, pp* **dealt**) *n* (*agreement*) сде́лка ▷ *vt* (*blow*) наноси́ть (*perf* нанести́); (*cards*) сдава́ть (*perf* сдать); **a great deal (of)** о́чень мно́го (*+gen*); **deal in** *vt fus* (*Comm, drugs*) торгова́ть (*impf*) *+instr*; **deal with** *vt fus* име́ть (*impf*) де́ло с *+instr*; (*problem*) реша́ть (*perf* реши́ть); (*subject*) занима́ться (*perf* заня́ться) *+instr*; **dealt** [dɛlt] *pt, pp of* **deal**

dean [di:n] *n* (*Scol*) дека́н

dear [dɪəʳ] *adj* дорого́й ▷ *n*: **(my) dear** (*to man, boy*) дорого́й (мой); (*to woman, girl*) дорога́я (моя́) ▷ *excl*: **dear me!** о, Го́споди!; **Dear Sir** уважа́емый господи́н; **Dear Mrs Smith** дорога́я *or* уважа́емая ми́ссис Смит; **dearly** *adv* (*love*) о́чень; (*pay*) до́рого

death [dɛθ] *n* смерть *f*; **death penalty** *n* сме́ртная казнь *f*

debate [dɪ'beɪt] *n* деба́ты *pl* ▷ *vt* (*topic*) обсужда́ть (*perf* обсуди́ть)

debit ['dɛbɪt] *vt*: **to debit a sum to sb** *or* **to sb's account** дебетова́ть (*impf/perf*) су́мму с кого́-н *or* с чьего́-н счёта; *see also* **direct debit**

d

debris ['dɛbri:] *n* обло́мки *mpl*, разва́лины *fpl*

debt [dɛt] *n* (*sum*) долг; **to be in debt** быть (*impf*) в долгу́

debug ['di:bʌg] *vt* (*Comput*) отла́живать (*perf* отла́дить) *+gen*

decade ['dɛkeɪd] *n* десятиле́тие

decaffeinated [dɪ'kæfɪneɪtɪd] *adj*: **decaffeinated coffee** ко́фе без кофеина

decay [dɪ'keɪ] *n* разруше́ние

deceased [dɪ'si:st] *n*: **the deceased** поко́йный(-ая) *m(f) adj*

deceit [dɪ'si:t] *n* обма́н

deceive [dɪ'si:v] *vt* обма́нывать (*perf* обману́ть)

December [dɪ'sɛmbəʳ] *n* дека́брь *m*

decency ['di:sənsɪ] *n* (*propriety*) благопристо́йность *f*

decent ['di:sənt] *adj* (*wages, meal*) прили́чный; (*behaviour, person*) поря́дочный

deception [dɪ'sɛpʃən] *n* обма́н

deceptive [dɪ'sɛptɪv] *adj* обма́нчивый

decide [dɪ'saɪd] *vt* (*settle*) реша́ть (*perf* реши́ть) ▷ *vi*: **to decide to do/that** реша́ть (*perf* реши́ть) *+infin*/, что; **to decide on** остана́вливаться (*perf* останови́ться) на *+prp*

листопа́дный

decision [dɪ'sɪʒən] *n* реше́ние

decisive [dɪ'saɪsɪv] *adj* реши́тельный

deck [dɛk] *n* (*Naut*) па́луба; (*of*

cards) колóда; (*also* **record deck**) проигрыватель *m*; **top deck** (*of bus*) вéрхний этáж; **deckchair** *n* шезлóнг

declaration [dɛklə'reɪʃən] *n* (*statement*) декларáция; (*of war*) объявлéние

declare [dɪ'klɛəʳ] *vt* (*state*) объявлять (*perf* объявить); (*for tax*) декларировать (*impf/perf*)

decline [dɪ'klaɪn] *n* (*drop*) падéние; (*in strength*) упáдок; (*lessening*) уменьшéние; **to be in** *or* **on the decline** быть (*impf*) в упáдке

decorate ['dɛkəreɪt] *vt* (*room etc*) отдéлывать (*perf* отдéлать); (*adorn*): **to decorate (with)** украшáть (*perf* укрáсить) *+instr*

decoration [dɛkə'reɪʃən] *n* (*on tree, dress*) украшéние; (*medal*) нагрáда

decorator ['dɛkəreɪtəʳ] *n* обóйщик

decrease ['di:kri:s] *vt* уменьшáть (*perf* умéньшить) ▷ *vi* уменьшáться (*perf* умéньшиться) ▷ *n*: **decrease (in)** уменьшéние (*+gen*)

decree [dɪ'kri:] *n* постановлéние

dedicate ['dɛdɪkeɪt] *vt*: **to dedicate to** посвящáть (*perf* посвятить) *+dat*

dedication [dɛdɪ'keɪʃən] *n* (*devotion*) прéданность *f*; (*in book etc*) посвящéние

deduction [dɪ'dʌkʃən] *n* (*conclusion*) умозаключéние; (*subtraction*) вычитáние; (*amount*) вычет

deed [di:d] *n* (*feat*) деяние, постýпок; (*Law*) акт

deep [di:p] *adj* глубóкий; (*voice*) низкий ▷ *adv*: **the spectators stood 20 deep** зрители стояли в 20 рядóв; **the lake is 4 metres deep** глубинá óзера — 4 мéтра; **deep blue** *etc* тёмно-синий *etc*; **deeply** *adv* глубокó

deer [dɪəʳ] *n inv* олéнь *m*

defeat [dɪ'fi:t] *n* поражéние ▷ *vt* наносить (*perf* нанести) поражéние *+dat*

defect ['di:fɛkt] *n* (*in product*) дефéкт; (*of plan*) недостáток; **defective** [dɪ'fɛktɪv] *adj* (*goods*) дефéктный

defence [dɪ'fɛns] (*US* **defense**) *n* защита; (*Mil*) оборóна

defend [dɪ'fɛnd] *vt* защищáть (*perf* защитить); (*Law*) защищáть (*impf*); **defendant** *n* подсудимый(-ая) *m(f) adj*, обвиняемый(-ая) *m(f) adj*; (*in civil case*) ответчик(-ица); **defender** *n* защитник

defense (*US*) = **defence**

defensive [dɪ'fɛnsɪv] *adj* (*weapons, measures*) оборонительный; (*behaviour, manner*) вызывáющий ▷ *n*: **he was on the defensive** он был готóв к оборóне

defer [dɪ'fə:ʳ] *vt* отсрóчивать (*perf* отсрóчить)

defiance [dɪ'faɪəns] *n* вызов; **in defiance of** вопреки *+dat*

defiant [dɪ'faɪənt] *adj* (*person, reply*) дéрзкий; (*tone*) вызывáющий

deficiency [dɪ'fɪʃənsɪ] *n* (*lack*) нехвáтка

deficient [dɪ'fɪʃənt] *adj*: **to be deficient in** (*lack*) испытывать (*impf*) недостáток в *+prp*

deficit ['dɛfɪsɪt] *n* (*Comm*) дефицит

define [dɪ'faɪn] *vt* определять (*perf* определить); (*word etc*) дава́ть (*perf* дать) определе́ние +*dat*

definite [ˈdɛfɪnɪt] *adj* определённый; **he was definite about it** его́ мне́ние на э́тот счёт бы́ло определённым; **definitely** *adv* определённо; (*certainly*) несомне́нно

definition [dɛfɪˈnɪʃən] *n* (*of word*) определе́ние

deflate [di:ˈfleɪt] *vt* (*tyre, balloon*) спуска́ть (*perf* спусти́ть)

deflect [dɪˈflɛkt] *vt* (*shot*) отража́ть (*perf* отрази́ть); (*criticism*) отклоня́ть (*perf* отклони́ть); (*attention*) отвлека́ть (*perf* отвле́чь)

defuse [di:ˈfju:z] *vt* разряжа́ть (*perf* разряди́ть)

defy [dɪˈfaɪ] *vt* (*resist*) оспа́ривать (*perf* оспо́рить); (*fig*: *description etc*) не поддава́ться (*impf*) +*dat*; **to defy sb to do** (*challenge*) призыва́ть (*perf* призва́ть) кого́-н +*infin*

degree [dɪˈgri:] *n* (*extent*) сте́пень *f*; (*unit of measurement*) гра́дус; (*Scol*) (учёная) сте́пень; **by degrees** постепе́нно; **to some degree, to a certain degree** до не́которой сте́пени

delay [dɪˈleɪ] *vt* (*decision, event*) откла́дывать (*perf* отложи́ть); (*person, plane etc*) заде́рживать (*perf* задержа́ть) ▷ *vi* ме́длить (*impf*) ▷ *n* заде́ржка; **to be delayed** заде́рживаться (*impf*); **without delay** незамедли́тельно

delegate [*n* ˈdɛlɪgɪt, *vb* ˈdɛlɪgeɪt] *n* делега́т ▷ *vt* (*task*) поруча́ть (*perf* поручи́ть)

deliberate [*adj* dɪˈlɪbərɪt, *vb* dɪˈlɪbəreɪt] *adj* (*intentional*) наме́ренный; (*slow*) неторопли́вый ▷ *vi* совеща́ться (*impf*); (*person*) разду́мывать (*impf*); **deliberately** *adv* (*see adj*) наме́ренно, наро́чно; неторопли́во

delicacy [ˈdɛlɪkəsɪ] *n* то́нкость *f*; (*food*) деликате́с

delicate [ˈdɛlɪkɪt] *adj* то́нкий; (*problem*) делика́тный; (*health*) хру́пкий

delicatessen [dɛlɪkəˈtɛsn] *n* гастроно́мия, магази́н деликате́сов

delicious [dɪˈlɪʃəs] *adj* о́чень вку́сный; (*smell*) восхити́тельный

delight [dɪˈlaɪt] *n* (*feeling*) восто́рг ▷ *vt* ра́довать (*perf* обра́довать); **to take (a) delight in** находи́ть (*impf*) удово́льствие в +*prp*; **delighted** *adj*: **(to be) delighted (at** *or* **with)** (быть (*impf*)) в восто́рге (от +*gen*); **he was delighted to see her** он был рад ви́деть её

delightful *adj* восхити́тельный

delinquent [dɪˈlɪŋkwənt] *adj* престу́пный

deliver [dɪˈlɪvəʳ] *vt* (*goods*) доставля́ть (*perf* доста́вить); (*letter*) вруча́ть (*perf* вручи́ть); (*message*) передава́ть (*perf* переда́ть); (*speech*) произноси́ть (*perf* произнести́); (*baby*) принима́ть (*perf* приня́ть); **delivery** *n* (*of goods*) доста́вка; (*of baby*) ро́ды *pl*; **to take delivery of** получа́ть (*perf* получи́ть)

delusion [dɪˈlu:ʒən] *n* заблужде́ние

demand [dɪˈmɑ:nd] *vt* тре́бовать (*perf* потре́бовать) +*gen* ▷ *n* (*request, claim*) тре́бование; (*Econ*): **demand (for)** спрос (на +*acc*); **to be in demand** (*commodity*) по́льзоваться (*impf*) спро́сом; **on demand** по требо́ванию; **demanding** *adj* (*boss*) требова́тельный; (*child*) тру́дный; (*work: requiring effort*) тяжёлый

demise [dɪ'maɪz] *n* (*fig*) упа́док

demo ['dɛməu] *n abbr* (*inf*) = **demonstration**

democracy [dɪ'mɔkrəsɪ] *n* (*system*) демокра́тия; (*country*) демократи́ческая страна́

democrat ['dɛməkræt] *n* демокра́т; **Democrat** (*US*) член па́ртии демокра́тов; **democratic** [dɛmə'krætɪk] *adj* демократи́ческий; **Democratic Party** (*US*) па́ртия демокра́тов

demolish [dɪ'mɔlɪʃ] *vt* сноси́ть (*perf* снести́); (*argument*) разгроми́ть (*perf*)

demolition [dɛmə'lɪʃən] *n* (*see vb*) снос; разгро́м

demon ['di:mən] *n* де́мон

demonstrate ['dɛmənstreɪt] *vt* демонстри́ровать (*perf* продемонстри́ровать) ▷ *vi*: **to demonstrate (for/against)** демонстри́ровать (*impf*) (за *+acc*/ про́тив *+gen*)

demonstration [dɛmən'streɪʃən] *n* демонстра́ция

den [dɛn] *n* (*of animal, person*) ло́гово

denial [dɪ'naɪəl] *n* отрица́ние; (*refusal*) отка́з

denim ['dɛnɪm] *n* джи́нсовая ткань *f*; **denims** *npl* (*jeans*) джи́нсы *pl*

Denmark ['dɛnma:k] *n* Да́ния

denounce [dɪ'nauns] *vt* (*condemn*) осужда́ть (*perf* осуди́ть); (*inform on*) доноси́ть (*perf* донести́) на *+acc*

dense [dɛns] *adj* (*smoke, foliage etc*) густо́й; (*inf: person*) тупо́й

density ['dɛnsɪtɪ] *n* пло́тность *f*; **single/double-density disk** диск с одина́рной/двойно́й пло́тностью

dent [dɛnt] *n* (*in metal*) вмя́тина ▷ *vt* (*also* **make a dent in**: *car etc*) оставля́ть (*perf* оста́вить) вмя́тину на *+acc*

dental ['dɛntl] *adj* зубно́й

dentist ['dɛntɪst] *n* зубно́й врач, стомато́лог

dentures ['dɛntʃəz] *npl* зубно́й проте́з *msg*

deny [dɪ'naɪ] *vt* отрица́ть (*impf*); (*allegation*) отверга́ть (*perf* отве́ргнуть); (*refuse*): **to deny sb sth** отка́зывать (*perf* отказа́ть) кому́-н в чём-н

deodorant [di:'əudərənt] *n* дезодора́нт

depart [dɪ'pa:t] *vi* (*person*) отбыва́ть (*perf* отбы́ть); (*bus, train*) отправля́ться (*perf* отпра́виться); (*plane*) улета́ть (*perf* улете́ть); **to depart from** (*fig*) отклоня́ться (*perf* отклони́ться) от *+gen*

department [dɪ'pa:tmənt] *n* (*in shop*) отде́л; (*Scol*) отделе́ние; (*Pol*) ве́домство, департа́мент; **department store** *n* универса́льный магази́н, универма́г

departure [dɪ'pa:tʃə[r]] *n* (*see vi*) отъе́зд; отправле́ние; вы́лет; **departure lounge** *n* зал вы́лета

depend [dɪ'pɛnd] *vi*: **to depend on** зави́сеть (*impf*) от *+gen*; (*trust*) полага́ться (*perf* положи́ться) на *+acc*; **it depends** смотря́ по обстоя́тельствам, как полу́чится; **depending on ...** в зави́симости от *+gen ...*; **dependent** *adj*: **dependent (on)** зави́симый (от *+gen*) ▷ *n* иждиве́нец(-нка)

depict [dɪ'pɪkt] *vt* изобража́ть (*perf* изобрази́ть)

deport [dɪ'pɔːt] *vt* депорти́ровать (*impf/perf*), высыла́ть (*perf* вы́слать)
deposit [dɪ'pɔzɪt] *n* (*in account*) депози́т, вклад; (*down payment*) пе́рвый взнос, зада́ток; (*of ore, oil*) за́лежь *f* ▷ *vt* (*money*) помеща́ть (*perf* помести́ть); (*bag*) сдава́ть (*perf* сдать); **deposit account** *n* депози́тный счёт
depot ['dɛpəu] *n* (*storehouse*) склад; (*for buses*) парк; (*for trains*) депо́ *nt ind*; (*US*: *station*) ста́нция
depress [dɪ'prɛs] *vt* (*Psych*) подавля́ть (*impf*), угнета́ть (*impf*); **depressed** *adj* (*person*) пода́вленный, угнетённый; (*prices*) сни́женный; **depressed area** райо́н, пережива́ющий экономи́ческий упа́док; **depressing** *adj* (*news, outlook*) удруча́ющий; **depression** [dɪ'prɛʃən] *n* депре́ссия; (*Meteorology*) о́бласть *f* ни́зкого давле́ния
deprive [dɪ'praɪv] *vt*: **to deprive sb of** лиша́ть (*perf* лиши́ть) кого́-н +*gen*; **deprived** *adj* бе́дный; (*family, child*) обездо́ленный
depth [dɛpθ] *n* глубина́; **in the depths of despair** в глубо́ком отча́янии; **to be out of one's depth** (*in water*) не достава́ть (*impf*) до дна
deputy ['dɛpjutɪ] *n* замести́тель *m*; (*Pol*) депута́т ▷ *cpd*: **deputy chairman** замести́тель председа́теля; **deputy head** (*Brit*: *Scol*) замести́тель дире́ктора
derelict ['dɛrɪlɪkt] *adj* забро́шенный
derive [dɪ'raɪv] *vt*: **to derive (from)** (*pleasure*) получа́ть (*perf* получи́ть) (от +*gen*); (*benefit*) извлека́ть (*perf* извле́чь) (из +*gen*)
descend [dɪ'sɛnd] *vt* (*stairs*) спуска́ться (*perf* спусти́ться) по +*dat*; (*hill*) спуска́ться (*perf* спусти́ться) с +*gen* ▷ *vi* (*go down*) спуска́ться (*perf* спусти́ться); **descendant** *n* пото́мок
descent [dɪ'sɛnt] *n* спуск; (*Aviat*) сниже́ние; (*origin*) происхожде́ние
describe [dɪs'kraɪb] *vt* опи́сывать (*perf* описа́ть)
description [dɪs'krɪpʃən] *n* описа́ние; (*sort*) род
desert [*n* 'dɛzət, *vb* dɪ'zəːt] *n* пусты́ня ▷ *vt* покида́ть (*perf* поки́нуть) ▷ *vi* (*Mil*) дезерти́ровать (*impf/perf*)
deserve [dɪ'zəːv] *vt* заслу́живать (*perf* заслужи́ть)
design [dɪ'zaɪn] *n* диза́йн; (*process*: *of dress*) модели́рование; (*sketch*: *of building*) прое́кт; (*pattern*) рису́нок ▷ *vt* (*house, kitchen*) проекти́ровать (*perf* спроекти́ровать); (*product, test*) разраба́тывать (*perf* разрабо́тать)
designate ['dɛzɪgneɪt] *vt* (*nominate*) назнача́ть (*perf* назна́чить); (*indicate*) обознача́ть (*perf* обозна́чить)
designer [dɪ'zaɪnə[r]] *n* (*also* **fashion designer**) моделье́р; (*Art*) диза́йнер; (*of machine*) констру́ктор
desirable [dɪ'zaɪərəbl] *adj* (*proper*) жела́тельный
desire [dɪ'zaɪə[r]] *n* жела́ние ▷ *vt* (*want*) жела́ть (*impf*)
desk [dɛsk] *n* (*in office, study*) (пи́сьменный) стол; (*for pupil*) па́рта; (*in hotel, at airport*) сто́йка; (*Brit*: *also* **cash desk**) ка́сса
despair [dɪs'pɛə[r]] *n* отча́яние ▷ *vi*: **to despair of sth/doing** отча́иваться (*perf* отча́яться) в чём-н/+*infin*

despatch [dɪs'pætʃ] *n, vt* = **dispatch**

desperate ['dɛspərɪt] *adj* (*action, situation*) отча́янный; (*criminal*) отъя́вленный; **to be desperate** (*person*) быть (*impf*) в отча́янии; **to be desperate to do** жа́ждать (*impf*) *+infin*; **to be desperate for money** кра́йне нужда́ться (*impf*) в деньга́х; **desperately** *adv* отча́янно; (*very*) чрезвыча́йно

desperation [dɛspə'reɪʃən] *n* отча́яние

despise [dɪs'paɪz] *vt* презира́ть (*impf*)

despite [dɪs'paɪt] *prep* несмотря́ на *+acc*

dessert [dɪ'zə:t] *n* десе́рт

destination [dɛstɪ'neɪʃən] *n* (*of person*) цель *f*; (*of mail*) ме́сто назначе́ния

destined ['dɛstɪnd] *adj*: **he is destined to do** ему́ суждено́ *+infin*; **to be destined for** предназнача́ться (*impf*) для *+gen*

destiny ['dɛstɪnɪ] *n* судьба́

destroy [dɪs'trɔɪ] *vt* уничтожа́ть (*perf* уничто́жить), разруша́ть (*perf* разру́шить)

destruction [dɪs'trʌkʃən] *n* уничтоже́ние, разруше́ние

destructive [dɪs'trʌktɪv] *adj* (*capacity, force*) разруши́тельный; (*criticism*) сокруши́тельный; (*emotion*) губи́тельный

detached [dɪ'tætʃt] *adj* беспристра́стный; **detached house** особня́к

detail ['di:teɪl] *n* подро́бность *f*, дета́ль *f* ▷ *vt* перечисля́ть (*perf* перечи́слить); **in detail** подро́бно, в дета́лях; **detailed** *adj* дета́льный, подро́бный

detain [dɪ'teɪn] *vt* заде́рживать (*perf* задержа́ть); (*in hospital*) оставля́ть (*perf* оста́вить)

detect [dɪ'tɛkt] *vt* обнару́живать (*perf* обнару́жить); (*sense*) чу́вствовать (*perf* почу́вствовать); **detection** [dɪ'tɛkʃən] *n* (*discovery*) обнаруже́ние; **detective** *n* сы́щик, детекти́в

detention [dɪ'tɛnʃən] *n* (*imprisonment*) содержа́ние под стра́жей; (*arrest*) задержа́ние; (*Scol*): **to give sb detention** оставля́ть (*perf* оста́вить) кого́-н по́сле уро́ков

DETENTION

В брита́нских шко́лах дете́й, наруша́ющих дисципли́ну, в ка́честве наказа́ния мо́гут оста́вить по́сле уро́ков в шко́ле.

deter [dɪ'tə:ʳ] *vt* уде́рживать (*perf* удержа́ть)

detergent [dɪ'tə:dʒənt] *n* мо́ющее сре́дство

deteriorate [dɪ'tɪərɪəreɪt] *vi* ухудша́ться (*perf* уху́дшиться)

determination [dɪtə:mɪ'neɪʃən] *n* (*resolve*) реши́мость *f*; (*establishment*) установле́ние

determine [dɪ'tə:mɪn] *vt* (*find out*) устана́вливать (*perf* установи́ть); (*establish, dictate*) определя́ть (*perf* определи́ть); **determined** *adj* реши́тельный, волево́й; **determined to do** по́лный реши́мости *+infin*

deterrent [dɪ'tɛrənt] *n* сре́дство сде́рживания, сде́рживающее сре́дство; **nuclear deterrent** сре́дство я́дерного сде́рживания

detour ['di:tuəʳ] *n* (*also US*) объе́зд

detract [dɪ'trækt] *vi*: **to detract from** умаля́ть (*perf* умали́ть)

detrimental [dɛtrɪ'mɛntl] *adj*: **detrimental to** вре́дный для *+gen*
devastating ['dɛvəsteɪtɪŋ] *adj* (*weapon, storm*) разруши́тельный; (*news, effect*) ошеломля́ющий
develop [dɪ'vɛləp] *vt* (*idea, industry*) развива́ть (*perf* разви́ть); (*plan, resource*) разраба́тывать (*perf* разрабо́тать); (*land*) застра́ивать (*perf* застро́ить); (*Phot*) проявля́ть (*perf* прояви́ть) ▷ *vi* (*evolve, advance*) развива́ться (*perf* разви́ться); (*appear*) проявля́ться (*perf* прояви́ться); **development** *n* разви́тие; (*of resources*) разрабо́тка; (*of land*) застро́йка
device [dɪ'vaɪs] *n* (*apparatus*) устро́йство, прибо́р
devil ['dɛvl] *n* дья́вол, чёрт
devious ['di:vɪəs] *adj* (*person*) лука́вый
devise [dɪ'vaɪz] *vt* разраба́тывать (*perf* разрабо́тать)
devote [dɪ'vəut] *vt*: **to devote sth to** посвяща́ть (*perf* посвяти́ть) что-н *+dat*; **devoted** *adj* (*admirer, partner*) пре́данный; **his book is devoted to Scotland** его́ кни́га посвящена́ Шотла́ндии
devotion [dɪ'vəuʃən] *n* пре́данность *f*; (*Rel*) поклоне́ние
devout [dɪ'vaut] *adj* (*Rel*) благочести́вый
dew [dju:] *n* роса́
diabetes [daɪə'bi:ti:z] *n* диабе́т
diabetic [daɪə'bɛtɪk] *n* диабе́тик
diagnose [daɪəg'nəuz] *vt* (*illness*) диагности́ровать (*impf/perf*); (*problem*) определя́ть (*perf* определи́ть)
diagnosis [daɪəg'nəusɪs] (*pl* **diagnoses**) *n* диа́гноз
diagonal [daɪ'ægənl] *adj* диагона́льный
diagram ['daɪəgræm] *n* схе́ма
dial ['daɪəl] *n* (*of clock*) цифербла́т; (*of radio*) регуля́тор настро́йки ▷ *vt* (*number*) набира́ть (*perf* набра́ть)
dialect ['daɪəlɛkt] *n* диале́кт
dialling tone ['daɪəlɪŋ-] (*US* **dial tone**) *n* непреры́вный гудо́к
dialogue ['daɪəlɔg] (*US* **dialog**) *n* диало́г
diameter [daɪ'æmɪtə^r] *n* диа́метр
diamond ['daɪəmənd] *n* алма́з; (*cut diamond*) бриллиа́нт; (*shape*) ромб; **diamonds** *npl* (*Cards*) бу́бны *fpl*
diaper ['daɪəpə^r] *n* (*US*) подгу́зник
diarrhoea [daɪə'ri:ə] (*US* **diarrhea**) *n* поно́с
diary ['daɪərɪ] *n* (*journal*) дневни́к; (*engagements book*) ежедне́вник
dice [daɪs] *npl inv* (*in game*) ку́бик ▷ *vt* ре́зать (*perf* наре́зать) ку́биками
dictate [dɪk'teɪt] *vt* диктова́ть (*perf* продиктова́ть)
dictator [dɪk'teɪtə^r] *n* дикта́тор
dictionary ['dɪkʃənrɪ] *n* слова́рь *m*
did [dɪd] *pt of* **do**
didn't ['dɪdnt] = **did not**
die [daɪ] *vi* (*person, emotion*) умира́ть (*perf* умере́ть); (*smile, light*) угаса́ть (*perf* уга́снуть); **to be dying for sth/to do** до́ смерти хоте́ть (*impf*) чего́-н/*+infin*
diesel ['di:zl] *n* ди́зель *m*; (*also* **diesel oil**) ди́зельное то́пливо
diet ['daɪət] *n* дие́та
differ ['dɪfə^r] *vi*: **to differ (from)** отлича́ться (*impf*) (от *+gen*); (*disagree*): **to differ about** расходи́ться (*perf* разойти́сь) в вопро́се *+gen*; **difference** *n*

различие; (*in size, age*) разница; (*disagreement*) разногласие; **different** *adj* другой, иной; (*various*) различный, разный; **to be different from** отличаться (*impf*) от *+gen*; **differentiate** [dɪfəˈrɛnʃɪeɪt] *vi*: **to differentiate (between)** проводить (*perf* провести) различие (между *+instr*); **differently** *adv* (*otherwise*) иначе, по-другому; (*in different ways*) по-разному

difficult [ˈdɪfɪkəlt] *adj* трудный, тяжёлый; **difficulty** *n* трудность *f*, затруднение

dig [dɪg] (*pt, pp* **dug**) *vt* (*hole*) копать (*perf* выкопать), рыть (*perf* вырыть); (*garden*) копать (*perf* вскопать) ▷ *n* (*prod*) толчок; (*excavation*) раскопки *fpl*; **to dig one's nails into** впиваться (*perf* впиться) ногтями в *+acc*; **dig up** *vt* (*plant*) выкапывать (*perf* выкопать); (*information*) раскапывать (*perf* раскопать)

digest [daɪˈdʒɛst] *vt* (*food*) переваривать (*perf* переварить); (*facts*) усваивать (*perf* усвоить); **digestion** [dɪˈdʒɛstʃən] *n* пищеварение

digit [ˈdɪdʒɪt] *n* (*number*) цифра; **digital** *adj*: **digital watch** электронные часы *mpl*

dignified [ˈdɪgnɪfaɪd] *adj* полный достоинства

dignity [ˈdɪgnɪtɪ] *n* достоинство

dilemma [daɪˈlɛmə] *n* дилемма

dilute [daɪˈluːt] *vt* (*liquid*) разбавлять (*perf* разбавить)

dim [dɪm] *adj* (*outline, memory*) смутный; (*light*) тусклый; (*room*) плохо освещённый ▷ *vt* (*light*) приглушать (*perf* приглушить)

dimension [daɪˈmɛnʃən] *n* (*measurement*) измерение; (*also pl*: *scale, size*) размеры *mpl*; (*aspect*) аспект

diminish [dɪˈmɪnɪʃ] *vi* уменьшаться (*perf* уменьшиться)

din [dɪn] *n* грохот

dine [daɪn] *vi* обедать (*perf* пообедать); **diner** *n* (*person*) обедающий(-ая) *m(f) adj*; (*US*) дешёвый ресторан

dinghy [ˈdɪŋgɪ] *n* (*also* **sailing dinghy**) шлюпка; (*also* **rubber dinghy**) надувная лодка

dingy [ˈdɪndʒɪ] *adj* (*streets, room*) мрачный; (*clothes, curtains etc*) замызганный

dining room [ˈdaɪnɪŋ-] *n* столовая *f adj*

dinner [ˈdɪnə^r] *n* (*evening meal*) ужин; (*lunch, banquet*) обед; **dinner jacket** *n* смокинг; **dinner party** *n* званый обед

dinosaur [ˈdaɪnəsɔː^r] *n* динозавр

dip [dɪp] *n* (*depression*) впадина; (*Culin*) соус ▷ *vt* (*immerse*) погружать (*perf* погрузить), окунать (*perf* окунуть); (: *in liquid*) макать (*perf* макнуть), обмакивать (*perf* обмакнуть); (*Brit*: *Aut*: *lights*) приглушать (*perf* приглушить) ▷ *vi* (*ground, road*) идти (*perf* пойти) под уклон; **to go for a dip** окунаться (*perf* окунуться)

diploma [dɪˈpləumə] *n* диплом

diplomacy [dɪˈpləuməsɪ] *n* дипломатия

diplomat [ˈdɪpləmæt] *n* дипломат; **diplomatic** [dɪpləˈmætɪk] *adj* (*Pol*) дипломатический; (*tactful*) дипломатичный

dire [daɪə^r] *adj* (*consequences*) зловещий; (*poverty, situation*) жуткий

direct [daɪˈrɛkt] *adj* прямой ▷ *adv* прямо ▷ *vt* (*company,* *project etc*) руководи́ть (*impf*) +*instr*; (*play, film*) ста́вить (*perf* поста́вить); **to direct (towards** *or* **at)** (*attention, remark*) направля́ть (*perf* напра́вить) (на +*acc*); **to direct sb to do** (*order*) веле́ть (*impf*) кому́-н +*infin*; **can you direct me to ...?** Вы не ука́жете, где нахо́дится ...?; **direct debit** *n* (*Brit*: *Comm*) прямо́е дебетова́ние

direction [dɪ'rɛkʃən] *n* (*way*) направле́ние; **directions** *npl* (*instructions*) указа́ния *ntpl*; **to have a good sense of direction** хорошо́ ориенти́роваться (*perf*); **directions for use** инстру́кция

directly [dɪ'rɛktlɪ] *adv* пря́мо; (*at once*) сейча́с же; (*as soon as*) как то́лько

director [dɪ'rɛktəʳ] *n* (*Comm*) дире́ктор; (*of project*) руководи́тель *m*; (*TV, Cinema*) режиссёр

directory [dɪ'rɛktərɪ] *n* спра́вочник

dirt [dəːt] *n* грязь *f*; **dirty** *adj* гря́зный ▷ *vt* па́чкать (*perf* испа́чкать)

disability [dɪsə'bɪlɪtɪ] *n*: **(physical) disability** инвали́дность *f no pl*; **mental disability** у́мственная неполноце́нность *f*

disabled [dɪs'eɪbld] *adj* (*mentally*) у́мственно неполноце́нный; (*physically*): **disabled person** инвали́д

disadvantage [dɪsəd'vɑːntɪdʒ] *n* недоста́ток

disagree [dɪsə'griː] *vi* (*differ*) расходи́ться (*perf* разойти́сь); **to disagree (with)** (*oppose*) не соглаша́ться (*perf* согласи́ться) (с +*instr*); **I disagree with you** я с Ва́ми не согла́сен; **disagreement** *n* разногла́сие; (*opposition*): **disagreement with** несогла́сие с +*instr*

disappear [dɪsə'pɪəʳ] *vi* исчеза́ть (*perf* исче́знуть); **disappearance** *n* исчезнове́ние

disappoint [dɪsə'pɔɪnt] *vt* разочаро́вывать (*perf* разочарова́ть); **disappointed** *adj* разочаро́ванный; **disappointing** *adj*: **the film is rather disappointing** э́тот фильм не́сколько разочаро́вывает; **disappointment** *n* разочарова́ние

disapproval [dɪsə'pruːvəl] *n* неодобре́ние

disapprove [dɪsə'pruːv] *vi*: **to disapprove (of)** не одобря́ть (*impf*) (+*acc*)

disarm [dɪs'ɑːm] *vt* (*Mil*) разоружа́ть (*perf* разоружи́ть); **disarmament** *n* разоруже́ние

disaster [dɪ'zɑːstəʳ] *n* (*natural*) бе́дствие; (*man-made, also fig*) катастро́фа

disastrous [dɪ'zɑːstrəs] *adj* губи́тельный

disbelief ['dɪsbə'liːf] *n* неве́рие

disc [dɪsk] *n* (*Anat*) межпозвоно́чный хрящ; (*Comput*) = **disk**

discard [dɪs'kɑːd] *vt* (*object*) выбра́сывать (*perf* вы́бросить); (*idea, plan*) отбра́сывать (*perf* отбро́сить)

discharge [*vb* dɪs'tʃɑːdʒ, *n* 'dɪstʃɑːdʒ] *vt* (*waste*) выбра́сывать (*perf* вы́бросить); (*patient*) выпи́сывать (*perf* вы́писать); (*employee*) увольня́ть (*perf* уво́лить); (*soldier*) демобилизова́ть (*impf/perf*) ▷ *n* (*Med*) выделе́ние; (*of patient*) вы́писка; (*of employee*)

увольне́ние; (*of soldier*) демобилиза́ция
discipline ['dɪsɪplɪn] *n* дисципли́на ▷ *vt* дисциплини́ровать (*impf/perf*); (*punish*) налага́ть (*perf* наложи́ть) дисциплина́рное взыска́ние на *+acc*
disclose [dɪs'kləuz] *vt* раскрыва́ть (*perf* раскры́ть)
disco ['dɪskəu] *n abbr* (= *discotheque*) дискоте́ка
discomfort [dɪs'kʌmfət] *n* (*unease*) нело́вкость *f*; (*pain*) недомога́ние
discontent [dɪskən'tɛnt] *n* недово́льство
discount [*n* 'dɪskaunt, *vb* dɪs'kaunt] *n* ски́дка ▷ *vt* (*Comm*) снижа́ть (*perf* сни́зить) це́ну на *+acc*; (*idea, fact*) не принима́ть (*perf* приня́ть) в расчёт
discourage [dɪs'kʌrɪdʒ] *vt* (*dishearten*) препя́тствовать (*perf* воспрепя́тствовать); **to discourage sb from doing** отгова́ривать (*perf* отговори́ть) кого́-н *+infin*
discover [dɪs'kʌvə^r] *vt* обнару́живать (*perf* обнару́жить); **discovery** *n* откры́тие
discredit [dɪs'krɛdɪt] *vt* дискредити́ровать (*impf/perf*)
discreet [dɪs'kri:t] *adj* (*tactful*) такти́чный; (*careful*) осмотри́тельный; (*barely noticeable*) неприме́тный
discrepancy [dɪs'krɛpənsɪ] *n* расхожде́ние
discretion [dɪs'krɛʃən] *n* (*tact*) такти́чность *f*; **use your (own) discretion** поступа́йте по своему́ усмотре́нию
discriminate [dɪs'krɪmɪneɪt] *vi*: **to discriminate between** различа́ть (*perf* различи́ть); **to discriminate against** дискримини́ровать (*impf/perf*)
discrimination [dɪskrɪmɪ'neɪʃən] *n* (*bias*) дискримина́ция; (*discernment*) разбо́рчивость *f*
discuss [dɪs'kʌs] *vt* обсужда́ть (*perf* обсуди́ть); **discussion** [dɪs'kʌʃən] *n* (*talk*) обсужде́ние; (*debate*) диску́ссия
disease [dɪ'zi:z] *n* боле́знь *f*
disgrace [dɪs'greɪs] *n* позо́р ▷ *vt* позо́рить (*perf* опозо́рить); **disgraceful** *adj* позо́рный
disgruntled [dɪs'grʌntld] *adj* недово́льный
disguise [dɪs'gaɪz] *n* маскиро́вка ▷ *vt* (*object*) маскирова́ть (*perf* замаскирова́ть); **in disguise** (*person*) переоде́тый; **to disguise (as)** (*dress up*) переодева́ть (*perf* переоде́ть) (*+instr*); (*make up*) гримирова́ть (*perf* загримирова́ть) (под *+acc*)
disgust [dɪs'gʌst] *n* отвраще́ние ▷ *vt* внуша́ть (*perf* внуши́ть) отвраще́ние *+dat*; **disgusting** *adj* отврати́тельный
dish [dɪʃ] *n* блю́до; **to do** *or* **wash the dishes** мыть (*perf* вы́мыть) посу́ду
dishonest [dɪs'ɔnɪst] *adj* нече́стный
dishwasher ['dɪʃwɔʃə^r] *n* посудомо́ечная маши́на
disillusion [dɪsɪ'lu:ʒən] *vt* разочаро́вывать (*perf* разочарова́ть)
disinfectant [dɪsɪn'fɛktənt] *n* дезинфици́рующее сре́дство
disintegrate [dɪs'ɪntɪgreɪt] *vi* (*break up*) распада́ться (*perf* распа́сться)
disk [dɪsk] *n* диск
dislike [dɪs'laɪk] *n* (*feeling*) неприя́знь *f* ▷ *vt* не люби́ть

(*impf*); **I dislike the idea** мне не нра́вится э́та иде́я; **he dislikes cooking** он не лю́бит гото́вить
dismal ['dɪzml] *adj* уны́лый, мра́чный; (*failure, performance*) жа́лкий
dismantle [dɪs'mæntl] *vt* разбира́ть (*perf* разобра́ть)
dismay [dɪs'meɪ] *n* трево́га, смяте́ние ▷ *vt* приводи́ть (*perf* привести́) в смяте́ние
dismiss [dɪs'mɪs] *vt* (*worker*) увольня́ть (*perf* уво́лить); (*pupils, soldiers*) распуска́ть (*perf* распусти́ть); (*Law*) прекраща́ть (*perf* прекрати́ть); (*possibility, idea*) отбра́сывать (*perf* отбро́сить); **dismissal** *n* (*sacking*) увольне́ние
disorder [dɪs'ɔːdəʳ] *n* беспоря́док; (*Med*) расстро́йство; **civil disorder** социа́льные беспоря́дки
dispatch [dɪs'pætʃ] *vt* (*send*) отправля́ть (*perf* отпра́вить) ▷ *n* (*sending*) отпра́вка; (*Press*) сообще́ние; (*Mil*) донесе́ние
dispel [dɪs'pɛl] *vt* рассе́ивать (*perf* рассе́ять)
dispense [dɪs'pɛns] *vt* (*medicines*) приготовля́ть (*perf* пригото́вить); **dispense with** *vt fus* обходи́ться (*perf* обойти́сь) без *+gen*; **dispenser** *n* торго́вый автома́т
disperse [dɪs'pəːs] *vt* (*objects*) рассе́ивать (*perf* рассе́ять); (*crowd*) разгоня́ть (*perf* разогна́ть) ▷ *vi* рассе́иваться (*perf* рассе́яться)
display [dɪs'pleɪ] *n* демонстра́ция; (*exhibition*) вы́ставка ▷ *vt* (*emotion, quality*) выка́зывать (*perf* вы́казать); (*goods, exhibits*) выставля́ть (*perf* вы́ставить)
disposable [dɪs'pəuzəbl] *adj* однора́зовый
disposal [dɪs'pəuzl] *n* (*of goods*) реализа́ция; (*of rubbish*) удале́ние; **to have sth at one's disposal** распола́гать (*impf*) чем-н
dispose [dɪs'pəuz] *vi*: **dispose of** избавля́ться (*perf* изба́виться) от *+gen*; (*problem, task*) справля́ться (*perf* спра́виться) с *+instr*
disposition [dɪspə'zɪʃən] *n* (*nature*) нрав
disproportionate [dɪsprə'pɔːʃənət] *adj* (*excessive*) неопра́вданно большо́й; **disproportionate to** несоизмери́мый с *+instr*
dispute [dɪs'pjuːt] *n* спор; (*domestic*) ссо́ра; (*Law*) тя́жба ▷ *vt* оспа́ривать (*perf* оспо́рить)
disregard [dɪsrɪ'gɑːd] *vt* пренебрега́ть (*perf* пренебре́чь)
disrupt [dɪs'rʌpt] *vt* наруша́ть (*perf* нару́шить); **disruption** [dɪs'rʌpʃən] *n* (*interruption*) наруше́ние
dissatisfaction [dɪssætɪs'fækʃən] *n* недово́льство, неудовлетворённость *f*
dissatisfied [dɪs'sætɪsfaɪd] *adj* неудовлетворённый; **dissatisfied (with)** недово́льный (*+instr*)
dissent [dɪ'sɛnt] *n* инакомы́слие
dissolve [dɪ'zɔlv] *vt* (*substance*) растворя́ть (*perf* раствори́ть); (*organization, parliament*) распуска́ть (*perf* распусти́ть); (*marriage*) расторга́ть (*perf* расто́ргнуть) ▷ *vi* растворя́ться (*perf* раствори́ться); **to dissolve in(to) tears** залива́ться (*perf* зали́ться) слеза́ми
distance ['dɪstns] *n* (*in space*) расстоя́ние; (*in sport*) диста́нция; (*in time*) отдалённость *f*; **in the**

d

distance вдалеке́, вдали́; **from a distance** издалека́, и́здали
distant [ˈdɪstnt] *adj* (*place, time*) далёкий; (*relative*) да́льний; (*manner*) отчуждённый
distinct [dɪsˈtɪŋkt] *adj* (*clear*) отчётливый; (*unmistakable*) определённый; (*different*): **distinct (from)** отли́чный (от +*gen*); **as distinct from** в отли́чие от +*gen*; **distinction** [dɪsˈtɪŋkʃən] *n* (*difference*) отли́чие; (*honour*) честь *f*; (*Scol*) ≈ "отли́чно"; **distinctive** *adj* своеобра́зный, характе́рный; (*feature*) отличи́тельный
distinguish [dɪsˈtɪŋgwɪʃ] *vt* различа́ть (*perf* различи́ть); **to distinguish o.s.** отлича́ться (*perf* отличи́ться); **distinguished** *adj* ви́дный
distort [dɪsˈtɔːt] *vt* искажа́ть (*perf* искази́ть)
distract [dɪsˈtrækt] *vt* отвлека́ть (*perf* отвле́чь); **distracted** *adj* (*dreaming*) невнима́тельный; (*anxious*) встрево́женный; **distraction** [dɪsˈtrækʃən] *n* (*diversion*) отвлече́ние; (*amusement*) развлече́ние
distraught [dɪsˈtrɔːt] *adj*: **distraught (with)** обезу́мевший (от +*gen*)
distress [dɪsˈtrɛs] *n* отча́яние; (*through pain*) страда́ние ▷ *vt* расстра́ивать (*perf* расстро́ить), приводи́ть (*perf* привести́) в отча́яние
distribute [dɪsˈtrɪbjuːt] *vt* (*prizes*) раздава́ть (*perf* разда́ть); (*leaflets*) распространя́ть (*perf* распространи́ть); (*profits, weight*) распределя́ть (*perf* распредели́ть)
distribution [dɪstrɪˈbjuːʃən] *n* (*of goods*) распростране́ние; (*of profits, weight*) распределе́ние
distributor [dɪsˈtrɪbjutə[r]] *n* (*Comm*) дистрибью́тер
district [ˈdɪstrɪkt] *n* райо́н
distrust [dɪsˈtrʌst] *n* недове́рие ▷ *vt* не доверя́ть (*impf*) +*dat*
disturb [dɪsˈtəːb] *vt* (*person*) беспоко́ить (*perf* побеспоко́ить); (*thoughts, peace*) меша́ть (*perf* помеша́ть) +*dat*; (*disorganize*) наруша́ть (*perf* нару́шить); **disturbance** *n* расстро́йство; (*violent event*) беспоря́дки *mpl*; **disturbed** *adj* (*person: upset*) расстро́енный; **emotionally disturbed** психи́чески неуравнове́шенный; **disturbing** *adj* трево́жный
ditch [dɪtʃ] *n* ров, кана́ва; (*for irrigation*) кана́л ▷ *vt* (*inf: person, car*) броса́ть (*perf* бро́сить); (*: plan*) забра́сывать (*perf* забро́сить)
dive [daɪv] *n* (*from board*) прыжо́к (*в во́ду*); (*underwater*) ныря́ние ▷ *vi* ныря́ть (*impf*); **to dive into** (*bag, drawer etc*) запуска́ть (*perf* запусти́ть) ру́ку в +*acc*; (*shop, car etc*) ныря́ть (*perf* нырну́ть) в +*acc*; **diver** *n* водола́з
diverse [daɪˈvəːs] *adj* разнообра́зный
diversion [daɪˈvəːʃən] *n* (*Brit: Aut*) объе́зд; (*of attention, funds*) отвлече́ние
diversity [daɪˈvəːsɪtɪ] *n* разнообра́зие, многообра́зие
divert [daɪˈvəːt] *vt* (*traffic*) отводи́ть (*perf* отвести́); (*funds, attention*) отвлека́ть (*perf* отвле́чь)
divide [dɪˈvaɪd] *vt* (*split*) разделя́ть (*perf* раздели́ть); (*Math*) дели́ть (*perf* раздели́ть); (*share out*) дели́ть (*perf* подели́ть) ▷ *vi*

делиться (*perf* разделиться); (*road*) разделяться (*perf* разделиться); **divided highway** *n* (*US*) автотрасса

divine [dɪ'vaɪn] *adj* божественный

diving ['daɪvɪŋ] *n* ныряние; (*Sport*) прыжки *mpl* в воду; **diving board** *n* вышка (*для прыжков в воду*)

division [dɪ'vɪʒən] *n* (*also Math*) деление; (*sharing out*) разделение; (*disagreement*) разногласие; (*Comm*) подразделение; (*Mil*) дивизия; (*Sport*) лига

divorce [dɪ'vɔːs] *n* развод ▷ *vt* (*Law*) разводиться (*perf* развестись) с +*instr*; **divorced** *adj* разведённый; **divorcee** [dɪvɔː'siː] *n* разведённый(-ая) *m(f) adj*

DIY *n abbr* (*Brit*) (= *do-it-yourself*) сделай сам

dizzy ['dɪzɪ] *adj*: **dizzy turn** *or* **spell** приступ головокружения

DJ *n abbr* (= *disc jockey*) диск-жокей

 **KEYWORD**

do [duː] (*pt* **did**, *pp* **done**) *aux vb*

1 (*in negative constructions and questions*): **I don't understand** я не понимаю; **she doesn't want it** она не хочет этого; **didn't you know?** разве Вы не знали?; **what do you think?** что Вы думаете?

2 (*for emphasis*) действительно; **she does look rather pale** она действительно выглядит очень бледной; **oh do shut up!** да, замолчи же!

3 (*in polite expressions*) пожалуйста; **do sit down** пожалуйста, садитесь; **do take care!** пожалуйста, береги себя!

4 (*used to avoid repeating vb*): **she swims better than I do** она плавает лучше меня *or*, чем я; **do you read newspapers? — yes, I do/ no, I don't** Вы читаете газеты? — да(, читаю)/нет(, не читаю); **she lives in Glasgow — so do I** она живёт в Глазго — и я тоже; **he didn't like it and neither did we** ему это не понравилось, и нам тоже; **who made this mess? — I did** кто здесь насорил? — я; **he asked me to help him and I did** он попросил меня помочь ему, что я и сделал

5 (*in tag questions*) не так *or* правда ли; **you like him, don't you?** он Вам нравится, не так *or* правда ли?; **I don't know him, do I?** я его не знаю, не так *or* правда ли?

▷ *vt* **1** делать (*perf* сделать); **what are you doing tonight?** что Вы делаете сегодня вечером?; **I've got nothing to do** мне нечего делать; **what can I do for you?** чем могу быть полезен?; **we're doing "Othello" at school** (*studying*) мы проходим "Отелло" в школе; (*performing*) мы ставим "Отелло" в школе; **to do one's teeth** чистить (*perf* почистить) зубы; **to do one's hair** причёсываться (*perf* причесаться); **to do the washing-up** мыть (*perf* помыть) посуду

2 (*Aut etc*): **the car was doing 100 (km/h)** машина шла со скоростью 100 км/ч; **we've done 200 km already** мы уже проехали 200 км; **he can do 100 km/h in that car** на этой машине он может ехать со скоростью 100 км/ч

▷ *vi* **1** (*act, behave*) делать (*perf* сделать); **do as I do** делайте, как я;

you did well to react so quickly ты молоде́ц, что так бы́стро среаги́ровал
2 (*get on, fare*): **he's doing well/ badly at school** он хорошо́/пло́хо у́чится; **the firm is doing well** дела́ в фи́рме иду́т успе́шно; **how do you do?** о́чень прия́тно
3 (*be suitable*) подходи́ть (*perf* подойти́); **will it do?** э́то подойдёт?
4 (*be sufficient*) хвата́ть (*perf* хвати́ть) *+gen*; **will ten pounds do?** десяти́ фу́нтов хва́тит?; **that'll do** э́того доста́точно; **that'll do!** (*in annoyance*) дово́льно!, хва́тит!; **to make do (with)** удовлетворя́ться (*perf* удовлетвори́ться) (*+instr*) ▷ *n* (*inf*): **we're having a bit of a do on Saturday** у нас бу́дет вечери́нка в суббо́ту; **it was a formal do** э́то был официа́льный приём
do away with *vt fus* (*abolish*) поко́нчить (*perf*) с *+instr*
do up *vt* (*laces*) завя́зывать (*perf* завяза́ть); (*dress, buttons*) застёгивать (*perf* застегну́ть); (*room, house*) ремонти́ровать (*perf* отремонти́ровать)
do with *vt fus*: **I could do with a drink** я бы вы́пил чего́-нибудь; **I could do with some help** по́мощь мне бы не помеша́ла; **what has it got to do with you?** како́е э́то име́ет к Вам отноше́ние?; **I won't have anything to do with it** я не жела́ю име́ть к э́тому никако́го отноше́ния; **it has to do with money** э́то каса́ется де́нег
do without *vt fus* обходи́ться (*perf* обойти́сь) без *+gen*

dock [dɔk] *n* (*Naut*) док; (*Law*) скамья́ подсуди́мых; **docks** *npl* (*Naut*) док *msg*, верфь *fsg*
doctor ['dɔktəʳ] *n* (*Med*) врач; (*Scol*) до́ктор
document ['dɔkjumənt] *n* докуме́нт; **documentary** [dɔkju'mɛntərɪ] *n* документа́льный фильм; **documentation** [dɔkjumən'teɪʃən] *n* документа́ция
dodge [dɔdʒ] *vt* увёртываться (*perf* увёрну́ться) от *+gen*
dodgy ['dɔdʒɪ] *adj* (*inf*): **dodgy character** подозри́тельный тип
does [dʌz] *vb see* **do**; **doesn't** ['dʌznt] = **does not**
dog [dɔg] *n* соба́ка ▷ *vt* пресле́довать (*impf*)
dole [dəul] *n* (*Brit*) посо́бие по безрабо́тице; **to be on the dole** получа́ть (*impf*) посо́бие по безрабо́тице
doll [dɔl] *n* (*also US*: *inf*) ку́кла
dollar ['dɔləʳ] *n* до́ллар
dolphin ['dɔlfɪn] *n* дельфи́н
dome [dəum] *n* ку́пол
domestic [də'mɛstɪk] *adj* дома́шний; (*trade, politics*) вну́тренний; (*happiness*) семе́йный
dominant ['dɔmɪnənt] *adj* (*share, role*) преоблада́ющий, домини́рующий; (*partner*) вла́стный
dominate ['dɔmɪneɪt] *vt* домини́ровать (*impf*) над *+instr*
dominoes ['dɔmɪnəuz] *n* (*game*) домино́ *nt ind*
donate [də'neɪt] *vt*: **to donate (to)** же́ртвовать (*perf* поже́ртвовать) (*+dat or* на *+acc*)
donation [də'neɪʃən] *n* поже́ртвование
done [dʌn] *pp of* **do**
donkey ['dɔŋkɪ] *n* осёл

donor ['dəunə^r] *n* (*Med*) до́нор; (*to charity*) же́ртвователь(ница) *m(f)*
don't [dəunt] = **do not**
donut ['dəunʌt] *n* (*US*) = **doughnut**
doom [du:m] *n* рок ▷ *vt*: **the plan was doomed to failure** план был обречён на прова́л
door [dɔ:^r] *n* дверь *f*; **doorbell** *n* (дверно́й) звоно́к; **door handle** *n* дверна́я ру́чка; (*of car*) ру́чка две́ри; **doorstep** *n* поро́г; **doorway** *n* дверно́й проём
dope [dəup] *n* (*inf*: *drug*) гаши́ш; (: *person*) приду́рок ▷ *vt* вводи́ть (*perf* ввести́) нарко́тик +*dat*
dormitory ['dɔ:mɪtrɪ] *n* (*room*) о́бщая спа́льня; (*US*: *building*) общежи́тие
DOS [dɔs] *n abbr* (*Comput*) (= *disk operating system*) ДОС (= *ди́сковая операцио́нная систе́ма*), DOS
dosage ['dəusɪdʒ] *n* до́за
dose [dəus] *n* (*of medicine*) до́за
dot [dɔt] *n* то́чка; (*speck*) кра́пинка, пя́тнышко ▷ *vt*: **dotted with** усе́янный +*instr*; **on the dot** мину́та в мину́ту
double ['dʌbl] *adj* двойно́й ▷ *adv*: **to cost double** сто́ить (*impf*) вдво́е доро́же ▷ *n* двойни́к ▷ *vt* удва́ивать (*perf* удво́ить) ▷ *vi* (*increase*) удва́иваться (*perf* удво́иться); **on the double**, *or* **at the double** (*Brit*) бего́м; **double bass** *n* контраба́с; **double bed** *n* двуспа́льная крова́ть *f*; **double-decker** *n* (*also* **double-decker bus**) двухэта́жный авто́бус; **double glazing** *n* (*Brit*) двойны́е ра́мы *fpl*; **double room** *n* (*in hotel*) двухме́стный но́мер; **doubles** *n* (*Tennis*) па́ры *fpl*
doubt [daut] *n* сомне́ние ▷ *vt* сомнева́ться (*impf*); (*mistrust*) сомнева́ться (*impf*) в +*prp*, не доверя́ть (*impf*) +*dat*; **I doubt whether** *or* **if she'll come** я сомнева́юсь, что она́ придёт; **doubtful** *adj* сомни́тельный; **doubtless** *adv* несомне́нно
dough [dəu] *n* (*Culin*) те́сто; **doughnut** (*US* **donut**) *n* по́нчик
dove [dʌv] *n* го́лубь *m*
down [daun] *n* (*feathers*) пух ▷ *adv* (*motion*) вниз; (*position*) внизу́ ▷ *prep* (*towards lower level*) (вниз) с +*gen or* по +*dat*; (*along*) (вдоль) по +*dat* ▷ *vt* (*inf*: *drink*) прогла́тывать (*perf* проглоти́ть); **down with the government!** доло́й прави́тельство!; **downfall** *n* паде́ние; (*from drinking etc*) ги́бель *f*; **downhill** *adv* (*face, look*) вниз; **to go downhill** (*person, business*) идти́ (*perf* пойти́) по́д гору; (*road*) идти́ (*perf* пойти́) под укло́н; **download** ['daunləud] *n* загру́зка ▷ *vt* загружа́ть (*perf* загрузи́ть) +*gen*; **downloadable** [daun'ləudəbl] *adj* (*Comput*) загружа́емый; **downright** *adj* я́вный; (*refusal*) по́лный ▷ *adv* соверше́нно
Down's syndrome *n* синдро́м Да́уна
down: **downstairs** *adv* (*position*) внизу́; (*motion*) вниз; **downtown** *adv* (*position*) в це́нтре; (*motion*) в центр; **downward** *adj* напра́вленный вниз ▷ *adv* вниз; **downward trend** тенде́нция на пониже́ние; **downwards** *adv* = **downward**
dozen ['dʌzn] *n* дю́жина; **a dozen books** дю́жина книг; **dozens of** деся́тки +*gen*

d

Dr *abbr* = **doctor**
drab [dræb] *adj* унылый
draft [drɑːft] *n* (*first version*) черновик; (*US*: *Mil*) призыв ▷ *vt* набрасывать (*perf* набросать); (*proposal*) составлять (*perf* составить); *see also* **draught**
drag [dræg] *vt* тащить (*impf*); (*lake, pond*) прочёсывать (*perf* прочесать) ▷ *vi* (*time, event etc*) тянуться (*impf*)
dragon ['drægn] *n* дракон; **dragonfly** *n* стрекоза
drain [dreɪn] *n* водосток, водоотвод; (*fig*): **drain on** (*on resources*) утечка +*gen*; (*on health, energy*) расход +*gen* ▷ *vt* (*land, glass*) осушать (*perf* осушить); (*vegetables*) сливать (*perf* слить); (*wear out*) утомлять (*perf* утомить) ▷ *vi* (*liquid*) стекать (*perf* стечь); **drainage** ['dreɪnɪdʒ] *n* (*system*) канализация; (*process*) дренаж, осушение; **draining board** (*US* **drainboard**) *n* сушка
drama ['drɑːmə] *n* (*also fig*) драма; **dramatic** [drə'mætɪk] *adj* драматический; (*increase etc*) резкий; (*change*) разительный; **dramatist** *n* драматург
drank [dræŋk] *pt of* **drink**
drastic ['dræstɪk] *adj* (*measure*) решительный; (*change*) коренной
draught [drɑːft] (*US* **draft**) *n* (*of air*) сквозняк; **on draught** (*beer*) бочковое; **draughts** *n* (*Brit*) шашки *pl*
draw [drɔː] (*pt* **drew**, *pp* **drawn**) *vt* (*Art*) рисовать (*perf* нарисовать); (*Tech*) чертить (*perf* начертить); (*pull*: *cart*) тащить (*impf*); (: *curtains*) задёргивать (*perf* задёрнуть); (*gun, tooth*) вырывать (*perf* вырвать); (*attention*) привлекать (*perf* привлечь); (*crowd*) собирать (*perf* собрать); (*money*) снимать (*perf* снять); (*wages*) получать (*perf* получить) ▷ *vi* (*Sport*) играть (*perf* сыграть) в ничью ▷ *n* (*Sport*) ничья; (*lottery*) лотерея; **to draw near** приближаться (*perf* приблизиться); **draw up** *vi* (*train, bus etc*) подъезжать (*perf* подъехать) ▷ *vt* (*chair etc*) придвигать (*perf* придвинуть); (*document*) составлять (*perf* составить); **drawback** *n* недостаток; **drawer** *n* ящик; **drawing** *n* (*picture*) рисунок; **drawing pin** *n* (*Brit*) (канцелярская) кнопка; **drawing room** *n* гостиная *f adj*
drawn [drɔːn] *pp of* **draw**
dread [drɛd] *n* ужас ▷ *vt* страшиться (*impf*) +*gen*; **dreadful** *adj* ужасный, страшный
dream [driːm] (*pt, pp* **dreamed** *or* **dreamt**) *n* сон; (*ambition*) мечта ▷ *vt*: **I must have dreamt it** мне это, наверное, приснилось ▷ *vi* видеть (*impf*) сон; (*wish*) мечтать (*impf*)
dreary ['drɪərɪ] *adj* тоскливый
dress [drɛs] *n* (*frock*) платье; (*no pl*: *clothing*) одежда ▷ *vt* одевать (*perf* одеть); (*wound*) перевязывать (*perf* перевязать) ▷ *vi* одеваться (*perf* одеться); **to get dressed** одеваться (*perf* одеться); **dress up** *vi* наряжаться (*perf* нарядиться); **dresser** *n* (*Brit*) буфет; (*US*: *chest of drawers*) туалетный столик; **dressing** *n* (*Med*) повязка; (*Culin*) заправка; **dressing gown** *n* (*Brit*) халат; **dressing room** *n* (*Theat*) (артистическая) уборная *f adj*; (*Sport*) раздевалка; **dressing table** *n* туалетный столик

drew [druː] *pt of* **draw**
dried [draɪd] *adj* (*fruit*) сушёный; (*milk*) сухо́й
drift [drɪft] *n* (*of current*) ско́рость *f*; (*of snow*) зано́с, сугро́б; (*meaning*) смысл ▷ *vi* (*boat*) дрейфова́ть (*impf*); **snow had drifted over the road** доро́гу занесло́ сне́гом
drill [drɪl] *n* (*drill bit*) сверло́; (*machine*) дрель *f*; (: *for mining etc*) бура́в; (*Mil*) уче́ние ▷ *vt* (*hole*) сверли́ть (*perf* просверли́ть) ▷ *vi* (*for oil*) working бури́ть (*impf*)
drink [drɪŋk] (*pt* **drank**, *pp* **drunk**) *n* напи́ток; (*alcohol*) (спиртно́й) напи́ток; (*sip*) глото́к ▷ *vt* пить (*perf* вы́пить) ▷ *vi* пить (*impf*); **to have a drink** попи́ть (*perf*); (*alcoholic*) вы́пить (*perf*); **I had a drink of water** я вы́пил воды́; **drink-driving** *n* вожде́ние в нетре́звом состоя́нии; **drinker** *n* пью́щий(-ая) *m(f) adj*; **drinking water** *n* питьева́я вода́
drip [drɪp] *n* ка́панье; (*one drip*) ка́пля; (*Med*) ка́пельница ▷ *vi* (*water, rain*) ка́пать (*impf*); **the tap is dripping** кран течёт
drive [draɪv] (*pt* **drove**, *pp* **driven**) *n* (*journey*) пое́здка; (*also* **driveway**) подъе́зд; (*energy*) напо́р; (*campaign*) кампа́ния; (*Comput*: *also* **disk drive**) дисково́д ▷ *vt* (*vehicle*) води́ть/ вести́ (*impf*); (*motor, wheel*) приводи́ть (*perf* привести́) в движе́ние ▷ *vi* води́ть (*perf* вести́) (маши́ну); (*travel*) е́здить/ е́хать (*impf*); **right-/left-hand drive** право-/левосторо́ннее управле́ние; **to drive sb to the airport** отвози́ть (*perf* отвезти́) кого́-н в аэропо́рт; **to drive sth into** (*nail, stake*) вбива́ть (*perf* вбить) что-н в *+acc*; **to drive sb mad** своди́ть (*perf* свести́) кого́-н с ума́; **driven** ['drɪvn] *pp of* **drive**; **driver** *n* води́тель *m*; (*of train*) машини́ст; **driver's license** *n* (*US*) (води́тельские) права́ *nt pl*; **driveway** *n* подъе́зд
driving ['draɪvɪŋ] *n* вожде́ние; **driving licence** *n* (*Brit*) (води́тельские) права́ *ntpl*
drizzle ['drɪzl] *n* и́зморось *f* ▷ *vi* мороси́ть (*impf*)
drop [drɔp] *n* (*of water*) ка́пля; (*reduction*) паде́ние; (*fall*: *distance*) расстоя́ние (*све́рху вниз*) ▷ *vt* (*object*) роня́ть (*perf* урони́ть); (*eyes*) опуска́ть (*perf* опусти́ть); (*voice, price*) понижа́ть (*perf* пони́зить); (*also* **drop off**: *passenger*) выса́живать (*perf* вы́садить) ▷ *vi* па́дать (*perf* упа́сть); (*wind*) стиха́ть (*perf* сти́хнуть); **drops** *npl* (*Med*) ка́пли *fpl*; **drop off** *vi* (*go to sleep*) засыпа́ть (*perf* засну́ть); **drop out** *vi* (*of game, deal*) выходи́ть (*perf* вы́йти)
drought [draut] *n* за́суха
drove [drəuv] *pt of* **drive**
drown [draun] *vt* топи́ть (*perf* утопи́ть); (*also* **drown out**: *sound*) заглуша́ть (*perf* заглуши́ть) ▷ *vi* тону́ть (*perf* утону́ть)
drug [drʌg] *n* (*Med*) лека́рство; (*narcotic*) нарко́тик ▷ *vt* (*person, animal*) вводи́ть (*perf* ввести́) нарко́тик *+dat*; **to be on drugs** быть (*impf*) на нарко́тиках; **hard/ soft drugs** си́льные/сла́бые нарко́тики

DRUGSTORE

Drugstore — апте́ка.
Америка́нские апте́ки сочета́ют

в себе́ апте́ки и кафе́. В них продаю́т не то́лько лека́рства, но и космети́ческие това́ры, напи́тки и заку́ски.

drum [drʌm] *n* бараба́н; (*for oil*) бо́чка; **drums** *npl* (*kit*) уда́рные инструме́нты *mpl*; **drummer** *n* (*in rock group*) уда́рник
drunk [drʌŋk] *pp of* **drink** ▷ *adj* пья́ный ▷ *n* пья́ный(-ая) *m(f) adj*; (*also* **drunkard**) пья́ница *m/f*; **drunken** *adj* пья́ный
dry [draɪ] *adj* сухо́й; (*lake, riverbed*) вы́сохший; (*humour*) сде́ржанный; (*lecture, subject*) ску́чный ▷ *vt* (*clothes, ground*) суши́ть (*perf* вы́сушить); (*surface*) вытира́ть (*perf* вы́тереть) ▷ *vi* со́хнуть (*perf* вы́сохнуть); **dry-cleaner's** *n* химчи́стка
DSS *n abbr* (*Brit*) (= *Department of Social Security*) Министе́рство социа́льного обеспе́чения
dual ['djuəl] *adj* двойно́й; (*function*) дво́йственный; **dual carriageway** *n* (*Brit*) автотра́сса
dubious ['dju:bɪəs] *adj* сомни́тельный
Dublin ['dʌblɪn] *n* Ду́блин
duck [dʌk] *n* у́тка ▷ *vi* (*also* **duck down**) пригиба́ться (*perf* пригну́ться)
due [dju:] *adj* (*expected*) предполага́емый; (*attention, consideration*) до́лжный; **I am due £20** мне должны́ *or* полага́ется £20 ▷ *n*: **to give sb his (*or* her) due** отдава́ть (*perf* отда́ть) кому́-н до́лжное ▷ *adv*: **due north** пря́мо на се́вер; **dues** *npl* (*for club etc*) взно́сы *mpl*; **in due course** в своё вре́мя; **due to** из-за +*gen*; **he is due to go** он до́лжен идти́
duel ['djuəl] *n* дуэ́ль *f*
duet [dju:'ɛt] *n* дуэ́т
dug [dʌg] *pt, pp of* **dig**
duke [dju:k] *n* ге́рцог
dull [dʌl] *adj* (*light, colour*) ту́склый, мра́чный; (*sound*) глухо́й; (*pain, wit*) тупо́й; (*event*) ску́чный ▷ *vt* притупля́ть (*perf* притупи́ть)
dumb [dʌm] *adj* (*inf, pej: person*) тупо́й; (: *idea*) дура́цкий
dummy ['dʌmɪ] *n* (*tailor's model*) манеке́н; (*Brit: for baby*) со́ска, пусты́шка ▷ *adj* (*bullet*) холосто́й
dump [dʌmp] *n* (*also* **rubbish dump**) сва́лка; (*inf, pej: place*) дыра́ ▷ *vt* (*put down*) сва́ливать (*perf* свали́ть), выбра́сывать (*perf* вы́бросить); (*car*) броса́ть (*perf* бро́сить)
dungarees [dʌŋgə'ri:z] *npl* комбинезо́н *msg*
duplicate [*n, adj* 'dju:plɪkət, *vb* 'dju:plɪkeɪt] *n* дублика́т, ко́пия ▷ *adj* запасно́й ▷ *vt* копи́ровать (*perf* скопи́ровать); (*repeat*) дубли́ровать (*perf* продубли́ровать); **in duplicate** в двойно́м экземпля́ре
durable ['djuərəbl] *adj* про́чный
duration [djuə'reɪʃən] *n* продолжи́тельность *f*
during ['djuərɪŋ] *prep* (*in the course of*) во вре́мя +*gen*, в тече́ние +*gen*; (*from beginning to end*) в тече́ние +*gen*
dusk [dʌsk] *n* су́мерки *pl*
dust [dʌst] *n* пыль *f* ▷ *vt* вытира́ть (*perf* вы́тереть) пыль с +*gen*; **to dust with** (*cake etc*) посыпа́ть (*perf* посы́пать) +*instr*; **dustbin** *n* (*Brit*) му́сорное ведро́; **dusty** *adj* пы́льный
Dutch [dʌtʃ] *adj* голла́ндский ▷ *npl*: **the Dutch** голла́ндцы *mpl*; **they decided to go Dutch** (*inf*) они́

решили, что каждый будет платить за себя

duty ['dju:tɪ] *n* (*responsibility*) обязанность *f*; (*obligation*) долг; (*tax*) пошлина; **on duty** на дежурстве; **off duty** вне службы; **duty-free** *adj* (*drink etc*) беспошлинный

duvet ['du:veɪ] *n* (*Brit*) одеяло

dwarf [dwɔ:f] (*pl* **dwarves**) *n* (*inf!*) карлик ▷ *vt* делать (*perf* сделать) крохотным; (*achievement*) умалять (*perf* умалить)

dwell [dwɛl] (*pt, pp* **dwelt**) *vi* проживать (*impf*); **dwell on** *vt fus* задерживаться (*perf* задержаться) на +*prp*

dye [daɪ] *n* краситель *m*, краска ▷ *vt* красить (*perf* покрасить)

dying ['daɪɪŋ] *adj* (*person, animal*) умирающий

dynamic [daɪ'næmɪk] *adj* (*leader, force*) динамичный

dynamite ['daɪnəmaɪt] *n* динамит

e

E [i:] *n* (*Mus*) ми *nt ind*

each [i:tʃ] *adj, pron* каждый; **each other** друг друга; **they hate each other** они ненавидят друг друга; **they think about each other** они думают друг о друге; **they have two books each** у каждого из них по две книги

eager ['i:gə^r] *adj* (*keen*) увлечённый; (*excited*) возбуждённый; **to be eager for/to do** жаждать (*impf*) +*gen*/+*infin*

eagle ['i:gl] *n* орёл

ear [ɪə^r] *n* (*Anat*) ухо; (*of corn*) колос; **earache** *n* ушная боль *f*; **I have earache** у меня болит ухо

earl [ə:l] *n* (*Brit*) граф

earlier ['ə:lɪə^r] *adj* более ранний ▷ *adv* раньше, ранее

early ['ə:lɪ] *adv* рано ▷ *adj* ранний; (*quick*: *reply*) незамедлительный; (*settlers*) пе́рвый; **early in the morning** ра́но у́тром; **to have an early night** ра́но ложи́ться (*perf* лечь) спать; **in the early spring, early in the spring** ра́нней весно́й; **in the early 19th century, early in the 19th century** в нача́ле 19-го ве́ка; **early retirement** *n*: **to take early retirement** ра́но уходи́ть (*perf* уйти́) на пе́нсию

earn [ə:n] *vt* (*salary*) зараба́тывать (*perf* зарабо́тать); (*interest*) приноси́ть (*perf* принести́); (*praise*) заслу́живать (*perf* заслужи́ть)

earnest ['ə:nɪst] *adj* (*person, manner*) серьёзный; (*wish, desire*) и́скренний; **in earnest** всерьёз

earnings ['ə:nɪŋz] *npl* за́работок *msg*

earring ['ɪərɪŋ] *n* серьга́

earth [ə:θ] *n* земля́; (*Brit*: *Elec*) заземле́ние ▷ *vt* (*Brit*: *Elec*) заземля́ть (*perf* заземли́ть); **Earth** (*planet*) Земля́; **earthquake** *n* землетрясе́ние

ease [i:z] *n* лёгкость *f*; (*comfort*) поко́й ▷ *vt* (*pain, problem*) облегча́ть (*perf* облегчи́ть); (*tension*) ослабля́ть (*perf* осла́бить); **to ease sth into** вставля́ть (*perf* вста́вить) что-н в *+acc*; **to ease sth out of** вынима́ть (*perf* вы́нуть) что-н из *+gen*; **to ease o.s. into** опуска́ться (*perf* опусти́ться) в *+acc*; **at ease!** (*Mil*) во́льно!

easily ['i:zɪlɪ] *adv* (*see adj*) легко́; непринуждённо; (*without doubt*) несомне́нно

east [i:st] *n* восто́к ▷ *adj* восто́чный ▷ *adv* на восто́к; **the East** Восто́к

Easter ['i:stə^r] *n* Па́сха; **Easter egg** *n* (*chocolate*) пасха́льное яйцо́

eastern ['i:stən] *adj* восто́чный

East Germany *n* (*formerly*) Восто́чная Герма́ния

easy ['i:zɪ] *adj* лёгкий; (*manner*) непринуждённый ▷ *adv*: **to take it** *or* **things easy** не напряга́ться (*impf*); **easy-going** *adj* (*person*) ужи́вчивый, покла́дистый

eat [i:t] (*pt* **ate**, *pp* **eaten**) *vt* есть (*perf* съесть) ▷ *vi* есть (*impf*)

EC *n abbr* (= *European Community*) ЕС (= *Европе́йское соо́бщество*)

ECB *n abbr* (= *European Central Bank*) Центра́льный банк Евро́пы

eccentric [ɪk'sɛntrɪk] *adj* эксцентри́чный

echo ['ɛkəu] (*pl* **echoes**) *n* э́хо ▷ *vt* (*repeat*) вто́рить (*impf*) *+dat* ▷ *vi* (*sound*) отдава́ться (*perf* отда́ться); **the room echoed with her laughter** в ко́мнате раздава́лся её смех

eclipse [ɪ'klɪps] *n* затме́ние

ecological [i:kə'lɔdʒɪkəl] *adj* экологи́ческий

ecology [ɪ'kɔlədʒɪ] *n* эколо́гия

economic [i:kə'nɔmɪk] *adj* экономи́ческий; (*profitable*) рента́бельный; **economical** *adj* экономи́чный; (*thrifty*) эконо́мный; **economics** *n* (*Scol*) эконо́мика

economist [ɪ'kɔnəmɪst] *n* экономи́ст

economy [ɪ'kɔnəmɪ] *n* эконо́мика, хозя́йство; (*financial prudence*) эконо́мия; **economy class** *n* (*Aviat*) *дешёвые поса́дочные места́*

ecstasy ['ɛkstəsɪ] *n* (*rapture*) экста́з

ecstatic [ɛks'tætɪk] *adj* восто́рженный

eczema ['ɛksɪmə] *n* экзе́ма

edge [ɛdʒ] *n* край; (*of knife etc*) остриё ▷ *vt* (*trim*) окаймля́ть (*perf* окаймить); **on edge** (*fig*) нервозный; **to edge away from** отходить (*perf* отойти) бочком от *+gen*

edgy ['ɛdʒɪ] *adj* нервозный

edible ['ɛdɪbl] *adj* съедобный

Edinburgh ['ɛdɪnbərə] *n* Эдинбург

edit ['ɛdɪt] *vt* редактировать (*perf* отредактировать); (*broadcast, film*) монтировать (*perf* смонтировать); **edition** [ɪ'dɪʃən] *n* (*of book*) издание; (*of newspaper, programme*) выпуск; **editor** *n* редактор; (*Press, TV*) обозреватель *m*; **editorial** [ɛdɪ'tɔ:rɪəl] *adj* редакционный ▷ *n* редакционная *f adj* (статья)

educate ['ɛdjukeɪt] *vt* (*teach*) давать (*perf* дать) образование *+dat*; (*instruct*) просвещать (*perf* просветить)

education [ɛdju'keɪʃən] *n* (*schooling*) просвещение, образование; (*teaching*) обучение; (*knowledge*) образование; **educational** *adj* (*institution*) учебный; (*staff*) преподавательский; **educational policy** политика в области просвещения; **educational system** система образования *or* просвещения

eel [i:l] *n* угорь *m*

eerie ['ɪərɪ] *adj* жуткий

effect [ɪ'fɛkt] *n* (*result*) эффект; **to take effect** (*drug*) действовать (*perf* подействовать); (*law*) вступать (*perf* вступить) в силу; **in effect** в сущности; **effective** *adj* (*successful*) эффективный; (*actual*) действительный; **effectively** *adv* (*successfully*) эффективно; (*in reality*) в сущности, фактически

efficiency [ɪ'fɪʃənsɪ] *n* эффективность *f*; дельность *f*

efficient [ɪ'fɪʃənt] *adj* эффективный; (*person*) дельный

effort ['ɛfət] *n* усилие; (*attempt*) попытка; **effortless** *adj* (*achievement*) лёгкий

e.g. *adv abbr* (*for example*) (= *exempli gratia*) например

egg [ɛg] *n* яйцо; **hard-boiled/ soft-boiled egg** яйцо вкрутую/ всмятку; **egg cup** *n* рюмка для яйца

ego ['i:gəu] *n* самолюбие

Egypt ['i:dʒɪpt] *n* Египет

eight [eɪt] *n* восемь; **eighteen** *n* восемнадцать; **eighteenth** [eɪ'ti:nθ] *adj* восемнадцатый; **eighth** [eɪtθ] *adj* восьмой; **eightieth** *adj* восьмидесятый; **eighty** *n* восемьдесят

Eire ['ɛərə] *n* Эйре *nt ind*

either ['aɪðə^r] *adj* (*one or other*) любой (*из двух*); (*both, each*) каждый ▷ *adv* также ▷ *pron*: **either (of them)** любой (из них) ▷ *conj*: **either yes or no** либо да, либо нет; **on either side** на обеих сторонах; **I don't smoke — I don't either** я не курю — я тоже; **I don't like either** мне не нравится ни тот, ни другой; **there was no sound from either of the flats** ни из одной из квартир не доносилось ни звука

elaborate [*adj* ɪ'læbərɪt, *vb* ɪ'læbəreɪt] *adj* сложный ▷ *vt* (*expand*) развивать (*perf* развить); (*refine*) разрабатывать (*perf* разработать) ▷ *vi*: **to elaborate on** (*idea, plan*) рассматривать (*perf* рассмотреть) в деталях

elastic [ɪ'læstɪk] *n* резинка ▷ *adj* (*stretchy*) эластичный

elbow ['ɛlbəu] *n* локоть *m*

elder [ˈɛldəʳ] *adj* ста́рший ▷ *n* (*tree*) бузина́; (*older person*): **elders** ста́ршие *pl adj*; **elderly** *adj* пожило́й ▷ *npl*: **the elderly** престаре́лые *pl adj*

eldest [ˈɛldɪst] *adj* (са́мый) ста́рший ▷ *n* ста́рший(-ая) *m(f) adj*

elect [ɪˈlɛkt] *vt* избира́ть (*perf* избра́ть) ▷ *adj*: **the president elect** и́збранный президе́нт; **to elect to do** предпочита́ть (*perf* предпоче́сть) *+infin*; **electoral** *adj* избира́тельный; **electorate** *n*: **the electorate** электора́т, избира́тели *mpl*

electric [ɪˈlɛktrɪk] *adj* электри́ческий; **electrical** *adj* электри́ческий; **electrician** [ɪlɛkˈtrɪʃən] *n* электромонтёр, эле́ктрик; **electricity** [ɪlɛkˈtrɪsɪtɪ] *n* электри́чество

electronic [ɪlɛkˈtrɔnɪk] *adj* электро́нный; **electronics** *n* электро́ника

elegance [ˈɛlɪgəns] *n* элега́нтность *f*

elegant [ˈɛlɪgənt] *adj* элега́нтный

element [ˈɛlɪmənt] *n* (*also Chem*) элеме́нт; (*of heater, kettle etc*) (электронагрева́тельный) элеме́нт; **the elements** стихи́я *fsg*; **he is in his element** он в свое́й стихи́и; **elementary** [ɛlɪˈmɛntərɪ] *adj* элемента́рный; (*school, education*) нача́льный

elephant [ˈɛlɪfənt] *n* слон(и́ха)

elevator [ˈɛlɪveɪtəʳ] *n* (*US*) лифт

eleven [ɪˈlɛvn] *n* оди́ннадцать; **eleventh** *adj* оди́ннадцатый

eligible [ˈɛlɪdʒəbl] *adj* (*for marriage*) подходя́щий; **to be eligible for** (*qualified*) име́ть (*impf*) пра́во на *+acc*; (*suitable*) подходи́ть (*perf* подойти́)

eliminate [ɪˈlɪmɪneɪt] *vt* исключа́ть (*perf* исключи́ть); (*team, contestant*) выбива́ть (*perf* вы́бить)

elm [ɛlm] *n* вяз

eloquent [ˈɛləkwənt] *adj* (*description, person*) красноречи́вый; (*speech*) я́ркий

else [ɛls] *adv* (*other*) ещё; **nothing else** бо́льше ничего́; **somewhere else** (*be*) где́-нибудь ещё; (*go*) куда́-нибудь ещё; (*come from*) отку́да-нибудь ещё; **everywhere else** везде́; **where else?** (*position*) где ещё?; (*motion*) куда́ ещё?; **everyone else** все остальны́е; **nobody else spoke** бо́льше никто́ не говори́л; **or else ...** а не то ...; **elsewhere** *adv* (*be*) в друго́м *or* ино́м ме́сте; (*go*) в друго́е *or* ино́е ме́сто

elusive [ɪˈluːsɪv] *adj* неуловимый

email [ˈiːmeɪl] *n* электро́нная по́чта ▷ *vt* (*message*) посыла́ть (*perf* посла́ть) по электро́нной по́чте; **to email sb** писа́ть (*perf* написа́ть) кому́-н по электро́нной по́чте; **email address** а́дрес электро́нной по́чты, электро́нный а́дрес

embankment [ɪmˈbæŋkmənt] *n* (*of road, railway*) на́сыпь *f*; (*of river*) на́бережная *f adj*

embargo [ɪmˈbɑːgəu] (*pl* **embargoes**) *n* эмба́рго *nt ind*

embark [ɪmˈbɑːk] *vi*: **to embark on** (*journey*) отправля́ться (*perf* отпра́виться) в *+acc*; (*task*) бра́ться (*perf* взя́ться); (*course of action*) предпринима́ть (*perf* предприня́ть)

embarrass [ɪmˈbærəs] *vt* смуща́ть (*perf* смути́ть); (*Pol*) ста́вить (*perf* поста́вить) в затрудни́тельное положе́ние;

embarrassed *adj* смущённый; **embarrassing** *adj* (*position*) нело́вкий, неудо́бный; **embarrassment** *n* (*feeling*) смуще́ние; (*problem*) затрудне́ние

embassy ['ɛmbəsɪ] *n* посо́льство

embrace [ɪm'breɪs] *vt* обнима́ть (*perf* обня́ть); (*include*) охва́тывать (*perf* охвати́ть) ▷ *vi* обнима́ться (*impf*)

embroidery *n* (*stitching*) вы́шивка; (*activity*) вышива́ние

embryo ['ɛmbrɪəu] *n* (*Bio*) эмбрио́н

emerald ['ɛmərəld] *n* изумру́д

emerge [ɪ'mə:dʒ] *vi* (*fact*) всплыва́ть (*perf* всплыть); (*industry, society*) появля́ться (*perf* появи́ться); **to emerge from** (*from room, imprisonment*) выходи́ть (*perf* вы́йти) из *+gen*

emergency [ɪ'mə:dʒənsɪ] *n* экстрема́льная ситуа́ция; **in an emergency** в экстрема́льной ситуа́ции; **state of emergency** чрезвыча́йное положе́ние; **emergency talks** э́кстренные перегово́ры; **emergency exit** *n* авари́йный вы́ход

emigrate ['ɛmɪgreɪt] *vi* эмигри́ровать (*impf/perf*)

emigration [ɛmɪ'greɪʃən] *n* эмигра́ция

eminent ['ɛmɪnənt] *adj* ви́дный, зна́тный

emission [ɪ'mɪʃən] *n* (*of gas*) вы́брос; (*of radiation*) излуче́ние

emoji [ɪ'məudʒɪ] *n* эмо́дзи *nt ind*

emoticon [ɪ'məutɪkən] *n* смайл

emotion [ɪ'məuʃən] *n* (*feeling*) чу́вство; **emotional** *adj* эмоциона́льный; (*issue*) волну́ющий

emphasis ['ɛmfəsɪs] (*pl* **emphases**) *n* значе́ние; (*in speaking*) ударе́ние, акце́нт

emphasize ['ɛmfəsaɪz] *vt* подчёркивать (*perf* подчеркну́ть)

empire ['ɛmpaɪə^r] *n* импе́рия

employ [ɪm'plɔɪ] *vt* нанима́ть (*perf* наня́ть); (*tool, weapon*) применя́ть (*perf* примени́ть); **employee** [ɪmplɔɪ'i:] *n* рабо́тник; **employer** *n* работода́тель *m*; **employment** *n* рабо́та; (*availability of jobs*) за́нятость *f*

emptiness ['ɛmptɪnɪs] *n* пустота́

empty ['ɛmptɪ] *adj* пусто́й ▷ *vt* (*container*) опорожня́ть (*perf* опорожни́ть); (*place, house etc*) опустоша́ть (*perf* опустоши́ть) ▷ *vi* (*house*) пусте́ть (*perf* опусте́ть); **empty-handed** *adj* с пусты́ми рука́ми

EMU *n abbr* = **European monetary union**

emulsion [ɪ'mʌlʃən] *n* (*also* **emulsion paint**) эму́льсия, эмульсио́нная кра́ска

enable [ɪ'neɪbl] *vt* (*make possible*) спосо́бствовать (*impf*) *+dat*; **to enable sb to do** (*allow*) дава́ть (*perf* дать) возмо́жность кому́-н *+infin*

enamel [ɪ'næməl] *n* эма́ль *f*

enchanting [ɪn'tʃɑ:ntɪŋ] *adj* обворожи́тельный

encl. *abbr* (*on letters etc*) (= *enclosed, enclosure*) приложе́ние

enclose [ɪn'kləuz] *vt* (*land, space*) огора́живать (*perf* огороди́ть); (*object*) заключа́ть (*perf* заключи́ть); **to enclose (with)** (*letter*) прилага́ть (*perf* приложи́ть) (к *+dat*); **please find enclosed a cheque for £100** здесь прилага́ется чек на £100

enclosure [ɪn'kləuʒə^r] *n* огоро́женное ме́сто

encore [ɔŋ'kɔːʳ] *excl* бис ▷ *n*: **as an encore** на бис
encounter [ɪn'kauntəʳ] *n* встре́ча ▷ *vt* встреча́ться (*perf* встре́титься) с *+instr*; (*problem*) ста́лкиваться (*perf* столкну́ться) с *+instr*
encourage [ɪn'kʌrɪdʒ] *vt* поощря́ть (*perf* поощри́ть); (*growth*) спосо́бствовать (*impf*) *+dat*; **to encourage sb to do** убежда́ть (*impf*) кого́-н *+infin*; **encouragement** *n* (*see vt*) поощре́ние; подде́ржка
encyclop(a)edia [ɛnsaɪkləu'piːdɪə] *n* энциклопе́дия
end [ɛnd] *n* коне́ц; (*aim*) цель *f* ▷ *vt* (*also* **bring to an end, put an end to**) класть (*perf* положи́ть) коне́ц *+dat*, прекраща́ть (*perf* прекрати́ть) ▷ *vi* (*situation, activity, period*) конча́ться (*perf* ко́нчиться); **in the end** в конце́ концо́в; **on end** (*object*) стоймя́; **for hours on end** часа́ми; **end up** *vi*: **to end up in** (*place*) оказываться (*perf* оказа́ться) в *+prp*; (*in prison*) угожда́ть (*perf* угоди́ть) в *+prp*; **we ended up taking a taxi** в конце́ концо́в мы взя́ли такси́
endanger [ɪn'deɪndʒəʳ] *vt* подверга́ть (*perf* подве́ргнуть) опа́сности; **an endangered species** вымира́ющий вид
endearing [ɪn'dɪərɪŋ] *adj* (*smile*) покоря́ющий; (*person, behaviour*) располага́ющий
endeavour [ɪn'dɛvəʳ] (*US* **endeavor**) *n* (*attempt*) попы́тка
ending ['ɛndɪŋ] *n* (*of book etc*) коне́ц
endless ['ɛndlɪs] *adj* бесконе́чный; (*forest, beach*) беskра́йний
endorse [ɪn'dɔːs] *vt* (*cheque*) распи́сываться (*perf* расписа́ться) на *+prp*; (*document*) де́лать (*perf* сде́лать) отме́тку на *+prp*; (*proposal, candidate*) подде́рживать (*perf* поддержа́ть); **endorsement** *n* (*approval*) подде́ржка; (*Brit*: *Aut*) отме́тка
endurance [ɪn'djuərəns] *n* выно́сливость *f*
endure [ɪn'djuəʳ] *vt* переноси́ть (*perf* перенести́) ▷ *vi* вы́стоять (*perf*)
enemy ['ɛnəmɪ] *adj* вра́жеский, неприя́тельский ▷ *n* враг; (*opponent*) проти́вник
energetic [ɛnə'dʒɛtɪk] *adj* энерги́чный
energy ['ɛnədʒɪ] *n* эне́ргия
enforce [ɪn'fɔːs] *vt* (*law*) следи́ть (*impf*) *or* проследи́ть *perf* за соблюде́нием (*+gen*)
engaged *adj* (*couple*) обручённый; (*Brit*: *busy*): **the line is engaged** ли́ния занята́; **he is engaged to** он обручён с *+instr*; **to get engaged** обруча́ться (*perf* обручи́ться)
engaged tone *n* (*Brit*: *Tel*) гудки́ *pl* "за́нято"
engagement *n* (*appointment*) договорённость *f*; (*to marry*) обруче́ние
engagement ring *n* обруча́льное кольцо́
engine ['ɛndʒɪn] *n* (*Aut*) дви́гатель *m*, мото́р; (*Rail*) локомоти́в
engineer [ɛndʒɪ'nɪəʳ] *n* (*designer*) инжене́р; (*for repairs*) меха́ник; (*US*: *Rail*) машини́ст; **engineering** *n* (*Scol*) инжене́рное де́ло; (*design*) техни́ческий диза́йн

England [ˈɪŋglənd] *n* Áнглия
English [ˈɪŋglɪʃ] *adj* англи́йский ▷ *n* (*Ling*) англи́йский язы́к; ▷ *npl*: **the English** (*people*) англича́не *mpl*; **Englishman** *irreg n* англича́нин
enhance [ɪnˈhɑːns] *vt* (*enjoyment, beauty*) уси́ливать (*perf* уси́лить); (*reputation*) повыша́ть (*perf* повы́сить)
enjoy [ɪnˈdʒɔɪ] *vt* люби́ть (*impf*); (*have benefit of*) облада́ть (*impf*) *+instr*; **to enjoy o.s.** хорошо́ проводи́ть (*perf* провести́) вре́мя; **to enjoy doing** люби́ть (*impf*) *+infin*; **enjoyable** *adj* прия́тный; **enjoyment** *n* удово́льствие
enlarge [ɪnˈlɑːdʒ] *vt* увели́чивать (*perf* увели́чить) ▷ *vi*: **to enlarge on** распространя́ться (*impf*) о *+prp*; **enlargement** *n* (*Phot*) увеличе́ние
enlist [ɪnˈlɪst] *vt* (*person*) вербова́ть (*perf* завербова́ть); (*support*) заруча́ться (*perf* заручи́ться) *+instr* ▷ *vi*: **to enlist in** (*Mil*) вербова́ться (*perf* завербова́ться) в *+acc*
enormous [ɪˈnɔːməs] *adj* грома́дный
enough [ɪˈnʌf] *adj* доста́точно *+gen* ▷ *pron* доста́точно ▷ *adv*: **big enough** доста́точно большо́й; **I've had enough!** с меня́ доста́точно *or* хва́тит!; **have you got enough work to do?** у Вас доста́точно рабо́ты?; **have you had enough to eat?** Вы нае́лись?; **that's enough, thanks** доста́точно, спаси́бо; **I've had enough of him** он мне надое́л; **enough!** дово́льно!; **strangely** *or* **oddly enough ...** как э́то ни стра́нно ...
enquire [ɪnˈkwaɪəʳ] *vt, vi* = **inquire**
enrich [ɪnˈrɪtʃ] *vt* обогаща́ть (*perf* обогати́ть)
en route [ɔnˈruːt] *adv* по пути́
ensure [ɪnˈʃuəʳ] *vt* обеспе́чивать (*perf* обеспе́чить)
entail [ɪnˈteɪl] *vt* влечь (*perf* повле́чь) за собо́й
enter [ˈɛntəʳ] *vt* (*room, building*) входи́ть (*perf* войти́) в *+acc*; (*university, college*) поступа́ть (*perf* поступи́ть) в *+acc*; (*club, profession, contest*) вступа́ть (*perf* вступи́ть) в *+acc*; (*in book*) заноси́ть (*perf* занести́); (*Comput*) вводи́ть (*perf* ввести́) ▷ *vi* входи́ть (*perf* войти́); **to enter sb in** (*competition*) запи́сывать (*perf* записа́ть) кого́-н в *+acc*; **enter into** *vt fus* (*discussion, deal*) вступа́ть (*perf* вступи́ть) в *+acc*
enterprise [ˈɛntəpraɪz] *n* (*company, undertaking*) предприя́тие; (*initiative*) предприи́мчивость *f*; **free/private enterprise** свобо́дное/ча́стное предпринима́тельство
enterprising [ˈɛntəpraɪzɪŋ] *adj* (*person*) предприи́мчивый; (*scheme*) предпринима́тельский
entertain [ɛntəˈteɪn] *vt* (*amuse*) развлека́ть (*perf* развле́чь); (*play host to*) принима́ть (*perf* приня́ть); (*idea*) разду́мывать (*impf*) над *+instr*; **entertainer** *n* эстра́дный арти́ст; **entertaining** *adj* занима́тельный, развлека́тельный; **entertainment** *n* (*amusement*) развлече́ние; (*show*) представле́ние
enthusiasm [ɪnˈθuːzɪæzəm] *n* энтузиа́зм
enthusiastic [ɪnθuːzɪˈæstɪk] *adj*: **enthusiastic (about)** по́лный энтузиа́зма (по по́воду *+gen*)

entire [ɪn'taɪəʳ] *adj* весь; **entirely** *adv* пóлностью; (*for emphasis*) совершéнно
entitled [ɪn'taɪtld] *adj*: **to be entitled to sth/to do** имéть (*impf*) прáво на что-н/*+infin*
entrance [*n* 'ɛntrns, *vb* ɪn'trɑːns] *n* (*way in*) вход; (*arrival*) появлéние ▷ *vt* обворáживать (*perf* обворожи́ть); **to gain entrance to** (*university*) поступáть (*perf* поступи́ть) в *+acc*; (*profession*) вступáть (*perf* вступи́ть) в *+acc*; **to make an entrance** появля́ться (*perf* появи́ться)
entrepreneur ['ɔntrəprə'nəːʳ] *n* предпринимáтель(ница) *m(f)*
entry ['ɛntrɪ] *n* вход; (*in register, accounts*) зáпись *f*; (*in reference book*) статья́; (*arrival*: *in country*) въезд; **"no entry"** "нет вхóда"; (*Aut*) "нет въéзда"
envelope ['ɛnvələup] *n* конвéрт
envious ['ɛnvɪəs] *adj* зави́стливый
environment [ɪn'vaɪərnmənt] *n* средá; **the environment** окружáющая средá; **environmental** [ɪnvaɪərn'mɛntl] *adj* экологи́ческий
envisage [ɪn'vɪzɪdʒ] *vt* предви́деть (*impf*)
envoy ['ɛnvɔɪ] *n* послáнник
envy ['ɛnvɪ] *n* зáвисть *f* ▷ *vt* зави́довать (*perf* позави́довать) *+dat*; **to envy sb sth** зави́довать (*perf* позави́довать) комý-н из-за чегó-н
epic ['ɛpɪk] *n* эпопéя; (*poem*) эпи́ческая поэ́ма ▷ *adj* эпохáльный
epidemic [ɛpɪ'dɛmɪk] *n* эпидéмия
epilepsy ['ɛpɪlɛpsɪ] *n* эпилéпсия
episode ['ɛpɪsəud] *n* эпизóд
equal ['iːkwl] *adj* рáвный; (*intensity, quality*) одинáковый ▷ *n* рáвный(-ая) *m(f) adj* ▷ *vt* (*number*) равня́ться (*impf*) *+dat*; **he is equal to** (*task*) емý по си́лам *or* по плечý; **equality** [iː'kwɔlɪtɪ] *n* рáвенство, равнопрáвие; **equally** *adv* одинáково; (*share*) пóровну
equation [ɪ'kweɪʃən] *n* (*Math*) уравнéние
equator [ɪ'kweɪtəʳ] *n* эквáтор
equip [ɪ'kwɪp] *vt*: **to equip (with)** (*person, army*) снаряжáть (*perf* снаряди́ть) (*+instr*); (*room, car*) оборýдовать (*impf/perf*) (*+instr*); **to equip sb for** (*prepare*) готóвить (*perf* подготóвить) когó-н к *+dat*; **equipment** *n* оборýдование
equivalent [ɪ'kwɪvələnt] *n* эквивалéнт ▷ *adj*: **equivalent (to)** эквивалéнтный (*+dat*)
era ['ɪərə] *n* э́ра
erase [ɪ'reɪz] *vt* стирáть (*perf* стерéть); **eraser** *n* рези́нка, лáстик
erect [ɪ'rɛkt] *adj* (*posture*) прямóй ▷ *vt* (*build*) воздвигáть (*perf* воздви́гнуть), возводи́ть (*perf* возвести́); (*assemble*) стáвить (*perf* постáвить); **erection** [ɪ'rɛkʃən] *n* (*see vt*) возведéние; установка; (*Physiol*) эрéкция
erosion [ɪ'rəuʒən] *n* эрóзия
erotic [ɪ'rɔtɪk] *adj* эроти́ческий
erratic [ɪ'rætɪk] *adj* (*attempts*) беспоря́дочный; (*behaviour*) сумасбрóдный
error ['ɛrəʳ] *n* оши́бка
erupt [ɪ'rʌpt] *vi* (*war, crisis*) разражáться (*perf* разрази́ться); **the volcano erupted** произошлó извержéние вулкáна; **eruption** [ɪ'rʌpʃən] *n* (*of volcano*)

извержéние; (*of fighting*) взрыв
escalator ['ɛskəleɪtə^r] *n* эскалáтор
escape [ɪs'keɪp] *n* (*from prison*) побéг; (*from person*) бéгство; (*of gas*) утéчка ▷ *vi* убегáть (*perf* убежáть); (*from jail*) бежáть (*impf/perf*); (*leak*) утекáть (*perf* утéчь) ▷ *vt* (*consequences etc*) избегáть (*perf* избежáть) +*gen*; **his name escapes me** егó имя вы́пало у меня́ из пáмяти; **to escape from** (*place*) сбегáть (*perf* сбежáть) из/с +*gen*; (*person*) сбегáть (*perf* сбежáть) от +*gen*; **he escaped with minor injuries** он отдéлался лёгкими уши́бами
escort [*n* 'ɛskɔːt, *vb* ɪs'kɔːt] *n* сопровождéние; (*Mil, Police*) конвóй; (: *one person*) конвои́р ▷ *vt* сопровождáть (*perf* сопроводи́ть)
especially [ɪs'pɛʃlɪ] *adv* осóбенно
espionage ['ɛspɪənɑːʒ] *n* шпионáж
essay ['ɛseɪ] *n* (*Scol*) сочинéние
essence ['ɛsns] *n* сýщность *f*; (*Culin*) эссéнция
essential [ɪ'sɛnʃl] *adj* обязáтельный, необходи́мый; (*basic*) сущéственный ▷ *n* необходи́мое *nt adj*; **essentials** *npl* (*of subject*) оснóвы; **it is essential to ...** необходи́мо +*infin* ...; **essentially** *adv* в сýщности
establish [ɪs'tæblɪʃ] *vt* (*organization*) учреждáть (*perf* учреди́ть); (*facts, contact*) устанáвливать (*perf* установи́ть); (*reputation*) утверждáть (*perf* утверди́ть) за собóй; **establishment** *n* (*see vb*) учреждéние; установлéние; утверждéние; (*shop etc*) заведéние; **the Establishment** истéблишмент
estate [ɪs'teɪt] *n* (*land*) помéстье; (*Brit*: *also* **housing estate**) жилóй кóмплекс; **estate agent** *n* (*Brit*) агéнт по продáже недви́жимости, риэ́лтер
estimate [*vb* 'ɛstɪmeɪt, *n* 'ɛstɪmət] *vt* (*reckon*) предвари́тельно подсчи́тывать (*perf* подсчитáть); (: *cost*) оцéнивать (*perf* оцени́ть) ▷ *n* (*calculation*) подсчёт; (*assessment*) оцéнка; (*builder's etc*) смéта
etc *abbr* (= *et cetera*) и т.д. (= *и так дáлее*)
eternal [ɪ'tɜːnl] *adj* вéчный
eternity [ɪ'tɜːnɪtɪ] *n* вéчность *f*
ethical ['ɛθɪkl] *adj* (*relating to ethics*) эти́ческий; (*morally right*) эти́чный
ethics ['ɛθɪks] *n, npl* э́тика *fsg*
Ethiopia [iːθɪ'əupɪə] *n* Эфиóпия
ethnic ['ɛθnɪk] *adj* этни́ческий
etiquette ['ɛtɪkɛt] *n* этикéт
EU *n abbr* (= *European Union*) ЕС, Евросою́з (= *Европéйский сою́з*)
euro ['juərəu] *n* éвро *m ind*
Europe ['juərəp] *n* Еврóпа; **European** [juərə'piːən] *adj* европéйский; **European Community** *n* Европéйское сообщество; **European Union** *n* Европéйский сою́з
evacuate [ɪ'vækjueɪt] *vt* (*people*) эвакуи́ровать (*impf/perf*); (*place*) освобождáть (*perf* освободи́ть)
evade [ɪ'veɪd] *vt* (*duties, question*) уклоня́ться (*perf* уклони́ться) от +*gen*; (*person*) избегáть (*impf*) +*gen*
evaluate [ɪ'væljueɪt] *vt* оцéнивать (*perf* оцени́ть)
eve [iːv] *n*: **on the eve of** наканýне +*gen*

even ['i:vn] *adj* (*level, smooth*) ро́вный; (*equal*) ра́вный; (*number*) чётный ▷ *adv* да́же; **even if** да́же е́сли; **even though** хотя́ и; **even more** ещё бо́льше; (*+adj*) ещё бо́лее; **even so** (и) всё же; **not even** да́же не; **I am even more likely to leave now** тепе́рь ещё бо́лее вероя́тно, что я уе́ду; **to break even** зака́нчивать (*perf* зако́нчить) без убы́тка; **to get even with sb** (*inf*) расквита́ться (*perf*) с кем-н

evening ['i:vnɪŋ] *n* ве́чер; **in the evening** ве́чером; **evening dress** *n* (*no pl*: *formal clothes*) вече́рний туале́т

event [ɪ'vɛnt] *n* (*occurrence*) собы́тие; (*Sport*) вид (соревнова́ния); **in the event of** в слу́чае *+gen*

eventual [ɪ'vɛntʃuəl] *adj* коне́чный; **eventually** *adv* в конце́ концо́в

ever ['ɛvəʳ] *adv* (*always*) всегда́; (*at any time*) когда́-либо, когда́-нибудь; **why ever not?** почему́ же нет?; **the best ever** са́мый лу́чший; **have you ever been to Russia?** Вы когда́-нибудь бы́ли в Росси́и?; **better than ever** лу́чше, чем когда́-либо; **ever since** с те́х пор; **ever since our meeting** со дня на́шей встре́чи; **ever since we met** с тех пор как мы встре́тились; **ever since that day** с того́ дня; **evergreen** *n* вечнозелёный

 **KEYWORD**

every ['ɛvrɪ] *adj* **1** (*each*) ка́ждый; (*all*) все; **every one of them** ка́ждый из них; **every shop in the town was closed** все магази́ны го́рода бы́ли закры́ты
2 (*all possible*) вся́кий, вся́ческий; **we wish you every success** мы жела́ем Вам вся́ческих успе́хов; **I gave you every assistance** я помо́г Вам всем, чем то́лько возмо́жно; **I tried every option** я испро́бовал все вариа́нты; **I have every confidence in him** я в нём соверше́нно уве́рен; **he's every bit as clever as his brother** он столь же умён, как и его́ брат
3 (*showing recurrence*) ка́ждый; **every week** ка́ждую неде́лю; **every other car** ка́ждая втора́я маши́на; **she visits me every other/third day** она́ прихо́дит ко мне че́рез день/ ка́ждые два дня; **every now and then** вре́мя от вре́мени

everybody ['ɛvrɪbɔdɪ] *pron* (*each*) ка́ждый; (*all*) все *pl*

everyday ['ɛvrɪdeɪ] *adj* (*daily*) ежедне́вный; (*common*) повседне́вный

everyone ['ɛvrɪwʌn] *pron* = **everybody**

everything ['ɛvrɪθɪŋ] *pron* всё

everywhere ['ɛvrɪwɛəʳ] *adv* везде́, повсю́ду

evidence ['ɛvɪdns] *n* (*proof*) доказа́тельство; (*testimony*) показа́ние; (*indication*) при́знаки *mpl*; **to give evidence** дава́ть (*perf* дать) (свиде́тельские) показа́ния

evident ['ɛvɪdnt] *adj* очеви́дный; **evidently** *adv* очеви́дно

evil ['i:vl] *adj* (*person, spirit*) злой; (*influence*) дурно́й; (*system*) ги́бельный ▷ *n* зло

evoke [ɪ'vəuk] *vt* вызыва́ть (*perf* вы́звать)

evolution [i:və'lu:ʃən] *n* эволю́ция

evolve [ɪ'vɔlv] *vi* (*animal, plant*)

эволюционировать (*impf/perf*); (*plan, idea*) развиваться (*perf* развиться)
ex- [ɛks] *prefix* (*former*) экс-, бывший
exact [ɪg'zækt] *adj* точный ▷ *vt*: **to exact sth from** (*payment*) взыскивать (*perf* взыскать) что-н с *+gen*; **exactly** *adv* точно
exaggerate [ɪg'zædʒəreɪt] *vt, vi* преувеличивать (*perf* преувеличить)
exaggeration [ɪgzædʒə'reɪʃən] *n* преувеличение
exam [ɪg'zæm] *n abbr* **= examination**
examination [ɪgzæmɪ'neɪʃən] *n* (*inspection*) изучение; (*consideration*) рассмотрение; (*Scol*) экзамен; (*Med*) осмотр
examine [ɪg'zæmɪn] *vt* (*scrutinize*) рассматривать (*perf* рассмотреть), изучать (*perf* изучить); (*inspect*) осматривать (*perf* осмотреть); (*Scol*) экзаменовать (*perf* проэкзаменовать); (*Med*) осматривать (*perf* осмотреть); **examiner** *n* (*Scol*) экзаменатор
example [ɪg'zɑ:mpl] *n* пример; **for example** например
exceed [ɪk'si:d] *vt* превышать (*perf* превысить); **exceedingly** *adv* весьма, чрезвычайно
excel [ɪk'sɛl] *vi*: **to excel (in** *or* **at)** отличаться (*perf* отличиться) (в *+prp*); **excellence** ['ɛksələns] *n* (*in sport, business*) мастерство; (*superiority*) превосходство; **excellent** ['ɛksələnt] *adj* отличный, превосходный
except [ɪk'sɛpt] *prep* (*also* **except for**) кроме *+gen* ▷ *vt*: **to except sb (from)** исключать (*perf* исключить) кого-н (из *+gen*); **except if/when** кроме тех случаев, если/когда; **except that** кроме того, что; **exception** [ɪk'sɛpʃən] *n* исключение; **to take exception to** обижаться (*perf* обидеться) на *+acc*; **exceptional** [ɪk'sɛpʃənl] *adj* исключительный
excess [ɪk'sɛs] *n* избыток; **excess baggage** *n* излишек багажа; **excessive** *adj* чрезмерный
exchange [ɪks'tʃeɪndʒ] *n* (*argument*) перепалка ▷ *vt*: **to exchange (for)** (*goods etc*) обменивать (*perf* обменять) (на *+acc*); **exchange (of)** обмен (*+instr*); **exchange rate** *n* валютный *or* обменный курс
excite [ɪk'saɪt] *vt* возбуждать (*perf* возбудить), волновать (*perf* взволновать); **to get excited** возбуждаться (*perf* возбудиться), волноваться (*perf* взволноваться); **excitement** *n* (*agitation*) возбуждение; (*exhilaration*) волнение
exciting [ɪk'saɪtɪŋ] *adj* (*news, opportunity*) волнующий
exclude [ɪks'klu:d] *vt* исключать (*perf* исключить)
exclusion [ɪks'klu:ʒən] *n* исключение
exclusive [ɪks'klu:sɪv] *adj* (*hotel, interview*) эксклюзивный; (*use, right*) исключительный; **exclusive of** исключая *+acc*; **exclusively** *adv* исключительно
excruciating [ɪks'kru:ʃɪeɪtɪŋ] *adj* мучительный
excursion [ɪks'kə:ʃən] *n* экскурсия
excuse [*n* ɪks'kju:s, *vb* ɪks'kju:z] *n* оправдание ▷ *vt* (*justify*) оправдывать (*perf* оправдать); (*forgive*) прощать (*perf* простить);

to make excuses for sb опра́вдываться (*impf*) за кого́-н; **that's no excuse!** э́то не оправда́ние!; **to excuse sb from sth** освобожда́ть (*perf* освободи́ть) кого́-н от чего́-н; **excuse me!** извини́те!, прости́те!; (*as apology*) извини́те *or* прости́те (меня́)!; **if you will excuse me, I have to ...** с Ва́шего разреше́ния я до́лжен ...

execute [ˈɛksɪkjuːt] *vt* (*kill*) казни́ть (*impf/perf*); (*carry out*) выполня́ть (*perf* вы́полнить)

execution [ɛksɪˈkjuːʃən] *n* (*see vb*) казнь *f*, выполне́ние

executive [ɪɡˈzɛkjutɪv] *n* (*person*) руководи́тель *m*; (*committee*) исполни́тельный о́рган ▷ *adj* (*board, role*) руководя́щий

exempt [ɪɡˈzɛmpt] *adj*: **exempt from** освобождённый от *+gen* ▷ *vt*: **to exempt sb from** освобожда́ть (*perf* освободи́ть) кого́-н от *+gen*

exercise [ˈɛksəsaɪz] *n* (*Sport*) заря́дка, гимна́стика; (: *for legs, stomach etc*) (физи́ческое) упражне́ние; (*also Scol, Mus*) упражне́ние; (*keep-fit*) заря́дка; (*physical*) гимна́стика ▷ *vt* (*patience*) проявля́ть (*perf* прояви́ть); (*authority, right*) применя́ть (*perf* примени́ть); (*dog*) выгу́ливать (*impf*) ▷ *vi* (*also* **to take exercise**) упражня́ться (*impf*); **military exercises** вое́нные уче́ния

exert [ɪɡˈzəːt] *vt* (*influence, pressure*) ока́зывать (*perf* оказа́ть); (*authority*) применя́ть (*perf* примени́ть); **to exert o.s.** напряга́ться (*perf* напря́чься); **exertion** [ɪɡˈzəːʃən] *n* (*effort*) уси́лие

exhaust [ɪɡˈzɔːst] *n* (*also* **exhaust pipe**) выхлопна́я труба́; (*fumes*) выхлопны́е га́зы *mpl* ▷ *vt* (*person*) изнуря́ть (*perf* изнури́ть); (*money, resources*) истоща́ть (*perf* истощи́ть); (*topic*) исче́рпывать (*perf* исче́рпать); **exhausted** *adj* изнурённый, изнеможённый; **exhaustion** [ɪɡˈzɔːstʃən] *n* изнеможе́ние; **nervous exhaustion** не́рвное истоще́ние

exhibit [ɪɡˈzɪbɪt] *n* экспона́т ▷ *vt* (*paintings*) экспони́ровать (*impf/perf*), выставля́ть (*perf* вы́ставить); (*quality, emotion*) проявля́ть (*perf* прояви́ть); **exhibition** [ɛksɪˈbɪʃən] *n* (*of paintings etc*) вы́ставка

exhilarating [ɪɡˈzɪləreɪtɪŋ] *adj* волну́ющий

exile [ˈɛksaɪl] *n* (*banishment*) ссы́лка, изгна́ние; (*person*) ссы́льный(-ая) *m(f) adj*, изгна́нник ▷ *vt* (*abroad*) высыла́ть (*perf* вы́слать)

exist [ɪɡˈzɪst] *vi* существова́ть (*impf*); **existence** *n* существова́ние; **existing** *adj* существу́ющий

exit [ˈɛksɪt] *n* (*way out*) вы́ход; (*on motorway*) вы́езд; (*departure*) ухо́д

exotic [ɪɡˈzɔtɪk] *adj* экзоти́ческий

expand [ɪksˈpænd] *vt* (*area, business, influence*) расширя́ть (*perf* расши́рить) ▷ *vi* (*gas, metal, business*) расширя́ться (*perf* расши́риться)

expansion [ɪksˈpænʃən] *n* расшире́ние; (*of economy*) рост

expect [ɪksˈpɛkt] *vt* ожида́ть (*impf*); (*baby*) ждать (*impf*); (*suppose*) полага́ть (*impf*) ▷ *vi*: **to be expecting** (*be pregnant*) ждать (*impf*) ребёнка; **expectation**

[ɛkspɛk'teɪʃən] *n* (*hope*) ожида́ние

expedition [ɛkspə'dɪʃən] *n* экспеди́ция; (*for pleasure*) похо́д

expel [ɪks'pɛl] *vt* (*from school etc*) исключа́ть (*perf* исключи́ть); (*from place*) изгоня́ть (*perf* изгна́ть)

expenditure [ɪks'pɛndɪtʃə^r] *n* (*money spent*) затра́ты *fpl*; (*of energy, time, money*) затра́та, расхо́д

expense [ɪks'pɛns] *n* (*cost*) сто́имость *f*; **expenses** *npl* (*travelling etc expenses*) расхо́ды *mpl*; (*expenditure*) затра́ты *fpl*; **at the expense of** за счёт *+gen*

expensive [ɪks'pɛnsɪv] *adj* дорого́й

experience [ɪks'pɪərɪəns] *n* (*in job, of situation*) о́пыт; (*event, activity*) слу́чай; (: *difficult, painful*) испыта́ние ▷ *vt* испы́тывать (*perf* испыта́ть), пережива́ть (*perf* пережи́ть); **experienced** *adj* о́пытный

experiment [ɪks'pɛrɪmənt] *n* экспериме́нт, о́пыт ▷ *vi*: **to experiment (with/on)** экспериме́нти́ровать (*impf*) (с *+instr*/на *+prp*); **experimental** [ɪkspɛrɪ'mɛntl] *adj* (*methods, ideas*) эксперимента́льный; (*tests*) про́бный

expert ['ɛkspə:t] *n* экспе́рт, специали́ст; **expert opinion/advice** мне́ние/сове́т экспе́рта *or* специали́ста; **expertise** [ɛkspə:'ti:z] *n* зна́ния *ntpl* и о́пыт

expire [ɪks'paɪə^r] *vi* (*run out*) истека́ть (*perf* истечь); **my passport expires in January** срок де́йствия моего́ па́спорта истека́ет в январе́

explain [ɪks'pleɪn] *vt* объясня́ть (*perf* объясни́ть)

explanation [ɛksplə'neɪʃən] *n* объясне́ние

explicit [ɪks'plɪsɪt] *adj* я́вный, очеви́дный; (*sex, violence*) открове́нный

explode [ɪks'pləud] *vi* (*bomb, person*) взрыва́ться (*perf* взорва́ться); (*population*) ре́зко возраста́ть (*perf* возрасти́)

exploit [*vb* ɪks'plɔɪt, *n* 'ɛksplɔɪt] *vt* эксплуати́ровать (*impf*); (*opportunity*) испо́льзовать (*impf/perf*) ▷ *n* дея́ние; **exploitation** [ɛksplɔɪ'teɪʃən] *n* (*see vt*) эксплуата́ция; испо́льзование

explore [ɪks'plɔ:^r] *vt* (*place*) иссле́довать (*impf/perf*); (*idea, suggestion*) изуча́ть (*perf* изучи́ть); **explorer** *n* иссле́дователь(ница) *m(f)*

explosion [ɪks'pləuʒən] *n* взрыв; **population explosion** демографи́ческий взрыв

explosive [ɪks'pləusɪv] *adj* (*device, effect*) взрывно́й; (*situation*) взрывоопа́сный; (*person*) вспы́льчивый ▷ *n* (*substance*) взры́вчатое вещество́; (*device*) взрывно́е устро́йство

export [*n, cpd* 'ɛkspɔ:t, *vb* ɛks'pɔ:t] *n* (*process*) э́кспорт, вы́воз; (*product*) предме́т э́кспорта ▷ *vt* экспорти́ровать (*impf/perf*), вывози́ть (*perf* вы́везти) ▷ *cpd* (*duty, licence*) э́кспортный

expose [ɪks'pəuz] *vt* (*object*) обнажа́ть (*perf* обнажи́ть); (*truth, plot*) раскрыва́ть (*perf* раскры́ть); (*person*) разоблача́ть (*perf* разоблачи́ть); **to expose sb to sth** подверга́ть (*perf* подве́ргнуть) кого́-н чему́-н; **exposed** *adj* (*place*): **exposed (to)** откры́тый (*+dat*)

exposure [ɪks'pəuʒə^r] *n* (*of*

culprit) разоблаче́ние; (*Phot*) вы́держка, экспози́ция; **to suffer from exposure** (*Med*) страда́ть (*perf* пострада́ть) от переохлажде́ния

express [ɪks'prɛs] *adj* (*clear*) чёткий; (*Brit*: *service*) сро́чный ▷ *n* экспре́сс ▷ *vt* выража́ть (*perf* вы́разить); **expression** [ɪks'prɛʃən] *n* выраже́ние

exquisite [ɛks'kwɪzɪt] *adj* (*perfect*) изы́сканный

extend [ɪks'tɛnd] *vt* (*visit, deadline*) продлева́ть (*perf* продли́ть); (*building*) расширя́ть (*perf* расши́рить); (*hand*) протя́гивать (*perf* протяну́ть); (*welcome*) ока́зывать (*perf* оказа́ть) ▷ *vi* (*land, road*) простира́ться (*impf*); (*period*) продолжа́ться (*perf* продо́лжиться); **to extend an invitation to sb** приглаша́ть (*perf* пригласи́ть) кого́-н

extension [ɪks'tɛnʃən] *n* (*of building*) пристро́йка; (*of time*) продле́ние; (*Elec*) удлини́тель *m*; (*Tel*: *in house*) паралле́льный телефо́н; (: *in office*) доба́вочный телефо́н

extensive [ɪks'tɛnsɪv] *adj* обши́рный; (*damage*) значи́тельный

extent [ɪks'tɛnt] *n* (*of area etc*) протяжённость *f*; (*of problem etc*) масшта́б; **to some extent** до не́которой сте́пени; **to go to the extent of ...** доходи́ть (*perf* дойти́) до того́, что ...; **to such an extent that ...** до тако́й сте́пени, что ...

exterior [ɛks'tɪərɪə^r] *adj* нару́жный ▷ *n* (*outside*) вне́шняя сторона́

external [ɛks'tə:nl] *adj* вне́шний

extinct [ɪks'tɪŋkt] *adj* (*animal*) вы́мерший; (*plant*) исчéзнувший; **to become extinct** (*animal*) вымира́ть (*perf* вы́мереть); (*plant*) исчеза́ть (*perf* исче́знуть); **extinction** [ɪks'tɪŋkʃən] *n* (*of animal*) вымира́ние; (*of plant*) исчезнове́ние

extra ['ɛkstrə] *adj* (*additional*) дополни́тельный; (*spare*) ли́шний ▷ *adv* (*in addition*) дополни́тельно; (*especially*) осо́бенно ▷ *n* (*luxury*) изли́шество; (*surcharge*) допла́та

extract [*vb* ɪks'trækt, *n* 'ɛkstrækt] *vt* извлека́ть (*perf* извле́чь); (*tooth*) удаля́ть (*perf* удали́ть); (*mineral*) добыва́ть (*perf* добы́ть); (*money, promise*) вытя́гивать (*perf* вы́тянуть) ▷ *n* (*from novel, recording*) отры́вок

extraordinary [ɪks'trɔ:dnrɪ] *adj* незауря́дный, необыча́йный

extravagance [ɪks'trævəgəns] *n* (*with money*) расточи́тельство

extravagant [ɪks'trævəgənt] *adj* (*lavish*) экстравага́нтный; (*wasteful*: *person*) расточи́тельный

extreme [ɪks'tri:m] *adj* кра́йний; (*situation*) экстрема́льный; (*heat, cold*) сильне́йший ▷ *n* (*of behaviour*) кра́йность *f*; **extremely** *adv* кра́йне

extrovert ['ɛkstrəvə:t] *n* экстрове́рт

eye [aɪ] *n* (*Anat*) глаз; (*of needle*) у́шко ▷ *vt* разгля́дывать (*perf* разгляде́ть); **to keep an eye on** (*person, object*) присма́тривать (*perf* присмотре́ть) за +*instr*; (*time*) следи́ть (*impf*) за +*instr*; **eyebrow** *n* бровь *f*; **eyelash** *n* ресни́ца; **eyelid** *n* ве́ко; **eyeliner** *n* каранда́ш для век; **eye shadow** *n* те́ни *fpl* (для век); **eyesight** *n* зре́ние

f

F [ɛf] *n* (*Mus*) фа
F *abbr* = **Fahrenheit**
fabric ['fæbrɪk] *n* (*cloth*) ткань *f*
fabulous ['fæbjuləs] *adj* (*inf*) ска́зочный; (*extraordinary*) невероя́тный
face [feɪs] *n* (*of person, organization*) лицо́; (*of clock*) цифербла́т; (*of mountain, cliff*) склон ▷ *vt* (*fact*) признава́ть (*perf* призна́ть); **the house faces the sea** дом обращён к мо́рю; **he was facing the door** он был обращён лицо́м к двери́; **we are facing difficulties** нам предстоя́т тру́дности; **face down** лицо́м вниз; **to lose/save face** теря́ть (*perf* потеря́ть)/спаса́ть (*perf* спасти́) репута́цию *or* лицо́; **to make** *or* **pull a face** де́лать (*perf* сде́лать) грима́су; **in the face of** (*difficulties etc*) пе́ред лицо́м +*gen*; **on the face of it** на пе́рвый взгляд; **face to face (with)** лицо́м к лицу́ (с +*instr*); **face up to** *vt fus* признава́ть (*perf* призна́ть); (*difficulties*) справля́ться (*perf* спра́виться) с +*instr*; **face cloth** *n* (*Brit*) махро́вая салфе́тка (*для лица́*)
facial ['feɪʃl] *adj*: **facial expression** выраже́ние лица́; **facial hair** во́лосы, расту́щие на лице́
facilitate [fə'sɪlɪteɪt] *vt* спосо́бствовать (*impf/perf*) +*dat*
facilities [fə'sɪlɪtɪz] *npl* усло́вия *ntpl*; (*buildings*) помеще́ние *ntsg*; (*equipment*) обору́дование *ntsg*; **cooking facilities** усло́вия для приготовле́ния пи́щи
fact [fækt] *n* факт; **in fact** факти́чески
faction ['fækʃən] *n* (*group*) фра́кция
factor ['fæktəʳ] *n* (*of problem*) фа́ктор
factory ['fæktərɪ] *n* (*for textiles*) фа́брика; (*for machinery*) заво́д
factual ['fæktjuəl] *adj* факти́ческий
faculty ['fækəltɪ] *n* спосо́бность *f*; (*of university*) факульте́т
fad [fæd] *n* причу́да
fade [feɪd] *vi* (*colour*) выцвета́ть (*perf* вы́цвести); (*light, hope, smile*) угаса́ть (*perf* уга́снуть); (*sound*) замира́ть (*perf* замере́ть); (*memory*) тускне́ть (*perf* потускне́ть)
fag [fæg] *n* (*Brit*: *inf*) сигаре́та
Fahrenheit ['færənhaɪt] *n* Фаренге́йт
fail [feɪl] *vt* (*exam, candidate*) прова́ливать (*perf* провали́ть); (*subj*: *memory*) изменя́ть (*perf* измени́ть) +*dat*; (: *person*) подводи́ть (*perf* подвести́); (: *courage*) покида́ть (*perf*

поки́нуть) ▷ *vi* (*candidate, attempt*) прова́ливаться (*perf* провали́ться); (*brakes*) отка́зывать (*perf* отказа́ть); **my eyesight/ health is failing** у меня́ слабе́ет зре́ние/здоро́вье; **to fail to do** (*be unable*) не мочь (*perf* смочь) *+infin*; **without fail** обяза́тельно, непреме́нно; **failing** *n* недоста́ток ▷ *prep* за неиме́нием *+gen*; **failure** *n* прова́л, неуда́ча; (*Tech*) ава́рия, вы́ход из стро́я; (*person*) неуда́чник(-ица)

faint [feɪnt] *adj* сла́бый; (*recollection*) сму́тный; (*mark*) едва́ заме́тный ▷ *vi* (*Med*) па́дать (*perf* упа́сть) в о́бморок; **to feel faint** чу́вствовать (*perf* почу́вствовать) сла́бость; **faintest** *adj*: **I haven't the faintest idea** я не име́ю ни мале́йшего поня́тия

fair [fɛəʳ] *adj* (*person, decision*) справедли́вый; (*size, number*) изря́дный; (*chance, guess*) хоро́ший; (*skin, hair*) све́тлый; (*weather*) хоро́ший, я́сный ▷ *n* (*also* **trade fair**) я́рмарка; (*Brit*: *also* **funfair**) аттракцио́ны *mpl* ▷ *adv*: **to play fair** вести́ (*impf*) дела́ че́стно; **fairground** *n* я́рмарочная пло́щадь *f*; **fairly** *adv* (*justly*) справедли́во; (*quite*) дово́льно

fairy ['fɛərɪ] *n* фе́я; **fairy tale** *n* ска́зка

faith [feɪθ] *n* (*also Rel*) ве́ра; **faithful** *adj*: **faithful (to)** ве́рный (*+dat*); **faithfully** *adv* ве́рно

fake [feɪk] *n* (*painting, document*) подде́лка ▷ *adj* фальши́вый, подде́льный ▷ *vt* (*forge*) подде́лывать (*perf* подде́лать); (*feign*) симули́ровать (*impf*)

fall [fɔːl] (*pt* **fell**, *pp* **fallen**) *n* паде́ние; (*US*: *autumn*) о́сень *f* ▷ *vi* па́дать (*perf* упа́сть); (*government*) пасть (*perf*); (*rain, snow*) па́дать (*impf*), выпада́ть (*perf* вы́пасть); **falls** *npl* (*waterfall*) водопа́д *msg*; **a fall of snow** снегопа́д; **to fall flat** (*plan*) прова́ливаться (*perf* провали́ться); **to fall flat (on one's face)** па́дать (*perf* упа́сть) ничко́м; **fall back on** *vt fus* прибега́ть (*perf* прибе́гнуть) к *+dat*; **fall down** *vi* (*person*) па́дать (*perf* упа́сть); (*building*) ру́шиться (*perf* ру́хнуть); **fall for** *vt fus* (*trick, story*) ве́рить (*perf* пове́рить) *+dat*; (*person*) влюбля́ться (*perf* влюби́ться) в *+acc*; **fall in** *vi* (*roof*) обва́ливаться (*perf* обвали́ться); **fall off** *vi* па́дать (*perf* упа́сть); (*handle, button*) отва́ливаться (*perf* отвали́ться); **fall out** *vi* (*hair, teeth*) выпада́ть (*perf* вы́пасть); **to fall out with sb** ссо́риться (*perf* поссо́риться) с кем-н

fallen ['fɔːlən] *pp of* **fall**

false [fɔːls] *adj* (*untrue, wrong*) ло́жный; (*insincere, artificial*) фальши́вый; **false teeth** *npl* (*Brit*) иску́сственные зу́бы *mpl*

fame [feɪm] *n* сла́ва

familiar [fə'mɪlɪəʳ] *adj* (*well-known*) знако́мый; (*intimate*) дру́жеский; **he is familiar with** (*subject*) он знако́м с *+instr*

family ['fæmɪlɪ] *n* семья́; (*children*) де́ти *pl*

famine ['fæmɪn] *n* го́лод

famous ['feɪməs] *adj* знамени́тый

fan [fæn] *n* (*folding*) ве́ер; (*Elec*) вентиля́тор; (*of famous person*) покло́нник(-ица); (*of sports team*) боле́льщик(-ица); (: *inf*) фан ▷ *vt* (*face*) обма́хивать (*perf*

обмахну́ть); (*fire*) раздува́ть (*perf* разду́ть)
fanatic [fə'nætɪk] *n* (*extremist*) фана́тик
fancy ['fænsɪ] *n* (*whim*) при́хоть *f* ▷ *adj* шика́рный ▷ *vt* (*want*) хоте́ть (*perf* захоте́ть); (*imagine*) вообража́ть (*perf* вообрази́ть); **to take a fancy to** увлека́ться (*perf* увле́чься) *+instr*; **he fancies her** (*inf*) она́ ему́ нра́вится; **fancy that!** представля́ете!; **fancy dress** *n* маскара́дный костю́м
fantastic [fæn'tæstɪk] *adj* фантасти́ческий; **that's fantastic!** замеча́тельно!, потряса́юще!
fantasy ['fæntəsɪ] *n* фанта́зия
far [fɑː[r]] *adj* (*distant*) да́льний ▷ *adv* (*a long way*) далеко́; (*much*) гора́здо; **at the far end** в да́льнем конце́; **at the far side** на друго́й стороне́; **the far left/right** (*Pol*) кра́йне ле́вый/пра́вый; **far away, far off** далеко́; **he was far from poor** он был далеко́ *or* отню́дь не бе́ден; **by far** намно́го; **go as far as the post office** дойди́те до по́чты; **as far as I know** наско́лько мне изве́стно; **how far?** (*distance*) как далеко́?
farce [fɑːs] *n* фарс
fare [fɛə[r]] *n* (*in taxi, train, bus*) сто́имость *f* прое́зда; **half/full fare** полсто́имости/по́лная сто́имость прое́зда
Far East *n*: **the Far East** Да́льний Восто́к
farm [fɑːm] *n* фе́рма ▷ *vt* (*land*) обраба́тывать (*perf* обрабо́тать); **farmer** *n* фе́рмер; **farmhouse** *n* фе́рмерская уса́дьба; **farming** *n* (*agriculture*) се́льское хозя́йство; (*of crops*) выра́щивание; (*of animals*) разведе́ние; **farmyard** *n* фе́рмерский двор
farther ['fɑːðə[r]] *adv* да́лее
fascinating ['fæsɪneɪtɪŋ] *adj* (*story*) захва́тывающий; (*person*) очарова́тельный
fascination [fæsɪ'neɪʃən] *n* очарова́ние
fashion ['fæʃən] *n* (*trend*) мо́да; **in/out of fashion** в/не в мо́де; **in a friendly fashion** по-дру́жески; **fashionable** *adj* мо́дный; **fashion show** *n* пока́з *or* демонстра́ция мод
fast [fɑːst] *adv* (*quickly*) бы́стро; (*firmly*: *stick*) про́чно; (: *hold*) кре́пко ▷ *n* (*Rel*) пост ▷ *adj* бы́стрый; (*progress*) стреми́тельный; (*car*) скоростно́й; (*colour*) про́чный; **to be fast** (*clock*) спеши́ть (*impf*); **he is fast asleep** он кре́пко спит
fasten ['fɑːsn] *vt* закрепля́ть (*perf* закрепи́ть); (*door*) запира́ть (*perf* запере́ть); (*shoe*) завя́зывать (*perf* завяза́ть); (*coat, dress*) застёгивать (*perf* застегну́ть); (*seat belt*) пристёгивать (*perf* пристегну́ть) ▷ *vi* (*coat, belt*) застёгиваться (*perf* застегну́ться); (*door*) запира́ться (*perf* запере́ться)
fast food *n* бы́стро пригото́вленная еда́
fat [fæt] *adj* то́лстый ▷ *n* жир
fatal ['feɪtl] *adj* (*mistake*) фата́льный, рокво́й; (*injury, illness*) смерте́льный; **fatally** *adv* (*injured*) смерте́льно
fate [feɪt] *n* судьба́, рок
father ['fɑːðə[r]] *n* оте́ц; **father-in-law** *n* (*wife's father*) свёкор; (*husband's father*) тесть *m*
fatigue [fə'tiːg] *n* утомле́ние
fatty ['fætɪ] *adj* (*food*) жи́рный
fault [fɔːlt] *n* (*blame*) вина́; (*defect*: *in person*) недоста́ток; (: *in*

f

machine) дефе́кт; (*Geo*) разло́м ▷ *vt* (*criticize*) придира́ться (*impf*) к +*dat*; **it's my fault** э́то моя́ вина́; **to find fault with** придира́ться (*perf* придра́ться) к +*dat*; **I am at fault** я винова́т; **faulty** *adj* (*goods*) испо́рченный; (*machine*) повреждённый
fauna ['fɔ:nə] *n* фа́уна
favour ['feɪvəʳ] (*US* **favor**) *n* (*approval*) расположе́ние; (*help*) одолже́ние ▷ *vt* (*prefer*: *solution*) ока́зывать (*perf* оказа́ть) предпочте́ние +*dat*; (: *pupil etc*) выделя́ть (*perf* вы́делить); (*assist*) благоприя́тствовать (*impf*) +*dat*; **to do sb a favour** ока́зывать (*perf* оказа́ть) кому́-н услу́гу; **in favour of** в по́льзу +*gen*; **favourable** *adj* благоприя́тный; **favourite** *adj* люби́мый ▷ *n* люби́мец; (*Sport*) фавори́т
fawn [fɔ:n] *n* молодо́й оле́нь *m*
fax [fæks] *n* факс ▷ *vt* посыла́ть (*perf* посла́ть) фа́ксом
FBI *n abbr* (*US*) (= *Federal Bureau of Investigation*) ФБР (= *Федера́льное бюро́ рассле́дований*)
fear [fɪəʳ] *n* страх; (*less strong*) боя́знь *f*; (*worry*) опасе́ние ▷ *vt* боя́ться (*impf*) +*gen*; **for fear of missing my flight** боя́сь опозда́ть на самолёт; **fearful** *adj* (*person*): **to be fearful of** боя́ться (*impf*) *or* страши́ться *impf* (+*gen*); **fearless** *adj* бесстра́шный
feasible ['fi:zəbl] *adj* осуществи́мый
feast [fi:st] *n* (*banquet*) пир
feat [fi:t] *n* по́двиг
feather ['fɛðəʳ] *n* перо́
feature ['fi:tʃəʳ] *n* осо́бенность *f*, черта́; (*Press*) о́черк; (*TV, Radio*) переда́ча ▷ *vi*: **to feature in** фигури́ровать (*impf*) в +*prp*; **features** *npl* (*of face*) черты́ *fpl* (лица́); **feature film** *n* худо́жественный фильм
February ['fɛbruərɪ] *n* февра́ль *m*
fed [fɛd] *pt, pp of* **feed**
federal ['fɛdərəl] *adj* федера́льный
federation [fɛdə'reɪʃən] *n* федера́ция
fee [fi:] *n* пла́та; **school fees** пла́та за обуче́ние
feeble ['fi:bl] *adj* хи́лый; (*excuse*) сла́бый
feed [fi:d] (*pt, pp* **fed**) *n* (*fodder*) корм; (*Comput*) ле́нта, френд-ле́нта ▷ *vt* корми́ть (*perf* накорми́ть); **to feed sth into** (*data*) загружа́ть (*perf* загрузи́ть) что-н в +*acc*; (*paper*) подава́ть (*perf* пода́ть) что-н в +*acc*; **feed on** *vt fus* пита́ться (*impf*) +*instr*
feel [fi:l] (*pt, pp* **felt**) *vt* (*touch*) тро́гать (*perf* потро́гать); (*experience*) чу́вствовать (*impf*), ощуща́ть (*perf* ощути́ть); **to feel (that)** (*believe*) счита́ть (*impf*), что; **he feels hungry** он го́лоден; **she feels cold** ей хо́лодно; **to feel lonely/better** чу́вствовать (*impf*) себя́ одино́ко/лу́чше; **I don't feel well** я пло́хо себя́ чу́вствую; **the material feels like velvet** э́тот материа́л на о́щупь как ба́рхат; **I feel like ...** (*want*) мне хо́чется ...; **feel about** *vi*: **to feel about for sth** иска́ть (*impf*) что-н о́щупью; **feeling** *n* чу́вство; (*physical*) ощуще́ние
feet [fi:t] *npl of* **foot**
fell [fɛl] *pt of* **fall**
fellow ['fɛləu] *n* (*man*) па́рень *m*; (*of society*) действи́тельный член ▷ *cpd*: **their fellow prisoners/**

students их сока́мерники/ сокýрсники; **fellowship** *n* (*Scol*) стипе́ндия (*для иссле́довательской рабо́ты*)
felt [fɛlt] *pt, pp of* **feel** ▷ *n* фетр
female ['fi:meɪl] *n* са́мка ▷ *adj* же́нский; (*child*) же́нского по́ла
feminine ['fɛmɪnɪn] *adj* (*clothes, behaviour*) же́нственный; (*Ling*) же́нского ро́да
feminist ['fɛmɪnɪst] *n* фемини́ст(ка)
fence [fɛns] *n* (*barrier*) забо́р, и́згородь *f*
fencing ['fɛnsɪŋ] *n* (*Sport*) фехтова́ние
fend [fɛnd] *vi*: **to fend for o.s.** забо́титься (*perf* позабо́титься) о себе́; **fend off** *vt* отража́ть (*perf* отрази́ть)
fender ['fɛndə^r] *n* (*US*: *of car*) крыло́
fern [fə:n] *n* па́поротник
ferocious [fə'rəuʃəs] *adj* (*animal, attack*) свире́пый; (*behaviour, heat*) ди́кий
ferry ['fɛrɪ] *n* (*also* **ferryboat**) паро́м ▷ *vt* перевози́ть (*perf* перевезти́)
fertile ['fə:taɪl] *adj* (*land, soil*) плодоро́дный; (*imagination*) бога́тый; (*woman*) спосо́бный к зача́тию
fertilizer ['fə:tɪlaɪzə^r] *n* удобре́ние
festival ['fɛstɪvəl] *n* (*Rel*) пра́здник; (*Art, Mus*) фестива́ль *m*
festive ['fɛstɪv] *adj* (*mood*) пра́здничный; **the festive season** (*Brit*) ≈ Свя́тки *pl*
fetch [fɛtʃ] *vt* (*object*) приноси́ть (*perf* принести́); (*person*) приводи́ть (*perf* привести́); (*by car*) привози́ть (*perf* привезти́)
fête [feɪt] *n* благотвори́тельный база́р
fetus ['fi:təs] *n* (*US*) = **foetus**
feud [fju:d] *n* вражда́
fever ['fi:və^r] *n* (*temperature*) жар; (*disease*) лихора́дка; **feverish** *adj* лихора́дочный; (*person*: *with excitement*) возбуждённый; **he is feverish** у него́ жар, его́ лихора́дит
few [fju:] *adj* (*not many*) немно́гие; (*some*) не́которые *pl adj* ▷ *pron*: **(a) few** немно́гие *pl adj*; **a few** (*several*) не́сколько *+gen*; **fewer** *adj* ме́ньше *+gen*
fiancé [fɪ'ã:ŋseɪ] *n* жени́х
fiancée *n* неве́ста
fiasco [fɪ'æskəu] *n* фиа́ско *nt ind*
fibre ['faɪbə^r] (*US* **fiber**) *n* волокно́; (*dietary*) клетча́тка
fickle ['fɪkl] *adj* непостоя́нный
fiction ['fɪkʃən] *n* (*Literature*) худо́жественная литерату́ра; **fictional** *adj* (*event, character*) вы́мышленный
fiddle ['fɪdl] *n* (*Mus*) скри́пка; (*swindle*) надува́тельство ▷ *vt* (*Brit*: *accounts*) подде́лывать (*perf* подде́лать)
fidelity [fɪ'dɛlɪtɪ] *n* (*loyalty*) ве́рность *f*
field [fi:ld] *n* по́ле; (*fig*) о́бласть *f*
fierce [fɪəs] *adj* свире́пый; (*fighting*) я́ростный
fifteen [fɪf'ti:n] *n* пятна́дцать; **fifteenth** *adj* пятна́дцатый
fifth [fɪfθ] *adj* пя́тый ▷ *n* (*fraction*) пя́тая *f adj*; (*Aut*: *also* **fifth gear**) пя́тая ско́рость *f*
fiftieth ['fɪftɪɪθ] *adj* пятидеся́тый
fifty ['fɪftɪ] *n* пятьдеся́т
fig [fɪg] *n* инжи́р
fight [faɪt] (*pt, pp* **fought**) *n* дра́ка; (*campaign, struggle*) борьба́ ▷ *vt* (*person*) дра́ться (*perf* подра́ться) с *+instr*; (*Mil*) вое́вать (*impf*) с *+instr*; (*illness,*

f

problem, emotion) боро́ться (*impf*) с +*instr* ▷ *vi* (*people*) дра́ться (*impf*); (*Mil*) воева́ть (*impf*); **to fight an election** уча́ствовать (*impf*) в предвы́борной борьбе́; **fighting** *n* (*battle*) бой; (*brawl*) дра́ка

figure [ˈfɪgəʳ] *n* фигу́ра; (*number*) ци́фра ▷ *vt* (*think*) счита́ть (*impf*) ▷ *vi* (*appear*) фигури́ровать (*impf*); **figure out** *vt* понима́ть (*perf* поня́ть)

file [faɪl] *n* (*dossier*) де́ло; (*folder*) скоросшива́тель *m*; (*Comput*) файл ▷ *vt* (*papers, document*) подшива́ть (*perf* подши́ть); (*Law*: *claim*) подава́ть (*perf* пода́ть); (*wood, fingernails*) шлифова́ть (*perf* отшлифова́ть) ▷ *vi*: **to file in/past** входи́ть (*perf* войти́)/ проходи́ть (*perf* пройти́) коло́нной; **in single file** в коло́нну по одному́

fill [fɪl] *vi* (*room etc*) наполня́ться (*perf* напо́лниться) ▷ *vt* (*vacancy*) заполня́ть (*perf* запо́лнить); (*need*) удовлетворя́ть (*perf* удовлетвори́ть) ▷ *n*: **to eat one's fill** наеда́ться (*perf* нае́сться); **to fill (with)** (*container*) наполня́ть (*perf* напо́лнить) (+*instr*); (*space, area*) заполня́ть (*perf* запо́лнить) (+*instr*); **fill in** *vt* заполня́ть (*perf* запо́лнить); **fill up** *vt* (*container*) наполня́ть (*perf* напо́лнить); (*space*) заполня́ть (*perf* запо́лнить) ▷ *vi* (*Aut*) заправля́ться (*perf* запра́виться)

fillet [ˈfɪlɪt] *n* филе́ *nt ind*

filling [ˈfɪlɪŋ] *n* (*for tooth*) пло́мба; (*of pie*) начи́нка; (*of cake*) просло́йка

film [fɪlm] *n* (*Cinema*) фильм; (*Phot*) плёнка; (*of powder, liquid etc*) то́нкий слой ▷ *vt, vi* снима́ть (*perf* снять); **film star** *n* кинозвезда́ *m/f*

filter [ˈfɪltəʳ] *n* фильтр ▷ *vt* фильтрова́ть (*perf* профильтрова́ть)

filth [fɪlθ] *n* грязь *f*; **filthy** *adj* гря́зный

fin [fɪn] *n* (*of fish*) плавни́к

final [ˈfaɪnl] *adj* (*last*) после́дний; (*Sport*) фина́льный; (*ultimate*) заключи́тельный; (*definitive*) оконча́тельный ▷ *n* (*Sport*) фина́л; **finals** *npl* (*Scol*) выпускны́е экза́мены *mpl*; **finale** [fɪˈnɑːlɪ] *n* фина́л; **finalist** *n* финали́ст; **finally** *adv* (*eventually*) в конце́ концо́в; (*lastly*) наконе́ц

finance [faɪˈnæns] *n* фина́нсы *pl* ▷ *vt* финанси́ровать (*impf/perf*); **finances** *npl* (*personal*) фина́нсы *pl*

financial [faɪˈnænʃəl] *adj* фина́нсовый

find [faɪnd] (*pt, pp* **found**) *vt* находи́ть (*perf* найти́); (*discover*) обнару́живать (*perf* обнару́жить) ▷ *n* нахо́дка; **to find sb at home** застава́ть (*perf* заста́ть) кого́-н до́ма; **to find sb guilty** (*Law*) признава́ть (*perf* призна́ть) кого́-н вино́вным(-ой); **find out** *vt* (*fact, truth*) узнава́ть (*perf* узна́ть); (*person*) разоблача́ть (*perf* разоблачи́ть) ▷ *vi*: **to find out about** узнава́ть (*perf* узна́ть) о +*prp*; **findings** *npl* (*Law*) заключе́ние *ntsg*; (*in research*) результа́ты *mpl*

fine [faɪn] *adj* прекра́сный; (*delicate*: *hair, features*) то́нкий; (*sand, powder, detail*) ме́лкий; (*adjustment*) то́чный ▷ *adv* (*well*) прекра́сно ▷ *n* штраф ▷ *vt* штрафова́ть (*perf* оштрафова́ть); **he's fine** (*well*) он чу́вствует себя́ хорошо́; (*happy*) у него́ всё в поря́дке; **the weather is fine** пого́да хоро́шая; **to cut it fine** (*of time*) оставля́ть (*perf* оста́вить) сли́шком ма́ло вре́мени

finger ['fɪŋgəʳ] *n* па́лец ▷ *vt* тро́гать (*perf* потро́гать); **little finger** мизи́нец

finish ['fɪnɪʃ] *n* коне́ц; (*Sport*) фи́ниш; (*polish etc*) отде́лка ▷ *vt* зака́нчивать (*perf* зако́нчить), конча́ть (*perf* ко́нчить) ▷ *vi* зака́нчиваться (*perf* зако́нчиться); (*person*) зака́нчивать (*perf* зако́нчить); **to finish doing** конча́ть (*perf* ко́нчить) *+infin*; **he finished third** (*in race etc*) он зако́нчил тре́тьим; **finish off** *vt* зака́нчивать (*perf* зако́нчить); (*kill*) прика́нчивать (*perf* прико́нчить); **finish up** *vt* (*food*) доеда́ть (*perf* дое́сть); (*drink*) допива́ть (*perf* допи́ть) ▷ *vi* (*end up*) конча́ть (*perf* ко́нчить)

Finland ['fɪnlənd] *n* Финля́ндия; **Gulf of Finland** Фи́нский зали́в

Finn [fɪn] *n* финн; **Finnish** *adj* фи́нский

fir [fəːʳ] *n* ель *f*

fire ['faɪəʳ] *n* (*flames*) ого́нь *m*, пла́мя *nt*; (*in hearth*) ого́нь *m*; (*accidental*) пожа́р; (*bonfire*) костёр ▷ *vt* (*gun etc*) вы́стрелить (*perf*) из *+gen*; (*arrow*) выпуска́ть (*perf* вы́пустить); (*stimulate*) разжига́ть (*perf* разже́чь); (*inf: dismiss*) увольня́ть (*perf* уво́лить) ▷ *vi* (*shoot*) вы́стрелить (*perf*); **the house is on fire** дом гори́т *or* в огне́; **fire alarm** *n* пожа́рная сигнализа́ция; **firearm** *n* огнестре́льное ору́жие *nt no pl*; **fire brigade** *n* пожа́рная кома́нда; **fire engine** *n* пожа́рная маши́на; **fire escape** *n* пожа́рная ле́стница; **fire-extinguisher** *n* огнетуши́тель *m*; **firefighter** *n* пожа́рный(-ая) *m(f) adj*, пожа́рник; **fireplace** *n* ками́н; **fire station** *n* пожа́рное депо́ *nt ind*; **firewood** *n* дрова́ *pl*; **fireworks** *npl* фейерве́рк *msg*

firm [fəːm] *adj* (*ground, decision, faith*) твёрдый; (*mattress*) жёсткий; (*grasp, body, muscles*) кре́пкий ▷ *n* фи́рма; **firmly** *adv* (*believe, stand*) твёрдо; (*grasp, shake hands*) кре́пко

first [fəːst] *adj* пе́рвый ▷ *adv* (*before all others*) пе́рвый; (*firstly*) во-пе́рвых ▷ *n* (*Aut: also* **first gear**) пе́рвая ско́рость *f*; (*Brit: Scol: degree*) дипло́м пе́рвой сте́пени; **at first** снача́ла; **first of all** пре́жде всего́; **first aid** *n* пе́рвая по́мощь *f*; **first-aid kit** *n* паке́т пе́рвой по́мощи; **first-class** *adj* (*excellent*) первокла́ссный; **first-class ticket** биле́т пе́рвого кла́сса; **first-class stamp** ма́рка пе́рвого кла́сса

FIRST-CLASS POSTAGE

В Великобрита́нии мо́жно приобрести́ почто́вые ма́рки пе́рвого и второ́го кла́сса. Пи́сьма с ма́ркой пе́рвого кла́сса доставля́ются по ме́сту назначе́ния на сле́дующий день.

first: **first-hand** *adj* непосре́дственный; **a first-hand account** расска́з очеви́дца; **first lady** *n* (*US*) пе́рвая ле́ди *f ind*; **firstly** *adv* во-пе́рвых; **first name** *n* и́мя *nt*; **first-rate** *adj* первокла́ссный

fiscal ['fɪskl] *adj* фиска́льный
fish [fɪʃ] *n inv* ры́ба ▷ *vt* (*river, area*) лови́ть (*impf*) ры́бу в *+prp*, рыба́чить (*impf*) в *+prp* ▷ *vi* (*commercially*) занима́ться (*impf*) рыболо́вством; (*as sport, hobby*) занима́ться (*impf*) ры́бной ло́влей; **to go fishing** ходи́ть/идти́ (*perf* пойти́) на рыба́лку; **fisherman** *irreg n* рыба́к

FISH AND CHIPS

Fish and chips — жа́реная ры́ба и карто́фель фри. Э́та традицио́ная брита́нская бы́страя еда́ продаётся в специа́льных магази́нах. Её мо́жно съесть тут же в магази́не или купи́ть на вы́нос в пла́стиковой коро́бке или завёрнутую в бума́жный паке́т.

fist [fɪst] *n* кула́к
fit [fɪt] *adj* (*suitable*) приго́дный; (*healthy*) в хоро́шей фо́рме ▷ *vt* (*subj: clothes etc*) подходи́ть (*perf* подойти́) по разме́ру *+dat*, быть (*impf*) впо́ру *+dat* ▷ *vi* (*clothes*) подходи́ть (*perf* подойти́) по разме́ру, быть (*impf*) впо́ру; (*parts*) подходи́ть (*perf* подойти́) ▷ *n* (*Med*) припа́док; (*of coughing, giggles*) при́ступ; **fit to do** (*ready*) гото́вый *+infin*; **fit for** (*suitable for*) приго́дный для *+gen*; **a fit of anger** при́ступ гне́ва; **this dress is a good fit** э́то пла́тье хорошо́ сиди́т; **by fits and starts** уры́вками; **fit in** *vi* (*person, object*) впи́сываться (*perf* вписа́ться); **fitness** *n* (*Med*) состоя́ние здоро́вья; **fitting** *adj* (*thanks*) надлежа́щий; **fittings** *npl*: **fixtures and fittings** обору́дование *ntsg*
five [faɪv] *n* пять; **fiver** *n* (*inf: Brit*) пять фу́нтов; (*: US*) пять до́лларов
fix [fɪks] *vt* (*arrange: date*) назнача́ть (*perf* назна́чить); (*: amount*) устана́вливать (*perf* установи́ть); (*mend*) нала́живать (*perf* нала́дить) ▷ *n* (*inf*): **to be in a fix** влипа́ть (*perf* вли́пнуть); **fixed** *adj* (*price*) твёрдый; (*ideas*) навя́зчивый; (*smile*) засты́вший
fixture ['fɪkstʃə^r] *n see* **fittings**
fizzy ['fɪzɪ] *adj* шипу́чий, газиро́ванный
flag [flæg] *n* флаг
flair [flɛə^r] *n* (*style*) стиль *m*; **a flair for** (*talent*) дар *or* тала́нт к *+dat*; **political flair** полити́ческий тала́нт
flak [flæk] *n* (*inf*) нахлобу́чка
flake [fleɪk] *n* (*of snow, soap powder*) хло́пья *pl*; (*of rust, paint*) слой
flamboyant [flæm'bɔɪənt] *adj* я́ркий, бро́ский; (*person*) колори́тный
flame [fleɪm] *n* (*of fire*) пла́мя *nt*
flank [flæŋk] *n* (*of animal*) бок; (*Mil*) фланг ▷ *vt*: **flanked by** ме́жду *+instr*
flannel ['flænl] *n* (*fabric*) флане́ль *f*; (*Brit: also* **face flannel**) махро́вая салфе́тка (*для лица́*)
flap [flæp] *n* (*of envelope*) отворо́т; (*of pocket*) кла́пан ▷ *vt* (*wings*) хло́пать *impf +instr*
flare [flɛə^r] *n* (*signal*) сигна́льная раке́та; **flare up** *vi* вспы́хивать (*perf* вспы́хнуть)
flash [flæʃ] *n* вспы́шка; (*also* **news flash**) мо́лния ▷ *vt* (*light*) (внеза́пно) освеща́ть (*perf* освети́ть); (*news, message*) посыла́ть (*perf* посла́ть) мо́лнией;

(*look*) мета́ть (*perf* метну́ть) ▷ *vi* (*lightning, light, eyes*) сверка́ть (*perf* сверкну́ть); (*light on ambulance etc*) мига́ть (*impf*); **in a flash** мгнове́нно; **to flash by** *or* **past (sth)** (*person*) мча́ться (*perf* промча́ться) ми́мо (чего́-н); **flashlight** *n* фона́рь *m*, проже́ктор

flask [flɑːsk] *n* (*also* **vacuum flask**) те́рмос

flat [flæt] *adj* (*surface*) пло́ский; (*tyre*) спу́щенный; (*battery*) се́вший; (*beer*) вы́дохшийся; (*refusal, denial*) категори́ческий; (*Mus*: *note*) бемо́льный; (*rate, fee*) еди́ный ▷ *n* (*Brit*: *apartment*) кварти́ра; (*Aut*: *also* **flat tyre**) спу́щенная ши́на; (*Mus*) бемо́ль *m*; **to work flat out** выкла́дываться (*perf* вы́ложиться) по́лностью

flatter ['flætəʳ] *vt* льсти́ть (*perf* польсти́ть) *+dat*

flavour ['fleɪvəʳ] (*US* **flavor**) *vt* (*soup*) приправля́ть (*perf* припра́вить) ▷ *n* (*taste*) вкус; (*of ice-cream etc*) при́вкус; **strawberry-flavoured** с клубни́чным при́вкусом

flaw [flɔː] *n* (*in argument, character*) недоста́ток, изъя́н; (*in cloth, glass*) дефе́кт; **flawless** *adj* безупре́чный

flea [fliː] *n* блоха́

flee [fliː] (*pt, pp* **fled**) *vt* (*danger, famine*) бежа́ть (*impf*) от *+gen*; (*country*) бежа́ть (*impf/perf*) из *+gen* ▷ *vi* спаса́ться (*impf*) бе́гством

fleece [fliːs] *n* (*sheep's coat*) (ове́чья) шку́ра; (*sheep's wool*) ове́чья шерсть *f*

fleet [fliːt] *n* (*of ships*) флот; (*of lorries, cars*) парк

fleeting ['fliːtɪŋ] *adj* мимолётный

Flemish ['flɛmɪʃ] *adj* фламáндский

flesh [flɛʃ] *n* (*Anat*) плоть *f*; (*of fruit*) мя́коть *f*

flew [fluː] *pt of* **fly**

flex [flɛks] *n* ги́бкий шнур ▷ *vt* (*leg, muscles*) размина́ть (*perf* размя́ть); **flexibility** [flɛksɪ'bɪlɪtɪ] *n* ги́бкость *f*; **flexible** ['flɛksɪbl] *adj* ги́бкий

flick [flɪk] *vt* (*with finger*) сма́хивать (*perf* смахну́ть); (*ash*) стря́хивать (*perf* стряхну́ть); (*whip*) хлестну́ть (*perf*) *+instr*; (*switch*) щёлкать (*perf* щёлкнуть) *+instr*

flicker ['flɪkəʳ] *vi* (*light, flame*) мерца́ть (*impf*)

flight [flaɪt] *n* полёт; (*of steps*) пролёт (*ле́стницы*)

flimsy ['flɪmzɪ] *adj* (*shoes, clothes*) лёгкий; (*structure*) непро́чный; (*excuse, evidence*) сла́бый

fling [flɪŋ] (*pt, pp* **flung**) *vt* (*throw*) швыря́ть (*perf* швырну́ть)

flip [flɪp] *vt* (*coin*) подбра́сывать (*perf* подбро́сить) щелчко́м

float [fləut] *n* (*for fishing*) поплаво́к; (*for swimming*) *пенопла́стовая доска́ для обуча́ющихся пла́вать*; (*money*) разме́нные де́ньги *pl* ▷ *vi* (*object, person*: *on water*) пла́вать (*impf*); (*sound, cloud*) плыть (*impf*) ▷ *vt* (*idea, plan*) пуска́ть (*perf* пусти́ть) в ход; **to float a company** выпуска́ть (*perf* вы́пустить) а́кции компа́нии на ры́нок

flock [flɔk] *n* (*of sheep*) ста́до; (*of birds*) ста́я ▷ *vi*: **to flock to** стека́ться (*perf* стёчься) в *+prp*

flood [flʌd] *n* (*of water*) наводне́ние; (*of letters, imports etc*) пото́к ▷ *vt* (*subj*: *water*) заливáть (*perf* залúть); (: *people*) наводнять (*perf* наводнúть) ▷ *vi* (*place*) наполняться (*perf* напóлниться) водóй; **to flood into** (*people, goods*) хлы́нуть (*perf*) в/на +*acc*; **flooding** *n* наводнéние

floor [flɔːʳ] *n* (*of room*) пол; (*storey*) этáж; (*of sea, valley*) дно ▷ *vt* (*subj*: *question, remark*) сражáть (*perf* сразúть); **ground** *or* (*US*) **first floor** пéрвый этáж; **floorboard** *n* половúца

flop [flɔp] *n* (*failure*) провáл

floppy [ˈflɔpɪ] *n* (*also* **floppy disk**) дискéта, гúбкий диск

flora [ˈflɔːrə] *n* флóра; **floral** [ˈflɔːrl] *adj* (*pattern*) цветúстый

flour [ˈflauəʳ] *n* мукá

flourish [ˈflʌrɪʃ] *vi* (*business*) процветáть (*impf*); (*plant*) пы́шно растú (*impf*) ▷ *n* (*bold gesture*): **with a flourish** демонстратúвно

flow [fləu] *n* (*also Elec*) потóк; (*of blood, river*) течéние ▷ *vi* течь (*impf*)

flower [ˈflauəʳ] *n* цветóк ▷ *vi* (*plant, tree*) цвестú (*impf*); **flowers** цветы́; **flowerpot** *n* цветóчный горшóк

flown [fləun] *pp of* **fly**

flu [fluː] *n* (*Med*) грипп

fluent [ˈfluːənt] *adj* (*linguist*) свобóдно говорящий; (*speech*) бéглый; (*writing*) свобóдный; **he speaks fluent Russian, he's fluent in Russian** он свобóдно говорúт по-рýсски

fluff [flʌf] *n* (*on jacket, carpet*) ворс; **fluffy** *adj* (*soft*) пушúстый

fluid [ˈfluːɪd] *adj* (*movement*) текýчий; (*situation*) перемéнчивый ▷ *n* жúдкость *f*

fluke [fluːk] *n* (*inf*) удáча, везéние

flung [flʌŋ] *pt, pp of* **fling**

fluorescent [fluəˈrɛsnt] *adj* (*dial, light*) флюоресцúрующий

fluoride [ˈfluəraɪd] *n* фторúд

flurry [ˈflʌrɪ] *n* (*of snow*) вихрь *m*; **a flurry of activity** бýрная дéятельность *f*

flush [flʌʃ] *n* (*on face*) румянец ▷ *vt* (*drains, pipe*) промывáть (*perf* промы́ть) ▷ *vi* (*redden*) зардéться (*perf*) ▷ *adj*: **flush with** (*level*) на однóм ýровне с +*instr*; **to flush the toilet** спускáть (*perf* спустúть) вóду в туалéте

flute [fluːt] *n* флéйта

flutter [ˈflʌtəʳ] *n* (*of wings*) взмах

fly [flaɪ] (*pt* **flew**, *pp* **flown**) *n* (*insect*) мýха; (*on trousers*: *also* **flies**) ширúнка ▷ *vt* (*plane*) летáть (*impf*) на +*prp*; (*passengers, cargo*) перевозúть (*perf* перевезтú); (*distances*) пролетáть (*perf* пролетéть), преодолевáть (*perf* преодолéть) ▷ *vi* (*also fig*) летáть/летéть (*impf*); (*flag*) развевáться (*impf*); **flying** *n* (*activity*) лётное дéло ▷ *adj*: **a flying visit** крáткий визúт; **with flying colours** блестяще

foal [fəul] *n* жеребёнок

foam [fəum] *n* пéна; (*also* **foam rubber**) поролóн

focus [ˈfəukəs] (*pl* **focuses**) *n* (*Phot*) фóкус; (*of attention, argument*) средотóчие ▷ *vt* (*camera*) настрáивать (*perf* настрóить) ▷ *vi*: **to focus (on)** (*Phot*) настрáиваться (*perf* настрóиться) (на +*acc*); **to focus on** (*fig*) сосредотáчиваться (*perf* сосредотóчиться) на +*prp*; **in focus** в фóкусе; **out of focus** не в фóкусе

foetus [ˈfiːtəs] (*US* **fetus**) *n* плод, зарóдыш

fog [fɔg] *n* тумáн; **foggy** *adj* тумáнный; **it's foggy** тумáнно

foil [fɔɪl] *n* (*metal*) фольга́
fold [fəuld] *n* (*crease*) скла́дка; (: *in paper*) сгиб ▷ *vt* (*clothes, paper*) скла́дывать (*perf* сложи́ть); (*arms*) скре́щивать (*perf* скрести́ть); **folder** *n* па́пка; (*ring-binder*) скоросшива́тель *m*; **folding** *adj* складно́й
foliage ['fəulɪɪdʒ] *n* листва́
folk [fəuk] *npl* лю́ди *pl*, наро́д *msg* ▷ *cpd* (*art, music*) наро́дный; **folks** *npl* (*inf*: *relatives*) бли́зкие *pl adj*; **folklore** ['fəuklɔːʳ] *n* фолькло́р
follow ['fɔləu] *vt* (*leader, person*) сле́довать (*perf* после́довать) за +*instr*; (*example, advice*) сле́довать (*perf* после́довать) +*dat*; (*event, story*) следи́ть (*impf*) за +*instr*; (*route, path*) держа́ться (*impf*) +*gen*; (*on Twitter*) чита́ть (*impf*), фо́лловить (*perf* зафо́лловить) (*inf*) ▷ *vi* сле́довать (*perf* после́довать); **to follow suit** (*fig*) сле́довать (*perf* после́довать) приме́ру; **follow up** *vt* (*letter, offer*) рассма́тривать (*perf* рассмотре́ть); (*case*) рассле́довать (*impf*); **follower** *n* (*of person, belief*) после́дователь(ница) *m(f)*; **following** *adj* сле́дующий
fond [fɔnd] *adj* (*smile, look, parents*) ла́сковый; (*memory*) прия́тный; **to be fond of** люби́ть (*impf*)
food [fuːd] *n* еда́, пи́ща; **food poisoning** *n* пищево́е отравле́ние; **food processor** *n* ку́хонный комба́йн
fool [fuːl] *n* дура́к ▷ *vt* (*deceive*) обма́нывать (*perf* обману́ть), одура́чивать (*perf* одура́чить); **foolish** *adj* глу́пый; (*rash*) неосмотри́тельный
foot [fut] (*pl* **feet**) *n* (*of person*) нога́, ступня́; (*of animal*) нога́; (*of bed*) коне́ц; (*of cliff*) подно́жие; (*measure*) фут ▷ *vt*: **to foot the bill** плати́ть (*perf* заплати́ть); **on foot** пешко́м

FOOT

Foot — ме́ра длины́ ра́вная 30,4 см.

foot: **footage** *n* (*Cinema*: *material*) ка́дры *mpl*; **football** *n* футбо́льный мяч; (*game*: *Brit*) футбо́л; (: *US*) америка́нский футбо́л; **footballer** *n* (*Brit*) футболи́ст; **foothills** *npl* предго́рья *ntpl*; **foothold** *n* (*on rock etc*) опо́ра; **footing** *n* (*fig*) осно́ва; **to lose one's footing** (*fall*) теря́ть (*perf* потеря́ть) опо́ру; **footnote** *n* сно́ска; **footpath** *n* тропи́нка, доро́жка; **footprint** *n* след; **footwear** *n* о́бувь *f*

KEYWORD

for [fɔːʳ] *prep* **1** (*indicating destination*) в/на +*acc*; (*indicating intention*) за +*instr*; **the train for London** по́езд в *or* на Ло́ндон; **he left for work** он уе́хал на рабо́ту; **he went for the paper/the doctor** он пошёл за газе́той/врачо́м; **is this for me?** э́то мне *or* для меня́?; **there's a letter for you** Вам письмо́; **it's time for lunch/bed** пора́ обе́дать/спать
2 (*indicating purpose*) для +*gen*; **what's it for?** для чего́ э́то?; **give it to me — what for?** да́йте мне э́то — заче́м *or* для чего́?; **to pray for peace** моли́ться (*impf*) за мир
3 (*on behalf of, representing*): **to speak for sb** говори́ть (*impf*) от

лицá когó-н; **MP for Brighton** член парлáмента от Брáйтона; **he works for the government** он на госудáрственной слýжбе; **he works for a local firm** он рабóтает на мéстную фи́рму; **I'll ask him for you** я спрошý егó от Вáшего и́мени; **to do sth for sb** (*on behalf of*) дéлать (*perf* сдéлать) что-н за когó-н

4 (*because of*) из-за *+gen*; **for lack of funds** из-за отсýтствия средств; **for this reason** по э́той причи́не; **for some reason, for whatever reason** по какóй-то причи́не; **for fear of being criticized** боя́сь кри́тики; **to be famous for sth** быть (*impf*) извéстным чем-н

5 (*with regard to*) для *+gen*; **it's cold for July** для иióля сейчáс хóлодно; **he's tall for his age** для своегó вóзраста он высóкий; **a gift for languages** спосóбности к языкáм; **for everyone who voted yes, 50 voted no** на кáждый гóлос "за", прихóдится 50 голосóв "прóтив"

6 (*in exchange for, in favour of*) за *+acc*; **I sold it for £5** я продáл э́то за £5; **I'm all for it** я целикóм и пóлностью за э́то

7 (*referring to distance*): **there are roadworks for five miles** на протяжéнии пяти́ миль произвóдятся дорóжные рабóты; **to stretch for miles** простирáться (*impf*) на мнóго миль; **we walked for miles/for ten miles** мы прошли́ мнóго миль/дéсять миль

8 (*referring to time*) на *+acc*; (: *in past*): **he was away for 2 years** он был в отъéзде 2 гóда, егó нé было 2 гóда; (: *in future*): **she will be away for a month** онá уезжáет на мéсяц; **can you do it for tomorrow?** Вы мóжете сдéлать э́то к зáвтрашнему дню?; **it hasn't rained for 3 weeks** ужé 3 недéли нé было дождя́; **for hours** часáми

9 (*with infinite clause*): **it is not for me to decide** не мне решáть; **there is still time for you to do it** у Вас ещё есть врéмя сдéлать э́то; **for this to be possible ...** чтóбы э́то осуществи́ть, ...

10 (*in spite of*) несмотря́ на *+acc*; **for all his complaints** несмотря́ на все егó жáлобы

11 (*in phrases*): **for the first/last time** в пéрвый/послéдний раз; **for the time being** покá

▷ *conj* (*rather formal*) и́бо

forbid [fəˈbɪd] (*pt* **forbad(e)**, *pp* **forbidden**) *vt* запрещáть (*perf* запрети́ть); **to forbid sb to do** запрещáть (*perf* запрети́ть) комý-н *+infin*

force [fɔːs] *n* (*also Phys*) си́ла ▷ *vt* (*compel*) вынуждáть (*perf* вы́нудить), принуждáть (*perf* принýдить); (*push*) толкáть (*perf* толкнýть); (*break open*) взлáмывать (*perf* взломáть); **the Forces** (*Brit: Mil*) вооружённые си́лы *fpl*; **in force** в большóм коли́честве; **to force o.s. to do** заставля́ть (*perf* застáвить) себя́ *+infin*; **forced** *adj* (*landing*) вы́нужденный; (*smile*) принуждённый; **forceful** *adj* си́льный

ford [fɔːd] *n* (*in river*) брод

fore [fɔːʳ] *n*: **to come to the fore** выдвигáться (*perf* вы́двинуться)

forecast [ˈfɔːkɑːst] *n* прогнóз ▷ *vt* (*irreg like* **cast**) предскáзывать (*perf* предсказáть)

forecourt [ˈfɔːkɔːt] *n* (*of garage*) перéдняя площáдка

forefinger ['fɔːfɪŋgəʳ] *n* указа́тельный па́лец
forefront ['fɔːfrʌnt] *n*: **in** *or* **at the forefront of** (*movement*) в аванга́рде +*gen*
foreground ['fɔːgraund] *n* пере́дний план
forehead ['fɔrɪd] *n* лоб
foreign ['fɔrɪn] *adj* (*language, tourist, firm*) иностра́нный; (*trade*) вне́шний; (*country*) зарубе́жный; **foreign person** иностра́нец(-нка); **foreigner** *n* иностра́нец(-нка); **foreign exchange** *n* (*system*) обме́н валю́ты; **Foreign Office** *n* (*Brit*) министе́рство иностра́нных дел; **Foreign Secretary** *n* (*Brit*) мини́стр иностра́нных дел
foreman ['fɔːmən] *irreg n* (*Industry*) ма́стер
foremost ['fɔːməust] *adj* (*most important*) важне́йший ▷ *adv*: **first and foremost** в пе́рвую о́чередь, пре́жде всего́
forensic [fə'rɛnsɪk] *adj* (*medicine, test*) суде́бный
foresee [fɔː'siː] (*irreg like* **see**) *vt* предви́деть (*impf/perf*); **foreseeable** *adj*: **in the foreseeable future** в обозри́мом бу́дущем
forest ['fɔrɪst] *n* лес; **forestry** *n* лесово́дство, лесни́чество
forever [fə'rɛvəʳ] *adv* (*for good*) навсегда́, наве́чно; (*endlessly*) ве́чно
foreword ['fɔːwəːd] *n* предисло́вие
forgave [fə'geɪv] *pt of* **forgive**
forge [fɔːdʒ] *vt* (*signature, money*) подде́лывать (*perf* подде́лать); **forgery** *n* подде́лка
forget [fə'gɛt] (*pt* **forgot**, *pp* **forgotten**) *vt* забыва́ть (*perf* забы́ть); (*appointment*) забыва́ть (*perf* забы́ть) о +*prp* ▷ *vi* забыва́ть (*perf* забы́ть); **forgetful** *adj* забы́вчивый
forgive [fə'gɪv] (*pt* **forgave**, *pp* **forgiven**) *vt* (*pardon*) проща́ть (*perf* прости́ть); **to forgive sb sth** проща́ть (*perf* прости́ть) кому́-н что-н; **to forgive sb for sth** (*excuse*) проща́ть (*perf* прости́ть) кого́-н за что-н; **I forgave him for doing it** я прости́л его́ за то, что он сде́лал э́то
forgot [fə'gɔt] *pt of* **forget**; **forgotten** *pp of* **forget**
fork [fɔːk] *n* ви́лка; (*for gardening*) ви́лы *pl*; (*in road, river, tree*) разветвле́ние
forlorn [fə'lɔːn] *adj* поки́нутый; (*hope, attempt*) тще́тный
form [fɔːm] *n* (*type*) вид; (*shape*) фо́рма; (*Scol*) класс; (*questionnaire*) анке́та; (*also* **booking form**) бланк ▷ *vt* (*make*) образо́вывать (*perf* образова́ть); (*organization, group*) формирова́ть (*perf* сформирова́ть); (*idea, habit*) выраба́тывать (*perf* вы́работать); **in top form** в прекра́сной фо́рме
formal ['fɔːməl] *adj* форма́льный; (*person, behaviour*) церемо́нный; (*occasion*) официа́льный; **formal clothes** официа́льная фо́рма оде́жды; **formality** [fɔː'mælɪtɪ] *n* форма́льность *f*; (*of person, behaviour*) церемо́нность *f*; (*of occasion*) официа́льность *f*
format ['fɔːmæt] *n* форма́т
formation [fɔː'meɪʃən] *n* формирова́ние
former ['fɔːməʳ] *adj* бы́вший; (*earlier*) пре́жний ▷ *n*: **the former ... the latter ...** пе́рвый ... после́дний ...; **formerly** *adv*

ра́нее, ра́ньше
formidable ['fɔːmɪdəbl] *adj* (*opponent*) гро́зный; (*task*) серьёзнейший
formula ['fɔːmjulə] (*pl* **formulae** *or* **formulas**) *n* (*Math, Chem*) фо́рмула; (*plan*) схе́ма
fort [fɔːt] *n* кре́пость *f*, форт
forthcoming *adj* предстоя́щии; (*person*) общи́тельный
fortieth ['fɔːtɪɪθ] *adj* сороково́й
fortnight ['fɔːtnaɪt] (*Brit*) *n* две неде́ли; **fortnightly** *adv* раз в две неде́ли ▷ *adj*: **fortnightly magazine** журна́л, выходя́щий раз в две неде́ли
fortress ['fɔːtrɪs] *n* кре́пость *f*
fortunate ['fɔːtʃənɪt] *adj* (*event, choice*) счастли́вый; (*person*) уда́чливый; **he was fortunate to get a job** на его́ сча́стье, он получи́л рабо́ту; **it is fortunate that ...** к сча́стью ...; **fortunately** *adv* к сча́стью; **fortunately for him** на его́ сча́стье
fortune ['fɔːtʃən] *n* (*wealth*) состоя́ние; (*also* **good fortune**) сча́стье, уда́ча; **ill fortune** невезе́ние, неуда́ча
forty ['fɔːtɪ] *n* со́рок
forum ['fɔːrəm] *n* фо́рум
forward ['fɔːwəd] *adv* вперёд ▷ *n* (*Sport*) напада́ющий(-ая) *m(f) adj*, фо́рвард ▷ *vt* (*letter, parcel*) пересыла́ть (*perf* пересла́ть) ▷ *adj* (*position*) пере́дний; (*not shy*) де́рзкий; **to move forward** (*progress*) продвига́ться (*perf* продви́нуться)
fossil ['fɔsl] *n* окамене́лость *f*, ископа́емое *nt adj*
foster ['fɔstə^r] *vt* (*child*) брать (*perf* взять) на воспита́ние
fought [fɔːt] *pt, pp of* **fight**
foul [faul] *adj* га́дкий, ме́рзкий; (*language*) непристо́йный; (*temper*) жу́ткий ▷ *n* (*Sport*) наруше́ние ▷ *vt* (*dirty*) га́дить (*perf* зага́дить)
found [faund] *pt, pp of* **find** ▷ *vt* (*establish*) осно́вывать (*perf* основа́ть); **foundation** *n* (*base*) осно́ва; (*organization*) о́бщество, фонд; (*also* **foundation cream**) крем под макия́ж; **foundations** *npl* (*of building*) фунда́мент *msg*; **founder** *n* основа́тель(ница) *m(f)*
fountain ['fauntɪn] *n* фонта́н
four [fɔː^r] *n* четы́ре; **on all fours** на четвере́ньках
fourteen ['fɔː'tiːn] *n* четы́рнадцать; **fourteenth** *adj* четы́рнадцатый
fourth ['fɔːθ] *adj* четвёртый ▷ *n* (*Aut*: *also* **fourth gear**) четвёртая ско́рость *f*
fowl [faul] *n* пти́ца
fox [fɔks] *n* лиса́ ▷ *vt* озада́чивать (*perf* озада́чить)
foyer ['fɔɪeɪ] *n* фойе́ *nt ind*
fraction ['frækʃən] *n* (*portion*) части́ца; (*Math*) дробь *f*; **a fraction of a second** до́ля секу́нды
fracture ['fræktʃə^r] *n* перело́м ▷ *vt* (*bone*) лома́ть (*perf* слома́ть)
fragile ['frædʒaɪl] *adj* хру́пкий
fragment ['frægmənt] *n* фрагме́нт; (*of glass*) оско́лок, обло́мок
fragrance ['freɪgrəns] *n* благоуха́ние
frail [freɪl] *adj* (*person*) сла́бый, не́мощный; (*structure*) хру́пкий
frame [freɪm] *n* (*of building, structure*) карка́с, о́стов; (*of person*) сложе́ние; (*of picture, window*) ра́ма; (*of spectacles*: *also* **frames**) опра́ва ▷ *vt* обрамля́ть (*perf* обра́мить); **frame of mind** настрое́ние; **framework** *n*

каркас; (*fig*) рамки *fpl*

France [frɑːns] *n* Франция

franchise ['fræntʃaɪz] *n* (*Pol*) право голоса; (*Comm*) франшиза

frank [fræŋk] *adj* (*discussion, person*) откровенный; (*look*) открытый; **frankly** *adv* откровенно

frantic ['fræntɪk] *adj* исступлённый; (*hectic*) лихорадочный

fraud [frɔːd] *n* (*person*) мошенник; (*crime*) мошенничество

fraught [frɔːt] *adj*: **fraught with** чреватый *+instr*

fray [freɪ] *vi* трепаться (*perf* истрепаться); **tempers were frayed** все были на грани срыва

freak [friːk] *adj* странный, ненормальный ▷ *n*: **he is a freak** он со странностями

freckle ['frɛkl] *n* (*usu pl*) веснушка

free [friː] *adj* свободный; (*costing nothing*) бесплатный ▷ *vt* (*prisoner etc*) освобождать (*perf* освободить), выпускать (*perf* выпустить) (на свободу); (*object*) высвобождать (*perf* высвободить); **free (of charge), for free** бесплатно; **freedom** *n* свобода; **free kick** *n* (*Football*) свободный удар; **freelance** *adj* внештатный, работающий по договорам; **freely** *adv* (*without restriction*) свободно; (*liberally*) обильно; **free-range** *adj*: **free-range eggs** *яйца от кур на свободном выгуле*; **free will** *n*: **of one's own free will** по (своей) доброй воле

freeze [friːz] (*pt* **froze**, *pp* **frozen**) *vi* (*weather*) холодать (*perf* похолодать); (*liquid, pipe, person*) замерзать (*perf* замёрзнуть); (*person*: *stop moving*) застывать (*perf* застыть) ▷ *vt* замораживать (*perf* заморозить) ▷ *n* (*on arms, wages*) замораживание; **freezer** *n* морозильник

freezing ['friːzɪŋ] *adj*: **freezing (cold)** ледяной ▷ *n*: **3 degrees below freezing** 3 градуса мороза *or* ниже нуля; **I'm freezing** я замёрз; **it's freezing** очень холодно

freight [freɪt] *n* фрахт

French [frɛntʃ] *adj* французский; ▷ *npl*: **the French** (*people*) французы *mpl*; **French fries** *npl* (*US*) картофель *msg* фри; **Frenchman** *irreg n* француз

frenzy ['frɛnzɪ] *n* (*of violence*) остервенение, бешенство

frequency ['friːkwənsɪ] *n* частота

frequent [*adj* 'friːkwənt, *vb* frɪ'kwɛnt] *adj* частый ▷ *vt* посещать (*impf*); **frequently** *adv* часто

fresh [frɛʃ] *adj* свежий; (*instructions, approach*) новый; **to make a fresh start** начинать (*perf* начать) заново; **fresh in one's mind** свежо в памяти; **fresher** *n* (*Brit*: *inf*) первокурсник; **freshly** *adv*: **freshly made** свежеприготовленный; **freshly painted** свежевыкрашенный; **freshwater** *adj* (*lake*) пресный; (*fish*) пресноводный

fret [frɛt] *vi* волноваться (*impf*)

friction ['frɪkʃən] *n* трение; (*fig*) трения *ntpl*

Friday ['fraɪdɪ] *n* пятница

fridge [frɪdʒ] *n* (*Brit*) холодильник

fried [fraɪd] *pt, pp of* **fry** ▷ *adj* жареный

f

friend [frɛnd] *n* (*male*) друг; (*female*) подру́га ▷ *vt* добавля́ть (*perf* доба́вить) в друзья́, зафре́ндить (*perf*) (*inf*); **friendly** *adj* (*person, smile etc*) дружелю́бный; (*government, country*) дру́жественный; (*place, restaurant*) прия́тный ▷ *n* (*also* **friendly match**) това́рищеский матч; **to be friendly with** дружи́ть (*impf*) с *+instr*; **to be friendly to sb** относи́ться (*perf* отнести́сь) к кому́-н дружелю́бно; **friendship** *n* дру́жба

fright [fraɪt] *n* испу́г; **to take fright** испуга́ться (*perf*); **frighten** *vt* пуга́ть (*perf* испуга́ть); **frightened** *adj* испу́ганный; **to be frightened (of)** боя́ться (*impf*) (*+gen*); **he is frightened by change** его́ пуга́ют измене́ния; **frightening** *adj* стра́шный, устраша́ющий

fringe [frɪndʒ] *n* (*Brit: of hair*) чёлка; (*on shawl, lampshade etc*) бахрома́; (*of forest etc*) край, окра́ина

frivolous ['frɪvələs] *adj* (*conduct, person*) легкомы́сленный; (*object, activity*) пустя́чный

frog [frɔg] *n* лягу́шка

KEYWORD

from [frɔm] *prep* **1** (*indicating starting place, origin etc*) из *+gen*, с *+gen*; (*from a person*) от *+gen*; **he is from Cyprus** он с Ки́пра; **from London to Glasgow** из Ло́ндона в Гла́зго; **a letter from my sister** письмо́ от мое́й сестры́; **a quotation from Dickens** цита́та из Ди́ккенса; **to drink from the bottle** пить (*impf*) из буты́лки; **where do you come from?** Вы отку́да?

2 (*indicating movement: from inside*) из *+gen*; (*: away from*) от *+gen*; (*: off*) с *+gen*; (*: from behind*) из-за *+gen*; **she ran from the house** она́ вы́бежала из до́ма; **the car drove away from the house** маши́на отъе́хала от до́ма; **he took the magazine from the table** он взял журна́л со стола́; **they got up from the table** они́ вста́ли из-за стола́

3 (*indicating time*) с *+gen*; **from two o'clock to** *or* **until** *or* **till three (o'clock)** с двух часо́в до трёх (часо́в); **from January (to August)** с января́ (по а́вгуст)

4 (*indicating distance: position*) от *+gen*; (*: motion*) до *+gen*; **the hotel is one kilometre from the beach** гости́ница нахо́дится в киломе́тре от пля́жа; **we're still a long way from home** мы ещё далеко́ от до́ма

5 (*indicating price, number etc: range*) от *+gen*; (*: change*) с *+gen*; **prices range from £10 to £50** це́ны коле́блются от £10 до £50; **the interest rate was increased from nine per cent to ten per cent** проце́нтные ста́вки повы́сились с девяти́ до десяти́ проце́нтов

6 (*indicating difference*) от *+gen*; **to be different from sb/sth** отлича́ться (*impf*) от кого́-н/чего́-н

7 (*because of, on the basis of*): **from what he says** су́дя по тому́, что он говори́т; **from what I understand** как я понима́ю; **to act from conviction** де́йствовать (*impf*) по убежде́нию; **he is weak from hunger** он слаб от го́лода

front [frʌnt] *n* (*of house, also fig*) фаса́д; (*of dress*) пе́ред; (*of train, car*) пере́дняя часть *f*; (*also* **sea**

front) на́бережная *f adj*; (*Mil, Meteorology*) фронт ▷ *adj* пере́дний; **in front** вперёд; **in front of** пе́ред +*instr*; **front door** *n* входна́я дверь *f*; **frontier** ['frʌntɪəʳ] *n* грани́ца; **front page** *n* пе́рвая страни́ца (*газе́ты*)
frost [frɔst] *n* моро́з; (*also* **hoarfrost**) и́ней; **frostbite** *n* обмороже́ние; **frosty** *adj* (*weather, night*) моро́зный; (*welcome, look*) ледяно́й
froth ['frɔθ] *n* (*on liquid*) пе́на
frown [fraun] *n* нахму́ренный взгляд
froze [frəuz] *pt of* **freeze**; **frozen** *pp of* **freeze**
fruit [fru:t] *n inv* фрукт; (*fig*) плод; **fruit machine** *n* (*Brit*) игрово́й автома́т
frustrate [frʌs'treɪt] *vt* (*person, plan*) расстра́ивать (*perf* расстро́ить)
fry [fraɪ] (*pt, pp* **fried**) *vt* жа́рить (*perf* пожа́рить); **frying pan** (*US* **fry-pan**) *n* сковорода́
ft *abbr* = **feet**; **foot**
fudge [fʌdʒ] *n* ≈ сли́вочная пома́дка
fuel ['fjuəl] *n* (*for heating*) то́пливо; (*for plane, car*) горю́чее *nt adj*
fulfil [ful'fɪl] (*US* **fulfill**) *vt* (*function, desire, promise*) исполня́ть (*perf* испо́лнить); (*ambition*) осуществля́ть (*perf* осуществи́ть)
full [ful] *adj* по́лный; (*skirt*) широ́кий ▷ *adv*: **to know full well that** прекра́сно знать (*impf*), что; **at full volume/power** на по́лную гро́мкость/мо́щность; **I'm full (up)** я сыт; **he is full of enthusiasm/hope** он по́лон энтузиа́зма/наде́жды; **full details** все дета́ли; **at full speed** на по́лной ско́рости; **a full two hours** це́лых два часа́; **in full** по́лностью; **full-length** *adj* (*film, novel*) полнометра́жный; (*coat*) дли́нный; (*mirror*) высо́кий; **full moon** *n* по́лная луна́; **full-scale** *adj* (*attack, war, search etc*) широкомасшта́бный; **full-time** *adj, adv* (*study*) на дневно́м отделе́нии; (*work*) на по́лной ста́вке; **fully** *adv* (*completely*) по́лностью, вполне́; **fully as big as** по кра́йней ме́ре тако́й же величины́, как
fumes [fju:mz] *npl* испаре́ния *ntpl*, пары́ *mpl*
fun [fʌn] *n*: **what fun!** как ве́село!; **to have fun** весели́ться (*perf* повесели́ться); **he's good fun (to be with)** с ним ве́село; **for fun** для заба́вы; **to make fun of** подшу́чивать (*perf* подшути́ть) над +*instr*
function ['fʌŋkʃən] *n* фу́нкция; (*product*) произво́дная *f adj*; (*social occasion*) приём ▷ *vi* (*operate*) функциони́ровать (*impf*)
fund [fʌnd] *n* фонд; (*of knowledge etc*) запа́с; **funds** *npl* (*money*) (де́нежные) сре́дства *ntpl*, фо́нды *mpl*
fundamental [fʌndə'mɛntl] *adj* фундамента́льный
funeral ['fju:nərəl] *n* по́хороны *pl*
fungus ['fʌŋgəs] (*pl* **fungi**) *n* (*plant*) гриб; (*mould*) пле́сень *f*
funnel ['fʌnl] *n* (*for pouring*) воро́нка; (*of ship*) труба́
funny ['fʌnɪ] *adj* (*amusing*) заба́вный; (*strange*) стра́нный, чудно́й
fur [fə:ʳ] *n* мех
furious ['fjuərɪəs] *adj* (*person*) взбешённый; (*exchange,*

argument) бу́рный; (*effort, speed*) неи́стовый

furnish ['fə:nɪʃ] *vt* (*room, building*) обставля́ть (*perf* обста́вить); **to furnish sb with sth** (*supply*) предоставля́ть (*perf* предоста́вить) что-н кому́-н; **furnishings** *npl* обстано́вка *fsg*

furniture ['fə:nɪtʃə^r] *n* ме́бель *f*; **piece of furniture** предме́т ме́бели

furry ['fə:rɪ] *adj* пуши́стый

further ['fə:ðə^r] *adj* дополни́тельный ▷ *adv* (*farther*) да́льше; (*moreover*) бо́лее того́ ▷ *vt* (*career, project*) продвига́ть (*perf* продви́нуть), соде́йствовать (*impf/perf*) +*dat*; **further education** *n* (*Brit*) профессиона́льно-техни́ческое образова́ние

FURTHER EDUCATION

Further education — сре́днее специа́льное образова́ние. Его́ мо́жно получи́ть в ко́лледжах. Обуче́ние прово́дится на осно́ве по́лного дневно́го ку́рса, почасово́го или вече́рнего ку́рса.

furthermore *adv* бо́лее того́

furthest ['fə:ðɪst] *superl of* **far**

fury ['fjuərɪ] *n* я́рость *f*, бе́шенство

fuse [fju:z] (*US* **fuze**) *n* (*Elec*) предохрани́тель *m*; (*on bomb*) фити́ль *m*

fusion ['fju:ʒən] *n* (*of ideas, qualities*) слия́ние; (*also* **nuclear fusion**) я́дерный си́нтез

fuss [fʌs] *n* (*excitement*) сумато́ха; (*anxiety*) суета́; (*trouble*) шум; **to make** *or* **kick up a fuss** поднима́ть (*perf* подня́ть) шум; **to make a fuss of sb** носи́ться (*impf*) с кем-н; **fussy** *adj* (*nervous*) суетли́вый; (*choosy*) ме́лочный, су́етный; (*elaborate*) вы́чурный

future ['fju:tʃə^r] *adj* бу́дущий ▷ *n* бу́дущее *nt adj*; (*Ling*: *also* **future tense**) бу́дущее вре́мя *nt*; **in (the) future** в бу́дущем; **in the near/immediate future** в недалёком/ближа́йшем бу́дущем

fuze [fju:z] *n* (*US*) = **fuse**

fuzzy ['fʌzɪ] *adj* (*thoughts, picture*) расплы́вчатый; (*hair*) пуши́стый

g

g *abbr* (= *gram*) г (= *грамм*)
gadget [ˈgædʒɪt] *n* приспособле́ние
Gaelic [ˈgeɪlɪk] *n* (*Ling*) га́льский язы́к
gag [gæg] *n* (*on mouth*) кляп ▷ *vt* вставля́ть (*perf* вста́вить) кляп *+dat*
gain [geɪn] *n* (*increase*) приро́ст ▷ *vt* (*confidence, experience*) приобрета́ть (*perf* приобрести́); (*speed*) набира́ть (*perf* набра́ть) ▷ *vi* (*benefit*): **to gain from sth** извлека́ть (*perf* извле́чь) вы́году из чего́-н; **to gain 3 pounds (in weight)** поправля́ться (*perf* попра́виться) на 3 фу́нта; **to gain on sb** догоня́ть (*perf* догна́ть) кого́-н
gala [ˈgɑːlə] *n* (*festival*) пра́зднество
galaxy [ˈgæləksɪ] *n* гала́ктика
gale [geɪl] *n* (*wind*) си́льный ве́тер; (*at sea*) штормово́й ве́тер
gallery [ˈgælərɪ] *n* (*also* **art gallery**) галере́я; (*in hall, church*) балко́н; (*in theatre*) галёрка
gallon [ˈgæln] *n* галло́н (*4,5 ли́тра*)
gallop [ˈgæləp] *vi* (*horse*) скака́ть (*impf*) (гало́пом), галопи́ровать (*impf*)
gamble [ˈgæmbl] *n* риско́ванное предприя́тие, риск ▷ *vt* (*money*) ста́вить (*perf* поста́вить) ▷ *vi* (*take a risk*) рискова́ть (*perf* рискну́ть); (*bet*) игра́ть (*impf*) в аза́ртные и́гры; **to gamble on sth** (*also fig*) де́лать (*perf* сде́лать) ста́вку на что-н; **gambler** *n* игро́к; **gambling** [ˈgæmblɪŋ] *n* аза́ртные и́гры *fpl*
game [geɪm] *n* игра́; (*match*) матч; (*esp Tennis*) гейм; (*also* **board game**) насто́льная игра́; (*Culin*) дичь *f* ▷ *adj* (*willing*): **game (for)** гото́вый (на *+acc*); **big game** кру́пный зверь
gammon [ˈgæmən] *n* (*bacon*) о́корок; (*ham*) ветчина́
gang [gæŋ] *n* ба́нда; (*of friends*) компа́ния
gangster [ˈgæŋstəʳ] *n* га́нгстер
gap [gæp] *n* (*space*) промежу́ток; (*: between teeth*) щерби́на; (*: in time*) интерва́л; (*difference*) расхожде́ние; **generation gap** разногла́сия ме́жду поколе́ниями
garage [ˈgærɑːʒ] *n* гара́ж; (*petrol station*) запра́вочная ста́нция, бензоколо́нка
garbage [ˈgɑːbɪdʒ] *n* (*US: rubbish*) му́сор; (*inf: nonsense*) ерунда́; **garbage can** *n* (*US*) помо́йный я́щик
garden [ˈgɑːdn] *n* сад;

gardens *npl* (*park*) парк *msg*; **gardener** *n* садово́д; (*employee*) садо́вник(-ица); **gardening** *n* садово́дство
garlic ['gɑ:lɪk] *n* чесно́к
garment ['gɑ:mənt] *n* наря́д
garnish ['gɑ:nɪʃ] *vt* украша́ть (*perf* укра́сить)
garrison ['gærɪsn] *n* гарнизо́н
gas [gæs] *n* газ; (*US*: *gasoline*) бензи́н ▷ *vt* (*kill*) удуша́ть (*perf* удуши́ть) (*газом*)
gasoline ['gæsəli:n] *n* (*US*) бензи́н
gasp [gɑ:sp] *n* (*breath*) вдох
gas station *n* (*US*) запра́вочная ста́нция, бензоколо́нка
gate [geɪt] *n* кали́тка; (*at airport*) вы́ход; **gates** *npl* воро́та; **gateway** *n* воро́та *pl*
gather ['gæðə^r] *vt* собира́ть (*perf* собра́ть); (*understand*) полага́ть (*impf*) ▷ *vi* собира́ться (*perf* собра́ться); **to gather speed** набира́ть (*perf* набра́ть) ско́рость; **gathering** *n* собра́ние
gauge [geɪdʒ] *n* (*instrument*) измери́тельный прибо́р ▷ *vt* (*amount, quantity*) измеря́ть (*perf* изме́рить); (*fig*) оце́нивать (*perf* оцени́ть)
gave [geɪv] *pt of* **give**
gay [geɪ] *adj* (*cheerful*) весёлый; (*homosexual*): **gay bar** бар для голубы́х *or* гомосексуали́стов ▷ *n* гомосексуали́ст, голубо́й *m adj*; **he is gay** он гомосексуали́ст *or* голубо́й
gaze [geɪz] *n* (при́стальный) взгляд ▷ *vi*: **to gaze at sth** разгля́дывать (*impf*) что-н
GB *abbr* = **Great Britain**
GCSE *n abbr* (*Brit*) (= *General Certificate of Secondary Education*)

GCSE

GCSE — аттеста́т о сре́днем образова́нии. Шко́льники сдаю́т экза́мены для получе́ния э́того аттеста́та в во́зрасте 15-16 лет. Часть предме́тов, по кото́рым сдаю́тся экза́мены обяза́тельна, часть - по вы́бору. Одна́ко э́того аттеста́та не доста́точно для поступле́ния в университе́т.

gear [gɪə^r] *n* (*equipment, belongings etc*) принадле́жности *fpl*; (*Aut*) ско́рость *f*; (: *mechanism*) переда́ча ▷ *vt* (*fig*): **to gear sth to** приспоса́бливать (*perf* приспосо́бить) что-н к *+dat*; **top** *or (US)* **high/low gear** вы́сшая/ни́зкая ско́рость; **in gear** в зацепле́нии; **gearbox** *n* коро́бка переда́ч *or* скоросте́й; **gear lever** (*US* **gear shift**) *n* переключа́тель *m* скоросте́й
geese [gi:s] *npl of* **goose**
gem [dʒɛm] *n* (*stone*) драгоце́нный ка́мень *m*, самоцве́т
Gemini ['dʒɛmɪnaɪ] *n* Близнецы́ *mpl*
gender ['dʒɛndə^r] *n* (*sex*) пол; (*Ling*) род
gene [dʒi:n] *n* ген
general ['dʒɛnərl] *n* (*Mil*) генера́л ▷ *adj* о́бщий; (*movement, interest*) всео́бщий; **in general** в о́бщем; **general election** *n* всео́бщие вы́боры *mpl*; **generally** *adv* вообще́; (*+vb*) обы́чно; **to become generally available** станови́ться (*perf* стать) общедосту́пным(-ой); **it is generally accepted that ...** общепри́знанно, что ...
generate ['dʒɛnəreɪt] *vt* (*power, electricity*) генери́ровать (*impf*),

вырабáтывать (*perf* вы́работать); (*excitement, interest*) вызывáть (*perf* вы́звать); (*jobs*) создавáть (*perf* создáть)

generation [dʒɛnəˈreɪʃən] *n* поколéние; (*of power*) генери́рование; **for generations** из поколéния в поколéние

generator [ˈdʒɛnəreɪtəʳ] *n* генерáтор

generosity [dʒɛnəˈrɔsɪtɪ] *n* щéдрость *f*

generous [ˈdʒɛnərəs] *adj* (*person: lavish*) щéдрый; (*: unselfish*) великоду́шный; (*amount of money*) значи́тельный

genetics [dʒɪˈnɛtɪks] *n* генéтика

Geneva [dʒɪˈniːvə] *n* Женéва

genitals [ˈdʒɛnɪtlz] *npl* половы́е óрганы *mpl*

genius [ˈdʒiːnɪəs] *n* (*skill*) талáнт; (*person*) гéний

gent [dʒɛnt] *n abbr* (*Brit: inf*) = **gentleman**

gentle [ˈdʒɛntl] *adj* нéжный, лáсковый; (*nature, movement, landscape*) мя́гкий

gentleman [ˈdʒɛntlmən] *irreg n* (*man*) джентльмéн

gently [ˈdʒɛntlɪ] *adv* (*smile, treat, speak*) нéжно, лáсково; (*curve, slope, move*) мя́гко

gents [dʒɛnts] *n*: **the gents** мужскóй туалéт

genuine [ˈdʒɛnjuɪn] *adj* (*sincere*) и́скренний; (*real*) пóдлинный

geographic(al) [dʒɪəˈgræfɪk(l)] *adj* географи́ческий

geography [dʒɪˈɔgrəfɪ] *n* геогрáфия

geology [dʒɪˈɔlədʒɪ] *n* геолóгия

geometry [dʒɪˈɔmətrɪ] *n* геомéтрия

Georgia [ˈdʒɔːdʒə] *n* Гру́зия; **Georgian** *adj* грузи́нский

geranium [dʒɪˈreɪnɪəm] *n* герáнь *f*

geriatric [dʒɛrɪˈætrɪk] *adj* гериатри́ческий

germ [dʒəːm] *n* (*Med*) микрóб

German [ˈdʒəːmən] *adj* немéцкий ▷ *n* нéмец(-мка); **German measles** *n* (*Brit*) красну́ха

Germany [ˈdʒəːmənɪ] *n* Гермáния

gesture [ˈdʒɛstjəʳ] *n* жест

KEYWORD

get [gɛt] (*pt, pp* **got**) (*US*) ▷ (*pp* **gotten**) *vi* **1** (*become*) станови́ться (*perf* стать); **it's getting late** станóвится пóздно; **to get old** старéть (*perf* постарéть); **to get tired** уставáть (*perf* устáть); **to get cold** мёрзнуть (*perf* замёрзнуть); **to get annoyed easily** легкó раздражáться (*impf*); **he was getting bored** емý стáло скýчно; **he gets drunk every weekend** он напивáется кáждый выходнóй

2 (*be*): **he got killed** егó уби́ли; **when do I get paid?** когдá мне заплáтят?

3 (*go*): **to get to/from** добирáться (*perf* добрáться) до *+gen*/из *+gen*/с *+gen*; **how did you get here?** как Вы сюдá добрали́сь?

4 (*begin*): **to get to know sb** узнавáть (*perf* узнáть) когó-н; **I'm getting to like him** он начинáет мне нрáвиться; **let's get started** давáйте начнём

▷ *modal aux vb*: **you've got to do it** Вы должны́ э́то сдéлать

▷ *vt* **1: to get sth done** сдéлать (*perf*) что-н; **to get the washing done** стирáть (*perf* постирáть); **to get the dishes done** мыть (помы́ть *or* вы́мыть *perf*) посýду; **to get the**

car started *or* **to start** заводи́ть (*perf* завести́) маши́ну; **to get sb to do** заставля́ть (*perf* заста́вить) кого́-н *+infin*; **to get sb ready** собира́ть (*perf* собра́ть) кого́-н; **to get sth ready** гото́вить (*perf* пригото́вить) что-н; **to get sb drunk** напа́ивать (*perf* напои́ть) кого́-н; **she got me into trouble** она́ вовлекла́ меня́ в неприя́тности
2 (*obtain*: *permission, results*) получа́ть (*perf* получи́ть); (*find*: *job, flat*) находи́ть (*perf* найти́); (*person*: *call*) звать (*perf* позва́ть); (: *pick up*) забира́ть (*perf* забра́ть); (*call out*: *doctor, plumber etc*) вызыва́ть (*perf* вы́звать); (*object*: *carry*) приноси́ть (*perf* принести́); (: *buy*) покупа́ть (*perf* купи́ть); (: *deliver*) доставля́ть (*perf* доста́вить); **we must get him to hospital** мы должны́ доста́вить его́ в больни́цу; **do you think we'll get the piano through the door?** как Вы ду́маете, мы протáщим пиани́но че́рез дверь?; **I'll get the car** я схожу́ за маши́ной; **can I get you something to drink?** Позво́льте предложи́ть Вам что́-нибудь вы́пить?
3 (*receive*) получа́ть (*perf* получи́ть); **to get a reputation for** приобрета́ть (*perf* приобрести́) дурну́ю репута́цию *+instr*; **what did you get for your birthday?** что Вам подари́ли на день рожде́ния?
4 (*grab*) хвата́ть (*perf* схвати́ть); (*hit*): **the bullet got him in the leg** пу́ля попа́ла ему́ в но́гу
5 (*catch, take*): **we got a taxi** мы взя́ли такси́; **did she get her plane?** она́ успе́ла на самолёт?; **what train are you getting?** каки́м по́ездом Вы е́дете?; **where do I get the train?** где мне сесть на по́езд?
6 (*understand*) понима́ть (*perf* поня́ть); (*hear*) расслы́шать (*perf*); **(do you) get it?** (*inf*) (тебе́) поня́тно?; **I've got it!** тепе́рь поня́тно!; **I'm sorry, I didn't get your name** прости́те, я не расслы́шал Ва́ше и́мя
7 (*have, possess*): **how many children have you got?** ско́лько у Вас дете́й?; **I've got very little time** у меня́ о́чень ма́ло вре́мени

get about *vi* (*news*) распространя́ться (*perf* распространи́ться); **I don't get about much now** (*go places*) тепе́рь я ма́ло где быва́ю

get along *vi*: **get along with** ла́дить (*impf*) с *+instr*; (*manage*) = **get by**; **I'd better be getting along** мне, пожа́луй, пора́ (идти́)

get at *vt fus* (*criticize*) придира́ться (*perf* придра́ться) к *+dat*; (*reach*) дотя́гиваться (*perf* дотяну́ться) до *+gen*

get away *vi* (*leave*) уходи́ть (*perf* уйти́); (*escape*) убега́ть (*perf* убежа́ть)

get away with *vt fus*: **he gets away with everything** ему́ всё схо́дит с рук

get back *vi* (*return*) возвраща́ться (*perf* возврати́ться), верну́ться (*perf*) ▷ *vt* получа́ть (*perf* получи́ть) наза́д *or* обра́тно

get by *vi* (*pass*) проходи́ть (*perf* пройти́); (*manage*): **to get by without** обходи́ться (*perf* обойти́сь) без *+gen*; **I will get by** (*manage*) я спра́влюсь

get down *vt* (*depress*) угнета́ть (*impf*) ▷ *vi*: **to get down from** слеза́ть (*perf* слезть) с *+gen*

get down to *vt fus* сади́ться (*perf* сесть) *or* бра́ться (*perf* взя́ться) за *+acc*

get in *vi* (*train*) прибыва́ть (*perf* прибы́ть), приходи́ть (*perf* прийти́); (*arrive home*) приходи́ть (*perf* прийти́); (*to concert, building*) попада́ть (*perf* попа́сть), проходи́ть (*perf* пройти́); **he got in by ten votes** он прошёл с большинство́м в де́сять голосо́в; **as soon as the bus arrived we all got in** как то́лько авто́бус подошёл, мы се́ли в него́
get into *vt fus* (*building*) входи́ть (*perf* войти́) в *+acc*; (*vehicle*) сади́ться (*perf* сесть) в *+acc*; (*clothes*) влеза́ть (*perf* влезть) в *+acc*; (*fight, argument*) вступа́ть (*perf* вступи́ть) в *+acc*; (*university, college*) поступа́ть (*perf* поступи́ть) в *+acc*; (*subj: train*) прибыва́ть (*perf* прибы́ть) в/на *+acc*; **to get into bed** ложи́ться (*perf* лечь) в посте́ль
get off *vi* (*escape*): **to get off lightly/with sth** отде́лываться (*perf* отде́латься) легко́/чем-н
▷ *vt* (*clothes*) снима́ть (*perf* снять)
▷ *vt fus* (*train, bus*) сходи́ть (*perf* сойти́) с *+gen*; (*horse, bicycle*) слеза́ть (*perf* слезть) с *+gen*
get on *vi* (*age*) старе́ть (*impf*); **how are you getting on?** как Ва́ши успе́хи?
get out *vi* (*leave*) выбира́ться (*perf* вы́браться); (*socialize*) выбира́ться (*perf* вы́браться) из до́ма
get out of *vt fus* (*duty*) отде́лываться (*perf* отде́латься) от *+gen*
get over *vt fus* (*illness*) преодолева́ть (*perf* преодоле́ть)
get round *vt fus* (*law, rule*) обходи́ть (*perf* обойти́); (*fig: person*) угова́ривать (*perf* уговори́ть)
get through *vi* (*Tel*) дозва́ниваться (*perf* дозвони́ться)
get through to *vt fus* (*Tel*) дозва́ниваться (*perf* дозвони́ться) до *+gen*
get together *vi* (*several people*) собира́ться (*perf* собра́ться)
▷ *vt* (*people*) собира́ть (*perf* собра́ть)
get up *vi* встава́ть (*perf* встать)
get up to *vt fus* (*Brit*) затева́ть (*perf* зате́ять); **they're always getting up to mischief** они́ всегда́ прока́зничают

ghastly ['gɑ:stlɪ] *adj* ме́рзкий, омерзи́тельный
ghetto ['gɛtəu] *n* ге́тто *nt ind*
ghost [gəust] *n* (*spirit*) привиде́ние, при́зрак
giant ['dʒaɪənt] *n* (*in myths*) велика́н; (*fig: Comm*) гига́нт
▷ *adj* огро́мный
gift [gɪft] *n* (*present*) пода́рок; (*ability*) дар, тала́нт; **gifted** *adj* одарённый
gigantic [dʒaɪ'gæntɪk] *adj* гига́нтский
giggle ['gɪgl] *vi* хихи́кать (*impf*)
gills [gɪlz] *npl* (*of fish*) жа́бры *fpl*
gilt [gɪlt] *adj* позоло́ченный
gimmick ['gɪmɪk] *n* уло́вка, трюк
gin [dʒɪn] *n* джин
ginger ['dʒɪndʒə^r] *n* (*spice*) имби́рь *m*
giraffe [dʒɪ'rɑ:f] *n* жира́ф
girl [gə:l] *n* (*child*) де́вочка; (*young unmarried woman*) де́вушка; (*daughter*) до́чка; **an English girl** молода́я англича́нка; **girlfriend** *n* подру́га
gist [dʒɪst] *n* суть *f*

 **KEYWORD**

give [gɪv] (*pt* **gave**, *pt* **given**) *vt*
1 (*hand over*): **to give sb sth** *or* **sth to sb** дава́ть (*perf* дать) кому́-н что-н; **they gave her a book for her birthday** они́ подари́ли ей кни́гу на день рожде́ния
2 (*used with noun to replace verb*): **to give a sigh** вздыха́ть (*perf* вздохну́ть); **to give a shrug** передёргивать (*perf* передёрнуть) плеча́ми; **to give a speech** выступа́ть (*perf* вы́ступить) с ре́чью; **to give a lecture** чита́ть (*perf* прочита́ть) ле́кцию; **to give three cheers** три́жды прокрича́ть (*perf*) "ура́"
3 (*tell*: *news*) сообща́ть (*perf* сообщи́ть); (*advice*) дава́ть (*perf* дать); **could you give him a message for me please? tell him that ...** переда́йте ему́, пожа́луйста, от меня́, что ...; **I've got a message to give you from your brother** я до́лжен переда́ть тебе́ что-то от твоего́ бра́та
4: to give sb sth (*clothing, food, right*) дава́ть (*perf* дать) кому́-н что-н; (*title*) присва́ивать (*perf* присво́ить) кому́-н что-н; (*honour, responsibility*) возлага́ть (*perf* возложи́ть) на кого́-н что-н; **to give sb a surprise** удивля́ть (*perf* удиви́ть) кого́-н; **that's given me an idea** э́то навело́ меня́ на мысль
5 (*dedicate*: *one's life*) отдава́ть (*perf* отда́ть); **you'll need to give me more time** Вы должны́ дать мне бо́льше вре́мени; **she gave it all her attention** она́ отнесла́сь к э́тому с больши́м внима́нием
6 (*organize*: *dinner etc*) дава́ть (*perf* дать)
▷ *vi* **1** (*stretch*: *fabric*) растя́гиваться (*perf* растяну́ться)
2 (*break, collapse*) = **give way**
give away *vt* (*money, object*) отдава́ть (*perf* отда́ть); (*bride*) отдава́ть (*perf* отда́ть) за́муж
give back *vt* отдава́ть (*perf* отда́ть) обра́тно
give in *vi* (*yield*) сдава́ться (*perf* сда́ться) ▷ *vt* (*essay etc*) сдава́ть (*perf* сдать)
give off *vt fus* (*smoke, heat*) выделя́ть (*impf*)
give out *vt* (*distribute*) раздава́ть (*perf* разда́ть)
give up *vi* (*stop trying*) сдава́ться (*perf* сда́ться) ▷ *vt* (*job, boyfriend*) броса́ть (*perf* бро́сить); (*idea, hope*) оставля́ть (*perf* оста́вить); **to give up smoking** броса́ть (*perf* бро́сить) кури́ть; **to give o.s. up** сдава́ться (*perf* сда́ться)
give way *vi* (*rope, ladder*) не выде́рживать (*perf* вы́держать); (*wall, roof*) обва́ливаться (*perf* обвали́ться); (*floor*) прова́ливаться (*perf* провали́ться); (*chair*) ру́хнуть (*perf*); (*Brit*: *Aut*) уступа́ть (*perf* уступи́ть) доро́гу; **his legs gave way beneath him** у него́ подкоси́лись но́ги

glacier ['glæsɪəʳ] *n* ледни́к
glad [glæd] *adj*: **I am glad** я рад; **gladly** *adv* (*willingly*) с ра́достью
glamorous ['glæmərəs] *adj* шика́рный, роско́шный
glance [glɑːns] *n* (*look*) взгляд ▷ *vi*: **to glance at** взгля́дывать (*perf* взгляну́ть) на *+acc*
gland [glænd] *n* железа́
glare [glɛəʳ] *n* взгляд; (*of light*) сия́ние

glaring ['glɛərɪŋ] *adj* я́вный, вопию́щий
glass [glɑːs] *n* (*substance*) стекло́; (*container, contents*) стака́н; **glasses** *npl* (*spectacles*) очки́ *ntpl*
glaze [gleɪz] *n* (*on pottery*) глазу́рь *f*
gleam [gliːm] *vi* мерца́ть (*impf*)
glen [glɛn] *n* речна́я доли́на
glide [glaɪd] *vi* скользи́ть (*impf*); (*Aviat*) плани́ровать (*impf*); (*bird*) пари́ть (*impf*); **glider** *n* планёр
glimmer ['glɪmə[r]] *n* (*of interest, hope*) про́блеск; (*of light*) мерца́ние
glimpse [glɪmps] *n*: **glimpse of** взгляд на +*acc* ▷ *vt* ви́деть (*perf* уви́деть) ме́льком, взгляну́ть (*perf*) на +*acc*
glint [glɪnt] *vi* блесте́ть (*perf* блесну́ть), мерца́ть (*impf*)
glitter ['glɪtə[r]] *vi* сверка́ть (*perf* сверкну́ть)
global ['gləubl] *adj* (*interest, attention*) глоба́льный; **global warming** *n* глоба́льное потепле́ние
globe [gləub] *n* (*world*) земно́й шар; (*model of world*) гло́бус
gloom [gluːm] *n* мрак; (*fig*) уны́ние
glorious ['glɔːrɪəs] *adj* (*sunshine, flowers*) великоле́пный
glory ['glɔːrɪ] *n* (*prestige*) сла́ва
gloss [glɔs] *n* гля́нец, лоск; (*also* **gloss paint**) гля́нцевая кра́ска
glossary ['glɔsərɪ] *n* глосса́рий
glossy ['glɔsɪ] *adj* (*photograph, magazine*) гля́нцевый; (*hair*) блестя́щий
glove [glʌv] *n* перча́тка; **glove compartment** *n* перча́точный я́щик, бардачо́к (*inf*)
glow [gləu] *vi* свети́ться (*impf*)
glucose ['gluːkəus] *n* глюко́за
glue [gluː] *n* клей ▷ *vt*: **to glue sth onto sth** прикле́ивать (*perf* прикле́ить) что-н на что-н

KEYWORD

go [gəu] (*pt* **went**, *pp* **gone**, *pl* **goes**) *vi* **1** (*move*: *on foot*) ходи́ть/идти́ (*perf* пойти́); (*travel*: *by transport*) е́здить/е́хать (*perf* пое́хать); **she went into the kitchen** она́ пошла́ на ку́хню; **he often goes to China** он ча́сто е́здит в Кита́й; **they are going to the theatre tonight** сего́дня ве́чером они́ иду́т в теа́тр
2 (*depart*: *on foot*) уходи́ть (*perf* уйти́); (: *by plane*) улета́ть (*perf* улете́ть); (: *by train, car*) уезжа́ть (*perf* уе́хать); **the plane goes at 6am** самолёт улетает в 6 часо́в утра́; **the train/bus goes at 6pm** по́езд/авто́бус ухо́дит в 6 часо́в; **I must go now** мне на́до идти́
3 (*attend*): **to go to** ходи́ть (*impf*) в/на +*acc*; **she doesn't go to lectures/school** она́ не хо́дит на ле́кции/в шко́лу; **she went to university** она́ учи́лась в университе́те
4 (*take part in activity*): **to go dancing** ходи́ть/идти́ (*perf* пойти́) танцева́ть
5 (*work*): **is your watch going?** Ва́ши часы́ иду́т?; **the bell went** прозвене́л звоно́к; **the tape recorder was still going** магнитофо́н всё ещё рабо́тал
6 (*become*): **to go pale** бледне́ть (*perf* побледне́ть); **to go mouldy** пле́сневеть (*perf* запле́сневеть)
7 (*be sold*) расходи́ться (*perf* разойти́сь); **the books went for £10** кни́ги разошли́сь по £10
8 (*fit, suit*): **to go with** подходи́ть

(*perf* подойти́) к *+dat*
9 (*be about to, intend to*): **to go to do** собира́ться (*perf* собра́ться) *+infin*
10 (*time*) идти́ (*impf*)
11 (*event, activity*) проходи́ть (*perf* пройти́); **how did it go?** как всё прошло́?
12 (*be given*) идти́ (*perf* пойти́); **the proceeds will go to charity** при́быль пойдёт на благотвори́тельные це́ли; **the job is to go to someone else** рабо́ту даду́т кому́-то друго́му
13 (*break etc*): **the fuse went** предохрани́тель перегоре́л; **the leg of the chair went** но́жка сту́ла litt слома́лась
14 (*be placed*): **the milk goes in the fridge** молоко́ быва́ет в холоди́льнике
▷ *n* **1** (*try*) попы́тка; **to have a go (at doing)** де́лать (*perf* сде́лать) попы́тку (*+infin*)
2 (*turn*): **whose go is it?** (*in board games*) чей ход?
3 (*move*): **to be on the go** быть (*impf*) на нога́х
go about *vi* (*also* **go around**: *rumour*) ходи́ть (*impf*)
go ahead *vi* (*event*) продолжа́ться (*perf* продо́лжиться); **to go ahead with** (*project*) приступа́ть (*perf* приступи́ть) к *+dat*; **may I begin? — yes, go ahead!** мо́жно начина́ть? — да, дава́йте!
go along *vi* идти́ (*perf* пойти́); **to go along with sb** (*accompany*) идти́ (*perf* пойти́) с кем-н; (*agree*) соглаша́ться (*perf* согласи́ться) с кем-н
go away *vi* (*leave*: *on foot*) уходи́ть (*perf* уйти́); (: *by transport*) уезжа́ть (*perf* уе́хать); **go away and think about it for a while** иди́ и поду́май об э́том
go back *vi* (*return, go again*) возвраща́ться (*perf* возврати́ться), верну́ться (*perf*); **we went back into the house** мы верну́лись в дом; **I am never going back to her house again** я никогда́ бо́льше не пойду́ к ней
go for *vt fus* (*fetch*: *paper, doctor*) идти́ (*perf* пойти́) за *+instr*; (*choose, like*) выбира́ть (*perf* вы́брать); (*attack*) набра́сываться (*perf* набро́ситься) на *+acc*; **that goes for me too** ко мне э́то то́же отно́сится
go in *vi* (*enter*) входи́ть (*perf* войти́), заходи́ть (*perf* зайти́)
go in for *vt fus* (*enter*) принима́ть (*perf* приня́ть) уча́стие в *+prp*; (*take up*) заня́ться (*perf*) *+instr*
go into *vt fus* (*enter*) входи́ть (*perf* войти́) в *+acc*; (*take up*) заня́ться (*perf*) *+instr*; **to go into details** входи́ть (*impf*) *or* вдава́ться (*impf*) в подро́бности
go off *vi* (*leave*: *on foot*) уходи́ть (*perf* уйти́); (: *by transport*) уезжа́ть (*perf* уе́хать); (*food*) по́ртиться (*perf* испо́ртиться); (*bomb*) взрыва́ться (*perf* взорва́ться); (*gun*) выстре́ливать (*perf* вы́стрелить); (*alarm*) звони́ть (*perf* зазвони́ть); (*event*) проходи́ть (*perf* пройти́); (*lights*) выключа́ться (*perf* вы́ключиться)
▷ *vt fus* разлюби́ть (*perf*)
go on *vi* (*discussion*) продолжа́ться (*impf*); (*continue*): **to go on (doing)** продолжа́ть (*impf*) (*+infin*); **life goes on** жизнь продолжа́ется; **what's going on here?** что здесь происхо́дит?; **we don't have enough information to go on** у нас недоста́точно

информáции
go on with *vt fus* продолжáть (*perf* продóлжить)
go out *vi* (*fire, light*) гáснуть (*perf* погáснуть); (*leave*): **to go out of** выходи́ть (*perf* вы́йти) из *+gen*; **are you going out tonight?** Вы сегóдня вéчером кудá-нибýдь идёте?
go over *vi* идти́ (*perf* пойти́) ▷ *vt fus* просмáтривать (*perf* просмотрéть)
go through *vt fus* (*town etc*: *by transport*) проезжáть (*perf* проéхать) чéрез *+acc*; (*files, papers*) просмáтривать (*perf* просмотрéть)
go up *vi* (*ascend*) поднимáться (*perf* подня́ться); (*price, level, buildings*) расти́ (*perf* вы́расти)
go without *vt fus* обходи́ться (*perf* обойти́сь) без *+gen*

goal [gəul] *n* (*Sport*) гол; (*aim*) цель *f*; **goalkeeper** *n* вратáрь *m*, голки́пер; **goalpost** *n* боковáя штáнга, стóйка ворóт
goat [gəut] *n* (*billy*) козёл; (*nanny*) козá
god [gɔd] *n* (*fig*) божествó, бог; God Бог; **godchild** *n* крéстник(-ица); **goddaughter** *n* крéстница; **goddess** *n* боги́ня; **godfather** *n* крёстный отéц; **godmother** *n* крёстная мать *f*; **godson** *n* крéстник
goggles ['gɔglz] *npl* защи́тные очки́ *ntpl*
going ['gəuɪŋ] *adj*: **the going rate** текýщие расцéнки *fpl*
gold [gəuld] *n* (*metal*) зóлото ▷ *adj* золотóй; **gold reserves** золотóй запáс; **goldfish** *n* серéбряный карáсь *m*
golf [gɔlf] *n* гольф; **golf club** *n* (*stick*) клю́шка (*в гóльфе*); **golf course** *n* пóле для игры́ в гольф
gone [gɔn] *pp of* **go**
gong [gɔŋ] *n* гонг
good [gud] *adj* хорóший; (*pleasant*) прия́тный; (*kind*) дóбрый ▷ *n* (*virtue*) добрó; (*benefit*) пóльза; **goods** *npl* (*Comm*) товáры *mpl*; **good!** хорошó!; **to be good at** имéть (*impf*) спосóбности к *+dat*; **it's good for you** э́то полéзно (для здорóвья); **would you be good enough to ...?** не бýдете ли Вы так добры́ *+perf infin* ...?; **a good deal (of)** большóе коли́чество (*+gen*); **a good many** мнóго *+gen*; **good afternoon/evening!** дóбрый день/ вéчер!; **good morning!** дóброе ýтро!; **good night!** (*on leaving*) до свидáния!; (*on going to bed*) спокóйной *or* дóброй нóчи!; **it's no good complaining** жáловаться бесполéзно; **for good** навсегдá; **goodbye** *excl* до свидáния; **to say goodbye (to)** прощáться (*perf* попрощáться) (с *+instr*); **Good Friday** *n* Страстнáя пя́тница; **good-looking** *adj* краси́вый; **good-natured** *adj* добродýшный; (*pet*) послýшный; **goodness** *n* добротá; **for goodness sake!** рáди Бóга!; **goodness gracious!** Бóже!, Гóсподи!; **goodwill** *n* (*of person*) дóбрая вóля
goose [gu:s] (*pl* **geese**) *n* гусь(-сы́ня) *m(f)*
gooseberry ['guzbərɪ] *n* крыжóвник *m no pl*
gorge [gɔ:dʒ] *n* тесни́на, (ýзкое) ущéлье ▷ *vt*: **to gorge o.s. (on)** наедáться (*perf* наéсться) (*+gen*)
gorgeous ['gɔ:dʒəs] *adj* прелéстный

g

gorilla [gə'rɪlə] *n* гори́лла
gospel ['gɔspl] *n* (*Rel*) Ева́нгелие
gossip ['gɔsɪp] *n* (*rumours*) спле́тня; (*chat*) разгово́ры *mpl*; (*person*) спле́тник(-ица)
got [gɔt] *pt, pp of* **get**; **gotten** *pp* (*US*) *of* **get**
govern ['gʌvən] *vt* (*country*) управля́ть (*impf*) *+instr*; (*event, conduct*) руководи́ть (*impf*) *+instr*
government ['gʌvnmənt] *n* прави́тельство; (*act*) управле́ние
governor ['gʌvənəʳ] *n* (*of state, colony*) губерна́тор; (*of school etc*) член правле́ния
gown [gaun] *n* (*dress*) пла́тье; (*of teacher, judge*) ма́нтия
GP *n abbr* (= *general practitioner*) участко́вый терапе́вт
grab [græb] *vt* хвата́ть (*perf* схвати́ть) ▷ *vi*: **to grab at** хвата́ться (*perf* схвати́ться) за *+acc*
grace [greɪs] *n* гра́ция, изя́щество; (*Rel*) моли́тва (*пе́ред едо́й*); **5 days' grace** 5 дней отсро́чки; **graceful** *adj* (*animal, person*) грацио́зный
gracious ['greɪʃəs] *adj* (*person, smile*) любе́зный ▷ *excl*: **(good) gracious!** Бо́же пра́вый!
grade [greɪd] *n* (*Comm*: *quality*) сорт; (*Scol*: *mark*) оце́нка; (*US*: *school year*) класс ▷ *vt* (*rank, class*) распределя́ть (*perf* распредели́ть); (*products*) сортирова́ть (*perf* рассортирова́ть); **grade crossing** *n* (*US*) железнодоро́жный перее́зд; **grade school** *n* (*US*) нача́льная шко́ла
gradient ['greɪdɪənt] *n* (*of hill*) укло́н
gradual ['grædjuəl] *adj* постепе́нный; **gradually** *adv* постепе́нно
graduate [*n* 'grædjuɪt, *vb* 'grædjueɪt] *n* выпускни́к(-и́ца) ▷ *vi*: **to graduate from** зака́нчивать (*perf* зако́нчить); **I graduated last year** я зако́нчил университе́т в про́шлом году́
graduation [grædju'eɪʃən] *n* (*ceremony*) выпускно́й ве́чер
graffiti [grə'fiːtɪ] *n, npl* графи́ти *nt ind*
grain [greɪn] *n* (*seed*) зерно́; (*no pl*: *cereals*) хле́бные зла́ки *mpl*; (*of sand*) песчи́нка; (*of salt*) крупи́нка; (*of wood*) волокно́
gram [græm] *n* грамм
grammar ['græməʳ] *n* грамма́тика; **grammar school** *n* (*Brit*) ≈ гимна́зия

GRAMMAR SCHOOL

В Великобрита́нии гимна́зии даю́т сре́днее образова́ние. Ученики́ поступа́ют в них на ко́нкурсной осно́ве. Число́ их невелико́. Одна́ко в США **grammar school** называ́ются нача́льные шко́лы.

gramme [græm] *n* = **gram**
grand [grænd] *adj* грандио́зный; (*gesture*) величе́ственный; **grandchild** (*pl* **grandchildren**) *n* внук(-у́чка); **granddad** *n* (*inf*) де́душка *m*; **granddaughter** *n* вну́чка; **grandfather** *n* дед; **grandma** *n* (*inf*) бабу́ля, ба́бушка; **grandmother** *n* ба́бушка; **grandparents** *npl* де́душка *m* и ба́бушка; **grandson** *n* внук
granite ['grænɪt] *n* грани́т
granny ['grænɪ] *n* (*inf*) = **grandma**

grant [grɑːnt] *vt* (*money, visa*) выдава́ть (*perf* вы́дать); (*request*) удовлетворя́ть (*perf* удовлетвори́ть); (*admit*) признава́ть (*perf* призна́ть) ▷ *n* (*Scol*) стипе́ндия; (*Admin*) грант; **to take sb/sth for granted** принима́ть (*perf* приня́ть) кого́-н/что-н как до́лжное
grape [greɪp] *n* виногра́д *m no pl*; **grapefruit** (*pl* **grapefruit** *or* **grapefruits**) *n* грейпфру́т
graph [grɑːf] *n* (*diagram*) гра́фик; **graphic** ['gr[ae]fɪk] *adj* (*explicit*) вырази́тельный; (*design*) изобрази́тельный; **graphics** *n* гра́фика
grasp [grɑːsp] *vt* хвата́ть (*perf* схвати́ть) ▷ *n* (*grip*) хва́тка; (*understanding*) понима́ние
grass [grɑːs] *n* трава́; (*lawn*) газо́н; **grasshopper** *n* кузне́чик
grate [greɪt] *n* ками́нная решётка ▷ *vt* (*Culin*) тере́ть (*perf* натере́ть) ▷ *vi* (*metal, chalk*): **to grate (on)** скрежета́ть (*impf*) (по +*dat*)
grateful ['greɪtful] *adj* благода́рный
grater ['greɪtə[r]] *n* тёрка
gratitude ['grætɪtjuːd] *n* благода́рность *f*
grave [greɪv] *n* моги́ла ▷ *adj* серьёзный
gravel ['grævl] *n* гра́вий
gravestone ['greɪvstəun] *n* надгро́бие
graveyard ['greɪvjɑːd] *n* кла́дбище
gravity ['grævɪtɪ] *n* тяготе́ние, притяже́ние; (*seriousness*) серьёзность *f*
gravy ['greɪvɪ] *n* (*sauce*) со́ус
gray [greɪ] *adj* (*US*) = **grey**
graze [greɪz] *vi* пасти́сь (*impf*) ▷ *vt* (*scrape*) цара́пать (*perf* оцара́пать)
grease [griːs] *n* (*lubricant*) сма́зка; (*fat*) жир ▷ *vt* сма́зывать (*perf* сма́зать)
greasy ['griːsɪ] *adj* жи́рный
great [greɪt] *adj* (*large*) большо́й; (*heat, pain*) си́льный; (*city, man*) вели́кий; (*inf*: *terrific*) замеча́тельный
Great Britain *n* Великобрита́ния

Great Britain

В Великобрита́нию вхо́дят А́нглия, Шотла́ндия и Уэльс. Э́ти стра́ны вме́сте с Се́верной Ирла́ндией образу́ют **United Kingdom** — Соединённое Короле́вство (Великобрита́нии и Се́верной Ирла́ндии).

greatly *adv* о́чень; (*influenced*) весьма́
Greece [griːs] *n* Гре́ция
greed [griːd] *n* жа́дность *f*; (*for power, wealth*) жа́жда; **greedy** *adj* жа́дный
Greek [griːk] *adj* гре́ческий
green [griːn] *adj* зелёный ▷ *n* (*colour*) зелёный цвет; (*grass*) лужа́йка; **greens** *npl* (*vegetables*) зе́лень *fsg*; **greengrocer** *n* (*Brit*) зеленщи́к; (*shop*) овощно́й магази́н; **greenhouse** *n* тепли́ца; **greenhouse effect** *n* парнико́вый эффе́кт
Greenland ['griːnlənd] *n* Гренла́ндия
greet [griːt] *vt* приве́тствовать (*perf* поприве́тствовать), здоро́ваться (*perf* поздоро́ваться); (*news*) встреча́ть (*perf* встре́тить); **greeting** *n* приве́тствие
grew [gruː] *pt of* **grow**
grey [greɪ] (*US* **gray**) *adj* се́рый; (*hair*) седо́й; **greyhound** *n*

борзая *f adj*
grid [grɪd] *n* (*pattern*) сéтка; (*grating*) решётка; (*Elec*) еди́ная энергосистéма
grief [gri:f] *n* гóре
grievance ['gri:vəns] *n* жáлоба
grieve [gri:v] *vi* горевáть (*impf*); **to grieve for** горевáть (*impf*) о +*prp*
grill [grɪl] *n* (*on cooker*) гриль *m*; (*grilled food*: *also* **mixed grill**) жáренные на гри́ле продýкты *mpl* ▷ *vt* (*Brit*) жáрить (*perf* пожáрить) (на гри́ле)
grim [grɪm] *adj* (*place, person*) мрáчный, угрю́мый; (*situation*) тяжёлый
grime [graɪm] *n* (*from soot, smoke*) кóпоть *f*; (*from mud*) грязь *f*
grin [grɪn] *n* ширóкая улы́бка ▷ *vi*: **to grin (at)** широкó улыбáться (*perf* улыбнýться) (+*dat*)
grind [graɪnd] (*pt, pp* **ground**) *vt* (*coffee, pepper*) молóть (*perf* смолóть); (*US*: *meat*) прокрýчивать (*perf* прокрути́ть); (*knife*) точи́ть (*perf* наточи́ть)
grip [grɪp] *n* хвáтка; (*of tyre*) сцеплéние ▷ *vt* (*object*) схвáтывать (*perf* схвати́ть); (*audience, attention*) захвáтывать (*perf* захвати́ть); **to come to grips with** занимáться (*perf* заня́ться) +*instr*; **gripping** *adj* захвáтывающий
grit [grɪt] *n* (*stone*) щéбень *m* ▷ *vt* (*road*) посыпáть (*perf* посы́пать) щéбнем; **to grit one's teeth** сти́скивать (*perf* сти́снуть) зýбы
groan [grəun] *n* (*of person*) стон
grocer ['grəusəʳ] *n* бакалéйщик; **groceries** *npl* бакалéя *fsg*; **grocer's (shop)** *n* бакалéйный магази́н, бакалéя
groin [grɔɪn] *n* пах
groom [gru:m] *n* (*for horse*) кóнюх; (*also* **bridegroom**) жени́х ▷ *vt* (*horse*) ухáживать (*impf*) за +*instr*; **to groom sb for** (*job*) готóвить (*perf* подготóвить) когó-н к +*dat*
groove [gru:v] *n* канáвка
gross [grəus] *adj* вульгáрный; (*neglect, injustice*) вопию́щий; (*Comm*: *income*) валовóй; **grossly** *adv* чрезмéрно
grotesque [grə'tɛsk] *adj* гротéскный
ground [graund] *pt, pp of* **grind** ▷ *n* (*earth, land*) земля́; (*floor*) пол; (*US*: *also* **ground wire**) заземлéние; (*usu pl*: *reason*) основáние ▷ *vt* (*US*: *Elec*) заземля́ть (*perf* заземли́ть); **grounds** *npl* (*of coffee*) гýща *fsg*; **school grounds** шкóльная площáдка; **sports ground** спорти́вная площáдка; **on the ground** на землé; **to the ground** (*burnt*) дотлá; **the plane was grounded by the fog** самолёт не мог подня́ться в вóздух из-за тумáна; **groundwork** *n* (*preparation*) фундáмент, оснóва; **to do the groundwork** заклáдывать (*perf* заложи́ть) фундáмент
group [gru:p] *n* грýппа
grouse [graus] *n inv* (*bird*) (шотлáндская) куропáтка
grow [grəu] (*pt* **grew**, *pp* **grown**) *vi* расти́ (*perf* вы́расти); (*become*) станови́ться (*perf* стать) ▷ *vt* (*roses, vegetables*) выращивать (*perf* вы́растить); (*beard, hair*) отрáщивать (*perf* отрасти́ть); **grow up** *vi* (*child*) расти́ (*perf*

вы́расти), взросле́ть (*perf* повзросле́ть)

growl [graul] *vi* (*dog*) рыча́ть (*impf*)

grown [grəun] *pp of* **grow**; **grown-up** *n* (*adult*) взро́слый(-ая) *m(f) adj* ▷ *adj* (*son, daughter*) взро́слый

growth [grəuθ] *n* рост; (*increase*) приро́ст; (*Med*) о́пухоль *f*

grub [grʌb] *n* (*larva*) личи́нка; (*inf: food*) жратва́

grubby ['grʌbɪ] *adj* гря́зный

grudge [grʌdʒ] *n* недово́льство; **to bear sb a grudge** зата́ивать (*perf* зата́ить) на кого́-н оби́ду

gruelling ['gruəlɪŋ] (*US* **grueling**) *adj* изнури́тельный, тя́жкий

gruesome ['gru:səm] *adj* жу́ткий

grumble ['grʌmbl] *vi* ворча́ть (*impf*)

grumpy ['grʌmpɪ] *adj* сварли́вый

grunt [grʌnt] *vi* (*pig*) хрю́кать (*perf* хрю́кнуть); (*person*) бурча́ть (*perf* бу́ркнуть)

guarantee [gærən'ti:] *n* (*assurance*) поручи́тельство; (*warranty*) гара́нтия ▷ *vt* гаранти́ровать (*impf/perf*); **he can't guarantee (that) he'll come** он не мо́жет поручи́ться, что он придёт

guard [gɑ:d] *n* (*one person*) охра́нник; (*squad*) охра́на; (*Brit: Rail*) конду́ктор; (*Tech*) предохрани́тельное устро́йство; (*also* **fireguard**) предохрани́тельная решётка (*пе́редками́ном*) ▷ *vt* (*prisoner*) охраня́ть (*impf*); (*secret*) храни́ть (*impf*); **to guard (against)** (*protect*) охраня́ть (*impf*) (от *+gen*); **to be on one's guard** быть (*impf*) насторо́же *or* начеку́; **guard against** *vt fus* (*prevent*) предохраня́ть (*impf*) от *+gen*; **guardian** *n* (*Law*) опеку́н

guerrilla [gə'rɪlə] *n* партиза́н(ка)

guess [gɛs] *vt* (*estimate*) счита́ть (*perf* сосчита́ть) приблизи́тельно; (*correct answer*) уга́дывать (*perf* угада́ть) ▷ *vi* дога́дываться (*perf* догада́ться) ▷ *n* дога́дка; **to take** *or* **have a guess** отга́дывать (*perf* отгада́ть)

guest [gɛst] *n* (*visitor*) гость(я) *m(f)*; (*in hotel*) постоя́лец(-лица); **guesthouse** *n* гости́ница

guidance ['gaɪdəns] *n* (*advice*) сове́т

guide [gaɪd] *n* (*in museum, on tour*) гид, экскурсово́д; (*also* **guidebook**) путеводи́тель *m*; (*handbook*) руково́дство ▷ *vt* (*show around*) води́ть (*impf*); (*direct*) направля́ть (*perf* напра́вить); **guidebook** *n* путеводи́тель *m*; **guide dog** *n* соба́ка-поводы́рь *f*; **guidelines** *npl* руково́дство *ntsg*

guild [gɪld] *n* ги́льдия

guilt [gɪlt] *n* (*remorse*) вина́; (*culpability*) вино́вность *f*; **guilty** *adj* (*person, expression*) винова́тый; (*of crime*) вино́вный

guinea pig ['gɪnɪ-] *n* морска́я сви́нка; (*fig*) подо́пытный кро́лик

guitar [gɪ'tɑ:[r]] *n* гита́ра

gulf [gʌlf] *n* (*Geo*) зали́в; (*fig*) про́пасть *f*

gull [gʌl] *n* ча́йка

gulp [gʌlp] *vi* не́рвно сгла́тывать (*perf* сглотну́ть) ▷ *vt* (*also* **gulp down**) прогла́тывать (*perf* проглоти́ть)

gum [gʌm] *n* (*Anat*) десна́; (*glue*) клей; (*also* **chewing-gum**) жва́чка (*inf*), жева́тельная рези́нка

gun [gʌn] *n* пистоле́т; (*rifle, airgun*) ружьё; **gunfire** *n*

стрельба́; **gunman** *irreg n* вооружённый банди́т; **gunpoint** *n*: **at gunpoint** под ду́лом пистоле́та; **gunshot** *n* вы́стрел
gust [gʌst] *n* (*of wind*) поры́в
gut [gʌt] *n* (*Anat*) кишка́; **guts** *npl* (*Anat*) кишки́ *fpl*, вну́тренности *fpl*; (*inf: courage*) му́жество *ntsg*
gutter ['gʌtəʳ] *n* (*in street*) сто́чная кана́ва; (*of roof*) водосто́чный жёлоб
guy [gaɪ] *n* (*inf: man*) па́рень *m*; (*also* **guyrope**) пала́точный шнур
gym [dʒɪm] *n* (*also* **gymnasium**) гимнасти́ческий зал; (*also* **gymnastics**) гимна́стика; **gymnastics** [dʒɪm'næstɪks] *n* гимна́стика
gynaecologist [gaɪnɪ'kɔlədʒɪst] (*US* **gynecologist**) *n* гинеко́лог
gypsy ['dʒɪpsɪ] *n* цыга́н(ка)

habit ['hæbɪt] *n* (*custom*) привы́чка; (*addiction*) пристра́стие; (*Rel*) облаче́ние
habitat ['hæbɪtæt] *n* среда́ обита́ния
hack [hæk] *vt* отруба́ть (*perf* отруби́ть) ▷ *n* (*pej: writer*) писа́ка *m/f*
had [hæd] *pt, pp of* **have**
haddock ['hædək] (*pl* **haddock** *or* **haddocks**) *n* треска́
hadn't ['hædnt] = **had not**
haemorrhage ['hɛmərɪdʒ] (*US* **hemorrhage**) *n* кровотече́ние; **brain haemorrhage** кровоизлия́ние (в мозг)
Hague [heɪg] *n*: **The Hague** Гаа́га
hail [heɪl] *n* град ▷ *vt* (*flag down*) подзыва́ть (*perf* подозва́ть) ▷ *vi*: **it's hailing** идёт град; **hailstone** *n* гра́дина
hair [hɛəʳ] *n* во́лосы *pl*; (*of animal*)

волосяно́й покро́в; **to do one's hair** причёсываться (*perf* причеса́ться); **hairbrush** *n* щётка для воло́с; **haircut** *n* стри́жка; **hairdresser** *n* парикма́хер; **hair dryer** [-draɪəʳ] *n* фен; **hair spray** *n* лак для воло́с; **hairstyle** *n* причёска; **hairy** *adj* (*person*) волоса́тый; (*animal*) мохна́тый

half [hɑːf] (*pl* **halves**) *n* полови́на; (*also* **half pint**: *of beer etc*) полпи́нты *f*; (*on train, bus*) биле́т за полцены́ ▷ *adv* наполови́ну; **one and a half** (*with m/nt nouns*) полтора́ *+gen sg*; (*with f nouns*) полторы́ *+gen sg*; **three and a half** три с полови́ной; **half a dozen (of)** полдю́жины *f* (*+gen*); **half a pound (of)** полфу́нта *m* (*+gen*); **a week and a half** полторы́ неде́ли; **half (of)** полови́на (*+gen*); **half the amount of** полови́на *+gen*; **to cut sth in half** разреза́ть (*perf* разре́зать) что-н попола́м; **half-hearted** *adj* лени́вый; **half-hour** *n* полчаса́ *m*; **half-price** *adj, adv* за полцены́; **half-time** *n* переры́в ме́жду та́ймами; **halfway** *adv* на полпути́

HALF TERM

Half term — коро́ткие кани́кулы. В середи́не триме́стров шко́льникам даю́т коро́ткий переры́в в 3-4 дня.

hall [hɔːl] *n* (*in house*) прихо́жая *f adj*, холл; (*for concerts, meetings etc*) зал

hallmark ['hɔːlmɑːk] *n* про́ба; (*fig*) отличи́тельная черта́

Hallowe'en ['hæləu'iːn] *n* кану́н Дня всех святы́х

HALLOWE'EN

Э́тот пра́здник отмеча́ют ве́чером 31 октября́. По тради́ции э́то день ведьм и ду́хов. Де́ти наряжа́ются в костю́мы ведьм и вампи́ров, де́лают ла́мпы из тыкв. С наступле́нием темноты́ они́ хо́дят по дома́м, игра́я в игру́ подо́бную ру́сским Коробе́йникам. Е́сли хозя́ева не даю́т де́тям конфе́т, они́ мо́гут сыгра́ть над ни́ми шу́тку.

hallucination [həluːsɪ'neɪʃən] *n* галлюцина́ция

hallway ['hɔːlweɪ] *n* прихо́жая *f adj*, холл

halo ['heɪləu] *n* (*Rel*) нимб

halt [hɔːlt] *n* остано́вка ▷ *vt* остана́вливать (*perf* останови́ть) ▷ *vi* остана́вливаться (*perf* останови́ться)

halve [hɑːv] *vt* (*reduce*) сокраща́ть (*perf* сократи́ть) наполови́ну; (*divide*) дели́ть (*perf* разде́ли́ть) попола́м

halves [hɑːvz] *pl of* **half**

ham [hæm] *n* (*meat*) ветчина́; **hamburger** *n* га́мбургер

hammer ['hæməʳ] *n* молото́к ▷ *vi* (*on door etc*) колоти́ть (*impf*) ▷ *vt* (*nail*): **to hammer in** забива́ть (*perf* заби́ть), вбива́ть (*perf* вбить); **to hammer sth into sb** (*fig*) вда́лбливать (*perf* вдолби́ть) что-н кому́-н

hamper ['hæmpəʳ] *vt* меша́ть (*perf* помеша́ть) *+dat* ▷ *n* (*basket*) больша́я корзи́на с кры́шкой

hamster ['hæmstəʳ] *n* хомя́к

hand [hænd] *n* (*Anat*) рука́, кисть *f*, (*of clock*) стре́лка; (*worker*) рабо́чий *m adj* ▷ *vt* (*give*)

h

вруча́ть (*perf* вручи́ть); **to give** *or* **lend sb a hand** протя́гивать (*perf* протяну́ть) кому́-н ру́ку (по́мощи); **at hand** под руко́й; **in hand** (*situation*) под контро́лем; (*time*) в распоряже́нии; **on hand** (*person, services etc*) в распоряже́нии; **I have the information to hand** я располага́ю информа́цией; **on the one hand ..., on the other hand ...** с одно́й стороны́ ..., с друго́й стороны́ ...; **hand in** *vt* (*work*) сдава́ть (*perf* сдать); **hand out** *vt* раздава́ть (*perf* разда́ть); **hand over** *vt* передава́ть (*perf* переда́ть), вруча́ть (*perf* вручи́ть); **handbag** *n* (да́мская) су́мочка; **handbrake** *n* ручно́й то́рмоз; **handcuffs** *npl* нару́чники *mpl*; **handful** *n* (*fig*: *of people*) го́рстка; **hand-held** *adj* ручно́й

handicap ['hændɪkæp] *n* (*inf!:disability*) физи́ческая неполноце́нность *f*; (*disadvantage*) препя́тствие ▷ *vt* препя́тствовать (*perf* воспрепя́тствовать) *+dat*

handkerchief ['hæŋkətʃɪf] *n* носово́й плато́к

handle ['hændl] *n* ру́чка ▷ *vt* (*touch*) держа́ть (*impf*) в рука́х; (*deal with*) занима́ться (*impf*) *+instr*; (: *successfully*) справля́ться (*perf* спра́виться) с *+instr*; (*treat*: *people*) обраща́ться (*impf*) с *+instr*; **to fly off the handle** (*inf*) срыва́ться (*perf* сорва́ться); **"handle with care"** "обраща́ться осторо́жно"

hand luggage *n* ручна́я кладь *f*

handmade ['hænd'meɪd] *adj* ручно́й рабо́ты; **it's handmade** э́то ручна́я рабо́та

handsome ['hænsəm] *adj* (*man*) краси́вый; (*woman*) интере́сный; (*building, profit, sum*) внуши́тельный

handwriting ['hændraɪtɪŋ] *n* по́черк

handy ['hændɪ] *adj* (*useful*) удо́бный; (*close at hand*) побли́зости

hang [hæŋ] (*pt, pp* **hung**) *vt* ве́шать (*perf* пове́сить) ▷ (*pt, pp* **hanged**) (*execute*) ве́шать (*perf* пове́сить) ▷ *vi* висе́ть (*impf*) ▷ *n*: **to get the hang of sth** (*inf*) разбира́ться (*perf* разобра́ться) в чём-н; **hang around** *vi* слоня́ться (*impf*), болта́ться (*impf*); **hang on** *vi* (*wait*) подожда́ть (*impf*); **hang up** *vi* (*Tel*) ве́шать (*perf* пове́сить) тру́бку ▷ *vt* ве́шать (*perf* пове́сить)

hangover ['hæŋəuvə^r] *n* (*after drinking*) похме́лье

happen ['hæpən] *vi* случа́ться (*perf* случи́ться), происходи́ть (*perf* произойти́); **I happened to meet him in the park** я случа́йно встре́тил его́ в па́рке; **as it happens** кста́ти

happily ['hæpɪlɪ] *adv* (*luckily*) к сча́стью; (*cheerfully, gladly*) ра́достно

happiness ['hæpɪnɪs] *n* (*cheerfulness*) сча́стье

happy ['hæpɪ] *adj* (*pleased*) счастли́вый; (*cheerful*) весёлый; **I am happy (with it)** (*content*) я дово́лен (э́тим); **he is always happy to help** он всегда́ рад помо́чь; **happy birthday!** с днём рожде́ния!

harassment ['hærəsmənt] *n* пресле́дование

harbour ['hɑːbə^r] (*US* **harbor**) *n* га́вань *f* ▷ *vt* (*hope, fear*) зата́ивать (*perf* затаи́ть); (*criminal, fugitive*) укрыва́ть (*perf* укры́ть)

hard [hɑːd] *adj* (*surface, object*) твёрдый; (*question, problem*) трýдный; (*work, life*) тяжёлый; (*person*) сурóвый; (*facts, evidence*) неопровержи́мый ▷ *adv*: **to work hard** мнóго и усéрдно рабóтать (*impf*); **I don't have any hard feelings** я не держý зла; **he is hard of hearing** он туг нá ухо; **to think hard** хорошó подýмать (*perf*); **to try hard to win** упóрно добивáться (*impf*) побéды; **to look hard at** смотрéть (*perf* посмотрéть) при́стально на *+acc*; **hardback** *n* кни́га в твёрдом переплёте; **hard disk** *n* жёсткий диск; **harden** *vt* (*substance*) дéлать (*perf* сдéлать) твёрдым(-ой); (*attitude, person*) ожесточáть (*perf* ожесточи́ть) ▷ *vi* (*see vt*) твердéть (*perf* затвердéть); ожесточáться (*perf* ожесточи́ться)

hardly ['hɑːdlɪ] *adv* едвá; **hardly ever/anywhere** почти́ никогдá/ нигдé

hardship ['hɑːdʃɪp] *n* тя́готы *pl*, трýдности *fpl*

hard up *adj* (*inf*) нуждáющийся; **I am hard up** я нуждáюсь

hardware ['hɑːdwɛəʳ] *n* (*tools*) скобяны́е издéлия *ntpl*

hard-working [hɑːd'wəːkɪŋ] *adj* усéрдный

hardy ['hɑːdɪ] *adj* выносливый; (*plant*) морозоустóйчивый

hare [hɛəʳ] *n* зáяц

harm [hɑːm] *n* (*injury*) телéсное повреждéние, трáвма; (*damage*) ущéрб ▷ *vt* (*thing*) повреждáть (*perf* повреди́ть); (*person*) наноси́ть (*perf* нанести́) вред *+dat*; **harmful** *adj* врéдный; **harmless** *adj* безоби́дный

harmony ['hɑːmənɪ] *n* гармóния

harness ['hɑːnɪs] *n* (*for horse*) ýпряжь *f*; (*for child*) пострóмки *fpl*; (*safety harness*) привязны́е ремни́ *mpl* ▷ *vt* (*horse*) запрягáть (*perf* запря́чь); (*resources, energy*) стáвить (*perf* постáвить) себé на слýжбу

harp [hɑːp] *n* áрфа

harsh [hɑːʃ] *adj* (*sound, light, criticism*) рéзкий; (*person, remark*) жёсткий; (*life, winter*) сурóвый

harvest ['hɑːvɪst] *n* (*time*) жáтва; (*of barley, fruit*) урожáй ▷ *vt* собирáть (*perf* собрáть) урожáй *+gen*

has [hæz] *vb see* **have**

hasn't ['hæznt] = **has not**

hassle ['hæsl] (*inf*) *n* морóка

haste [heɪst] *n* спéшка; **hasten** ['heɪsn] *vt* торопи́ть (*perf* поторопи́ть) ▷ *vi*: **to hasten to do** торопи́ться (*perf* поторопи́ться) *+infin*

hastily ['heɪstɪlɪ] *adv* (*see adj*) поспéшно; опромéтчиво

hasty ['heɪstɪ] *adj* поспéшный; (*rash*) опромéтчивый

hat [hæt] *n* шля́па; (*woolly*) шáпка

hatch [hætʃ] *n* (*Naut*: *also* **hatchway**) люк; (*also* **service hatch**) раздáточное окнó ▷ *vi* (*also* **hatch out**) вылуплúться (*perf* вы́лупиться)

hate [heɪt] *vt* ненави́деть (*impf*)

hatred ['heɪtrɪd] *n* нéнависть *f*

haul [hɔːl] *vt* (*pull*) таскáть/ тащи́ть (*impf*) ▷ *n* (*of stolen goods etc*) добы́ча

haunt [hɔːnt] *vt* (*fig*) преслéдовать (*impf*); **to haunt sb/a house** явля́ться (*perf* яви́ться) комý-н/в дóме; **haunted** *adj*: **this house is haunted** в э́том дóме есть привидéния

h

KEYWORD

have [hæv] (*pt, pp* **had**) *aux vb*
1 to have arrived приéхать (*perf*); **have you already eaten?** ты ужé поéл?; **he has been kind to me** он был добр ко мне; **he has been promoted** он получи́л повышéние по слу́жбе; **has he told you?** он Вам сказáл?; **having finished** *or* **when he had finished ...** закóнчив *or* когдá он закóнчил ...
2 (*in tag questions*) не так ли; **you've done it, haven't you?** Вы сдéлали э́то, не так ли?
3 (*in short answers and questions*): **you've made a mistake — no I haven't/so I have** Вы оши́блись — нет, не оши́бся/да, оши́бся; **we haven't paid — yes we have!** мы не заплати́ли — нет, заплати́ли!; **I've been there before, have you?** я там ужé был, а Вы?
▷ *modal aux vb* (*be obliged*): **I have (got) to finish this work** я дóлжен закóнчить э́ту рабóту; **I haven't got** *or* **I don't have to wear glasses** мне не нáдо носи́ть очки́; **this has to be a mistake** э́то, наверняка́, оши́бка
▷ *vt* **1** (*possess*): **I** *etc* **have** у меня́ (есть) *etc +nom*; **he has (got) blue eyes/dark hair** у негó голубы́е глазá/тёмные вóлосы; **do you have** *or* **have you got a car?** у Вас есть маши́на?
2 (*referring to meals etc*): **to have dinner** обéдать (*perf* пообéдать); **to have breakfast** зáвтракать (*perf* позáвтракать); **to have a cigarette** выку́ривать (*perf* вы́курить) сигарéту; **to have a glass of wine** выпивáть (*perf* вы́пить) бокáл винá
3 (*receive, obtain etc*): **may I have your address?** Вы мóжете дать мне свой áдрес?; **you can have the book for £5** бери́те кни́гу за £5; **I must have the report by tomorrow** доклáд дóлжен быть у меня́ к зáвтрашнему дню; **she is having a baby in March** онá бу́дет рожáть в мáрте
4 (*allow*) допускáть (*perf* допусти́ть); **I won't have it!** я э́того не допущу́!
5: I am having my television repaired мне должны́ почини́ть телеви́зор; **to have sb do** проси́ть (*perf* попроси́ть) когó-н *+infin*; **he soon had them all laughing** вскóре он застáвил всех смея́ться
6 (*experience, suffer*): **I have flu/a headache** у меня́ грипп/боли́т головá; **to have a cold** простужáться (*perf* простуди́ться); **she had her bag stolen** у неё укрáли су́мку; **he had an operation** ему́ сдéлали оперáцию
7 (*+n*): **to have a swim** плáвать (*perf* поплáвать); **to have a rest** отдыхáть (*perf* отдохну́ть); **let's have a look** давáйте посмóтрим; **we are having a meeting tomorrow** зáвтра у нас бу́дет собрáние; **let me have a try** дáйте мне попрóбовать
have out *vt*: **to have it out with sb** объясня́ться (*perf* объясни́ться) с кем-н; **she had her tooth out** ей удали́ли зуб; **she had her tonsils out** ей вы́резали глáнды

haven ['heɪvn] *n* (*fig*) убéжище
haven't ['hævnt] = **have not**
havoc ['hævək] *n* (*chaos*) хáос
hawk [hɔːk] *n* я́стреб
hay [heɪ] *n* сéно; **hay fever** *n* сеннáя лихорáдка; **haystack** *n* стог сéна

hazard [ˈhæzəd] *n* опа́сность *f* ▷ *vt*: **to hazard a guess** осме́ливаться (*perf* осме́литься) предположи́ть; **hazardous** *adj* опа́сный

haze [heɪz] *n* ды́мка; **heat haze** ма́рево

hazy [ˈheɪzɪ] *adj* тума́нный

he [hiː] *pron* он

head [hɛd] *n* (*Anat*) голова́; (*mind*) ум; (*of list, queue*) нача́ло; (*of table*) глава́; (*Comm*) руководи́тель(ница) *m(f)*; (*Scol*) дире́ктор ▷ *vt* возглавля́ть (*perf* возгла́вить); **heads or tails** ≈ орёл или ре́шка; **he is head over heels in love** он влюблён по́ уши; **head for** *vt fus* (*place*) направля́ться (*perf* напра́виться) в/на *+acc or* к *+dat*; (*disaster*) обрека́ть (*perf* обре́чь) себя́ на *+acc*; **headache** *n* (*Med*) головна́я боль *f*; **heading** *n* заголо́вок; **headlight** *n* фа́ра; **headline** *n* заголо́вок; **head office** *n* управле́ние; **headphones** *npl* нау́шники *mpl*; **headquarters** *npl* штаб-кварти́ра *fsg*; **headscarf** *n* косы́нка, (головно́й) плато́к; **head teacher** *n* дире́ктор шко́лы

heal [hiːl] *vt* выле́чивать (*perf* вы́лечить); (*damage*) поправля́ть (*perf* попра́вить) ▷ *vi* (*injury*) зажива́ть (*perf* зажи́ть); (*damage*) восстана́вливаться (*perf* восстанови́ться)

health [hɛlθ] *n* здоро́вье; **health care** *n* здравоохране́ние; **Health Service** *n* (*Brit*): **the Health Service** слу́жба здравоохране́ния; **healthy** *adj* здоро́вый; (*pursuit*) поле́зный; (*profit*) доста́точно хоро́ший

heap [hiːp] *n* (*small*) ку́ча; (*large*) гру́да ▷ *vt*: **to heap (up)** (*stones, sand*) сва́ливать (*perf* свали́ть) в ку́чу; **to heap with sth** (*plate, sink*) наполня́ть (*perf* напо́лнить) чем-н; **heaps of** (*inf*) ку́ча *fsg +gen*

hear [hɪəʳ] (*pt, pp* **heard**) *vt* слы́шать (*perf* услы́шать); (*lecture, concert, case*) слу́шать (*impf*); **to hear about** слы́шать (*perf* услы́шать) о *+prp*; **to hear from sb** слы́шать (*perf* услы́шать) от кого́-н; **I can't hear you** Вас не слы́шно; **heard** [həːd] *pt, pp of* **hear**; **hearing** *n* (*sense*) слух; (*Law, Pol*) слу́шание; **hearing aid** *n* слухово́й аппара́т

heart [hɑːt] *n* се́рдце; (*of problem, matter*) суть *f*; **hearts** *npl* (*Cards*) че́рви *fpl*; **to lose/take heart** пасть (*perf*)/не па́дать (*impf*) ду́хом; **at heart** в глубине́ души́; **(off) by heart** наизу́сть; **heart attack** *n* серде́чный при́ступ, инфа́ркт; **heartbeat** *n* (*rhythm*) сердцебие́ние; **heartbroken** *adj*: **he is heartbroken** он уби́т го́рем

hearth [hɑːθ] *n* оча́г

heartless [ˈhɑːtlɪs] *adj* бессерде́чный

hearty [ˈhɑːtɪ] *adj* (*person, laugh*) задо́рный, весёлый; (*welcome, support*) серде́чный; (*appetite*) здоро́вый

heat [hiːt] *n* тепло́; (*extreme*) жар; (*of weather*) жара́; (*excitement*) пыл; (*also* **qualifying heat**: *in race*) забе́г; (: *in swimming*) заплы́в ▷ *vt* (*water, food*) греть (*perf* нагре́ть); (*house*) ота́пливать (*perf* отопи́ть); **heat up** *vi* (*water, house*) согрева́ться (*perf* согре́ться) ▷ *vt* (*food, water*) подогрева́ть (*perf* подогре́ть); (*room*) обогрева́ть (*perf* обогре́ть); **heated** *adj* (*argument*) горя́чий; (*pool*) обогрева́емый; **heater** *n* обогрева́тель *m*

heather ['hɛðə^r] *n* ве́реск

heating ['hi:tɪŋ] *n* отопле́ние

heat wave *n* пери́од си́льной жары́

heaven ['hɛvn] *n* рай; **heavenly** *adj* (*fig*) ра́йский

heavily ['hɛvɪlɪ] *adv* (*fall, sigh*) тяжело́; (*drink, smoke, depend*) си́льно; (*sleep*) кре́пко

heavy ['hɛvɪ] *adj* тяжёлый; (*rain, blow, fall*) си́льный; (*build*: *of person*) гру́зный; **he is a heavy drinker/smoker** он мно́го пьёт/ку́рит

Hebrew ['hi:bru:] *adj* древнеевре́йский

Hebrides ['hɛbrɪdi:z] *npl*: **the Hebrides** Гебри́дские острова́ *mpl*

hectic ['hɛktɪk] *adj* (*day*) сумато́шный; (*activities*) лихора́дочный

he'd [hi:d] = **he would**; **he had**

hedge [hɛdʒ] *n* жива́я и́згородь *f*

hedgehog ['hɛdʒhɔg] *n* ёж

heed [hi:d] *vt* (*also* **take heed of**) принима́ть (*perf* приня́ть) во внима́ние

heel [hi:l] *n* (*of foot*) пя́тка; (*of shoe*) каблу́к

hefty ['hɛftɪ] *adj* (*person, object*) здорове́нный; (*profit, fine*) изря́дный

height [haɪt] *n* (*of tree, of plane*) высота́; (*of person*) рост; (*of power*) верши́на; (*of season*) разга́р; (*of luxury, taste*) верх; **heighten** *vt* уси́ливать (*perf* уси́лить)

heir [ɛə^r] *n* насле́дник; **heiress** *n* насле́дница

held [hɛld] *pt, pp of* **hold**

helicopter ['hɛlɪkɔptə^r] *n* вертолёт

hell [hɛl] *n* (*also fig*) ад; **hell!** (*inf*) чёрт!

he'll [hi:l] = **he will**; **he shall**

hello [hə'ləu] *excl* здра́вствуйте; (*informal*) приве́т; (*Tel*) алло́

helmet ['hɛlmɪt] *n* (*of policeman, miner*) ка́ска; (*also* **crash helmet**) шлем

help [hɛlp] *n* по́мощь *f* ▷ *vt* помога́ть (*perf* помо́чь) *+dat*; **help!** на по́мощь!, помоги́те!; **help yourself** угоща́йтесь; **he can't help it** он ничего́ не мо́жет поде́лать с э́тим; **helper** *n* помо́щник(-ица); **helpful** *adj* поле́зный; **helpless** *adj* беспо́мощный; **helpline** *n* телефо́н дове́рия

hem [hɛm] *n* (*of dress*) подо́л

hemorrhage ['hɛmərɪdʒ] *n* (*US*) = **haemorrhage**

hen [hɛn] *n* (*chicken*) ку́рица

hence [hɛns] *adv* (*therefore*) сле́довательно, всле́дствие э́того; **2 years hence** (*from now*) по истече́нии двух лет

hepatitis [hɛpə'taɪtɪs] *n* гепати́т, боле́знь *f* Бо́ткина

her [hə:^r] *pron* (*direct*) её; (*indirect*) ей; (*after prep*: *+gen*) неё; (: *+instr, +dat, +prp*) ней; *see also* **me** ▷ *adj* её; (*referring to subject of sentence*) свой; *see also* **my**

herb [hə:b] *n* трава́; (*as medicine*) лека́рственная трава́; **herbs** *npl* (*Culin*) зе́лень *fsg*

herd [hə:d] *n* ста́до

here [hɪə^r] *adv* (*location*) здесь; (*destination*) сюда́; (*at this point*: *in past*) тут; **from here** отсю́да; **"here!"** (*present*) "здесь!"; **here is ..., here are ...** вот ...

hereditary [hɪ'rɛdɪtrɪ] *adj* насле́дственный

heritage ['hɛrɪtɪdʒ] *n* насле́дие

hernia ['hə:nɪə] *n* гры́жа

hero ['hɪərəu] (*pl* **heroes**) *n* герóй; **heroic** [hɪ'rəuɪk] *adj* героúческий
heroin ['hɛrəuɪn] *n* герóин
heroine ['hɛrəuɪn] *n* герóиня
heron ['hɛrən] *n* цáпля
herring ['hɛrɪŋ] *n* (*Zool*) сельдь *f*; (*Culin*) селёдка
hers [hə:z] *pron* её; (*referring to subject of sentence*) свой; *see also* **mine**[1]
herself [hə:'sɛlf] *pron* (*reflexive, after prep*: *+acc, +gen*) себя́; (: *+dat, +prp*) себé; (: *+instr*) собóй; (*emphatic*) самá; (*alone*): **by herself** однá; *see also* **myself**
he's [hi:z] = **he is**; **he has**
hesitant ['hɛzɪtənt] *adj* нерешúтельный; **to be hesitant to do** не решáться (*impf*) *+infin*
hesitate ['hɛzɪteɪt] *vi* колебáться (*perf* поколебáться); (*be unwilling*) не решáться (*impf*)
hesitation [hɛzɪ'teɪʃən] *n* колебáние
heterosexual ['hɛtərəu'sɛksjuəl] *adj* гетеросексуáльный
heyday ['heɪdeɪ] *n*: **the heyday of** расцвéт *+gen*
hi [haɪ] *excl* (*as greeting*) привéт
hiccoughs ['hɪkʌps] *npl* = **hiccups**
hiccups ['hɪkʌps] *npl*: **she's got (the) hiccups** у неё икóта
hide [haɪd] (*pt* **hid**, *pp* **hidden**) *n* (*skin*) шкýра ▷ *vt* (*object, person*) прятать (*perf* спря́тать); (*feeling, information*) скрывáть (*perf* скрыть); (*sun, view*) закрывáть (*perf* закры́ть) ▷ *vi*: **to hide (from sb)** прятаться (*perf* спря́таться) (от когó-н)
hideous ['hɪdɪəs] *adj* жýткий; (*face*) омерзúтельный
hiding ['haɪdɪŋ] *n* (*beating*) пóрка; **to be in hiding** скрывáться (*impf*)
hi-fi ['haɪfaɪ] *n* стереосистéма
high [haɪ] *adj* высóкий; (*wind*) сúльный ▷ *adv* высокó; **the building is 20 m high** высотá здáния — 20 м; **to be high** (*inf*: *on drugs etc*) кайфовáть (*impf*); **high risk** высóкая стéпень рúска; **high in the air** (*position*) высокó в вóздухе; **highchair** *n* высóкий стýльчик (*для мáленьких детéй*); **higher education** *n* вы́сшее образовáние; **high jump** *n* прыжóк в высотý; **Highlands** *npl*: **the Highlands** Высокогóрья *ntpl* (*Шотлáндии*); **highlight** *n* (*of event*) кульминáция ▷ *vt* (*problem, need*) выявля́ть (*perf* вы́явить); **highly** *adv* óчень; (*paid*) высокó; **to speak highly of** высокó отзывáться (*perf* отозвáться) о *+prp*; **to think highly of** быть (*impf*) высóкого мнéния о *+prp*; **highness** *n*: **Her/His Highness** Её/Егó Высóчество; **high-rise** *adj* высóтный; **high school** *n* (*Brit*) срéдняя шкóла (*для 11-18ти лéтних*); (*US*) срéдняя шкóла (*для 14-18ти лéтних*)

HIGH SCHOOL

В Британии дéти посещáют срéднюю шкóлу в вóзрасте от 11 до 18 лет. В США шкóльники вначáле посещáют млáдшую срéднюю шкóлу, а затéм, в вóзрасте от 14 до 18 лет, срéднюю шкóлу. Шкóльное образовáние обязáтельно до 16 лет.

high: **high season** *n* (*Brit*) разгáр

сезо́на; **high street** *n* (*Brit*) центра́льная у́лица; **highway** *n* (*US*) тра́сса, автостра́да; (*main road*) автостра́да

hijack ['haɪdʒæk] *vt* (*plane, bus*) угоня́ть (*perf* угна́ть)

hike [haɪk] *n*: **to go for a hike** идти́ (*perf* пойти́) в похо́д

hilarious [hɪ'lɛərɪəs] *adj* чрезвыча́йно смешно́й

hill [hɪl] *n* (*small*) холм; (*fairly high*) гора́; (*slope*) склон; **hillside** *n* склон; **hilly** *adj* холми́стый

him [hɪm] *pron* (*direct*) его́; (*indirect*) ему́; (*after prep*: *+gen*) него́; (: *+dat*) нему́; (: *+instr*) ним; (: *+prp*) нём; *see also* **me**; **himself** *pron* (*reflexive, after prep*: *+acc, +gen*) себя́; (: *+dat, +prp*) себе́; (: *+instr*) собо́й; (*emphatic*) сам; (*alone*): **by himself** оди́н; *see also* **myself**

hinder ['hɪndə^r] *vt* препя́тствовать (*perf* воспрепя́тствовать) *or* меша́ть (*perf* помеша́ть) *+dat*

hindsight ['haɪndsaɪt] *n*: **with hindsight** ретроспекти́вным взгля́дом

Hindu ['hɪndu:] *adj* инду́сский

hinge [hɪndʒ] *n* (*on door*) петля́

hint [hɪnt] *n* (*suggestion*) намёк; (*tip*) сове́т; (*sign, glimmer*) подо́бие

hip [hɪp] *n* бедро́

hippopotamus [hɪpə'pɔtəməs] (*pl* **hippopotamuses** *or* **hippopotami**) *n* гиппопота́м

hire ['haɪə^r] *vt* (*Brit*: *car, equipment*) брать (*perf* взять) напрока́т; (*venue*) снима́ть (*perf* снять), арендова́ть (*impf/perf*); (*worker*) нанима́ть (*perf* наня́ть) ▷ *n* (*Brit*: *of car*) прока́т; **for hire** напрока́т; **hire-purchase** *n* (*Brit*): **to buy sth on hire-purchase** покупа́ть (*perf* купи́ть) что-н в рассро́чку

his [hɪz] *adj* его́; (*referring to subject of sentence*) свой; *see also* **my** ▷ *pron* его́; *see also* **mine**[1]

hiss [hɪs] *vi* (*snake, gas*) шипе́ть (*impf*)

historian [hɪ'stɔ:rɪən] *n* исто́рик

historic(al) [hɪ'stɔrɪk(l)] *adj* истори́ческий

history ['hɪstərɪ] *n* (*of town, country*) исто́рия

hit [hɪt] (*pt* **hit**) *vt* ударя́ть (*perf* уда́рить); (*target*) попада́ть (*perf* попа́сть) в *+acc*; (*collide with*: *car*) ста́лкиваться (*perf* столкну́ться) с *+instr*; (*affect*: *person, services*) ударя́ть (*perf* уда́рить) по *+dat* ▷ *n* (*Comput*) посеще́ние; (*success*): **the play was a big hit** пье́са по́льзовалась больши́м успе́хом; **to hit it off (with sb)** (*inf*) находи́ть (*perf* найти́) о́бщий язы́к (с кем-н)

hitch [hɪtʃ] *vt* (*also* **hitch up**: *trousers, skirt*) подтя́гивать (*perf* подтяну́ть) ▷ *n* (*difficulty*) поме́ха; **to hitch sth to** (*fasten*) привя́зывать (*perf* привяза́ть) что-н к *+dat*; (*hook*) прицепля́ть (*perf* прицепи́ть) что-н к *+dat*; **to hitch (a lift)** лови́ть (*perf* пойма́ть) попу́тку

hi-tech ['haɪ'tɛk] *adj* высокотехни́ческий

HIV *n abbr* (= *human immunodeficiency virus*) ВИЧ (= *ви́рус иммунодефици́та челове́ка*); **HIV-negative/positive** с отрица́тельной/положи́тельной реа́кцией на ВИЧ

hive [haɪv] *n* (*of bees*) у́лей

hoard [hɔ:d] *n* (*of food*) (та́йный) запа́с; (*of treasure*) клад ▷ *vt* (*provisions*) запаса́ть (*perf* запасти́); (*money*) копи́ть (*perf* скопи́ть)

hoarse [hɔːs] *adj* (*voice*) хри́плый

hoax [həuks] *n* (*false alarm*) ло́жная трево́га

hob [hɔb] *n* *ве́рхняя часть плиты́ с конфо́рками*

hobby ['hɔbɪ] *n* хо́бби *nt ind*

hockey ['hɔkɪ] *n* хокке́й (на траве́)

hog [hɔg] *vt* (*inf*) завладева́ть (*perf* завладе́ть) *+instr*

hoist [hɔɪst] *n* подъёмник, лебёдка ▷ *vt* поднима́ть (*perf* подня́ть); **to hoist sth on to one's shoulders** взва́ливать (*perf* взвали́ть) что-н на пле́чи

hold [həuld] (*pt, pp* **held**) *vt* (*grip*) держа́ть (*impf*); (*contain*) вмеща́ть (*impf*); (*detain*) содержа́ть (*impf*); (*power, qualification*) облада́ть (*impf*) *+instr*; (*post*) занима́ть (*perf* заня́ть); (*conversation, meeting*) вести́ (*perf* провести́); (*party*) устра́ивать (*perf* устро́ить) ▷ *vi* (*withstand pressure*) выде́рживать (*perf* вы́держать); (*be valid*) остава́ться (*perf* оста́ться) в си́ле ▷ *n* (*grasp*) захва́т; (*Naut*) трюм; (*Aviat*) грузово́й отсе́к; **to hold one's head up** высоко́ держа́ть (*impf*) го́лову; **to hold sb hostage** держа́ть (*impf*) кого́-н в ка́честве зало́жника; **hold the line!** (*Tel*) не клади́те *or* ве́шайте тру́бку!; **he holds you responsible for her death** он счита́ет Вас вино́вным в её сме́рти; **to catch** *or* **grab hold of** хвата́ться (*perf* схвати́ться) за *+acc*; **to have a hold over sb** держа́ть (*impf*) кого́-н в рука́х; **hold back** *vt* (*thing*) приде́рживать (*perf* придержа́ть); (*person*) уде́рживать (*perf* удержа́ть); (*information*) скрыва́ть (*perf* скрыть); **hold down** *vt* (*person*) уде́рживать (*perf* удержа́ть); **to hold down a job** уде́рживаться (*perf* удержа́ться) на рабо́те; **hold on** *vi* (*grip*) держа́ться (*impf*); (*wait*) ждать (*perf* подожда́ть); **hold on!** (*Tel*) не клади́те *or* ве́шайте тру́бку!; **hold on to** *vt fus* (*for support*) держа́ться (*impf*) за *+acc*; (*keep: object*) приде́рживать (*perf* придержа́ть); (*: beliefs*) сохраня́ть (*perf* сохрани́ть); **hold out** *vt* (*hand*) протя́гивать (*perf* протяну́ть); (*hope, prospect*) сохраня́ть (*perf* сохрани́ть) ▷ *vi* (*resist*) держа́ться (*perf* продержа́ться); **hold up** *vt* (*raise*) поднима́ть (*perf* подня́ть); (*support*) подде́рживать (*perf* поддержа́ть); (*delay*) заде́рживать (*perf* задержа́ть); (*rob*) гра́бить (*perf* огра́бить); **holder** *n* (*container*) держа́тель *m*; (*of ticket, record*) облада́тель(ница) *m(f)*; **title holder** нося́щий(-ая) *m(f) adj* ти́тул

hole [həul] *n* (*in wall*) дыра́; (*in road*) я́ма; (*burrow*) нора́; (*in clothing*) ды́рка; (*in argument*) брешь *f*

holiday ['hɔlɪdeɪ] *n* (*Brit: from school*) кани́кулы *pl*; (*: from work*) о́тпуск; (*day off*) выходно́й день *m*; (*also* **public holiday**) пра́здник; **on holiday** (*from school*) на кани́кулах; (*from work*) в о́тпуске

Holland ['hɔlənd] *n* Голла́ндия

hollow ['hɔləu] *adj* (*container*) по́лый; (*log, tree*) дупли́стый; (*cheeks*) впа́лый; (*laugh*) неи́скренний; (*claim, sound*) пусто́й ▷ *n* (*in ground*) впа́дина;

(*in tree*) дупло́ ▷ *vt*: **to hollow out** выка́пывать (*perf* вы́копать)
holly ['hɔlɪ] *n* остроли́ст
holocaust ['hɔləkɔ:st] *n* (*nuclear*) истребле́ние; (*Jewish*) холоко́ст
holy ['həulɪ] *adj* свято́й
home [həum] *n* дом; (*area, country*) ро́дина ▷ *cpd* дома́шний; (*Econ, Pol*) вну́тренний; (*Sport*): **home team** хозя́ева *mpl* по́ля ▷ *adv* (*go, come*) домо́й; (*hammer etc*) в то́чку; **at home** до́ма; (*in country*) на ро́дине; (*in situation*) как у себя́ до́ма; **make yourself at home** чу́вствуйте себя́ как до́ма; **homeland** *n* ро́дина; **homeless** *adj* бездо́мный ▷ *npl*: **the homeless** бездо́мные *pl adj*; **homely** *adj* ую́тный; **home-made** *adj* (*food*) дома́шний; (*bomb*) самоде́льный; **Home Office** *n* (*Brit*): **the Home Office** ≈ Министе́рство вну́тренних дел; **home page** *n* электро́нная страни́ца *or* страни́чка; **Home Secretary** *n* (*Brit*) ≈ мини́стр вну́тренних дел; **homesick** *adj*: **to be homesick** (*for family*) скуча́ть (*impf*) по до́му; (*for country*) скуча́ть (*impf*) по ро́дине; **homework** *n* дома́шняя рабо́та, дома́шнее зада́ние
homicide ['hɔmɪsaɪd] *n* (*esp US*) уби́йство
homosexual [hɔməu'sɛksjuəl] *adj* гомосексуа́льный ▷ *n* гомосексуали́ст(ка)
honest ['ɔnɪst] *adj* че́стный; **honestly** *adv* че́стно; **honesty** *n* че́стность *f*
honey ['hʌnɪ] *n* (*food*) мёд; **honeymoon** *n* медо́вый ме́сяц; **honeysuckle** *n* жи́молость *f*
honorary ['ɔnərərɪ] *adj* почётный
honour ['ɔnə^r] (*US* **honor**) *vt* (*person*) почита́ть (*impf*), чтить (*impf*); (*commitment*) выполня́ть (*perf* вы́полнить) ▷ *n* (*pride*) честь *f*; (*tribute, distinction*) по́честь *f*; **honourable** *adj* (*person, action*) благоро́дный

HONOURS DEGREE

Honours degree — (учёная) сте́пень. Большинство́ студе́нтов университе́та получа́ют учёную сте́пень. Така́я сте́пень вы́ше по у́ровню, чем так называ́емая "обы́чная сте́пень" или "зачёт".

hood [hud] *n* капюшо́н; (*US*: *Aut*) капо́т; (*of cooker*) вытяжно́й колпа́к
hoof [hu:f] (*pl* **hooves**) *n* копы́то
hook [huk] *n* крючо́к ▷ *vt* прицепля́ть (*perf* прицепи́ть)
hooligan ['hu:lɪgən] *n* хулига́н
hoop [hu:p] *n* о́бруч
hoover ['hu:və^r] (*Brit*) *n* пылесо́с ▷ *vt* пылесо́сить (*perf* пропылесо́сить)
hooves [hu:vz] *npl of* **hoof**
hop [hɔp] *vi* скака́ть (*impf*) на одно́й ноге́
hope [həup] *vt, vi* наде́яться (*impf*) ▷ *n* наде́жда; **to hope that/ to do** наде́яться (*impf*), что/+*infin*; **I hope so/not** наде́юсь, что да/нет; **hopeful** *adj* (*person*) по́лный наде́жд; (*situation*) обнадёживающий; **to be hopeful of sth** наде́яться (*impf*) на что-н; **hopefully** *adv* (*expectantly*) с наде́ждой; **hopefully, he'll come back** бу́дем наде́яться, что он вернётся; **hopeless** *adj*

(*situation, person*) безнадёжный; **I'm hopeless at names** я не в состоя́нии запомина́ть имена́
hops [hɔps] *npl* хмель *msg*
horizon [həˈraɪzn] *n* горизо́нт; **horizontal** [hɔrɪˈzɔntl] *adj* горизонта́льный
hormone [ˈhɔːməun] *n* гормо́н
horn [hɔːn] *n* (*of animal*) рог; (*also* **French horn**) валто́рна; (*Aut*) гудо́к
horoscope [ˈhɔrəskəup] *n* гороско́п
horrendous [həˈrɛndəs] *adj* ужаса́ющий
horrible [ˈhɔrɪbl] *adj* ужа́сный
horrid [ˈhɔrɪd] *adj* проти́вный, ме́рзкий
horror [ˈhɔrəʳ] *n* (*alarm*) у́жас; (*dislike*) отвраще́ние; (*of war*) у́жасы *mpl*
horse [hɔːs] *n* ло́шадь *f*; **horseback** *adv*: **on horseback** верхо́м; **horsepower** *n* лошади́ная си́ла; **horse racing** *n* ска́чки *fpl*; **horseradish** *n* хрен
hose [həuz] *n* (*also* **hosepipe**) шланг
hospital [ˈhɔspɪtl] *n* больни́ца
hospitality [hɔspɪˈtælɪtɪ] *n* гостеприи́мство
host [həust] *n* (*at party, dinner*) хозя́ин; (*TV, Radio*) веду́щий *m adj*; **a host of** ма́сса *+gen*, мно́жество *+gen*
hostage [ˈhɔstɪdʒ] *n* зало́жник(-ица)
hostel [ˈhɔstl] *n* общежи́тие; (*for homeless*) прию́т; (*also* **youth hostel**) молодёжная гости́ница
hostess [ˈhəustɪs] *n* (*at party, dinner etc*) хозя́йка; (*TV, Radio*) веду́щая *f adj*; (*Brit*: *also* **air hostess**) стюарде́сса
hostile [ˈhɔstaɪl] *adj* (*person, attitude*) вражде́бный; (*conditions, environment*) неблагоприя́тный; (*troops*) вра́жеский
hostility [hɔˈstɪlɪtɪ] *n* вражде́бность *f*
hot [hɔt] *adj* (*object, temper, argument*) горя́чий; (*weather*) жа́ркий; (*spicy*: *food*) о́стрый; **she is hot** ей жа́рко; **it's hot** (*weather*) жа́рко
hotel [həuˈtɛl] *n* гости́ница, оте́ль *m*
hotspot [ˈhɔtspɔt] *n* (*Comput*: *also* **wireless hotspot**) хо́т-спо́т *m*
hot-water bottle [hɔtˈwɔːtə-] *n* гре́лка
hound [haund] *vt* трави́ть (*perf* затрави́ть) ▷ *n* го́нчая *f adj*
hour [ˈauəʳ] *n* час; **hourly** *adj* (*rate*) почасово́й; (*service*) ежеча́сный
house [*n* haus, *vb* hauz] *n* дом; (*Theat*) зал ▷ *vt* (*person*) сели́ть (*perf* посели́ть); (*collection*) размеща́ть (*perf* размести́ть); **at my house** у меня́ до́ма; **the House of Commons/Lords** (*Brit*) Пала́та о́бщин/ло́рдов; **on the house** (*inf*) беспла́тно; **household** *n* (*inhabitants*) домоча́дцы *mpl*; (*home*) дом; **housekeeper** *n* эконо́мка; **housewife** *irreg n* дома́шняя хозя́йка, домохозя́йка; **housework** *n* дома́шние дела́ *ntpl*

House of Lords

House of Lords — Пала́та ло́рдов. Брита́нский парла́мент состои́т из двух пала́т: из Пала́ты о́бщин, чле́ны кото́рой избира́ются и Пала́ты ло́рдов, кото́рая в настоя́щее вре́мя переживáет периóд реформ. До недáвнего врéмени её члéны не избирáлись.

housing ['hauzɪŋ] *n* жильё; **housing estate** (*US* **housing project**) *n* жилищный кóмплекс; (*larger*) жилóй массив
hover ['hɔvəʳ] *vi* (*bird, insect*) парить (*impf*); **hovercraft** *n* сýдно на воздýшной подýшке

 **KEYWORD**

how [hau] *adv* **1** (*in what way*) как; **to know how to do** умéть (*impf*) +*infin*, знать (*impf*), как +*infin*; **how did you like the film?** как Вам понрáвился фильм?; **how are you?** как делá *or* Вы?
2 скóлько; **how much milk/many people?** скóлько молокá/человéк?; **how long?** как дóлго?, скóлько врéмени?; **how old are you?** скóлько Вам лет?; **how tall is he?** какóго он рóста?; **how lovely/awful!** как чудéсно/ужáсно!

howl [haul] *vi* (*animal, wind*) выть (*impf*); (*baby, person*) ревéть (*impf*)
HP *n abbr* (*Brit*) = **hire-purchase**
h.p. *abbr* (*Aut*) (= *horsepower*) л.с. (= *лошадиная сила*)
HQ *abbr* = **headquarters**
HTML *abbr* (= *hypertext markup language*) гипертекст
hug [hʌg] *vt* обнимáть (*perf* обнять); (*object*) обхвáтывать (*perf* обхватить)
huge [hju:dʒ] *adj* огрóмный, громáдный
hull [hʌl] *n* (*Naut*) кóрпус
hum [hʌm] *vt* напевáть (*impf*) (*без слов*) ▷ *vi* (*person*) напевáть (*impf*); (*machine*) гудéть (*perf* прогудéть)
human ['hju:mən] *adj* человéческий ▷ *n* (*also* **human being**) человéк
humane [hju:'meɪn] *adj* (*treatment*) человéчный
humanitarian [hju:mænɪ'tɛərɪən] *adj* (*aid*) гуманитáрный; (*principles*) гумáнный
humanity [hju:'mænɪtɪ] *n* (*mankind*) человéчество; (*humaneness*) человéчность *f*, гумáнность *f*
human rights *npl* правá *ntpl* человéка
humble ['hʌmbl] *adj* скрóмный ▷ *vt* сбивáть (*perf* сбить) спесь с +*gen*
humidity [hju:'mɪdɪtɪ] *n* влáжность *f*
humiliate [hju:'mɪlɪeɪt] *vt* унижáть (*perf* унизить)
humiliation [hju:mɪlɪ'eɪʃən] *n* унижéние
humorous ['hju:mərəs] *adj* (*book*) юмористический; (*remark*) шутливый; **humorous person** человéк с юмором
humour ['hju:məʳ] (*US* **humor**) *n* юмор; (*mood*) настроéние ▷ *vt* ублажáть (*perf* ублажить)
hump [hʌmp] *n* (*in ground*) бугóр; (*on back*) горб
hunch [hʌntʃ] *n* догáдка
hundred ['hʌndrəd] *n* сто; **hundredth** *adj* сóтый
hung [hʌŋ] *pt, pp of* **hang**
Hungarian [hʌŋ'gɛərɪən] *adj* венгéрский
Hungary ['hʌŋgərɪ] *n* Вéнгрия
hunger ['hʌŋgəʳ] *n* гóлод
hungry ['hʌŋgrɪ] *adj* голóдный; (*keen*): **hungry for** жáждущий +*gen*; **he is hungry** он гóлоден

hunt [hʌnt] *vt* (*animal*) охо́титься (*impf*) на *+acc*; (*criminal*) охо́титься (*impf*) за *+instr* ▷ *vi* (*Sport*) охо́титься (*impf*) ▷ *n* охо́та; (*for criminal*) ро́зыск; **to hunt (for)** (*search*) иска́ть (*impf*); **hunter** *n* охо́тник(-ица); **hunting** *n* охо́та

hurdle ['hə:dl] *n* препя́тствие; (*Sport*) барье́р

hurricane ['hʌrɪkən] *n* урага́н

hurry ['hʌrɪ] *n* спе́шка ▷ *vi* спеши́ть (*perf* поспеши́ть), торопи́ться (*perf* поторопи́ться) ▷ *vt* (*person*) подгоня́ть (*perf* подогна́ть), торопи́ть (*perf* поторопи́ть); **to be in a hurry** спеши́ть (*impf*), торопи́ться (*impf*); **hurry up** *vt* (*person*) подгоня́ть (*perf* подогна́ть), торопи́ть (*perf* поторопи́ть); (*process*) ускоря́ть (*perf* ускорить) ▷ *vi* торопи́ться (*perf* поторопи́ться); **hurry up!** поторопи́сь!, скоре́е!

hurt [hə:t] (*pt, pp* **hurt**) *vt* причиня́ть (*perf* причини́ть) боль *+dat*; (*injure*) ушиба́ть (*perf* ушиби́ть); (*feelings*) задева́ть (*perf* заде́ть) ▷ *vi* (*be painful*) боле́ть (*impf*) ▷ *adj* (*offended*) оби́женный; (*injured*) ушибленный; **to hurt o.s.** ушиба́ться (*perf* ушиби́ться)

husband ['hʌzbənd] *n* муж

hush [hʌʃ] *n* тишина́; **hush!** ти́хо!, ти́ше!

husky ['hʌskɪ] *adj* (*voice*) хри́плый ▷ *n* ездова́я соба́ка

hut [hʌt] *n* (*house*) избу́шка, хи́жина; (*shed*) сара́й

hyacinth ['haɪəsɪnθ] *n* гиаци́нт

hydrogen ['haɪdrədʒən] *n* водоро́д

hygiene ['haɪdʒi:n] *n* гигие́на

hygienic [haɪ'dʒi:nɪk] *adj* (*product*) гигиени́ческий

hymn [hɪm] *n* церко́вный гимн

hype [haɪp] *n* (*inf*) ажиота́ж

hyperlink ['haɪpəlɪŋk] *n* гиперссы́лка

hypocritical [hɪpə'krɪtɪkl] *adj* лицеме́рный

hypothesis [haɪ'pɔθɪsɪs] (*pl* **hypotheses**) *n* гипо́теза

I

I [aɪ] *pron* я
ice [aɪs] *n* лёд; (*ice cream*) моро́женое *nt adj* ▷ *vt* покрыва́ть (*perf* покры́ть) глазу́рью; **iceberg** *n* а́йсберг; **ice cream** *n* моро́женое *nt adj*; **ice hockey** *n* хокке́й (*на льду*)
Iceland ['aɪslənd] *n* Исла́ндия
icing ['aɪsɪŋ] *n* глазу́рь *f*; **icing sugar** *n* (*Brit*) са́харная пу́дра (*для приготовле́ния глазу́ри*)
icon ['aɪkɔn] *n* (*Rel*) ико́на; (*Comput*) ико́нка
icy ['aɪsɪ] *adj* (*cold*) ледяно́й; (*road*) обледене́лый
I'd [aɪd] = **I would**; **I had**
idea [aɪ'dɪə] *n* иде́я
ideal [aɪ'dɪəl] *n* идеа́л ▷ *adj* идеа́льный
identical [aɪ'dɛntɪkl] *adj* иденти́чный
identification [aɪdɛntɪfɪ'keɪʃən] *n* определе́ние, идентифика́ция; (*of person, body*) опозна́ние; **(means of) identification** удостовере́ние ли́чности
identify [aɪ'dɛntɪfaɪ] *vt* определя́ть (*perf* определи́ть); (*person*) узнава́ть (*perf* узна́ть); (*body*) опознава́ть (*perf* опозна́ть); (*distinguish*) выявля́ть (*perf* вы́явить)
identity [aɪ'dɛntɪtɪ] *n* (*of person*) ли́чность *f*; (*of group, nation*) самосозна́ние
ideology [aɪdɪ'ɔlədʒɪ] *n* идеоло́гия
idiom ['ɪdɪəm] *n* (*phrase*) идио́ма
idiot ['ɪdɪət] *n* идио́т(ка)
idle ['aɪdl] *adj* пра́здный; (*lazy*) лени́вый; (*unemployed*) безрабо́тный; (*machinery, factory*) безде́йствующий; **to be idle** безде́йствовать (*impf*)
idol ['aɪdl] *n* куми́р; (*Rel*) и́дол
idyllic [ɪ'dɪlɪk] *adj* идилли́ческий
i.e. *abbr* (*that is*) (= *id est*) т.е. (= *то есть*)

KEYWORD

if [ɪf] *conj* **1** (*conditional use*) е́сли; **if I finish early, I will ring you** е́сли я зако́нчу ра́но, я тебе́ позвоню́; **if I were you (I would ...)** на Ва́шем ме́сте (я бы ...)
2 (*whenever*) когда́
3 (*although*): **(even) if** да́же е́сли; **I'll get it done, (even) if it takes all night** я сде́лаю э́то, да́же е́сли э́то займёт у меня́ всю ночь
4 (*whether*) ли; **I don't know if he is here** я не зна́ю, здесь ли он; **ask him if he can stay** спроси́те, смо́жет ли он оста́ться
5: if so/not е́сли да/нет; **if only** е́сли бы то́лько; **if only I could** е́сли бы я то́лько мог; *see also* **as**

ignite [ɪg'naɪt] *vt* (*set fire to*) зажига́ть (*perf* зажéчь) ▷ *vi* загора́ться (*perf* загорéться)
ignition [ɪg'nɪʃən] *n* (*Aut*) зажига́ние
ignorance ['ɪgnərəns] *n* невéжество
ignorant ['ɪgnərənt] *adj* невéжественный; **ignorant of** (*a subject*) несвéдущий в +*prp*; (*unaware of*): **he is ignorant of that fact** он не зна́ет об э́том
ignore [ɪg'nɔːʳ] *vt* игнори́ровать (*impf/perf*); (*disregard*) пренебрега́ть (*perf* пренебрéчь)
I'll [aɪl] = **I will; I shall**
ill [ɪl] *adj* больно́й; (*effects*) дурно́й ▷ *adv*: **to speak ill (of sb)** ду́рно говори́ть (*impf*) (о ком-н); **he is ill** он бо́лен; **to be taken ill** заболева́ть (*perf* заболéть)
illegal [ɪ'liːgl] *adj* незако́нный; (*organization*) нелега́льный
illegible [ɪ'lɛdʒɪbl] *adj* неразбо́рчивый
illegitimate [ɪlɪ'dʒɪtɪmət] *adj* (*child*) внебра́чный; (*activities*) незако́нный, нелегити́мный
ill health [ɪl'hɛlθ] *n* плохо́е здоро́вье
illiterate [ɪ'lɪtərət] *adj* негра́мотный
illness ['ɪlnɪs] *n* болéзнь *f*
illuminate [ɪ'luːmɪneɪt] *vt* (*light up*) освеща́ть (*perf* освети́ть)
illusion [ɪ'luːʒən] *n* (*false idea*) иллю́зия; (*trick*) фо́кус
illustrate ['ɪləstreɪt] *vt* иллюстри́ровать (*perf* проиллюстри́ровать)
illustration [ɪlə'streɪʃən] *n* иллюстра́ция
I'm [aɪm] = **I am**
image ['ɪmɪdʒ] *n* (*picture*) о́браз; (*public face*) и́мидж; (*reflection*) изображéние
imaginary [ɪ'mædʒɪnərɪ] *adj* (*creature, land*) вообража́емый
imagination [ɪmædʒɪ'neɪʃən] *n* воображéние
imaginative [ɪ'mædʒɪnətɪv] *adj* (*solution*) хитроу́мный; **he is very imaginative** он облада́ет бога́тым воображéнием
imagine [ɪ'mædʒɪn] *vt* (*visualize*) представля́ть (*perf* предста́вить) (себé), вообража́ть (*perf* вообрази́ть); (*dream*) вообража́ть (*perf* вообрази́ть); (*suppose*) предполага́ть (*perf* предположи́ть)
imitate ['ɪmɪteɪt] *vt* подража́ть (*impf*) +*dat*, имити́ровать (*impf*)
imitation [ɪmɪ'teɪʃən] *n* подража́ние, имита́ция
immaculate [ɪ'mækjulət] *adj* безупрéчный
immature [ɪmə'tjuəʳ] *adj* незрéлый
immediate [ɪ'miːdɪət] *adj* (*reaction, answer*) немéдленный; (*need*) безотлага́тельный; (*family*) ближа́йший; **immediately** *adv* (*at once*) немéдленно; (*directly*) сра́зу
immense [ɪ'mɛns] *adj* огро́мный, грома́дный
immigrant ['ɪmɪgrənt] *n* иммигра́нт(ка)
immigration [ɪmɪ'greɪʃən] *n* иммигра́ция; (*also* **immigration control**) иммигра́цио́нный контро́ль
imminent ['ɪmɪnənt] *adj* (*arrival, departure*) немину́емый
immoral [ɪ'mɔrl] *adj* амора́льный, безнра́вственный
immortal [ɪ'mɔːtl] *adj* бессмéртный
immune [ɪ'mjuːn] *adj*: **he is**

immune to (*disease*) у негó иммунитéт прóтив *+gen*; (*flattery, criticism etc*) он невосприймчив к *+dat*; **immune system** *n* иммýная систéма

immunize [ˈɪmjunaɪz] *vt*: **to immunize sb (against)** дéлать (*perf* сдéлать) комý-н привúвку (прóтив *+gen*)

impact [ˈɪmpækt] *n* (*of crash*) удáр; (*force*) удáрная сúла; (*of law, measure*) воздéйствие

impartial [ɪmˈpɑːʃl] *adj* беспристрáстный

impatience [ɪmˈpeɪʃəns] *n* нетерпéние

impatient [ɪmˈpeɪʃənt] *adj* нетерпелúвый; **to get** *or* **grow impatient** терять (*perf* потерять) терпéние; **she was impatient to leave** ей не терпéлось уйтú

impeccable [ɪmˈpɛkəbl] *adj* безупрéчный

impending [ɪmˈpɛndɪŋ] *adj* грядýщий

imperative [ɪmˈpɛrətɪv] *adj*: **it is imperative that ...** необходúмо, чтóбы ...

imperfect [ɪmˈpəːfɪkt] *adj* (*system*) несовершéнный; (*goods*) дефéктный

imperial [ɪmˈpɪərɪəl] *adj* (*history, power*) импéрский; (*Brit*: *measure*): **imperial system** *британская систéма единúц измерéния и вéса*

impersonal [ɪmˈpəːsənl] *adj* (*organization, place*) безлúкий

impersonate [ɪmˈpəːsəneɪt] *vt* выдавáть (*perf* вы́дать) себя за *+acc*

implement [*vb* ˈɪmplɪmɛnt, *n* ˈɪmplɪmənt] *vt* проводúть (*perf* провестú) в жизнь ▷ *n* (*for gardening*) орýдие

implication [ɪmplɪˈkeɪʃən] *n* (*inference*) слéдствие

implicit [ɪmˈplɪsɪt] *adj* (*inferred*) невы́раженный, имплицúтный; (*unquestioning*) безоговóрочный

imply [ɪmˈplaɪ] *vt* (*hint*) намекáть (*perf* намекнýть); (*mean*) означáть (*impf*)

import [*vb* ɪmˈpɔːt, *n, cpd* ˈɪmpɔːt] *vt* импортúровать (*impf/perf*), ввозúть (*perf* ввезтú) ▷ *n* (*article*) импортúруемый товáр; (*importation*) úмпорт ▷ *cpd*: **import duty/licence** пóшлина/лицéнзия на ввоз

importance [ɪmˈpɔːtns] *n* вáжность *f*

important [ɪmˈpɔːtnt] *adj* вáжный; **it's not important** э́то невáжно

impose [ɪmˈpəuz] *vt* (*restrictions, fine*) налагáть (*perf* наложúть); (*discipline, rules*) вводúть (*perf* ввестú) ▷ *vi* навя́зываться (*perf* навязáться)

imposing [ɪmˈpəuzɪŋ] *adj* велúчественный

impossible [ɪmˈpɔsɪbl] *adj* (*task, demand*) невыполнúмый; (*situation, person*) невыносúмый

impotent [ˈɪmpətnt] *adj* бессúльный

impractical [ɪmˈpræktɪkl] *adj* (*plan etc*) нереáльный; (*person*) непрактúчный

impress [ɪmˈprɛs] *vt* (*person*) производúть (*perf* произвестú) впечатлéние на *+acc*; **to impress sth on sb** внушáть (*perf* внушúть) что-н комý-н

impression [ɪmˈprɛʃən] *n* впечатлéние; (*of stamp, seal*) отпечáток; (*imitation*) имитáция; **he is under the impression that ...** у негó создалóсь впечатлéние, что ...

impressive [ɪm'prɛsɪv] *adj* впечатля́ющий
imprison [ɪm'prɪzn] *vt* заключа́ть (*perf* заключи́ть) в тюрьму́; **imprisonment** *n* (тюре́мное) заключе́ние
improbable [ɪm'prɔbəbl] *adj* невероя́тный
improve [ɪm'pru:v] *vt* улучша́ть (*perf* улу́чшить) ▷ *vi* улучша́ться (*perf* улу́чшиться); (*pupil*) станови́ться (*perf* стать) лу́чше; **the patient improved** больно́му ста́ло лу́чше; **improvement** *n*: **improvement (in)** улучше́ние (+*gen*)
improvise ['ɪmprəvaɪz] *vt, vi* импровизи́ровать (*impf/perf*)
impulse ['ɪmpʌls] *n* (*urge*) поры́в; **to act on impulse** поддава́ться (*perf* подда́ться) поры́ву
impulsive [ɪm'pʌlsɪv] *adj* (*person*) импульси́вный; (*gesture*) поры́вистый

 **KEYWORD**

in [ɪn] *prep* **1** (*indicating position*) в/на +*prp*; **in the house/garden** в до́ме/саду́; **in the street/Ukraine** на у́лице/Украи́не; **in London/Canada** в Ло́ндоне/Кана́де; **in the country** в дере́вне; **in town** в го́роде; **in here** здесь; **in there** там
2 (*indicating motion*) в/на +*acc*; **in the house/room** в дом/ко́мнату
3 (*indicating time: during*): **in spring/summer/autumn/winter** весно́й/ле́том/о́сенью/зимо́й; **in the morning/afternoon/evening** у́тром/днём/ве́чером; **in the evenings** по вечера́м; **at 4 o'clock in the afternoon** в 4 часа́ дня
4 (*indicating time: in the space of*) за +*acc*; (: *after a period of*) че́рез +*acc*; **I did it in 3 hours** я сде́лал э́то за 3 часа́; **I'll see you in 2 weeks** уви́димся че́рез 2 неде́ли
5 (*indicating manner etc*): **in a loud/quiet voice** гро́мким/ти́хим го́лосом; **in English/Russian** по-англи́йски/по-ру́сски, на англи́йском/ру́сском языке́
6 (*wearing*) в +*prp*; **the boy in the blue shirt** ма́льчик в голубо́й руба́шке
7 (*indicating circumstances*): **in the sun** на со́лнце; **in the rain** под дождём; **in the shade** в тени́; **a rise in prices** повыше́ние цен
8 (*indicating mood, state*) в +*prp*; **in despair** в отча́янии
9 (*with ratios, numbers*): **one in ten households** одна́ из десяти́ семе́й; **20 pence in the pound** 20 пе́нсов с ка́ждого фу́нта; **they lined up in twos** они́ вы́строились по́ двое; **a gradient of one in five** укло́н оди́н к пяти́
10 (*referring to people, works*) у +*gen*; **the disease is common in children** э́то заболева́ние ча́сто встреча́ется у дете́й; **in Dickens** у Ди́ккенса; **you have a good friend in him** он тебе́ хоро́ший друг
11 (*indicating profession etc*): **to be in publishing/advertising** занима́ться (*impf*) изда́тельским де́лом/рекла́мным би́знесом; **to be in teaching** рабо́тать (*impf*) учи́телем; **to be in the army** быть (*impf*) в а́рмии
12 (*with present participle*): **in saying this** говоря́ э́то; **in behaving like this, she ...** поступа́я таки́м о́бразом, она́ ...
▷ *adv*: **to be in** (*train, ship, plane*) прибыва́ть (*perf* прибы́ть); (*in fashion*) быть (*impf*) в мо́де; **is he**

in today? он сего́дня здесь?; **he is not in today** его́ сего́дня нет; **he wasn't in yesterday** его́ вчера́ не́ было; **he'll be in later today** он бу́дет по́зже сего́дня; **to ask sb in** предлага́ть (*perf* предложи́ть) кому́-н войти́; **to run/walk in** вбега́ть (*perf* вбежа́ть)/входи́ть (*perf* войти́)
▷ *n*: **to know all the ins and outs** знать (*impf*) все ходы́ и вы́ходы

in. *abbr* = **inch**
inability [ɪnəˈbɪlɪtɪ] *n*: **inability (to do)** неспосо́бность *f* (+*infin*)
inaccurate [ɪnˈækjurət] *adj* нето́чный
inadequate [ɪnˈædɪkwət] *adj* недоста́точный; (*work*) неудовлетвори́тельный; (*person*) некомпете́нтный; **to feel inadequate** чу́вствовать (*impf*) себя́ не на у́ровне
inadvertently [ɪnədˈvəːtntlɪ] *adv* неча́янно, неумы́шленно
inappropriate [ɪnəˈprəuprɪət] *adj* (*unsuitable*) неподходя́щий; (*improper*) неуме́стный
inbox [ˈɪnbɔks] *n* па́пка "Входя́щие"
Inc. *abbr* = **incorporated**
incapable [ɪnˈkeɪpəbl] *adj* (*helpless*) беспо́мощный; **incapable of sth/doing** неспосо́бный на что-н/+*infin*
incense [*n* ˈɪnsɛns, *vb* ɪnˈsɛns] *n* ла́дан ▷ *vt* приводи́ть (*perf* привести́) в я́рость
incentive [ɪnˈsɛntɪv] *n* сти́мул
inch [ɪntʃ] *n* дюйм

INCH

Inch – ме́ра длины́ ра́вная 2,54 см.

incidence [ˈɪnsɪdns] *n* число́; **high incidence** высо́кий у́ровень
incident [ˈɪnsɪdnt] *n* (*event*) слу́чай; **without incident** без происше́ствий; **incidentally** [ɪnsɪˈdɛntəlɪ] *adv* (*by the way*) кста́ти, ме́жду про́чим
inclination [ɪnklɪˈneɪʃən] *n* (*desire*) располо́женность *f*; (*tendency*) скло́нность *f*
incline [*n* ˈɪnklaɪn, *vb* ɪnˈklaɪn] *n* (*slope*) укло́н, накло́н ▷ *vi*: **he is inclined to ...** он скло́нен +*infin* ....; **he is inclined to depression** он скло́нен к депре́ссиям
include [ɪnˈkluːd] *vt* включа́ть (*perf* включи́ть)
including [ɪnˈkluːdɪŋ] *prep* включа́я +*acc*
inclusion [ɪnˈkluːʒən] *n* включе́ние
inclusive [ɪnˈkluːsɪv] *adj*: **inclusive of** включа́я +*acc*; **the price is fully inclusive** цена́ включа́ет в себя́ всё; **from March 1st to 5th inclusive** с 1-ого до 5-ого ма́рта включи́тельно
income [ˈɪnkʌm] *n* дохо́д; **income support** *n* де́нежное посо́бие (*се́мьям с ни́зким дохо́дом*); **income tax** *n* подохо́дный нало́г
incompatible [ɪnkəmˈpætɪbl] *adj* несовмести́мый
incompetence [ɪnˈkɔmpɪtns] *n* некомпете́нтность *f*
incompetent [ɪnˈkɔmpɪtnt] *adj* (*person*) некомпете́нтный; (*work*) неуме́лый
incomplete [ɪnkəmˈpliːt] *adj* (*unfinished*) незавершённый; (*partial*) непо́лный
inconsistent [ɪnkənˈsɪstnt] *adj* (*actions*) непосле́довательный; (*statement*) противоречи́вый;

(*work*) неро́вный; **inconsistent with** (*beliefs, values*) несовмести́мый с *+instr*

inconvenience [ɪnkənˈviːnjəns] *n* (*problem*) неудо́бство ▷ *vt* причиня́ть (*perf* причини́ть) беспоко́йство *+dat*

inconvenient [ɪnkənˈviːnjənt] *adj* неудо́бный

incorporate [ɪnˈkɔːpəreɪt] *vt* (*contain*) включа́ть (*impf*) в себя́, содержа́ть (*impf*); **to incorporate (into)** включа́ть (*perf* включи́ть) (в *+acc*)

incorrect [ɪnkəˈrɛkt] *adj* неве́рный, непра́вильный

increase [*n* ˈɪnkriːs, *vb* ɪnˈkriːs] *n*: **increase (in), increase (of)** увеличе́ние (*+gen*) ▷ *vi* увели́чиваться (*perf* увели́читься) ▷ *vt* увели́чивать (*perf* увели́чить); (*price*) поднима́ть (*perf* подня́ть)

increasingly *adv* (*with comparative*) всё; (*more intensely*) всё бо́лее; (*more often*) всё ча́ще

incredible [ɪnˈkrɛdɪbl] *adj* невероя́тный

incur [ɪnˈkəːʳ] *vt* (*expenses, loss*) нести́ (*perf* понести́); (*debt*) накопи́ть (*perf*); (*disapproval, anger*) навлека́ть (*perf* навле́чь) на себя́

indecent [ɪnˈdiːsnt] *adj* непристо́йный

indeed [ɪnˈdiːd] *adv* (*certainly*) действи́тельно, в са́мом де́ле; (*in fact, furthermore*) бо́лее того́; **this book is very interesting indeed** э́та кни́га весьма́ интере́сная; **thank you very much indeed** большо́е Вам спаси́бо; **he is indeed very talented** он на са́мом де́ле о́чень тала́нтлив; **yes indeed!** да, действи́тельно *or* коне́чно!

indefinitely *adv* (*continue, wait*) бесконе́чно; (*be closed, delayed*) на неопределённое вре́мя

independence [ɪndɪˈpɛndns] *n* незави́симость *f*

independent [ɪndɪˈpɛndnt] *adj* незави́симый

index [ˈɪndɛks] (*pl* **indexes**) *n* (*in book*) указа́тель *m*; (*in library etc*) катало́г; **price index** и́ндекс цен

India [ˈɪndɪə] *n* И́ндия; **Indian** *adj* инди́йский ▷ *n* инди́ец

indicate [ˈɪndɪkeɪt] *vt* ука́зывать (*perf* указа́ть) на *+acc*; (*mention*) ука́зывать (*perf* указа́ть)

indication [ɪndɪˈkeɪʃən] *n* знак; **all the indications are that ...** всё ука́зывает на то, что ...

indicative [ɪnˈdɪkətɪv] *adj*: **to be indicative of** свиде́тельствовать (*impf*) о *+prp*, ука́зывать (*impf*) на *+acc*

indicator [ˈɪndɪkeɪtəʳ] *n* (*Aut*) указа́тель *m* поворо́та; (*fig*) показа́тель *m*

indifference [ɪnˈdɪfrəns] *n* безразли́чие, равноду́шие

indifferent [ɪnˈdɪfrənt] *adj* безразли́чный, равноду́шный; (*mediocre*) посре́дственный

indigestion [ɪndɪˈdʒɛstʃən] *n* несваре́ние желу́дка

indignant [ɪnˈdɪgnənt] *adj*: **indignant at sth/with sb** возмущённый чем-н/кем-н

indirect [ɪndɪˈrɛkt] *adj* (*way*) око́льный, обхо́дный; (*answer*) уклóнчивый; (*effect*) побо́чный; **indirect object** (*Ling*) ко́свенное дополне́ние

indispensable [ɪndɪsˈpɛnsəbl] *adj* (*object*) необходи́мый; (*person*) незамени́мый

individual [ɪndɪˈvɪdjuəl] *n*

личность *f*, индивидуум ▷ *adj* индивидуальный; **certain individuals** отдельные личности; **individually** *adv* в отдельности; (*responsible*) лично

indoor [ˈɪndɔːʳ] *adj* (*plant*) комнатный; (*pool*) закрытый; **indoors** *adv* (*go*) в помещение; (*be*) в помещении; **he stayed indoors all morning** он просидел дома всё утро

induce [ɪnˈdjuːs] *vt* (*cause*) вызывать (*perf* вызвать); (*persuade*) побуждать (*perf* побудить); (*Med*: *birth*) стимулировать (*impf/perf*)

indulge [ɪnˈdʌldʒ] *vt* (*desire, whim etc*) потворствовать (*impf*) +*dat*, потакать (*impf*) +*dat*; (*person, child*) баловать (*perf* избаловать) ▷ *vi*: **to indulge in** баловаться (*perf* побаловаться) +*instr*

industrial [ɪnˈdʌstrɪəl] *adj* индустриальный, промышленный; **industrial accident** несчастный случай на производстве; **industrial estate** *n* (*Brit*) индустриальный парк

industry [ˈɪndəstrɪ] *n* (*manufacturing*) индустрия, промышленность *f no pl*; **industries** *npl* отрасли *pl* промышленности; **tourist/fashion industry** индустрия туризма/моды

inefficient [ɪnɪˈfɪʃənt] *adj* неэффективный; (*machine*) непроизводительный

inequality [ɪnɪˈkwɔlɪtɪ] *n* (*of system*) неравенство

inevitable [ɪnˈɛvɪtəbl] *adj* неизбежный, неотвратимый

inevitably [ɪnˈɛvɪtəblɪ] *adv* неизбежно

inexpensive [ɪnɪkˈspɛnsɪv] *adj* недорогой

inexperienced [ɪnɪkˈspɪərɪənst] *adj* неопытный

inexplicable [ɪnɪkˈsplɪkəbl] *adj* необъяснимый

infamous [ˈɪnfəməs] *adj* (*person*) бесчестный

infant [ˈɪnfənt] *n* (*baby*) младенец; (*young child*) ребёнок

INFANT SCHOOL

Infant school — подготовительная школа. В Великобритании такую школу посещают дети в возрасте от 5 (иногда 4) до 7 лет.

infantry [ˈɪnfəntrɪ] *n* пехота

infect [ɪnˈfɛkt] *vt* заражать (*perf* заразить); **infection** [ɪnˈfɛkʃən] *n* зараза, инфекция; **infectious** [ɪnˈfɛkʃəs] *adj* (*disease*) инфекционный; (*fig*) заразительный

inferior [ɪnˈfɪərɪəʳ] *adj* (*position, status*) подчинённый; (*goods*) низкого качества

infertile [ɪnˈfəːtaɪl] *adj* бесплодный

infertility [ɪnfəːˈtɪlɪtɪ] *n* бесплодие

infested [ɪnˈfɛstɪd] *adj*: **the house is infested with rats** дом кишит крысами

infinite [ˈɪnfɪnɪt] *adj* бесконечный

infirmary [ɪnˈfəːmərɪ] *n* больница

inflammation [ɪnfləˈmeɪʃən] *n* воспаление

inflation [ɪnˈfleɪʃən] *n* инфляция

inflexible [ɪnˈflɛksɪbl] *adj* (*rule, timetable*) жёсткий; (*person*) негибкий

inflict [ɪnˈflɪkt] *vt*: **to inflict sth on sb** причиня́ть (*perf* причини́ть) что-н кому́-н
influence [ˈɪnfluəns] *n* (*power*) влия́ние; (*effect*) возде́йствие ▷ *vt* влия́ть (*perf* повлия́ть) на *+acc*; **under the influence of alcohol** под возде́йствием алкого́ля
influential [ɪnfluˈɛnʃl] *adj* влия́тельный
influx [ˈɪnflʌks] *n* прито́к
inform [ɪnˈfɔːm] *vt*: **to inform sb of sth** сообща́ть (*perf* сообщи́ть) кому́-н о чём-н ▷ *vi*: **to inform on sb** доноси́ть (*perf* донести́) на кого́-н
informal [ɪnˈfɔːml] *adj* (*visit, invitation*) неофициа́льный; (*discussion, manner*) непринуждённый; (*clothes*) бу́дничный
information [ɪnfəˈmeɪʃən] *n* информа́ция, сообще́ние; **a piece of information** сообще́ние
informative [ɪnˈfɔːmətɪv] *adj* содержа́тельный
infrastructure [ˈɪnfrəstrʌktʃəʳ] *n* инфраструкту́ра
infuriating [ɪnˈfjuərɪeɪtɪŋ] *adj* возмути́тельный
ingenious [ɪnˈdʒiːnjəs] *adj* хитроу́мный; (*person*) изобрета́тельный
ingredient [ɪnˈgriːdɪənt] *n* ингредие́нт; (*fig*) составна́я часть *f*
inhabit [ɪnˈhæbɪt] *vt* населя́ть (*impf*); **inhabitant** *n* жи́тель(ница) *m(f)*
inhale [ɪnˈheɪl] *vt* вдыха́ть (*perf* вдохну́ть) ▷ *vi* де́лать (*perf* сде́лать) вдох; (*when smoking*) затя́гиваться (*perf* затяну́ться)
inherent [ɪnˈhɪərənt] *adj*: **inherent in** *or* **to** прису́щий *+dat*
inherit [ɪnˈhɛrɪt] *vt* насле́довать (*impf/perf*), унасле́довать (*perf*); **inheritance** *n* насле́дство
inhibit [ɪnˈhɪbɪt] *vt* ско́вывать (*perf* скова́ть); (*growth*) заде́рживать (*perf* задержа́ть); **inhibition** [ɪnhɪˈbɪʃən] *n* ско́ванность *f no pl*
initial [ɪˈnɪʃl] *adj* первонача́льный, нача́льный ▷ *n* (*also* **initial letter**) нача́льная бу́ква ▷ *vt* ста́вить (*perf* поста́вить) инициа́лы на *+prp*; **initials** *npl* (*of name*) инициа́лы *mpl*; **initially** *adv* (*at first*) внача́ле, снача́ла
initiate [ɪˈnɪʃɪeɪt] *vt* (*talks etc*) класть (*perf* положи́ть) нача́ло *+dat*, зачина́ть (*impf*); (*new member*) посвяща́ть (*perf* посвяти́ть)
initiative [ɪˈnɪʃətɪv] *n* инициати́ва, начина́ние; (*enterprise*) инициати́вность *f*; **to take the initiative** брать (*perf* взять) на себя́ инициати́ву
inject [ɪnˈdʒɛkt] *vt* (*drugs, poison*) вводи́ть (*perf* ввести́); (*patient*): **to inject sb with sth** де́лать (*perf* сде́лать) уко́л чего́-н кому́-н; **to inject into** (*money*) влива́ть (*perf* влить) в *+acc*; **injection** [ɪnˈdʒɛkʃən] *n* уко́л; (*of money*) влива́ние
injure [ˈɪndʒəʳ] *vt* (*person, limb, feelings*) ра́нить (*impf/perf*); **injured** *adj* ра́неный
injury [ˈɪndʒərɪ] *n* ра́на; (*industrial, sports*) тра́вма
injustice [ɪnˈdʒʌstɪs] *n* несправедли́вость *f*
ink [ɪŋk] *n* (*in pen*) черни́ла *pl*
inland [ˈɪnlənd] *adv* (*travel*) вглубь; **Inland Revenue** *n* (*Brit*) ≈ (Гла́вное) нало́говое управле́ние
in-laws [ˈɪnlɔːz] *npl* (*of woman*)

i

роднá со стороны мýжа; (*of man*) *роднá со стороны жены*
inmate ['ɪnmeɪt] *n* (*of prison*) заключённый(-ая) *m(f) adj*; (*of asylum*) пациéнт(ка)
inn [ɪn] *n* трактир
inner ['ɪnəʳ] *adj* внýтренний; **inner city** *n* центрáльная часть *f* гóрода
innocence ['ɪnəsns] *n* невинóвность *f*; (*naivety*) невинность *f*
innocent ['ɪnəsnt] *adj* невинóвный; (*naive*) невинный
innovation [ɪnəu'veɪʃən] *n* нóвшество
input ['ɪnput] *n* (*resources, money*) вложéние
inquest ['ɪnkwɛst] *n* (*into death*) (судéбное) расслéдование
inquire [ɪn'kwaɪəʳ] *vi*: **to inquire (about)** наводить (*perf* навести) спрáвки (о *+prp*); (*health*) справля́ться (*perf* спрáвиться) о *+prp*; **to inquire when/where** осведомля́ться (*perf* осведóмиться) когдá/где; **inquire into** *vt fus* расслéдовать (*impf/perf*)
ins. *abbr* = **inches**
insane [ɪn'seɪn] *adj* безýмный, сумасшéдший
insect ['ɪnsɛkt] *n* насекóмое *nt adj*
insecure [ɪnsɪ'kjuəʳ] *adj* (*person*) неувéренный в себé
insecurity [ɪnsɪ'kjuərɪtɪ] *n* неувéренность *f* в себé
insensitive [ɪn'sɛnsɪtɪv] *adj* бесчýвственный
insert [ɪn'sə:t] *vt*: **to insert (into)** вставля́ть (*perf* встáвить) (в *+acc*); (*piece of paper*) вклáдывать (*perf* вложить) (в *+acc*)
inside ['ɪn'saɪd] *n* внýтренняя часть *f* ▷ *adj* внýтренний ▷ *adv* (*be*) внутри; (*go*) внутрь ▷ *prep* (*position*) внутри *+gen*; (*motion*) внутрь *+gen*; **inside ten minutes** в предéлах десяти минýт; **insides** *npl* (*inf*: *stomach*) внýтренности *fpl*; **inside out** *adv* наизнáнку; (*know*) вдоль и поперёк
insight ['ɪnsaɪt] *n*: **insight (into)** понимáние (*+gen*)
insignificant [ɪnsɪg'nɪfɪknt] *adj* незначительный
insist [ɪn'sɪst] *vi*: **to insist (on)** настáивать (*perf* настоя́ть) (на *+prp*); **he insisted that I came** он настоя́л на том, чтóбы я пришёл; **he insisted that all was well** он утверждáл, что всё в поря́дке; **insistent** *adj* настóйчивый
insomnia [ɪn'sɔmnɪə] *n* бессóнница
inspect [ɪn'spɛkt] *vt* (*equipment, premises*) осмáтривать (*perf* осмотрéть); **inspection** [ɪn'spɛkʃən] *n* осмóтр; **inspector** *n* (*Admin, Police*) инспéктор; (*Brit*: *on buses, trains*) контролёр
inspiration [ɪnspə'reɪʃən] *n* вдохновéние
inspire [ɪn'spaɪəʳ] *vt* (*workers, troops*) вдохновля́ть (*perf* вдохновить); **to inspire sth (in sb)** внушáть (*perf* внушить) что-н (комý-н)
instability [ɪnstə'bɪlɪtɪ] *n* нестабильность *f*
install [ɪn'stɔ:l] *vt* (*machine*) устанáвливать (*perf* установить); (*official*) стáвить (*perf* постáвить); **installation** [ɪnstə'leɪʃən] *n* (*of machine, plant*) установка
instalment [ɪn'stɔ:lmənt] (*US* **installment**) *n* (*of payment*) взнос; (*of story*) часть *f*; **to pay in instalments** платить (*perf*

заплати́ть) в рассро́чку
instance [ˈɪnstəns] *n* приме́р; **for instance** наприме́р; **in the first instance** в пе́рвую о́чередь
instant [ˈɪnstənt] *n* мгнове́ние, миг ▷ *adj* (*reaction, success*) мгнове́нный; (*coffee*) раствори́мый; **come here this instant!** иди́ сюда́ сию́ же мину́ту!; **instantly** *adv* неме́дленно, сра́зу
instead [ɪnˈstɛd] *adv* взаме́н ▷ *prep*: **instead of** вме́сто *or* взаме́н *+gen*
instinct [ˈɪnstɪŋkt] *n* инсти́нкт; **by instinct** инстинкти́вно; **instinctive** [ɪnˈstɪŋktɪv] *adj* инстинкти́вный
institute [ˈɪnstɪtjuːt] *n* (*for research, teaching*) институ́т; (*professional body*) ассоциа́ция ▷ *vt* (*system, rule*) учрежда́ть (*perf* учреди́ть)
institution [ɪnstɪˈtjuːʃən] *n* учрежде́ние; (*custom, tradition*) институ́т
instruct [ɪnˈstrʌkt] *vt*: **to instruct sb in sth** обуча́ть (*perf* обучи́ть) кого́-н чему́-н; **to instruct sb to do** поруча́ть (*perf* поручи́ть) кому́-н *+infin*; **instruction** [ɪnˈstrʌkʃən] *n* (*teaching*) обуче́ние; **instructions** *npl* (*orders*) указа́ния *ntpl*; **instructions (for use)** инстру́кция *or* руково́дство (по примене́нию); **instructor** *n* (*for driving etc*) инстру́ктор
instrument [ˈɪnstrumənt] *n* инструме́нт; **instrumental** [ɪnstruˈmɛntl] *adj*: **to be instrumental in** игра́ть (*perf* сыгра́ть) суще́ственную роль в *+prp*
insufficient [ɪnsəˈfɪʃənt] *adj* недоста́точный
insulation [ɪnsjuˈleɪʃən] *n* (*against cold*) (тепло)изоля́ция
insulin [ˈɪnsjulɪn] *n* инсули́н
insult [*vb* ɪnˈsʌlt, *n* ˈɪnsʌlt] *vt* оскорбля́ть (*perf* оскорби́ть) ▷ *n* оскорбле́ние; **insulting** [ɪnˈsʌltɪŋ] *adj* оскорби́тельный
insurance [ɪnˈʃuərəns] *n* страхова́ние; **insurance policy** *n* страхово́й по́лис
insure [ɪnˈʃuəʳ] *vt*: **to insure (against)** страхова́ть (*perf* застрахова́ть) (от *+gen*); **to insure (o.s.) against** страхова́ться (*perf* застрахова́ться) от *+gen*
intact [ɪnˈtækt] *adj* (*unharmed*) неповреждённый; (*whole*) нетро́нутый
intake [ˈɪnteɪk] *n* (*of food, drink*) потребле́ние; (*Brit*: *of pupils, recruits*) набо́р
integral [ˈɪntɪgrəl] *adj* неотъе́млемый
integrate [ˈɪntɪgreɪt] *vt* интегри́ровать (*impf/perf*) ▷ *vi* (*groups, individuals*) объединя́ться (*perf* объедини́ться)
integrity [ɪnˈtɛgrɪtɪ] *n* (*morality*) че́стность *f*, поря́дочность *f*
intellect [ˈɪntəlɛkt] *n* интелле́кт; **intellectual** [ɪntəˈlɛktjuəl] *adj* интеллектуа́льный ▷ *n* интеллектуа́л
intelligence [ɪnˈtɛlɪdʒəns] *n* ум; (*thinking power*) у́мственные спосо́бности *fpl*; (*Mil etc*) разве́дка
intelligent [ɪnˈtɛlɪdʒənt] *adj* у́мный; (*animal*) разу́мный
intend [ɪnˈtɛnd] *vt*: **to intend sth for** предназнача́ть (*perf* предназна́чить) что-н для *+gen*; **to intend to do** намерева́ться (*impf*) *+infin*
intense [ɪnˈtɛns] *adj* (*heat,*

emotion) си́льный; (*noise, activity*) интенси́вный
intensify [ɪn'tɛnsɪfaɪ] *vt* уси́ливать (*perf* уси́лить)
intensity [ɪn'tɛnsɪtɪ] *n* (*of effort, sun*) интенси́вность *f*
intensive [ɪn'tɛnsɪv] *adj* интенси́вный; **intensive care** интенси́вная терапи́я
intent [ɪn'tɛnt] *adj*: **intent (on)** сосредото́ченный (на +*prp*); **to be intent on doing** (*determined*) стреми́ться (*impf*) +*infin*
intention [ɪn'tɛnʃən] *n* наме́рение; **intentional** *adj* наме́ренный
interact [ɪntər'ækt] *vi*: **to interact (with)** взаимоде́йствовать (*impf*) (с +*instr*); **interaction** [ɪntər'ækʃən] *n* взаимоде́йствие
intercom ['ɪntəkɔm] *n* селе́ктор
intercourse ['ɪntəkɔ:s] *n* (*sexual*) полово́е snoше́ние
interest ['ɪntrɪst] *n*: **interest (in)** интере́с (к +*dat*); (*Comm*: *sum of money*) проце́нты *mpl* ▷ *vt* интересова́ть (*impf*); **to interest sb in sth** заинтересо́вывать (*perf* заинтересова́ть) кого́-н в чем-н; **interested** *adj* заинтересо́ванный; **to be interested (in sth)** (*music etc*) интересова́ться (*impf*) (чем-н); **interesting** *adj* интере́сный
interfere [ɪntə'fɪə^r] *vi*: **to interfere in** вме́шиваться (*perf* вмеша́ться) в +*acc*; **to interfere with** (*hinder*) меша́ть (*perf* помеша́ть) +*dat*; **interference** *n* вмеша́тельство
interim ['ɪntərɪm] *adj* (*government*) вре́менный; (*report*) промежу́точный ▷ *n*: **in the interim** тем вре́менем
interior [ɪn'tɪərɪə^r] *n* (*of building*) интерье́р; (*of car, box etc*) вну́тренность *f* ▷ *adj* (*door, room etc*) вну́тренний; **interior department/minister** департа́мент/мини́стр вну́тренних дел
intermediate [ɪntə'mi:dɪət] *adj* (*stage*) промежу́точный
internal [ɪn'tə:nl] *adj* вну́тренний
international [ɪntə'næʃənl] *adj* междунаро́дный
Internet ['ɪntənɛt] *n* Интерне́т; **Internet café** *n* интерне́т-кафе́ *nt ind*; **Internet Service Provider** *n* интерне́т-прова́йдер
interpret [ɪn'tə:prɪt] *vt* (*explain*) интерпрети́ровать (*impf/perf*), толкова́ть (*impf*); (*translate*) переводи́ть (*perf* перевести́) (*у́стно*) ▷ *vi* переводи́ть (*perf* перевести́) (*у́стно*); **interpretation** [ɪntə:prɪ'teɪʃən] *n* интерпрета́ция, толкова́ние; **interpreter** *n* перево́дчик(-ица) (*устный*)
interrogation [ɪntɛrəu'geɪʃən] *n* допро́с
interrupt [ɪntə'rʌpt] *vt, vi* прерыва́ть (*perf* прерва́ть); **interruption** [ɪntə'rʌpʃən] *n* (*act*) прерыва́ние
interval ['ɪntəvl] *n* интерва́л; (*Brit*: *Sport*) переры́в; (: *Theat*) антра́кт; **at intervals** вре́мя от вре́мени
intervene [ɪntə'vi:n] *vi* (*in conversation, situation*) вме́шиваться (*perf* вмеша́ться); (*event*) меша́ть (*perf* помеша́ть)
interview ['ɪntəvju:] *n* (*see vt*) собесе́дование; интервью́ *nt ind* ▷ *vt* (*for job*) проводи́ть (*perf* провести́) собесе́дование с +*instr*; (*Radio, TV etc*) интервью́ировать (*impf/perf*), брать (*perf* взять)

интервью у *+gen*

intimate ['ɪntɪmət] *adj* (*friend, relationship*) близкий; (*conversation, atmosphere*) интимный; (*knowledge*) глубокий, непосредственный

intimidate [ɪn'tɪmɪdeɪt] *vt* запугивать (*perf* запугать)

 **KEYWORD**

into ['ɪntu] *prep* **1** (*indicating motion*) в/на *+acc*; **into the house/garden** в дом/сад; **into the post office/factory** на почту/фабрику; **research into cancer** исследования в области раковых заболеваний; **he worked late into the night** он работал до поздней ночи **2** (*indicating change of condition, result*): **she has translated the letter into Russian** она перевела письмо на русский язык; **the vase broke into pieces** ваза разбилась на мелкие кусочки; **they got into trouble for it** им попало за это; **he lapsed into silence** он погрузился в молчание; **to burst into tears** расплакаться (*perf*); **to burst into flames** вспыхивать (*perf* вспыхнуть)

intolerant [ɪn'tɔlərnt] *adj* нетерпимый

intranet ['ɪntrənɛt] *n* интранет, локальная вычислительная сеть

intricate ['ɪntrɪkət] *adj* (*pattern*) замысловатый; (*relationship*) сложный

intriguing [ɪn'triːgɪŋ] *adj* (*fascinating*) интригующий

introduce [ɪntrə'djuːs] *vt* (*new idea, measure etc*) вводить (*perf* ввести); (*speaker, programme*) представлять (*perf* представить); **to introduce sb (to sb)** представлять (*perf* представить) кого-н (кому-н); **to introduce sb to** (*pastime etc*) знакомить (*perf* познакомить) кого-н с *+instr*

introduction [ɪntrə'dʌkʃən] *n* введение; (*to person, new experience*) знакомство

introductory [ɪntrə'dʌktərɪ] *adj* (*lesson*) вступительный

intrude [ɪn'truːd] *vi*: **to intrude (on)** вторгаться (*perf* вторгнуться) (в/на *+acc*); **intruder** *n*: **there is an intruder in our house** к нам в дом кто-то вторгся

intuition [ɪntjuː'ɪʃən] *n* интуиция

inundate ['ɪnʌndeɪt] *vt*: **to inundate with** (*calls etc*) засыпать (*perf* засыпать) *+instr*

invade [ɪn'veɪd] *vt* (*Mil*) вторгаться (*perf* вторгнуться) в *+acc*

invalid [*n* 'ɪnvəlɪd, *adj* ɪn'vælɪd] *n* инвалид ▷ *adj* недействительный

invaluable [ɪn'væljuəbl] *adj* неоценимый

invariably [ɪn'vɛərɪəblɪ] *adv* неизменно

invasion [ɪn'veɪʒən] *n* (*Mil*) вторжение

invent [ɪn'vɛnt] *vt* изобретать (*perf* изобрести); (*fabricate*) выдумывать (*perf* выдумать); **invention** [ɪn'vɛnʃən] *n* (*see vt*) изобретение; выдумка; **inventor** *n* изобретатель *m*

inventory ['ɪnvəntrɪ] *n* (*of house etc*) (инвентаризационная) опись *f*

inverted commas [ɪn'vəːtɪd-] *npl* (*Brit*: *Ling*) кавычки *fpl*

invest [ɪn'vɛst] *vt* вкладывать (*perf* вложить) ▷ *vi*: **to invest in** вкладывать (*perf* вложить) деньги в *+acc*

investigate [ɪn'vɛstɪgeɪt] *vt* (*accident, crime*) рассле́довать (*impf/perf*)
investigation [ɪnvɛstɪ'geɪʃən] *n* рассле́дование
investment [ɪn'vɛstmənt] *n* (*activity*) инвести́рование; (*amount of money*) инвести́ция, вклад
investor [ɪn'vɛstə^r] *n* инве́стор, вкла́дчик
invigilator [ɪn'vɪdʒɪleɪtə^r] *n* *экзамена́тор, следя́щий за тем, что́бы студе́нты не спи́сывали во вре́мя экза́менов*
invisible [ɪn'vɪzɪbl] *adj* неви́димый
invitation [ɪnvɪ'teɪʃən] *n* приглаше́ние
invite [ɪn'vaɪt] *vt* приглаша́ть (*perf* пригласи́ть); (*discussion, criticism*) побужда́ть (*perf* побуди́ть) к *+dat*; **to invite sb to do** предлага́ть (*perf* предложи́ть) кому́-н *+infin*
inviting [ɪn'vaɪtɪŋ] *adj* соблазни́тельный
invoice ['ɪnvɔɪs] *n* счёт, факту́ра ▷ *vt* выпи́сывать (*perf* вы́писать) счёт *or* факту́ру *+dat*
involve [ɪn'vɔlv] *vt* (*include*) вовлека́ть (*perf* вовле́чь); (*concern, affect*) каса́ться (*impf*) *+gen*; **to involve sb (in sth)** вовлека́ть (*perf* вовле́чь) кого́-н (во что-н); **involvement** *n* (*participation*) прича́стность *f*; (*enthusiasm*) увлече́ние
iPod® ['aɪpɔd] *n* айпод *m* (*inf*)
IQ *n abbr* (= *intelligence quotient*) коэффицие́нт у́мственного разви́тия
IRA *n abbr* (= *Irish Republican Army*) ИРА (= *Ирла́ндская республика́нская а́рмия*)
Iran [ɪ'rɑːn] *n* Ира́н; **Iranian** [ɪ'reɪnɪən] *adj* ира́нский
Iraq [ɪ'rɑːk] *n* Ира́к; **Iraqi** *adj* ира́кский
Ireland ['aɪələnd] *n* Ирла́ндия
iris ['aɪrɪs] (*pl* **irises**) *n* (*Anat*) ра́дужная оболо́чка (гла́за)
Irish ['aɪrɪʃ] *adj* ирла́ндский ▷ *npl*: **the Irish** ирла́ндцы; **Irishman** *irreg n* ирла́ндец
iron ['aɪən] *n* (*metal*) желе́зо; (*for clothes*) утю́г ▷ *cpd* желе́зный ▷ *vt* (*clothes*) гла́дить (*perf* погла́дить); **iron out** *vt* (*fig: problems*) ула́живать (*perf* ула́дить)
ironic(al) [aɪ'rɔnɪk(l)] *adj* ирони́ческий
ironing board *n* глади́льная доска́
irony ['aɪrənɪ] *n* иро́ния
irrational [ɪ'ræʃənl] *adj* неразу́мный, нерациона́льный
irregular [ɪ'rɛgjulə^r] *adj* (*pattern*) непра́вильной фо́рмы; (*surface*) неро́вный; (*Ling*) непра́вильный
irrelevant [ɪ'rɛləvənt] *adj*: **this fact is irrelevant** э́тот факт к де́лу не отно́сится
irresistible [ɪrɪ'zɪstɪbl] *adj* (*urge, desire*) непреодоли́мый; (*person, thing*) неотрази́мый
irresponsible [ɪrɪ'spɔnsɪbl] *adj* безотве́тственный
irrigation [ɪrɪ'geɪʃən] *n* ороше́ние, ирригáция
irritable ['ɪrɪtəbl] *adj* раздражи́тельный
irritate ['ɪrɪteɪt] *vt* раздража́ть (*perf* раздражи́ть)
irritating ['ɪrɪteɪtɪŋ] *adj* (*sound etc*) доса́дный; (*person*) неприя́тный
irritation [ɪrɪ'teɪʃən] *n* раздраже́ние

is [ɪz] *vb see* **be**
Islam [ˈɪzlɑːm] *n* (*Rel*) ислáм; **Islamic** [ɪzˈlæmɪk] *adj* ислáмский, мусульмáнский
island [ˈaɪlənd] *n* (*Geo*) óстров
isn't [ˈɪznt] = **is not**
isolated *adj* (*place, person*) изолúрованный; (*incident*) отдéльный
isolation [aɪsəˈleɪʃən] *n* изолЯ́ция
ISP *n abbr* = **Internet Service Provider**
Israel [ˈɪzreɪl] *n* Изрáиль *m*; **Israeli** [ɪzˈreɪlɪ] *adj* изрáильский
issue [ˈɪʃuː] *n* (*problem, subject*) вопрóс, проблéма; (*of book, stamps etc*) вы́пуск; (*most important part*): **the issue** суть *f* ▷ *vt* (*newspaper*) выпускáть (*perf* вы́пустить); (*statement*) дéлать (*perf* сдéлать); (*equipment, documents*) выдавáть (*perf* вы́дать); **to be at issue** быть (*impf*) предмéтом обсуждéния; **to make an issue of sth** дéлать (*perf* сдéлать) проблéму из чегó-н

KEYWORD

it [ɪt] *pron* **1** (*specific subject*) он (*f* онá, *nt* онó) (*direct object*) егó (*f* её) (*indirect object*) ему́ (*f* ей) (*after prep*: *+gen*) негó (*f* неё) (: *+dat*) нему́ (*f* ней) (: *+instr*) ним (*f* ней) (: *+prp*) нём (*f* ней); **where is your car? — it's in the garage** где Вáша маши́на? — онá в гаражé; **I like this hat, whose is it?** мне нрáвится э́та шля́па, чья онá?
2 э́то; (: *indirect object*) э́тому; **what kind of car is it? — it's a Lada** какáя э́то маши́на? — э́то Лáда; **who is it? — it's me** кто э́то? — э́то я
3 (*after prep*: *+gen*) э́того; (: *+dat*) э́тому; (: *+instr*) э́тим; (: *+prp*) э́том; **I spoke to him about it** я говори́л с ним об э́том; **why is it that ...?** отчегó ...?; **what is it?** (*what's wrong*) что такóе?
4 (*impersonal*): **it's raining** идёт дождь; **it's cold today** сегóдня хóлодно; **it's interesting that ...** интерéсно, что ...; **it's 6 o'clock** сейчáс 6 часóв; **it's the 10th of August** сегóдня 10-ое áвгуста

Italian [ɪˈtæljən] *adj* итальЯ́нский
italics [ɪˈtælɪks] *npl* (*Typ*) курси́в *msg*
Italy [ˈɪtəlɪ] *n* Итáлия
itch [ɪtʃ] *vi* чесáться (*impf*); **he was itching to know our secret** ему́ не терпéлось узнáть наш секрéт; **itchy** *adj*: **I feel all itchy** у меня́ всё чéшется
it'd [ˈɪtd] = **it had**; **it would**
item [ˈaɪtəm] *n* предмéт; (*on agenda*) пункт; (*also* **news item**) сообщéние
itinerary [aɪˈtɪnərərɪ] *n* маршру́т
it'll [ˈɪtl] = **it shall**; **it will**
its [ɪts] *adj, pron* егó (*f* её) (*referring to subject of sentence*) свой (*f* своя́, *nt* своё) *see also* **my**; **mine**[1]
it's [ɪts] = **it has**; **it is**
itself [ɪtˈsɛlf] *pron* (*reflexive*) себя́; (*emphatic*: *masculine*) сам по себé; (: *feminine*) самá по себé; (: *neuter*) самó по себé
ITV *n abbr* (*Brit*: *TV*) = **Independent Television**
I've [aɪv] = **I have**
ivory [ˈaɪvərɪ] *n* (*substance*) слонóвая кость *f*
ivy [ˈaɪvɪ] *n* (*Bot*) плющ

j

jab [dʒæb] *n* (*Brit: inf: Med*) укóл
jack [dʒæk] *n* (*Aut*) домкрáт; (*Cards*) валéт
jacket ['dʒækɪt] *n* кýртка; (*of suit*) пиджáк; (*of book*) суперoблóжка
jackpot ['dʒækpɔt] *n* джек-пот, куш
jagged ['dʒægɪd] *adj* зубчáтый
jail [dʒeɪl] *n* тюрьмá ▷ *vt* сажáть (*perf* посадить) (в тюрьмý)
jam [dʒæm] *n* (*preserve*) джем; (*also* **traffic jam**) прóбка ▷ *vt* (*passage*) забивáть (*perf* забить); (*mechanism*) заклинивать (*perf* заклинить) ▷ *vi* (*drawer*) застревáть (*perf* застрять); **to jam sth into** запихивать (*perf* запихнýть) что-н в +*acc*
janitor ['dʒænɪtə^r] *n* вахтёр
January ['dʒænjuərɪ] *n* январь *m*
Japan [dʒə'pæn] *n* Япóния
Japanese [dʒæpə'ni:z] *n* япóнец(-нка)
jar [dʒɑ:^r] *n* бáнка
jargon ['dʒɑ:gən] *n* жаргóн
javelin ['dʒævlɪn] *n* копьё
jaw [dʒɔ:] *n* чéлюсть *f*
jazz [dʒæz] *n* джаз
jealous ['dʒɛləs] *adj* ревнивый; **to be jealous of** (*possessive*) ревновáть (*impf*) к +*dat*; (*envious*) завидовать (*impf*) +*dat*; **jealousy** *n* (*resentment*) ревность *f*; (*envy*) зáвисть *f*
jeans [dʒi:nz] *npl* джинсы *pl*
jelly ['dʒɛlɪ] *n* желé *nt ind*; (*US*) джем; **jellyfish** *n* медýза
jerk [dʒə:k] *n* (*jolt*) рывóк ▷ *vt* дёргать (*perf* дёрнуть), рванýть (*perf*) ▷ *vi* дёргаться (*perf* дёрнуться); **the car jerked to a halt** машина рéзко затормозила
jersey ['dʒə:zɪ] *n* (*pullover*) свитер
Jesus ['dʒi:zəs] *n* (*Rel*) Исýс
jet [dʒɛt] *n* (*of gas, liquid*) струя; (*Aviat*) реактивный самолёт; **jet lag** *n* *нарушéние сýточного режима организма пóсле длительного полёта*
jetty ['dʒɛtɪ] *n* причáл
Jew [dʒu:] *n* еврéй(ка)
jewel ['dʒu:əl] *n* драгоцéнный кáмень *m*; **jeweller** (*US* **jeweler**) *n* ювелир; **jewellery** (*US* **jewelry**) *n* драгоцéнности *fpl*, ювелирные издéлия *ntpl*
Jewish ['dʒu:ɪʃ] *adj* еврéйский
jigsaw ['dʒɪgsɔ:] *n* (*also* **jigsaw puzzle**) головолóмка
job [dʒɔb] *n* рабóта; (*task*) дéло; (*inf: difficulty*): **I had a job getting here!** я с трудóм добрáлся сюдá!; **it's not my job** это не моё дéло; **it's a good job that ...** хорошó ещё, что ...; **jobless** *adj* безрабóтный
jockey ['dʒɔkɪ] *n* жокéй

jog [dʒɔg] *vt* толкáть (*perf* толкнýть) ▷ *vi* бéгать (*impf*) трусцóй; **to jog sb's memory** подстёгивать (*perf* подстегнýть) чью-н пáмять; **jogging** *n* бег трусцóй
join [dʒɔɪn] *vt* (*organization*) вступáть (*perf* вступи́ть) в *+acc*; (*put together*) соединя́ть (*perf* соедини́ть); (*group, queue*) присоединя́ться (*perf* присоедини́ться) к *+dat* ▷ *vi* (*rivers*) сливáться (*perf* сли́ться); (*roads*) сходи́ться (*perf* сойти́сь); **join in** *vi* присоединя́ться (*perf* присоедини́ться) ▷ *vt fus* (*work, discussion etc*) принимáть (*perf* приня́ть) учáстие в *+prp*; **join up** *vi* (*meet*) соединя́ться (*perf* соедини́ться); (*Mil*) поступáть (*perf* поступи́ть) на воéнную слýжбу
joiner ['dʒɔɪnəʳ] *n* (*Brit*) столя́р
joint [dʒɔɪnt] *n* (*Tech*) стык; (*Anat*) сустáв; (*Brit*: *Culin*) кусóк (*мя́са*); (*inf*: *place*) притóн; (: *of cannabis*) скрýтка с марихуáной, кося́к ▷ *adj* совмéстный
joke [dʒəuk] *n* (*gag*) шýтка, анекдóт; (*also* **practical joke**) рóзыгрыш ▷ *vi* шути́ть (*perf* пошути́ть); **to play a joke on** шути́ть (*perf* пошути́ть) над *+instr*, сыгрáть (*perf*) шýтку с *+instr*; **joker** *n* шутни́к; (*Cards*) джóкер
jolly ['dʒɔlɪ] *adj* весёлый ▷ *adv* (*Brit*: *inf*) óчень
jolt [dʒəult] *n* (*jerk*) рывóк ▷ *vt* встря́хивать (*perf* встряхнýть); (*emotionally*) потрясáть (*perf* потрясти́)
journal ['dʒə:nl] *n* журнáл; (*diary*) дневни́к; **journalism** *n* журнали́стика; **journalist** *n* журнали́ст(ка)
journey ['dʒə:nɪ] *n* поéздка; (*distance covered*) путь *m*, дорóга
joy [dʒɔɪ] *n* рáдость *f*; **joyrider** *n* *человéк, угоня́ющий маши́ны рáди развлечéния*
Jr *abbr* (*in names*) = **junior**
judge [dʒʌdʒ] *n* судья́ *m* ▷ *vt* (*competition, person etc*) суди́ть (*impf*); (*consider, estimate*) оцéнивать (*perf* оцени́ть)
judo ['dʒu:dəu] *n* дзюдó *nt ind*
jug [dʒʌg] *n* кувши́н
juggle ['dʒʌgl] *vi* жонгли́ровать (*impf*) ▷ *vt* (*fig*) жонгли́ровать (*impf*) *+instr*
juice [dʒu:s] *n* сок; **juicy** ['dʒu:sɪ] *adj* сóчный
July [dʒu:'laɪ] *n* ию́ль *m*
jumble ['dʒʌmbl] *n* (*muddle*) нагромождéние ▷ *vt* (*also* **jumble up**) перемéшивать (*perf* перемешáть); **jumble sale** *n* (*Brit*) *благотвори́тельная распродáжа подéржанных вещéй*
jumbo ['dʒʌmbəu] *n* (*also* **jumbo jet**) реакти́вный аэрóбус
jump [dʒʌmp] *vi* пры́гать (*perf* пры́гнуть); (*start*) подпры́гивать (*perf* подпры́гнуть); (*increase*) подскáкивать (*perf* подскочи́ть) ▷ *vt* (*fence*) перепры́гивать (*perf* перепры́гнуть) (чéрез *+acc*), перескáкивать (*perf* перескочи́ть) (чéрез *+acc*) ▷ *n* прыжóк; (*increase*) скачóк; **to jump the queue** (*Brit*) идти́ (*perf* пойти́) без óчереди
jumper ['dʒʌmpəʳ] *n* (*Brit*) сви́тер, джéмпер; (*US*: *dress*) сарафáн
junction ['dʒʌŋkʃən] *n* (*Brit*: *of roads*) перекрёсток; (: *Rail*) ýзел
June [dʒu:n] *n* ию́нь *m*
jungle ['dʒʌŋgl] *n* джýнгли *pl*
junior ['dʒu:nɪəʳ] *adj* млáдший

▷ *n* мла́дший(-ая) *m(f) adj*; **he's junior to me (by 2 years), he's my junior (by 2 years)** он мла́дше меня́ (на 2 го́да)

junk [dʒʌŋk] *n* барахло́, хлам; **junk food** *n еда́, содержа́щая ма́ло пита́тельных веще́ств*; **junkie** *n* (*inf*) наркома́н; **junk mail** *n* незапро́шенная почто́вая рекла́ма

jurisdiction [dʒuərɪs'dɪkʃən] *n* (*Law*) юрисди́кция; (*Admin*) сфе́ра полномо́чий

jury ['dʒuərɪ] *n* прися́жные *pl adj* (заседа́тели)

just [dʒʌst] *adj* справедли́вый ▷ *adv* (*exactly*) как раз, и́менно; (*only*) то́лько; (*barely*) едва́; **he's just left** он то́лько что ушёл; **it's just right** э́то как раз то, что на́до; **just two o'clock** ро́вно два часа́; **she's just as clever as you** она́ столь же умна́, как и ты; **it's just as well (that) ...** и хорошо́, (что) ...; **just as he was leaving** как раз когда́ он собра́лся уходи́ть; **just before Christmas** пе́ред са́мым Рождество́м; **there was just enough petrol** бензи́на едва́ хвати́ло; **just here** вот здесь; **he (only) just missed** он чуть не попа́л; **just listen!** ты то́лько послу́шай!

justice ['dʒʌstɪs] *n* (*Law*: *system*) правосу́дие; (*fairness*) справедли́вость *f*; (*US*: *judge*) судья́ *m*; **to do justice to** (*fig*) отдава́ть (*perf* отда́ть) до́лжное *+dat*

justification [dʒʌstɪfɪ'keɪʃən] *n* основа́ние; (*of action*) оправда́ние

justify ['dʒʌstɪfaɪ] *vt* опра́вдывать (*perf* оправда́ть); **to justify o.s.** опра́вдываться (*perf* оправда́ться)

juvenile ['dʒu:vənaɪl] *n* несовершенноле́тний(-яя) *m(f) adj*, подро́сток ▷ *adj* де́тский

k

K *abbr* = **one thousand**; (*Comput*) (= *kilobyte*) K (= *килоба́йт*)
kangaroo [kæŋgə'ruː] *n* кенгуру́ *m ind*
karaoke [kɑːrə'əukɪ] *n* карио́ки *ind*
karate [kə'rɑːtɪ] *n* карате́ *nt ind*
kebab [kə'bæb] *n* ≈ шашлы́к
keel [kiːl] *n* киль *m*
keen [kiːn] *adj* о́стрый; (*eager*) стра́стный, увлечённый; (*competition*) напряжённый; **to be keen to do** *or* **on doing** о́чень хоте́ть (*impf*) +*infin*; **to be keen on sth** увлека́ться (*impf*) чем-н
keep [kiːp] (*pt, pp* **kept**) *vt* (*receipt, money*) оставля́ть (*perf* оста́вить) себе́; (*store*) храни́ть (*impf*); (*preserve*) сохраня́ть (*perf* сохрани́ть); (*house, shop, family*) содержа́ть (*impf*); (*prisoner, chickens*) держа́ть (*impf*); (*accounts, diary*) вести́ (*impf*); (*promise*) сде́рживать (*perf* сдержа́ть) ▷ *vi* (*in certain state or place*) остава́ться (*perf* оста́ться); (*food*) сохраня́ться (*impf*); (*continue*): **to keep doing** продолжа́ть (*impf*) +*impf infin* ▷ *n*: **he has enough for his keep** ему́ доста́точно на прожи́тие; **where do you keep the salt?** где у вас соль?; **he tries to keep her happy** он де́лает всё для того́, что́бы она́ была́ дово́льна; **to keep the house tidy** содержа́ть (*impf*) дом в поря́дке; **to keep sth to o.s.** держа́ть (*impf*) что-н при себе́; **to keep sth (back) from sb** скрыва́ть (*perf* скрыть) что-н от кого́-н; **to keep sth from happening** не дава́ть (*perf* дать) чему́-н случи́ться; **to keep time** (*clock*) идти́ (*impf*) то́чно; **keep on** *vi*: **to keep on doing** продолжа́ть (*impf*) +*impf infin*; **to keep on (about)** не перестава́я говори́ть (*impf*) (о +*prp*); **keep out** *vt* не впуска́ть (*perf* впусти́ть); **"keep out"** "посторо́нним вход воспрещён"; **keep up** *vt* (*payments, standards*) подде́рживать (*impf*) ▷ *vi*: **to keep up (with)** поспева́ть (*perf* поспе́ть) (за +*instr*), идти́ (*impf*) в но́гу (с +*instr*); **keep fit** *n* аэро́бика
kennel ['kɛnl] *n* конура́
Kenya ['kɛnjə] *n* Ке́ния
kept [kɛpt] *pt, pp of* **keep**
kerb [kəːb] *n* (*Brit*) бордю́р
kettle ['kɛtl] *n* ча́йник
key [kiː] *n* ключ; (*of piano, computer*) кла́виша ▷ *cpd* ключево́й ▷ *vt* (*also* **key in**) набира́ть (*perf* набра́ть) (на клавиату́ре); **keyboard** *n* клавиату́ра; **keyring** *n* брело́к

khaki ['kɑːkɪ] *n, adj* хáки *nt, adj ind*
kick [kɪk] *vt* (*person, table*) ударя́ть (*perf* удáрить) ногóй; (*ball*) ударя́ть (*perf* удáрить) ногóй по *+dat*; (*inf*: *habit, addiction*) побoрóть (*perf*) ▷ *vi* (*horse*) лягáться (*impf*) ▷ *n* удáр; **kick off** *vi*: **the match kicks off at 3pm** матч начинáется в 3 часá (*в футбóле*)
kid [kɪd] *n* (*inf*: *child*) ребёнок; (*goat*) козлёнок
kidnap ['kɪdnæp] *vt* похищáть (*perf* похи́тить)
kidney ['kɪdnɪ] *n* (*Med*) пóчка; (*Culin*) пóчки *fpl*
kill [kɪl] *vt* убивáть (*perf* уби́ть); **to kill o.s.** покóнчить (*perf*) с собóй; **to be killed** (*in war, accident*) погибáть (*perf* поги́бнуть); **killer** *n* убийца *m/f*
kilo ['kiːləu] *n* килогрáмм, килó *nt ind* (*inf*); **kilogram(me)** ['kɪləugræm] *n* килогрáмм; **kilometre** ['kɪləmiːtə[r]] (*US* **kilometer**) *n* киломéтр
kind [kaɪnd] *adj* дóбрый ▷ *n* тип, род; **in kind** (*Comm*) натýрой; **a kind of** род *+gen*; **two of a kind** две вéщи одногó ти́па; **what kind of ...?** какóй ...?
kindergarten ['kɪndəgɑːtn] *n* дéтский сад
kindly ['kaɪndlɪ] *adj* (*smile*) дóбрый; (*person, tone*) доброжелáтельный ▷ *adv* (*smile, behave*) любéзно, доброжелáтельно; **will you kindly give me his address** бýдьте добры́, дáйте мне егó áдрес
kindness ['kaɪndnɪs] *n* (*quality*) добротá
king [kɪŋ] *n* корóль *m*; **kingdom** *n* королéвство; **the animal/plant kingdom** живóтное/расти́тельное цáрство; **kingfisher** *n* зиморóдок
kiosk ['kiːɔsk] *n* киóск; (*Brit*: *Tel*) телефóнная бýдка
kipper ['kɪpə[r]] *n* ≈ копчёная селёдка
kiss [kɪs] *n* поцелýй ▷ *vt* целовáть (*perf* поцеловáть) ▷ *vi* целовáться (*perf* поцеловáться)
kit [kɪt] *n* (*also* **sports kit**) (спорти́вный) костю́м; (*equipment*) снаряжéние; (*set of tools*) набóр; (*for assembly*) комплéкт
kitchen ['kɪtʃɪn] *n* кýхня
kite [kaɪt] *n* (*toy*) воздýшный змей
kitten ['kɪtn] *n* котёнок
kitty ['kɪtɪ] *n* (*pool of money*) óбщая кáсса
kiwi ['kiːwiː] *n* ки́ви *f ind*
km *abbr* (= *kilometre*) км (= *киломéтр*)
knack [næk] *n* спосóбность *f*
knee [niː] *n* колéно
kneel [niːl] (*pt, pp* **knelt**) *vi* (*also* **kneel down**: *action*) вставáть (*perf* встать) на колéни; (: *state*) стоя́ть (*impf*) на колéнях
knew [njuː] *pt of* **know**
knickers ['nɪkəz] *npl* (*Brit*) (жéнские) трýсики *mpl*
knife [naɪf] (*pl* **knives**) *n* нож ▷ *vt* рáнить (*impf*) ножóм
knight [naɪt] *n* ры́царь *m*; (*Chess*) конь *m*
knit [nɪt] *vt* (*garment*) вязáть (*perf* связáть) ▷ *vi* вязáть (*impf*); (*bones*) срастáться (*perf* срасти́сь); **to knit one's brows** хмýрить (*perf* нахмýрить) брóви; **knitting** *n* вязáнье; **knitting needle** *n* вязáльная спи́ца
knives [naɪvz] *npl of* **knife**

knob [nɔb] *n* (*on door*) ру́чка; (*on radio etc*) кно́пка
knock [nɔk] *vt* (*strike*) ударя́ть (*perf* уда́рить); (*bump into*) ста́лкиваться (*perf* столкну́ться) с +*instr*; (*inf: criticize*) критикова́ть (*impf*) ▷ *n* (*blow, bump*) уда́р, толчо́к; (*on door*) стук; **to knock some sense into sb** учи́ть (*perf* научи́ть) кого́-н уму́-ра́зуму; **he knocked at** *or* **on the door** он постуча́л в дверь; **knock down** *vt* (*person, price*) сбива́ть (*perf* сбить); **knock out** *vt* (*subj: person, drug*) оглуша́ть (*perf* оглуши́ть); (*Boxing*) нокаути́ровать (*perf*); (*defeat*) выбива́ть (*perf* вы́бить); **knock over** *vt* сбива́ть (*perf* сбить)
knot [nɔt] *n* (*also Naut*) у́зел; (*in wood*) сучо́к ▷ *vt* завя́зывать (*perf* завяза́ть) узло́м
know [nəu] (*pt* **knew**, *pp* **known**) *vt* (*facts, people*) знать (*impf*); **to know how to do** уме́ть (*impf*) +*infin*; **to know about** *or* **of** знать (*impf*) о +*prp*; **know-all** *n* (*Brit: inf: pej*) всезна́йка *m/f*; **know-how** *n* но́у-ха́у *nt ind*; **knowingly** *adv* (*purposely*) созна́тельно; (*smile, look*) понима́юще
knowledge ['nɔlɪdʒ] *n* зна́ние; (*things learnt*) зна́ния *ntpl*; (*awareness*) представле́ние; **knowledgeable** *adj* зна́ющий; **he is very knowledgeable about art** он большо́й знато́к иску́сства
known [nəun] *pp of* **know**
knuckle ['nʌkl] *n* костя́шка
Korea [kə'rɪə] *n* Коре́я
Kosovan ['kɔsəvən] *n* косова́р
Kosovar ['kɔsəvɑːʳ] *n* косова́р
Kosovo ['kɔsəvəu] *n* Ко́сово

L *abbr* (*Brit: Aut*) (= *learner*) учени́к
l *abbr* (= *litre*) л (= *литр*)
lab [læb] *n abbr* = **laboratory**
label ['leɪbl] *n* этике́тка, ярлы́к; (*on suitcase*) би́рка ▷ *vt* (*see n*) прикрепля́ть (*perf* прикрепи́ть) ярлы́к на +*acc*; прикрепля́ть (*perf* прикрепи́ть) би́рку к +*dat*
labor ['leɪbəʳ] *n* (*US*) = **labour**
laboratory [lə'bɔrətərɪ] *n* лаборато́рия
labour ['leɪbəʳ] (*US* **labor**) *n* (*work*) труд; (*workforce*) рабо́чая си́ла; (*Med*) ро́ды *mpl*; **to be in labour** рожа́ть (*impf*); **labourer** *n* неквалифици́рованный рабо́чий *m adj*
lace [leɪs] *n* (*fabric*) кру́жево; (*of shoe*) шнуро́к ▷ *vt* (*shoe: also* **lace up**) шнурова́ть (*perf* зашнурова́ть)
lack [læk] *n* (*absence*) отсу́тствие;

(*shortage*) недоста́ток, нехва́тка ▷ *vt*: **she lacked self-confidence** ей не хвата́ло *or* не достава́ло уве́ренности в себе́; **through** *or* **for lack of** из-за недоста́тка *+gen*
lacquer ['lækəʳ] *n* лак
lad [læd] *n* па́рень *m*
ladder ['lædəʳ] *n* ле́стница; (*Brit*: *in tights*) спусти́вшиеся пе́тли *fpl*
ladle ['leɪdl] *n* поло́вник
lady ['leɪdɪ] *n* (*woman*) да́ма; **ladies and gentlemen ...** да́мы и господа́ ...; **young/old lady** молода́я/пожила́я же́нщина; **the ladies' (room)** же́нский туале́т; **ladybird** (*US* **ladybug**) *n* бо́жья коро́вка
lag [læg] *n* (*period of time*) заде́ржка
lager ['lɑːgəʳ] *n* све́тлое пи́во
laid [leɪd] *pt, pp of* **lay**
lain [leɪn] *pp of* **lie**
lake [leɪk] *n* о́зеро
lamb [læm] *n* (*Zool*) ягнёнок; (*Culin*) (молода́я) бара́нина
lame [leɪm] *adj* (*person, animal*) хромо́й; (*excuse, argument*) сла́бый
lament [lə'mɛnt] *n* плач ▷ *vt* опла́кивать (*perf* опла́кать)
lamp [læmp] *n* ла́мпа; (*street lamp*) фона́рь *m*; **lamppost** *n* (*Brit*) фона́рный столб; **lampshade** *n* абажу́р
land [lænd] *n* земля́ ▷ *vi* (*from ship*) выса́живаться (*perf* вы́садиться); (*Aviat*) приземля́ться (*perf* приземли́ться) ▷ *vt* (*plane*) сажа́ть (*perf* посади́ть); (*goods*) выгружа́ть (*perf* вы́грузить); **to land sb with sth** (*inf*) нава́ливать (*perf* навали́ть) что-н на кого́-н; **landing** *n* (*of house*) ле́стничная площа́дка; (*of plane*) поса́дка, приземле́ние; **landlady** *n* (*of house, flat*) домовладе́лица, хозя́йка; (*of pub*) хозя́йка; **landlord** *n* (*of house, flat*) домовладе́лец, хозя́ин; (*of pub*) хозя́ин; **landmark** *n* (назе́мный) ориенти́р; (*fig*) ве́ха; **landowner** *n* землевладе́лец(-лица); **landscape** *n* (*view, painting*) пейза́ж; (*terrain*) ландша́фт; **landslide** *n* (*Geo*) о́ползень *m*; (*Pol*: *also* **landslide victory**) реши́тельная побе́да
lane [leɪn] *n* (*in country*) тропи́нка; (*of road*) полоса́; (*Sport*) доро́жка
language ['læŋgwɪdʒ] *n* язы́к; **bad language** скверносло́вие
lantern ['læntən] *n* фона́рь *m*
lap [læp] *n* коле́ни *ntpl*; (*Sport*) круг
lapel [lə'pɛl] *n* ла́цкан
lapse [læps] *n* (*bad behaviour*) про́мах; (*of time*) промежу́ток; (*of concentration*) поте́ря
laptop ['læptɔp] *n* (*also* **laptop computer**) портати́вный компью́тер, ноутбу́к *m*
lard [lɑːd] *n* свино́й жир
larder ['lɑːdəʳ] *n* кладова́я *f adj*
large [lɑːdʒ] *adj* большо́й; (*major*) кру́пный; **at large** (*as a whole*) в це́лом; (*at liberty*) на во́ле; **largely** *adv* по бо́льшей ча́сти; **largely because ...** в основно́м, потому́ что ...; **large-scale** *adj* крупномасшта́бный
lark [lɑːk] *n* (*bird*) жа́воронок
laryngitis [lærɪn'dʒaɪtɪs] *n* ларинги́т
laser ['leɪzəʳ] *n* ла́зер; **laser printer** *n* ла́зерный при́нтер
lash [læʃ] *n* (*eyelash*) ресни́ца; (*of whip*) уда́р (*хлыста́*) ▷ *vt* (*also* **lash against**: *subj*: *rain, wind*)

хлеста́ть (*impf*) о *+acc*; (*tie*): **to lash to** привя́зывать (*perf* привяза́ть) к *+dat*

last [lɑ:st] *adj* (*most recent*) про́шлый; (*final*) после́дний ▷ *adv* в после́дний раз; (*finally*) в конце́ ▷ *vi* (*continue*) дли́ться (*perf* продли́ться), продолжа́ться (*impf*); (*keep*: *thing*) сохраня́ться (*perf* сохрани́ться); (: *person*) держа́ться (*perf* продержа́ться); (*suffice*): **we had enough money to last us** нам хвати́ло де́нег; **last year** в про́шлом году́; **last week** на про́шлой неде́ле; **last night** (*early*) вчера́ ве́чером; (*late*) про́шлой но́чью; **at last** наконе́ц; **last but one** предпосле́дний; **lastly** *adv* наконе́ц; **last-minute** *adj* после́дний

latch [lætʃ] *n* (*on gate*) задви́жка; (*on front door*) замо́к *m*

late [leɪt] *adj* по́здний; (*dead*) поко́йный ▷ *adv* по́здно; (*behind time*) с опозда́нием; **to be late** опа́здывать (*perf* опозда́ть); **of late** в после́днее вре́мя; **in late May** в конце́ ма́я; **latecomer** *n* опозда́вший(-ая) *m(f) adj*; **lately** *adv* в после́днее вре́мя

later ['leɪtəʳ] *adj* (*time, date*) бо́лее по́здний; (*meeting, version*) после́дующий ▷ *adv* по́зже, поздне́е; **later on** впосле́дствии, по́зже; **he arrived later than me** он пришёл по́зже меня́

latest ['leɪtɪst] *adj* са́мый по́здний; (*most recent*) (са́мый) после́дний; (*news*) после́дний; **at the latest** са́мое по́зднее

lather ['lɑ:ðəʳ] *n* (мы́льная) пе́на

Latin ['lætɪn] *n* (*Ling*) лати́нский язы́к ▷ *adj*: **Latin languages** рома́нские языки́; **Latin countries** стра́ны ю́жной Евро́пы; **Latin America** *n* Лати́нская Аме́рика

latitude ['lætɪtju:d] *n* (*Geo*) широта́

latter ['lætəʳ] *adj* после́дний ▷ *n*: **the latter** после́дний(-яя) *m(f) adj*

Latvia ['lætvɪə] *n* Ла́твия; **Latvian** *adj* латви́йский ▷ *n* (*Ling*) латы́шский язы́к

laugh [lɑ:f] *n* смех ▷ *vi* смея́ться (*impf*); **for a laugh** (*inf*) для сме́ха; **laugh at** *vt fus* смея́ться (*perf* посмея́ться) над *+instr*; **laughter** *n* смех

launch [lɔ:ntʃ] *n* (*of rocket, product*) за́пуск ▷ *vt* (*ship*) спуска́ть (*perf* спусти́ть) на́ воду; (*rocket*) запуска́ть (*perf* запусти́ть); (*attack, campaign*) начина́ть (*perf* нача́ть); (*product*) пуска́ть (*perf* пусти́ть) в прода́жу, запуска́ть (*perf* запусти́ть)

laundry ['lɔ:ndrɪ] *n* (*washing*) сти́рка

lava ['lɑ:və] *n* ла́ва

lavatory ['lævətərɪ] *n* туале́т

lavender ['lævəndəʳ] *n* лава́нда

lavish ['lævɪʃ] *adj* (*amount, hospitality*) ще́дрый ▷ *vt*: **to lavish sth on sb** осыпа́ть (*perf* осы́пать) кого́-н чем-н

law [lɔ:] *n* зако́н; (*professions*): **(the) law** юриспруде́нция; (*Scol*) пра́во; **it's against the law** э́то противозако́нно; **lawful** *adj* зако́нный

lawn [lɔ:n] *n* газо́н; **lawn mower** *n* газонокоси́лка

lawsuit ['lɔ:su:t] *n* суде́бный иск

lawyer ['lɔ:jəʳ] *n* (*solicitor, barrister*) юри́ст

lax [læks] *adj* (*discipline*) сла́бый; (*standards*) ни́зкий; (*morals, behaviour*) распу́щенный

laxative ['læksətɪv] *n* слаби́тельное *nt adj*

lay [leɪ] *pt of* **lie** ▷ *adj* (*not expert*) непрофессиона́льный; (*Rel*) мирско́й ▷ (*pt, pp* **laid**) *vt* (*place*) класть (*perf* положи́ть); (*table*) накрыва́ть (*perf* накры́ть) (на *+acc*); (*carpet*) стлать (*perf* постели́ть); (*cable*) прокла́дывать (*perf* проложи́ть); (*egg*) откла́дывать (*perf* отложи́ть); **lay down** *vt* (*object*) класть (*perf* положи́ть); (*rules etc*) устана́вливать (*perf* установи́ть); (*weapons*) скла́дывать (*perf* сложи́ть); **to lay down the law** прика́зывать (*perf* приказа́ть); **lay off** *vt* (*workers*) увольня́ть (*perf* уво́лить); **lay on** *vt* (*meal etc*) устра́ивать (*perf* устро́ить); **lay out** *vt* раскла́дывать (*perf* разложи́ть)

lay-by ['leɪbaɪ] *n* (*Brit*) площа́дка для вре́менной стоя́нки (*на автодоро́ге*)

layer ['leɪə^r] *n* слой

layout ['leɪaut] *n* (*of garden, building*) планиро́вка

lazy ['leɪzɪ] *adj* лени́вый

lb *abbr* (= *pound*) (*weight*) фунт

LB

Pound — ме́ра ве́са ра́вная 0,454 кг.

lead¹ [li:d] (*pt, pp* **led**) *n* (*front position*) пе́рвенство, ли́дерство; (*clue*) нить *f*; (*in play, film*) гла́вная роль *f*; (*for dog*) поводо́к; (*Elec*) про́вод ▷ *vt* (*competition, market*) лиди́ровать (*impf*) в *+prp*; (*opponent*) опережа́ть (*impf*); (*person, group: guide*) вести́ (*perf* повести́); (*activity, organization etc*) руководи́ть (*impf*) *+instr* ▷ *vi* (*road, pipe*) вести́ (*impf*); (*Sport*) лиди́ровать (*impf*); **to lead the way** ука́зывать (*perf* указа́ть) путь; **lead away** *vt* уводи́ть (*perf* увести́); **lead on** *vt* води́ть (*impf*) за́ нос; **lead to** *vt fus* вести́ (*perf* привести́) к *+dat*; **lead up to** *vt fus* (*events*) приводи́ть (*perf* привести́) к *+dat*; (*topic*) подводи́ть (*perf* подвести́) к *+dat*

lead² [lɛd] *n* (*metal*) свине́ц; (*in pencil*) графи́т

leader ['li:də^r] *n* (*of group, Sport*) ли́дер; **leadership** *n* руково́дство; (*quality*) ли́дерские ка́чества *ntpl*

lead-free ['lɛdfri:] *adj* не содержа́щий свинца́

leading ['li:dɪŋ] *adj* (*most important*) веду́щий; (*first, front*) пере́дний

lead singer [li:d-] *n* соли́ст(ка)

leaf [li:f] (*pl* **leaves**) *n* лист

leaflet ['li:flɪt] *n* листо́вка

league [li:g] *n* ли́га; **to be in league with sb** быть (*impf*) в сго́воре с кем-н

leak [li:k] *n* уте́чка; (*hole*) течь *f* ▷ *vi* протека́ть (*perf* проте́чь); (*liquid, gas*) проса́чиваться (*perf* просочи́ться) ▷ *vt* (*information*) разглаша́ть (*perf* разгласи́ть)

lean [li:n] (*pt, pp* **leaned** *or* **leant**) *adj* (*person*) сухоща́вый; (*meat*) по́стный ▷ *vt*: **to lean sth on** *or* **against** прислоня́ть (*perf* прислони́ть) что-н к *+dat* ▷ *vi*: **to lean forward/back** наклоня́ться (*perf* наклони́ться) вперёд/наза́д; **to lean against** (*wall*) прислоня́ться (*perf* прислони́ться) к *+dat*; (*person*) опира́ться (*perf* опере́ться) на *+acc*; **to lean on** (*chair*) опира́ться (*perf* опере́ться) о *+acc*; (*rely on*) опира́ться (*perf* опере́ться) на *+acc*; **leant** [lɛnt] *pt, pp of* **lean**

leap [li:p] (*pt, pp* **leaped** *or* **leapt**) *n* скачо́к ▷ *vi* пры́гать (*perf* пры́гнуть); (*price, number*) подска́кивать (*perf* подскочи́ть); **leapt** [lɛpt] *pp, pt of* **leap**; **leap year** *n* високо́сный год

learn [lə:n] (*pt, pp* **learned** *or* **learnt**) *vt* (*skill*) учи́ться (*perf* научи́ться) +*dat*; (*facts, poem*) учи́ть (*perf* вы́учить) ▷ *vi* учи́ться (*impf*); **to learn about** *or* **of/that ...** (*hear, read*) узнава́ть (*perf* узна́ть) о +*prp*/, что ...; **to learn about sth** (*study*) изуча́ть (*perf* изучи́ть) что-н; **to learn (how) to do** учи́ться (*perf* научи́ться) +*impf infin*; **learnt** [lə:nt] *pt, pp of* **learn**

lease [li:s] *n* аре́ндный догово́р, аре́нда ▷ *vt*: **to lease sth (to sb)** сдава́ть (*perf* сдать) что-н в аре́нду (кому́-н); **to lease sth from sb** арендова́ть (*impf/perf*) *or* брать (взять *perf*) в аре́нду у кого́-н

leash [li:ʃ] *n* поводо́к

least [li:st] *adj*: **the least** (+*noun*: *smallest*) наиме́ньший; (: *slightest*: *difficulty*) мале́йший ▷ *adv* (+*vb*) ме́ньше всего́; (+*adj*) наиме́нее; **at least** по кра́йней ме́ре; **not in the least** (*as response*) отню́дь нет; (+*vb*, +*adj*) ниско́лько *or* во́все не

leather ['lɛðə^r] *n* ко́жа

leave [li:v] (*pt, pp* **left**) *vt* оставля́ть (*perf* оста́вить), покида́ть (*perf* поки́нуть); (*go away from*: *on foot*) уходи́ть (*perf* уйти́) из +*gen*; (: *by transport*) уезжа́ть (*perf* уе́хать) из +*gen*; (*party, committee*) выходи́ть (*perf* вы́йти) из +*gen* ▷ *vi* (*on foot*) уходи́ть (*perf* уйти́); (*by transport*) уезжа́ть (*perf* уе́хать); (*bus, train*) уходи́ть (*perf* уйти́) ▷ *n* о́тпуск; **to leave sth to sb** (*money, property*) оставля́ть (*perf* оста́вить) что-н кому́-н; **to be left (over)** остава́ться (*perf* оста́ться); **on leave** в о́тпуске; **leave behind** *vt* оставля́ть (*perf* оста́вить); **leave out** *vt* (*omit*) пропуска́ть (*perf* пропусти́ть); **he was left out** его́ пропусти́ли

leaves [li:vz] *npl of* **leaf**

lecture ['lɛktʃə^r] *n* ле́кция ▷ *vi* чита́ть (*impf*) ле́кции ▷ *vt* (*scold*): **to lecture sb on** *or* **about** чита́ть (*perf* прочита́ть) кому́-н ле́кцию по по́воду +*gen*; **to give a lecture on** чита́ть (*perf* прочита́ть) ле́кцию о +*prp*; **lecturer** *n* (*Brit*: *Scol*) преподава́тель(ница) *m(f)*

led [lɛd] *pt, pp of* **lead**[1]

ledge [lɛdʒ] *n* вы́ступ; (*of window*) подоко́нник

leek [li:k] *n* лук-поре́й *no pl*

left [lɛft] *pt, pp of* **leave** ▷ *adj* (*of direction, position*) ле́вый ▷ *n* ле́вая сторона́ ▷ *adv* (*motion*): **(to the) left** нале́во; (*position*): **(on the) left** сле́ва; **the Left** (*Pol*) ле́вые *pl adj*; **left-handed** *adj*: **he/she is left-handed** он/она́ левша́; **left-wing** *adj* (*Pol*) ле́вый

leg [lɛg] *n* (*Anat*) нога́; (*of insect, furniture*) но́жка; (*also* **trouser leg**) штани́на; (*of journey, race*) эта́п

legacy ['lɛgəsɪ] *n* (*in will*) насле́дство; (*fig*) насле́дие

legal ['li:gl] *adj* (*advice, requirement*) юриди́ческий; (*system, action*) суде́бный; (*lawful*) зако́нный; **legalize** *vt* узако́нивать (*perf* узако́нить); **legally** *adv* юриди́чески; (*by law*) по зако́ну

legend ['lɛdʒənd] *n* (*story*) леге́нда; (*person*) легенда́рная ли́чность *f*; **legendary** *adj*

легенда́рный
legislation [lɛdʒɪs'leɪʃən] *n* законода́тельство
legislative ['lɛdʒɪslətɪv] *adj* (*Pol*) законода́тельный
legitimate [lɪ'dʒɪtɪmət] *adj* зако́нный, легити́мный
leisure ['lɛʒə^r] *n* (*also* **leisure time**) досу́г, свобо́дное вре́мя *nt*; **at (one's) leisure** не спеша́; **leisure centre** *n* спорти́вно-оздорови́тельный ко́мплекс; **leisurely** *adj* нетороплѝвый
lemon ['lɛmən] *n* (*fruit*) лимо́н; **lemonade** [lɛmə'neɪd] *n* лимона́д
lend [lɛnd] (*pt, pp* **lent**) *vt*: **to lend sth to sb, lend sb sth** ода́лживать (*perf* одолжи́ть) что-н кому́-н
length [lɛŋθ] *n* (*measurement*) длина́; (*distance*) протяжённость *f*; (*piece*: *of wood, cloth etc*) отре́зок; (*duration*) продолжи́тельность *f*; **at length** (*for a long time*) простра́нно; **lengthy** *adj* (*text*) дли́нный; (*meeting*) продолжи́тельный; (*explanation*) простра́нный
lens [lɛnz] *n* (*of glasses, camera*) ли́нза
Lent [lɛnt] *n* Вели́кий Пост
lent [lɛnt] *pt, pp of* **lend**
lentil ['lɛntl] *n* чечеви́ца *no pl*
Leo ['li:əu] *n* Лев
leopard ['lɛpəd] *n* леопа́рд
leotard ['li:əta:d] *n* трико́ *nt ind*
lesbian ['lɛzbɪən] *adj* лесби́йский ▷ *n* лесбия́нка
less [lɛs] *adj* (*attention, money*) ме́ньше *+gen* ▷ *adv* (*beautiful, clever*) ме́нее ▷ *prep* ми́нус *+nom*; **less than** ме́ньше *or* ме́нее *+gen*; **less than half** ме́ньше полови́ны; **less than ever** ме́ньше, чем когда́-либо; **less and less** всё ме́ньше и ме́ньше; (*+adj*) всё ме́нее и ме́нее; **the less ... the more ...** чем ме́ньше ..., тем бо́льше ...; **lesser** *adj*: **to a lesser extent** в ме́ньшей сте́пени
lesson ['lɛsn] *n* уро́к; **to teach sb a lesson** (*fig*) проучи́ть (*perf*) кого́-н
let [lɛt] (*pt, pp* **let**) *vt* (*Brit*: *lease*) сдава́ть (*perf* сдать) (внаём); (*allow*): **to let sb do** разреша́ть (*perf* разреши́ть) *or* позволя́ть (*perf* позво́лить) кому́-н *+infin*; **let me try** да́йте я попро́бую; **to let sb know about ...** дава́ть (*perf* дать) кому́-н знать о *+prp* ...; **let's go there** дава́й(те) пойдём туда́; **let's do it!** дава́й(те) сде́лаем э́то; **"to let"** "сдаётся внаём"; **to let go of** отпуска́ть (*perf* отпусти́ть); **let down** *vt* (*tyre etc*) спуска́ть (*perf* спусти́ть); (*fig*: *person*) подводи́ть (*perf* подвести́); **let in** *vt* (*water, air*) пропуска́ть (*perf* пропусти́ть); (*person*) впуска́ть (*perf* впусти́ть); **let off** *vt* (*culprit, child*) отпуска́ть (*perf* отпусти́ть); (*bomb*) взрыва́ть (*perf* взорва́ть); **let out** *vt* выпуска́ть (*perf* вы́пустить); (*sound*) издава́ть (*perf* изда́ть)
lethal ['li:θl] *adj* (*weapon, chemical*) смертоно́сный; (*dose*) смерте́льный
letter ['lɛtə^r] *n* письмо́; (*of alphabet*) бу́ква; **letter box** *n* (*Brit*) почто́вый я́щик

LETTER BOX

Поми́мо почто́вого я́щика да́нное сло́во та́кже обознача́ет про́резь во входно́й две́ри, в кото́рую опуска́ется корреспонде́нция.

lettuce ['lɛtɪs] *n* сала́т лату́к
leukaemia [lu:'ki:mɪə] (*US* **leukemia**) *n* белокро́вие, лейкеми́я
level ['lɛvl] *adj* (*flat*) ро́вный ▷ *n* у́ровень *m* ▷ *adv*: **to draw level with** (*person, vehicle*) поравня́ться (*perf*) с *+instr*; **to be level with** быть (*impf*) на одно́м у́ровне с *+instr*
lever ['li:və^r] *n* рыча́г; (*bar*) лом; **leverage** *n* (*fig*: *influence*) влия́ние
levy ['lɛvɪ] *n* нало́г ▷ *vt* налага́ть (*perf* наложи́ть)
liability [laɪə'bɪlətɪ] *n* (*responsibility*) отве́тственность *f*; (*person, thing*) обу́за *m/f*; **liabilities** *npl* (*Comm*) обяза́тельства *ntpl*
liable ['laɪəbl] *adj*: **liable for** (*legally responsible*) подсу́дный за *+acc*; **to be liable to** подлежа́ть (*impf*) *+dat*; **he's liable to take offence** возмо́жно, что он оби́дится
liar ['laɪə^r] *n* лжец, лгун(ья)
libel ['laɪbl] *n* клевета́
liberal ['lɪbərl] *adj* (*also Pol*) либера́льный; (*large, generous*) ще́дрый; **Liberal Democrat** *n* либера́л-демокра́т; **the Liberal Democrats** (*party*) па́ртия либера́л-демокра́тов
liberate ['lɪbəreɪt] *vt* освобожда́ть (*perf* освободи́ть)
liberation [lɪbə'reɪʃən] *n* освобожде́ние
liberty ['lɪbətɪ] *n* свобо́да; **to be at liberty** (*criminal*) быть (*impf*) на свобо́де; **I'm not at liberty to comment** я не во́лен комменти́ровать; **to take the liberty of doing** позволя́ть (*perf* позво́лить) себе́ *+infin*
Libra ['li:brə] *n* Весы́ *pl*
librarian [laɪ'brɛərɪən] *n* библиоте́карь *m*
library ['laɪbrərɪ] *n* библиоте́ка
lice [laɪs] *npl of* **louse**
licence ['laɪsns] (*US* **license**) *n* (*permit*) лице́нзия; (*Aut*: *also* **driving licence**) (води́тельские) права́ *ntpl*
license ['laɪsns] *n* (*US*) = **licence** ▷ *vt* выдава́ть (*perf* вы́дать) лице́нзию на *+acc*; **licensed** *adj* (*restaurant*) с лице́нзией на прода́жу спиртны́х напи́тков
lick [lɪk] *vt* (*stamp, fingers etc*) лиза́ть (*impf*), обли́зывать (*perf* облиза́ть); **to lick one's lips** обли́зываться (*perf* облиза́ться)
lid [lɪd] *n* кры́шка; (*also* **eyelid**) ве́ко
lie [laɪ] (*pt* **lay**, *pp* **lain**) *vi* (*be horizontal*) лежа́ть (*impf*); (*be situated*) лежа́ть (*impf*), находи́ться (*impf*); (*problem, cause*) заключа́ться (*impf*) ▷ (*pt, pp* **lied**) (*be untruthful*) лгать (*perf* солга́ть), врать (*perf* совра́ть) ▷ *n* (*untrue statement*) ложь *f no pl*; **to lie** *or* **be lying in first/last place** занима́ть (*impf*) пе́рвое/после́днее ме́сто; **lie down** *vi* (*motion*) ложи́ться (*perf* лечь); (*position*) лежа́ть (*impf*); **lie-in** *n* (*Brit*): **to have a lie-in** встава́ть (*perf* встать) попо́зже
lieutenant [lɛf'tɛnənt, (*US*) lu:'tɛnənt] *n* лейтена́нт
life [laɪf] (*pl* **lives**) *n* жизнь *f*; **lifeboat** *n* спаса́тельное су́дно; (*on ship*) спаса́тельная шлю́пка; **lifeguard** *n* спаса́тель *m*; **life jacket** *n* спаса́тельный жиле́т; **life preserver** *n* (*US*) = **life jacket**; **lifestyle** *n* о́браз жи́зни; **lifetime** *n* (*of person*) жизнь *f*; (*of*

institution) вре́мя *nt* существова́ния
lift [lɪft] *vt* поднима́ть (*perf* подня́ть); (*ban, sanctions*) снима́ть (*perf* снять) ▷ *vi* (*fog*) рассе́иваться (*perf* рассе́яться) ▷ *n* (*Brit*) лифт; **to give sb a lift** (*Brit*: *Aut*) подвози́ть (*perf* подвезти́) кого́-н
light [laɪt] (*pt, pp* **lit**) *n* свет; (*Aut*) фа́ра ▷ *vt* (*candle, fire*) зажига́ть (*perf* заже́чь); (*place*) освеща́ть (*perf* освети́ть) ▷ *adj* (*pale, bright*) све́тлый; (*not heavy*) лёгкий; **lights** *npl* (*also* **traffic lights**) светофо́р *msg*; **have you got a light?** (*for cigarette*) мо́жно у Вас прикури́ть?; **to come to light** выясня́ться (*perf* вы́ясниться); **in the light of** (*discussions etc*) в свете *+gen*; **light up** *vi* (*face*) светле́ть (*perf* просветле́ть) ▷ *vt* (*illuminate*) освеща́ть (*perf* освети́ть); **light-hearted** *adj* (*person*) беспе́чный; (*question, remark*) несерьёзный; **lighthouse** *n* мая́к; **lighting** *n* освеще́ние; **lightly** *adv* (*touch, kiss*) слегка́; (*eat, treat*) легко́; (*sleep*) чу́тко; **to get off lightly** легко́ отде́лываться (*perf* отде́латься)
lightning ['laɪtnɪŋ] *n* мо́лния
like [laɪk] *prep* как *+acc*; (*similar to*) похо́жий на *+acc* ▷ *vt* (*sweets, reading*) люби́ть (*impf*) ▷ *n*: **and the like** и тому́ подо́бное; **he looks like his father** он похо́ж на своего́ отца́; **what does she look like?** как она́ вы́глядит?; **what's he like?** что он за челове́к?; **there's nothing like ...** ничто́ не мо́жет сравни́ться с *+instr* ...; **do it like this** де́лайте э́то так; **that's just like him** (*typical*) э́то на него́ похо́же; **it is nothing like ...** э́то совсе́м не то, что ...; **I like/liked him** он мне нра́вится/понра́вился; **I would like, I'd like** мне хоте́лось бы, я бы хоте́л; **would you like a coffee?** хоти́те ко́фе?; **his likes and dislikes** его́ вку́сы; **likeable** *adj* симпати́чный
likelihood ['laɪklɪhud] *n* вероя́тность *f*
likely ['laɪklɪ] *adj* вероя́тный; **she is likely to agree** она́, вероя́тно, согласи́тся; **not likely!** (*inf*) ни за что!
likewise ['laɪkwaɪz] *adv* та́кже; **to do likewise** поступа́ть (*perf* поступи́ть) таки́м же о́бразом
lilac ['laɪlək] *n* сире́нь *f no pl*
lily ['lɪlɪ] *n* ли́лия
limb [lɪm] *n* (*Anat*) коне́чность *f*
lime [laɪm] *n* (*fruit*) лайм; (*tree*) ли́па; (*chemical*) и́звесть *f*
limelight ['laɪmlaɪt] *n*: **to be in the limelight** быть (*impf*) в це́нтре внима́ния
limestone ['laɪmstəun] *n* известня́к
limit ['lɪmɪt] *n* преде́л; (*restriction*) лими́т, ограниче́ние ▷ *vt* (*production, expense etc*) лимити́ровать (*impf/perf*), ограни́чивать (*perf* ограни́чить); **limited** *adj* ограни́ченный
limousine ['lɪməzi:n] *n* лимузи́н
limp [lɪmp] *vi* хрома́ть (*impf*) ▷ *adj* (*person, limb*) бесси́льный; (*material*) мя́гкий
line [laɪn] *n* ли́ния; (*row*) ряд; (*of writing, song*) строка́, стро́чка; (*wrinkle*) морщи́на; (*wire*) про́вод; (*fig*: *of thought*) ход; (*of business, work*) о́бласть *f* ▷ *vt* (*road*) выстра́иваться (*perf* вы́строиться) вдоль *+gen*; (*clothing*) подбива́ть (*perf* подби́ть); (*container*) выкла́дывать (*perf* вы́ложить)

изнутри́; **hold the line please!** (*Tel*) пожа́луйста, не клади́те тру́бку!; **to cut in line** (*US*) идти́ (*perf* пойти́) без о́череди; **in line with** (*in keeping with*) в соотве́тствии с *+instr*; **line up** *vi* выстра́иваться (*perf* вы́строиться) ▷ *vt* (*order*) выстра́ивать (*perf* вы́строить)

linen ['lɪnɪn] *n* (*sheets etc*) бельё

liner ['laɪnəʳ] *n* (*ship*) ла́йнер; (*also* **bin liner**) *целофа́новый мешо́к для му́сорного ведра́*

linger ['lɪŋgəʳ] *vi* уде́рживаться (*perf* удержа́ться); (*person*) заде́рживаться (*perf* задержа́ться)

lingerie ['lænʒəri:] *n* же́нское (ни́жнее) бельё

linguist ['lɪŋgwɪst] *n* (*language specialist*) лингви́ст; **linguistics** [lɪŋ'gwɪstɪks] *n* языкозна́ние, лингви́стика

lining ['laɪnɪŋ] *n* (*cloth*) подкла́дка

link [lɪŋk] *n* связь *f*; (*of chain*) звено́ ▷ *vt* (*join*) соединя́ть (*perf* соедини́ть); (*associate*): **to link with** *or* **to** свя́зывать (*perf* связа́ть) с *+instr*; **link up** *vt* (*systems*) соединя́ть (*perf* соедини́ть) ▷ *vi* соединя́ться (*perf* соедини́ться)

lion ['laɪən] *n* лев

lip [lɪp] *n* (*Anat*) губа́; **lip-read** *vi* чита́ть (*impf*) с губ; **lipstick** *n* (губна́я) пома́да

liqueur [lɪ'kjuəʳ] *n* ликёр

liquid ['lɪkwɪd] *n* жи́дкость *f* ▷ *adj* жи́дкий

liquor ['lɪkəʳ] *n* (*esp US*) спиртно́е *nt adj*, спиртно́й напи́ток

Lisbon ['lɪzbən] *n* Лиссабо́н

lisp [lɪsp] *n* шепеля́вость *f*

list [lɪst] *n* спи́сок ▷ *vt* (*enumerate*) перечисля́ть (*perf* перечи́слить); (*write down*) составля́ть (*perf* соста́вить) спи́сок *+gen*

listen ['lɪsn] *vi*: **to listen (to sb/sth)** слу́шать (*impf*) (кого́-н/что-н)

lit [lɪt] *pt, pp of* **light**

liter ['li:təʳ] *n* (*US*) = **litre**

literacy ['lɪtərəsɪ] *n* гра́мотность *f*

literal ['lɪtərl] *adj* буква́льный; **literally** *adv* буква́льно

literary ['lɪtərərɪ] *adj* литерату́рный

literate ['lɪtərət] *adj* (*able to read and write*) гра́мотный

literature ['lɪtrɪtʃəʳ] *n* литерату́ра

Lithuania [lɪθju'eɪnɪə] *n* Литва́; **Lithuanian** *adj* лито́вский

litre ['li:təʳ] (*US* **liter**) *n* литр

litter ['lɪtəʳ] *n* (*rubbish*) му́сор; (*Zool*) помёт, вы́водок

little ['lɪtl] *adj* ма́ленький; (*younger*) мла́дший; (*short*) коро́ткий ▷ *adv* ма́ло; **a little (bit)** немно́го; **little by little** понемно́гу

live [*vb* lɪv, *adj* laɪv] *vi* жить (*impf*) ▷ *adj* (*animal, plant*) живо́й; (*broadcast*) прямо́й; (*performance*) пе́ред пу́бликой; (*bullet*) боево́й; (*Elec*) под напряже́нием; **to live with sb** жить (*impf*) с кем-н; **he lived to (be) a hundred** он дожи́л до ста лет; **live on** *vt fus* (*food*) жить (*impf*) на *+prp*; (*salary*) жить (*impf*) на *+acc*; **live up to** *vt fus* опра́вдывать (*perf* оправда́ть)

livelihood ['laɪvlɪhud] *n* сре́дства *ntpl* к существова́нию

lively ['laɪvlɪ] *adj* живо́й; (*place, event*) оживлённый

liver ['lɪvəʳ] *n* (*Anat*) пе́чень *f*; (*Culin*) печёнка

lives [laɪvz] *npl of* **life**

livestock ['laɪvstɔk] *n* скот

living ['lɪvɪŋ] *adj* живо́й ▷ *n*: **to earn** *or* **make a living** зараба́тывать (*perf* зарабо́тать) на

жизнь; **living room** *n* гости́ная *f adj*
lizard ['lɪzəd] *n* я́щерица
load [ləud] *n* (*of person, animal*) но́ша; (*of vehicle*) груз; (*weight*) нагру́зка ▷ *vt* (*also* **load up (with)**: *goods*) грузи́ть (*perf* погрузи́ть); (*gun, camera*) заряжа́ть (*perf* заряди́ть); **to load (with)** (*also* **load up**: *vehicle, ship*) загружа́ть (*perf* загрузи́ть) (+*instr*); **loads of, a load of** (*inf*) ку́ча +*gen*; **a load of rubbish** (*inf*) сплошна́я чепуха́; **loaded** *adj* (*gun*) заря́женный; **loaded question** вопро́с с подте́кстом *or* подво́хом
loaf [ləuf] (*pl* **loaves**) *n* (*bread*) буха́нка
loan [ləun] *n* заём; (*money*) ссу́да ▷ *vt* дава́ть (*perf* дать) взаймы́; (*money*) ссужа́ть (*perf* ссуди́ть); **to take sth on loan** брать (*perf* взять) что-н на вре́мя
loathe [ləuð] *vt* ненави́деть (*impf*)
loaves [ləuvz] *npl of* **loaf**
lobby ['lɔbɪ] *n* (*of building*) вестибю́ль *m*; (*pressure group*) ло́бби *nt ind* ▷ *vt* склоня́ть (*perf* склони́ть) на свою́ сто́рону
lobster ['lɔbstə^r] *n* ома́р
local ['ləukl] *adj* ме́стный; **locals** *npl* ме́стные *pl adj* (жи́тели); **local authorities** *npl* ме́стные вла́сти *fpl*; **local government** *n* ме́стное управле́ние; **locally** *adv* (*live, work*) побли́зости
locate [ləu'keɪt] *vt* определя́ть (*perf* определи́ть) расположе́ние *or* местонахожде́ние +*gen*; **to be located in** (*situated*) располага́ться (*impf*), находи́ться (*impf*) в/на +*prp*
location [ləu'keɪʃən] *n* (*place*) расположе́ние, местонахожде́ние; **on location** (*Cinema*) на нату́ре
loch [lɔx] *n* (*Scottish*) о́зеро
lock [lɔk] *n* (*on door etc*) замо́к; (*on canal*) шлюз; (*of hair*) ло́кон ▷ *vt* запира́ть (*perf* запере́ть) ▷ *vi* (*door*) запира́ться (*perf* запере́ться); (*wheels*) тормози́ть (*perf* затормози́ть); **lock in** *vt*: **to lock sb in** запира́ть (*perf* запере́ть) кого́-н; **lock up** *vt* (*criminal etc*) упря́тывать (*perf* упря́тать); (*house*) запира́ть (*perf* запере́ть) ▷ *vi* запира́ться (*perf* запере́ться)
locker ['lɔkə^r] *n* шка́фчик
locomotive [ləukə'məutɪv] *n* локомоти́в
lodge [lɔdʒ] *n* привра́тницкая *f adj*; **lodger** *n* квартира́нт(ка)
loft [lɔft] *n* черда́к
log [lɔg] *n* бревно́; (*for fire*) поле́но; (*account*) журна́л ▷ *vt* (*event, fact*) регистри́ровать (*perf* зарегистри́ровать); **log in** *vi* (*Comput*) входить (*perf* войти); **log off** *vi* (*Comput*) выходи́ть (*perf* вы́йти) из систе́мы; **log on** *vi* (*Comput*) входи́ть (*perf* войти́) в систе́му
logic ['lɔdʒɪk] *n* ло́гика; **logical** *adj* (*based on logic*) логи́ческий; (*reasonable*) логи́чный
login ['lɔgɪn] *n* (*Comput*) и́мя (*nt*) по́льзователя
logo ['ləugəu] *n* эмбле́ма
London ['lʌndən] *n* Ло́ндон
lone [ləun] *adj* (*person*) одино́кий
loneliness ['ləunlɪnɪs] *n* одино́чество
lonely ['ləunlɪ] *adj* (*person, childhood*) одино́кий; (*place*) уединённый
long [lɔŋ] *adj* дли́нный; (*in time*) до́лгий ▷ *adv* (*see adj*) дли́нно; до́лго ▷ *vi*: **to long for sth/to do** жа́ждать (*impf*) чего́-н/+*infin*; **so** *or*

as long as you don't mind если только Вы не возража́ете; **don't be long!** не задéрживайтесь!; **how long is the street?** каковá длинá э́той у́лицы?; **how long is the lesson?** скóлько дли́тся урóк?; **6 metres long** длинóй в 6 мéтров; **6 months long** продолжи́тельностью в 6 мéсяцев; **all night (long)** всю ночь (напролёт); **he no longer comes** он бóльше не прихóдит; **long before** задóлго до *+gen*; **long after** дóлгое врéмя пóсле *+gen*; **before long** вскóре; **at long last** наконéц; **long-distance** *adj* (*travel*) дáльний

longitude [ˈlɔŋgɪtjuːd] *n* долготá

long: **long jump** *n* прыжóк в длину́; **long-life** *adj* консерви́рованный; (*battery*) продлённого дéйствия; **long-standing** *adj* долголéтний; **long-term** *adj* долгосрóчный

look [luk] *vi* (*see*) смотрéть (*perf* посмотрéть); (*glance*) взгляну́ть (*perf*); (*seem, appear*) вы́глядеть (*impf*) ▷ *n* (*glance*) взгляд; (*appearance*) вид; (*expression*) выражéние; **looks** *npl* (*also* **good looks**) краси́вая внéшность *fsg*; **to look south/(out) onto the sea** (*face*) выходи́ть (*impf*) на юг/на мóре; **look after** *vt fus* (*care for*) уха́живать (*impf*) за *+instr*; (*deal with*) забóтиться (*impf*) о *+prp*; **look around** *vt fus* = **look round**; **look at** *vt fus* смотрéть (*perf* посмотрéть) на *+acc*; (*read quickly*) просмáтривать (*perf* просмотрéть); **look back** *vi* (*turn around*): **to look back (at)** огля́дываться (*perf* огляну́ться) (на *+acc*); **look down on** *vt fus* (*fig*) смотрéть (*impf*) свысокá на *+acc*; **look for** *vt fus* искáть (*impf*); **look forward to** *vt fus*: **to look forward to sth** ждать (*impf*) чегó-н с нетерпéнием; **we look forward to hearing from you** (с нетерпéнием) ждём Вáшего отвéта; **look into** *vt fus* расслéдовать (*impf/perf*); **look on** *vi* (*watch*) наблюдáть (*impf*); **look out** *vi* (*beware*): **to look out (for)** остерегáться (*impf*) (*+gen*); **to look out (of)** (*glance out*) выгля́дывать (*perf* вы́глянуть) (в *+acc*); **look out for** *vt fus* (*search for*) старáться (*perf* постарáться) найти́; **look round** *vt fus* (*museum etc*) осмáтривать (*perf* осмотрéть); **look through** *vt fus* (*papers*) просмáтривать (*perf* просмотрéть); (*window*) смотрéть (*perf* посмотрéть) в *+acc*; **look to** *vt fus* (*rely on*) ждать (*impf*) от *+gen*; **look up** *vi* поднимáть (*perf* подня́ть) глазá; (*situation*) идти́ (*perf* пойти́) к лу́чшему ▷ *vt* (*fact*) смотрéть (*perf* посмотрéть); **lookout** *n* (*person*) наблюдáтель(ница) *m(f)*; (*point*) наблюдáтельный пункт; **to be on the lookout for sth** присмáтривать (*impf*) что-н

loop [luːp] *n* пéтля ▷ *vt*: **to loop sth round sth** завя́зывать (*perf* завязáть) что-н пéтлей вокру́г чегó-н

loose [luːs] *adj* свобóдный; (*knot, grip, connection*) слáбый; (*hair*) распу́щенный ▷ *n*: **to be on the loose** быть (*impf*) в бегáх; **the handle is loose** ру́чка расшатáлась; **to set loose** (*prisoner*) освобождáть (*perf* освободи́ть); **loosen** *vt* (*belt, screw, grip*) ослабля́ть (*perf* ослáбить)

loot [luːt] *n* (*inf*) нагрáбленное *nt*

adj ▷ *vt* (*shops, homes*) разграблять (*perf* разграбить)
lord [lɔːd] *n* (*Brit*: *peer*) лорд; (*Rel*): **the Lord** Господь *m*; **my Lord** милорд; **good Lord!** Боже правый!
lorry [ˈlɔrɪ] *n* (*Brit*) грузовик
lose [luːz] (*pt, pp* **lost**) *vt* терять (*perf* потерять); (*contest, argument*) проигрывать (*perf* проиграть) ▷ *vi* (*in contest, argument*) проигрывать (*perf* проиграть); **loser** *n* (*in contest*) проигравший(-ая) *m(f) adj*
loss [lɔs] *n* потеря; (*sense of bereavement*) утрата; (*Comm*) убыток; **heavy losses** тяжёлые потери *fpl*; **to be at a loss** теряться (*perf* растеряться)
lost [lɔst] *pt, pp of* **lose** ▷ *adj* пропавший; **to get lost** заблудиться (*perf*)
lot [lɔt] *n* (*of people, goods*) партия; (*at auction*) лот; **a lot (of)** (*many*) много (*+gen*); **the lot** (*everything*) всё; **lots of ...** много *+gen* ...; **I see a lot of him** мы с ним часто видимся; **I read/don't read a lot** я много/мало читаю; **a lot bigger/more expensive** намного *or* гораздо больше/дороже; **to draw lots (for sth)** тянуть (*impf*) жребий (для чего-н)
lotion [ˈləuʃən] *n* лосьон
lottery [ˈlɔtərɪ] *n* лотерея
loud [laud] *adj* (*noise, voice, laugh*) громкий; (*support, condemnation*) громогласный; (*clothes*) кричащий ▷ *adv* громко; **out loud** вслух; **loudly** *adv* (*speak, laugh*) громко; (*support*) громогласно; **loudspeaker** *n* громкоговоритель *m*
lounge [laundʒ] *n* (*in house, hotel*) гостиная *f adj*; (*at airport*) зал ожидания
louse [laus] (*pl* **lice**) *n* (*insect*) вошь *f*
love [lʌv] *vt* любить (*impf*) ▷ *n*: **love (for)** любовь *f* (к *+dat*); **to love to do** любить (*impf*) *+infin*; **I'd love to come** я бы с удовольствием пришёл; **"love (from) Anne"** "любящая Вас Анна"; **to fall in love with** влюбляться (*perf* влюбиться) в *+acc*; **he is in love with her** он в неё влюблён; **to make love** заниматься (*perf* заняться) любовью; **"fifteen love"** (*Tennis*) "пятнадцать — ноль"; **love affair** *n* роман; **love life** *n* интимная жизнь *f*
lovely [ˈlʌvlɪ] *adj* (*beautiful*) красивый; (*delightful*) чудесный
lover [ˈlʌvə^r] *n* любовник(-ица); (*of art etc*) любитель(ница) *m(f)*
loving [ˈlʌvɪŋ] *adj* нежный
low [ləu] *adj* низкий; (*quiet*) тихий; (*depressed*) подавленный ▷ *adv* (*fly*) низко; (*sing*: *quietly*) тихо ▷ *n* (*Meteorology*) низкое давление; **we are (running) low on milk** у нас осталось мало молока; **an all-time low** небывало низкий уровень
lower [ˈləuə^r] *adj* (*bottom*: *of two things*) нижний; (*less important*) низший ▷ *vt* (*object*) спускать (*perf* спустить); (*level, price*) снижать (*perf* снизить); (*voice*) понижать (*perf* понизить); (*eyes*) опускать (*perf* опустить)

LOWER SIXTH

Lower sixth — нижняя ступень школьного квалификационного курса. Этот курс длится два года, в течение которых школьники готовятся к квалификацио́нным экза́менам, даю́щим пра́во поступле́ния в университе́т.

low-fat ['ləu'fæt] *adj* обезжи́ренный
loyal ['lɔɪəl] *adj* ве́рный; (*Pol*) лоя́льный; **loyalty** *n* ве́рность *f*; (*Pol*) лоя́льность *f*; **loyalty card** *n* ≈ диско́нтная ка́рта
LP *n abbr* (= *long-playing record*) долгоигра́ющая пласти́нка

L-PLATES

L-plates — бе́лая табли́чка, на кото́рую нанесена́ кра́сная бу́ква **L**, обознача́ющая **Learner** – Учени́к. Таки́е табли́чки помеща́ются на за́днем или ветрово́м стекле́ автомоби́лей, води́тели кото́рых прохо́дят курс по вожде́нию.

Ltd *abbr* (*Comm*) (= *limited (liability) company*) компа́ния с ограни́ченной отве́тственностью
luck [lʌk] *n* (*also* **good luck**) уда́ча; **bad luck** неуда́ча; **good luck!** уда́чи (Вам)!; **hard** *or* **tough luck!** не повезло́!; **luckily** *adv* к сча́стью; **lucky** *adj* (*situation, object*) счастли́вый; (*person*) уда́чливый; **he is lucky at cards/in love** ему́ везёт в ка́ртах/любви́
lucrative ['lu:krətɪv] *adj* при́быльный, дохо́дный; (*job*) высокоопла́чиваемый
ludicrous ['lu:dɪkrəs] *adj* смехотво́рный
luggage ['lʌgɪdʒ] *n* бага́ж
lukewarm ['lu:kwɔ:m] *adj* слегка́ тёплый; (*fig*) прохла́дный
lull [lʌl] *n* зати́шье ▷ *vt*: **to lull sb to sleep** убаю́кивать (*perf* убаю́кать) кого́-н; **to lull sb into a false sense of security** усыпля́ть (*perf* усыпи́ть) чью-н бди́тельность
lullaby ['lʌləbaɪ] *n* колыбе́льная *f adj*
luminous ['lu:mɪnəs] *adj* (*digit, star*) светя́щийся
lump [lʌmp] *n* (*of clay, snow*) ком; (*of butter, sugar*) кусо́к; (*bump*) ши́шка; (*growth*) о́пухоль *f* ▷ *vt*: **to lump together** меша́ть (*perf* смеша́ть) в (одну́) ку́чу; **a lump sum** единовре́менно выпла́чиваемая су́мма; **lumpy** *adj* (*sauce*) комкова́тый
lunatic ['lu:nətɪk] *adj* (*behaviour*) безу́мный
lunch [lʌntʃ] *n* обе́д; **lunch time** *n* обе́денное вре́мя *nt*, обе́д
lung [lʌŋ] *n* лёгкое *nt adj*; **lung cancer** рак лёгких
lure [luə^r] *vt* зама́нивать (*perf* замани́ть); **to lure sb away from** отвлека́ть (*perf* отвле́чь) кого́-н от +*gen*
lush [lʌʃ] *adj* (*healthy*) пы́шный
lust [lʌst] *n* (*sexual desire*) по́хоть *f*; (*greed*): **lust (for)** жа́жда (к +*dat*)
Luxembourg ['lʌksəmbə:g] *n* Люксембу́рг
luxurious [lʌg'zjuərɪəs] *adj* роско́шный
luxury ['lʌkʃərɪ] *n* (*great comfort*) ро́скошь *f*; (*treat*) роско́шество
lyrics ['lɪrɪks] *npl* текст *msg* (*пе́сни*)

m *abbr* (= *metre*) м (= *метр*); = **mile**; **million**
MA *n abbr* = **Master of Arts**
mac [mæk] *n* (*Brit*: *inf*) макинто́ш
macaroni [mækəˈrəunɪ] *n* макаро́ны *pl*
Macedonia [mæsɪˈdəunɪə] *n* Македо́ния
machine [məˈʃiːn] *n* маши́на; (*also* **sewing machine**) маши́нка; **machine gun** *n* пулемёт; **machinery** [məˈʃiːnərɪ] *n* обору́дование; (*Pol*) механи́зм
mackerel [ˈmækrl] *n inv* ску́мбрия
mackintosh [ˈmækɪntɔʃ] *n* = **mac**
mad [mæd] *adj* сумасше́дший, поме́шанный; (*angry*) бе́шеный; (*keen*): **he is mad about** он поме́шан на +*prp*
madam [ˈmædəm] *n* (*form of address*) мада́м *f ind*, госпожа́
made [meɪd] *pt, pp of* **make**
madman [ˈmædmən] *irreg n* сумасше́дший *m adj*
madness [ˈmædnɪs] *n* безу́мие
Madrid [məˈdrɪd] *n* Мадри́д
Mafia [ˈmæfɪə] *n*: **the Mafia** ма́фия
magazine [mægəˈziːn] *n* журна́л
maggot [ˈmægət] *n* личи́нка (насеко́мых)
magic [ˈmædʒɪk] *n* ма́гия; **magical** *adj* маги́ческий; (*experience, evening*) волше́бный; **magician** [məˈdʒɪʃən] *n* (*conjurer*) фо́кусник
magistrate [ˈmædʒɪstreɪt] *n* (*Law*) мирово́й судья́ *m*
magnet [ˈmægnɪt] *n* магни́т; **magnetic** [mægˈnɛtɪk] *adj* магни́тный; (*personality*) притяга́тельный
magnificent [mægˈnɪfɪsnt] *adj* великоле́пный
magnify [ˈmægnɪfaɪ] *vt* увели́чивать (*perf* увели́чить); (*sound*) уси́ливать (*perf* уси́лить); **magnifying glass** *n* увеличи́тельное стекло́, лу́па
mahogany [məˈhɔgənɪ] *n* кра́сное де́рево
maid [meɪd] *n* (*in house*) служа́нка; (*in hotel*) го́рничная *f adj*
maiden name *n* де́вичья фами́лия
mail [meɪl] *n* по́чта ▷ *vt* отправля́ть (*perf* отпра́вить) по по́чте; (*Comput*): **to mail sb** писа́ть (*perf* написа́ть) кому́-н по электро́нной по́чте; **mailbox** *n* (*US*: *letter box*) почто́вый я́щик; **mail order** *n* *зака́з това́ров по по́чте*
main [meɪn] *adj* гла́вный ▷ *n*: **gas/water main** газопрово́дная/

водопрово́дная магистра́ль *f*; **mains** *npl* сеть *fsg*; **main meal** обе́д; **mainland** *n*: **the mainland** матери́к; **mainly** *adv* гла́вным о́бразом; **mainstream** *n* госпо́дствующая направле́ние

maintain [meɪn'teɪn] *vt* (*friendship, system, momentum*) подде́рживать (*perf* поддержа́ть); (*building*) обслу́живать (*impf*); (*affirm*: *belief, opinion*) утвержда́ть (*impf*)

maintenance ['meɪntənəns] *n* (*of friendship, system*) поддержа́ние; (*of building*) обслу́живание; (*Law*: *alimony*) алиме́нты *pl*

maize [meɪz] *n* кукуру́за, маи́с

majesty ['mædʒɪstɪ] *n*: **Your Majesty** Ва́ше Вели́чество

major ['meɪdʒə^r] *adj* (*important*) суще́ственный

majority [mə'dʒɔrɪtɪ] *n* большинство́

make [meɪk] (*pt, pp* **made**) *vt* де́лать (*perf* сде́лать); (*clothes*) шить (*perf* сшить); (*manufacture*) изготовля́ть (*perf* изгото́вить); (*meal*) гото́вить (*perf* пригото́вить); (*money*) зараба́тывать (*perf* зарабо́тать); (*profit*) получа́ть (*perf* получи́ть) ▷ *n* (*brand*) ма́рка; **to make sb do** (*force*) заставля́ть (*perf* заста́вить) кого́-н +*infin*; **2 and 2 make 4** (*equal*) 2 плюс 2 равня́ется четырём; **to make sb unhappy** расстра́ивать (*perf* расстро́ить) кого́-н; **to make a noise** шуме́ть (*impf*); **to make the bed** стели́ть (*perf* постели́ть) посте́ль; **to make a fool of sb** де́лать (*perf* сде́лать) из кого́-н дурака́; **to make a profit** получа́ть (*perf* получи́ть) при́быль; **to make a loss** нести́ (*perf* понести́) убы́ток; **to make it** (*arrive*) успева́ть (*perf* успе́ть); **let's make it Monday** дава́йте договори́мся на понеде́льник; **to make do with/without** обходи́ться (*perf* обойти́сь) +*instr*/без +*gen*; **make for** *vt fus* (*place*) направля́ться (*perf* напра́виться) к +*dat*/в +*acc*; **make out** *vt* (*decipher*) разбира́ть (*perf* разобра́ть); (*see*) различа́ть (*perf* различи́ть); (*write out*) выпи́сывать (*perf* вы́писать); (*understand*) разбира́ться (*perf* разобра́ться) в +*prp*; **make up** *vt fus* (*constitute*) составля́ть (*perf* соста́вить) ▷ *vt* (*invent*) выду́мывать (*perf* вы́думать) ▷ *vi* (*after quarrel*) мири́ться (*perf* помири́ться); (*with cosmetics*): **to make (o.s.) up** де́лать (*perf* сде́лать) макия́ж; **make up for** *vt fus* (*mistake*) загла́живать (*perf* загла́дить); (*loss*) восполня́ть (*perf* воспо́лнить); **maker** *n* (*of goods*) изготови́тель *m*; **makeshift** *adj* вре́менный; **make-up** *n* косме́тика, макия́ж; (*Theat*) грим

making ['meɪkɪŋ] *n* (*of programme*) созда́ние; **to have the makings of** име́ть (*impf*) зада́тки +*gen*

malaria [mə'lɛərɪə] *n* маляри́я

male [meɪl] *n* (*human*) мужчи́на *m*; (*animal*) саме́ц ▷ *adj* мужско́й; (*child*) мужско́го по́ла

malicious [mə'lɪʃəs] *adj* зло́бный, злой

malignant [mə'lɪgnənt] *adj* (*Med*) злока́чественный

mall [mɔːl] *n* (*also* **shopping mall**) ≈ торго́вый центр

mallet ['mælɪt] *n* деревя́нный молото́к

malnutrition [mælnjuː'trɪʃən] *n* недоеда́ние

m

malt [mɔːlt] *n* (*grain*) со́лод; (*also* **malt whisky**) солодо́вое ви́ски *nt ind*
mammal ['mæml] *n* млекопита́ющее *nt adj*
mammoth ['mæməθ] *adj* (*task*) колосса́льный
man [mæn] (*pl* **men**) *n* мужчи́на *m*; (*person, mankind*) челове́к ▷ *vt* (*machine*) обслу́живать (*impf*); (*post*) занима́ть (*perf* заня́ть); **an old man** стари́к; **man and wife** муж и жена́
manage ['mænɪdʒ] *vi* (*get by*) обходи́ться (*perf* обойти́сь) ▷ *vt* (*business, organization*) руководи́ть (*impf*) *+instr*, управля́ть (*impf*) *+instr*; (*shop, restaurant*) заве́довать (*impf*) *+instr*; (*economy*) управля́ть (*impf*) *+instr*; (*workload, task*) справля́ться (спра́виться (*impf*)) с *+instr*; **I managed to convince him** мне удало́сь убеди́ть его́; **management** *n* (*body*) руково́дство; (*act*): **management (of)** управле́ние (*+instr*); **manager** *n* (*of business, organization*) управля́ющий *m adj*, ме́неджер; (*of shop*) заве́дующий *m adj*; (*of pop star*) ме́неджер; (*Sport*) гла́вный тре́нер; **manageress** [mænɪdʒə'rɛs] *n* (*of shop*) заве́дующая *f adj*; **managerial** [mænɪ'dʒɪərɪəl] *adj* (*role*) руководя́щий; **managerial staff** руководя́щий аппара́т
managing director ['mænɪdʒɪŋ-] *n* управля́ющий дире́ктор
mandarin ['mændərɪn] *n* (*also* **mandarin orange**) мандари́н
mandate ['mændeɪt] *n* (*Pol*) полномо́чие
mandatory ['mændətərɪ] *adj* обяза́тельный
mane [meɪn] *n* гри́ва
maneuver [mə'nuːvə^r] *n, vb* (*US*) = **manoeuvre**
mango ['mæŋgəu] (*pl* **mangoes**) *n* ма́нго *nt ind*
mania ['meɪnɪə] *n* (*also Psych*) ма́ния
maniac ['meɪnɪæk] *n* манья́к
manic ['mænɪk] *adj* безу́мный, маниака́льный
manifest ['mænɪfɛst] *vt* проявля́ть (*perf* прояви́ть) ▷ *adj* очеви́дный, я́вный
manifesto [mænɪ'fɛstəu] *n* манифе́ст
manipulate [mə'nɪpjuleɪt] *vt* манипули́ровать (*impf*) *+instr*
mankind [mæn'kaɪnd] *n* челове́чество
manly ['mænlɪ] *adj* му́жественный
man-made ['mæn'meɪd] *adj* иску́сственный
manner ['mænə^r] *n* (*way*) о́браз; (*behaviour*) мане́ра; **manners** *npl* (*conduct*) мане́ры *fpl*; **all manner of things/people** всевозмо́жные ве́щи/лю́ди; **in a manner of speaking** в не́котором ро́де
manoeuvre [mə'nuːvə^r] (*US* **maneuver**) *vt* передвига́ть (*perf* передви́нуть); (*manipulate*) маневри́ровать (*impf*) *+instr* ▷ *vi* маневри́ровать (*impf*) ▷ *n* манёвр
manpower ['mænpauə^r] *n* рабо́чая си́ла
mansion ['mænʃən] *n* особня́к
manslaughter ['mænslɔːtə^r] *n* непредумы́шленное уби́йство
mantelpiece ['mæntlpiːs] *n* ками́нная доска́
manual ['mænjuəl] *adj* ручно́й ▷ *n* посо́бие; **manual worker**

чернорабо́чий(-ая) *m(f) adj*
manufacture [mænju'fæktʃəʳ] *vt* (*goods*) изготовля́ть (*perf* изгото́вить), производи́ть (*perf* произвести́) ▷ *n* изготовле́ние, произво́дство; **manufacturer** *n* изготови́тель *m*, производи́тель *m*
manure [mə'njuəʳ] *n* наво́з
manuscript ['mænjuskrɪpt] *n* (*old text*) манускри́пт; (*before printing*) ру́копись *f*
many ['mɛnɪ] *adj* (*a lot of*) мно́го *+gen* ▷ *pron* (*several*) мно́гие *pl adj*; **a great many** о́чень мно́го *+gen*, мно́жество *+gen*; **how many?** ско́лько?; **many a time** мно́го раз; **in many cases** во мно́гих слу́чаях; **many of us** мно́гие из нас
map [mæp] *n* ка́рта; (*of town*) план
maple ['meɪpl] *n* клён
mar [mɑːʳ] *vt* по́ртить (*perf* испо́ртить)
marathon ['mærəθən] *n* марафо́н
marble ['mɑːbl] *n* (*stone*) мра́мор
March [mɑːtʃ] *n* март
march [mɑːtʃ] *vi* марширова́ть (*perf* промарширова́ть) ▷ *n* марш
mare [mɛəʳ] *n* кобы́ла
margarine [mɑːdʒə'riːn] *n* маргари́н
margin ['mɑːdʒɪn] *n* (*on page*) поля́ *ntpl*; (*of victory*) преиму́щество; (*of defeat*) меньшинство́; (*also* **profit margin**) ма́ржа, чи́стая при́быль *f no pl*; **marginal** *adj* незначи́тельный
marigold ['mærɪgəuld] *n* ноготки́ *mpl*
marijuana [mærɪ'wɑːnə] *n* марихуа́на
marina [mə'riːnə] *n* мари́на, при́стань *f* для яхт
marine [mə'riːn] *adj* морско́й; (*engineer*) судово́й ▷ *n* (*Brit*) слу́жащий *m adj* вое́нно-морско́го фло́та; (*US*) морско́й пехоти́нец
marital ['mærɪtl] *adj* супру́жеский; **marital status** семе́йное положе́ние
maritime ['mærɪtaɪm] *adj* морско́й
mark [mɑːk] *n* (*symbol*) значо́к, поме́тка; (*stain*) пятно́; (*of shoes etc*) след; (*token*) знак; (*Brit: Scol*) отме́тка, оце́нка ▷ *vt* (*occasion*) отмеча́ть (*perf* отме́тить); (*with pen*) помеча́ть (*perf* поме́тить); (*subj: shoes, tyres*) оставля́ть (*perf* оста́вить) след на *+prp*; (*furniture*) поврежда́ть (*perf* повреди́ть); (*clothes, carpet*) ста́вить (*perf* поста́вить) пятно́ на *+prp*; (*place, time*) ука́зывать (*perf* указа́ть); (*Brit: Scol*) проверя́ть (*perf* прове́рить); **marked** *adj* заме́тный; **marker** *n* (*sign*) знак; (*bookmark*) закла́дка; (*pen*) флома́стер
market ['mɑːkɪt] *n* ры́нок ▷ *vt* (*promote*) реклами́ровать (*impf*); (*sell*) выпуска́ть (*perf* вы́пустить) в прода́жу; **marketing** *n* ма́ркетинг; **market research** *n* ма́ркетинговые иссле́дования *ntpl*
marmalade ['mɑːməleɪd] *n* джем (*ци́трусовый*)
maroon [mə'ruːn] *vt*: **we were marooned** мы бы́ли отре́заны от вне́шнего ми́ра
marquee [mɑː'kiː] *n* марки́за, пала́точный павильо́н
marriage ['mærɪdʒ] *n* брак; (*wedding*) сва́дьба; **marriage certificate** *n* свиде́тельство о бра́ке

m

married ['mærɪd] *adj* (*man*) жена́тый; (*woman*) заму́жняя; (*couple*) жена́тые; (*life*) супру́жеский
marrow ['mærəu] *n* (*Bot*) кабачо́к; (*also* **bone marrow**) ко́стный мозг
marry ['mærɪ] *vt* (*subj*: *man*) жени́ться (*impf/perf*) на +*prp*; (: *woman*) выходи́ть (*perf* вы́йти) за́муж за +*acc*; (: *priest*) венча́ть (*perf* обвенча́ть); (*also* **marry off**: *son*) жени́ть (*impf/perf*); (: *daughter*) выдава́ть (*perf* вы́дать) за́муж ▷ *vi*: **to get married** (*man*) жени́ться (*impf*); (*woman*) выходи́ть (*perf* вы́йти) за́муж; (*couple*) жени́ться (*perf* пожени́ться)
Mars [mɑːz] *n* Марс
marsh [mɑːʃ] *n* боло́то
marshal ['mɑːʃl] *n* (*at public event*) распоряди́тель(ница) *m(f)* ▷ *vt* (*support*) упоря́дочивать (*perf* упоря́дочить); **police marshal** (*US*) нача́льник полице́йского уча́стка
martyr ['mɑːtəʳ] *n* му́ченик(-ица)
marvellous (*US* **marvelous**) ['mɑːvləs] *adj* восхити́тельный, изуми́тельный
Marxist ['mɑːksɪst] *adj* маркси́стский ▷ *n* маркси́ст(ка)
marzipan ['mɑːzɪpæn] *n* марципа́н
mascara [mæs'kɑːrə] *n* тушь *f* для ресни́ц
mascot ['mæskət] *n* талисма́н
masculine ['mæskjulɪn] *adj* мужско́й; (*Ling*) мужско́го ро́да
mash [mæʃ] *vt* де́лать (*perf* сде́лать) пюре́ из +*gen*
mask [mɑːsk] *n* ма́ска ▷ *vt* (*feelings*) маскирова́ть (*impf*)
mason ['meɪsn] *n* (*also* **stone mason**) ка́менщик; (*also* **freemason**) масо́н, во́льный ка́менщик; **masonry** *n* (ка́менная) кла́дка
mass [mæs] *n* (*also Phys*) ма́сса; (*Rel*): **Mass** прича́стие ▷ *cpd* ма́ссовый; **masses** *npl* (наро́дные) ма́ссы *fpl*; **masses of** (*inf*) ма́сса *fsg* +*gen*, у́йма *fsg* +*gen*
massacre ['mæsəkəʳ] *n* ма́ссовое уби́йство, резня́
massage ['mæsɑːʒ] *n* масса́ж ▷ *vt* (*rub*) масси́ровать (*impf*)
massive ['mæsɪv] *adj* масси́вный; (*support, changes*) огро́мный
mass media *n inv* сре́дства *ntpl* ма́ссовой информа́ции
mast [mɑːst] *n* ма́чта
master ['mɑːstəʳ] *n* (*also fig*) хозя́ин ▷ *vt* (*control*) владе́ть (*perf* овладе́ть) +*instr*; (*learn, understand*) овладева́ть (*perf* овладе́ть) +*instr*; **Master Smith** (*title*) господи́н *or* ма́стер Смит; **Master of Arts/Science** ≈ маги́стр гуманита́рных/есте́ственных нау́к; **masterpiece** *n* шеде́вр
masturbation [mæstə'beɪʃən] *n* мастурба́ция
mat [mæt] *n* ко́врик; (*also* **doormat**) дверно́й ко́врик; (*also* **table mat**) подста́вка ▷ *adj* = **matt**
match [mætʃ] *n* спи́чка; (*Sport*) матч; (*equal*) ро́вня *m/f* ▷ *vt* (*subj*: *colours*) сочета́ться (*impf*) с +*instr*; (*correspond to*) соотве́тствовать (*impf*) +*dat* ▷ *vi* (*colours, materials*) сочета́ться (*impf*); **to be a good match** (*colours, clothes*) хорошо́ сочета́ться (*impf*); **they make** *or* **are a good match** они́ хоро́шая па́ра; **matching** *adj*

сочета́ющийся
mate [meɪt] *n* (*inf: friend*) друг; (*animal*) саме́ц(-мка); (*Naut*) помо́щник капита́на ▷ *vi* спа́риваться (*perf* спа́риться)
material [məˈtɪərɪəl] *n* материа́л ▷ *adj* материа́льный; **materials** *npl* (*equipment*) принадле́жности *fpl*; **building materials** строи́тельные материа́лы; **materialize** *vi* материализова́ться (*impf/perf*), осуществля́ться (*perf* осуществи́ться)
maternal [məˈtəːnl] *adj* матери́нский
maternity [məˈtəːnɪtɪ] *n* матери́нство
mathematics [mæθəˈmætɪks] *n* матема́тика
maths [mæθs] *n abbr* = **mathematics**
matron [ˈmeɪtrən] *n* (*in hospital*) ста́ршая медсестра́; (*in school*) (шко́льная) медсестра́
matt [mæt] *adj* ма́товый
matter [ˈmætəʳ] *n* де́ло, вопро́с; (*substance, material*) вещество́ ▷ *vi* име́ть (*impf*) значе́ние; **matters** *npl* (*affairs, situation*) дела́ *ntpl*; **reading matter** (*Brit*) материа́л для чте́ния; **what's the matter?** в чём де́ло?; **no matter what** несмотря́ ни на что́; **as a matter of course** как само́ собо́й разуме́ющееся; **as a matter of fact** со́бственно говоря́; **it doesn't matter** э́то не ва́жно
mattress [ˈmætrɪs] *n* матра́с
mature [məˈtjuəʳ] *adj* (*person*) зре́лый; (*cheese, wine*) вы́держанный ▷ *vi* (*develop*) развива́ться (*perf* разви́ться); (*grow up*) взросле́ть (*perf* повзросле́ть); (*cheese*) зреть *or* созрева́ть (*perf* созре́ть); (*wine*) выста́иваться (*perf* вы́стояться)
maturity [məˈtjuərɪtɪ] *n* зре́лость *f*
maximum [ˈmæksɪməm] (*pl* **maxima** *or* **maximums**) *adj* максима́льный ▷ *n* ма́ксимум
May [meɪ] *n* май

MAY DAY

May Day — Первома́й. По тради́ции в э́тот день пра́зднуется нача́ло весны́.

may [meɪ] (*conditional* **might**) *vi* (*to show possibility*): **I may go to Russia** я, мо́жет быть, пое́ду в Росси́ю; (*to show permission*): **may I smoke/come?** мо́жно закури́ть/мне прийти́?; **it may** *or* **might rain** мо́жет пойти́ дождь; **you may** *or* **might as well go now** Вы, пожа́луй, мо́жете идти́ сейча́с; **come what may** будь что бу́дет
maybe [ˈmeɪbiː] *adv* мо́жет быть
mayhem [ˈmeɪhɛm] *n* погро́м
mayonnaise [meɪəˈneɪz] *n* майоне́з
mayor [mɛəʳ] *n* мэр

KEYWORD

me [miː] *pron* **1** (*direct*) меня́; **he loves me** он лю́бит меня́; **it's me** э́то я
2 (*indirect*) мне; **give me them** *or* **them to me** да́йте их мне
3 (*after prep*: *+gen*) меня́; (: *+dat*, *+prp*) мне; (: *+instr*) мной; **it's for me** (*on answering phone*) э́то мне
4 (*referring to subject of sentence*: *after prep*: *+gen*) себя́: (: *+dat*) себе́: (: *+instr*) собо́й: (: *+prp*) себе́; **I took him with me** я взял его́ с собо́й

m

meadow ['mɛdəu] *n* луг
meagre ['mi:gə^r] (*US* **meager**) *adj* скýдный
meal [mi:l] *n* едá *no pl*; (*afternoon*) обéд; (*evening*) ýжин; **during meals** во врéмя еды́, за едóй
mean [mi:n] (*pt, pp* **meant**) *adj* (*miserly*) скупóй; (*unkind*) врéдный; (*vicious*) пóдлый ▷ *vt* (*signify*) знáчить (*impf*), означáть (*impf*); (*refer to*) имéть (*impf*) в видý ▷ *n* (*average*) серéдина; **means** *npl* (*way*) спóсоб *msg*, срéдство *ntsg*; (*money*) срéдства *ntpl*; **by means of** посрéдством +*gen*, с пóмощью +*gen*; **by all means!** пожáлуйста!; **do you mean it?** Вы э́то серьёзно?; **to mean to do** (*intend*) намеревáться (*impf*) +*infin*; **to be meant for** предназначáться (*impf*) для +*gen*; **meaning** *n* (*purpose, value*) смысл; (*definition*) значéние; **meaningful** *adj* (*result, occasion*) знач́ительный; (*glance, remark*) многознач́ительный; **meaningless** *adj* бессмы́сленный; **meant** [mɛnt] *pt, pp of* **mean**; **meantime** *adv* (*also* **in the meantime**) тем врéменем, мéжду тем; **meanwhile** *adv* = **meantime**
measles ['mi:zlz] *n* корь *f*
measure ['mɛʒə^r] *vt* измеря́ть (*perf* измéрить) ▷ *n* мéра; (*of whisky etc*) пóрция; (*also* **tape measure**) рулéтка, сантимéтр ▷ *vi*: **the room measures 10 feet by 20** плóщадь кóмнаты 10 фýтов на 20; **measurements** *npl* мéрки *fpl*, размéры *mpl*
meat [mi:t] *n* мя́со; **cold meats** (*Brit*) холóдные мясны́е закýски *fpl*
mechanic [mɪ'kænɪk] *n* механ́ик; **mechanical** *adj* механ́ический
mechanism ['mɛkənɪzəm] *n* механ́изм
medal ['mɛdl] *n* медáль *f*; **medallist** (*US* **medalist**) *n* медал́ист(ка)
meddle ['mɛdl] *vi*: **to meddle in** вмéшиваться (*perf* вмешáться) в +*acc*; **to meddle with sth** вторгáться (*perf* втóргнуться) во что-н
media ['mi:dɪə] *n or npl*: **the media** срéдства *ntpl* мáссовой информáции, мéдия ▷ *npl see* **medium**
mediaeval [mɛdɪ'i:vl] *adj* = **medieval**
mediate ['mi:dɪeɪt] *vi* (*arbitrate*) посрéдничать (*impf*)
medical ['mɛdɪkl] *adj* медиц́инский ▷ *n* медосмóтр
medication [mɛdɪ'keɪʃən] *n* лекáрство, лекáрственный препарáт
medicine ['mɛdsɪn] *n* (*science*) медиц́ина; (*drug*) лекáрство
medieval [mɛdɪ'i:vl] *adj* средневекóвый
mediocre [mi:dɪ'əukə^r] *adj* заýря́дный, посрéдственный
meditation [mɛdɪ'teɪʃən] *n* (*Rel*) медитáция
Mediterranean [mɛdɪtə'reɪnɪən] *adj*: **the Mediterranean (Sea)** Средизéмное мóре
medium ['mi:dɪəm] (*pl* **media** *or* **mediums**) *adj* срéдний ▷ *n* (*means*) срéдство
meek [mi:k] *adj* крóткий
meet [mi:t] (*pt, pp* **met**) *vt* встречáть (*perf* встрéтить);

(*obligations*) выполня́ть (*perf* вы́полнить); (*problem*) ста́лкиваться (*perf* столкну́ться) с +*instr*; (*need*) удовлетворя́ть (*perf* удовлетвори́ть) ▷ *vi* (*people*) встреча́ться (*perf* встре́титься); (*lines, roads*) пересека́ться (*perf* пересе́чься); **meet with** *vt fus* (*difficulty*) ста́лкиваться (*perf* столкну́ться) с +*instr*; (*success*) по́льзоваться (*impf*) +*instr*; (*approval*) находи́ть (*perf* найти́); **meeting** *n* встре́ча; (*at work, of committee etc*) заседа́ние, собра́ние; (*Pol*: *also* **mass meeting**) ми́тинг; **she's at a meeting** она́ на заседа́нии

melancholy ['mɛlənkəlɪ] *adj* (*smile*) меланхоли́ческий

melody ['mɛlədɪ] *n* мело́дия

melon ['mɛlən] *n* ды́ня

melt [mɛlt] *vi* та́ять (*perf* раста́ять) ▷ *vt* (*snow, butter*) топи́ть (*perf* растопи́ть)

member ['mɛmbə^r] *n* (*also Anat*) член; **Member of Parliament** (*Brit*) член парла́мента; **membership** *n* (*members*) чле́ны *mpl*; (*status*) чле́нство; **membership card** *n* чле́нский биле́т

meme [mi:m] *n* мем

memento [mə'mɛntəu] *n* сувени́р

memo ['mɛməu] *n* (*Admin*: *instruction*) директи́ва

memorable ['mɛmərəbl] *adj* па́мятный

memorial [mɪ'mɔ:rɪəl] *n* па́мятник ▷ *cpd* мемориа́льный

memorize ['mɛməraɪz] *vt* зау́чивать (*perf* заучи́ть) (наизу́сть)

memory ['mɛmərɪ] *n* па́мять *f*; (*recollection*) воспомина́ние; **in memory of** в па́мять о +*prp*; **memory card** *n* (*Comput*) ка́рта па́мяти

men [mɛn] *npl of* **man**

menace ['mɛnɪs] *n* (*threat*) угро́за

mend [mɛnd] *vt* ремонти́ровать (*perf* отремонти́ровать), чини́ть (*perf* почини́ть); (*clothes*) чини́ть (*perf* почини́ть) ▷ *n*: **to be on the mend** идти́ (*impf*) на попра́вку; **to mend one's ways** исправля́ться (*perf* испра́виться)

meningitis [mɛnɪn'dʒaɪtɪs] *n* менинги́т

menopause ['mɛnəupɔ:z] *n* климактери́ческий пери́од, кли́макс

menstruation [mɛnstru'eɪʃən] *n* менструа́ция

menswear ['mɛnzwɛə^r] *n* мужска́я оде́жда

mental ['mɛntl] *adj* (*ability, exhaustion*) у́мственный; (*image*) мы́сленный; (*illness*) душе́вный, психи́ческий; (*arithmetic, calculation*) в уме́; **mentality** [mɛn'tælɪtɪ] *n* менталите́т, умонастрое́ние

mention ['mɛnʃən] *n* упомина́ние ▷ *vt* упомина́ть (*perf* упомяну́ть); **don't mention it!** не́ за что!

menu ['mɛnju:] *n* (*also Comput*) меню́ *nt ind*

MEP *n abbr* (*Brit*) (= *Member of the European Parliament*) член Европе́йского парла́мента

mercenary ['mə:sɪnərɪ] *adj* коры́стный ▷ *n* наёмник

merchant ['mə:tʃənt] *n* торго́вец

merciless ['mə:sɪlɪs] *adj* беспоща́дный

mercury ['mə:kjurɪ] *n* (*metal*) ртуть *f*

mercy ['mə:sɪ] *n* милосе́рдие;

m

to be at sb's mercy быть (*impf*) во власти кого-н
mere [mɪəʳ] *adj*: **she's a mere child** она́ всего́ лишь ребёнок; **his mere presence irritates her** само́ его́ прису́тствие раздража́ет её; **merely** *adv* (*simply*) про́сто; (*just*) то́лько
merge [mə:dʒ] *vt* слива́ть (*perf* слить), объединя́ть (*perf* объедини́ть) ▷ *vi* (*also Comm*) слива́ться (*perf* сли́ться); (*roads*) сходи́ться (*perf* сойти́сь); **merger** *n* (*Comm*) слия́ние
meringue [mə'ræŋ] *n* безе́ *nt ind*
merit ['mɛrɪt] *n* досто́инство ▷ *vt* заслу́живать (*perf* заслужи́ть)
merry ['mɛrɪ] *adj* весёлый; **Merry Christmas!** С Рождество́м!, Счастли́вого Рождества́!
mesh [mɛʃ] *n* (*net*) сеть *f*
mess [mɛs] *n* (*in room*) беспоря́док; (*of situation*) неразбери́ха; (*Mil*) столо́вая *f adj*; **to be in a mess** (*untidy*) быть (*impf*) в беспоря́дке; **mess up** *vt* (*spoil*) по́ртить (*perf* испо́ртить)
message ['mɛsɪdʒ] *n* сообще́ние; (*note*) запи́ска; (*of play, book*) иде́я; **to leave sb a message** (*note*) оставля́ть (*perf* оста́вить) кому́-н запи́ску; **can I give him a message?** ему́ что́-нибудь переда́ть?
messenger ['mɛsɪndʒəʳ] *n* курье́р, посы́льный *m adj*
Messrs *abbr* (*on letters*) (= *messieurs*) гг. (= *господа́*)
messy ['mɛsɪ] *adj* (*untidy*) неу́бранный
met [mɛt] *pt, pp of* **meet**
metabolism [mɛ'tæbəlɪzəm] *n* метаболи́зм, обме́н веще́ств
metal ['mɛtl] *n* мета́лл
metaphor ['mɛtəfəʳ] *n* мета́фора
meteor ['mi:tɪəʳ] *n* метео́р
meteorology [mi:tɪə'rɔlədʒɪ] *n* метеороло́гия
meter ['mi:təʳ] *n* (*instrument*) счётчик; (*US*: *unit*) = **metre**
method ['mɛθəd] *n* (*way*) ме́тод, спо́соб; **methodical** [mɪ'θɔdɪkl] *adj* методи́чный
meticulous [mɪ'tɪkjuləs] *adj* тща́тельный
metre ['mi:təʳ] (*US* **meter**) *n* метр
metric ['mɛtrɪk] *adj* метри́ческий
metropolitan [mɛtrə'pɔlɪtn] *adj* столи́чный
Mexico ['mɛksɪkəu] *n* Ме́ксика
mice [maɪs] *npl of* **mouse**
micro: **microphone** *n* микрофо́н; **microscope** *n* микроско́п; **microwave** *n* (*also* **microwave oven**) микроволно́вая печь *f*
mid [mɪd] *adj*: **in mid May/afternoon** в середи́не ма́я/дня; **in mid air** в во́здухе; **midday** *n* по́лдень *m*
middle ['mɪdl] *n* середи́на ▷ *adj* сре́дний; **in the middle of** посреди́ *+gen*; **middle-aged** *adj* сре́дних лет; **Middle Ages** *npl*: **the Middle Ages** сре́дние века́ *mpl*; **middle-class** *adj*: **middle-class people/values** лю́ди/це́нности сре́днего кла́сса; **Middle East** *n*: **the Middle East** Бли́жний Восто́к
midge [mɪdʒ] *n* мо́шка
midnight ['mɪdnaɪt] *n* по́лночь *f*
midst [mɪdst] *n*: **in the midst of** посреди́ *+gen*
midway [mɪd'weɪ] *adv*: **midway (between)** на полпути́ (ме́жду *+instr*); **midway through** в середи́не *+gen*
midweek [mɪd'wi:k] *adv* в середи́не неде́ли
midwife ['mɪdwaɪf] (*pl*

midwives) *n* акушéрка
might [maɪt] *vb see* **may**
mighty [maɪtɪ] *adj* мóщный
migraine ['mi:greɪn] *n* мигрéнь *f*
migrant ['maɪgrənt] *adj*: **migrant worker** рабóчий-мигрáнт
migration [maɪ'greɪʃən] *n* мигрáция
mike [maɪk] *n abbr* = **microphone**
mild [maɪld] *adj* мягкий; (*interest*) слáбый; (*infection*) лёгкий; **mildly** ['maɪldlɪ] *adv* (*see adj*) мягко; слегкá; легкó; **to put it mildly** мягко говоря
mile [maɪl] *n* миля; **mileage** *n* колúчество миль; **milestone** *n* ≈ километрóвый столб; (*fig*) вéха

MILE

В Великобритáнии и Амéрике расстоя́ние измеряется в ми́лях, а не в киломéтрах. Однá ми́ля равня́ется 1 609 мéтрам.

military ['mɪlɪtərɪ] *adj* воéнный ▷ *n*: **the military** воéнные *pl adj*
militia [mɪ'lɪʃə] *n* (нарóдное) ополчéние
milk [mɪlk] *n* молокó ▷ *vt* (*cow*) дои́ть (*perf* подои́ть); (*fig*) эксплуати́ровать (*impf*); **milky** *adj* молóчный
mill [mɪl] *n* (*factory*: *making cloth*) фáбрика; (: *making steel*) завóд; (*for coffee, pepper*) мéльница
millimetre (*US* **millimeter**) ['mɪlɪmi:tə^r] *n* миллимéтр
million ['mɪljən] *n* миллиóн; **millionaire** [mɪljə'nɛə^r] *n* миллионéр
mime [maɪm] *n* пантоми́ма ▷ *vt* изображáть (*perf* изобрази́ть) жéстами
mimic ['mɪmɪk] *vt* (*subj*: *comedian*) пароди́ровать (*impf/perf*)
min. *abbr* (= *minute*) мин(.) (= *минýта*)
mince [mɪns] *vt* (*meat*) пропускáть (*perf* пропусти́ть) чéрез мясорýбку ▷ *n* (*Brit*) (мяснóй) фарш

MINCE PIE

Mince pie — пирожóк с сухофрýктами. Хотя́ э́то выражéние буквáльно означáет "пирожóк с фáршем", начи́нка такóго пирожкá состои́т из сухофрýктов, а не из мя́са.

mind [maɪnd] *n* (*intellect*) ум ▷ *vt* (*look after*) смотрéть (*impf*) за +*instr*; (*object to*): **I don't mind the noise** шум меня́ не беспокóит; **it's always on my mind** э́то не выхóдит у меня́ из головы́; **to keep** *or* **bear sth in mind** имéть (*impf*) что-н в видý; **to make up one's mind** решáться (*perf* реши́ться); **to my mind ...** по моемý мнéнию ...; **I don't mind** мне всё равнó; **mind you, ...** имéйте в видý ...; **never mind!** ничегó!; **mindless** *adj* (*violence*) бездýмный; (*job*) механи́ческий

 **KEYWORD**

mine[1] [maɪn] *pron* **1** мой (*f* моя́, *nt* моё, *pl* мои́); **that book is mine** э́та кни́га моя́; **that house is mine** э́тот дом мой; **this is mine** э́то моё; **an uncle of mine** мой дя́дя
2 (*referring back to subject*) свой (*f* своя́, *nt* своё, *pl* свои́); **may I borrow your pen? I have forgotten mine** мóжно взять Вáшу рýчку? я забы́л свою́

m

mine[2] [maɪn] *n* (*for coal*) ша́хта; (*explosive*) ми́на ▷ *vt* (*coal*) добыва́ть (*perf* добы́ть); **minefield** *n* ми́нное по́ле; **miner** *n* шахтёр

mineral ['mɪnərəl] *n* минера́л; (*ore*) поле́зное ископа́емое *nt adj*; **mineral water** *n* минера́льная вода́

miniature ['mɪnətʃə^r] *adj* миниатю́рный

minibus ['mɪnɪbʌs] *n* микроавто́бус

MINICAB

Minicab — такси́. Э́тот тип такси́ регули́руется зако́ном в ме́ньшей сте́пени. В отли́чие от традицио́нного чёрного такси́ его́ вызыва́ют по телефо́ну, а не остана́вливают на у́лице.

minimal ['mɪnɪml] *adj* минима́льный

minimize ['mɪnɪmaɪz] *vt* (*reduce*) своди́ть (*perf* свести́) к ми́нимуму; (*play down*) преуменьша́ть (*perf* преуме́ньшить)

minimum ['mɪnɪməm] (*pl* **minima**) *n* ми́нимум ▷ *adj* минима́льный

mining ['maɪnɪŋ] *n* (*industry*) у́гольная промы́шленность *f*

minister ['mɪnɪstə^r] *n* (*Brit*) мини́стр; (*Rel*) свяще́нник

ministry ['mɪnɪstrɪ] *n* (*Brit*: *Pol*) министе́рство

minor ['maɪnə^r] *adj* (*injuries*) незначи́тельный; (*repairs*) ме́лкий ▷ *n* (*Law*) несовершенноле́тний(-яя) *m(f) adj*; **minority** [maɪ'nɔrɪtɪ] *n* меньшинство́

mint [mɪnt] *n* (*Bot*) мя́та; (*sweet*) мя́тная конфе́та ▷ *vt* чека́нить (*perf* отчека́нить); **in mint condition** в прекра́сном состоя́нии

minus ['maɪnəs] *n* (*also* **minus sign**) ми́нус ▷ *prep*: **12 minus 6 equals 6** 12 ми́нус 6 равня́ется 6; **minus 24 (degrees)** ми́нус 24 гра́дуса

minute[1] [maɪ'nju:t] *adj* (*tiny*) тща́тельный

minute[2] ['mɪnɪt] *n* мину́та; **minutes** *npl* (*of meeting*) протоко́л *msg*; **at the last minute** в после́днюю мину́ту

miracle ['mɪrəkl] *n* чу́до

miraculous [mɪ'rækjuləs] *adj* чуде́сный

mirror ['mɪrə^r] *n* зе́ркало

misbehave [mɪsbɪ'heɪv] *vi* пло́хо себя́ вести́ (*impf*)

miscarriage ['mɪskærɪdʒ] *n* (*Med*) вы́кидыш; **miscarriage of justice** суде́бная оши́бка

miscellaneous [mɪsɪ'leɪnɪəs] *adj* (*subjects, items*) разнообра́зный

mischief ['mɪstʃɪf] *n* озорство́; (*maliciousness*) зло

mischievous ['mɪstʃɪvəs] *adj* (*naughty, playful*) озорно́й

misconception ['mɪskən'sɛpʃən] *n* заблужде́ние, ло́жное представле́ние

misconduct [mɪs'kɔndʌkt] *n* дурно́е поведе́ние; **professional misconduct** наруше́ние служе́бной дисципли́ны

miserable ['mɪzərəbl] *adj* (*unhappy*) несча́стный; (*unpleasant*) скве́рный; (*donation, conditions*) жа́лкий; (*failure*) позо́рный

misery ['mɪzərɪ] *n* (*unhappiness*) невзго́да; (*wretchedness*) жа́лкое существова́ние

misfortune [mɪs'fɔ:tʃən] *n* несча́стье

misguided [mɪsˈgaɪdɪd] *adj* (*person*) неве́рно ориенти́рованный; (*ideas*) оши́бочный
misinterpret [mɪsɪnˈtəːprɪt] *vt* неве́рно интерпрети́ровать (*impf/perf*) *or* толкова́ть (истолкова́ть *perf*)
mislead [mɪsˈliːd] (*irreg like* **lead**[1]) *vt* вводи́ть (*perf* ввести́) в заблужде́ние; **misleading** *adj* обма́нчивый
misprint [ˈmɪsprɪnt] *n* опеча́тка
Miss [mɪs] *n* мисс *f ind*
miss [mɪs] *vt* (*train, bus etc*) пропуска́ть (*perf* пропусти́ть); (*target*) не попада́ть (*perf* попа́сть) в *+acc*; (*person, home*) скуча́ть (*impf*) по *+dat*; (*chance, opportunity*) упуска́ть (*perf* упусти́ть) ▷ *vi* (*person*) прома́хиваться (*perf* промахну́ться) ▷ *n* про́мах; **you can't miss my house** мой дом невозмо́жно не заме́тить; **miss out** *vt* (*Brit*) пропуска́ть (*perf* пропусти́ть)
missile [ˈmɪsaɪl] *n* (*Mil*) раке́та
missing [ˈmɪsɪŋ] *adj* пропа́вший; (*tooth, wheel*) недостаю́щий; **to be missing** (*absent*) отсу́тствовать (*impf*); **to be missing, go missing** пропада́ть (*perf* пропа́сть) бе́з вести
mission [ˈmɪʃən] *n* (*also Pol, Rel*) ми́ссия; **missionary** *n* миссионе́р(ка)
mist [mɪst] *n* (*light*) ды́мка
mistake [mɪsˈteɪk] (*irreg like* **take**) *n* оши́бка ▷ *vt* (*be wrong about*) ошиба́ться (*perf* ошиби́ться) в *+prp*; **by mistake** по оши́бке; **to make a mistake** ошиба́ться (*perf* ошиби́ться), де́лать (*perf* сде́лать) оши́бку; **to mistake A for B** принима́ть (*perf* приня́ть) А за Б; **mistaken** *pp of* **mistake** ▷ *adj*: **to be mistaken** ошиба́ться (*perf* ошиби́ться)
mistletoe [ˈmɪsltəu] *n* оме́ла

MISTLETOE

В Великобрита́нии и США э́то расте́ние испо́льзуется как рожде́ственское украше́ние. По обы́чаю под оме́лой полага́ется целова́ться.

mistook [mɪsˈtuk] *pt of* **mistake**
mistress [ˈmɪstrɪs] *n* (*also fig*) хозя́йка; (*lover*) любо́вница
mistrust [mɪsˈtrʌst] *vt* не доверя́ть (*impf*) *+dat* ▷ *n*: **mistrust (of)** недове́рие (к *+dat*)
misty [ˈmɪstɪ] *adj* (*day*) тума́нный
misunderstand [mɪsʌndəˈstænd] (*irreg like* **stand**) *vt* непра́вильно понима́ть (*perf* поня́ть) ▷ *vi* не понима́ть (*perf* поня́ть); **misunderstanding** *n* недоразуме́ние
misuse [*n* mɪsˈjuːs, *vb* mɪsˈjuːz] *n* (*of power, funds*) злоупотребле́ние ▷ *vt* злоупотребля́ть (*perf* злоупотреби́ть) *+instr*
mix [mɪks] *vt* (*cake, cement*) заме́шивать (*perf* замеси́ть) ▷ *n* смесь *f* ▷ *vi* (*people*): **to mix (with)** обща́ться (*impf*) (с *+instr*); **to mix sth (with sth)** сме́шивать (*perf* смеша́ть) что-н (с чем-н); **mix up** *vt* (*combine*) переме́шивать (*perf* перемеша́ть); (*confuse*: *people*) пу́тать (*perf* спу́тать); (: *things*) пу́тать (*perf* перепу́тать); **mixer** *n* (*for food*) ми́ксер; **mixture** [ˈmɪkstʃə[r]] *n* смесь *f*; **mix-up** *n* пу́таница

m

mm *abbr* (= *millimetre*) мм (= *миллиме́тр*)
moan [məun] *n* (*cry*) стон ▷ *vi* (*inf: complain*): **to moan (about)** ныть (*impf*) (о +*prp*)
moat [məut] *n* ров
mob [mɔb] *n* (*crowd*) толпа́
mobile ['məubaɪl] *adj* подви́жный ▷ *n* (*toy*) подвесно́е декорати́вное украше́ние; (*phone*) моби́льный телефо́н, моби́льник (*inf*); **mobile phone** *n* моби́льный телефо́н
mobility [məu'bɪlɪtɪ] *n* подви́жность *f*
mobilize ['məubɪlaɪz] *vt* мобилизова́ть (*impf/perf*)
mock [mɔk] *vt* (*ridicule*) издева́ться (*impf*) над +*instr* ▷ *adj* (*fake*) ло́жный; **mockery** *n* издева́тельство; **to make a mockery of sb/sth** выставля́ть (*perf* вы́ставить) кого́-н/что-н на посме́шище
mod cons *npl abbr* (*Brit*) = **modern conveniences**
mode [məud] *n* (*of life*) о́браз; (*of transport*) вид
model ['mɔdl] *n* моде́ль *f*, маке́т; (*also* **fashion model**) моде́ль, манеке́нщик(-ица); (*also* **artist's model**) нату́рщик(-ица) ▷ *adj* (*ideal*) образцо́вый
modem ['məudɛm] *n* (*Comput*) моде́м
moderate [*adj* 'mɔdərət, *vb* 'mɔdəreɪt] *adj* (*views, amount*) уме́ренный; (*change*) незначи́тельный ▷ *vt* умеря́ть (*perf* уме́рить)
moderation [mɔdə'reɪʃən] *n* уме́ренность *f*
modern ['mɔdən] *adj* совреме́нный
modest ['mɔdɪst] *adj* скро́мный; **modesty** *n* скро́мность *f*
modification [mɔdɪfɪ'keɪʃən] *n* (*see vt*) модифика́ция; видоизмене́ние
modify ['mɔdɪfaɪ] *vt* (*vehicle, engine*) модифици́ровать (*impf/perf*); (*plan*) видоизменя́ть (*perf* видоизмени́ть)
moist [mɔɪst] *adj* вла́жный; **moisture** *n* вла́га
mold [məuld] *n, vb* (*US*) = **mould**
mole [məul] *n* (*spot*) ро́динка; (*Zool*) крот
molecule ['mɔlɪkju:l] *n* моле́кула
mom [mɔm] *n* (*US*) = **mum**
moment ['məumənt] *n* моме́нт, мгнове́ние; **for a moment** на мгнове́ние; **at that moment** в э́тот моме́нт; **at the moment** в настоя́щий моме́нт; **momentary** *adj* мгнове́нный
momentous [məu'mɛntəs] *adj* знамена́тельный
momentum [məu'mɛntəm] *n* (*fig*) дви́жущая си́ла; **to gather** *or* **gain momentum** набира́ть (*perf* набра́ть) си́лу
mommy ['mɔmɪ] *n* (*US*) = **mummy**
monarch ['mɔnək] *n* мона́рх; **monarchy** *n* мона́рхия
monastery ['mɔnəstərɪ] *n* монасты́рь *m*
Monday ['mʌndɪ] *n* понеде́льник
monetary ['mʌnɪtərɪ] *adj* де́нежный
money ['mʌnɪ] *n* де́ньги *pl*; **to make money** (*person*) зараба́тывать (*perf* зарабо́тать) де́ньги; (*make a profit*) де́лать (*perf* сде́лать) де́ньги
mongrel ['mʌŋgrəl] *n* дворня́га
monitor ['mɔnɪtə[r]] *n* монито́р; (*Comput*) монито́р ▷ *vt*

(*broadcasts, pulse*) следи́ть (*impf*) за *+instr*
monk [mʌŋk] *n* мона́х
monkey ['mʌŋkɪ] *n* обезья́на
monopoly [mə'nɔpəlɪ] *n* монопо́лия
monotonous [mə'nɔtənəs] *adj* однообра́зный, моното́нный
monster ['mɔnstə^r] *n* чудо́вище, монстр
month [mʌnθ] *n* ме́сяц; **monthly** *adj* ежеме́сячный; (*ticket*) ме́сячный ▷ *adv* ежеме́сячно
monument ['mɔnjumənt] *n* (*memorial*) па́мятник, монуме́нт
mood [mu:d] *n* настрое́ние; (*of crowd*) настро́й; **to be in a good/bad mood** быть (*impf*) в хоро́шем/плохо́м настрое́нии; **moody** *adj* (*temperamental*): **she is a very moody person** у неё о́чень переме́нчивое настрое́ние
moon [mu:n] *n* луна́; **moonlight** *n* лу́нный свет
moor [muə^r] *n* ве́ресковая пу́стошь *f*
moose [mu:s] *n inv* лось *m*
mop [mɔp] *n* (*for floor*) шва́бра; (*of hair*) копна́ ▷ *vt* (*floor*) мыть (вы́мыть *or* помы́ть *perf*) (*шва́брой*); (*eyes, face*) вытира́ть (*perf* вы́тереть)
moped ['məupɛd] *n* мопе́д
moral ['mɔrl] *adj* мора́льный; (*person*) нра́вственный ▷ *n* (*of story*) мора́ль *f*; **morals** *npl* (*values*) нра́вы *mpl*
morale [mɔ'rɑ:l] *n* мора́льный дух
morality [mə'rælɪtɪ] *n* нра́вственность *f*
morbid ['mɔ:bɪd] *adj* (*imagination*) ненорма́льный; (*ideas*) жу́ткий

KEYWORD

more [mɔ:^{r}] *adj* **1** (*greater in number etc*) бо́льше *+gen*; **I have more friends than enemies** у меня́ бо́льше друзе́й, чем враго́в
2 (*additional*) ещё; **do you want (some) more tea?** хоти́те ещё ча́ю?; **is there any more wine?** вино́ ещё есть?; **I have no** *or* **I don't have any more money** у меня́ бо́льше нет де́нег; **it'll take a few more weeks** э́то займёт ещё не́сколько неде́ль
▷ *pron* **1** (*greater amount*): **more than ten** бо́льше десяти́; **we've sold more than a hundred tickets** мы прода́ли бо́лее ста биле́тов; **it costs more than we expected** э́то сто́ит бо́льше, чем мы ожида́ли
2 (*further or additional amount*): **is there any more?** ещё есть?; **there's no more** бо́льше ничего́ нет; **a little more** ещё немно́го *or* чуть-чуть; **many/much more** намно́го/гора́здо бо́льше
▷ *adv* **1** (*+vb*) бо́льше; **I like this picture more** э́та карти́на мне нра́вится бо́льше
2: more dangerous/difficult (than) бо́лее опа́сный/тру́дный(, чем)
3: more economically (than) бо́лее экономи́чно(, чем); **more easily/quickly (than)** ле́гче/быстре́е(, чем); **more and more** (*excited, friendly*) всё бо́лее и бо́лее; **he grew to like her more and more** она́ нра́вилась ему́ всё бо́льше и бо́льше; **more or less** бо́лее и́ли ме́нее; **she is more beautiful than ever** она́ прекра́снее, чем когда́-либо; **he loved her more than ever** он люби́л её бо́льше, чем

m

когда́-либо; **the more …, the better** чем бо́льше …, тем лу́чше; **once more** ещё раз; **I'd like to see more of you** мне хоте́лось бы ви́деть тебя́ ча́ще

moreover [mɔːˈrəuvəʳ] *adv* бо́лее того́

morgue [mɔːg] *n* морг

morning [ˈmɔːnɪŋ] *n* у́тро; (*between midnight and 3 a.m.*) ночь *f* ▷ *cpd* у́тренний; **in the morning** у́тром; **3 o'clock in the morning** 3 часа́ но́чи; **7 o'clock in the morning** 7 часо́в утра́

Morse [mɔːs] *n* (*also* **Morse code**) а́збука Мо́рзе

mortal [ˈmɔːtl] *adj* (*man, sin*) сме́ртный; (*deadly*) смерте́льный

mortar [ˈmɔːtəʳ] *n* (*cement*) цеме́нтный раство́р

mortgage [ˈmɔːgɪdʒ] *n* ипоте́чный креди́т ▷ *vt* закла́дывать (*perf* заложи́ть)

Moscow [ˈmɔskəu] *n* Москва́

Moslem [ˈmɔzləm] *adj, n* = **Muslim**

mosque [mɔsk] *n* мече́ть *f*

mosquito [mɔsˈkiːtəu] (*pl* **mosquitoes**) *n* кома́р

moss [mɔs] *n* мох

 **KEYWORD**

most [məust] *adj* **1** (*almost all*: *countable nouns*) большинство́ *+gen*; (: *uncountable and collective nouns*) бо́льшая часть *+gen*; **most cars** большинство́ маши́н; **most milk** бо́льшая часть молока́; **in most cases** в большинстве́ слу́чаев

2 (*largest, greatest*): **who has the most money?** у кого́ бо́льше всего́ де́нег?; **this book has attracted the most interest among the critics** э́та кни́га вы́звала наибо́льший интере́с у кри́тиков

▷ *pron* (*greatest quantity, number*: *countable nouns*) большинство́; (: *uncountable and collective nouns*) бо́льшая часть *f*; **most of the houses** большинство́ домо́в; **most of the cake** бо́льшая часть то́рта; **do the most you can** де́лайте всё, что Вы мо́жете; **I ate the most** я съел бо́льше всех; **to make the most of sth** максима́льно испо́льзовать (*impf/perf*) что-н; **at the (very) most** са́мое бо́льшее

▷ *adv* (*+vb*: *with inanimate objects*) бо́льше всего́; (: *with animate objects*) бо́льше всех; (*+adv*) исключи́тельно; (*+adj*) са́мый, наибо́лее; **I liked him the most** он понра́вился мне бо́льше всех; **what do you value most, wealth or health?** что Вы бо́льше всего́ це́ните, бога́тство и́ли здоро́вье?

mostly [ˈməustlɪ] *adv* бо́льшей ча́стью, в основно́м

MOT *n abbr* (*Brit*) = **Ministry of Transport**; **MOT (test)** техосмо́тр

MOT

По зако́ну автомоби́ли, кото́рым бо́льше трёх лет, должны́ ежего́дно проходи́ть техосмо́тр.

motel [məuˈtɛl] *n* моте́ль *m*

moth [mɔθ] *n* мотылёк

mother [ˈmʌðəʳ] *n* мать *f* ▷ *vt* (*pamper*) ня́нчиться (*impf*) с *+instr* ▷ *adj*: **mother country** ро́дина, родна́я страна́; **motherhood** *n* материнство; **mother-in-law** *n* (*wife's mother*) тёща; (*husband's mother*) свекро́вь *f*; **mother tongue** *n* родно́й язы́к

Mother's Day

Mother's Day — День Ма́тери. Отмеча́ется в четвёртое воскресе́нье Вели́кого Поста́. В э́тот день поздравле́ния и пода́рки получа́ют то́лько ма́мы.

motif [məu'tiːf] *n* (*design*) орна́мент

motion ['məuʃən] *n* (*movement, gesture*) движе́ние; (*proposal*) предложе́ние; **motionless** *adj* неподви́жный

motivation [məutɪ'veɪʃən] *n* (*drive*) целеустремлённость *f*

motive ['məutɪv] *n* моти́в, побужде́ние

motor ['məutə^r] *n* мото́р ▷ *cpd* (*trade*) автомоби́льный; **motorbike** *n* мотоци́кл; **motorcycle** *n* мотоци́кл; **motorist** *n* автомобили́ст; **motorway** *n* (*Brit*) автомагистра́ль *f*, автостра́да

motto ['mɔtəu] (*pl* **mottoes**) *n* деви́з

mould [məuld] (*US* **mold**) *n* (*cast*) фо́рма; (*mildew*) пле́сень *f* ▷ *vt* (*substance*) лепи́ть (*perf* вы́лепить); (*fig*: *opinion, character*) формирова́ть (*perf* сформирова́ть); **mouldy** *adj* (*food*) запле́сневелый

mound [maund] *n* (*heap*) ку́ча

mount [maunt] *vt* (*horse*) сади́ться (*perf* сесть) на *+acc*; (*display*) устра́ивать (*perf* устро́ить); (*jewel*) оправля́ть (*perf* опра́вить); (*picture*) обрамля́ть (*perf* обра́мить); (*stair*) всходи́ть (*perf* взойти́) по *+dat* ▷ *vi* (*increase*) расти́ (*impf*) ▷ *n*: **Mount Ararat** гора́ Арара́т; **mount up** *vi* нака́пливаться (*perf* накопи́ться)

mountain ['mauntɪn] *n* гора́ ▷ *cpd* го́рный; **mountain bike** *n* *велосипе́д, для езды́ по пересечённой ме́стности*; **mountainous** *adj* го́рный, гори́стый

mourn [mɔːn] *vt* (*death*) опла́кивать (*impf*) ▷ *vi*: **to mourn for** скорбе́ть (*impf*) по *+dat or* о *+prp*; **mourning** *n* тра́ур; **in mourning** в тра́уре

mouse [maus] (*pl* **mice**) *n* (*also Comput*) мышь *f*; **mouse mat** *n* ко́врик для мы́ши; **mouse pad** *n* = **mouse mat**

moustache [məs'tɑːʃ] (*US* **mustache**) *n* усы́ *mpl*

mouth [mauθ] *n* рот; (*of cave, hole*) вход; (*of river*) у́стье; **mouthful** *n* (*of food*) кусо́чек; (*of drink*) глото́к; **mouth organ** *n* губна́я гармо́шка; **mouthpiece** *n* (*Mus*) мундшту́к; (*Tel*) микрофо́н

move [muːv] *n* (*movement*) движе́ние; (*in game*) ход; (*of house*) перее́зд; (*of job*) перехо́д ▷ *vt* передвига́ть (*perf* передви́нуть); (*piece*: *in game*) ходи́ть (*perf* пойти́) *+instr*; (*arm etc*) двига́ть (*perf* дви́нуть) *+instr*; (*person*: *emotionally*) тро́гать (*perf* тро́нуть), растро́гать (*perf*) ▷ *vi* дви́гаться (*perf* дви́нуться); (*things*) дви́гаться (*impf*); (*also* **move house**) переезжа́ть (*perf* перее́хать); **get a move on!** потора́пливайтесь!; **move about** *vi* (*change position*)

передвига́ться (*perf* передви́нуться), перемеща́ться (*perf* перемести́ться); (*travel*) переезжа́ть (*impf*) с ме́ста на ме́сто; **move around** *vi* = **move about**; **move away** *vi*: **to move away (from)** (*leave*) уезжа́ть (*perf* уе́хать) (из +*gen*); (*step away*) отходи́ть (*perf* отойти́) (от +*gen*); **move in** *vi* (*police, soldiers*) входи́ть (*perf* войти́); **to move in(to)** (*house*) въезжа́ть (*perf* въе́хать) (в +*acc*); **move out** *vi* (*of house*) выезжа́ть (*perf* вы́ехать); **move over** *vi* (*to make room*) подвига́ться (*perf* подви́нуться); **move up** *vi* (*be promoted*) продвига́ться (*perf* продви́нуться) по слу́жбе;
movement *n* движе́ние; (*between fixed points*) передвиже́ние; (*in attitude, policy*) сдвиг

movie [ˈmuːvɪ] *n* (кино)фи́льм; **to go to the movies** ходи́ть/идти́ (*perf* пойти́) в кино́

moving [ˈmuːvɪŋ] *adj* (*emotional*) тро́гательный; (*mobile*) подви́жный

mow [məu] (*pt* **mowed**, *pp* **mowed** *or* **mown**) *vt* (*grass*) подстрига́ть (*perf* подстри́чь)

MP *n abbr* = **Member of Parliament**

MP3 *abbr* MP3; **MP3 player** *n* MP3-пле́ер *m*

mph *abbr* = **miles per hour**

Mr [ˈmɪstəʳ] *n*: **Mr Smith** (*informal*) ми́стер Смит; (*formal*) г-н Смит (= *господи́н Смит*)

Mrs [ˈmɪsɪz] *n*: **Mrs Smith** (*informal*) ми́ссис Смит; (*formal*) г-жа Смит (= *госпожа́ Смит*)

Ms [mɪz] *n* = **Miss**; **Mrs**

Ms

Да́нное сокраще́ние употребля́ется гла́вным о́бразом в пи́сьменном языке́ и заменя́ет **Miss** и **Mrs.** Употребля́я его́, вы не ука́зываете, за́мужем же́нщина или нет.

MSP *n abbr* (= *Member of the Scottish Parliament*) член шотла́ндского парла́мента

 **KEYWORD**

much [mʌtʃ] *adj* мно́го +*gen*; **we haven't got much time** у нас не так мно́го вре́мени; **how much** ско́лько +*gen*; **how much money do you need?** ско́лько де́нег Вам ну́жно?; **he's spent so much money today** он сего́дня потра́тил так мно́го де́нег; **I have as much money as you (do)** у меня́ сто́лько же де́нег, ско́лько у Вас; **I don't have as much time as you (do)** у меня́ нет сто́лько вре́мени, ско́лько у Вас
▷ *pron* мно́го, мно́гое; **much is still unclear** мно́гое ещё нея́сно; **there isn't much to do here** здесь не́чего де́лать; **how much does it cost? — too much** ско́лько э́то сто́ит? — сли́шком до́рого; **how much is it?** ско́лько э́то сто́ит?, почём э́то? (*разг*)
▷ *adv* **1** (*greatly, a great deal*) о́чень; **thank you very much** большо́е спаси́бо; **we are very much looking forward to your visit** мы о́чень ждём Ва́шего прие́зда; **he is very much a gentleman** он настоя́щий джентельме́н; **however much he tries** ско́лько бы

он ни старался; **I try to help as much as possible** *or* **as I can** я стара́юсь помога́ть как мо́жно бо́льше *or* ско́лько могу́; **I read as much as ever** я чита́ю сто́лько же, ско́лько пре́жде; **he is as much a member of the family as you** он тако́й же член семьи́, как и Вы
2 (*by far*) намно́го, гора́здо; **I'm much better now** мне сейча́с намно́го *or* гора́здо лу́чше; **it's much the biggest publishing company in Europe** э́то са́мое кру́пное изда́тельство в Евро́пе
3 (*almost*) почти́; **the view today is much as it was 10 years ago** вид сего́дня почти́ тако́й же, как и 10 лет наза́д; **how are you feeling? — much the same** как Вы себя́ чу́вствуете? — всё так же

muck [mʌk] *n* (*dirt*) грязь *f*
mud [mʌd] *n* грязь *f*
muddle ['mʌdl] *n* (*mix-up*) пу́таница, неразбери́ха; (*mess*) беспоря́док ▷ *vt* (*also* **muddle up**: *person*) запу́тывать (*perf* запу́тать); (: *things*) переме́шивать (*perf* перемеша́ть)
muddy ['mʌdɪ] *adj* гря́зный
muffled ['mʌfld] *adj* приглушённый
mug [mʌg] *n* кру́жка; (*inf*: *face*) мо́рда; (: *fool*) ду́рень *m* ▷ *vt* гра́бить (*perf* огра́бить) (*на у́лице*)
mule [mju:l] *n* (*Zool*) мул
multinational [mʌltɪ'næʃənl] *adj* междунаро́дный
multiple ['mʌltɪpl] *adj* (*injuries*) многочи́сленный ▷ *n* (*Math*) кра́тное число́; **multiple collision** столкнове́ние не́скольких автомоби́лей; **multiple sclerosis** *n* рассе́янный склеро́з
multiplication [mʌltɪplɪ'keɪʃən] *n* умноже́ние
multiply ['mʌltɪplaɪ] *vt* умножа́ть (*perf* умно́жить) ▷ *vi* размножа́ться (*perf* размно́житься)
multistorey ['mʌltɪ'stɔ:rɪ] *adj* (*Brit*) многоэта́жный
mum [mʌm] (*Brit*: *inf*) *n* ма́ма ▷ *adj*: **to keep mum about sth** пома́лкивать (*impf*) о чём-н
mumble ['mʌmbl] *vt* бормота́ть (*perf* пробормота́ть) ▷ *vi* бормота́ть (*impf*)
mummy ['mʌmɪ] *n* (*Brit*: *inf*) маму́ля, ма́ма; (*corpse*) му́мия
mumps [mʌmps] *n* сви́нка
munch [mʌntʃ] *vt, vi* жева́ть (*impf*)
municipal [mju:'nɪsɪpl] *adj* муниципа́льный
mural ['mjuərl] *n* фре́ска, насте́нная ро́спись *f*
murder ['mə:də^r] *n* убийство (*умы́шленное*) ▷ *vt* убива́ть (*perf* уби́ть) (*умы́шленно*); **murderer** *n* уби́йца *m/f*
murky ['mə:kɪ] *adj* (*street, night*) мра́чный; (*water*) му́тный
murmur ['mə:mə^r] *n* (*of voices, waves*) ро́пот ▷ *vt, vi* шепта́ть (*impf*)
muscle ['mʌsl] *n* мы́шца, му́скул
muscular ['mʌskjulə^r] *adj* (*pain, injury*) мы́шечный; (*person*) му́скулистый
museum [mju:'zɪəm] *n* музе́й
mushroom ['mʌʃrum] *n* гриб
music ['mju:zɪk] *n* му́зыка; **musical** *adj* музыка́льный; (*sound, tune*) мелоди́чный ▷ *n* мю́зикл; **musician** [mju:'zɪʃən] *n* музыка́нт
Muslim ['mʌzlɪm] *n* мусульма́нин(-нка) ▷ *adj* мусульма́нский

mussel ['mʌsl] *n* мидия
must [mʌst] *n* (*need*) необходи́мость *f* ▷ *aux vb* (*necessity*): **I must go** мне на́до *or* ну́жно идти́; (*obligation*): **I must do it** я до́лжен э́то сде́лать; (*probability*): **he must be there by now** он до́лжен уже́ быть там; **you must come and see me soon** Вы обяза́тельно должны́ ско́ро ко мне зайти́; **why must he behave so badly?** отчего́ он так пло́хо себя́ ведёт?
mustache ['mʌstæʃ] *n* (*US*) = **moustache**
mustard ['mʌstəd] *n* горчи́ца
mustn't ['mʌsnt] = **must not**
mute [mju:t] *adj* (*silent*) безмо́лвный
mutilate ['mju:tɪleɪt] *vt* (*person*) уве́чить (*perf* изуве́чить); (*thing*) уро́довать (*perf* изуро́довать)
mutiny ['mju:tɪnɪ] *n* мятёж, бунт
mutter ['mʌtə[r]] *vt, vi* бормота́ть (*impf*)
mutton ['mʌtn] *n* бара́нина
mutual ['mju:tʃuəl] *adj* (*feeling, help*) взаи́мный; (*friend, interest*) о́бщий; **mutual understanding** взаимопонима́ние
muzzle ['mʌzl] *n* (*of dog*) мо́рда; (*of gun*) ду́ло; (*for dog*) намо́рдник ▷ *vt* (*dog*) надева́ть (*perf* наде́ть) намо́рдник на *+acc*

 **KEYWORD**

my [maɪ] *adj* **1** мой; (*referring back to subject of sentence*) свой; **this is my house/car** э́то мой дом/моя́ маши́на; **is this my pen or yours?** э́то моя́ ру́чка или Ва́ша?; **I've lost my key** я потеря́л свой ключ
2 (*with parts of the body etc*): **I've washed my hair/cut my finger** я помы́л го́лову/поре́зал па́лец

 **KEYWORD**

myself [maɪ'sɛlf] *pron*
1 (*reflexive*): **I've hurt myself** я ушйбся; **I consider myself clever** я счита́ю себя́ у́мным; **I am ashamed of myself** мне сты́дно за моё поведе́ние
2 (*complement*): **she's the same age as myself** она́ одного́ во́зраста со мной
3 (*after prep*: *+gen*) себя́; (: *+dat, +prp*) себе́; (: *+instr*) собо́й; **I wanted to keep the book for myself** я хоте́л оста́вить кни́гу себе́; **I sometimes talk to myself** иногда́ я сам с собо́й разгова́риваю; **(all) by myself** (*alone*) сам; **I made it all by myself** я всё э́то сде́лал сам
4 (*emphatic*) сам; **I myself chose the flowers** я сам выбира́л цветы́

mysterious [mɪs'tɪərɪəs] *adj* таи́нственный
mystery ['mɪstərɪ] *n* (*puzzle*) зага́дка
mystical ['mɪstɪkl] *adj* мисти́ческий
myth [mɪθ] *n* миф; **mythology** [mɪ'θɔlədʒɪ] *n* мифоло́гия

n/a *abbr* (= *not applicable*) не применяется
nag [næg] *vt* (*scold*) пили́ть (*impf*)
nail [neɪl] *n* но́готь *m*; (*Tech*) гвоздь *m* ▷ *vt*: **to nail sth to** прибива́ть (*perf* приби́ть) что-н к +*dat*; **nail polish** *n* лак для ногте́й
naive [naɪ'i:v] *adj* наи́вный
naked ['neɪkɪd] *adj* го́лый
name [neɪm] *n* (*of person*) и́мя *nt*; (*of place, object*) назва́ние; (*of pet*) кли́чка ▷ *vt* называ́ть (*perf* назва́ть); **what's your name?** как Вас зову́т?; **my name is Peter** меня́ зову́т Пи́тер; **what's the name of this place?** как называ́ется э́то ме́сто?; **by name** по и́мени; **in the name of** (*for the sake of*) во и́мя +*gen*; (*representing*) от и́мени +*gen*; **namely** *adv* а и́менно
nanny ['nænɪ] *n* ня́ня
nap [næp] *n* (*sleep*) коро́ткий сон
napkin ['næpkɪn] *n* (*also* **table napkin**) салфе́тка
nappy ['næpɪ] *n* (*Brit*) подгу́зник
narrative ['nærətɪv] *n* исто́рия, по́весть *f*
narrator [nə'reɪtə^r] *n* (*in book*) расска́зчик(-ица); (*in film*) ди́ктор
narrow ['nærəu] *adj* у́зкий; (*majority, advantage*) незначи́тельный ▷ *vi* (*road*) сужа́ться (*perf* су́зиться); (*gap, difference*) уменьша́ться (*perf* уме́ньшиться) ▷ *vt*: **to narrow sth down to** своди́ть (*perf* свести́) что-н к +*dat*; **to have a narrow escape** едва́ спасти́сь (*perf*)
nasal ['neɪzl] *adj* (*voice*) гнуса́вый
nasty ['nɑ:stɪ] *adj* (*unpleasant*) проти́вный; (*malicious*) зло́бный; (*situation, wound*) скве́рный
nation ['neɪʃən] *n* наро́д; (*state*) страна́; (*native population*) на́ция
national ['næʃənl] *adj* национа́льный; **National Health Service** *n* (*Brit*) госуда́рственная слу́жба здравоохране́ния; **National Insurance** *n* (*Brit*) госуда́рственное страхова́ние; **nationalist** *adj* национлисти́ческий; **nationality** [næʃə'nælɪtɪ] *n* (*status*) гражда́нство; (*ethnic group*) наро́дность *f*
nationwide ['neɪʃənwaɪd] *adj* общенаро́дный ▷ *adv* по всей стране́
native ['neɪtɪv] *n* (*local inhabitant*) ме́стный(-ая) жи́тель(ница) *m(f)* ▷ *adj* (*indigenous*) коренно́й, иско́нный; (*of one's birth*) родно́й; (*innate*) врождённый; **a native of Russia** уроже́нец(-нка) Росси́и; **a native**

speaker of Russian носи́тель(ница) *m(f)* ру́сского языка́
NATO ['neɪtəu] *n abbr* (= *North Atlantic Treaty Organization*) НАТО
natural ['nætʃrəl] *adj* (*behaviour*) есте́ственный; (*aptitude, materials*) приро́дный; (*disaster*) стихи́йный; **naturally** *adv* есте́ственно; (*innately*) от приро́ды; (*in nature*) есте́ственным о́бразом; **naturally, I refused** есте́ственно, я отказа́лся
nature ['neɪtʃə^r] *n* (*also* **Nature**) приро́да; (*character*) нату́ра; (*sort*) хара́ктер; **by nature** (*person*) по нату́ре; (*event, thing*) по приро́де
naughty ['nɔ:tɪ] *adj* (*child*) непослу́шный, озорно́й
nausea ['nɔ:sɪə] *n* тошнота́
naval ['neɪvl] *adj* вое́нно-морско́й
navel ['neɪvl] *n* пупо́к
navigate ['nævɪgeɪt] *vt* (*Naut, Aviat*) управля́ть (*impf*) +*instr* ▷ *vi* определя́ть (*perf* определи́ть) маршру́т
navigation [nævɪ'geɪʃən] *n* (*science*) навига́ция; (*action*): **navigation (of)** управле́ние (+*instr*)
navy ['neɪvɪ] *n* вое́нно-морско́й флот; **navy(-blue)** *adj* тёмно-си́ний
Nazi ['nɑ:tsɪ] *n* наци́ст(ка)
NB *abbr* (*note well*) (= *nota bene*) нотабе́не
near [nɪə^r] *adj* бли́зкий ▷ *adv* бли́зко ▷ *prep* (*also* **near to**: *space*) во́зле +*gen*, о́коло +*gen*; (: *time*) к +*dat*, о́коло +*gen*; **nearby** *adj* близлежа́щий ▷ *adv* побли́зости; **nearly** *adv* почти́; **I nearly fell** я чуть (бы́ло) не упа́л
neat [ni:t] *adj* (*person, place*) опря́тный; (*work*) аккура́тный; (*clear*: *categories*) чёткий; (*esp US*: *inf*) кла́ссный; **neatly** *adv* (*dress*) опря́тно; (*work*) аккура́тно; (*sum up*) чётко
necessarily ['nɛsɪsrɪlɪ] *adv* неизбе́жно
necessary ['nɛsɪsrɪ] *adj* необходи́мый; (*inevitable*) обяза́тельный, неизбе́жный; **it's not necessary** э́то не обяза́тельно; **it is necessary to/that ...** необходи́мо +*infin*/что́бы ...
necessity [nɪ'sɛsɪtɪ] *n* необходи́мость *f*; **necessities** *npl* (*essentials*) предме́ты *mpl* пе́рвой необходи́мости
neck [nɛk] *n* (*Anat*) ше́я; (*of garment*) во́рот; (*of bottle*) го́рлышко; **necklace** ['nɛklɪs] *n* ожере́лье
need [ni:d] *n* потре́бность *f*; (*deprivation*) нужда́; (*necessity*): **need (for)** нужда́ (в +*prp*) ▷ *vt*: **I need time/money** мне ну́жно вре́мя/нужны́ де́ньги; **there's no need to worry** не́зачем волнова́ться; **I need to see him** мне на́до *or* ну́жно с ним уви́деться; **you don't need to leave yet** Вам ещё не пора́ уходи́ть
needle ['ni:dl] *n* игла́, иго́лка; (*for knitting*) спи́ца ▷ *vt* (*fig*: *inf*) подка́лывать (*perf* подколо́ть)
needless ['ni:dlɪs] *adj* изли́шний; **needless to say** само́ собо́й разуме́ется
needn't ['ni:dnt] = **need not**
needy ['ni:dɪ] *adj* нужда́ющийся
negative ['nɛgətɪv] *adj* (*also Elec*) отрица́тельный ▷ *n* (*Phot*) негати́в
neglect [nɪ'glɛkt] *vt* (*child, work*) забра́сывать (*perf* забро́сить); (*garden, health*) запуска́ть (*perf* запусти́ть); (*duty*) пренебрега́ть (*perf* пренебре́чь) ▷ *n*: **neglect (of)** невнима́ние (к +*dat*); **in a state of neglect** в запусте́нии

negotiate [nɪ'gəuʃɪeɪt] *vt* (*treaty, deal*) заключа́ть (*perf* заключи́ть); (*obstacle*) преодолева́ть (*perf* преодоле́ть); (*corner*) огиба́ть (*perf* обогну́ть) ▷ *vi*: **to negotiate (with sb for sth)** вести́ (*impf*) перегово́ры (с кем-н о чём-н)
negotiation [nɪgəuʃɪ'eɪʃən] *n* (*of treaty, deal*) заключе́ние; (*of obstacle*) преодоле́ние; **negotiations** перегово́ры *mpl*
negotiator [nɪ'gəuʃɪeɪtə^r] *n* уча́стник перегово́ров
neighbour ['neɪbə^r] (*US* **neighbor**) *n* сосе́д(ка); **neighbourhood** *n* (*place*) райо́н; (*people*) сосе́ди *mpl*; **neighbouring** *adj* сосе́дний
neither ['naɪðə^r] *adj* ни тот, ни друго́й ▷ *conj*: **I didn't move and neither did John** ни я, ни Джон не дви́нулись с ме́ста ▷ *pron*: **neither of them came** ни тот ни друго́й не пришли́, ни оди́н из них не пришёл; **neither version is true** ни та ни друга́я ве́рсия не верна́; **neither ... nor ...** ни ..., ни ...; **neither good nor bad** ни хорошо́, ни пло́хо
neon ['ni:ɔn] *n* нео́н
nephew ['nɛvju:] *n* племя́нник
nerve [nə:v] *n* (*Anat*) нерв; (*courage*) вы́держка; (*impudence*) на́глость *f*
nervous ['nə:vəs] *adj* не́рвный; **to be** *or* **feel nervous** не́рвничать (*impf*); **nervous breakdown** *n* не́рвный срыв
nest [nɛst] *n* гнездо́
net [nɛt] *n* (*also fig*) сеть *f*; (*Sport*) се́тка; (*Comput*): **the Net** Сеть *f* ▷ *adj* (*Comm*) чи́стый ▷ *vt* (*fish*) лови́ть (*perf* пойма́ть) в сеть; (*profit*) приноси́ть (*perf* принести́)
Netherlands ['nɛðələndz] *npl*: **the Netherlands** Нидерла́нды *pl*
nett [nɛt] *adj* = **net**
nettle ['nɛtl] *n* крапи́ва
network ['nɛtwə:k] *n* сеть *f*
neurotic [njuə'rɔtɪk] *adj* неврастени́чный
neutral ['nju:trəl] *adj* нейтра́льный ▷ *n* (*Aut*) холосто́й ход
never ['nɛvə^r] *adv* никогда́; **never in my life** никогда́ в жи́зни; **nevertheless** *adv* тем не ме́нее
new [nju:] *adj* (*brand new*) но́вый; (*recent*) неда́вний; **newborn** *adj* новоро́жденный; **newcomer** *n* новичо́к; **newly** *adv* неда́вно
news [nju:z] *n* (*good, bad*) но́вость *f*, изве́стие; **a piece of news** но́вость; **the news** (*Radio, TV*) но́вости *fpl*; **news agency** *n* информацио́нное аге́нтство; **newsletter** *n* информацио́нный бюллете́нь *m*; **newsreader** *n* ди́ктор (*програ́ммы новосте́й*)
New Year *n* Но́вый год; **Happy New Year!** С Но́вым го́дом!; **New Year's Day** *n* пе́рвое января́; **New Year's Eve** *n* кану́н Но́вого го́да
New Zealand [nju:'zi:lənd] *n* Но́вая Зела́ндия
next [nɛkst] *adj* сле́дующий; (*adjacent*) сосе́дний ▷ *adv* пото́м, зате́м ▷ *prep*: **next to** ря́дом с *+instr*, во́зле *+gen*; **next time** в сле́дующий раз; **the next day** на сле́дующий день; **next year** в бу́дущем *or* сле́дующем году́; **in the next 15 minutes** в ближа́йшие 15 мину́т; **next to nothing** почти́ ничего́; **next please!** сле́дующий, пожа́луйста!; **next door** *adv* по сосе́дству, ря́дом ▷ *adj* (*neighbour*) ближа́йший; **next of**

kin *n* ближáйший рóдственник
NHS *n abbr* (*Brit*) = **National Health Service**
nibble [ˈnɪbl] *vt* надкýсывать (*perf* надкуси́ть)
nice [naɪs] *adj* прия́тный, хорóший; (*attractive*) симпати́чный; **to look nice** хорошó вы́глядеть (*impf*); **that's very nice of you** óчень ми́ло с Вáшей стороны́
nick [nɪk] *n* (*in skin*) порéз; (*in surface*) зарýбка ▷ *vt* (*inf*: *steal*) утáскивать (*perf* утащи́ть); **in the nick of time** как раз вóвремя
nickel [ˈnɪkl] *n* ни́кель *m*; (*US*: *coin*) *монéта в 5 цéнтов*
nickname [ˈnɪkneɪm] *n* кли́чка, прóзвище ▷ *vt* прозывáть (*perf* прозвáть)
nicotine [ˈnɪkəti:n] *n* никоти́н
niece [ni:s] *n* племя́нница
night [naɪt] *n* ночь *f*; (*evening*) вéчер; **at night, by night** нóчью; **all night long** всю ночь напролёт; **in** *or* **during the night** нóчью; **last night** вчерá нóчью; (*evening*) вчерá вéчером; **the night before last** позапрóшлой нóчью; (*evening*) позавчерá вéчером; **nightdress** *n* ночнáя рубáшка
nightlife [ˈnaɪtlaɪf] *n* ночнáя жизнь *f*
nightly [ˈnaɪtlɪ] *adj* (*every night*) еженóщный ▷ *adv* еженóщно
nightmare [ˈnaɪtmɛəʳ] *n* кошмáр
nil [nɪl] *n* нуль *m*; (*Brit*: *score*) ноль *m*
nine [naɪn] *n* дéвять; **nineteen** *n* девятнáдцать; **nineteenth** *adj* девятнáдцатый; **ninetieth** *adj* девянóстый; **ninety** *n* девянóсто; **ninth** [naɪnθ] *adj* девя́тый
nip [nɪp] *vt* (*pinch*) щипáть (*perf* ущипнýть); (*bite*) кусáть (*perf* укуси́ть) ▷ *vi* (*Brit*: *inf*): **to nip out** выскáкивать (*perf* вы́скочить)
nipple [ˈnɪpl] *n* (*Anat*) сосóк
nitrogen [ˈnaɪtrədʒən] *n* азóт

 **KEYWORD**

no [nəu] (*pl* **noes**) *adv* (*opposite of "yes"*) нет; **are you coming? — no (I'm not)** Вы придёте? — нет(, не придý); **no thank you** нет, спаси́бо
▷ *adj* (*not any*): **I have no money/books** у меня́ нет дéнег/книг; **it is of no importance at all** э́то не имéет никакóго значéния; **no system is totally fair** никакáя систéма не явля́ется пóлностью справедли́вой; **"no entry"** "вход воспрещён"; **"no smoking"** "не кури́ть"
▷ *n*: **there were twenty noes** двáдцать голосóв бы́ло "прóтив"

nobility [nəuˈbɪlɪtɪ] *n* (*class*) знать *f*, дворя́нство
noble [ˈnəubl] *adj* (*aristocratic*) дворя́нский, знáтный; (*high-minded*) благорóдный
nobody [ˈnəubədɪ] *pron* никтó; **there is nobody here** здесь никогó нет
nod [nɔd] *vi* кивáть (*impf*) ▷ *n* кивóк ▷ *vt*: **to nod one's head** кивáть (*perf* кивнýть) головóй; **nod off** *vi* задремáть (*perf*)
noise [nɔɪz] *n* шум
noisy [ˈnɔɪzɪ] *adj* шýмный
nominal [ˈnɔmɪnl] *adj* номинáльный
nominate [ˈnɔmɪneɪt] *vt* (*propose*): **to nominate sb (for)** выставля́ть (*perf* вы́ставить) кандидатýру когó-н (на +*acc*);

(*appoint*): **to nominate sb (to/as)** назнача́ть (*perf* назна́чить) кого́-н (на *+acc*/*+instr*)
nomination [nɔmɪ'neɪʃən] *n* (*see vb*) выставле́ние; назначе́ние
nominee [nɔmɪ'ni:] *n* кандида́т
non- [nɔn] *prefix* не-
none [nʌn] *pron* (*person*) никто́, ни оди́н; (*thing*: *countable*) ничто́, ни оди́н; (: *uncountable*) ничего́; **none of you** никто́ *or* ни оди́н из вас; **I've none left** у меня́ ничего́ не оста́лось
nonetheless ['nʌnðə'lɛs] *adv* тем не ме́нее, всё же
nonfiction [nɔn'fɪkʃən] *n* документа́льная литерату́ра
nonsense ['nɔnsəns] *n* ерунда́, чепуха́
non-smoker [nɔn'sməukə^r] *adj* некуря́щий *m adj*
noodles ['nu:dlz] *npl* вермише́ль *fsg*
noon [nu:n] *n* по́лдень *m*
no-one ['nəuwʌn] *pron* = **nobody**
nor [nɔ:^r] *conj* = **neither** ▷ *adv see* **neither**
norm [nɔ:m] *n* но́рма
normal ['nɔ:ml] *adj* норма́льный; **normally** *adv* (*usually*) обы́чно; (*properly*) норма́льно
north [nɔ:θ] *n* се́вер ▷ *adj* се́верный ▷ *adv* (*go*) на се́вер; (*be*) к се́веру; **North Africa** *n* Се́верная А́фрика; **North America** *n* Се́верная Аме́рика; **northeast** *n* се́веро-восто́к; **northern** ['nɔ:ðən] *adj* се́верный; **Northern Ireland** *n* Се́верная Ирла́ндия; **North Pole** *n* Се́верный по́люс; **North Sea** *n* Се́верное мо́ре; **northwest** *n* се́веро-за́пад
Norway ['nɔ:weɪ] *n* Норве́гия
Norwegian [nɔ:'wi:dʒən] *adj* норве́жский
nose [nəuz] *n* нос; (*sense of smell*) нюх, чутьё; **nosebleed** *n* носово́е кровотече́ние; **nosey** ['nəuzɪ] *adj* (*inf*) = **nosy**
nostalgia [nɔs'tældʒɪə] *n* ностальги́я
nostalgic [nɔs'tældʒɪk] *adj* (*memory, film*) ностальги́ческий; **to be nostalgic (for)** испы́тывать (*impf*) ностальги́ю (по *+dat*), тоскова́ть (*impf*) по *+dat*
nostril ['nɔstrɪl] *n* ноздря́
nosy ['nəuzɪ] *adj* (*inf*): **to be nosy** сова́ть (*impf*) нос в чужи́е дела́
not [nɔt] *adv* нет; (*before verbs*) не; **he is not** *or* **isn't at home** его́ нет до́ма; **he asked me not to do it** он попроси́л меня́ не де́лать э́того; **you must not** *or* **you mustn't do that** (*forbidden*) э́того нельзя́ де́лать; **it's too late, isn't it?** уже́ сли́шком по́здно, не пра́вда ли?; **not that ...** не то, что́бы ...; **not yet** нет ещё, ещё нет; **not now** не сейча́с; *see also* **all**; **only**
notably ['nəutəblɪ] *adv* (*particularly*) осо́бенно; (*markedly*) заме́тно
notch [nɔtʃ] *n* насе́чка
note [nəut] *n* (*record*) за́пись *f*; (*letter*) запи́ска; (*also* **footnote**) сно́ска; (*also* **banknote**) банкно́та; (*Mus*) но́та; (*tone*) тон ▷ *vt* (*observe*) замеча́ть (*perf* заме́тить); (*also* **note down**) запи́сывать (*perf* записа́ть); **notebook** *n* записна́я кни́жка; **noted** *adj* изве́стный; **notepad** *n* блокно́т; **notepaper** *n* пи́счая бума́га
nothing ['nʌθɪŋ] *n* ничто́; (*zero*) ноль *m*; **he does nothing** он ничего́ не де́лает; **there is nothing to do/be said** де́лать/сказа́ть не́чего;

nothing new/much/of the sort ничегó нóвого/осóбенного/подóбного; **for nothing** дáром
notice ['nəutɪs] *n* (*announcement*) объявлéние; (*warning*) предупреждéние ▷ *vt* замечáть (*perf* замéтить); **to take notice of** обращáть (*perf* обратúть) внимáние на *+acc*; **at short notice** без предупреждéния; **until further notice** впредь до дальнéйшего уведомлéния; **noticeable** *adj* замéтный; **notice board** *n* доскá объявлéний
notification [nəutɪfɪ'keɪʃən] *n* уведомлéние
notify ['nəutɪfaɪ] *vt*: **to notify sb (of sth)** уведомля́ть (*perf* увéдомить) когó-н (о чём-н)
notion ['nəuʃən] *n* (*idea*) поня́тие; (*opinion*) представлéние
notorious [nəu'tɔ:rɪəs] *adj* печáльно извéстный
noun [naun] *n* (úмя *nt*) существúтельное *nt adj*
nourish ['nʌrɪʃ] *vt* питáть (*impf*); (*fig*) взрáщивать (*perf* взрастúть); **nourishment** *n* (*food*) питáние
novel ['nɔvl] *n* ромáн ▷ *adj* оригинáльный; **novelist** *n* романúст(ка); **novelty** *n* (*newness*) новизнá; (*object*) новúнка
November [nəu'vɛmbə^r] *n* ноя́брь *m*
novice ['nɔvɪs] *n* (*in job*) новичóк
now [nau] *adv* тепéрь, сейчáс ▷ *conj*: **now (that) ...** тепéрь, когдá ...; **right now** пря́мо сейчáс; **by now** к настоя́щему врéмени; **now and then** *or* **again** врéмя от врéмени; **from now on** отны́не, впредь; **until now** до сих пор; **nowadays** *adv* в нáши дни
nowhere ['nəuwɛə^r] *adv* (*be*) нигдé; (*go*) никудá
nuclear ['nju:klɪə^r] *adj* я́дерный
nucleus ['nju:klɪəs] (*pl* **nuclei**) *n* ядрó
nude [nju:d] *adj* обнажённый, нагóй ▷ *n*: **in the nude** в обнажённом вúде
nudge [nʌdʒ] *vt* подтáлкивать (*perf* подтолкнýть)
nuisance ['nju:sns] *n* досáда; (*person*) занýда; **what a nuisance!** какáя досáда!
numb [nʌm] *adj* онемéвший; **to go numb** немéть (*perf* онемéть)
number ['nʌmbə^r] *n* нóмер; (*Math*) числó; (*written figure*) цúфра; (*quantity*) кóличество ▷ *vt* (*pages etc*) нумеровáть (*perf* пронумеровáть); (*amount to*) насчúтывать (*impf*); **a number of** нéсколько *+gen*, ряд *+gen*; **numberplate** *n* (*Brit*) номернóй знак
numerical [nju:'mɛrɪkl] *adj* (*value*) числовóй; **in numerical order** по номерáм
numerous ['nju:mərəs] *adj* многочúсленный; **on numerous occasions** многокрáтно
nun [nʌn] *n* монáхиня
nurse [nə:s] *n* медсестрá; (*also* **male nurse**) медбрáт ▷ *vt* (*patient*) ухáживать (*impf*) за *+instr*
nursery ['nə:sərɪ] *n* (*institution*) я́сли *pl*; (*room*) дéтская *f adj*; (*for plants*) питóмник; **nursery rhyme** *n* дéтская пéсенка; **nursery school** *n* дéтский сад
nursing ['nə:sɪŋ] *n* (*profession*) профéссия медсестры́; **nursing home** *n* чáстный дом для престарéлых
nurture ['nə:tʃə^r] *vt* (*child, plant*)

выра́щивать (*perf* вы́растить)
nut [nʌt] *n* (*Bot*) оре́х; (*Tech*) га́йка; **nutmeg** *n* муска́тный оре́х
nutrient ['nju:trɪənt] *n* пита́тельное вещество́
nutrition [nju:'trɪʃən] *n* (*nourishment*) пита́тельность *f*; (*diet*) пита́ние
nutritious [nju:'trɪʃəs] *adj* пита́тельный
nylon ['naɪlɔn] *n* нейло́н ▷ *adj* нейло́новый

oak [əuk] *n* дуб ▷ *adj* дубо́вый
OAP *n abbr* (*Brit*) = **old age pensioner**
oar [ɔ:ʳ] *n* весло́
oasis [əu'eɪsɪs] (*pl* **oases**) *n* оа́зис
oath [əuθ] *n* (*promise*) кля́тва; (: *Law*) прися́га; (*swear word*) прокля́тие; **on** (*Brit*) *or* **under oath** под прися́гой
oats [əuts] *npl* овёс *msg*
obedience [ə'bi:dɪəns] *n* повинове́ние, послуша́ние
obedient [ə'bi:dɪənt] *adj* послу́шный
obese [əu'bi:s] *adj* ту́чный
obey [ə'beɪ] *vt* подчиня́ться (*perf* подчини́ться) +*dat*, повинова́ться (*impf/perf*) +*dat*
obituary [ə'bɪtjuərɪ] *n* некроло́г
object [*n* 'ɔbdʒɪkt, *vb* əb'dʒɛkt] *n* (*thing*) предме́т; (*aim, purpose*) цель *f*; (*of affection, desires*)

объе́кт; (*Ling*) дополне́ние ▷ *vi*: **to object (to)** возража́ть (*perf* возрази́ть) (про́тив *+gen*); **money is no object** де́ньги — не пробле́ма; **objection** [əb'dʒɛkʃən] *n* возраже́ние; **I have no objection to ...** я не име́ю никаки́х возраже́ний про́тив *+gen ...*; **objective** [əb'dʒɛktɪv] *adj* объекти́вный ▷ *n* цель *f*

obligation [ɔblɪ'geɪʃən] *n* обяза́тельство

obligatory [ə'blɪgətərɪ] *adj* обяза́тельный

oblige [ə'blaɪdʒ] *vt* обя́зывать (*perf* обяза́ть); (*force*): **to oblige sb to do** обя́зывать (*perf* обяза́ть) кого́-н *+infin*; **I'm much obliged to you for your help** (*grateful*) я о́чень обя́зан Вам за Ва́шу по́мощь

oblivious [ə'blɪvɪəs] *adj*: **to be oblivious of** *or* **to** не сознава́ть (*impf*) *+gen*

obnoxious [əb'nɔkʃəs] *adj* отврати́тельный

oboe ['əubəu] *n* гобо́й

obscene [əb'si:n] *adj* непристо́йный

obscure [əb'skjuəʳ] *adj* (*little known*) неприме́тный; (*incomprehensible*) сму́тный ▷ *vt* (*view etc*) загора́живать (*perf* загороди́ть); (*truth etc*) затемня́ть (*perf* затемни́ть)

observant [əb'zə:vnt] *adj* наблюда́тельный

observation [ɔbzə'veɪʃən] *n* наблюде́ние; (*remark*) замеча́ние

observe [əb'zə:v] *vt* (*watch*) наблюда́ть (*impf*) за *+instr*; (*comment*) замеча́ть (*perf* заме́тить); (*abide by*) соблюда́ть (*perf* соблюсти́); **observer** *n* наблюда́тель *m*

obsession [əb'sɛʃən] *n* страсть *f*, одержи́мость *f*

obsessive [əb'sɛsɪv] *adj* стра́стный, одержи́мый

obsolete ['ɔbsəli:t] *adj* устаре́вший

obstacle ['ɔbstəkl] *n* препя́тствие

obstinate ['ɔbstɪnɪt] *adj* упря́мый

obstruct [əb'strʌkt] *vt* (*road, path*) загора́живать (*perf* загороди́ть); (*traffic, progress*) препя́тствовать (*perf* воспрепя́тствовать) *+dat*; **obstruction** [əb'strʌkʃən] *n* (*of law*) обстру́кция; (*object*) препя́тствие

obtain [əb'teɪn] *vt* приобрета́ть (*perf* приобрести́)

obvious ['ɔbvɪəs] *adj* очеви́дный; **obviously** *adv* очеви́дно; (*of course*) разуме́ется; **obviously not** разуме́ется, нет

occasion [ə'keɪʒən] *n* (*time*) раз; (*case, opportunity*) слу́чай; (*event*) собы́тие; **occasional** *adj* ре́дкий, неча́стый; **occasionally** *adv* и́зредка

occupant ['ɔkjupənt] *n* (*long-term*) обита́тель(ница) *m(f)*

occupation [ɔkju'peɪʃən] *n* заня́тие; (*Mil*) оккупа́ция

occupy ['ɔkjupaɪ] *vt* занима́ть (*perf* заня́ть); (*country, attention*) захва́тывать (*perf* захвати́ть); **to occupy o.s. with sth** занима́ться (*perf* заня́ться) чем-н

occur [ə'kə:ʳ] *vi* происходи́ть (*perf* произойти́), случа́ться (*perf* случи́ться); (*exist*) встреча́ться (*perf* встре́титься); **to occur to sb** приходи́ть (*perf* прийти́) кому́-н в го́лову; **occurrence** *n* (*event*) происше́ствие

ocean ['əuʃən] *n* океа́н
o'clock [ə'klɔk] *adv*: **it is five o'clock** сейча́с пять часо́в
October [ɔk'təubə^r] *n* октя́брь *m*
octopus ['ɔktəpəs] *n* осьмино́г
odd [ɔd] *adj* (*strange*) стра́нный, необы́чный; (*uneven*) нечётный; (*not paired*) непа́рный; **60-odd** шестьдеся́т с ли́шним; **at odd times** времена́ми; **I was the odd one out** я был ли́шний; **oddly** *adv* (*behave, dress*) стра́нно; *see also* **enough**; **odds** *npl* (*in betting*) ста́вки *fpl*; **to be at odds (with)** быть (*impf*) не в лада́х (с +*instr*)
odour ['əudə^r] (*US* **odor**) *n* за́пах

KEYWORD

of [ɔv, əv] *prep* **1** (*expressing belonging*): **the history of Russia** исто́рия Росси́и; **a friend of ours** наш друг; **a boy of 10** ма́льчик десяти́ лет; **that was kind of you** э́то бы́ло о́чень любе́зно с Ва́шей стороны́; **a man of great ability** челове́к больши́х спосо́бностей; **the city of New York** го́род Нью-Йо́рк; **south of London** к ю́гу от Ло́ндона
2 (*expressing quantity, amount, dates etc*): **a kilo of flour** килогра́мм муки́; **how much of this material do you need?** ско́лько тако́й тка́ни Вам ну́жно?; **there were three of them** (*people*) их бы́ло тро́е; (*objects*) их бы́ло три; **three of us stayed** тро́е из нас оста́лись; **the 5th of July** 5-ое ию́ля; **on the 5th of July** 5-ого ию́ля
3 (*from*) из +*gen*; **the house is made of wood** дом сде́лан из де́рева

KEYWORD

off [ɔf] *adv* **1** (*referring to distance, time*): **it's a long way off** э́то далеко́ отсю́да; **the city is 5 miles off** до го́рода 5 миль; **the game is 3 days off** до игры́ оста́лось 3 дня
2 (*departure*): **to go off to Paris/Italy** уезжа́ть (*perf* уе́хать) в Пари́ж/Ита́лию; **I must be off** мне пора́ (идти́)
3 (*removal*): **to take off one's hat/clothes** снима́ть (*perf* снять) шля́пу/оде́жду; **the button came off** пу́говица оторвала́сь; **ten per cent off** (*Comm*) ски́дка в де́сять проце́нтов
4: to be off (*on holiday*) быть (*impf*) в о́тпуске; **I'm off on Fridays** (*day off*) у меня́ выходно́й по пя́тницам; **he was off on Friday** (*absent*) в пя́тницу его́ не́ было на рабо́те; **I have a day off** у меня́ отгу́л; **to be off sick** не рабо́тать (*impf*) по боле́зни
▷ *adj* **1** (*not on*) вы́ключенный; (: *tap*) закры́тый; (*disconnected*) отключённый
2 (*cancelled*: *meeting, match*) отменённый; (: *agreement*) растóргнутый
3 (*Brit*): **to go off** (*milk*) прокиса́ть (*perf* проки́снуть); (*cheese, meat*) по́ртиться (*perf* испо́ртиться)
4: on the off chance на вся́кий слу́чай; **to have an off day** встава́ть (*perf* встать) с ле́вой ноги́
▷ *prep* **1** (*indicating motion*) с +*gen*; **to fall off a cliff** упа́сть (*perf*) со скалы́
2 (*distant from*) от +*gen*; **it's just off the M1** э́то недалеко́ от автостра́ды M1; **it's five km off the main road** э́то в пяти́ км от шоссе́

3: to be off meat (*dislike*) разлюби́ть (*perf*) мя́со

offence [ə'fɛns] (*US* **offense**) *n* (*crime*) правонаруше́ние; **to take offence at** обижа́ться (*perf* оби́деться) на *+acc*
offend [ə'fɛnd] *vt* (*person*) обижа́ть (*perf* оби́деть); **offender** *n* правонаруши́тель(ница) *m(f)*
offense [ə'fɛns] *n* (*US*) = **offence**
offensive [ə'fɛnsɪv] *adj* (*remark, behaviour*) оскорби́тельный ▷ *n* (*Mil*) наступле́ние; **offensive weapon** ору́дие нападе́ния
offer ['ɔfəʳ] *n* предложе́ние ▷ *vt* предлага́ть (*perf* предложи́ть)
office ['ɔfɪs] *n* о́фис; (*room*) кабине́т; **doctor's office** (*US*) кабине́т врача́; **to take office** (*person*) вступа́ть (*perf* вступи́ть) в до́лжность
officer ['ɔfɪsəʳ] *n* (*Mil*) офице́р; (*also* **police officer**) полице́йский *m adj*; (: *in Russia*) милиционе́р
official [ə'fɪʃl] *adj* официа́льный ▷ *n* (*of organization*) должностно́е лицо́; **government official** официа́льное лицо́
off-licence ['ɔflaɪsns] *n* (*Brit*) ви́нный магази́н
off-line [ɔf'laɪn] *adj* (*Comput*) в оффла́йн (*m ind*), оффла́йнобый; (: *работать*) автоно́мный; (*switched off*) отключённый
off-peak ['ɔf'pi:k] *adj* (*heating, electricity*) непи́ковый
offset ['ɔfsɛt] *irreg vt* уравнове́шивать (*perf* уравнове́сить)
offshore [ɔf'ʃɔ:ʳ] *adj* (*oilrig, fishing*) морско́й; (*Comm*) оффшо́рный; **offshore wind** ве́тер с бе́рега
offspring ['ɔfsprɪŋ] *n inv* о́тпрыск
often ['ɔfn] *adv* ча́сто; **how often ...?** как ча́сто ...?; **more often than not** ча́ще всего́; **as often as not** дово́льно ча́сто; **every so often** вре́мя от вре́мени
oil [ɔɪl] *n* ма́сло; (*petroleum*) нефть *f*; (*for heating*) печно́е то́пливо ▷ *vt* сма́зывать (*perf* сма́зать); **oily** *adj* (*rag*) прома́сленный; (*skin*) жи́рный
ointment ['ɔɪntmənt] *n* мазь *f*
O.K. ['əu'keɪ] *excl* (*inf*) хорошо́, ла́дно
old [əuld] *adj* ста́рый; **how old are you?** ско́лько Вам лет?; **he's 10 years old** ему́ 10 лет; **old man** стари́к; **old woman** стару́ха; **older brother** ста́рший брат; **old age** *n* ста́рость *f*; **old-fashioned** *adj* старомо́дный
olive ['ɔlɪv] *n* (*fruit*) масли́на, оли́вка ▷ *adj* оли́вковый; **olive oil** *n* оли́вковое ма́сло
Olympic Games® *npl* (*also* **the Olympics**) Олимпи́йские и́гры *fpl*
omelet(te) ['ɔmlɪt] *n* омле́т
omen ['əumən] *n* предзнаменова́ние
ominous ['ɔmɪnəs] *adj* злове́щий
omit [əu'mɪt] *vt* пропуска́ть (*perf* пропусти́ть)

 **KEYWORD**

on [ɔn] *prep* **1** (*position*) на *+prp*; (*motion*) на *+acc*; **the book is on the table** кни́га на столе́; **to put the book on the table** класть (*perf* положи́ть) кни́гу на стол; **on the left** сле́ва; **the house is on the main road** дом стои́т у шоссе́
2 (*indicating means, method, condition etc*): **on foot** пешко́м; **on**

the plane/train (*go*) на самолёте/поезде; (*be*) в самолёте/поезде; **on the radio/television** по радио/телевизору; **she's on the telephone** она разговаривает по телефону; **to be on medication** принимать (*impf*) лекарства; **to be on holiday/business** быть (*impf*) в отпуске/командировке
3 (*referring to time*): **on Friday** в пятницу; **on Fridays** по пятницам; **on June 20th** 20-ого июня; **a week on Friday** через неделю, считая с пятницы; **on arrival** по приезде; **on seeing this** увидев это
4 (*about, concerning*) о *+prp*; **information on train services** информация о расписании поездов; **a book on physics** книга по физике
▷ *adv* **1** (*referring to dress*) в *+prp*; **to have one's coat on** быть (*impf*) в пальто; **what's she got on?** во что она была одета?; **she put her boots/hat on** она надела сапоги/шляпу
2 (*further, continuously*) дальше, далее; **to walk on** идти (*impf*) дальше
▷ *adj* **1** (*functioning, in operation*) включённый; (: *tap*) открытый; **is the meeting still on?** (*not cancelled*) собрание состоится?; **there's a good film on at the cinema** в кинотеатре идёт хороший фильм
2: that's not on! (*inf*: *of behaviour*) так не пойдёт *or* не годится!

once [wʌns] *adv* (один) раз; (*formerly*) когда-то, однажды ▷ *conj* как только; **at once** сразу же; (*simultaneously*) вместе; **once a week** (один) раз в неделю; **once more** ещё раз; **once and for all** раз и навсегда

oncoming ['ɔnkʌmɪŋ] *adj* встречный

 **KEYWORD**

one [wʌn] *n* один (*f* одна, *nt* одно, *pl* одни); **one hundred and fifty** сто пятьдесят; **one day there was a knock at the door** однажды раздался стук в дверь; **one by one** один за другим
▷ *adj* **1** (*sole*) единственный; **the one book which ...** единственная книга, которая ...
2 (*same*) один; **they all belong to the one family** они все из одной семьи
▷ *pron* **1: I'm the one who told him** это я сказал ему; **this one** этот (*f* эта, *nt* это); **that one** тот (*f* та, *nt* то); **I've already got one** у меня уже есть
2: one another друг друга; **do you ever see one another?** Вы когда-нибудь видитесь?; **they didn't dare look at one another** они не смели взглянуть друг на друга
3 (*impersonal*): **one never knows** никогда не знаешь; **one has to do it** надо сделать это; **to cut one's finger** порезать (*perf*) (себе) палец

one: **one-off** *n* (*Brit*: *inf*) единичный случай; **oneself** *pron* (*reflexive*) себя; (*emphatic*) сам; (*after prep*: *+acc, +gen*) себя; (: *+dat*) себе; (: *+instr*) собой; (: *+prp*) себе; **to hurt oneself** ушибаться (*perf* ушибиться); **to keep sth for oneself** держать (*impf*) что-н при себе; **to talk to oneself** разговаривать (*impf*) с (самим) собой; **one-sided** *adj* односторонний; (*contest*) неравный; **one-way** *adj*: **one-way street** у́лица с односторо́нним движе́нием

ongoing ['ɔngəuɪŋ] *adj* продолжа́ющийся

onion ['ʌnjən] *n* лук

on-line [ɔn'laɪn] *adj* онла́йновый; **to go on-line** включа́ться (*perf* включи́ться) в сеть

only ['əunlɪ] *adv* то́лько ▷ *adj* еди́нственный ▷ *conj* то́лько; **not only ... but also ...** не то́лько ..., но и ...

onset ['ɔnsɛt] *n* наступле́ние

onward(s) ['ɔnwəd(z)] *adv* вперёд, да́льше; **from that time onward(s)** с тех пор

opaque [əu'peɪk] *adj* ма́товый

open ['əupn] *adj* откры́тый ▷ *vt* открыва́ть (*perf* откры́ть) ▷ *vi* открыва́ться (*perf* откры́ться); (*book, debate etc*) начина́ться (*perf* нача́ться); **in the open (air)** на откры́том во́здухе; **open up** *vt* открыва́ть (*perf* откры́ть) ▷ *vi* открыва́ться (*perf* откры́ться); **opening** *adj* (*speech, remarks etc*) вступи́тельный ▷ *n* (*gap, hole*) отве́рстие; (*job*) вака́нсия; **openly** *adv* откры́то; **open-minded** *adj* (*person*) откры́тый; **open-plan** *adj*: **open-plan office** о́фис с откры́той планиро́вкой

opera ['ɔpərə] *n* о́пера

operate ['ɔpəreɪt] *vt* управля́ть (*impf*) *+instr* ▷ *vi* де́йствовать (*impf*); (*Med*): **to operate (on sb)** опери́ровать (*perf* прооперúровать) (кого́-н)

operation [ɔpə'reɪʃən] *n* опера́ция; (*of machine*: *functioning*) рабо́та; (: *controlling*) управле́ние; **to be in operation** де́йствовать (*impf*); **he had an operation** (*Med*) ему́ сде́лали опера́цию; **operational** [ɔpə'reɪʃənl] *adj*: **the machine was operational** маши́на функциони́ровала

operative ['ɔpərətɪv] *adj* (*law etc*) де́йствующий

operator ['ɔpəreɪtə^r] *n* (*Tel*) телефони́ст(ка); (*Tech*) опера́тор

opinion [ə'pɪnjən] *n* мне́ние; **in my opinion** по моему́ мне́нию, по-мо́ему; **opinion poll** *n* опро́с обще́ственного мне́ния

opponent [ə'pəunənt] *n* оппоне́нт, проти́вник(-ница); (*Sport*) проти́вник

opportunity [ɔpə'tju:nɪtɪ] *n* возмо́жность *f*; **to take the opportunity of doing** по́льзоваться (*perf* воспо́льзоваться) слу́чаем, что́бы *+infin*

oppose [ə'pəuz] *vt* проти́виться (*perf* воспроти́виться) *+dat*; **to be opposed to sth** проти́виться (*impf*) чему́-н; **as opposed to** в противополо́жность *+dat*

opposite ['ɔpəzɪt] *adj* противополо́жный ▷ *adv* напро́тив ▷ *prep* напро́тив *+gen* ▷ *n*: **the opposite** (*say, think, do etc*) противополо́жное *nt adj*

opposition [ɔpə'zɪʃən] *n* оппози́ция; **the Opposition** (*Pol*) оппозицио́нная па́ртия

oppress [ə'prɛs] *vt* угнета́ть (*impf*)

opt [ɔpt] *vi*: **to opt for** избира́ть (*perf* избра́ть); **to opt to do** реша́ть (*perf* реши́ть) *+infin*; **opt out** *vi*: **to opt out of** выходи́ть (*perf* вы́йти) из *+gen*

optician [ɔp'tɪʃən] *n* окули́ст

optimism ['ɔptɪmɪzəm] *n* оптими́зм

optimistic [ɔptɪ'mɪstɪk] *adj*

оптимисти́чный
optimum [ˈɔptɪməm] *adj* оптима́льный
option [ˈɔpʃən] *n* (*choice*) возмо́жность *f*, вариа́нт; **optional** *adj* необяза́тельный
or [ɔːʳ] *conj* и́ли; (*otherwise*): **or (else)** а то, ина́че; (*with negative*): **he hasn't seen or heard anything** он ничего́ не ви́дел и не слы́шал
oral [ˈɔːrəl] *adj* у́стный; (*medicine*) ора́льный ▷ *n* у́стный экза́мен
orange [ˈɔrɪndʒ] *n* апельси́н ▷ *adj* (*colour*) ора́нжевый
orbit [ˈɔːbɪt] *n* орби́та ▷ *vt* обраща́ться (*perf* обрати́ться) вокру́г *+gen*
orchard [ˈɔːtʃəd] *n* сад (*фрукто́вый*)
orchestra [ˈɔːkɪstrə] *n* орке́стр
orchid [ˈɔːkɪd] *n* орхиде́я
ordeal [ɔːˈdiːl] *n* испыта́ние
order [ˈɔːdəʳ] *n* зака́з; (*command*) прика́з; (*sequence, discipline*) поря́док ▷ *vt* зака́зывать (*perf* заказа́ть); (*command*) прика́зывать (*perf* приказа́ть) *+dat*; (*also* **put in order**) располага́ть (*perf* расположи́ть) по поря́дку; **in order** в поря́дке; **in order to do** для того́ что́бы *+infin*; **out of order** (*not in sequence*) не по поря́дку; (*not working*) неиспра́вный; **to order sb to do** прика́зывать (*perf* приказа́ть) кому́-н *+infin*; **order form** *n* бланк зака́за; **orderly** *n* (*Med*) санита́р ▷ *adj* (*room*) опря́тный; (*system*) упоря́доченный
ordinary [ˈɔːdnrɪ] *adj* обы́чный, обыкнове́нный; (*mediocre*) зауря́дный; **out of the ordinary** необыкнове́нный
ore [ɔːʳ] *n* руда́
organ [ˈɔːgən] *n* (*Anat*) о́рган; (*Mus*) орга́н; **organic** [ɔːˈgænɪk] *adj* (*fertilizer*) органи́ческий; (*food*) экологи́чески чи́стый; **organism** *n* органи́зм
organization [ɔːgənaɪˈzeɪʃən] *n* организа́ция
organize [ˈɔːgənaɪz] *vt* организо́вывать (*impf/perf*), устра́ивать (*perf* устро́ить)
orgasm [ˈɔːgæzəm] *n* орга́зм
oriental [ɔːrɪˈɛntl] *adj* восто́чный
origin [ˈɔrɪdʒɪn] *n* происхожде́ние; **original** [əˈrɪdʒɪnl] *adj* первонача́льный; (*new*) оригина́льный; (*genuine*) по́длинный; (*imaginative*) самобы́тный ▷ *n* по́длинник, оригина́л; **originally** [əˈrɪdʒɪnəlɪ] *adv* первонача́льно; **originate** [əˈrɪdʒɪneɪt] *vi*: **to originate from** происходи́ть (*perf* произойти́) от/из *+gen*; **to originate in** зарожда́ться (*perf* зароди́ться) в *+prp*
ornament [ˈɔːnəmənt] *n* (*decorative object*) украше́ние; **ornamental** [ɔːnəˈmɛntl] *adj* декорати́вный
ornate [ɔːˈneɪt] *adj* декорати́вный
orphan [ˈɔːfn] *n* сирота́ *m/f*
orthodox [ˈɔːθədɔks] *adj* ортодокса́льный; **the Russian Orthodox Church** Ру́сская правосла́вная це́рковь
orthopaedic [ɔːθəˈpiːdɪk] (*US* **orthopedic**) *adj* ортопеди́ческий
ostrich [ˈɔstrɪtʃ] *n* стра́ус
other [ˈʌðəʳ] *adj* друго́й ▷ *pron*: **the other (one)** друго́й(-а́я) *m(f) adj*, друго́е *nt adj* ▷ *adv*: **other than** кро́ме *+gen*; **others** *npl* (*other people*) други́е *pl adj*; **the others** остальны́е *pl adj*; **the other day** на днях; **otherwise** *adv* (*differently*) ина́че, по-друго́му;

(*apart from that*) в остальнóм
▷ *conj* а то, инáче

otter ['ɔtəʳ] *n* вы́дра

ought [ɔ:t] (*pt* **ought**) *aux vb*: **I ought to do it** мне слéдует э́то сдéлать; **this ought to have been corrected** э́то слéдовало испрáвить; **he ought to win** он дóлжен вы́играть

ounce [auns] *n* ýнция

OUNCE

Ounce — мéра вéса рáвная 28,349 г.

our ['auəʳ] *adj* наш; *see also* **my**; **ours** *pron* наш; (*referring to subject of sentence*) свой; *see also* **mine**[1]; **ourselves** *pl pron* (*reflexive, complement*) себя́; (*after prep*: *+acc, +gen*) себя́; (: *+dat, +prp*) себé; (: *+instr*) собóй; (*emphatic*) сáми; (*alone*): **(all) by ourselves** сáми; **let's keep it between ourselves** давáйте остáвим э́то мéжду нáми; *see also* **myself**

oust [aust] *vt* изгоня́ть (*perf* изгнáть)

 **KEYWORD**

out [aut] *adv* **1** (*not in*): **they're out in the garden** они́ в садý; **out in the rain/snow** под дождём/ снéгом; **out here** здесь; **out there** там; **to go out** выходи́ть (*perf* вы́йти); **out loud** грóмко
2 (*not at home, absent*): **he is out at the moment** егó сейчáс нет (дóма); **let's have a night out on Friday** давáйте пойдём кудá-нибудь в пя́тницу вéчером!
3 (*indicating distance*) в *+prp*; **the boat was ten km out (from the shore)** корáбль находи́лся в десяти́ км от бéрега
4 (*Sport*): **the ball is out** мяч за предéлами пóля
▷ *adj* **1**: **to be out** (*unconscious*) быть (*impf*) без сознáния; (*out of game*) выбывáть (*perf* вы́быть); (*flowers*) распускáться (*perf* распусти́ться); (*news, secret*) станови́ться (*perf* стать) извéстным(-ой); (*fire, light, gas*) тýхнуть (*perf* потýхнуть), гáснуть (*perf* погáснуть); **to go out of fashion** выходи́ть (*perf* вы́йти) из мóды
2 (*finished*): **before the week was out** до окончáния недéли
3: **to be out to do** (*intend*) намеревáться (*impf*) *+infin*; **to be out in one's calculations** (*wrong*) ошибáться (*perf* ошиби́ться) в расчётах
▷ *prep* **1** (*outside, beyond*) из *+gen*; **to go out of the house** выходи́ть (*perf* вы́йти) из дóма; **to be out of danger** (*safe*) быть (*impf*) вне опáсности
2 (*cause, motive*): **out of curiosity** из любопы́тства; **out of fear/joy/ boredom** от стрáха/рáдости/скýки; **out of grief** с гóря; **out of necessity** по необходи́мости
3 (*from, from among*) из *+gen*
4 (*without*): **we are out of sugar/ petrol** у нас кóнчился сáхар/ бензи́н

outbreak ['autbreɪk] *n* (*of disease, violence*) вспы́шка; (*of war*) начáло

outburst ['autbə:st] *n* взрыв

outcast ['autkɑ:st] *n* изгóй

outcome ['autkʌm] *n* исхóд

outcry ['autkraɪ] *n* негодовáние, протéст

outdated [aut'deɪtɪd] *adj* (*customs, ideas*) отжи́вший; (*technology*) устаре́лый
outdoor [aut'dɔːʳ] *adj* на откры́том во́здухе; (*pool*) откры́тый; **outdoors** *adv* на у́лице, на откры́том во́здухе
outer ['autəʳ] *adj* нару́жный; **outer space** *n* косми́ческое простра́нство
outfit ['autfɪt] *n* (*clothes*) костю́м
outgoing ['autgəuɪŋ] *adj* (*extrovert*) общи́тельный; (*president, mayor etc*) уходя́щий
outing ['autɪŋ] *n* похо́д
outlaw ['autlɔː] *vt* объявля́ть (*perf* объяви́ть) вне зако́на
outlay ['autleɪ] *n* затра́ты *fpl*
outlet ['autlɛt] *n* (*hole*) выходно́е отве́рстие; (*pipe*) сток; (*Comm*: *also* **retail outlet**) торго́вая то́чка; (*for emotions*) вы́ход
outline ['autlaɪn] *n* (*shape*) ко́нтур, очерта́ния *ntpl*; (*sketch, explanation*) набро́сок ▷ *vt* (*fig*) опи́сывать (*perf* описа́ть)
outlook ['autluk] *n* (*attitude*) взгля́ды *mpl*, воззре́ния *ntpl*; (*prospects*) перспекти́вы *fpl*
outnumber [aut'nʌmbəʳ] *vt* чи́сленно превосходи́ть (*perf* превзойти́)
out-of-date [autəv'deɪt] *adj* (*clothes*) немо́дный; (*equipment*) устаре́лый
out-of-the-way ['autəvðə'weɪ] *adj* (*place*) глуби́нный
outpatient ['autpeɪʃənt] *n* амбулато́рный(-ая) пацие́нт(ка)
output ['autput] *n* вы́работка, проду́кция; (*Comput*) выходны́е да́нные *pl*
outrage ['autreɪdʒ] *n* (*emotion*) возмуще́ние ▷ *vt* возмуща́ть (*perf* возмути́ть); **outrageous** [aut'reɪdʒəs] *adj* возмути́тельный
outright [*adv* aut'raɪt, *adj* 'autraɪt] *adv* (*win, own*) абсолю́тно; (*refuse, deny*) наотре́з; (*ask*) пря́мо ▷ *adj* (*winner, victory*) абсолю́тный; (*refusal, hostility*) откры́тый; **to be killed outright** погиба́ть (*perf* поги́бнуть) сра́зу
outset ['autsɛt] *n* нача́ло
outside [aut'saɪd] *n* нару́жная сторона́ ▷ *adj* нару́жный, вне́шний ▷ *adv* (*be*) снару́жи; (*go*) нару́жу ▷ *prep* вне *+gen*, за преде́лами *+gen*; (*building*) у *+gen*; (*city*) под *+instr*; **outsider** *n* (*stranger*) посторо́нний(-яя) *m(f) adj*
outskirts ['autskəːts] *npl* окра́ины *fpl*
outspoken [aut'spəukən] *adj* открове́нный
outstanding [aut'stændɪŋ] *adj* (*exceptional*) выдаю́щийся; (*unfinished*) незако́нченный; (*unpaid*) неопла́ченный
outward ['autwəd] *adj* вне́шний; **the outward journey** пое́здка туда́
outweigh [aut'weɪ] *vt* переве́шивать (*perf* переве́сить)
oval ['əuvl] *adj* ова́льный
ovary ['əuvərɪ] *n* я́ичник
oven ['ʌvn] *n* (*domestic*) духо́вка

 **KEYWORD**

over ['əuvəʳ] *adv* **1** (*across*): **to cross over** переходи́ть (*perf* перейти́); **over here** здесь; **over there** там; **to ask sb over** (*to one's house*) приглаша́ть (*perf* пригласи́ть) кого́-н в го́сти *or* к себе́
2 (*indicating movement from upright*): **to knock/turn sth over** сбива́ть (*perf* сбить)/

перевора́чивать (*perf* переверну́ть) что-н; **to fall over** па́дать (*perf* упа́сть); **to bend over** нагиба́ться (*perf* нагну́ться) **3** (*finished*): **the game is over** игра́ око́нчена; **his life is over** его́ зако́нчилась жизнь **4** (*excessively*) сли́шком, чересчу́р **5** (*remaining*: *money, food etc*): **there are 3 over** оста́лось 3 **6: all over** (*everywhere*) везде́, повсю́ду; **over and over (again)** сно́ва и сно́ва ▷ *prep* **1** (*on top of*) на *+prp*; (*above, in control of*) над *+instr* **2** (*on(to) the other side of*) че́рез *+acc*; **the pub over the road** паб че́рез доро́гу **3** (*more than*) свы́ше *+gen*, бо́льше *+gen*; **she is over 40** ей бо́льше 40; **over and above** намно́го бо́льше, чем **4** (*in the course of*) в тече́ние *+gen*, за *+acc*; **over the winter** за́ зиму, в тече́ние зимы́; **let's discuss it over dinner** дава́йте обсу́дим э́то за обе́дом; **the work is spread over two weeks** рабо́та рассчи́тана на две неде́ли

overall [*adj, n* 'əuvərɔ:l, *adv* əuvə'rɔ:l] *adj* о́бщий ▷ *adv* (*in general*) в це́лом *or* о́бщем; (*altogether*) целико́м ▷ *n* (*Brit*) хала́т; **overalls** *npl* (*clothing*) комбинезо́н *msg*; **overall majority** подавля́ющее большинство́

overboard ['əuvəbɔ:d] *adv*: **to fall overboard** па́дать (*perf* упа́сть) за́ борт

overcast ['əuvəkɑ:st] *adj* хму́рый, па́смурный

overcoat ['əuvəkəut] *n* пальто́ *nt ind*

overcome [əuvə'kʌm] (*irreg like* **come**) *vt* (*problems*) преодолева́ть (*perf* преодоле́ть)

overcrowded [əuvə'kraudɪd] *adj* перепо́лненный

overdo [əuvə'du:] (*irreg like* **do**) *vt* (*work, exercise*) перестара́ться (*perf*) в *+prp*; (*interest, concern*) утри́ровать (*impf*)

overdose ['əuvədəus] *n* передозиро́вка

overdraft ['əuvədrɑ:ft] *n* перерасхо́д, овердра́фт

overdrawn [əuvə'drɔ:n] *adj*: **he is overdrawn** он превы́сил креди́т своего́ теку́щего счёта

overdue [əuvə'dju:] *adj* (*change, reform etc*) запозда́лый

overgrown [əuvə'grəun] *adj* (*garden*) заро́сший

overhead [*adv* əuvə'hɛd, *adj, n* 'əuvəhɛd] *adv* наверху́, над голово́й; (*in the sky*) в не́бе ▷ *adj* (*lighting*) ве́рхний; (*cable, railway*) надзе́мный ▷ *n* (*US*) = **overheads**; **overheads** *npl* (*expenses*) накладны́е расхо́ды *mpl*

overhear [əuvə'hɪə[r]] (*irreg like* **hear**) *vt* (случа́йно) подслу́шать (*perf*)

overlap [əuvə'læp] *vi* находи́ть (*impf*) оди́н на друго́й; (*fig*) части́чно совпада́ть (*perf* совпа́сть)

overleaf [əuvə'li:f] *adv* на оборо́те

overload [əuvə'ləud] *vt* (*also Elec, fig*) перегружа́ть (*perf* перегрузи́ть)

overlook [əuvə'luk] *vt* (*place*) выходи́ть (*impf*) на *+acc*; (*problem*) упуска́ть (*perf* упусти́ть) из ви́ду; (*behaviour*) закрыва́ть (*perf* закры́ть) глаза́ на *+acc*

overnight [əuvə'naɪt] *adv* (*during the night*) зá ночь; (*fig*) в одночáсье, срáзу; **to stay overnight** ночевáть (*perf* переночевáть)
overpowering [əuvə'pauərɪŋ] *adj* (*heat, stench*) невыносúмый
overrun [əuvə'rʌn] *irreg vi* (*meeting*) затя́гиваться (*perf* затяну́ться)
overseas [əuvə'si:z] *adv* (*live, work*) за рубежóм *or* грани́цей; (*go*) за рубéж *or* грани́цу ▷ *adj* (*market, trade*) внéшний; (*student, visitor*) инострáнный
oversee [əuvə'si:] (*irreg like* **see**) *vt* следи́ть (*impf*) за *+instr*
overshadow [əuvə'ʃædəu] *vt* (*place, building etc*) возвышáться (*impf*) над *+instr*; (*fig*) затмевáть (*perf* затми́ть)
oversight ['əuvəsaɪt] *n* недосмóтр
overt [əu'və:t] *adj* откры́тый
overtake [əuvə'teɪk] (*irreg like* **take**) *vt* (*Aut*) обгоня́ть (*perf* обогнáть)
overthrow [əuvə'θrəu] (*irreg like* **throw**) *vt* свергáть (*perf* свéргнуть)
overtime ['əuvətaɪm] *n* сверхурóчное врéмя *nt*
overturn [əuvə'tə:n] *vt* (*car, chair*) переворáчивать (*perf* переверну́ть); (*decision, plan*) отвергáть (*perf* отвéргнуть); (*government, system*) свергáть (*perf* свéргнуть)
overweight [əuvə'weɪt] *adj* ту́чный
overwhelm [əuvə'wɛlm] *vt* (*subj: feelings, emotions*) переполня́ть (*perf* перепóлнить); **overwhelming** *adj* (*victory, defeat*) пóлный; (*majority*) подавля́ющий; (*feeling, desire*) всепобеждáющий
owe [əu] *vt*: **she owes me £500** онá должнá мне £500; **he owes his life to that man** он обя́зан своéй жи́знью э́тому человéку
owing to ['əuɪŋ-] *prep* вслéдствие *+gen*
owl [aul] *n* совá
own [əun] *vt* владéть (*impf*) *+instr* ▷ *adj* сóбственный; **he lives on his own** он живёт оди́н; **to get one's own back** оты́грываться (*perf* отыгрáться); **own up** *vi*: **to own up to sth** признавáться (*perf* признáться) в чём-н; **owner** *n* владéлец(-лица); **ownership** *n*: **ownership (of)** владéние (*+instr*)
ox [ɔks] (*pl* **oxen**) *n* бык
oxygen ['ɔksɪdʒən] *n* кислорóд
oyster ['ɔɪstə[r]] *n* у́стрица
oz. *abbr* = **ounce**
ozone ['əuzəun] *n* озóн

O

p

p *abbr* (*Brit*) = **penny, pence**

PA *n abbr* (= *personal assistant*) референ́т, ли́чный секрета́рь *m*

pa [pɑː] *n* (*inf*) па́па *m*

p.a. *abbr* = **per annum**

pace [peɪs] *n* (*step*) шаг; (*speed*) темп ▷ *vi*: **to pace up and down** ходи́ть (*impf*) взад вперёд; **to keep pace with** идти́ (*impf*) в но́гу с *+instr*; **pacemaker** *n* (*Med*) ритмиза́тор се́рдца

Pacific [pəˈsɪfɪk] *n*: **the Pacific (Ocean)** Ти́хий океа́н

pack [pæk] *n* (*packet*) па́чка; (*of wolves*) ста́я; (*also* **backpack**) рюкза́к; (*of cards*) коло́да ▷ *vt* (*fill*) пакова́ть (*perf* упакова́ть); (*cram*): **to pack into** набива́ть (*perf* наби́ть) в *+acc* ▷ *vi*: **to pack (one's bags)** укла́дываться (*perf* уложи́ться)

package [ˈpækɪdʒ] *n* паке́т; (*also* **package deal**: *Comm*) паке́т предложе́ний; **package holiday** *n* (*Brit*) организо́ванный о́тдых по путёвке

packet [ˈpækɪt] *n* (*of cigarettes etc*) па́чка; (*of crisps*) паке́т

packing [ˈpækɪŋ] *n* прокла́дочный материа́л; (*act*) упако́вка

pact [pækt] *n* пакт

pad [pæd] *n* (*of paper*) блокно́т; (*soft material*) прокла́дка ▷ *vt* (*cushion, soft toy etc*) набива́ть (*perf* наби́ть)

paddle [ˈpædl] *n* (*oar*) байда́рочное весло́; (*US*: *bat*) раке́тка ▷ *vt* управля́ть (*impf*) *+instr* ▷ *vi* (*in sea*) шлёпать (*impf*)

paddock [ˈpædək] *n* (*field*) вы́гон

padlock [ˈpædlɔk] *n* (вися́чий) замо́к

paedophile [ˈpiːdəufaɪl] (*US* **pedophile**) *n* педофи́л

page [peɪdʒ] *n* страни́ца; (*also* **pageboy**) паж ▷ *vt* (*in hotel etc*) вызыва́ть (*perf* вы́звать) (по селе́ктору)

paid [peɪd] *pt, pp of* **pay**

pain [peɪn] *n* боль *f*; **to be in pain** страда́ть (*impf*) от бо́ли; **to take pains to do** стара́ться (*perf* постара́ться) изо всех сил *+infin*; **painful** *adj* мучи́тельный; **my back is painful** у меня́ боли́т спина́; **painkiller** *n* болеутоля́ющее *nt adj* (сре́дство); **painstaking** *adj* кропотли́вый

paint [peɪnt] *n* кра́ска ▷ *vt* кра́сить (*perf* покра́сить); (*picture, portrait*) рисова́ть (*perf* нарисова́ть), писа́ть (*perf* написа́ть); **to paint the door blue** кра́сить (*perf* покра́сить) дверь в голубо́й цвет; **painter** *n* (*artist*) худо́жник(-ица); (*decorator*) маля́р; **painting** *n* карти́на; (*activity*: *of artist*) жи́вопись *f*; (: *of decorator*) маля́рное де́ло

pair [pɛəʳ] *n* па́ра

pajamas [pəˈdʒɑːməz] *npl* (*US*) = **pyjamas**

pal [pæl] *n* (*inf*) дружо́к

palace [ˈpæləs] *n* дворе́ц

pale [peɪl] *adj* бле́дный

Palestine [ˈpælɪstaɪn] *n* Палести́на

palm [pɑːm] *n* (*also* **palm tree**) па́льма; (*of hand*) ладо́нь *f* ▷ *vt*: **to palm sth off on sb** (*inf*) подсо́вывать (*perf* подсу́нуть) что-н кому́-н

pamphlet [ˈpæmflət] *n* брошю́ра; (*political, literary etc*) памфле́т

pan [pæn] *n* (*also* **saucepan**) кастрю́ля; (*also* **frying pan**) сковорода́

pancake [ˈpænkeɪk] *n* (*thin*) блин; (*thick*) ола́дья

panda [ˈpændə] *n* па́нда, бамбу́ковый медве́дь *m*

pane [peɪn] *n*: **pane (of glass)** (*in window*) око́нное стекло́

panel [ˈpænl] *n* (*of wood, glass etc*) пане́ль *f*; (*of experts*) коми́ссия; **panel of judges** жюри́ *nt ind*

panic [ˈpænɪk] *n* па́ника ▷ *vi* паникова́ть (*impf*)

panorama [pænəˈrɑːmə] *n* панора́ма

pansy [ˈpænzɪ] *n* аню́тины гла́зки *pl*

panther [ˈpænθəʳ] *n* панте́ра

pantomime [ˈpæntəmaɪm] *n* (*Brit*) *рожде́ственское театрализо́ванное представле́ние*

PANTOMIME

Pantomime — рожде́ственское представле́ние. Коме́дии с бога́тым музыка́льным оформле́нием, напи́санные по моти́вам изве́стных ска́зок, таки́х как "Зо́лушка", "Кот в сапога́х" и др. Они́ предназна́чены гла́вным о́бразом для дете́й. Теа́тры ста́вят их в Рождество́.

pants [pænts] *npl* (*Brit*: *underwear*) трусы́ *pl*; (*US*: *trousers*) брю́ки *pl*

paper [ˈpeɪpəʳ] *n* бума́га; (*also* **newspaper**) газе́та; (*exam*) пи́сьменный экза́мен; (*essay*: *at conference*) докла́д; (: *in journal*) статья́; (*also* **wallpaper**) обо́и *pl* ▷ *adj* бума́жный ▷ *vt* окле́ивать (*perf* окле́ить) обо́ями; **papers** *npl* (*also* **identity papers**) докуме́нты *mpl*; **paperback** *n* кни́га в мя́гкой обло́жке; **paperclip** *n* (канцеля́рская) скре́пка; **paperwork** *n* бума́жная волоки́та

paprika [ˈpæprɪkə] *n* кра́сный мо́лотый пе́рец

par [pɑːʳ] *n*: **to be on a par with** быть (*impf*) на ра́вных с +*instr*

parachute [ˈpærəʃuːt] *n* парашю́т

parade [pəˈreɪd] *n* ше́ствие; (*Mil*) пара́д ▷ *vi* (*Mil*) идти́ (*impf*) стро́ем

paradise [ˈpærədaɪs] *n* (*also fig*) рай

paradox [ˈpærədɔks] *n* парадо́кс

paraffin [ˈpærəfɪn] *n* (*Brit*: *also* **paraffin oil**) кероси́н

paragraph [ˈpærəgrɑːf] *n* абза́ц

parallel [ˈpærəlɛl] *adj*

P

паралле́льный; (*fig*: *similar*) аналоги́чный ▷ *n* паралле́ль *f*
paralysis [pəˈrælɪsɪs] *n* (*Med*) парали́ч
paranoid [ˈpærənɔɪd] *adj* (*person*) парано́идный
parasite [ˈpærəsaɪt] *n* парази́т
parcel [ˈpɑːsl] *n* (*package*) свёрток; (*sent by post*) посы́лка
pardon [ˈpɑːdn] *n* (*Law*) поми́лование ▷ *vt* (*Law*) ми́ловать (*perf* поми́ловать); **pardon me!, I beg your pardon!** прошу́ проще́ния!; **(I beg your) pardon?**, *(US)* **pardon me?** (*what did you say?*) прости́те, не расслы́шал
parent [ˈpɛərənt] *n* роди́тель(ница) *m(f)*; **parents** *npl* (*mother and father*) роди́тели *mpl*; **parental** [pəˈrɛntl] *adj* роди́тельский
Paris [ˈpærɪs] *n* Пари́ж
parish [ˈpærɪʃ] *n* (*Rel*) прихо́д
park [pɑːk] *n* парк ▷ *vt* ста́вить (*perf* поста́вить), паркова́ть (*perf* припаркова́ть) ▷ *vi* паркова́ться (*perf* припаркова́ться)
parking [ˈpɑːkɪŋ] *n* (*of vehicle*) парко́вка; (*space to park*) стоя́нка; **"no parking"** "стоя́нка запрещена́"; **parking lot** *n* (*US*) (авто)стоя́нка
parliament [ˈpɑːləmənt] *n* парла́мент; **parliamentary** [pɑːləˈmɛntərɪ] *adj* парла́ментский
parole [pəˈrəul] *n*: **he was released on parole** (*Law*) он был освобождён под че́стное сло́во
parrot [ˈpærət] *n* попуга́й
parsley [ˈpɑːslɪ] *n* петру́шка
parsnip [ˈpɑːsnɪp] *n* пастерна́к (посевно́й)
part [pɑːt] *n* (*section, division*) часть *f*; (*component*) дета́ль *f*; (*role*) роль *f*; (*episode*) се́рия; (*US*: *in hair*) пробо́р ▷ *adv* = **partly** ▷ *vt* разделя́ть (*perf* раздели́ть); (*hair*) расчёсывать (*perf* расчеса́ть) на пробо́р ▷ *vi* (*people*) расстава́ться (*perf* расста́ться); (*crowd*) расступа́ться (*perf* расступи́ться); **to take part in** принима́ть (*perf* приня́ть) уча́стие в +*prp*; **to take sb's part** (*support*) станови́ться (*perf* стать) на чью-н сто́рону; **for my part** с мое́й стороны́; **for the most part** бо́льшей ча́стью; **part with** *vt fus* расстава́ться (*perf* расста́ться) с +*instr*
partial [ˈpɑːʃl] *adj* (*incomplete*) части́чный; **I am partial to chocolate** (*like*) у меня́ пристра́стие к шокола́ду
participant [pɑːˈtɪsɪpənt] *n* уча́стник(-ица)
participate [pɑːˈtɪsɪpeɪt] *vi*: **to participate in** уча́ствовать (*impf*) в +*prp*
particle [ˈpɑːtɪkl] *n* части́ца
particular [pəˈtɪkjuləʳ] *adj* (*distinct, special*) осо́бый; (*fussy*) привере́дливый; **particulars** *npl* (*personal details*) да́нные *pl adj*; **in particular** в ча́стности; **particularly** *adv* осо́бенно
parting [ˈpɑːtɪŋ] *n* разделе́ние; (*farewell*) проща́ние; (*Brit*: *in hair*) пробо́р ▷ *adj* проща́льный
partition [pɑːˈtɪʃən] *n* (*wall, screen*) перегоро́дка
partly [ˈpɑːtlɪ] *adv* части́чно
partner [ˈpɑːtnəʳ] *n* партнёр(ша); (*spouse*) супру́г(а); (*Comm, Sport, Cards*) партнёр; **partnership** *n* (*Comm*: *company*) това́рищество; (: *with person*) партнёрство; (*Pol*) сою́з

part-time ['pɑ:t'taɪm] *adj* (*work*) почасово́й; (*staff*) на почасово́й ста́вке ▷ *adv*: **to work part-time** быть (*impf*) на почасово́й ста́вке; **to study part-time** обуча́ться (*impf*) по непо́лной програ́мме

party ['pɑ:tɪ] *n* па́ртия; (*celebration*: *formal*) ве́чер; (: *informal*) вечери́нка; (*group*: *rescue*) отря́д; (: *of tourists etc*) гру́ппа ▷ *cpd* (*Pol*) парти́йный; **birthday party** пра́зднование дня рожде́ния, день рожде́ния

pass [pɑ:s] *vt* (*time*) проводи́ть (*perf* провести́); (*hand over*) передава́ть (*perf* переда́ть); (*go past*: *on foot*) проходи́ть (*perf* пройти́); (: *by transport*) проезжа́ть (*perf* прое́хать); (*overtake*: *vehicle*) обгоня́ть (*perf* обогна́ть); (*exam*) сдава́ть (*perf* сдать); (*law, proposal*) принима́ть (*perf* приня́ть) ▷ *vi* (*go past*: *on foot*) проходи́ть (*perf* пройти́); (: *by transport*) проезжа́ть (*perf* прое́хать); (*in exam*) сдава́ть (*perf* сдать) экза́мен ▷ *n* (*permit*) про́пуск; (*Geo*) перева́л; (*Sport*) пас, переда́ча; (*Scol*: *also* **pass mark**): **to get a pass** получа́ть (*perf* получи́ть) зачёт; **pass by** *vi* (*on foot*) проходи́ть (*perf* пройти́); (*by transport*) проезжа́ть (*perf* прое́хать); **pass on** *vt* передава́ть (*perf* переда́ть)

passage ['pæsɪdʒ] *n* (*also Anat*) прохо́д; (*in book*) отры́вок; (*journey*) путеше́ствие

passenger ['pæsɪndʒə^r] *n* пассажи́р(ка)

passer-by [pɑ:sə'baɪ] (*pl* **passers-by**) *n* прохо́жий(-ая) *m(f) adj*

passion ['pæʃən] *n* страсть *f*; **passionate** *adj* стра́стный

passive ['pæsɪv] *adj* пасси́вный

passport ['pɑ:spɔ:t] *n* па́спорт

password ['pɑ:swə:d] *n* паро́ль *m*

past [pɑ:st] *prep* ми́мо +*gen*; (*beyond*) за +*instr*; (*later than*) по́сле +*gen* ▷ *adj* (*government etc*) пре́жний; (*week, month etc*) про́шлый ▷ *n* про́шлое *nt adj*; (*Ling*): **the past (tense)** проше́дшее вре́мя ▷ *adv*: **to run past** пробега́ть (*perf* пробежа́ть) ми́мо; **ten/quarter past eight** де́сять мину́т/че́тверть девя́того; **for the past few days** за после́дние не́сколько дней

pasta ['pæstə] *n* макаро́нные изде́лия *ntpl*

paste [peɪst] *n* (*wet mixture*) па́ста; (*glue*) кле́йстер; (*Culin*) паште́т ▷ *vt* (*paper etc*) наноси́ть (*perf* нанести́) клей на +*acc*

pastel ['pæstl] *adj* пасте́льный

pastime ['pɑ:staɪm] *n* времяпрепровожде́ние

pastry ['peɪstrɪ] *n* (*dough*) те́сто

pasture ['pɑ:stʃə^r] *n* па́стбище

pat [pæt] *vt* (*dog*) ласка́ть (*perf* приласка́ть) ▷ *n*: **to give sb/o.s. a pat on the back** (*fig*) хвали́ть (*perf* похвали́ть) кого́-н/себя́

patch [pætʃ] *n* (*of material*) запла́та; (*also* **eye patch**) повя́зка; (*area*) пятно́; (*repair*) запла́та ▷ *vt* (*clothes*) лата́ть (*perf* залата́ть); **to go through a bad patch** пережива́ть (*impf*) тру́дные времена́; **bald patch** лы́сина; **patchy** *adj* (*colour*) пятни́стый; (*information, knowledge etc*) отры́вочный

pâté ['pæteɪ] *n* (*Culin*) паште́т

patent ['peɪtnt] *n* пате́нт ▷ *vt* (*Comm*) патентова́ть (*perf* запатентова́ть)

P

paternal [pəˈtəːnl] *adj* (*love, duty*) отцо́вский
path [pɑːθ] *n* (*trail, track*) тропа́, тропи́нка; (*concrete, gravel etc*) доро́жка; (*trajectory*) ли́ния движе́ния
pathetic [pəˈθɛtɪk] *adj* жа́лостный; (*very bad*) жа́лкий
patience [ˈpeɪʃns] *n* (*quality*) терпе́ние
patient [ˈpeɪʃnt] *n* пацие́нт(ка) ▷ *adj* терпели́вый
patio [ˈpætɪəu] *n* па́тио *m ind*, вну́тренний дво́рик
patriotic [pætrɪˈɔtɪk] *adj* патриоти́чный; (*song etc*) патриоти́ческий
patrol [pəˈtrəul] *n* патру́ль *m* ▷ *vt* патрули́ровать (*impf*)
patron [ˈpeɪtrən] *n* (*client*) (постоя́нный) клие́нт; (*benefactor: of charity*) шеф, покрови́тель *m*; **patron of the arts** покрови́тель(ница) *m(f)* иску́сств
pattern [ˈpætən] *n* (*design*) узо́р; (*Sewing*) вы́кройка
pause [pɔːz] *n* переры́в; (*in speech*) па́уза ▷ *vi* де́лать (*perf* сде́лать) переры́в; (*in speech*) де́лать (*perf* сде́лать) па́узу
pave [peɪv] *vt* мости́ть (*perf* вы́мостить); **to pave the way for** (*fig*) прокла́дывать (*perf* проложи́ть) путь для *+gen*; **pavement** *n* (*Brit*) тротуа́р
pavilion [pəˈvɪlɪən] *n* (*Sport*) павильо́н
paw [pɔː] *n* (*of animal*) ла́па
pawn [pɔːn] *n* (*Chess, fig*) пе́шка ▷ *vt* закла́дывать (*perf* заложи́ть); **pawnbroker** *n* ростовщи́к(-и́ца)
pay [peɪ] (*pt, pp* **paid**) *n* зарпла́та ▷ *vt* (*sum of money, wage*) плати́ть (*perf* заплати́ть); (*debt, bill*) плати́ть (*perf* уплати́ть) ▷ *vi* (*be profitable*) окупа́ться (*perf* окупи́ться); **to pay attention (to)** обраща́ть (*perf* обрати́ть) внима́ние (на *+acc*); **to pay sb a visit** наноси́ть (*perf* нанести́) кому́-н визи́т; **pay back** *vt* возвраща́ть (*perf* возврати́ть), верну́ть (*perf*); (*person*) отпла́чивать (*perf* отплати́ть); **pay for** *vt fus* плати́ть (*perf* заплати́ть) за *+acc*; (*fig*) поплати́ться (*perf*) за *+acc*; **pay in** *vt* вноси́ть (*perf* внести́); **pay off** *vt* (*debt*) выпла́чивать (*perf* вы́платить); (*creditor*) рассчи́тываться (*perf* рассчита́ться) с *+instr*; (*person*) рассчи́тывать (*perf* рассчита́ть) ▷ *vi* окупа́ться (*perf* окупи́ться); **pay up** *vi* рассчи́тываться (*perf* рассчита́ться) (сполна́); **payable** *adj* (*cheque*): **payable to** подлежа́щий упла́те на и́мя *+gen*; **payment** *n* (*act*) платёж, упла́та; (*amount*) вы́плата
PC *n abbr* (= *personal computer*) ПК (= *персона́льный компью́тер*); (*Brit*) = **police constable**; **politically correct**
pc *abbr* = **per cent**
pea [piː] *n* (*Bot, Culin*) горо́х *m no pl*
peace [piːs] *n* (*not war*) мир; (*calm*) поко́й; **peaceful** *adj* (*calm*) ми́рный
peach [piːtʃ] *n* пе́рсик
peacock [ˈpiːkɔk] *n* павли́н
peak [piːk] *n* верши́на, пик; (*of cap*) козырёк
peanut [ˈpiːnʌt] *n* ара́хис
pear [pɛəʳ] *n* гру́ша
pearl [pəːl] *n* жемчу́жина; **pearls** *npl* же́мчуг
peasant [ˈpɛznt] *n* крестья́нин(-нка)

peat [pi:t] *n* торф
pebble ['pɛbl] *n* га́лька *no pl*
peck [pɛk] *vt* (*subj*: *bird*) клева́ть (*impf*); (: *once*) клю́нуть (*perf*) ▷ *n* (*kiss*) поцелу́й
peculiar [pɪ'kju:lɪə^r] *adj* (*strange*) своеобра́зный; (*unique*): **peculiar to** сво́йственный *+dat*
pedal ['pɛdl] *n* педа́ль *f* ▷ *vi* крути́ть (*impf*) педа́ли
pedestal ['pɛdəstl] *n* пьедеста́л
pedestrian [pɪ'dɛstrɪən] *n* пешехо́д
pedigree ['pɛdɪgri:] *n* родосло́вная *f adj* ▷ *cpd* поро́дистый
pedophile ['pi:dəufaɪl] *n* (*US*) = **paedophile**
pee [pi:] *vi* (*inf*) пи́сать (*perf* попи́сать)
peel [pi:l] *n* кожура́ ▷ *vt* (*vegetables, fruit*) чи́стить (*perf* почи́стить) ▷ *vi* (*paint*) лупи́ться (*perf* облупи́ться); (*wallpaper*) отстава́ть (*perf* отста́ть); (*skin*) шелуши́ться (*impf*)
peep [pi:p] *n* (*look*) взгляд укра́дкой ▷ *vi* взгля́дывать (*perf* взгляну́ть)
peer [pɪə^r] *n* (*Brit*: *noble*) пэр; (*equal*) ро́вня *m/f*; (*contemporary*) рове́сник(-ица) ▷ *vi*: **to peer at** всма́триваться (*perf* всмотре́ться) в *+acc*
peg [pɛg] *n* (*for coat etc*) крючо́к; (*Brit*: *also* **clothes peg**) прище́пка
pejorative [pɪ'dʒɔrətɪv] *adj* уничижи́тельный
pelvis ['pɛlvɪs] *n* таз
pen [pɛn] *n* ру́чка; (*felt-tip*) флома́стер; (*enclosure*) заго́н
penalty ['pɛnltɪ] *n* наказа́ние; (*fine*) штраф; (*Sport*) пена́льти *m ind*
pence [pɛns] *npl of* **penny**
pencil ['pɛnsl] *n* каранда́ш
pending ['pɛndɪŋ] *prep* впредь до *+gen*, в ожида́нии *+gen* ▷ *adj* (*lawsuit, exam etc*) предстоя́щий
penetrate ['pɛnɪtreɪt] *vt* (*subj*: *person, light*) проника́ть (*perf* прони́кнуть) в/на *+acc*
penguin ['pɛŋgwɪn] *n* пингви́н
penicillin [pɛnɪ'sɪlɪn] *n* пеницилли́н
peninsula [pə'nɪnsjulə] *n* полуо́стров
penis ['pi:nɪs] *n* пе́нис, полово́й член
penknife ['pɛnnaɪf] *n* перочи́нный нож
penniless ['pɛnɪlɪs] *adj* без гроша́
penny ['pɛnɪ] (*pl* **pennies** *or* **pence**) *n* (*Brit*) пе́нни *nt ind*, пенс
pension ['pɛnʃən] *n* пе́нсия; **pensioner** *n* (*Brit*: *also* **old age pensioner**) пенсионе́р(ка)
pentagon ['pɛntəgən] *n* (*US*): **the Pentagon** Пентаго́н
penultimate [pɛ'nʌltɪmət] *adj* предпосле́дний
people ['pi:pl] *npl* (*persons*) лю́ди *pl*; (*nation, race*) наро́д; **several people came** пришло́ не́сколько челове́к; **people say that ...** говоря́т, что ...
pepper ['pɛpə^r] *n* пе́рец ▷ *vt* (*fig*): **to pepper with** забра́сывать (*perf* заброса́ть) *+instr*; **peppermint** *n* (*sweet*) мя́тная конфе́та
per [pə:^r] *prep* (*of amounts*) на *+acc*; (*of price*) за *+acc*; (*of charge*) с *+gen*; **per annum/day** в год/день; **per person** на челове́ка
perceive [pə'si:v] *vt* (*realize*) осознава́ть (*perf* осозна́ть)
per cent *n* проце́нт
percentage [pə'sɛntɪdʒ] *n* проце́нт

perception [pə'sɛpʃən] *n* (*insight*) понима́ние
perch [pə:tʃ] *vi*: **to perch (on)** (*bird*) сади́ться (*perf* сесть) (на +*acc*); (*person*) приса́живаться (*perf* присе́сть) (на +*acc*)
percussion [pə'kʌʃən] *n* уда́рные инструме́нты *mpl*
perennial [pə'rɛnɪəl] *adj* (*fig*) ве́чный
perfect [*adj* 'pə:fɪkt, *vb* pə'fɛkt] *adj* соверше́нный, безупре́чный; (*weather*) прекра́сный; (*utter*: *nonsense etc*) соверше́нный ▷ *vt* (*technique*) соверше́нствовать (*perf* усоверше́нствовать); **perfection** [pə'fɛkʃən] *n* соверше́нство; **perfectly** ['pə:fɪktlɪ] *adv* (*well, all right*) вполне́
perform [pə'fɔ:m] *vt* (*task, operation*) выполня́ть (*perf* вы́полнить); (*piece of music*) исполня́ть (*perf* испо́лнить); (*play*) игра́ть (*perf* сыгра́ть) ▷ *vi* (*well, badly*) справля́ться (*perf* спра́виться); **performance** *n* (*of actor, athlete etc*) выступле́ние; (*of musical work*) исполне́ние; (*of play, show*) представле́ние; (*of car, engine, company*) рабо́та; **performer** *n* исполни́тель(ница) *m(f)*
perfume ['pə:fju:m] *n* духи́ *pl*
perhaps [pə'hæps] *adv* мо́жет быть, возмо́жно
perimeter [pə'rɪmɪtə^r] *n* пери́метр
period ['pɪərɪəd] *n* (*length of time*) пери́од; (*Scol*) уро́к; (*esp US*: *full stop*) то́чка; (*Med*) менструа́ция ▷ *adj* (*costume, furniture*) стари́нный; **periodical** [pɪərɪ'ɔdɪkl] *n* (*magazine*) периоди́ческое изда́ние ▷ *adj* периоди́ческий
perish ['pɛrɪʃ] *vi* (*person*) погиба́ть (*perf* поги́бнуть)
perk [pə:k] *n* (*inf*) дополни́тельное преиму́щество
perm [pə:m] *n* перманéнт, хими́ческая зави́вка
permanent ['pə:mənənt] *adj* постоя́нный; (*dye, ink*) сто́йкий
permission [pə'mɪʃən] *n* позволе́ние, разреше́ние
permit [*vb* pə'mɪt, *n* 'pə:mɪt] *vt* позволя́ть (*perf* позво́лить) ▷ *n* разреше́ние
persecute ['pə:sɪkju:t] *vt* пресле́довать (*impf*)
persecution [pə:sɪ'kju:ʃən] *n* пресле́дование
persevere [pə:sɪ'vɪə^r] *vi* упо́рствовать (*impf*)
persist [pə'sɪst] *vi*: **to persist (in doing)** наста́ивать (*perf* настоя́ть) (на том, что́бы +*infin*); **persistent** *adj* непрекраща́ющийся; (*smell*) сто́йкий; (*person*) упо́рный
person ['pə:sn] *n* челове́к; **in person** ли́чно; **personal** *adj* ли́чный; **personal computer** *n* персона́льный компью́тер; **personality** [pə:sə'nælɪtɪ] *n* хара́ктер; (*famous person*) знамени́тость *f*; **personally** *adv* ли́чно; **to take sth personally** принима́ть (*perf* приня́ть) что-н на свой счёт
personnel [pə:sə'nɛl] *n* персона́л, штат; (*Mil*) ли́чный соста́в
perspective [pə'spɛktɪv] *n* (*Archit, Art*) перспекти́ва; (*way of thinking*) ви́дение; **to get sth into perspective** (*fig*) смотре́ть (*perf* посмотре́ть) на что-н в и́стинном све́те
perspiration [pə:spɪ'reɪʃən] *n* пот

persuade [pəˈsweɪd] *vt*: **to persuade sb to do** убеждáть (*perf* убедúть) *or* уговáривать (*perf* уговорúть) когó- н *+infin*
persuasion [pəˈsweɪʒən] *n* убеждéние
persuasive [pəˈsweɪsɪv] *adj* (*argument*) убедúтельный; (*person*) настóйчивый
perverse [pəˈvəːs] *adj* (*contrary*) врéдный
pervert [*vb* pəˈvəːt, *n* ˈpəːvəːt] *vt* (*person, mind*) развращáть (*perf* развратúть), растлевáть (*perf* растлúть); (*truth, sb's words*) извращáть (*perf* извратúть) ▷ *n* (*also* **sexual pervert**) (половóй) извращéнец
pessimism [ˈpɛsɪmɪzəm] *n* пессимúзм
pessimistic [pɛsɪˈmɪstɪk] *adj* пессимистúчный
pest [pɛst] *n* (*insect*) вредúтель *m*; (*fig: nuisance*) занýда *m/f*
pester [ˈpɛstə[r]] *vt* приставáть (*perf* пристáть) к *+dat*
pesticide [ˈpɛstɪsaɪd] *n* пестицúд
pet [pɛt] *n* домáшнее живóтное *nt adj*
petal [ˈpɛtl] *n* лепестóк
petite [pəˈtiːt] *adj* миниатю́рный
petition [pəˈtɪʃən] *n* (*signed document*) петúция
petrified [ˈpɛtrɪfaɪd] *adj* (*fig*) оцепенéвший; **I was petrified** я оцепенéл
petrol [ˈpɛtrəl] (*Brit*) *n* бензúн; **two/four-star petrol** нúзкооктáновый/ высóкооктáновый бензúн
petroleum [pəˈtrəulɪəm] *n* нефть *f*
petty [ˈpɛtɪ] *adj* (*trivial*) мéлкий; (*small-minded*) ограничéнный
pew [pjuː] *n* скамья́ (*в цéркви*)
phantom [ˈfæntəm] *n* фантóм
pharmacist [ˈfɑːməsɪst] *n* фармацéвт
pharmacy [ˈfɑːməsɪ] *n* (*shop*) аптéка
phase [feɪz] *n* фáза ▷ *vt*: **to phase sth in** поэтáпно вводúть (*perf* ввестú) что-н; **to phase sth out** поэтáпно ликвидúровать (*impf/perf*) что-н
PhD *n abbr* (= *Doctor of Philosophy*) дóктор филосóфии
pheasant [ˈfɛznt] *n* фазáн
phenomena [fəˈnɔmɪnə] *npl of* **phenomenon**
phenomenal [fəˈnɔmɪnl] *adj* феноменáльный
phenomenon [fəˈnɔmɪnən] (*pl* **phenomena**) *n* явлéние, феномéн
philosopher [fɪˈlɔsəfə[r]] *n* филóсоф
philosophical [fɪləˈsɔfɪkl] *adj* филосóфский
philosophy [fɪˈlɔsəfɪ] *n* филосóфия
phobia [ˈfəubjə] *n* фóбия, страх
phone [fəun] *n* телефóн ▷ *vt* звонúть (*perf* позвонúть) *+dat*; **to be on the phone** говорúть (*impf*) по телефóну; (*possess phone*) имéть (*impf*) телефóн; **phone back** *vt* перезвáнивать (*perf* перезвонúть) *+dat* ▷ *vi* перезвáнивать (*perf* перезвонúть); **phone up** *vt* звонúть (*perf* позвонúть) *+dat*; **phone book** *n* телефóнная кнúга; **phone box** *n* (*Brit*) телефóнная бýдка; **phone call** *n* телефóнный звонóк; **phonecard** *n* телефóнная кáрта
phonetics [fəˈnɛtɪks] *n* фонéтика
phoney [ˈfəunɪ] *adj* фальшúвый

P

photo ['fəutəu] *n* фотогра́фия; **photocopier** ['fəutəukɔpɪə^r] *n* (*machine*) ксе́рокс, копирова́льная маши́на; **photocopy** *n* ксероко́пия, фотоко́пия ▷ *vt* фотокопи́ровать (*perf* сфотокопи́ровать), ксерокопи́ровать (*impf/perf*); **photograph** *n* фотогра́фия ▷ *vt* фотографи́ровать (*perf* сфотографи́ровать); **photographer** [fə'tɔgrəfə^r] *n* фото́граф; **photography** [fə'tɔgrəfɪ] *n* фотогра́фия

phrase [freɪz] *n* фра́за ▷ *vt* формули́ровать (*perf* сформули́ровать)

physical ['fɪzɪkl] *adj* физи́ческий; (*world, object*) материа́льный; **physically** *adv* физи́чески

physician [fɪ'zɪʃən] *n* (*esp US*) врач

physicist ['fɪzɪsɪst] *n* фи́зик

physics ['fɪzɪks] *n* фи́зика

physiotherapy [fɪzɪəu'θɛrəpɪ] *n* физиотерапи́я

physique [fɪ'zi:k] *n* телосложе́ние

pianist ['pi:ənɪst] *n* piани́ст(ка)

piano [pɪ'ænəu] *n* пиани́но, фортепья́но *nt ind*

pick [pɪk] *n* (*also* **pickaxe**) кирка́ ▷ *vt* (*select*) выбира́ть (*perf* вы́брать); (*gather: fruit, flowers*) собира́ть (*perf* собра́ть); (*remove*) рвать (*impf*); (*lock*) взла́мывать (*perf* взлома́ть); **take your pick** выбира́йте; **to pick one's nose/teeth** ковыря́ть (*impf*) в носу́/зуба́х; **to pick a quarrel (with sb)** иска́ть (*impf*) по́вод для ссо́ры (с кем-н); **pick out** *vt* (*distinguish*) разгляде́ть (*perf*); (*select*) отбира́ть (*perf* отобра́ть); **pick up** *vi* (*improve*) улучша́ться (*perf* улу́чшиться) ▷ *vt* (*lift*) поднима́ть (*perf* подня́ть); (*arrest*) забира́ть (*perf* забра́ть); (*collect: person: by car*) заезжа́ть (*perf* зае́хать) за +*instr*; (*passenger*) подбира́ть (*perf* подобра́ть); (*language, skill etc*) усва́ивать (*perf* усво́ить); (*Radio*) лови́ть (*perf* пойма́ть); **to pick up speed** набира́ть (*perf* набра́ть) ско́рость; **to pick o.s. up** (*after falling*) поднима́ться (*perf* подня́ться)

pickle ['pɪkl] *n* (*also* **pickles**) соле́нья *ntpl* ▷ *vt* (*in vinegar*) мариноваа́ть (*perf* замаринова́ть); (*in salt water*) соли́ть (*perf* засоли́ть)

pickpocket ['pɪkpɔkɪt] *n* вор-карма́нник

picnic ['pɪknɪk] *n* пикни́к

picture ['pɪktʃə^r] *n* карти́на; (*photo*) фотогра́фия; (*TV*) изображе́ние ▷ *vt* (*imagine*) рисова́ть (*perf* нарисова́ть) карти́ну +*gen*; **pictures** *npl*: **the pictures** (*Brit: inf*) кино́ *nt ind*

picturesque [pɪktʃə'rɛsk] *adj* живопи́сный

pie [paɪ] *n* пиро́г; (*small*) пирожо́к

piece [pi:s] *n* (*portion, part*) кусо́к; (*component*) дета́ль *f* ▷ *vt*: **to piece together** (*information*) свя́зывать (*perf* связа́ть); (*object*) соединя́ть (*perf* соедини́ть); **a piece of clothing** вещь, предме́т оде́жды; **a piece of advice** сове́т; **to take to pieces** (*dismantle*) разбира́ть (*perf* разобра́ть)

pier [pɪə^r] *n* пирс

pierce [pɪəs] *vt* протыка́ть (*perf* проткну́ть), прока́лывать (*perf* проколо́ть)

pig [pɪg] *n* (*also fig*) свинья́

pigeon ['pɪdʒən] *n* го́лубь *m*
pigtail ['pɪgteɪl] *n* коси́чка
pike [paɪk] *n inv* (*fish*) щу́ка
pile [paɪl] *n* (*large heap*) ку́ча, гру́да; (*neat stack*) сто́пка; (*of carpet*) ворс ▷ *vi*: **to pile into** (*vehicle*) набива́ться (*perf* наби́ться) в *+acc*; **to pile out of** (*vehicle*) выва́ливаться (*perf* вы́валиться) из *+gen*; **pile up** *vt* (*objects*) сва́ливать (*perf* свали́ть) в ку́чу ▷ *vi* громозди́ться (*impf*); (*problems, work*) нака́пливаться (*perf* накопи́ться)
piles [paɪlz] *npl* (*Med*) геморро́й *msg*
pilgrimage ['pɪlgrɪmɪdʒ] *n* пало́мничество
pill [pɪl] *n* табле́тка; **the pill** (*contraceptive*) противозача́точные *pl adj* (табле́тки)
pillar ['pɪlə^r] *n* (*Archit*) столб, коло́нна
pillow ['pɪləu] *n* поду́шка; **pillowcase** *n* на́волочка
pilot ['paɪlət] *n* (*Aviat*) пило́т, лётчик ▷ *cpd* (*scheme, study etc*) эксперимента́льный ▷ *vt* (*aircraft*) управля́ть (*impf*) *+instr*
pimple ['pɪmpl] *n* прыщ, пры́щик
PIN [pɪn] *n* (= *personal identification number*) (*also* **PIN number**) персона́льный идентификацио́нный но́мер
pin [pɪn] *n* (*for clothes, papers*) була́вка ▷ *vt* прика́лывать (*perf* приколо́ть); **pins and needles** (*fig*) колотьё; **to pin sth on sb** (*fig*) возлага́ть (*perf* возложи́ть) что-н на кого́-н; **pin down** *vt*: **to pin sb down** (*fig*) принужда́ть (*perf* прину́дить) кого́-н
pinch [pɪntʃ] *n* (*small amount*) щепо́тка ▷ *vt* щипа́ть (*perf* ущипну́ть); (*inf*: *steal*) стащи́ть (*perf*); **at a pinch** в кра́йнем слу́чае
pine [paɪn] *n* (*tree, wood*) сосна́
pineapple ['paɪnæpl] *n* анана́с
pink [pɪŋk] *adj* ро́зовый
pint [paɪnt] *n* пи́нта

PINT

Одна́ пи́нта равна́ 0,568 л.

pioneer [paɪə'nɪə^r] *n* (*of science, method*) первооткрыва́тель *m*, нова́тор
pious ['paɪəs] *adj* на́божный
pip [pɪp] *n* (*of grape, melon*) ко́сточка; (*of apple, orange*) зёрнышко
pipe [paɪp] *n* (*for water, gas*) труба́; (*for smoking*) тру́бка ▷ *vt* (*water, gas, oil*) подава́ть (*perf* пода́ть); **pipes** *npl* (*also* **bagpipes**) волы́нка *fsg*
pirate ['paɪərət] *n* (*sailor*) пира́т ▷ *vt* (*video tape, cassette*) незако́нно распространя́ть (*perf* распространи́ть)
Pisces ['paɪsi:z] *n* Ры́бы *fpl*
pistol ['pɪstl] *n* пистоле́т
pit [pɪt] *n* (*in ground*) я́ма; (*also* **coal pit**) ша́хта; (*quarry*) карье́р ▷ *vt*: **to pit one's wits against sb** состяза́ться (*impf*) в уме́ с кем-н
pitch [pɪtʃ] *n* (*Brit*: *Sport*) по́ле; (*Mus*) высота́; (*level*) у́ровень *m*
pitiful ['pɪtɪful] *adj* жа́лкий
pity ['pɪtɪ] *n* жа́лость *f* ▷ *vt* жале́ть (*perf* пожале́ть)
pizza ['pi:tsə] *n* пи́цца
placard ['plækɑ:d] *n* плака́т
place [pleɪs] *vt* (*put*) помеща́ть (*perf* помести́ть); (*identify*: *person*) вспомина́ть (*perf* вспо́мнить) ▷ *n* ме́сто; (*home*): **at his place** у него́

(до́ма); **to place an order with sb for sth** (*Comm*) зака́зывать (*perf* заказа́ть) что-н у кого́-н; **to take place** происходи́ть (*perf* произойти́); **out of place** (*inappropriate*) неуме́стный; **in the first place** (*first of all*) во-пе́рвых; **to change places with sb** меня́ться (*perf* поменя́ться) места́ми с кем-н

placid ['plæsɪd] *adj* (*person*) ти́хий

plague [pleɪg] *n* (*Med*) чума́; (*fig: of locusts etc*) наше́ствие ▷ *vt* (*fig: subj: problems*) осажда́ть (*perf* осади́ть)

plaice [pleɪs] *n inv* ка́мбала

plain [pleɪn] *adj* просто́й; (*unpatterned*) гла́дкий; (*clear*) я́сный, поня́тный ▷ *adv* (*wrong, stupid etc*) я́вно ▷ *n* (*Geo*) равни́на; **plainly** *adv* я́сно

plan [plæn] *n* план ▷ *vt* плани́ровать (*perf* заплани́ровать); (*draw up plans for*) плани́ровать (*impf*) ▷ *vi* плани́ровать (*impf*)

plane [pleɪn] *n* (*Aviat*) самолёт; (*fig: level*) план

planet ['plænɪt] *n* плане́та

plank [plæŋk] *n* (*of wood*) доска́

planning ['plænɪŋ] *n* (*of future, event*) плани́рование; (*also* **town planning**) планиро́вка

plant [plɑ:nt] *n* (*Bot*) расте́ние; (*factory*) заво́д; (*machinery*) устано́вка ▷ *vt* (*seed, garden*) сажа́ть (*perf* посади́ть); (*field*) засе́ивать (*perf* засе́ять); (*bomb, evidence*) подкла́дывать (*perf* подложи́ть); **plantation** [plæn'teɪʃən] *n* (*of tea, sugar etc*) планта́ция; (*of trees*) лесонасажде́ние

plaque [plæk] *n* (*on teeth*) налёт; (*on building*) мемориа́льная доска́

plaster ['plɑ:stə^r^] *n* (*for walls*) штукату́рка; (*also* **plaster of Paris**) гипс; (*Brit: also* **sticking plaster**) пла́стырь *m* ▷ *vt* (*wall, ceiling*) штукату́рить (*perf* оштукату́рить); (*cover*): **to plaster with** заштукату́ривать (*perf* заштукату́рить) *+instr*

plastic ['plæstɪk] *n* пластма́сса ▷ *adj* (*made of plastic*) пластма́ссовый

plate [pleɪt] *n* (*dish*) таре́лка

plateau ['plætəu] (*pl* **plateaus** *or* **plateaux**) *n* плато́ *nt ind*

platform ['plætfɔ:m] *n* (*at meeting*) трибу́на; (*at concert*) помо́ст; (*for landing, loading on etc*) площа́дка; (*Rail, Pol*) платфо́рма

plausible ['plɔ:zɪbl] *adj* убеди́тельный

play [pleɪ] *n* пье́са ▷ *vt* (*subj: children: game*) игра́ть (*impf*) в *+acc*; (*sport, cards*) игра́ть (*perf* сыгра́ть) в *+acc*; (*opponent*) игра́ть (*perf* сыгра́ть) с *+instr*; (*part, piece of music*) игра́ть (*perf* сыгра́ть); (*instrument*) игра́ть (*impf*) на *+prp*; (*tape, record*) ста́вить (*perf* поста́вить) ▷ *vi* игра́ть (*impf*); **play down** *vt* не заостря́ть (*impf*) внима́ние на *+prp*; **player** *n* (*Sport*) игро́к; **playful** *adj* (*person*) игри́вый; **playground** *n* (*in park*) де́тская площа́дка; (*in school*) игрова́я площа́дка; **playgroup** *n* де́тская гру́ппа; **playtime** *n* (*Scol*) переме́на; **playwright** *n* драмату́рг

plc *abbr* (*Brit*) (= *public limited company*) публи́чная компа́ния с ограни́ченной отве́тственностью

plea [pli:] *n* (*personal request*) мольба́; (*public request*) призы́в;

(*Law*) заявле́ние
plead [pli:d] *vt* (*ignorance, ill health etc*) ссыла́ться (*perf* сосла́ться) на *+acc* ▷ *vi* (*Law*): **to plead guilty/not guilty** признава́ть (*perf* призна́ть) себя́ вино́вным(-ой)/невино́вным(-ой); (*beg*): **to plead with sb** умоля́ть (*impf*) кого́-н
pleasant ['plɛznt] *adj* прия́тный
please [pli:z] *excl* пожа́луйста ▷ *vt* угожда́ть (*perf* угоди́ть) *+dat*; **please yourself!** (*inf*) как Вам уго́дно!; **do as you please** де́лайте как хоти́те; **he is difficult/easy to please** ему́ тру́дно/легко́ угоди́ть; **pleased** *adj*: **pleased (with)** дово́льный (*+instr*); **pleased to meet you** о́чень прия́тно
pleasure ['plɛʒə^r] *n* удово́льствие; **it's a pleasure** не сто́ит; **to take pleasure in** получа́ть (*perf* получи́ть) удово́льствие от *+gen*
pleat [pli:t] *n* скла́дка
pledge [plɛdʒ] *n* обяза́тельство ▷ *vt* (*money*) обя́зываться (*perf* обяза́ться) дать; (*support*) обя́зываться (*perf* обяза́ться) оказа́ть
plentiful ['plɛntɪful] *adj* оби́льный
plenty ['plɛntɪ] *n* (*enough*) изоби́лие; **plenty of** (*food, money etc*) мно́го *+gen*; (*jobs, people, houses*) мно́жество *+gen*; **we've got plenty of time to get there** у нас доста́точно вре́мени, что́бы туда́ добра́ться
pliers ['plaɪəz] *npl* плоскогу́бцы *pl*
plight [plaɪt] *n* му́ки *fpl*
plot [plɔt] *n* (*conspiracy*) за́говор; (*of story*) сюже́т; (*of land*) уча́сток ▷ *vt* (*plan*) замышля́ть (замы́слить *impf*); (*Math*) наноси́ть (*perf* нанести́) ▷ *vi* (*conspire*) составля́ть (*perf* соста́вить) за́говор
plough [plau] (*US* **plow**) *n* плуг ▷ *vt* паха́ть (*perf* вспаха́ть)
ploy [plɔɪ] *n* уло́вка
pluck [plʌk] *vt* (*eyebrows*) выщи́пывать (*perf* вы́щипать); (*instrument*) перебира́ть (*impf*) стру́ны *+gen*; **to pluck up courage** набира́ться (*perf* набра́ться) хра́брости *or* му́жества
plug [plʌg] *n* (*Elec*) ви́лка, ште́псель *m*; (*in sink, bath*) про́бка ▷ *vt* (*hole*) затыка́ть (*perf* заткну́ть); (*inf*: *advertise*) реклами́ровать (*perf* разреклами́ровать); **plug in** *vt* (*Elec*) включа́ть (*perf* включи́ть) в розе́тку
plum [plʌm] *n* сли́ва
plumber ['plʌmə^r] *n* водопрово́дчик, сле́сарь-санте́хник
plumbing ['plʌmɪŋ] *n* (*piping*) водопрово́д и канализа́ция; (*trade, work*) сле́сарное де́ло
plummet ['plʌmɪt] *vi*: **to plummet (down)** (*price, amount*) ре́зко па́дать (*perf* упа́сть)
plump [plʌmp] *adj* по́лный, пу́хлый ▷ *vi*: **to plump for** (*inf*) выбира́ть (*perf* вы́брать)
plunge [plʌndʒ] *n* (*fig*: *of prices etc*) ре́зкое паде́ние ▷ *vt* (*knife*) мета́ть (*perf* метну́ть); (*hand*) выбра́сывать (*perf* вы́бросить) ▷ *vi* (*fall*) ру́хнуть (*perf*); (*dive*) броса́ться (*perf* бро́ситься); (*fig*: *prices etc*) ре́зко па́дать (*perf* упа́сть); **to take the plunge** (*fig*) отва́живаться (*perf* отва́житься)
plural ['pluərl] *n* мно́жественное число́

P

plus [plʌs] *n, adj* плюс *ind* ▷ *prep*: **ten plus ten is twenty** десять плюс десять — двадцать; **ten/twenty plus** (*more than*) десять/двадцать с лишним
plywood ['plaɪwud] *n* фанéра
PM *abbr* (*Brit*) = **Prime Minister**
p.m. *adv abbr* (= *post meridiem*) пóсле полýдня
pneumonia [nju:'məunɪə] *n* воспалéние лёгких, пневмонúя
PO Box *n abbr* (= *Post Office Box*) абонéнтский *or* почтóвый я́щик
pocket ['pɔkɪt] *n* кармáн; (*fig*: *small area*) уголóк ▷ *vt* класть (*perf* положúть) себé в кармáн; **to be out of pocket** (*Brit*) быть (*impf*) в убы́тке
podcast ['pɔdkæst] *n* подкаст ▷ *vi* выпускáть (*perf* вы́пустить) подкáст
poem ['pəuɪm] *n* (*long*) поэ́ма; (*short*) стихотворéние
poet ['pəuɪt] *n* (*male*) поэ́т; (*female*) поэтéсса; **poetic** [pəu'ɛtɪk] *adj* поэтúческий; **poetry** *n* поэ́зия
poignant ['pɔɪnjənt] *adj* пронзúтельный
point [pɔɪnt] *n* (*of needle, knife etc*) остриё, кóнчик; (*purpose*) смысл; (*significant part*) суть *f*; (*particular position*) тóчка; (*detail, moment*) момéнт; (*stage in development*) стáдия; (*score*) очкó; (*Elec*: *also* **power point**) розéтка ▷ *vt* (*show, mark*) укáзывать (*perf* указáть) ▷ *vi*: **to point at** укáзывать (*perf* указáть) на *+acc*; **points** *npl* (*Rail*) стрéлка *fsg*; **to be on the point of doing** собирáться (*impf*) *+infin*; **I made a point of visiting him** я счёл необходúмым посетúть егó; **to get/miss the point** понимáть (*perf* поня́ть)/не понимáть (*perf* поня́ть) суть; **to come to the point** доходúть (*perf* дойтú) до сýти; **there's no point in doing** нет смы́сла *+infin*; **to point sth at sb** (*gun etc*) нацéливать (*perf* нацéлить) что-н на когó-н; **point out** *vt* укáзывать (*perf* указáть) на *+acc*; **point to** *vt fus* укáзывать (*perf* указáть) на *+acc*; **point-blank** *adv* (*refuse*) наотрéз; (*say, ask*) напрямúк ▷ *adj*: **at point-blank range** в упóр; **pointed** *adj* óстрый; (*fig*: *remark*) язвúтельный; **pointless** *adj* бессмы́сленный; **point of view** *n* тóчка зрéния
poison ['pɔɪzn] *n* яд ▷ *vt* отравля́ть (*perf* отравúть); **poisonous** *adj* (*toxic*) ядовúтый
poke [pəuk] *vt* (*with stick etc*) ты́кать (*perf* ткнуть); **to poke sth in(to)** (*put*) втыкáть (*perf* воткнýть) что-н в *+acc*
poker ['pəukə^r] *n* кочергá; (*Cards*) пóкер
Poland ['pəulənd] *n* Пóльша
polar ['pəulə^r] *adj* поля́рный; **polar bear** *n* бéлый медвéдь *m*
pole [pəul] *n* (*stick*) шест; (*telegraph pole*) столб; (*Geo*) пóлюс; **pole vault** *n* прыжкú *mpl* с шестóм
police [pə'li:s] *npl* полúция *fsg*; (*in Russia*) милúция *fsg* ▷ *vt* патрулúровать (*impf*); **policeman** *irreg n* полицéйский *m adj*; **police officer** *n* полицéйский *m adj*; **police station** *n* полицéйский учáсток; (*in Russia*) отделéние милúции; **policewoman** *irreg n* (жéнщина-)полицéйский *m adj*
policy ['pɔlɪsɪ] *n* полúтика; (*also* **insurance policy**) пóлис
polio ['pəulɪəu] *n* полиомиелúт

Polish ['pəulɪʃ] *adj* по́льский
polish ['pɔlɪʃ] *n* (*for furniture*) (полирова́льная) па́ста; (*for shoes*) гутали́н; (*for floor*) мастика; (*shine, also fig*) лоск ▷ *vt* (*furniture etc*) полирова́ть (*perf* отполирова́ть); (*floors, shoes*) натира́ть (*perf* натере́ть); **polished** *adj* (*style*) отто́ченный
polite [pə'laɪt] *adj* ве́жливый
political [pə'lɪtɪkl] *adj* полити́ческий; (*person*) полити́чески акти́вный, политизи́рованный; **politically** *adv* полити́чески; **politically correct** полити́чески корре́ктный
politician [pɔlɪ'tɪʃən] *n* поли́тик, полити́ческий де́ятель *m*
politics ['pɔlɪtɪks] *n* поли́тика; (*Scol*) политоло́гия
poll [pəul] *n* (*also* **opinion poll**) опро́с; (*usu pl*: *election*) вы́боры *mpl* ▷ *vt* (*number of votes*) набира́ть (*perf* набра́ть)
pollen ['pɔlən] *n* пыльца́
pollute [pə'lu:t] *vt* загрязня́ть (*perf* загрязни́ть)
pollution [pə'lu:ʃən] *n* загрязне́ние; (*substances*) загрязни́тель *m*
polo neck ['pəuləu-] *n* (*also* **polo neck sweater** *or* **jumper**) сви́тер с кру́глым воротнико́м
polyester [pɔlɪ'ɛstə^r] *n* (*fabric*) полиэфи́рное волокно́
polystyrene [pɔlɪ'staɪri:n] *n* пенопла́ст
polythene ['pɔlɪθi:n] *n* полиэтиле́н
pomegranate ['pɔmɪgrænɪt] *n* (*Bot*) грана́т
pompous ['pɔmpəs] *adj* (*pej*: *person, style*) напы́щенный, чва́нный
pond [pɔnd] *n* пруд
ponder ['pɔndə^r] *vt* обду́мывать (*perf* обду́мать)
pony ['pəunɪ] *n* по́ни *m ind*; **ponytail** *n* (*hairstyle*) хвост, хво́стик
poodle ['pu:dl] *n* пу́дель *m*
pool [pu:l] *n* (*puddle*) лу́жа; (*pond*) пруд; (*also* **swimming pool**) бассе́йн; (*fig*: *of light, paint*) пятно́; (*Sport, Comm*) пул ▷ *vt* объединя́ть (*perf* объедини́ть); **pools** *npl* (*also* **football pools**) футбо́льный тотализа́тор; **typing pool**, *(US)* **secretary pool** машинопи́сное бюро́ *nt ind*
poor [puə^r] *adj* (*not rich*) бе́дный; (*bad*) плохо́й; ▷ *npl*: **the poor** (*people*) беднота́ *fsg*, бе́дные *pl adj*; **poor in** (*resources etc*) бе́дный *+instr*; **poorly** *adv* пло́хо ▷ *adj*: **she is feeling poorly** она́ пло́хо себя́ чу́вствует
pop [pɔp] *n* (*also* **pop music**) поп-му́зыка; (*inf*: *US*: *father*) па́па *m*; (*sound*) хлопо́к ▷ *vi* (*balloon*) ло́паться (*perf* ло́пнуть) ▷ *vt* (*put quickly*): **to pop sth into/onto** забра́сывать (*perf* забро́сить) что-н в *+acc*/на *+acc*; **pop in** *vi* загля́дывать (*perf* загляну́ть), заска́кивать (*perf* заскочи́ть); **pop up** *vi* вылеза́ть (*perf* вы́лезти); **popcorn** *n* возду́шная кукуру́за, попко́рн
pope [pəup] *n*: **the Pope** Па́па *m* ри́мский
poplar ['pɔplə^r] *n* то́поль *m*
poppy ['pɔpɪ] *n* мак
pop star *n* поп-звезда́ *m/f*
popular ['pɔpjulə^r] *adj* популя́рный; **popularity** [pɔpju'lærɪtɪ] *n* популя́рность *f*
population [pɔpju'leɪʃən] *n* (*of town, country*) населе́ние
porcelain ['pɔ:slɪn] *n* фарфо́р

porch [pɔːtʃ] *n* крыльцо́; (*US*) вера́нда
pore [pɔːʳ] *n* по́ра
pork [pɔːk] *n* свини́на
porn [pɔːn] *n* (*inf*) порногра́фия
pornographic [pɔːnəˈgræfɪk] *adj* порнографи́ческий
pornography [pɔːˈnɔgrəfɪ] *n* порногра́фия
porridge [ˈpɔrɪdʒ] *n* овся́ная ка́ша
port [pɔːt] *n* (*harbour*) порт; (*wine*) портве́йн; **port of call** порт захо́да
portable [ˈpɔːtəbl] *adj* портати́вный
porter [ˈpɔːtəʳ] *n* (*doorkeeper*) портье́ *m ind*, швейца́р; (*for luggage*) носи́льщик
portfolio [pɔːtˈfəulɪəu] *n* (*Art*) па́пка
portion [ˈpɔːʃən] *n* (*part*) часть *f*; (*equal part*) до́ля; (*of food*) по́рция
portrait [ˈpɔːtreɪt] *n* портре́т
portray [pɔːˈtreɪ] *vt* изобража́ть (*perf* изобрази́ть)
Portugal [ˈpɔːtjugl] *n* Португа́лия
Portuguese [pɔːtjuˈgiːz] *adj* португа́льский
pose [pəuz] *n* по́за ▷ *vt* (*question*) ста́вить (*perf* поста́вить); (*problem, danger*) создава́ть (*perf* созда́ть) ▷ *vi* (*pretend*): **to pose as** выдава́ть (*perf* вы́дать) себя́ за *+acc*; **to pose for** пози́ровать (*impf*) для *+gen*
posh [pɔʃ] *adj* (*inf*: *hotel etc*) фешене́бельный; (: *person, behaviour*) великосве́тский
position [pəˈzɪʃən] *n* положе́ние; (*of house, thing*) расположе́ние, ме́сто; (*job*) до́лжность *f*; (*in competition, race*) ме́сто; (*attitude*) пози́ция ▷ *vt* располага́ть (*perf* расположи́ть)
positive [ˈpɔzɪtɪv] *adj* (*affirmative*) положи́тельный; (*certain*) уве́ренный, убеждённый; (*definite*: *decision, policy*) определённый
possess [pəˈzɛs] *vt* владе́ть (*impf*) *+instr*; (*quality, ability*) облада́ть (*impf*) *+instr*; **possession** [pəˈzɛʃən] *n* (*state of possessing*) владе́ние; **possessions** *npl* (*belongings*) ве́щи *fpl*; **to take possession of** вступа́ть (*perf* вступи́ть) во владе́ние *+instr*; **possessive** *adj* (*quality*) со́бственнический; (*person*) ревни́вый; (*Ling*) притяжа́тельный
possibility [pɔsɪˈbɪlɪtɪ] *n* возмо́жность *f*
possible [ˈpɔsɪbl] *adj* возмо́жный; **it's possible** э́то возмо́жно; **as soon as possible** как мо́жно скоре́е
possibly [ˈpɔsɪblɪ] *adv* (*perhaps*) возмо́жно; **if you possibly can** е́сли то́лько Вы мо́жете; **I cannot possibly come** я ника́к не смогу́ прийти́
post [pəust] *n* (*Brit*: *mail*) по́чта; (*pole*) столб; (*job, situation, also Comput*) пост ▷ *vt* (*Brit*: *mail*) посыла́ть (*perf* посла́ть), отправля́ть (*perf* отпра́вить) (по по́чте); **postage** *n* почто́вые расхо́ды *mpl*; **postal** *adj* почто́вый; **postcard** *n* (почто́вая) откры́тка; **postcode** *n* (*Brit*) почто́вый и́ндекс
poster [ˈpəustəʳ] *n* афи́ша, плака́т; (*for advertising*) по́стер
postgraduate [ˈpəustˈgrædjuət] *n* аспира́нт(ка) ▷ *adj*: **postgraduate study** аспиранту́ра

postman ['pəustmən] *irreg n* почтальо́н
post office *n* почто́вое отделе́ние, отделе́ние свя́зи; (*organization*): **the Post Office** ≈ Министе́рство свя́зи
postpone [pəus'pəun] *vt* откла́дывать (*perf* отложи́ть)
posture ['pɔstʃəʳ] *n* (*of body*) оса́нка
pot [pɔt] *n* (*for cooking, flowers*) горшо́к; (*also* **teapot**) (зава́рочный) ча́йник; (*also* **coffeepot**) кофе́йник; (*bowl, container*) ба́нка ▷ *vt* (*plant*) сажа́ть (*perf* посади́ть); **a pot of tea** ча́йник ча́я
potato [pə'teɪtəu] (*pl* **potatoes**) *n* карто́фель *m no pl*, карто́шка (*inf*); (*single potato*) карто́фелина
potent ['pəutnt] *adj* мо́щный; (*drink*) кре́пкий
potential [pə'tɛnʃl] *adj* потенциа́льный ▷ *n* потенциа́л
pottery ['pɔtərɪ] *n* кера́мика; (*factory*) фа́брика керами́ческих изде́лий; (*small*) керами́ческий цех
potty ['pɔtɪ] *adj* (*inf*: *mad*) чо́кнутый ▷ *n* (*for child*) горшо́к
pouch [pautʃ] *n* (*for tobacco*) кисе́т; (*for coins*) кошелёк; (*Zool*) су́мка
poultry ['pəultrɪ] *n* (*birds*) дома́шняя пти́ца; (*meat*) пти́ца
pounce [pauns] *vi*: **to pounce on** набра́сываться (*perf* набро́ситься) на *+acc*
pound [paund] *n* (*money, weight*) фунт; **pound sterling** фунт сте́рлингов

POUND

Pound — ме́ра ве́са ра́вная 0,454 кг

pour [pɔːʳ] *vt* (*liquid*) налива́ть (*perf* нали́ть); (*dry substance*) насыпа́ть (*perf* насы́пать) ▷ *vi* (*water etc*) ли́ться (*impf*); (*rain*) лить (*impf*); **to pour sb some tea** налива́ть (*perf* нали́ть) кому́-н чай; **pour in** *vi* (*people*) вали́ть (*perf* повали́ть); (*news, letters etc*) сы́паться (*perf* посы́паться); **pour out** *vi* (*people*) вали́ть (*perf* повали́ть) ▷ *vt* (*drink*) налива́ть (*perf* нали́ть); (*fig*: *thoughts etc*) излива́ть (*perf* изли́ть)
pout [paut] *vi* надува́ть (*perf* наду́ть) гу́бы, ду́ться (*perf* наду́ться)
poverty ['pɔvətɪ] *n* бе́дность *f*
powder ['paudəʳ] *n* порошо́к; (*also* **face powder**) пу́дра
power ['pauəʳ] *n* (*authority*) власть *f*; (*ability, opportunity*) возмо́жность *f*; (*legal right*) полномо́чие; (*of engine*) мо́щность *f*; (*electricity*) (электро) эне́ргия; **to be in power** находи́ться (*impf*) у вла́сти; **powerful** *adj* могу́чий; (*person, organization*) могу́щественный; (*argument, engine*) мо́щный; **powerless** *adj* беси́льный; **power station** *n* электроста́нция
pp *abbr* = **pages**
PR *n abbr* = **public relations**
practical ['præktɪkl] *adj* (*not theoretical*) практи́ческий; (*sensible, viable*) практи́чный; (*good with hands*) уме́лый; **practically** *adv* практи́чески
practice ['præktɪs] *n* пра́ктика; (*custom*) привы́чка ▷ *vt, vi* (*US*) = **practise**; **in practice** на пра́ктике; **I am out of practice** я разучи́лся
practise ['præktɪs] (*US* **practice**) *vt* (*piano etc*) упражня́ться (*impf*)

P

на *+acc*; (*sport, language*) отрабатывать (*perf* отработать); (*custom*) придерживаться (*impf*) *+gen*; (*craft*) заниматься (*impf*) *+instr*; (*religion*) исповедовать (*impf*) ▷ *vi* (*Mus*) упражняться (*impf*); (*Sport*) тренироваться (*impf*); (*lawyer, doctor*) практиковать (*impf*); **to practise law/medicine** заниматься (*impf*) адвокатской/врачебной практикой

practising ['præktɪsɪŋ] *adj* (*Christian etc*) набожный; (*doctor, lawyer*) практикующий

practitioner [præk'tɪʃənə^r] *n* терапевт

pragmatic [præg'mætɪk] *adj* (*reason etc*) прагматический

praise [preɪz] *n* (*approval*) похвала ▷ *vt* хвалить (*perf* похвалить)

pram [præm] *n* (*Brit*) детская коляска

prawn [prɔ:n] *n* креветка

pray [preɪ] *vi* молиться (*perf* помолиться); **to pray for/that** молиться (*impf*) за *+acc*/, чтобы; **prayer** [prɛə^r] *n* молитва

preach [pri:tʃ] *vi* проповедовать (*impf*) ▷ *vt* (*sermon*) произносить (*perf* произнести); **preacher** *n* проповедник(-ица)

precarious [prɪ'kɛərɪəs] *adj* рискованный

precaution [prɪ'kɔ:ʃən] *n* предосторожность *f*

precede [prɪ'si:d] *vt* предшествовать (*impf*) *+dat*; **precedent** ['prɛsɪdənt] *n* прецедент

preceding [prɪ'si:dɪŋ] *adj* предшествующий

precinct ['pri:sɪŋkt] *n* (*US: in city*) район, префектура; **pedestrian precinct** (*Brit*) пешеходная зона; **shopping precinct** (*Brit*) торговый центр

precious ['prɛʃəs] *adj* ценный; (*stone*) драгоценный

precise [prɪ'saɪs] *adj* точный; **precisely** *adv* (*accurately*) точно; (*exactly*) ровно

precision [prɪ'sɪʒən] *n* точность *f*

predator ['prɛdətə^r] *n* хищник

predecessor ['pri:dɪsɛsə^r] *n* предшественник(-ица)

predicament [prɪ'dɪkəmənt] *n* затруднительное положение

predict [prɪ'dɪkt] *vt* предсказывать (*perf* предсказать); **predictable** *adj* предсказуемый; **prediction** [prɪ'dɪkʃən] *n* предсказание

predominantly [prɪ'dɔmɪnəntlɪ] *adv* преимущественно

preface ['prɛfəs] *n* предисловие

PREFECT

Prefect — староста школы. Старостами могут быть только старшеклассники. Они помогают учителям поддерживать в школе дисциплину.

prefer [prɪ'fə:^{r}] *vt* предпочитать (*perf* предпочесть); **preferable** ['prɛfrəbl] *adj* предпочтительный; **preferably** ['prɛfrəblɪ] *adv* предпочтительно; **preference** ['prɛfrəns] *n* (*liking*): **to have a preference for** предпочитать (*impf*)

prefix ['pri:fɪks] *n* приставка

pregnancy ['prɛgnənsɪ] *n* беременность *f*

pregnant ['prɛgnənt] *adj* беременная; (*remark, pause*)

многозначи́тельный; **she is 3 months pregnant** она́ на четвёртом ме́сяце бере́менности
prehistoric ['pri:hɪs'tɔrɪk] *adj* доистори́ческий
prejudice ['prɛdʒudɪs] *n* (*dislike*) предрассу́док; (*preference*) предвзя́тость *f*, предубежде́ние
preliminary [prɪ'lɪmɪnərɪ] *adj* предвари́тельный
prelude ['prɛlju:d] *n* прелю́дия
premature ['prɛmətʃuəʳ] *adj* преждевре́менный; (*baby*) недоно́шенный
premier ['prɛmɪəʳ] *adj* лу́чший ▷ *n* премье́р(-мини́стр)
première ['prɛmɪɛəʳ] *n* премье́ра
premises ['prɛmɪsɪz] *npl* (*of business*) помеще́ние *ntsg*; **on the premises** в помеще́нии
premium ['pri:mɪəm] *n* пре́мия; **to be at a premium** по́льзоваться (*impf*) больши́м спро́сом
premonition [prɛmə'nɪʃən] *n* предчу́вствие
preoccupied [pri:'ɔkjupaɪd] *adj* озабо́ченный
preparation [prɛpə'reɪʃən] *n* (*activity*) подгото́вка; (*of food*) приготовле́ние; **preparations** *npl* (*arrangements*) приготовле́ния *ntpl*
prepare [prɪ'pɛəʳ] *vt* подгота́вливать (*perf* подгото́вить); (*meal*) гото́вить (*perf* пригото́вить) ▷ *vi*: **to prepare for** гото́виться (*perf* подгото́виться) к +*dat*; **prepared** *adj* гото́вый; **prepared for** (*ready*) гото́вый к +*dat*
preposition [prɛpə'zɪʃən] *n* предло́г
prescribe [prɪ'skraɪb] *vt* (*Med*) пропи́сывать (*perf* прописа́ть)
prescription [prɪ'skrɪpʃən] *n* (*Med*: *slip of paper*) реце́пт; (: *medicine*) лека́рство (*назна́ченное врачо́м*)
presence ['prɛzns] *n* прису́тствие; (*fig*) нару́жность *f*; **in sb's presence** в прису́тствии кого́-н
present [*adj, n* 'prɛznt, *vb* prɪ'zɛnt] *adj* (*current*) ны́нешний, настоя́щий; (*in attendance*) прису́тствующий ▷ *n* (*gift*) пода́рок ▷ *vt* представля́ть (*perf* предста́вить); (*Radio, TV*) вести́ (*impf*); **the present** (*time*) настоя́щее *nt adj*; **at present** в настоя́щее вре́мя; **to give sb a present** дари́ть (*perf* подари́ть) кому́-н пода́рок; **to present sth to sb, present sb with sth** (*prize etc*) вруча́ть (*perf* вручи́ть) что-н кому́-н; (*gift*) преподноси́ть (*perf* преподнести́) что-н кому́-н; **to present sb (to)** (*introduce*) представля́ть (*perf* предста́вить) кого́-н (+*dat*)
presentation [prɛzn'teɪʃən] *n* (*of report etc*) изложе́ние; (*appearance*) вне́шний вид; (*also* **presentation ceremony**) презента́ция
present-day *adj* сего́дняшний, ны́нешний
presenter [prɪ'zɛntəʳ] *n* (*Radio, TV*) веду́щий(-ая) *m(f) adj*; (: *of news*) ди́ктор
presently *adv* вско́ре; (*now*) в настоя́щее вре́мя
preservation [prɛzə'veɪʃən] *n* (*act*: *of building, democracy*) сохране́ние
preservative [prɪ'zə:vətɪv] *n* (*for food*) консерва́нт; (*for wood*) пропи́точный соста́в
preserve [prɪ'zə:v] *vt* сохраня́ть (*perf* сохрани́ть); (*food*)

P

консерви́ровать (*perf* законсерви́ровать) ▷ *n* (*usu pl*: *jam*) варе́нье
preside [prɪ'zaɪd] *vi*: **to preside (over)** председа́тельствовать (*impf*) (на +*prp*)
president ['prɛzɪdənt] *n* (*Pol, Comm*) президе́нт; **presidential** [prɛzɪ'dɛnʃl] *adj* президе́нтский; **presidential candidate** кандида́т в президе́нты; **presidential adviser** сове́тник президе́нта
press [prɛs] *n* (*also* **printing press**) печа́тный стано́к ▷ *vt* (*hold together*) прижима́ть (*perf* прижа́ть); (*push*) нажима́ть (*perf* нажа́ть); (*iron*) гла́дить (*perf* погла́дить); (*pressurize*: *person*) вынужда́ть (*perf* вы́нудить); **the press** (*newspapers, journalists*) пре́сса; **to press sth on sb** (*insist*) навя́зывать (*perf* навяза́ть) что-н кому́-н; **to press sb to do** *or* **into doing** вынужда́ть (*perf* вы́нудить) кого́-н +*infin*; **to press for** (*change etc*) наста́ивать (*perf* настоя́ть) на +*prp*; **press ahead** *vi*: **press ahead with** продолжа́ть (*perf* продо́лжить); **press on** *vi* продолжа́ть (*impf*); **press conference** *n* пресс-конфере́нция; **pressing** *adj* (*urgent*) неотло́жный
pressure ['prɛʃəʳ] *n* давле́ние; (*stress*) напряже́ние; **to put pressure on sb (to do)** ока́зывать (*perf* оказа́ть) давле́ние *or* нажи́м на кого́-н (+*infin*); **pressure group** *n* инициати́вная гру́ппа
prestige [prɛs'tiːʒ] *n* прести́ж
prestigious [prɛs'tɪdʒəs] *adj* прести́жный
presumably [prɪ'zjuːməblɪ] *adv* на́до полага́ть
presume [prɪ'zjuːm] *vt*: **to presume (that)** (*suppose*) предполага́ть (*perf* предположи́ть), что
pretence [prɪ'tɛns] (*US* **pretense**) *n* притво́рство; **under false pretences** под ло́жным предло́гом
pretend [prɪ'tɛnd] *vi*: **to pretend that** притворя́ться (*perf* притвори́ться), что; **he pretended to help** он сде́лал вид, что помога́ет; **he pretended to be asleep** он притвори́лся, что спит
pretense [prɪ'tɛns] *n* (*US*) = **pretence**
pretentious [prɪ'tɛnʃəs] *adj* претенцио́зный
pretext ['priːtɛkst] *n* предло́г
pretty ['prɪtɪ] *adj* (*person*) хоро́шенький; (*thing*) краси́вый ▷ *adv* (*quite*) дово́льно
prevail [prɪ'veɪl] *vi* (*be current*) преоблада́ть (*impf*), превали́ровать (*impf*); (*gain influence*) оде́рживать (*perf* одержа́ть) верх; **prevailing** *adj* (*wind*) преоблада́ющий
prevent [prɪ'vɛnt] *vt* (*accident etc*) предотвраща́ть (*perf* предотврати́ть), предупрежда́ть (*perf* предупреди́ть); **to prevent sb from doing** меша́ть (*perf* помеша́ть) кому́-н +*infin*; **prevention** [prɪ'vɛnʃən] *n* предотвраще́ние, предупрежде́ние; **preventive** *adj* (*Pol*: *measures*) превенти́вный; (*medicine*) профилакти́ческий
preview ['priːvjuː] *n* (*of film*) (закры́тый) просмо́тр; (*of exhibition*) верниса́ж
previous ['priːvɪəs] *adj* предыду́щий; **previous to** до +*gen*; **previously** *adv* (*before*) ра́нее; (*in the past*) пре́жде
prey [preɪ] *n* добы́ча

price [praɪs] *n* цена́ ▷ *vt* оце́нивать (*perf* оцени́ть); **priceless** *adj* (*diamond, painting etc*) бесце́нный; **price list** *n* прейскура́нт

prick [prɪk] *n* (*pain*) уко́л ▷ *vt* (*make hole in*) прока́лывать (*perf* проколо́ть); (*finger*) коло́ть (*perf* уколо́ть); **to prick up one's ears** навостри́ть (*perf*) у́ши

prickly ['prɪklɪ] *adj* колю́чий

pride [praɪd] *n* го́рдость *f*; (*pej*: *arrogance*) горды́ня ▷ *vt*: **to pride o.s. on** горди́ться (*impf*) *+instr*

priest [pri:st] *n* свяще́нник

primarily ['praɪmərɪlɪ] *adv* в пе́рвую о́чередь

primary ['praɪmərɪ] *adj* (*task*) первостепе́нный, первоочередно́й ▷ *n* (*US*: *Pol*) предвари́тельные вы́боры *mpl*; **primary school** *n* (*Brit*) нача́льная шко́ла

prime [praɪm] *adj* (*most important*) гла́вный, основно́й; (*best quality*) первосо́ртный; (*example*) я́ркий ▷ *n* расцве́т ▷ *vt* (*fig*: *person*) подгота́вливать (*perf* подгото́вить); **Prime Minister** *n* премье́р-мини́стр

primitive ['prɪmɪtɪv] *adj* (*early*) первобы́тный; (*unsophisticated*) примити́вный

primrose ['prɪmrəuz] *n* первоцве́т

prince [prɪns] *n* принц; (*Russian*) князь *m*; **princess** [prɪn'sɛs] *n* принце́сса; (*Russian*: *wife*) княги́ня; (: *daughter*) княжна́

principal ['prɪnsɪpl] *adj* гла́вный, основно́й ▷ *n* (*of school, college*) дире́ктор; (*of university*) ре́ктор

principle ['prɪnsɪpl] *n* при́нцип; (*scientific law*) зако́н; **in principle** в при́нципе; **on principle** из при́нципа

print [prɪnt] *n* (*Typ*) шрифт; (*Art*) эста́мп, гравю́ра; (*Phot, fingerprint*) отпеча́ток; (*footprint*) след ▷ *vt* (*book etc*) печа́тать (*perf* напеча́тать); (*cloth*) набива́ть (*perf* наби́ть); (*write in capitals*) писа́ть (*perf* написа́ть) печа́тными бу́квами; **this book is out of print** э́та кни́га бо́льше не издаётся; **printer** *n* (*machine*) при́нтер; (*firm*: *also* **printer's**) типогра́фия

prior ['praɪə^r] *adj* (*previous*) пре́жний; (*more important*) главне́йший; **to have prior knowledge of sth** знать (*impf*) о чём-н зара́нее; **prior to** до́ *+gen*

priority [praɪ'ɔrɪtɪ] *n* (*most urgent task*) первоочередна́я зада́ча; (*most important thing, task*) приорите́т; **to have priority (over)** име́ть (*impf*) преиму́щество (пе́ред *+instr*)

prison ['prɪzn] *n* тюрьма́ ▷ *cpd* тюре́мный; **prisoner** *n* (*in prison*) заключённый(-ая) *m(f) adj*; (*captured person*) пле́нный(-ая) *m(f) adj*; **prisoner of war** *n* военнопле́нный *m adj*

privacy ['prɪvəsɪ] *n* уедине́ние

private ['praɪvɪt] *adj* (*property, industry*) ча́стный; (*discussion, club*) закры́тый; (*belongings, life*) ли́чный; (*thoughts, plans*) скры́тый; (*secluded*) уединённый; (*secretive, reserved*) за́мкнутый; (*confidential*) конфиденциа́льный; **"private"** (*on door*) "посторо́нним вход воспрещён"; **in private** конфиденциа́льно

privatize ['praɪvɪtaɪz] *vt* приватизи́ровать (*impf/perf*)

privilege ['prɪvɪlɪdʒ] *n* привиле́гия

P

prize [praɪz] *n* приз ▷ *adj* первокла́ссный ▷ *vt* (высоко́) цени́ть (*impf*)
pro [prəu] *prep* за +*acc* ▷ *n*: **the pros and cons** за и про́тив
probability [prɔbə'bɪlɪtɪ] *n*: **probability of/that** вероя́тность *f* +*gen*/того́, что; **in all probability** по всей вероя́тности
probable ['prɔbəbl] *adj* вероя́тный
probably ['prɔbəblɪ] *adv* вероя́тно
probation [prə'beɪʃən] *n* (*Law*) усло́вное осужде́ние; (*employee*) испыта́тельный срок
probe [prəub] *vt* (*investigate*) рассле́довать (*impf/perf*); (*poke*) прощу́пывать (*perf* прощу́пать)
problem ['prɔbləm] *n* пробле́ма
procedure [prə'si:dʒə^r] *n* процеду́ра
proceed [prə'si:d] *vi* (*activity, event, process*) продолжа́ться (*perf* продо́лжиться); (*person*) продвига́ться (*perf* продви́нуться); **to proceed with** (*continue*) продолжа́ть (*perf* продо́лжить); **to proceed to do** продолжа́ть (*perf* продо́лжить) +*infin*; **proceedings** *npl* (*events*) мероприя́тия *ntpl*; (*Law*) суде́бное разбира́тельство *ntsg*; **proceeds** ['prəusi:dz] *npl* поступле́ния *ntpl*
process ['prəusɛs] *n* проце́сс ▷ *vt* обраба́тывать (*perf* обрабо́тать); **in the process** в проце́ссе
procession [prə'sɛʃən] *n* проце́ссия
proclaim [prə'kleɪm] *vt* провозглаша́ть (*perf* провозгласи́ть)
prod [prɔd] *vt* (*push*) ты́кать (*perf* ткнуть) ▷ *n* тычо́к
produce [*vb* prə'dju:s, *n* 'prɔdju:s] *vt* производи́ть (*perf* произвести́); (*Chem*) выраба́тывать (*perf* вы́работать); (*evidence, argument*) представля́ть (*perf* предста́вить); (*bring or take out*) предъявля́ть (*perf* предъяви́ть); (*play, film*) ста́вить (*perf* поста́вить) ▷ *n* (*Agr*) (сельскохозя́йственная) проду́кция; **producer** [prə'du:sə^r] *n* (*of film, play*) режиссёр-постано́вщик, продю́сер
product ['prɔdʌkt] *n* (*thing*) изде́лие; (*food, result*) проду́кт
production [prə'dʌkʃən] *n* (*process*) произво́дство; (*amount produced*) проду́кция; (*Theat*) постано́вка
productive [prə'dʌktɪv] *adj* производи́тельный, продукти́вный
productivity [prɔdʌk'tɪvɪtɪ] *n* производи́тельность *f*, продукти́вность *f*
profession [prə'fɛʃən] *n* профе́ссия; **professional** *adj* профессиона́льный
professor [prə'fɛsə^r] *n* (*Brit*) профе́ссор; (*US*) преподава́тель(ница) *m(f)*
profile ['prəufaɪl] *n* (*of face, also Comput*) про́филь *m*; (*article*) о́черк; **profile picture** *n* фотогра́фия про́филя, фо́то про́филя (*inf*)
profit ['prɔfɪt] *n* при́быль *f*, дохо́д ▷ *vi*: **to profit by** *or* **from** (*fig*) извлека́ть (*perf* извле́чь) вы́году из +*gen*; **profitable** *adj* при́быльный; (*fig*) вы́годный
profound [prə'faund] *adj* глубо́кий
program(me) ['prəugræm] *n* програ́мма ▷ *vt* программи́ровать (*perf* запрограмми́ровать); **programmer** *n* программи́ст(ка)

progress [*n* 'prəugrɛs, *vb* prə'grɛs] *n* (*advances, changes*) прогрéсс; (*development*) развйтие ▷ *vi* прогрессйровать (*impf*); (*continue*) продолжáться (*perf* продóлжиться); **the match is in progress** матч идёт; **progressive** [prə'grɛsɪv] *adj* прогрессйвный; (*gradual*) постепéнный

prohibit [prə'hɪbɪt] *vt* запрещáть (*perf* запретйть)

project [*n* 'prɔdʒɛkt, *vb* prə'dʒɛkt] *n* проéкт ▷ *vt* (*plan, estimate*) проектйровать (*perf* запроектйровать) ▷ *vi* (*jut out*) выступáть (*perf* вы́ступить); **projection** [prə'dʒɛkʃən] *n* (*estimate*) перспектйвная оцéнка; **projector** [prə'dʒɛktə[r]] *n* (*Cinema*) кинопроéктор; (*also* **slide projector**) проéктор

prolific [prə'lɪfɪk] *adj* плодовйтый

prolong [prə'lɔŋ] *vt* продлевáть (*perf* продлйть)

promenade [prɔmə'nɑ:d] *n* променáд

prominent ['prɔmɪnənt] *adj* выдаю́щийся

promiscuous [prə'mɪskjuəs] *adj* разврáтный

promise ['prɔmɪs] *n* (*vow*) обещáние; (*talent*) потенциáл; (*hope*) надéжда ▷ *vi* (*vow*) давáть (*perf* дать) обещáние ▷ *vt*: **to promise sb sth, promise sth to sb** обещáть (*perf* пообещáть) что-н комý-н; **to promise (sb) to do/that** обещáть (*perf* пообещáть) (комý-н) *+infin*/, что; **to promise well** подавáть (*impf*) большие надéжды; **promising** ['prɔmɪsɪŋ] *adj* многообещáющий

promote [prə'məut] *vt* (*employee*) повышáть (*perf* повы́сить) (в дóлжности); (*product, pop star*) реклами́ровать (*impf/perf*); (*ideas*) поддéрживать (*perf* поддержáть); **promotion** [prə'məuʃən] *n* (*at work*) повышéние (в дóлжности); (*of product, event*) реклáма

prompt [prɔmpt] *adj* незамедлйтельный ▷ *vt* (*cause*) побуждáть (*perf* побудйть); (*when talking*) подскáзывать (*perf* подсказáть) ▷ *adv*: **at 8 o'clock prompt** рóвно в 8 часóв; **to prompt sb to do** побуждáть (*perf* побудйть) когó-н *+infin*; **promptly** *adv* (*immediately*) незамедлйтельно; (*exactly*) тóчно

prone [prəun] *adj*: **prone to** (*inclined to*) склóнный к *+dat*

pronoun ['prəunaun] *n* местоимéние

pronounce [prə'nauns] *vt* (*word*) произносйть (*perf* произнестй); (*declaration, verdict*) объявля́ть (*perf* объявйть); (*opinion*) выскáзывать (*perf* вы́сказать)

pronunciation [prənʌnsɪ'eɪʃən] *n* (*of word*) произношéние

proof [pru:f] *n* (*evidence*) доказáтельство ▷ *adj*: **this vodka is 70% proof** э́то семидесятигрáдусная вóдка

prop [prɔp] *n* (*support*) подпóрка ▷ *vt* (*also* **prop up**) подпирáть (*perf* подперéть); **to prop sth against** прислоня́ть (*perf* прислонйть) что-н к *+dat*; **props** *npl* (*Theat*) реквизйт *msg*

propaganda [prɔpə'gændə] *n* пропагáнда

propeller *n* пропéллер

proper ['prɔpə[r]] *adj* (*real*) настоя́щий; (*correct*) дóлжный, надлежáщий; (*socially acceptable*)

p

прили́чный; **properly** *adv* (*eat, study*) как сле́дует; (*behave*) прили́чно, до́лжным о́бразом

property ['prɔpətɪ] *n* (*possessions*) со́бственность *f*; (*building and land*) недви́жимость *f*; (*quality*) сво́йство

prophecy ['prɔfɪsɪ] *n* проро́чество

proportion [prə'pɔ:ʃən] *n* (*part*) часть *f*, до́ля; (*ratio*) пропо́рция, соотноше́ние; **proportional** *adj*: **proportional (to)** пропорциона́льный (+*dat*)

proposal [prə'pəuzl] *n* предложе́ние

propose [prə'pəuz] *vt* (*plan, toast*) предлага́ть (*perf* предложи́ть); (*motion*) выдвига́ть (*perf* вы́двинуть) ▷ *vi* (*offer marriage*): **to propose (to sb)** де́лать (*perf* сде́лать) предложе́ние (кому́-н); **to propose sth/to do** *or* **doing** предполага́ть (*impf*) что-н/+*infin*

proposition [prɔpə'zɪʃən] *n* (*statement*) утвержде́ние; (*offer*) предложе́ние

proprietor [prə'praɪətə^r] *n* владе́лец(-лица)

prose [prəuz] *n* (*not poetry*) про́за

prosecute ['prɔsɪkju:t] *vt*: **to prosecute sb** пресле́довать (*impf*) кого́-н в суде́бном поря́дке

prosecution [prɔsɪ'kju:ʃən] *n* (*Law*: *action*) суде́бное пресле́дование; (: *accusing side*) обвине́ние

prosecutor ['prɔsɪkju:tə^r] *n* обвини́тель *m*

prospect ['prɔspɛkt] *n* перспекти́ва; **prospects** *npl* (*for work etc*) перспекти́вы *fpl*; **prospective** [prə'spɛktɪv] *adj* (*future*) бу́дущий; (*potential*) возмо́жный; **prospectus** [prə'spɛktəs] *n* проспе́кт

prosper ['prɔspə^r] *vi* преуспева́ть (*perf* преуспе́ть); **prosperity** [prɔ'spɛrɪtɪ] *n* процвета́ние; **prosperous** *adj* преуспева́ющий

prostitute ['prɔstɪtju:t] *n* проститу́тка

protect [prə'tɛkt] *vt* защища́ть (*perf* защити́ть); **protection** [prə'tɛkʃən] *n* защи́та; **protective** *adj* защи́тный; (*person*) забо́тливый, бе́режный

protein ['prəuti:n] *n* бело́к, протеи́н

protest [*n* 'prəutɛst, *vb* prə'tɛst] *n* проте́ст ▷ *vi*: **to protest about/against** протестова́ть (*impf*) по по́воду +*gen*/про́тив +*gen* ▷ *vt* (*insist*): **to protest that** заявля́ть (*perf* заяви́ть), что

Protestant ['prɔtɪstənt] *n* протеста́нт(ка)

proud [praud] *adj*: **proud (of)** го́рдый (+*instr*)

prove [pru:v] *vt* дока́зывать (*perf* доказа́ть) ▷ *vi*: **to prove (to be)** оказа́ться (*impf/perf*) +*instr*; **to prove o.s.** проявля́ть (*perf* прояви́ть) себя́

proverb ['prɔvə:b] *n* посло́вица

provide [prə'vaɪd] *vt* обеспе́чивать (*perf* обеспе́чить) +*instr*; **to provide sb with sth** обеспе́чивать (*perf* обеспе́чить) кого́-н чем-н; **provide for** *vt fus* (*person*) обеспе́чивать (*perf* обеспе́чить); **provided (that)** *conj* при усло́вии, что

providing [prə'vaɪdɪŋ] *conj* = **provided (that)**

province ['prɔvɪns] *n* о́бласть *f*

provincial [prə'vɪnʃəl] *adj* провинциа́льный

provision [prəˈvɪʒən] *n* (*supplying*) обеспе́чение; (*of contract, agreement*) положе́ние; **provisions** *npl* (*food*) прови́зия *fsg*; **provisional** *adj* вре́менный
provocative [prəˈvɔkətɪv] *adj* (*remark, gesture*) провокацио́нный
provoke [prəˈvəuk] *vt* провоци́ровать (*perf* спровоци́ровать)
proximity [prɔkˈsɪmɪtɪ] *n* бли́зость *f*
proxy [ˈprɔksɪ] *n*: **by proxy** по дове́ренности
prudent [ˈpru:dnt] *adj* благоразу́мный
prune [pru:n] *n* черносли́в *m no pl* ▷ *vt* подреза́ть (*perf* подре́зать)
PS *abbr* = **postscript**
pseudonym [ˈsju:dənɪm] *n* псевдони́м
psychiatric [saɪkɪˈætrɪk] *adj* психиатри́ческий
psychiatrist [saɪˈkaɪətrɪst] *n* психиа́тр
psychic [ˈsaɪkɪk] *adj* (*person*) яснови́дящий
psychological [saɪkəˈlɔdʒɪkl] *adj* психологи́ческий
psychologist [saɪˈkɔlədʒɪst] *n* психо́лог
psychology [saɪˈkɔlədʒɪ] *n* психоло́гия
PTO *abbr* (= *please turn over*) смотри́ на оборо́те
pub [pʌb] *n* паб, пивна́я *f adj*
puberty [ˈpju:bətɪ] *n* полова́я зре́лость *f*
public [ˈpʌblɪk] *adj* обще́ственный; (*statement, action etc*) публи́чный ▷ *n*: **the public** (*everyone*) обще́ственность *f*, наро́д; **to make public** предава́ть (*perf* преда́ть) гла́сности; **in public** публи́чно
publication [pʌblɪˈkeɪʃən] *n* публика́ция, изда́ние
publicity [pʌbˈlɪsɪtɪ] *n* (*information*) рекла́ма, пабли́сити *nt ind*; (*attention*) шуми́ха
publicize [ˈpʌblɪsaɪz] *vt* предава́ть (*perf* преда́ть) гла́сности
public: **publicly** *adv* публи́чно; **public opinion** *n* обще́ственное мне́ние; **public relations** *npl* вне́шние свя́зи *fpl*, свя́зи с обще́ственностью; **public school** *n* (*Brit*) ча́стная шко́ла; (*US*) госуда́рственная шко́ла
publish [ˈpʌblɪʃ] *vt* издава́ть (*perf* изда́ть); (*Press*: *letter, article*) публикова́ть (*perf* опубликова́ть); **publisher** *n* (*company*) изда́тельство; **publishing** *n* (*profession*) изда́тельское де́ло
pudding [ˈpudɪŋ] *n* пу́динг; (*Brit*: *dessert*) сла́дкое *nt adj*; **black pudding**, *(US)* **blood pudding** кровяна́я колбаса́
puddle [ˈpʌdl] *n* лу́жа
puff [pʌf] *n* (*of wind*) дунове́ние; (*of cigarette, pipe*) затя́жка; (*of smoke*) клуб
pull [pul] *vt* тяну́ть (*perf* потяну́ть); (*trigger*) нажима́ть (*perf* нажа́ть) на *+acc*; (*curtains etc*) задёргивать (*perf* задёрнуть) ▷ *vi* (*tug*) тяну́ть (*impf*) ▷ *n*: **to give sth a pull** (*tug*) тяну́ть (*perf* потяну́ть) что-н; **to pull to pieces** разрыва́ть (*perf* разорва́ть) на ча́сти; **to pull o.s. together** брать (*perf* взять) себя́ в ру́ки; **to pull sb's leg** (*fig*) разы́грывать (*perf* разыгра́ть) кого́-н; **pull down** *vt* (*building*) сноси́ть (*perf* снести́); **pull in** *vt* (*crowds, people*) привлека́ть (*perf* привле́чь); **pull out** *vt* (*extract*) выта́скивать (*perf*

вы́тащить) ▷ *vi*: **to pull out (from)** (*Aut*: *from kerb*) отъезжа́ть (*perf* отъе́хать) (от +*gen*); **pull up** *vi* (*stop*) остана́вливаться (*perf* останови́ться) ▷ *vt* (*plant*) вырыва́ть (*perf* вы́рвать) (с ко́рнем)

pulley ['pulɪ] *n* шкив

pullover ['puləuvə^r] *n* свитер, пуло́вер

pulpit ['pulpɪt] *n* ка́федра

pulse [pʌls] *n* (*Anat*) пульс

puma ['pju:mə] *n* пу́ма

pump [pʌmp] *n* насо́с; (*also* **petrol pump**) бензоколо́нка ▷ *vt* кача́ть (*perf* накача́ть); (*extract*: *oil, water, gas*) выка́чивать (*perf* вы́качать)

pumpkin ['pʌmpkɪn] *n* ты́ква

pun [pʌn] *n* каламбу́р

punch [pʌntʃ] *n* уда́р; (*for making holes*) дыроко́л; (*drink*) пунш ▷ *vt* (*hit*): **to punch sb/sth** ударя́ть (*perf* уда́рить) кого́-н/что-н кулако́м

punctual ['pʌŋktjuəl] *adj* пунктуа́льный

punctuation [pʌŋktju'eɪʃən] *n* пунктуа́ция

puncture ['pʌŋktʃə^r] *n* (*Aut*) проко́л ▷ *vt* прока́лывать (*perf* проколо́ть)

punish ['pʌnɪʃ] *vt*: **to punish sb (for sth)** нака́зывать (*perf* наказа́ть) кого́-н (за что-н); **punishment** *n* наказа́ние

pupil ['pju:pl] *n* (*Scol*) учени́к(-и́ца); (*of eye*) зрачо́к

puppet ['pʌpɪt] *n* марионе́тка

puppy ['pʌpɪ] *n* (*young dog*) щено́к

purchase ['pə:tʃɪs] *n* поку́пка ▷ *vt* покупа́ть (*perf* купи́ть)

pure [pjuə^r] *adj* чи́стый; **purely** *adv* чи́сто; **purify** ['pjuərɪfaɪ] *vt* очища́ть (*perf* очи́стить); **purity** ['pjuərɪtɪ] *n* чистота́

purple ['pə:pl] *adj* фиоле́товый

purpose ['pə:pəs] *n* цель *f*; **on purpose** наме́ренно

purr [pə:^r] *vi* мурлы́кать (*impf*)

purse [pə:s] *n* (*Brit*) кошелёк; (*US*: *handbag*) су́мка ▷ *vt*: **to purse one's lips** поджима́ть (*perf* поджа́ть) гу́бы

pursue [pə'sju:] *vt* пресле́довать (*impf*); (*fig*: *policy*) проводи́ть (*impf*); (: *interest*) проявля́ть (*impf*)

pursuit [pə'sju:t] *n* (*of person, thing*) пресле́дование; (*of happiness, wealth etc*) по́иски *mpl*; (*pastime*) заня́тие

push [puʃ] *n* (*shove*) толчо́к ▷ *vt* (*press*) нажима́ть (*perf* нажа́ть); (*shove*) толка́ть (*perf* толкну́ть); (*promote*) прота́лкивать (*perf* протолкну́ть) ▷ *vi* (*press*) нажима́ть (*perf* нажа́ть); (*shove*) толка́ться (*impf*); (*fig*): **to push for** тре́бовать (*perf* потре́бовать) +*acc* or +*gen*; **push through** *vt* (*measure, scheme*) прота́лкивать (*perf* протолкну́ть); **push up** *vt* (*prices*) повыша́ть (*perf* повы́сить)

put [put] (*pt, pp* **put**) *vt* ста́вить (*perf* поста́вить); (*thing*: *horizontally*) класть (*perf* положи́ть); (*person*: *in institution*) помеща́ть (*perf* помести́ть); (: *in prison*) сажа́ть (*perf* посади́ть); (*idea, feeling*) выража́ть (*perf* вы́разить); (*case, view*) излага́ть (*perf* изложи́ть); **I put it to you that …** я говорю́ Вам, что …; **put across** *vt* (*ideas etc*) объясня́ть (*perf* объясни́ть); **put away** *vt* (*store*) убира́ть (*perf* убра́ть); **put back** *vt* (*replace*) класть (*perf* положи́ть) на ме́сто; (*postpone*) откла́дывать (*perf* отложи́ть);

(*delay*) задéрживать (*perf* задержáть); **put by** *vt* отклáдывать (*perf* отложи́ть); **put down** *vt* (*place*) стáвить (*perf* постáвить); (: *horizontally*) класть (*perf* положи́ть); (*note down*) запи́сывать (*perf* записáть); (*suppress, humiliate*) подавля́ть (*perf* подави́ть); (*animal*: *kill*) умерщвля́ть (*perf* умертви́ть); **to put sth down to** (*attribute*) объясня́ть (*perf* объясни́ть) что-н +*instr*; **put forward** *vt* (*ideas*) выдвигáть (*perf* вы́двинуть); **put in** *vt* (*application, complaint*) подавáть (*perf* подáть); (*time, effort*) вклáдывать (*perf* вложи́ть); **put off** *vt* (*delay*) отклáдывать (*perf* отложи́ть); (*discourage*) оттáлкивать (*perf* оттолкну́ть); (*switch off*) выключáть (*perf* вы́ключить); **put on** *vt* (*clothes*) надевáть (*perf* надéть); (*make-up, ointment etc*) наклáдывать (*perf* наложи́ть); (*light etc*) включáть (*perf* включи́ть); (*kettle, record, dinner*) стáвить (*perf* постáвить); (*assume*: *look*) напускáть (*perf* напусти́ть) на себя́; (*behaviour*) принимáть (*perf* приня́ть); **to put on weight** поправля́ться (*perf* попрáвиться); **put out** *vt* (*fire*) туши́ть (*perf* потуши́ть); (*candle, cigarette, light*) гаси́ть (*perf* погаси́ть); (*rubbish*) выноси́ть (*perf* вы́нести); (*one's hand*) вытя́гивать (*perf* вы́тянуть); **put through** *vt* (*person, call*) соединя́ть (*perf* соедини́ть); (*plan, agreement*) выполня́ть (*perf* вы́полнить); **put up** *vt* (*building, tent*) стáвить (*perf* постáвить); (*umbrella*) раскрывáть (*perf* раскры́ть); (*hood*) надевáть (*perf* надéть); (*poster, sign*) вывéшивать (*perf* вы́весить); (*price, cost*) поднимáть (*perf* подня́ть); (*guest*) помещáть (*perf* помести́ть); **put up with** *vt fus* мири́ться (*impf*) с +*instr*

puzzle ['pʌzl] *n* (*game, toy*) головолóмка

puzzling ['pʌzlɪŋ] *adj* запу́танный

pyjamas [pɪ'dʒɑːməz] (*US* **pajamas**) *npl*: **(a pair of) pyjamas** пижáма *fsg*

pylon ['paɪlən] *n* пилóн, опóра

pyramid ['pɪrəmɪd] *n* (*Geom*) пирами́да

p

q

quadruple [kwɔ'dru:pl] *vt* увели́чивать (*perf* увели́чить) в четы́ре ра́за ▷ *vi* увели́чиваться (*perf* увели́читься) в четы́ре ра́за
quaint [kweɪnt] *adj* чудно́й
quake [kweɪk] *vi* трепета́ть (*impf*)
qualification [kwɔlɪfɪ'keɪʃən] *n* (*usu pl*: *academic, vocational*) квалифика́ция; (*skill, quality*) ка́чество; **what are your qualifications?** кака́я у Вас квалифика́ция?
qualified ['kwɔlɪfaɪd] *adj* (*trained*) квалифици́рованный; **I'm not qualified to judge that** я не компете́нтен суди́ть об э́том
qualify ['kwɔlɪfaɪ] *vt* (*modify*: *make more specific*) уточня́ть (*perf* уточни́ть); (: *express reservation*) огова́ривать (*perf* оговори́ть) ▷ *vi*: **to qualify as an engineer** получа́ть (*perf* получи́ть) квалифика́цию инжене́ра; **to qualify (for)** (*benefit etc*) име́ть (*impf*) пра́во (на *+acc*); (*in competition*) выходи́ть (*perf* вы́йти) в *+acc*
quality ['kwɔlɪtɪ] *n* ка́чество; (*property*: *of wood, stone*) сво́йство
quantity ['kwɔntɪtɪ] *n* коли́чество
quarantine ['kwɔrnti:n] *n* каранти́н
quarrel ['kwɔrl] *n* ссо́ра ▷ *vi*: **to quarrel (with)** ссо́риться (*perf* поссо́риться) (с *+instr*)
quarry ['kwɔrɪ] *n* карье́р; (*for stone*) каменоло́мня
quarter ['kwɔ:tə^r] *n* че́тверть *f*; (*of year, town*) кварта́л; (*US*: *coin*) два́дцать пять це́нтов ▷ *vt* дели́ть (*perf* раздели́ть) на четы́ре ча́сти; **quarters** *npl* (*for living*) помеще́ние *ntsg*; (: *Mil*) каза́рмы *fpl*; **a quarter of an hour** че́тверть *f* ча́са; **quarterly** *adj* (*meeting*) (еже)кварта́льный; (*payment*) (по)кварта́льный ▷ *adv* (*see adj*) ежекварта́льно; покварта́льно
quartz [kwɔ:ts] *n* кварц
quay [ki:] *n* (*also* **quayside**) при́стань *f*
queasy ['kwi:zɪ] *adj*: **I feel a bit queasy** меня́ немно́го мути́т
queen [kwi:n] *n* короле́ва; (*Cards*) да́ма; (*Chess*) ферзь *m*
queer [kwɪə^r] *adj* (*odd*) стра́нный
quench [kwɛntʃ] *vt*: **to quench one's thirst** утоля́ть (*perf* утоли́ть) жа́жду
query ['kwɪərɪ] *n* вопро́с ▷ *vt* подверга́ть (*perf* подве́ргнуть) сомне́нию
quest [kwɛst] *n* по́иск
question ['kwɛstʃən] *n* вопро́с;

(*doubt*) сомнение ▷ *vt* (*interrogate*) допрашивать (*perf* допросить); (*doubt*) усомниться (*perf*) в +*prp*; **beyond question** бесспорно; **that's out of the question** об этом не может быть и речи; **questionable** *adj* сомнительный; **question mark** *n* вопросительный знак; **questionnaire** [kwɛstʃə'nɛəʳ] *n* анкета

queue [kju:] (*Brit*) *n* очередь *f* ▷ *vi* (*also* **queue up**) стоять (*impf*) в очереди

quick [kwɪk] *adj* быстрый; (*clever*: *person*) сообразительный; (: *mind*) живой; (*brief*) краткий; **be quick!** быстро!; **quickly** *adv* быстро

quid [kwɪd] *n inv* (*Brit*: *inf*) фунт (*стерлингов*)

quiet ['kwaɪət] *adj* тихий; (*peaceful, not busy*) спокойный; (*without fuss*) сдержанный ▷ *n* (*silence*) тишина; (*peace*) покой; **quietly** *adv* тихо; (*calmly*) спокойно

quilt [kwɪlt] *n* (*also* **continental quilt**) стёганое одеяло

quit [kwɪt] (*pt, pp* **quit** *or* **quitted**) *vt* бросать (*perf* бросить) ▷ *vi* (*give up*) сдаваться (*perf* сдаться); (*resign*) увольняться (*perf* уволиться)

quite [kwaɪt] *adv* (*rather*) довольно; (*entirely*) совершенно; (*almost*): **the flat's not quite big enough** квартира недостаточно большая; **quite a few** довольно много; **quite (so)!** верно!, (вот) именно!

quits [kwɪts] *adj*: **let's call it quits** будем квиты

quiver ['kwɪvəʳ] *vi* трепетать (*impf*)

quiz [kwɪz] *n* (*game*) викторина ▷ *vt* расспрашивать (*perf* расспросить)

quota ['kwəutə] *n* квота

quotation [kwəu'teɪʃən] *n* цитата; (*estimate*) цена (продавца)

quote [kwəut] *n* цитата; (*estimate*) цена ▷ *vt* цитировать (*perf* процитировать); (*figure, example*) приводить (*perf* привести); (*price*) назначать (*perf* назначить); **quotes** *npl* (*quotation marks*) кавычки *fpl*

rabbi ['ræbaɪ] *n* равви́н
rabbit ['ræbɪt] *n* (*male*) кро́лик; (*female*) крольчи́ха
rabies ['reɪbi:z] *n* бе́шенство, водобоя́знь *f*
RAC *n abbr* (*Brit*) (= *Royal Automobile Club*) *Короле́вская автомоби́льная ассоциа́ция*
race [reɪs] *n* (*species*) ра́са; (*competition*) го́нки *fpl*; (: *running*) забе́г; (: *swimming*) заплы́в; (: *horse race*) ска́чки *fpl*; (*for power, control*) борьба́ ▷ *vt* (*horse*) гнать (*impf*) ▷ *vi* (*compete*) принима́ть (*perf* приня́ть) уча́стие в соревнова́нии; (*hurry*) мча́ться (*impf*); (*pulse*) учаща́ться (*perf* участи́ться); **racecourse** *n* ипподро́м; **racehorse** *n* скакова́я ло́шадь *f*
racial ['reɪʃl] *adj* ра́совый
racing ['reɪsɪŋ] *n* (*horse racing*) ска́чки *fpl*; (*motor racing*) го́нки *fpl*
racism ['reɪsɪzəm] *n* раси́зм
racist ['reɪsɪst] *adj* раси́стский ▷ *n* раси́ст(ка)
rack [ræk] *n* (*shelf*) по́лка; (*also* **luggage rack**) бага́жная по́лка; (*also* **roof rack**) бага́жник (*на кры́ше автомоби́ля*); (*for dishes*) суши́лка для посу́ды ▷ *vt*: **she was racked by pain** её терза́ла боль; **to rack one's brains** лома́ть (*impf*) го́лову
racket ['rækɪt] *n* (*Sport*) раке́тка; (*noise*) гвалт; (*con*) жу́льничество; (*extortion*) ре́кет
radar ['reɪdɑ:ʳ] *n* рада́р
radiation [reɪdɪ'eɪʃən] *n* (*radioactive*) радиа́ция, радиоакти́вное излуче́ние; (*of heat, light*) излуче́ние
radiator ['reɪdɪeɪtəʳ] *n* радиа́тор, батаре́я; (*Aut*) радиа́тор
radical ['rædɪkl] *adj* радика́льный
radio ['reɪdɪəu] *n* (*broadcasting*) ра́дио *nt ind*; (*for transmitting and receiving*) радиопереда́тчик ▷ *vt* (*person*) свя́зываться (*perf* связа́ться) по ра́дио с +*instr*; **on the radio** по ра́дио; **radioactive** *adj* радиоакти́вный; **radio station** *n* радиоста́нция
radish ['rædɪʃ] *n* реди́ска; **radishes** реди́с *msg*
RAF *n abbr* (*Brit*) (= *Royal Air Force*) ≈ ВВС (= *Вое́нно-возду́шные си́лы Великобрита́нии*)
raffle ['ræfl] *n* (вещева́я) лотере́я
raft [rɑ:ft] *n* плот
rag [ræg] *n* тря́пка; (*pej*: *newspaper*) газетёнка; **rags** *npl* (*clothes*) лохмо́тья *pl*
rage [reɪdʒ] *n* (*fury*) бе́шенство, я́рость *f* ▷ *vi* (*person*)

свирéпствовать (*impf*); (*storm, debate*) бушевáть (*impf*); **it's all the rage** (*in fashion*) все помешáлись на э́том

ragged ['rægɪd] *adj* (*edge*) зазу́бренный; (*clothes*) потрёпанный

raid [reɪd] *n* (*Mil*) рейд; (*criminal*) налёт; (*by police*) облáва, рейд ▷ *vt* (*see n*) совершáть (*perf* соверши́ть) рейд на *+acc*; совершáть (*perf* соверши́ть) налёт на *+acc*

rail [reɪl] *n* (*on stairs, bridge etc*) пери́ла *pl*; **rails** *npl* (*Rail*) рéльсы *mpl*; **by rail** пóездом; **railing(s)** *n(pl)* (*iron fence*) решётка *fsg*; **railroad** *n* (*US*) = **railway**; **railway** *n* (*Brit*) желéзная дорóга ▷ *cpd* железнодорóжный; **railway line** *n* (*Brit*) железнодорóжная ли́ния; **railway station** *n* (*Brit*: *large*) железнодорóжный вокзáл; (: *small*) железнодорóжная стáнция

rain [reɪn] *n* дождь *m* ▷ *vi*: **it's raining** идёт дождь; **in the rain** под дождём, в дождь; **rainbow** *n* рáдуга; **raincoat** *n* плащ; **rainfall** *n* (*measurement*) у́ровень *m* осáдков; **rainy** *adj* (*day*) дождли́вый

raise [reɪz] *n* (*esp US*) повышéние ▷ *vt* (*lift, produce*) поднимáть (*perf* поднять́); (*increase, improve*) повышáть (*perf* повы́сить); (*doubts*: *subj*: *person*) выскáзывать (*perf* вы́сказать); (: *results*) вызывáть (*perf* вы́звать); (*rear*: *family*) воспи́тывать (*perf* воспитáть); (*get together*: *army, funds*) собирáть (*perf* собрáть); (: *loan*) изы́скивать (*perf* изыскáть); **to raise one's voice** повышáть (*perf* повы́сить) гóлос

raisin ['reɪzn] *n* изю́минка; **raisins** *npl* изю́м *m no pl*

rake [reɪk] *n* (*tool*) грáбли *pl* ▷ *vt* (*garden*) разрáвнивать (*perf* разровня́ть) (грáблями); (*leaves, hay*) сгребáть (*perf* сгрести́)

rally ['rælɪ] *n* (*Pol etc*) манифестáция; (*Aut*) (авто)рáлли *nt ind*; (*Tennis*) рáлли *nt ind* ▷ *vt* (*supporters*) сплáчивать (*perf* сплоти́ть) ▷ *vi* (*supporters*) сплáчиваться (*perf* сплоти́ться)

ram [ræm] *n* барáн ▷ *vt* (*crash into*) тарáнить (*perf* протарáнить); (*push*: *bolt*) задвигáть (*perf* задви́нуть); (: *fist*) дви́нуть (*perf*) *+instr*

RAM *n abbr* (*Comput*) (= *random access memory*) ЗУПВ (= *запоминáющее устрóйство с произвóльной вы́боркой*)

ramble ['ræmbl] *vi* (*walk*) броди́ть (*impf*); (*talk*: *also* **ramble on**) зану́дствовать (*impf*)

rambling ['ræmblɪŋ] *adj* (*speech*) несвя́зный

ramp [ræmp] *n* скат, уклóн; **on ramp** (*US*: *Aut*) въезд на автострáду; **off ramp** (*US*: *Aut*) съезд с автострáды

rampage [ræm'peɪdʒ] *n*: **to be on the rampage** бу́йствовать (*impf*)

ran [ræn] *pt of* **run**

ranch [rɑːntʃ] *n* рáнчо *nt ind*

random ['rændəm] *adj* случáйный ▷ *n*: **at random** наугáд

rang [ræŋ] *pt of* **ring**

range [reɪndʒ] *n* (*series*: *of proposals*) ряд; (: *of products*) ассортимéнт *m no pl*; (: *of colours*) гáмма; (*of mountains*) цепь *f*; (*of missile*) дáльность *f*, рáдиус дéйствия; (*of voice*) диапазóн;

r

(*Mil*: *also* **shooting range**) стрéльбище ▷ *vt* (*place in a line*) выстрáивать (*perf* вы́строить) ▷ *vi*: **to range over** (*extend*) простирáться (*impf*); **to range from ... to ...** колебáться (*impf*) от +*gen* ... до +*gen* ...

ranger [ˈreɪndʒəʳ] *n* (*in forest*) лесни́к; (*in park*) смотри́тель(ница) *m(f)*

rank [ræŋk] *n* (*row*) ряд; (*Mil*) шерéнга; (*status*) чин, ранг; (*Brit*: *also* **taxi rank**) стоя́нка такси́ ▷ *vi*: **to rank among** чи́слиться (*impf*) среди́ +*gen* ▷ *vt*: **I rank him sixth** я стáвлю егó на шестóе мéсто; **the rank and file** (*fig*) рядовы́е чле́ны *mpl*

ransom [ˈrænsəm] *n* вы́куп; **to hold to ransom** (*fig*) держáть (*impf*) в залóжниках

rant [rænt] *vi*: **to rant and rave** рвать (*impf*) и метáть (*impf*)

rap [ræp] *vi*: **to rap on a door/table** стучáть (*perf* постучáть) в дверь/по столу́

rape [reɪp] *n* изнаси́лование ▷ *vt* наси́ловать (*perf* изнаси́ловать)

rapid [ˈræpɪd] *adj* стреми́тельный; **rapidly** *adv* стреми́тельно

rapist [ˈreɪpɪst] *n* наси́льник

rapport [ræˈpɔːʳ] *n* взаимопонимáние

rare [rɛəʳ] *adj* рéдкий; (*steak*) кровáвый; **rarely** *adv* рéдко, нечáсто

rash [ræʃ] *adj* опромéтчивый ▷ *n* (*Med*) сыпь *f no pl*

raspberry [ˈrɑːzbərɪ] *n* мали́на *f no pl*

rat [ræt] *n* (*also fig*) кры́са

rate [reɪt] *n* (*speed*) скóрость *f*; (: *of change, inflation*) темп; (*of interest*) стáвка; (*ratio*) у́ровень *m*; (*price*: *at hotel etc*) расцéнка ▷ *vt* (*value*) оцéнивать (*perf* оцени́ть); (*estimate*) расцéнивать (*perf* расцени́ть); **rates** *npl* (*Brit*: *property tax*) налóг *msg* на недви́жимость; **to rate sb as** считáть (*impf*) когó-н +*instr*; **to rate sth as** расцéнивать (*perf* расцени́ть) что-н как

rather [ˈrɑːðəʳ] *adv* (*quite, somewhat*) довóльно; (*to some extent*) нéсколько; (*more accurately*): **or rather** вернéе сказáть; **it's rather expensive** (*quite*) э́то довóльно дóрого; **there's rather a lot** довóльно мнóго; **I would rather go** я, пожáлуй, пойду́; **I'd rather not leave** я бы не хотéл уходи́ть; **rather than** (+*n*) а не +*nom*, вмéсто +*gen*; **rather than go to the park, I went to the cinema** вмéсто тогó чтóбы идти́ в парк, я пошёл в кинó

rating [ˈreɪtɪŋ] *n* оцéнка, рéйтинг; **ratings** *npl* (*Radio, TV*) рéйтинг *msg*

ratio [ˈreɪʃɪəu] *n* соотношéние; **in the ratio of one hundred to one** в соотношéнии сто к одномý

ration [ˈræʃən] *n* (*allowance*: *of food*) рациóн, паёк; (: *of petrol*) нóрма ▷ *vt* норми́ровать (*impf/perf*); **rations** *npl* (*Mil*) рациóн *msg*

rational [ˈræʃənl] *adj* разу́мный, рационáльный

rattle [ˈrætl] *n* дребезжáние; (*of train, car*) громыхáние; (*for baby*) погремýшка ▷ *vi* (*small objects*) дребезжáть (*impf*) ▷ *vt* (*shake noisily*) сотрясáть (*perf* сотрясти́); (*fig*: *unsettle*) нерви́ровать (*impf*); **to rattle along** (*car, bus*) прогромыхáть (*impf*); **the wind**

rattled the windows óкна дребезжáли от вéтра
rave [reɪv] *vi* (*in anger*) бесновáться (*impf*), бушевáть (*impf*); (*Med*) брéдить (*impf*); (*with enthusiasm*): **to rave about** восторгáться (*impf*) +*instr*
raven ['reɪvən] *n* вóрон
ravine [rə'vi:n] *n* ущéлье
raw [rɔ:] *adj* сырóй; (*unrefined*: *sugar*) нерафинúрованный; (*sore*) свéжий; (*inexperienced*) зелёный; (*weather, day*) промóзглый; **raw material** *n* сырьё *nt no pl*
ray [reɪ] *n* луч; (*of heat*) потóк
razor ['reɪzə^r] *n* брúтва; **safety razor** безопáсная брúтва; **electric razor** электробрúтва
Rd *abbr* = **road**
re [ri:] *prep* относúтельно +*gen*
reach [ri:tʃ] *vt* (*place, end, agreement*) достигáть (достúгнуть *or* достúчь *perf*) +*gen*; (*conclusion, decision*) приходúть (*perf* прийтú) к +*dat*; (*be able to touch*) доставáть (*perf* достáть); (*by telephone*) свя́зываться (*perf* связáться) с +*instr* ▷ *vi*: **to reach into** запускáть (*perf* запустúть) рýку в +*acc*; **out of/within reach** вне/в предéлах досягáемости; **within reach of the shops** недалекó от магазúнов; **"keep out of the reach of children"** "берéчь от детéй"; **to reach for** протя́гивать (*perf* протянýть) рýку к +*dat*; **to reach up** протя́гивать (*perf* протянýть) рýку вверх; **reach out** *vt* протя́гивать (*perf* протянýть) ▷ *vi*: **to reach out for sth** протя́гивать (*perf* протянýть) рýку за чем-н
react [ri:'ækt] *vi* (*Chem*): **to react (with)** вступáть (*perf* вступúть) в реáкцию (с +*instr*); (*Med*): **to react (to)** реагúровать (*impf*) (на +*acc*); (*respond*) реагúровать (*perf* отреагúровать) (на +*acc*); (*rebel*): **to react (against)** восставáть (*perf* восстáть) (прóтив +*gen*); **reaction** [ri:'ækʃən] *n* (*Chem*) реáкция; (*also Med, Pol*): **reaction (to/against)** реáкция (на +*acc*/прóтив +*gen*); **reactions** *npl* (*reflexes*) реáкция *fsg*; **reactor** *n* (*also* **nuclear reactor**) реáктор
read[1] [rɛd] *pt, pp of* **read**[2]
read[2] [ri:d] (*pt, pp* **read**) *vt* читáть (прочитáть *or* прочéсть *perf*); (*mood*) определя́ть (*perf* определúть); (*thermometer etc*) снимáть (*perf* снять) показáния с +*gen*; (*Scol*) изучáть (*impf*) ▷ *vi* (*person*) читáть (*impf*); (*text etc*) читáться (*impf*); **read out** *vt* зачúтывать (*perf* зачитáть); **reader** *n* (*of book, newspaper etc*) читáтель(ница) *m(f)*
readily ['rɛdɪlɪ] *adv* (*willingly*) с готóвностью; (*easily*) легкó
reading ['ri:dɪŋ] *n* (*of books etc*) чтéние; (*on thermometer etc*) показáние
ready ['rɛdɪ] *adj* готóвый ▷ *vt*: **to get sb/sth ready** готóвить (*perf* подготóвить) когó-н/что-н; **to get ready** готóвиться (*perf* приготóвиться)
real [rɪəl] *adj* настоя́щий; (*leather*) натурáльный; **in real terms** реáльно; **real estate** *n* недвúжимость *f*; **realistic** [rɪə'lɪstɪk] *adj* реалистúческий; **reality** [ri:'ælɪtɪ] *n* реáльность *f*, действúтельность *f*; **in reality** на сáмом дéле, в реáльности
realization [rɪəlaɪ'zeɪʃən] *n* (*see vt*) осознáние; осуществлéние
realize ['rɪəlaɪz] *vt* (*understand*) осознавáть (*perf* осознáть); (*fulfil*) осуществля́ть (*perf* осуществúть)

r

really [ˈrɪəlɪ] *adv* (*very*) о́чень; (*actually*): **what really happened?** что произошло́ в действи́тельности *or* на са́мом де́ле?; **really?** (*with interest*) действи́тельно?, пра́вда?; (*expressing surprise*) неуже́ли?
realm [rɛlm] *n* (*fig*: *of activity, study*) о́бласть *f*, сфе́ра
reappear [ri:əˈpɪəʳ] *vi* сно́ва появля́ться (*perf* появи́ться)
rear [rɪəʳ] *adj* за́дний ▷ *n* (*back*) за́дняя часть *f* ▷ *vt* (*cattle, family*) выра́щивать (*perf* вы́растить) ▷ *vi* (*also* **rear up**) станови́ться (*perf* стать) на дыбы́
rearrange [ri:əˈreɪndʒ] *vt* (*objects*) переставля́ть (*perf* переста́вить); (*order*) изменя́ть (*perf* измени́ть)
reason [ˈri:zn] *n* (*cause*) причи́на; (*ability to think*) ра́зум, рассу́док; (*sense*) смысл ▷ *vi*: **to reason with sb** убежда́ть (*impf*) кого́-н; **it stands to reason that …** разуме́ется, что …; **reasonable** *adj* разу́мный; (*quality*) неплохо́й; (*price*) уме́ренный; **reasonably** *adv* (*sensibly*) разу́мно; (*fairly*) дово́льно; **reasoning** *n* рассужде́ние
reassurance [ri:əˈʃuərəns] *n* (*comfort*) подде́ржка
reassure [ri:əˈʃuəʳ] *vt* (*comfort*) утеша́ть (*perf* уте́шить); **to reassure sb of** заверя́ть (*perf* заве́рить) кого́-н в +*prp*
rebate [ˈri:beɪt] *n* обра́тная вы́плата
rebel [*n* ˈrɛbl, *vb* rɪˈbɛl] *n* бунта́рь(-рка) *m(f)* ▷ *vi* восстава́ть (*perf* восста́ть); **rebellion** [rɪˈbɛljən] *n* восста́ние; **rebellious** [rɪˈbɛljəs] *adj* (*child, behaviour*) стропти́вый; (*troops*) мяте́жный
rebuild [ri:ˈbɪld] (*irreg like* **build**) *vt* (*town, building*) перестра́ивать (*perf* перестро́ить); (*fig*) восстана́вливать (*perf* восстанови́ть)
recall [rɪˈkɔ:l] *vt* вспомина́ть (*perf* вспо́мнить); (*parliament, ambassador etc*) отзыва́ть (*perf* отозва́ть)
receipt [rɪˈsi:t] *n* (*document*) квита́нция; (*act of receiving*) получе́ние; **receipts** *npl* (*Comm*) де́нежные поступле́ния *ntpl*, платежи́ *mpl*
receive [rɪˈsi:v] *vt* получа́ть (*perf* получи́ть); (*criticism*) встреча́ть (*perf* встре́тить); (*visitor, guest*) принима́ть (*perf* приня́ть); **receiver** *n* (*Tel*) (телефо́нная) тру́бка; (*Comm*) ликвида́тор (*неплатёжеспосо́бной компа́нии*)
recent [ˈri:snt] *adj* неда́вний; **recently** *adv* неда́вно
reception [rɪˈsɛpʃən] *n* (*in hotel*) регистра́ция; (*in office, hospital*) приёмная *f adj*; (*in health centre*) регистрату́ра; (*party, also Radio, TV*) приём; **receptionist** *n* (*in hotel, hospital*) регистра́тор; (*in office*) секрета́рь *m*
recession [rɪˈsɛʃən] *n* (*Econ*) спад
recipe [ˈrɛsɪpɪ] *n* (*also fig*) реце́пт
recipient [rɪˈsɪpɪənt] *n* получа́тель *m*
recital [rɪˈsaɪtl] *n* (*concert*) со́льный конце́рт
recite [rɪˈsaɪt] *vt* (*poem*) деклами́ровать (*perf* продеклами́ровать)
reckless [ˈrɛkləs] *adj* безотве́тственный
reckon [ˈrɛkən] *vt* (*calculate*) счита́ть (посчита́ть *or* сосчита́ть *perf*); (*think*): **I reckon that …** я

считаю, что ...

reclaim [rɪ'kleɪm] *vt* (*demand back*) требовать (*perf* потребовать) обратно; (*land*: *from sea*) отвоёвывать (*perf* отвоевать)

recognition [rɛkəg'nɪʃən] *n* признание; (*of person, place*) узнавание; **he has changed beyond recognition** он изменился до неузнаваемости

recognize ['rɛkəgnaɪz] *vt* признавать (*perf* признать); (*symptom*) распознавать (*perf* распознать); **to recognize (by)** (*person, place*) узнавать (*perf* узнать) (по *+dat*)

recollection [rɛkə'lɛkʃən] *n* воспоминание, память *f*

recommend [rɛkə'mɛnd] *vt* рекомендовать (*perf* порекомендовать); **recommendation** [rɛkəmɛn'deɪʃən] *n* рекомендация

reconcile ['rɛkənsaɪl] *vt* (*people*) мирить (*perf* помирить); (*facts, beliefs*) примирять (*perf* примирить); **to reconcile o.s. to sth** смиряться (*perf* смириться) с чем-н

reconsider [ri:kən'sɪdə^{r}] *vt* пересматривать (*perf* пересмотреть)

reconstruct [ri:kən'strʌkt] *vt* перестраивать (*perf* перестроить); (*event, crime*) воспроизводить (*perf* воспроизвести), реконструировать (*impf/perf*)

record [*vb* rɪ'kɔ:d, *n, adj* 'rɛkɔ:d] *vt* (*in writing, on tape*) записывать (*perf* записать); (*register*: *temperature, speed etc*) регистрировать (*perf* зарегистрировать) ▷ *n* (*written account*) запись *f*; (*of meeting*) протокол; (*of attendance*) учёт; (*Mus*) пластинка; (*history*: *of person, company*) репутация; (*also* **criminal record**) судимость *f*; (*Sport*) рекорд ▷ *adj*: **in record time** в рекордное время; **off the record** (*speak*) неофициально; **recorder** [rɪ'kɔ:də^{r}] *n* (*Mus*) английская флейта; **recording** [rɪ'kɔ:dɪŋ] *n* запись *f*; **record player** [-'pleɪə^{r}] *n* проигрыватель *m*

recount [rɪ'kaunt] *vt* (*story*) поведать (*perf*); (*event*) поведать (*perf*) о *+prp*

recover [rɪ'kʌvə^{r}] *vt* получать (*perf* получить) обратно; (*Comm*) возмещать (*perf* возместить) ▷ *vi* (*get better*): **to recover (from)** поправляться (*perf* поправиться) (после *+gen*); **recovery** *n* (*Med*) выздоровление; (*Comm*) подъём; (*of stolen items*) возвращение; (*of lost items*) обнаружение

recreation [rɛkrɪ'eɪʃən] *n* (*leisure activities*) развлечение

recruit [rɪ'kru:t] *n* (*Mil*) новобранец, призывник ▷ *vt* (*into organization, army*) вербовать (*perf* завербовать); (*into company*) нанимать (*perf* нанять); **(new) recruit** (*in company*) новый сотрудник; (*in organization*) новый член; **recruitment** *n* (*Mil*) вербовка; (*by company*) набор (*на работу*)

rectangle ['rɛktæŋgl] *n* прямоугольник

rectangular [rɛk'tæŋgjulə^{r}] *adj* прямоугольный

rectify ['rɛktɪfaɪ] *vt* исправлять (*perf* исправить)

recur [rɪ'kə:^{r}] *vi* повторяться (*perf* повториться)

recycle [ri:'saɪkl] *vt*

r

перерабáтывать (*perf* переработать)
red [rɛd] *n* крáсный цвет; (*pej*: *Pol*) крáсный(-ая) *m(f) adj* ▷ *adj* крáсный; (*hair*) рыжий; **to be in the red** имéть (*impf*) задóлженность; **Red Cross** *n* Крáсный Крест; **redcurrant** *n* крáсная сморóдина *f no pl*
redeem [rɪ'di:m] *vt* (*situation, reputation*) спасáть (*perf* спастú); (*debt*) выплáчивать (*perf* вы́платить)
redhead ['rɛdhɛd] *n* рыжий(-ая) *m(f) adj*
reduce [rɪ'dju:s] *vt* сокращáть (*perf* сократúть); **to reduce sb to tears** доводúть (*perf* довестú) когó-н до слёз; **to reduce sb to silence** заставлять (*perf* застáвить) когó-н замолчáть; **he was reduced to stealing** он дошёл до тогó, что стал воровáть
reduction [rɪ'dʌkʃən] *n* (*in price*) скúдка; (*in numbers*) сокращéние
redundancy [rɪ'dʌndənsɪ] (*Brit*) *n* сокращéние (штáтов)
redundant [rɪ'dʌndnt] *adj* (*Brit*: *unemployed*) увóленный; (*useless*) излúшний; **he was made redundant** егó сократúли
reed [ri:d] *n* (*Bot*) тростнúк
reef [ri:f] *n* риф
reel [ri:l] *n* катýшка; (*of film, tape*) бобúна
ref [rɛf] *n abbr* (*Sport*: *inf*) = **referee**
refer [rɪ'fə:ʳ] *vt*: **to refer sb to** (*book etc*) отсылáть (*perf* отослáть) когó-н к *+dat*; (*doctor*) направлять (*perf* напрáвить) когó-н к *+dat*; **refer to** *vt fus* упоминáть (*perf* упомянýть) о *+prp*; (*relate to*) относúться (*impf*) к *+dat*; (*consult*) обращáться (*perf* обратúться) к *+dat*
referee [rɛfə'ri:] *n* (*Sport*) реферú *m ind*, судья *m*; (*Brit*: *for job*) лицó, дающее рекомендáцию ▷ *vt* судúть (*impf*)
reference ['rɛfrəns] *n* (*mention*) упоминáние; (*in book, paper*) ссы́лка; (*for job*: *letter*) рекомендáция; **with reference to** (*in letter*) ссылáясь на *+acc*
refine [rɪ'faɪn] *vt* (*sugar*) рафинúровать (*impf/perf*); (*oil*) очищáть (*perf* очúстить); (*theory, task*) совершéнствовать (*perf* усовершéнствовать); **refined** *adj* (*person, taste*) утончённый
reflect [rɪ'flɛkt] *vt* отражáть (*perf* отразúть) ▷ *vi* (*think*) раздýмывать (*impf*); **reflect on** *vt* (*discredit*) отражáться (*perf* отразúться) на *+acc*; **reflection** [rɪ'flɛkʃən] *n* отражéние; (*thought*) раздýмье; (*comment*): **reflection on** суждéние о *+prp*; **on reflection** взвéсив все обстоятельства
reflex ['ri:flɛks] *n* рефлéкс
reform [rɪ'fɔ:m] *n* (*of law, system*) рефóрма ▷ *vt* (*character*) преобразовáть (*impf/perf*); (*system*) реформúровать (*impf/perf*)
refrain [rɪ'freɪn] *n* (*of song*) припéв ▷ *vi*: **to refrain from commenting** воздéрживаться (*perf* воздержáться) от комментáриев
refresh [rɪ'frɛʃ] *vt* освежáть (*perf* освежúть); **refreshing** *adj* (*sleep*) освежáющий; (*drink*) тонизúрующий; **refreshments** *npl* закýски *fpl* и напúтки *mpl*
refrigerator [rɪ'frɪdʒəreɪtəʳ] *n* холодúльник
refuge ['rɛfju:dʒ] *n* (*shelter*) убéжище, прибéжище; **to take**

refuge in находи́ть (*perf* найти́) прибе́жище в *+prp*
refugee [rɛfju'dʒiː] *n* бе́женец(-нка)
refund [*n* 'riːfʌnd, *vb* rɪ'fʌnd] *n* возмеще́ние ▷ *vt* возмеща́ть (*perf* возмести́ть)
refurbish [riː'fəːbɪʃ] *vt* ремонти́ровать (*perf* отремонти́ровать)
refusal [rɪ'fjuːzəl] *n* отка́з
refuse[1] [rɪ'fjuːz] *vt* (*offer, gift*) отка́зываться (*perf* отказа́ться) от *+gen*; (*permission*) отка́зывать (*perf* отказа́ть) в *+prp* ▷ *vi* отка́зываться (*perf* отказа́ться); **to refuse to do** отка́зываться (*perf* отказа́ться) *+infin*
refuse[2] ['rɛfjuːs] *n* му́сор
regain [rɪ'geɪn] *vt* (*power, position*) вновь обрета́ть (*perf* обрести́)
regard [rɪ'gɑːd] *n* (*esteem*) уваже́ние ▷ *vt* (*consider*) счита́ть (*impf*); (*view, look on*): **to regard with** относи́ться (*perf* отнести́сь) с *+instr*; **to give one's regards to** передава́ть (*perf* переда́ть) покло́ны *+dat*; **as regards, with regard to** что каса́ется *+gen*, относи́тельно *+gen*; **regarding** *prep* относи́тельно *+gen*; **regardless** *adv* (*continue*) несмотря́ ни на что́; **regardless of** несмотря́ на *+acc*, не счита́ясь с *+instr*
reggae ['rɛgeɪ] *n* рэ́гги *m ind*
regiment ['rɛdʒɪmənt] *n* полк
region ['riːdʒən] *n* (*area*: *of country*) регио́н; (: *smaller*) райо́н; (*Admin, Anat*) о́бласть *f*; **in the region of** (*fig*) в райо́не *+gen*; **regional** *adj* (*organization*) областно́й, регио́нальный; (*accent*) ме́стный
register ['rɛdʒɪstə^r] *n* (*census, record*) за́пись *f*; (*Scol*) журна́л; (*also* **electoral register**) спи́сок избира́телей ▷ *vt* регистри́ровать (*perf* зарегистри́ровать); (*subj*: *meter etc*) пока́зывать (*perf* показа́ть) ▷ *vi* регистри́роваться (*perf* зарегистри́роваться); (*as student*) запи́сываться (*perf* записа́ться); (*make impression*) запечатлева́ться (*perf* запечатле́ться) в па́мяти; **registered** *adj* (*letter*) заказно́й; **Registered Trademark** *n* зарегистри́рованный това́рный знак
registrar ['rɛdʒɪstrɑː^r] *n* регистра́тор
registration [rɛdʒɪs'treɪʃən] *n* регистра́ция; (*Aut*: *also* **registration number**) (регистрацио́нный) но́мер автомоби́ля
registry office ['rɛdʒɪstrɪ-] *n* (*Brit*) ≈ ЗАГС (*отде́л за́писей гражда́нского состоя́ния*)
regret [rɪ'grɛt] *n* сожале́ние ▷ *vt* сожале́ть (*impf*) о *+prp*; (*death*) скорбе́ть (*impf*) о *+prp*; **regrettable** *adj* приско́рбный, досто́йный сожале́ния
regular ['rɛgjulə^r] *adj* регуля́рный; (*even*) ро́вный; (*symmetrical*) пра́вильный; (*usual*: *time*) обы́чный ▷ *n* (*in café, restaurant*) завсегда́тай; (*in shop*) клие́нт; **regularly** *adv* регуля́рно; (*symmetrically*: *shaped etc*) пра́вильно
regulate ['rɛgjuleɪt] *vt* регули́ровать (*perf* отрегули́ровать)
regulation [rɛgju'leɪʃən] *n* регули́рование; (*rule*) пра́вило

r

rehabilitation [ˈriːəbɪlɪˈteɪʃən] *n* (*of addict*) реабилитáция; (*of criminal*) интегрáция

rehearsal [rɪˈhəːsəl] *n* репетúция

rehearse [rɪˈhəːs] *vt* репетúровать (*perf* отрепетúровать)

reign [reɪn] *n* цáрствование ▷ *vi* (*monarch*) цáрствовать (*impf*); (*fig*) царúть (*impf*)

reimburse [riːɪmˈbəːs] *vt* возмещáть (*perf* возместúть)

rein [reɪn] *n* (*for horse*) вожжá

reincarnation [riːɪnkɑːˈneɪʃən] *n* (*belief*) переселéние душ

reindeer [ˈreɪndɪəʳ] *n inv* сéверный олéнь *m*

reinforce [riːɪnˈfɔːs] *vt* (*strengthen*) укреплять (*perf* укрепúть); (*back up*) подкреплять (*perf* подкрепúть)

reinstate [riːɪnˈsteɪt] *vt* восстанáвливать (*perf* восстановúть) в прéжнем положéнии

reject [*vb* rɪˈdʒɛkt, *n* ˈriːdʒɛkt] *vt* отклонять (*perf* отклонúть), отвергáть (*perf* отвéргнуть); (*political system*) отвергáть (*perf* отвéргнуть); (*candidate*) отклонять (*perf* отклонúть); (*goods*) браковáть (*perf* забраковáть) ▷ *n* (*product*) некондициóнное издéлие; **rejection** [rɪˈdʒɛkʃən] *n* отклонéние

rejoice [rɪˈdʒɔɪs] *vi*: **to rejoice at** *or* **over** ликовáть (*impf*) по пóводу *+gen*

relate [rɪˈleɪt] *vt* (*tell*) перескáзывать (*perf* пересказáть); (*connect*): **to relate sth to** относúть (*perf* отнестú) что-н к *+dat* ▷ *vi*: **to relate to** (*person*) сходúться (*perf* сойтúсь) с *+instr*; (*subject, thing*) относúться (*perf* отнестúсь) к *+dat*; **related** *adj*: **related (to)** (*person*) состоящий в родствé (с *+instr*); (*animal, language*) рóдственный (с *+instr*); **they are related** онú состоят в родствé; **relating to** [rɪˈleɪtɪŋ-] *prep* относúтельно *+gen*

relation [rɪˈleɪʃən] *n* (*member of family*) рóдственник(-ица); (*connection*) отношéние; **relations** *npl* (*dealings*) сношéния *ntpl*; (*relatives*) рóдственники *mpl*, родня *fsg*; **relationship** *n* (*between two people, countries*) (взаимо-)отношéния *ntpl*; (*between two things, affair*) связь *f*

relative [ˈrɛlətɪv] *n* (*family member*) рóдственник(-ица) ▷ *adj* (*comparative*) относúтельный; **relative to** (*in relation to*) относящийся к *+dat*; **relatively** *adv* относúтельно

relax [rɪˈlæks] *vi* расслабляться (*perf* расслáбиться) ▷ *vt* (*grip, rule, control*) ослаблять (*perf* ослáбить); (*person*) расслаблять (*perf* расслáбить); **relaxation** [riːlækˈseɪʃən] *n* óтдых; (*of muscle*) расслаблéние; (*of grip, rule, control*) ослаблéние; **relaxed** *adj* непринуждённый, расслáбленный; **relaxing** *adj* (*holiday*) расслабляющий

relay [*n* ˈriːleɪ, *vb* rɪˈleɪ] *n* (*race*) эстафéта ▷ *vt* передавáть (*perf* передáть)

release [rɪˈliːs] *n* (*from prison*) освобождéние; (*of gas, book, film*) вы́пуск ▷ *vt* (*see n*) освобождáть (*perf* освободúть); выпускáть (*perf* вы́пустить); (*Tech: catch, spring etc*) отпускáть (*perf* отпустúть)

relentless [rɪˈlɛntlɪs] *adj* (*effort*) неослáбный; (*rain*) продолжи́тельный; (*determined*) неуста́нный

relevant ['rɛləvənt] *adj* актуа́льный; **relevant to** относя́щийся к *+dat*

reliable [rɪ'laɪəbl] *adj* надёжный; (*information*) достове́рный

relic ['rɛlɪk] *n* (*of past etc*) рели́квия

relief [rɪ'li:f] *n* облегче́ние; (*aid*) по́мощь *f*

relieve [rɪ'li:v] *vt* (*pain, suffering*) облегча́ть (*perf* облегчи́ть); (*fear, worry*) уменьша́ть (*perf* уме́ньшить); (*colleague, guard*) сменя́ть (*perf* смени́ть); **to relieve sb of sth** освобожда́ть (*perf* освободи́ть) кого́-н от чего́-н; **relieved** *adj*: **to feel relieved** чу́вствовать (*perf* почу́вствовать) облегче́ние

religion [rɪ'lɪdʒən] *n* рели́гия

religious [rɪ'lɪdʒəs] *adj* религио́зный

relish ['rɛlɪʃ] *n* (*Culin*) припра́ва; (*enjoyment*) наслажде́ние ▷ *vt* наслажда́ться (*perf* наслади́ться) *+instr*, смакова́ть (*impf*)

reluctance [rɪ'lʌktəns] *n* нежела́ние

reluctant [rɪ'lʌktənt] *adj* неохо́тный; (*person*): **he is reluctant to go there** он идёт туда́ неохо́тно; **reluctantly** *adv* неохо́тно

rely on [rɪ'laɪ-] *vt fus* (*count on*) расчи́тывать (*impf*) на *+acc*; (*trust*) полага́ться (*perf* положи́ться) на *+acc*

remain [rɪ'meɪn] *vi* остава́ться (*perf* оста́ться); **remainder** *n* оста́ток; **remaining** *adj* сохрани́вшийся, оста́вшийся; **remains** *npl* (*of meal*) оста́тки *mpl*; (*of building*) разва́лины *fpl*; (*of body*) оста́нки *mpl*

remand [rɪ'mɑ:nd] *n*: **on remand** взя́тый под стра́жу ▷ *vt*: **he was remanded in custody** он был взят под стра́жу

remark [rɪ'mɑ:k] *n* замеча́ние ▷ *vt* замеча́ть (*perf* заме́тить); **remarkable** *adj* замеча́тельный

remedy ['rɛmədɪ] *n* (*cure*) сре́дство ▷ *vt* исправля́ть (*perf* испра́вить)

remember [rɪ'mɛmbə[r]] *vt* (*recall*) вспомина́ть (*perf* вспо́мнить); (*bear in mind*) по́мнить (*impf*)

Remembrance Day

Remembrance Day — День па́мяти. Отмеча́ется в ближа́йшее к 11 ноября́ воскресе́нье. В э́тот день лю́ди чтят па́мять тех, кто поги́б в двух мировы́х во́йнах. Они́ покупа́ют кра́сные бума́жные ма́ки и но́сят их в петли́цах. Де́ньги, вы́рученные от прода́жи ма́ков, иду́т на благотвори́тельные це́ли.

remind [rɪ'maɪnd] *vt*: **to remind sb to do** напомина́ть (*perf* напо́мнить) кому́-н *+infin*; **to remind sb of sth** напомина́ть (*perf* напо́мнить) кому́-н о чём-н; **she reminds me of her mother** она́ напомина́ет мне свою́ мать; **reminder** *n* напомина́ние

reminiscent [rɛmɪ'nɪsənt] *adj*: **to be reminiscent of sth** напомина́ть (*perf* напо́мнить) что-н

remnant ['rɛmnənt] *n* оста́ток

remorse [rɪ'mɔ:s] *n* раска́яние

remote [rɪ'məut] *adj* (*place, time*) отдалённый; **remote control** *n* дистанцио́нное управле́ние; **remotely** *adv* отдалённо; **I'm not remotely interested** я нисколько не заинтересо́ван

removal [rɪ'mu:vəl] *n* удале́ние; (*Brit: of furniture*) перево́зка

remove [rɪ'mu:v] *vt* (*take away*) убира́ть (*perf* убра́ть); (*clothing, employee*) снима́ть (*perf* снять); (*stain*) удаля́ть (*perf* удали́ть); (*problem, doubt*) устраня́ть (*perf* устрани́ть)

Renaissance [rɪ'neɪsɑ̃:s] *n*: **the Renaissance** (*History*) Возрожде́ние

render ['rɛndəʳ] *vt* (*assistance*) ока́зывать (*perf* оказа́ть); (*harmless, useless*) де́лать (*perf* сде́лать) *+instr*

rendezvous ['rɔndɪvu:] *n* (*meeting*) свида́ние; (*place*) ме́сто свида́ния

renew [rɪ'nju:] *vt* возобновля́ть (*perf* возобнови́ть); **renewable** [ri:'nju:əbl] *adj* (*energy*) возобновля́емый

renovate ['rɛnəveɪt] *vt* модернизи́ровать (*impf/perf*); (*building*) де́лать (*perf* сде́лать) капита́льный ремо́нт в *+prp*

renowned [rɪ'naund] *adj* просла́вленный

rent [rɛnt] *n* кварти́рная пла́та ▷ *vt* (*take for rent: house*) снима́ть (*perf* снять); (*: television, car*) брать (*perf* взять) напрока́т; (*also* **rent out**: *house*) сдава́ть (*perf* сдать) (внаём); (*: television, car*) дава́ть (*perf* дать) напрока́т; **rental** *n* (*charge*) пла́та за прока́т

rep [rɛp] *n abbr* (*Comm*) = **representative**

repair [rɪ'pɛəʳ] *n* ремо́нт ▷ *vt* (*clothes, shoes*) чини́ть (*perf* почини́ть); (*car*) ремонти́ровать (*perf* отремонти́ровать); **in good/bad repair** в хоро́шем/плохо́м состоя́нии

repay [ri:'peɪ] (*irreg like* **pay**) *vt* (*money, debt*) выпла́чивать (*perf* вы́платить); (*person*) упла́чивать (*perf* уплати́ть) *+dat*; **to repay sb (for sth)** (*favour*) отпла́чивать (*perf* отплати́ть) кому́-н (за что-н); **repayment** *n* вы́плата

repeat [rɪ'pi:t] *vt* повторя́ть (*perf* повтори́ть) ▷ *vi* повторя́ться (*perf* повтори́ться) ▷ *n* (*Radio, TV*) повторе́ние; **repeatedly** *adv* неоднокра́тно

repellent [ri'pɛlənt] *n*: **insect repellent** репелле́нт

repercussions [ri:pə'kʌʃənz] *npl* после́дствия *ntpl*

repetition [rɛpɪ'tɪʃən] *n* (*repeat*) повторе́ние

repetitive [rɪ'pɛtɪtɪv] *adj* повторя́ющийся

replace [rɪ'pleɪs] *vt* (*put back*) класть (*perf* положи́ть) обра́тно; (*: vertically*) ста́вить (*perf* поста́вить) обра́тно; (*take the place of*) заменя́ть (*perf* замени́ть); **replacement** *n* заме́на

replay [*n* 'ri:pleɪ, *vb* ri:'pleɪ] *n* (*of match*) переигро́вка; (*of film*) повто́рный пока́з ▷ *vt* (*match, game*) переи́грывать (*perf* переигра́ть); (*part of tape*) повто́рно прои́грывать (*perf* проигра́ть)

replica ['rɛplɪkə] *n* (*copy*) ко́пия

reply [rɪ'plaɪ] *n* отве́т ▷ *vi* отвеча́ть (*perf* отве́тить)

report [rɪ'pɔ:t] *n* (*account*) докла́д, отчёт; (*Press, TV etc*) репорта́ж; (*statement*) сообще́ние; (*Brit: also* **school report**) отчёт об успева́емости

▷ *vt* сообща́ть (*perf* сообщи́ть) о *+prp*; (*event, meeting*) докла́дывать (*perf* доложи́ть) о *+prp*; (*person*) доноси́ть (*perf* донести́) на *+acc* ▷ *vi* (*make a report*) докла́дывать (*perf* доложи́ть); **to report to sb** (*present o.s.*) явля́ться (*perf* яви́ться) к кому́-н; (*be responsible to*) быть (*impf*) под нача́лом кого́-н; **to report that** сообща́ть (*perf* сообщи́ть), что; **reportedly** *adv* как сообща́ют; **reporter** *n* репортёр

represent [rɛprɪ'zɛnt] *vt* (*person, nation*) представля́ть (*perf* предста́вить); (*view, belief*) излага́ть (*perf* изложи́ть); (*constitute*) представля́ть (*impf*) собо́й; (*idea, emotion*) символизи́ровать (*impf/perf*); (*describe*): **to represent sth as** изобража́ть (*perf* изобрази́ть) что-н как; **representation** [rɛprɪzɛn'teɪʃən] *n* (*state*) представи́тельство; (*picture, statue*) изображе́ние; **representative** *n* представи́тель *m* ▷ *adj* представи́тельный

repress [rɪ'prɛs] *vt* подавля́ть (*perf* подави́ть); **repression** [rɪ'prɛʃən] *n* подавле́ние

reprimand ['rɛprɪmɑ:nd] *n* вы́говор ▷ *vt* де́лать (*perf* сде́лать) вы́говор *+dat*

reproduce [ri:prə'dju:s] *vt* воспроизводи́ть (*perf* воспроизвести́) ▷ *vi* размножа́ться (*perf* размно́житься)

reproduction [ri:prə'dʌkʃən] *n* воспроизведе́ние; (*Art*) репроду́кция

reptile ['rɛptaɪl] *n* пресмыка́ющееся *nt adj* (живо́тное)

republic [rɪ'pʌblɪk] *n* респу́блика; **Republican** *n* (*US: Pol*) республика́нец(-нка)

reputable ['rɛpjutəbl] *adj* (*person*) уважа́емый; **reputable company** компа́ния с хоро́шей репута́цией

reputation [rɛpju'teɪʃən] *n* репута́ция

request [rɪ'kwɛst] *n* (*polite demand*) про́сьба; (*formal demand*) зая́вка ▷ *vt*: **to request sth of** *or* **from sb** проси́ть (*perf* попроси́ть) что-н у кого́-н

require [rɪ'kwaɪə[r]] *vt* (*subj: person*) нужда́ться (*impf*) в *+prp*; (*: thing, situation*) тре́бовать (*impf*); (*order*): **to require sth of sb** тре́бовать (*perf* потре́бовать) что-н от кого́-н; **we require you to complete the task** мы тре́буем, что́бы Вы заверши́ли рабо́ту; **requirement** *n* (*need, want*) потре́бность *f*

rescue ['rɛskju:] *n* спасе́ние ▷ *vt*: **to rescue (from)** спаса́ть (*perf* спасти́) (от *+gen*); **to come to sb's rescue** приходи́ть (*perf* прийти́) кому́-н на по́мощь

research [rɪ'sə:tʃ] *n* иссле́дование ▷ *vt* иссле́довать (*impf/perf*)

resemblance [rɪ'zɛmbləns] *n* схо́дство

resemble [rɪ'zɛmbl] *vt* походи́ть (*impf*) на *+acc*

resent [rɪ'zɛnt] *vt* (*fact*) негодова́ть (*impf*) про́тив *+gen*; (*person*) негодова́ть (*impf*) на *+acc*; **resentful** *adj* негоду́ющий; **I am resentful of his behaviour** его́ поведе́ние приво́дит меня́ в негодова́ние; **resentment** *n* негодова́ние

reservation [rɛzə'veɪʃən] *n*

(*booking*) предвари́тельный зака́з; (*doubt*) сомне́ние; (*for tribe*) резерва́ция
reserve [rɪ'zəːv] *n* (*store*) резе́рв, запа́с; (*also* **nature reserve**) запове́дник; (*Sport*) запасно́й игро́к; (*restraint*) сде́ржанность *f* ▷ *vt* (*look, tone*) сохраня́ть (*perf* сохрани́ть); (*seats, table etc*) зака́зывать (*perf* заказа́ть); **in reserve** в резе́рве *or* запа́се; **reserved** *adj* (*restrained*) сде́ржанный
reservoir ['rɛzəvwɑːʳ] *n* (*of water*) водохрани́лище
reshuffle [riː'ʃʌfl] *n*: **Cabinet reshuffle** перетасо́вка *or* перестано́вки *fpl* в кабине́те мини́стров
residence ['rɛzɪdəns] *n* (*home*) резиде́нция; (*length of stay*) пребыва́ние
resident ['rɛzɪdənt] *n* (*of country, town*) (постоя́нный(-ая)) жи́тель(ница) *m(f)*; (*in hotel*) прожива́ющий(-ая) *m(f) adj* ▷ *adj* (*population*) постоя́нный
residential [rɛzɪ'dɛnʃəl] *adj* (*area*) жило́й; (*course, college*) с прожива́нием
resign [rɪ'zaɪn] *vi* (*from post*) уходи́ть (*perf* уйти́) в отста́вку ▷ *vt* (*one's post*) оставля́ть (*perf* оста́вить) с *+gen*; **to resign o.s. to** смиря́ться (*perf* смири́ться) с *+instr*; **resignation** [rɛzɪg'neɪʃən] *n* отста́вка; (*acceptance*) поко́рность *f*, смире́ние
resin ['rɛzɪn] *n* смола́
resist [rɪ'zɪst] *vt* сопротивля́ться (*impf*) *+dat*; (*temptation*) устоя́ть (*perf*) пе́ред *+instr*; **resistance** *n* (*opposition*) сопротивле́ние; (*to illness*) сопротивля́емость *f*
resolution [rɛzə'luːʃən] *n* (*decision*) реше́ние; (: *formal*) резолю́ция; (*determination*) реши́мость *f*; (*of problem, difficulty*) разреше́ние
resolve [rɪ'zɔlv] *n* реши́тельность *f* ▷ *vt* (*problem, difficulty*) разреша́ть (*perf* разреши́ть) ▷ *vi*: **to resolve to do** реша́ть (*perf* реши́ть) *+infin*
resort [rɪ'zɔːt] *n* (*town*) куро́рт; (*recourse*) прибега́ние ▷ *vi*: **to resort to** прибега́ть (*perf* прибе́гнуть) к *+dat*; **the last resort** после́дняя наде́жда; **in the last resort** в кра́йнем слу́чае
resource [rɪ'sɔːs] *n* ресу́рс; **resourceful** *adj* изобрета́тельный, нахо́дчивый
respect [rɪs'pɛkt] *n* уваже́ние ▷ *vt* уважа́ть (*impf*); **respects** *npl* (*greetings*) почте́ние *ntsg*; **with respect to, in respect of** в отноше́нии *+gen*; **in this respect** в э́том отноше́нии; **respectable** *adj* прили́чный; (*morally correct*) респекта́бельный; **respectful** *adj* почти́тельный
respective [rɪs'pɛktɪv] *adj*: **he drove them to their respective homes** он отвёз их обо́их по дома́м; **respectively** *adv* соотве́тственно
respond [rɪs'pɔnd] *vi* (*answer*) отвеча́ть (*perf* отве́тить); (*react*): **to respond to** (*pressure, criticism*) реаги́ровать (*perf* отреаги́ровать) на *+acc*
response [rɪs'pɔns] *n* (*answer*) отве́т; (*reaction*) резона́нс, о́тклик
responsibility [rɪspɔnsɪ'bɪlɪtɪ] *n* (*liability*) отве́тственность *f*; (*duty*) обя́занность *f*
responsible [rɪs'pɔnsɪbl] *adj*: **responsible (for)** отве́тственный (за *+acc*)

responsive [rɪs'pɔnsɪv] *adj* (*child, nature*) отзы́вчивый; **responsive to** (*demand, treatment*) восприи́мчивый к *+dat*

rest [rɛst] *n* (*relaxation, pause*) о́тдых; (*stand, support*) подста́вка ▷ *vi* (*relax, stop*) отдыха́ть (*perf* отдохну́ть) ▷ *vt* (*head, eyes etc*) дава́ть (*perf* дать) о́тдых *+dat*; (*lean*): **to rest sth against** прислоня́ть (*perf* прислони́ть) что-н к *+dat*; **the rest** (*remainder*) остально́е *nt adj*; **the rest of them** остальны́е (из них); **to rest on** (*person*) опира́ться (*perf* опере́ться) на *+acc*; (*idea*) опира́ться (*impf*) на *+acc*; (*object*) лежа́ть (*impf*) на *+prp*; **rest assured that ...** бу́дьте уве́рены, что ...; **it rests with him to ...** на нём лежи́т обя́занность *+infin* ...; **to rest one's eyes** *or* **gaze on** остана́вливать (*perf* останови́ть) (свой) взгляд на *+acc*

restaurant ['rɛstərɔŋ] *n* рестора́н

restless ['rɛstlɪs] *adj* беспоко́йный

restoration [rɛstə'reɪʃən] *n* (*of building etc*) реставра́ция; (*of order, health*) восстановле́ние

restore [rɪ'stɔːʳ] *vt* (*see n*) реставри́ровать (*perf* отреставри́ровать); восстана́вливать (*perf* восстанови́ть); (*stolen property*) возвраща́ть (*perf* возврати́ть); (*to power*) верну́ть (*perf*)

restrain [rɪs'treɪn] *vt* сде́рживать (*perf* сдержа́ть); (*person*): **to restrain sb from doing** не дава́ть (*perf* дать) кому́-н *+infin*; **restraint** *n* (*moderation*) сде́ржанность *f*; (*restriction*) ограниче́ние

restrict [rɪs'trɪkt] *vt* ограни́чивать (*perf* ограни́чить); **restriction** [rɪs'trɪkʃən] *n*: **restriction (on)** ограниче́ние (на *+acc*)

result [rɪ'zʌlt] *n* результа́т ▷ *vi*: **to result in** зака́нчиваться (*perf* зако́нчиться) *+instr*; **as a result of** в результа́те *+gen*

resume [rɪ'zjuːm] *vt* (*work, journey*) возобновля́ть (*perf* возобнови́ть) ▷ *vi* продолжа́ть (*perf* продо́лжить)

résumé ['reɪzjuːmeɪ] *n* резюме́ *nt ind*; (*US*: *for job*) автобиогра́фия

retail ['riːteɪl] *adj* ро́зничный ▷ *adv* в ро́зницу; **retailer** *n* ро́зничный торго́вец

retain [rɪ'teɪn] *vt* (*keep*) сохраня́ть (*perf* сохрани́ть)

retaliation [rɪtælɪ'eɪʃən] *n* (*against attack*) отве́тный уда́р; (*against ill-treatment*) возме́здие

retarded [rɪ'tɑːdɪd] *adj* (*development, growth*) заме́дленный

retire [rɪ'taɪəʳ] *vi* (*give up work*) уходи́ть (*perf* уйти́) на пе́нсию; (*withdraw*) удаля́ться (*perf* удали́ться); (*go to bed*) удаля́ться (*perf* удали́ться) на поко́й; **retired** *adj*: **he is retired** он на пе́нсии; **retirement** *n* вы́ход *or* ухо́д на пе́нсию

retreat [rɪ'triːt] *n* (*place*) убе́жище; (*withdrawal*) ухо́д; (*Mil*) отступле́ние ▷ *vi* отступа́ть (*perf* отступи́ть)

retrieve [rɪ'triːv] *vt* (*object*) получа́ть (*perf* получи́ть) обра́тно; (*honour*) восстана́вливать (*perf* восстанови́ть); (*situation*) спаса́ть (*perf* спасти́)

retrospect ['rɛtrəspɛkt] *n*: **in retrospect** в ретроспе́кции;

retrospective [rɛtrə'spɛktɪv] *adj* (*law, tax*) имéющий обрáтную сúлу

return [rɪ'tə:n] *n* (*from, to place*) возвращéние; (*of sth stolen etc*) возврáт; (*Comm*) дохóд ▷ *cpd* (*journey, ticket*) обрáтный ▷ *vi* возвращáться (*perf* возвратúться), вернýться (*perf*) ▷ *vt* возвращáть (*perf* возвратúть), вернýть (*perf*); (*Law: verdict*) выносúть (*perf* вы́нести); (*Pol: candidate*) избирáть (*perf* избрáть); (*ball*) отбивáть (*perf* отбúть); **in return (for)** в отвéт (на +*acc*); **many happy returns (of the day)!** с днём рождéния!; **to return to** (*consciousness*) приходúть (*perf* прийтú) в +*acc*; (*power*) вернýться (*perf*) к +*dat*

reunion [ri:'ju:nɪən] *n* (*reuniting*) воссоединéние; (*party*) встрéча

revamp [ri:'væmp] *vt* обновлять (*perf* обновúть)

reveal [rɪ'vi:l] *vt* (*make known*) обнарýживать (*perf* обнарýжить); (*make visible*) открывáть (*perf* откры́ть); **revealing** *adj* (*action, statement*) показáтельный; (*dress*) откры́тый

revel ['rɛvl] *vi*: **to revel in sth** упивáться (*impf*) чем-н; **to revel in doing** обожáть (*impf*) +*infin*

revelation [rɛvə'leɪʃən] *n* (*fact*) откры́тие

revenge [rɪ'vɛndʒ] *n* месть *f*; **to take revenge on, revenge o.s. on** мстить (*perf* отомстúть) +*dat*

revenue ['rɛvənju:] *n* дохóды *mpl*

Reverend ['rɛvərənd] *adj*: **the Reverend** егó преподóбие

reversal [rɪ'və:sl] *n* радикáльное изменéние; (*of roles*) перемéна

reverse [rɪ'və:s] *n* (*opposite*) противополóжность *f*; (*of coin, medal*) оборóтная сторонá; (*of paper*) оборóт; (*Aut: also* **reverse gear**) обрáтный ход ▷ *adj* (*opposite*) обрáтный ▷ *vt* (*order, position, decision*) изменя́ть (*perf* изменúть); (*process, policy*) поворáчивать (*perf* повернýть) вспять ▷ *vi* (*Brit: Aut*) давáть (*perf* дать) зáдний ход; **in reverse order** в обрáтном поря́дке; **to reverse a car** давáть (*perf* дать) зáдний ход; **to reverse roles** меня́ться (*perf* поменя́ться) роля́ми

revert [rɪ'və:t] *vi*: **to revert to** (*to former state*) возвращáться (*perf* возвратúться) к +*dat*; (*Law: money, property*) переходúть (*perf* перейтú) к +*dat*

review [rɪ'vju:] *n* (*of situation, policy etc*) пересмóтр; (*of book, film etc*) рецéнзия; (*magazine*) обозрéние ▷ *vt* (*situation, policy etc*) пересмáтривать (*perf* пересмотрéть); (*book, film etc*) рецензúровать (*perf* отрецензúровать)

revise [rɪ'vaɪz] *vt* (*manuscript*) перерабáтывать (*perf* переработать); (*opinion, law*) пересмáтривать (*perf* пересмотрéть) ▷ *vi* (*Scol*) повторя́ть (*perf* повторúть)

revision [rɪ'vɪʒən] *n* (*see vb*) переработка; пересмóтр; повторéние

revival [rɪ'vaɪvəl] *n* (*recovery*) оживлéние; (*of interest, faith*) возрождéние

revive [rɪ'vaɪv] *vt* (*person*) возвращáть (*perf* возвратúть) к жúзни; (*economy, industry*) оживля́ть (*perf* оживúть); (*tradition, interest etc*) возрождáть (*perf* возродить) ▷ *vi* (*see vt*) приходить (*perf* прийти) в сознание; оживляться (*perf* оживиться); возрождаться (*perf* возродиться)

revolt [rɪ'vəult] *n* (*rebellion*) восстание ▷ *vi* (*rebel*) восставать (*perf* восстать) ▷ *vt* вызывать (*perf* вызвать) отвращение у *+gen*; **revolting** *adj* отвратительный

revolution [rɛvə'lu:ʃən] *n* революция; (*of wheel, earth etc*) оборот; **revolutionary** *adj* революционный ▷ *n* революционер(ка)

revolve [rɪ'vɔlv] *vi* (*turn*) вращаться (*impf*); (*fig*): **to revolve (a)round** вращаться (*impf*) вокруг *+gen*

revolver [rɪ'vɔlvə^r] *n* револьвер

reward [rɪ'wɔ:d] *n* награда ▷ *vt*: **to reward (for)** (*effort*) вознаграждать (*perf* вознаградить) (за *+acc*); **rewarding** *adj*: **this work is rewarding** эта работа приносит удовлетворение

rewind [ri:'waɪnd] (*irreg like* **wind**[2]) *vt* перематывать (*perf* перемотать)

rewrite [ri:'raɪt] (*irreg like* **write**) *vt* (*rework*) переписывать (*perf* переписать)

rheumatism ['ru:mətɪzəm] *n* ревматизм

rhinoceros [raɪ'nɔsərəs] *n* носорог

rhubarb ['ru:bɑ:b] *n* ревень *m*

rhyme [raɪm] *n* рифма; (*in poetry*) размер

rhythm ['rɪðm] *n* ритм

rib [rɪb] *n* (*Anat*) ребро

ribbon ['rɪbən] *n* лента; **in ribbons** (*torn*) в клочья

rice [raɪs] *n* рис

rich [rɪtʃ] *adj* богатый; (*clothes, jewels*) роскошный; (*food, colour, life*) насыщенный; (*abundant*): **rich in** богатый *+instr*; ▷ *npl*: **the rich** (*rich people*) богатые *pl adj*

rid [rɪd] (*pt, pp* **rid**) *vt*: **to rid sb of sth** избавлять (*perf* избавить) кого-н от чего-н; **to get rid of** избавляться (*perf* избавиться) *or* отделываться (*perf* отделаться) от *+gen*

ridden ['rɪdn] *pp of* **ride**

riddle ['rɪdl] *n* (*conundrum*) загадка ▷ *vt*: **riddled with** (*holes, bullets*) изрешечённый *+instr*; (*guilt, doubts*) полный *+gen*; (*corruption*) пронизанный *+instr*

ride [raɪd] (*pt* **rode**, *pp* **ridden**) *n* поездка ▷ *vi* (*as sport*) ездить (*impf*) верхом; (*go somewhere, travel*) ездить/ехать (поехать *perf*) ▷ *vt* (*horse*) ездить/ехать (*impf*) верхом на *+prp*; (*bicycle, motorcycle*) ездить/ехать (*impf*) на *+prp*; (*distance*) проезжать (*perf* проехать); **a 5 mile ride** поездка в 5 миль; **to take sb for a ride** (*fig*) прокатить (*perf*) кого-н; **rider** *n* (*on horse*) наездник(-ица); (*on bicycle*) велосипедист(ка); (*on motorcycle*) мотоциклист(ка)

ridge [rɪdʒ] *n* (*of hill*) гребень *m*

ridicule ['rɪdɪkju:l] *vt* высмеивать (*perf* высмеять)

ridiculous [rɪ'dɪkjuləs] *adj* смехотворный; **it's ridiculous** это смешно

riding ['raɪdɪŋ] *n* верховая езда

rife [raɪf] *adj*: **to be rife** (*corruption*) процветать (*impf*); **to be rife with** (*rumours, fears*) изобиловать (*impf*) *+instr*

rifle ['raɪfl] *n* (*Mil*) винтовка; (*for hunting*) ружьё

rift [rɪft] *n* (*also fig*) трещина

rig [rɪg] *n* (*also* **oil rig**) буровая́ установка ▷ *vt* подтасо́вывать (*perf* подтасова́ть) результа́ты *+gen*

right [raɪt] *adj* пра́вильный; (*person, time, size*) подходя́щий; (*fair, just*) справедли́вый; (*not left*) пра́вый ▷ *n* (*entitlement*) пра́во; (*not left*) пра́вая сторона́ ▷ *adv* (*correctly*) пра́вильно; (*not to the left*) напра́во ▷ *vt* (*ship*) выра́внивать (*perf* вы́ровнять); (*car*) ста́вить (*perf* поста́вить) на колёса; (*fault, situation*) исправля́ть (*perf* испра́вить); (*wrong*) устраня́ть (*perf* устрани́ть) ▷ *excl* так, хорошо́; **she's right** она́ права́; **that's right!** (*answer*) пра́вильно!; **is that clock right?** э́ти часы́ пра́вильно иду́т?; **on the right** спра́ва; **you are in the right** пра́вда за Ва́ми; **by rights** по справедли́вости; **right and wrong** хоро́шее и дурно́е; **right now** сейча́с же; **right away** сра́зу же; **rightful** *adj* зако́нный; **rightly** *adv* (*with reason*) справедли́во; **right of way** *n* (*path etc*) пра́во прохо́да; (*Aut*) пра́во прое́зда; **right-wing** *adj* (*Pol*) пра́вый

rigid ['rɪdʒɪd] *adj* (*structure, control*) жёсткий; (*fig: attitude etc*) ко́сный

rigorous ['rɪgərəs] *adj* жёсткий; (*training*) серьёзный

rim [rɪm] *n* (*of glass, dish*) край; (*of spectacles*) ободо́к; (*of wheel*) о́бод

rind [raɪnd] *n* (*of bacon, cheese*) ко́рка; (*of lemon, orange etc*) кожура́

ring [rɪŋ] (*pt* **rang**, *pp* **rung**) *n* (*of metal, smoke*) кольцо́; (*of people, objects, light*) круг; (*of spies, drug dealers etc*) сеть *f*; (*for boxing*) ринг; (*of circus*) аре́на; (*of doorbell, telephone*) звоно́к ▷ *vi* звони́ть (*perf* позвони́ть); (*doorbell*) звене́ть (*impf*); (*also* **ring out**: *voice, shot*) раздава́ться (*perf* разда́ться) ▷ *vt* (*Brit: Tel*) звони́ть (*perf* позвони́ть) *+dat*; **to give sb a ring** (*Brit: Tel*) звони́ть (*perf* позвони́ть) кому́-н; **my ears are ringing** у меня́ звени́т в уша́х; **to ring the bell** звони́ть (*impf*) в звоно́к; **ring up** *vt* (*Brit*) звони́ть (*perf* позвони́ть) *+dat*; **ringtone** ['rɪŋtəun] *n* (*on mobile*) *мело́дия для моби́льного телефо́на*

rink [rɪŋk] *n* (*for skating*) като́к

rinse [rɪns] *vt* полоска́ть (*perf* прополоска́ть) ▷ *n*: **to give sth a rinse** опола́скивать (*perf* ополосну́ть) что-н

riot ['raɪət] *n* (*disturbance*) беспоря́дки *mpl*, бесчи́нства *ntpl* ▷ *vi* бесчи́нствовать (*impf*); **to run riot** бу́йствовать (*impf*)

rip [rɪp] *n* разры́в ▷ *vt* (*paper, cloth*) разрыва́ть (*perf* разорва́ть) ▷ *vi* разрыва́ться (*perf* разорва́ться)

ripe [raɪp] *adj* спе́лый, зре́лый

ripple ['rɪpl] *n* рябь *f no pl*, зыбь *f no pl*; (*of laughter, applause*) волна́

rise [raɪz] (*pt* **rose**, *pp* **risen**) *n* (*slope*) подъём; (*increase*) повыше́ние; (*fig: of state, leader*) возвыше́ние ▷ *vi* поднима́ться (*perf* подня́ться); (*prices, numbers, voice*) повыша́ться (*perf* повы́ситься); (*sun, moon*) всходи́ть (*perf* взойти́); (*also* **rise up**: *rebels*) восстава́ть (*perf* восста́ть); (*in rank*) продвига́ться (*perf* продви́нуться); **rise to power** прихо́д к вла́сти; **to give rise to** вызыва́ть (*perf* вы́звать); **to rise to the occasion** ока́зываться (*perf*

оказа́ться) на высоте́ положе́ния;
risen [rɪzn] *pp of* **rise**
rising ['raɪzɪŋ] *adj* (*number, prices*) расту́щий; (*sun, moon*) восходя́щий
risk [rɪsk] *n* риск ▷ *vt* (*endanger*) рискова́ть (*impf*) *+instr*, (*chance*) рискова́ть (*perf* рискну́ть) *+instr*; **to take a risk** рискова́ть (*perf* рискну́ть), идти́ (*perf* пойти́) на риск; **to run the risk of doing** рискова́ть (*impf*) *+infin*; **at risk** в опа́сной ситуа́ции; **to put sb/sth at risk** подверга́ть (*perf* подве́ргнуть) кого́-н/что-н ри́ску; **at one's own risk** на свой (страх и) риск; **risky** *adj* риско́ванный
rite [raɪt] *n* обря́д; **last rites** после́днее прича́стие
ritual ['rɪtjuəl] *adj* ритуа́льный ▷ *n* (*Rel*) обря́д; (*procedure*) ритуа́л
rival ['raɪvl] *n* сопе́рник(-ица); (*in business*) конкуре́нт ▷ *adj* (*business*) конкури́рующий ▷ *vt* сопе́рничать (*impf*) с *+instr*; **rival team** кома́нда сопе́рника; **rivalry** *n* (*in sport, love*) сопе́рничество; (*in business*) конкуре́нция
river ['rɪvə^r] *n* река́ ▷ *cpd* (*port, traffic*) речно́й; **up/down river** вверх/вниз по реке́
road [rəud] *n* доро́га, путь *m*; (*in town*) доро́га; (*motorway etc*) доро́га, шоссе́ *nt ind* ▷ *cpd* (*accident*) доро́жный; **major/minor road** гла́вная/второстепе́нная доро́га; **road sense** чу́вство доро́ги; **road junction** пересече́ние доро́г, перекрёсток; **roadblock** *n* доро́жное загражде́ние; **road rage** *n* хулига́нское поведе́ние на автодоро́ге; **roadside** *n* обо́чина
roam [rəum] *vi* скита́ться (*impf*)
roar [rɔː^r] *n* рёв; (*of laughter*) взрыв ▷ *vi* реве́ть (*impf*); **to roar with laughter** хохота́ть (*impf*)
roast [rəust] *n* (*of meat*) жарко́е *nt adj* ▷ *vt* (*meat, potatoes*) жа́рить (*perf* зажа́рить)
rob [rɔb] *vt* гра́бить (*perf* огра́бить); **to rob sb of sth** красть (*perf* укра́сть) что-н у кого́-н; (*fig*) лиша́ть (*perf* лиши́ть) кого́-н чего́-н; **robber** *n* граби́тель *m*; **robbery** *n* ограбле́ние, грабёж
robe [rəub] *n* (*for ceremony etc*) ма́нтия; (*also* **bath robe**) ба́нный хала́т; (*US*) плед
robin ['rɔbɪn] *n* (*Zool*) заря́нка
robot ['rəubɔt] *n* ро́бот
robust [rəu'bʌst] *adj* (*person*) кре́пкий
rock [rɔk] *n* (*substance*) (го́рная) поро́да; (*boulder*) валу́н; (*US: small stone*) ка́мешек; (*Mus: also* **rock music**) рок ▷ *vt* (*swing*) кача́ть (*impf*); (*shake*) шата́ть (*impf*) ▷ *vi* (*object*) кача́ться (*impf*), шата́ться (*impf*); (*person*) кача́ться (*impf*); **on the rocks** (*drink*) со льдом; (*marriage etc*) на гра́ни распа́да; **rock and roll** *n* рок-н-ро́лл
rocket ['rɔkɪt] *n* раке́та
rocky ['rɔkɪ] *adj* (*hill*) скали́стый; (*path, soil*) камени́стый; (*unstable*) ша́ткий
rod [rɔd] *n* прут; (*also* **fishing rod**) у́дочка
rode [rəud] *pt of* **ride**
rodent ['rəudnt] *n* грызу́н
rogue [rəug] *n* плут
role [rəul] *n* роль *f*; **role model** *n* приме́р (для подража́ния)
roll [rəul] *n* (*of paper, cloth etc*) руло́н; (*of banknotes*) сви́ток; (*also* **bread roll**) бу́лочка; (*register, list*) спи́сок; (*of drums*) бой; (*of*

r

thunder) раскáт ▷ *vt* (*ball, stone etc*) катáть/катúть (*impf*); (*also* **roll up**: *string*) скрýчивать (*perf* скрутúть); (: *sleeves, eyes*) закáтывать (*perf* закатáть); (*cigarette*) свёртывать (*perf* свернýть); (*also* **roll out**: *pastry*) раскáтывать (*perf* раскатáть) ▷ *vi* (*also* **roll along**: *ball, car etc*) катúться (*impf*); (*ship*) качáться (*impf*); **roll up** *vt* (*carpet, newspaper*) сворáчивать (*perf* свернýть); **roller** *n* (*for hair*) бигудú *pl ind*; **roller skates** *npl* рóлики *mpl*, рóликовые конькú *mpl*; **rolling pin** *n* скáлка

ROM [rɔm] *n abbr* (*Comput*) (= *read-only memory*) ПЗУ (= *постоя́нное запоминáющее устрóйство*)

Roman ['rəumən] *adj* рúмский; **Roman Catholic** *adj* (рúмско-) католúческий ▷ *n* катóлик(-ичка)

romance [rə'mæns] *n* (*love affair, novel*) ромáн; (*charm*) ромáнтика

Romania [rəu'meɪnɪə] *n* Румы́ния; **Romanian** *adj* румы́нский

romantic [rə'mæntɪk] *adj* романтúчный; (*play, story etc*) романтúческий

Rome [rəum] *n* Рим

roof [ru:f] (*pl* **roofs**) *n* кры́ша; **the roof of the mouth** нёбо

room [ru:m] *n* (*in house*) кóмната; (*in school*) класс; (*in hotel*) нóмер; (*space*) мéсто; **rooms** *npl* (*lodging*) квартúра *fsg*; **"rooms to let"**, *(US)* **"rooms for rent"** "сдаю́тся кóмнаты"; **single/double room** (*in hotel*) одномéстный/двухмéстный нóмер

root [ru:t] *n* кóрень *m*; **roots** *npl* (*family origins*) кóрни *mpl*

rope [rəup] *n* верёвка ▷ *vt* (*also* **rope off**: *area*) отгорáживать (*perf* отгородúть) верёвкой; **to know the ropes** (*fig*) знать (*impf*), что к чемý; **to rope to** привя́зывать (*perf* привязáть) верёвкой к +*dat*; **to rope together** свя́зывать (*perf* связáть) верёвкой

rose [rəuz] *pt of* **rise** ▷ *n* рóза

rosemary ['rəuzmərɪ] *n* розмарúн

rosy ['rəuzɪ] *adj* (*face, cheeks*) румя́ный; (*situation*) рáдостный; (*future*) рáдужный

rot [rɔt] *n* (*result*) гниль *f* ▷ *vt* гноúть (*perf* сгноúть) ▷ *vi* гнить (*perf* сгнúть)

rota ['rəutə] *n* расписáние дежýрств

rotate [rəu'teɪt] *vt* вращáть (*impf*); (*crops, jobs*) чередовáть (*impf*) ▷ *vi* вращáться (*impf*)

rotten ['rɔtn] *adj* гнилóй; (*meat, eggs*) тýхлый; (*fig*: *unpleasant*) мéрзкий; (*inf*: *bad*) погáный; **to feel rotten** (*ill*) чýвствовать (*impf*) себя́ погáно

rouble ['ru:bl] (*US* **ruble**) *n* рубль *m*

rough [rʌf] *adj* грýбый; (*surface*) шероховáтый; (*terrain*) пересечённый; (*person, manner*) рéзкий; (*sea*) бýрный; (*town, area*) опáсный; (*plan, work*) черновóй; (*guess*) приблизúтельный ▷ *vt*: **to rough it** ограничивать (*perf* ограничить) себя́ ▷ *adv*: **to sleep rough** (*Brit*) ночевáть (*impf*) где придётся; **roughly** *adv* грýбо; (*approximately*) приблизúтельно

Roumania *etc* = **Romania** *etc*

round [raund] *adj* крýглый ▷ *n* (*duty*: *of policeman, doctor*) обхóд; (*game*: *of cards, golf*) пáртия; (*in competition*) тур; (*of ammunition*) компле́кт; (*of talks, also Boxing*) ра́унд ▷ *vt* огиба́ть (*perf* обогну́ть) ▷ *prep* (*surrounding*) вокру́г *+gen*; (*approximately*): **round about three hundred** где-то о́коло трёхсот ▷ *adv*: **all round** круго́м, вокру́г; **a round of applause** взрыв аплодисме́нтов; **a round of drinks** по бока́лу на ка́ждого; **round his neck/the table** вокру́г его́ ше́и/стола́; **the shop is just round the corner** (*fig*) до магази́на руко́й пода́ть; **to go round the back** обходи́ть (*perf* обойти́) сза́ди; **to walk round the room** ходи́ть (*impf*) по ко́мнате; **to go round to sb's (house)** ходи́ть/ идти́ (*impf*) к кому́-н; **there's enough to go round** хва́тит на всех; **round off** *vt* (*speech etc*) заверша́ть (*perf* заверши́ть); **round up** *vt* (*cattle, people*) сгоня́ть (*perf* согна́ть); (*price, figure*) округля́ть (*perf* округли́ть); **roundabout** *n* (*Brit*: *Aut*) кольцева́я тра́нспортная развя́зка; (: *at fair*) карусе́ль *f* ▷ *adj*: **in a roundabout way** око́льным путём; **roundup** *n* (*of information*) сво́дка

rouse [rauz] *vt* (*wake up*) буди́ть (*perf* разбуди́ть); (*stir up*) возбужда́ть (*perf* возбуди́ть)

route [ru:t] *n* (*way*) путь *m*, доро́га; (*of bus, train etc*) маршру́т

routine [ru:'ti:n] *adj* (*work*) повседне́вный; (*procedure*) обы́чный ▷ *n* (*habits*) распоря́док; (*drudgery*) рути́на; (*Theat*) но́мер

row¹ [rəu] *n* ряд ▷ *vi* грести́ (*impf*) ▷ *vt* управля́ть (*impf*) *+instr*; **in a row** (*fig*) подря́д

row² [rau] *n* (*noise*) шум; (*dispute*) сканда́л; (*inf*: *scolding*) нагоня́й ▷ *vi* сканда́лить (*perf* посканда́лить)

rowing ['rəuɪŋ] *n* гре́бля

royal ['rɔɪəl] *adj* короле́вский; **royalty** *n* (*royal persons*) чле́ны *mpl* короле́вской семьи́; (*payment*) (а́вторский) гонора́р

rpm *abbr* (= *revolutions per minute*) оборо́ты в мину́ту

RSVP *abbr* (= *répondez s'il vous plaît*) *про́сим отве́тить на приглаше́ние*

rub [rʌb] *vt* (*part of body*) тере́ть (*perf* потере́ть); (*object*: *to clean*) тере́ть (*impf*); (: *to dry*) вытира́ть (*perf* вы́тереть); (*hands*: *also* **rub together**) потира́ть (*perf* потере́ть) ▷ *n*: **to give sth a rub** (*polish*) натира́ть (*perf* натере́ть) что-н; **to rub sb up** *or* (*US*) **rub sb the wrong way** раздража́ть (*perf* раздражи́ть) кого́-н

rubber ['rʌbə^r] *n* (*substance*) рези́на, каучу́к; (*Brit*: *eraser*) рези́нка, ла́стик

rubbish ['rʌbɪʃ] *n* му́сор; (*junk*) хлам; (*fig*: *pej*: *nonsense*) ерунда́, чушь *f*; (: *goods*) дрянь *f*

rubble ['rʌbl] *n* обло́мки *mpl*

ruble ['ru:bl] *n* (*US*) = **rouble**

ruby ['ru:bɪ] *n* руби́н

rucksack ['rʌksæk] *n* рюкза́к

rudder ['rʌdə^r] *n* руль *m*

rude [ru:d] *adj* (*impolite*) гру́бый; (*unexpected*) жесто́кий

rug [rʌg] *n* ко́врик; (*Brit*: *blanket*) плед

rugby ['rʌgbɪ] *n* (*also* **rugby football**) ре́гби *nt ind*

rugged ['rʌgɪd] *adj* (*landscape*) скали́стый; (*features*) гру́бый; (*character*) прямо́й

ruin ['ru:ɪn] *n* (*destruction*: *of building, plans*) разруше́ние; (*downfall*) ги́бель *f*; (*bankruptcy*) разоре́ние ▷ *vt* (*building, hopes, plans*) разруша́ть (*perf* разру́шить); (*future, health, reputation*) губи́ть (*perf* погуби́ть); (*person*: *financially*) разоря́ть (*perf* разори́ть); (*spoil*: *clothes*) по́ртить (*perf* испо́ртить); **ruins** *npl* (*of building*) разва́лины *fpl*, руи́ны *fpl*

rule [ru:l] *n* (*norm, regulation*) пра́вило; (*government*) правле́ние ▷ *vt* (*country, people*) пра́вить (*impf*) +*instr* ▷ *vi* (*leader, monarch etc*) пра́вить (*impf*); **as a rule** как пра́вило; **rule out** *vt* (*exclude*) исключа́ть (*perf* исключи́ть); **ruler** *n* прави́тель(ница) *m(f)*; (*instrument*) лине́йка

ruling ['ru:lɪŋ] *adj* (*party*) пра́вящий ▷ *n* (*Law*) постановле́ние

rum [rʌm] *n* ром

Rumania *etc* = **Romania** *etc*

rumble ['rʌmbl] *n* (*of traffic, thunder*) гул

rumour ['ru:mə[r]] (*US* **rumor**) *n* слух ▷ *vt*: **it is rumoured that ...** хо́дят слу́хи, что ...

run [rʌn] (*pt* **ran**, *pp* **run**) *n* (*fast pace*) бег; (*journey*) пое́здка; (*Skiing*) тра́сса; (*Cricket, Baseball*) очко́; (*in tights etc*) спусти́вшиеся пе́тли *fpl* ▷ *vi* бе́гать/бежа́ть (*impf*); (*flee*) бежа́ть (*impf/perf*), сбега́ть (*perf* сбежа́ть); (*work*: *machine*) рабо́тать (*impf*); (*bus, train*) ходи́ть (*impf*); (*play, show*) идти́ (*impf*); (: *contract*) дли́ться (*impf*); (*in election*) баллоти́роваться (*perf*) ▷ *vt* (*race, distance*) пробега́ть (*perf* пробежа́ть); (*business, hotel*) управля́ть (*impf*) +*instr*; (*competition, course*) организова́ть (*impf/perf*); (*house*) вести́ (*impf*); (*Comput*: *program*) выполня́ть (*perf* вы́полнить); (*water*) пуска́ть (*perf* пусти́ть); (*bath*) наполня́ть (*perf* напо́лнить); (*Press*: *feature*) печа́тать (*perf* напеча́тать); **in the long run** в коне́чном ито́ге; **to be on the run** скрыва́ться (*impf*); **to run sth along** *or* **over** (*hand, fingers*) проводи́ть (*perf* провести́) чем-н по +*dat*; **I'll run you to the station** я подвезу́ Вас до ста́нции; **run about** *vi* бе́гать (*impf*); **run around** *vi* = **run about**; **run away** *vi* убега́ть (*perf* убежа́ть); **run down** *vt* (*production, industry*) свора́чивать (*perf* сверну́ть); (*Aut*: *hit*) сбива́ть (*perf* сбить); (*criticize*) поноси́ть (*impf*); **to be run down** (*person*) выбива́ться (*perf* вы́биться) из сил; **run in** *vt* (*Brit*: *car*) обка́тывать (*perf* обката́ть); **run into** *vt fus* (*meet*: *person*) ста́лкиваться (*perf* столкну́ться) с +*instr*; (: *trouble*) ната́лкиваться (*perf* натолкну́ться) на +*acc*; (*collide with*) вреза́ться (*perf* вре́заться) в +*acc*; **run off** *vt* (*copies*) де́лать (*perf* сде́лать), отсня́ть (*perf*) ▷ *vi* (*person, animal*) сбега́ть (*perf* сбежа́ть); **run out** *vi* (*person*) выбега́ть (*perf* вы́бежать); (*liquid*) вытека́ть (*perf* вы́течь); (*lease, visa*) истека́ть (*perf* исте́чь); (*money*) иссяка́ть (*perf* исся́кнуть); **my passport runs out in July** срок де́йствия моего́ па́спорта истека́ет в ию́ле; **run out of** *vt fus*: **I've run out of money/petrol** *or (US)* **gas** у меня́ ко́нчились де́ньги/ко́нчился бензи́н; **run over** *vt* (*Aut*) дави́ть (*perf* задави́ть); **run through** *vt fus* пробега́ть (*perf* пробежа́ть); (*rehearse*) прогоня́ть (*perf* прогна́ть); **run up** *vt*: **to run up a**

debt аккумули́ровать (*impf/perf*) долги́; **to run up against** (*difficulties*) ста́лкиваться (*perf* столкну́ться) с *+instr*; **runaway** *adj* (*truck, horse etc*) потеря́вший управле́ние

rung [rʌŋ] *pp of* **ring** ▷ *n* (*of ladder*) ступе́нька

runner ['rʌnəʳ] *n* (*in race: person*) бегу́н(ья); (: *horse*) скаку́н; (*on sledge, for drawer etc*) по́лоз; **runner-up** *n* финали́ст (*заня́вший второ́е ме́сто*)

running ['rʌnɪŋ] *n* (*sport*) бег; (*of business*) руково́дство ▷ *adj* (*water: to house*) водопрово́дный; **he is in/out of the running for sth** ему́ сули́т/не сули́т что-н; **6 days running** 6 дней подря́д

runny ['rʌnɪ] *adj* (*honey, egg*) жи́дкий; (*nose*) сопли́вый

run-up ['rʌnʌp] *n* (*to event*) преддве́рие

runway ['rʌnweɪ] *n* взлётно-поса́дочная полоса́

rupture ['rʌptʃəʳ] *n* (*Med*) гры́жа

rural ['ruərl] *adj* се́льский

rush [rʌʃ] *n* (*hurry*) спе́шка; (*Comm: sudden demand*) большо́й спрос; (*of water*) пото́к; (*of emotion*) прили́в ▷ *vt*: **to rush one's meal/work** второпя́х съеда́ть (*perf* съесть)/де́лать (*perf* сде́лать) рабо́ту ▷ *vi* (*person*) бежа́ть (*impf*); (*air, water*) хлы́нуть (*perf*); **rushes** *npl* (*Bot*) камы́ши́ *mpl*; **rush hour** *n* час пик

Russia ['rʌʃə] *n* Росси́я; **Russian** *adj* (*native Russian*) ру́сский; (*belonging to Russian Federation*) росси́йский ▷ *n* ру́сский(-ая) *m(f) adj*; (*Ling*) ру́сский язы́к

rust [rʌst] *n* ржа́вчина ▷ *vi* ржаве́ть (*perf* заржаве́ть)

rusty ['rʌstɪ] *adj* ржа́вый; (*fig: skill*) подзабы́тый

ruthless ['ru:θlɪs] *adj* беспоща́дный

rye [raɪ] *n* рожь *f*

S

Sabbath ['sæbəθ] *n* (*Christian*) воскресе́нье

sabotage ['sæbətɑːʒ] *n* сабота́ж ▷ *vt* (*machine, building*) выводи́ть (*perf* вы́вести) из стро́я; (*plan, meeting*) саботи́ровать (*impf/perf*)

sachet ['sæʃeɪ] *n* паке́тик

sack [sæk] *n* (*bag*) мешо́к ▷ *vt* (*dismiss*) увольня́ть (*perf* уво́лить); **to give sb the sack** увольня́ть (*perf* уво́лить) кого́-н (с рабо́ты); **I got the sack** меня́ уво́лили (с рабо́ты)

sacred ['seɪkrɪd] *adj* свяще́нный; (*place*) свято́й

sacrifice ['sækrɪfaɪs] *n* же́ртва; (*Rel*) жертвоприноше́ние ▷ *vt* (*fig*) же́ртвовать (*perf* поже́ртвовать) +*instr*

sad [sæd] *adj* печа́льный

saddle ['sædl] *n* седло́

sadistic [sə'dɪstɪk] *adj* сади́стский

sadly ['sædlɪ] *adv* (*unhappily*) печа́льно, гру́стно; (*unfortunately*) к сожале́нию; (*seriously*: *mistaken, neglected*) серьёзно

sadness ['sædnɪs] *n* печа́ль *f*, грусть *f*

s.a.e. *abbr* (*Brit*) (= *stamped addressed envelope*) *надпи́санный конве́рт с ма́ркой*

safari [sə'fɑːrɪ] *n*: **to go on safari** проводи́ть (*perf* провести́) о́тпуск в сафа́ри

safe [seɪf] *adj* (*place, subject*) безопа́сный; (*return, journey*) благополу́чный; (*bet*) надёжный ▷ *n* сейф; **to be safe** находи́ться (*impf*) в безопа́сности; **safe from** (*attack*) защищённый от +*gen*; **safe and sound** цел и невреди́м; **(just) to be on the safe side** на вся́кий слу́чай; **safely** *adv* (*assume, say*) с уве́ренностью; (*drive, arrive*) благополу́чно; **safety** *n* безопа́сность *f*; **safety pin** англи́йская була́вка

sage [seɪdʒ] *n* (*herb*) шалфе́й

Sagittarius [sædʒɪ'tɛərɪəs] *n* Стреле́ц

said [sɛd] *pt, pp of* **say**

sail [seɪl] *n* па́рус ▷ *vt* (*boat*) пла́вать/плыть (*impf*) на +*prp* ▷ *vi* (*passenger, ship*) пла́вать/плыть (*impf*); (*also* **set sail**) отплыва́ть (*perf* отплы́ть); **to go for a sail** е́хать (*perf* пое́хать) ката́ться на ло́дке; **sailing** *n* (*Sport*) па́русный спорт; **sailor** *n* моря́к, матро́с

saint [seɪnt] *n* свято́й(-а́я) *m(f) adj*

sake [seɪk] *n*: **for the sake of sb/sth, for sb's/sth's sake** ра́ди кого́-н/чего́-н

salad ['sæləd] *n* сала́т

salami [sə'lɑːmɪ] *n* саля́ми *f ind*

salary ['sælərɪ] *n* зарпла́та (= *за́работная пла́та*)

sale [seɪl] *n* (*act*) прода́жа; (*with discount*) распрода́жа; (*auction*) то́рги *mpl*; **sales** *npl* (*amount sold*) объём *msg* прода́жи; **"for sale"** "продаётся"; **on sale** в прода́же; **salesman** *irreg n* (*also* **travelling salesman**) торго́вый аге́нт

saliva [sə'laɪvə] *n* слюна́

salmon ['sæmən] *n inv* (*Zool*) лосо́сь *m*; (*Culin*) лососи́на

salon ['sælɔn] *n* сало́н; **beauty salon** космети́ческий сало́н

salt [sɔ:lt] *n* соль *f*; **salty** *adj* солёный

salute [sə'lu:t] *n* (*Mil*) салю́т ▷ *vt* (*Mil*) отдава́ть (*perf* отда́ть) честь *+dat*; (*fig*) приве́тствовать (*impf*)

salvage ['sælvɪdʒ] *n* (*saving*) спасе́ние ▷ *vt* (*also fig*) спаса́ть (*perf* спасти́)

same [seɪm] *adj* тако́й же; (*identical*) одина́ковый ▷ *pron*: **the same** тот же (са́мый) (*f* та же (са́мая), *nt* то же (са́мое), *pl* те же (са́мые)); **the same book as** та же (са́мая) кни́га, что и; **at the same time** (*simultaneously*) в э́то же вре́мя; (*yet*) в то же вре́мя; **all** *or* **just the same** всё равно́; **to do the same (as sb)** де́лать (*perf* сде́лать) то же (са́мое) (, что и кто-н); **Happy New Year! — the same to you!** С Но́вым Го́дом! — Вас та́кже!

sample ['sɑ:mpl] *n* (*of work, goods*) образе́ц ▷ *vt* (*food, wine*) про́бовать (*perf* попро́бовать); **to take a blood/urine sample** брать (*perf* взять) кровь/мочу́ на ана́лиз

sanction ['sæŋkʃən] *n* (*approval*) са́нкция ▷ *vt* (*approve*) санкциони́ровать (*impf/perf*); **sanctions** *npl* (*severe measures*) са́нкции *fpl*

sanctuary ['sæŋktjuərɪ] *n* (*for animals*) запове́дник; (*for people*) убе́жище

sand [sænd] *n* песо́к ▷ *vt* (*also* **sand down**) ошку́ривать (*perf* ошку́рить)

sandal ['sændl] *n* санда́лия

sandpaper ['sændpeɪpə^r] *n* нажда́чная бума́га

sandstone ['sændstəun] *n* песча́ник

sandwich ['sændwɪtʃ] *n* бутербро́д ▷ *vt*: **sandwiched between** зажа́тый ме́жду *+instr*; **cheese/ham sandwich** бутербро́д с сы́ром/ветчино́й

sandy ['sændɪ] *adj* песча́ный

sane [seɪn] *adj* разу́мный

sang [sæŋ] *pt of* **sing**

sanity ['sænɪtɪ] *n* (*of person*) рассу́док; (*sense*) разу́мность *f*

sank [sæŋk] *pt of* **sink**

Santa Claus [sæntə'klɔ:z] *n* (*in Britain etc*) Са́нта-Кла́ус; (*in Russia*) ≈ Дед Моро́з

sap [sæp] *n* (*Bot*) сок ▷ *vt* (*strength*) выса́сывать (*perf* вы́сосать); (*confidence*) отбира́ть (*perf* отобра́ть)

sapphire ['sæfaɪə^r] *n* сапфи́р

sarcasm ['sɑ:kæzm] *n* сарка́зм

sarcastic [sɑ:'kæstɪk] *adj* саркасти́чный

sardine [sɑ:'di:n] *n* сарди́на

sat [sæt] *pt, pp of* **sit**

satellite ['sætəlaɪt] *n* спу́тник; (*Pol: country*) сателли́т; **satellite dish** *n* спу́тниковая анте́нна

satin ['sætɪn] *adj* атла́сный

satire ['sætaɪə^r] *n* сати́ра

satisfaction [sætɪs'fækʃən] *n* (*pleasure*) удовлетворе́ние; (*refund, apology etc*) возмеще́ние

satisfactory [sætɪs'fæktərɪ] *adj* удовлетвори́тельный
satisfy ['sætɪsfaɪ] *vt* удовлетворя́ть (*perf* удовлетвори́ть); (*convince*) убежда́ть (*perf* убеди́ть); **to satisfy sb (that)** убежда́ть (*perf* убеди́ть) кого́-н (в том, что)
Saturday ['sætədɪ] *n* суббо́та

Saturday job

Saturday job — суббо́тняя рабо́та. Брита́нские шко́льники в суббо́ту не у́чатся, поэ́тому мно́гие подро́стки устра́иваются на суббо́тнюю рабо́ту в кафе́ и́ли магази́н.

sauce [sɔːs] *n* со́ус; **saucepan** *n* кастрю́ля
saucer ['sɔːsə^r] *n* блю́дце
Saudi Arabia [saudɪə'reɪbɪə] *n* Сау́довская Ара́вия
sauna ['sɔːnə] *n* са́уна, фи́нская ба́ня
sausage ['sɔsɪdʒ] *n* (*for cooking*) сарде́лька, соси́ска
savage ['sævɪdʒ] *adj* свире́пый
save [seɪv] *vt* (*rescue*) спаса́ть (*perf* спасти́); (*economize on*) эконо́мить (*perf* сэконо́мить); (*put by*) сберега́ть (*perf* сбере́чь); (*keep*: *receipts, file*) сохраня́ть (*perf* сохрани́ть); (: *seat, place*) занима́ть (*perf* заня́ть); (*work, trouble*) избавля́ть (*perf* изба́вить) от *+gen*; (*Sport*) отбива́ть (*perf* отби́ть), отража́ть (*perf* отрази́ть) ▷ *vi* (*also* **save up**) копи́ть (*perf* скопи́ть) де́ньги ▷ *prep* поми́мо *+gen*
savings ['seɪvɪŋz] *npl* (*money*) сбереже́ния *ntpl*
savour ['seɪvə^r] (*US* **savor**) *vt* (*food, drink*) смакова́ть (*impf*); (*experience*) наслажда́ться (*perf* наслади́ться) *+instr*; **savoury** *adj* несла́дкий
saw [sɔː] (*pt* **sawed**, *pp* **sawed** *or* **sawn**) *vt* пили́ть (*impf*) ▷ *n* пила́ ▷ *pt of* **see**; **sawdust** *n* опи́лки *pl*
saxophone ['sæksəfəun] *n* саксофо́н
say [seɪ] (*pt, pp* **said**) *vt* говори́ть (*perf* сказа́ть) ▷ *n*: **to have one's say** выража́ть (*perf* вы́разить) своё мне́ние; **to say yes** соглаша́ться (*perf* согласи́ться); **to say no** отка́зываться (*perf* отказа́ться); **could you say that again?** повтори́те, пожа́луйста; **that is to say** то есть; **that goes without saying** э́то само́ собо́й разуме́ется; **saying** *n* погово́рка
scab [skæb] *n* (*on wound*) струп
scaffolding ['skæfəldɪŋ] *n* леса́ *mpl*
scald [skɔːld] *n* ожо́г ▷ *vt* ошпа́ривать (*perf* ошпа́рить)
scale [skeɪl] *n* шкала́; (*usu pl*: *of fish*) чешуя́ *f no pl*; (*Mus*) га́мма; (*of map, project etc*) масшта́б ▷ *vt* взбира́ться (*perf* взобра́ться) на *+acc*; **scales** *npl* (*for weighing*) весы́ *pl*; **on a large scale** в широ́ком масшта́бе
scalp [skælp] *n* скальп
scalpel ['skælpl] *n* ска́льпель *m*
scampi ['skæmpɪ] *npl* (*Brit*) паниро́ванные креве́тки *fpl*
scan [skæn] *vt* (*examine*) обсле́довать (*perf*); (*read quickly*) просма́тривать (*perf* просмотре́ть); (*Radar*) скани́ровать (*impf*) ▷ *n* (*Med*) скани́рование; **ultrasound scan** ультразву́к
scandal ['skændl] *n* сканда́л;

(*gossip*) спле́тни *fpl*; (*disgrace*) позо́р

Scandinavia [skændɪ'neɪvɪə] *n* Скандина́вия

scapegoat ['skeɪpɡəut] *n* козёл отпуще́ния

scar [skɑ:] *n* шрам; (*fig*) тра́вма ▷ *vt* травми́ровать (*impf/perf*); **his face is scarred** у него́ на лице́ шрам

scarce [skɛəs] *adj* ре́дкий; **to make o.s. scarce** (*inf*) исчеза́ть (*perf* исче́знуть); **scarcely** *adv* (*hardly*) едва́ ли; (*with numbers*) то́лько

scare [skɛə^r] *n* (*fright*) испу́г; (*public fear*) трево́га, па́ника ▷ *vt* пуга́ть (*perf* испуга́ть); **there was a bomb scare at the station** опаса́лись, что на ста́нции подло́жена бо́мба; **scarecrow** *n* (огоро́дное) чу́чело; **scared** *adj* испу́ганный, напу́ганный; **he was scared** он испуга́лся *or* был испу́ган

scarf [skɑ:f] (*pl* **scarfs** *or* **scarves**) *n* шарф; (*also* **headscarf**) плато́к

scarves [skɑ:vz] *npl of* **scarf**

scary ['skɛərɪ] *adj* стра́шный

scatter ['skætə^r] *vt* (*papers, seeds*) разбра́сывать (*perf* разброса́ть) ▷ *vi* рассыпа́ться (*perf* рассы́паться)

scenario [sɪ'nɑ:rɪəu] *n* сцена́рий

scene [si:n] *n* (*Theat, fig*) сце́на; (*of crime, accident*) ме́сто; (*sight, view*) карти́на; **scenery** *n* (*Theat*) декора́ции *fpl*; (*landscape*) пейза́ж

scenic ['si:nɪk] *adj* живопи́сный

scent [sɛnt] *n* (*smell*) за́пах; (*track, also fig*) след; (*perfume*) духи́ *pl*

sceptical ['skɛptɪkl] (*US* **skeptical**) *adj* (*person*) скепти́чный; (*remarks*) скепти́ческий

schedule ['ʃɛdju:l, (*US*) 'skɛdju:l] *n* (*timetable*) расписа́ние, гра́фик; (*list of prices, details etc*) пе́речень *m* ▷ *vt* (*timetable*) распи́сывать (*perf* расписа́ть); (*visit*) назнача́ть (*perf* назна́чить); **on schedule** по расписа́нию *or* гра́фику; **to be ahead of schedule** опережа́ть (*perf* опереди́ть) гра́фик; **to be behind schedule** отстава́ть (*perf* отста́ть) от гра́фика

scheme [ski:m] *n* (*plan, idea*) за́мысел; (*plot*) про́иски *pl*, ко́зни *pl*; (*pension plan etc*) план

schizophrenic [skɪtsə'frɛnɪk] *adj* шизофрени́ческий

scholar ['skɔlə^r] *n* (*learned person*) учёный *m adj*; **scholarship** *n* (*grant*) стипе́ндия

school [sku:l] *n* шко́ла; (*US*: *inf*) университе́т; (*Brit*: *college*) институ́т ▷ *cpd* шко́льный; **schoolboy** *n* шко́льник; **schoolchildren** *npl* шко́льники *mpl*; **schoolgirl** *n* шко́льница; **schooling** *n* шко́льное образова́ние

science ['saɪəns] *n* нау́ка; (*in school*) естествозна́ние; **science fiction** *n* нау́чная фанта́стика

scientific [saɪən'tɪfɪk] *adj* нау́чный

scientist ['saɪəntɪst] *n* учёный *m adj*

scissors ['sɪzəz] *npl*: **(a pair of) scissors** но́жницы *pl*

scold [skəuld] *vt* брани́ть (*perf* вы́бранить), руга́ть (*perf* отруга́ть)

scone [skɔn] *n* (*Culin*) кекс

scooter ['sku:tə^r] *n* (*also* **motor scooter**) мопе́д; (*toy*) самока́т

scope [skəup] *n* (*opportunity*) просто́р; (*of plan, undertaking*) масшта́б

score [skɔːʳ] *n* (*in game, test*) счёт ▷ *vt* (*goal*) забива́ть (*perf* заби́ть); (*point*) набира́ть (*perf* набра́ть); (*in test*) получа́ть (*perf* получи́ть) ▷ *vi* (*in game*) набира́ть (*perf* набра́ть) очки́; (*Football*) забива́ть (*perf* заби́ть) гол; **scores of** деся́тки *+gen*; **on that score** на э́тот счёт; **to score six out of ten** набира́ть (*perf* набра́ть) шесть ба́ллов из десяти́; **score out** *vt* вычёркивать (*perf* вы́черкнуть); **scoreboard** *n* табло́ *nt ind*

scorn [skɔːn] *n* презре́ние ▷ *vt* презира́ть (*impf*)

Scorpio ['skɔːpɪəu] *n* Скорпио́н

scorpion ['skɔːpɪən] *n* скорпио́н

Scot [skɔt] *n* шотла́ндец(-дка)

Scotch [skɔtʃ] *n* (шотла́ндское) ви́ски *nt ind*

Scotland ['skɔtlənd] *n* Шотла́ндия

Scots [skɔts] *adj* шотла́ндский

Scottish ['skɔtɪʃ] *adj* шотла́ндский

scout [skaut] *n* (*Mil*) разве́дчик; (*also* **boy scout**) (бой)ска́ут

scramble ['skræmbl] *vi*: **to scramble out of** выкара́бкиваться (*perf* вы́карабкаться) из *+gen*; **to scramble for** дра́ться (*perf* подра́ться) за *+acc*; **scrambled eggs** *npl* яи́чница-болту́нья

scrap [skræp] *n* (*of paper*) клочо́к; (*of information*) обры́вок; (*of material*) лоску́т; (*also* **scrap metal**) металлоло́м, металли́ческий лом ▷ *vt* (*machines etc*) отдава́ть (*perf* отда́ть) на слом; (*plans etc*) отка́зываться (*perf* отказа́ться) от *+gen*; **scraps** *npl* (*of food*) объе́дки *mpl*

scrape [skreɪp] *vt* (*remove*) соска́бливать (*perf* соскобли́ть); (*rub against*) цара́пать (*perf* поцара́пать), обдира́ть (*perf* ободра́ть) ▷ *vi*: **to scrape through** (*exam etc*) пролеза́ть (*perf* проле́зть) на *+prp*

scratch [skrætʃ] *n* цара́пина ▷ *vt* цара́пать (*perf* поцара́пать); (*an itch*) чеса́ть (*perf* почеса́ть) ▷ *vi* чеса́ться (*perf* почеса́ться); **from scratch** с нуля́; **to be up to scratch** быть (*impf*) на до́лжном у́ровне

scream [skriːm] *n* вопль *m*, крик ▷ *vi* вопи́ть (*impf*), крича́ть (*impf*)

screen [skriːn] *n* экра́н; (*barrier, also fig*) ши́рма ▷ *vt* (*protect, conceal*) заслоня́ть (*perf* заслони́ть); (*show: film etc*) выпуска́ть (*perf* вы́пустить) на экра́н; (*check: candidates etc*) проверя́ть (*perf* прове́рить); **screening** *n* (*Med*) профилакти́ческий осмо́тр; **screenplay** *n* сцена́рий; **screen saver** *n* скринсе́йвер

screw [skruː] *n* винт ▷ *vt* (*fasten*) приви́нчивать (*perf* привинти́ть); **to screw sth in** зави́нчивать (*perf* завинти́ть) что-н; **screwdriver** *n* отвёртка

scribble ['skrɪbl] *vt* черкну́ть (*perf*) ▷ *vi* исчёркивать (*perf* исчёркать)

script [skrɪpt] *n* (*Cinema etc*) сцена́рий; (*Arabic etc*) шрифт

scroll [skrəul] *n* сви́ток ▷ *vt*: **to scroll up/down** перемеща́ть (*perf* перемести́ть) наве́рх/вниз

scrub [skrʌb] *vt* скрести́ (*impf*)

scruffy ['skrʌfɪ] *adj* потрёпанный

scrutiny ['skruːtɪnɪ] *n* тща́тельное изуче́ние *or* рассмотре́ние

sculptor ['skʌlptəʳ] *n* ску́льптор

sculpture ['skʌlptʃəʳ] *n* скульптýра
scum [skʌm] *n* пéна; (*inf: pej: people*) подóнки *mpl*
sea [siː] *n* мóре ▷ *cpd* морскóй; **by sea** (*travel*) мóрем; **on the sea** (*town*) на мóре; **out to sea, out at sea** в мóре; **seafood** *n* рыбные блюда *ntpl*; **seafront** *n* нáбережная *f adj*; **seagull** *n* чáйка
seal [siːl] *n* (*Zool*) тюлéнь *m*; (*stamp*) печáть *f* ▷ *vt* (*envelope*) запечáтывать (*perf* запечáтать); (*opening*) задéлывать (*perf* задéлать)
sea level *n* ýровень *m* мóря
seam [siːm] *n* (*of garment*) шов
search [səːtʃ] *n* пóиск; (*for criminal*) рóзыск; (*of sb's home etc*) óбыск ▷ *vt* обыскивать (*perf* обыскáть) ▷ *vi*: **to search for** искáть (*impf*); **in search of** в пóисках *+gen*
seasick ['siːsɪk] *adj*: **to be seasick** страдáть (*impf*) морскóй болéзнью
seaside ['siːsaɪd] *n* взмóрье
season ['siːzn] *n* врéмя *nt* гóда; (*for football, of films etc*) сезóн ▷ *vt* (*food*) заправлять (*perf* заправить); **seasonal** *adj* сезóнный; **seasoning** *n* приправа
seat [siːt] *n* (*chair, place*) сидéнье; (*in theatre, parliament*) мéсто; (*of trousers*) зад ▷ *vt* (*subj: venue*) вмещáть (*perf* вместить); **to be seated** сидéть (*impf*); **seat belt** *n* привязнóй ремéнь *m*
seaweed ['siːwiːd] *n* вóдоросли *fpl*
sec. *abbr* = **second²**
secluded [sɪ'kluːdɪd] *adj* уединённый

second¹ [sɪ'kɔnd] *vt* (*Brit: employee*) командировáть (*impf*)
second² ['sɛkənd] *adj* вторóй ▷ *adv* (*come*) вторым; (*when listing*) во-вторых ▷ *n* (*unit of time*) секýнда; (*Aut: also* **second gear**) вторáя скóрость *f*; (*Comm*) некондициóнный товáр; (*Brit: Scol*) диплóм вторóго клáсса ▷ *vt* (*motion*) поддéрживать (*perf* поддержáть); **secondary** *adj* вторичный; **secondary school** *n* срéдняя шкóла; **second-class** *adj* второразрядный; **second-class stamp** мáрка вторóго клáсса

SECOND-CLASS POSTAGE

В Великобритáнии мóжно приобрести почтóвые мáрки пéрвого и вторóго клáсса. Мáрки вторóго клáсса дешéвле. Письма с такими мáрками доставляются по мéсту назначéния чéрез 2-3 дня.

second: **second-hand** *adj* подéржанный, сэ́конд-хэнд *ind*; **secondly** *adv* во-вторых; **second-rate** *adj* (*film*) посрéдственный; (*restaurant*) второразрядный; **second thoughts** *npl*: **to have second thoughts (about doing)** сомневáться (*impf*) (слéдует ли *+infin*); **on second thoughts** *or (US)* **thought** по зрéлом размышлéнии
secrecy ['siːkrəsɪ] *n* секрéтность *f*
secret ['siːkrɪt] *adj* секрéтный, тáйный; (*admirer*) тáйный ▷ *n* секрéт, тáйна; **in secret** (*do, meet*) секрéтно, тáйно
secretary ['sɛkrətərɪ] *n* секретáрь

S

m; **Secretary of State (for)** (*Brit*) ≈ мини́стр (+*gen*)
secretive ['si:krətɪv] *adj* (*pej*: *person*) скры́тный; **he is secretive about his plans** он де́ржит свои́ пла́ны в секре́те
secret service *n* секре́тная слу́жба
sect [sɛkt] *n* се́кта
section ['sɛkʃən] *n* (*part*) часть *f*; (*of population, company*) се́ктор; (*of document, book*) разде́л
sector ['sɛktə^r] *n* (*part*) се́ктор
secular ['sɛkjulə^r] *adj* све́тский
secure [sɪ'kjuə^r] *adj* (*safe*: *person, money, job*) надёжный; (*firmly fixed*: *rope, shelf*) про́чный ▷ *vt* (*fix*: *rope, shelf etc*) (про́чно) закрепля́ть (*perf* закрепи́ть); (*get*: *job, loan etc*) обеспе́чивать (*perf* обеспе́чить)
security [sɪ'kjuərɪtɪ] *n* (*protection*) безопа́сность *f*; (*for one's future*) обеспе́ченность *f*
sedate [sɪ'deɪt] *adj* (*person*) степе́нный; (*pace*) разме́ренный ▷ *vt* дава́ть (*perf* дать) седати́вное *or* успокои́тельное сре́дство
sedative ['sɛdɪtɪv] *n* седати́вное *or* успокои́тельное сре́дство
seduce [sɪ'dju:s] *vt* соблазня́ть (*perf* соблазни́ть)
seductive [sɪ'dʌktɪv] *adj* (*look, voice*) обольсти́тельный; (*offer*) соблазни́тельный
see [si:] (*pt* **saw**, *pp* **seen**) *vt* ви́деть (*perf* уви́деть) ▷ *vi* ви́деть (*impf*); (*find out*) выясня́ть (*perf* вы́яснить); **to see that** (*ensure*) следи́ть (*perf* проследи́ть), что́бы; **see you soon!** пока́!, до ско́рого!; **see off** *vt* провожа́ть (*perf* проводи́ть); **see through** *vt* доводи́ть (*perf* довести́) до конца́ ▷ *vt fus* ви́деть (*impf*) наскво́зь +*acc*; **see to** *vt fus* позабо́титься (*perf*) о +*prp*
seed [si:d] *n* се́мя *nt*; **to go to seed** (*fig*) сдать (*perf*)
seeing ['si:ɪŋ] *conj*: **seeing (that)** поско́льку, так как
seek [si:k] (*pt, pp* **sought**) *vt* иска́ть (*impf*)
seem [si:m] *vi* каза́ться (*perf* показа́ться); **there seems to be ...** ка́жется, что име́ется ...; **he seems to be tired** он ка́жется уста́лым; **seemingly** *adv* по-ви́димому; (*important*) как представля́ется
seen [si:n] *pp of* **see**
segment ['sɛgmənt] *n* (*of population*) се́ктор; (*of orange*) до́лька
seize [si:z] *vt* хвата́ть (*perf* схвати́ть); (*power, hostage, territory*) захва́тывать (*perf* захвати́ть); (*opportunity*) по́льзоваться (*perf* воспо́льзоваться) +*instr*
seizure ['si:ʒə^r] *n* (*Med*) при́ступ; (*of power*) захва́т; (*of goods*) конфиска́ция
seldom ['sɛldəm] *adv* ре́дко
select [sɪ'lɛkt] *adj* (*school, area*) эли́тный ▷ *vt* (*choose*) выбира́ть (*perf* вы́брать); **selection** [sɪ'lɛkʃən] *n* (*process*) отбо́р; (*range*) вы́бор; (*medley*) подбо́рка; **selective** *adj* (*person*) разбо́рчивый; (*not general*) избира́тельный
self [sɛlf] (*pl* **selves**) *n*: **he became his usual self again** он стал опя́ть сами́м собо́й ▷ *prefix* само-; **self-assured** *adj* самоуве́ренный; **self-catering** *adj* (*Brit*): **self-catering holiday** *туристи́ческая путёвка, в кото́рую включа́ется прое́зд и жильё*;

self-centred (*US* **self-centered**) *adj* эгоцентри́чный; **self-confidence** *n* уве́ренность *f* в себе́; **self-conscious** *adj* (*nervous*) засте́нчивый; **self-control** *n* самооблада́ние; **self-defence** (*US* **self-defense**) *n* самозащи́та, самооборо́на; **in self-defence** защища́я себя́; **self-employed** *adj* рабо́тающий на себя́; **selfie** *n* се́лфи *nt ind*; **self-interest** *n* коры́сть *f*; **selfish** *adj* эгоисти́ческий; **self-pity** *n* жа́лость *f* к (самому́) себе́; **self-respect** *n* самоуваже́ние; **self-service** *adj*: **self-service restaurant** кафе́ *nt ind* с самообслу́живанием

sell [sɛl] (*pt, pp* **sold**) *vt* продава́ть (*perf* прода́ть) ▷ *vi* продава́ться (*impf*); **to sell at** *or* **for 10 pounds** продава́ться (*impf*) по 10 фу́нтов; **sell off** *vt* распродава́ть (*perf* распрода́ть); **sell out** *vi* (*book etc*) расходи́ться (*perf* разойти́сь); (*shop*): **to sell out of sth** распродава́ть (*perf* распрода́ть) что-н; **the tickets are sold out** все биле́ты про́даны

Sellotape ['sɛləuteɪp] *n* (*Brit*) кле́йкая ле́нта

selves [sɛlvz] *pl of* **self**

semester [sɪ'mɛstə^r] *n* (*esp US*) семе́стр

semi- ['sɛmɪ] *prefix* полу-

SEMI

Semi — полуособня́к. В Великобрита́нии мно́гие се́мьи живу́т в полуособняка́х - два двухэта́жных до́ма име́ют одну́ о́бщую сте́ну, но отде́льный вход и сад.

semi: **semicircle** *n* полукру́г; **semicolon** *n* то́чка с запято́й; **semifinal** *n* полуфина́л

seminar ['sɛmɪnɑː^r] *n* семина́р

senate ['sɛnɪt] *n* сена́т

senator ['sɛnɪtə^r] *n* (*US etc*) сена́тор

send [sɛnd] (*pt, pp* **sent**) *vt* посыла́ть (*perf* посла́ть); **send away** *vt* (*letter, goods*) отсыла́ть (*perf* отосла́ть); (*visitor*) прогоня́ть (*perf* прогна́ть); **send back** *vt* посыла́ть (*perf* посла́ть) обра́тно; **send for** *vt fus* (*by post*) зака́зывать (*perf* заказа́ть); (*person*) посыла́ть (*perf* посла́ть) за *+instr*; **send off** *vt* (*letter*) отправля́ть (*perf* отпра́вить); (*Brit: Sport*) удаля́ть (*perf* удали́ть); **send out** *vt* (*invitation*) рассыла́ть (*perf* разосла́ть); (*signal*) посыла́ть (*perf* посла́ть); **sender** *n* отправи́тель *m*

senile ['siːnaɪl] *adj* маразмати́ческий

senior ['siːnɪə^r] *adj* (*staff, officer*) ста́рший; (*manager, consultant*) гла́вный; **to be senior to sb** (*in rank*) быть (*impf*) вы́ше кого́-н по положе́нию; **she is 15 years his senior** она́ ста́рше его́ на 15 лет; **senior citizen** *n* (*esp Brit*) пожило́й челове́к, челове́к пенсио́нного во́зраста

sensation [sɛn'seɪʃən] *n* (*feeling*) ощуще́ние; (*great success*) сенса́ция; **sensational** *adj* (*wonderful*) потряса́ющий; (*dramatic*) сенсацио́нный

sense [sɛns] *vt* чу́вствовать (*perf* почу́вствовать), ощуща́ть (*perf* ощути́ть) ▷ *n* (*feeling*) чу́вство, ощуще́ние; **it makes sense** в э́том есть смысл; **the senses** пять чувств; **senseless** *adj* бессмы́сленный; (*unconscious*) бесчу́вственный; **sense of humour** (*US* **sense of humor**) *n* чу́вство ю́мора

sensible ['sɛnsɪbl] *adj* разу́мный; (*shoes*) практи́чный

sensitive ['sɛnsɪtɪv] *adj* чувстви́тельный; (*understanding*) чу́ткий; (*issue*) щекотли́вый

sensual ['sɛnsjuəl] *adj* чу́вственный

sensuous ['sɛnsjuəs] *adj* (*lips*) чу́вственный; (*material*) не́жный

sent [sɛnt] *pt, pp of* **send**

sentence ['sɛntns] *n* (*Ling*) предложе́ние; (*Law*) пригово́р ▷ *vt*: **to sentence sb to** пригова́ривать (*perf* приговори́ть) кого́-н к *+dat*

sentiment ['sɛntɪmənt] *n* (*tender feelings*) чу́вство; (*opinion*) настрое́ние; **sentimental** [sɛntɪ'mɛntl] *adj* сентимента́льный

separate [*adj* 'sɛprɪt, *vb* 'sɛpəreɪt] *adj* отде́льный; (*ways*) ра́зный ▷ *vt* (*split up*: *people*) разлуча́ть (*perf* разлучи́ть); (: *things*) разделя́ть (*perf* раздели́ть); (*distinguish*) различа́ть (*perf* различи́ть) ▷ *vi* расходи́ться (*perf* разойти́сь); **separately** ['sɛprɪtlɪ] *adv* отде́льно, по отде́льности; **separation** [sɛpə'reɪʃən] *n* (*being apart*) разлу́ка; (*Law*) разде́льное прожива́ние

September [sɛp'tɛmbə[r]] *n* сентя́брь *m*

septic ['sɛptɪk] *adj* заражённый

sequel ['si:kwl] *n* продолже́ние

sequence ['si:kwəns] *n* после́довательность *f*

Serbia ['sə:bɪə] *n* Се́рбия

Serbo-Croat ['sə:bəu'krəuæt] *adj* се́рбо-хорва́тский

sergeant ['sɑ:dʒənt] *n* сержа́нт

serial ['sɪərɪəl] *n* (*TV, Radio*) сериа́л; (*Press*) *произведе́ние в не́скольких частя́х*

series ['sɪərɪz] *n inv* се́рия

serious ['sɪərɪəs] *adj* серьёзный; **are you serious (about it)?** Вы (э́то) серьёзно?; **seriously** *adv* серьёзно

sermon ['sə:mən] *n* про́поведь *f*

servant ['sə:vənt] *n* слуга́(-ужа́нка) *m(f)*

serve [sə:v] *vt* (*company, country*) служи́ть (*impf*) *+dat*; (*customer*) обслу́живать (*perf* обслужи́ть); (*subj*: *train etc*) обслу́живать (*impf*); (*apprenticeship*) проходи́ть (*perf* пройти́); (*prison term*) отбыва́ть (*perf* отбы́ть) ▷ *vi* (*Tennis*) подава́ть (*perf* пода́ть) ▷ *n* (*Tennis*) пода́ча; **it serves him right**подело́м ему́; **to serve on** (*jury, committee*) состоя́ть (*impf*) в *+prp*; **to serve as/for** служи́ть (*perf* послужи́ть) *+instr*/вме́сто *+gen*

service ['sə:vɪs] *n* (*help*) услу́га; (*in hotel*) обслу́живание, се́рвис; (*Rel*) слу́жба; (*Aut*) техобслу́живание; (*Tennis*) пода́ча ▷ *vt* (*car*) проводи́ть (*perf* провести́) техобслу́живание *+gen*; **services** *npl*: **the Services** (*Mil*) Вооружённые си́лы *fpl*; **military** *or* **national service** вое́нная слу́жба; **train service** железнодоро́жное сообще́ние; **postal service** почто́вая связь

serviette [sə:vɪ'ɛt] *n* (*Brit*) салфе́тка

session ['sɛʃən] *n* (*of treatment*) сеа́нс; **recording session** за́пись *f*; **to be in session** (*court etc*) заседа́ть (*impf*)

set [sɛt] (*pt, pp* **set**) *n* (*collection*) набóр; (*of pans, clothes*) комплéкт; (*also* **television set**) телевúзор; (*Tennis*) сет; (*Math*) мнóжество; (*Cinema, Theat*: *stage*) сцéна ▷ *adj* (*fixed*) установленный; (*ready*) готóвый ▷ *vt* (*place*: *vertically*) стáвить (*perf* постáвить); (: *horizontally*) класть (*perf* положúть); (*table*) накрывáть (*perf* накрыть); (*time*) назначáть (*perf* назнáчить); (*price, record*) устанáвливать (*perf* установúть); (*alarm, task*) стáвить (*perf* постáвить); (*exam*) составлять (*perf* состáвить) ▷ *vi* (*sun*) садúться (*perf* сесть), заходúть (*perf* зайтú); (*jam*) густéть (*perf* загустéть); (*jelly, concrete*) застывáть (*perf* застыть); **to set to music** класть (*perf* положúть) на мýзыку; **to set on fire** поджигáть (*perf* поджéчь); **to set free** освобождáть (*perf* освободúть); **set about** *vt fus* (*task*) приступáть (*perf* приступúть) к +*dat*; **set aside** *vt* (*money*) откладывать (*perf* отложúть); (*time*) выделять (*perf* вы́делить); **set back** *vt* (*progress*) задéрживать (*perf* задержáть); **to set sb back £5** обходúться (*perf* обойтúсь) комý-н в £5; **set off** *vi* отправляться (*perf* отпрáвиться) ▷ *vt* (*bomb*) взрывáть (*perf* взорвáть); (*alarm*) приводúть (*perf* привестú) в дéйствие; (*events*) повлекáть (*perf* повлéчь) (за собóй); **set out** *vt* выставлять (*perf* вы́ставить) ▷ *vi* (*depart*): **to set out (from)** отправляться (*perf* отпрáвиться) (из +*gen*); **to set out to do** намеревáться (*impf*) +*infin*; **set up** *vt* (*organization*) учреждáть (*perf* учредúть);

setback *n* неудáча

settee [sɛ'ti:] *n* дивáн

setting ['sɛtɪŋ] *n* (*background*) обстанóвка; (*position*: *of controls*) положéние

settle ['sɛtl] *vt* (*argument, problem*) разрешáть (*perf* разрешúть); (*matter*) улáживать (*perf* улáдить); (*bill*) рассчúтываться (*perf* рассчитáться) с +*instr* ▷ *vi* (*dust, sediment*) оседáть (*perf* осéсть); (*also* **settle down**) обоснóвываться (*perf* обосновáться); (: *live sensibly*) остепеняться (*perf* остепенúться); (: *calm down*) успокáиваться (*perf* успокóиться); **to settle for sth** соглашáться (*perf* согласúться) на что-н; **to settle on sth** останáвливаться (*perf* остановúться) на чём-н; **settle in** *vi* освáиваться (*perf* освóиться); **settlement** *n* (*payment*) уплáта; (*agreement*) соглашéние; (*village, colony*) поселéние; (*of conflict*) урегулúрование

seven ['sɛvn] *n* семь; **seventeen** *n* семнáдцать; **seventeenth** *adj* семнáдцатый; **seventh** *adj* седьмóй; **seventieth** *adj* семидесятый; **seventy** *n* сéмьдесят

sever ['sɛvə^r] *vt* (*artery, pipe*) перерезáть (*perf* перерéзать); (*relations*) прерывáть (*perf* прервáть)

several ['sɛvərl] *adj* нéсколько +*gen* ▷ *pron* нéкоторые *pl adj*; **several of us** нéкоторые из нас

severe [sɪ'vɪə^r] *adj* (*shortage, pain, winter*) жестóкий; (*damage*) серьёзный; (*stern*) жёсткий

sew [səu] (*pt* **sewed**, *pp* **sewn**) *vt, vi* шить (*impf*)

S

sewage ['su:ɪdʒ] *n* сто́чные во́ды *fpl*; **sewage system** канализа́ция
sewer ['su:əʳ] *n* канализацио́нная труба́
sewing ['səuɪŋ] *n* шитьё; **sewing machine** *n* шве́йная маши́нка
sewn [səun] *pp of* **sew**
sex [sɛks] *n* (*gender*) пол; (*lovemaking*) секс; **to have sex with sb** переспа́ть (*perf*) с кем-н; **sexist** *adj* секси́стский; **he is sexist** он — секси́ст; **sexual** *adj* полово́й; **sexual equality** ра́венство поло́в; **sexual harassment** сексуа́льное пресле́дование; **sexy** *adj* сексуа́льный; (*woman*) сексопи́льная
shabby ['ʃæbɪ] *adj* потрёпанный; (*treatment*) недосто́йный
shack [ʃæk] *n* лачу́га
shade [ʃeɪd] *n* (*shelter*) тень *f*; (*for lamp*) абажу́р; (*of colour*) отте́нок ▷ *vt* (*shelter*) затеня́ть (*perf* затени́ть); (*eyes*) заслоня́ть (*perf* заслони́ть); **in the shade** в тени́
shadow ['ʃædəu] *n* тень *f* ▷ *vt* (*follow*) сле́довать (*impf*) как тень за *+instr*; **shadow cabinet** *n* (*Brit*) тенево́й кабине́т
shady ['ʃeɪdɪ] *adj* (*place, trees*) тени́стый; (*fig*: *dishonest*) тёмный
shaft [ʃɑ:ft] *n* (*of mine, lift*) ша́хта; (*of light*) сноп
shake [ʃeɪk] (*pt* **shook**, *pp* **shaken**) *vt* трясти́ (*impf*); (*bottle*) взба́лтывать (*perf* взболта́ть); (*building*) сотряса́ть (*perf* сотрясти́); (*weaken*: *beliefs, resolve*) пошатну́ть (*perf*); (*upset, surprise*) потряса́ть (*perf* потрясти́) ▷ *vi* (*voice*) дрожа́ть (*impf*); **to shake one's head** кача́ть (*perf* покача́ть) голово́й; **to shake hands with sb** жать (*perf* пожа́ть) кому́-н ру́ку; **to shake with** трясти́сь (*impf*) от *+gen*; **shake off** *vt* стря́хивать (*perf* стряхну́ть); (*fig*: *pursuer*) избавля́ться (*perf* изба́виться) от *+gen*; **shake up** *vt* (*fig*: *organization*) встря́хивать (*perf* встряхну́ть)
shaky ['ʃeɪkɪ] *adj* (*hand, voice*) дрожа́щий
shall [ʃæl] *aux vb*: **I shall go** я пойду́; **shall I open the door?** (мне) откры́ть дверь?; **I'll get some water, shall I?** я принесу́ воды́, да?
shallow ['ʃæləu] *adj* (*water*) ме́лкий; (*box*) неглубо́кий; (*breathing, also fig*) пове́рхностный
sham [ʃæm] *n* притво́рство
shambles ['ʃæmblz] *n* неразбери́ха
shame [ʃeɪm] *n* (*embarrassment*) стыд; (*disgrace*) позо́р ▷ *vt* позо́рить (*perf* опозо́рить); **it is a shame that/to do** жаль, что/*+infin*; **what a shame!** кака́я жа́лость!, как жаль!; **shameful** *adj* позо́рный; **shameless** *adj* бессты́дный
shampoo [ʃæm'pu:] *n* шампу́нь *m* ▷ *vt* мыть (помы́ть *or* вы́мыть *perf*) шампу́нем
shan't [ʃɑ:nt] = **shall not**
shape [ʃeɪp] *n* фо́рма ▷ *vt* (*ideas, events*) формирова́ть (*perf* сформирова́ть); (*clay*) лепи́ть (*perf* слепи́ть); **to take shape** обрета́ть (*perf* обрести́) фо́рму
share [ʃɛəʳ] *n* до́ля; (*Comm*) а́кция ▷ *vt* (*books, cost*) дели́ть (*perf* подели́ть); (*toys*) дели́ться (*perf* подели́ться) *+instr*; (*features, qualities*) разделя́ть (*impf*); (*opinion, concern*) разделя́ть (*perf* раздели́ть); **share out** *vt* дели́ть

(*perf* разделить); **shareholder** *n* акционер
shark [ʃɑ:k] *n* акула
sharp [ʃɑ:p] *adj* острый; (*sound*) резкий; (*Mus*) диез *ind* ▷ *adv* (*precisely*): **at 2 o'clock sharp** ровно в два часа; **he is very sharp** у него очень острый ум; **sharpen** *vt* (*pencil, knife*) точить (*perf* поточить); **sharpener** *n* (*also* **pencil sharpener**) точилка; **sharply** *adv* резко
shatter [ˈʃætəʳ] *vt* (*vase, hopes*) разбивать (*perf* разбить); (*upset: person*) потрясать (*perf* потрясти) ▷ *vi* биться (*perf* разбиться)
shave [ʃeɪv] *vt* брить (*perf* побрить) ▷ *vi* бриться (*perf* побриться) ▷ *n*: **to have a shave** бриться (*perf* побриться)
shawl [ʃɔ:l] *n* шаль *f*
she [ʃi:] *pron* она
shed [ʃɛd] (*pt, pp* **shed**) *n* (*in garden*) сарай ▷ *vt* (*skin, load*) сбрасывать (*perf* сбросить); (*tears*) лить (*impf*)
she'd [ʃi:d] = **she had**; **she would**
sheep [ʃi:p] *n inv* овца; **sheepdog** *n* овчарка
sheer [ʃɪəʳ] *adj* (*utter*) сущий; (*steep*) отвесный
sheet [ʃi:t] *n* (*on bed*) простыня; (*of paper, glass etc*) лист; (*of ice*) полоса
sheik(h) [ʃeɪk] *n* шейх
shelf [ʃɛlf] (*pl* **shelves**) *n* полка
shell [ʃɛl] *n* (*of mollusc*) раковина; (*of egg, nut*) скорлупа; (*explosive*) снаряд; (*of building*) каркас; (*of ship*) корпус ▷ *vt* (*peas*) лущить (*perf* облущить); (*Mil*) обстреливать (*perf* обстрелять)
she'll [ʃi:l] = **she will**; **she shall**
shellfish [ˈʃɛlfɪʃ] *n inv* (*crab*) рачки *pl*; (*scallop*) моллюски *mpl*
shelter [ˈʃɛltəʳ] *n* (*refuge*) приют; (*protection*) укрытие ▷ *vt* (*protect*) укрывать (*perf* укрыть); (*hide*) давать (*perf* дать) приют +*dat* ▷ *vi* укрываться (*perf* укрыться); **sheltered** *adj* (*life*) беззаботный; (*spot*) защищённый
shelves [ʃɛlvz] *npl of* **shelf**
shepherd [ˈʃɛpəd] *n* пастух
sheriff [ˈʃɛrɪf] *n* (*US*) шериф
sherry [ˈʃɛrɪ] *n* херес
she's [ʃi:z] = **she is**; **she has**
shield [ʃi:ld] *n* щит; (*trophy*) трофей ▷ *vt*: **to shield (from)** заслонять (*perf* заслонить) (от +*gen*)
shift [ʃɪft] *n* (*in direction, conversation*) перемена; (*in policy, emphasis*) сдвиг; (*at work*) смена ▷ *vt* передвигать (*perf* передвинуть), перемещать (*perf* переместить) ▷ *vi* перемещаться (*perf* переместиться)
shin [ʃɪn] *n* голень *f*
shine [ʃaɪn] (*pt, pp* **shone**) *n* блеск ▷ *vi* (*sun, light*) светить (*impf*); (*eyes, hair*) блестеть (*impf*) ▷ *vt*: **to shine a torch on sth** направлять (*perf* направить) фонарь на что-н
shiny [ˈʃaɪnɪ] *adj* блестящий
ship [ʃɪp] *n* корабль *m* ▷ *vt* (*by ship*) перевозить (*perf* перевезти) по морю; (*send*) отправлять (*perf* отправить), экспедировать (*impf/perf*); **shipment** *n* (*goods*) партия; **shipping** *n* (*of cargo*) перевозка; **shipwreck** *n* (*ship*) судно, потерпевшее крушение ▷ *vt*: **to be shipwrecked** терпеть (*perf* потерпеть) кораблекрушение; **shipyard** *n* (судостроительная) верфь *f*
shirt [ʃə:t] *n* (*man's*) рубашка;

S

(*woman's*) блу́зка; **in (one's) shirt sleeves** в одно́й руба́шке
shit [ʃɪt] *excl* (*inf!*) чёрт!, блин!
shiver [ˈʃɪvəʳ] *n* дрожь *f* ▷ *vi* дрожа́ть (*impf*)
shock [ʃɔk] *n* (*start, impact*) толчо́к; (*Elec, Med*) шок; (*emotional*) потрясе́ние ▷ *vt* (*upset*) потряса́ть (*perf* потрясти́); (*offend*) возмуща́ть (*perf* возмути́ть), шоки́ровать (*impf/perf*); **shocking** *adj* (*outrageous*) возмути́тельный; (*dreadful*) кошма́рный
shoe [ʃuː] *n* (*for person*) ту́фля; (*for horse*) подко́ва; **shoes** (*footwear*) о́бувь *fsg*; **shoelace** *n* шнуро́к
shone [ʃɔn] *pt, pp of* **shine**
shook [ʃuk] *pt of* **shake**
shoot [ʃuːt] (*pt, pp* **shot**) *n* (*Bot*) росто́к, побе́г ▷ *vt* (*gun*) стреля́ть (*impf*) из +*gen*; (*bird, robber etc: kill*) застре́ливать (*perf* застрели́ть); (*: wound*) вы́стрелить (*perf*) в +*acc*; (*film*) снима́ть (*perf* снять) ▷ *vi*: **to shoot (at)** стреля́ть (*perf* вы́стрелить) (в +*acc*); (*Football etc*) бить (*impf*) (по +*dat*); **shoot down** *vt* (*plane*) сбива́ть (*perf* сбить); **shooting** *n* (*shots, attack*) стрельба́; (*Hunting*) охо́та
shop [ʃɔp] *n* магази́н; (*also* **workshop**) мастерска́я *f adj* ▷ *vi* (*also* **go shopping**) ходи́ть (*impf*) по магази́нам, де́лать (*perf* сде́лать) поку́пки; **shopkeeper** *n* владе́лец(-лица) магази́на; **shoplifting** *n* кра́жа това́ров (*из магази́нов*); **shopping** *n* (*goods*) поку́пки *fpl*; **shopping centre** (*US* **shopping center**) *n* торго́вый центр; **shopping mall** *n* (*esp US*) = **shopping centre**
shore [ʃɔːʳ] *n* бе́рег
short [ʃɔːt] *adj* коро́ткий; (*in height*) невысо́кий; (*curt*) ре́зкий; (*insufficient*) ску́дный; **we are short of milk** у нас ма́ло молока́; **in short** коро́че говоря́; **it is short for ...** э́то сокраще́ние от +*gen* ...; **to cut short** (*speech, visit*) прерыва́ть (*perf* прерва́ть); **everything short of ...** всё, кро́ме +*gen* ...; **short of doing** кро́ме как +*infin*; **to fall short of** не выполня́ть (*perf* вы́полнить); **we're running short of time** у нас зака́нчивается вре́мя; **to stop short** застыва́ть (*perf* засты́ть) на ме́сте; **to stop short of doing** не осме́ливаться (*perf* осме́литься) +*infin*; **shortage** *n*: **a shortage of** нехва́тка +*gen*, дефици́т +*gen*; **short cut** *n* (*on journey*) коро́ткий путь *m*; **shortfall** *n* недоста́ток; **shorthand** *n* (*Brit*) стеногра́фия; **short-lived** *adj* кратковре́менный, недо́лгий; **shortly** *adv* вско́ре; **shorts** *npl*: **(a pair of) shorts** шо́рты *pl*; **short-sighted** *adj* (*Brit*) близору́кий; **short story** *n* расска́з; **short-term** *adj* (*effect*) кратковре́менный
shot [ʃɔt] *pt, pp of* **shoot** ▷ *n* (*of gun*) вы́стрел; (*Football*) уда́р; (*injection*) уко́л; (*Phot*) сни́мок; **a good/poor shot** (*person*) ме́ткий/ плохо́й стрело́к; **like a shot** ми́гом; **shotgun** *n* дробови́к
should [ʃud] *aux vb*: **I should go now** я до́лжен идти́; **I should go if I were you** на Ва́шем ме́сте я бы пошёл; **I should like to** я бы хоте́л
shoulder [ˈʃəuldəʳ] *n* (*Anat*) плечо́ ▷ *vt* (*fig*) принима́ть (*perf* приня́ть) на себя́; **shoulder blade** *n* лопа́тка

shouldn't ['ʃudnt] = **should not**
shout [ʃaut] *n* крик ▷ *vt* выкри́кивать (*perf* вы́крикнуть) ▷ *vi* (*also* **shout out**) крича́ть (*impf*)
shove [ʃʌv] *vt* толка́ть (*perf* толкну́ть); (*inf: put*): **to shove sth in** запи́хивать (запиха́ть *or* запихну́ть *perf*) что-н в *+acc*
shovel ['ʃʌvl] *n* лопа́та ▷ *vt* (*snow, coal*) грести́ (*impf*) (*лопа́той*)
show [ʃəu] (*pt* **showed**, *pp* **shown**) *n* (*of emotion*) проявле́ние; (*semblance*) подо́бие; (*exhibition*) вы́ставка; (*Theat*) спекта́кль *m*; (*TV*) програ́мма, шо́у *nt ind* ▷ *vt* пока́зывать (*perf* показа́ть); (*courage etc*) проявля́ть (*perf* прояви́ть) ▷ *vi* (*be evident*) проявля́ться (*perf* прояви́ться); **for show** для ви́ду; **to be on show** (*exhibits etc*) выставля́ться (*impf*); **show in** *vt* (*person*) проводи́ть (*perf* провести́); **show off** *vi* хва́статься (*impf*) ▷ *vt* (*display*) хва́статься (*perf* похва́статься) *+instr*; **show out** *vt* (*person*) провожа́ть (*perf* проводи́ть) к вы́ходу; **show up** *vi* (*against background*) видне́ться (*impf*); (*fig*) обнару́живаться (*perf* обнару́житься); (*inf: turn up*) явля́ться (*perf* яви́ться) ▷ *vt* (*uncover*) выявля́ть (*perf* вы́явить); **show business** *n* шо́у-би́знес
shower ['ʃauə[r]] *n* (*also* **shower bath**) душ; (*of rain*) кратковре́менный дождь *m* ▷ *vi* принима́ть (*perf* приня́ть) душ ▷ *vt*: **to shower sb with** (*gifts, abuse etc*) осыпа́ть (*perf* осы́пать) кого́-н *+instr*; **to have** *or* **take a shower** принима́ть (*perf* приня́ть) душ; **shower gel** *n* гель *m* для ду́ша
show: **showing** *n* (*of film*) пока́з, демонстра́ция; **show jumping** *n* конку́р; **shown** *pp of* **show**; **show-off** *n* (*inf*) хвасту́н(ья); **showroom** *n* демонстрацио́нный зал
shrank [ʃræŋk] *pt of* **shrink**
shred [ʃrɛd] *n* (*usu pl*) клочо́к ▷ *vt* кроши́ть (*perf* накроши́ть)
shrewd [ʃru:d] *adj* проница́тельный
shriek [ʃri:k] *n* визг ▷ *vi* визжа́ть (*impf*)
shrimp [ʃrɪmp] *n* (ме́лкая) креве́тка
shrine [ʃraɪn] *n* святы́ня; (*tomb*) ра́ка
shrink [ʃrɪŋk] (*pt* **shrank**, *pp* **shrunk**) *vi* (*cloth*) сади́ться (*perf* сесть); (*profits, audiences*) сокраща́ться (*perf* сократи́ться); (*also* **shrink away**) отпря́нуть (*perf*)
shrivel ['ʃrɪvl] (*also* **shrivel up**) *vt* высу́шивать (*perf* вы́сушить) ▷ *vi* высыха́ть (*perf* вы́сохнуть)
shroud [ʃraud] *vt*: **shrouded in mystery** оку́танный та́йной

Shrove Tuesday

Shrove Tuesday — Ма́сленица. За Ма́сленицей сле́дует пе́рвый день Вели́кого Поста́. По тради́ции на Ма́сленицу пеку́т блины́.

shrub [ʃrʌb] *n* куст
shrug [ʃrʌg] *vi*: **to shrug (one's shoulders)** пожима́ть (*perf* пожа́ть) плеча́ми; **shrug off** *vt* отма́хиваться (*perf* отмахну́ться) от *+gen*

S

shrunk [ʃrʌŋk] *pp of* **shrink**
shudder [ˈʃʌdəʳ] *vi* содрога́ться (*perf* содрогну́ться)
shuffle [ˈʃʌfl] *vt* тасова́ть (*perf* стасова́ть) ▷ *vi*: **to shuffle (one's feet)** волочи́ть (*impf*) но́ги
shun [ʃʌn] *vt* избега́ть (*impf*) *+gen*
shut [ʃʌt] (*pt, pp* **shut**) *vt* закрыва́ть (*perf* закры́ть) ▷ *vi* (*factory*) закрыва́ться (*perf* закры́ться); **shut down** *vt* (*factory etc*) закрыва́ть (*perf* закры́ть) ▷ *vi* (*factory*) закрыва́ться (*perf* закры́ться); **shut off** *vt* (*supply etc*) перекрыва́ть (*perf* перекры́ть); **shut up** *vi* (*keep quiet*) заткну́ться (*perf*) ▷ *vt* (*keep quiet*) затыка́ть (*perf* заткну́ть) рот *+dat*; **shutter** *n* (*on window*) ста́вень *m*; (*Phot*) затво́р
shuttle [ˈʃʌtl] *n* (*plane*) самолёт-челно́к; (*also* **space shuttle**) шатл; (*also* **shuttle service**) регуля́рное сообще́ние
shy [ʃaɪ] *adj* (*timid*) засте́нчивый, стесни́тельный; (*reserved*) осторо́жный
Siberia [saɪˈbɪərɪə] *n* Сиби́рь *f*
sick [sɪk] *adj* (*ill*) больно́й; (*humour*) скве́рный; **he is/was sick** (*vomiting*) его́ рвёт/вы́рвало; **I feel sick** меня́ тошни́т; **I'm sick of arguing/school** меня́ тошни́т от спо́ров/шко́лы; **sickening** *adj* проти́вный, тошнотво́рный
sickly [ˈsɪklɪ] *adj* (*child*) хи́лый; (*smell*) тошнотво́рный
sickness [ˈsɪknɪs] *n* (*illness*) боле́знь *f*; (*vomiting*) рво́та
side [saɪd] *n* сторона́; (*of body*) бок; (*team*) кома́нда, сторона́; (*of hill*) склон ▷ *adj* (*door etc*) боково́й; **sideboard** *n* буфе́т; **side effect** *n* побо́чное де́йствие; **side street** *n* переу́лок; **sidewalk** *n* (*US*) тротуа́р; **sideways** *adv* (*go in, lean*) бо́ком; (*look*) и́скоса
siege [si:dʒ] *n* оса́да
sieve [sɪv] *n* (*Culin*) си́то ▷ *vt* просе́ивать (*perf* просе́ять)
sift [sɪft] *vt* просе́ивать (*perf* просе́ять)
sigh [saɪ] *n* вздох ▷ *vi* вздыха́ть (*perf* вздохну́ть)
sight [saɪt] *n* (*faculty*) зре́ние; (*spectacle*) зре́лище, вид; (*on gun*) прице́л; **in sight** в по́ле зре́ния; **out of sight** из ви́да; **sightseeing** *n*: **to go sightseeing** осма́тривать (*perf* осмотре́ть) достопримеча́тельности
sign [saɪn] *n* (*notice*) вы́веска; (*with hand*) знак; (*indication, evidence*) при́знак ▷ *vt* (*document*) подпи́сывать (*perf* подписа́ть); **to sign sth over to sb** передава́ть (*perf* переда́ть) что-н кому́-н; **sign on** *vi* (*Brit*: *as unemployed*) отмеча́ться (*perf* отме́титься) как безрабо́тный; (*for course*) регистри́роваться (*perf* зарегистри́роваться); **sign up** *vi* (*Mil*) нанима́ться (*perf* наня́ться); (*for course*) регистри́роваться (*perf* зарегистри́роваться) ▷ *vt* нанима́ть (*perf* наня́ть)
signal [ˈsɪgnl] *n* сигна́л ▷ *vi* сигнализи́ровать (*impf/perf*); **to signal to** подава́ть (*perf* пода́ть) знак *+dat*
signature [ˈsɪgnətʃəʳ] *n* по́дпись *f*
significance [sɪgˈnɪfɪkəns] *n* значе́ние
significant [sɪgˈnɪfɪkənt] *adj* (*amount, discovery*) значи́тельный
signify [ˈsɪgnɪfaɪ] *vt* (*represent*) означа́ть (*impf*)

silence ['saɪləns] *n* тишина́ ▷ *vt* заставля́ть (*perf* заста́вить) замолча́ть
silent ['saɪlənt] *adj* безмо́лвный; (*taciturn*) молчали́вый; (*film*) немо́й; **to remain silent** молча́ть (*impf*)
silhouette [sɪluː'ɛt] *n* силуэ́т
silk [sɪlk] *n* шёлк ▷ *adj* шёлковый
silly ['sɪlɪ] *adj* глу́пый
silver ['sɪlvəʳ] *n* серебро́ ▷ *adj* серебри́стый
SIM card ['sɪm-] *n* (*Tel*) СИМ-ка́рта
similar ['sɪmɪləʳ] *adj*: **similar (to)** схо́дный (с *+instr*), подо́бный (*+dat*); **similarity** [sɪmɪ'lærɪtɪ] *n* схо́дство; **similarly** *adv* (*in a similar way*) подо́бным о́бразом
simmer ['sɪməʳ] *vi* (*Culin*) туши́ться (*impf*)
simple ['sɪmpl] *adj* просто́й; (*foolish*) недалёкий
simplicity [sɪm'plɪsɪtɪ] *n* (*see adj*) простота́; недалёкость *f*
simplify ['sɪmplɪfaɪ] *vt* упроща́ть (*perf* упрости́ть)
simply ['sɪmplɪ] *adv* про́сто
simulate ['sɪmjuleɪt] *vt* изобража́ть (*perf* изобрази́ть)
simultaneous [sɪməl'teɪnɪəs] *adj* одновре́менный; **simultaneously** *adv* одновре́менно
sin [sɪn] *n* грех ▷ *vi* греши́ть (*perf* согреши́ть)
since [sɪns] *adv* с тех пор ▷ *conj* (*time*) с тех пор как; (*because*) так как ▷ *prep*: **since July** с ию́ля; **since then, ever since** с тех пор; **it's two weeks since I wrote** уже́ две неде́ли с (тех пор) как я написа́л; **since our last meeting** со вре́мени на́шей после́дней встре́чи
sincere [sɪn'sɪəʳ] *adj* и́скренний
sing [sɪŋ] (*pt* **sang**, *pp* **sung**) *vt, vi* петь (*perf* спеть)
singer ['sɪŋəʳ] *n* певе́ц(-ви́ца)
singing ['sɪŋɪŋ] *n* пе́ние
single ['sɪŋgl] *adj* (*person*) одино́кий; (*individual*) одино́чный; (*not double*) одина́рный ▷ *n* (*Brit*: *also* **single ticket**) биле́т в оди́н коне́ц; (*record*) *со́льник*; **not a single person** ни оди́н челове́к; **single out** *vt* (*choose*) выделя́ть (*perf* вы́делить); **single-minded** *adj* целеустремлённый; **single room** *n* (*in hotel*) одноме́стный но́мер
singular ['sɪŋgjuləʳ] *adj* необыкнове́нный ▷ *n* (*Ling*) еди́нственное число́
sinister ['sɪnɪstəʳ] *adj* злове́щий
sink [sɪŋk] (*pt* **sank**, *pp* **sunk**) *n* ра́ковина ▷ *vt* (*ship*) топи́ть (*perf* потопи́ть); (*well*) рыть (*perf* вы́рыть); (*foundations*) врыва́ть (*perf* врыть) ▷ *vi* (*ship*) тону́ть (потону́ть *perf or* затону́ть *perf*); (*heart, spirits*) па́дать (*perf* упа́сть); (*also* **sink back, sink down**) отки́дываться (*perf* отки́нуться); **to sink sth into** (*teeth, claws etc*) вонза́ть (*perf* вонзи́ть) что-н в *+acc*; **sink in** *vi* (*fig*): **it took a long time for her words to sink in** её слова́ дошли́ до меня́ нескоро
sinus ['saɪnəs] *n* (*Anat*) па́зуха
sip [sɪp] *n* ма́ленький глото́к ▷ *vt* потя́гивать *impf*
sir [səʳ] *n* сэр, господи́н; **Sir John Smith** Сэр Джон Смит
siren ['saɪərn] *n* сире́на
sister ['sɪstəʳ] *n* сестра́; (*Brit*: *Med*) (медици́нская *or* мед-) сестра́; **sister-in-law** *n* (*brother's wife*) неве́стка; (*husband's sister*) золо́вка; (*wife's sister*) своя́ченица

sit [sɪt] (*pt, pp* **sat**) *vi* (*sit down*) сади́ться (*perf* сесть); (*be sitting*) сиде́ть (*impf*); (*assembly*) заседа́ть (*impf*) ▷ *vt* (*exam*) сдава́ть (*perf* сдать); **sit down** *vi* сади́ться (*perf* сесть); **sit up** *vi* (*after lying*) сади́ться (*perf* сесть)

sitcom ['sɪtkɔm] *n abbr* (*TV*) (= *situation comedy*) коме́дия положе́ний

site [saɪt] *n* (*place*) ме́сто; (*also* **building site**) строи́тельная площа́дка

sitting ['sɪtɪŋ] *n* (*of assembly etc*) заседа́ние; (*in canteen*) сме́на; **sitting room** *n* гости́ная *f adj*

situated ['sɪtjueɪtɪd] *adj*: **to be situated** находи́ться (*impf*), располага́ться (*impf*)

situation [sɪtju'eɪʃən] *n* ситуа́ция, положе́ние; (*job*) ме́сто; (*location*) положе́ние; **"situations vacant"** (*Brit*) "вака́нтные места́"

six [sɪks] *n* шесть; **sixteen** *n* шестна́дцать; **sixteenth** *adj* шестна́дцатый; **sixth** *adj* шесто́й; **sixtieth** *adj* шестидеся́тый; **sixty** *n* шестьдеся́т

SIXTH FORM

Sixth form — квалификацио́нный курс. Э́тот курс состои́т из двух ступе́ней – ни́жней и ве́рхней. Курс дли́тся два го́да и предлага́ется на вы́бор шко́льникам, кото́рые к 16 года́м заверши́ли обяза́тельную шко́льную програ́мму. В тече́ние двух лет ученики́ гото́вятся к выпускны́м экза́менам, даю́щим пра́во на поступле́ние в университе́т.

size [saɪz] *n* разме́р; (*extent*) величина́, масшта́б; **sizeable** *adj* поря́дочный

skate [skeɪt] *n* (*also* **ice skate**) конёк; (*also* **roller skate**) ро́ликовый конёк, ро́лик ▷ *vi* ката́ться (*impf*) на конька́х

skating ['skeɪtɪŋ] *n* (*for pleasure*) ката́ние на конька́х

skeleton ['skɛlɪtn] *n* (*Anat*) скеле́т; (*outline*) схе́ма

sketch [skɛtʃ] *n* эски́з, набро́сок; (*outline*) набро́сок; (*Theat, TV*) сце́нка, скетч ▷ *vt* (*draw*) наброса́ть (*impf*); (*also* **sketch out**) обрисо́вывать (*perf* обрисова́ть) в о́бщих черта́х

ski [ski:] *n* лы́жа ▷ *vi* ката́ться (*impf*) на лы́жах

skid [skɪd] *vi* (*Aut*) идти́ (*perf* пойти́) ю́зом

skier ['ski:ə[r]] *n* лы́жник(-ица)

skiing ['ski:ɪŋ] *n* (*for pleasure*) ката́ние на лы́жах

skilful ['skɪlful] (*US* **skillful**) *adj* иску́сный, уме́лый; (*player*) техни́чный

skill [skɪl] *n* (*ability, dexterity*) мастерство́; (*in computing etc*) на́вык; **skilled** *adj* (*able*) иску́сный; (*worker*) квалифици́рованный

skim [skɪm] *vt* (*milk*) снима́ть (*perf* снять) сли́вки с +*gen*; (*glide over*) скользи́ть (*impf*) над +*instr* ▷ *vi*: **to skim through** пробега́ть (*perf* пробежа́ть)

skin [skɪn] *n* (*of person*) ко́жа; (*of animal*) шку́ра; (*of fruit, vegetable*) кожура́; (*of grape, tomato*) ко́жица ▷ *vt* (*animal*) снима́ть (*perf* снять) шку́ру с +*gen*; **skinny** *adj* то́щий

skip [skɪp] *n* (*Brit: container*) скип ▷ *vi* подпры́гивать (*perf* подпры́гнуть); (*with rope*) скака́ть (*impf*) ▷ *vt* (*miss out*) пропуска́ть (*perf* пропусти́ть)

skipper ['skɪpəʳ] *n* (*Naut*) шки́пер, капита́н; (*Sport*) капита́н

skirt [skəːt] *n* ю́бка ▷ *vt* обходи́ть (*perf* обойти́)

skull [skʌl] *n* че́реп

skunk [skʌŋk] *n* (*animal*) скунс

sky [skaɪ] *n* не́бо; **skyscraper** *n* небоскрёб

slab [slæb] *n* плита́

slack [slæk] *adj* (*rope*) прови́сший; (*discipline*) сла́бый; (*security*) плохо́й

slam [slæm] *vt* (*door*) хло́пать (*perf* хло́пнуть) +*instr* ▷ *vi* (*door*) захло́пываться (*perf* захло́пнуться)

slang [slæŋ] *n* (*informal language*) сленг; (*jargon*) жарго́н

slant [slɑːnt] *n* накло́н; (*fig*: *approach*) укло́н

slap [slæp] *n* шлепо́к ▷ *vt* шлёпать (*perf* шлёпнуть); **to slap sb across the face** дава́ть (*perf* дать) кому́-н пощёчину; **to slap sth on sth** (*paint etc*) ля́пать (*perf* наля́пать) что-н на что-н

slash [slæʃ] *vt* ре́зать (*perf* поре́зать); (*fig*: *prices*) уре́зывать (*perf* уре́зать)

slate [sleɪt] *n* (*material*) сла́нец; (*tile*) кро́вельная пли́тка (*из гли́нистого сла́нца*) ▷ *vt* (*fig*) разноси́ть (*perf* разнести́) в пух и прах

slaughter ['slɔːtəʳ] *n* (*of animals*) убо́й; (*of people*) резня́, бо́йня ▷ *vt* (*see n*) забива́ть (*perf* заби́ть); истребля́ть (*perf* истреби́ть)

slave [sleɪv] *n* раб(ы́ня); **slavery** *n* ра́бство

Slavonic [slə'vɔnɪk] *adj* славя́нский

sleazy ['sliːzɪ] *adj* (*place*) запу́щенный

sledge [slɛdʒ] *n* са́ни *pl*; (*for children*) са́нки *pl*

sleek [sliːk] *adj* (*fur*) лосня́щийся; (*hair*) блестя́щий

sleep [sliːp] (*pt, pp* **slept**) *n* сон ▷ *vi* спать (*impf*); (*spend night*) ночева́ть (*perf* переночева́ть); **to go to sleep** засыпа́ть (*perf* засну́ть); **sleep in** *vi* просыпа́ть (*perf* проспа́ть); **sleeper** *n* (*Rail*: *train*) по́езд со спа́льными ваго́нами; (: *berth*) спа́льное ме́сто; **sleeping bag** *n* спа́льный мешо́к; **sleepy** *adj* со́нный

sleet [sliːt] *n* мо́крый снег

sleeve [sliːv] *n* (*of jacket etc*) рука́в; (*of record*) конве́рт

slender ['slɛndəʳ] *adj* (*figure*) стро́йный; (*majority*) небольшо́й

slept [slɛpt] *pt, pp of* **sleep**

slice [slaɪs] *n* (*of meat*) кусо́к; (*of bread, lemon*) ло́мтик ▷ *vt* (*bread, meat etc*) нареза́ть (*perf* наре́зать)

slick [slɪk] *adj* (*performance*) гла́дкий; (*salesman, answer*) бо́йкий ▷ *n* (*also* **oil slick**) плёнка не́фти

slide [slaɪd] (*pt, pp* **slid**) *n* (*in playground*) де́тская го́рка; (*Phot*) слайд; (*Brit*: *also* **hair slide**) зако́лка ▷ *vt* задвига́ть (*perf* задви́нуть) ▷ *vi* скользи́ть (*impf*)

slight [slaɪt] *adj* хру́пкий; (*small*) незначи́тельный; (: *error*) ме́лкий; (*accent, pain*) сла́бый ▷ *n* униже́ние; **not in the slightest** нисколько; **slightly** *adv* (*rather*) слегка́

slim [slɪm] *adj* (*figure*) стро́йный; (*chance*) сла́бый ▷ *vi* худе́ть (*perf* похуде́ть)

slimy ['slaɪmɪ] *adj* (*pond*) и́листый

S

sling [slɪŋ] (*pt, pp* **slung**) *n* (*Med*) пéревязь *f* ▷ *vt* (*throw*) швыря́ть (*perf* швырну́ть)

slip [slɪp] *n* (*mistake*) прóмах; (*underskirt*) ни́жняя ю́бка; (*of paper*) полóска ▷ *vt* сова́ть (*perf* су́нуть) ▷ *vi* (*slide*) скользи́ть (скользну́ть *f*); (*lose balance*) поскользну́ться (*perf*); (*decline*) снижа́ться (*perf* сни́зиться); **to give sb the slip** ускольза́ть (*perf* ускользну́ть) от когó-н; **a slip of the tongue** оговóрка; **to slip sth on/off** надева́ть (*perf* наде́ть)/ сбра́сывать (*perf* сбрóсить) что-н; **to slip into** (*room etc*) скользну́ть (*perf*) в *+acc*; **to slip out of** (*room etc*) выска́льзывать (*perf* вы́скользнуть) из *+gen*; **slip away** *vi* ускольза́ть (*perf* ускользну́ть); **slip in** *vt* сова́ть (*perf* су́нуть) ▷ *vi* (*errors*) закра́дываться (*perf* закра́сться)

slipper ['slɪpə^r] *n* та́почка

slippery ['slɪpərɪ] *adj* скóльзкий

slit [slɪt] (*pt, pp* **slit**) *n* (*cut*) разре́з; (*in skirt*) шли́ца; (*opening*) щель *f* ▷ *vt* разреза́ть (*perf* разре́зать)

slog [slɔg] *n*: **it was a hard slog** э́то была́ тяжёлая рабóта

slogan ['sləugən] *n* лóзунг

slope [sləup] *n* склон; (*gentle hill*) уклóн; (*slant*) наклóн

sloppy ['slɔpɪ] *adj* (*work*) халту́рный

slot [slɔt] *n* (*in machine*) прóрезь *f*, паз ▷ *vt*: **to slot sth into** опуска́ть (*perf* опусти́ть) что-н в *+acc*

Slovakia [sləu'vækɪə] *n* Слова́кия

slow [sləu] *adj* ме́дленный; (*stupid*) тупóй ▷ *adv* ме́дленно ▷ *vt* (*also* **slow down, slow up**: *vehicle*) замедля́ть (*perf* заме́длить) ▷ *vi* (*traffic*) замедля́ться (*perf* заме́длиться); (*car, train etc*) сбавля́ть (*perf* сба́вить) ход; **my watch is (20 minutes) slow** мой часы́ отстаю́т (на 20 мину́т); **slowly** *adv* ме́дленно; **slow motion** *n*: **in slow motion** в заме́дленном де́йствии

slug [slʌg] *n* (*Zool*) сли́зень *m*

sluggish ['slʌgɪʃ] *adj* вя́лый

slum [slʌm] *n* трущóба

slump [slʌmp] *n* (*economic*) спад; (*in profits, sales*) паде́ние

slung [slʌŋ] *pt, pp of* **sling**

slur [slə:^r] *vt* (*words*) мя́млить (*perf* промя́млить) ▷ *n* (*fig*): **slur (on)** пятнó (на *+prp*)

sly [slaɪ] *adj* лука́вый

smack [smæk] *n* (*slap*) шлепóк ▷ *vt* хлóпать (*perf* хлóпнуть); (*child*) шлёпать (*perf* отшлёпать) ▷ *vi*: **to smack of** отдава́ть (*impf*) *+instr*

small [smɔ:l] *adj* ма́ленький; (*quantity, amount*) небольшóй, ма́лый

smart [smɑ:t] *adj* (*neat, tidy*) опря́тный; (*clever*) толкóвый ▷ *vi* (*also fig*) жечь (*impf*); **smart phone** *n* смартфóн

smash [smæʃ] *n* (*collision*: *also* **smash-up**) ава́рия ▷ *vt* разбива́ть (*perf* разби́ть); (*Sport*: *record*) побива́ть (*perf* поби́ть) ▷ *vi* (*break*) разбива́ться (*perf* разби́ться); **to smash against** *or* **into** (*collide*) вреза́ться (*perf* вре́заться) в *+acc*; **smashing** *adj* (*inf*) потрясáющий

smear [smɪə^r] *n* (*trace*) след; (*Med*: *also* **smear test**) мазóк ▷ *vt* (*spread*) ма́зать (*perf* нама́зать)

smell [smɛl] (*pt, pp* **smelt** *or* **smelled**) *n* зáпах; (*sense*) обоня́ние ▷ *vt* чу́вствовать (*perf* почу́вствовать) зáпах *+gen* ▷ *vi* (*food etc*) пáхнуть (*impf*); **to smell (of)** (*unpleasant*) воня́ть (*impf*) (*+instr*); **smelly** *adj* вонючий, злово́нный
smelt [smɛlt] *pt, pp of* **smell**
smile [smaɪl] *n* улы́бка ▷ *vi* улыбáться (*perf* улыбну́ться)
smirk [smə:k] *n* (*pej*) ухмы́лка
smog [smɔg] *n* смог
smoke [sməuk] *n* дым ▷ *vi* (*person*) кури́ть (*impf*); (*chimney*) дыми́ться (*impf*) ▷ *vt* (*cigarettes*) кури́ть (*perf* вы́курить); **smoked** *adj* (*bacon, fish*) копчёный; (*glass*) ды́мчатый; **smoker** *n* (*person*) куря́щий(-ая) *m(f) adj*, кури́льщик(-щица)
smoking ['sməukɪŋ] *n* (*act*) куре́ние; **"no smoking"** "не кури́ть"
smoky ['sməukɪ] *adj* ды́мный
smooth [smu:ð] *adj* глáдкий; (*sauce*) одноро́дный; (*flavour*) мя́гкий; (*movement*) плáвный; **smoothie** *n* смýзи *m ind*
smother ['smʌðəʳ] *vt* (*fire*) туши́ть (*perf* потуши́ть); (*person*) души́ть (*perf* задуши́ть); (*emotions*) подавля́ть (*perf* подави́ть)
smudge [smʌdʒ] *n* пятно́ ▷ *vt* размáзывать (*perf* размáзать)
smug [smʌg] *adj* дово́льный
smuggle ['smʌgl] *vt* (*goods*) провози́ть (*perf* провезти́) (*контрабáндой*)
smuggling ['smʌglɪŋ] *n* контрабáнда
snack [snæk] *n* закýска
snag [snæg] *n* помéха
snail [sneɪl] *n* ули́тка
snake [sneɪk] *n* змея́
snap [snæp] *adj* (*decision etc*) моментáльный ▷ *vt* (*break*) разлáмывать (*perf* разломи́ть); (*fingers*) щёлкать (*perf* щёлкнуть) *+instr* ▷ *vi* (*break*) разлáмываться (*perf* разломи́ться); (*speak sharply*) кричáть (*impf*); **to snap shut** (*trap, jaws etc*) защёлкиваться (*perf* защёлкнуться); **snap up** *vt* расхвáтывать (*perf* расхватáть); **snapshot** *n* сни́мок
snarl [snɑ:l] *vi* рычáть (*impf*)
snatch [snætʃ] *n* обры́вок ▷ *vt* (*grab*) хватáть (*perf* схвати́ть); (*handbag*) вырывáть (*perf* вы́рвать); (*child*) похищáть (*perf* похи́тить); (*opportunity*) урывáть (*perf* урвáть)
sneak [sni:k] *vi*: **to sneak into** прокрáльзывать (*perf* проскользну́ть) в *+acc*; **to sneak out of** выскáльзывать (*perf* вы́скользнуть) из *+gen*; **to sneak up on** я́бедничать (*perf* ная́бедничать) на *+acc*; **sneakers** *npl* кроссо́вки *fpl*
sneer [snɪəʳ] *vi* (*mock*): **to sneer at** глуми́ться (*impf*) над *+instr*
sneeze [sni:z] *vi* чихáть (*perf* чихну́ть)
sniff [snɪf] *n* (*sound*) сопéние ▷ *vi* шмы́гать (*perf* шмыгну́ть) но́сом; (*when crying*) всхли́пывать (*impf*) ▷ *vt* ню́хать (*impf*)
snip [snɪp] *vt* рéзать (*perf* порéзать)
sniper ['snaɪpəʳ] *n* снáйпер
snob [snɔb] *n* сноб
snooker ['snu:kəʳ] *n* сну́кер
snore [snɔ:ʳ] *vi* храпéть (*impf*)
snorkel ['snɔ:kl] *n* трýбка (*ныря́льщика*)
snow [snəu] *n* снег ▷ *vi*: **it's snowing** идёт снег; **snowball** *n*

снежóк; **snowdrift** *n* сугрóб; **snowman** *n irreg* снеговúк, снéжная бáба

SNP *n abbr* = **Scottish National Party**

snub [snʌb] *vt* пренебрежúтельно обходúться (*perf* обойтúсь) с *+instr*

snug [snʌg] *adj* (*place*) уютный; (*well-fitting*) облегáющий

KEYWORD

so [səu] *adv* **1** (*thus, likewise*) так; **if this is so** éсли э́то так; **if so** éсли так; **while she was so doing, he ...** покá онá э́то дéлала, он ...; **I didn't do it — you did so!** я не дéлал э́того — а вот и сдéлал!; **you weren't there — I was so!** тебя́ там нé было — а вот и был!; **I like him — so do I** он мне нрáвится — мне тóже; **I'm still at school — so is he** я ещё учу́сь в шкóле — он тóже; **so it is!** и действúтельно!, и прáвда!; **I hope/think so** надéюсь/дýмаю, что так; **so far** покá; **how do you like the book so far?** ну, как Вам кнúга?

2 (*in comparisons*: *+adv*) настóлько, так; (: *+adj*) настóлько, такóй; **so quickly (that)** настóлько *or* так бы́стро(, что); **so big (that)** такóй большóй(, что); **she's not so clever as her brother** онá не так умнá, как её брат

3 (*describing degree, extent*) так; **I've got so much work** у меня́ так мнóго рабóты; **I love you so much** я тебя́ так люблю́; **thank you so much** спасúбо Вам большóе; **I'm so glad to see you** я так рад Вас вúдеть; **there are so many books I would like to read** есть так мнóго книг, котóрые я бы хотéл прочéсть; **so ... that ...** так ... что ...

4 (*about*) óколо *+gen*; **ten or so** óколо десятú; **I only have an hour or so** у меня́ есть óколо чáса

5 (*phrases*): **so long!** (*inf*: *goodbye*) покá!

▷ *conj* **1** (*expressing purpose*): **so as to do** чтóбы *+infin*; **I brought this wine so that you could try it** я принёс э́то винó, чтóбы Вы моглú егó попрóбовать

2 (*expressing result*) так что; **so I was right** так что, я был прав; **so you see, I could have stayed** так что, вúдите, я мог бы остáться

soak [səuk] *vt* (*drench*) промочúть (*perf*); (*steep*) замáчивать (*perf* замочúть) ▷ *vi* (*steep*) отмокáть (*impf*); **soak up** *vt* впúтывать (*perf* впитáть) (в себя́)

soap [səup] *n* мы́ло; **soap opera** *n* (*TV*) мы́льная óпера

soar [sɔːʳ] *vi* (*price, temperature*) подскáкивать (*perf* подскочúть)

sob [sɔb] *n* рыдáние ▷ *vi* рыдáть (*impf*)

sober ['səubəʳ] *adj* трéзвый; (*colour, style*) сдéржанный

soccer ['sɔkəʳ] *n* футбóл

sociable ['səuʃəbl] *adj* общúтельный

social ['səuʃl] *adj* (*history, structure etc*) общéственный, социáльный; **he has a good social life** он мнóго общáется с людьмú; **socialism** *n* социалúзм; **socialist** *n* социалúст ▷ *adj* социалистúческий; **socialize** *vi*: **to socialize (with)** общáться (*impf*) (с *+instr*); **socially** *adv*: **to visit sb socially** заходúть (*perf* зайтú) к комý-н по-дрýжески; **socially**

acceptable социа́льно прие́млемый; **social media** *n* социа́льные се́ти; **social networking** [-'nɛtwə:kɪŋ] *n* *взаимоде́йствие посре́дством социа́льных сете́й с други́ми их уча́стниками*; **social security** (*Brit*) *n* социа́льная защи́та; **social work** *n* социа́льная рабо́та

society [sə'saɪətɪ] *n* о́бщество

sociology [səusɪ'ɔlədʒɪ] *n* социоло́гия

sock [sɔk] *n* носо́к

socket ['sɔkɪt] *n* глазни́ца; (*Brit*: *Elec*: *in wall*) розе́тка

soda ['səudə] *n* (*also* **soda water**) со́довая *f adj*; (*US*: *also* **soda pop**) газиро́вка

sodium ['səudɪəm] *n* на́трий

sofa ['səufə] *n* дива́н

soft [sɔft] *adj* мя́гкий; **soft drink** *n* безалкого́льный напи́ток; **softly** *adv* (*gently*) мя́гко; (*quietly*) ти́хо; **software** *n* програ́мма, програ́ммное обеспе́чение

soggy ['sɔgɪ] *adj* (*ground*) сыро́й

soil [sɔɪl] *n* (*earth*) по́чва; (*territory*) земля́ ▷ *vt* па́чкать (*perf* запа́чкать)

solar ['səulə[r]] *adj* со́лнечный

sold [səuld] *pt, pp of* **sell**

soldier ['səuldʒə[r]] *n* (*Mil*) солда́т

sole [səul] *n* (*of foot*) подо́шва; (*of shoe*) подо́шва, подмётка ▷ *n inv* (*fish*) па́лтус ▷ *adj* (*unique*) еди́нственный; **solely** *adv* то́лько

solemn ['sɔləm] *adj* торже́ственный

solicitor [sə'lɪsɪtə[r]] *n* (*Brit*) адвока́т

solid ['sɔlɪd] *adj* (*not hollow*) це́льный; (*not liquid*) твёрдый; (*reliable*) про́чный; (*entire*) це́лый; (*gold*) чи́стый ▷ *n* твёрдое те́ло; **solids** *npl* твёрдая пи́ща *fsg*

solitary ['sɔlɪtərɪ] *adj* одино́кий; (*empty*) уединённый; (*single*) едини́чный

solitude ['sɔlɪtju:d] *n* уедине́ние, одино́чество

solo ['səuləu] *n* со́ло *nt ind* ▷ *adv* (*fly*) в одино́чку; (*play*) со́ло; **soloist** *n* соли́ст(ка)

soluble ['sɔljubl] *adj* раствори́мый

solution [sə'lu:ʃən] *n* (*answer*) реше́ние; (*liquid*) раство́р

solve [sɔlv] *vt* (*problem*) разреша́ть (*perf* разреши́ть); (*mystery*) раскрыва́ть (*perf* раскры́ть)

solvent ['sɔlvənt] *adj* платёжеспосо́бный ▷ *n* раствори́тель *m*

sombre ['sɔmbə[r]] (*US* **somber**) *adj* мра́чный

 **KEYWORD**

some [sʌm] *adj* **1** (*a certain amount or number of*): **would you like some tea/biscuits?** хоти́те ча́ю/пече́нья?; **there's some milk in the fridge** в холоди́льнике есть молоко́; **he asked me some questions** он за́дал мне не́сколько вопро́сов; **there are some people waiting to see you** Вас ждут каки́е-то лю́ди

2 (*certain*: *in contrasts*) не́который; **some people say that ...** не́которые говоря́т, что ...

3 (*unspecified*) како́й-то; **some woman phoned you** Вам звони́ла кака́я-то же́нщина; **we'll meet again some day** мы когда́-нибудь опя́ть встре́тимся; **shall we meet some day next week?** дава́йте

S

встре́тимся ка́к-нибудь на сле́дующей неде́ле!
▷ *pron* (*a certain number: people*) не́которые *pl*, одни́ *pl*; **some took the bus, and some walked** не́которые пое́хали на авто́бусе, а не́которые пошли́ пешко́м; **I've got some** (*books etc*) у меня́ есть не́сколько; **who would like a piece of cake? — I'd like some** кто хо́чет кусо́к то́рта? — я хочу́; **I've read some of the book** я прочёл часть кни́ги
▷ *adv* о́коло; **some ten people** о́коло десяти́ челове́к

somebody ['sʌmbədɪ] *pron* **= someone**

somehow ['sʌmhau] *adv* (*in some way: in future*) ка́к-нибудь; (: *in past*) ка́к-то; (*for some reason*) почему́-то, каки́м-то о́бразом

someone ['sʌmwʌn] *pron* (*specific person*) кто́-то; (*unspecified person*) кто́-нибудь; **I saw someone in the garden** я ви́дел кого́-то в саду́; **someone will help you** Вам кто́-нибудь помо́жет

something ['sʌmθɪŋ] *pron* (*something specific*) что́-то; (*something unspecified*) что́-нибудь; **there's something wrong with my car** что́-то случи́лось с мое́й маши́ной; **would you like something to eat/drink?** хоти́те чего́-нибудь пое́сть/вы́пить?; **I have something for you** у меня́ ко́е-что для Вас есть

sometime ['sʌmtaɪm] *adv* (*in future*) когда́-нибудь; (*in past*) когда́-то, как-то

sometimes ['sʌmtaɪmz] *adv* иногда́

somewhat ['sʌmwɔt] *adv* не́сколько

somewhere ['sʌmwɛə[r]] *adv* (*be: somewhere specific*) где́-то; (: *anywhere*) где́-нибудь; (*go: somewhere specific*) куда́-то; (: *anywhere*) куда́-нибудь; (*come from*) отку́да-то; **it's somewhere or other in Scotland** э́то где́-то в Шотла́ндии; **is there a post office somewhere around here?** здесь где́-нибудь есть по́чта?; **let's go somewhere else** дава́йте пое́дем куда́-нибудь в друго́е ме́сто

son [sʌn] *n* сын

song [sɔŋ] *n* пе́сня

son-in-law ['sʌnɪnlɔ:] *n* зять *m*

soon [su:n] *adv* (*in a short time*) ско́ро; (*early*) ра́но; **soon (afterwards)** вско́ре; *see also* **as**; **sooner** *adv* скоре́е; **I would sooner do that** я бы скоре́е сде́лал э́то; **sooner or later** ра́но или по́здно

soothe [su:ð] *vt* успока́ивать (*perf* успоко́ить)

sophisticated [sə'fɪstɪkeɪtɪd] *adj* изощрённый; (*refined*) изы́сканный

soprano [sə'prɑ:nəu] *n* сопра́но *f ind*

sordid ['sɔ:dɪd] *adj* (*place*) убо́гий; (*story etc*) гну́сный

sore [sɔ:[r]] *n* я́зва, боля́чка ▷ *adj* (*esp US: offended*) оби́женный; (*painful*): **my arm is sore, I've got a sore arm** у меня́ боли́т рука́; **it's a sore point** (*fig*) э́то больно́е ме́сто

sorrow ['sɔrəu] *n* печа́ль *f*, грусть *f*

sorry ['sɔrɪ] *adj* плаче́вный; **I'm sorry** мне жаль; **sorry!** извини́те, пожа́луйста!; **sorry?** (*pardon*) прости́те?; **I feel sorry for him** мне его́ жаль *or* жа́лко

sort [sɔːt] *n* (*type*) сорт ▷ *vt* (*mail*) сортировáть (*perf* рассортировáть); (*also* **sort out**: *papers, belongings etc*) разбирáть (*perf* разобрáть); (: *problems*) разбирáться (*perf* разобрáться) в *+prp*
so-so ['səusəu] *adv* так себé
sought [sɔːt] *pt, pp of* **seek**
soul [səul] *n* (*spirit, person*) душá
sound [saund] *adj* (*healthy*) здорóвый; (*safe, not damaged*) цéлый; (*secure*: *investment*) надёжный; (*reliable, thorough*) солúдный; (*sensible*: *advice*) разýмный ▷ *n* звук ▷ *vt* (*alarm*) поднимáть (*perf* поднять) ▷ *vi* звучáть (*impf*) ▷ *adv*: **he is sound asleep** он крéпко спит; **I don't like the sound of it** мне э́то не нрáвится; **soundtrack** *n* мýзыка (*из кинофúльма*)
soup [suːp] *n* суп
sour ['sauə[r]] *adj* кúслый; (*fig*: *bad-tempered*) угрю́мый
source [sɔːs] *n* (*also fig*) истóчник
south [sauθ] *n* юг ▷ *adj* ю́жный ▷ *adv* (*go*) на юг; (*be*) на ю́ге; **South America** *n* Ю́жная Амéрика; **southeast** *n* ю́го-востóк; **southern** ['sʌðən] *adj* ю́жный; **South Pole** *n*: **the South Pole** Ю́жный пóлюс; **southwest** *n* ю́го-зáпад
souvenir [suːvə'nɪə[r]] *n* сувенúр
sovereign ['sɔvrɪn] *n* (*ruler*) государь(-рыня) *m(f)*
Soviet ['səuvɪət] *adj* совéтский; **the Soviet Union** (*formerly*) Совéтский Сою́з
sow[1] [sau] *n* (*pig*) свинья́
sow[2] [səu] (*pt* **sowed**, *pp* **sown**) *vt* (*also fig*) сéять (*perf* посéять)
soya ['sɔɪə] (*US* **soy**) *adj* сóевый

spa [spɑː] *n* (*US*: *also* **health spa**) вóды *fpl*
space [speɪs] *n* прострáнство; (*small place, room*) мéсто; (*beyond Earth*) кóсмос; (*interval, period*) промежýток ▷ *cpd* космúческий ▷ *vt* (*also* **space out**: *payments, visits*) распределя́ть (*perf* распределúть); **spacecraft** *n* космúческий корáбль *m*; **spaceship** *n* = **spacecraft**
spacious ['speɪʃəs] *adj* простóрный
spade [speɪd] *n* (*tool*) лопáта; (*child's*) лопáтка; **spades** *npl* (*Cards*) пúки *fpl*
spaghetti [spə'gɛtɪ] *n* спагéтти *pl ind*
Spain [speɪn] *n* Испáния
spam [spæm] *vt* (*Comput*) спам (*бесполезная информация, обычно реклама, по электронной почте*), на Интернéте
span [spæn] *pt of* **spin** ▷ *n* (*of hand, wings*) размáх; (*in time*) промежýток ▷ *vt* охвáтывать (*perf* охватúть)
Spanish ['spænɪʃ] *adj* испáнский; ▷ *npl*: **the Spanish** испáнцы *mpl*
spank [spæŋk] *vt* шлёпать (*perf* отшлёпать)
spanner ['spænə[r]] *n* (*Brit*) (гáечный) ключ
spare [spɛə[r]] *adj* (*free*: *time, seat*) свобóдный; (*surplus*) лúшний; (*reserve*) запаснóй ▷ *vt* (*trouble, expense*) избавля́ть (*perf* избáвить) от *+gen*; (*make available*) выделя́ть (*perf* вы́делить); (*refrain from hurting*) щадúть (*perf* пощадúть); **I have some time to spare** у меня́ есть немнóго свобóдного врéмени; **to have money to spare** имéть (*impf*) лúшние дéньги; **spare time** *n* свобóдное врéмя *nt*

S

spark [spɑ:k] *n* (*also fig*) и́скра
sparkle ['spɑ:kl] *n* блеск ▷ *vi* (*diamonds, water, eyes*) сверка́ть (*impf*)
sparkling ['spɑ:klɪŋ] *adj* (*wine*) игри́стый
sparrow ['spærəu] *n* воробе́й
sparse [spɑ:s] *adj* ре́дкий
spasm ['spæzəm] *n* (*Med*) спазм
spat [spæt] *pt, pp of* **spit**
spate [speɪt] *n* (*fig*): **a spate of** пото́к *+gen*
speak [spi:k] (*pt* **spoke**, *pp* **spoken**) *vi* говори́ть (*impf*); (*make a speech*) выступа́ть (*perf* вы́ступить) ▷ *vt* (*truth*) говори́ть (*perf* сказа́ть); **to speak to sb** разгова́ривать (*impf*) *or* говори́ть (*impf*) с кем-н; **to speak of** *or* **about** говори́ть (*impf*) о *+prp*; **speaker** *n* (*in public*) ора́тор; (*also* **loudspeaker**) громкоговори́тель *m*
spear [spɪə^r] *n* копьё
special ['spɛʃl] *adj* (*important*) осо́бый, осо́бенный; (*edition, adviser, school*) специа́льный; **specialist** *n* специали́ст; **speciality** [spɛʃɪ'ælɪtɪ] *n* (*dish*) фи́рменное блю́до; (*subject*) специализа́ция; **specialize** *vi*: **to specialize (in)** специализи́роваться (*impf/perf*) (в/на *+prp*); **specially** *adv* (*especially*) осо́бенно
species ['spi:ʃi:z] *n inv* вид
specific [spə'sɪfɪk] *adj* специфи́ческий, определённый; **specifically** *adv* (*exactly*) точне́е; (*specially*) специа́льно
specify ['spɛsɪfaɪ] *vt* уточня́ть (*perf* уточни́ть)
specimen ['spɛsɪmən] *n* (*example*) экземпля́р; (*sample*) образе́ц; **a specimen of urine** моча́ для ана́лиза
speck [spɛk] *n* (*of dirt*) пя́тнышко; (*of dust*) крупи́ца, крупи́нка
spectacle ['spɛktəkl] *n* (*scene, event*) зре́лище; **spectacles** *npl* (*glasses*) очки́ *pl*
spectacular [spɛk'tækjulə^r] *adj* впечатля́ющий, порази́тельный
spectator [spɛk'teɪtə^r] *n* зри́тель(ница) *m(f)*
spectrum ['spɛktrəm] (*pl* **spectra**) *n* спектр
speculate ['spɛkjuleɪt] *vi* (*Comm*) спекули́ровать (*impf*); (*guess*): **to speculate about** стро́ить (*impf*) предположе́ния о *+prp*
sped [spɛd] *pt, pp of* **speed**
speech [spi:tʃ] *n* речь *f*; **speechless** *adj*: **I was speechless with anger** от гне́ва я лиши́лся да́ра ре́чи; **she looked at him, speechless** она́ посмотре́ла на него́ в онеме́нии
speed [spi:d] (*pt, pp* **sped**) *n* (*rate*) ско́рость *f*; (*promptness*) быстрота́ ▷ *vi* (*move*): **to speed along/by** мча́ться (*perf* промча́ться) по *+dat*/ми́мо *+gen*; **at full** *or* **top speed** на по́лной *or* преде́льной ско́рости; **speed up** ▷ (*pt, pp* **speeded up**) *vi* ускоря́ться (*perf* уско́риться) ▷ *vt* ускоря́ть (*perf* уско́рить); **speeding** *n* превыше́ние ско́рости; **speed limit** *n* преде́л ско́рости; **speedometer** [spɪ'dɔmɪtə^r] *n* спидо́метр; **speedy** *adj* (*prompt*) ско́рый
spell [spɛl] (*pt, pp* **spelt** *or* **spelled**) *n* (*also* **magic spell**) колдовство́; (*period of time*) пери́од ▷ *vt* (*also* **spell out**) произноси́ть (*perf* произнести́) по бу́квам; (*fig*: *explain*) разъясня́ть

(*perf* разъяснить) ▷ *vi*: **he can't spell** у него плохая орфография; **spelling** *n* орфография, правописание

spend [spɛnd] (*pt, pp* **spent**) *vt* (*money*) тратить (*perf* потратить); (*time, life*) проводить (*perf* провести)

sperm [spə:m] *n* сперма

sphere [sfɪəʳ] *n* сфера

spice [spaɪs] *n* (*pepper, salt etc*) специя

spicy ['spaɪsɪ] *adj* (*food*) острый; (: *with a strong flavour*) пряный

spider ['spaɪdəʳ] *n* паук

spike [spaɪk] *n* (*point*) остриё

spill [spɪl] (*pt, pp* **spilt** *or* **spilled**) *vt* (*liquid*) проливать (*perf* пролить), разливать (*perf* разлить) ▷ *vi* (*liquid*) проливаться (*perf* пролиться), разливаться (*perf* разлиться)

spin [spɪn] (*pt* **spun** *or* **span**, *pp* **spun**) *n* (*trip in car*) катание; (*Aviat*) штопор; (*Pol*) уклон, тенденция ▷ *vt* (*Brit*: *clothes*) выжимать (*perf* выжать) (в стиральной машине) ▷ *vi* (*make thread*) прясть (*impf*); (*person, head*) кружиться (*impf*)

spinach ['spɪnɪtʃ] *n* шпинат

spinal ['spaɪnl] *adj* (*relating to the spine*) позвоночный; (*relating to the spinal cord*) спинномозговой; **spinal injury** повреждение позвоночника; **spinal cord** *n* спинной мозг

spine [spaɪn] *n* (*Anat*) позвоночник; (*thorn*) колючка, игла

spiral ['spaɪərl] *n* спираль *f*

spire ['spaɪəʳ] *n* шпиль *m*

spirit ['spɪrɪt] *n* дух; (*soul*) душа; **spirits** *npl* (*alcohol*) спиртные напитки *mpl*, спиртное *ntsg adj*; **in good/low spirits** в хорошем/подавленном настроении

spiritual ['spɪrɪtjuəl] *adj* духовный

spit [spɪt] (*pt, pp* **spat**) *n* вертел; (*saliva*) слюна ▷ *vi* (*person*) плевать (*perf* плюнуть); (*fire, hot oil*) брызгать (*impf*); (*inf*: *rain*) моросить (*impf*)

spite [spaɪt] *n* злоба, злость *f* ▷ *vt* досаждать (*perf* досадить) *+dat*; **in spite of** несмотря на *+acc*; **spiteful** *adj* злобный

splash [splæʃ] *n* (*sound*) всплеск ▷ *vt* брызгать (*perf* брызнуть) ▷ *vi* (*also* **splash about**) плескаться (*impf*)

splendid ['splɛndɪd] *adj* великолепный

splinter ['splɪntəʳ] *n* (*of wood*) щепка; (*of glass*) осколок; (*in finger*) заноза

split [splɪt] (*pt, pp* **split**) *n* (*crack, tear*) трещина; (*Pol, fig*) раскол ▷ *vt* (*atom, piece of wood*) расщеплять (*perf* расщепить); (*Pol, fig*) раскалывать (*perf* расколоть); (*work, profits*) делить (*perf* разделить) ▷ *vi* (*divide*) расщепляться (*perf* расщепиться), разделяться (*perf* разделиться); **split up** *vi* (*couple*) расходиться (*perf* разойтись); (*group*) разделяться (*perf* разделиться)

spoil [spɔɪl] (*pt, pp* **spoilt** *or* **spoiled**) *vt* портить (*perf* испортить)

spoke [spəuk] *pt of* **speak** ▷ *n* (*of wheel*) спица; **spoken** *pp of* **speak**

spokesman ['spəuksmən] *irreg n* представитель *m*

spokeswoman ['spəukswumən] *irreg n* представительница

sponge [spʌndʒ] *n* губка; (*also* **sponge cake**) бисквит

sponsor ['spɔnsəʳ] *n* спо́нсор ▷ *vt* финанси́ровать (*impf/perf*), спонси́ровать (*impf/perf*); (*applicant*) поруча́ться (*perf* поручи́ться) за *+acc*; **sponsorship** *n* спо́нсорство

SPONSORSHIP

В Великобрита́нии спонси́рование явля́ется распространённым спо́собом сбо́ра де́нег на благотвори́тельность. При́нято выполня́ть ра́зного ро́да зада́чи, наприме́р, пла́вание, ходьба́ на дли́нную диста́нцию или да́же похуде́ние. Предполо́жим, вы хоти́те собра́ть де́ньги для благотвори́тельной организа́ции, финанси́рующей иссле́дования ра́ковых заболева́ний. Вы заявля́ете, что пройдёте пешко́м 10 миль и про́сите знако́мых, друзе́й и тд спонси́ровать ва́ше реше́ние, же́ртвуя де́ньги в по́льзу э́той благотвори́тельной организа́ции.

spontaneous [spɔn'teɪnɪəs] *adj* (*gesture*) спонта́нный, непосре́дственный; (*demonstration*) стихи́йный

spoon [spuːn] *n* ло́жка; **spoonful** *n* (по́лная) ло́жка

sport [spɔːt] *n* (*game*) спорт *m no pl*; **sportsman** *irreg n* спортсме́н; **sportswoman** *irreg n* спортсме́нка; **sporty** *adj* спорти́вный

spot [spɔt] *n* (*mark*) пятно́; (*dot: on pattern*) кра́пинка; (*on skin*) пры́щик; (*place*) ме́сто ▷ *vt* замеча́ть (*perf* заме́тить); **a spot of bother** ме́лкая неприя́тность *f*; **spots of rain** ка́пли дождя́; **on the spot** (*in that place*) на ме́сте; (*immediately*) в тот же моме́нт; **spotless** *adj* чисте́йший; **spotlight** *n* проже́ктор

spouse [spaus] *n* супру́г(а)

sprang [spræŋ] *pt of* **spring**

sprawl [sprɔːl] *vi* (*person*) разва́ливаться (*perf* развали́ться); (*place*) раски́дываться (*perf* раски́нуться)

spray [spreɪ] *n* (*drops of water*) бры́зги *pl*; (*hair spray*) аэрозо́ль *m* ▷ *vt* опры́скивать (*perf* опры́скать)

spread [sprɛd] (*pt, pp* **spread**) *n* (*range*) спектр; (*distribution*) распростране́ние; (*Culin: butter*) бутербро́дный маргари́н; (*inf: food*) пир ▷ *vt* (*lay out*) расстила́ть (*perf* расстели́ть); (*scatter*) разбра́сывать (*perf* разброса́ть); (*butter*) нама́зывать (*perf* нама́зать); (*wings*) расправля́ть (*perf* распра́вить); (*arms*) раскрыва́ть (*perf* раскры́ть); (*workload, wealth*) распределя́ть (*perf* распредели́ть) ▷ *vi* (*disease, news*) распространя́ться (*perf* распространи́ться); **spread out** *vi* (*move apart*) рассыпа́ться (*perf* рассы́паться); **spreadsheet** *n* (крупноформа́тная) электро́нная табли́ца

spree [spriː] *n* разгу́л

spring [sprɪŋ] (*pt* **sprang**, *pp* **sprung**) *n* (*coiled metal*) пружи́на; (*season*) весна́; (*of water*) исто́чник, родни́к ▷ *vi* (*leap*) пры́гать (*perf* пры́гнуть); **in spring** весно́й; **to spring from** (*stem from*) происходи́ть (*perf*

произойти́) из *+gen*
sprinkle ['sprɪŋkl] *vt* (*salt, sugar*) посыпа́ть (*perf* посы́пать) *+instr*; **to sprinkle water on sth, sprinkle sth with water** опры́скивать (*perf* опры́скать) что-н водо́й
sprint [sprɪnt] *n* (*race*) спринт ▷ *vi* (*run fast*) стреми́тельно бе́гать/бежа́ть (*impf*)
sprung [sprʌŋ] *pp of* **spring**
spun [spʌn] *pt, pp of* **spin**
spur [spəːʳ] *n* (*fig*) сти́мул ▷ *vt* (*also* **spur on**) пришпо́ривать (*perf* пришпо́рить); **to spur sb on to** побужда́ть (*perf* побуди́ть) кого́-н к *+dat*; **on the spur of the moment** вдруг, не разду́мывая
spy [spaɪ] *n* шпио́н ▷ *vi*: **to spy on** шпио́нить (*impf*) за *+instr*
Sq. *abbr* = **square**
squabble ['skwɔbl] *vi* вздо́рить (*perf* повздо́рить)
squad [skwɔd] *n* (*Mil, Police*) отря́д; (*Sport*) кома́нда
squadron ['skwɔdrn] *n* (*Aviat*) эскадри́лья
square [skwɛəʳ] *n* (*shape*) квадра́т; (*in town*) пло́щадь *f* ▷ *adj* квадра́тный ▷ *vt* (*reconcile, settle*) ула́живать (*perf* ула́дить); **a square meal** соли́дный обе́д; **2 metres square** 2 ме́тра в ширину́, 2 ме́тра в длину́; **2 square metres** 2 квадра́тных ме́тра
squash [skwɔʃ] *n* (*Brit: drink*) напи́ток; (*Sport*) сквош ▷ *vt* дави́ть (*perf* раздави́ть)
squat [skwɔt] *adj* призе́мистый ▷ *vi* (*also* **squat down**: *position*) сиде́ть (*impf*) на ко́рточках; (: *motion*) сади́ться (*perf* сесть) на ко́рточки
squeak [skwiːk] *vi* (*door*) скрипе́ть (*perf* скри́пнуть); (*mouse*) пища́ть (*perf* пи́скнуть)
squeal [skwiːl] *vi* визжа́ть (*impf*)
squeeze [skwiːz] *n* (*of hand*) пожа́тие; (*Econ*) ограниче́ние ▷ *vt* сжима́ть (*perf* сжать); (*juice*) выжима́ть (*perf* вы́жать)
squid [skwɪd] *n* кальма́р
squint [skwɪnt] *n* (*Med*) косогла́зие
squirrel ['skwɪrəl] *n* бе́лка
squirt [skwəːt] *vi* бры́згать (*perf* бры́знуть) ▷ *vt* бры́згать (*perf* бры́знуть) *+instr*
Sr *abbr* (*in names*) = **senior**
St *abbr* (= *saint*) св.; (= *street*) ул. (= *у́лица*)
stab [stæb] *vt* наноси́ть (*perf* нанести́) уда́р *+dat*; (*kill*): **to stab sb (to death)** заре́зать (*perf*) кого́-н ▷ *n* (*of pain*) уко́л; (*inf: try*): **to have a stab at doing** пыта́ться (*perf* попыта́ться) *+infin*
stability [stə'bɪlɪtɪ] *n* усто́йчивость *f*, стаби́льность *f*
stable ['steɪbl] *adj* стаби́льный, усто́йчивый ▷ *n* (*for horse*) коню́шня
stack [stæk] *n* (*of wood, plates*) шта́бель *m*; (*of papers*) ки́па ▷ *vt* (*also* **stack up**: *chairs etc*) скла́дывать (*perf* сложи́ть)
stadium ['steɪdɪəm] (*pl* **stadia** *or* **stadiums**) *n* (*Sport*) стадио́н
staff [stɑːf] *n* (*workforce*) штат, сотру́дники *mpl*; (*Brit: Scol: also* **teaching staff**) преподава́тельский соста́в *or* коллекти́в ▷ *vt*: **the firm is staffed by 5 people** на фи́рму рабо́тает 5 челове́к
stag [stæg] *n* (*Zool*) саме́ц оле́ня
stage [steɪdʒ] *n* (*in theatre*) сце́на; (*platform*) подмо́стки *pl*; (*point, period*) ста́дия ▷ *vt* (*play*) ста́вить (*perf* поста́вить); (*demonstration*) устра́ивать (*perf*

S

устро́ить); **in stages** поэта́пно, по эта́пам
stagger ['stægəʳ] *vt* (*amaze*) потряса́ть (*perf* потрясти́); (*holidays etc*) распи́сывать (*perf* расписа́ть) ▷ *vi*: **he staggered along the road** он шёл по доро́ге шата́ясь; **staggering** *adj* потряса́ющий, порази́тельный
stagnant ['stægnənt] *adj* (*water*) стоя́чий; (*economy*) засто́йный
stain [steɪn] *n* пятно́ ▷ *vt* (*mark*) ста́вить (*perf* поста́вить) пятно́ на +*acc*; **stainless steel** *n* нержаве́ющая сталь *f*
stair [stɛəʳ] *n* (*step*) ступе́нь *f*, ступе́нька; **stairs** *npl* (*steps*) ле́стница *fsg*; **staircase** *n* ле́стница; **stairway** = **staircase**
stake [steɪk] *n* (*post*) кол; (*investment*) до́ля ▷ *vt* (*money, reputation*) рискова́ть (*perf* рискну́ть) +*instr*; **his reputation was at stake** его́ репута́ция была́ поста́влена на ка́рту; **to stake a claim (to)** притяза́ть (*impf*) (на +*acc*)
stale [steɪl] *adj* (*bread*) чёрствый; (*food*) несве́жий; (*air*) за́тхлый
stalk [stɔ:k] *n* (*of flower*) сте́бель *m*; (*of fruit*) черешо́к
stall [stɔ:l] *n* (*in market*) прила́вок; (*in stable*) сто́йло ▷ *vi*: **I stalled (the car)** у меня́ загло́хла маши́на; **stalls** *npl* (*Brit*: *Theat*) парте́р *msg*
stamina ['stæmɪnə] *n* сто́йкость *f*, вы́держка
stammer ['stæməʳ] *n* заика́ние
stamp [stæmp] *n* (*Post*) ма́рка; (*rubber stamp*) печа́ть *f*, штамп; (*mark, also fig*) печа́ть ▷ *vi* (*also* **stamp one's foot**) то́пать (*perf* то́пнуть) (ного́й) ▷ *vt* (*mark*) клейми́ть (*perf* заклейми́ть); (: *with rubber stamp*) штампова́ть (*perf* проштампова́ть)
stampede [stæm'pi:d] *n* да́вка
stance [stæns] *n* (*also fig*) пози́ция
stand [stænd] (*pt, pp* **stood**) *n* (*stall*) ларёк, кио́ск; (*at exhibition*) стенд; (*Sport*) трибу́на; (*for umbrellas*) сто́йка; (*for coats, hats*) ве́шалка ▷ *vi* (*be upright*) стоя́ть (*impf*); (*rise*) встава́ть (*perf* встать); (*remain*: *decision, offer*) остава́ться (*perf* оста́ться) в си́ле; (*in election etc*) баллоти́роваться (*impf*) ▷ *vt* (*place*: *object*) ста́вить (*perf* поста́вить); (*tolerate, withstand*) терпе́ть (*perf* стерпе́ть), выноси́ть (*perf* вы́нести); **to make a stand against sth** выступа́ть (*perf* вы́ступить) про́тив чего́-н; **to stand for parliament** (*Brit*) баллоти́роваться (*impf*) в парла́мент; **to stand at** (*value, score etc*) составля́ть (*perf* соста́вить) на +*prp*; **stand by** *vi* (*be ready*) быть (*impf*) нагото́ве ▷ *vt fus* не отступа́ть (*perf* отступи́ть) от +*gen*; **stand for** *vt fus* (*signify*) обознача́ть (*impf*); (*represent*) представля́ть (*impf*); **I won't stand for it** я э́того не потерплю́; **stand out** *vi* (*be obvious*) выделя́ться (*perf* вы́делиться); **stand up** *vi* (*rise*) встава́ть (*perf* встать); **stand up for** *vt fus* (*defend*) стоя́ть (*perf* постоя́ть) за +*acc*; **stand up to** *vt fus* ока́зывать (*perf* оказа́ть) сопротивле́ние +*dat*
standard ['stændəd] *n* (*level*) у́ровень *m*; (*norm, criterion*) станда́рт ▷ *adj* (*normal*: *size etc*) станда́ртный; **standards** *npl* (*morals*) нра́вы *mpl*; **standard of living** *n* у́ровень *m* жи́зни

standpoint ['stændpɔɪnt] *n* позиция

standstill ['stændstɪl] *n*: **to be at a standstill** (*negotiations*) быть (*impf*) в тупике́; **to come to a standstill** (*negotiations*) заходи́ть (*perf* зайти́) в тупи́к; (*traffic*) стать (*perf*)

stank [stæŋk] *pt of* **stink**

staple ['steɪpl] *n* (*for papers*) скоба́ ▷ *adj* (*food etc*) основно́й ▷ *vt* (*fasten*) сшива́ть (*perf* сшить)

star [stɑːʳ] *n* звезда́ ▷ *vi*: **to star in** игра́ть (*perf* сыгра́ть) гла́вную роль в *+prp* ▷ *vt*: **the film stars my brother** гла́вную роль в фи́льме игра́ет мой брат; **stars** *npl*: **the stars** (*horoscope*) звёзды *fpl*

starch [stɑːtʃ] *n* (*also Culin*) крахма́л

stare [stɛəʳ] *vi*: **to stare at** (*deep in thought*) при́стально смотре́ть (*impf*) на *+acc*; (*amazed*) тара́щиться (*impf*) на *+acc*

stark [stɑːk] *adj* (*bleak*) го́лый ▷ *adv*: **stark naked** соверше́нно го́лый

start [stɑːt] *n* нача́ло; (*Sport*) старт; (*in fright*) вздра́гивание; (*advantage*) преиму́щество ▷ *vt* (*begin, found*) начина́ть (*perf* нача́ть); (*cause*) вызыва́ть (*perf* вы́звать); (*engine*) заводи́ть (*perf* завести́) ▷ *vi* (*begin*) начина́ться (*perf* нача́ться); (*begin moving*) отправля́ться (*perf* отпра́виться); (*engine, car*) заводи́ться (*perf* завести́сь); (*jump*: *in fright*) вздра́гивать (*perf* вздро́гнуть); **to start doing** *or* **to do** начина́ть (*perf* нача́ть) *+impf infin*; **start off** *vi* (*begin*) начина́ться (*perf* нача́ться); (*begin moving*) тро́гаться (*perf* тро́нуться); (*leave*) отправля́ться (*perf* отпра́виться); **start out** *vi* (*leave*) отправля́ться (*perf* отпра́виться); **start up** *vi* (*engine, car*) заводи́ться (*perf* завести́сь) ▷ *vt* (*business*) начина́ть (*perf* нача́ть); (*car, engine*) заводи́ть (*perf* завести́); **starter** *n* (*Brit*: *Culin*) заку́ска; **starting point** *n* (*for journey*) отправно́й пункт

startle ['stɑːtl] *vt* вспу́гивать (*perf* вспугну́ть)

startling ['stɑːtlɪŋ] *adj* порази́тельный

starvation [stɑː'veɪʃən] *n* го́лод

starve [stɑːv] *vi* (*to death*) умира́ть (*perf* умере́ть) от го́лода; (*be very hungry*) голода́ть (*impf*) ▷ *vt* (*person, animal*) мори́ть (*perf* замори́ть) го́лодом

state [steɪt] *n* (*condition*) состоя́ние; (*government*) госуда́рство ▷ *vt* (*say, declare*) констати́ровать (*impf/perf*); **the States** (*Geo*) Соединённые Шта́ты *mpl*; **to be in a state** быть (*impf*) в па́нике

statement ['steɪtmənt] *n* (*declaration*) заявле́ние

statesman ['steɪtsmən] *irreg n* госуда́рственный де́ятель *m*

static ['stætɪk] *adj* (*not moving*) стати́чный, неподви́жный

station ['steɪʃən] *n* ста́нция; (*larger railway station*) вокза́л; (*also* **police station**) полице́йский уча́сток ▷ *vt* (*position*: *guards etc*) выставля́ть (*perf* вы́ставить)

stationary ['steɪʃnərɪ] *adj* (*vehicle*) неподви́жный

stationery ['steɪʃnərɪ] *n* канцеля́рские принадле́жности *fpl*

statistic [stə'tɪstɪk] *n* стати́стик;

S

statistics *n* (*science*) стати́стика

statue ['stætju:] *n* ста́туя

stature ['stætʃəʳ] *n* (*size*) рост

status ['steɪtəs] *n* ста́тус; (*importance*) значе́ние; **the status quo** ста́тус-кво *m ind*

statutory ['stætjutrɪ] *adj* устано́вленный зако́ном

staunch [stɔ:ntʃ] *adj* пре́данный, непоколеби́мый

stay [steɪ] *n* пребыва́ние ▷ *vi* (*remain*) остава́ться (*perf* оста́ться); (*with sb, as guest*) гости́ть (*impf*); (*in place*) остана́вливаться (*perf* останови́ться); **to stay at home** остава́ться (*perf* оста́ться) до́ма; **to stay put** не дви́гаться (*perf* дви́нуться) с ме́ста; **to stay the night** ночева́ть (*perf* переночева́ть); **stay in** *vi* (*at home*) остава́ться (*perf* оста́ться) до́ма; **stay on** *vi* остава́ться (*perf* оста́ться); **stay out** *vi* (*of house*) отсу́тствовать (*impf*); **stay up** *vi* (*at night*) не ложи́ться (*impf*) (спать)

steadily ['stɛdɪlɪ] *adv* (*firmly*) про́чно; (*constantly, fixedly*) постоя́нно

steady ['stɛdɪ] *adj* (*constant*) стаби́льный; (*boyfriend, speed*) постоя́нный; (*person*) уравнове́шенный; (*firm: hand etc*) твёрдый; (*look, voice*) ро́вный ▷ *vt* (*object*) придава́ть (*perf* прида́ть) усто́йчивость *+dat*; (*nerves, voice*) совлада́ть (*perf*) с *+instr*

steak [steɪk] *n* филе́ *nt ind*; (*fried beef*) бифште́кс

steal [sti:l] (*pt* **stole**, *pp* **stolen**) *vt* ворова́ть (*perf* сворова́ть), красть (*perf* укра́сть) ▷ *vi* ворова́ть (*impf*), красть (*impf*); (*creep*) кра́сться (*impf*)

steam [sti:m] *n* пар ▷ *vt* (*Culin*) па́рить (*impf*) ▷ *vi* (*give off steam*) выделя́ть (*impf*) пар

steel [sti:l] *n* сталь *f* ▷ *adj* стально́й

steep [sti:p] *adj* круто́й; (*price*) высо́кий ▷ *vt* (*food*) выма́чивать (*perf* вы́мочить); (*clothes*) зама́чивать (*perf* замочи́ть)

steeple ['sti:pl] *n* шпиль *m*

steer [stɪəʳ] *vt* (*vehicle, person*) направля́ть (*perf* напра́вить) ▷ *vi* маневри́ровать (*impf*); **steering wheel** *n* руль *m*

stem [stɛm] *n* (*of plant*) сте́бель *m*; (*of glass*) но́жка ▷ *vt* (*stop*) остана́вливать (*perf* останови́ть); **stem from** *vt fus* произраста́ть (*perf* произрасти́) из *+gen*

step [stɛp] *n* (*also fig*) шаг; (*of stairs*) ступе́нь *f*, ступе́нька ▷ *vi* (*forward, back*) ступа́ть (*perf* ступи́ть); **steps** *npl* (*Brit*) = **stepladder**; **to be in/out of step (with)** идти́ (*impf*) в но́гу/не в но́гу (с *+instr*); **step down** *vi* (*fig: resign*) уходи́ть (*perf* уйти́) в отста́вку; **step on** *vt fus* (*walk on*) наступа́ть (*perf* наступи́ть) на *+acc*; **step up** *vt* (*increase*) уси́ливать (*perf* уси́лить); **stepbrother** *n* сво́дный брат; **stepdaughter** *n* па́дчерица; **stepfather** *n* о́тчим; **stepladder** *n* (*Brit*) стремя́нка; **stepmother** *n* ма́чеха; **stepsister** *n* сво́дная сестра́; **stepson** *n* па́сынок

stereo ['stɛrɪəu] *n* (*system*) стереосисте́ма

stereotype ['stɪərɪətaɪp] *n* стереоти́п

sterile ['stɛraɪl] *adj* беспло́дный; (*clean*) стери́льный

sterilize ['stɛrɪlaɪz] *vt*

стерилизова́ть (*impf/perf*)
sterling ['stə:lɪŋ] *n* (*Econ*) фунт сте́рлингов; **sterling silver** серебро́ 925-ой про́бы
stern [stə:n] *adj* суро́вый
stew [stju:] *n* (*meat*) тушёное мя́со ▷ *vt* туши́ть (*perf* потуши́ть)
steward ['stju:əd] *n* (*on plane*) бортпроводни́к; **stewardess** *n* (*on plane*) стюарде́сса, бортпроводни́ца
stick [stɪk] (*pt, pp* **stuck**) *n* (*of wood*) па́лка; (*walking stick*) трость *f* ▷ *vt* (*with glue etc*) кле́ить (*perf* прикле́ить); (*inf*: *put*) сова́ть (*perf* су́нуть); (*thrust*) втыка́ть (*perf* воткну́ть) ▷ *vi* (*become attached*) прикле́иваться (*perf* прикле́иться); (*in mind*) засе́сть (*perf*); **stick out** *vi* (*ears*) торча́ть (*impf*); **stick up for** *vt fus* (*person*) заступа́ться (*perf* заступи́ться) за +*acc*; (*principle*) отста́ивать (*perf* отстоя́ть); **sticker** *n* накле́йка; **sticky** *adj* (*hands etc*) ли́пкий; (*label*) кле́йкий; (*situation*) щекотли́вый
stiff [stɪf] *adj* (*brush*) жёсткий; (*person*) деревя́нный; (*zip*) туго́й; (*manner, smile*) натя́нутый; (*competition*) жёсткий; (*severe*: *sentence*) суро́вый; (*strong*: *drink*) кре́пкий; (: *breeze*) си́льный ▷ *adv* до́ смерти
stifling ['staɪflɪŋ] *adj* (*heat*) удý шливый
stigma ['stɪgmə] *n* (*fig*) клеймо́
still [stɪl] *adj* ти́хий ▷ *adv* (*up to this time*) всё ещё; (*even, yet*) ещё; (*nonetheless*) всё-таки, тем не ме́нее
stimulate ['stɪmjuleɪt] *vt* стимули́ровать (*impf/perf*)
stimulus ['stɪmjuləs] (*pl* **stimuli**) *n* (*encouragement*) сти́мул
sting [stɪŋ] (*pt, pp* **stung**) *n* (*from insect*) уку́с; (*from plant*) ожо́г; (*organ*: *of wasp etc*) жа́ло ▷ *vt* (*also fig*) уязвля́ть (*perf* уязви́ть) ▷ *vi* (*insect, animal*) жа́литься (*impf*); (*plant*) же́чься (*impf*); (*eyes, ointment etc*) жечь (*impf*)
stink [stɪŋk] (*pt* **stank**, *pp* **stunk**) *vi* смерде́ть (*impf*), воня́ть (*impf*) (*inf*)
stir [stə:ʳ] *n* (*fig*) шум, сенса́ция ▷ *vt* (*tea etc*) меша́ть (*perf* помеша́ть); (*fig*: *emotions*) волнова́ть (*perf* взволнова́ть) ▷ *vi* (*move*) шевели́ться (*perf* пошевели́ться); **stir up** *vt* (*trouble*) вызыва́ть (*perf* вы́звать); **stir-fry** *vt* бы́стро обжа́ривать (*perf* обжа́рить)
stitch [stɪtʃ] *n* (*Sewing*) стежо́к; (*Knitting*) петля́; (*Med*) шов ▷ *vt* (*sew*) шить (*perf* сшить); (*Med*) зашива́ть (*perf* заши́ть); **I have a stitch in my side** у меня́ ко́лет в боку́
stock [stɔk] *n* (*supply*) запа́с; (*Agr*) поголо́вье; (*Culin*) бульо́н; (*Finance*: *usu pl*) це́нные бума́ги *fpl* ▷ *adj* (*reply, excuse etc*) дежу́рный ▷ *vt* (*have in stock*) име́ть (*impf*) в нали́чии; **stocks and shares** а́кции и це́нные бума́ги; **to be in/out of stock** име́ться (*impf*)/не име́ться (*impf*) в нали́чии; **to take stock of** (*fig*) оце́нивать (*perf* оцени́ть); **stockbroker** *n* (*Comm*) фо́ндовый бро́кер; **stock exchange** *n* фо́ндовая би́ржа
stocking ['stɔkɪŋ] *n* чуло́к
stock market *n* (*Brit*) фо́ндовая би́ржа
stole [stəul] *pt of* **steal**; **stolen** *pp of* **steal**
stomach ['stʌmək] *n* (*Anat*)

S

желу́док; (*belly*) живо́т ▷ *vt* (*fig*) переноси́ть (*perf* перенести́)
stone [stəun] *n* (*also Med*) ка́мень *m*; (*pebble*) ка́мешек; (*in fruit*) ко́сточка; (*Brit*: *weight*) сто́ун (*14 фу́нтов*) ▷ *adj* ка́менный

STONE

Stone — ме́ра ве́са ра́вная 6,35 кг.

stood [stud] *pt, pp of* **stand**
stool [stu:l] *n* табуре́т(ка)
stoop [stu:p] *vi* (*also* **stoop down**: *bend*) наклоня́ться (*perf* наклони́ться), нагиба́ться (*perf* нагну́ться)
stop [stɔp] *n* остано́вка; (*Ling*: *also* **full stop**) то́чка ▷ *vt* остана́вливать (*perf* останови́ть); (*prevent*: *also* **put a stop to**) прекраща́ть (*perf* прекрати́ть) ▷ *vi* (*person, clock*) остана́вливаться (*perf* останови́ться); (*rain, noise etc*) прекраща́ться (*perf* прекрати́ться); **to stop doing** перестава́ть (*perf* переста́ть) +*infin*; **stop by** *vi* заходи́ть (*perf* зайти́); **stoppage** ['stɔpɪdʒ] *n* (*strike*) забасто́вка
storage ['stɔ:rɪdʒ] *n* хране́ние
store [stɔ:ʳ] *n* (*stock, reserve*) запа́с; (*depot*) склад; (*Brit*: *large shop*) универма́г; (*esp US*: *shop*) магази́н ▷ *vt* храни́ть (*impf*); **in store** в бу́дущем
storey ['stɔ:rɪ] (*US* **story**) *n* эта́ж
storm [stɔ:m] *n* (*also fig*) бу́ря; (*of criticism*) шквал; (*of laughter*) взрыв ▷ *vt* (*attack*: *place*) штурмова́ть (*impf*); **stormy** *adj* (*fig*) бу́рный; **stormy weather** нена́стье
story ['stɔ:rɪ] *n* исто́рия; (*lie*) вы́думка, ска́зка; (*US*) = **storey**
stout [staut] *adj* (*strong*: *branch etc*) кре́пкий; (*fat*) доро́дный; (*resolute*: *friend, supporter*) сто́йкий
stove [stəuv] *n* печь *f*, пе́чка
St Petersburg [sənt'pi:təzbə:g] *n* Санкт-Петербу́рг
straight [streɪt] *adj* прямо́й; (*simple*: *choice*) я́сный ▷ *adv* пря́мо; **to put** *or* **get sth straight** (*make clear*) вноси́ть (*perf* внести́) я́сность во что-н; **straight away, straight off** (*at once*) сра́зу (же); **straighten** *vt* (*skirt, tie, bed*) поправля́ть (*perf* попра́вить); **straightforward** *adj* (*simple*) просто́й; (*honest*) прямо́й
strain [streɪn] *n* (*pressure*) нагру́зка; (*Med*: *physical*) растяже́ние; (: *mental*) напряже́ние ▷ *vt* (*back etc*) растя́гивать (*perf* растяну́ть); (*voice*) напряга́ть (*perf* напря́чь); (*stretch*: *resources*) перенапряга́ть (*perf* перенапря́чь) по +*dat*; (*Culin*) проце́живать (*perf* процеди́ть); **strained** *adj* (*muscle*) растя́нутый; (*laugh, relations*) натя́нутый
strand [strænd] *n* нить *f*; (*of hair*) прядь *f*; **stranded** *adj*: **to be stranded** застрева́ть (*perf* застря́ть)
strange [streɪndʒ] *adj* стра́нный; (*not known*) незнако́мый; **strangely** *adv* (*act, laugh*) стра́нно; *see also* **enough**; **stranger** *n* (*unknown person*) незнако́мец, посторо́нний(-яя) *m(f) adj*
strangle ['stræŋgl] *vt* (*also fig*) души́ть (*perf* задуши́ть)
strap [stræp] *n* реме́нь *m*; (*of*

dress) брете́лька; (*of watch*) ремешо́к

strategic [strəˈtiːdʒɪk] *adj* стратеги́ческий

strategy [ˈstrætɪdʒɪ] *n* страте́гия

straw [strɔː] *n* соло́ма; (*drinking straw*) соло́минка; **that's the last straw!** э́то после́дняя ка́пля!

strawberry [ˈstrɔːbərɪ] *n* клубни́ка *f no pl*; (*wild*) земляни́ка *f no pl*

stray [streɪ] *adj* (*animal*) бродя́чий; (*bullet*) шально́й ▷ *vi* заблуди́ться (*perf*); (*thoughts*) блужда́ть (*impf*)

streak [striːk] *n* (*stripe*) полоса́

stream [striːm] *n* руче́й; (*of people, vehicles, questions*) пото́к ▷ *vi* (*liquid*) течь (*impf*), ли́ться (*impf*); **to stream in/out** (*people*) вали́ть (*perf* повали́ть) толпо́й в *+acc*/из *+gen*

street [striːt] *n* у́лица

strength [strɛŋθ] *n* си́ла; (*of girder, knot etc*) про́чность *f*; **strengthen** *vt* (*building, machine*) укрепля́ть (*perf* укрепи́ть); (*fig*: *group*) пополня́ть (*perf* попо́лнить); (: *argument*) подкрепля́ть (*perf* подкрепи́ть)

strenuous [ˈstrɛnjuəs] *adj* (*exercise*) уси́ленный; (*efforts*) напряжённый

stress [strɛs] *n* (*pressure*) давле́ние, напряже́ние; (*mental strain*) стресс; (*emphasis*) ударе́ние ▷ *vt* (*point, need etc*) де́лать (*perf* сде́лать) ударе́ние на *+acc*; (*syllable*) ста́вить (*perf* поста́вить) ударе́ние на *+acc*

stretch [strɛtʃ] *n* (*area*) отре́зок, простра́нство ▷ *vt* (*pull*) натя́гивать (*perf* натяну́ть) ▷ *vi* (*person, animal*) потя́гиваться (*perf* потяну́ться); (*extend*): **to stretch to** *or* **as far as** простира́ться (*impf*) до *+gen*; **stretch out** *vi* растя́гиваться (*perf* растяну́ться) ▷ *vt* (*arm etc*) протя́гивать (*perf* протяну́ть)

stretcher [ˈstrɛtʃəʳ] *n* носи́лки *pl*

strict [strɪkt] *adj* стро́гий; (*precise*: *meaning*) то́чный; **strictly** *adv* (*severely*) стро́го; (*exactly*) то́чно

stride [straɪd] (*pt* **strode**, *pp* **stridden**) *n* (*step*) шаг ▷ *vi* шага́ть (*impf*)

strike [straɪk] (*pt, pp* **struck**) *n* (*of workers*) забасто́вка; (*Mil*: *attack*) уда́р ▷ *vt* (*hit*: *person, thing*) ударя́ть (*perf* уда́рить); (*subj*: *idea, thought*) осеня́ть (*perf* осени́ть); (*oil etc*) открыва́ть (*perf* откры́ть) месторожде́ние *+gen*; (*bargain, deal*) заключа́ть (*perf* заключи́ть) ▷ *vi* (*workers*) бастова́ть (*impf*); (*disaster, illness*) обру́шиваться (*perf* обру́шиться); (*clock*) бить (*perf* проби́ть); **to be on strike** (*workers*) бастова́ть (*impf*); **to strike a match** зажига́ть (*perf* заже́чь) спи́чку; **striker** *n* забасто́вщик(-ица); (*Sport*) напада́ющий(-ая) *m(f) adj*

striking [ˈstraɪkɪŋ] *adj* порази́тельный

string [strɪŋ] (*pt, pp* **strung**) *n* верёвка; (*Mus*: *for guitar etc*) струна́; (*of beads*) ни́тка ▷ *vt*: **to string together** свя́зывать (*perf* связа́ть); **strings** *npl* (*Mus*) стру́нные инструме́нты *mpl*; **to string out** растя́гивать (*perf* растяну́ть)

strip [strɪp] *n* полоса́, поло́ска ▷ *vt* (*undress*) раздева́ть (*perf* разде́ть); (*paint*) обдира́ть (*perf* ободра́ть), сдира́ть (*perf* содра́ть); (*also* **strip down**: *machine*)

S

разбирáть (*perf* разобрáть) ▷ *vi* раздевáться (*perf* раздéться)
stripe [straɪp] *n* полóска; (*Police, Mil*) петлúца; **striped** *adj* полосáтый
stripper ['strɪpəʳ] *n* стриптизёрка
strive [straɪv] (*pt* **strove**, *pp* **striven**) *vi*: **to strive for sth/to do** стремúться (*impf*) к чемý-н/+*infin*
strode [strəud] *pt of* **stride**
stroke [strəuk] *n* (*also Med*) удáр; (*Swimming*) стиль *m* ▷ *vt* глáдить (*perf* поглáдить); **at a stroke** однúм мáхом
stroll [strəul] *n* прогýлка ▷ *vi* прогýливаться (*perf* прогуля́ться), прохáживаться (*perf* пройтúсь)
strong [strɔŋ] *adj* сúльный; **they are 50 strong** их 50; **stronghold** *n* (*fig*) оплóт, тверды́ня
strove [strəuv] *pt of* **strive**
struck [strʌk] *pt, pp of* **strike**
structure ['strʌktʃəʳ] *n* структýра
struggle ['strʌgl] *n* (*fight*) борьбá ▷ *vi* (*try hard*) сúлиться (*impf*), прилагáть (*perf* приложúть) большúе усúлия; (*fight*) борóться (*impf*); (: *to free o.s.*) сопротивля́ться (*impf*)
strung [strʌŋ] *pt, pp of* **string**
stub [stʌb] *n* (*of cheque, ticket etc*) корешóк; (*of cigarette*) окýрок ▷ *vt*: **to stub one's toe** бóльно спотыкáться (*perf* споткнýться)
stubble ['stʌbl] *n* (*on chin*) щетúна
stubborn ['stʌbən] *adj* (*determination, child*) упря́мый, упóрный
stuck [stʌk] *pt, pp of* **stick** ▷ *adj*: **to be stuck** застря́ть (*perf*)
stud [stʌd] *n* (*on clothing etc*) кнóпка, заклёпка; (*earring*) серьгá со штифтóм; (*on sole of boot*) шип ▷ *vt* (*fig*): **studded with** усы́панный +*instr*
student ['stju:dənt] *n* (*at university*) студéнт(ка); (*at school*) учáщийся(-аяся) *m(f) adj* ▷ *adj* студéнческий; (*at school*) ученúческий
studio ['stju:dɪəu] *n* стýдия
study ['stʌdɪ] *n* (*activity*) учёба; (*room*) кабинéт ▷ *vt* изучáть (*perf* изучúть) ▷ *vi* учúться (*perf*)
stuff [stʌf] *n* (*things*) вéщи *fpl*; (*substance*) веществó ▷ *vt* набивáть (*perf* набúть); (*Culin*) начиня́ть (*perf* начинúть), фаршировáть (*perf* нафаршировáть); (*inf*: *push*) запúхивать (*perf* запихáть); **stuffing** *n* набúвка; (*Culin*) начúнка, фарш; **stuffy** *adj* (*room*) дýшный; (*person, ideas*) чóпорный
stumble ['stʌmbl] *vi* спотыкáться (*perf* споткнýться); **to stumble across** *or* **on** (*fig*) натыкáться (*perf* наткнýться) на +*acc*
stump [stʌmp] *n* (*of tree*) пень *m*; (*of limb*) обрýбок ▷ *vt* озадáчивать (*perf* озадáчить)
stun [stʌn] *vt* (*subj*: *news*) потрясáть (*perf* потрястú), ошеломля́ть (*perf* ошеломúть); (: *blow on head*) оглушáть (*perf* оглушúть)
stung [stʌŋ] *pt, pp of* **sting**
stunk [stʌŋk] *pp of* **stink**
stunning ['stʌnɪŋ] *adj* (*fabulous*) потрясáющий
stupid ['stju:pɪd] *adj* глýпый; **stupidity** [stju:'pɪdɪtɪ] *n* глýпость *f*
sturdy ['stə:dɪ] *adj* крéпкий
stutter ['stʌtəʳ] *n* заикáние ▷ *vi* заикáться (*impf*)
style [staɪl] *n* стиль *m*
stylish ['staɪlɪʃ] *adj* стúльный, элегáнтный

subconscious [sʌbˈkɔnʃəs] *adj* подсозна́тельный
subdued [sʌbˈdjud] *adj* (*light*) приглушённый; (*person*) пода́вленный
subject [*n* ˈsʌbdʒɪkt, *vb* səbˈdʒɛkt] *n* (*topic*) те́ма; (*Scol*) предме́т; (*Ling*) подлежа́щее *nt adj* ▷ *vt*: **to subject sb to sth** подверга́ть (*perf* подве́ргнуть) кого́-н чему́-н; **to be subject to** (*tax*) подлежа́ть (*impf*) *+dat*; (*law*) подчиня́ться (*impf*) *+dat*; **subjective** [səbˈdʒɛktɪv] *adj* субъекти́вный
submarine [sʌbməˈri:n] *n* подво́дная ло́дка
submission [səbˈmɪʃən] *n* (*state*) подчине́ние, повинове́ние; (*of plan etc*) пода́ча
submit [səbˈmɪt] *vt* (*proposal, application etc*) представля́ть (*perf* предста́вить) на рассмотре́ние ▷ *vi*: **to submit to sth** подчиня́ться (*perf* подчини́ться) чему́-н
subordinate [səˈbɔ:dɪnət] *adj*: **to be subordinate to** (*in rank*) подчиня́ться (*impf*) *+dat* ▷ *n* подчинённый(-ая) *m(f) adj*
subscribe [səbˈskraɪb] *vi*: **to subscribe to** (*opinion, fund*) подде́рживать (*perf* поддержа́ть); (*magazine etc*) подпи́сываться (*perf* подписа́ться) на *+acc*
subscription [səbˈskrɪpʃən] *n* (*to magazine etc*) подпи́ска
subsequent [ˈsʌbsɪkwənt] *adj* после́дующий; **subsequent to** вслед *+dat*; **subsequently** *adv* впосле́дствии
subside [səbˈsaɪd] *vi* (*feeling, wind*) утиха́ть (*perf* ути́хнуть); (*flood*) убыва́ть (*perf* убы́ть)
subsidiary [səbˈsɪdɪərɪ] *n* (*also* **subsidiary company**) доче́рняя компа́ния
subsidy [ˈsʌbsɪdɪ] *n* субси́дия, дота́ция
substance [ˈsʌbstəns] *n* (*product, material*) вещество́
substantial [səbˈstænʃl] *adj* (*solid*) про́чный, основа́тельный; (*fig*: *reward, meal*) соли́дный
substitute [ˈsʌbstɪtju:t] *n* (*person*) заме́на; (: *Football etc*) запасно́й *m adj* (игро́к); (*thing*) замени́тель *m* ▷ *vt*: **to substitute A for B** заменя́ть (*perf* замени́ть) А на Б
substitution [sʌbstɪˈtju:ʃən] *n* (*act*) заме́на
subtitle [ˈsʌbtaɪtl] *n* (*in film*) субти́тр
subtle [ˈsʌtl] *adj* (*change*) то́нкий, едва́ улови́мый; (*person*) то́нкий, иску́сный
subtract [səbˈtrækt] *vt* вычита́ть (*perf* вы́честь)
suburb [ˈsʌbə:b] *n* при́город; **the suburbs** (*area*) при́город *msg*; **suburban** [səˈbə:bən] *adj* при́городный
subway [ˈsʌbweɪ] *n* (*US*) метро́ *nt ind*, подзе́мка (*inf*); (*Brit*: *underpass*) подзе́мный перехо́д
succeed [səkˈsi:d] *vi* (*plan etc*) удава́ться (*perf* уда́ться), име́ть (*impf*) успе́х; (*person*: *in career etc*) преуспева́ть (*perf* преуспе́ть) ▷ *vt* (*in job, order*) сменя́ть (*perf* смени́ть); **he succeeded in finishing the article** ему́ удало́сь зако́нчить статью́
success [səkˈsɛs] *n* успе́х, уда́ча; **the book was a success** кни́га име́ла успе́х; **he was a success** он доби́лся успе́ха; **successful** *adj* (*venture*) успе́шный; **he was successful in convincing her** ему́ удало́сь убеди́ть её; **successfully** *adv* успе́шно

S

succession [sək'sɛʃən] *n* (*series*) чередá, ряд; (*to throne etc*) наслéдование; **in succession** подря́д
successive [sək'sɛsɪv] *adj* (*governments*) слéдующий оди́н за други́м
successor [sək'sɛsə^r] *n* преéмник(-ица); (*to throne*) наслéдник(-ица)
succumb [sə'kʌm] *vi* (*to temptation*) поддавáться (*perf* поддáться)
such [sʌtʃ] *adj* такóй ▷ *adv*: **such a long trip** такáя дли́нная поéздка; **such a book** такáя кни́га; **such books** таки́е кни́ги; **such a lot of** такóе мнóжество *+gen*; **such as** (*like*) таки́е как; **as such** как таковóй; **such-and-such** *adj* таки́е-то и таки́е-то
suck [sʌk] *vt* (*bottle, sweet*) сосáть (*impf*)
sudden ['sʌdn] *adj* внезáпный; **all of a sudden** внезáпно, вдруг; **suddenly** *adv* внезáпно, вдруг
sudoku [su'dəuku:] *n* судóку *nt ind*
sue [su:] *vt* предъявля́ть (*perf* предъяви́ть) иск *+dat*
suede [sweɪd] *n* зáмша
suffer ['sʌfə^r] *vt* (*hardship etc*) переноси́ть (*perf* перенести́); (*pain*) страдáть (*impf*) от *+gen* ▷ *vi* (*person, results etc*) страдáть (*perf* пострадáть); **to suffer from** страдáть (*impf*) *+instr*; **suffering** *n* (*hardship*) страдáние
suffice [sə'faɪs] *vi*: **this suffices to ...** э́того достáточно, ...
sufficient [sə'fɪʃənt] *adj* достáточный
suffocate ['sʌfəkeɪt] *vi* задыхáться (*perf* задохну́ться)
sugar ['ʃugə^r] *n* сáхар
suggest [sə'dʒɛst] *vt* (*propose*) предлагáть (*perf* предложи́ть); (*indicate*) предполагáть (*perf* предположи́ть); **suggestion** [sə'dʒɛstʃən] *n* (*see vt*) предложéние; предположéние
suicide ['suɪsaɪd] *n* (*death*) самоуби́йство; *see also* **commit**
suit [su:t] *n* костю́м; (*Law*) иск; (*Cards*) масть *f* ▷ *vt* (*be convenient, appropriate*) подходи́ть (*perf* подойти́) *+dat*; (*colour, clothes*) идти́ (*impf*) *+dat*; **to suit sth to** (*adapt*) приспосáбливать (*perf* приспосóбить) что-н к *+dat*; **they are well suited** (*couple*) они́ хорошó друг дру́гу подхóдят; **suitable** *adj* подходя́щий
suitcase ['su:tkeɪs] *n* чемодáн
suite [swi:t] *n* (*of rooms*) апартамéнты *mpl*; (*furniture*): **bedroom/dining room suite** спáльный/столóвый гарниту́р
sulfur ['sʌlfə^r] *n* (*US*) = **sulphur**
sulk [sʌlk] *vi* злóбствовать (*impf*), ду́ться (*impf*) (*inf*)
sulphur ['sʌlfə^r] (*US* **sulfur**) *n* сéра
sultana [sʌl'tɑ:nə] *n* кишми́ш
sum [sʌm] *n* (*calculation*) арифмéтика, вычислéние; (*amount*) су́мма; **sum up** *vt* (*describe*) сумми́ровать (*impf/perf*) ▷ *vi* подводи́ть (*perf* подвести́) итóг
summarize ['sʌməraɪz] *vt* сумми́ровать (*impf/perf*)
summary ['sʌmərɪ] *n* (*of essay etc*) крáткое изложéние
summer ['sʌmə^r] *n* лéто ▷ *adj* лéтний; **in summer** лéтом; **summertime** *n* (*season*) лéто, лéтняя порá
summit ['sʌmɪt] *n* (*of mountain*)

вершина, пик; (*also* **summit meeting**) встреча на высшем уровне, саммит

sun [sʌn] *n* солнце; **sunbathe** *vi* загорать (*impf*); **sunburn** *n* солнечный ожог

Sunday ['sʌndɪ] *n* воскресенье

sunflower ['sʌnflauə^r] *n* (*Bot*) подсолнечник

sung [sʌŋ] *pp of* **sing**

sunglasses ['sʌnglɑ:sɪz] *npl* солнцезащитные очки *pl*

sunk [sʌŋk] *pp of* **sink**

sun: **sunlight** *n* солнечный свет; **sunny** *adj* (*weather, place*) солнечный; **sunrise** *n* восход (солнца); **sunset** *n* закат, заход (солнца); **sunshine** *n* солнечный свет; **in the sunshine** на солнце; **sunstroke** *n* солнечный удар; **suntan** *n* загар

super ['su:pə^r] *adj* мировой, потрясающий

superb [su:'pə:b] *adj* превосходный, великолепный

superficial [su:pə'fɪʃəl] *adj* поверхностный; (*wound*) лёгкий

superintendent [su:pərɪn'tɛndənt] *n* (*Police*) начальник

superior [su'pɪərɪə^r] *adj* (*better*) лучший; (*more senior*) вышестоящий; (*smug*) высокомерный ▷ *n* начальник

supermarket ['su:pəmɑ:kɪt] *n* супермаркет, универсам

supernatural [su:pə'nætʃərəl] *adj* сверхъестественный

superpower ['su:pəpauə^r] *n* (*Pol*) великая держава, сверхдержава

superstition [su:pə'stɪʃən] *n* суеверие

superstitious [su:pə'stɪʃəs] *adj* суеверный

supervise ['su:pəvaɪz] *vt* (*person, activity*) курировать (*impf*); (*dissertation*) руководить (*impf*)

supervision [su:pə'vɪʒən] *n* руководство, надзор

supervisor ['su:pəvaɪzə^r] *n* (*of workers*) начальник; (*Scol*) научный(-ая) руководитель(ница) *m(f)*

supper ['sʌpə^r] *n* ужин

supple ['sʌpl] *adj* (*person, body*) гибкий; (*leather*) упругий

supplement ['sʌplɪmənt] *n* (*of vitamins*) добавка, дополнение; (*of book, newspaper etc*) приложение ▷ *vt* добавлять (*perf* добавить) к +*dat*

supplier [sə'plaɪə^r] *n* поставщик

supply [sə'plaɪ] *n* (*see vt*) поставка; снабжение; (*stock*) запас ▷ *vt* (*goods*) поставлять (*perf* поставить); (*gas*) снабжать (*perf* снабдить); **to supply sb/sth with sth** (*see vt*) поставлять (*perf* поставить) что-н кому-н/чему-н; снабжать (*perf* снабдить) кого-н/что-н чем-н; **supplies** *npl* (*food*) запасы *mpl* продовольствия

support [sə'pɔ:t] *n* (*moral, financial etc*) поддержка; (*Tech*) опора ▷ *vt* (*morally*) поддерживать (*perf* поддержать); (*financially: family etc*) содержать (*impf*); (*football team etc*) болеть (*impf*) за +*acc*; (*hold up*) поддерживать (*impf*); (*theory etc*) подтверждать (*perf* подтвердить); **supporter** *n* (*Pol etc*) сторонник(-ица); (*Sport*) болельщик(-ица)

suppose [sə'pəuz] *vt* полагать (*impf*), предполагать (*perf* предположить); **he was supposed to do it** (*duty*) он должен был это сделать; **supposedly** [sə'pəuzɪdlɪ] *adv* якобы

supposing [sə'pəuzɪŋ] *conj* предполо́жим, допу́стим

suppress [sə'prɛs] *vt* (*revolt*) подавля́ть (*perf* подави́ть)

supreme [su'pri:m] *adj* (*in titles*) Верхо́вный; (*effort, achievement*) велича́йший

surcharge ['sə:tʃɑ:dʒ] *n* дополни́тельный сбор

sure [ʃuəʳ] *adj* (*certain*) уве́ренный; (*reliable*) ве́рный; **to make sure of sth/that** удостоверя́ться (*perf* удостове́риться) в чём-н/, что; **sure!** (*okay*) коне́чно!; **sure enough** и пра́вда *or* впра́вду; **surely** *adv* (*certainly*) наверняка́

surf [sə:f] *vt* (*Comput*) ла́зить (*impf*) по +*dat*, серфить (*impf*)

surface ['sə:fɪs] *n* пове́рхность *f* ▷ *vi* всплыва́ть (*perf* всплы́ть)

surfing ['sə:fɪŋ] *n* сёрфинг

surge [sə:dʒ] *n* (*increase*) рост; (*fig: of emotion*) прили́в

surgeon ['sə:dʒən] *n* (*Med*) хиру́рг

surgery ['sə:dʒərɪ] *n* (*treatment*) хирурги́я, хирурги́ческое вмеша́тельство; (*Brit: room*) кабине́т; (*: time*) приём; **to undergo surgery** переноси́ть (*perf* перенести́) опера́цию

surname ['sə:neɪm] *n* фами́лия

surpass [sə:'pɑ:s] *vt* (*person, thing*) превосходи́ть (*perf* превзойти́)

surplus ['sə:pləs] *n* избы́ток, изли́шек; (*of trade, payments*) акти́вное са́льдо *nt ind* ▷ *adj* (*stock, grain*) избы́точный

surprise [sə'praɪz] *n* удивле́ние; (*unexpected event*) неожи́данность *f* ▷ *vt* (*astonish*) удивля́ть (*perf* удиви́ть); (*catch unawares*) застава́ть (*perf* заста́ть) враспло́х

surprising [sə'praɪzɪŋ] *adj* (*situation, announcement*) неожи́данный; **surprisingly** *adv* удиви́тельно

surrender [sə'rɛndəʳ] *n* сда́ча, капитуля́ция ▷ *vi* (*army, hijackers etc*) сдава́ться (*perf* сда́ться)

surround [sə'raund] *vt* (*subj: walls, hedge etc*) окружа́ть (*impf*); (*Mil, Police etc*) окружа́ть (*perf* окружи́ть); **surrounding** *adj* (*countryside*) окружа́ющий, окре́стный; **surroundings** *npl* (*place*) окре́стности *fpl*; (*conditions*) окруже́ние *ntsg*

surveillance [sə:'veɪləns] *n* наблюде́ние

survey [*vb* sə:'veɪ, *n* 'sə:veɪ] *vt* (*scene, work etc*) осма́тривать (*perf* осмотре́ть) ▷ *n* (*of land*) геодези́ческая съёмка; (*of house*) инспе́кция; (*of habits etc*) обзо́р; **surveyor** [sə'veɪəʳ] *n* (*of land*) геодези́ст; (*of house*) инспе́ктор

survival [sə'vaɪvl] *n* выжива́ние

survive [sə'vaɪv] *vi* выжива́ть (*perf* вы́жить), уцеле́ть (*perf*); (*custom etc*) сохраня́ться (*perf* сохрани́ться) ▷ *vt* (*person*) пережива́ть (*perf* пережи́ть); (*illness*) переноси́ть (*perf* перенести́)

survivor [sə'vaɪvəʳ] *n* (*of illness, accident*) вы́живший(-ая) *m(f) adj*

suspect [*vb* səs'pɛkt, *n, adj* 'sʌspɛkt] *vt* подозрева́ть (*impf*) ▷ *n* подозрева́емый(-ая) *m(f) adj* ▷ *adj* подозри́тельный

suspend [səs'pɛnd] *vt* (*delay*) приостана́вливать (*perf* приостанови́ть); (*stop*) прерыва́ть (*perf* прерва́ть); (*from employment*) отстраня́ть (*perf* отстрани́ть); **suspenders** *npl* (*Brit*) подвя́зки *fpl*; (*US*)

подтя́жки *fpl*
suspense [səs'pɛns] *n* трево́га, напряже́ние; **to keep sb in suspense** держа́ть (*impf*) кого́-н во взве́шенном состоя́нии
suspension [səs'pɛnʃən] *n* (*from job, team*) отстране́ние; (*Aut*) амортиза́тор; (*of payment*) приостановле́ние
suspicion [səs'pɪʃən] *n* подозре́ние
suspicious [səs'pɪʃəs] *adj* подозри́тельный
sustain [səs'teɪn] *vt* подде́рживать (*perf* поддержа́ть); (*losses*) нести́ (*perf* понести́); (*injury*) получа́ть (*perf* получи́ть); **sustainable** *adj* (*development, progress*) стаби́льный, усто́йчивый
swallow ['swɔləu] *n* (*Zool*) ла́сточка ▷ *vt* (*food, pills*) глота́ть (*perf* проглоти́ть); (*fig*) подавля́ть (*perf* подави́ть)
swam [swæm] *pt of* **swim**
swamp [swɔmp] *n* топь *f* ▷ *vt* (*with water*) залива́ть (*perf* зали́ть); (*fig*: *person*) зава́ливать (*perf* завали́ть)
swan [swɔn] *n* ле́бедь *m*
swap [swɔp] *n* обме́н ▷ *vt*: **to swap (for)** (*exchange (for)*) меня́ть (*perf* обменя́ть) (на *+acc*); (*replace (with)*) меня́ть (*perf* поменя́ть) (на *+acc*)
swarm [swɔ:m] *n* (*of bees*) рой; (*of people*) тьма
sway [sweɪ] *vi* кача́ться (*perf* качну́ться) ▷ *vt*: **to be swayed by** поддава́ться (*perf* подда́ться) на *+acc*
swear [swɛə[r]] (*pt* **swore**, *pp* **sworn**) *vi* (*curse*) скверносло́вить (*impf*), руга́ться (*perf* вы́ругаться) ▷ *vt* кля́сться (*perf* покля́сться)
sweat [swɛt] *n* пот ▷ *vi* поте́ть (*perf* вспоте́ть); **sweater** *n* сви́тер; **sweatshirt** *n* спорти́вный сви́тер; **sweaty** *adj* (*clothes*) пропоте́вший; (*hands*) по́тный
swede [swi:d] *n* (*Brit*) брю́ква
Sweden ['swi:dn] *n* Шве́ция
Swedish ['swi:dɪʃ] *adj* шве́дский; ▷ *npl*: **the Swedish** шве́ды
sweep [swi:p] (*pt, pp* **swept**) *vt* (*with brush*) мести́ *or* подмета́ть (*perf* подмести́); (*with arm*) сма́хивать (*perf* смахну́ть); (*subj*: *current*) сноси́ть (*perf* снести́), смыва́ть (*perf* смыть) ▷ *vi* (*wind*) бушева́ть (*impf*)
sweet [swi:t] *n* (*candy*) конфе́та; (*Brit*: *Culin*) сла́дкое *nt adj no pl*, сла́дости *fpl* ▷ *adj* сла́дкий; (*kind, attractive*) ми́лый; **sweet corn** *n* кукуру́за
swell [swɛl] (*pt* **swelled**, *pp* **swollen** *or* **swelled**) *n* (*of sea*) волне́ние ▷ *adj* (*US*: *inf*) мирово́й ▷ *vi* (*numbers*) расти́ (*perf* вы́расти); (*also* **swell up**: *face, ankle etc*) опуха́ть (*perf* опу́хнуть), вздува́ться (*perf* взду́ться); **swelling** *n* (*Med*) о́пухоль *f*, взду́тие
swept [swɛpt] *pt, pp of* **sweep**
swift [swɪft] *adj* стреми́тельный
swim [swɪm] (*pt* **swam**, *pp* **swum**) *vi* пла́вать/плыть (*impf*); (*as sport*) пла́вать (*impf*); (*head*) идти́ (*perf* пойти́) кру́гом; (*room*) плыть (*perf* поплы́ть) ▷ *vt* переплыва́ть (*perf* переплы́ть); (*a length*) проплыва́ть (*perf* проплы́ть); **swimmer** *n* пловéц(-вчи́ха); **swimming** *n* пла́вание; **swimming costume** *n* (*Brit*) купа́льный костю́м; **swimming pool** *n* пла́вательный

S

бассе́йн; **swimming trunks** *npl* пла́вки *pl*; **swimsuit** *n* купа́льник

swing [swɪŋ] (*pt, pp* **swung**) *n* (*in playground*) каче́ли *pl*; (*change*: *in opinions etc*) крен, поворо́т ▷ *vt* (*arms*) разма́хивать (*impf*) +*instr*; (*legs*) болта́ть (*impf*) +*instr*; (*also* **swing round**: *vehicle etc*) развора́чивать (*perf* разверну́ть) ▷ *vi* кача́ться (*impf*); (*also* **swing round**: *vehicle etc*) развора́чиваться (*perf* разверну́ться); **to be in full swing** (*party etc*) быть (*impf*) в по́лном разга́ре

swirl [swəːl] *vi* кружи́ться (*impf*)

Swiss [swɪs] *adj* швейца́рский

switch [swɪtʃ] *n* (*for light, radio etc*) выключа́тель *m*; (*change*) переключе́ние ▷ *vt* (*change*) переключа́ть (*perf* переключи́ть); **switch off** *vt* выключа́ть (*perf* вы́ключить); **switch on** *vt* включа́ть (*perf* включи́ть); **switchboard** *n* (*Tel*) коммута́тор

Switzerland [ˈswɪtsələnd] *n* Швейца́рия

swivel [ˈswɪvl] *vi* (*also* **swivel round**) повора́чиваться (*impf*)

swollen [ˈswəulən] *pp of* **swell**

sword [sɔːd] *n* меч

swore [swɔːʳ] *pt of* **swear**

sworn [swɔːn] *pp of* **swear** ▷ *adj* (*statement, evidence*) да́нный под прися́гой; (*enemy*) закля́тый

swum [swʌm] *pp of* **swim**

swung [swʌŋ] *pt, pp of* **swing**

syllable [ˈsɪləbl] *n* слог

syllabus [ˈsɪləbəs] *n* (учёбная) програ́мма

symbol [ˈsɪmbl] *n* (*sign*) знак; (*representation*) си́мвол; **symbolic(al)** [sɪmˈbɔlɪk(l)] *adj* символи́ческий

symmetrical [sɪˈmɛtrɪkl] *adj* симметри́чный

symmetry [ˈsɪmɪtrɪ] *n* симме́трия

sympathetic [sɪmpəˈθɛtɪk] *adj* (*person*) уча́стливый; (*remark, opinion*) сочу́вственный; (*likeable*: *character*) прия́тный, симпати́чный; **to be sympathetic to(wards)** (*supportive of*) сочу́вствовать (*impf*) +*dat*

sympathize [ˈsɪmpəθaɪz] *vi*: **to sympathize with** сочу́вствовать (*impf*) +*dat*

sympathy [ˈsɪmpəθɪ] *n* (*pity*) сочу́вствие, уча́стие; **with our deepest sympathy** с глубоча́йшими соболе́знованиями; **to come out in sympathy** (*workers*) бастова́ть (*impf*) в знак солида́рности

symphony [ˈsɪmfənɪ] *n* симфо́ния

symptom [ˈsɪmptəm] *n* симпто́м

synagogue [ˈsɪnəgɔg] *n* синаго́га

syndicate [ˈsɪndɪkɪt] *n* (*of people, businesses*) синдика́т

syndrome [ˈsɪndrəum] *n* синдро́м

synonym [ˈsɪnənɪm] *n* сино́ним

synthetic [sɪnˈθɛtɪk] *adj* (*materials*) синтети́ческий, иску́сственный

syringe [sɪˈrɪndʒ] *n* шприц

syrup [ˈsɪrəp] *n* (*juice*) сиро́п; (*also* **golden syrup**) (све́тлая *or* жёлтая) па́тока

system [ˈsɪstəm] *n* систе́ма; **systematic** [sɪstəˈmætɪk] *adj* системати́ческий

t

ta [tɑː] *excl* (*Brit: inf*) спаси́бо
table ['teɪbl] *n* (*furniture*) стол; (*Math, Chem etc*) табли́ца; **to lay** *or* **set the table** накрыва́ть (*perf* накры́ть) на стол; **table of contents** оглавле́ние; **tablecloth** *n* ска́терть *f*; **table lamp** *n* насто́льная ла́мпа; **tablemat** *n* подста́вка (*под столовые приборы*); **tablespoon** *n* столо́вая ло́жка
tablet ['tæblɪt] *n* (*Comput*) планше́т
table tennis *n* насто́льный те́ннис
tabloid ['tæblɔɪd] *n* табло́ид, малоформа́тная газе́та

TABLOID

Так называ́ют популя́рные малоформа́тные газе́ты. Они́ соде́ржат мно́го фотогра́фий, больши́е заголо́вки и коро́ткие статьи́. Табло́иды освеща́ют сканда́льные исто́рии, жизнь звёзд шо́у-би́знеса и спорти́вные но́вости.

taboo [tə'buː] *n* табу́ *nt ind* ▷ *adj* запрещённый
tack [tæk] *n* (*nail*) гвоздь *m* с широ́кой шля́пкой
tackle ['tækl] *n* (*for fishing etc*) снасть *f*; (*for lifting*) сло́жный блок; (*Sport*) блокиро́вка ▷ *vt* (*difficulty*) справля́ться (*perf* спра́виться) с *+instr*; (*fight, challenge*) схвати́ться (*perf*) с *+instr*; (*Sport*) блоки́ровать (*impf/perf*)
tacky ['tækɪ] *adj* (*sticky*) ли́пкий; (*pej: cheap*) дешёвый
tact [tækt] *n* такт, такти́чность *f*; **tactful** *adj* такти́чный
tactics ['tæktɪks] *npl* та́ктика *fsg*
tactless ['tæktlɪs] *adj* беста́ктный
tag [tæg] *n* (*label*) этике́тка, ярлы́к
tail [teɪl] *n* (*of animal, plane*) хвост; (*of shirt*) коне́ц; (*of coat*) пола́ ▷ *vt* сади́ться (*perf* сесть) на хвост *+dat*; **tails** *npl* (*suit*) фрак *msg*
tailor ['teɪlə^r] *n* (мужско́й) портно́й *m adj*
take [teɪk] (*pt* **took**, *pp* **taken**) *vt* брать (*perf* взять); (*photo, measures*) снима́ть (*perf* снять); (*shower, decision, drug*) принима́ть (*perf* приня́ть); (*notes*) де́лать (*perf* сде́лать); (*grab: sb's arm etc*) хвата́ть (*perf* схвати́ть); (*require: courage, time*) тре́бовать (*perf* потре́бовать); (*tolerate: pain etc*) переноси́ть (*perf* перенести́); (*hold: passengers etc*) вмеща́ть

(*perf* вмести́ть); (*on foot: person*) отводи́ть (*perf* отвести́); (*: thing*) относи́ть (*perf* отнести́); (*by transport: person, thing*) отвози́ть (*perf* отвезти́); (*exam*) сдава́ть (*perf* сдать); **to take sth from** (*drawer etc*) вынима́ть (*perf* вы́нуть) что-н из *+gen*; (*steal from: person*) брать (*perf* взять) что-н у *+gen*; **I take it that ...** как я понима́ю, ...; **take apart** *vt* разбира́ть (*perf* разобра́ть); **take away** *vt* (*remove*) убира́ть (*perf* убра́ть); (*carry off*) забира́ть (*perf* забра́ть); (*Math*) отнима́ть (*perf* отня́ть); **take back** *vt* (*return: thing*) относи́ть (*perf* отнести́) обра́тно; (*: person*) отводи́ть (*perf* отвести́) обра́тно; (*one's words*) брать (*perf* взять) наза́д; **take down** *vt* (*building*) сноси́ть (*perf* снести́); (*note*) запи́сывать (*perf* записа́ть); **take in** *vt* (*deceive*) обма́нывать (*perf* обману́ть); (*understand*) воспринима́ть (*perf* восприня́ть); (*lodger, orphan*) брать (*perf* взять); **take off** *vi* (*Aviat*) взлета́ть (*perf* взлете́ть) ▷ *vt* (*remove*) снима́ть (*perf* снять); **take on** *vt* (*work, employee*) брать (*perf* взять); (*opponent*) сража́ться (*perf* срази́ться) с *+instr*; **take out** *vt* (*invite*) води́ть/вести́ (*perf* повести́); (*remove*) вынима́ть (*perf* вы́нуть); **to take sth out of** (*drawer, pocket etc*) вынима́ть (*perf* вы́нуть) что-н из *+gen*; **don't take your anger out on me!** не вымеща́й свой гнев на мне!; **take over** *vt* (*business*) поглоща́ть (*perf* поглоти́ть); (*country*) захва́тывать (*perf* захвати́ть) власть в *+prp* ▷ *vi*: **to take over from sb** сменя́ть (*perf* смени́ть) кого́-н; **take to** *vt fus*: **she took to him at once** он ей сра́зу понра́вился; **take up** *vt* (*hobby*) заня́ться (*perf*) *+instr*; (*job*) бра́ться (*perf* взя́ться) за *+acc*; (*idea, story*) подхва́тывать (*perf* подхвати́ть); (*time, space*) занима́ть (*perf* заня́ть); **I'll take you up on that!** ловлю́ Вас на сло́ве!; **takeaway** *n* (*Brit: food*) еда́ на вы́нос; **takeoff** *n* (*Aviat*) взлёт; **takeover** *n* (*Comm*) поглоще́ние

takings ['teɪkɪŋz] *npl* (*Comm*) вы́ручка *fsg*

tale [teɪl] *n* расска́з; **to tell tales** (*fig*) я́бедничать (*perf* ная́бедничать)

talent ['tælnt] *n* тала́нт; **talented** *adj* тала́нтливый

talk [tɔ:k] *n* (*speech*) докла́д; (*conversation, interview*) бесе́да, разгово́р; (*gossip*) разгово́ры *mpl* ▷ *vi* (*speak*) говори́ть (*impf*); (*to sb*) разгова́ривать (*impf*); **talks** *npl* (*Pol etc*) перегово́ры *pl*; **to talk about** говори́ть (*perf* поговори́ть) *or* разгова́ривать *impf* о (*+prp*); **to talk sb into doing** угова́ривать (*perf* уговори́ть) кого́-н *+infin*; **to talk sb out of sth** отгова́ривать (*perf* отговори́ть) кого́-н от чего́-н; **to talk shop** говори́ть (*impf*) о дела́х; **talk over** *vt* (*problem*) обгова́ривать (*perf* обговори́ть)

tall [tɔ:l] *adj* высо́кий; **he is 6 feet tall** его́ рост — 6 фу́тов

tambourine [tæmbə'ri:n] *n* (*Mus*) тамбури́н, бу́бен

tame [teɪm] *adj* ручно́й; (*fig*) вя́лый

tampon ['tæmpɔn] *n* тампо́н

tan [tæn] *n* (*also* **suntan**) зага́р

tandem ['tændəm] *n* (*cycle*) танде́м; **in tandem** (*together*)

совме́стно, вме́сте
tangerine [tændʒəˈriːn] *n* мандари́н
tank [tæŋk] *n* (*water tank*) бак; (: *large*) цисте́рна; (*for fish*) аква́риум; (*Mil*) танк
tanker [ˈtæŋkə^r] *n* (*ship*) та́нкер; (*truck, Rail*) цисте́рна
tanned [tænd] *adj* загоре́лый
tantrum [ˈtæntrəm] *n* исте́рика
tap [tæp] *n* (водопрово́дный) кран; (*gentle blow*) стук ▷ *vt* (*hit*) стуча́ть (*perf* постуча́ть) по *+dat*; (*resources*) испо́льзовать (*impf/perf*); (*telephone, conversation*) прослу́шивать (*impf*)
tape [teɪp] *n* (*also* **magnetic tape**) (магни́тная) плёнка; (*cassette*) кассе́та; (*sticky tape*) кле́йкая ле́нта ▷ *vt* (*record*) запи́сывать (*perf* записа́ть); (*stick*) закле́ивать (*perf* закле́ить) кле́йкой ле́нтой; **tape recorder** *n* магнитофо́н
tapestry [ˈtæpɪstrɪ] *n* (*object*) гобеле́н
tar [tɑː] *n* дёготь *m*
target [ˈtɑːgɪt] *n* цель *f*
tariff [ˈtærɪf] *n* (*on goods*) тари́ф; (*Brit: in hotels etc*) прейскура́нт
tarmac [ˈtɑːmæk] *n* (*Brit: on road*) асфа́льт
tart [tɑːt] *n* (*Culin: large*) пиро́г ▷ *adj* (*flavour*) те́рпкий
tartan [ˈtɑːtn] *adj* (*rug, scarf etc*) кле́тчатый
task [tɑːsk] *n* зада́ча; **to take sb to task** отчи́тывать (*perf* отчита́ть) кого́-н
taste [teɪst] *n* вкус; (*sample*) про́ба; (*fig: glimpse, idea*) представле́ние ▷ *vt* про́бовать (*perf* попро́бовать) ▷ *vi*: **to taste of** *or* **like** име́ть (*impf*) вкус *+gen*; **you can taste the garlic (in the dish)** (в блю́де) чу́вствуется чесно́к; **in bad/good taste** в дурно́м/хоро́шем вку́се; **tasteful** *adj* элега́нтный; **tasteless** *adj* безвку́сный
tasty [ˈteɪstɪ] *adj* (*food*) вку́сный
tatters [ˈtætəz] *npl*: **in tatters** (*clothes*) изо́рванный в кло́чья
tattoo [təˈtuː] *n* (*on skin*) татуиро́вка
taught [tɔːt] *pt, pp of* **teach**
taunt [tɔːnt] *n* издева́тельство ▷ *vt* (*person*) издева́ться (*impf*) над *+instr*
Taurus [ˈtɔːrəs] *n* Теле́ц
taut [tɔːt] *adj* (*thread etc*) туго́й; (*skin*) упру́гий
tax [tæks] *n* нало́г ▷ *vt* (*earnings, goods etc*) облага́ть (*perf* обложи́ть) нало́гом; (*fig: memory, patience*) напряга́ть (*perf* напря́чь); **tax-free** *adj* (*goods, services*) не облага́емый нало́гом
taxi [ˈtæksɪ] *n* такси́ *nt ind*
taxpayer [ˈtækspeɪə^r] *n* налогоплате́льщик(-щица)
TB *n abbr* = **tuberculosis**
tea [tiː] *n* чай; (*Brit: meal*) у́жин; **high tea** (*Brit*) (по́здний) обе́д
teach [tiːtʃ] (*pt, pp* **taught**) *vi* преподава́ть (*impf*) ▷ *vt*: **to teach sb sth, teach sth to sb** учи́ть (*perf* научи́ть) кого́-н чему́-н; (*in school*) преподава́ть (*impf*) что-н кому́-н; **teacher** *n* учи́тель(ница) *m(f)*; **teaching** *n* (*work*) преподава́ние
team [tiːm] *n* (*of people*) кома́нда
teapot [ˈtiːpɔt] *n* (зава́рочный) ча́йник
tear[1] [tɛə^r] (*pt* **tore**, *pp* **torn**) *n* дыра́, ды́рка ▷ *vt* (*rip*) рвать (*perf* порва́ть) ▷ *vi* (*rip*) рва́ться (*perf* порва́ться)
tear[2] [tɪə^r] *n* слеза́; **in tears** в

t

слезах; **tearful** *adj* заплаканный
tease [ti:z] *vt* дразнить (*impf*)
teaspoon ['ti:spu:n] *n* чайная ложка
teatime ['ti:taɪm] *n* ужин
tea towel *n* (*Brit*) посудное полотенце
technical ['tɛknɪkl] *adj* (*terms, advances*) технический
technician [tɛk'nɪʃən] *n* техник
technique [tɛk'ni:k] *n* техника
technology [tɛk'nɔlədʒɪ] *n* техника; (*in particular field*) технология
teddy (bear) ['tɛdɪ(-)] *n* (плюшевый) мишка
tedious ['ti:dɪəs] *adj* нудный
tee [ti:] *n* подставка для мяча (*в гольфе*)
teenage ['ti:neɪdʒ] *adj* (*problems*) подростковый; (*fashion*) тинейджеровский; **teenage children** подростки *mpl*; **teenager** *n* подросток, тинейджер
teens [ti:nz] *npl*: **to be in one's teens** быть (*impf*) в подростковом возрасте
teeth [ti:θ] *npl of* **tooth**
teetotal ['ti:'təutl] *adj* непьющий, трезвый
telecommunications ['tɛlɪkəmju:nɪ'keɪʃənz] *n* телекоммуникации *fpl*
telegram ['tɛlɪgræm] *n* телеграмма
telephone ['tɛlɪfəun] *n* телефон ▷ *vt* (*person*) звонить (*perf* позвонить) +*dat*; **he is on the telephone** (*talking*) он говорит по телефону; **are you on the telephone?** (*possessing phone*) у Вас есть телефон?; **telephone call** *n* телефонный звонок; **there is a telephone call for Peter** Питера просят к телефону; **telephone directory** *n* телефонный справочник; **telephone number** *n* номер телефона, телефон (*inf*)
telesales ['tɛlɪseɪlz] *n* телефонная реклама
telescope ['tɛlɪskəup] *n* телескоп
television ['tɛlɪvɪʒən] *n* телевидение; (*set*) телевизор; **on television** по телевидению
tell [tɛl] (*pt, pp* **told**) *vt* (*say*) говорить (*perf* сказать); (*relate*) рассказывать (*perf* рассказать); (*distinguish*): **to tell sth from** отличать (*perf* отличить) что-н от +*gen* ▷ *vi* (*have an effect*): **to tell (on)** сказываться (*perf* сказаться) (на +*prp*); **to tell sb to do** говорить (*perf* сказать) кому-н +*infin*; **tell off** *vt*: **to tell sb off** отчитывать (*perf* отчитать) кого-н; **teller** *n* (*in bank*) кассир
telly ['tɛlɪ] *n abbr* (*Brit*: *inf*) (= *television*) телик
temper ['tɛmpə[r]] *n* (*nature*) нрав; (*mood*) настроение; (*fit of anger*) гнев; **to be in a temper** быть (*impf*) в раздражённом состоянии; **to lose one's temper** выходить (*perf* выйти) из себя
temperament ['tɛmprəmənt] *n* темперамент; **temperamental** [tɛmprə'mɛntl] *adj* темпераментный; (*fig*) капризный
temperature ['tɛmprətʃə[r]] *n* температура; **he has** *or* **is running a temperature** у него температура, он температурит (*inf*)
temple ['tɛmpl] *n* (*Rel*) храм; (*Anat*) висок
temporary ['tɛmpərərɪ] *adj* временный
tempt [tɛmpt] *vt* соблазнять (*perf* соблазнить), искушать

(*impf*); **to tempt sb into doing** соблазня́ть (*perf* соблазни́ть) кого́-н +*infin*; **temptation** [tɛmp'teɪʃən] *n* собла́зн, искуше́ние; **tempting** *adj* (*offer*) соблазни́тельный

ten [tɛn] *n* де́сять

tenant ['tɛnənt] *n* съёмщик(-мщица)

tend [tɛnd] *vt* (*crops, patient*) уха́живать (*impf*) за +*instr* ▷ *vi*: **to tend to do** име́ть (*impf*) скло́нность +*infin*

tendency ['tɛndənsɪ] *n* (*habit*) скло́нность *f*; (*trend*) тенде́нция

tender ['tɛndəʳ] *adj* не́жный; (*sore*) чувстви́тельный ▷ *n* (*Comm*: *offer*) предложе́ние ▷ *vt* (*apology*) приноси́ть (*perf* принести́); **legal tender** (*money*) зако́нное платёжное сре́дство; **to tender one's resignation** подава́ть (*perf* пода́ть) в отста́вку

tendon ['tɛndən] *n* сухожи́лие

tennis ['tɛnɪs] *n* те́ннис

tenor ['tɛnəʳ] *n* (*Mus*) те́нор

tense [tɛns] *adj* напряжённый

tension ['tɛnʃən] *n* напряже́ние

tent [tɛnt] *n* пала́тка

tentative ['tɛntətɪv] *adj* (*person, smile*) осторо́жный; (*conclusion, plans*) сде́ржанный

tenth [tɛnθ] *adj* деся́тый ▷ *n* (*fraction*) одна́ деся́тая *f adj*

tepid ['tɛpɪd] *adj* (*liquid*) теплова́тый

term [tə:m] *n* (*expression*) те́рмин; (*period in power etc*) срок; (*Scol*: *in school*) че́тверть *f*; (: *at university*) триме́стр ▷ *vt* (*call*) называ́ть (*perf* назва́ть); **terms** *npl* (*conditions*) усло́вия *ntpl*; **in abstract terms** в абстра́ктных выраже́ниях; **in the short term** в ближа́йшем бу́дущем; **in the long term** в перспекти́ве; **to be on good terms with sb** быть (*impf*) в хоро́ших отноше́ниях с кем-н; **to come to terms with** примиря́ться (*perf* примири́ться) с +*instr*

terminal ['tə:mɪnl] *adj* неизлечи́мый ▷ *n* (*Elec*) кле́мма, зажи́м; (*Comput*) термина́л; (*also* **air terminal**) аэровокза́л, термина́л; (*Brit*: *also* **coach terminal**) авто́бусный вокза́л

terminate ['tə:mɪneɪt] *vt* прекраща́ть (*perf* прекрати́ть)

terminology [tə:mɪ'nɔlədʒɪ] *n* терминоло́гия

terrace ['tɛrəs] *n* терра́са; **the terraces** (*Brit*: *standing areas*) трибу́ны *fpl*; **terraced** *adj* (*garden*) терра́сный; **terraced house** *дом в ряду́ примыка́ющих друг к дру́гу однoти́пных домо́в*

terrain [tɛ'reɪn] *n* ландша́фт

terrible ['tɛrɪbl] *adj* ужа́сный

terribly ['tɛrɪblɪ] *adv* ужа́сно

terrific [tə'rɪfɪk] *adj* (*thunderstorm, speed etc*) колосса́льный; (*time, party etc*) потряса́ющий

terrify ['tɛrɪfaɪ] *vt* ужаса́ть (*perf* ужасну́ть)

territorial [tɛrɪ'tɔ:rɪəl] *adj* территориа́льный

territory ['tɛrɪtərɪ] *n* террито́рия; (*fig*) о́бласть *f*

terror ['tɛrəʳ] *n* у́жас; **terrorism** *n* террори́зм; **terrorist** *n* террори́ст(ка)

test [tɛst] *n* (*trial, check*) прове́рка, тест; (*of courage etc*) испыта́ние; (*Med*) ана́лиз; (*Chem*) о́пыт; (*Scol*) контро́льная рабо́та, тест; (*also* **driving test**) экза́мен на води́тельские права́ ▷ *vt* проверя́ть (*perf* прове́рить); (*courage*) испы́тывать (*perf* испыта́ть); (*Med*) анализи́ровать (*perf* проанализи́ровать)

testicle ['tɛstɪkl] *n* яи́чко

testify ['tɛstɪfaɪ] *vi* (*Law*) дава́ть (*perf* дать) показа́ния; **to testify to sth** свиде́тельствовать (*impf*) о чём-н

testimony ['tɛstɪmənɪ] *n* (*Law*) показа́ние, свиде́тельство; (*clear proof*): **to be (a) testimony to** явля́ться (*perf* яви́ться) свиде́тельством *+gen*

test tube *n* проби́рка

text [tɛkst] *n* текст; (*on mobile phone*) SMS *nt* ▷ *vt* писа́ть (*perf* написа́ть) SMS; **textbook** *n* учéбник; **text message** *n* тéкстовое сообщéние, SMS *nt ind*

texture ['tɛkstʃə^r] *n* (*structure*) строéние, структу́ра; (*feel*) факту́ра

than [ðæn] *conj* чем; (*with numerals*) бо́льше *+gen*, бо́лее *+gen*; **I have less work than you** у меня́ мéньше рабо́ты, чем у Вас; **more than once** не раз; **more than three times** бо́лее *or* бо́льше трёх раз

thank [θæŋk] *vt* благодари́ть (*perf* поблагодари́ть); **thank you (very much)** (большо́е) спаси́бо; **thank God**! сла́ва Бо́гу!; **thanks** *npl* благода́рность *fsg* ▷ *excl* спаси́бо; **many thanks, thanks a lot** большо́е спаси́бо; **thanks to** благодаря́ *+dat*

KEYWORD

that [ðæt] (*pl* **those**) *adj* (*demonstrative*) тот (*f* та, *nt* то); **that man** тот мужчи́на; **which book would you like? — that one over there** каку́ю кни́гу Вы хоти́те? — вон ту; **I like this film better than that one** мне э́тот фильм нра́вится бо́льше, чем тот
▷ *pron* **1** (*demonstrative*) э́то; **who's/what's that?** кто/что э́то?; **is that you?** э́то Вы?; **we talked of this and that** мы говори́ли об э́том и о том *or* сём; **that's what he said** вот что он сказа́л; **what happened after that?** а что произошло́ по́сле э́того?; **that is (to say)** то́ есть
2 (*direct object*) кото́рый (*f* кото́рую, *nt* кото́рое, *pl* кото́рые) (*indirect object*) кото́рому (*f* кото́рой, *pl* кото́рым) (*after prep*: *+acc*) кото́рый (*f* кото́рую, *nt* кото́рое, *pl* кото́рые) (: *+gen*) кото́рого (*f* кото́рой, *pl* кото́рых) (: *+dat*) кото́рому (*f* кото́рой, *pl* кото́рым) (: *+instr*) кото́рым (*f* кото́рой, *pl* кото́рыми) (: *+prp*) кото́ром (*f* кото́рой, *pl* кото́рых); **the theory that we discussed** тео́рия, кото́рую мы обсужда́ли; **all (that) I have** всё, что у меня́ есть
3 (*of time*) когда́; **the day (that) he died** день, когда́ он умер
▷ *conj* что; (*introducing purpose*) что́бы; **he thought that I was ill** он ду́мал, что я был бо́лен; **she suggested that I phone you** она́ предложи́ла, что́бы я Вам позвони́л
▷ *adv* (*demonstrative*): **I can't work that much** я не могу́ так мно́го рабо́тать; **it can't be that bad** не так уж всё пло́хо; **the wall's about that high** стена́ приме́рно вот тако́й высоты́

thaw [θɔː] *n* о́ттепель *f*

KEYWORD

the [ðiː, ðə] *def art* **1**: **the books/**

children are at home книги/дети дома; **the rich and the poor** богатые *pl adj* и бедные *pl adj*; **to attempt the impossible** пытаться (*perf* попытаться) сделать невозможное
2 (*in titles*): **Elizabeth the First** Елизавета Первая
3 (*in comparisons*): **the more ... the more ...** чем больше ..., тем больше ...; (*+adj*) чем более ..., тем более ...

theatre ['θɪətə^r] (*US* **theater**) *n* театр; (*Med*: *also* **operating theatre**) операционная *f adj*
theft [θɛft] *n* кража
their [ðɛə^r] *adj* их; (*referring to subject of sentence*) свой; *see also* **my**; **theirs** *pron* их; (*referring to subject of sentence*) свой; *see also* **mine**[1]
them [ðɛm] *pron* (*direct*) их; (*indirect*) им; (*after prep*: *+gen, +prp*) них; (: *+dat*) ним; (: *+instr*) ними; **a few of them** некоторые из них; **give me a few of them** дайте мне несколько из них; *see also* **me**
theme [θi:m] *n* тема
themselves [ðəm'sɛlvz] *pl pron* (*reflexive*) себя; (*emphatic*) сами; (*after prep*: *+gen*) себя; (: *+dat, +prp*) себе; (: *+instr*) собой; (*alone*): **(all) by themselves** одни; **they shared the money between themselves** они разделили деньги между собой; *see also* **myself**
then [ðɛn] *adv* потом; (*at that time*) тогда ▷ *conj* (*therefore*) тогда ▷ *adj* (*at the time*) тогдашний; **from then on** с тех пор; **by then** к тому времени; **if ... then ...** если ... то ...
theology [θɪ'ɔlədʒɪ] *n* теология, богословие
theory ['θɪərɪ] *n* теория; **in theory** теоретически
therapist ['θɛrəpɪst] *n* врач
therapy ['θɛrəpɪ] *n* терапия

 **KEYWORD**

there [ðɛə^r] *adv* **1: there is some milk in the fridge** в холодильнике есть молоко; **there is someone in the room** в комнате кто-то есть; **there were many problems** было много проблем; **there will be a lot of people at the concert** на концерте будет много народу; **there was a book/there were flowers on the table** на столе лежала книга/стояли цветы; **there has been an accident** произошла авария
2 (*referring to place*: *motion*) туда; (: *position*) там; (: *closer*) тут; **I agree with you there** тут *or* в этом я с тобой согласен; **there you go!** (*inf*) вот!; **there he is!** вот он!; **get out of there!** уходи оттуда!

thereabouts ['ðɛərə'bauts] *adv* (*place*) поблизости; (*amount*) около этого
thereafter [ðɛər'ɑ:ftə^r] *adv* с того времени
thereby ['ðɛəbaɪ] *adv* таким образом
therefore ['ðɛəfɔ:^r] *adv* поэтому
there's ['ðɛəz] = **there is**; **there has**
thermal ['θə:ml] *adj* (*springs*) горячий; (*underwear*) утеплённый
thermometer [θə'mɔmɪtə^r] *n* термометр, градусник
these [ði:z] *pl adj, pron* эти
thesis ['θi:sɪs] (*pl* **theses**) *n* (*Scol*) диссертация
they [ðeɪ] *pron* они; **they say that**

t

... говоря́т, что ...; **they'd** = **they had**; **they would**; **they'll** = **they shall**; **they will**; **they're** = **they are**; **they've** = **they have**

thick [θɪk] *adj* (*in shape*) то́лстый; (*in consistency*) густо́й; (*inf*: *stupid*) тупо́й ▷ *n*: **in the thick of the battle** в са́мой гу́ще би́твы; **the wall is 20 cm thick** толщина́ стены́ — 20 см; **thicken** *vi* (*plot*) усложня́ться (*perf* усложни́ться) ▷ *vt* (*sauce etc*) де́лать (*perf* сде́лать) гу́ще; **thickness** *n* (*size*) толщина́

thief [θi:f] (*pl* **thieves**) *n* вор(о́вка)

thigh [θaɪ] *n* бедро́

thin [θɪn] *adj* то́нкий; (*person, animal*) худо́й; (*soup, sauce*) жи́дкий ▷ *vt*: **to thin (down)** (*sauce, paint*) разбавля́ть (*perf* разба́вить)

thing [θɪŋ] *n* вещь *f*; **things** *npl* (*belongings*) ве́щи *fpl*; **poor thing** бедня́жка *m/f*; **the best thing would be to ...** са́мое лу́чшее бы́ло бы *+infin* ...; **how are things?** как дела́?

think [θɪŋk] (*pt, pp* **thought**) *vt* (*reflect, believe*) ду́мать (*impf*); **to think of** (*come up with*) приводи́ть (*perf* привести́); (*consider*) ду́мать (*perf* поду́мать) о *+prp*; **what did you think of them?** что Вы о них ду́маете?; **to think about** ду́мать (*perf* поду́мать) о *+prp*; **I'll think about it** я поду́маю об э́том; **I am thinking of starting a business** я ду́маю нача́ть би́знес; **I think so/not** я ду́маю, что да/нет; **to think well of sb** ду́мать (*impf*) о ком-н хорошо́; **think over** *vt* обду́мывать (*perf* обду́мать); **think up** *vt* приду́мывать (*perf* приду́мать)

third [θə:d] *adj* тре́тий ▷ *n* (*fraction*) треть *f*, одна́ тре́тья *f adj*; (*Aut*: *also* **third gear**) тре́тья ско́рость *f*; (*Brit*: *Scol*) дипло́м тре́тьей сте́пени; **thirdly** *adv* в-тре́тьих; **Third World** *n*: **the Third World** Тре́тий мир

thirst [θə:st] *n* жа́жда; **thirsty** *adj*: **I am thirsty** я хочу́ *or* мне хо́чется пить

thirteen [θə:'ti:n] *n* трина́дцать; **thirteenth** *adj* трина́дцатый

thirtieth ['θə:tɪɪθ] *adj* тридца́тый

thirty ['θə:tɪ] *n* три́дцать

 **KEYWORD**

this [ðɪs] (*pl* **these**) *adj* (*demonstrative*) э́тот (*f* э́та, *nt* э́то); **this man** э́тот мужчи́на; **which book would you like? — this one please** каку́ю кни́гу Вы хоти́те? — вот э́ту, пожа́луйста
▷ *pron* (*demonstrative*) э́тот (*f* э́та, *nt* э́то); **who/what is this?** кто/что э́то?; **this is where I live** вот здесь я живу́; **this is what he said** вот, что он сказа́л; **this is Mr Brown** э́то ми́стер Бра́ун
▷ *adv* (*demonstrative*): **this high/long** вот тако́й высоты́/длины́; **the dog was about this big** соба́ка была́ вот така́я больша́я; **we can't stop now we've gone this far** тепе́рь, когда́ мы так далеко́ зашли́, мы не мо́жем останови́ться

thistle ['θɪsl] *n* чертополо́х

thorn [θɔ:n] *n* шип, колю́чка

thorough ['θʌrə] *adj* (*search, wash*) тща́тельный; (*knowledge, research*) основа́тельный; (*person*) скрупулёзный; **thoroughly** *adv* по́лностью, тща́тельно; (*very*:

satisfied) совершённо вполне́; (: *ashamed*) совершённо
those [ðəuz] *pl adj, pron* те
though [ðəu] *conj* хотя́ ▷ *adv* впро́чем, одна́ко
thought [θɔ:t] *pt, pp of* **think** ▷ *n* мысль *f*; (*reflection*) размышле́ние; (*opinion*) соображе́ние; **thoughtful** *adj* (*deep in thought*) заду́мчивый; (*serious*) поду́манный, глубо́кий; (*considerate*) внима́тельный; **thoughtless** *adj* безду́мный
thousand ['θauzənd] *n* ты́сяча; **two thousand** две ты́сячи; **five thousand** пять ты́сяч; **thousands of** ты́сячи *+gen*; **thousandth** *adj* ты́сячный
thrash [θræʃ] *vt* поро́ть (*perf* вы́пороть); (*inf*: *defeat*) громи́ть (*perf* разгроми́ть)
thread [θrɛd] *n* (*yarn*) нить *f*, ни́тка; (*of screw*) резьба́; (*Comput*) ве́тка диску́ссии ▷ *vt* (*needle*) продева́ть (*perf* проде́ть) ни́тку в *+acc*
threat [θrɛt] *n* угро́за; **threaten** *vi* (*storm, danger*) грози́ть (*impf*) ▷ *vt*: **to threaten sb with** угрожа́ть (*impf*) *or* грози́ть (пригрози́ть *perf*) кому́-н *+instr*; **to threaten to do** угрожа́ть (*impf*) *or* грози́ть (пригрози́ть *perf*) *+infin*
three [θri:] *n* три; **three-dimensional** *adj* (*object*) трёхме́рный; **three-piece suite** *n* мя́гкая ме́бель *f*
threshold ['θrɛʃhəuld] *n* поро́г
threw [θru:] *pt of* **throw**
thrill [θrɪl] *n* (*excitement*) восто́рг; (*fear*) тре́пет ▷ *vt* приводи́ть (*perf* привести́) в тре́пет, восхища́ть (*perf* восхити́ть); **to be thrilled** быть (*impf*) в восто́рге; **thriller** *n* три́ллер; **thrilling** *adj* захва́тывающий
throat [θrəut] *n* го́рло; **I have a sore throat** у меня́ боли́т го́рло
throne [θrəun] *n* трон
through [θru:] *prep* (*space*) че́рез *+acc*; (*time*) в тече́ние *+gen*; (*by means of*) че́рез *+acc*, посре́дством *+gen*; (*because of*) из-за *+gen* ▷ *adj* (*ticket, train*) прямо́й ▷ *adv* насквозь; **he is absent through illness** он отсу́тствовал по боле́зни; **to put sb through to sb** (*Tel*) соединя́ть (*perf* соедини́ть) кого́-н с кем-н; **to be through with** поко́нчить (*perf*) с *+instr*; **"no through road"** (*Brit*) "нет сквозно́го прое́зда"; **throughout** *prep* (*place*) по *+dat*; (*time*) в тече́ние *+gen* ▷ *adv* везде́, повсю́ду
throw [θrəu] (*pt* **threw**, *pp* **thrown**) *n* бросо́к ▷ *vt* (*object*) броса́ть (*perf* бро́сить); (*fig*: *person*) сбива́ть (*perf* сбить) с то́лку; **to throw a party** зака́тывать (*perf* закати́ть) ве́чер; **throw away** *vt* (*rubbish*) выбра́сывать (*perf* вы́бросить); (*money*) броса́ть (*impf*) на ве́тер; **throw off** *vt* сбра́сывать (*perf* сбро́сить); **throw out** *vt* (*rubbish, person*) выбра́сывать (*perf* вы́бросить); (*idea*) отверга́ть (*perf* отве́ргнуть); **throw up** *vi* (*vomit*): **he threw up** его́ вы́рвало
thrush [θrʌʃ] *n* (*Zool*) дрозд
thrust [θrʌst] (*pt, pp* **thrust**) *n* (*Tech*) дви́жущая си́ла ▷ *vt* толка́ть (*perf* толкну́ть)
thud [θʌd] *n* глухо́й стук
thug [θʌg] *n* (*criminal*) хулига́н
thumb [θʌm] *n* (*Anat*) большо́й па́лец (*ки́сти*) ▷ *vt*: **to thumb a lift** (*inf*) голосова́ть (*impf*) (*на доро́ге*)
thump [θʌmp] *n* (*blow*) уда́р;

t

(*sound*) глухо́й стук ▷ *vt* (*person*) сту́кнуть (*perf*) ▷ *vi* (*heart etc*) стуча́ть (*impf*)

thunder ['θʌndəʳ] *n* гром; **thunderstorm** *n* гроза́

Thursday ['θəːzdɪ] *n* четве́рг

thus [ðʌs] *adv* ита́к, таки́м о́бразом

thwart [θwɔːt] *vt* (*person*) чини́ть (*impf*) препя́тствия *+dat*; (*plans*) расстра́ивать (*perf* расстро́ить)

thyme [taɪm] *n* тимья́н, чабре́ц

tick [tɪk] *n* (*of clock*) ти́канье; (*mark*) га́лочка, пти́чка; (*Zool*) клещ ▷ *vi* (*clock*) ти́кать (*impf*) ▷ *vt* отмеча́ть (*perf* отме́тить) га́лочкой; **in a tick** (*Brit*: *inf*) ми́гом

ticket ['tɪkɪt] *n* биле́т; (*price tag*) этике́тка; (*also* **parking ticket**) штраф за наруше́ние пра́вил паркова́ния

tickle ['tɪkl] *vt* щекота́ть (*perf* пощекота́ть) ▷ *vi* щекота́ть (*impf*)

ticklish ['tɪklɪʃ] *adj* (*problem*) щекотли́вый; (*person*): **to be ticklish** боя́ться (*impf*) щеко́тки

tide [taɪd] *n* прили́в и отли́в; (*fig*: *of events*) волна́; (*of fashion, opinion*) направле́ние; **high tide** по́лная вода́, вы́сшая то́чка прили́ва; **low tide** ма́лая вода́, ни́зшая то́чка отли́ва; **tide over** *vt*: **this money will tide me over till Monday** на э́ти де́ньги я смогу́ продержа́ться до понеде́льника

tidy ['taɪdɪ] *adj* опря́тный; (*mind*) аккура́тный ▷ *vt* (*also* **tidy up**) прибира́ть (*perf* прибра́ть)

tie [taɪ] *n* (*string etc*) шнуро́к; (*Brit*: *also* **necktie**) га́лстук; (*fig*: *link*) связь *f*; (*Sport*) ничья́ ▷ *vt* завя́зывать (*perf* завяза́ть) ▷ *vi* (*Sport*) игра́ть (*perf* сыгра́ть) вничью́; **to tie sth in a bow** завя́зывать (*perf* завяза́ть) что-н ба́нтом; **to tie a knot in sth** завя́зывать (*perf* завяза́ть) что-н узло́м; **tie up** *vt* (*dog, boat*) привя́зывать (*perf* привяза́ть); (*prisoner, parcel*) свя́зывать (*perf* связа́ть); **I'm tied up at the moment** (*busy*) сейча́с я за́нят

tier [tɪəʳ] *n* (*of stadium etc*) я́рус; (*of cake*) слой

tiger ['taɪgəʳ] *n* тигр

tight [taɪt] *adj* (*rope*) туго́й; (*shoes, bend, clothes*) у́зкий; (*security*) уси́ленный; (*schedule, budget*) жёсткий ▷ *adv* (*hold, squeeze*) кре́пко; (*shut*) пло́тно; **money is tight** у меня́ ту́го с деньга́ми; **tighten** *vt* (*rope*) натя́гивать (*perf* натяну́ть); (*screw*) затя́гивать (*perf* затяну́ть); (*grip*) сжима́ть (*perf* сжать); (*security*) уси́ливать (*perf* уси́лить) ▷ *vi* (*grip*) сжима́ться (*perf* сжа́ться); (*rope*) натя́гиваться (*perf* натяну́ться); **tightly** *adv* (*grasp*) кре́пко; **tights** *npl* (*Brit*) колго́тки *pl*

tile [taɪl] *n* (*on roof*) черепи́ца; (*on floor*) пли́тка

till [tɪl] *n* ка́сса ▷ *prep, conj* = **until**

tilt [tɪlt] *vt* наклоня́ть (*perf* наклони́ть); (*head*) склоня́ть (*perf* склони́ть) ▷ *vi* наклоня́ться (*perf* наклони́ться)

timber ['tɪmbəʳ] *n* (*wood*) древеси́на

time [taɪm] *n* вре́мя *nt*; (*occasion*) раз ▷ *vt* (*measure time of*) засека́ть (*perf* засе́чь) вре́мя *+gen*; (*fix moment for*) выбира́ть (*perf* вы́брать) вре́мя для *+gen*; **a long time** до́лго; **a long time ago** давно́; **for the time being** пока́; **four at a time** по четы́ре; **from time to time** вре́мя от вре́мени; **at times**

временáми; **in time** (*soon enough*) вóвремя; (*after some time*) со врéменем; (*Mus: play*) в такт; **in a week's time** чéрез недéлю; **in no time** в два счёта; **any time** (*whenever*) в любóе врéмя; (*as response*) нé за что; **on time** вóвремя; **five times five** пятью пять; **what time is it?** котóрый час?; **to have a good time** хорошó проводи́ть (*perf* провести́) врéмя; **time limit** *n* предéльный срок; **timely** *adj* своеврéменный; **timer** *n* (*time switch*) тáймер; **timetable** *n* расписáние

timid ['tɪmɪd] *adj* рóбкий

timing ['taɪmɪŋ] *n*: **the timing of his resignation was unfortunate** вы́бор врéмени для егó отстáвки был неудáчен

tin [tɪn] *n* (*material*) óлово; (*container*) (жестянáя) бáнка; (: *Brit: can*) консéрвная бáнка; **tinfoil** *n* фольгá

tinker ['tɪŋkəʳ] *n* (*infl*) бродя́чий луди́льщик

tinned [tɪnd] *adj* (*Brit*) консерви́рованный

tin-opener ['tɪnəupnəʳ] *n* (*Brit*) консéрвный нож

tinted ['tɪntɪd] *adj* (*hair*) подкрáшеный; (*spectacles, glass*) ды́мчатый

tiny ['taɪnɪ] *adj* крóшечный

tip [tɪp] *n* (*of pen etc*) кóнчик; (*gratuity*) чаевы́е *pl adj*; (*Brit: for rubbish*) свáлка; (*advice*) совéт ▷ *vt* (*waiter*) давáть (*perf* дать) на чай *+dat*; (*tilt*) наклоня́ть (*perf* наклони́ть); (*also* **tip over**) опроки́дывать (*perf* опроки́нуть); (*also* **tip out**) вывáливать (*perf* вы́валить)

tiptoe ['tɪptəu] *n*: **on tiptoe** на цы́почках

tire ['taɪəʳ] *n* (*US*) = **tyre** ▷ *vt* утомля́ть (*perf* утоми́ть) ▷ *vi* уставáть (*perf* устáть); **tired** *adj* устáлый; **to be tired of sth** уставáть (*perf* устáть) от чегó-н

tiring ['taɪərɪŋ] *adj* утоми́тельный

tissue ['tɪʃuː] *n* бумáжная салфéтка; (*Anat, Bio*) ткань *f*

tit [tɪt] *n* (*Zool*) сини́ца; **tit for tat** зуб за зуб

title ['taɪtl] *n* (*of book etc*) назвáние; (*rank, in sport*) ти́тул

KEYWORD

to [tuː, tə] *prep* **1** (*direction*) в/на *+acc*; **to drive to school/the station** éздить/éхать (*perf* поéхать) в шкóлу/на стáнцию; **to the left** налéво; **to the right** напрáво

2 (*as far as*) до *+gen*; **from Paris to London** от Пари́жа до Лóндона; **to count to ten** считáть (*perf* посчитáть) до десяти́

3 (*with expressions of time*): **a quarter to five** без чéтверти пять

4 (*for, of*) к *+dat*; **the key to the front door** ключ (к) входнóй двéри; **a letter to his wife** письмó женé; **she is secretary to the director** онá секретáрь дирéктора

5 (*expressing indirect object*): **to give sth to sb** давáть (*perf* дать) что-н комý-н; **to talk to sb** разговáривать (*impf*) *or* говори́ть (*impf*) с кем-н; **what have you done to your hair?** что Вы сдéлали со свои́ми волосáми?

6 (*in relation to*) к *+dat*; **three goals to two** три: два; **X miles to the gallon** ≈ X ли́тров на киломéтр; **30 roubles to the dollar** 30 рублéй за дóллар

7 (*purpose, result*) к *+dat*; **to my surprise** к моемý удивлéнию; **to**

come to sb's aid приходи́ть (*perf* прийти́) кому́-н на по́мощь
▷ *with vb* **1: to want/try to do** хоте́ть (*perf* захоте́ть)/пыта́ться (*perf* попыта́ться) *+infin*; **he has nothing to lose** ему́ не́чего теря́ть; **I am happy to ...** я сча́стлив *+infin* ...; **ready to use** гото́вый к употребле́нию; **too old/young to ...** сли́шком стар/мо́лод, что́бы *+infin* ...
2 (*with vb omitted*): **I don't want to** я не хочу́; **I don't feel like going — you really ought to** мне не хо́чется идти́ — но, Вы должны́
3 (*purpose, result*) что́бы *+infin*; **I did it to help you** я сде́лал э́то, что́бы помо́чь Вам
▷ *adv*: **to push the door to, pull the door to** закрыва́ть (*perf* закры́ть) дверь

toad [təud] *n* (*Zool*) жа́ба; **toadstool** *n* (*Bot*) пога́нка
toast [təust] *n* тост ▷ *vt* (*Culin*) поджа́ривать (*perf* поджа́рить); (*drink to*) пить (*perf* вы́пить) за *+acc*; **toaster** *n* то́стер
tobacco [tə'bækəu] *n* таба́к
today [tə'deɪ] *adv, n* сего́дня
toddler ['tɔdlə^r] *n* малы́ш
toe [təu] *n* (*of foot*) па́лец (*ноги́*); (*of shoe, sock*) носо́к ▷ *vt*: **to toe the line** (*fig*) соотве́тствовать (*impf*)
toffee ['tɔfɪ] *n* ири́ска, тяну́чка
together [tə'gɛðə^r] *adv* вме́сте; (*at same time*) одновреме́нно; **together with** вме́сте с *+instr*
toilet ['tɔɪlət] *n* унита́з; (*Brit*: *room*) туале́т ▷ *cpd* туале́тный; **toiletries** *npl* туале́тные принадле́жности *fpl*
token ['təukən] *n* (*sign, souvenir*) знак; (*substitute coin*) жето́н ▷ *adj* (*strike, payment etc*) символи́ческий; **book/gift token** (*Brit*) кни́жный/пода́рочный тало́н; **record token** (*Brit*) тало́н на пласти́нку
told [təuld] *pt, pp of* **tell**
tolerant ['tɔlərnt] *adj*: **tolerant (of)** терпи́мый (к *+dat*)
tolerate ['tɔləreɪt] *vt* терпе́ть (*impf*)
toll [təul] *n* (*of casualties etc*) число́; (*tax, charge*) сбор, пла́та
tomato [tə'mɑːtəu] (*pl* **tomatoes**) *n* помидо́р
tomb [tuːm] *n* моги́ла; **tombstone** *n* надгро́бная плита́, надгро́бие
tomorrow [tə'mɔrəu] *adv, n* за́втра; **the day after tomorrow** послеза́втра; **tomorrow morning** за́втра у́тром
ton [tʌn] *n* (*Brit*) дли́нная то́нна; (*US*: *also* **short ton**) коро́ткая то́нна; (*also* **metric ton**) метри́ческая то́нна; **tons of** (*inf*) у́йма *+gen*
tone [təun] *n* (*of voice, colour*) тон ▷ *vi* (*colours*: *also* **tone in**) сочета́ться (*impf*); **tone up** *vt* (*muscles*) укрепля́ть (*perf* укрепи́ть)
tongue [tʌŋ] *n* язы́к
tonic ['tɔnɪk] *n* (*Med*) тонизи́рующее сре́дство; (*also* **tonic water**) то́ник
tonight [tə'naɪt] *adv* (*this evening*) сего́дня ве́чером; (*this night*) сего́дня но́чью ▷ *n* (*see adv*) сего́дняшний ве́чер; сего́дняшняя ночь *f*
tonsil ['tɔnsl] *n* (*usu pl*) минда́лина; **tonsillitis** [tɔnsɪ'laɪtɪs] *n* тонзилли́т
too [tuː] *adv* (*excessively*) сли́шком; (*also*: *referring to*

subject) та́кже, то́же; (: *referring to object*) та́кже; **too much, too many** сли́шком мно́го
took [tuk] *pt of* **take**
tool [tu:l] *n* (*instrument*) инструме́нт
tooth [tu:θ] (*pl* **teeth**) *n* (*Anat*) зуб; (*Tech*) зубе́ц; **toothache** *n* зубна́я боль *f*; **toothbrush** *n* зубна́я щётка; **toothpaste** *n* зубна́я па́ста
top [tɔp] *n* (*of mountain*) верши́на; (*of tree*) верху́шка; (*of head*) маку́шка; (*of page, list etc*) нача́ло; (*of ladder, cupboard, table, box*) верх; (*lid*: *of box, jar*) кры́шка; (: *of bottle*) про́бка; (*also* **spinning top**) юла́, волчо́к ▷ *adj* (*shelf, step*) ве́рхний; (*marks*) вы́сший; (*scientist*) веду́щий ▷ *vt* (*poll, vote*) лиди́ровать (*impf*) в +*prp*; (*list*) возглавля́ть (*perf* возгла́вить); (*exceed*: *estimate etc*) превыша́ть (*perf* превы́сить); **on top of** (*above*: *be*) на +*prp*; (: *put*) на +*acc*; (*in addition to*) сверх +*gen*; **from top to bottom** све́рху до́низу; **top up** (*US* **top off**) *vt* (*bottle*) долива́ть (*perf* доли́ть)
topic ['tɔpɪk] *n* те́ма; **topical** *adj* актуа́льный
topless ['tɔplɪs] *adj* обнажённый до по́яса
topple ['tɔpl] *vt* (*overthrow*) ски́дывать (*perf* ски́нуть) ▷ *vi* опроки́дываться (*perf* опроки́нуться)
torch [tɔ:tʃ] *n* (*with flame*) фа́кел; (*Brit*: *electric*) фона́рь *m*
tore [tɔ:ʳ] *pt of* **tear**[1]
torment [*n* 'tɔ:mɛnt, *vb* tɔ:'mɛnt] *n* муче́ние ▷ *vt* му́чить (*impf*)
torn [tɔ:n] *pp of* **tear**[1]
tornado [tɔ:'neɪdəu] (*pl* **tornadoes**) *n* смерч
torpedo [tɔ:'pi:dəu] (*pl* **torpedoes**) *n* торпе́да
torrent ['tɔrnt] *n* пото́к; **torrential** [tɔ'rɛnʃl] *adj* проливно́й
tortoise ['tɔ:təs] *n* черепа́ха
torture ['tɔ:tʃəʳ] *n* пы́тка ▷ *vt* пыта́ть (*impf*)
Tory ['tɔ:rɪ] (*Brit*: *Pol*) *adj* консервати́вный ▷ *n* то́ри *m/f ind*, консерва́тор
toss [tɔs] *vt* (*throw*) подки́дывать (*perf* подки́нуть), подбра́сывать (*perf* подбро́сить); (*head*) отки́дывать (*perf* отки́нуть) ▷ *vi*: **to toss and turn** воро́чаться (*impf*); **to toss a coin** подбра́сывать (*perf* подбро́сить) моне́ту; **to toss up to do** подбра́сывать (*perf* подбро́сить) моне́ту, что́бы +*infin*
total ['təutl] *adj* (*number, workforce etc*) о́бщий; (*failure, wreck etc*) по́лный ▷ *n* о́бщая су́мма ▷ *vt* (*add up*) скла́дывать (*perf* сложи́ть); (*add up to*) составля́ть (*perf* соста́вить)
totalitarian [təutælɪ'tɛərɪən] *adj* (*Pol*) тоталита́рный
totally ['təutəlɪ] *adv* по́лностью; (*unprepared*) соверше́нно
touch [tʌtʃ] *n* (*sense*) осяза́ние; (*approach*) мане́ра; (*detail*) штрих; (*contact*) прикоснове́ние ▷ *vt* (*with hand, foot*) каса́ться (*perf* косну́ться) +*gen*, тро́гать (*perf* тро́нуть); (*tamper with*) тро́гать (*impf*); (*make contact with*) прикаса́ться (*perf* прикосну́ться) к +*dat*, дотра́гиваться (*perf* дотро́нуться) до +*gen*; (*move*: *emotionally*) тро́гать (*perf* тро́нуть); **there's been a touch of frost** подморо́зило; **to get in touch with sb** свя́зываться (*perf*

связа́ться) с кем-н; **to lose touch** (*friends*) теря́ть (*perf* потеря́ть) связь; **touch on** *vt fus* каса́ться (*perf* косну́ться) *+gen*; **touched** *adj* (*moved*) тро́нутый; **touching** *adj* тро́гательный; **touchline** *n* бокова́я ли́ния

tough [tʌf] *adj* (*hard-wearing*) кре́пкий, про́чный; (*person*: *physically*) выно́сливый; (: *mentally*) сто́йкий; (*difficult*) тяжёлый

tour ['tuəʳ] *n* (*journey*) пое́здка; (*of town, factory etc*) экску́рсия; (*by pop group etc*) гастро́ли *pl* ▷ *vt* (*country, city*) объезжа́ть (*perf* объе́хать); (*factory*) обходи́ть (*perf* обойти́)

tourism ['tuərɪzm] *n* тури́зм

tourist ['tuərɪst] *n* тури́ст(ка) ▷ *cpd* (*attractions, season*) туристи́ческий

tournament ['tuənəmənt] *n* турни́р

tow [təu] *vt* вози́ть/везти́ (*impf*) на букси́ре; **"on** *or* *(US)* **in tow"** (*Aut*) "на букси́ре"

toward(s) [tə'wɔːd(z)] *prep* к *+dat*; **toward(s) doing** с тем что́бы *+infin*

towel ['tauəl] *n* (*also* **hand towel**) полоте́нце для рук; (*also* **bath towel**) ба́нное полоте́нце

tower ['tauəʳ] *n* ба́шня; **tower block** *n* (*Brit*) ба́шня, высо́тный дом

town [taun] *n* го́род; **to go to town** (*fig*) разоря́ться (*perf* разори́ться); **town centre** *n* центр (го́рода); **town hall** *n* ра́туша

toxic ['tɔksɪk] *adj* токси́чный

toy [tɔɪ] *n* игру́шка

trace [treɪs] *n* след ▷ *vt* (*draw*) переводи́ть (*perf* перевести́); (*follow*) просле́живать (*perf* проследи́ть); (*find*) разы́скивать (*perf* разыска́ть)

track [træk] *n* след; (*path*) тропа́; (*of bullet etc*) траекто́рия; (*Rail*) (железнодоро́жный) путь *m*; (*song, also Sport*) доро́жка ▷ *vt* (*follow*) идти́ (*impf*) по сле́ду *+gen*; **to keep track of** следи́ть (*impf*) за *+instr*; **track down** *vt* (*prey*) высле́живать (*perf* вы́следить); (*person*) оты́скивать (*perf* отыска́ть); **tracksuit** *n* трениро́вочный костю́м

tractor ['træktəʳ] *n* тра́ктор

trade [treɪd] *n* (*activity*) торго́вля; (*skill, job*) ремесло́ ▷ *vi* (*do business*) торгова́ть (*impf*) ▷ *vt*: **to trade sth (for sth)** обме́нивать (*perf* обменя́ть) что-н (на что-н); **trade in** *vt* (*car etc*) предлага́ть (*perf* предложи́ть) для встре́чной прода́жи; **trademark** *n* торго́вый знак; **trader** *n* торго́вец; **tradesman** *irreg n* (*shopkeeper*) торго́вец, ла́вочник; **trade union** *n* профсою́з (= *профессиона́льный сою́з*)

tradition [trə'dɪʃən] *n* тради́ция; **traditional** *adj* (*also fig*) традицио́нный

traffic ['træfɪk] *n* движе́ние; (*of drugs*) нелега́льная торго́вля; **traffic jam** *n* про́бка, зато́р; **traffic lights** *npl* светофо́р *msg*; **traffic warden** *n* (*Brit*) *регулиро́вщик паркова́ния маши́н на городски́х у́лицах*

tragedy ['trædʒədɪ] *n* траге́дия

tragic ['trædʒɪk] *adj* траги́ческий

trail [treɪl] *n* (*path*) доро́жка, тропи́нка; (*track*) след; (*of smoke, dust*) шлейф ▷ *vt* (*drag*) волочи́ть (*impf*); (*follow*) сле́довать (*impf*) по пята́м за *+instr* ▷ *vi* (*hang* *loosely*) волочи́ться (*impf*); (*in game, contest*) волочи́ться (*impf*) в хвосте́, отстава́ть (*impf*); **trailer** *n* (*Aut*) прице́п; (*US*: *caravan*) автоприце́п; (*Cinema*) рекла́мный ро́лик, ано́нс

train [treɪn] *n* по́езд; (*of dress*) шлейф ▷ *vt* (*apprentice, doctor etc*) обуча́ть (*perf* обучи́ть), гото́вить (*impf*); (*athlete, mind*) тренирова́ть (*impf*); (*dog*) дрессирова́ть (*perf* вы́дрессировать) ▷ *vi* учи́ться (*perf* обучи́ться); (*Sport*) тренирова́ться (*impf*); **one's train of thought** ход чьих-н мы́слей; **to train sb as** учи́ть (*perf* обучи́ть) кого́-н на +*acc*; **to train sth on** (*camera etc*) направля́ть (*perf* напра́вить) что-н на +*acc*; **trainee** *n* (*hairdresser*) учени́к; **trainee teacher** практика́нт(ка); **trainer** *n* (*coach*) тре́нер; (*of animals*) дрессиро́вщик(-щица); **trainers** *npl* (*shoes*) кроссо́вки *fpl*; **training** *n* (*for occupation*) обуче́ние, подгото́вка; (*Sport*) трениро́вка; **to be in training** (*Sport*) тренирова́ться (*impf*)

trait [treɪt] *n* черта́

traitor ['treɪtəʳ] *n* преда́тель(ница) *m(f)*

tram [træm] *n* (*Brit*) трамва́й

tramp [træmp] *n* (*person*) бродя́га *m/f*

trample ['træmpl] *vt*: **to trample (underfoot)** раста́птывать (*perf* растопта́ть)

trampoline ['træmpəliːn] *n* бату́т

tranquil ['træŋkwɪl] *adj* безмяте́жный

transaction [træn'zækʃən] *n* опера́ция

transatlantic ['trænzət'læntɪk] *adj* трансатланти́ческий

transcript ['trænskrɪpt] *n* (*typed*) распеча́тка; (*hand-written*) ру́копись *f*

transfer ['trænsfəʳ] *n* перево́д; (*Pol*: *of power*) переда́ча; (*Sport*) перехо́д; (*design*) переводна́я карти́нка ▷ *vt* (*employees, money*) переводи́ть (*perf* перевести́); (*Pol*: *power*) передава́ть (*perf* переда́ть)

transform [træns'fɔːm] *vt* (*completely*) преобразо́вывать (*perf* преобразова́ть); (*alter*) преобража́ть (*perf* преобрази́ть); **transformation** [trænsfə'meɪʃən] *n* (*see vt*) преобразова́ние; преображе́ние

transfusion [træns'fjuːʒən] *n* (*also* **blood transfusion**) перелива́ние кро́ви

transit ['trænzɪt] *n* транзи́т; **in transit** (*people, things*) при перево́зке, в транзи́те

transition [træn'zɪʃən] *n* перехо́д

translate [trænz'leɪt] *vt*: **to translate (from/into)** переводи́ть (*perf* перевести́) (с +*gen*/на +*acc*)

translation [trænz'leɪʃən] *n* перево́д

translator [trænz'leɪtəʳ] *n* перево́дчик(-ица)

transmission [trænz'mɪʃən] *n* переда́ча

transmit [trænz'mɪt] *vt* передава́ть (*perf* переда́ть); **transmitter** *n* переда́тчик

transparent [træns'pærnt] *adj* прозра́чный

transplant [*n* 'trænsplɑːnt, *vb* træns'plɑːnt] *n* переса́дка ▷ *vt* (*Med, Bot*) переса́живать (*perf* пересади́ть)

transport [*n* 'trænspɔːt, *vb*

træns'pɔ:t] *n* тра́нспорт; (*of people, goods*) перево́зка ▷ *vt* (*carry*) перевози́ть (*perf* перевезти́)

transportation ['trænspɔ:'teɪʃən] *n* транспортиро́вка, перево́зка; (*means of transport*) тра́нспорт

transvestite [trænz'vɛstaɪt] *n* трансвести́т

trap [træp] *n* лову́шка, западня́ ▷ *vt* лови́ть (*perf* пойма́ть) в лову́шку; (*confine*) запира́ть (*perf* запере́ть)

trash [træʃ] *n* му́сор; (*pej, fig*) дрянь *f*

trauma ['trɔ:mə] *n* тра́вма; **traumatic** [trɔ:'mætɪk] *adj* (*fig*) мучи́тельный

travel ['trævl] *n* (*travelling*) путеше́ствия *ntpl* ▷ *vi* (*for pleasure*) путеше́ствовать (*impf*); (*commute*) е́здить (*impf*); (*news, sound*) распространя́ться (*perf* распространи́ться) ▷ *vt* (*distance: by transport*) проезжа́ть (*perf* прое́хать); **travels** *npl* (*journeys*) разъе́зды *mpl*; **travel agent** *n* тураге́нт; **traveller** (*US* **traveler**) *n* путеше́ственник(-ица); **traveller's cheque** (*US* **traveler's check**) *n* доро́жный чек

tray [treɪ] *n* (*for carrying*) подно́с; (*on desk*) корзи́нка

treacherous ['trɛtʃərəs] *adj* (*person*) вероло́мный; (*look, action*) преда́тельский; (*ground, tide*) кова́рный

treacle ['tri:kl] *n* па́тока

tread [trɛd] (*pt* **trod**, *pp* **trodden**) *n* (*of stair*) ступе́нь *f*; (*of tyre*) проте́ктор ▷ *vi* ступа́ть (*impf*)

treason ['tri:zn] *n* изме́на

treasure ['trɛʒə^r] *n* сокро́вище ▷ *vt* дорожи́ть (*impf*) +*instr*; (*thought*) леле́ять (*impf*); **treasures** *npl* (*art treasures etc*) сокро́вища *ntpl*; **treasurer** *n* казначе́й

treasury ['trɛʒərɪ] *n*: **the Treasury,** *(US)* **the Treasury Department** Госуда́рственное Казначе́йство

treat [tri:t] *n* (*present*) удово́льствие ▷ *vt* (*person, object*) обраща́ться (*impf*) с +*instr*; (*patient, illness*) лечи́ть (*impf*); **to treat sb to sth** угоща́ть (*perf* угости́ть) кого́-н чем-н; **treatment** *n* (*attention, handling*) обраще́ние; (*Med*) лече́ние

treaty ['tri:tɪ] *n* соглаше́ние

treble ['trɛbl] *vt* утра́ивать (*perf* утро́ить) ▷ *vi* утра́иваться (*perf* утро́иться)

tree [tri:] *n* де́рево

trek [trɛk] *n* (*trip*) похо́д, перехо́д

tremble ['trɛmbl] *vi* дрожа́ть (*impf*)

tremendous [trɪ'mɛndəs] *adj* (*enormous*) грома́дный; (*excellent*) великоле́пный

trench [trɛntʃ] *n* кана́ва; (*Mil*) транше́я, око́п

trend [trɛnd] *n* (*tendency*) тенде́нция; (*of events, fashion*) направле́ние; **trendy** *adj* мо́дный

trespass ['trɛspəs] *vi*: **to trespass on** (*private property*) вторга́ться (*perf* вто́ргнуться) в +*acc*; **"no trespassing"** "прохо́д воспрещён"

trial ['traɪəl] *n* (*Law*) проце́сс, суд; (*of machine etc*) испыта́ние; **trials** *npl* (*bad experiences*) перипети́и *fpl*; **on trial** (*Law*) под судо́м; **by trial and error** ме́тодом проб и оши́бок

triangle ['traɪæŋgl] *n* (*Math, Mus*) треуго́льник

triangular [traɪ'æŋgjulə^r] *adj* треуго́льный

tribe [traɪb] *n* племя *nt*
tribunal [traɪ'bju:nl] *n* трибунал
tribute ['trɪbju:t] *n* (*compliment*) дань *f*; **to pay tribute to** отдавать (*perf* отдать) дань *+dat*
trick [trɪk] *n* (*magic trick*) фокус; (*prank*) подвох; (*skill, knack*) приём ▷ *vt* проводить (*perf* провести); **to play a trick on sb** разыгрывать (*perf* разыграть) кого-н; **that should do the trick** это должно сработать
trickle ['trɪkl] *n* (*of water etc*) струйка ▷ *vi* (*water, rain etc*) струиться (*impf*)
tricky ['trɪkɪ] *adj* (*job*) непростой; (*business*) хитрый; (*problem*) каверзный
trifle ['traɪfl] *n* (*small detail*) пустяк ▷ *adv*: **a trifle long** чуть длинноват
trigger ['trɪgə^r] *n* (*of gun*) курок
trim [trɪm] *adj* (*house, garden*) ухоженный; (*figure*) подтянутый ▷ *vt* (*cut*) подравнивать (*perf* подровнять); (*decorate*): **to trim (with)** отделывать (*perf* отделать) (*+instr*) ▷ *n*: **to give sb a trim** подравнивать (*perf* подровнять) волосы кому-н
trip [trɪp] *n* (*journey*) поездка; (*outing*) экскурсия ▷ *vi* (*stumble*) спотыкаться (*perf* споткнуться); **on a trip** на экскурсии; **trip up** *vi* (*stumble*) спотыкаться (*perf* споткнуться) ▷ *vt* (*person*) ставить (*perf* подставить) подножку *+dat*
triple ['trɪpl] *adj* тройной
tripod ['traɪpɔd] *n* тренога
triumph ['traɪʌmf] *n* (*satisfaction*) торжество; (*achievement*) триумф ▷ *vi*: **to triumph (over)** торжествовать (*perf* восторжествовать) (над *+instr*); **triumphant** [traɪ'ʌmfənt] *adj* (*team, wave*) торжествующий; (*return*) победный
trivial ['trɪvɪəl] *adj* тривиальный
trod [trɔd] *pt of* **tread**; **trodden** *pp of* **tread**
trolley ['trɔlɪ] *n* тележка; (*also* **trolley bus**) троллейбус
trombone [trɔm'bəun] *n* тромбон
troop [tru:p] *n* (*of soldiers*) отряд; (*of people*) группа; **troops** *npl* (*Mil*) войска *ntpl*
trophy ['trəufɪ] *n* трофей
tropical ['trɔpɪkl] *adj* тропический
trot [trɔt] *n* рысь *f* (*способ бега*)
trouble ['trʌbl] *n* (*difficulty*) затруднение; (*worry, unrest*) беспокойство; (*bother, effort*) хлопоты *pl* ▷ *vt* (*worry*) беспокоить (*impf*); (*disturb*) беспокоить (*perf* побеспокоить) ▷ *vi*: **to trouble to do** побеспокоиться (*perf*) *+infin*; **troubles** *npl* (*personal*) неприятности *fpl*; **to be in trouble** (*ship, climber etc*) быть (*impf*) в беде; **I am in trouble** у меня неприятности; **to have trouble doing** с трудом *+infin*; **troubled** *adj* (*person*) встревоженный; (*times*) смутный; (*country*) многострадальный; **troublemaker** *n* смутьян; **troublesome** *adj* (*child*) озорной
trough [trɔf] *n* (*also* **drinking trough**) корыто; (*also* **feeding trough**) кормушка; (*low point*) впадина
trousers ['trauzəz] *npl* брюки *pl*; **short trousers** шорты
trout [traut] *n inv* (*Zool*) форель *f*
truant ['truənt] *n* (*Brit*): **to play**

truant прогу́ливать (*perf* прогуля́ть) уро́ки
truce [tru:s] *n* переми́рие
truck [trʌk] *n* (*lorry*) грузови́к; (*Rail*) платфо́рма
true [tru:] *adj* и́стинный; (*accurate*: *likeness*) то́чный; (*loyal*) ве́рный; **to come true** сбыва́ться (*perf* сбы́ться); **it is true** э́то пра́вда *or* ве́рно
truly ['tru:lɪ] *adv* по-настоя́щему; (*truthfully*) по пра́вде говоря́; **yours truly** (*in letter*) и́скренне Ваш
trumpet ['trʌmpɪt] *n* (*Mus*) труба́
trunk [trʌŋk] *n* (*of tree*) ствол; (*of elephant*) хо́бот; (*case*) доро́жный сунду́к; (*US*: *Aut*) бага́жник; **trunks** *npl* (*also* **swimming trunks**) пла́вки *pl*
trust [trʌst] *n* (*faith*) дове́рие; (*responsibility*) долг; (*Law*) довери́тельная со́бственность *f* ▷ *vt* (*rely on, have faith in*) доверя́ть (*impf*) +*dat*; (*hope*): **to trust (that)** полага́ть (*impf*), что; (*entrust*): **to trust sth to sb** доверя́ть (*perf* дове́рить) что-н кому́-н; **to take sth on trust** принима́ть (*perf* приня́ть) что-н на ве́ру; **trusted** *adj* пре́данный; **trustworthy** *adj* надёжный
truth [tru:θ] *n* пра́вда; (*principle*) и́стина; **truthful** *adj* правди́вый
try [traɪ] *n* (*attempt*) попы́тка; (*Rugby*) прохо́д с мячо́м ▷ *vt* (*test*) про́бовать (*perf* попро́бовать); (*Law*) суди́ть (*impf*); (*patience*) испы́тывать (*impf*); (*key, door*) про́бовать (*perf* попро́бовать); (*attempt*): **to try to do** стара́ться (*perf* постара́ться) *or* пыта́ться (*perf* попыта́ться) +*infin* ▷ *vi* (*make effort*) стара́ться (*impf*); **to have a try** про́бовать (*perf* попро́бовать); **try on** *vt* (*dress etc*) примеря́ть (*perf* приме́рить); **trying** *adj* утоми́тельный
tsar [zɑ:ʳ] *n* царь *m*
T-shirt ['ti:ʃə:t] *n* футбо́лка
tub [tʌb] *n* (*container*) бо́чка; (*bath*) ва́нна
tube [tju:b] *n* (*pipe*) тру́бка; (*container*) тю́бик; (*Brit*: *underground train*) метро́ *nt ind*; (*for tyre*) ка́мера
tuberculosis [tjubə:kju'ləusɪs] *n* туберкулёз
tuck [tʌk] *vt* (*put*) су́нуть (*perf*)
Tuesday ['tju:zdɪ] *n* вто́рник
tug [tʌg] *n* (*ship*) букси́р ▷ *vt* дёргать (*perf* дёрнуть)
tuition [tju:'ɪʃən] *n* (*Brit*) обуче́ние; (*US*: *fees*) пла́та за обуче́ние; **private tuition** ча́стные уро́ки
tulip ['tju:lɪp] *n* тюльпа́н
tumble ['tʌmbl] *n* паде́ние ▷ *vi* (*fall*: *person*) вали́ться (*perf* свали́ться)
tumbler ['tʌmbləʳ] *n* бока́л
tummy ['tʌmɪ] *n* (*inf*) живо́т
tumour ['tju:məʳ] (*US* **tumor**) *n* (*Med*) о́пухоль *f*
tuna ['tju:nə] *n inv* (*also* **tuna fish**) туне́ц
tune [tju:n] *n* (*melody*) моти́в ▷ *vt* настра́ивать (*perf* настро́ить); (*Aut*) нала́живать (*perf* нала́дить); **the guitar is in/out of tune** гита́ра настро́ена/расстро́ена; **to sing in tune** петь (*impf*) в лад; **to sing out of tune** фальши́вить (*impf*); **to be in/out of tune with** (*fig*) быть (*impf*) в ладу́/не в ладу́ с +*instr*; **tune in** *vi* (*Radio, TV*): **to tune in (to)** настра́иваться (*perf* настро́иться) (на +*acc*)
tunic ['tju:nɪk] *n* ту́ника

tunnel [ˈtʌnl] *n* (*passage*) туннéль *m*
turf [tə:f] *n* (*grass*) дёрн
Turkey [ˈtə:kɪ] *n* Тýрция
turkey [ˈtə:kɪ] *n* индéйка
Turkish [ˈtə:kɪʃ] *adj* турéцкий
turmoil [ˈtə:mɔɪl] *n* смятéние; **in turmoil** в смятéнии
turn [tə:n] *n* поворóт; (*chance*) óчередь *f*; (*inf*: *Med*) вы́вих ▷ *vt* поворáчивать (*perf* повернýть) ▷ *vi* (*object*) поворáчиваться (*perf* повернýться); (*person*: *look back*) оборáчиваться (*perf* обернýться); (*reverse direction*) разворáчиваться (*perf* развернýться); (*become*): **he's turned forty** емý испóлнилось сóрок; **a good/bad turn** дóбрая/плохáя услýга; **"no left turn"** (*Aut*) "нет лéвого поворóта"; **it's your turn** твоя́ óчередь; **in turn** по óчереди; **to take turns at sth** дéлать (*impf*) что-н по óчереди; **to turn nasty** озлобля́ться (*perf* озлóбиться); **turn away** *vi* отворáчиваться (*perf* отвернýться) ▷ *vt* (*business, applicant*) отклоня́ть (*perf* отклони́ть); **turn back** *vi* поворáчивать (*perf* повернýть) назáд ▷ *vt* (*person*) вернýть (*perf*); (*vehicle*) разворáчивать (*perf* развернýть); **to turn back the clock** (*fig*) повернýть (*perf*) врéмя вспять; **turn down** *vt* (*request*) отклоня́ть (*perf* отклони́ть); (*heating*) уменьшáть (*perf* умéньшить) подáчу *+gen*; **turn in** *vi* (*inf*) идти́ (*perf* пойти́) на боковýю; **turn off** *vi* сворáчивать (*perf* свернýть) ▷ *vt* выключáть (*perf* вы́ключить); **turn on** *vt* включáть (*perf* включи́ть); **turn out** *vt* (*light, gas*) выключáть (*perf* вы́ключить); (*produce*) выпускáть (*perf* вы́пустить) ▷ *vi* (*troops, voters*) прибывáть (*perf* прибы́ть); **to turn out to be** окáзываться (*perf* оказáться) *+instr*; **turn over** *vi* (*person*) переворáчиваться (*perf* перевернýться) ▷ *vt* (*object, page*) переворáчивать (*perf* перевернýть); **turn round** *vi* (*person, vehicle*) разворáчиваться (*perf* развернýться); **turn up** *vi* (*person*) объявля́ться (*perf* объяви́ться); (*lost object*) находи́ться (*perf* найти́сь) ▷ *vt* (*collar*) поднимáть (*perf* подня́ть); (*radio*) дéлать (*perf* сдéлать) грóмче; (*heater*) увели́чивать (*perf* увели́чить) подáчу *+gen*; **turning** *n* поворóт; **turning point** *n* (*fig*) поворóтный пункт, перелóмный момéнт
turnip [ˈtə:nɪp] *n* (*Bot, Culin*) рéпа
turnout [ˈtə:naut] *n*: **there was a high turnout for the local elections** в мéстных вы́борах при́няло учáстие мнóго людéй
turnover [ˈtə:nəuvəʳ] *n* (*Comm*) оборóт; (: *of staff*) текýчесть *f*
turquoise [ˈtə:kwɔɪz] *adj* (*colour*) бирюзóвый
turtle [ˈtə:tl] *n* черепáха
tutor [ˈtju:təʳ] *n* преподавáтель(ница) *m(f)*; (*private tutor*) репети́тор; **tutorial** [tju:ˈtɔ:rɪəl] *n* (*Scol*) семинáр
TV *n abbr* (= *television*) ТВ (= *телеви́дение*)
tweed [twi:d] *n* твид
tweet [twi:t] *vi* писáть (*perf* написáть) твит, тви́тить (*perf* тви́тнуть) (*inf*) ▷ *n* твит
twelfth [twɛlfθ] *adj* двенáдцатый
twelve [twɛlv] *n* двенáдцать; **at twelve (o'clock)** в двенáдцать (часóв)

t

twentieth ['twɛntɪɪθ] *adj* двадца́тый
twenty ['twɛntɪ] *n* два́дцать
twice [twaɪs] *adv* два́жды; **twice as much** вдво́е бо́льше
twig [twɪg] *n* сучо́к
twilight ['twaɪlaɪt] *n* (*evening*) су́мерки *mpl*
twin [twɪn] *adj* (*towers*) па́рный ▷ *n* близне́ц ▷ *vt*: **to be twinned with** (*towns etc*) быть (*impf*) побрати́мами с *+instr*; **twin sister** сестра́-близне́ц; **twin brother** брат-близне́ц
twinkle ['twɪŋkl] *vi* мерца́ть (*impf*); (*eyes*) сверка́ть (*impf*)
twist [twɪst] *n* (*action*) закру́чивание; (*in road, coil, flex*) вито́к; (*in story*) поворо́т ▷ *vt* (*turn*) изгиба́ть (*perf* изогну́ть); (*injure*: *ankle etc*) выви́хивать (*perf* вы́вихнуть); (*fig*: *meaning, words*) искажа́ть (*perf* искази́ть), кове́ркать (*perf* искове́ркать) ▷ *vi* (*road, river*) извива́ться (*impf*)
twitch [twɪtʃ] *n* (*nervous*) подёргивание
two [tu:] *n* два *m/nt* (*f* две); **to put two and two together** (*fig*) сообража́ть (*perf* сообрази́ть) что к чему́
type [taɪp] *n* тип; (*Typ*) шрифт ▷ *vt* (*letter etc*) печа́тать (*perf* напеча́тать); **typewriter** *n* пи́шущая маши́нка
typhoid ['taɪfɔɪd] *n* брюшно́й тиф
typhoon [taɪ'fu:n] *n* тайфу́н
typical ['tɪpɪkl] *adj*: **typical (of)** типи́чный (для *+gen*)
typing ['taɪpɪŋ] *n* машино́пись *f*
typist ['taɪpɪst] *n* машини́стка
tyre ['taɪə[r]] (*US* **tire**) *n* ши́на
tzar [zɑ:[r]] *n* = **tsar**

u

UFO *n abbr* (= *unidentified flying object*) НЛО (= *неопо́знанный лета́ющий объе́кт*)
ugly ['ʌglɪ] *adj* (*person, dress etc*) уро́дливый, безобра́зный; (*dangerous*: *situation*) скве́рный
UK *n abbr* = **United Kingdom**
Ukraine [ju:'kreɪn] *n* Украи́на
Ukrainian [ju:'kreɪnɪən] *adj* украи́нский
ulcer ['ʌlsə[r]] *n* я́зва
ultimate ['ʌltɪmət] *adj* (*final*) оконча́тельный, коне́чный; (*greatest*) преде́льный; **ultimately** *adv* в коне́чном ито́ге; (*basically*) в преде́льном счёте
ultimatum [ʌltɪ'meɪtəm] (*pl* **ultimatums** *or* **ultimata**) *n* ультима́тум
ultraviolet ['ʌltrə'vaɪəlɪt] *adj* (*light etc*) ультрафиоле́товый

umbrella [ʌm'brɛlə] *n* (*for rain, sun*) зонт, зо́нтик
umpire ['ʌmpaɪəʳ] *n* судья́ *m*, рефери́ *m ind*
UN *n abbr* = **United Nations**
unable [ʌn'eɪbl] *adj* неспосо́бный; **he is unable to pay** он неспосо́бен заплати́ть
unanimous [ju:'nænɪməs] *adj* единоду́шный
unarmed [ʌn'ɑ:md] *adj* безору́жный
unattached [ʌnə'tætʃt] *adj* (*person*) одино́кий
unattractive [ʌnə'træktɪv] *adj* непривлека́тельный
unavoidable [ʌnə'vɔɪdəbl] *adj* (*delay*) неизбе́жный
unaware [ʌnə'wɛəʳ] *adj*: **to be unaware of** не подозрева́ть (*impf*) о *+prp*; (*fail to notice*) не осознава́ть (*impf*)
unbearable [ʌn'bɛərəbl] *adj* невыноси́мый
unbeatable [ʌn'bi:təbl] *adj* (*price, quality*) непревзойдённый
unbelievable [ʌnbɪ'li:vəbl] *adj* невероя́тный
uncanny [ʌn'kænɪ] *adj* (*resemblance, knack*) необъясни́мый; (*silence*) жу́ткий
uncertain [ʌn'sə:tn] *adj* (*unsure*): **uncertain about** неуве́ренный относи́тельно *+gen*; **in no uncertain terms** без обиняко́в, вполне́ определённо; **uncertainty** *n* (*not knowing*) неопределённость *f*; (*often pl*: *doubt*) сомне́ние
unchanged [ʌn'tʃeɪndʒd] *adj* (*orders, habits*) неизме́нный
uncle ['ʌŋkl] *n* дя́дя *m*
uncomfortable [ʌn'kʌmfətəbl] *adj* неудо́бный; (*unpleasant*) гнету́щий
uncommon [ʌn'kɔmən] *adj* (*rare, unusual*) необы́чный
unconditional [ʌnkən'dɪʃənl] *adj* (*acceptance, obedience*) безусло́вный; (*discharge, surrender*) безоговоро́чный
unconscious [ʌn'kɔnʃəs] *adj* без созна́ния; (*unaware*): **unconscious of** не сознаю́щий *+gen*
uncontrollable [ʌnkən'trəuləbl] *adj* (*child, animal*) неуправля́емый; (*laughter*) неудержи́мый
unconventional [ʌnkən'vɛnʃənl] *adj* нетрадицио́нный
uncover [ʌn'kʌvəʳ] *vt* открыва́ть (*perf* откры́ть); (*plot, secret*) раскрыва́ть (*perf* раскры́ть)
undecided [ʌndɪ'saɪdɪd] *adj* (*person*) колеблющийся; **he is undecided as to whether he will go** он не реши́л пойдёт ли он
undeniable [ʌndɪ'naɪəbl] *adj* (*fact, evidence*) неоспори́мый
under ['ʌndəʳ] *adv* (*go, fly etc*) вниз ▷ *prep* (*position*) под *+instr*; (*motion*) под *+acc*; (*less than*: *cost, pay*) ме́ньше *+gen*; (*according to*) по *+dat*; (*during*) при *+prp*; **children under 16** де́ти до 16-ти лет; **under there** там внизу́; **under repair** в ремо́нте
undercover [ʌndə'kʌvəʳ] *adj* та́йный
underestimate ['ʌndər'ɛstɪmeɪt] *vt* недооце́нивать (*perf* недооцени́ть)
undergo [ʌndə'gəu] (*irreg like* **go**) *vt* (*repair*) проходи́ть (*perf* пройти́); (*operation*) переноси́ть (*perf* перенести́); (*change*) претерпева́ть (*perf* претерпе́ть)
undergraduate [ʌndə'grædjuɪt] *n* студе́нт(ка)
underground ['ʌndəgraund] *adv*

(*work*) под землёй ▷ *adj* (*car park*) подзéмный; (*activities*) подпóльный ▷ *n*: **the underground** (*Brit*: *Rail*) метрó *nt ind*; (*Pol*) подпóлье

underline [ʌndəˈlaɪn] *vt* подчёркивать (*perf* подчеркнýть)

undermine [ʌndəˈmaɪn] *vt* (*authority*) подрывáть (*perf* подорвáть)

underneath [ʌndəˈniːθ] *adv* внизý ▷ *prep* (*position*) под *+instr*; (*motion*) под *+acc*

underpants [ˈʌndəpænts] *npl* (*men's*) трусы́ *pl*

underprivileged [ʌndəˈprɪvɪlɪdʒd] *adj* (*family*) неимýщий

understand [ʌndəˈstænd] (*irreg like* **stand**) *vt* понимáть (*perf* поня́ть); (*believe*): **to understand that** полагáть (*impf*), что; **understandable** *adj* поня́тный; **understanding** *adj* понимáющий ▷ *n* понимáние; (*agreement*) договорённость *f*

understatement [ˈʌndəsteɪtmənt] *n*: **that's an understatement!** э́то сли́шком мя́гко скáзано!

understood [ʌndəˈstud] *pt, pp of* **understand** ▷ *adj* (*agreed*) согласóванный; (*implied*) подразумевáемый

undertake [ʌndəˈteɪk] (*irreg like* **take**) *vt* (*task, duty*) брать (*perf* взять) на себя́; **to undertake to do** обя́зываться (*perf* обязáться) *+infin*

undertaker [ˈʌndəteɪkə^r] *n* владéлец похорóнного бюрó

underwater [ʌndəˈwɔːtə^r] *adv* под водóй ▷ *adj* подвóдный

underwear [ˈʌndəwɛə^r] *n* ни́жнее бельё

underworld [ˈʌndəwəːld] *n* (*of crime*) престýпный мир

undesirable [ʌndɪˈzaɪərəbl] *adj* нежелáтельный

undisputed [ˈʌndɪsˈpjuːtɪd] *adj* неоспори́мый

undo [ʌnˈduː] (*irreg like* **do**) *vt* (*laces, strings*) развя́зывать (*perf* развязáть); (*buttons*) расстёгивать (*perf* расстегнýть); (*spoil*) губи́ть (*perf* погуби́ть)

undoubtedly *adv* несомнéнно, бесспóрно

undress [ʌnˈdrɛs] *vt* раздевáть (*perf* раздéть) ▷ *vi* раздевáться (*perf* раздéться)

uneasy [ʌnˈiːzɪ] *adj* (*feeling*) тревóжный; (*peace, truce*) напряжённый; **he is** *or* **feels uneasy** он неспокóен

unemployed [ʌnɪmˈplɔɪd] *adj* безрабóтный ▷ *npl*: **the unemployed** безрабóтные *pl adj*

unemployment [ʌnɪmˈplɔɪmənt] *n* безрабóтица

uneven [ʌnˈiːvn] *adj* нерóвный

unexpected [ʌnɪksˈpɛktɪd] *adj* неожи́данный; **unexpectedly** *adv* неожи́данно

unfair [ʌnˈfɛə^r] *adj*: **unfair (to)** несправедли́вый (к *+dat*)

unfaithful [ʌnˈfeɪθful] *adj* невéрный

unfamiliar [ʌnfəˈmɪlɪə^r] *adj* незнакóмый

unfashionable [ʌnˈfæʃnəbl] *adj* немóдный

unfavourable [ʌnˈfeɪvrəbl] (*US* **unfavorable**) *adj* неблагоприя́тный

unfinished [ʌnˈfɪnɪʃt] *adj* незакóнченный

unfit [ʌnˈfɪt] *adj* (*physically*): **she is unfit** онá в плохóй спорти́вной фóрме; **he is unfit for the job** он непригóден для э́той рабóты

unfold [ʌn'fəuld] *vt* (*sheets, map*) разворáчивать (*perf* разверну́ть) ▷ *vi* (*situation*) разворáчиваться (*perf* разверну́ться)
unfollow [ʌn'fɔləu] *vt* отпи́сываться (*perf* отписáться) от *+gen*, отменя́ть (*perf* отмени́ть) подпи́ску на *+acc*
unforgettable [ʌnfə'gɛtəbl] *adj* незабывáемый
unfortunate [ʌn'fɔ:tʃənət] *adj* (*unlucky*) несчáстный; (*regrettable*) неудáчный; **unfortunately** *adv* к сожалéнию
unfriend [ʌn'frɛnd] *vt* удаля́ть (*perf* удали́ть) из спи́ска друзе́й; отфрéндить (*perf*) (*inf*)
unfriendly [ʌn'frɛndlɪ] *adj* недружелю́бный
unhappy [ʌn'hæpɪ] *adj* несчáстный; **unhappy with** (*dissatisfied*) недовóльный *+instr*
unhealthy [ʌn'hɛlθɪ] *adj* нездорóвый
unhurt [ʌn'hə:t] *adj* невреди́мый
unidentified [ʌnaɪ'dɛntɪfaɪd] *adj* анони́мный; *see also* **UFO**
uniform ['ju:nɪfɔ:m] *n* фóрма ▷ *adj* единообрáзный; (*temperature*) постоя́нный
uninhabited [ʌnɪn'hæbɪtɪd] *adj* необитáемый
unintentional [ʌnɪn'tɛnʃənəl] *adj* неумы́шленный
union ['ju:njən] *n* (*unification*) объединéние; (*also* **trade union**) профсою́з ▷ *cpd* профсою́зный
unique [ju:'ni:k] *adj* уникáльный
unit ['ju:nɪt] *n* (*single whole*) цéлое *nt adj*; (*measurement*) едини́ца; (*of furniture etc*) сéкция
unite [ju:'naɪt] *vt* объединя́ть (*perf* объедини́ть) ▷ *vi* объединя́ться (*perf* объедини́ться); **united** *adj* объединённый; (*effort*) совмéстный; **United Kingdom** *n* Соединённое Королéвство; **United Nations (Organization)** *n* (Организáция) Объединённых Нáций; **United States (of America)** *n* Соединённые Штáты (Амéрики)
unity ['ju:nɪtɪ] *n* еди́нство
universal [ju:nɪ'və:sl] *adj* универсáльный
universe ['ju:nɪvə:s] *n* вселéнная *f adj*
university [ju:nɪ'və:sɪtɪ] *n* университéт
unjust [ʌn'dʒʌst] *adj* несправедли́вый
unkind [ʌn'kaɪnd] *adj* недóбрый; (*behaviour*) злóбный
unknown [ʌn'nəun] *adj* неизвéстный
unlawful [ʌn'lɔ:ful] *adj* незакóнный
unleash [ʌn'li:ʃ] *vt* (*fig: feeling*) давáть (*perf* дать) вóлю *+dat*; (*: force*) развя́зывать (*perf* развязáть)
unless [ʌn'lɛs] *conj* éсли не; **he won't come, unless we ask** он не придёт, éсли мы не попрóсим
unlike [ʌn'laɪk] *adj* (*not alike*) непохóжий ▷ *prep* (*different from*) в отли́чие от *+gen*
unlikely [ʌn'laɪklɪ] *adj* (*not likely*) маловероя́тный
unlimited [ʌn'lɪmɪtɪd] *adj* неограни́ченный
unload [ʌn'ləud] *vt* (*box, car*) разгружáть (*perf* разгрузи́ть)
unlucky [ʌn'lʌkɪ] *adj* невезу́чий; (*object*) несчастли́вый; **he is unlucky** он невезу́чий, ему́ не везёт
unmarried [ʌn'mærɪd] *adj* (*man*) нежена́тый, холостóй; (*woman*) незаму́жняя
unmistak(e)able [ʌnmɪs'teɪkəbl]

adj (*voice, sound*) характе́рный
unnatural [ʌnˈnætʃrəl] *adj* неесте́ственный
unnecessary [ʌnˈnɛsəsərɪ] *adj* нену́жный
UNO *n abbr* (= *United Nations Organization*) ОО́Н (= *Организа́ция Объединённых На́ций*)
unofficial [ʌnəˈfɪʃl] *adj* неофициа́льный
unpack [ʌnˈpæk] *vi* распако́вываться (*perf* распакова́ться) ▷ *vt* распако́вывать (*perf* распакова́ть)
unpleasant [ʌnˈplɛznt] *adj* неприя́тный
unpopular [ʌnˈpɔpjuləʳ] *adj* непопуля́рный
unprecedented [ʌnˈprɛsɪdəntɪd] *adj* беспрецеде́нтный
unpredictable [ʌnprɪˈdɪktəbl] *adj* непредсказу́емый
unqualified [ʌnˈkwɔlɪfaɪd] *adj* неквалифици́рованный; (*total*) соверше́нный
unravel [ʌnˈrævl] *vt* (*fig: mystery*) разга́дывать (*perf* разгада́ть)
unreal [ʌnˈrɪəl] *adj* (*not real*) нереа́льный
unrealistic [ˈʌnrɪəˈlɪstɪk] *adj* нереалисти́чный
unreasonable [ʌnˈriːznəbl] *adj* неразу́мный; (*length of time*) нереа́льный
unrelated [ʌnrɪˈleɪtɪd] *adj* (*incident*) изоли́рованный, отде́льный; **to be unrelated** (*people*) не состоя́ть (*impf*) в родстве́
unreliable [ʌnrɪˈlaɪəbl] *adj* ненадёжный
unrest [ʌnˈrɛst] *n* волне́ния *ntpl*
unruly [ʌnˈruːlɪ] *adj* неуправля́емый
unsafe [ʌnˈseɪf] *adj* опа́сный
unsatisfactory [ˈʌnsætɪsˈfæktərɪ] *adj* неудовлетвори́тельный
unsettled [ʌnˈsɛtld] *adj* (*person*) беспоко́йный; **the weather is unsettled** пого́да не установи́лась
unsightly [ʌnˈsaɪtlɪ] *adj* непригля́дный
unskilled [ʌnˈskɪld] *adj* неквалифици́рованный
unstable [ʌnˈsteɪbl] *adj* (*government*) нестаби́льный; (*person: mentally*) неуравнове́шенный
unsteady [ʌnˈstɛdɪ] *adj* нетвёрдый
unsuccessful [ʌnsəkˈsɛsful] *adj* (*attempt*) безуспе́шный; (*writer*) неуда́вшийся; **to be unsuccessful (in sth)** терпе́ть (*perf* потерпе́ть) неуда́чу (в чём-н); **your application was unsuccessful** Ва́ше заявле́ние не при́нято
unsuitable [ʌnˈsuːtəbl] *adj* неподходя́щий
unsure [ʌnˈʃuəʳ] *adj* неуве́ренный; **he is unsure of himself** он неуве́рен в себе́
untidy [ʌnˈtaɪdɪ] *adj* неопря́тный
until [ənˈtɪl] *prep* до +*gen* ▷ *conj* пока́ не; **until he comes** пока́ он не придёт; **until now/then** до сих/тех пор
unused¹ [ʌnˈjuːzd] *adj* (*not used*) неиспо́льзованный
unused² [ʌnˈjuːst] *adj*: **he is unused to it** он к э́тому не привы́к; **she is unused to flying** она́ не привы́кла лета́ть
unusual [ʌnˈjuːʒuəl] *adj* необы́чный; (*exceptional*) необыкнове́нный
unveil [ʌnˈveɪl] *vt* (*statue*) открыва́ть (*perf* откры́ть)
unwanted [ʌnˈwɔntɪd] *adj* (*child, pregnancy*) нежела́нный

unwell [ʌn'wɛl] *adj*: **to feel unwell** чу́вствовать (*impf*) себя́ пло́хо; **he is unwell** он пло́хо себя́ чу́вствует, он нездоро́в
unwilling [ʌn'wɪlɪŋ] *adj*: **to be unwilling to do** не хоте́ть (*impf*) *+infin*
unwind [ʌn'waɪnd] (*irreg like* **wind**[2]) *vi* (*relax*) расслабля́ться (*perf* рассла́биться)
unwise [ʌn'waɪz] *adj* неблагоразу́мный

KEYWORD

up [ʌp] *prep* (*motion*) на *+acc*; (*position*) на *+prp*; **he went up the stairs/the hill** он подня́лся по ле́стнице/на́ гору; **the cat was up a tree** ко́шка была́ на де́реве; **they live further up this street** они́ живу́т да́льше на э́той у́лице; **he has gone up to Scotland** он пое́хал в Шотла́ндию
▷ *adv* **1** (*upwards, higher*): **up in the sky/the mountains** высоко́ в не́бе/в гора́х; **put the picture a bit higher up** пове́сьте карти́ну повы́ше; **up there** (*up above*) там наверху́
2: to be up (*out of bed*) встава́ть (*perf* встать); (*prices, level*) поднима́ться (*perf* подня́ться); **the tent is up** пала́тка устано́влена
3: up to (*as far as*) до *+gen*; **up to now** до сих пор
4: to be up to (*depending on*) зави́сеть (*impf*) от *+gen*; **it's not up to me to decide** не мне реша́ть; **it's up to you** э́то на Ва́ше усмотре́ние
5: to be up to (*inf: be doing*) затева́ть (*impf*); (*be satisfactory*) соотве́тствовать (*impf*) *+dat*, отвеча́ть (*impf*) *+dat*; **he's not up to the job** он не справля́ется с э́той рабо́той; **his work is not up to the required standard** его́ рабо́та не соотве́тствует тре́буемым станда́ртам; **what's she up to these days?** а что она́ тепе́рь поде́лывает?
▷ *n*: **ups and downs** (*in life, career*) взлёты *mpl* и паде́ния *ntpl*

upbringing ['ʌpbrɪŋɪŋ] *n* воспита́ние
update [ʌp'deɪt] *vt* (*records*) обновля́ть (*perf* обнови́ть)
upgrade [ʌp'greɪd] *vt* (*house, equipment*) модернизи́ровать (*impf/perf*); (*employee*) повыша́ть (*perf* повы́сить) (в до́лжности)
upheaval [ʌp'hi:vl] *n* переворо́т
uphill [ʌp'hɪl] *adj* (*fig*) тяжёлый, напряжённый ▷ *adv* вверх; **to go uphill** поднима́ться (*perf* подня́ться) в го́ру
upholstery [ʌp'həulstərɪ] *n* оби́вка
upload [ʌp'ləud] *vt* загружа́ть (*perf* загрузи́ть), выкла́дывать (*perf* вы́ложить)
upon [ə'pɔn] *prep* (*position*) на *+prp*; (*motion*) на *+acc*
upper ['ʌpə^r] *adj* ве́рхний
upright ['ʌpraɪt] *adj* (*vertical*) вертика́льный
uprising ['ʌpraɪzɪŋ] *n* восста́ние
uproar ['ʌprɔ:^r] *n* (*protest*) возмуще́ние; (*shouts*) го́мон, кри́ки *mpl*
upset [*vb, adj* ʌp'sɛt, *n* 'ʌpsɛt] (*irreg like* **set**) *vt* (*glass etc*) опроки́дывать (*perf* опроки́нуть); (*routine*) наруша́ть (*perf* нару́шить); (*person, plan*) расстра́ивать (*perf* расстро́ить) ▷ *adj* расстро́енный ▷ *n*: **I have a stomach upset** (*Brit*) у меня́ расстро́йство желу́дка

u

upside down ['ʌpsaɪd-] *adv* вверх нога́ми; (*turn*) вверх дном
upstairs [ʌp'stɛəz] *adv* (*be*) наверху́; (*go*) наве́рх ▷ *adj* ве́рхний ▷ *n* ве́рхний эта́ж
up-to-date ['ʌptə'deɪt] *adj* (*information*) после́дний; (*equipment*) нове́йший
upward ['ʌpwəd] *adj*: **upward movement/glance** движе́ние/взгляд вверх ▷ *adv* = **upwards**; **upwards** *adv* вверх; (*more than*): **upwards of** свы́ше *+gen*
uranium [juə'reɪnɪəm] *n* ура́н
urban ['ə:bən] *adj* городско́й
urge [ə:dʒ] *n* потре́бность *f* ▷ *vt*: **to urge sb to do** настоя́тельно проси́ть (*perf* попроси́ть) кого́-н *+infin*
urgency ['ə:dʒənsɪ] *n* (*of task etc*) неотло́жность *f*; (*of tone*) насто́йчивость *f*
urgent ['ə:dʒənt] *adj* (*message*) сро́чный; (*need*) насу́щный, неотло́жный; (*voice*) насто́йчивый
urine ['juərɪn] *n* моча́
US *n abbr* (= *United States*) США (= *Соединённые Шта́ты Аме́рики*)
us [ʌs] *pron* (*direct*) нас; (*indirect*) нам; (*after prep*: *+gen, +prp*) нас; (: *+dat*) нам; (: *+instr*) на́ми; **a few of us** не́которые из нас; *see also* **me**
USA *n abbr* (= *United States of America*) США (= *Соединённые Шта́ты Аме́рики*)
USB stick [ju: ɛs bi:-] *n* (USB-) флеш-накопи́тель *m*, флеш-ди́ск, флёшка (*inf*)
use [*vb* ju:z, *n* ju:s] *vt* (*object, tool*) по́льзоваться (*impf*) *+instr*, испо́льзовать (*impf/perf*); (*phrase*) употребля́ть (*perf* употреби́ть) ▷ *n* (*using*) испо́льзование, употребле́ние; (*usefulness*) по́льза; (*purpose*) примене́ние; **she used to do it** она́ когда́-то занима́лась э́тим; **what's this used for?** для чего́ э́то испо́льзуется?; **to be used to** привы́кнуть (*perf*) к *+dat*; **to be in use** употребля́ться (*impf*), быть (*impf*) в употребле́нии; **to be out of use** не употребля́ться (*impf*); **of use** поле́зный; **it's no use** (э́то) бесполе́зно; **use up** *vt* (*food*) расхо́довать (*perf* израсхо́довать); **used** [ju:zd] *adj* (*car*) поде́ржанный; **useful** ['ju:sful] *adj* поле́зный; **useless** ['ju:slɪs] *adj* (*unusable*) неприго́дный; (*pointless*) бесполе́зный; **user** ['ju:zə[r]] *n* по́льзователь *m*; **user-friendly** *adj* просто́й в испо́льзовании
USSR *n abbr* (*formerly*) (= *Union of Soviet Socialist Republics*) СССР (= *Сою́з Сове́тских Социалисти́ческих Респу́блик*)
usual ['ju:ʒuəl] *adj* (*time, place etc*) обы́чный; **as usual** как обы́чно; **usually** *adv* обы́чно
utensil [ju:'tɛnsl] *n* инструме́нт; (*for cooking*) принадле́жность *f*
utility [ju:'tɪlɪtɪ] *n*: **public utilities** коммуна́льные услу́ги *fpl*
utilize ['ju:tɪlaɪz] *vt* утилизи́ровать (*impf/perf*)
utmost ['ʌtməust] *adj* велича́йший ▷ *n*: **to do one's utmost** де́лать (*perf* сде́лать) всё возмо́жное
utter ['ʌtə[r]] *adj* (*amazement*) по́лный; (*conviction*) глубо́кий; (*rubbish*) соверше́нный ▷ *vt* (*words*) произноси́ть (*perf* произнести́); **utterly** *adv* соверше́нно
U-turn ['ju:'tə:n] *n* (*Aut*) разворо́т на 180 гра́дусов

vacancy ['veɪkənsɪ] *n* (*Brit*: *job*) вака́нсия; (*room*) свобо́дный но́мер
vacant ['veɪkənt] *adj* (*room, seat*) свобо́дный; (*look*) пусто́й
vacation [və'keɪʃən] *n* (*esp US*: *holiday*) о́тпуск; (*Brit*: *Scol*) кани́кулы *pl*
vaccine ['væksi:n] *n* вакци́на
vacuum ['vækjum] *n* (*empty space*) ва́куум ▷ *vt* пылесо́сить (*perf* пропылесо́сить); **vacuum cleaner** *n* пылесо́с
vagina [və'dʒaɪnə] *n* влага́лище
vague [veɪg] *adj* (*blurred*: *memory, outline*) сму́тный; (*look*) рассе́янный; (*idea, instructions, answer*) неопределённый
vain [veɪn] *adj* тщесла́вный; (*useless*) тще́тный; **in vain** тще́тно, напра́сно
valid ['vælɪd] *adj* (*ticket, document*) действи́тельный; (*reason, argument*) ве́ский
valley ['vælɪ] *n* доли́на
valuable ['væljuəbl] *adj* це́нный; (*time*) драгоце́нный; **valuables** *npl* (*jewellery etc*) це́нности *fpl*
value ['vælju:] *n* це́нность *f* ▷ *vt* оце́нивать (*perf* оцени́ть); (*appreciate*) цени́ть (*impf*); **values** *npl* (*principles*) це́нности *fpl*
valve [vælv] *n* (*also Med*) кла́пан
vampire ['væmpaɪə[r]] *n* вампи́р
van [væn] *n* (*Aut*) фурго́н
vandalism ['vændəlɪzəm] *n* вандали́зм
vanilla [və'nɪlə] *n* вани́ль *f*
vanish ['vænɪʃ] *vi* исчеза́ть (*perf* исче́знуть)
vanity ['vænɪtɪ] *n* тщесла́вие
vape [veɪp] *vi* кури́ть (*impf*) электро́нную сигаре́ту, па́рить (*impf*), ве́йпить (*impf*) (*inf*)
vapour ['veɪpə[r]] (*US* **vapor**) *n* пар
variable ['vɛərɪəbl] *adj* (*likely to change*) изме́нчивый; (*able to be changed*: *speed*) переме́нный
variation [vɛərɪ'eɪʃən] *n* (*change*) измене́ние; (*different form*) вариа́ция
varied ['vɛərɪd] *adj* разнообра́зный
variety [və'raɪətɪ] *n* разнообра́зие; (*type*) разнови́дность *f*
various ['vɛərɪəs] *adj* (*different, several*) разли́чный
varnish ['vɑ:nɪʃ] *n* (*product*) лак; (*also* **nail varnish**) лак для ногте́й ▷ *vt* (*wood, table*) лакирова́ть (*perf* отлакирова́ть); (*nails*) кра́сить (*perf* покра́сить)
vary ['vɛərɪ] *vt* разнообра́зить (*impf*) ▷ *vi* (*sizes, colours*) различа́ться (*impf*); (*become different*): **to vary with** (*weather etc*)

меня́ться (*impf*) в зави́симости от +*gen*
vase [vɑ:z] *n* ва́за
vast [vɑ:st] *adj* (*knowledge, area*) обши́рный; (*expense*) грома́дный
VAT [væt] *n abbr* (*Brit*) (= *value-added tax*) НДС (= *нало́г на доба́вленную сто́имость*)
vault [vɔ:lt] *n* (*tomb*) склеп; (*in bank*) сейф, храни́лище ▷ *vt* (*also* **vault over**) перепры́гивать (*perf* перепры́гнуть) че́рез +*acc*
VCR *n abbr* = **video cassette recorder**
VDU ['vi:di:yu] *n abbr* (= *visual display unit*) монито́р, диспле́й *m*
veal [vi:l] *n* (*Culin*) теля́тина
veer [vɪə^r] *vi* (*vehicle*) свора́чивать (*perf* сверну́ть); (*wind*) меня́ть (*perf* поменя́ть) направле́ние
vegetable ['vɛdʒtəbl] *n* (*Bot*) о́вощ ▷ *adj* (*oil etc*) расти́тельный; (*dish*) овощно́й
vegetarian [vɛdʒɪ'tɛərɪən] *n* вегетариа́нец(-а́нка) ▷ *adj* вегетариа́нский
vegetation [vɛdʒɪ'teɪʃən] *n* (*plants*) расти́тельность *f*
vehicle ['vi:ɪkl] *n* автотра́нспортное сре́дство; (*fig*) сре́дство, ору́дие
veil [veɪl] *n* вуа́ль *f*
vein [veɪn] *n* (*of leaf*) жи́лка; (*Anat*) ве́на; (*of ore*) жи́ла
velvet ['vɛlvɪt] *n* ба́рхат ▷ *adj* ба́рхатный
vendor ['vɛndə^r] *n*: **street vendor** у́личный(-ая) торго́вец(-вка)
vengeance ['vɛndʒəns] *n* мще́ние, возме́здие; **with a vengeance** (*fig*) отча́янно
venison ['vɛnɪsn] *n* олени́на
venom ['vɛnəm] *n* (*also fig*) яд
vent [vɛnt] *n* (*also* **air vent**) вентиляцио́нное отве́рстие ▷ *vt* (*fig*) дава́ть (*perf* дать) вы́ход +*dat*
ventilation [vɛntɪ'leɪʃən] *n* вентиля́ция
venture ['vɛntʃə^r] *n* предприя́тие ▷ *vt* (*opinion*) осме́ливаться (*perf* осме́литься) на +*acc* ▷ *vi* осме́ливаться (*perf* осме́литься); **business venture** предприя́тие
venue ['vɛnju:] *n* ме́сто проведе́ния
verb [və:b] *n* глаго́л
verbal ['və:bl] *adj* (*spoken*) у́стный
verdict ['və:dɪkt] *n* (*Law*) верди́кт; (*fig*: *opinion*) заключе́ние
verge [və:dʒ] *n* (*Brit*: *of road*) обо́чина; **to be on the verge of sth** быть (*impf*) на гра́ни чего́-н
verify ['vɛrɪfaɪ] *vt* (*confirm*) подтвержда́ть (*perf* подтверди́ть); (*check*) сверя́ть (*perf* све́рить)
versatile ['və:sətaɪl] *adj* (*person*) разносторо́нний; (*substance, machine etc*) универса́льный
verse [və:s] *n* (*poetry, in Bible*) стих; (*part of poem*) строфа́
version ['və:ʃən] *n* (*form*) вариа́нт; (*account*: *of events*) ве́рсия
versus ['və:səs] *prep* про́тив +*gen*
vertical ['və:tɪkl] *adj* вертика́льный
very ['vɛrɪ] *adv* о́чень ▷ *adj* са́мый; **the very book which ...** та са́мая кни́га, кото́рая ...; **thank you very much** большо́е (Вам) спаси́бо; **very much better** гора́здо лу́чше; **I very much hope so** я о́чень наде́юсь на э́то; **the very last** са́мый после́дний; **at the very least** как ми́нимум
vessel ['vɛsl] *n* су́дно; (*bowl*) сосу́д; **blood vessel** кровено́сный сосу́д
vest [vɛst] *n* (*Brit*: *underwear*)

ма́йка; (*US*: *waistcoat*) жиле́т
vet [vɛt] *n abbr* (*Brit*) (= *veterinary surgeon*) ветерина́р ▷ *vt* (*check*) проверя́ть (*perf* прове́рить); (*approve*) одобря́ть (*perf* одобри́ть)
veteran ['vɛtərn] *n* (*of war*) ветера́н
veterinary ['vɛtrɪnərɪ] *adj* ветерина́рный
veto ['vi:təu] (*pl* **vetoes**) *n* ве́то *nt ind* ▷ *vt* (*Pol, Law*) налага́ть (*perf* наложи́ть) ве́то на *+acc*
via ['vaɪə] *prep* че́рез *+acc*
viable ['vaɪəbl] *adj* жизнеспосо́бный
vibrate [vaɪ'breɪt] *vi* вибри́ровать (*impf*)
vibration [vaɪ'breɪʃən] *n* вибра́ция
vicar ['vɪkə^r] *n* (*Rel*) прихо́дский свяще́нник
vice [vaɪs] *n* поро́к; (*Tech*) тиски́ *pl*
vice-chairman [vaɪs'tʃɛəmən] *irreg n* замести́тель *m* председа́теля
vice versa ['vaɪsɪ'və:sə] *adv* наоборо́т
vicinity [vɪ'sɪnɪtɪ] *n*: **in the vicinity (of)** вблизи́ (от *+gen*)
vicious ['vɪʃəs] *adj* (*attack, blow*) жесто́кий; (*words, look, dog*) злой; **vicious circle** поро́чный круг
victim ['vɪktɪm] *n* же́ртва
victor ['vɪktə^r] *n* победи́тель(ница) *m(f)*
victorious [vɪk'tɔ:rɪəs] *adj* (*team*) победоно́сный; (*shout*) побе́дный
victory ['vɪktərɪ] *n* побе́да
video ['vɪdɪəu] *cpd* ви́део *ind* ▷ *n* (*also* **video film**) видеофи́льм; (*also* **video cassette**) видеокассе́та; (*also* **video cassette recorder**) видеомагнитофо́н; (*also* **video camera**) видеока́мера; **video game** *n* видеоигра́; **videophone** *n* видеотелефо́н; **video recorder** *n* видеомагнитофо́н; **video tape** *n* видеоле́нта
vie [vaɪ] *vi*: **to vie with sb/for sth** состяза́ться (*impf*) с кем-н/в чём-н
Vienna [vɪ'ɛnə] *n* Ве́на
view [vju:] *n* (*sight, outlook*) вид; (*opinion*) взгляд ▷ *vt* рассма́тривать (*perf* рассмотре́ть); **in full view (of)** на виду́ (у *+gen*); **in view of the bad weather/the fact that** ввиду́ плохо́й пого́ды/того́, что; **in my view** на мой взгляд; **viewer** *n* (*person*) зри́тель(ница) *m(f)*; **viewfinder** *n* (*Phot*) видоиска́тель *m*; **viewpoint** *n* (*attitude*) то́чка зре́ния; (*place*) ме́сто обозре́ния
vigilant ['vɪdʒɪlənt] *adj* бди́тельный
vigorous ['vɪgərəs] *adj* (*action, campaign*) энерги́чный
vile [vaɪl] *adj* гну́сный, омерзи́тельный
villa ['vɪlə] *n* ви́лла
village ['vɪlɪdʒ] *n* дере́вня
villain ['vɪlən] *n* (*in novel etc*) злоде́й; (*Brit*: *criminal*) престу́пник
vine [vaɪn] *n* (*with grapes*) (виногра́дная) лоза́
vinegar ['vɪnɪgə^r] *n* у́ксус
vineyard ['vɪnjɑ:d] *n* виногра́дник
vintage ['vɪntɪdʒ] *cpd* (*comedy, performance etc*) класси́ческий; (*wine*) ма́рочный
vinyl ['vaɪnl] *n* вини́л
viola [vɪ'əulə] *n* (*Mus*) альт
violation [vaɪə'leɪʃən] *n* (*of agreement etc*) наруше́ние
violence ['vaɪələns] *n* (*brutality*) наси́лие
violent ['vaɪələnt] *adj* (*behaviour*)

жесто́кий; (*death*) наси́льственный; (*debate, criticism*) ожесточённый

violet ['vaɪələt] *adj* фиоле́товый ▷ *n* (*plant*) фиа́лка

violin [vaɪə'lɪn] *n* (*Mus*) скри́пка

VIP *n abbr* (= *very important person*) осо́бо ва́жное лицо́

virgin ['və:dʒɪn] *n* де́вственница ▷ *adj* (*snow, forest etc*) де́вственный

Virgo ['və:gəu] *n* Де́ва

virtually ['və:tjuəlɪ] *adv* факти́чески, практи́чески

virtual reality ['və:tjuəl-] *n* (*Comput*) виртуа́льная реа́льность *f*

virtue ['və:tju:] *n* (*moral correctness*) доброде́тель *f*; (*advantage*) преиму́щество; (*good quality*) досто́инство; **by virtue of** благодаря́ *+dat*

virus ['vaɪərəs] *n* (*Med*) ви́рус

visa ['vi:zə] *n* (*for travel*) ви́за

visibility [vɪzɪ'bɪlɪtɪ] *n* ви́димость *f*

visible ['vɪzəbl] *adj* ви́димый; (*results, growth*) очеви́дный

vision ['vɪʒən] *n* (*sight*) зре́ние; (*foresight*) прови́дение, ви́дение

visit ['vɪzɪt] *n* посеще́ние, визи́т ▷ *vt* (*person, place*) посеща́ть (*perf* посети́ть); (*elderly, patient*) навеща́ть (*perf* навести́ть); **visitor** *n* (*person visiting*) гость(я) *m(f)*; (*in public place*) посети́тель(ница) *m(f)*; (*in town etc*) прие́зжий(-ая) *m(f) adj*

visual ['vɪzjuəl] *adj* (*image*) зри́тельный; **visualize** *vt* представля́ть (*perf* предста́вить)

vital ['vaɪtl] *adj* (*question*) жи́зненный; (*problem*) насу́щный; (*full of life: person*) де́ятельный, по́лный жи́зни; (*organization*) жизнеде́ятельный; **it is vital ...** необходи́мо ...; **vitality** [vaɪ'tælɪtɪ] *n* (*liveliness*) жи́вость *f*

vitamin ['vɪtəmɪn] *n* витами́н

vivid ['vɪvɪd] *adj* (*description, colour*) я́ркий; (*memory*) отчётливый; (*imagination*) живо́й

vlog [vlɔg] *n* видеобло́г, влог; **vlogger** *n* видеобло́гер

vocabulary [vəu'kæbjulərɪ] *n* (*words known*) слова́рный запа́с

vocal ['vəukl] *adj* (*articulate*) речи́стый

vocation [vəu'keɪʃən] *n* призва́ние

vodka ['vɔdkə] *n* во́дка

voice [vɔɪs] *n* го́лос ▷ *vt* (*opinion*) выска́зывать (*perf* вы́сказать); **voice mail** *n* (*system*) голосова́я по́чта; (*device*) автоотве́тчик

void [vɔɪd] *n* (*emptiness*) пустота́; (*hole*) прова́л ▷ *adj* (*invalid*) недействи́тельный

volatile ['vɔlətaɪl] *adj* (*situation*) изме́нчивый; (*person*) неусто́йчивый; (*liquid*) лету́чий

volcano [vɔl'keɪnəu] (*pl* **volcanoes**) *n* вулка́н

volleyball ['vɔlɪbɔ:l] *n* волейбо́л

voltage ['vəultɪdʒ] *n* (*Elec*) напряже́ние

volume ['vɔlju:m] *n* (*amount*) объём; (*book*) том; (*sound level*) гро́мкость *f*

voluntarily ['vɔləntrɪlɪ] *adv* доброво́льно

voluntary ['vɔləntərɪ] *adj* (*willing*) доброво́льный; (*unpaid*) обще́ственный

volunteer [vɔlən'tɪə[r]] *n* (*unpaid helper*) доброво́льный(-ая) помо́щник(-ица), волонтёр; (*to army etc*) доброво́лец ▷ *vt* (*information*) предлага́ть (*perf* предложи́ть) ▷ *vi* (*for army etc*) идти́ (*perf* пойти́) доброво́льцем; **to volunteer to do** вызыва́ться (*perf* вы́зваться) *+infin*

vomit ['vɔmɪt] *n* рво́та ▷ *vi*: **he vomited** его́ вы́рвало

vote [vəut] *n* (*indication of opinion*) голосова́ние; (*votes cast*) число́ по́данных голосо́в; (*right to vote*) пра́во го́лоса ▷ *vi* голосова́ть (*perf* проголосова́ть) ▷ *vt* (*Labour etc*) голосова́ть (*perf* проголосова́ть) за *+acc*; (*elect*): **he was voted chairman** он был и́збран председа́телем; (*propose*): **to vote that** предлага́ть (*perf* предложи́ть), что́бы; **to put sth to the vote, take a vote on sth** ста́вить (*perf* поста́вить) что-н на голосова́ние; **vote of thanks** благода́рственная речь *f*; **to pass a vote of confidence/no confidence** выража́ть (*perf* вы́разить) во́тум дове́рия/недове́рия; **to vote for** *or* **in favour of/against** голосова́ть (*perf* проголосова́ть) за *+acc*/ про́тив *+gen*; **voter** *n* избира́тель(ница) *m(f)*

voting ['vəutɪŋ] *n* голосова́ние

voucher ['vautʃəʳ] *n* (*with petrol, cigarettes etc*) ва́учер

vow [vau] *n* кля́тва ▷ *vt*: **to vow to do/that** кля́сться (*perf* покля́сться) *+infin*/, что; **vows** *npl* (*Rel*) обе́т *msg*

vowel ['vauəl] *n* гла́сный *m adj*

voyage ['vɔɪɪdʒ] *n* (*by ship*) пла́вание; (*by spacecraft*) полёт

vulgar ['vʌlgəʳ] *adj* (*rude*) вульга́рный; (*tasteless*) по́шлый

vulnerable ['vʌlnərəbl] *adj* (*position*) уязви́мый; (*person*) рани́мый; **he is vulnerable to …** он подве́ржен *+dat* …

vulture ['vʌltʃəʳ] *n* (*Zool*) гриф

W

wade [weɪd] *vi*: **to wade through** (*water*) пробира́ться (*perf* пробра́ться) че́рез *+acc*

wage [weɪdʒ] *n* (*also* **wages**) зарпла́та ▷ *vt*: **to wage war** вести́ (*impf*) войну́

wail [weɪl] *n* (*of person*) вопль *m* ▷ *vi* (*person*) вопи́ть (*impf*); (*siren*) выть (*impf*)

waist [weɪst] *n* та́лия; **waistcoat** *n* (*Brit*) жиле́т

wait [weɪt] *vi* ждать (*impf*) ▷ *n* ожида́ние; **to keep sb waiting** заставля́ть (*perf* заста́вить) кого́-н ждать; **I can't wait to go home** (*fig*) мне не те́рпится пойти́ домо́й; **to wait for sb/sth** ждать (*impf*) кого́-н/чего́-н; **we had a long wait for the bus** мы до́лго жда́ли авто́буса; **wait on** *vt fus* (*serve*) обслу́живать (*perf* обслужи́ть); **waiter** *n* официа́нт; **waiting**

list *n* óчередь *f*, спи́сок очередникóв; **waiting room** *n* (*in surgery*) приёмная *f adj*; (*in station*) зал ожидáния; **waitress** *n* официáнтка

wake [weɪk] (*pt* **woke** *or* **waked**, *pp* **woken** *or* **waked**) *vt* (*also* **wake up**) буди́ть (*perf* разбуди́ть) ▷ *vi* (*also* **wake up**) просыпáться (*perf* проснýться) ▷ *n* бдéние (у грóба); (*Naut*) кильвáтер; **in the wake of** (*fig*) вслéдствие *+gen*

Wales [weɪlz] *n* Уэ́льс

walk [wɔːk] *n* (*hike*) похóд; (*shorter*) прогýлка; (*gait*) похóдка; (*path*) тропá ▷ *vi* (*go on foot*) ходи́ть/идти́ (*impf*) (пешкóм); (*baby*) ходи́ть (*impf*); (*for pleasure, exercise*) гуля́ть (*impf*) ▷ *vt* (*distance*) проходи́ть (*perf* пройти́); (*dog*) выгýливать (*perf* вы́гулять); **10 minutes' walk from here** в 10-ти́ минýтах ходьбы́ отсю́да; **walk out** *vi* (*audience*) демонстрати́вно покидáть (*perf* поки́нуть) зал; (*workers*) забастовáть (*perf*); **walker** *n* (*hiker*) тури́ст(ка); **walking stick** *n* трость *f*

wall [wɔːl] *n* стенá

wallet [ˈwɔlɪt] *n* бумáжник

wallpaper [ˈwɔːlpeɪpəʳ] *n* обóи *pl* ▷ *vt* оклéивать (*perf* оклéить) обóями

walnut [ˈwɔːlnʌt] *n* (*nut*) грéцкий орéх; (*wood*) орéх

walrus [ˈwɔːlrəs] (*pl* **walrus** *or* **walruses**) *n* морж

waltz [wɔːlts] *n* вальс

wander [ˈwɔndəʳ] *vi* (*person*) броди́ть (*impf*); (*mind, thoughts*) блуждáть (*impf*) ▷ *vt* броди́ть (*impf*) по *+dat*

want [wɔnt] *vt* (*wish for*) хотéть (*impf*) *+acc* or *+gen*; (*need*) нуждáться (*impf*) в *+prp* ▷ *n*: **for want of** за недостáтком *+gen*; **to want to do** хотéть (*impf*) *+infin*; **I want you to apologize** я хочý, чтóбы Вы извини́лись; **wanted** *adj* (*criminal etc*) разы́скиваемый

war [wɔːʳ] *n* войнá; **to declare war (on)** объявля́ть (*perf* объяви́ть) войнý (*+dat*)

ward [wɔːd] *n* (*Med*) палáта; (*Brit*: *Pol*) óкруг; (*Law*) *ребёнок, под опéкой*; **ward off** *vt* (*attack, enemy*) отражáть (*perf* отрази́ть); (*danger, illness*) отвращáть (*perf* отврати́ть)

warden [ˈwɔːdn] *n* (*of park, reserve*) смотри́тель(ница) *m(f)*; (*of prison*) начáльник; (*of youth hostel*) комендáнт

wardrobe [ˈwɔːdrəub] *n* шифоньéр, платянóй шкаф; (*clothes*) гардерóб; (*Theat*) костюмéрная *f adj*

warehouse [ˈwɛəhaus] *n* склад

warfare [ˈwɔːfɛəʳ] *n* воéнные *or* боевы́е дéйствия *ntpl*

warm [wɔːm] *adj* тёплый; (*thanks, supporter*) горя́чий; (*heart*) дóбрый; **it's warm today** сегóдня теплó; **I'm warm** мне теплó; **warm up** *vi* (*person, room*) согревáться (*perf* согрéться); (*water*) нагревáться (*perf* нагрéться); (*athlete*) разминáться (*perf* размя́ться) ▷ *vt* разогревáть (*perf* разогрéть); **the weather warmed up** на ýлице потеплéло; **warmly** *adv* (*applaud*) горячó; (*dress, welcome*) теплó; **warmth** *n* теплó

warn [wɔːn] *vt*: **to warn sb (not) to do/of/that** предупреждáть (*perf* предупреди́ть) когó-н (не) *+infin*/о *+prp*/, что; **warning** *n* предупреждéние

warrant ['wɔrnt] *n* (*also* **search warrant**) о́рдер на о́быск; **warranty** *n* гара́нтия
Warsaw ['wɔːsɔː] *n* Варша́ва
warship ['wɔːʃɪp] *n* вое́нный кора́бль *m*
wart [wɔːt] *n* борода́вка
wartime ['wɔːtaɪm] *n*: **in wartime** в вое́нное вре́мя
wary ['wɛərɪ] *adj*: **to be wary of sb/sth** относи́ться (*impf*) к кому́-н/ чему́-н с опа́ской
was [wɔz] *pt of* **be**
wash [wɔʃ] *n* мытьё; (*clothes*) сти́рка; (*washing programme*) режи́м сти́рки (*в стира́льной маши́не*); (*of ship*) пе́нистый след ▷ *vt* (*hands, body*) мыть (*perf* помы́ть); (*clothes*) стира́ть (*perf* постира́ть); (*face*) умыва́ть (*perf* умы́ть) ▷ *vi* (*person*) мы́ться (*perf* помы́ться); (*sea etc*): **to wash over sth** перека́тываться (*perf* перекати́ться) че́рез что-н; **to have a wash** помы́ться (*perf*); **to give sth a wash** помы́ть (*perf*) что-н; (*clothes*) постира́ть (*perf*) что-н; **wash off** *vi* отмыва́ться (*perf* отмы́ться); (*stain*) отсти́рываться (*perf* отстира́ться); **wash up** *vi* (*Brit*) мыть (*perf* вы́мыть) посу́ду; (*US*) мы́ться (*perf* помы́ться); **washer** *n* ша́йба; **washing** *n* сти́рка; **washing-up** *n* (гря́зная) посу́да
wasn't ['wɔznt] = **was not**
wasp [wɔsp] *n* оса́
waste [weɪst] *n* (*act*) тра́та; (*rubbish*) отхо́ды *mpl*; (*also* **waste land**: *in city*) пусты́рь *m* ▷ *adj* (*rejected, damaged*) брако́ванный; (*left over*) отрабо́танный ▷ *vt* растра́чивать (*perf* растра́тить); (*opportunity*) упуска́ть (*perf* упусти́ть); **wastes** *npl* (*area*) пусты́ня *fsg*; **waste paper** испо́льзованная бума́га; **wastepaper basket** *n* корзи́на для (нену́жных) бума́г
watch [wɔtʃ] *n* (*also* **wristwatch**) (нару́чные) часы́ *pl*; (*act of watching*) наблюде́ние ▷ *vt* (*look at*) наблюда́ть (*impf*) за +*instr*; (*match, programme*) смотре́ть (*perf* посмотре́ть); (*events, weight, language*) следи́ть (*impf*) за +*instr*; (*be careful of: person*) остерега́ться (*impf*) +*gen*; (*look after*) смотре́ть (*impf*) за +*instr* ▷ *vi* (*take care*) смотре́ть (*impf*); (*keep guard*) дежу́рить (*impf*); **watch out** *vi* остерега́ться (*perf* остере́чься)
water ['wɔːtə^r] *n* вода́ ▷ *vt* полива́ть (*perf* поли́ть) ▷ *vi* (*eyes*) слези́ться (*impf*); **in British waters** в брита́нских во́дах; **water down** *vt* разбавля́ть (*perf* разба́вить) (водо́й); (*fig*) смягча́ть (*perf* смягчи́ть); **watercolour** (*US* **watercolor**) *n* (*picture*) акваре́ль *f*; **waterfall** *n* водопа́д; **watering can** *n* ле́йка; **watermelon** *n* арбу́з; **waterproof** *adj* непромока́емый
watt [wɔt] *n* ватт
wave [weɪv] *n* волна́; (*of hand*) взмах ▷ *vi* (*signal*) маха́ть (*impf*); (*branches*) кача́ться (*impf*); (*flag*) развева́ться (*impf*) ▷ *vt* маха́ть (*impf*) +*instr*; (*stick, gun*) разма́хивать (*impf*) +*instr*; **wavelength** *n* (*Radio*) длина́ волны́; **they are on the same wavelength** (*fig*) они́ смо́трят на ве́щи одина́ково
wax [wæks] *n* (*polish*) воск; (: *for floor*) масти́ка; (*for skis*) мазь *f*; (*in ear*) се́ра ▷ *vt* (*floor*) натира́ть (*perf* натере́ть) масти́кой; (*car*)

натирáть (*perf* натерéть) вóском; (*skis*) мáзать (*perf* смáзать) мáзью

way [weɪ] *n* (*route*) путь *m*, дорóга; (*manner, method*) спóсоб; (*usu pl*: *habit*) привы́чка; **which way? — this way** кудá? — сюдá; **is it a long way from here?** э́то далекó отсю́да?; **which way do we go now?** кудá нам тепéрь идти́?; **on the way** (*en route*) по пути́ *or* дорóге; **to be on one's way** быть (*impf*) в пути́; **to go out of one's way to do** старáться (*perf* постарáться) изо всех сил *+infin*; **to be in sb's way** стоя́ть (*impf*) на чьём-н пути́; **to lose one's way** заблуди́ться (*perf*); **the plan is under way** план осуществля́ется; **in a way** в извéстном смы́сле; **in some ways** в нéкоторых отношéниях; **no way!** (*inf*) ни за что!; **by the way ...** кстáти ..., мéжду прóчим ...; **"way in"** (*Brit*) "вход"; **"way out"** (*Brit*) "вы́ход"; **"give way"** (*Brit*: *Aut*) "уступи́те дорóгу"

WC *n abbr* (= *water closet*) туалéт

we [wi:] *pron* мы

weak [wi:k] *adj* слáбый; **to grow weak** слабéть (*perf* ослабéть); **weaken** *vi* (*person*) смягчáться (*perf* смягчи́ться) ▷ *vt* (*government, person*) ослабля́ть (*perf* ослáбить); **weakness** *n* слáбость *f*; **to have a weakness for** имéть (*impf*) слáбость к *+dat*

wealth [wɛlθ] *n* (*money, resources*) богáтство; (*of details, knowledge etc*) оби́лие; **wealthy** *adj* богáтый

weapon ['wɛpən] *n* орýжие

wear [wɛəʳ] (*pt* **wore**, *pp* **worn**) *n* (*use*) нóска; (*damage*) изнóс ▷ *vi* (*last*) носи́ться (*impf*); (*rub through*) изнáшиваться (*perf* износи́ться) ▷ *vt* (*generally*) носи́ть (*impf*); (*put on*) надевáть (*perf* надéть); (*damage*) изнáшивать (*perf* износи́ть); **he was wearing his new shirt** на нём былá егó нóвая рубáшка; **wear down** *vt* (*resistance*) сломи́ть (*perf*); **wear out** *vt* (*shoes, clothing*) изнáшивать (*perf* износи́ть)

weary ['wɪərɪ] *adj* утомлённый ▷ *vi*: **to weary of** утомля́ться (*perf* утоми́ться) от *+gen*

weasel ['wi:zl] *n* (*Zool*) лáска

weather ['wɛðəʳ] *n* погóда ▷ *vt* (*crisis*) выдéрживать (*perf* вы́держать); **I am under the weather** мне нездорóвится; **weather forecast** *n* прогнóз погóды

weave [wi:v] (*pt* **wove**, *pp* **woven**) *vt* (*cloth*) ткать (*perf* соткáть)

web [wɛb] *n* паути́на; (*fig*) сеть *f*; **web address** *n* áдрес в Интернéт, веб-áдрес; **webcam** *n* Интернéт-кáмера, веб-кáмера; **web page** *n* электрóнная страни́ца, страни́ца на интернéте; **website** *n* сайт

wed [wɛd] (*pt, pp* **wedded**) *vi* венчáться (*perf* обвенчáться)

we'd [wi:d] = **we had**; **we would**

wedding [wɛdɪŋ] *n* свáдьба; (*in church*) венчáние; **silver/golden wedding** серéбряная/золотáя свáдьба

wedge [wɛdʒ] *n* клин ▷ *vt* закрепля́ть (*perf* закрепи́ть) кли́ном; (*pack tightly*): **to wedge in** вти́скивать (*perf* вти́снуть) в *+acc*

Wednesday ['wɛdnzdɪ] *n* средá

wee [wi:] *adj* (*Scottish*) мáленький

weed [wi:d] *n* сорня́к ▷ *vt*

полóть (*perf* вы́полоть)

week [wiːk] *n* недéля; **a week today** чéрез недéлю; **a week on Friday** в слéдующую пя́тницу; **weekday** *n* бу́дний день *m*; **weekend** *n* выходны́е *pl adj* (дни), суббóта и воскресéнье; **weekly** *adv* еженедéльно ▷ *adj* еженедéльный

weep [wiːp] (*pt, pp* **wept**) *vi* (*person*) плáкать (*impf*)

weigh [weɪ] *vt* взвéшивать (*perf* взвéсить) ▷ *vi* вéсить (*impf*); **weigh down** *vt* отягощáть (*perf* отяготи́ть); (*fig*) тяготи́ть (*impf*)

weight [weɪt] *n* вес; (*for scales*) ги́ря; **to lose weight** худéть (*perf* похудéть); **to put on weight** поправля́ться (*perf* попрáвиться)

weir [wɪəʳ] *n* (*in river*) запру́да

weird [wɪəd] *adj* (*strange*) стрáнный, дикóвинный

welcome [ˈwɛlkəm] *adj* желáнный ▷ *n* (*hospitality*) приём; (*greeting*) привéтствие ▷ *vt* (*also* **bid welcome**) привéтствовать (*impf*); **thank you — you're welcome!** спаси́бо — пожáлуйста!

weld [wɛld] *vt* свáривать (*perf* свари́ть)

welfare [ˈwɛlfɛəʳ] *n* (*well-being*) благополу́чие; (*US: social aid*) социáльное посóбие; **welfare state** *n* госудáрство всеóбщего благосостоя́ния

well [wɛl] *n* (*for water*) колóдец; (*also* **oil well**) (нефтянáя) сквáжина ▷ *adv* хорошó ▷ *excl* (*anyway*) ну; (*so*) ну вот ▷ *adj*: **he is well** он здорóв; **as well** тáкже; **I woke well before dawn** я просну́лся задóлго до рассвéта; **I've brought my anorak as well as a jumper** крóме сви́тера я взял ещё и ку́ртку; **well done!** молодéц!; **get well soon!** поправля́йтесь скорéе!; **he is doing well at school** в шкóле он успевáет; **the business is doing well** би́знес процветáет; **well up** *vi* (*tears*) наверну́ться (*perf*)

we'll [wiːl] = **we will**; **we shall**

well-dressed [ˈwɛlˈdrɛst] *adj* хорошó одéтый

wellies [ˈwɛlɪz] *npl* = **wellingtons**

wellingtons [ˈwɛlɪŋtənz] *npl* (*also* **wellington boots**) рези́новые сапоги́ *mpl*

well-known [ˈwɛlˈnəun] *adj* извéстный

well-off [ˈwɛlˈɔf] *adj* обеспéченный

Welsh [wɛlʃ] *adj* уэ́льский; ▷ *npl*: **the Welsh** (*people*) уэ́льсцы *mpl*, валли́йцы *mpl*; **Welshman** *irreg n* уэ́льсец, валли́ец; **Welshwoman** *n irreg* валли́йка, жи́тельница Уэ́льса

went [wɛnt] *pt of* **go**

wept [wɛpt] *pt, pp of* **weep**

were [wəːʳ] *pt of* **be**

we're [wɪəʳ] = **we are**

weren't [wəːnt] = **were not**

west [wɛst] *n* зáпад ▷ *adj* зáпадный ▷ *adv* на зáпад; **the West** (*Pol*) Зáпад; **western** *adj* зáпадный ▷ *n* (*Cinema*) вéстерн

wet [wɛt] *adj* (*damp, rainy*) влáжный, сырóй; (*soaking*) мóкрый; **to get wet** мóкнуть (*perf* промóкнуть)

we've [wiːv] = **we have**

whale [weɪl] *n* кит

wharf [wɔːf] (*pl* **wharves**) *n* при́стань *f*

KEYWORD

what [wɔt] *adj* **1** (*interrogative: direct, indirect*) какóй (*f* какáя, *nt*

W

какóе, *pl* какúе); **what books do you need?** какúе кнúги Вам нужны́?; **what size is the dress?** какóго размéра э́то плáтье?
2 (*emphatic*) какóй (*f* какáя, *nt* какóе, *pl* какúе); **what a lovely day!** какóй чудéсный день!; **what a fool I am!** какóй же я дурáк!
▷ *pron* **1** (*interrogative*) что; **what are you doing?** что Вы дéлаете?; **what are you talking about?** о чём Вы говорúте?; **what is it called?** как э́то называ́ется?; **what about me?** а как же я?; **what about doing ...?** как насчёт тогó, чтóбы *+infin* ...?
2 (*relative*) что; **I saw what was on the table** я вúдел, что бы́ло на столé; **tell me what you're thinking about** скажúте мне, о чём Вы дýмаете; **what you say is wrong** то, что Вы говорúте, невéрно
▷ *excl* (*disbelieving*) что; **I've crashed the car — what!** я разбúл машúну — что!

whatever [wɔt'ɛvəʳ] *adj* (*any*) любóй; **whatever book** любáя кнúга ▷ *pron* (*any*) всё; (*regardless of*) что бы ни; **whatever you do ...** что бы ты не дéлал ...; **whatever the reason ...** каковá бы ни былá причúна ...; **do whatever is necessary/you want** дéлайте всё, что необходúмо/хотúте; **whatever happens** что бы ни случúлось; **there is no reason whatever** нет никакóй причúны; **nothing whatever** абсолю́тно ничегó

whatsoever [wɔtsəu'ɛvəʳ] *adj*: **there is no reason whatsoever** нет никакóй причúны

wheat [wi:t] *n* пшенúца

wheel [wi:l] *n* (*of car etc*) колесó; (*also* **steering wheel**) руль *m*; **wheelbarrow** *n* тáчка; **wheelchair** *n* инвалúдная коля́ска

wheeze [wi:z] *vi* хрипéть (*impf*)

when [wɛn] *adv, conj* когдá; **when you've read the book ...** когдá Вы прочитáете кнúгу ...

whenever [wɛn'ɛvəʳ] *adv* в любóе врéмя ▷ *conj* (*any time*) когдá тóлько; (*every time that*) кáждый раз, когдá

where [wɛəʳ] *adv* (*position*) где; (*motion*) кудá ▷ *conj* где; **where ... from?** откýда ...?; **this is where ...** э́то там, где ...; **whereabouts** [*adv* wɛərə'bauts, *n* 'wɛərəbauts] *adv* (*position*) где; (*motion*) кудá ▷ *n* местонахождéние; **whereas** *conj* тогдá *or* в то врéмя как; **whereby** *adv* (*formal*) посрéдством чегó; **wherever** [wɛər'ɛvəʳ] *conj* (*no matter where*): **wherever he was** где бы он нú был; (*not knowing where*): **wherever that is** где бы то нú было ▷ *adv* (*interrogative: position*) где же; (*: motion*) кудá же; **wherever he goes** кудá бы он ни шёл

whether ['wɛðəʳ] *conj* ли; **I doubt whether she loves me** я сомневáюсь, лю́бит ли онá меня́; **I don't know whether to accept this proposal** я не знáю, приня́ть ли э́то предложéние; **whether you go or not** пойдёте Вы úли нет

KEYWORD

which [wɪtʃ] *adj* **1** (*interrogative: direct, indirect*) какóй (*f* какáя, *nt* какóе, *pl* какúе); **which picture would you like?** какýю картúну Вы хотúте?; **which books are yours?** какúе кнúги Вáши?; **which one?**

какой? (*f* какая, *nt* какое); **I've got two pens, which one do you want?** у меня есть две ручки, какую Вы хотите?; **which one of you did it?** кто из Вас это сделал?
2: in which case в таком случае; **by which time** к тому времени ▷ *pron* **1** (*interrogative*) какой (*f* какая, *nt* какое, *pl* какие); **there are several museums, which shall we visit first?** здесь есть несколько музеев. В какой мы пойдём сначала?; **which do you want, the apple or the banana?** что Вы хотите — яблоко или банан?; **which of you are staying?** кто из Вас остаётся?
2 (*relative*) который (*f* которая, *nt* которое, *pl* которые); **the apple which is on the table** яблоко, которое лежит на столе; **the news was bad, which is what I had feared** вести были плохие, чего я и опасался; **I had lunch, after which I decided to go home** я пообедал, после чего я решил пойти домой; **I made a speech, after which nobody spoke** я выступил с речью, после которой никто ничего не сказал

whichever [wɪtʃ'ɛvə^r] *adj* (*any*) любой; (*regardless of*) какой бы ни; **take whichever book you prefer** возьмите любую книгу; **whichever book you take** какую бы книгу Вы ни взяли
while [waɪl] *n* (*period of time*) время *nt* ▷ *conj* пока, в то время как; (*although*) хотя; **for a while** ненадолго; **while away** *vt*: **to while away the time** коротать (*perf* скоротать) время
whim [wɪm] *n* прихоть *f*
whine [waɪn] *vi* (*person, animal*) скулить (*impf*); (*engine, siren*) выть (*impf*)
whip [wɪp] *n* кнут, хлыст; (*Pol*: *person*) организатор парламентской фракции ▷ *vt* (*person, animal*) хлестать (*impf*); (*cream, eggs*) взбивать (*perf* взбить); **to whip sth out** выхватывать (*perf* выхватить) что-н; **to whip sth away** вырывать (*perf* вырвать) что-н
whirl [wə:l] *vi* кружиться (*impf*), вращаться (*impf*)
whisk [wɪsk] *n* (*Culin*) венчик ▷ *vt* (*Culin*) взбивать (*perf* взбить); **to whisk sb away** *or* **off** увозить (*perf* увезти) кого-н
whiskers ['wɪskəz] *npl* (*of animal*) усы *mpl*; (*of man*) бакенбарды *fpl*
whisky ['wɪskɪ] (*US, Ireland* **whiskey**) *n* виски *nt ind*
whisper ['wɪspə^r] *n* шёпот ▷ *vi* шептаться (*impf*) ▷ *vt* шептать (*impf*)
whistle ['wɪsl] *n* (*sound*) свист; (*object*) свисток ▷ *vi* свистеть (*perf* свистнуть)
white [waɪt] *adj* белый ▷ *n* (*colour*) белый цвет; (*person*) белый(-ая) *m(f) adj*; (*of egg, eye*) белок; **whitewash** *n* (*paint*) известковый раствор (*для побелки*) ▷ *vt* (*building*) белить (*perf* побелить); (*fig*: *incident*) обелять (*perf* обелить)
whiting ['waɪtɪŋ] *n inv* хек
whizz [wɪz] *vi*: **to whizz past** *or* **by** проноситься (*perf* пронестись) мимо

 **KEYWORD**

who [hu:] *pron* **1** (*interrogative*) кто; **who is it?, who's there?** кто это *or* там?; **who did you see there?** кого Вы там видели?

W

2 (*relative*) который (*f* которая, *nt* которое, *pl* которые); **the woman who spoke to me** женщина, которая говорила со мной

whole [həul] *adj* целый ▷ *n* (*entire unit*) целое *nt adj*; (*all*): **the whole of Europe** вся Европа; **on the whole, as a whole** в целом; **wholemeal** *adj* (*Brit*): **wholemeal flour** мука грубого помола; **wholemeal bread** хлеб из муки грубого помола; **wholesale** *adj* (*price*) оптовый; (*destruction*) массовый ▷ *adv* (*buy, sell*) оптом
wholly ['həulɪ] *adv* полностью, целиком

 **KEYWORD**

whom [hu:m] *pron*
1 (*interrogative*: *+acc*, *+gen*) кого; (: *+dat*) кому; (: *+instr*) кем; (: *+prp*) ком; **whom did you see there?** кого Вы там видели?; **to whom did you give the book?** кому Вы отдали книгу?
2 (*relative*: *+acc*) которого (*f* которую, *pl* которых) (: *+gen*) которого (*f* которой, *pl* которых) (: *+dat*) которому (*f* которой, *pl* которым) (: *+instr*) которым (*f* которой, *pl* которыми) (: *+prp*) котором (*f* которой, *pl* которых); **the man whom I saw/to whom I spoke** человек, которого я видел/с которым я говорил

whore [hɔ:ʳ] *n* (*inf*: *pej*) шлюха

 **KEYWORD**

whose [hu:z] *adj* **1** (*possessive*: *interrogative*) чей (*f* чья, *nt* чьё, *pl* чьи); **whose book is this?, whose is this book?** чья это книга?
2 (*possessive*: *relative*) который (*f* которая, *nt* которое, *pl* которые); **the woman whose son you rescued** женщина, сына которой Вы спасли
▷ *pron* чей (*f* чья, *nt* чьё, *pl* чьи); **whose is this?** это чьё?; **I know whose it is** я знаю, чьё это

why [waɪ] *adv, conj* почему
▷ *excl*: **why, it's you!** как, это Вы?; **why is he always late?** почему он всегда опаздывает?; **I'm not going — why not?** я не пойду — почему?; **why not do it now?** почему бы не сделать это сейчас?; **I wonder why he said that** интересно, почему он это сказал; **that's not why I'm here** я здесь не по этой причине; **that's why** вот почему; **there is a reason why I want to see him** у меня есть причина для встречи с ним; **why, it's obvious/that's impossible!** но ведь это же очевидно/невозможно!
wicked ['wɪkɪd] *adj* злобный, злой; (*mischievous*: *smile*) лукавый
wide [waɪd] *adj* широкий ▷ *adv*: **to open wide** широко открывать (*perf* открыть); **to shoot wide** стрелять (*impf*) мимо цели; **the bridge is 3 metres wide** ширина моста — 3 метра; **widely** *adv* (*believed, known*) широко; (*travelled*) много; (*differing*) значительно; **widen** *vt* расширять (*perf* расширить) ▷ *vi* расширяться (*perf* расшириться); **wide open** *adj* широко раскрытый; **widespread** *adj* (*belief etc*) широко распространённый

widow ['wɪdəu] *n* вдова́; **widower** *n* вдове́ц
width [wɪdθ] *n* ширина́
wield [wi:ld] *vt* (*power*) облада́ть (*impf*) *+instr*
wife [waɪf] (*pl* **wives**) *n* жена́
Wi-Fi ['waɪfaɪ] *n* беспроводна́я связь
wig [wɪg] *n* пари́к
wild [waɪld] *adj* (*animal, plant, guess*) ди́кий; (*weather, sea*) бу́рный; (*person, behaviour*) бу́йный; **wilds** *npl*: **the wilds** (*remote area*) ди́кие места́ *ntpl*; **in the wilds of** в де́брях *+gen*; **wilderness** ['wɪldənɪs] *n* ди́кая ме́стность *f*; (*desert*) пусты́ня; **wildlife** *n* ди́кая приро́да; **wildly** *adv* (*behave*) бу́йно, ди́ко; (*applaud*) бу́рно; (*hit*) неистово; (*guess*) наобу́м

KEYWORD

will [wɪl] *aux vb* **1** (*forming future tense*): **I will finish it tomorrow** я зако́нчу э́то за́втра; **I will be working all morning** я бу́ду рабо́тать всё у́тро; **I will have finished it by tomorrow** я зако́нчу э́то к за́втрашнему дню; **I will always remember you** я бу́ду по́мнить тебя́ всегда́; **will you do it? — yes, I will/no, I won't** Вы сде́лаете э́то? — да, сде́лаю/нет, не сде́лаю; **the car won't start** маши́на ника́к не заво́дится
2 (*in conjectures, predictions*): **he will** *or* **he'll be there by now** он, наве́рное, уже́ там; **mistakes will happen** оши́бки неизбе́жны
3 (*in commands, requests, offers*): **will you be quiet!** а ну́-ка, поти́ше!; **will you help me?** Вы мне не помо́жете?; **will you have a cup of tea?** не хоти́те ли ча́шку ча́я?
▷ *vt* (*pt, pp* **willed**): **to will o.s. to do** заставля́ть (*perf* заста́вить) себя́ *+infin*; **to will sb to do** заклина́ть (*impf*) кого́-н *+infin*
▷ *n* (*volition*) во́ля; (*testament*) завеща́ние

willing ['wɪlɪŋ] *adj* (*agreed*) согла́сный; (*enthusiastic*) усе́рдный; **he's willing to do it** он гото́в сде́лать э́то; **willingly** *adv* с гото́вностью, охо́тно
willow ['wɪləu] *n* (*tree*) и́ва
willpower ['wɪlpauə^r] *n* си́ла во́ли
wilt [wɪlt] *vi* ни́кнуть (*perf* пони́кнуть)
win [wɪn] (*pt, pp* **won**) *n* побе́да ▷ *vt* выи́грывать (*perf* вы́играть); (*support, popularity*) завоёвывать (*perf* завоева́ть) ▷ *vi* побежда́ть (*perf* победи́ть), выи́грывать (*perf* вы́играть); **win over** *vt* (*person*) покоря́ть (*perf* покори́ть)
wind[1] [wɪnd] *n* ве́тер; (*Med*) га́зы *mpl* ▷ *vt*: **the blow winded him** от уда́ра у него́ захвати́ло дух
wind[2] [waɪnd] (*pt, pp* **wound**) *vt* (*rope, thread*) мота́ть (*perf* смота́ть); (*toy, clock*) заводи́ть (*perf* завести́) ▷ *vi* (*road, river*) ви́ться (*impf*); **wind up** *vt* (*toy, clock*) заводи́ть (*perf* завести́); (*debate*) заверша́ть (*perf* заверши́ть)
windfall ['wɪndfɔ:l] *n* (*money*) неожи́данный дохо́д
wind farm *n* ветряна́я электроста́нция
windmill ['wɪndmɪl] *n* ветряна́я ме́льница
window ['wɪndəu] *n* окно́; (*in shop*) витри́на; **windowsill** [-sɪl] *n* подоко́нник

windscreen ['wɪndskri:n] *n* ветровóе стеклó
windy ['wɪndɪ] *adj* вéтреный; **it's windy today** сегóдня вéтрено
wine [waɪn] *n* винó
wing [wɪŋ] *n* (*also Aut*) крылó; **wings** *npl* (*Theat*) кулисы *fpl*
wink [wɪŋk] *n* подмигивание ▷ *vi* подмигивать (*perf* подмигнýть), мигáть (*perf* мигнýть); (*light*) мигáть (*perf* мигнýть)
winner ['wɪnəʳ] *n* победитель(ница) *m(f)*
winter ['wɪntəʳ] *n* (*season*) зимá; **in winter** зимóй
wipe [waɪp] *n*: **to give sth a wipe** протирáть (*perf* протерéть) что-н ▷ *vt* (*rub*) вытирáть (*perf* вытереть); (*erase*) стирáть (*perf* стерéть); **wipe out** *vt* (*city, population*) стирáть (*perf* стерéть) с лицá земли
wire ['waɪəʳ] *n* прóволока; (*Elec*) прóвод; (*telegram*) телегрáмма ▷ *vt* (*person*) телеграфировать (*impf/perf*) +*dat*; (*Elec*: *also* **wire up**) подключáть (*perf* подключить); **to wire a house** дéлать (*perf* сдéлать) (электро) провóдку в дóме
wireless ['waɪəlɪs] *adj* беспроводный
wiring ['waɪərɪŋ] *n* (электро) провóдка
wisdom ['wɪzdəm] *n* мýдрость *f*
wise [waɪz] *adj* мýдрый
...wise [waɪz] *suffix*: **timewise** в смысле врéмени
wish [wɪʃ] *n* желáние ▷ *vt* желáть (*perf* пожелáть); **best wishes** (*for birthday etc*) всегó наилýчшего; **with best wishes** (*in letter*) с наилýчшими пожелáниями; **to wish sb goodbye** прощáться (*perf* попрощáться) с кем-н; **he wished me well** он пожелáл мне всегó хорóшего; **to wish to do** хотéть (*impf*) +*infin*; **I wish him to come** я хочý, чтóбы он пришёл; **to wish for** желáть (*perf* пожелáть) +*acc* or +*gen*
wistful ['wɪstful] *adj* тоскливый
wit [wɪt] *n* (*wittiness*) остроýмие; (*intelligence*: *also* **wits**) ум, рáзум
witch [wɪtʃ] *n* вéдьма

 **KEYWORD**

with [wɪð, wɪθ] *prep*
1 (*accompanying, in the company of*) с +*instr*; **I spent the day with him** я провёл с ним день; **we stayed with friends** мы остановились у друзéй; **I'll be with you in a minute** я освобожýсь чéрез минýту; **I'm with you** (*I understand*) я Вас понимáю; **she is really with it** (*inf*: *fashionable*) онá óчень стильная; (: *aware*) онá всё соображáет
2 (*descriptive*) с +*instr*; **a girl with blue eyes** дéвушка с голубыми глазáми; **a skirt with a silk lining** юбка на шёлковой подклáдке
3 (*indicating manner*) с +*instr*; (*indicating cause*) от +*gen*; (*indicating means*): **to write with a pencil** писáть (*impf*) карандашóм; **with tears in her eyes** со слезáми на глазáх; **red with anger** крáсный от гнéва; **you can open the door with this key** Вы мóжете открыть дверь этим ключём; **to fill sth with water** наполнять (*perf* напóлнить) что-н водóй

withdraw [wɪθ'drɔ:] (*irreg like* **draw**) *vt* (*object*) извлекáть (*perf* извлéчь); (*remark*) брать (*perf* взять) наза́д; (*offer*) снима́ть (*perf* снять) ▷ *vi* (*troops, person*) уходи́ть (*perf* уйти́); **to withdraw money from an account** снима́ть (*perf* снять) де́ньги со счёта; **withdrawal** *n* (*of offer, remark*) отка́з; (*of troops*) вы́вод; (*of money*) сня́тие; **withdrawn** *pp of* **withdraw** ▷ *adj* за́мкнутый

wither ['wɪðəʳ] *vi* (*plant*) вя́нуть (*perf* завя́нуть)

withhold [wɪθ'həuld] (*irreg like* **hold**) *vt* (*money*) уде́рживать (*perf* удержа́ть); (*information*)ута́ивать (*perf* утаи́ть)

within [wɪð'ɪn] *prep* (*place, distance, time*) внутри́ *+gen*, в преде́лах *+gen* ▷ *adv* внутри́; **within reach** в преде́лах досяга́емости; **within sight (of)** в по́ле зре́ния (*+gen*); **the finish is within sight** коне́ц не за гора́ми

without [wɪð'aut] *prep* без *+gen*; **without a hat** без ша́пки; **without saying a word** не говоря́ ни сло́ва; **without looking** не гля́дя; **to go without sth** обходи́ться (*perf* обойти́сь) без чего́-н

withstand [wɪθ'stænd] (*irreg like* **stand**) *vt* выде́рживать (*perf* вы́держать)

witness ['wɪtnɪs] *n* свиде́тель(ница) *m(f)* ▷ *vt* (*event*) быть (*impf*) свиде́телем(-льницей) *+gen*; (*document*) заверя́ть (*perf* заве́рить)

witty ['wɪtɪ] *adj* остроу́мный

wives [waɪvz] *npl of* **wife**

wobble ['wɔbl] *vi* (*legs*) трясти́сь (*impf*); (*chair*) шата́ться (*impf*)

woe [wəu] *n* го́ре

woke [wəuk] *pt of* **wake**; **woken** *pp of* **wake**

wolf [wulf] (*pl* **wolves**) *n* волк

woman ['wumən] (*pl* **women**) *n* же́нщина

womb [wu:m] *n* ма́тка

women ['wɪmɪn] *npl of* **woman**

won [wʌn] *pt, pp of* **win**

wonder ['wʌndəʳ] *n* (*feeling*) изумле́ние ▷ *vi*: **I wonder whether you could tell me ...** не мо́жете ли Вы сказа́ть мне ...; **I wonder why he is late** интере́сно, почему́ он опозда́л; **to wonder at** удивля́ться (*impf*) *+dat*; **to wonder about** разду́мывать (*impf*) о *+prp*; **it's no wonder (that)** не удиви́тельно(, что); **wonderful** *adj* (*excellent*) чуде́сный

won't [wəunt] = **will not**

wood [wud] *n* (*timber*) де́рево; (*forest*) лес; **wooden** *adj* (*object*) деревя́нный; (*fig*) дубо́вый; **woodwork** *n* (*skill*) столя́рное де́ло

wool [wul] *n* (*material, yarn*) шерсть *f*; **to pull the wool over sb's eyes** (*fig*) пуска́ть (*impf*) пыль в глаза́ кому́-н; **woollen** (*US* **woolen**) *adj* шерстяно́й; **woolly** (*US* **wooly**) *adj* шерстяно́й; (*fig*: *ideas*) расплы́вчатый; (: *person*) вя́лый

word [wə:d] *n* сло́во; (*news*) слух ▷ *vt* формули́ровать (*perf* сформули́ровать); **in other words** други́ми слова́ми; **to break/keep one's word** наруша́ть (*perf* нару́шить)/держа́ть (*perf* сдержа́ть) своё сло́во; **to have words with sb** име́ть (*impf*) кру́пный разгово́р с кем-н; **wording** *n* формулиро́вка; **word processor** *n* те́кстовый проце́ссор

wore [wɔ:ʳ] *pt of* **wear**

work [wə:k] *n* рабо́та; (*Art, Literature*) произведе́ние ▷ *vi* рабо́тать (*impf*); (*medicine etc*) действовать (*perf* подействовать) ▷ *vt* (*clay*) работать (*impf*) с +*instr*; (*wood, metal*) работать (*impf*) по +*dat*; (*land*) обрабатывать (*perf* обработать); (*mine*) разрабатывать (*perf* разработать); (*machine*) управлять (*impf*) +*instr*; (*miracle*) совершать (*perf* совершить); **he has been out of work for three months** он был без работы три месяца; **to work loose** (*part*) расшатываться (*perf* расшататься); (*knot*) слабнуть (*perf* ослабнуть); **work on** *vt fus* (*task*) работать (*impf*) над +*instr*; (*person*) работать (*impf*) с +*instr*; (*principle*) исходить (*impf*) из +*gen*; **work out** *vi* (*plans etc*) удаваться (*perf* удаться) ▷ *vt* (*problem*) разрешать (*perf* разрешить); (*plan*) разрабатывать (*perf* разработать); **it works out at £100** (*cost*) выходит £100; **worker** *n* (*in factory*) рабочий(-ая) *m(f) adj*; (*in community etc*) работник(-ница); **workforce** *n* рабочая сила; **working-class** *adj* рабочий; **workman** *irreg n* (квалифицированный) рабочий *m adj*; **workshop** *n* мастерская *f adj*, цех; (*session*) семинар; (*Theat, Mus*) студия

world [wəːld] *n* мир ▷ *adj* мировой; **to think the world of sb** быть (*impf*) очень высокого мнения о ком-н; **world champion** чемпион мира; **World Wide Web** *n* Всемирная Паутина

worm [wəːm] *n* (*Zool*) червь *m*

worn [wɔːn] *pp of* **wear** ▷ *adj* (*carpet*) потёртый; **worn-out** *adj* (*object*) изношенный; (*person*) измотанный

worried ['wʌrɪd] *adj* обеспокоенный, встревоженный

worry ['wʌrɪ] *n* (*anxiety*) беспокойство, волнение ▷ *vi* беспокоиться (*impf*), волноваться (*impf*) ▷ *vt* (*person*) беспокоить (*perf* обеспокоить), волновать (*perf* взволновать); **worrying** *adj* тревожный

worse [wəːs] *adj* худший ▷ *adv* хуже ▷ *n* худшее *nt adj*; **a change for the worse** ухудшение; **worsen** *vi* ухудшаться (*perf* ухудшиться); **worse off** *adj* (*financially*) более бедный

worship ['wəːʃɪp] *n* поклонение, преклонение ▷ *vt* поклоняться (*impf*) +*dat*, преклоняться (*impf*) перед +*instr*

worst [wəːst] *adj* наихудший ▷ *adv* хуже всего ▷ *n* наихудшее *nt adj*; **at worst** в худшем случае

worth [wəːθ] *adj*: **to be worth** стоить (*impf*); **it's worth it** это того стоит; **worthless** *adj* никчёмный; **worthwhile** *adj* стоящий

worthy [wəːðɪ] *adj*: **worthy (of)** достойный (+*gen*)

KEYWORD

would [wud] *aux vb*

1 (*conditional tense*): **I would tell you if I could** я бы сказал Вам, если бы мог; **if you asked him he would do it** если Вы его попросите, (то) он сделает это; **if you had asked him he would have done it** если бы Вы попросили его, (то) он бы сделал это

2 (*in offers, invitations, requests*): **would you like a cake?** не хотите (ли) пирога?; **would you ask him to come in?** пожалуйста, пригласите его войти!; **would you**

open the window please? откро́йте, пожа́луйста, окно́!
3 (*in indirect speech*): **I said I would do it** я сказа́л, что сде́лаю э́то; **he asked me if I would stay with him** он попроси́л меня́ оста́ться с ним; **he asked me if I would resit the exam if I failed** он спроси́л меня́, бу́ду ли я пересдава́ть экза́мен, е́сли я провалю́сь
4 (*emphatic*): **it WOULD have to snow today!** и́менно сего́дня до́лжен пойти́ снег!; **you WOULD say that, wouldn't you!** Вы, коне́чно, э́то ска́жете!
5 (*insistence*): **she wouldn't behave** она́ никак не хоте́ла хорошо́ себя́ вести́
6 (*conjecture*): **it would have been midnight** должно́ быть, была́ по́лночь; **it would seem so** должно́ быть, так; **it would seem that ...** похо́же, что ...
7 (*indicating habit*): **he would come here on Mondays** он (обы́чно) приходи́л сюда́ по понеде́льникам

wouldn't ['wudnt] = **would not**
wound[1] [waund] *pt, pp of* **wind**[2]
wound[2] [wu:nd] *n* ра́на ▷ *vt* ра́нить (*impf/perf*)
wove [wəuv] *pt of* **weave**; **woven** *pp of* **weave**
wrap [ræp] *vt* (*also* **wrap up**) завора́чивать (*perf* заверну́ть); (*wind*): **to wrap sth round sth** (*tape etc*) обора́чивать (*perf* оберну́ть) что-н вокру́г чего́-н; **wrapper** *n* (*on chocolate*) обёртка
wreath [ri:θ] *n* (*for dead*) вено́к
wreck [rɛk] *n* (*vehicle, ship*) обло́мки *mpl* ▷ *vt* (*car*) разбива́ть (*perf* разби́ть); (*stereo*) лома́ть (*perf* слома́ть); (*weekend*) по́ртить (*perf* испо́ртить); (*relationship*) разруша́ть (*perf* разру́шить); (*life, health*) губи́ть (*perf* погуби́ть); **wreckage** *n* обло́мки *mpl*; (*of building*) разва́лины *fpl*
wren [rɛn] *n* крапи́вник
wrench [rɛntʃ] *n* (*Tech*) га́ечный ключ; (*tug*) рыво́к; (*fig*) тоска́ ▷ *vt* (*twist*) вывёртывать (*perf* вы́вернуть); **to wrench sth from sb** вырыва́ть (*perf* вы́рвать) что-н у кого́-н
wrestle ['rɛsl] *vi* (*Sport*): **to wrestle (with sb)** боро́ться (*impf*) (с кем-н)
wrestling ['rɛslɪŋ] *n* борьба́
wretched ['rɛtʃɪd] *adj* несча́стный
wriggle ['rɪgl] *vi* (*also* **wriggle about**: *worm*) извива́ться (*impf*); (: *person*) ёрзать (*impf*)
wring [rɪŋ] (*pt, pp* **wrung**) *vt* (*hands*) лома́ть (*impf*); (*also* **wring out**: *clothes*) выжима́ть (*perf* вы́жать); (*fig*): **to wring sth out of sb** выжима́ть (*perf* вы́жать) что-н из кого́-н
wrinkle ['rɪŋkl] *n* (*on face*) морщи́на ▷ *vt* (*nose etc*) мо́рщить (*perf* смо́рщить) ▷ *vi* (*skin etc*) мо́рщиться (*perf* смо́рщиться)
wrist [rɪst] *n* (*Anat*) запя́стье
write [raɪt] (*pt* **wrote**, *pp* **written**) *vt* (*letter, novel etc*) писа́ть (*perf* написа́ть); (*cheque, receipt*) выпи́сывать (*perf* вы́писать) ▷ *vi* писа́ть (*impf*); **to write to sb** писа́ть (*perf* написа́ть) кому́-н; **write down** *vt* (*note*) писа́ть (*perf* написа́ть); **write off** *vt* (*debt*) спи́сывать (*perf* списа́ть); (*plan*) отменя́ть (*perf* отмени́ть); **writer** *n* писа́тель *m*

writing ['raɪtɪŋ] *n* (*words written*) на́дпись *f*; (*of letter, article*) (на) писа́ние; (*also* **handwriting**) по́черк; **writing is his favourite occupation** бо́льше всего́ он лю́бит писа́ть; **in writing** в пи́сьменном ви́де

written ['rɪtn] *pp of* **write**

wrong [rɔŋ] *adj* непра́вильный; (*information*) неве́рный; (*immoral*) дурно́й ▷ *adv* непра́вильно ▷ *n* (*injustice*) несправедли́вость *f* ▷ *vt* нехорошо́ поступа́ть (*perf* поступи́ть) с *+instr*; **you are wrong to do it** э́то нехорошо́ с Ва́шей стороны́; **you are wrong about that, you've got it wrong** Вы непра́вы; **who is in the wrong?** чья э́то вина́?; **what's wrong?** в чём де́ло?; **to go wrong** (*plan*) не удава́ться (*perf* уда́ться); **right and wrong** хоро́шее и дурно́е

wrote [rəut] *pt of* **write**

wrung [rʌŋ] *pt, pp of* **wring**

WWW *n abbr* = **World Wide Web**

Xmas ['ɛksməs] *n abbr* = **Christmas**

X-ray ['ɛksreɪ] *n* (*ray*) рентге́новские лучи́ *mpl*; (*photo*) рентге́новский сни́мок ▷ *vt* просве́чивать (*perf* просвети́ть) (рентге́новскими луча́ми)

xylophone ['zaɪləfəun] *n* ксилофо́н

Y

yacht [jɔt] *n* я́хта
yard [jɑ:d] *n* (*of house etc*) двор; (*measure*) ярд

YARD

Yard — ме́ра длины́ ра́вная 90,14 см.

yawn [jɔ:n] *n* зево́к ▷ *vi* зева́ть (*perf* зевну́ть)
year [jɪə^r] *n* год; **he is eight years old** ему́ во́семь лет; **an eight-year-old child** восьмиле́тний ребёнок; **yearly** *adj* ежего́дный ▷ *adv* ежего́дно
yearn [jə:n] *vi*: **to yearn for sth** тоскова́ть (*impf*) по чему́-н; **to yearn to do** жа́ждать (*impf*) +*infin*
yeast [ji:st] *n* дро́жжи *pl*
yell [jɛl] *vi* вопи́ть (*impf*)
yellow ['jɛləu] *adj* жёлтый
yes [jɛs] *particle* да; (*in reply to negative*) нет ▷ *n* проголосова́вший(-ая) *m(f) adj* "за"; **to say yes** говори́ть (*perf* сказа́ть) да
yesterday ['jɛstədɪ] *adv* вчера́ ▷ *n* вчера́шний день *m*; **yesterday morning/evening** вчера́ у́тром/ве́чером; **all day yesterday** вчера́ весь день
yet [jɛt] *adv* ещё, до сих пор ▷ *conj* одна́ко, всё же; **the work is not finished yet** рабо́та ещё не око́нчена; **the best yet** са́мый лу́чший на сего́дняшний день; **as yet** ещё пока́
yew [ju:] *n* (*tree*) тис
yield [ji:ld] *n* (*Agr*) урожа́й *m* ▷ *vt* (*surrender*) сдава́ть (*perf* сдать); (*produce*) приноси́ть (*perf* принести́) ▷ *vi* (*surrender*) отступа́ть (*perf* отступи́ть); (*US*: *Aut*) уступа́ть (*perf* уступи́ть) доро́гу
yog(h)ourt ['jəugət] *n* йо́гурт
yog(h)urt ['jəugət] *n* = **yog(h)ourt**
yolk [jəuk] *n* желто́к

 **KEYWORD**

you [ju:] *pron* **1** (*subject*: *familiar*) ты; (: *polite*) Вы; (: *2nd person pl*) вы; **you English are very polite** вы, англича́не, о́чень ве́жливы; **you and I will stay here** мы с тобо́й/Ва́ми оста́немся здесь
2 (*direct*: *familiar*) тебя́; (: *polite*) Вас; (: *2nd person pl*) вас; **I love you** я тебя́/Вас люблю
3 (*indirect*: *familiar*) тебе́; (: *polite*) Вам; (: *2nd person pl*) вам; **I'll give you a present** я тебе́/Вам что́-нибудь подарю
4 (*after prep*: +*gen*: *familiar*) тебя́;

(: *polite*) Вас; (: *2nd person pl*) вас; (: *+dat*: *familiar*) тебé; (: *polite*) Вам; (: *2nd person pl*) вам; (: *+instr*: *familiar*) тобóй; (: *polite*) Вáми; (: *2nd person pl*) вáми; (: *+prp*: *familiar*) тебé; (: *polite*) Вас; (: *2nd person pl*) вас; **they've been talking about you** они́ говори́ли о тебé/Вас
5 (*after prep*: *referring to subject of sentence*: *+gen*) себя́; (: *+dat*, *+prp*) себé; (: *+instr*) собóй; **will you take the children with you?** Вы возьмёте детéй с собóй?; **she's younger than you** онá молóже тебя́/Вас
6 (*impersonal*: *one*): **you never know what can happen** никогдá не знáешь, что мóжет случи́ться; **you can't do that!** так нельзя́!; **fresh air does you good** свéжий вóздух полéзен для здорóвья

you'd [ju:d] = **you had**; **you would**
you'll [ju:l] = **you shall**; **you will**
young [jʌŋ] *adj* молодóй; (*child*) мáленький ▷ *npl* (*of animal*) молодня́к *msg*; **the young** (*people*) молодёжь *f*; **youngster** *n* ребёнок
your [jɔːʳ] *adj* (*familiar*) твой; (*polite*) Ваш; (*2nd person pl*) ваш; *see also* **my**
you're [juəʳ] = **you are**
yours [jɔːz] *pron* (*familiar*) твой; (*polite*) Ваш; (*2nd person pl*) ваш; (*referring to subject of sentence*) свой; **is this yours?** э́то твоё/Вáше?; **yours sincerely, yours faithfully** и́скренне Ваш; *see also* **mine**[1]
yourself [jɔːˈsɛlf] *pron* (*reflexive*) себя́; (*after prep*: *+gen*) себя́; (: *+dat*, *+prp*) себé; (: *+instr*) собóй; (*emphatic*) сам (*f* самá, *pl* сáми) (*alone*) сам, оди́н; **(all) by yourself** ты сам *or* оди́н; **you yourself told me** Вы сáми сказáли мне; *see also* **myself**
yourselves [jɔːˈsɛlvz] *pl pron* (*reflexive*) себя́; (*after prep*: *+gen*) себя́; (: *+dat*, *+prp*) себé; (: *+instr*) собóй; (*emphatic*) сáми; (*alone*) сáми, одни́; **(all) by yourselves** сáми, одни́; **talk amongst yourselves for a moment** поговори́те мéжду собóй покá; *see also* **myself**
youth [ju:θ] *n* (*young days*) ю́ность *f*, мóлодость *f*; (*young people*) молодёжь *f*; (*young man*) ю́ноша *m*; **youthful** *adj* ю́ношеский; (*person*, *looks*) ю́ный
you've [ju:v] = **you have**

Z

zeal [zi:l] *n* рвéние
zebra ['zi:brə] *n* зéбра; **zebra crossing** *n* (*Brit*) зéбра, пешехóдный перехóд
zero ['zɪərəu] *n* ноль *m*, нуль *m*
zest [zɛst] *n* (*for life*) жáжда; (*of orange*) цéдра
zigzag ['zɪgzæg] *n* зигзáг
zinc [zɪŋk] *n* цинк
zip [zɪp] *n* (*also* **zip fastener**) мóлния ▷ *vt* (*also* **zip up**) застёгивать (*perf* застегнýть) на мóлнию; **zipper** *n* (*US*) = **zip**
zodiac ['zəudɪæk] *n* зодиáк
zone [zəun] *n* зóна
zoo [zu:] *n* зоопáрк
zoology [zu:'ɔlədʒɪ] *n* зоолóгия
zoom [zu:m] *vi*: **to zoom past** мелькáть (*perf* промелькнýть) мíмо; **zoom lens** *n* объектíв с перемéнным фóкусным расстоя́нием

Glossary of General Business Terms

account *n* счёт
account number *n* но́мер счёта
accounting *n* бухга́лтерский учёт
accounting period *n* бюдже́тный год
accounts payable *npl* счета́, подлежа́щие упла́те
accounts receivable *npl* ожида́емые поступле́ния
acid-test ratio *n* отноше́ние теку́щих акти́вов к теку́щим пасси́вам
acquisition *n* приобрете́ние
active partner *n* акти́вный партнёр
advertising *n* рекла́ма
advertising agency *n* рекла́мное аге́нтство
affiliate *n* аффили́рованное ли́цо
after-tax *adj* по́сле упла́ты нало́гов
aftermarket *n* внебиржево́й ры́нок це́нных бума́г
after-sales service *n* гаранти́йное обслу́живание
AGM *n* ежего́дное о́бщее собра́ние
agribusiness *n* агроби́знес, сельскохозя́йственный би́знес
amortization *n* амортиза́ция
annual general meeting = **AGM**
annual percentage rate *n* годова́я проце́нтная ста́вка
annual report *n* годово́й отчёт
annuity *n* ежего́дная ре́нта
antitrust law *n* антитре́стовский зако́н
arbitration *n* арбитра́ж
arrears *npl* задо́лженность
asking price *n* запра́шиваемая цена́
assets *npl* акти́вы
asset-stripping *n* распрода́жа непри́быльных акти́вов
audit *n* ауди́т
audited statement *n* одо́бренный ауди́тором отчёт
auditor *n* ауди́тор
authorized capital *n* уставно́й капита́л

bad debt *n* спи́санный долг (по несостоя́тельности)
balance due *n* су́мма к упла́те
balance of trade *n* торго́вый бала́нс
balance sheet *n* сво́дный бала́нс, бала́нсовая ве́домость
bank draft, banker's draft *n* ба́нковская тра́тта
bank giro *n* креди́тный перево́д (жи́ро)
bankrupt *adj* обанкро́тившийся
bankruptcy *n* банкро́тство
bargaining unit *n* си́льный аргуме́нт
basic rate *n* ба́зисный курс, тари́фная ста́вка
basis point *n* ба́зисный пункт
basket of currencies *n* валю́тная корзи́на
bear market *n* ры́нок "медве́дей"
benchmark *n* ориенти́р
bid price *n* цена́ покупа́теля
bidder *n* покупа́тель
bill of exchange *n* переводно́й ве́ксель
bill of lading *n* коноса́мент
bill of sale *n* ку́пчая
black market *n* чёрный ры́нок
bond *n* облига́ция
bonded warehouse *n* тамо́женный склад
boom-bust cycle *n* цикл, характеризи́рующийся подъёмом и спа́дом
borrower *n* заёмщик
borrowing capacity *n* заёмная спосо́бность
borrowing requirement *n* потре́бности в за́ймах
brand *n* (торго́вая) ма́рка
brand awareness *n* зна́ние торго́вой ма́рки
brand image *n* и́мидж торго́вой ма́рки
brand leader *n* веду́щая ма́рка
brand name *n* торго́вая ма́рка, фи́рменная ма́рка
break-even point *n* то́чка "при свои́х", то́чка самоокупа́емости
bridge loan, bridging loan *n*

промежу́точный креди́т
brokerage *n* бро́керская коми́ссия
budget *n* бюдже́т
budget deficit *n* дефици́т бюдже́та
budget surplus бюдже́тный избы́ток
building society *n* ипоте́чный банк, строи́тельное о́бщество
bull market *n* ры́нок "быко́в"
business *n* предприя́тие, фи́рма
business card *n* визи́тная ка́рточка
business class *n* би́знес-класс
business man *n* бизнесме́н, предпринима́тель
business plan *n* би́знес-план
business woman *n* бизнесме́нка, делова́я же́нщина
buyer's market *n* ры́нок покупа́теля
by-laws *npl* вну́тренние пра́вила де́ятельности корпора́ции
by-product *n* побо́чный проду́кт

calendar year *n* календа́рный год
capital *n* капита́л
capital account *n* бала́нс движе́ния капита́лов
capital assets *npl* основно́й капита́л
capital expenditure *n* расхо́ды на приобрете́ние основно́го капита́ла
capital gains tax *n* нало́г на реализо́ванный приро́ст капита́ла
capital goods *npl* капита́льные това́ры
capital investment *n* капиталовложе́ние
capitalization *n* капитализа́ция
cartel *n* карте́ль
cash account *n* нали́чный счёт
cash cow *n* би́знес, даю́щий прито́к нали́чных де́нег
cash discount *n* ски́дка с цены́ при поку́пке за нали́чные
cash on delivery *n* нало́женный платёж
CEO *n* гла́вный исполни́тельный ди́ректор
certificate of origin *n* сертифика́т происхожде́ния това́ра
certified public accountant *n* диплом́ированный бухга́лтер
chamber of commerce *n* торго́вая пала́та
charge account *n* креди́т по откры́тому счёту
clearing account *n* кли́ринговый счёт
clearing bank *n* кли́ринговый банк
COD *n* нало́женный платёж
collateral *n* фина́нсовое поручи́тельство, гара́нтия
collective bargaining *n* коллекти́вные перегово́ры
command economy *n* администрати́вно-кома́ндная эконо́мика
commercial bank *n* комме́рческий банк
commercial loan *n* краткосро́чная ссу́да
commission *n* комиссио́нное вознагражде́ние, коми́ ссия
commodities *npl* това́ры
commodity market *n* това́рный ры́нок
common stock *n* обыкнове́нная а́кция
conference call *n* конфере́нц-связь
conference room *n* конфере́нц-за́л
consortium *n* консо́рциум
consumer *n* потреби́тель
consumer credit *n* потреби́тельский креди́т
consumer durables *npl* долгосро́чные потреби́тельские това́ры
consumer goods *npl* потреби́тельские това́ры
consumer price index *n* = **CPI**
contract *n* контра́кт
copyright *n* а́вторское пра́во, копира́йт
cooperative *n* кооперати́в
corporate identity *n* корпорати́вное созна́ние
corporate image *n* корпорати́вный и́мидж
corporation *n* корпора́ция
cost of living *n* сто́имость жи́зни
cost, insurance and freight *n* сто́имость, страхова́ние и фрахт
cost-benefit analysis *n* ана́лиз изде́ржек и при́былей
cottage industry *n* куста́рная промы́шленность
counteroffer *n* встре́чное

предложе́ние
cover letter, covering letter *n* сопроводи́тельное письмо́
CPI *n* и́ндекс потреби́тельских цен
credit *n* креди́т
credit card *n* креди́тная ка́рточка
credit limit *n* креди́тный лими́т
credit note *n* креди́тный биле́т
credit rating *n* показа́тель кредитоспосо́бности
credit risk *n* креди́тный риск
credit union *n* креди́тный сою́з
creditor *n* кредито́р
crisis management *n* разреше́ние кри́зиса
currency unit *n* валю́тная едини́ца
current account *n* теку́щий счёт
customs clearance *n* тамо́женная очи́стка
customs duty *n* тамо́женная по́шлина

data capture *n* сбор информа́ции
data entry *n* ввод информа́ции
data processing *n* обрабо́тка информа́ции
daybook *n* журна́л, дневни́к
debit card *n* де́бетовая ка́рточка
debt *n* долг
debtor *n* должни́к
deflation *n* дефля́ция
deposit account *n* депози́тный счёт
depreciation *n* (*of assets*) сниже́ние сто́имости акти́вов (*of currency*) девальва́ция
derivatives market *n* ры́нок деривати́вов
direct debit *n* прямо́е дебетова́ние
discount *n* ски́дка
distribution *n* распределе́ние
distributor *n* дистрибью́тор
down payment *n* взнос нали́чных де́нег

early retirement *n* ра́нний ухо́д на пе́нсию
earned income *n* зарабо́танный дохо́д
earnings *npl* за́работок
e-business *n* би́знес уерез Интерне́ту
ECB *n* Европе́йский центра́льный банк
e-commerce *n* би́знес по интерне́ту
Economic and Monetary Union *n* = **EMU**
economies of scale *npl* сниже́ние сто́имости за счёт увеличе́ния объёма произво́дства
electronic funds transfer *n* систе́ма электро́нных платеже́й
EMS *n* ЕВС
EMU *n* Экономи́ческий и валю́тный сою́з
end product *n* коне́чный проду́кт
end user *n* коне́чный по́льзователь
enterprise *n* предприя́тие
entrepreneur *n* предпринима́тель
equities market *n* фо́ндовый ры́нок
escape clause *n* пункт догово́ра, освобожда́ющий от отве́тственности
escrow account *n* контра́кт, депони́рованный у тре́тьего лица́
e-tailer *n* интерне́т-продаве́ц
e-tailing *n* интерне́т-прода́жа
Eurozone *n* еврозо́на
European Central Bank *n* = **ECB**
European Monetary System *n* = **EMS**
exchange rate *n* валю́тный курс
excise tax *n* акци́з
expense account *n* счёт подотчётных сумм
export duty *n* э́кспортная по́шлина
export licence *n* э́кспортная лице́нзия

feasibility study *n* те́хнико-экономи́ческое обоснова́ние, ТЭО
finance company *n* фина́нсовая компа́ния
financial advisor *n* фина́нсовый консульта́нт
financial services *npl* фина́нсовые услу́ги
financial statement *n* фина́нсовый отчёт
financial year *n* (отчётно-)фина́нсовый год
fiscal policy *n* бюдже́тная и нало́говая поли́тика
fiscal year *n* фина́нсовый год
fixed assets *npl* основно́й капита́л

flat rate *n* единообра́зная ста́вка
floating capital *n* оборо́тный капита́л
floating currency *n* пла́вающая валю́та
foreign exchange *n* иностра́нная валю́та
foreign trade *n* вне́шняя торго́вля
forex *n* иностра́нная валю́та
franchise agreement *n* франши́зный догово́р
freehold *n* по́лное пра́во на владе́ние
fringe benefits *npl* дополни́тельные льго́ты

GDP *n* ВВП , вало́вый вну́тренний проду́кт
global economy *n* глоба́льная эконо́мика
globalization *n* глобализа́ция
GNP *n* ВНП, вало́вый национа́льный проду́кт
going concern *n* де́йствующее предприя́тие
goods on consignment *npl* па́ртия това́ров к отпра́вке
goodwill *n* до́брая во́ля
grievance procedure *n* поря́док рассмотре́ния жа́лоб
gross domestic product *n* = **GDP**
gross profit *n* о́бщая при́быль
gross national product *n* = **GNP**
Group of Eight *n* Больша́я Восьмёрка
guaranteed loan *n* гаранти́рованный заём

hard currency *n* твёрдая валю́та
headhunting *n* подбо́р высококвалифици́рованных ка́дров
hedge fund *n* хе́джевый фонд
hidden reserves *npl* скры́тые резе́рвы
holding company *n* хо́лдинговая компа́ния
hostile takeover bid *n* поглоще́ние компа́нии путём ску́пки её а́кций на ры́нке
HR *n* отде́л ка́дров

import duty *n* и́мпортная тамо́женная по́шлина
import licence *n* и́мпортная лице́нзия
income *n* дохо́д
income tax *n* подохо́дный нало́г
indemnity *n* гара́нтия возмеще́ния убы́тка
indexation *n* индекса́ция
industrial action *n* забасто́вка
industrial espionage *n* промы́шленный шпиона́ж
inflation *n* инфля́ция
information technology *n* информацио́нная техноло́гия
insider dealing, insider trading *n* незако́нные опера́ции с це́нными бума́гами ли́цами, располага́ющими конфиденциа́льной информа́цией
insolvency *n* неплатежеспосо́бность
insurance *n* страхова́ние
insurance company *n* страхова́я компа́ния
insurance policy *n* страхово́й по́лис
intangible assets *npl* "неосяза́емые" акти́вы
interest payment *n* опла́та проце́нтов
interest-free loan *n* беспроце́нтный займ
interest rate *n* проце́нтная ста́вка
Internet business *n* интерне́т-би́знес
Internet Service Provider *n* = **ISP**
investment *n* инвести́рование
investment income *n* дохо́д от инвести́ций
invoice *n* счёт-факту́ра
ISP *n* прова́йдер сетевы́х услу́г
issue price *n* цена́ эми́ссии

job description *n* описа́ние служе́бных обя́занностей
job sharing *n* разделе́ние рабо́чего ме́ста на двои́х или бо́лее сотру́дников
job title *n* наименова́ние служе́бного положе́ния
joint ownership *n* совме́стное владе́ние
joint stock company *n* акционе́рная компа́ния

joint venture *n* совме́стное предприя́тие
junk bond *n* бро́совая облига́ция

key account *n* ключево́й клие́нт

labour market *n* ры́нок рабо́чей си́лы
labour relations *npl* трудовы́е отноше́ния
lead time *n* вре́мя реализа́ции зака́за
leaseback *n* лиз-бэ́к
leasehold *n* арендо́ванная со́бственность
legal fees *npl* суде́бные изде́ржки
legal tender *n* зако́нное сре́дство платежа́
lender *n* кредито́р, заимода́вец
lending rate *n* ссу́дный проце́нт
letter of credit *n* аккредити́в
letter of intent *n* письмо́ о наме́рении соверши́ть сде́лку
leveraged buyout *n* поку́пка контро́льного паке́та а́кций
liabilities *npl* обяза́тельства
limited liability company *n* компа́ния с ограни́ченной отве́тственностью
limited partnership *n* ограни́ченное това́рищество
liquid assets *npl* ликви́дные акти́вы
liquidation *n* ликвида́ция
liquidator *n* ликвида́тор
liquidity ratio *n* коэффицие́нт ликви́дных акти́вов
listed company *n* официа́льно зарегистри́рованная компа́ния
list price *n* катало́жная цена́
loss leader *n* това́р, продава́емый в убы́ток для привлече́ния покупа́телей
lump sum *n* пауша́льная су́мма

management buyout *n* = **MBO**
managing director *n* = **MD**
man management *n* руково́дство ка́драми
manpower *n* рабо́чая си́ла
manufactured goods *npl* произведённые това́ры
manufacturing industry *n* произво́дственная сфе́ра
man-year *n* челове́ко-год
markdown *n* сниже́ние цены́
market *n* ры́нок
market economy *n* ры́ночная эконо́мика
market leader *n* веду́щий игро́к на ры́нке
market research *n* ана́лиз ры́нка
market share *n* до́ля на ры́нке *or* уде́льный вес в оборо́те ры́нка
marketing *n* ма́ркетинг
marketing strategy *n* ма́ркетинговая страте́гия
mark-up *n* надба́вка, маржа́
mass market *n* ма́ссовый спрос
mass production *n* ма́ссовое произво́дство
MBO *n* вы́куп контро́льного паке́та а́кций компа́нии её управля́ющими
MD *n* дире́ктор-распоряди́тель
merger *n* слия́ние
middleman *n* посре́дник
middle management *n* сре́днее звено́ управле́ния
mission statement *n* изло́жение це́лей
money market *n* де́нежный ры́нок
monopoly *n* монопо́лия
mortgage *n* ипоте́чный креди́т
mortgage lender *n* ипоте́чная компа́ния
mutual fund *n* паево́й фонд

natural wastage *n* есте́ственная у́быль
net income *n* чи́стый дохо́д
net profit *n* чи́стая при́быль
nominal interest rate *n* номина́льная проце́нтная ста́вка
non-cash payment *n* безнали́чная опла́та
non-profit-making organization *n* некомме́рческая организа́ция

offer price *n* цена́ продавца́
offshore *n* оффшорная зона, оффшора
offshore bank *n* оффшо́рный банк
online banking *n* веде́ние ба́нковских дел через Интерне́т
online business *n* интерне́т-би́знес

on-the-job training *n* обучéние по мéсту рабóты (*без отрыва от производства*)
open economy *n* открытая эконóмика
open market *n* открытый рынок
operating costs *npl* операциóнные издéржки
operating profit *n* операциóнная прибыль
order book *n* книга закáзов
order form *n* бланк закáза
ordinary share *n* обыкновéнная áкция
outgoings *npl* расхóды
outsourcing *n* закýпка на сторонé
outstanding debt *n* неуплáченный долг
overcapacity *n* изли́шний потенциáл
overdraft *n* перерасхóд, овердрáфт
overhead(s) *n(pl)* накладныe расхóды
overproduction *n* перепроизвóдство
overstaffing *n* изли́шек кáдров
own brand, own label *n* товáр, несýщий торгóвую мáрку самогó магази́на

paper profit *n* бумáжная при́быль, при́быль на бумáге
par value *n* номинáльная стóимость
parent company *n* матери́нская компáния
partnership *n* партнёрство
patent *n* патéнт
payment in kind *n* оплáта натýрой
penny stock(s) *n(pl)* áкция ценóй мéньше дóллара
pension fund *n* пенсиóнный фонд
pension plan, pension scheme *n* пенсиóнный план
people management *n* руковóдство кáдрами
per capita *adj* на дýшу (населéния)
per diem *adj* ежеднéвно, кáждый день
performance-related pay *n* оплáта по результáтам трудá
personal identification number *n* = **PIN**
petty cash *n* небольшáя нали́чность
piece rate *n* сдéльный тари́ф
piecework *n* сдéльная рабóта
PIN *n* ПИН
planned economy *n* плáновая эконóмика
point of sale *n* торгóвая тóчка
policy statement *n* изложéние поли́тики
PR *n* свя́зи с общéственностью
preference shares *npl* привилеги́рованная áкция
preferred stock *n* привилеги́рованная áкция
price fixing *n* фикси́рование цен
price freeze *n* заморáживание цен
price war *n* войнá цен
price-earnings ratio *n* отношéние ры́ночной цены́ áкции к её чи́стой при́были
private company *n* чáстная компáния
private investor *n* чáстный инвéстор
private sector *n* чáстный сéктор
privatization *n* приватизáция
product development *n* разрабóтка продýкта/товáра
product launch *n* зáпуск продýкта/товáра
product line *n* ли́ния товáров
product placement *n* позициони́рование продýкта/товáра
profit *n* при́быль
profit margin *n* размéр при́были
profit sharing *n* учáстие в при́былях
profit-making *adj* при́быльный
profitability *n* при́быльность
proforma invoice *adj* счёт-профóрма
promissory note *n* простóй вéксель
public relations *npl* = **PR**
public sector *n* общéственный сéктор
purchase order *n* закáз на товáры
purchasing power *n* покупáтельная спосóбность
pyramid selling *n* пирамидáльная продáжа

quality control *n* контрóль кáчества
quota *n* квóта

rebranding *n* переименовáние торгóвой мáрки

recommended retail price *n* = **RRP**
redundancy *n* увольне́ние
redundancy package *n* вы́плата при увольне́нии
relaunch *n* повто́рный за́пуск проду́кта/това́ра
relocation expenses *npl* расхо́ды по перее́зду
remuneration *n* вознагражде́ние
replacement value *n* сто́имость замеще́ния
research and development *n* нау́чно-иссле́довательские и о́пытно-констру́кторские рабо́ты
reserve price *n* резе́рвная цена́
retail *n* ро́зничная торго́вля, ро́зница
retail price index *n* и́ндекс ро́зничных цен
retailer *n* ро́зничный торго́вец
retirement plan *n* пенсио́нный план
return (on investment) *n* дохо́д (от инвести́ции)
risk management *n* управле́ние ри́ском
royalty *n* гонора́р
RRP *n* рекоменду́емая ро́зничная цена́

salary *n* окла́д, за́работная пла́та
salary scale *n* шкала́ окла́дов
sales *npl* прода́жи
sales force *n* сбы́тчики
sales tax *n* нало́г с прода́ж
savings account *n* сберега́тельный счёт
savings bank *n* сберега́тельный банк
second mortgage *n* дополни́тельный ипоте́чный креди́т
secondary market *n* втори́чный ры́нок
securities *npl* це́нные облига́ции
self-financing *adj* самофинанси́руемый
seller's market *n* ры́нок продавца́
selling point *n* наибо́лее привлека́тельный аспе́кт това́ра
selling price *n* цена́ реализации
service charge *n* ба́нковская коми́ссия
service industry *n* индустри́я обслу́живания
settlement of accounts *n* погаше́ние счето́в
severance pay *n* вы́плата при увольне́нии
share capital *n* акционе́рный капита́л
share index *n* фо́ндовый и́ндекс
share option *n* предоставле́ние слу́жащим компа́нии пра́ва на поку́пку а́кции да́нной компа́нии
shell company *n* зарегистри́рованная компа́ния с небольши́ми акти́вами
sick pay *n* больни́чные
silent partner *n* пасси́вный член това́рищества
single currency *n* еди́ная валю́та
Single Market *n* о́бщий ры́нок
sinking fund *n* фонд погаше́ния
sleeping partner *n* пасси́вный член това́рищества
soft currency *n* сла́бая валю́та
spot price *n* нали́чная цена́
spreadsheet *n* электро́нная табли́ца
stagflation *n* стагфля́ция
stakeholder pension *n* пе́нсия, получа́емая при уча́стии в капита́ле акционе́рной компа́нии
stamp duty *n* ге́рбовый сбор
standing order *n* постоя́нное поруче́ние
start-up capital *n* нача́льный капита́л
start-up cost *n* сто́имость первонача́льного вложе́ния
statement of account *n* вы́писка с ба́нковского счёта
state-owned enterprise *n* госуда́рственное предприя́тие
stock certificate *n* сертифика́т депони́рования а́кции
stock company *n* акционе́рная компа́ния
stock exchange *n* фо́ндовая би́ржа
stock market *n* фо́ндовый ры́нок
stock market index *n* и́ндекс фо́ндового ры́нка
stock option *n* фо́ндовый опцио́н
subcontractor *n* субподря́дчик
subcontracting *n* субконтра́кт

sublease *n* субаре́нда
subletting *n* субаре́нда
subsidiary *n* доче́рняя компа́ния
subsidy *n* субси́дия
sunrise industry *n* но́вая о́трасль эконо́мики
superannuation fund *n* пенсио́нный фонд (предприя́тия)
supplier *n* поставщи́к
supply and demand *n* спрос и предложе́ние
suspense account *n* промежу́точный счёт

takeover *n* поглоще́ние
takeover bid *n* предложе́ние поглоще́ния
tangible assets, tangibles *npl* реа́льные акти́вы
tariff *n* тари́ф
tariff barrier *n* тари́фный барье́р
tax *n* нало́г
taxable income *n* дохо́д, подлежа́щий налогообложе́нию
taxation *n* налогообложе́ние
tax bracket *n* ме́сто в нало́говой шкале́
tax evasion *n* уклоне́ние от упла́ты нало́гов
tax incentive *n* нало́говое стимули́рование
tax loophole *n* нало́говая лазе́йка
tax shelter *n* нало́говая защи́та
technology transfer *n* переда́ча техноло́гии
telecommuting *n* рабо́та на дому́ через компью́терную связь
teleconferencing *n* телеконфере́нция
telemarketing *n* телефо́нный ма́ркетинг
teleworking *n* рабо́та на дому́ через компью́терную связь
tender *n* те́ндер
terms and conditions *npl* те́рмины и усло́вия
time management *n* рациона́льное испо́льзование вре́мени
trade *n* торго́вля
trade agreement *n* торго́вое соглаше́ние
trade discount *n* торго́вая ски́дка
trade relations *npl* торго́вые отноше́ния
trade secret *n* торго́вый секре́т
trade surplus *n* акти́вное са́льдо
trade war *n* торго́вая война́
trademark *n* торго́вый знак
trading partner *n* торго́вый партнёр
treasury bill *n* казначе́йский ве́ксель
treasury bond *n* казначе́йская облига́ция
turnover *n* оборо́т

underinvestment *n* недоинвести́рование
underwriter *n* гара́нт (размеще́ния це́нных бума́г)
unique selling point *n* = **USP**
unit cost *n* себесто́имость едини́цы проду́кции
unit price *n* сто́имость това́рной едини́цы
unit sales *npl* объём прода́ж едини́цы проду́кции
unsecured loan *n* необеспе́ченный заём
upset price *n* резерви́рованная цена́, ни́зшая ста́ртовая цена́
USP *n* УТП, уника́льное торго́вое предложе́ние
usury *n* ростовщи́чество

value-added tax *n* = **VAT**
VAT *n* НДС, Нало́г на доба́вленную сто́имость
venture capital *n* ри́сковый капита́л
venture capitalist *n* ри́сковый капитали́ст
videoconferencing *n* телеконфере́нция

wage freeze *n* замора́живание зарпла́ты
waybill *n* коноса́мент
wholesale price *n* о́птовая цена́
wholesale price index *n* и́ндекс о́птовых цен
wholesaler *n* оптови́к
wholly-owned subsidiary *n* доче́рняя компа́ния, находя́щаяся в индивидуа́льном владе́нии
windfall profit *n* неожи́данный дохо́д

withholding tax *n* налогообложе́ние путём вы́четов
working capital *n* рабо́чий капита́л
World Bank *n* Мирово́й банк, Всеми́рный банк
World Trade Organization *n* = **WTO**
WTO *n* ВТО (Всеми́рная торго́вая организа́ция)

zero growth *n* нулево́й рост

Деловая терминология

ава́нс *м* advance
ави́зо *ср* advice, notification
а́вторское пра́во *ср* copyright
аву́ары *мн* assets
администрати́вно-кома́ндная эконо́мика *ж* command economy
аккредити́в *м* letter of credit
акти́вное са́льдо *ср* surplus account, trade surplus
акти́вы *мн* assets
акци́з *м* excise tax
акционе́рная компа́ния *ж* joint stock company, stock company
акционе́рный капита́л *м* share capital
амортиза́ция ж amortization
ана́лиз ры́нка *м* market research
арбитра́ж *м* arbitration
арендо́ванная со́бственность *ж* leasehold
ассортиме́нт това́ров *м* product range
ауди́т *м* audit
ауди́тор *м* auditor
аукцио́н *м* auction

ба́зисный курс *м* basic rate
бала́нс *м* balance
бала́нс нали́чности *м* cash balance
бала́нсовая ве́домость *ж* balance sheet
ба́нковская коми́ссия *ж* service charge
ба́нковская тра́тта *ж* bank draft, banker's draft
банкома́т *м* ATM
банкома́тная ка́рточка *ж* ATM card
ба́ртер *м* barter
безнали́чная опла́та *ж* non-cash payment
беспроце́нтный займ *м* interest-free loan
би́знес в Сети́ *м* Internet business
бизнесме́н *м* business man
бизнесме́нка *ж* business woman
би́знес-класс *м* business class
би́знес-план *м* business plan
би́ржа *ж* exchange
бланк зака́за *м* order form
больни́чные *мн* sick pay
Больша́я Восьмёрка *ж* Group of Eight
бро́керская коми́ссия *ж* brokerage
бро́совая облига́ция *ж* junk bond
бухга́лтерский учёт *м* accounting
бюдже́т *м* budget
бюдже́тная и нало́говая поли́тика *ж* fiscal policy
бюдже́тный избы́ток *м* budget surplus

валово́й вну́тренний проду́кт *м* gross domestic product
валово́й национа́льный проду́кт *м* gross national product
валю́тная едини́ца *ж* currency unit
валю́тная корзи́на *ж* basket of currencies
валю́тный курс *м* exchange rate
ввод информа́ции *м* data entry
ВВП *м* GDP
визи́тная ка́рточка *ж* business card
вне́шняя торго́вля *ж* foreign trade
ВНП *м* GNP
Всеми́рная торго́вая организа́ция *ж* World Trade Organization
Всеми́рный банк *м* World Bank
встре́чное предложе́ние *ср* counteroffer
ВТО *ж* WTO
втори́чный ры́нок *м* secondary market
вы́писка с ба́нковского счёта *ж* statement of account

гара́нт *м* guarantor
гаранти́йный срок *м* guarantee period
гаранти́йное обслу́живание *ср* after sales service
гара́нтия *ж* guarantee
гара́нтия возмеще́ния убы́тка *ж* indemnity
ГАТТ, Генера́льное соглаше́ние по

тари́фам и торго́вле *ср* GATT
ге́рбовый сбор *м* stamp duty
гла́вный исполни́тельный дире́ктор *м* chief executive, CEO
гла́вный, центра́льный о́фис *м* headquarters
глобализа́ция *ж* globalization
годова́я проце́нтная ста́вка *ж* annual percentage rate
годово́й отчёт *м* annual report
гонора́р *м* royalty
госуда́рственное предприя́тие *ср* state-owned enterprise

дебето́вая за́пись *ж* debit entry
дебето́вая ка́рточка *ж* debit card
девальва́ция *ж* depreciation (*of currency*)
де́йствующее предприя́тие *ср* going concern
делова́я же́нщина *ж* business woman
де́нежный ры́нок *м* money market
депози́тный счёт *м* deposit account
дефици́т бюдже́та *м* budget deficit
дефля́ция *ж* deflation
дефо́лт *м* default
дивиде́нд *м* dividend
дире́ктор-распоряди́тель *м* managing director, MD
диско́нт *м* discount
диско́нтная ка́рта *ж* discount card
дистрибью́тор *м* distributor
долг *м* debt
долгосро́чный контра́кт *м* long-term contract
должни́к *м* debtor
дохо́д *м* income
дохо́д от инвести́ций *м* investment income
доче́рняя компа́ния *ж* subsidiary

Европе́йский валю́тный сою́з *м* European Monetary System, EMD
Европе́йский центра́льный банк *м* European Central Bank, ECB
ЕВС *м* EMS
еди́ная валю́та *ж* single currency
единообра́зная ста́вка *ж* flat rate
ежего́дное о́бщее собра́ние *ср* annual general meeting

жирорасчёт *м* giro
жироче́к *м* giro (cheque)

забасто́вка *ж* industrial action
задо́лженность *ж* arrears
заёмщик *м* borrower, mortgagor
займ *м* loan
займ с фикси́рованной ста́вкой *м* fixed-rate loan
зака́з на това́ры *м* purchase order
зако́нное сре́дство платежа́ *ср* legal tender
замора́живание цен *ср* price freeze
за́пись в прихо́дной ча́сти *ж* credit entry
запра́шиваемая цена́ *ж* asking price
за́пуск това́ра *м* product launch
зарабо́танный дохо́д *м* earned income
за́работная пла́та *ж* salary
за́работок *м* earnings
застро́йщик *м* developer (*of property*)
защи́та потреби́теля *ж* consumer protection
зо́на свобо́дного предпринима́тельства *ж* free enterprise zone

избежа́ние нало́гов *ср* tax avoidance
избы́ток *м* surplus
и́мпортная лице́нзия *ж* import licence
и́мпортная тамо́женная по́шлина *ж* import duty
инвести́рование *ср* investment
и́ндекс о́птовых цен *м* wholesale price index
и́ндекс потреби́тельских цен *м* consumer price index, CPI
и́ндекс ро́зничных цен *м* retail price index
и́ндекс фо́ндового ры́нка *м* stock market index
индекса́ция *ж* indexation
индосса́мент *м* endorsement
индустри́я обслу́живания *ж* service industry
иностра́нная валю́та *ж* foreign exchange, forex
интеллектуа́льная со́бственность

ж intellectual property
интерне́т-би́знес *м* Internet business
интерне́т-шо́пинг *м* Internet shopping
инфля́ция *ж* inflation
информацио́нная техноло́гия *ж* information technology
ипоте́чная компа́ния *ж* mortgage lender
ипоте́чный банк *м* building society
ипоте́чный креди́т *м* mortgage
ипоте́ка *ж* mortgage

казначе́йская облига́ция *ж* treasury bond
казначе́йский ве́ксель *м* treasury bill
календа́рный год *м* calendar year
капита́л *м* capital
капитализа́ция *ж* capitalization
капиталовложе́ние *ср* capital investment
карте́ль *ж* cartel
катало́жная цена́ *ж* list price
кво́та *ж* quota
клие́нт *м* client
кли́ринговый банк *м* clearing bank
кли́ринговый счёт *м* clearing account
ключево́й клие́нт *м* key account
кни́га зака́зов *м* order book
коллекти́вные перегово́ры *мн* collective bargaining
кома́ндная эконо́мика *ж* command economy
комиссио́нное вознагражде́ние *ср* commission
коми́ссия *ж* commission
комите́нт *м* consigner
комме́рческий банк *м* commercial bank
компа́ния с ограни́ченной отве́тственностью *ж* limited liability company
конве́рсия *ж* conversion
коне́чный по́льзователь *м* end user
коне́чный потреби́тель *м* end consumer
коне́чный проду́кт *м* end product
конса́лтинг *м* consultation
коноса́мент *м* bill of lading, waybill
консо́рциум *м* consortium
контра́кт *м* contract
контра́кт без оговорённого сро́ка де́йствия *м* open-ended contract
кооперати́в *м* cooperative
копира́йт *м* copyright
корпорати́вная организа́ция *ж* corporate body
корпорати́вное созна́ние *ср* corporate identity
корпорати́вный и́мидж *м* corporate image
корпора́ция *ж* corporation
корреспонде́нт *м* correspondent
краткосро́чная ссу́да *ж* commercial loan
креди́т *м* credit
креди́т по откры́тому счёту *м* charge account
креди́тная ка́рточка *ж* credit card
креди́тный биле́т *м* credit note
креди́тный лими́т *м* credit limit
креди́тный перево́д (жи́ро) *м* bank giro
креди́тный риск *м* credit risk
кредито́р *м* creditor, lender
ку́пчая *ж* bill of sale

лиз-бэ́к *м* leaseback
ли́зинг *м* leasing
ликвида́тор *м* liquidator
ликвида́ция *ж* liquidation
ликви́дные акти́вы *мн* liquid assets
ли́ния това́ров *ж* product line
логоти́п *м* logo
лот *м* lot

маржа́ *ж* premium, mark-up
ма́ркетинг *м* marketing
ма́ссовое потребле́ние *ср* mass consumption
ма́ссовое произво́дство *ср* mass production
ма́ссовый спрос *м* mass market
Мирово́й банк *м* World Bank
монопо́лия *ж* monopoly

на ду́шу (населе́ния) *прил* per capita
надба́вка *ж* mark-up
накладны́е расхо́ды *мн* overhead(s)
нали́чная цена́ *ж* spot price

нали́чный счёт *м* cash account
нало́г *м* tax
нало́г на доба́вленную сто́имость *м* value-added tax
нало́г на реализо́ванный приро́ст капита́ла *м* capital gains tax
нало́г с прода́ж *м* sales tax
нало́говая деклара́ция *ж* tax declaration
нало́говая защи́та *ж* tax shelter
нало́говая лазе́йка *ж* tax loophole
нало́говое стимули́рование *ср* tax incentive
нало́говое убе́жище *ср* tax haven
налогообложе́ние *ср* taxation
нало́женный платёж *м* cash on delivery, COD
нау́чно-иссле́довательские и о́пытно-констру́кторские рабо́ты *ср* research and development
нача́льный капита́л *м* start-up capital
НДС *м* VAT
недоинвести́рование *ср* underinvestment
недоста́ча *ж* shortfall
некомме́рческая организа́ция *ж* non-profit-making organization
необеспе́ченный заём *м* unsecured loan
неплатежеспосо́бность *ж* insolvency
неупла́ченный долг *м* outstanding debt
неусто́йка *ж* forfeit
но́вый за́пуск (*проду́кта*) *м* relaunch
но́мер счёта *м* account number
номина́л *м* par value
номина́льная сто́имость *ж* par value

обанкро́титься *сов* to go bankrupt
обеспече́ние креди́та *ср* collateral
облига́ция *ж* bond
оборо́т *м* turnover
оборо́тные докуме́нты *мн* negotiable instruments
оборо́тный капита́л *м* floating capital
обрабо́тка информа́ции *ж* data processing
о́бщая при́быль *ж* gross profit
обще́ственный пра́здник *м* public holiday
обще́ственный се́ктор *м* public sector
о́бщий ры́нок *м* Single Market
обыкнове́нная а́кция *ж* ordinary share
обяза́тельства *мн* liabilities
овердра́фт *м* overdraft
ограни́ченное това́рищество *ср* limited partnership
окла́д *м* salary
операцио́нная при́быль *ж* operating profit
операцио́нные изде́ржки *мн* operating costs
опера́ция *ж* transaction
опла́та в рассро́чку *ж* instalment payment
опла́та нату́рой *ж* payment in kind
опла́та проце́нтов *ж* interest payment
о́птовая цена́ *ж* wholesale price
оптови́к *м* wholesaler
основно́й капита́л *м* capital assets, fixed assets
отгру́зка *ж* shipment
отде́л ка́дров *м* HR, human resources
откры́тая эконо́мика *ж* open economy
откры́тый ры́нок *м* open market
отчётно-финансовый год *м* financial year
официа́льно зарегистри́рованная компа́ния *ж* listed company
оффшорная зо́на = оффшор
оффшор *ж* offshore
оффшо́рный банк *м* offshore bank
оце́нка *ж* appraisal

паево́й фонд *м* mutual fund
па́ртия това́ров к отпра́вке *ж* goods on consignment
партнёрство *ср* partnership
пате́нт *м* patent
пауша́льная су́мма *ж* lump sum
пенсио́нный план *м* pension plan, pension scheme, retirement plan
пенсио́нный фонд *м* pension fund
переводно́й ве́ксель *м* bill of exchange

переговóры *мн* negotiations
передáча технолóгии *ж* technology transfer
переименовáние торгóвой мáрки *ср* rebranding
перепроизвóдство *ср* overproduction
перерасхóд *м* overdraft
персонáльный идентификациóнный нóмер *м* personal identification number
ПИН *м* PIN
плáвающая валюта *ж* floating currency
плáновая эконóмика *ж* planned economy
платёжеспосóбность *ж* creditworthiness
платёжный балáнс *м* balance of payments
побóчный продýкт *м* by-product
погашéние счетóв *ср* settlement of accounts
поглощéние *ср* takeover
подохóдный налóг *м* income tax
подрядчик *м* contractor
покупáтельная способность *ж* purchasing power
порядок рассмотрéния жáлоб *м* grievance procedure
посрéдник *м* middleman
посрéдничество *ср* mediation
поставщик *м* supplier
постановлéния и услóвия *мн* terms and conditions
постоянное поручéние *ср* standing order
поступлéния *мн* proceeds
потребитель *м* consumer
потребительские товáры *мн* consumer goods
потребительский кредит *м* consumer credit
правительственная цéнная бумáга *ж* government security
предварительный счёт-фактýра *м* proforma invoice
предложéние поглощéния *ср* takeover bid
предоплáта *ж* prepayment
предпринимáтель *м* entrepreneur, businessman
предприятие *ср* enterprise, business
прейскурáнт *м* price list
прибыль *ж* profit
прибыльность *ж* profitability
прибыльный *прил* profit-making
приватизáция *ж* privatization
привилегирóванная áкция *ж* preference shares, preferred stock
провáйдер сетевых услýг *м* Internet service provider, ISP
произвóдственная сфéра *ж* manufacturing industry
промежýточный кредит *м* bridge loan, bridging loan
промышленный шпионáж *м* industrial espionage
простóй вéксель *м* promissory note
процéнтная стáвка *ж* interest rate
прямóе дебетовáние *ср* direct debit

рабóтник *м* employee
работодáтель *м* employer
рабóчая сила *ж* labour force, manpower
рабóчее мéсто *ср* workplace
рабóчий капитáл *м* working capital
размéр прибыли *м* profit margin
разрешéние на рабóту *ср* work permit
распределéние *ср* distribution
расхóды *мн* outgoings
реáльные активы *мн* tangible assets, tangibles
резéрвная ценá *ж* reserve price
рекомендýемая рóзничная ценá *ж* recommended retail price, RRP
рéнта *ж* annuity
рентáбельность *ж* cost-effectiveness
рентáбельный *прил* cost-effective
рисковый капитáл *м* venture capital
рóзница *ж* retailing
рóзничная торгóвля *ж* retail
рóзничный торгóвец *м* retailer
ростовщичество *ср* usury
руковóдство кáдрами *ср* man management, people management
рынок *м* market
рынок деривативов *м* derivatives market
рынок недвижимости *м* property market
рынок облигáций *м* bond market

ры́нок покупа́теля *м* buyer's market
ры́нок рабо́чей си́лы *м* labour market
ры́нок "быко́в" *м* bull market
ры́нок "медве́дей" *м* bear market
ры́ночная цена́ *ж* market price
ры́ночная эконо́мика *ж* market economy
рэ́кет *м* racketeering

самофинанси́руемый *прил* self-financing
сберега́тельный банк *м* savings bank
сберега́тельный счёт *м* savings account
сбереже́ния *мн* savings
сбо́рочная ли́ния *ж* assembly line
сво́дный бала́нс *м* balance sheet
свя́зи с обще́ственностью *мн* PR
сде́льная рабо́та *ж* piecework
сде́льный тари́ф *м* piece rate
себесто́имость едини́цы проду́кции *ж* unit cost
сельскохозя́йственный би́знес *м* agribusiness
сертифика́т происхожде́ния това́ра *м* certificate of origin
систе́ма электро́нных платеже́й *ж* electronic funds transfer
ски́дка *ж* discount
сла́бая валю́та *ж* soft currency
слия́ние *ср* merger
сниже́ние сто́имости акти́вов *ср* depreciation (of assets)
совме́стное владе́ние *ср* joint ownership
совме́стное предприя́тие *ср* joint venture
сопроводи́тельное письмо́ *ср* cover letter, covering letter
социа́льная защи́та *ж* social security
со-дире́ктор *м* co-manager
спад *м* recession
спрос и предложе́ние *м* supply and demand
срок го́дности *м* shelf life
ссу́дный проце́нт *м* lending rate
стагфля́ция *ж* stagflation
сто́имость жи́зни *ж* cost of living
сто́имость, страхова́ние и фрахт *ж* cost, insurance and freight
сто́имость това́рной едини́цы *ж* unit price
страхова́ние *ср* insurance
страхова́я компа́ния *ж* insurance company
страхово́й аге́нт *м* insurance agent
страхово́й по́лис *м* insurance policy
строи́тельное о́бщество *ср* building society
субаре́нда *ж* sublease, subletting
субконтра́кт *м* subcontracting
субподря́дчик *м* subcontractor
субси́дия *ж* subsidy
суде́бные изде́ржки *мн* legal fees
су́мма к упла́те *ж* balance due
сумма́рная вы́писка с ба́нковского счёта *ж* summary statement
счёт *м* account
счёт подотчётных сумм *м* expense account
счёт-факту́ра *м* invoice

тамо́женная очи́стка *ж* customs clearance
тамо́женная по́шлина *ж* customs duty
тари́ф *м* tariff
тари́фная ста́вка *ж* basic rate
тари́фный барье́р *м* tariff barrier
твёрдая валю́та *ж* hard currency
теку́щий счёт *м* current account
телеконфере́нция *ж* teleconferencing
телефо́нный ма́ркетинг *м* telemarketing
те́ндер *м* tender
теневая́ эконо́мика *ж* underground economy
те́хника безопа́сности на произво́дстве *ж* occupational health and safety
те́хнико-экономи́ческое обоснова́ние *ср* feasibility study
това́рные запа́сы *мн* inventory
това́рный ры́нок *м* commodity market
торго́вая война́ *ж* trade war
торго́вая ма́рка *ж* brand name
торго́вая пала́та *ж* chamber of commerce
торго́вая ски́дка *ж* trade discount

торгóвая тóчка *ж* point of sale
торгóвая ярмарка *ж* trade show
торгóвля *ж* trade
торгóвое соглашéние *ср* trade agreement
торгóвое эмбáрго *ср* trade embargo
торгóвые отношéния *мн* trade relations
торгóвые сáнкции *мн* trade sanctions
торгóвый балáнс *м* balance of trade
торгóвый знак *м* trademark
торгóвый партнёр *м* trading partner
торгóвый секрéт *м* trade secret
тóчка "при своúх" *ж* break-even point
тóчка самоокупáемости *ж* break-even point
трáтта *ж* draft
трудовы́е отношéния *мн* labour relations

увольнéние *ср* redundancy
удéльный вес в оборóте ры́нка *м* market share
уклонéние от налóгов *ср* tax evasion
уникáльная характерúстика товáра *ж* unique selling point
услóвия трудá *мн* working conditions
уставнóй капитáл *м* authorized capital
учáстие в прúбылях *ср* profit sharing
учáстник переговóров *м* negotiator

ФАС FAS, free alongside ship
финáнсовая компáния *ж* finance company
финáнсовые услýги *мн* financial services
финáнсовый год *м* financial year, fiscal year
финáнсовый консультáнт *м* financial advisor
финáнсовый отчёт *м* financial statement
фúрма *ж* business, firm
фúрменная мáрка *ж* brand name
фúрменное наименовáние *ср* proprietary name

ФОБ FOB, free on board
фóндовая бúржа *ж* stock exchange
фóндовый úндекс *м* share index
фóндовый ры́нок *м* equities market, stock market
ФОР FOR, free on rail
фрáнко *прил* free
франшúзный договóр *м* franchise agreement

хéджевый фонд *м* hedge fund
хóлдинговая компáния *ж* holding company

ценá покупáтеля *ж* bid price
ценá продавцá *ж* offer price
цéнник *м* price tag
цéнные облигáции *мн* securities
цéновый контрóль *ж* price control

чáртер *м* charter
чáстная компáния *ж* private company
чáстный инвéстор *м* private investor
чáстный сéктор *м* private sector
человéко-год *м* man-year
человéко-час *м* man-hour
чёрный ры́нок *м* black market
чúстая прúбыль *ж* net profit
чúстый дохóд *м* net income

шкалá оклáдов *ж* salary scale
штáтное расписáние *ср* payroll

Экономúческий и валю́тный сою́з *м* Economic and Monetary Union, EMU
э́кспортная пóшлина *ж* export duty
э́кспортная лицéнзия *ж* export licence
электрóнная связь для совершéния платежéй *ж* wire transfer (system)
электрóнная таблúца *ж* spreadsheet

ярлы́к *м* price tag

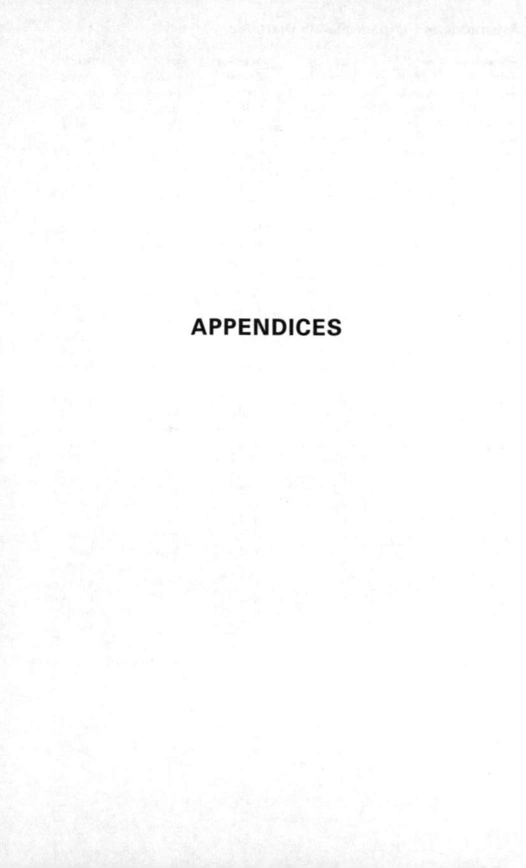

APPENDICES

Английские Неправильные Глаголы

present	pt	pp
arise	arose	arisen
awake	awoke	awoken
be (am, is, are; being)	was, were	been
bear	bore	born(e)
beat	beat	beaten
behold	beheld	beheld
become	became	become
begin	began	begun
bend	bent	bent
beseech	besought	besought
beset	beset	beset
bet	bet, betted	bet, betted
bid	bid, bade	bid, bidden
bind	bound	bound
bite	bit	bitten
bleed	bled	bled
blow	blew	blown
break	broke	broken
breed	bred	bred
bring	brought	brought
build	built	built
burn	burnt, burned	burnt, burned
burst	burst	burst
buy	bought	bought
can	could	(been able)
cast	cast	cast
catch	caught	caught
choose	chose	chosen
cling	clung	clung
come	came	come
cost	cost	cost
creep	crept	crept
cut	cut	cut
deal	dealt	dealt
dig	dug	dug
do (3rd person he/she/it does)	did	done
draw	drew	drawn
dream	dreamed, dreamt	dreamed, dreamt
drink	drank	drunk
drive	drove	driven

present	pt	pp
dwell	dwelt	dwelt
eat	ate	eaten
fall	fell	fallen
feed	fed	fed
feel	felt	felt
fight	fought	fought
find	found	found
flee	fled	fled
fling	flung	flung
fly (flies)	flew	flown
forbid	forbade	forbidden
forecast	forecast	forecast
forget	forgot	forgotten
forgive	forgave	forgiven
forsake	forsook	forsaken
freeze	froze	frozen
get	got	got, (US) gotten
give	gave	given
go (goes)	went	gone
grind	ground	ground
grow	grew	grown
hang	hung, hanged	hung, hanged
have (has; having)	had	had
hear	heard	heard
hide	hid	hidden
hit	hit	hit
hold	held	held
hurt	hurt	hurt
keep	kept	kept
kneel	knelt, kneeled	knelt, kneeled
know	knew	known
lay	laid	laid
lead	led	led
lean	leant, leaned	leant, leaned
leap	leapt, leaped	leapt, leaped
learn	learnt, learned	learnt, learned
leave	left	left
lend	lent	lent
let	let	let
lie (lying)	lay	lain

present	pt	pp
light	lit, lighted	lit, lighted
lose	lost	lost
make	made	made
may	might	—
mean	meant	meant
meet	met	met
mistake	mistook	mistaken
mow	mowed	mown, mowed
must	(had to)	(had to)
pay	paid	paid
put	put	put
quit	quit, quitted	quit, quitted
read	read	read
rid	rid	rid
ride	rode	ridden
ring	rang	rung
rise	rose	risen
run	ran	run
saw	sawed	sawed, sawn
say	said	said
see	saw	seen
seek	sought	sought
sell	sold	sold
send	sent	sent
set	set	set
sew	sewed	sewn
shake	shook	shaken
shed	shed	shed
shine	shone	shone
shoot	shot	shot
show	showed	shown
shrink	shrank	shrunk
shut	shut	shut
sing	sang	sung
sink	sank	sunk
sit	sat	sat
slay	slew	slain
sleep	slept	slept
slide	slid	slid
sling	slung	slung
slit	slit	slit
smell	smelt, smelled	smelt, smelled
sow	sowed	sown, sowed
speak	spoke	spoken
speed	sped, speeded	sped, speeded
spell	spelt, spelled	spelt, spelled
spend	spent	spent
spill	spilt, spilled	spilt, spilled
spin	spun	spun
spit	spat	spat
split	split	split
spoil	spoiled, spoilt	spoiled, spoilt
spread	spread	spread
spring	sprang	sprung
stand	stood	stood
steal	stole	stolen
stick	stuck	stuck
sting	stung	stung
stink	stank	stunk
stride	strode	stridden
strike	struck	struck, stricken
strive	strove	striven
swear	swore	sworn
sweep	swept	swept
swell	swelled	swollen, swelled
swim	swam	swum
swing	swung	swung
take	took	taken
teach	taught	taught
tear	tore	torn
tell	told	told
think	thought	thought
throw	threw	thrown
thrust	thrust	thrust
tread	trod	trodden
wake	woke, waked	woken, waked
wear	wore	worn
weave	wove, weaved	woven, weaved
wed	wedded, wed	wedded, wed
weep	wept	wept
win	won	won
wind	wound	wound
wring	wrung	wrung
write	wrote	written

Tables of Russian Irregular Forms

For all tables, where there are alternatives given under the accusative, these are the animate forms which are identical with the genitive.

Nouns

Table 1 **мать**

	Singular	*Plural*
Nom	мать	ма́тери
Acc	мать	матере́й
Gen	ма́тери	матере́й
Dat	ма́тери	матеря́м
Instr	ма́терью	матеря́ми
Prp	о ма́тери	о матеря́х

Table 2 **дочь**

	Singular	*Plural*
Nom	дочь	до́чери
Acc	дочь	дочере́й
Gen	до́чери	дочере́й
Dat	до́чери	дочеря́м
Instr	до́черью	дочерьми́
Prp	о до́чери	о дочеря́х

Table 3 **путь**

	Singular	*Plural*
Nom	путь	пути́
Acc	путь	пути́
Gen	пути́	путе́й
Dat	пути́	путя́м
Instr	путём	путя́ми
Prp	о пути́	о путя́х

Table 4 **вре́мя**

	Singular	*Plural*
Nom	вре́мя	времена́
Acc	вре́мя	времена́
Gen	вре́мени	времён
Dat	вре́мени	времена́м
Instr	вре́менем	времена́ми
Prp	о вре́мени	о времена́х

(Similarly with nouns like и́мя, пле́мя etc)

Table 5	*m*	*f*	*nt*	*pl*
Nom	чей	чья	чьё	чьи
Acc	чей/чьегó	чью	чьё	чьи/чьих
Gen	чьегó	чьей	чьегó	чьих
Dat	чьемý	чьей	чьемý	чьим
Instr	чьим	чьей	чьим	чьи́ми
Prp	о чьём	о чьей	о чьём	о чьих

(The instrumental form чьей has the alternative чьéю)

Table 6a

Nom	я	ты	он	онá	онó
Acc/Gen	меня́	тебя́	егó	её	егó
Dat	мне	тебé	емý	ей	емý
Instr	мной	тобóй	им	ей	им
Prp	обо мне	о тебé	о нём	о ней	о нём

(The instrumental forms мной, тобóй, ей have alternatives мнóю, тобóю and éю respectively. The reflexive personal pronoun себя́ declines like тебя́)

Table 6b

Nom	мы	вы	они́
Acc/Gen	нас	вас	их
Dat	нам	вам	им
Instr	нáми	вáми	и́ми
Prp	о нас	о вас	о них

Table 7

Nom	кто	что
Acc	когó	что
Gen	когó	чегó
Dat	комý	чемý
Instr	кем	чем
Prp	о ком	о чём

Table 8	*m*	*f*	*nt*	*pl*
Nom	мой	моя́	моё	мои́
Acc	мой/моегó	мою́	моё	мои́/мои́х
Gen	моегó	моéй	моегó	мои́х
Dat	моемý	моéй	моемý	мои́м
Instr	мои́м	моéй	мои́м	мои́ми
Prp	о моём	о моéй	о моём	о мои́х

(твой declines like мой, as does the reflexive possessive pronoun свой. The instrumental form моéй has the alternative моéю)

Table 9	*m*	*f*	*nt*	*pl*
Nom	наш	нáша	нáше	нáши
Acc	наш/нáшего	нáшу	нáше	нáши/нáших
Gen	нáшего	нáшей	нáшего	нáших
Dat	нáшему	нáшей	нáшему	нáшим
Instr	нáшим	нáшей	нáшим	нáшими
Prp	о нáшем	о нáшей	о нáшем	о нáших

(ваш declines like наш. The instrumental form нáшей has the alternative нáшею. The possessive pronouns егó, её and их are invariable)

Table 10	*m*	*f*	*nt*	*pl*
Nom	э́тот	э́та	э́то	э́ти
Acc	э́тот/э́того	э́ту	э́то	э́ти/э́тих
Gen	э́того	э́той	э́того	э́тих
Dat	э́тому	э́той	э́тому	э́тим
Instr	э́тим	э́той	э́тим	э́тими
Prp	об э́том	об э́той	об э́том	об э́тих

(The instrumental form э́той has the alternative э́тою)

Table 11	*m*	*f*	*nt*	*pl*
Nom	тот	та	то	те
Acc	тот/тогó	ту	то	те/тех
Gen	тогó	той	тогó	тех
Dat	томý	той	томý	тем
Instr	тем	той	тем	тéми
Prp	о тóм	о той	о тóм	о тéх

(The instrumental form той has the alternative тóю)

Table 12	*m*	*f*	*nt*	*pl*
Nom	сей	сия́	сиé	сии́
Acc	сей/сегó	сию́	сиé	сии́/сих
Gen	сегó	сей	сегó	сих
Dat	семý	сей	семý	сим
Instr	сим	сей	сим	си́ми
Prp	о сём	о сей	о сём	о сих

(The instrumental form сей has the alternative сéю)

Table 13	*m*	*f*	*nt*	*pl*
Nom	весь	вся	всё	все
Acc	весь/всегó	всю	всё	все/всех
Gen	всегó	всей	всегó	всех
Dat	всемý	всей	всемý	всем
Instr	всем	всей	всем	всéми
Prp	обо всём	обо всей	обо всём	обо всех

(The instrumental form всей has the alternative всéю)

Table 14	хотеть
я	хочу́
ты	хо́чешь
он/она́	хо́чет
мы	хоти́м
вы	хоти́те
они́	хотя́т
Past tense:	хоте́л, хоте́ла, хоте́ло, хоте́ли

(Similarly with verbs such as расхоте́ть, захоте́ть etc)

Table 15	есть
я	ем
ты	ешь
он/она́	ест
мы	еди́м
вы	еди́те
они́	едя́т
Past tense:	ел, е́ла, е́ло, е́ли
Imperative:	е́шь(те)!

(Similarly with verbs such as съесть, пое́сть, перее́сть etc)

Table 16	дать
я	дам
ты	дашь
он/она́	даст
мы	дади́м
вы	дади́те
они́	даду́т
Past tense:	дал, дала́, дало́, да́ли
Imperative:	да́й(те)!

(Similarly with verbs such as переда́ть, изда́ть, отда́ть, разда́ть etc)

Table 17	чтить
я	чту
ты	чтишь
он/она́	чтит
мы	чтим
вы	чти́те
они́	чтут/чтят
Past tense:	чтил, чти́ла, чти́ло, чти́ли
Imperative:	чти́(те)!

(Similarly with verbs such as почти́ть etc)

Table 18 **идти́**

я иду́
ты идёшь
он/она́ идёт
мы идём
вы идёте
они́ иду́т
Past tense: шёл, шла, шло, шли
Imperative: иди́(те)!
(Similarly with verbs such as прийти́, уйти́, отойти́, зайти́ etc)

Table 19 **ехать**

я е́ду
ты е́дешь
он/она́ е́дет
мы е́дем
вы е́дете
они́ е́дут
Past tense: е́хал, е́хала, е́хало, е́хали
Imperative: поезжа́й(те)!
(Similarly with verbs such as прие́хать, пере́ехать, уе́хать, въе́хать etc)

Table 20 **бежа́ть**

я бегу́
ты бежи́шь
он/она́ бежи́т
мы бежи́м
вы бежи́те
они́ бегу́т
Past tense: бежа́л, бежа́ла, бежа́ло, бежа́ли
Imperative: беги́(те)!
(Similarly with verbs such as побежа́ть, убежа́ть, прибежа́ть etc)

Table 21 **быть**

я бу́ду
ты бу́дешь
он/она́ бу́дет
мы бу́дем
вы бу́дете
они́ бу́дут
Past tense: был, была́, бы́ло, бы́ли
Imperative: бу́дь(те)!
(Not used in the present tense, except есть in certain cases)

Table 22	*m*	*f*	*nt*	*pl*
Nom	оди́н	одна́	одно́	одни́
Acc	оди́н/одного́	одну́	одно́	одни́/одни́х
Gen	одного́	одно́й	одного́	одни́х
Dat	одному́	одно́й	одному́	одни́м
Instr	одни́м	одно́й	одни́м	одни́ми
Prp	об одно́м	об одно́й	об одно́м	об одни́х

(The instrumental form одно́й has the alternative одно́ю)

Table 23	*m*	*f*	*nt*
Nom	два	две	два
Acc	два/двух	две/двух	два/двух
Gen	двух	двух	двух
Dat	двум	двум	двум
Instr	двумя́	двумя́	двумя́
Prp	о двух	о двух	о двух

Table 24		
Nom	три	четы́ре
Acc	три/трёх	четы́ре/четырёх
Gen	трёх	четырёх
Dat	трём	четырём
Instr	тремя́	четырьмя́
Prp	о трёх	о четырёх

Table 25	*m/nt*	*f*
Nom	о́ба	о́бе
Acc	о́ба/обо́их	о́бе/обе́их
Gen	обо́их	обе́их
Dat	обо́им	обе́им
Instr	обо́ими	обе́ими
Prp	об обо́их	об обе́их

Table 26		
Nom/ Acc	пять	пятьдеся́т
Gen/ Dat	пяти́	пяти́десяти
Instr	пятью́	пятью́десятью
Prp	о пяти́	о пяти́десяти

(шесть to два́дцать and три́дцать decline like пять; шестьдеся́т, во́семьдесят and се́мьдесят decline like пятьдеся́т)

Table 27

Nom/Acc	сóрок	сто
Gen/Dat/Instr	сорокá	ста
Prp	о сорокá	о ста

девянóсто declines like сто. After много and несколько the genitive plural is сот, the dative plural is стам, the instrumental plural is стáми and the prepositional plural is стах)

Table 28

Nom/Acc	двéсти	трúста	четы́реста	пятьсóт
Gen	двухсóт	трёхсóт	четырёхсóт	пятисóт
Dat	двумстáм	трёмстáм	четырёмстáм	пятистáм
Instr	двумястáми	тремястáми	четырьмястáми	пятьюстáми
Prp	о двумстáх	о трёхстáх	о четырёхстáх	о пятистáх

(шестьсóт, семьсóт, восемьсóт and девятьсóт decline like пятьсóт)

Table 29

	Singular	*Plural*
Nom	ты́сяча	ты́сячи
Acc	ты́сячу	ты́сячи
Gen	ты́сячи	ты́сяч
Dat	ты́сяче	ты́сячам
Instr	ты́сячей	ты́сячами
Prp	о ты́сяче	о ты́сячах

(The instrumental singular form ты́сячью also exists)

Table 30a

Nom	двóе	трóе	чéтверо
Acc	двóе/двои́х	трóе/трои́х	чéтверо/ четверы́х
Gen	двои́х	трои́х	четверы́х
Dat	двои́м	трои́м	четверы́м
Instr	двои́ми	трои́ми	четверы́ми
Prp	о двои́х	о трои́х	о четверы́х

Table 30b

Nom	пя́теро	шéстеро	сéмеро
Acc	пя́теро/ пятеры́х	шéстеро/ шестеры́х	сéмеро/ семеры́х
Gen	пятеры́х	шестеры́х	семеры́х
Dat	пятеры́м	шестеры́м	семеры́м
Instr	пятеры́ми	шестеры́ми	семеры́ми
Prp	о пятеры́х	о шестеры́х	о семеры́х

Количественные Числительные | Cardinal Numbers

Количественные Числительные		Cardinal Numbers
оди́н (одна́, одно́, одни́)	1	one
два (две)	2	two
три	3	three
четы́ре	4	four
пять	5	five
шесть	6	six
семь	7	seven
во́семь	8	eight
де́вять	9	nine
де́сять	10	ten
оди́ннадцать	11	eleven
двена́дцать	12	twelve
трина́дцать	13	thirteen
четы́рнадцать	14	fourteen
пятна́дцать	15	fifteen
шестна́дцать	16	sixteen
семна́дцать	17	seventeen
восемна́дцать	18	eighteen
девятна́дцать	19	nineteen
два́дцать	20	twenty
два́дцать оди́н (одна́, одно́, одни́)	21	twenty-one
два́дцать два (две)	22	twenty-two
три́дцать	30	thirty
со́рок	40	forty
пятьдеся́т	50	fifty
шестьдеся́т	60	sixty
се́мьдесят	70	seventy
во́семьдесят	80	eighty
девяно́сто	90	ninety
сто	100	a hundred
сто оди́н (одна́, одно́)	101	a hundred and one
две́сти	200	two hundred
две́сти оди́н (одна́, одно́)	201	two hundred and one
три́ста	300	three hundred
четы́реста	400	four hundred
пятьсо́т	500	five hundred
ты́сяча	1 000	a thousand
миллио́н	1 000 000	a million

Собирательные Числительные/Collective Numerals

дво́е
тро́е
че́тверо
пя́теро
ше́стеро
се́меро

Дроби / Fractions

Дроби	Fractions	
полови́на	a half	$^1/_2$
треть (*f*)	a third	$^1/_3$
че́тверть (*f*)	a quarter	$^1/_4$
одна́ пя́тая	a fifth	$^1/_5$
три че́тверти	three quarters	$^3/_4$
две тре́ти	two thirds	$^2/_3$
полтора́ (полторы́)	one and a half	$1^1/_2$
ноль це́лых (и) пять деся́тых	(nought) point five	0.5
три це́лых (и) четы́ре деся́тых	three point four	3.4
шесть це́лых (и) во́семьдесят де́вять со́тых	six point eight nine	6.89
де́сять проце́нтов	ten per cent	10%
сто проце́нтов	a hundred per cent	100%

Порядковые Числительные / Ordinal Numbers

Порядковые Числительные		Ordinal Numbers	
пе́рвый	1-й	first	1st
второ́й	2-й	second	2nd
тре́тий	3-й	third	3rd
четвёртый	4-й	fourth	4th
пя́тый	5-й	fifth	5th
шесто́й	6-й	sixth	6th
седьмо́й	7-й	seventh	7th
восьмо́й	8-й	eighth	8th
девя́тый	9-й	ninth	9th
деся́тый	10-й	tenth	10th
оди́ннадцатый		eleventh	
двена́дцатый		twelfth	
трина́дцатый		thirteenth	
четы́рнадцатый		fourteenth	
пятна́дцатый		fifteenth	
шестна́дцатый		sixteenth	
семна́дцатый		seventeenth	
восемна́дцатый		eighteenth	
девятна́дцатый		nineteenth	
двадца́тый		twentieth	
два́дцать пе́рвый		twenty-first	
два́дцать второ́й		twenty-second	
тридца́тый		thirtieth	
сороково́й		fortieth	
пятидеся́тый		fiftieth	
восьмидеся́тый		eightieth	
девяно́стый		ninetieth	
со́тый		hundredth	
сто пе́рвый		hundred-and-first	
ты́сячный		thousandth	
миллио́нный		millionth	

Даты и Время	**Date and Time**
котóрый час?	what time is it?
сейчáс 5 часóв	it is *or* it's 5 o'clock
в какóе врéмя	at what time?
в *+acc* ...	at...
в час дня	at one p.m.
пóлночь (*f*)	00.00 midnight
дéсять минýт пéрвого, двáцать четы́ре (часá) дéсять (минýт)	00.10, ten past midnight, ten past twelve a.m.
дéсять минýт вторóго, час дéсять	01.10, ten past one, one ten
чéтверть вторóго, час пятнáдцать	01.15, a quarter past one, one fifteen
половúна вторóго, час трúдцать	01.30, half past one, one thirty
без чéтверти два, час сóрок пять	01.45, a quarter to two, one forty-five
без десятú два, час пятьдеся́т	01.50, ten to two, one fifty
двенáдцать часóв дня, пóлдень (*m*)	12.00, midday
половúна пéрвого, двенáдцать трúдцать	12.30, half past twelve, twelve thirty p.m.
тринáдцать часóв, час дня	13.00, one (o'clock) (in the afternoon), one p.m.
девятнáдцать часóв, семь часóв вéчера	19.00, seven (o'clock) (in the evening), seven p.m.
двáдцать одúн (час) трúдцать (минýт), дéвять трúдцать вéчера	21.30, nine thirty (p.m. *or* at night)
двáдцать три (часá) сóрок пять (минýт), без чéтверти двенáдцать, одúннадцать сóрок пять	23.25, a quarter to twelve, eleven forty-five p.m.
чéрез двáдцать минýт	in twenty minutes
двáдцать минýт назáд	twenty minutes ago
в ближáйшие двáдцать минýт	in the next twenty minutes
за двáдцать минýт	within twenty minutes
спустя́ двáдцать минýт	after twenty minutes
сейчáс двáдцать минýт четвёртого	it's twenty past *or* after (*US*) three
полчасá	half an hour
чéтверть часá	quarter of an hour
полторá часá	an hour and a half
час с чéтвертью	an hour and a quarter
чéрез час	in an hour's time
чéрез час, кáждый час	every hour, on the hour
кáждый час	hourly
чéрез час	in an hour from now
разбудúте меня́ в семь часóв	wake me up at seven

с девятѝ до пятѝ	from nine to five
с двух до трех (часо́в)	between two and three (o'clock)
сего́дня с девятѝ утра́	since nine o'clock this morning
до десятѝ часо́в ве́чера	till ten o'clock tonight
о́коло трёх часо́в дня	at about three o'clock in the afternoon
три часа́ по Грѝнвичу	three o'clock GMT
уже́ нача́ло пя́того	it's just gone four
после четырёх	at the back of four
сего́дня	today
ка́ждый день/вто́рник	every day/Tuesday
вчера́	yesterday
сего́дня у́тром	this morning
за́втра днём/ве́чером	tomorrow afternoon/night
позавчера́ ве́чером, позапро́шлой но́чью	the night before last
позавчера́	the day before yesterday
вчера́ ве́чером, про́шлой но́чью	last night
два дня/шесть лет наза́д	two days/six years ago
послеза́втра	the day after tomorrow
в сре́ду	on Wednesday
он хо́дит туда́ по сре́дам	he goes there on Wednesdays
«закры́то по пя́тницам»	"closed on Fridays"
с понеде́льника до пя́тницы	from Monday to Friday
к четвергу́	by Thursday
как-то в ма́рте, в суббо́ту	one Saturday in March
че́рез неде́лю	in a week's time
во вто́рник на сле́дующей неде́ле	a week on *or* next Thursday
в воскресе́нье на про́шлой неде́ле	a week last Sunday
че́рез понеде́льник	Monday week
на э́той/сле́дующей/про́шлой неде́ле	this/next/last week
че́рез две неде́ли	in two weeks *or* a fortnight
в понеде́льник че́рез две неде́ли	two weeks on Monday
в э́тот день шесть лет наза́д	six years to the day
пе́рвая/после́дняя пя́тница ме́сяца	the first/last Friday of the month
в сле́дующем ме́сяце	next month
в про́шлом году́	last year
в конце́ ме́сяца	at the end of the month
два раза́ в неде́лю/ме́сяц/год	twice a week/month/year
како́е сего́дня число́?	what's the date?, what date is it today?
сего́дня 28-е	today's date is the 28th, today is the 28th
пе́рвое января́	the first of January, January the first

две ты́сячи трина́дцатый год	2013, two thousand and thirteen *or* twenty thirteen
роди́лся в 1980-м году́	I was born in 1980
у него́ день рожде́ния 5 ию́ня	his birthday is on 5th June (*Brit*) *or* June 5th
18 а́вгуста 2018	on 18th August (*Brit*) *or* August 18th 2018
с 19-го по 3-е	from the 19th to the 3rd
в 99-м году́	in '99
весна́ 97-го го́да	the Spring of '97
в 1930-х года́х	in (*or* during) the 1930s
в 1940-х года́х	in 1940 something
в 2019-м году́	in the year 2019
в XIII ве́ке	in the 13th century
4 год до н.э.	4 BC
70 год н.э.	70 AD